Microsoft®  Office 2007

Post-Advanced Concepts and Techniques

Gary B. Shelly

Thomas J. Cashman

Misty E. Vermaat

Contributing Authors

Mary Z. Last

Philip J. Pratt

Jeffrey J. Quasney

Susan L. Sebok

Jeffrey J. Webb

THOMSON COURSE TECHNOLOGY   25 THOMSON PLACE   BOSTON MA 02210

Australia • Canada • Denmark • Japan • Mexico • New Zealand • Philippines • Puerto Rico • Singapore • South Africa • Spain • United Kingdom • United States

THOMSON
COURSE TECHNOLOGY

Microsoft Office 2007
Post-Advanced Concepts and Techniques

Gary B. Shelly

Thomas J. Cashman

Misty E. Vermaat

Executive Editor
Alexandra Arnold

Senior Product Managers
Reed Curry, Mali Jones

Product Manager
Heather Hawkins

Associate Product Manager
Klenda Martinez

Editorial Assistant
Jon Farnham

Senior Marketing Manager
Joy Stark-Vancs

Marketing Coordinator
Julie Schuster

Print Buyer
Julio Esperas

Director of Production
Patty Stephan

Lead Production Editor
Matthew Hutchinson

Production Editors
Cathie DiMassa,
Jill Klaffky, Phillipa Lehar

Developmental Editors
Jill Batistick, Amanda Brodkin,
Laurie Brown, Lyn Markowicz

Proofreaders
John Bosco,
Kim Kosmatka

Indexer
Rich Carlson

QA Manuscript Reviewers
John Freitas, Serge Palladino,
Chris Scriver, Danielle Shaw,
Marianne Snow, Teresa Storch

Art Director
Bruce Bond

Cover and Text Design
Joel Sadagursky

Cover Photo
Jon Chomitz

Compositor
GEX Publishing Services

Printer
Banta Menasha

Contents

Microsoft Office **Word 2007**

CHAPTER SEVEN
Working with Document Sharing Tools, a Master Document, a Table of Contents, and an Index

Microsoft Office Excel® 2007

CHAPTER EIGHT
Formula Auditing, Data Validation, and Complex Problem Solving

Microsoft Office Access™ 2007

Microsoft Office PowerPoint® 2007

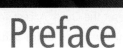

Preface

The Shelly Cashman Series® offers the finest textbooks in computer education. We are proud of the fact that our series of Microsoft Office 4.3, Microsoft Office 95, Microsoft Office 97, Microsoft Office 2000, Microsoft Office XP, and Microsoft Office 2003 textbooks have been the most widely used books in education. With each new edition of our Office books, we have made significant improvements based on the software and comments made by instructors and students.

Microsoft Office 2007 contains more changes in the user interface and feature set than all other previous versions combined. Recognizing that the new features and functionality of Microsoft Office 2007 would impact the way that students are taught skills, the Shelly Cashman Series development team carefully reviewed our pedagogy and analyzed its effectiveness in teaching today's Office student. An extensive customer survey produced results confirming what the series is best known for: its step-by-step, screen-by-screen instructions, its project-oriented approach, and the quality of its content.

We learned, though, that students entering computer courses today are different than students taking these classes just a few years ago. Students today read less, but need to retain more. They need not only to be able to perform skills, but to retain those skills and know how to apply them to different settings. Today's students need to be continually engaged and challenged to retain what they're learning.

As a result, we've renewed our commitment to focusing on the user and how they learn best. This commitment is reflected in every change we've made to our Office 2007 books.

Objectives of This Textbook

Microsoft Office 2007: Post-Advanced Concepts and Techniques is intended for a third course on Office 2007 applications. This book assumes that students are familiar with the fundamentals and some advanced features of Microsoft Windows Vista, Microsoft Office Word 2007, Microsoft Office Excel 2007, Microsoft Office Access 2007, Microsoft Office PowerPoint 2007, and Microsoft Office Outlook 2007. These features are covered in the companion textbooks *Microsoft Office 2007: Introductory Concepts and Techniques, Windows Vista Edition*, and *Microsoft Office 2007: Advanced Concepts and Techniques*. The objectives of this book are:

- To offer a comprehensive presentation of Microsoft Office Word 2007, Microsoft Office Excel 2007, Microsoft Office Access 2007, and Microsoft Office PowerPoint 2007

- To expose students to practical examples of the computer as a useful tool

- To acquaint students with the proper procedures to create and enhance documents, worksheets, databases, and presentations suitable for coursework, professional purposes, and personal use

- To help students discover the underlying functionality of Office 2007 so they can become more productive

- To develop an exercise-oriented approach that allows learning by doing

The Shelly Cashman Approach

Features of the Shelly Cashman Series Microsoft Office 2007 books include:

- **Project Orientation** Each chapter in the book presents a project with a practical problem and complete solution in an easy-to-understand approach.

- **Plan Ahead Boxes** The project orientation is enhanced by the inclusion of Plan Ahead boxes. These new features prepare students to create successful projects by encouraging them to think strategically about what they are trying to accomplish before they begin working.

- **Step-by-Step, Screen-by-Screen Instructions** Each of the tasks required to complete a project is clearly identified throughout the chapter. Now, the step-by-step instructions provide a context beyond point-and-click. Each step explains why students are performing a task, or the result of performing a certain action. Found on the screens accompanying each step, call-outs give students the information they need to know when they need to know it. Now, we've used color to distinguish the content in the call-outs. The Explanatory call-outs (in black) summarize what is happening on the screen and the Navigational call-outs (in red) show students where to click.

- **Q&A** Found within many of the step-by-step sequences, Q&As raise the kinds of questions students may ask when working through a step sequence and provide answers about what they are doing, why they are doing it, and how that task might be approached differently.

- **Experimental Steps** These new steps, within our step-by-step instructions, encourage students to explore, experiment, and take advantage of the features of the Office 2007 new user interface. These steps are not necessary to complete the projects, but are designed to increase the confidence with the software and build problem-solving skills.

- **Thoroughly Tested Projects** Unparalleled quality is ensured because every screen in the book is produced by the author only after performing a step, and then each project must pass Thomson Course Technology's Quality Assurance program.

- **Other Ways Boxes and Quick Reference Summary** The Other Ways boxes displayed at the end of most of the step-by-step sequences specify the other ways to do the task completed in the steps. Thus, the steps and the Other Ways box make a comprehensive reference unit. A Quick Reference Summary at the end of the book contains all of the tasks presented in the chapters, and all ways identified of accomplishing the tasks.

- **BTW** These marginal annotations provide background information, tips, and answers to common questions that complement the topics covered, adding depth and perspective to the learning process.

- **Integration of the World Wide Web** The World Wide Web is integrated into the Office 2007 learning experience by (1) BTW annotations that send students to Web sites for up-to-date information and alternative approaches to tasks; (2) a Microsoft Business Certification Program Web page so students can prepare for the certification examinations; (3) a Quick Reference Summary Web page that summarizes the ways to complete tasks (mouse, Ribbon, shortcut menu, and keyboard); and (4) the Learn It Online section at the end of each chapter, which has chapter reinforcement exercises, learning games, and other types of student activities.

- **End-of-Chapter Student Activities** Extensive student activities at the end of each chapter provide the student with plenty of opportunities to reinforce the materials learned in the chapter through hands-on assignments. Several new types of activities have been added that challenge the student in new ways to expand their knowledge, and to apply their new skills to a project with personal relevance.

Q&A

What is a maximized window?

A maximized window fills the entire screen. When you maximize a window, the Maximize button changes to a Restore Down button.

Other Ways

1. Click Italic button on Mini toolbar
2. Right-click selected text, click Font on shortcut menu, click Font tab, click Italic in Font style list, click OK button
3. Click Font Dialog Box Launcher, click Font tab, click Italic in Font style list, click OK button
4. Press CTRL+I

BTW

Minimizing the Ribbon
If you want to minimize the Ribbon, right-click the Ribbon and then click Minimize the Ribbon on the shortcut menu, double-click the active tab, or press CTRL+F1. To restore a minimized Ribbon, right-click the Ribbon and then click Minimize the Ribbon on the shortcut menu, double-click any top-level tab, or press CTRL+F1. To use commands on a minimized Ribbon, click the top-level tab.

Organization of This Textbook

Microsoft Office 2007: Post-Advanced Concepts and Techniques consists of three chapters each on Microsoft Office Word 2007, Microsoft Office Excel 2007, and Microsoft Office Access 2007, two chapters on Microsoft Office PowerPoint 2007, four special features emphasizing integration and collaboration, seven appendices, and a Quick Reference Summary.

End-of-Chapter Student Activities

A notable strength of the Shelly Cashman Series Microsoft Office 2007 books is the extensive student activities at the end of each chapter. Well-structured student activities can make the difference between students merely participating in a class and students retaining the information they learn. The activities in the Shelly Cashman Series Office books include the following.

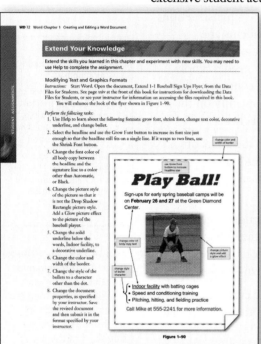

Figure 1–90

CHAPTER SUMMARY A concluding paragraph, followed by a listing of the tasks completed within a chapter together with the pages on which the step-by-step, screen-by-screen explanations appear.

LEARN IT ONLINE Every chapter features a Learn It Online section that is comprised of six exercises. These exercises include True/False, Multiple Choice, Short Answer, Flash Cards, Practice Test, and Learning Games.

APPLY YOUR KNOWLEDGE This exercise usually requires students to open and manipulate a file from the Data Files that parallels the activities learned in the chapter. To obtain a copy of the Data Files for Students, follow the instructions on the inside back cover of this text.

EXTEND YOUR KNOWLEDGE This exercise allows students to extend and expand on the skills learned within the chapter.

MAKE IT RIGHT This exercise requires students to analyze a document, identify errors and issues, and correct those errors and issues using skills learned in the chapter.

IN THE LAB Three all new in-depth assignments per chapter require students to utilize the chapter concepts and techniques to solve problems on a computer.

CASES AND PLACES Five unique real-world case-study situations, including Make It Personal, an open-ended project that relates to student's personal lives, and one small-group activity.

Instructor Resources CD-ROM

The Shelly Cashman Series is dedicated to providing you with all of the tools you need to make your class a success. Information about all supplementary materials is available through your Thomson Course Technology representative or by calling one of the following telephone numbers: Colleges, Universities, and Continuing Ed departments, 1-800-648-7450; High Schools, 1-800-824-5179; and Career Colleges, Business, Government, Library and Resellers, 1-800-477-3692.

The Instructor Resources CD-ROM for this textbook include both teaching and testing aids. The contents of each item on the Instructor Resources CD-ROM (ISBN 1-4239-1226-8) are described on the following pages.

INSTRUCTOR'S MANUAL The Instructor's Manual consists of Microsoft Word files, which include chapter objectives, lecture notes, teaching tips, classroom activities, lab activities, quick quizzes, figures and boxed elements summarized in the chapters, and a glossary page. The new format of the Instructor's Manual will allow you to map through every chapter easily.

LECTURE SUCCESS SYSTEM The Lecture Success System consists of intermediate files that correspond to certain figures in the book, allowing you to step through the creation of a project in a chapter during a lecture without entering large amounts of data.

SYLLABUS Sample syllabi, which can be customized easily to a course, are included. The syllabi cover policies, class and lab assignments and exams, and procedural information.

FIGURE FILES Illustrations for every figure in the textbook are available in electronic form. Use this ancillary to present a slide show in lecture or to print transparencies for use in lecture with an overhead projector. If you have a personal computer and LCD device, this ancillary can be an effective tool for presenting lectures.

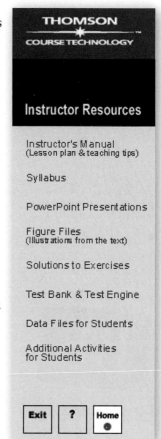

POWERPOINT PRESENTATIONS PowerPoint Presentations is a multimedia lecture presentation system that provides slides for each chapter. Presentations are based on chapter objectives. Use this presentation system to present well-organized lectures that are both interesting and knowledge based. PowerPoint Presentations provides consistent coverage at schools that use multiple lecturers.

SOLUTIONS TO EXERCISES Solutions are included for the end-of-chapter exercises, as well as the Chapter Reinforcement exercises. Rubrics and annotated solution files, as described below, are also included.

RUBRICS AND ANNOTATED SOLUTION FILES The grading rubrics provide a customizable framework for assigning point values to the laboratory exercises. Annotated solution files that correspond to the grading rubrics make it easy for you to compare students' results with the correct solutions whether you receive their homework as hard copy or via e-mail.

TEST BANK & TEST ENGINE In the ExamView test bank, you will find our standard question types (40 multiple-choice, 25 true/false, 20 completion) and new objective-based question types (5 modified multiple-choice, 5 modified true/false and 10 matching). Critical Thinking questions are also included (3 essays and 2 cases with 2 questions each) totaling the test bank to 112 questions for every chapter with page number references, and when appropriate, figure references. A version of the test bank you can print also is included. The test bank comes with a copy of the test engine, ExamView, the ultimate tool for your objective-based testing needs. ExamView is a state-of-the-art test builder that is easy to use. ExamView enables you to create paper-, LAN-, or Web-based tests from test banks designed specifically for your Thomson Course Technology textbook. Utilize the ultra-efficient QuickTest Wizard to create tests in less than five minutes by taking advantage of Thomson Course Technology's question banks, or customize your own exams from scratch.

LAB TESTS/TEST OUT The Lab Tests/Test Out exercises parallel the In the Lab assignments and are supplied for the purpose of testing students in the laboratory on the material covered in the chapter or testing students out of the course.

DATA FILES FOR STUDENTS All the files that are required by students to complete the exercises are included. You can distribute the files on the Instructor Resources CD-ROM to your students over a network, or you can have them follow the instructions on the inside back cover of this book to obtain a copy of the Data Files for Students.

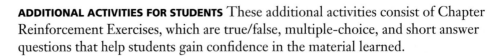

ADDITIONAL ACTIVITIES FOR STUDENTS These additional activities consist of Chapter Reinforcement Exercises, which are true/false, multiple-choice, and short answer questions that help students gain confidence in the material learned.

Assessment & Training Solutions
SAM 2007

SAM 2007 helps bridge the gap between the classroom and the real world by allowing students to train and test on important computer skills in an active, hands-on environment.

SAM 2007's easy-to-use system includes powerful interactive exams, training or projects on critical applications such as Word, Excel, Access, PowerPoint, Outlook, Windows, the Internet, and much more. SAM simulates the application environment, allowing students to demonstrate their knowledge and think through the skills by performing real-world tasks.

Designed to be used with the Shelly Cashman series, SAM 2007 includes built-in page references so students can print helpful study guides that match the Shelly Cashman series textbooks used in class. Powerful administrative options allow instructors to schedule exams and assignments, secure tests, and run reports with almost limitless flexibility.

Student Edition Labs

Our Web-based interactive labs help students master hundreds of computer concepts, including input and output devices, file management and desktop applications, computer ethics, virus protection, and much more. Featuring up-to-the-minute content, eye-popping graphics, and rich animation, the highly interactive Student Edition Labs offer students an alternative way to learn through dynamic observation, step-by-step practice, and challenging review questions.

Online Content

Blackboard is the leading distance learning solution provider and class-management platform today. Thomson Course Technology has partnered with Blackboard to bring you premium online content. Instructors: Content for use with *Microsoft Office 2007: Post-Advanced Concepts and Techniques*, is available in a Blackboard Course Cartridge and may include topic reviews, case projects, review questions, test banks, practice tests, custom syllabi, and more.

Thomson Course Technology also has solutions for several other learning management systems. Please visit http://www.course.com today to see what's available for this title.

CourseCasts Learning on the Go. Always Available...Always Relevant.

Want to keep up with the latest technology trends relevant to you? Visit our site to find a library of podcasts, CourseCasts, featuring a "CourseCast of the Week," and download them to your portable media player at http://coursecasts.course.com.

Our fast-paced world is driven by technology. You know because you are an active participant — always on the go, always keeping up with technological trends, and always learning new ways to embrace technology to power your life.

Ken Baldauf, a faculty member of the Florida State University (FSU) Computer Science Department, is responsible for teaching technology classes to thousands of FSU students each year. He knows what you know; he knows what you want to learn. He is also an expert in the latest technology and will sort through and aggregate the most pertinent news and information so you can spend your time enjoying technology, rather than trying to figure it out.

Visit us at http://coursecasts.course.com to learn on the go!

CourseNotes

Course Technology's CourseNotes are six-panel quick reference cards that reinforce the most important and widely used features of a software application in a visual and user-friendly format. CourseNotes will serve as a great reference tool during and after the student completes the course. CourseNotes for Microsoft Office 2007, Word 2007, Excel 2007, Access 2007, PowerPoint 2007, Windows Vista, and more are available now!

To the Student . . . Getting the Most Out of Your Book

Welcome to *Microsoft Office 2007: Post-Advanced Concepts and Techniques*. You can save yourself a lot of time and gain a better understanding of the Office 2007 programs if you spend a few minutes reviewing the figures and callouts in this section.

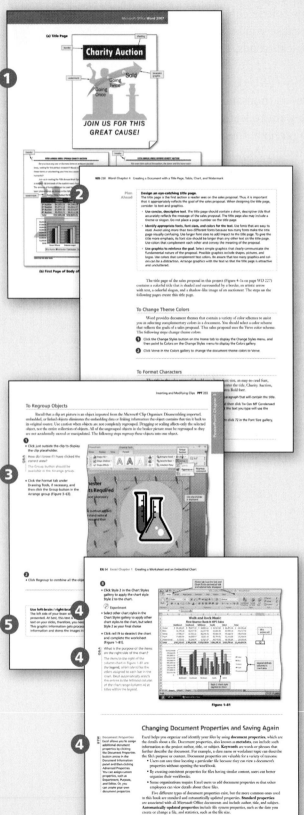

1 PROJECT ORIENTATION

Each chapter's project presents a practical problem and shows the solution in the first figure of the chapter. The project orientation lets you see firsthand how problems are solved from start to finish using application software and computers.

2 PROJECT PLANNING GUIDELINES AND PLAN AHEAD BOXES

Overall planning guidelines at the beginning of a chapter and Plan Ahead boxes throughout encourage you to think critically about how to accomplish the next goal before you actually begin working.

3 CONSISTENT STEP-BY-STEP, SCREEN-BY-SCREEN PRESENTATION

Chapter solutions are built using a step-by-step, screen-by-screen approach. This pedagogy allows you to build the solution on a computer as you read through the chapter. Generally, each step includes an explanation that indicates the result of the step.

4 MORE THAN JUST STEP-BY-STEP

BTW annotations in the margins of the book, Q&As in the steps, and substantive text in the paragraphs provide background information, tips, and answers to common questions that complement the topics covered, adding depth and perspective. When you finish with this book, you will be ready to use the Office programs to solve problems on your own. Experimental steps provide you with opportunities to step out on your own to try features of the programs, and pick up right where you left off in the chapter.

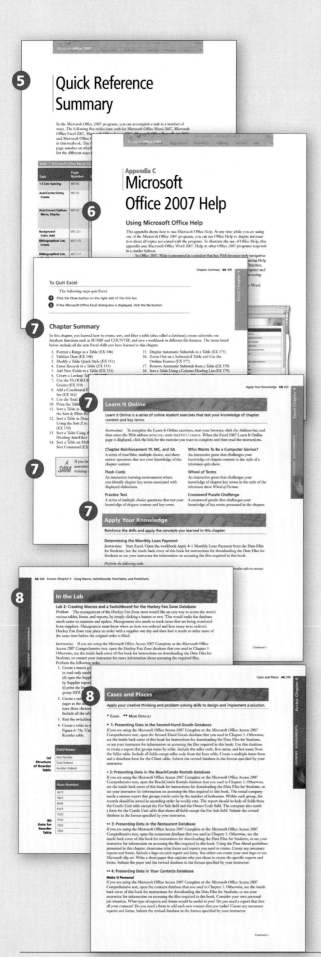

5 OTHER WAYS BOXES AND QUICK REFERENCE SUMMARY
Other Ways boxes that follow many of the step sequences and
a Quick Reference Summary at the back of the book explain the
other ways to complete the task presented, such as using the
mouse, Ribbon, shortcut menu, and keyboard.

6 EMPHASIS ON GETTING HELP WHEN YOU NEED IT
The first project of each application and Appendix C show you
how to use all the elements of Office Help. Being able to answer
your own questions will increase your productivity and reduce
your frustrations by minimizing the time it takes to learn how to
complete a task.

7 REVIEW, REINFORCEMENT, AND EXTENSION
After you successfully step through a project in a chapter, a
section titled Chapter Summary identifies the tasks with which you
should be familiar. Terms you should know for test purposes are
bold in the text. The SAM Training feature provides the opportunity
for addional reinforcement on important skills covered in each
chapter. The Learn It Online section at the end of each chapter
offers reinforcement in the form of review questions, learning
games, and practice tests. Also included are exercises that require
you to extend your learning beyond the book.

8 LABORATORY EXERCISES
If you really want to learn how to use the programs, then you
must design and implement solutions to problems on your own.
Every chapter concludes with several carefully developed
laboratory assignments that increase in complexity.

About Our New Cover Look

Learning styles of students have changed, but the
Shelly Cashman Series' dedication to their success has
remained steadfast for over 30 years. We are committed
to continually updating our approach and content to
reflect the way today's students learn and experience new
technology.

This focus on the user is reflected in our bold new cover
design, which features photographs of real students
using the Shelly Cashman Series in their courses. Each
book features a different user, reflecting the many ages,
experiences, and backgrounds of all of the students
learning with our books. When you use the Shelly
Cashman Series, you can be assured that you are learning
computer skills using the most effective courseware

Microsoft Office 2007

7 | Working with Document Sharing Tools, a Master Document, a Table of Contents, and an Index

Objectives

You will have mastered the material in this chapter when you can:

- Insert comments
- Track changes
- Review tracked changes
- Compare documents and combine documents
- Add and modify a caption
- Create a cross-reference
- Use the Building Blocks Organizer
- Link text boxes

- Compress pictures
- Work with a master document and subdocuments
- Insert a cover page
- Create and modify a table of contents
- Use the Document Map
- Create a table of figures
- Build and modify an index

7 | Working with Document Sharing Tools, a Master Document, a Table of Contents, and an Index

Introduction

During the course of your academic studies and professional activities, you may find it necessary to compose a document that is many pages in length or even hundreds of pages in length. When composing a long document, you must ensure that the document is organized so that a reader easily can locate material in that document. Sometimes a document of this nature is called a **reference document**.

Project Planning Guidelines

> The process of developing a document that communicates specific information requires careful analysis and planning. As a starting point, establish why the document is needed. Once the purpose is determined, analyze the intended readers of the document and their unique needs. Then, gather information about the topic and decide what to include in the document. Finally, determine the document design and style that will be most successful at delivering the message. Details of these guidelines are provided in Appendix A. In addition, each chapter in this book provides practical applications of these planning considerations.

Project — Reference Document

A reference document is any multipage document organized so that users easily can locate material and navigate through the document. Examples of reference documents include user guides, term papers, pamphlets, manuals, proposals, and plans.

The project in this chapter uses Word to produce the reference document shown in Figure 7–1. This reference document, titled the *Internet Post*, is a multipage information guide that is distributed by Donner County Library to library patrons. Notice that the inner margin between facing pages has extra space to allow duplicated copies of the document to be bound (i.e., stapled or fastened in some manner) — without the binding covering the words.

The *Internet Post* reference document begins with a title page designed to entice the target audience to open the document and read it. Next is the table of contents, followed by an introduction. The document then discusses five types of Web sites: portal, news, informational, business/marketing, and personal. The end of this reference document has a table of figures and an index to assist readers in locating information contained within the document. A miniature version of the *Internet Post* reference document is shown in Figure 7–1; for a more readable view, visit scsite.com/wd2007/ch7.

The section of the *Internet Post* reference document that is titled, Types of Web Sites, contains content written by someone other than you. After reviewing and editing the content, you will incorporate it in the reference document. The draft of this content is located on the Data Files for Students in a file called Types of Web Sites Draft. See the inside back cover of this book for instructions on downloading the Data Files for Students, or contact your instructor for information about accessing the required files.

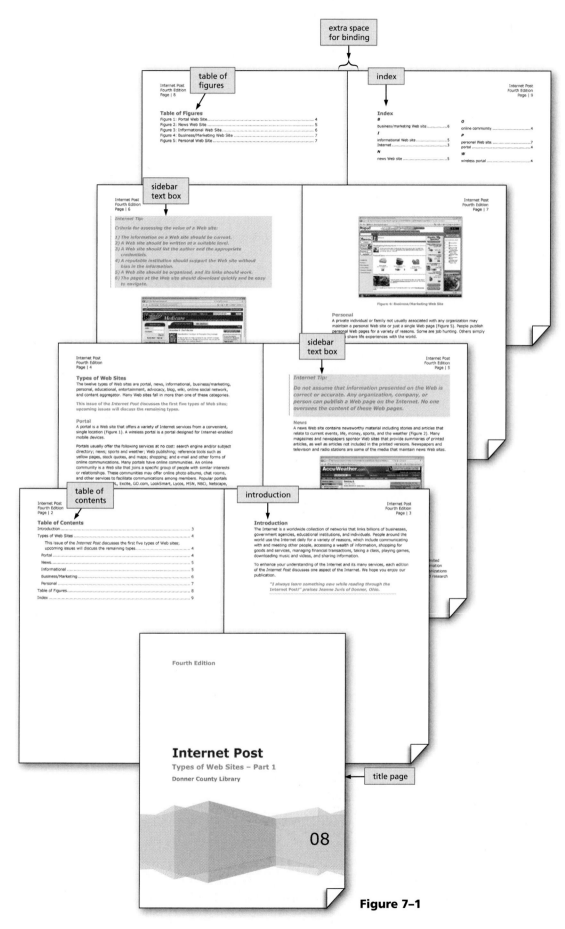

Figure 7–1

Overview

As you read through this chapter, you will learn how to create the reference document shown in Figure 7–1 on the previous page by performing these general tasks:

- Review the draft document.
- Modify the reviewed document.
- Create a master document for the reference document.
- Organize the reference document with a table of contents, a table of figures, and an index.
- Print the reference document.

Plan Ahead

General Project Guidelines

When creating a Word document, the actions you perform and decisions you make will affect the appearance and characteristics of the finished document. As you create a reference document, such as the project shown in Figure 7–1, you should follow these general guidelines:

1. **Prepare a document to be included in a longer document.** If a document contains multiple illustrations (figures), each figure should have a caption. In addition, each figure should be referenced from within the text. Any terms to be included in an index should be marked as an index entry.

2. **Include elements common to a reference document.** Most reference documents contain a title page, a table of contents, and an index. The title page entices passersby to take a copy of the document. By placing a table of contents at the beginning of the document and an index at the end, you help a reader locate topics within the document. If a document contains several illustrations, you also should include a table of figures.

3. **Prepare the document for distribution.** The reference document in Figure 7–1 prints on nine separate sheets of paper. When it is duplicated back to back, however, the document uses only five sheets of paper. The top of the first sheet of paper shows the title page, and the back of the same sheet contains the table of contents; the top of the second sheet of paper shows the introduction, and so on. The table of contents and introduction pages are called facing pages when duplicated in this manner. Be sure to allow enough room in the margins for binding (i.e., stapling) the document.

   For long documents that will be viewed online, incorporate bookmarks and/or hyperlinks so that a user can navigate quickly and easily through the document while viewing it on a computer.

When necessary, more specific details concerning the above guidelines are presented at appropriate points in the chapter. The chapter also will identify the actions performed and decisions made regarding these guidelines during the creation of the newsletter shown in Figure 7–1.

To Start Word

If you are using a computer to step through the project in this chapter and you want your screens to match the figures in this book, you should change your computer's resolution to 1024 × 768. For information about how to change a computer's resolution, read Appendix D.

The following steps start Word and verify Word settings.

Note: If you are using Windows XP, see Appendix F for alternate steps.

1 Click the Start button on the Windows Vista taskbar to display the Start menu.

2 Click All Programs at the bottom of the left pane on the Start menu to display the All Programs list and then click Microsoft Office in the All Programs list to display the Microsoft Office list.

3 Click Microsoft Office Word 2007 in the Microsoft Office list to start Word and display a new blank document in the Word window.

4 If the Word window is not maximized, click the Maximize button on its title bar to maximize the window.

5 If the Print Layout button on the status bar is not selected, click it so that Word is in Print Layout view.

6 If the rulers are displayed on the screen, click the View Ruler button at the top vertical scroll bar to remove the rulers from the Word window.

Reviewing a Document

Word provides many tools that allow users to work with others, or **collaborate**, on a document. One set of collaboration tools within Word allows you to track changes in a document and review the changes. That is, one computer user can create a document and another user(s) can make changes and insert comments in the same document. Those changes then appear on the screen with options that allow the originator (author) to accept or reject the changes and delete the comments. With another collaboration tool, you can compare and/or merge two or more documents to determine the differences between them.

To illustrate Word collaboration tools, this section follows these general steps:

1. Open the document to be reviewed.
2. Insert comments in the document for the originator (author).
3. Track changes in the document.
4. Accept and reject the tracked changes and delete all comments. For illustration purposes, you assume the role of originator (author) of the document in this step.
5. Compare the reviewed document to the original to view the differences.
6. Merge the original document with the reviewed document and with another reviewer's suggestions.

To Open a Word Document and Save It with a New File Name

The first step is to open the file called Types of Web Sites Draft on the Data Files for Students, so that you can review it. See the inside back cover of this book for instructions on downloading the Data Files for Students, or contact your instructor for information about accessing the required files. To preserve the contents of the original Types of Web Sites Draft file, you will save it with a new file name. The following steps open a document and save it with a new file name.

1 Click the Office Button and then click Open to display the Open dialog box.

2 Locate and then select the file with the name, Types of Web Sites Draft, and then click the Open button to display the document in the Word window.

3 Click the Office Button and then click Save As on the Office Button menu to display the Save As dialog box.

4 Type `Types of Web Sites Reviewed` in the File name text box to change the file name.

5 Locate and select your USB flash drive in the list of available drives.

6 Click the Save button in the Save As dialog box to save the document on the USB flash drive with the new file name, Types of Web Sites Reviewed.

7 If your zoom level is not 100%, click the Zoom Out or Zoom In button as many times as necessary until the Zoom level button displays 100% on its face.

8 Display the top of page 2 in the document window because this is the page that will contain the comments and tracked changes.

To Hide White Space

To display more content on the screen in Print Layout view, you can hide the white space if it is displayed at the top and bottom of the pages and the space between pages. Because the reference document in this chapter has several short pages, you hide white space. The following steps hide white space, if your screen displays it.

1

• Position the mouse pointer in the document window above the page (in the space between pages) until the mouse pointer changes to a Hide White Space button (Figure 7–2).

Q&A

My mouse pointer will not change to show the Hide White Space button. Why not?

You may not be in Print Layout view. Click the Print Layout button on the status bar.

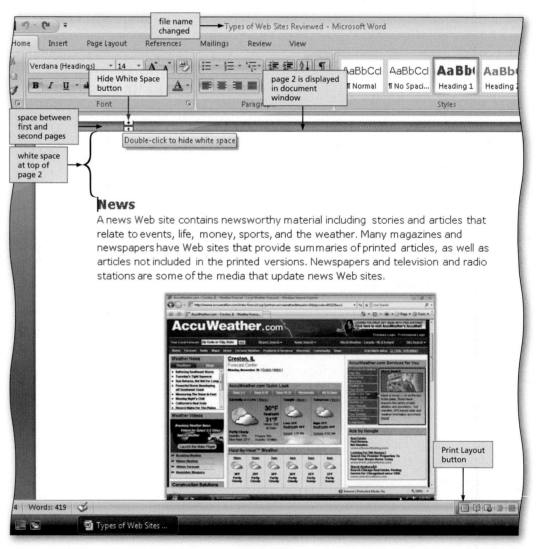

Figure 7–2

2

- Double-click the Hide White Space button to remove the white space, which causes the white space at the top and bottom of each page and the space between pages to disappear from the screen (Figure 7–3).

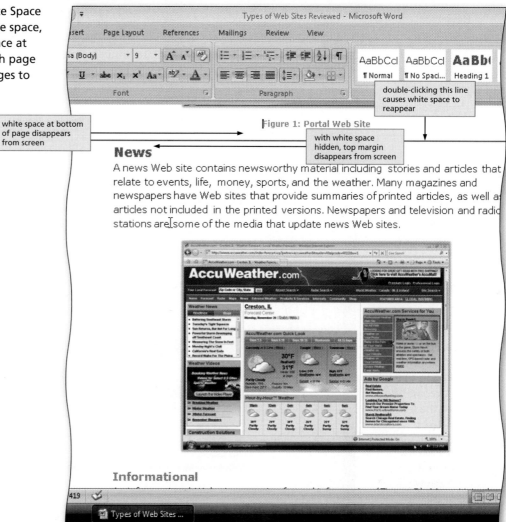

Figure 1: Portal Web Site

white space at bottom of page disappears from screen

double-clicking this line causes white space to reappear

with white space hidden, top margin disappears from screen

News

A news Web site contains newsworthy material including stories and articles that relate to events, life, money, sports, and the weather. Many magazines and newspapers have Web sites that provide summaries of printed articles, as well as articles not included in the printed versions. Newspapers and television and radio stations are some of the media that update news Web sites.

Informational

Figure 7–3

Q&A Does hiding white space have any affect on the printed document?
No.

Q&A What if I wanted white space to show again?
You would point between two pages and then double-click when the mouse pointer changes to a Show White Space button.

Other Ways

1. Click Office Button, click Word Options button, click Display in left pane, remove check mark from 'Show white space between pages in Print Layout view' check box

To Insert a Comment

Reviewers often use comments to communicate suggestions, tips, and other messages to the author of a document. A **comment** is a note inserted in a document. Comments do not affect the text of the document.

After reading through the Types of Web Sites Reviewed document, you have two comments for the originator (author) of the document. The first comment requests that the author insert an Internet tip at the top of the second and third pages in the document. The following steps insert this comment in the document.

- Display the Review tab.

- If the Display for Review setting is not Final Showing Markup, click the Display for Review box arrow and then click Final Showing Markup.

- Position the insertion point at the location where the comment should be located, in this case, at the top of page 2 to the left of the N in News.

- Click the Insert Comment button on the Review tab to display a comment balloon in the Markup Area in the document window (Figure 7–4).

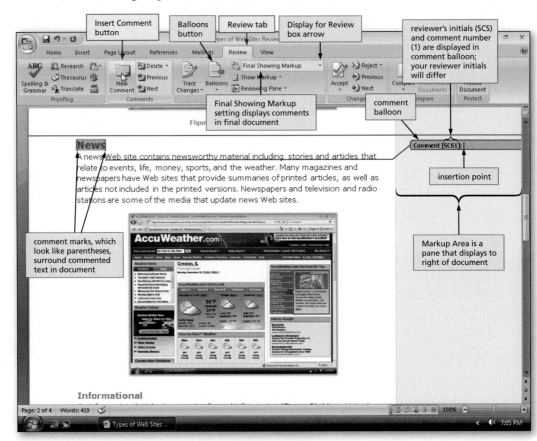

Figure 7–4

Q&A

What if the Markup Area does not appear with the comment balloon?

The balloons setting has been turned off. Click the Balloons button on the Review tab and then click Show Only Comments and Formatting in Balloons, which is the default setting.

Q&A

Why do comment marks surround selected text?

A comment is associated with text. If you do not select text on which you wish to comment, Word automatically selects the text to the right or left of the insertion point for the comment.

2

- In the comment balloon, type this text (Figure 7–5): Insert the Internet tip, which will discuss the accuracy of information on Web sites, at the top of this page and the next page.

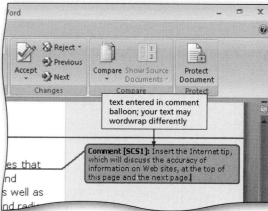

Figure 7–5

To Insert Another Comment

The second comment you want to insert in the document is to request that a figure reference be added to the end of the first sentence in the News section. The following steps insert another comment in the document.

1 Position the insertion point at the location where the comment should be located, in this case, at the end of the first sentence below the News heading.

2 Click the Insert Comment button on the Review tab to display a second comment balloon in the Markup Area in the document window.

3 In the new comment balloon, type this text (Figure 7–6): Insert a figure reference at the end of this sentence.

Q&A

Can I see the name of the reviewer that entered a comment?

Yes. Point to the comment marks in the document window to display a ScreenTip that identifies the reviewer's name, the date and time the comment was entered, as well as the text of the comment itself.

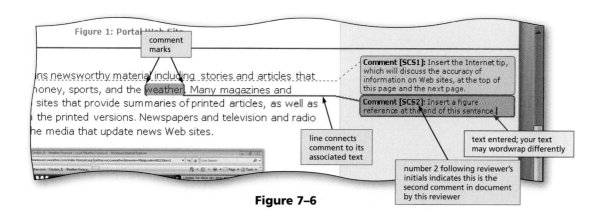

Figure 7–6

To Change Reviewer Information

Word uses predefined settings for the reviewer's initials and/or name that appears in the document window, the comment balloon, and the Reviewing Pane. If the reviewer's name or initials are not correct, you would change them by performing the following steps.

1a. Click the Track Changes button arrow on the Review tab to display the Track Changes menu. Click Change User Name on the Track Changes menu to display the Word Options dialog box.

or

1b. Display the Office Button menu and then click the Word Options button to display the Word Options dialog box. If necessary, click Popular in the left pane.

2. Enter the correct name in the User name text box, and enter the correct initials in the Initials text box.

3. Click the OK button.

To Enable Tracked Changes

When you edit a document that has the Track Changes feature enabled, Word marks all text or graphics that you insert, delete, or modify and refers to the revisions as **markup**. An author can identify the changes a reviewer has made by looking at the markup in a document. The author also has the ability to accept or reject any change that a reviewer has made to a document.

To track changes in a document, you must enable (turn on) the Track Changes feature. The following steps enable tracked changes.

• If the status bar does not show the Tracking Changes button, right-click anywhere on the status bar to display the Customize Status Bar menu and then click Track Changes on the menu to place a check mark beside the command and to display the Tracking Changes button on the status bar (Figure 7–7).

• To remove the Customize Status Bar menu from the screen, press the ESCAPE key.

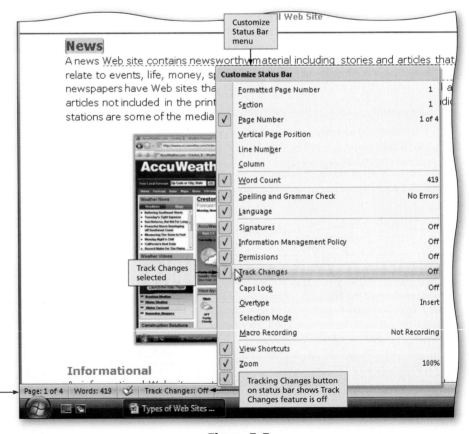

Figure 7–7

2

- If the Tracking Changes button on the status bar shows that the Track Changes feature is off, click the Tracking Changes button on the status bar to enable the Track Changes feature (Figure 7–8).

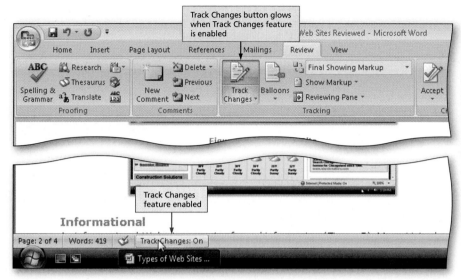

Figure 7–8

Other Ways
1. Click Track Changes button arrow on Review tab, click Track Changes   2. Press CTRL+SHIFT+E

To Track Changes

You have three suggested changes for the Types of Web Sites Reviewed document:

1. Insert the word, current, before the word, events, so that it reads: …that relate to current events.
2. Change the word, have, to the word, sponsor, in the second sentence.
3. Delete the word, stations, after radio.

The following steps track these changes as you enter them in the document.

1

- Position the insertion point immediately to the left of the word, events, in the first sentence below the News heading.
- Type current and then press the SPACEBAR to insert the word and a space (Figure 7–9).

Q&A

Why is the inserted text in color and underlined?

When the Track Changes feature is enabled, Word marks (signals) all text inserts by underlining them and marks all deletions by striking through them.

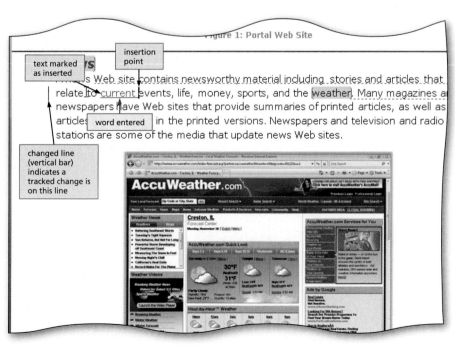

Figure 7–9

- In the next sentence, double-click the word, have, to select it.

- Type sponsor as the replacement text (Figure 7–10).

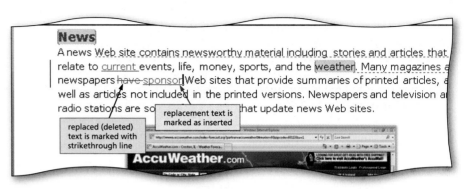

Figure 7–10

- In the last line of the News section, select the word, stations, and then press the DELETE key to delete the selection (Figure 7–11).

Q&A

Can I see the name of the person that tracked a change?

Yes. If you point to a tracked change in the document window, Word displays a ScreenTip that identifies the reviewer's name and the type of change made by that reviewer.

Figure 7–11

TO CHANGE HOW MARKUPS ARE DISPLAYED

The tracked changes, sometimes called **revision marks**, entered in the previous steps appeared inline instead of in markup balloons. Inline means that the inserts are underlined and the deletions are shown as strikethroughs. The default word setting on the Balloons menu, Show Only Comments and Formatting in Balloons, instructs Word to display comments and formatting changes in balloons and all other changes inline. If you wanted all changes to appear in balloons or all changes to appear inline, you would perform the following steps.

1. Click the Balloons button on the Review tab.

2. If you want all revisions to appear in balloons, click Show Revisions in Balloons. If you want all revisions to appear inline, click Show All Revisions Inline.

To Disable Tracked Changes

When you have finished tracking changes, you should disable (turn off) the Track Changes feature so that Word stops marking your revisions. The next step disables tracked changes.

1 To turn the Track Changes feature off, click Tracking Changes button on the status bar, or click the Track Changes button arrow on the Review tab and then click Track Changes, or press CTRL+SHIFT+E.

To Edit a Comment in a Comment Balloon

You modify comments in a comment balloon by clicking inside the comment balloon and editing the same way you edit text in the document window. The following steps edit a comment in a balloon.

1 Click at the end of the text in the second comment balloon to place the insertion point after the period.

2 Press the SPACEBAR and then type this sentence (Figure 7–12): `Also, add a caption to the figure.`

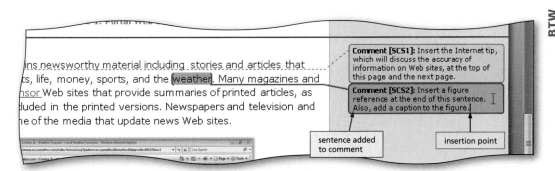

Figure 7–12

BTW

Responding to Comments
To respond to a comment, click the comment balloon and then click the Insert Comment button on the Review tab. Type your response in the new comment balloon.

To Use the Reviewing Pane

As an alternative to reading through tracked changes in the document window and comment balloons in the Markup Area, some users prefer to view tracked changes and comments in the **Reviewing Pane**. The Reviewing Pane can be displayed either at the left edge (vertically) or the bottom (horizontally) of the screen. The following steps display the Reviewing Pane on the screen.

1

• Click the Reviewing Pane button arrow on the Review tab to display the Reviewing Pane menu (Figure 7–13).

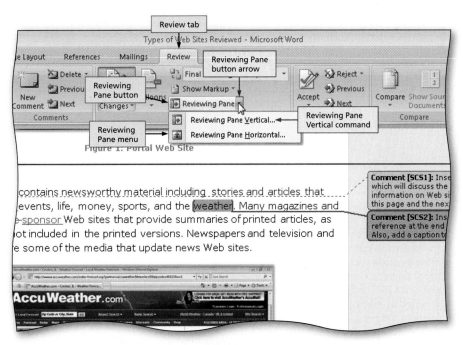

Figure 7–13

②

- Click Reviewing Pane Vertical on the Reviewing Pane menu to display the Reviewing Pane on the left side of the Word window.

③

- Click the Balloons button on the Review tab to display the Balloons menu (Figure 7–14).

Q&A

Why click the Balloons button?

Because the Reviewing Pane shows all comments, you do not need the Markup Area to display comment balloons. Thus, you will display all revisions inline.

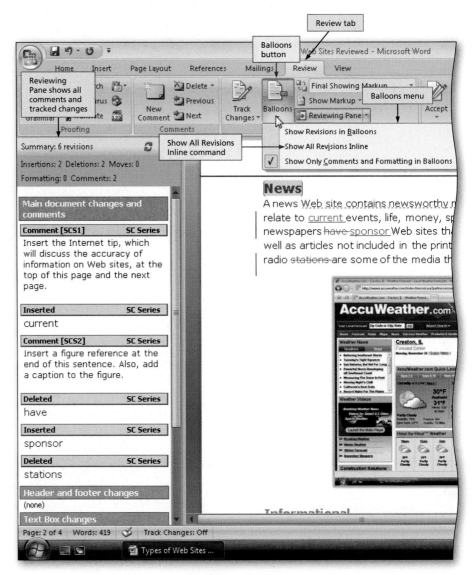

Figure 7–14

BTW

Certification
The Microsoft Certified Application Specialist (MCAS) program provides an opportunity for you to obtain a valuable industry credential — proof that you have the Word 2007 skills required by employers. For more information see Appendix G or visit the Word 2007 Certification Web page (scsite.com/wd2007/cert).

4

- Click Show All Revisions Inline to remove the Markup Area from the Word window and place all markups inline (Figure 7–15).

Can I edit revisions in the Reviewing Pane?

Yes. Simply click in the Reviewing Pane and edit the text the same way you edit in the document window.

5

- Click the Close button on the Reviewing Pane to close the pane.

- Click the Balloons button on the Review tab and then click Show Only Comments and Formatting in Balloons, so that the Markup Area reappears.

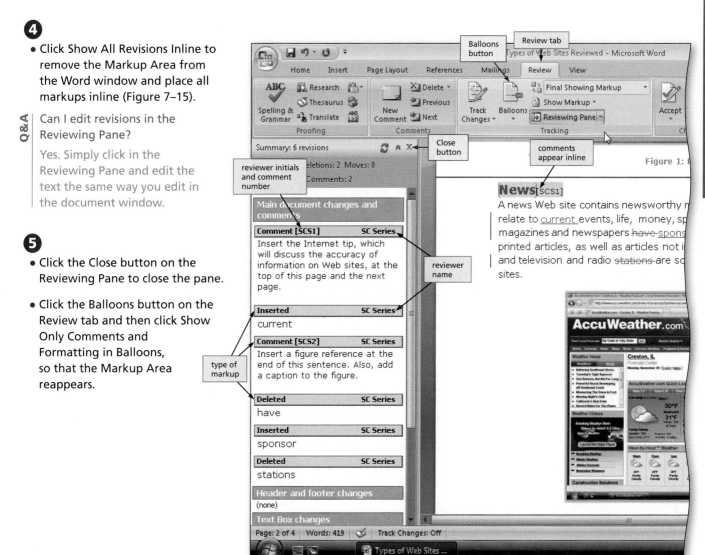

Figure 7–15

To Print Markups

When you print a document with comments and tracked changes, Word chooses the zoom percentage and page orientation to best display the comments in the printed document. You can print the document and the markups, which looks similar to how the Word window shows the markups on the screen, or you can print just the list of the markups. If you wanted to print markups, you would perform the following steps.

1. Click the Office Button, point to Print, and then click Print to display the Print dialog box.

2. To print the document and the markups, click the Print what box arrow and then click Document showing markup. To print just the markups (without printing the document), click the Print what box arrow and then click List of markup.

3. Click the OK button.

BTW

Locating Comments by Reviewer
You can find a comment through the Go To dialog box. Click the Find button arrow on the Home tab and then click Go To or press CTRL+G to display the Go To dialog box. Click Comment in the 'Go to what' list. Select the reviewer whose comments you wish to find and then click the Next button. You also can click the Select Browse Object button on the vertical scroll bar and then click Comment to scroll through comments.

Reviewing Tracked Changes and Comments

After tracking changes and entering comments in a document, you send the document to the originator for his or her review. For demonstration purposes in this chapter, you assume the role of originator and review the tracked changes and comments in the document.

To do this, be sure the markups are displayed on the screen. Click the Show Markup button on the Review tab and verify that Comments, Insertions and Deletions, and Formatting each have a check mark beside them. Ensure the Display for Review is Final Showing Markup; if it is not, click the Display for Review box arrow and then click Final Showing Markup.

The default Display for Review view is Final Showing Markup. This option shows the final document with tracked changes. To see how a document will look if you accept all the changes, without actually accepting them, click the Display for Review button arrow and then click Final. If you print this document, it will show how the document will look if you accept all the changes.

To see how the document looked before any changes were made, click the Display for Review button arrow and then click Original. The Original Showing Markup option shows the original document with tracked changes.

When finished reviewing the different options, click the Display for Review button arrow and then click Final Showing Markup.

To Review Tracked Changes and View Comments

The next step is to review the tracked changes and read the comments in the marked up document. You could scroll through the document and point to each markup to read it, but you might overlook one or more changes using this technique. A more efficient method is to use the Review tab to review the changes and comments one at a time, deciding whether to accept, modify, or delete them. The next steps review the changes and comments in the document.

1

• Press CTRL+HOME to position the insertion point at the beginning of the document, so that Word begins the review of tracked changes from the top of the document.

• Click the Next Change button on the Review tab, which causes Word to locate and select the first markup in the document, a comment, in this case (Figure 7–16).

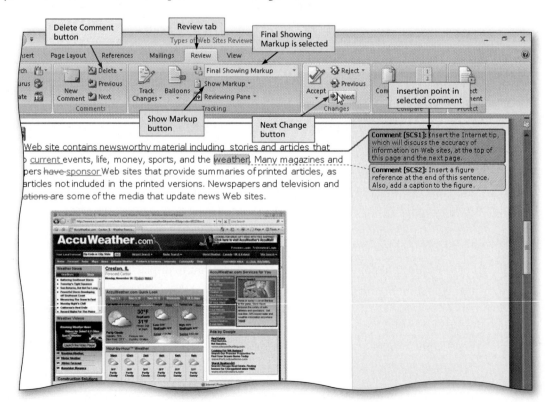

Figure 7–16

2

• Read through the comment and then click the Delete Comment button on the Review tab to remove the comment balloon from the Markup Area and comment marks in the document window (Figure 7–17).

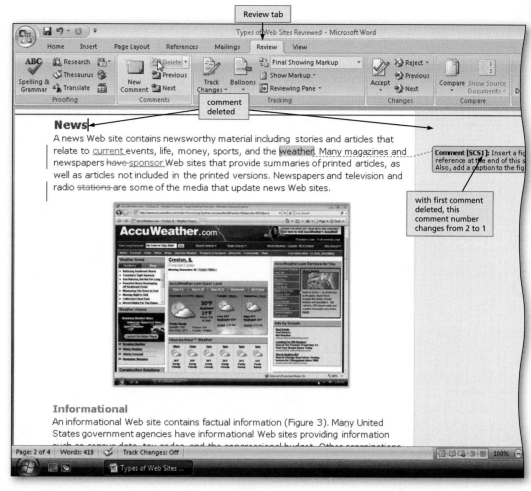

Figure 7–17

3

• Click the Next Change button on the Review tab again, so that Word locates and selects the next tracked change or comment, in this case, the inserted word, current (Figure 7–18).

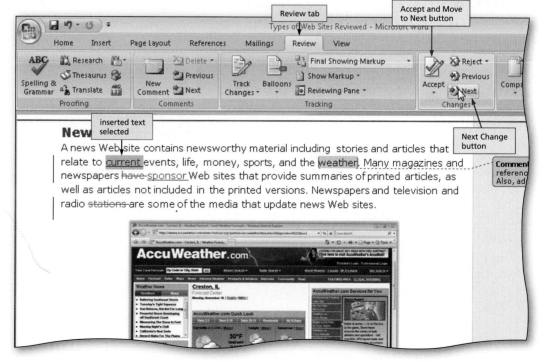

Figure 7–18

4

- Because you agree with this change, click the Accept and Move to Next button on the Review tab to accept the insertion of the word, current, and instruct Word to locate and select the next tracked change or comment, in this case, the remaining comment in the Markup Area (Figure 7–19).

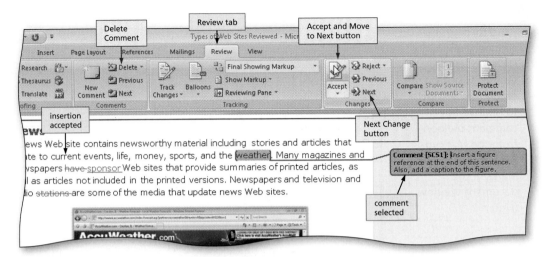

Figure 7–19

5

- Read the comment and then click the Delete Comment button on the Review tab.

- Click the Next Change button on the Review tab, so that Word locates and selects the next tracked change or comment.

- Click the Accept and Move to Next button on the Review tab to accept the deletion of the word, have, and instruct Word to locate and select the next tracked change or comment.

- Click the Accept and Move to Next button on the Review tab to accept the insertion of the word, sponsor, and instruct Word to locate and select the next tracked change or comment, in this case, the deletion of the word, stations (Figure 7–20).

6

- Because you do not agree with this change, click the Reject and Move to Next button on the Review tab to reject the marked deletion.

- Click the OK button in the dialog box that appears, which indicates the document contains no more comments or tracked changes.

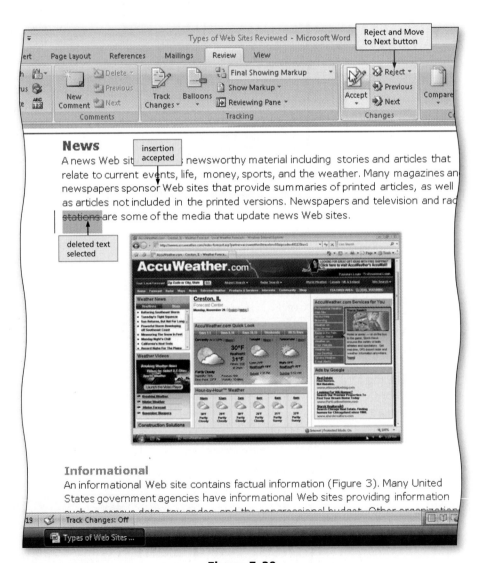

Figure 7–20

Other Ways

1. Right-click comment or tracked change, click   desired command on shortcut menu

TO DELETE ALL COMMENTS

If you wanted to delete all comments in the document at once, you would perform these steps.

1. Click the Delete Comment button arrow on the Review tab to display the Delete Comment menu.

2. Click Delete All Comments in Document on the Delete Comment menu.

Changing Tracking Options

If you wanted to change the color and markings reviewers use for tracked changes and comments or change how balloons are displayed, use the Track Changes Options dialog box (Figure 7–21). To display the Track Changes Options dialog box, click the Track Changes button arrow on the Review tab and then click Change Tracking Options on the Track Changes menu.

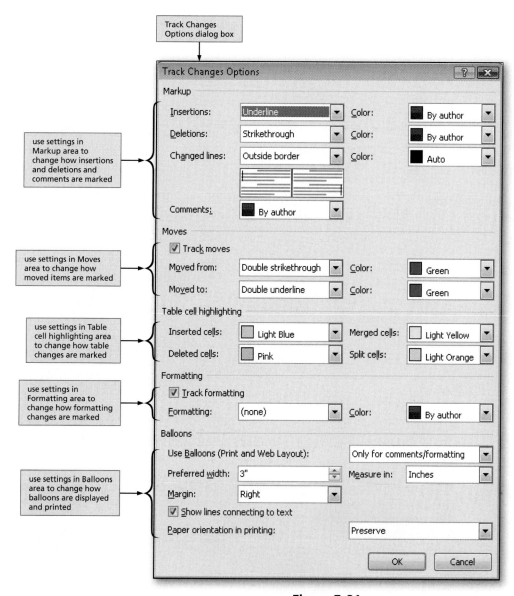

Figure 7–21

- To change how insertions and deletions are marked, modify the settings in the Markup area of the Track Changes Options dialog box.
- To change how moved items are marked, modify the settings in the Moves area of the Track Changes Options dialog box.
- To change how table changes are marked, modify the settings in the 'Table cell highlighting' area of the Track Changes Options dialog box.
- To change how formatting changes are marked, modify the settings in the Formatting area of the Track Changes Options dialog box.
- To change how balloons are displayed and printed, modify the settings in the Balloons area of the Track Changes Options dialog box.

To Save a Document Again

You have completed reviewing the document. Thus, you should save the document again.

 Save the document again with the same file name, Types of Web Sites Reviewed.

To Compare Documents

With Word, you can compare two documents to each other, which allows you easily to identify any differences between the two files. Word displays the differences between the documents as tracked changes for your review. By comparing files, you can verify that two separate files have the same or different content. If no tracked changes are found, then the two documents are identical.

Assume you want to compare the original Types of Web Sites Draft document with the Types of Web Sites Reviewed document so that you can identify the changes made to the document. The following steps compare two documents.

- Click the Compare button on the Review tab to display the Compare menu (Figure 7–22).

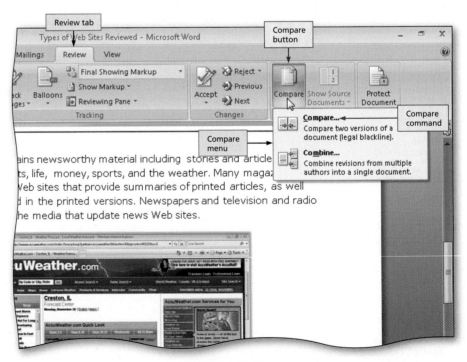

Figure 7–22

2

- Click Compare on the Compare menu to display the Compare Documents dialog box.

- Click the Original document box arrow and then click the file, Types of Web Sites Draft, in the Original document list.

Q&A What if the file is not in the Original document list?

Click the Browse for Original button, locate the file, and then click the Open button.

- Click the Revised document box arrow and then click the file, Types of Web Sites Reviewed, in the Revised document list.

Q&A What if the file is not in the Revised document list?

Click the Browse for Revised button, locate the file, and then click the Open button.

- If a More button appears in the dialog box, click it to expand the dialog box.

- If necessary, in the 'Show changes in' area, click New document so that tracked changes are marked in a new document. Ensure that all your settings in the expanded dialog box (below the Less button) match those in Figure 7–23.

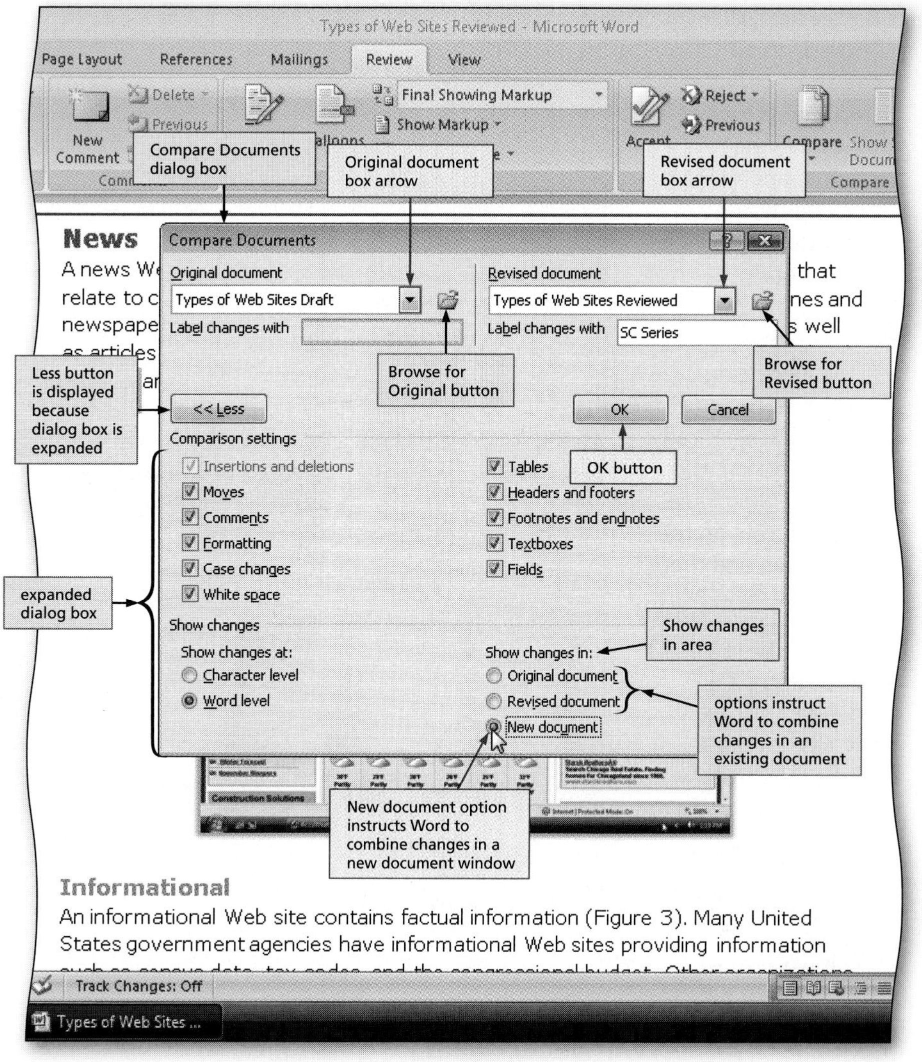

3

- Click the OK button to open a new document window and display the differences between the two documents as tracked changes in the new document window.

- Because you want to see the original document (Types of Web Sites Draft) and the revised document (Types of Web Sites Reviewed) on the screen along with the new document, verify that these documents are displayed on the screen by clicking the Show Source Documents button on the Review tab to display the Show Source Documents menu (Figure 7–24).

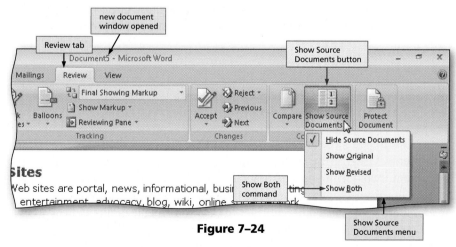

Figure 7–23

Figure 7–24

Q&A What if my screen already displays the original and revised documents?

You can skip Step 4 on the next page.

4

- If necessary, click Show Both on the Show Source Documents menu to display the original and revised documents, each in a separate window on the screen.

5

- If the Reviewing Pane does not appear automatically on your screen, click the Reviewing Pane button arrow on the Review tab and then click Reviewing Pane Vertical.

- Click the Next Change button on the Review tab to display the first tracked change in the compared document. If necessary, scroll to see the changes (Figure 7–25).

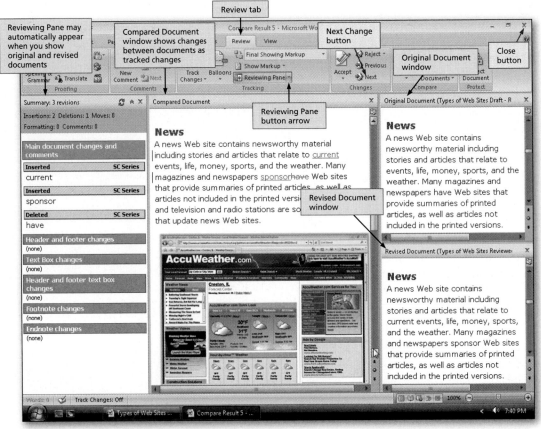

Figure 7–25

 Experiment

- Scroll through the Compared Document window and watch the Original Document window and Revised Document window scroll synchronously.

6

- When finished comparing the documents, click the Close button in the document window and then click the No button when Word asks if you want to save the compare results.

To Combine Revisions from Multiple Authors

Often, you have multiple reviewers that send you their markups (tracked changes) for the same original documents. Using Word, you can combine the tracked changes from multiple reviewers' documents into a single document, two documents at a time, until all documents are combined. Combining documents allows you to review all markups from a single document, from which you can accept and reject changes and read comments. Each reviewer's markups are shaded in a different color to help you visually differentiate among multiple reviewers' markups.

Assume you want to combine the original Types of Web Sites Draft document with the Types of Web Sites Reviewed document and also with a document called Types of Web Sites Reviewed by R. Smith, which is on the Data Files for Students. See the inside back cover of this book for instructions on downloading the Data Files for Students, or contact your instructor for information about accessing the required files. The next steps combine the three documents, two at a time.

1

- Click the Compare button on the Review tab to display the Compare menu (Figure 7–26).

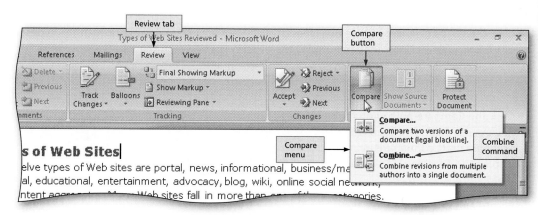

Figure 7–26

2

- Click Combine on the Compare menu to display the Combine Documents dialog box.

- Click the Original document box arrow and then click the file, Types of Web Sites Draft, in the Original document list.

Q&A What if the file is not in the Original document list?

Click the Browse for Original button, locate the file, and then click the Open button.

- Click the Revised document box arrow and then click the file, Types of Web Sites Reviewed, in the Revised document list.

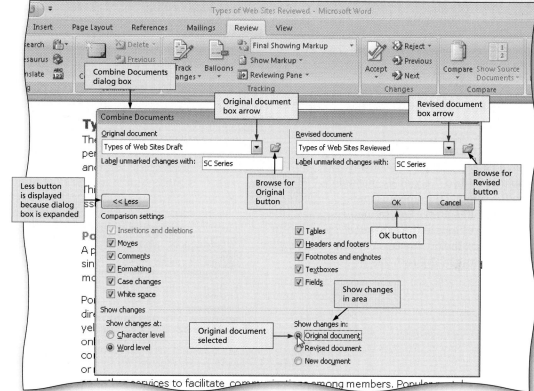

Figure 7–27

Q&A What if the file is not in the Revised document list?

Click the Browse for Revised button, locate the file, and then click the Open button.

- If a More button appears in the dialog box, click it to expand the dialog box.

- In the 'Show changes in' area, click Original document so that tracked changes are marked in the original document (Types of Web Sites Draft). Ensure that all your settings in the expanded dialog box (below the Less button) match those in Figure 7–27.

3

- Click the OK button to combine the Types of Web Sites Reviewed document with the Types of Web Sites Draft document and display the differences between the two documents as tracked changes in the Types of Web Sites Draft document.

4

- Click the Compare button on the Review tab again and then click Combine on the Compare menu to display the Combine Documents dialog box.

- Locate and display the file name, Types of Web Sites Draft, in the Original document text box.

- Locate and display the file name, Types of Web Sites Reviewed by R. Smith, in the Revised document text box.

- If a More button appears in the dialog box, click it to expand the dialog box.

- If necessary, in the 'Show changes in' area, click Original document so that tracked changes are marked in the original document (Types of Web Sites Draft). Ensure that all your settings in the expanded dialog box (below the Less button) match those in Figure 7–28.

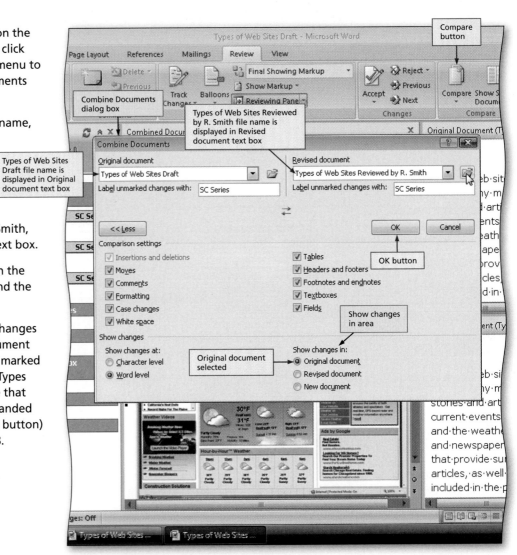

Figure 7–28

5
- Click the OK button to combine the Types of Web Sites Reviewed by R. Smith document with the currently combined document and display the differences between the three documents as tracked changes in the Types of Web Sites Draft document.

- If the source documents are displayed in the document window, click the Show Source Documents button on the Review tab to display the Show Source Documents menu (Figure 7–29).

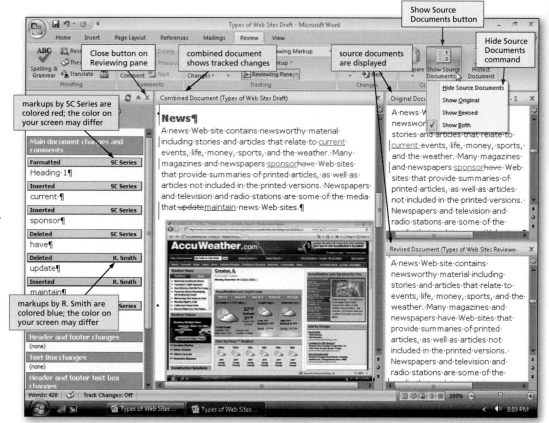

Figure 7–29

6
- Click the Hide Source Documents to close the Original Document window and the Revised Document window.

- If the Reviewing Pane is displayed, click its Close button.

BTW

Compare and Merge
If you wanted to compare two documents and merge the changes into an existing document instead of into a new document, you would do the following: click the Compare button on the Review tab, click Compare on the Compare menu, locate the original and revised documents via the dialog box, click 'Original document' to merge into the original document or click 'Revised document' to merge into the revised document, and then click the OK button.

To Show Tracked Changes and Comments by a Single Reviewer

In the documents just combined, you previously have seen all the SC Series (red) markups. R. Smith had this additional markup (in blue): replace the word, update, with the word, maintain. Instead of looking through a document for a particular reviewer's markups, you can show markups by reviewer. The following steps show the markups by the reviewer named R. Smith.

- Click the Show Markup button on the Review tab and then point to Reviewers on the Show Markup menu to display the Reviewers submenu (Figure 7–30).

Q&A What if my Reviewers submenu differs?

Your submenu may have additional or different reviewer names or colors, depending on your Word settings.

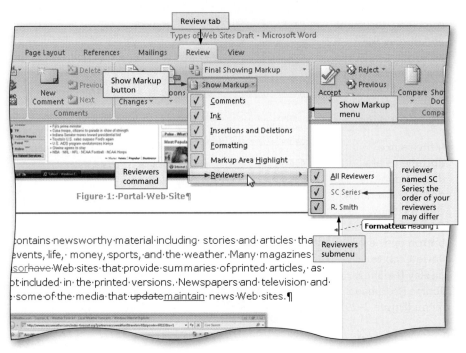

Figure 7–30

- Click SC Series on the Reviewers submenu to hide SC Series markups, which leaves markups by R. Smith displaying on the screen.

Q&A Are the SC Series reviewer markups deleted?

No. They are hidden from view.

- If necessary, scroll to redisplay the remaining markups in the document window (Figure 7–31).

- Redisplay all reviewer comments by clicking the Show Markup button on the Review tab, pointing to Reviewers, and then clicking All Reviewers on the Reviewers submenu.

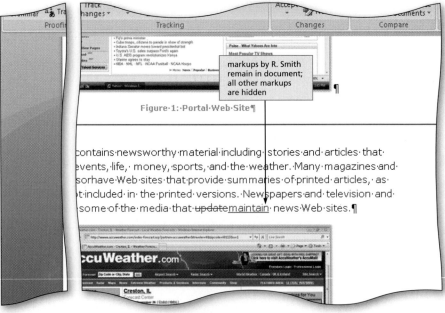

Figure 7–31

To Accept All Changes in a Document

If you are certain you plan to accept all changes in a document that contains tracked changes, you can accept all the changes at once. Doing this instructs Word that you agree with all changes in the combined document. Thus, the following steps reject the first change and then accept all remaining changes in a document.

1
- Click the Next Change button on the Review tab to locate the next change in the document (the formatting change) and then click the Reject and Move to Next button to reject the change.

2
- Click the Accept and Move to Next button arrow on the Review tab to display the Accept and Move to Next menu (Figure 7–32).

3
- Click Accept All Changes in Document, which instructs Word to accept all changes.

Q&A Can I reject all changes in a document?

Yes. You would click the Reject and Move to Next button arrow and then click Reject All Changes in Document.

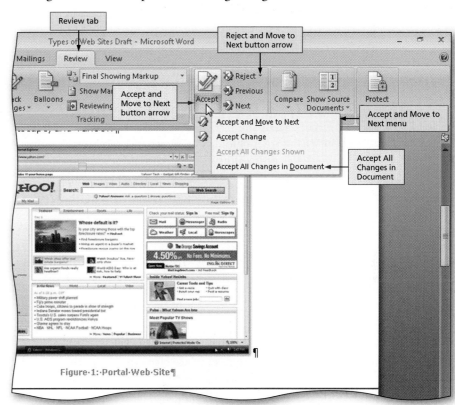

Figure 7–32

To Customize the Status Bar

You are finished working with tracked changes in this chapter. The following steps remove the Tracking Changes button from the status bar.

1 Right-click anywhere on the status bar to display the Customize Status Bar menu.

2 Remove the check mark beside the Track Changes command, which removes the Tracking Changes button from the status bar.

3 Press the ESCAPE key to remove the Customize Status Bar menu from the screen.

To Save a Document with a New File Name and Close It

The next step is to save the draft document with a new file name.

1 Click the Office Button and then click Save As on the Office Button menu to display the Save As dialog box.

2 Type Types of Web Sites Combined in the File name text box to change the file name.

3 Locate and select your USB flash drive in the list of available drives.

4 Click the Save button in the Save As dialog box to save the document on the USB flash drive with the new file name, Types of Web Sites Combined.

5 Close any open documents.

Preparing a Document To Be Included in a Reference Document

Before including the Types of Web Sites document in a longer document, you will make several modifications to the document:

1. Open the document to be modified.
2. Add a caption to the figure in the News section.
3. Insert a reference to the figure in the text.
4. Mark an index entry.
5. Insert text boxes that contain Internet tips.
6. Compress the pictures.

The following pages outline these changes.

Plan Ahead

> **Prepare a document to be included in a longer document.**
> Ensure that reference elements in a document, such as captions and index entries, are formatted properly and entered consistently.
>
> - **Captions.** A **caption** is text that appears outside of an illustration, usually below it. If the illustration is identified with a number, the caption may include the word, Figure, along with the illustration number (i.e., Figure 1). In the caption, separate the figure number from the text of the figure by a space or punctuation mark such as a period or colon (Figure 1: Portal Web Site).
>
> - **Index Entries.** If your document will include an index, read through the document and mark any terms or headings that you want to appear in the index. Include any term that the reader may want to locate quickly. Omit figures from index entries if the document will have a table of figures; otherwise, include figures in the index if appropriate.

To Open a Word Document and Save It with a New File Name

The first step is to open the file called Types of Web Sites Draft 2 on the Data Files for Students, so that you can modify it. See the inside back cover of this book for instructions on downloading the Data Files for Students, or contact your instructor for information about accessing the required files. To preserve the contents of the original Types of Web Sites Draft 2 file, you will save it with a new file name. The following steps open a document and save it with a new file name.

1 Click the Office Button and then click Open to display the Open dialog box.

2 Locate and then select the file with the name Types of Web Sites Draft 2 and then click the Open button to display the document in the Word window.

3 Click the Office Button and then click Save As on the Office Button menu to display the Save As dialog box.

4 Type `Types of Web Sites Final` in the File name text box to change the file name.

5 Locate and select your USB flash drive in the list of available drives.

6 Click the Save button in the Save As dialog box to save the document on the USB flash drive with the new file name, Types of Web Sites Final.

7 If your zoom level is not 100%, click the Zoom Out or Zoom In button as many times as necessary until the Zoom level button displays 100% on its face.

8 Display the top of page 2 in the document window because this is the page that will contain the modifications.

To Add a Caption

In this reference document, the captions contain the word, Figure, followed by the figure number, followed by a figure description. In Word, you can add a caption to an equation, a figure, and a table. If you move, delete, or add captions in a document, Word renumbers remaining captions in the document automatically. In the Types of Web Sites document, the illustration in the News section is missing its caption. The following steps add a caption to the illustration.

1

• Click the graphic to select it.

• Display the References tab.

• Click the Insert Caption button on the References tab to display the Caption dialog box with a figure number automatically assigned to the selected graphic (Figure 7–33).

Q&A Why is the figure number a 2?

The document already contains a Figure 1 as a caption. When you insert a new caption, or move or delete items containing captions, Word automatically updates caption numbers throughout the document.

Q&A What if the Caption text box has the label Table or Equation instead of Figure?

Click the Label box arrow in the Caption dialog box and then click Figure.

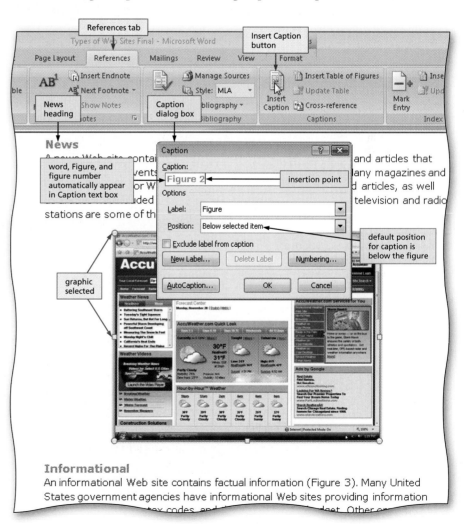

Figure 7–33

- Press the COLON (:) key and then press the SPACEBAR.

- Type News as the caption description (Figure 7–34).

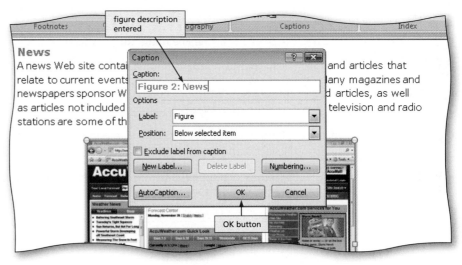

Figure 7–34

- Click the OK button to insert the caption below the selected graphic.

- If necessary, scroll to display the caption in the document window (Figure 7–35).

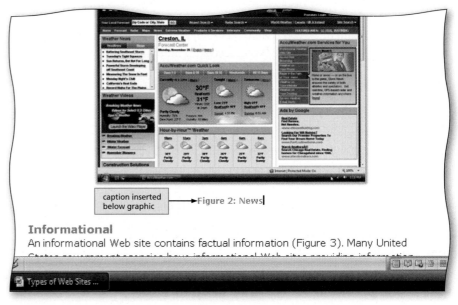

Figure 7–35

Caption Numbers

Each caption number contains a field. In Word, a **field** is a placeholder for data that might change in a document. Examples of fields you have used in previous projects are page numbers, merge fields, IF fields, form fields, and the current date. You update caption numbers using the same technique used to update any other field. That is, to update all caption numbers, select the entire document and then press the F9 key or right-click the field and click Update Field on the shortcut menu. When you print a document, Word updates the caption numbers automatically, regardless of whether the document window displays the updated caption numbers.

To Create a Cross-Reference

In reference documents, the text should reference a particular figure and explain the contents of the figure. The next step in this project is to add a reference to the new Figure 2. Because figures may be inserted, deleted, or moved, you may not know the actual figure number in the final document. For this reason, Word provides a method of creating a **cross-reference**, which is a link to an item such as a heading, caption, or footnote in a document. By creating a cross-reference to the caption, the text that mentions the figure will be updated whenever the caption to the figure is updated. The following steps create a cross-reference.

- At the end of the first sentence below the News heading, position the insertion point to the left of the period, press the SPACEBAR, and then press the LEFT PARENTHESIS key.

- Click the Cross-reference button on the References tab to display the Cross-reference dialog box (Figure 7–36).

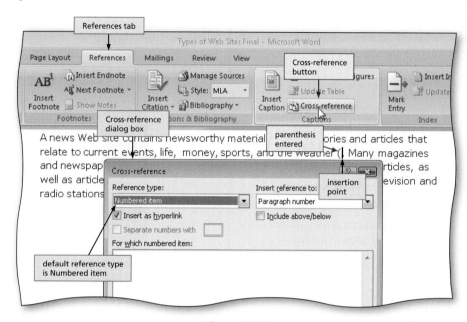

Figure 7–36

- Click the Reference type box arrow; scroll to and then click Figure, which displays a list of figures from the document in the 'For which caption' list.

- In the 'For which caption' list, click Figure 2: News.

- Click the 'Insert reference to' box arrow and then click 'Only label and number' to instruct Word that the cross-reference in the document should list just the label, Figure, followed by the number 2 (Figure 7–37).

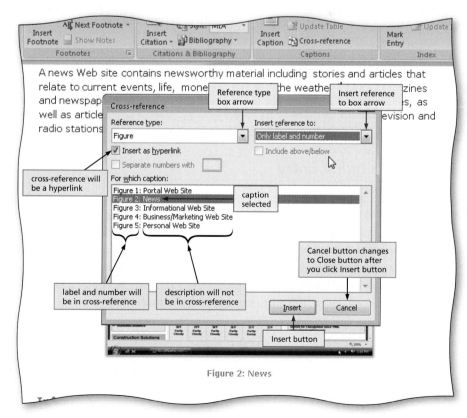

Figure 7–37

• Click the Insert button to insert the cross-reference in the document at the location of the insertion point.

Q&A What if my cross-reference is shaded gray?

The cross-reference is a field. Depending on your Word settings, fields may appear shaded in gray to help you identify them on the screen.

• Click the Close button in the Cross-reference dialog box.

• Press the RIGHT PARENTHESIS key to close off the cross-reference (Figure 7–38).

Q&A How do I update a cross-reference if a caption is added, deleted, or moved?

In many cases, Word automatically updates cross-references in a document if the item it refers to changes. To update a cross-reference manually, select the cross-reference and then press the F9 key, or right-click the cross-reference and then click Update Field on the shortcut menu.

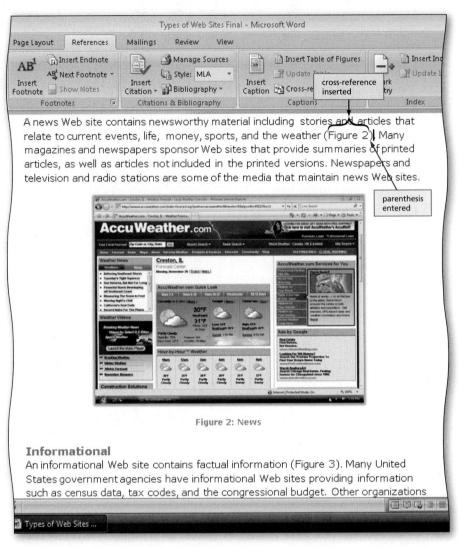

Figure 2: News

Figure 7–38

To Mark an Index Entry

The last page of the reference document in this project is an index, which lists important terms discussed in the document along with each term's corresponding page number. For Word to generate the index, you first must mark any text you wish to appear in the index. When you mark an index entry, Word creates a field that it uses to build the index. Index entry fields are hidden and are displayed on the screen only when you show formatting marks, that is, when the Show/Hide ¶ button on the Home tab is selected.

In this document, you want the text, news Web site, in the first sentence below the News heading to be marked as an index entry. The next steps mark an index entry.

1

- Select the text you wish to appear in the index (the words, news Web site, in this case).

- Click the Mark Entry button on the References tab to display the Mark Index Entry dialog box (Figure 7–39).

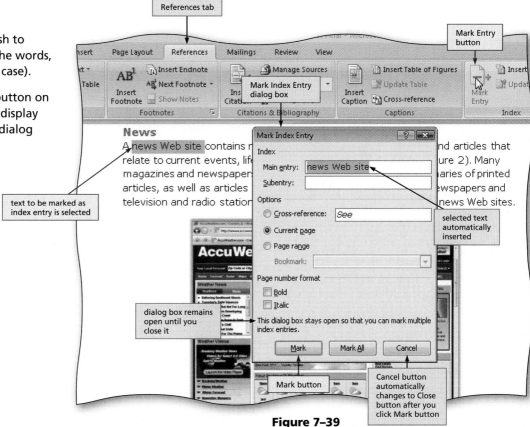

Figure 7–39

2

- Click the Mark button to mark the selected text in the document as an index entry (Figure 7–40).

- Click the Close button in the Mark Index Entry dialog box.

Q&A

Why do formatting marks now appear on the screen?

When you mark an index entry, Word automatically shows formatting marks so that you can see the index entry field. To hide the formatting marks, click the Show/Hide ¶ button on the Home tab.

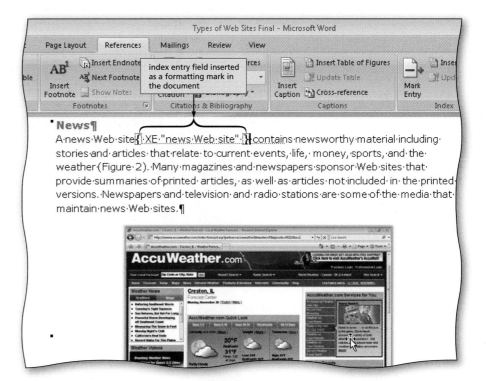

Figure 7–40

Other Ways

1. Select text, press ALT+SHIFT+X

BTW

Index Entries
Index entries may include a switch, which is a slash followed by a letter inserted after the field text. Switches include \b to apply bold formatting to the entry's page number, \f to define an entry type, \i to make the entry's page number italic, \r to insert a range of pages numbers, \t to insert specified text in place of a page number, and \y to specify that the subsequent text defines the pronunciation for the index entry. A colon in an index entry precedes a subentry keyword in the index.

TO MARK MULTIPLE INDEX ENTRIES

Word leaves the Mark Index Entry dialog box open until you close it, which allows you to mark multiple index entries without having to reopen the dialog box repeatedly. To mark multiple index entries, you would perform the following steps.

1. With the Mark Index Entry dialog box displayed, click in the document window; scroll to and select the next index entry.

2. If necessary, click the Main entry text box in the Mark Index Entry dialog box to display the selected text in the Main entry text box.

3. Click the Mark button.

4. Repeat Steps 1 through 3 for all entries. When finished, click the Close button in the dialog box.

To Search for and Highlight Specific Text

This document contains several marked index entries. Notice that the marked index entry begins with the letters, XE. You could scroll through the document, scanning for all occurrences of XE, to locate all the index entries. Or, you could use Word to highlight all occurrences of XE in the document so that you easily can locate them. The following steps search for and highlight all occurrences of XE in the document.

1

- Display the Home tab.

- Click the Find button on the Home tab to display the Find and Replace dialog box.

- Type XE in the Find what text box.

- Click the Reading Highlight button to display the Reading Highlight menu (Figure 7–41).

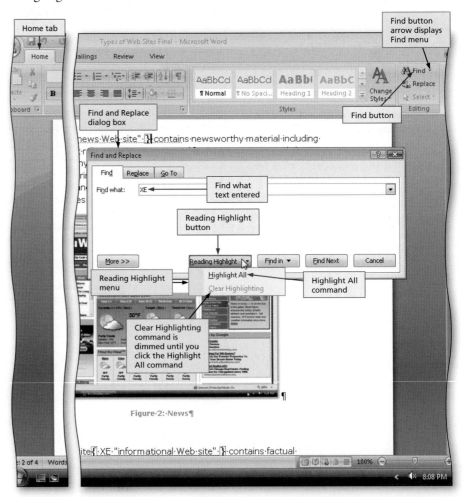

Figure 7–41

- Click Highlight All on the Reading Highlight menu to highlight in yellow all occurrences of the text, XE, in the document (Figure 7–42).

Experiment

- Scroll through the document to see other occurrences of the highlighted text.

- Turn off the highlighting by clicking the Reading Highlight button again and then clicking Clear Highlighting on the Reading Highlight menu (shown in Figure 7–41).

- Close the Find and Replace dialog box.

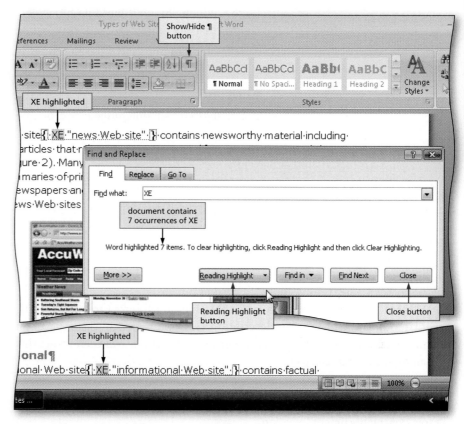

Figure 7–42

To Hide Formatting Marks

To remove the clutter of index entry fields from the document, you should hide formatting marks.

1 If the Show/Hide ¶ button on the Home tab is selected, click it to hide formatting marks.

Q&A What if the index entries still appear after clicking the Show/Hide ¶ button?

Click the Office Button, click the Word Options button, click Display in the left pane, remove the check mark from the Hidden text check box, and then click the OK button.

Building Blocks

Word includes many predefined **building blocks**, which are reusable formatted objects that are stored in galleries. Examples of building blocks include cover pages, headers, footers, page numbers, and text boxes. When you inserted a formatted header, for instance, you are working with a building block.

You can see a list of every available building block in the **Building Blocks Organizer**. From the Building Blocks Organizer, you can sort building blocks, change their properties, or insert them in a document. The project in this chapter uses a text box building block, specifically the Sideline Sidebar building block. The next pages follow these general steps to insert and format the building block.

1. Sort the building blocks in the Building Block Organizer.

2. Insert the Sideline Sidebar text box building block in the document.

3. Enter text in the text box.

4. Insert another Sideline Sidebar text box building block in the document.

5. Link the two text boxes together so that the text flows automatically from one text box to the other.

To Sort Building Blocks and Insert a Sidebar Text Box Building Block Using the Building Blocks Organizer

A **sidebar text box** is a text box that runs across the top or bottom of a page or along the edge of the right or left of a page. As an alternative to inserting a text box using the Text Box gallery, you can insert a text box (or any building block) using the Building Blocks Organizer.

To easily locate building blocks in the Building Blocks Organizer, you can sort its contents by name, gallery, category, template, behavior, or description. The following steps sort the Building Blocks Organizer by gallery, so that all the text box building blocks are grouped together, and then insert the Sideline Sidebar building block in the document on the current page.

- Be sure the insertion point is on page 2 of the document; building blocks are inserted on the current page.

- Display the Insert tab.

- Click the Quick Parts button on the Insert tab to display the Quick Parts menu (Figure 7–43).

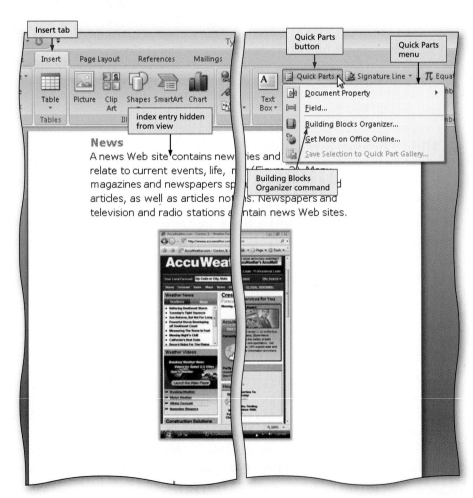

Figure 7–43

2

• Click Building Blocks Organizer on the Quick Parts menu to display the Building Blocks Organizer dialog box.

Experiment

• Drag the horizontal scroll bar in the Building Blocks Organizer dialog box to the right so that you can look at all the columns. When finished, drag the horizontal scroll bar back to the left in the Building Blocks Organizer dialog box.

3

• Click the Gallery heading in the Building blocks list to sort the building blocks by gallery (Figure 7–44).

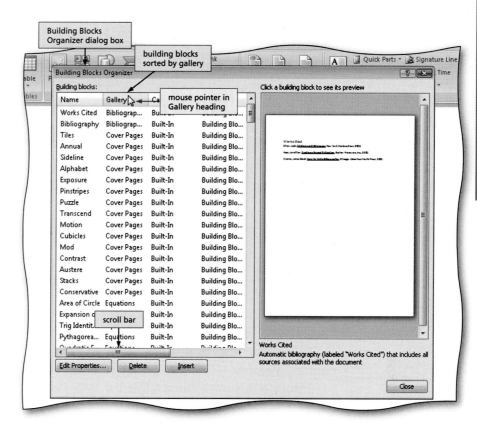

Figure 7–44

4

• Position the mouse pointer between the Name and Gallery column headings and double-click when the mouse pointer changes to a two-headed arrow, so that you can see the entire name in the first column of the list.

Experiment

• Click various names in the Building blocks list and notice a preview of the selected building block appears in the dialog box.

5

• Scroll through the Building blocks list to the Text Boxes group in the Gallery column and then click Sideline Sidebar to select it (Figure 7–45).

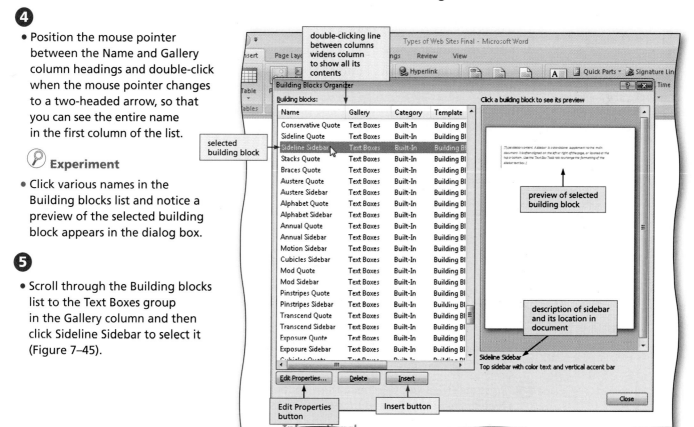

Figure 7–45

6

- Click the Insert button to insert the selected building block in the document on the current page (Figure 7–46).

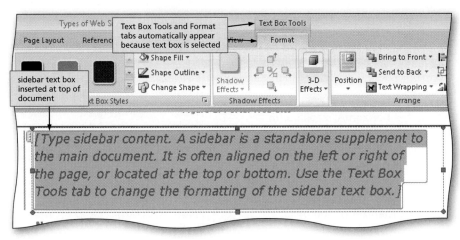

Figure 7–46

BTW

Equations
Word includes several predefined mathematical equations that you can insert in a document and then edit, if desired. You insert an equation, such as the quadratic equation, using the Building Blocks Organizer. Or, you can click the Equation button on the Insert tab to display the Equation Tools Design tab, which enables you to insert and customize equations.

TO EDIT PROPERTIES OF BUILDING BLOCK ELEMENTS

Properties of a building block include its name, gallery, category, description, location where it is saved, and how it is inserted in the document. If you wanted to change any of these building block properties for a particular building block, you would perform these steps.

1. Click the Quick Parts button on the Insert tab to display the Quick Parts menu.
2. Click Building Blocks Organizer on the Quick Parts menu to display the Building Blocks Organizer dialog box.
3. Select the building block you wish to edit.
4. Click the Edit Properties button (shown in Figure 7–45 on the previous page) to display the Modify Building Block dialog box.
5. Edit any property in the dialog box and then click the OK button. Close the Building Blocks Organizer dialog box.

To Enter Text in the Sidebar Text Box

The next step is to enter the text in the sidebar text box, up to the numbered list.

1 If necessary, click the sidebar text box to select it.

2 Press the DELETE key to delete the current content of the sidebar text box.

3 In a 14-point bold italic font, type `Internet Tip:` and then press the ENTER key.

4 Type the following paragraph: `Do not assume that information presented on the Web is correct or accurate. Any organization, company, or person can publish a Web page on the Internet. No one oversees the content of these Web pages.`

5 Press the ENTER key. Use the buttons on the Home tab to change the font size to 12 point. Type `Internet Tip:` and then press the ENTER key.

6 Type `Criteria for assessing the value of a Web site:` and then press the ENTER key (Figure 7–47).

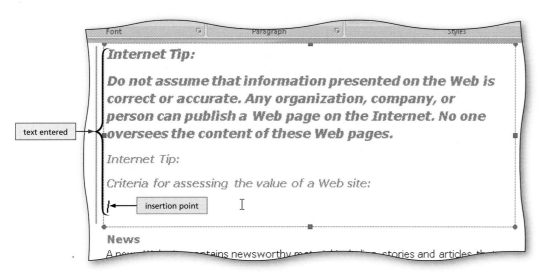

Figure 7–47

To Enter and Format a Numbered List

The last part of the text in the text box is a numbered list. After entering the numbered list, you change the format of the numbers so that they are followed by parentheses instead of periods. Also, a numbered list, by default, is indented. Because the sidebar text box has a vertical line along its left edge, you remove the indent so that the vertical line is not broken. The following steps enter and format a numbered list.

- If necessary, display the Home tab.

- Click the Numbering button on the Home tab to turn on numbering, which automatically displays a number 1 followed by a period.

- Type The information on a Web site should be current. and then press the ENTER key.

- Enter the remaining text for numbers 2 through 6, as shown in Figure 7–48, pressing the ENTER key at the end of each line, except for the last one.

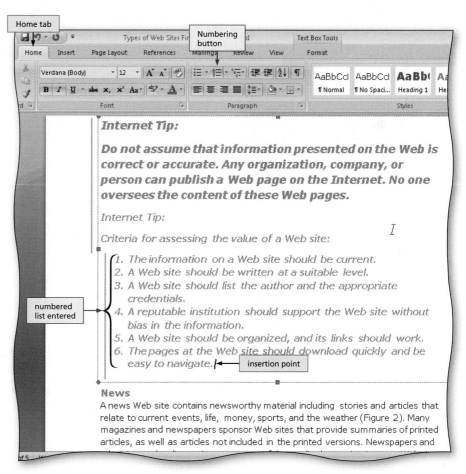

Figure 7–48

- Select the numbered list by dragging through it.

- Click the Numbering button arrow on the Home tab to display the Numbering gallery (Figure 7–49).

- Select Number alignment: Left (third format in first row in Numbering Library area) to change the numbering format of the selected text.

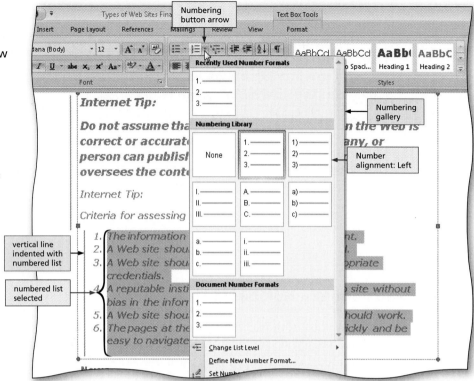

Figure 7–49

- Click the View Ruler button on the vertical scroll bar to display the rulers.

- Drag the Left Indent marker from the ½" mark on the ruler to the ¼" mark, so that the vertical line to the left of the numbered list is aligned with the rest of the text box vertical line (Figure 7–50).

- Click the View Ruler button on the vertical scroll bar to hide the rulers.

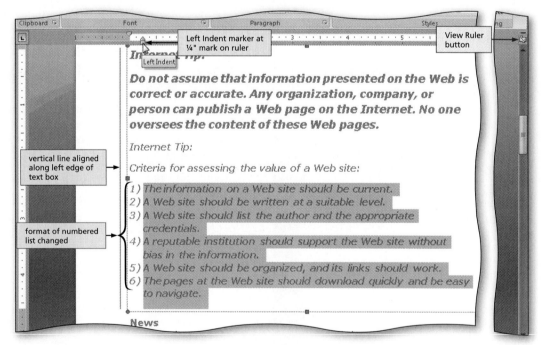

Figure 7–50

To Link Text Boxes

The text box above the News heading is too long. Instead of one long text box, this project splits the text box across the top of two pages. Word allows you to link two separate text boxes, so that the text automatically flows from one text box into the other. The following steps link text boxes.

1

- Display Figure 3 in the document window.

- Position the insertion point to the left of the figure and then press the ENTER key.

- Position the insertion point on the blank line above the figure.

- If necessary, display the Insert tab.

- Click the Quick Parts button on the Insert tab to display the Quick Parts menu.

- Click Building Blocks Organizer on the Quick Parts menu to display the Building Blocks Organizer dialog box.

- Locate the Sideline Sidebar building block and then click the Insert button to insert the sideline text box in the document.

- If necessary, click the text box to select it and then press the DELETE key to delete its contents (Figure 7–51).

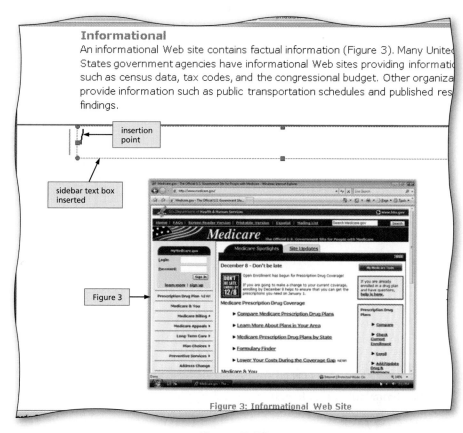

Figure 7–51

2

- Scroll to display the first text box in the document window.

- Click the text box to select it.

- Click the Create Link button on the Format tab (Figure 7–52).

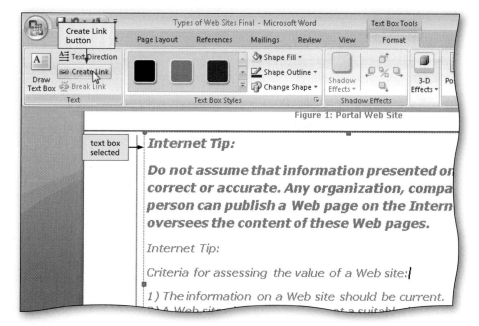

Figure 7–52

3

- Scroll to display the second (empty) text box in the document window, noticing that the mouse pointer now has the shape of a cup.

- Position the mouse pointer in the empty text box, so that the mouse pointer shape changes to a pouring cup (Figure 7–53).

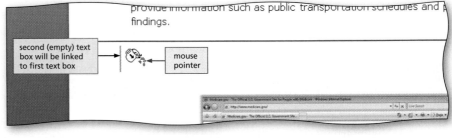

provide information such as public transportation schedules and findings.

second (empty) text box will be linked to first text box → mouse pointer

Figure 7–53

4

- Click the empty text box to link it to the first text box, which causes text from the first text box to flow into the second (linked) text box (Figure 7–54).

Q&A

How would I remove a link?

Select the text box in which you created the link and then click the Break Link button on the Format tab.

oversees the content of these Web pages. ← text from the first text box flows to second (linked) text box

Internet Tip:

Criteria for assessing the value of a Web site:

Figure 7–54

5

- Display the first text box in the document window and then select the text box.

- Resize the text box by dragging its bottom-middle sizing handle until the amount of text that is displayed in the text box is similar to Figure 7–55.

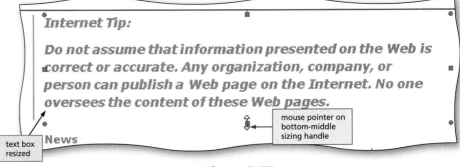

Internet Tip:

Do not assume that information presented on the Web is correct or accurate. Any organization, company, or person can publish a Web page on the Internet. No one oversees the content of these Web pages.

text box resized → News

mouse pointer on bottom-middle sizing handle

Figure 7–55

6

- Display the second text box in the document window and then select the text box.

- Resize the text box by dragging its bottom-middle sizing handle until the amount of text that is displayed in the text box is similar to Figure 7–56.

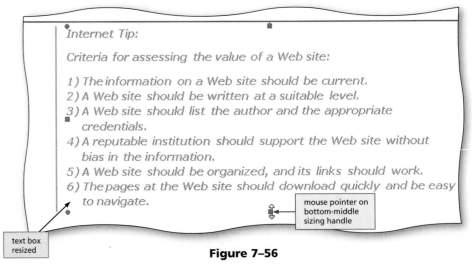

Internet Tip:

Criteria for assessing the value of a Web site:

1) The information on a Web site should be current.
2) A Web site should be written at a suitable level.
3) A Web site should list the author and the appropriate credentials.
4) A reputable institution should support the Web site without bias in the information.
5) A Web site should be organized, and its links should work.
6) The pages at the Web site should download quickly and be easy to navigate.

text box resized

mouse pointer on bottom-middle sizing handle

Figure 7–56

To Fill Text Boxes with Color

To make the sidebar text boxes more eye-catching, they are filled with a light orange color. The following steps fill a text box.

- With the second text box selected, click the Shape Fill button arrow on the Format tab to display the Shape Fill gallery.

Q&A What if the Format tab is not active?

Click Format on the Ribbon to display the Format tab.

- Point to Orange, Accent 1, Lighter 80% (fifth color in the second row) to display a live preview of this fill color (Figure 7–57).

Experiment

- Point to various colors in the Shape Fill gallery and watch the text box fill color change in the document window.

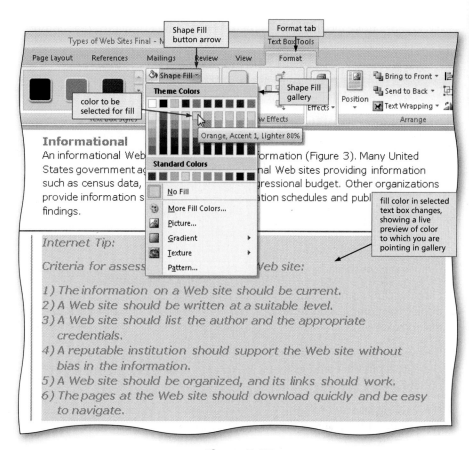

Figure 7–57

- Click Orange, Accent 1, Lighter 80% (fifth color in second row) to change fill color of the text box.

- Display the first text box in the document window and then click the text box to select it.

- Click the Shape Fill button to fill this text box with the most recently defined fill color (Orange, Accent 1, Lighter 80%), as shown in Figure 7–58.

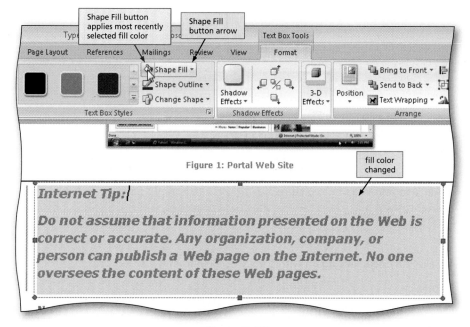

Figure 7–58

To Compress Pictures

Pictures and other illustrations in documents can increase the size of your Word documents. If you plan to e-mail a document or post it for downloading, you may want to reduce its file size to speed up file transmission time. In Word, you can compress pictures, which reduces the size of the Word document. Compressing the pictures in Word does not cause any loss in their quality. The following steps compress pictures in the document.

1

- Click any figure in the document to select it, so that the Picture Tools and Format tabs appear. If necessary, click Format to display the Format tab.

- Click the Compress Pictures button on the Format tab to display the Compress Pictures dialog box.

- If the 'Apply to selected pictures only' check box contains a check mark, click the check box to remove the check mark.

- Click the Options button to display the Compression Settings dialog box.

- If necessary, select the first two check boxes in the Compression options area.

- If necessary, select Print in the Target output area (Figure 7–59).

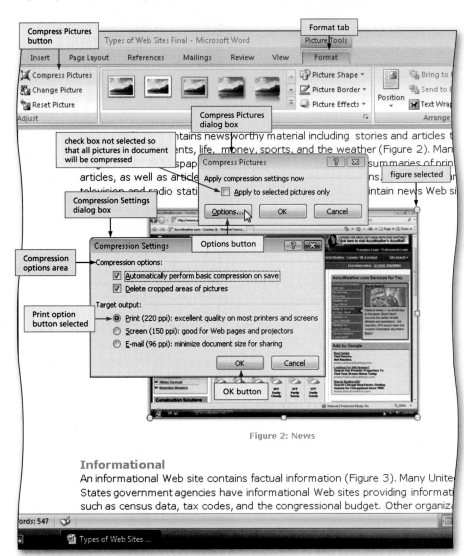

Figure 7–59

2

- Click the OK button in each dialog box to compress all pictures in the document.

Q&A

Can I compress a single picture?

Yes. Select the picture and then place a check mark in the 'Apply to selected pictures only' check box.

- Save the document again with the same file name.

Other Ways
1. Click the Tools button in the Save As dialog box, click Compress Pictures on the Tools menu

To Close a Document

You are finished modifying the Types of Web Sites Final document. Thus, you close it.

 Click the Office Button and then click Close on the Office Button menu.

Working with a Master Document

When you are creating a document that includes other files, you may want to create a master document to organize the documents. A **master document** is simply a document that contains links to one or more other documents, each of which are called a **subdocument**. In addition to subdocuments, a master document can contain its own text and graphics.

In this project, the master document file is named Internet Post - Fourth Edition. This master document file contains a link to one subdocument: the Types of Web Sites Final file. The master document also contains other items: a title page, a table of contents, a table of figures, and an index. The following pages create this master document and insert the necessary elements in the document to create the finished Internet Post - Fourth Edition document.

Outlines

To create a master document, you must be in Outline view. You then enter the headings of the document as an outline using Word's built-in heading styles. In an outline, the major heading is displayed at the left margin with each subordinate, or lower-level, heading indented. In Word, the built-in Heading 1 style is displayed at the left margin in outline view. Heading 2 style is indented below Heading 1 style, Heading 3 style is indented further, and so on.

You do not want to use a built-in heading style for the paragraphs of text within the document because when you create a table of contents, Word places all lines formatted using the built-in heading styles in the table of contents. Thus, the text below each heading is formatted using the Body Text style.

Each heading should print at the top of a new page. Because you might want to format the pages within a heading differently from those pages in other headings, you insert next page section breaks between each heading.

To Create an Outline

The Internet Post - Fourth Edition document contains these four major headings: Overview (which later is changed to Introduction), Types of Web Sites, Table of Figures, and Index. The heading, Types of Web Sites, is not entered in the outline; instead, it is part of the subdocument inserted in the master document.

The Overview section contains three paragraphs of body text, which you enter directly in the outline. The Types of Web Sites content is inserted from the subdocument. You will instruct Word to create the content for the Table of Figures and Index later in this chapter. The steps on the next pages create an outline that contains headings and body text to be used in the master document.

BTW

Master Documents
Master documents can be used when multiple people prepare different sections of a document or when a document contains separate elements such as the chapters in a book. If multiple people in a network need to work on the same document simultaneously, individual people each can work on a section (subdocument), all of which can be stored together collectively in a master document on the network server.

- To display a new blank document window, click the Office Button, click New on the Office Button menu, click Blank document in the New Document dialog box, if necessary, and then click the Create button.

- To switch to Outline view, click the Outline button on the status bar, which displays the Outlining tab on the Ribbon.

- Be sure the Show Text Formatting check box is selected on the Outlining tab.

- Type Overview as the first heading in the outline and then press the ENTER key.

- Click the Demote to Body Text button, so that you can enter the Overview paragraphs of text (Figure 7–60).

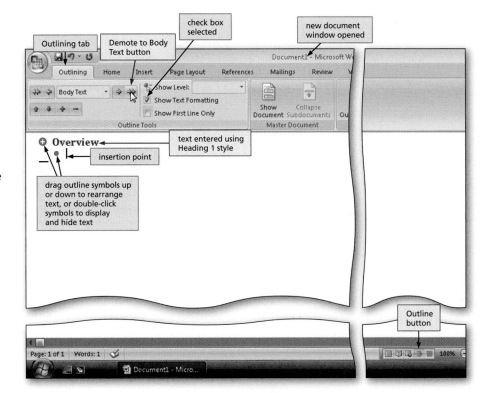

Figure 7–60

- Type the first overview paragraph shown in Figure 7–61 and then press the ENTER key.

Q&A Why is only my first line of text in the paragraph displayed?

Remove the check mark from the Show First Line Only check box on the Outlining tab.

- Type the second overview paragraph shown in Figure 7–61 and then press the ENTER key.

- Type the third overview paragraph shown in Figure 7–61 and then press the ENTER key.

- Click the Promote to Heading 1 button on the Outlining tab because you are finished entering body text and will enter the remaining headings in the outline.

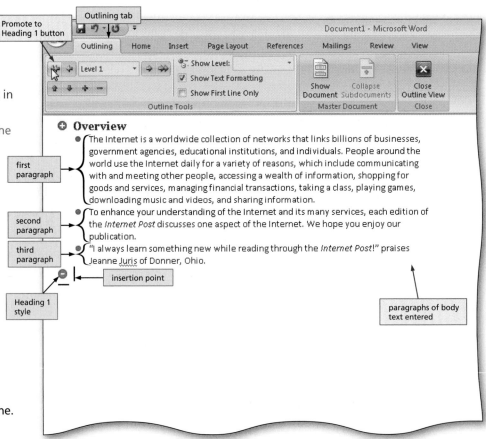

Figure 7–61

3

- Display the Page Layout tab.

- To enter a next page section break before the next heading, click the Breaks button on the Page Layout tab and then click Next Page on the Breaks menu.

4

- Type `Table of Figures` and then press the ENTER key.

- Repeat Step 3.

5

- Type `Index` as the last entry (Figure 7–62).

Q&A

Why do some outline symbols contain a plus and others a minus?

The plus means the outline level has subordinate levels; the minus means the outline level does not have any subordinate levels.

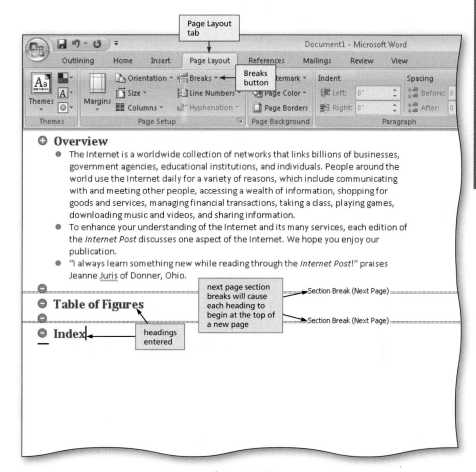

Figure 7–62

Other Ways

1. Click Outline View button on View tab

To Show First Line Only

With the Show First Line only button not selected, the content of each paragraph of body text is displayed in outline view. To make the outline more readable, users often instruct Word to display just the first line of each paragraph of body text. The following step displays only the first line of body text paragraphs.

1

- Display the Outlining tab.

- Place a check mark in the Show First Line Only check box on the Outlining tab, so that Word displays only the first line of each paragraph (Figure 7–63).

Q&A

How would I redisplay all lines of the paragraphs of body text?

Remove the check mark from the Show First Line Only check box.

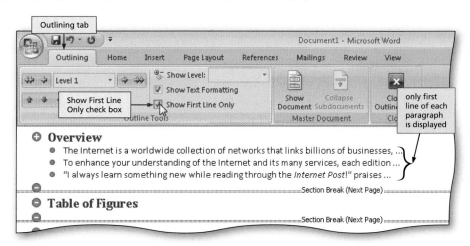

Figure 7–63

To Insert a Subdocument

The next step is to insert a subdocument in the master document. Word places the first line of text in the subdocument at the first heading level because it is defined using the Heading 1 style. The subdocument to be inserted is the Types of Web Sites Final file you modified earlier in this chapter. The following steps insert a subdocument in a master document.

- If formatting marks do not appear, click the Show/Hide ¶ button on the Home tab.

- Position the insertion point where you want to insert the subdocument (on the section break between the Overview and Table of Figures headings).

- Click the Show Document button on the Outlining tab so that all commands in the Master Document group appear.

- With the USB flash drive that contains the Types of Web Sites Final file connected to one of the computer's USB ports, click the Insert Subdocument button on the Outlining tab.

- When Word displays the Insert Subdocument dialog box, locate and select your USB flash drive in the list of available drives and then click the Types of Web Sites Final file (Figure 7–64).

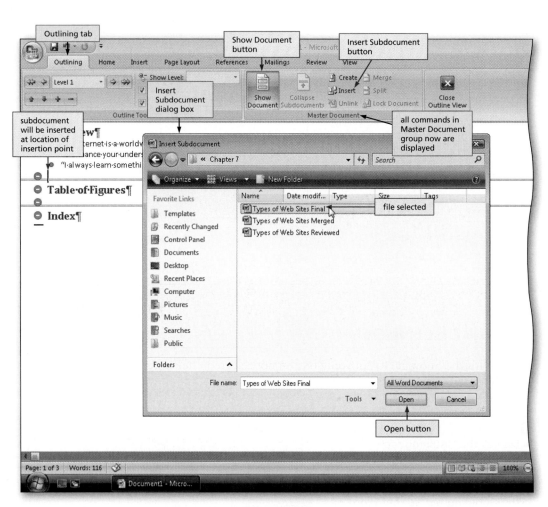

Figure 7–64

3

- Click the Open button in the dialog box to insert the selected file as a subdocument.

- If Word displays a dialog box about styles, click the No to All button.

- Press CTRL+HOME to position the insertion point at the top of the document (Figure 7–65).

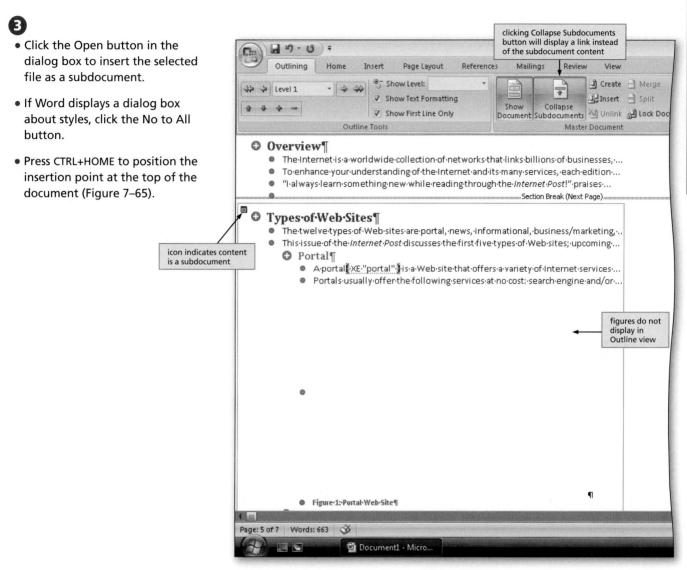

Figure 7–65

___

To Save a Document

With the headings entered and subdocument inserted, you are finished in Outline view with the master document. When you save a master document, Word also saves any subdocument files on the disk. Thus, the Types of Web Sites Final file automatically will be saved along with the master document. The following steps save the master document.

1 Click the Save button on the Quick Access Toolbar to display the Save As dialog box.

2 Type Internet Post - Fourth Edition in the File name text box to change the file name.

3 Locate and select your USB flash drive in the list of available drives.

4 Click the Save button in the Save As dialog box to save the document on the USB flash drive with the new file name, Internet Post - Fourth Edition.

Master Documents and Subdocuments

When you open the master document, the subdocuments initially are collapsed, that is, displayed as hyperlinks (Figure 7–66). To work with the contents of a master document after you open it, switch to Outline view and then expand the subdocuments by clicking the Expand Subdocuments button.

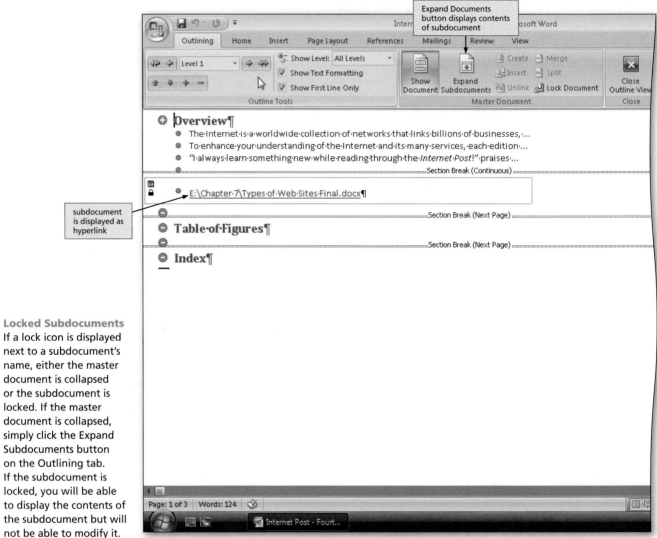

Figure 7–66

BTW

Locked Subdocuments
If a lock icon is displayed next to a subdocument's name, either the master document is collapsed or the subdocument is locked. If the master document is collapsed, simply click the Expand Subdocuments button on the Outlining tab. If the subdocument is locked, you will be able to display the contents of the subdocument but will not be able to modify it.

You can open a subdocument in a separate document window and modify it. To open a collapsed subdocument, click the hyperlink. To open an expanded subdocument, double-click the subdocument icon to the left of the document heading (shown in Figure 7-65 on the previous page).

If, for some reason, you wanted to remove a subdocument from a master document, you would expand the subdocuments, click the subdocument icon to the left of the subdocument's first heading, and then press the DELETE key. Although Word removes the subdocument from the master document, the subdocument file remains on disk.

Occasionally, you may want to convert a subdocument to part of the master document — breaking the connection between the text in the master document and the subdocument. To do this, expand the subdocuments, click the subdocument icon, and then click the Remove Subdocument button on the Outlining tab.

Organizing a Reference Document

Reference documents are organized and formatted so that users easily can navigate through and read the document. The reference document in this chapter includes the following elements: a formatted quotation, a title page, a table of contents, a table of figures, an index, alternating headers, and a gutter margin. This section illustrates the tasks required to include these elements.

Include elements common to a reference document.
Be sure to include all essential information on the title page, table of contents, table of figures or list of tables (if one exists), and index.

- **Title Page.** A title page should contain, at a minimum, the title of the document and name of the author. Some also contain a subtitle, edition or volume number, and date written.

- **Table of Contents.** The table of contents should list the title (heading) of each chapter or section and the starting page number of the chapter or section. You may use a leader character, such as a dot or hyphen, to fill the space between the heading and the page number. Sections prior to the table of contents are not listed in it — only list material that follows the table of contents.

- **Table of Figures or List of Tables.** If you have multiple figures or tables in a document, consider identifying all of them in a table of figures or a list of tables. The format of the table of figures or list of tables should match the table of contents.

- **Index.** The index normally is set in two columns, although one column is acceptable. The index can contain any item a reader might want to look up, such as a heading or a key term. If the document does not have a table of figures or list of tables, also include figures and tables in the index.

Plan
Ahead

To Change the View and the Document Theme

The first step in this section is to switch to Print Layout view and change the document theme to Aspect.

1 Click the Print Layout button on the status bar so that Word switches from Outline view to Print Layout view.

2 Display the Page Layout tab.

3 Click the Themes button on the Page Layout tab and then click Aspect in the Themes gallery to change the document theme to Aspect.

4 Display the Home tab. If formatting marks are showing, click the Show/Hide ¶ button to hide them.

BTW

Readability Statistics
You can instruct Word to display readability statistics when it has finished a spelling and grammar check on a document. Three readability statistics presented are the percent of passive sentences, the Flesch Reading Ease score, and the Flesch-Kincaid Grade Level score. The Flesch Reading Ease score uses a 100-point scale to rate the ease with which a reader can understand the text in a document. A higher score means the document is easier to understand. The Flesch-Kincaid Grade Level score rates the text in a document on a U.S. school grade level. For example, a score of 10.0 indicates a student in the tenth grade can understand the material. To show readability statistics when the spelling check is complete, click the Office Button, click the Word Options button, click Proofing in the left pane, place a check mark in the 'Show readability statistics' check box, and then click the OK button.

To Apply a Quote Style

Word provides two different styles for quotations (Quote and Intense Quote), so that a reader easily can identify a quotation. In the Overview section of this document, the last paragraph is a quotation. The following steps format the paragraph using the Intense Quote style.

- Position the insertion point somewhere in the paragraph containing the quotation.

- If necessary, display the Home tab.

- Click the More button in the Styles group to display the Styles gallery (Figure 7–67).

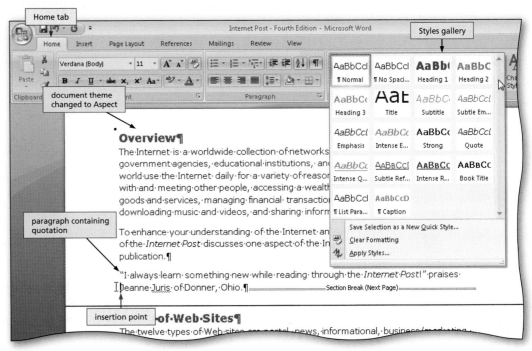

Figure 7–67

- Point to Intense Quote in the Styles gallery to display a live preview in the document of the Intense Quote style (Figure 7–68).

Experiment

- Point to Quote in the Styles gallery and watch the paragraph containing the insertion point (the quotation) show a live preview of the Quote style, so that you can see the differences between the Intense Quote and Quote styles.

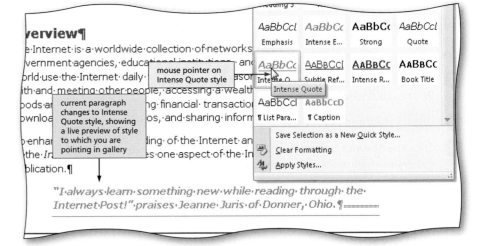

Figure 7–68

- Click Intense Quote in the Styles gallery to apply the Intense Quote style to the paragraph containing the quotation.

Other Ways

1. Click Styles Dialog Box Launcher, click Intense Quote or Quote style in Styles task pane
2. Press CTRL+SHIFT+S, click Style Name box arrow in Apply Styles task pane, click Intense Quote or Quote in the list

To Change the Format of Text

The name of a publication, such as the *Internet Post*, usually is italicized. Because the Intense Quote style italicizes the text in the quotation, the name of the publication in the quote no longer is set apart. In this situation, you use a contrafont for the publication; that is, you remove the italic from the publication name. The following steps remove the italic format from text.

1 Select the text, Internet Post, in the quotation.

2 Click the Italic button on the Home tab to remove the italic format from the selected text.

To Insert a Cover Page

The reference document in this chapter includes a title page. Word has many predefined cover page formats that you can use for the title page in a document. The following steps insert a cover page.

1

- Display the Insert tab.

- Click the Cover Page button on the Insert tab to display the Cover Page gallery (Figure 7–69).

 Experiment

- Scroll through the Cover Page gallery to see the variety of available predefined cover pages.

Q&A Does it matter where I position the insertion point?

No. By default, Word inserts the cover page as the first page in a document.

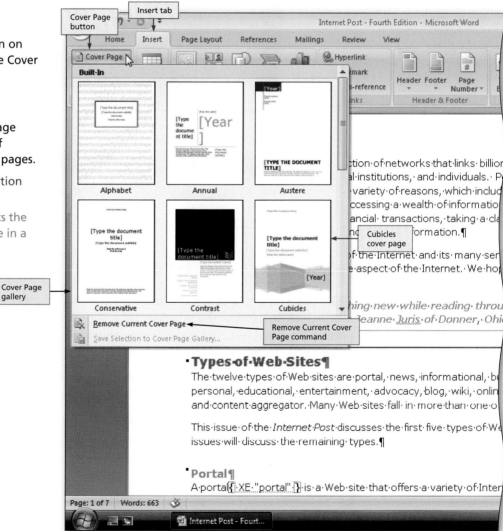

Figure 7–69

2

• Click Cubicles in the Cover Page gallery to insert the Cubicles cover page as the first page in the current document.

• Change the zoom level to 60% so that the entire cover page is displayed in the document window (Figure 7–70).

Q&A   Does the cover page have to be the first page?

No. You can right-click the desired cover page and then click the desired location from the submenu.

Q&A   How would I delete a cover page?

You would click the Cover Page button on the Insert tab and then click Remove Current Cover Page in the Cover Page gallery.

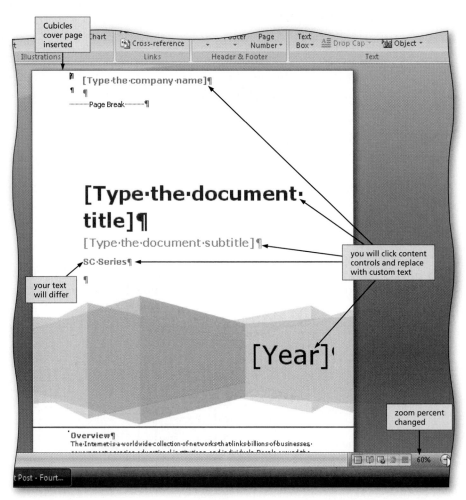

Figure 7–70

To Enter Text in Content Controls

The next step is to select content controls on the cover page and replace their instructions or text with the title page information. Keep in mind that the content controls present suggested text. You can enter any appropriate text in any content control. The following steps enter title page text on the cover page.

1 Because formatting marks clutter the title page, if necessary, click the Show/Hide ¶ button on the Home tab to turn off formatting marks.

2 Click the content control with the instruction, Type the company name. Type `Fourth Edition` in the content control.

3 Click the content control with the instruction, Type the document title. Type `Internet Post` in the content control.

4 Click the content control with the instruction, Type the document subtitle. Type `Types of Web Sites - Part 1` in the content control.

5 Replace the text in the user name content control, SC Series in this case, with the text `Donner County Library`.

6 Type `08` in the Year content control (Figure 7–71).

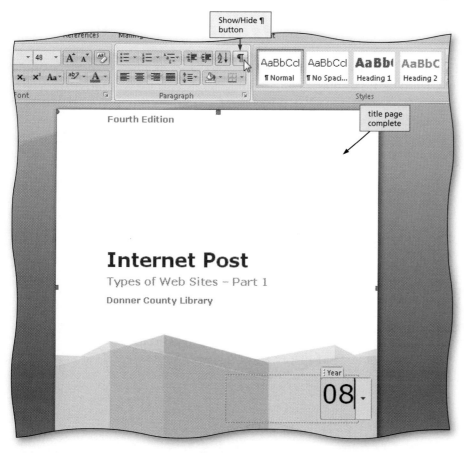

Figure 7–71

To Insert a Blank Page

In the reference document in this chapter, the table of contents is on a page between the title page and the Overview page. Thus, the next step inserts a blank page before the current second page.

1

- Change the zoom back to 100%.

- Position the insertion point to the left of the word, Overview, on page 2.

- Display the Insert tab.

- Click the Blank Page button on the Insert tab to insert a blank page at the location of the insertion point.

- If necessary, hide white space again by positioning the mouse pointer above the page (in the space between pages) and double-clicking when the mouse pointer changes to a Hide White Space button.

- If necessary, scroll to display the blank page in the document window (Figure 7–72).

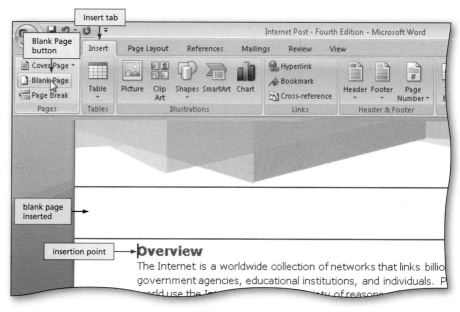

Figure 7–72

To Create a Table of Contents

A table of contents lists all headings in a document and their associated page numbers. When you use Word's built-in heading styles (for example, Heading 1, Heading 2, and so on), you can instruct Word to create a table of contents from these headings. In the reference document in this chapter, the heading of each section uses the Heading 1 style, and subheadings use the Heading 2 style.

Word has many predefined table of contents formats. The following steps use a predefined building block to create a table of contents.

- Position the insertion point at the top of the blank page 2, which is the location for the table of contents.

- Display the References tab.

- Ensure that formatting marks do not show.

Q&A
Why should I hide formatting marks?

Formatting marks, especially those for index entries, sometimes can cause wrapping to occur on the screen that will be different from how the printed document will wrap. These differences could cause a heading to move to the next page. To ensure that the page references in the table of contents reflect the printed pages, be sure that formatting marks are hidden when you create a table of contents.

2

- Click the Table of Contents button on the References tab to display the Table of Contents gallery (Figure 7–73).

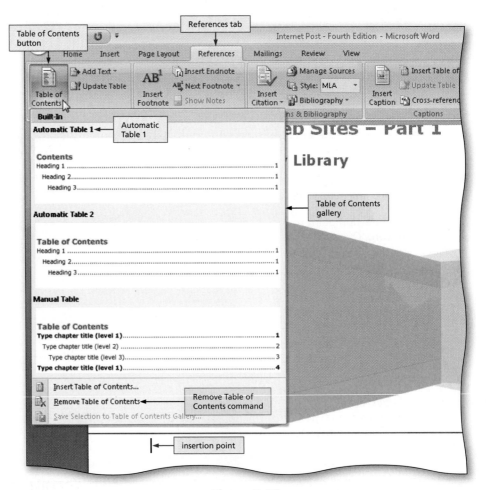

Figure 7–73

3

- Click Automatic Table 1 in the Table of Contents gallery to insert the table of contents at the location of the insertion point (Figure 7–74).

Q&A How would I delete a table of contents?

You would click the Table of Contents button on the References tab and then click Remove Table of Contents in the Table of Contents gallery.

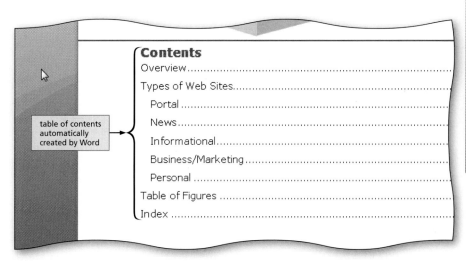

Figure 7–74

Other Ways

1. Click Table of Contents button on References tab, click Insert Table of Contents, select table of contents options, click OK button

To Use the Document Map

When you use Word's built-in heading styles in a document, you can use the Document Map to navigate quickly through the document. The Document Map is a pane at the left edge of the Word window that displays in an outline format any text formatted using Word's heading styles. When you click a heading in the Document Map, Word displays the page associated with that heading in the document window. The following steps show the Document Map and then navigate to a heading using the Document Map.

1

- Display the View tab.

- Place a check mark in the Document Map check box on the View tab to display the Document Map in a separate pane at the left edge of the Word window (Figure 7–75).

Q&A What if all the headings do not display?

Right-click the Document Map and then click All on the shortcut menu to ensure that all headings are displayed. If a heading still does not display, verify that the heading is formatted with a heading style. To display subheadings below a heading in the Document Map, click the plus sign (+) to the left of the heading. Likewise, to hide subheadings, click the minus sign (–) to the left of the heading.

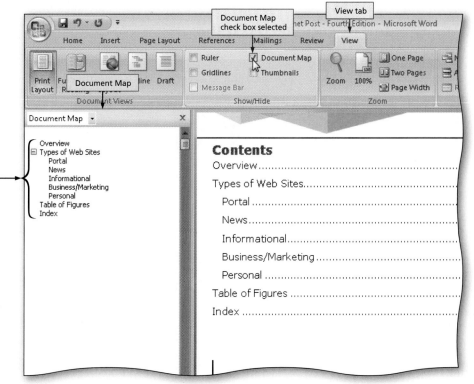

Figure 7–75

● Click the heading, Types of Web Sites, in the Document Map to display the page containing the Types of Web Sites heading in the Word window (Figure 7–76).

Q&A Can I adjust the width of the Document Map?

Yes. You can change the width of the Document Map by dragging its resize bar to the left or right. If a heading is too wide for the Document Map, you can point to the heading to display a ScreenTip that shows the complete title.

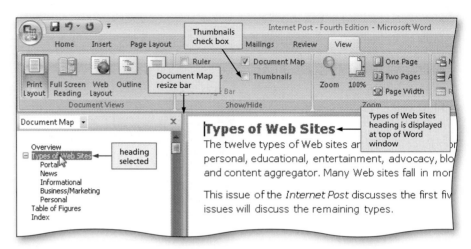

Figure 7–76

TO DISPLAY THUMBNAILS

Instead of headings, you can display **thumbnails**, which are miniature images of each page, on the left side of the Word window. You then can scroll through and click any thumbnail to display the associated page in the document window. If you wanted to display thumbnails, you would perform these steps.

1. Display the View tab.

2. Place a check mark in the Thumbnails check box (shown in Figure 7–76) to display the Thumbnails pane.

To Add Text to the Table of Contents

Occasionally, you may want to add a paragraph of text, which normally is not formatted using a heading style, to a table of contents. The following steps add a paragraph of text to the table of contents by formatting it as Level 3.

● Position the insertion point in the paragraph of text that you want to add to the table of contents, as shown in Figure 7–77.

● Display the References tab.

● Click the Add Text button on the References tab to display the Add Text menu (Figure 7–77).

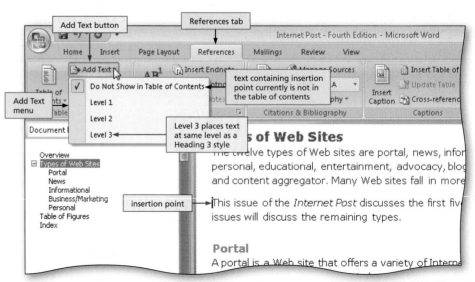

Figure 7–77

• Click Level 3 in the Add Text menu, which changes the format of the current paragraph to a Heading 3 style and adds the paragraph of text to the table of contents (Figure 7–78).

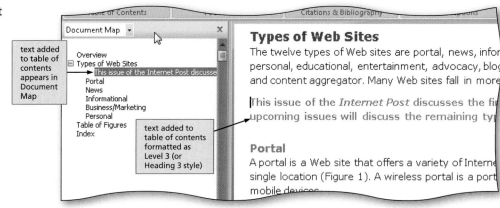

text added to table of contents appears in Document Map

text added to table of contents formatted as Level 3 (or Heading 3 style)

Types of Web Sites

The twelve types of Web sites are portal, news, infor personal, educational, entertainment, advocacy, blog and content aggregator. Many Web sites fall in more

This issue of the *Internet Post* discusses the fir upcoming issues will discuss the remaining ty

Portal

A portal is a Web site that offers a variety of Interne single location (Figure 1). A wireless portal is a port mobile devices

Figure 7–78

To Modify Heading Text

Instead of the term, Overview, you decide to use the term, Introduction, as the heading for the page that follows the table of contents. The following steps modify the heading text.

1 Click the heading, Overview, in the Document Map to display the Overview heading in the document window.

2 Replace the word, Overview, with the word, Introduction (Figure 7–79).

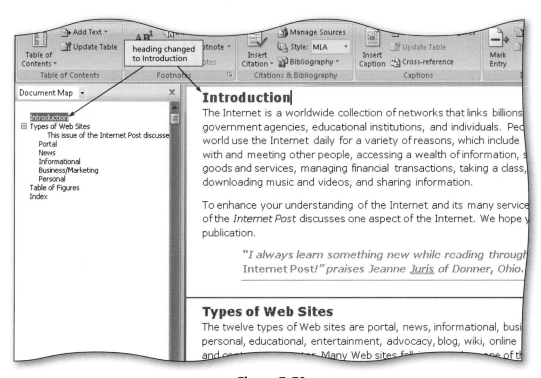

Figure 7–79

To Update a Table of Contents

When you change headings or text in a document, you should update the associated table of contents. You have made two changes that will affect the table of contents: changed a heading and added a paragraph of text. Thus, the following steps update the table of contents.

- Display the table of contents in the document window.

- Click the table of contents to select it (Figure 7–80).

Q&A

Why does the ScreenTip say Ctrl+Click to follow link?

Each entry in the table of contents is a link. If you hold down the CTRL key while clicking an entry in the table of contents, Word will display the associated heading in the document window.

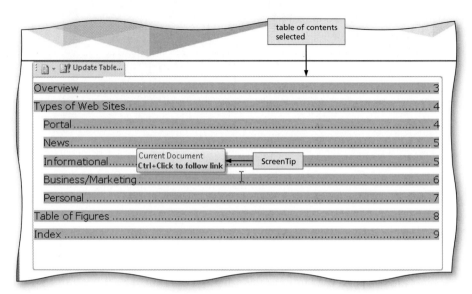

Figure 7–80

- Click the Update Table button that is attached to the table to update the table of contents (Figure 7–81).

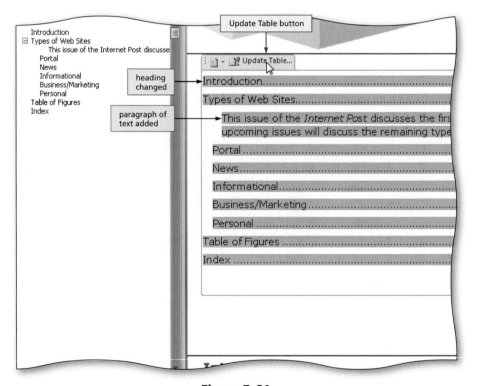

Figure 7–81

To Change the Format of a Table of Contents

You can change the format of the table of contents to any of the predefined table of contents styles. The following steps change the table of contents to the Automatic Table 2 style.

1
• Click the Table of Contents button that is attached to the selected table of contents, which displays the Table of Contents gallery (Figure 7–82).

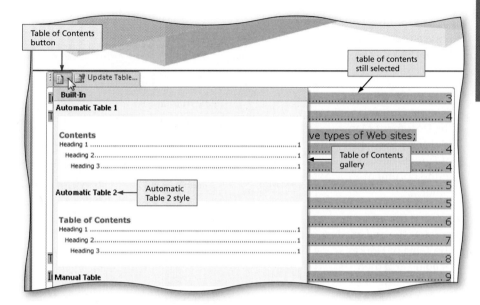

Figure 7–82

2
• Click Automatic Table 2 in the Table of Contents gallery to change the table of contents style (Figure 7–83).

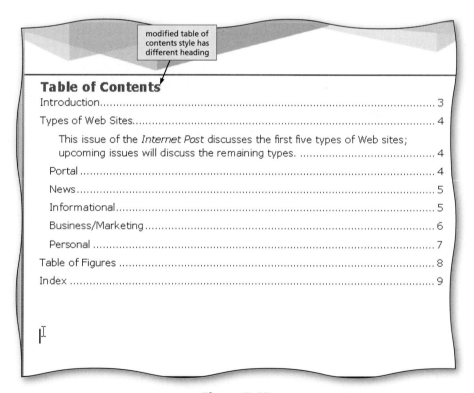

Figure 7–83

Other Ways
1. Click Table of Contents button on References tab

To Create a Table of Figures

At the end of the reference document is a table of figures, which lists all figures and their corresponding page numbers. Word generates this table of figures from the captions in the document. The following steps create a table of figures.

- Ensure that formatting marks are not displayed.

- Click the heading, Table of Figures, in the Document Map to display the Table of Figures heading in the document window.

- Position the insertion point at the end of the Table of Figures heading and then press the ENTER key, so that the insertion point is on the line below the heading.

- Click the Insert Table of Figures button on the References tab to display the Table of Figures dialog box.

- Be sure that all settings in your dialog box match those in Figure 7–84.

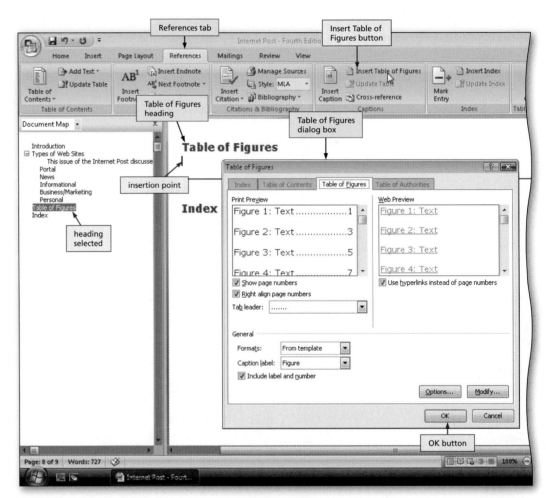

Figure 7–84

- Click the OK button to create a table of figures at the location of the insertion point (Figure 7–85).

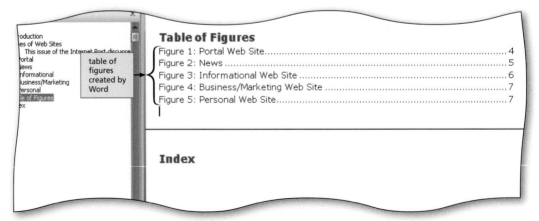

Figure 7–85

To Change the Format of the Table of Figures

If you wanted to change the format of the table of figures, you would perform the following steps.

1. Click the table of figures to select it.
2. Click the Insert Table of Figures button on the References tab to display the Table of Figures dialog box.
3. Change settings in the dialog box as desired.
4. Click the OK button to apply the changed settings.
5. Click the OK button when Word asks if you want to replace the selected table of figures.

To Edit a Caption and Update the Table of Figures

When you modify captions in a document or move illustrations to a different location in the document, you will have to update the table of figures. The following steps change the Figure 2 caption and then update the table of figures.

- Click the heading, News, in the Document Pane to display the News heading in the document window.

- Scroll to display the Figure 2 caption in the document window.

- Add the words, Web Site, to the Figure 2 caption so that it reads: News Web Site (Figure 7–86).

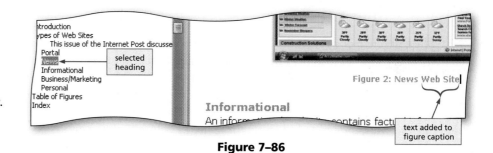

Figure 7–86

- Click the heading, Table of Figures, in the Document Map to display the Table of Figures heading in the document window.

- Click the table of figures to select it.

- Click the Update Table of Figures button on the References tab to display the Update Table of Figures dialog box.

- Click 'Update entire table', so that Word updates the contents of the entire table of figures instead of updating only the page numbers (Figure 7–87).

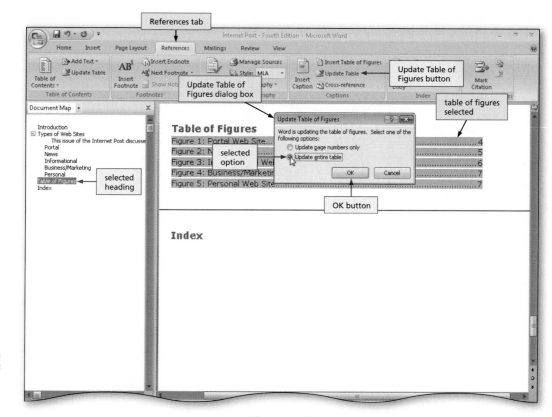

Figure 7–87

3
- Click the OK button to update the table of figures (Figure 7–88).

Q&A

Are the entries in the table of figures links?

Yes. As with the table of contents, you can CTRL+click any entry in the table of figures and Word will display the associated figure in the document window.

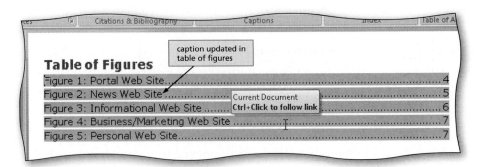

Figure 7–88

Other Ways

1. Select table, press F9 key

To Build an Index

   The reference document in this chapter ends with an index. For Word to generate the index, you first must mark any text you wish to appear in the index. Earlier, this chapter showed how to mark index entries.

   Once all index entries are marked, Word can build the index from the index entry fields in the document. Recall that index entry fields begin with XE, which appear on the screen when formatting marks are displayed. When index entry fields show on the screen, the document's pagination probably will be altered because of the extra text in the index entries. Thus, be sure to hide formatting marks before building an index. The following steps build an index.

1

- Click the heading, Index, in the Document Map to display the Index heading in the document window.

- Click to the right of the Index heading and then press the ENTER key.

- Ensure that formatting marks are not displayed.

- Click the Insert Index button on the References tab to display the Index dialog box.

- If necessary, click the Formats box arrow in the dialog box; scroll to and then click Formal in the list, to select the Formal index format (Figure 7–89).

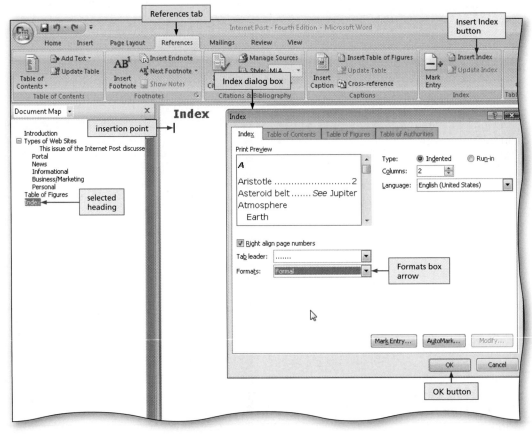

Figure 7–89

2

● Click the OK button to create an index at the location of the insertion point (Figure 7–90).

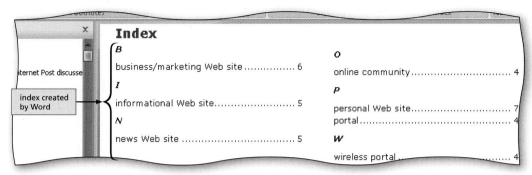

Figure 7–90

To Mark Another Index Entry

The following steps mark an index entry in the Introduction section.

1 Click the heading, Introduction, in the Document Map to display the Introduction heading in the document window.

2 Select the word, Internet, in the first sentence below the heading.

3 Click the Mark Entry button on the References tab to display the Mark Index Entry dialog box (Figure 7–91).

4 Click the Mark button to mark the entry.

5 Close the dialog box.

6 Hide formatting marks.

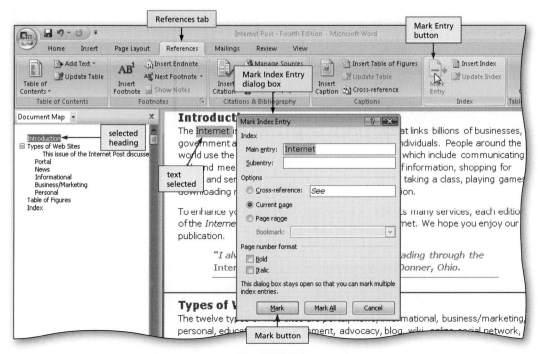

Figure 7–91

To EDIT AN INDEX ENTRY

At some time, you may want to change an index entry. For example, the entry, online community, might need to change to the entry, online user community. If you wanted to change an index entry, you would perform the following steps.

1. Display formatting marks.
2. Locate the XE field for the index entry you wish to change (i.e., { XE "online community"}).
3. Change the text inside the quotation marks (i.e., { XE "online user community"}).
4. Update the index as described in the steps at the bottom of this page.

To DELETE AN INDEX ENTRY

If you wanted to delete an index entry, you would perform the following steps.

1. Display formatting marks.
2. Select the XE field for the index entry you wish to delete (i.e., { XE "online community"}).
3. Press the DELETE key.
4. Update the index as described in the next steps.

To Update an Index

After marking a new index entry, you must update the index. The following step updates the index.

- Click the heading, Index, in the Document Map to display the Index heading in the document window.

- In the document window, click the index to select it.

- Click the Update Index button on the References tab to update the index (Figure 7–92).

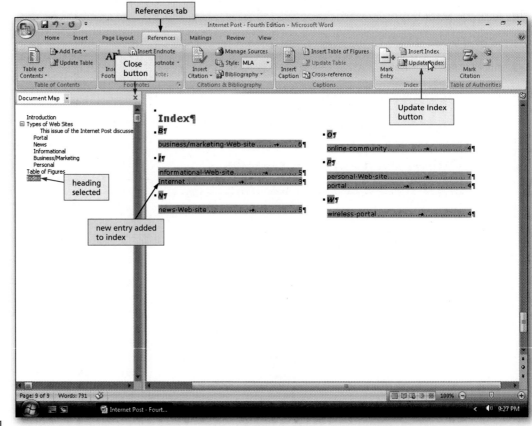

Figure 7–92

Other Ways

1. Select index, press F9 key

To Change the Format of the Index

If you wanted to change the format of the index, you would perform the following steps.

1. Click the index to select it.
2. Click the Insert Index button on the References tab to display the Index dialog box.
3. Change settings in the dialog box as desired. If you want to modify the style used for the index, click the Modify button.
4. Click the OK button to apply the changed settings.
5. Click the OK button when Word asks if you want to replace the selected index.

To Delete an Index

If you wanted to delete an index, you would perform the following steps.

1. Click the index to select it.
2. Press SHIFT+F9 to display field codes.
3. Drag through the entire field code, including the braces, and then press the DELETE key.

Table of Authorities

In addition to creating an index, table of figures, and table of contents, you can use Word to create a table of authorities. Legal documents often include a **table of authorities** to list references to cases, rules, statutes, etc. To create a table of authorities, mark the citations first and then build the table of authorities.

The procedures for marking citations, editing citations, creating the table of authorities, changing the format of the table of authorities, and updating the table of authorities are the same as those for indexes. The only difference is you use the buttons in the Table of Authorities group instead of the buttons in the Index group.

To Close the Document Map

You are finished using the Document Map. Thus, the following step closes the Document Map.

1 Click the Close button in the Document Map to close it.

BTW

Field Codes
If your index, table of contents, or table of figures displays odd characters inside curly braces {}, then Word is displaying field codes instead of field results. Press ALT+F9 to display the index or table correctly. If Word prints field codes for your index or table, click the Office Button, click the Word Options button, click Advanced in the left pane, scroll to the Print section, remove the check mark from the 'Print field codes instead of their values' check box, click the OK button, and then print the document again.

To Create Alternating Headers

The *Internet Post* documents are designed so that they can be duplicated back-to-back. That is, the document prints on nine separate pages. When they are duplicated, however, pages one and two are printed on opposite sides of the same sheet of paper. Thus, the nine-page document when printed back-to-back uses only five sheets of paper.

In many books and documents that have facing pages, the page number is on the outside edges of the pages. In Word, you accomplish this task by specifying one type of header for even-numbered pages and another type of header for odd-numbered pages. The following steps create alternating headers beginning on the second page of the document.

1

- Press CTRL+HOME to position the insertion point at the top of the document.

- Display the Insert tab.

- Click the Header button on the Insert tab and then click Edit Header to display the header area.

- Be sure the Different First Page check box contains a check mark.

- Place a check mark in the Different Odd & Even Pages check box, so that you can enter a different header for odd and even pages.

2

- Click the Next Section button to display the Even Page Header -Section 1-.

- Type Internet Post and then press the ENTER key. Type Fourth Edition and then press the ENTER key.

- Click the Insert Page Number button, point to Current Position, and then select Accent Bar 3 in the Current Position gallery. Press the ENTER key (Figure 7–93).

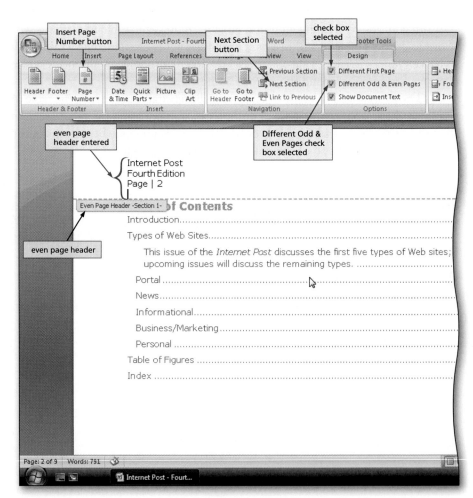

Figure 7–93

3

- Click the Next Section button to display the Odd Page Header.

- Right-align the insertion point.

- Type Internet Post and then press the ENTER key. Type Fourth Edition and then press the ENTER key.

- Click the Insert Page Number button, point to Current Position, and then select Accent Bar 3 in the Current Position gallery. Press the ENTER key (Figure 7–94).

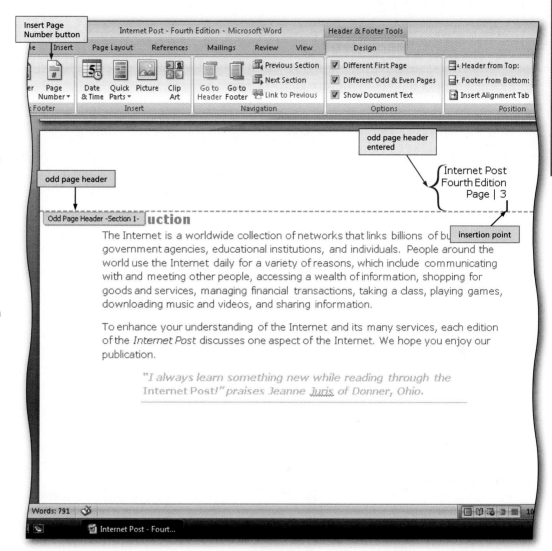

Figure 7–94

What if some pages do not have a header?

Click the header and then click the Link to Previous button on the Design tab. If a dialog box appears, click the Yes button. If the header still does not appear, re-enter the header text in that section.

4

- Click the Close Header and Footer button.

Can I create alternating footers?

Yes. Follow the same basic procedure, except enter text in the footer instead of the header.

To Set a Gutter Margin

The reference document in this chapter is designed so that the inner margin between facing pages has extra space to allow printed versions of the documents to be bound (such as stapled) — without the binding covering the words. This extra space in the inner margin is called the **gutter margin**. The following steps set a three-quarter-inch left and right margin and a one-half-inch gutter margin.

- Display the Page Layout tab.

- Click the Margins button and then click Custom Margins to display the Page Setup dialog box.

- Type .75 in the Left text box, .75 in the Right text box, and .5 in the Gutter text box.

- Click the Apply to box arrow and then click Whole document (Figure 7–95).

- Click the OK button to set the new margins for the entire document.

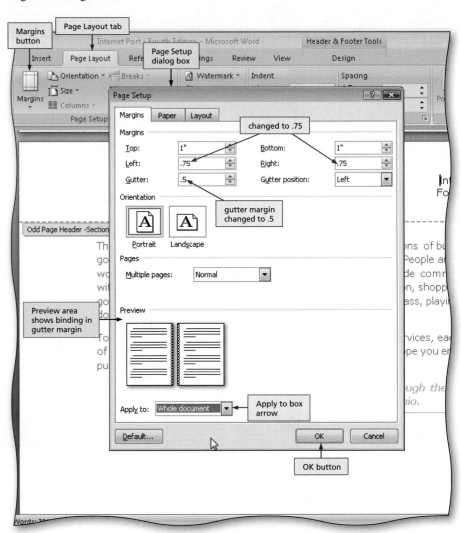

Figure 7–95

To Display the Document in Print Preview

To view the layout of all the pages in the document, the following steps display all the pages in print preview.

1. Click the Office Button, point to Print, and then click Print Preview.

2. Change the zoom level to 10% to display all the pages in the reference document, as shown in Figure 7–96.

3. Click the Close Print Preview button on the Print Preview tab.

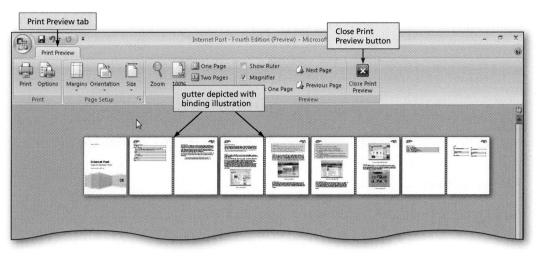

Figure 7–96

To Add Bookmarks

To assist users in navigating through a document online, you can add bookmarks. A **bookmark** is an item in a document that you name for future reference. For example, you could bookmark the headings in the document, so that users easily could jump to these areas of the document. The following steps add bookmarks.

- Display the Portal heading in the document window and then select the heading.

- Display the Insert tab.

- Click the Bookmark button on the Insert tab to display the Bookmark dialog box.

- Type Portal in the Bookmark name text box (Figure 7–97).

Q&A

Are there any rules for bookmark names?

Bookmark names can contain only letters, numbers, and the underscore character (_). They also must begin with a letter and cannot contain spaces.

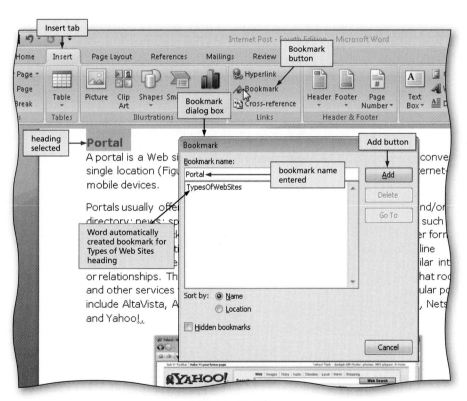

Figure 7–97

- Click the Add button to add the bookmark name to the list of existing bookmarks in the document.

- Repeat Steps 1 and 2 for these headings in the document: News, Informational, Business/Marketing (note: use Business as the bookmark name because the slash is not a valid character in bookmark names), and Personal.

To Go To a Bookmark

Once you have added bookmarks, you can jump to them by performing these steps.

1. Display the Bookmark dialog box (Figure 7–97 on the previous page).
2. Click the bookmark name in the list and then click the Go To button.

   or

1. Press the F5 key to display the Go To sheet in the Find and Replace dialog box.
2. Click Bookmark in the list, select the bookmark name, and then click the Go To button.

To Insert a Hyperlink

Instead of or in addition to bookmarks in online documents, you can insert hyperlinks. For example, the Types of Web Sites section lists the Web sites discussed in the paper. You could convert each of the listed Web sites to a hyperlink, so that a user could click the link to display that section of the paper in the document window. If you wanted to insert a hyperlink that links to a heading or bookmark in the document, you would follow these steps.

1. Select the text to be a hyperlink.
2. Click the Insert Hyperlink button on the Insert tab.
3. In the Link to bar, click Place in This Document, so that Word displays all the headings and bookmarks in the document.
4. Click the heading or bookmark to which you want to link.
5. Click the OK button.

To Save and Print a Document and Quit Word

The reference document for this project now is complete. Save the document, print it, and then quit Word.

1 Save the document with the same file name.

2 Print the finished document (shown in Figure 7–1 on page WD 483).

3 Quit Word.

BTW

Conserving Ink and Toner
You can instruct Word to print draft quality documents to conserve ink or toner by clicking the Office Button, clicking the Word Options button, clicking Advanced in the left pane of the Word Options dialog box, scrolling to the Print area, placing a check mark in the 'Use draft quality' check box, and then clicking the OK button. Click the Office Button, point to Print, and then click Quick Print.

Chapter Summary

In this chapter, you have learned how to insert comments, track changes, review tracked changes, compare documents and combine documents, use the Building Blocks Organizer, work with master documents and subdocuments, and create a table of contents, a table of figures, and an index. The items listed below include all the new Word skills you have learned in this chapter.

1. Hide White Space (WD 486)
2. Insert a Comment (WD 488)
3. Change Reviewer Information (WD 490)
4. Enable Tracked Changes (WD 490)
5. Track Changes (WD 491)
6. Change How Markups Are Displayed (WD 492)
7. Disable Tracked Changes (WD 492)
8. Edit a Comment in a Comment Balloon (WD 493)
9. Use the Reviewing Pane (WD 493)
10. Print Markups (WD 495)
11. Review Tracked Changes and View Comments (WD 496)
12. Delete All Comments (WD 499)
13. Compare Documents (WD 500)
14. Combine Revisions from Multiple Authors (WD 502)
15. Show Tracked Changes and Comments by a Single Reviewer (WD 506)
16. Accept All Changes in a Document (WD 507)
17. Customize the Status Bar (WD 507)
18. Add a Caption (WD 509)
19. Create a Cross-Reference (WD 511)
20. Mark an Index Entry (WD 512)
21. Mark Multiple Index Entries (WD 514)
22. Search for and Highlight Specific Text (WD 514)
23. Sort Building Blocks and Insert a Sidebar Text Box Building Block Using the Building Blocks Organizer (WD 516)
24. Edit Properties of Building Block Elements (WD 518)
25. Enter and Format a Numbered List (WD 519)
26. Link Text Boxes (WD 521)
27. Fill Text Boxes with Color (WD 523)
28. Compress Pictures (WD 524)
29. Create an Outline (WD 525)
30. Show First Line Only (WD 527)
31. Insert a Subdocument (WD 528)
32. Apply a Quote Style (WD 532)
33. Insert a Cover Page (WD 533)
34. Insert a Blank Page (WD 535)
35. Create a Table of Contents (WD 536)
36. Use the Document Map (WD 537)
37. Display Thumbnails (WD 538)
38. Add Text to the Table of Contents (WD 538)
39. Update a Table of Contents (WD 540)
40. Change the Format of a Table of Contents (WD 541)
41. Create a Table of Figures (WD 542)
42. Change the Format of the Table of Figures (WD 543)
43. Edit a Caption and Update the Table of Figures (WD 543)
44. Build an Index (WD 544)
45. Edit an Index Entry (WD 546)
46. Delete an Index Entry (WD 546)
47. Update an Index (WD 546)
48. Change the Format of the Index (WD 547)
49. Delete an Index (WD 547)
50. Create Alternating Headers (WD 548)
51. Set a Gutter Margin (WD 550)
52. Add Bookmarks (WD 551)
53. Go To a Bookmark (WD 552)
54. Insert a Hyperlink (WD 552)

 If you have a SAM user profile, you may have access to hands-on instruction, practice, and assessment. Log in to your SAM account (http://sam2007.course.com) to launch any assigned training activities or exams that relate to the skills covered in this chapter.

BTW

Quick Reference
For a table that lists how to complete the tasks covered in this book using the mouse, Ribbon, shortcut menu, and keyboard, see the Quick Reference Summary at the back of this book, or visit the Word 2007 Quick Reference Web page (scsite.com/wd2007/qr).

Learn It Online

Test your knowledge of chapter content and key terms.

Instructions: To complete the Learn It Online exercises, start your browser, click the Address bar, and then enter the Web address scsite.com/wd2007/learn. When the Word 2007 Learn It Online page is displayed, click the link for the exercise you want to complete and then read the instructions.

Chapter Reinforcement TF, MC, and SA
A series of true/false, multiple choice, and short answer questions that test your knowledge of the chapter content.

Flash Cards
An interactive learning environment where you identify chapter key terms associated with displayed definitions.

Practice Test
A series of multiple choice questions that test your knowledge of chapter content and key terms.

Who Wants To Be a Computer Genius?
An interactive game that challenges your knowledge of chapter content in the style of a television quiz show.

Wheel of Terms
An interactive game that challenges your knowledge of chapter key terms in the style of the television show *Wheel of Fortune.*

Crossword Puzzle Challenge
A crossword puzzle that challenges your knowledge of key terms presented in the chapter.

Apply Your Knowledge

Reinforce the skills and apply the concepts you learned in this chapter.

Working with Word's Collaboration Features
Instructions: Start Word. Open the document, Apply 7-1 E-Commerce Draft, from the Data Files for Students. See the inside back cover of this book for instructions on downloading the Data Files for Students, or contact your instructor for information about accessing the required files.

The document includes several paragraphs of text that contain tracked changes and comments. You are to insert additional tracked changes and comments, accept and reject tracked changes, delete comments, and compare documents.

Perform the following tasks:
1. Save the document with Apply 7-1 E-Commerce Reviewed as the file name.
2. If necessary, customize the status bar so that it displays the Tracking Changes button.
3. Enable (turn on) tracked changes.
4. If approved by your instructor, change the user name and initials so that your name and initials are displayed in the tracked changes and comments.
5. Use the Review tab to navigate to the first comment. Follow the instruction in the comment. Be sure tracked changes are on when you add the required text to the document.
6. When finished making the change, reply to the comment with a new comment that includes a message you completed the requested task. What color are the SCS markups? What color are your markups?
7. With tracked changes on, insert the words, or service, after the word, product, in the second sentence of the third paragraph so that the sentence reads: Users can purchase just about any type of product or service on the Web.

8. Insert the following comment for the word, Internet, in the first sentence: Should the word, Internet, be in all lowercase?

9. With tracked changes on, change the word, difference, in the last paragraph to the word, different.

10. Edit the comment entered in Step 8 to add the word, letters, at the end of the comment — immediately to the left of the question mark.

11. Print the document with tracked changes. *Hint*: In the Print dialog box, select 'Document showing markup' in Print what list.

12. Print just the tracked changes. *Hint*: In the Print dialog box, select 'List of markup' in Print what list.

13. Save the document again with the same name, Apply 7-1 E-Commerce Reviewed (Figure 7–98).

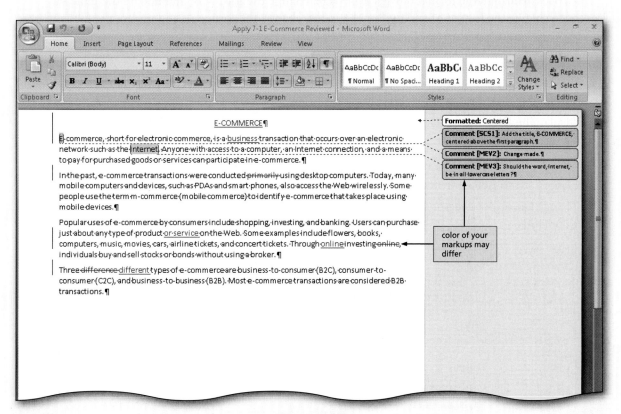

Figure 7–98

14. Reject the deletion of the word, primarily, in the second paragraph.

15. Accept all the remaining edits in the document.

16. Delete all the comments.

17. Disable (turn off) tracked changes. Remove the Tracking Changes button from the status bar.

18. Change the document properties as specified by your instructor. Save the document with a new file name, Apply 7-1 E-Commerce Final.

19. Submit the revised document in the format specified by your instructor.

20. Close all open documents.

21. Compare the Apply 7-1 E-Commerce Draft (original document) with the Apply 7-1 E-Commerce Final (revised document) file. Show changes in a new document. Show both source documents. Save the compare result document with the name, Apply 7-1 E-Commerce Compared.

22. Compare the Apply 7-1 E-Commerce Draft with the Apply 7-1 E-Commerce Final file. Show changes in the original document (Apply 7-1 E-Commerce Draft). Close the document without saving.

Extend Your Knowledge

Extend the skills you learned in this chapter and experiment with new skills. You may need to use Help to complete the assignment.

Working with a Reference Document

Instructions: Start Word. Open the document, Extend 7-1 Certification Draft, from the Data Files for Students. See the inside back cover of this book for instructions on downloading the Data Files for Students, or contact your instructor for information about accessing the required files.

You will change the format of the cover page, change the format of and update the table of contents, change the format of and update the index, change the format of and update the table of figures, insert a sidebar, link text boxes, and format text boxes.

Perform the following tasks:

1. Use Help to review and expand your knowledge about these topics: cover page, table of contents, index, table of figures, and text boxes.

2. Display the Document Map. Use the Document Map to navigate to areas of the reference document for the tasks in this exercise.

3. Change the title page to a cover page format other than Pinstripes.

4. Change the format of the table of contents to Automatic Table 1.

5. Change the leader character in the table of contents to hyphens (Figure 7–99).

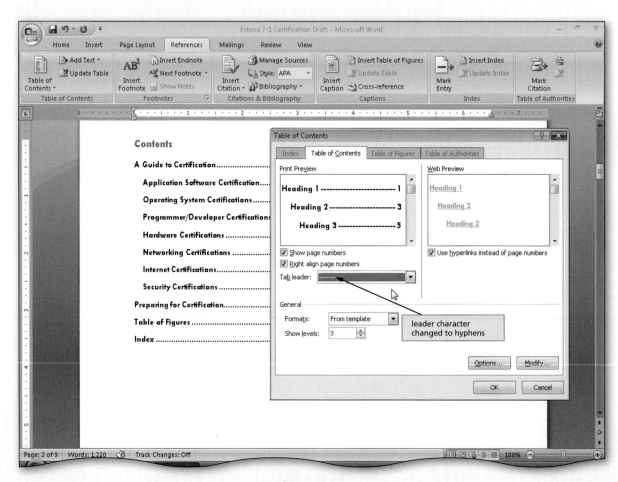

Figure 7–99

6. Change the format of the table of figures to a format other than the From template format. Change the leader character in the table of figures to hyphens.

7. Change the format of the index to a format other than From template.

8. The document currently has eight terms marked as index entries. Read through the document and mark 10 more terms as index entries.

9. Change the index entry, software certifications, to read as follows: application software certifications.

10. Update the index.

11. Modify the caption for Figure 5 to insert the word, usually, between the words, certifications test, so that it reads as follows: Networking certifications usually test knowledge of a company-specific network.

12. Update the table of figures.

13. Change the heading, Application Software Certification, to Application Software Certifications (add an s to Certification).

14. Update the table of contents.

15. Display the Building Blocks Organizer. Sort the building blocks by category. Sort the building blocks by gallery.

16. Use the Building Blocks Organizer to insert a second Exposure Sidebar text box in the document on a page other than page 3.

17. Link the two text boxes together. Resize the text boxes so that the text in the first paragraph is in the first text box and the text in the second paragraph is in the second text box.

18. Format the text boxes using a style other than the default.

19. Make any other necessary formatting changes to the document.

20. Change the document properties as specified by your instructor.

21. Save the revised document with a new file name and then submit it in the format specified by your instructor.

Make It Right

Analyze a document and correct all errors and/or improve the design.

Formatting a Reference Document

Instructions: Start Word. Open the document, Make It Right 7-1 IT Job Descriptions Draft, from the Data Files for Students. See the inside back cover of this book for instructions on downloading the Data Files for Students, or contact your instructor for information about accessing the required files.

The document is a reference document whose elements are not formatted properly (Figure 7–100 on the next page). You are to insert a page break, delete a section break, reformat headings for the table of contents, add text to the table of contents, format a quote, insert bookmarks, and add a header and footer with a page number.

Continued >

Make It Right *continued*

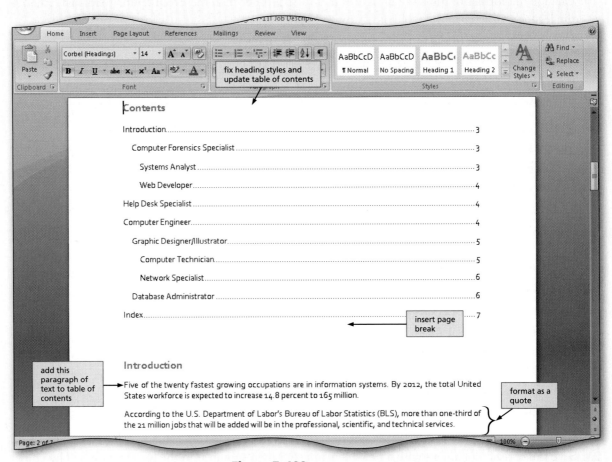

Figure 7–100

Perform the following tasks:

1. Hide white space between pages.

2. Insert a page break between the table of contents and the introduction.

3. Delete the next page section break above the Graphic Designer/Illustrator heading.

4. All entries in the table of contents should be a Heading 1. Reformat all headings to Heading 1.

5. Add the first paragraph in the Introduction as text in the table of contents. Convert it to a Level 3.

6. Update the table of contents.

7. In the Introduction section, format the second paragraph that begins with the word, According, to either the Quote Style or the Intense Quote Style.

8. The index currently contains 3 entries. Mark at least 15 more entries and then update the index. Change the index to a format of your choice.

9. Search for and highlight all occurrences of the word, degree. How many occurrences were located? Clear the highlighting.

10. Insert a bookmark for each heading in the document.

11. Use the Go To command to practice locating bookmarks in the document.

12. Add a built-in header to the document. Add the same style of built-in footer to the document. Fill in the appropriate text in the header and footer. Be sure to include a page number.

13. Change the document properties, as specified by your instructor. Save the revised document with a new file name and then submit it in the format specified by your instructor.

In the Lab

Design and/or create a document using the guidelines, concepts, and skills presented in this chapter. Labs are listed in order of increasing difficulty.

Lab 1: Working with a Cover Page, a Table of Contents, and an Index

Problem: As a computer technician in the Computer Systems department at your school, you have been asked to prepare a guide outlining backup procedures. A miniature version of this document is shown in Figure 7–101. For a more readable view, visit scsite.com/wd2007/ch7 or see your instructor.

A draft of the body of the document is on the Data Files for Students. See the inside back cover of this book for instructions on downloading the Data Files for Students, or contact your instructor for information about accessing the required files.

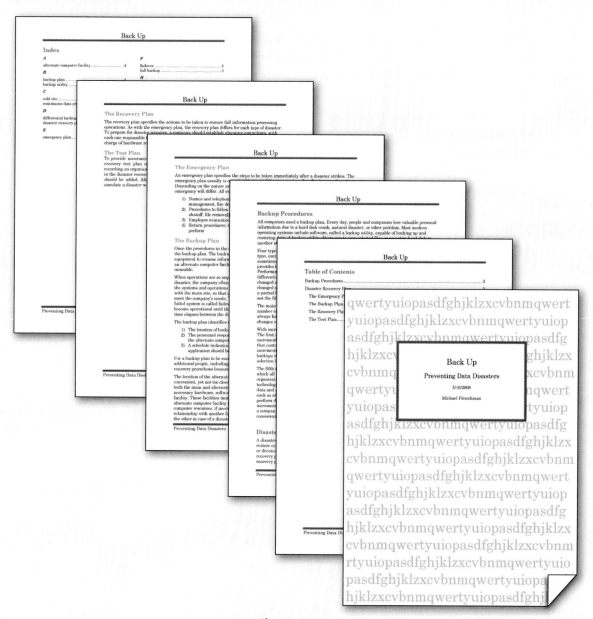

Figure 7–101

Continued >

In the Lab *continued*

Perform the following tasks:

1. Open the document, Lab 7-1 Backup Procedures Draft, from the Data Files for Students. Save the document with a new file name, Lab 7-1 Backup Procedures Final.

2. Create a title page by inserting the Alphabet style cover page. Use the following information on the title page: title - Back Up; subtitle - Preventing Data Disasters; date - *use today's date*; author - *use your name*.

3. Insert a blank page between the title page and the heading, Backup Procedures.

4. Create a table of contents on the blank page using the Automatic Table 2 style.

5. Change the format of the numbered lists in the Emergency Plan and Backup Plan sections to Number alignment: Left.

6. Insert the Alphabet header on all pages but the title page.

7. Insert the Alphabet footer on all pages but the title page. Replace the content control with the text, Preventing Data Disasters.

8. Mark the following terms in the document as index entries: alternate computer facility, backup plan, backup utility, cold site, continuous data protection, differential backup, disaster recovery plan, emergency plan, failover, full backup, hot site, incremental backup, recovery plan, selective backup, test plan.

9. Build an index for the document. Remember to hide formatting marks prior to building the index. Use the Formal format, with right-aligned page numbers.

10. Save the document again and then submit it in the format specified by your instructor.

In the Lab

Lab 2: Working with a Cover Page, a Table of Contents, a Table of Figures, and an Index

Problem: As a laboratory assistant for the computer department at your school, you have been asked to prepare a guide outlining the basics of software use. A miniature version of this document is shown in Figure 7–102. For a more readable view, visit scsite.com/wd2007/ch7 or see your instructor.

A draft of the body of the document is on the Data Files for Students. See the inside back cover of this book for instructions on downloading the Data Files for Students, or contact your instructor for information about accessing the required files.

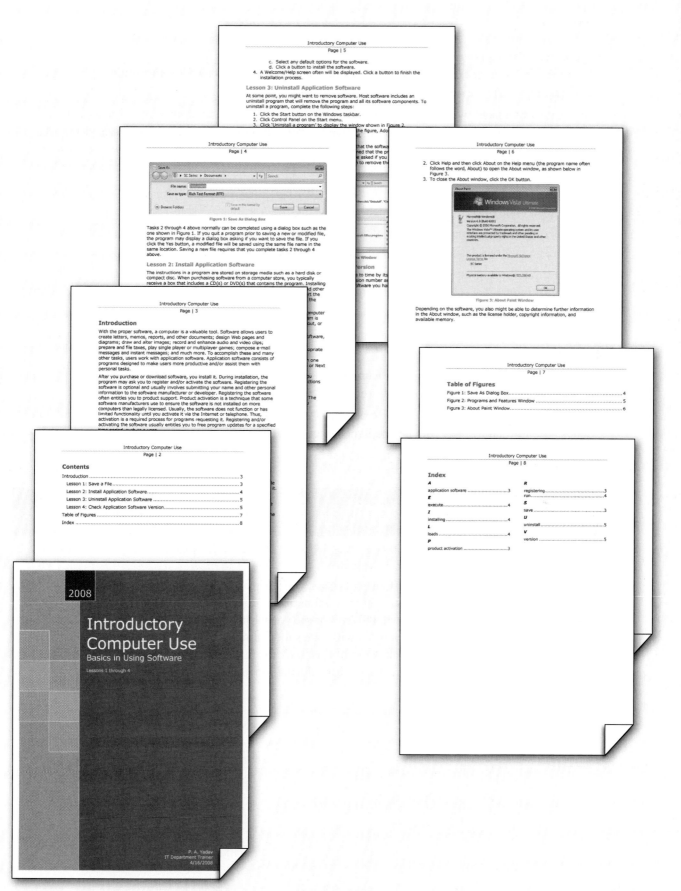

Figure 7–102

Continued >

In the Lab *continued*

Perform the following tasks:

1. Open the document, Lab 7-2 Using Software Draft, from the Data Files for Students. Save the document with a new file name, Lab 7-2 Using Software Final.

2. Create a title page by inserting the Puzzle style cover page. Use the following information on the title page: year - *use current year*; title - Introductory Computer Use; subtitle - Basics in Using Software; abstract - Lessons 1 through 4; author - *use your name*; company - *use your instructor's name*; date - *use today's date*. If necessary, reduce the size of the year so that it fits on a single line.

3. Insert a blank page between the title page and the heading, Introduction.

4. Create a table of contents on the blank page using the Automatic Table 1 style.

5. Insert the Conservative header on all pages but the title page. Delete the date and replace it with the page number. Use the Accent Bar 3 page number style.

6. Add the following caption to the figures: first figure - Figure 1: Save As Dialog Box; second figure - Figure 2: Programs and Features Window; third figure - Figure 3: About Paint Window.

7. Replace the occurrences of xx in the document with cross-references to the figure captions.

8. At the end of the document, create a table of figures on a separate page. Use the From template format.

9. Mark the following terms in the document as index entries: application software, execute, installing, loads, product activation, registering, run, save, uninstall, version.

10. Build an index for the document. Remember to hide formatting marks prior to building the index. Use the Formal format, with right-aligned page numbers.

11. Save the document again and then submit it in the format specified by your instructor.

In the Lab

Lab 3: Working with a Linked Text Box, a Master Document, a Cover Page, a Table of Contents, a Table of Figures, and an Index

Problem: As part of your Computer Concepts class, your instructor has asked you to prepare a reference document about detailed analysis. A miniature version of this document is shown in Figure 7–103. For a more readable view, visit scsite.com/wd2007/ch7 or see your instructor.

The document is a master document with one subdocument. The subdocument is on the Data Files for Students. See the inside back cover of this book for instructions on downloading the Data Files for Students, or contact your instructor for information about accessing the required files.

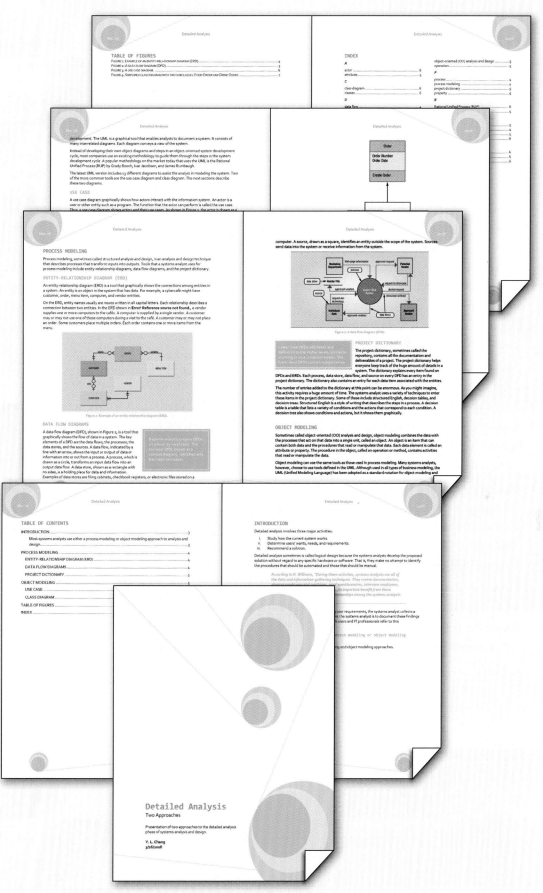

Figure 7–103

Continued >

STUDENT ASSIGNMENTS

Perform the following tasks:

1. Open the file Lab 7-3 Process and Object Modeling Subdocument Draft, from the Data Files for Students. Save the document with the name, Lab 7-3 Process and Object Modeling Subdocument Final.

2. Insert a simple text box to the right of the DATA FLOW DIAGRAMS heading. Enter this text in the text box: `Systems analysts prepare DFDs on a level-by-level basis. The top level DFD, known as a context diagram, identifies only the major processes.` Press the ENTER key. Continue entering this text in the text box: `Lower-level DFDs add detail and definition to the higher levels, similar to zooming in on a computer screen. The lower-level DFDs contain subprocesses.` Format the text box using the Solid Fill, Compound Outline - Accent 1 style. Change the font color of the text to white in the text box and bold the text. Change its wrapping style to Square.

3. On the next page, to the left of the PROJECT DICTIONARY heading, insert another simple text box. Format it using the Solid Fill, Compound Outline - Accent 1 style. Change its wrapping style to Square.

4. Link the two text boxes together. Resize each text box so that each one contains just one paragraph. Save and close the document.

5. Start a new document. In Outline view, enter the following headings: INTRODUCTION, TABLE OF FIGURES, and INDEX. Insert a next page section break between each heading.

6. Save the master document with the file name, Lab 7-3 Detailed Analysis Master Document.

7. Between the INTRODUCTION and TABLE OF FIGURES headings, insert the subdocument named Lab 7-3 Process and Object Modeling Subdocument Final.

8. Switch to Print Layout view.

9. Create a title page by inserting the Mod style cover page. Use the following information on the title page: title - Detailed Analysis; subtitle - Two Approaches; abstract - Presentation of two approaches to the detailed analysis phase of systems analysis and design.; author - *use your name*; date - *use today's date*.

10. Insert a blank page between the title page and the heading, Introduction.

11. Create a table of contents on the blank page using the Automatic Table 2 style. Change the heading to all uppercase using the Change Case button on the Ribbon.

12. Enter the text for the INTRODUCTION page as shown in Figure 7–104. Change the format of the numbered list as shown in the figure.

Detailed analysis involves three major activities:

   i.   Study how the current system works.
   ii.   Determine users' wants, needs, and requirements.
   iii. Recommend a solution.

Detailed analysis sometimes is called logical design because the systems analysts develop the proposed solution without regard to any specific hardware or software. That is, they make no attempt to identify the procedures that should be automated and those that should be manual.

According to R. Williams, "During these activities, systems analysts use all of the data and information-gathering techniques. They review documentation, observe employees and machines, send questionnaires, interview employees, conduct JAD sessions, and do research. An important benefit from these activities is that they build valuable relationships among the systems analysts and users."

While studying the current system and identifying user requirements, the systems analyst collects a great deal of data and information. A major task for the systems analyst is to document these findings in a way that can be understood by everyone. Both users and IT professionals refer to this documentation.

Most systems analysts use either a process modeling or object modeling approach to analysis and design.

The following sections discuss the process modeling and object modeling approaches.

Figure 7–104

13. On the INTRODUCTION page, format the quotation paragraph using the Intense Quote style.

14. Add the text in the second to last paragraph on the INTRODUCTION page to the table of contents, as a Level 3.

15. Update the table of contents.

16. At the end of the document, create a table of figures on the page with the TABLE OF FIGURES heading. Use the Formal format.

17. Build an index for the document. Remember to hide formatting marks prior to building the index. Use the Formal format with right-aligned page numbers.

18. Beginning on the second page (the table of contents), create alternating headers and footers. Use the Mod (Even Page) header style for the even page header. Use the Mod (Odd Page) header style for the odd page header. Use the current date in the header. Use the Mod (Even Page) footer style for the even page footer. Use the Mod (Odd Page) footer style for the odd page footer. The title page does not have a header or footer.

19. For the entire document, set the left and right margins to .75" and set a gutter margin of .5".

20. Insert a bookmark for each Heading 1 in the document.

21. Compress the pictures in the document.

22. Save the document again and then submit it in the format specified by your instructor.

23. Make any additional adjustments so that the document looks like Figure 7–103 on page WD 563.

24. Save the document again. Print the document. If you have access to a copy machine, duplicate the document back-to-back.

Cases and Places

Apply your creative thinking and problem solving skills to design and implement a solution.

• Easier •• More Difficult

• 1: Create the Next Edition of this Chapter's Master Document and Subdocument

As an assistant at the public library, you have been asked to create a series of documents for distribution to patrons in the computer laboratory. The IT director asked you to create handouts that discuss various types of Web sites. The first document you created is shown in Figure 7–1 on page WD 483. The next reference document will be a continuation of this topic. Use the file named, Case 1 - Other Types of Web Sites, as the subdocument. This file is on the Data Files for Students. See the inside back cover of this book for instructions on downloading the Data Files for Students, or contact your instructor for information about accessing the required files. For each section in the subdocument, insert the appropriate figure. The figures are on the Data Files for Students, and their file names reflect the section in which they should be inserted. For example, the file named, Case 1 - Types of Web Sites - Blog, contains the figure that should be inserted in the Blog section; the file named, Case 1 - Types of Web Sites - Advocacy, contains the figure that should be inserted in the Advocacy section; and so on. Insert an appropriate caption below each figure, and then insert a cross-reference to each figure. At a minimum, mark the following terms as index entries: educational Web site, entertainment Web site, advocacy Web site, blog, vlog, vlogosphere, vlogger, wiki, online social networks, social networking Web site, and content aggregator. Once the figures are inserted and the index entries marked, close the subdocument file. Create a master document that contains the subdocument file. The master document also should have a title page (cover page), an introduction, a table of contents, a table of figures, and an index. Format the document with alternating headers and a gutter margin. Compress the pictures. Use the concepts and techniques presented in this chapter to organize and format the document.

• 2: Create a Reference Document about Using Word (No Master Document)

As a laboratory assistant at your school's computer facility, your supervisor has asked you to create a document for distribution to students in the lab that outlines some of the features of Microsoft Office Word 2007. To compose the document, you can use any text in this textbook. The document should contain at least three figures, which can be created by capturing screen shots. To capture a screen shot, display the screen on your computer and then press the PRINT SCREEN key. Use Paint or another graphic program to paste the screen shot and then save it. Insert the graphic files (screen shots) in the Word document. Use Word's Callouts shapes to add bubbles to the figures, if necessary. Add captions to the figures. Insert cross-references to the figures. The finished document should have a title page, an introduction, a table of contents, a table of figures, and an index. Format the document with alternating headers and a gutter margin. Compress the pictures. The entire document should be at least nine pages in length. Use the concepts and techniques presented in this chapter to organize and format the document.

•• 3: Create a Legal Reference Document (No Master Document)

Your aunt has hired you this summer to work as an office assistant for her law firm. The firm is expanding, and your aunt has found what she believes to be an ideal location, complete with a suitable building that needs minor repair and remodeling. She has asked you to help her create a document she will present to the other partners. The document must outline the various considerations involved in expanding to a second location on the city's west side. In addition to an introduction, she needs four additional sections included: need/reason for expansion, location, building contractor estimates, and inspector findings. You must obtain estimates, reports, and expert input using public records from building contractors and the inspectors. In addition, you will need to obtain legal documents from the city containing zoning restrictions and a description of the property. Use Word to create a reference document with an introduction section and headings for each of the four additional sections. The town's legal documents, along with the building contractor's and inspector's reports, should be cited as authorities so that you can generate a table of authorities in the final document. Once you have created the table of authorities, practice changing its format and updating its content. Also include a title page, a table of contents, an index, and — if you use digital photographs, charts, SmartArt graphics, or tables — a table of figures. Use the concepts and techniques presented in this chapter to format the document.

●● 4: Create a Reference Document from your Experiences (No Master Document)

Make It Personal

For this assignment, you will create a reference document that highlights a recent trip you took, an event you attended, or an activity in which you participate (or just enjoy). For example, you could create a document that lists your last vacation's destination, itinerary, and pictures. If you play a sport, the document might discuss the sport in general or your team in particular. Create subheadings for pertinent areas about your topic. For instance, if football is your chosen sport, you could include sections about history of the game, favorite team, players, owner, division, statistics, draft picks, and so forth. If you recently took a trip to Spain, you could include a section about the country's geography, your itinerary, sites you visited, hotel accommodations, food, etc. The document should have a minimum of four figures. For the figures, you can use digital photographs, scanned images, SmartArt graphics, tables, or charts. Include a title page, a table of contents, a table of figures, and an index. Format the document with alternating headers and a gutter margin. Compress the pictures. Use the concepts and techniques presented in this chapter to organize and format the document.

●● 5: Create a Master Document that contains Subdocuments Reviewed by Classmates

Working Together

Virtually every student has spent hours pouring over school course catalogues trying to determine which classes to take. Sometimes it is helpful to talk to someone who has taken the class you are considering, for a more personal perspective. For this assignment, do the following:

1. Assign each team member an area or category of classes to describe (i.e., have one member write about math classes, another about English or literature classes, another history classes, another science classes, etc.). Each member should write course descriptions for three classes he or she currently is taking or has taken in the past in his or her assigned area. For each class, include a section about class description, credit hours, topics/material covered, likes/dislikes, and a recommendation for taking (or not taking) the class.

2. Each team member should use tracked changes to review the other's documents. Change your reviewer's ink colors for all markup options: insertions, deletions, formatting, changed lines, comments, and moves. Also, change the width of the balloons to 2". On each document, make at least five tracked changes and insert at least two comments. Then, obtain the files from your teammates containing tracked changes for the document you wrote. Compare the documents. Then, combine them into your document. Show reviewer markups one at a time. Accept and reject that reviewer's changes, as you deem appropriate. Save the final document.

3. Each of the final documents from your teammates should become a subdocument in a master document. The master document should include a title page (cover page), a table of contents, an index, and if appropriate, a table of figures. Insert a hyperlink to each heading in the document. Use the concepts and techniques presented in this chapter to format the document.

8 | Creating an Online Form

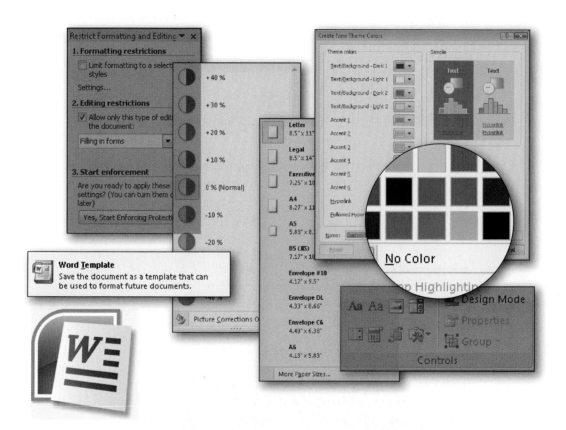

Objectives

You will have mastered the material in this chapter when you can:

- Design an online form
- Change paper size
- Save a document as a template
- Insert a borderless table in a form
- Insert plain text, drop-down list, combo box, date, and rich text content controls
- Edit placeholder text
- Change properties of content controls

- Use the Format Painter
- Insert and format a rectangle shape
- Modify a theme
- Protect a form
- Open a new document based on a template
- Fill in a form

8 | Creating an Online Form

Introduction

During your personal and professional life, you undoubtedly have filled in countless forms. Whether a federal tax form, a time card, a job application, an order, a deposit slip, or a survey, a form is designed to collect information. In the past, forms were printed; that is, you received the form on a piece of paper, filled it in with a pen or pencil, and then returned it manually. With an **online form**, you use a computer to access, fill in, and then return the form. In Word, you easily can create an online form for distribution electronically; you also can fill in that same form using Word.

Project Planning Guidelines

> The process of developing a document that communicates specific information requires careful analysis and planning. As a starting point, establish why the document is needed. Once the purpose is determined, analyze the intended readers of the document and their unique needs. Then, gather information about the topic and decide what to include in the document. Finally, determine the document design and style that will be most successful at delivering the message. Details of these guidelines are provided in Appendix A. In addition, each chapter in this book provides practical applications of these planning considerations.

Project — Online Form

Today, people are concerned with using resources efficiently. To minimize paper waste, protect the environment, enhance office efficiency, and improve access to data, many businesses have moved toward a paperless office. Thus, online forms have replaced many paper forms. You access online forms at a Web site, on your company's intranet, or from your inbox if you receive the form via e-mail.

The project in this chapter uses Word to produce the online form shown in Figure 8–1. Universal Travel is a travel agency that offers weekly specials to its customers. Instead of receiving the specials via the postal service, Universal Travel will e-mail the specials to customers who would like to receive them electronically. To request the weekly specials, customers fill out the form shown in Figure 8–1, save it, and then e-mail it back to Universal Travel.

Figure 8–1a shows how the form is displayed on a user's screen initially; Figure 8–1b shows the form partially filled in by one user; and Figure 8–1c shows how the user filled in the entire form.

The data entry area of the form contains four text boxes (First Name, Last Name, E-Mail Address, and Favorite Destinations), one drop-down list box (Preferred Airline Ticket), a combination text box/drop-down list box (Preferred Rental Vehicle), and a date (Today's Date).

The form is designed so that it fits completely within a Word window that is set at a predefined zoom level — without a user having to scroll while filling in the form. The data entry area of the form is enclosed by a rectangle that is outlined with a dotted gray line. The rectangle also has a shadow on its bottom and right edges. The line of text above the data entry area is covered with the color gray, giving it the look of text that has been marked with a highlighter pen.

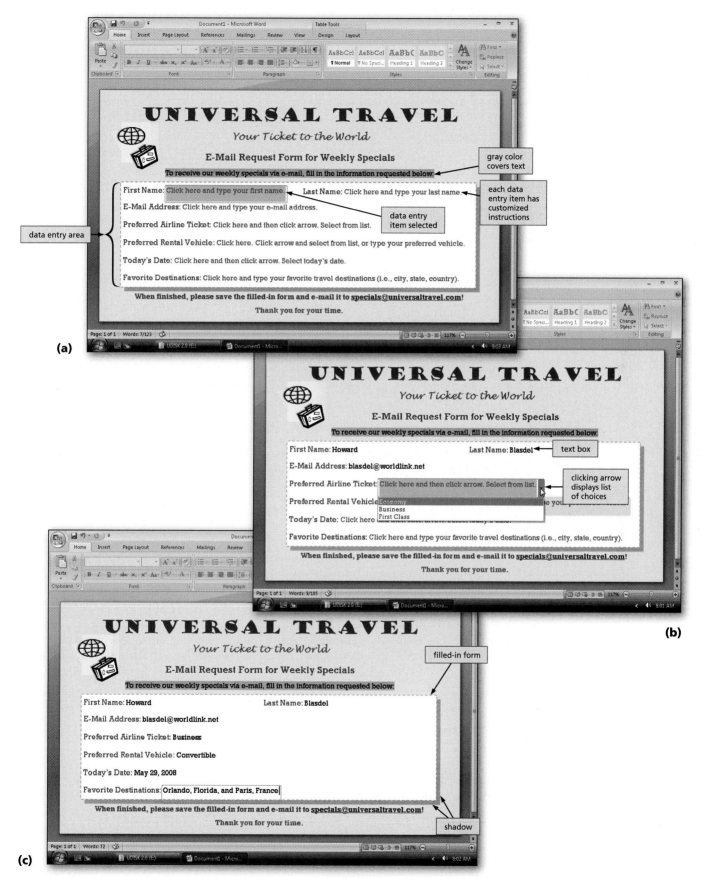

Figure 8–1

Overview

As you read through this chapter, you will learn how to create the online form shown in Figure 8–1 on the previous page by performing these general tasks:

- Save a document as a template.
- Set document formats.
- Enter text, graphics, and content controls in the form.
- Protect the form.

Plan Ahead

General Project Guidelines

When creating a Word document, the actions you perform and decisions you make will affect the appearance and characteristics of the finished document. As you create an online form, such as the project shown in Figure 8–1, you should follow these general guidelines:

1. **Design the form.** To minimize the time spent creating a form while at the computer, you should sketch the form on a piece of paper first. Design a well-thought-out draft of the form — being sure to include all essential form elements. These elements include the form's title, text and graphics, data entry fields, and data entry instructions. A **data entry field** is a placeholder for data that a user enters in the form.

2. **Determine the correct field type for each data entry field.** For each data entry field, decide its specifications, such as its type and/or a list of possible values that it can contain.

3. **Save the form as a template.** By saving a form as a Word template, instead of as a Word document, you will simplify the data entry process for users of the form.

4. **Create a functional and visually appealing form.** Use colors that complement one another. Draw the user's attention to important sections. Arrange data entry fields in logical groups on the form and in an order that users would expect. Data entry instructions should be succinct and easy to understand. Ensure that users can change and enter data only in designated areas of the form.

5. **Determine how the form data will be analyzed.** If the data entered in the form will be analyzed by a program outside of Word, create the data entry fields so that the entries are stored in separate fields that can be shared with other programs.

6. **Test the form.** Be sure that the form works as you intended. Fill in the form as if you are a user. Have others fill in the form to be sure it is organized in a logical manner and is easy to understand and complete. If any errors or weaknesses in the form are identified, correct them and test the form again.

7. **Publish or distribute the form.** Not only does an online form reduce the need for paper, it saves the time spent making copies of the form and distributing it. When the form is complete, post it on the Web or your company's intranet, or e-mail it to targeted recipients.

When necessary, more specific details concerning the above guidelines are presented at appropriate points in the chapter. The chapter also will identify the actions performed and decisions made regarding these guidelines during the creation of the online form shown in Figure 8–1.

To Start Word

If you are using a computer to step through the project in this chapter and you want your screens to match the figures in this book, you should change your computer's resolution to 1024 × 768. For information about how to change a computer's resolution, read Appendix D.

The following steps start Word and verify Word settings.

1 Start Word.

2 If the Word window is not maximized, click its Maximize button.

3 If the Print Layout button on the status bar is not selected, click it so that Word is in Print Layout view.

4 If your zoom level is not 100%, click the Zoom Out or Zoom In button as many times as necessary until the Zoom level button displays 100% on its face.

5 If the rulers are displayed, click the View Ruler button on the vertical scroll bar because you will not use the rulers to perform tasks in this project.

To Display Formatting Marks

It is helpful to display formatting marks that indicate where in the online form you pressed the ENTER key, SPACEBAR, and other keys. The following steps display formatting marks.

1 If necessary, display the Home tab.

2 If the Show/Hide ¶ button on the Home tab is not selected already, click it to display formatting marks on the screen.

Saving a Document as a Template

A **template** is a file that contains the definition of the appearance of a Word document, including items such as default font, font size, margin settings, and line spacing; available styles; and even placement of text. Every Word document you create is based on a template. When you select Blank document in the New Document dialog box, Word creates a document based on the Normal template. Word also provides other templates for more specific types of documents such as memos, letters, and fax cover sheets. Creating a document based on these templates can improve your productivity because Word has defined much of the document's appearance for you.

In this chapter, you create an online form. If you create and save an online form as a Word document, users will be required to open that Word document to display the form on the screen. Next, they will fill in the form. Then, to preserve the content of the original form, they will have to save the form with a new file name. If they accidentally click the Save button on the Quick Access Toolbar during the process of filling in the form, Word will replace the original blank form with a filled-in form.

If you create and save the online form as a template instead, users will open a new document window that is based on that template. This displays the form on the screen as a brand new Word document; that is, the document does not have a file name. Thus, the user fills in the form and then clicks the Save button to save his or her filled-in form. By creating a Word template for the form, instead of a Word document, the original template for the form remains intact when the user clicks the Save button.

To Save a Document as a Template

The following steps save a document as a template, which will be used for the online form.

1

- If necessary, display a new blank document in the Word window.

- With a USB flash drive connected to one of the computer's USB ports, click the Office Button and then point to Save As on the Office Button menu to display the Save As submenu (Figure 8–2).

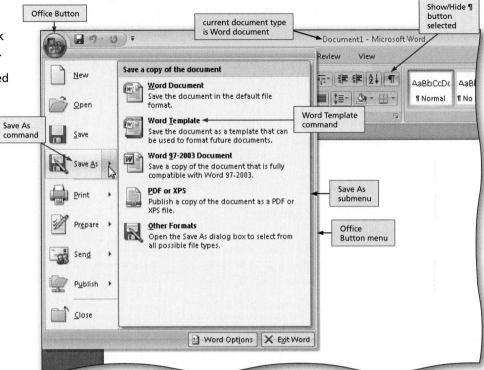

Figure 8–2

2

- Click Word Template on the Save As submenu to display the Save As dialog box with the file type automatically changed to Word Template (Figure 8–3).

Q&A
How does Word differentiate between a saved Word template and a saved Word document?

Files typically have a file name and a file extension. The file extension identifies the file type. The source program often assigns a file type to a file. A Word document has an extension of .docx, whereas a Word template has an extension of .dotx. Thus, a file named July Report.docx is a Word document, and a file named Fitness Form.dotx is a Word template.

Figure 8–3

- Type Universal Travel in the File name text box to change the file name.

- Change the save location to the USB flash drive (Figure 8–4).

4

- Click the Save button in the Save As dialog box to save the document as a Word template with the name Universal Travel.

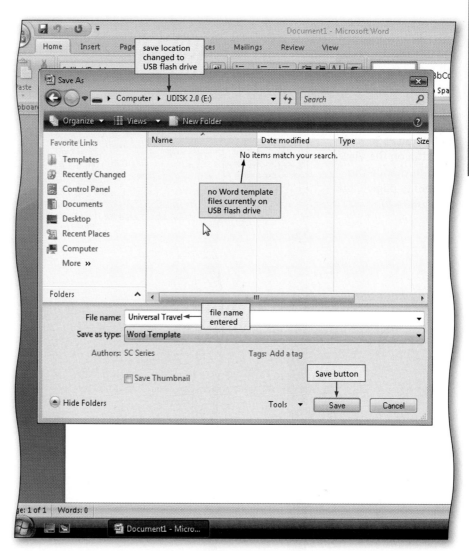

Figure 8–4

Other Ways

1. Press F12; change document type to Word Template

Changing Document Settings

To enhance the look of the form, you change several default settings in Word:

1. Display the page as wide as possible in the document window to maximize the amount of space for text and graphics on the form.

2. Change the size of the paper so that it fits completely within the document window.

3. Adjust the margins so that as much text as possible will fit in the document.

4. Change the document theme to Foundry.

5. Change the page color to light blue.

The following pages make these changes to the document.

To Zoom Page Width

In the online form in this chapter, the form is to appear as wide as possible in the document window. When you change the zoom to page width, Word extends the edges of the page to the edge of the document window. The following step zooms page width.

1

- Display the View tab.

- Click the Page Width button on the View tab to change the zoom to page width (Figure 8–5).

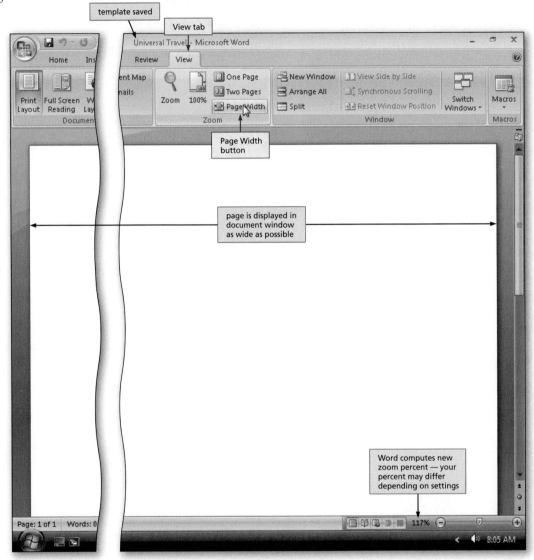

Figure 8–5

BTW

Certification
The Microsoft Certified Application Specialist (MCAS) program provides an opportunity for you to obtain a valuable industry credential — proof that you have the Word 2007 skills required by employers. For more information see Appendix G or visit the Word 2007 Certification Web page (scsite.com/wd2007/cert).

To Change Paper Size

For the online form in this chapter, all edges of the paper appear in the document window. Currently, the top, left, and right edges are displayed in the document window. To display the bottom edge also, change the height of the paper from 11 inches to 4.75 inches. The following steps change paper size.

1

- Display the Page Layout tab.

- Click the Page Size button on the Page Layout tab to display the Page Size gallery (Figure 8–6).

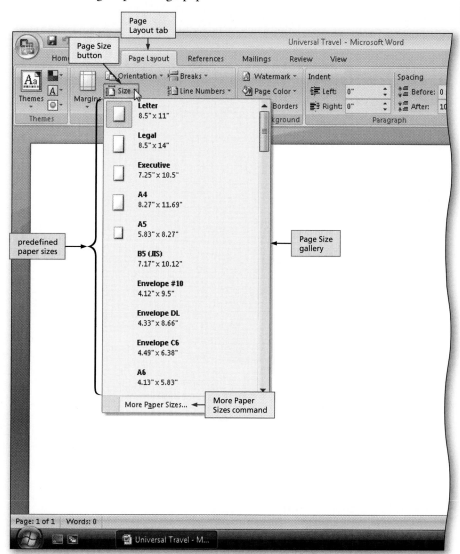

Figure 8–6

2

- Click More Paper Sizes in the Page Size gallery to display the Paper sheet in the Page Setup dialog box.

- In the Height text box, type 4.75 as the new height (Figure 8–7).

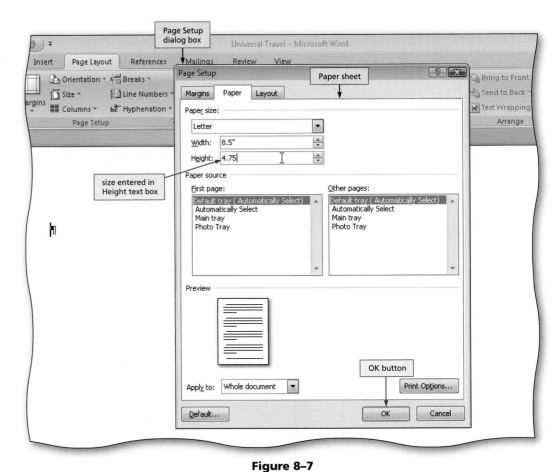

Figure 8–7

3

- Click the OK button to change the paper size to 8.5 inches wide by 4.75 inches tall (Figure 8–8).

 Q&A What if the height of my document does not match the figure?

It is possible that you need to show white space. Position the mouse pointer above the top of the page below the Ribbon and then double-click when the mouse pointer changes to a Show White Space button.

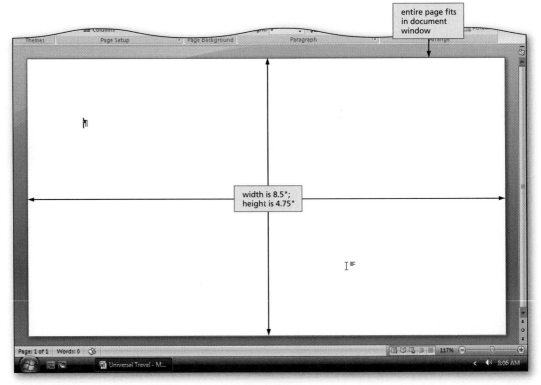

Figure 8–8

To Set Custom Margins

Recall that Word is preset to use 1-inch top, bottom, left, and right margins. To maximize the space for the contents of the form, this chapter sets the left and right margins to .5 inches, the top margin to .25 inches, and the bottom margin to 0 inches. The following steps set custom margins.

1 Click the Margins button on the Page Layout tab to display the Margins gallery.

2 Click Custom Margins in the Margins gallery to display the Margins sheet in Page Setup dialog box.

3 Type .25 in the Top text box to change the top margin setting and then press the TAB key to position the insertion point in the Bottom text box.

4 Type 0 (zero) in the Bottom text box to change the bottom margin setting and then press the TAB key.

Q&A — Why set the bottom margin to zero?

This allows you to place form contents at the bottom of the page, if necessary.

5 Type .5 in the Left text box to change the left margin setting and then press the TAB key.

6 Type .5 in the Right box to change the right margin setting (Figure 8–9).

7 Click the OK button to set the custom margins for this document.

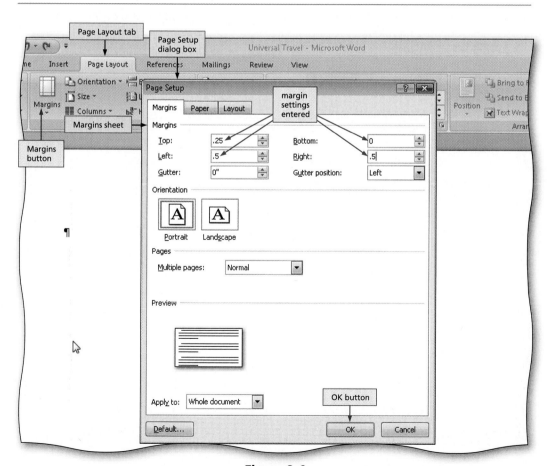

Figure 8–9

To Change the Document Theme

The next step in this section is to change the document theme to Foundry.

1 Click the Themes button on the Page Layout tab and then click Foundry in the Themes gallery to change the document theme to Foundry, which causes the face of the buttons in the Themes group to show colors, fonts, and effects associated with the Foundry theme.

To Change the Page Color

The next step is to change the page color of the online form so that it is visually appealing. This online form uses a light shade of blue. The following steps change the page color.

1 Click the Page Color button on the Page Layout tab to display the Page Color gallery.

2 Point to the seventh color in the second row (Sky Blue, Accent 3, Lighter 80%) to display a live preview of the selected page color (Figure 8–10).

3 Click the seventh color in the second row to change the page color to a light shade of blue.

Q&A Do page colors print?

When you change the page color, it appears only on screen. Changing the background color has no effect on a printed document.

4 If the rulers appear on the screen, click the View Ruler button at the top of the vertical scroll bar to hide the rulers.

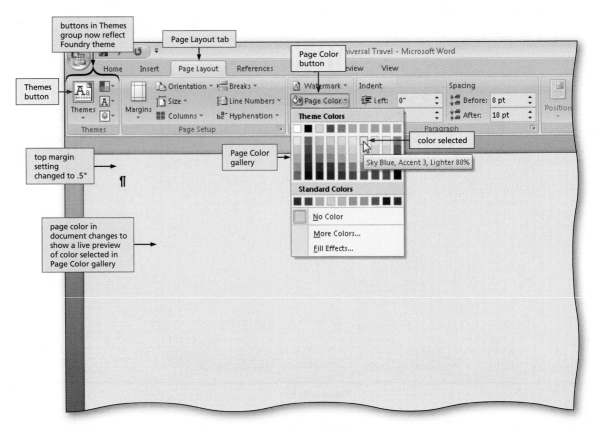

Figure 8–10

Enter Content in the Online Form

The next step in creating the online form in this chapter is to enter the text, graphics, and content controls in the document. The following pages outline this process.

To Enter Text

The next step is to enter the text at the top of the online form.

1 Type UNIVERSAL TRAVEL and then press the ENTER key.

2 Type Your Ticket to the World and then press the ENTER key.

3 Type E-Mail Request Form for Weekly Specials and then press the ENTER key.

4 Type To receive our weekly specials via e-mail, fill in the information requested below: and then press the ENTER key (Figure 8–11).

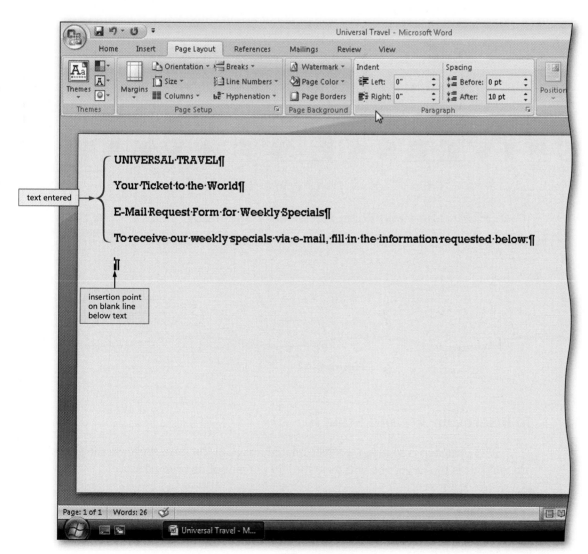

Figure 8–11

To Format Text

The following steps format the text at the top of the online form.

1 Center the four lines of text just entered.

2 Format the characters on the first line to 26-point Goudy Stout font with the color of Rose, Accent 6, Darker 50%.

3 Format the characters on the second line to 14-point bold Lucida Handwriting font with the color of Sky Blue, Accent 3, Darker 50%.

4 Format the characters on the third line to 14-point bold font with the color of Black, Text 1, Lighter 35%.

5 Change the spacing after the first line to 0 point.

6 Change the spacing after the third line to 6 point (Figure 8–12).

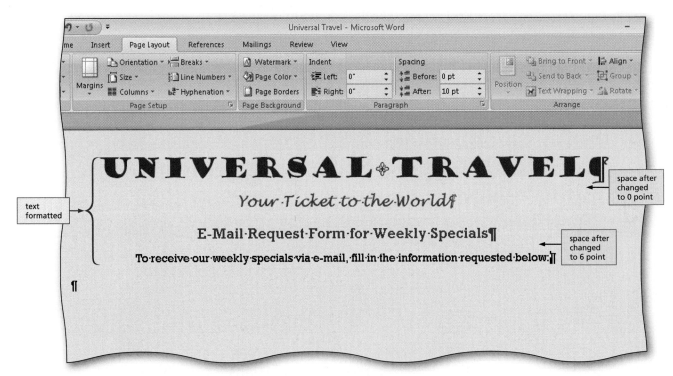

Figure 8–12

To Insert Clip Art and Scale It

The next step is to insert a travel-related image in the form. Because the graphic's original size is too large, you will scale it to 50 percent of its original size.

1 Display the Insert tab. Click the Clip Art button on the Insert tab to display the Clip Art task pane.

2 In the Clip Art task pane, if necessary, click the Search for text box. Type `travel` in the Search for text box.

3 Click the Go button to display a list of clips that match the description, travel.

4 Scroll to and then click the travel-related clip art that matches the one in Figure 8–13.

5 Close the Clip Art task pane.

Q&A What if my clip art image is not in the same location as in Figure 8–13?

The clip art image may be in a different location, depending on the position of the insertion point when you inserted the image. In a later section, you will move the image to a different location.

6 With the graphic still selected, click the Size Dialog Box Launcher on the Picture Tools Format tab to display the Size dialog box.

Q&A What if the Format tab is not the active tab on my Ribbon?

Double-click the graphic or click Format on the Ribbon to display the Format tab.

7 Change the values in the Height and Width text boxes in the Scale area to 50% (Figure 8–13).

Q&A Why does the width value change to match the height value?

When the 'Lock aspect ratio' check box is selected, Word automatically keeps the proportion of the height and width the same.

8 Click the Close button in the Size dialog box to close the dialog box.

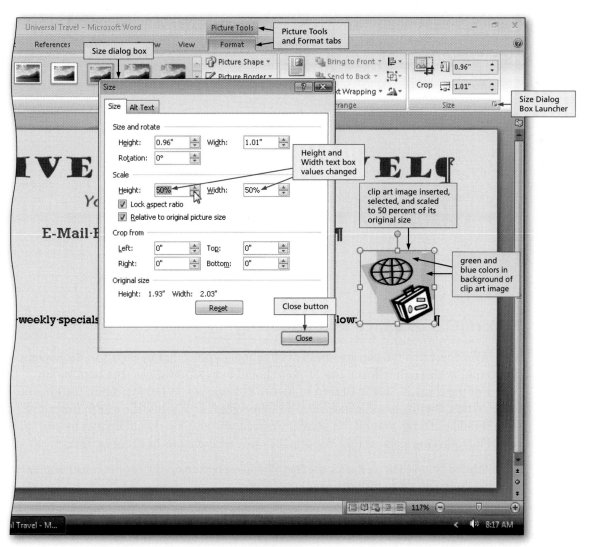

Figure 8–13

To Adjust the Contrast of a Graphic

In this online form, the blue and green background colors in the clip art image are too dark. You would like to soften the colors, that is, increase the contrast in the graphic. The following steps adjust a graphic's contrast.

- Click the Contrast button on the Format tab to display the Contrast gallery.

- Point to +40 % in the Contrast gallery to display a live preview of that contrast applied to the selected clip art image (Figure 8–14).

Experiment

- Point to various percentages in the Contrast gallery and watch the clip art image's contrast change.

- Click +40 % in the Contrast gallery to increase the contrast in the clip art image.

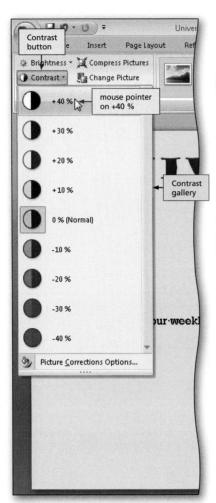

Figure 8–14

Other Ways

1. Right-click image, click Format Picture on short-cut menu, click Picture in left pane, drag Contrast slider, click Close button

To Format a Graphic's Text Wrapping

Word inserted the clip art image as an inline graphic, that is, as part of the current paragraph. In this online form, the graphic should be positioned near the bottom-left corner of the company name (shown in Figure 8–1 on page WD 571). Thus, the graphic needs to be a floating graphic instead of an inline graphic. That is, the text in the online form should not wrap around the graphic; instead, the graphic should float in front of the text. The following steps change the graphic's text wrapping to In Front of Text.

1. With the graphic selected, click the Text Wrapping button on the Format tab to display the Text Wrapping menu (Figure 8–15).

2. Click In Front of Text on the Text Wrapping menu to change the graphic from inline to floating with In Front of Text wrapping.

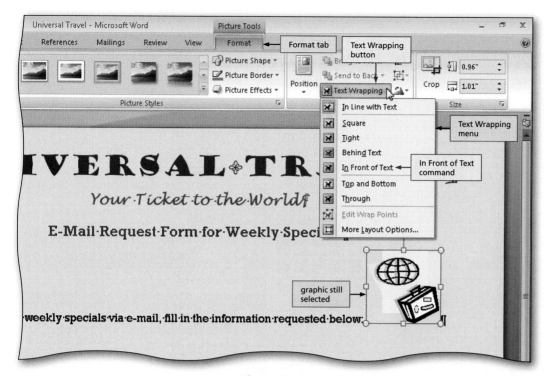

Figure 8–15

To Move a Graphic

The final step associated with the graphic is to move it so that it is positioned on the left side of the online form.

1 Point inside the selected graphic, and when the mouse pointer has a four-headed arrow attached to it, drag the graphic to the location shown in Figure 8–16.

Figure 8–16

To Highlight Text

You want to emphasize the fourth line of text that instructs the user to fill in the information in the form. To emphasize text in an online document, you can highlight it. **Highlighting** alerts a reader to online text's importance, much like a highlighter pen does in a textbook. Word provides 15 colors you can use to highlight text, including the traditional yellow and green, as well as some nontraditional highlight colors such as gray, dark blue, and dark red. The following steps highlight the fourth line of text in the color gray.

1

- Select the text to be highlighted, which, in this case, is the fourth line of text.

- Display the Home tab.

- Click the Text Highlight Color button arrow to display the Text Highlight Color gallery (Figure 8–17).

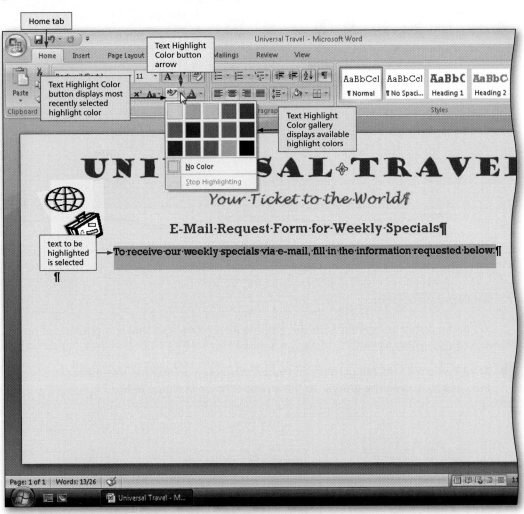

Figure 8–17

Q&A The Text Highlight Color gallery did not appear. Why not?

You clicked the Text Highlight Color button instead of the Text Highlight Color button arrow. Click the Undo button on the Quick Access Toolbar and then repeat Step 1.

Q&A What if the icon on the Text Highlight Color button already displays the color I want to use?

You can click the Text Highlight Color button instead of the button arrow.

2

• Point to Gray-25% in the Text Highlight Color gallery to display a live preview of this highlight color applied to the selected text (Figure 8–18).

 Experiment

• Point to various colors in the Text Highlight Color gallery and watch the highlight color on the selected text change.

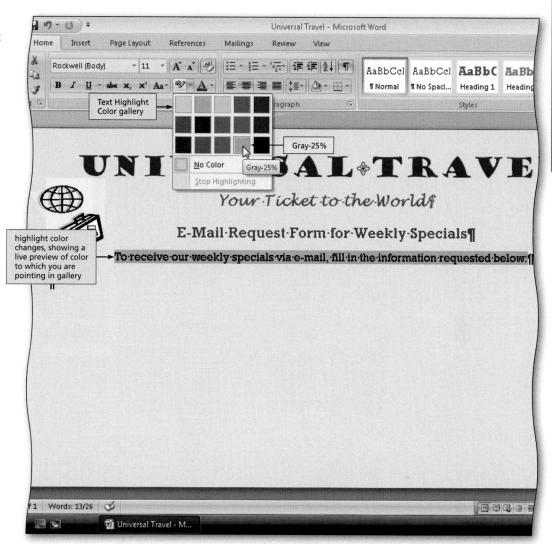

Figure 8–18

3

• Click Gray-25% in the Text Highlight Color gallery to highlight the selected text in gray.

Q&A How would I remove a highlight from text?

Select the highlighted text, click the Text Highlight Color button arrow, and then click No Color in the Text Highlight Color gallery.

Other Ways

1. Click Text Highlight Color button arrow, select desired color, select text to be highlighted in document, select any additional text to be highlighted, click Text Highlight Color button to turn off highlighting

BTW | **Highlighter**
If you click the Text Highlight Color button without first selecting any text, the highlighter remains active until you turn it off. This allows you to continue selecting text that you want to be highlighted. To deactivate the highlighter, click the Text Highlight Color button, click Stop Highlighting on the Text Highlight Color menu, or press the ESC key.

To Show the Developer Tab

To create a form in Word, you need to use buttons on the Developer tab. Because it allows you to perform more advanced tasks not required by everyday Word users, the Developer tab does not appear on the Ribbon by default. The following steps display the Developer tab on the Ribbon.

1

- Click the Office Button to display the Office Button menu (Figure 8–19).

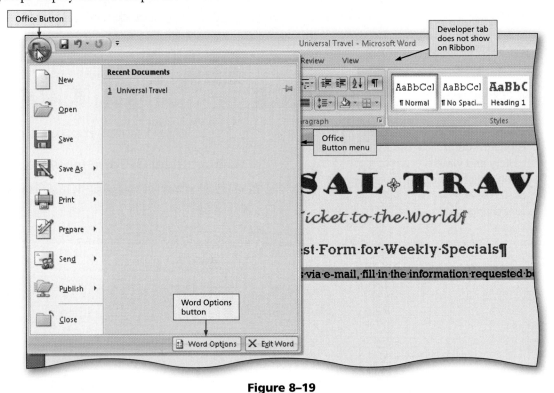

Figure 8–19

2

- Click the Word Options button on the Office Button menu to display the Word Options dialog box.

- If necessary, click Popular in the left pane.

- If it is not selected already, place a check mark in the Show Developer tab in the Ribbon check box (Figure 8–20).

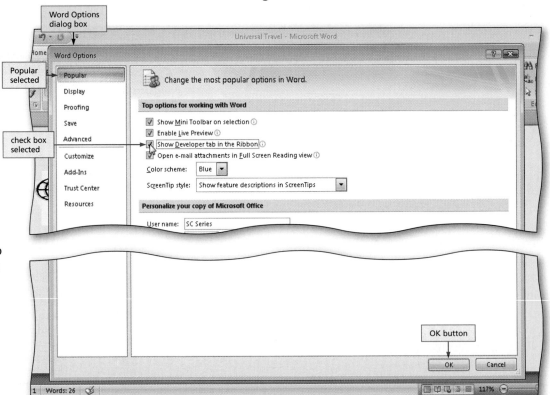

Figure 8–20

3

- Click the OK button to show the Developer tab on the Ribbon (Figure 8–21).

How do I remove the Developer tab from the Ribbon?

Follow these same steps, except remove the check mark from the Show Developer tab in the Ribbon check box in the Word Options dialog box.

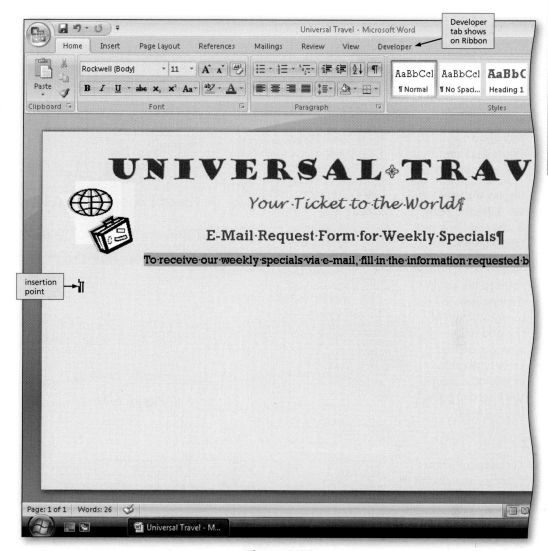

Figure 8–21

To Insert a Borderless Table in a Form

The first line of data entry in the form consists of the First Name content control, which begins at the left margin, and the Last Name content control, which begins at the center point of the same line. At first glance, you might decide to set a tab stop at each content control location. This, however, can be a complex task. For example, to place two content controls evenly across a row, you must calculate the location of each tab stop. If you insert a 2×1 table instead, Word automatically calculates the size of two evenly spaced columns. Thus, to enter multiple content controls on a single line, insert a table.

In this online form, the line containing the First Name and Last Name content controls will be a 2×1 table, that is, a table with two columns and one row. By inserting a 2×1 table, Word automatically positions the second column at the center point.

When you insert a table, Word automatically surrounds it with a border. You do not want borders on tables in forms. Also, to maintain consistent formatting throughout the form, you also will place 10 points after the table. The steps on the next page enter a 2×1 table in the form, remove its border, and add space after it.

1

- If necessary, position the insertion point on the blank paragraph mark below the gray highlighted text (shown in Figure 8–21 on the previous page).

- Display the Insert tab. Click the Table button on the Insert tab to display the Table gallery.

- Point to the cell in the first row and second column of the grid to preview the desired table dimension at the location of the insertion point (Figure 8–22).

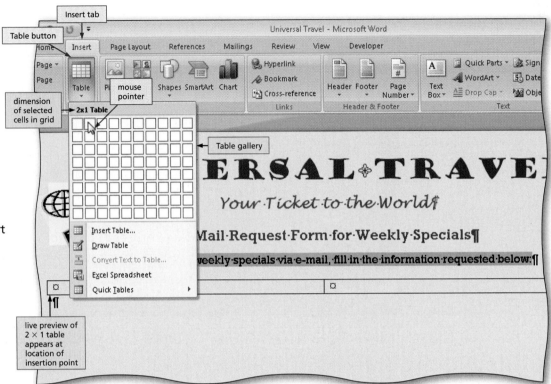

Figure 8–22

2

- Click the cell in the first row and second column of the grid to insert an empty 2 × 1 table.

3

- Point to the first cell in the table to display the table move handle.

- Click the table move handle to select the table.

- Click the Borders button arrow on the Design tab to display the Borders gallery (Figure 8–23).

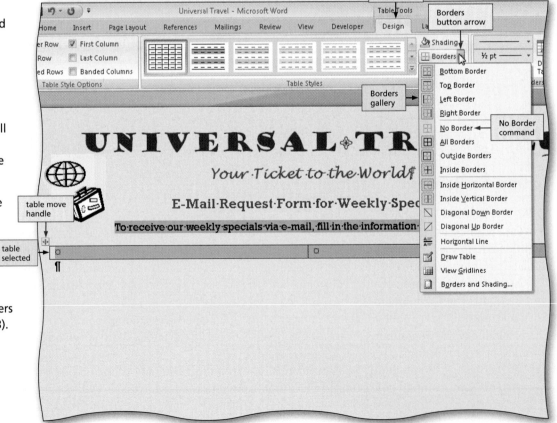

Figure 8–23

4

- Click No Border in the Borders gallery to remove the borders from the table.

- Click the first cell of the table to remove the selection.

5

- Display the Page Layout tab.

- Change the value in the Spacing After text box to 10 pt (Figure 8–24).

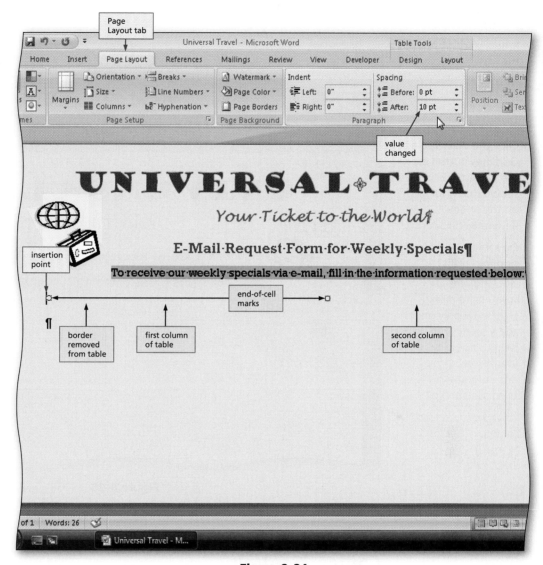

Figure 8–24

Q&A My screen does not display the end-of-cell marks. Why not?

You can display formatting marks by clicking the Show/Hide ¶ button on the Home tab.

Other Ways

1. Click Table button on Insert tab, click Insert Table in Table gallery, enter number of columns and rows, click OK button

To Show Gridlines

When you remove the borders from the table, you no longer can see the individual cells in the table. To help identify the location of cells, you can display **gridlines**, which show cell outlines on the screen. The following step shows gridlines.

- If necessary, position the insertion point in a table cell.

- Display the Layout tab.

- Click the View Table Gridlines button on the Layout tab to show table gridlines on the screen (Figure 8–25).

Q&A

Do table gridlines print?

No. Gridlines are formatting marks that show only on the screen. Gridlines help users easily identify cells, rows, and columns in borderless tables.

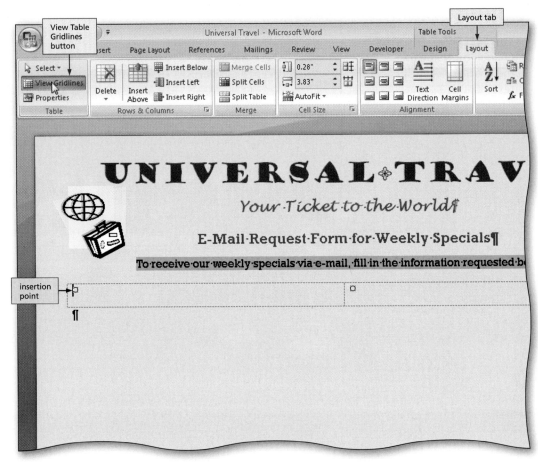

Figure 8–25

Content Controls

To add data entry fields in a Word form, you insert content controls. The Developer tab in Word includes seven different content controls you can insert in your online forms. Table 8–1 outlines the use of each of these controls.

Table 8–1 Content Controls	
Type	**Use**
Rich Text	User enters text, and if desired, may format the entered text.
Plain Text (or Text)	User enters text, which may not be formatted.
Picture	User inserts drawing, shape, picture, clip art, or SmartArt graphic.
Combo Box	User types text entry or selects one item from a list of choices.
Drop-Down List	User selects one item from a list of choices.
Date	User interacts with a calendar to select a date or types a date in the placeholder.
Building Block Gallery	User selects built-in building block from gallery.

Determine the correct field type for each data entry field.
Word uses content controls for data entry fields. For each data entry field, decide which content control best maps to the type of data the field will contain. The field specifications for the fields in this chapter's online form are listed below:

**Plan
Ahead**

- The First Name, Last Name, E-Mail Address, and Favorite Destinations data entry fields will contain text. The first three will be plain text content controls and the last will be a rich text content control.

- The Preferred Airline Ticket data entry field must contain one of these three values: Economy, Business, or First Class. This field will be a drop-down list content control.

- The Preferred Rental Vehicle data entry field can contain one of these five values: Compact Car, Full-Size Car, SUV, Minivan, or All-Terrain Vehicle. In addition, users should be able to enter their own value in this data entry field if none of these five values are applicable. A combo box content control will be used for this field.

- The Today's Date data entry field should contain only a valid date value. Thus, this field will be a date content control.

The following pages insert content controls in the online form.

To Insert a Plain Text Content Control

The first item that a user enters in the E-Mail Request Form for Weekly Specials is his or her first name. Because the first name entry contains text that the user should not format, this online form uses a plain text content control for the first name data entry field. The label, First Name, displays to the left of the plain text content control. To improve readability, a colon or some other character often separates a label from the content control. The following steps enter the label, First Name:, and a plain text content control.

- With the insertion point in the first cell of the table as shown in Figure 8–25, type First Name: as the label for the content control.

- Press the SPACEBAR (Figure 8–26).

Figure 8–26

- Display the Developer tab.

- Click the Text button on the Developer tab to insert a plain text content control at the location of the insertion point (Figure 8–27).

Q&A

Is the plain text content control similar to the content controls that I have used in Word installed templates, such as the memo and resume templates?

Yes. The content controls you insert through the Developer tab have the same functionality as the content controls in the Word installed templates.

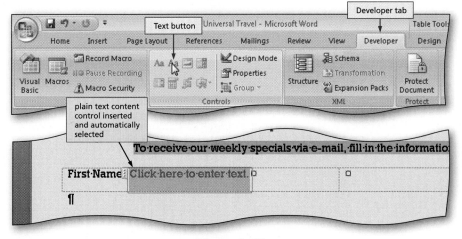

Figure 8–27

To Edit Placeholder Text

A content control displays **placeholder text**, which instructs the user how to enter values in the content control. The default placeholder text for a plain text content control is the instruction, Click here to enter text. You can change the wording in the placeholder text to be more instructional. The following steps edit the placeholder text for the plain text content control just entered.

- With the plain text content control selected, click the Design Mode button on the Developer tab to turn on design mode (Figure 8–28).

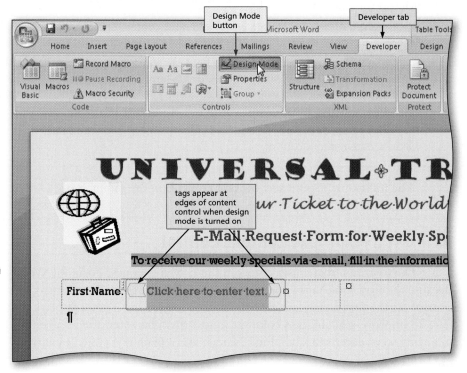

Figure 8–28

- If necessary, click the placeholder text to position the insertion point in it (Figure 8–29).

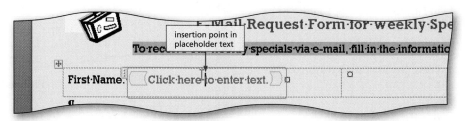

Figure 8–29

- Edit the placeholder text so that it contains this instruction (Figure 8–30): Click here and type your first name.

Q&A

What if the placeholder text wraps to the next line?

Because of the tags at each edge of the placeholder text, the entered text may wrap in the table cell. Once you turn off design mode, the placeholder text should fit on a single line.

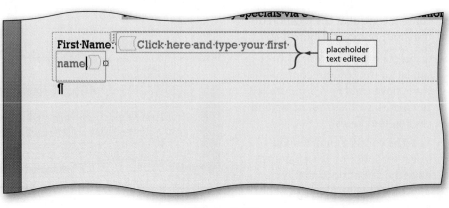

Figure 8–30

4

- Click the Design Mode button on the Developer tab to turn off design mode (Figure 8–31).

Q&A When users enter data in the content control, how will their entry be formatted?

It will look just like the placeholder text. If you want the format of data that the user enters to be different from the format of the current placeholder text, simply change the format of the placeholder text when design mode is turned on.

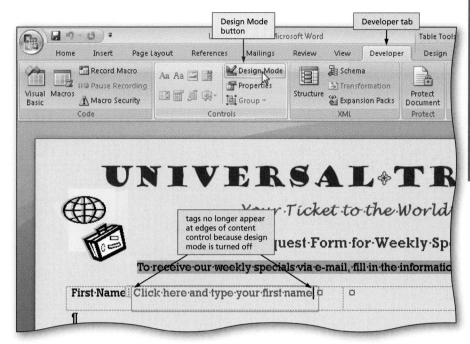

Figure 8–31

To Change the Properties of a Plain Text Content Control

When you click a content control in a Word installed template, the content control may display an identifier in its top-left corner. For templates that you create, you can instruct Word to display this identifier, called the title, by changing the properties of the content control. In addition, you can lock the content control so that a user cannot delete the content control during the data entry process. The following steps change properties of a plain text content control.

1

- With content control selected, click the Control Properties button on the Developer tab to display the Content Control Properties dialog box (Figure 8–32).

Q&A How do I know the content control is selected?

A selected content control is surrounded by a blue outline. It also may be shaded or contain the insertion point.

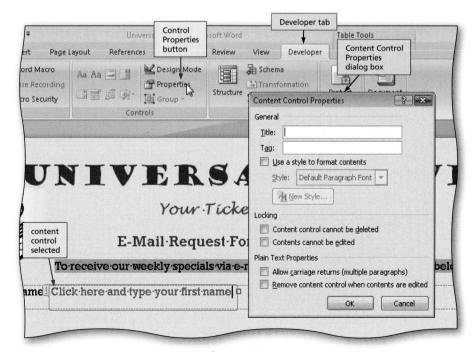

Figure 8–32

- Type First Name in the Title text box.

- Place a check mark in the 'Content control cannot be deleted' check box (Figure 8–33).

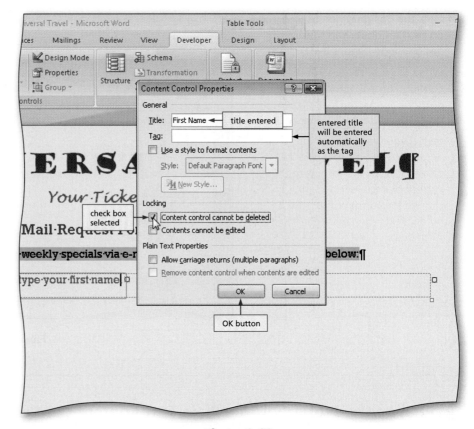

Figure 8–33

- Click the OK button to assign the modified properties to the content control (Figure 8–34).

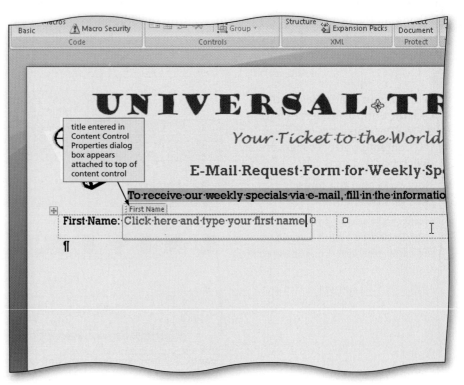

Figure 8–34

To Insert Another Plain Text Content Control and Edit Its Placeholder Text

The second item that a user enters in the E-Mail Request Form for Weekly Specials is his or her last name. The steps for entering the last name content control are similar to those for the first name because the last name also is a plain text content control. The following steps enter the label, Last Name:, and a plain text content control and edit its placeholder text.

1 Position the insertion point in the second cell (column) in the table.

2 With the insertion point in the second cell of the table, type `Last Name:` as the label for the content control and then press the SPACEBAR.

3 Click the Text button on the Developer tab to insert a plain text content control at the location of the insertion point.

4 With the plain text content control selected, click the Design Mode button on the Developer tab to turn on design mode.

5 If necessary, click the placeholder text to position the insertion point in it.

6 Edit the placeholder text so that it contains this instruction (Figure 8-35): Click here and type your last name.

7 Click the Design Mode button on the Developer tab to turn off design mode.

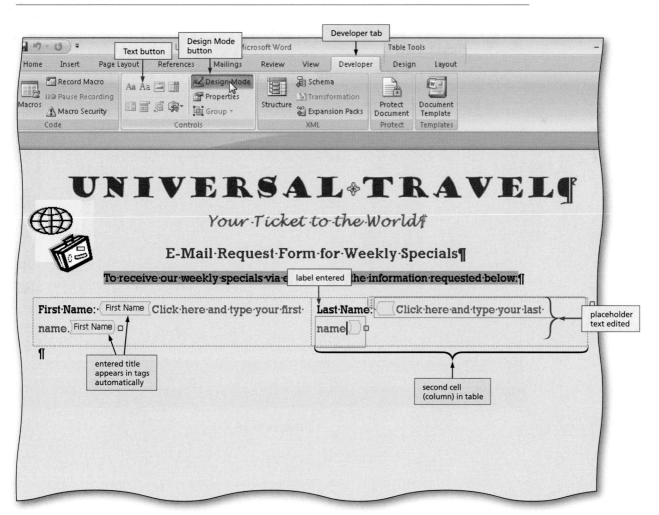

Figure 8–35

To Change the Properties of a Plain Text Content Control

The next step is to change the title and locking properties of the Last Name content control, as you did for the First Name content control. The following steps change properties of a plain text content control.

1 With content control selected, click the Control Properties button on the Developer tab to display the Content Control Properties dialog box.

2 Type `Last Name` in the Title text box.

3 Place a check mark in the 'Content control cannot be deleted' check box (Figure 8–36).

4 Click the OK button to assign the properties to the content control.

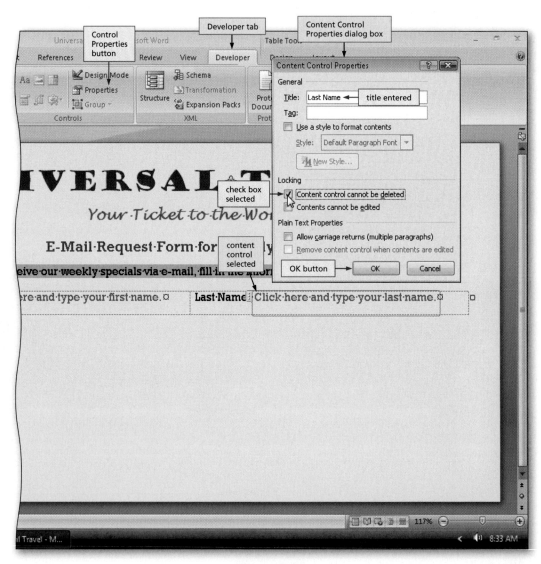

Figure 8–36

To Hide Gridlines

Because you are finished with the table in this form and will not enter any additional tables, you will hide the gridlines. The following steps hide gridlines.

1 If necessary, position the insertion point in a table cell.

2 Display the Layout tab.

3 Click the View Table Gridlines button on the Layout tab to hide table gridlines on the screen (Figure 8–37).

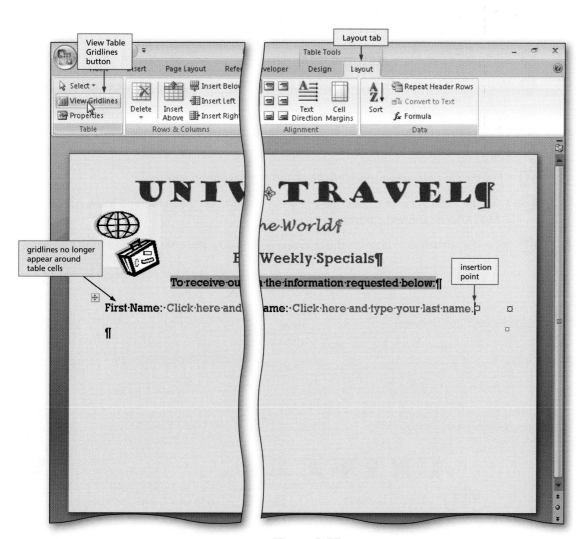

Figure 8–37

To Insert Another Plain Text Content Control, Edit Its Placeholder Text, and Change Its Properties

The third item that a user enters in the E-Mail Request Form is his or her e-mail address. You use similar steps to enter the e-mail address content control as for the first name and last name; that is, the e-mail address also is a plain text content control. The steps on the next page enter a plain text content control, edit its placeholder text, and then change its properties.

1 Position the insertion point on the blank paragraph mark below the First Name content control.

2 Type E-Mail Address: as the label for the content control and then press the SPACEBAR.

3 If necessary, display the Developer tab. Click the Text button on the Developer tab to insert a plain text content control at the location of the insertion point.

4 With the plain text content control selected, click the Design Mode button on the Developer tab to turn on design mode.

5 If necessary, click the placeholder text to position the insertion point in it.

6 Edit the placeholder text so that it contains this instruction: Click here and type your e-mail address.

7 Click the Design Mode button on the Developer tab to turn off design mode.

8 With content control selected, click the Control Properties button on the Developer tab to display the Content Control Properties dialog box.

9 Type E-Mail Address in the Title text box.

10 Place a check mark in the 'Content control cannot be deleted' check box (Figure 8–38).

11 Click the OK button to assign the properties to the content control.

12 Press the END key twice to position the insertion point on the paragraph mark after the E-Mail Address content control.

13 Press the ENTER key to position the insertion point below the E-Mail Address content control.

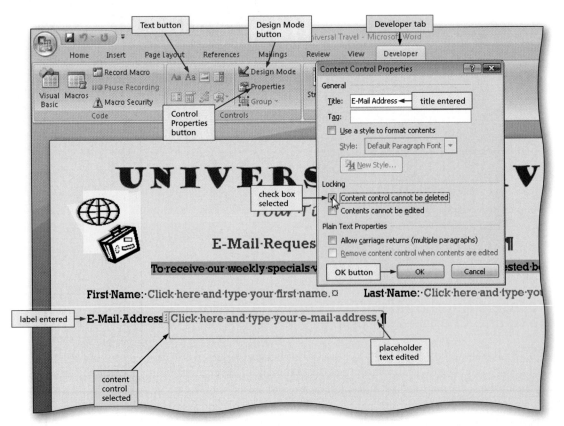

Figure 8–38

To Insert a Drop-Down List Content Control

In the online form in this chapter, the user selects from one of these three choices for the Preferred Airline Ticket content control: Economy, Business, or First Class. To present a set of choices to a user in the form of a drop-down list, from which the user selects one, insert a drop-down list content control. To view the set of choices, the user clicks the arrow at the right edge of the content control. The following steps insert a drop-down list content control.

1

- With the insertion point positioned on the blank para-graph mark below the E-Mail Address content control, type `Preferred Airline Ticket:` and then press the SPACEBAR.

2

- Click the Drop-Down List button on the Developer tab to insert a drop-down list content control at the location of the insertion point (Figure 8–39).

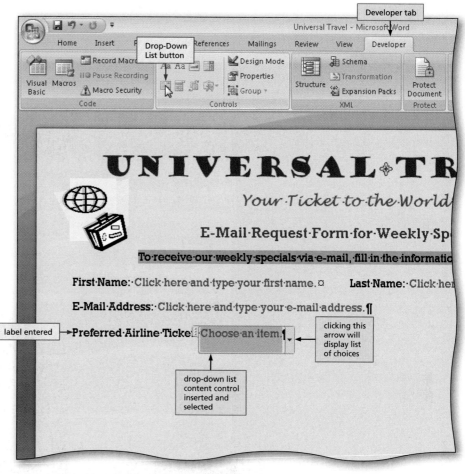

Figure 8–39

To Edit Placeholder Text

The following steps edit the placeholder text for the drop-down list content control.

1 With the drop-down list content control selected, click the Design Mode button on the Developer tab to turn on design mode.

2 If necessary, click the placeholder text to position the insertion point in it.

3 Edit the placeholder text so that it contains this instruction: Click here and then click arrow. Select from list.

4 Click the Design Mode button on the Developer tab to turn off design mode.

To Change the Properties of a Drop-Down List Content Control

In addition to identifying a title and locking the drop-down list content control, you need to specify the choices that will be displayed when a user clicks the arrow to the right of the content control. The following steps change the properties of a drop-down list content control.

- With content control selected, click the Control Properties button on the Developer tab to display the Content Control Properties dialog box.

- Type Airline Ticket in the Title text box.

- Place a check mark in the 'Content control cannot be deleted' check box.

- In the Drop-Down List Properties area, click 'Choose an item.' to select it (Figure 8–40).

- Click the Remove button to delete the 'Choose an item' entry.

Q&A Why delete the 'Choose an item' entry?

If you leave it in the list, it will appear as the first item in the list when the user clicks the content control arrow. You do not want it in the list, so you delete it.

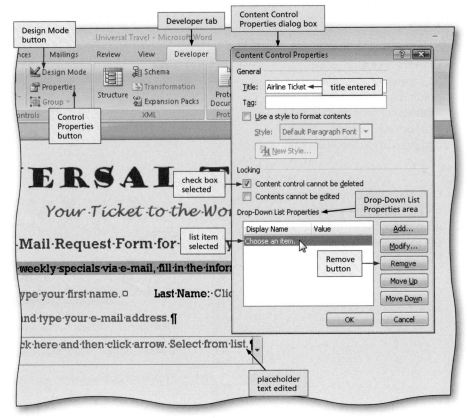

Figure 8–40

- Click the Add button to display the Add Choice dialog box.

- Type Economy in the Display Name text box (Figure 8–41).

Q&A What is the difference between a display name and a value?

In many cases, such as the example shown here, they are the same. Sometimes, however, you want to store a shorter or different value. For example, if the user selects a state such as Illinois as the display name, you may wish to store the value as the state code of IL. Using shorter values, such as IL, makes it easier for separate programs to analyze and interpret entered data.

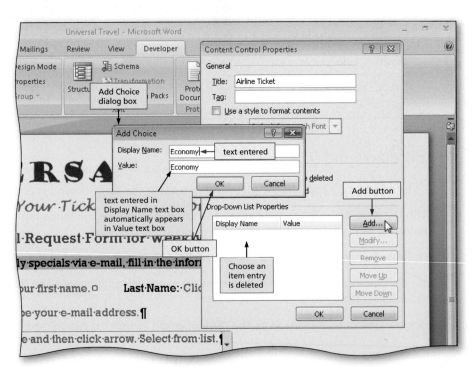

Figure 8–41

4

- Click the OK button or press the ENTER key to add the entered display name to the list of choices in the Drop-Down List Properties area in the Content Control Properties dialog box.

- Click the Add button to display the Add Choice dialog box.

- Type Business in the Display Name text box.

- Click the OK button or press the ENTER key to add the entry to the list.

- Click the Add button to display the Add Choice dialog box.

- Type First Class in the Display Name text box.

- Click the OK button or press the ENTER key to add the entry to the list (Figure 8–42).

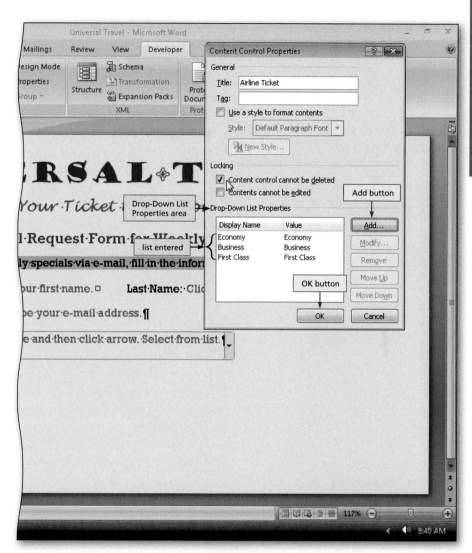

Figure 8–42

5

- Click the OK button to change the content control properties.

- Press the END key twice to position the insertion point at the end of the current line and then press the ENTER key to position the insertion point below the Preferred Airline Ticket content control.

To Insert a Combo Box Content Control

In the online form in this chapter, users can type their own entry in the Preferred Rental Vehicle content control or select from one of these five choices: Compact Car, Full-Size Car, SUV, Minivan, All-Terrain Vehicle. In Word, a combo box content control allows a user to type text or select from a list. The following steps insert a combo box content control.

1
- With the insertion point positioned on the blank paragraph mark below the Preferred Airline Ticket content control, type Preferred Rental Vehicle: and then press the SPACEBAR.

2
- Click the Combo Box button on the Developer tab to insert a combo box content control at the location of the insertion point (Figure 8–43).

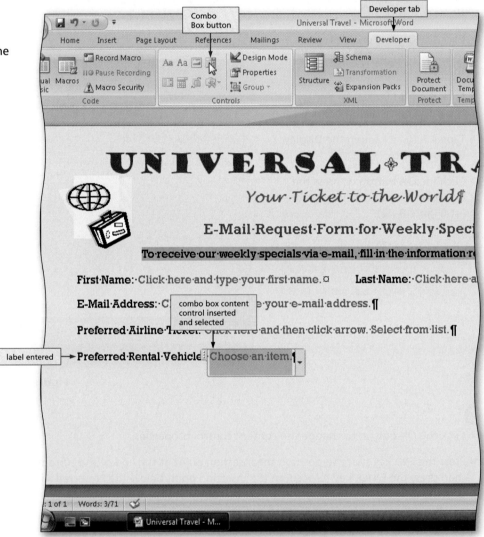

Figure 8–43

To Edit Placeholder Text

The following steps edit the placeholder text for the combo box content control.

1 With the combo box content control selected, click the Design Mode button on the Developer tab to turn on design mode.

2 If necessary, click in the placeholder text to position the insertion point in it.

3 Edit the placeholder text so that it contains this instruction: Click here. Click arrow and select from list, or type your preferred vehicle.

4 Click the Design Mode button on the Developer tab to turn off design mode.

To Change the Properties of a Combo Box Content Control

You follow similar steps to enter the list for a combo box content control as you do for the drop-down list content control. The following steps change the properties of a combo box content control.

1
- With content control selected, click the Control Properties button on the Developer tab to display the Content Control Properties dialog box.

- Type `Rental Vehicle` in the Title text box.

- Place a check mark in the 'Content control cannot be deleted' check box.

- In the Drop-Down List Properties area, click 'Choose an item.' to select it (Figure 8–44).

2
- Click the Remove button to delete the 'Choose an item.' entry.

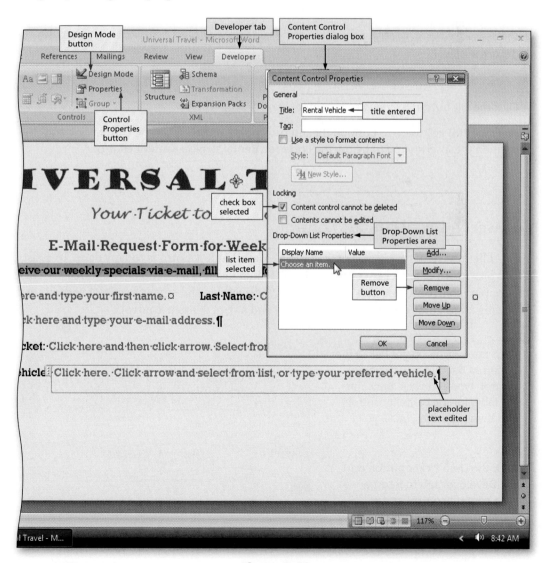

Figure 8–44

- Click the Add button to display the Add Choice dialog box.

- Type Compact Car in the Display Name text box.

- Click the OK button to add the entered display name to the list of choices in the Drop-Down List Properties area in the Content Control Properties dialog box.

- Click the Add button and add Full-Size Car to the list.

- Click the Add button and add SUV to the list.

- Click the Add button and add Minivan to the list.

- Click the Add button and add All-Terrain Vehicle to the list (Figure 8–45).

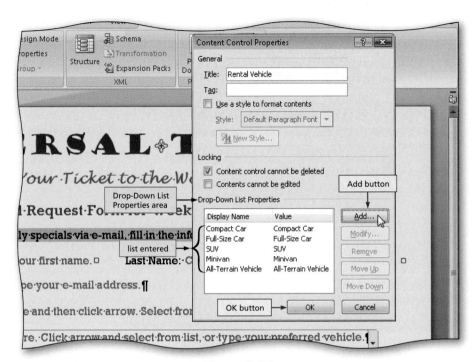

Figure 8–45

- Click the OK button to change the content control properties.

- Press the END key twice to position the insertion point at the end of the current line and then press the ENTER key to position the insertion point below the Preferred Rental Vehicle content control.

To Insert a Date Content Control

The next item that users enter in the E-Mail Request Form is today's date. To assist users with entering dates, Word provides a date picker content control, which displays a calendar when the user clicks the arrow to the right of the content control. Users also can enter a date directly in the content control without using the calendar. The following steps enter the label, Today's Date:, and a date content control.

1

- With the insertion point below the Preferred Rental Vehicle content control, type Today's Date: as the label for the content control and then press the SPACEBAR.

2

- Click the Date Picker button on the Developer tab to insert a date content control at the location of the insertion point (Figure 8–46).

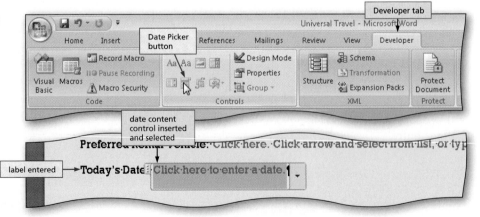

Figure 8–46

To Edit Placeholder Text

The following steps edit the placeholder text for the date content control.

1 With the date content control selected, click the Design Mode button on the Developer tab to turn on design mode.

2 If necessary, click the placeholder text to position the insertion point in it.

3 Edit the placeholder text so that it contains this instruction: Click here and then click arrow. Select today's date.

4 Click the Design Mode button on the Developer tab to turn off design mode.

To Change the Properties of a Date Content Control

In addition to identifying a title for a date content control and locking the control, you can specify how the date will be displayed when the user selects it from the calendar. The following steps change these properties of a date content control.

1

- With content control selected, click the Control Properties button on the Developer tab to display the Content Control Properties dialog box.

- Type Today's Date in the Title text box.

- Place a check mark in the 'Content control cannot be deleted' check box.

- In the 'Display the date like this' area, click the desired format in this list (Figure 8–47).

2

- Click the OK button to change the content control properties.

- Press the END key twice to position the insertion point at the end of the current line and then press the ENTER key to position the insertion point below the Today's Date content control.

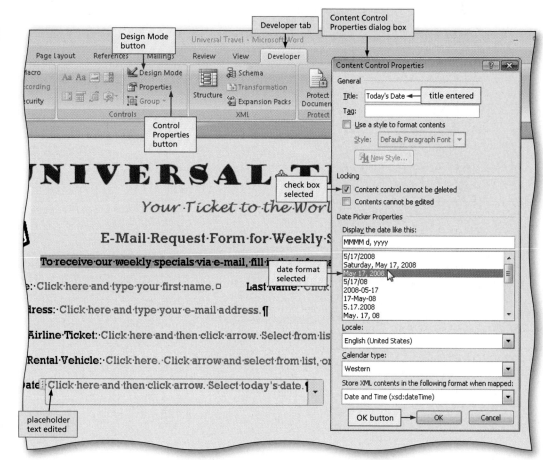

Figure 8–47

To Insert a Rich Text Content Control

The last item that users enter in the E-Mail Request Form for Weekly Specials is their favorite destinations. Because you want to allow users to format the text they enter in this content control, you use the rich text content control. The difference between a plain text and rich text content control is that the users can format text as they enter it in the rich text content control. The following step enters the label, Favorite Destinations:, and a rich text content control.

- With the insertion point on the paragraph mark below the Today's Date content control, type Favorite Destinations: as the label for the content control and then press the SPACEBAR.

- Click the Rich Text button on the Developer tab to insert a rich text content control at the location of the insertion point (Figure 8–48).

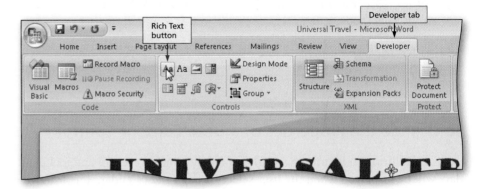

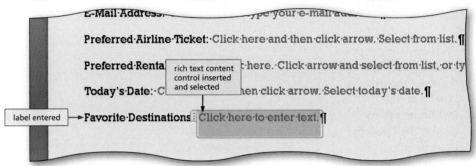

Figure 8–48

To Edit Placeholder Text

The following steps edit placeholder text for the rich text content control.

1 With the rich text content control selected, click the Design Mode button on the Developer tab to turn on design mode.

2 If necessary, scroll to page 2 to display the rich text content control.

Q&A Why did the content control move to another page (Figure 8–49)?

Because design mode displays tags, the content controls and placeholder text are not displayed in their proper positions on the screen. When you turn off design mode, the content controls will return to their original locations and the extra page should disappear.

3 If necessary, click the placeholder text to position the insertion point in it.

4 Edit the placeholder text so that it contains this instruction (Figure 8–49): Click here and type your favorite travel destinations (i.e., city, state, country).

5 Click the Design Mode button on the Developer tab to turn off design mode.

6 Scroll to display the top of the form in the document window.

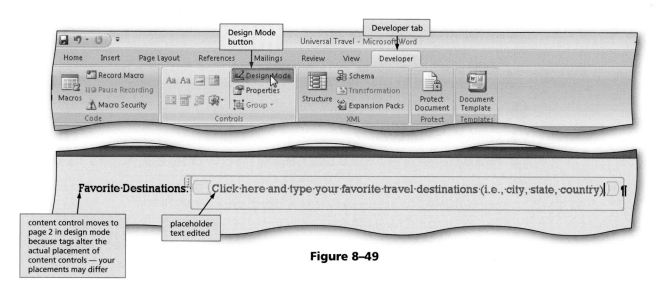

Figure 8–49

To Change the Properties of a Rich Text Content Control

In the online form in this chapter, you change the same two properties for the rich text content control as for the plain text content control. That is, you enter a title and lock the content control. The following steps change the properties of the rich text content control.

1 With content control selected, click the Control Properties button on the Developer tab to display the Content Control Properties dialog box.

2 Type Favorite Destinations in the Title text box.

3 Place a check mark in the 'Content control cannot be deleted' check box (Figure 8–50).

4 Click the OK button to assign the properties to the content control.

5 Press the END key twice to position the insertion point on the paragraph mark after the Favorite Destinations content control and then press the ENTER key to position the insertion point below the Favorite Destinations content control.

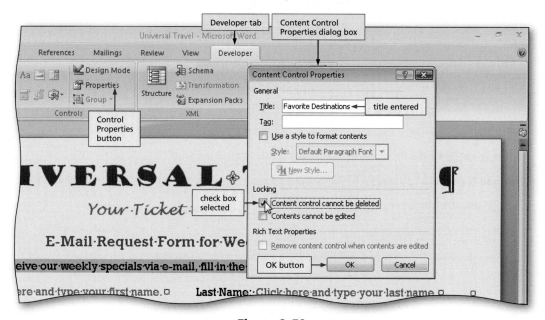

Figure 8–50

To Enter and Format Text

The next step is to enter and format the two lines of text at the bottom of the online form.

1 Be sure the insertion point is on the line below the Favorite Destinations content control.

2 Center the paragraph mark.

3 Format the text to be typed in bold font with the color of Sky Blue, Accent 3, Darker 50%.

4 Type When finished, please save the filled-in form and e-mail it to specials@universaltravel.com! and then press the ENTER key.

Q&A Why did the e-mail address change color?

In this document theme, the color for a hyperlink is a shade of rose. When you pressed the ENTER key, Word automatically formatted the hyperlink in this color.

5 Format the text to be typed in bold with the color of Black, Text 1, Lighter 50%.

6 Type Thank you for your time.

7 Position the insertion point in the line containing the hyperlink. Change the space before the paragraph to 12 point and the space after to 6 point (Figure 8–51).

8 If the text flows to a second page, reduce spacing before paragraphs in the form so that all lines fit on a single page.

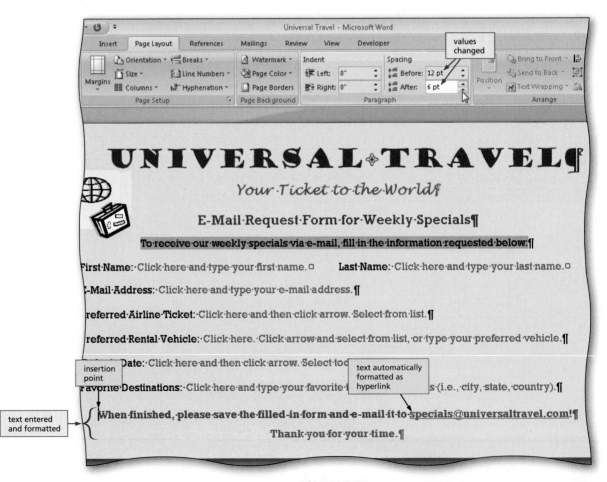

Figure 8–51

To Use the Format Painter Button

The labels for the content controls in the online form in this chapter are to be formatted to 12-point font with the color of Sky Blue, Accent 3, Darker 50%. Instead of selecting each label one at a time and then formatting it, you will format the First Name: label and then copy its format to the remaining labels on the form. The following steps copy formatting.

- Format the First Name: label in the form to 12-point with a color of Sky Blue, Accent 3, Darker 50%.

- Select the text that contains the formatting you wish to copy, in this case, the First Name: label.

- If necessary, display the Home tab.

- Double-click the Format Painter button on the Home tab to turn on the format painter (Figure 8–52).

Q&A Why double-click the Format Painter button?

To copy selected formats from one location to another, click the Format Painter button on the Home tab once. If you want to copy formatting to multiple locations, however, double-click the Format Painter button so that the format painter remains active until you turn it off.

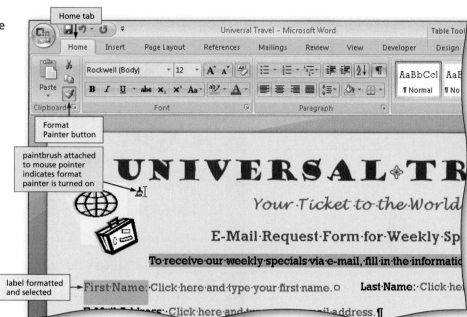

Figure 8–52

- Drag through the Last Name: label on the form to paste the formatting from the First Name: label to this text (Figure 8–53).

- Drag through these remaining labels on the form to paste formatting from the First Name: label to these labels: E-Mail Address:, Preferred Airline Ticket:, Preferred Rental Vehicle:, Today's Date:, and Favorite Destinations:.

Q&A What if the Format Painter button no longer is selected?

Repeat Step 1.

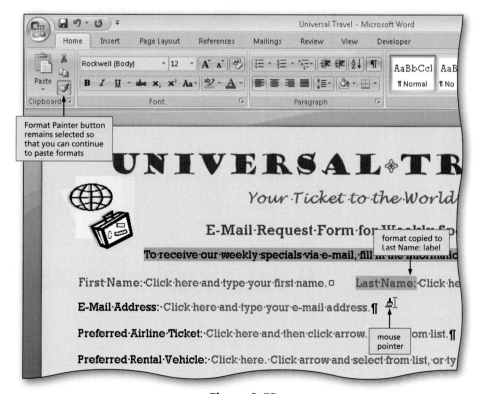

Figure 8–53

4

- Click the Format Painter button on the Home tab to turn off the format painter (Figure 8–54).

Q&A

What if my form now spills onto a second page?

Adjust the spacing above and/or below the paragraphs so that all form contents fit on a single page.

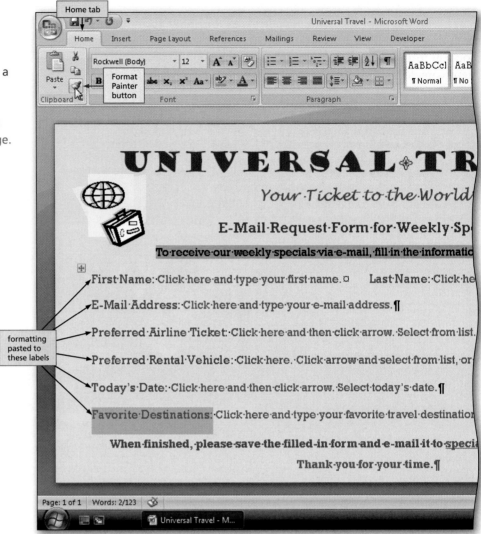

Figure 8–54

To Hide Formatting Marks

You are finished with entering and formatting text on the screen. To make the form more pleasing to view, you hide formatting marks. The following steps hide formatting marks.

1 If necessary, display the Home tab.

2 If the Show/Hide ¶ button on the Home tab is selected, click it to remove formatting marks from the screen.

BTW

Format Painter
If you also want to copy paragraph formatting, such as alignment and line spacing, select the paragraph mark at the end of the paragraph prior to clicking the Format Painter button. If you want to copy only character formatting, such as fonts and font sizes, do not include the paragraph mark in your selected text.

To Draw a Rectangle

The next step is to emphasize the data entry area of the form. The data entry area includes all the content controls in which a user enters data. To call attention to this area of the form, this online form places a rectangle around the data entry area, changes the style rectangle, and then adds a shadow to the rectangle. The first of the following steps draws the rectangle, and the subsequent steps format the rectangle.

- Position the insertion point on the line below the Favorite Destinations content control.

- Display the Insert tab.

- Click the Shapes button on the Insert tab to display the Shapes gallery (Figure 8–55).

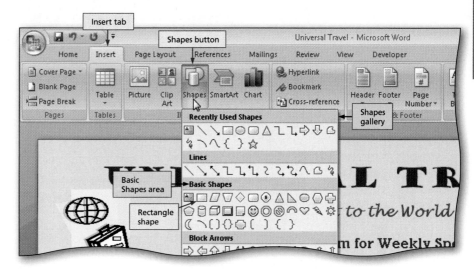

Figure 8–55

- Click Rectangle in the Basic Shapes area of the Shapes gallery, so that you can draw a rectangle on the screen.

- Position the crosshair mouse pointer as shown in Figure 8–56.

Figure 8–56

- Drag the mouse pointer downward and rightward to form a rectangle around the data entry area, as shown in Figure 8–57.

Figure 8–57

4

- Release the mouse button to draw the rectangle shape on top of the data entry area (Figure 8–58).

What happened to all the text in the data entry area?

When you draw a shape in a document, Word initially places the shape in front of, or on top of, any text in the same area. You can change the stacking order of the shape so that it is displayed behind the text. Thus, the next steps place a shape behind text.

Figure 8–58

To Send a Graphic Behind Text

You want the shape graphic to be positioned behind the data entry area text, so that you can see the text in the data entry area along with the shape. The following steps send a graphic behind text.

1

- If necessary, display the Format tab.

- With the rectangle shape selected, click the Send to Back button arrow on the Format tab to display the Send to Back menu (Figure 8–59).

My Send to Back menu did not appear. Why not?

You clicked the Send to Back button instead of the Send to Back button arrow. Repeat Step 1.

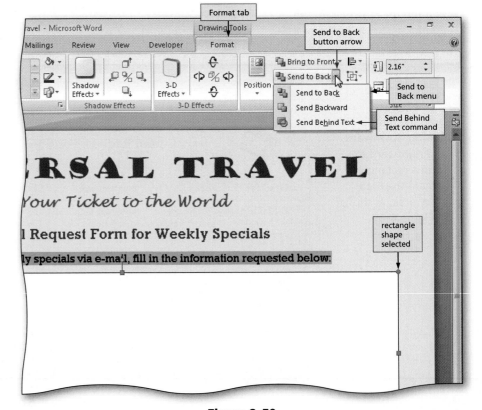

Figure 8–59

2

• Click Send Behind Text on the Send to Back menu to position the rectangle shape behind the text (Figure 8–60).

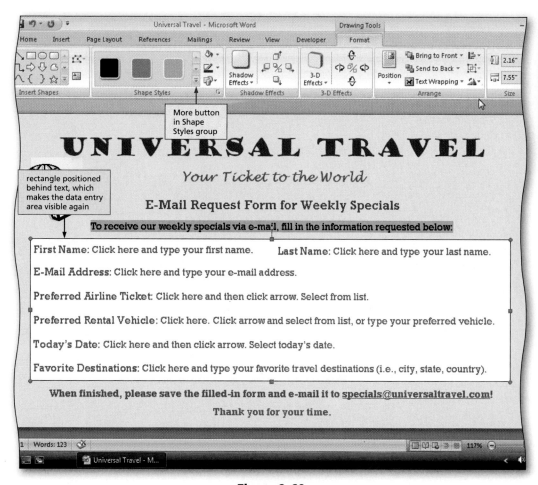

Figure 8–60

Q&A

What if I want a shape to cover text?

You would click the Bring to Front button arrow on the Format tab and then click Bring in Front of Text on the Bring to Front menu.

Other Ways

1. Right-click selected graphic, point to Order on shortcut menu, click Send Behind Text on submenu

BTW

Ordering Graphics

If you have multiple graphics displaying on the screen and would like them to overlap, you can change their stacking order by using commands on the Bring to Front and Send to Back menus. The Bring to Front command on the Bring to Front menu displays the selected object at the top of the stack, and the Send to Back command on the Send to Back menu displays the selected object at the bottom of the stack. The Bring Forward and Send Backward commands each move the graphic forward or backward one layer in the stack. These commands also are available through the shortcut menu that is displayed when you right-click a graphic.

To Apply a Shape Style

The next step is to apply a shape style to the rectangle, so that it is more colorful. Word provides a Shape Styles gallery, allowing you to change the look of the shape to a more visually appealing style. The following steps apply a style to the rectangle.

- With the shape still selected, click the More button in the Shape Styles gallery (shown in Figure 8–60 on the previous page) on the Format tab to expand the Shape Styles gallery.

- Point to Dashed Outline - Accent 4 in the Shape Styles gallery to display a live preview of that style applied to the rectangle shape in the document (Figure 8–61).

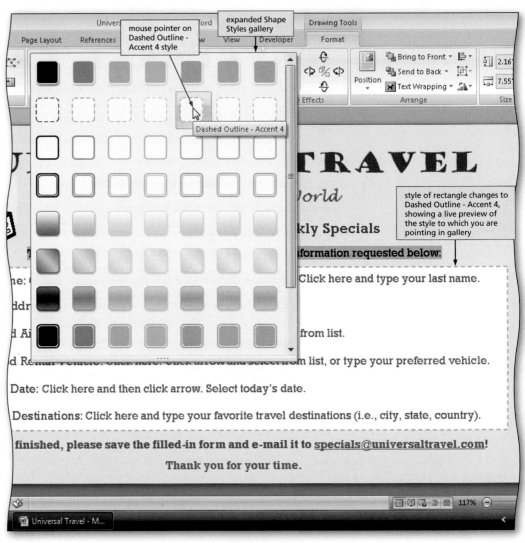

Figure 8–61

Experiment

- Point to various shape styles in the Shape Styles gallery and watch the style of the rectangle shape change.

❸

- Click Dashed Outline - Accent 4 in the Shape Styles gallery to apply the selected style to the rectangle shape.

Other Ways
1. Click Advanced Tools Dialog Box Launcher in Shape Styles group, select desired colors, click OK button   2. Click Format AutoShape on shortcut menu, select desired colors, click OK button

To Add a Shadow to a Shape

To further offset the data entry area of the form, this online form has a shadow on the bottom and right edges of the rectangle shape. The following steps add a shadow to the rectangle shape.

1
- With the shape still selected, click the Shadow Effects button on the Format tab to display the Shadow Effects gallery.

2
- Point to Shadow Style 4 in the Shadow Effects gallery to display a live preview of that shadow effect applied to the rectangle shape in the document (Figure 8–62).

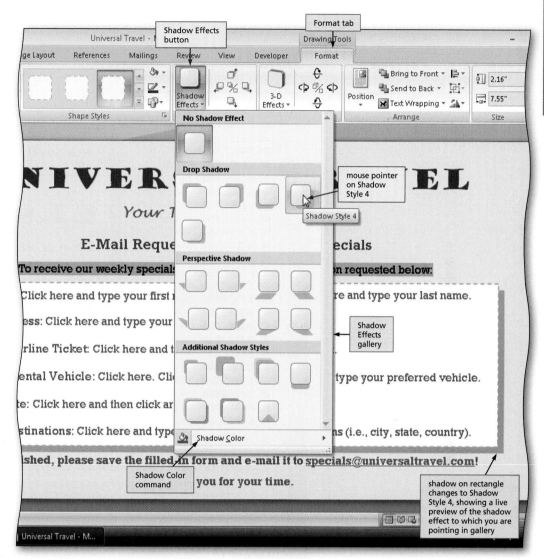

Figure 8–62

 Experiment
- Point to various shadows in the Shadow Effects gallery and watch the shadow on the rectangle shape change.

3
- Click Shadow Style 4 in the Shadow Effects gallery to apply the selected shadow to the rectangle shape.

Q&A

Can I change the color of a shadow?

Yes. Click Shadow Color in the Shadow Effects gallery and then select the desired color in the Shadow Color gallery.

To Customize a Theme Color and Save It with a New Theme Name

The final step in formatting the online form in this chapter is to change the color of the hyperlink. You would like the hyperlink to be darker, to match the company name. A document theme has twelve predefined colors for various on-screen objects including text, backgrounds, and hyperlinks. You can change any of the theme colors. The following steps customize the Foundry theme, changing its designated theme color for hyperlinks.

- Display the Page Layout tab.

- Click the Theme Colors button on the Page Layout tab to display the Theme Colors gallery (Figure 8–63).

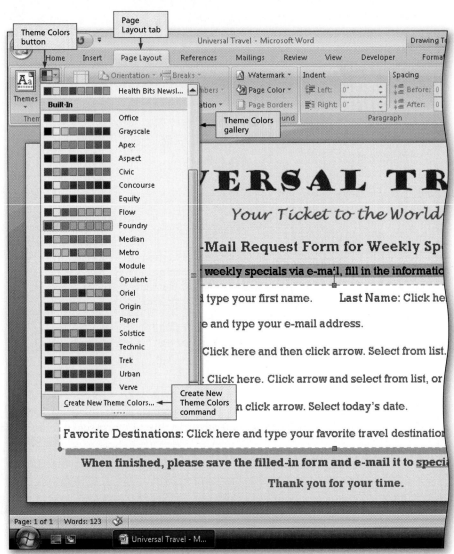

Figure 8–63

2

- Click Create New Theme Colors in the Theme Colors gallery to display the Create New Theme Colors dialog box.

- Click the Hyperlink button to display the Theme Colors gallery (Figure 8–64).

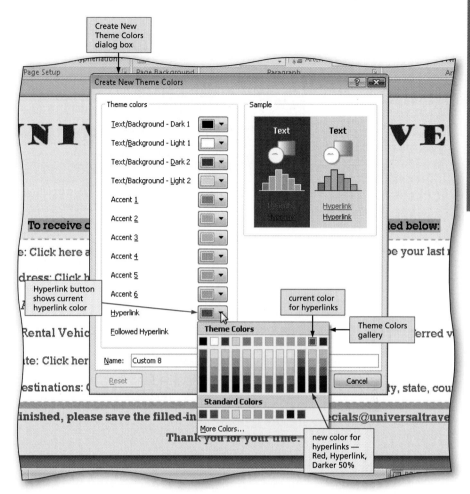

Figure 8–64

3

- Click the bottom color in the Hyperlink column (Red, Hyperlink, Darker 50%) as the new hyperlink color.

Q&A

Do I have to select colors in the specified column?

No. Word organizes suggested colors in columns. You can select any color for any item in this dialog box.

- Type Universal Travel Form in the Name text box (Figure 8–65).

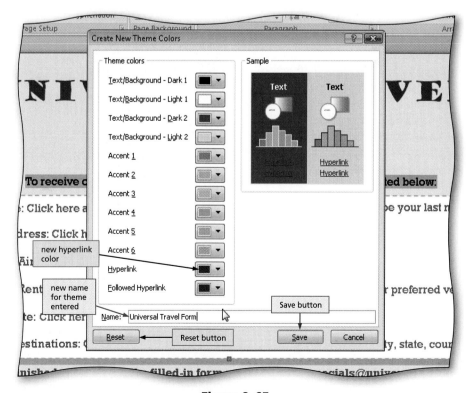

Figure 8–65

4

- Click the Save button in the Create New Theme Colors dialog box to save the modified theme with the name, Universal Travel Form, which is positioned at the top of the Theme Color gallery for future access (Figure 8–66).

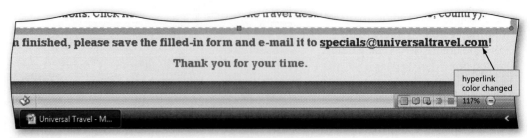

n finished, please save the filled-in form and e-mail it to **specials@universaltravel.com**! Thank you for your time.

hyperlink color changed

Universal Travel - M...

117%

Figure 8–66

Q&A What if I do not enter a name for the modified theme?

Word assigns a name that begins with the letters, Custom, followed by a number (i.e., Custom8).

Q&A What if I wanted to reset all the original theme colors?

You would click the Reset button in the Create New Theme Colors dialog box before clicking the Save button.

Other Ways

1. Make changes to theme colors, fonts, and/or effects; click Themes on | Page Layout tab, click Save Current Theme in Themes gallery

To Protect a Form

It is crucial that you protect a form before making it available to users. When you **protect a form**, you are allowing users to enter data only in designated areas — specifically, the content controls. The following steps protect the online form.

1

- Display the Developer tab.

- Click the Protect Document button on the Developer tab to display the Restrict Formatting and Editing task pane (Figure 8–67). (If a menu appears instead of the task pane, click Restrict Formatting and Editing on the menu to display the task pane.)

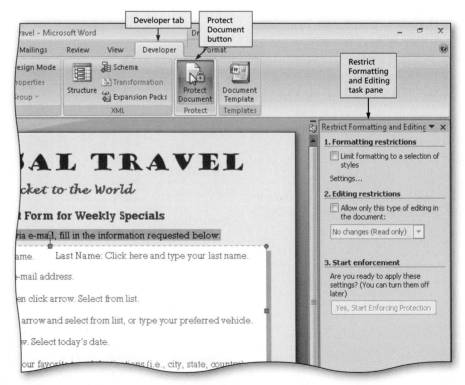

Figure 8–67

2

• In the Editing restrictions area, place a check mark in the 'Allow only this type of editing in the document' check box and then click its box arrow to display a list of types of allowed restrictions (Figure 8–68).

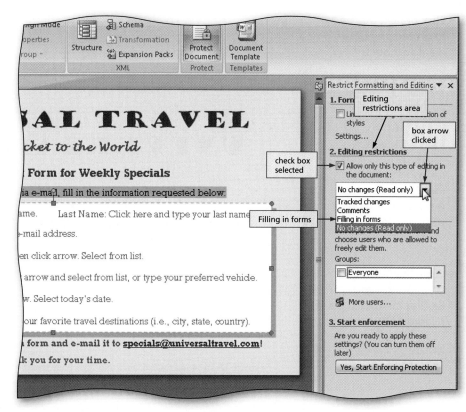

Figure 8–68

3

• Click 'Filling in forms' to instruct Word that the only editing allowed is to content controls in forms.

• In the Start enforcement area, click the Yes, Start Enforcing Protection button, which displays the Start Enforcing Protection dialog box (Figure 8–69).

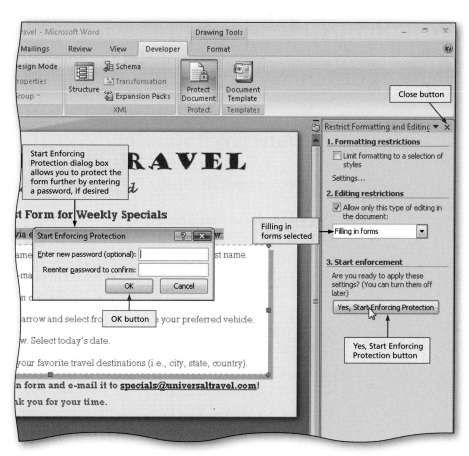

Figure 8–69

4

- Click the OK button to protect the document without a password.

Q&A

What if I enter a password?

If you enter a password, only a user who knows the password will be able to unprotect the document. Chapter 9 discusses passwords in more depth.

- Close the Restrict Formatting and Editing task pane (Figure 8–70).

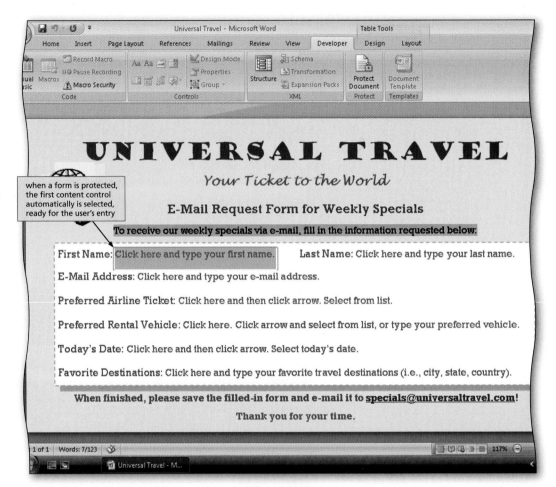

Figure 8–70

Protecting Documents

In addition to protecting a form so that it only can be filled in, Word provides several other options in the Restrict Formatting and Editing task pane.

To Set Formatting Restrictions

If you wanted to restrict users from making certain types of formatting changes to a document, you would perform the following steps.

1. Click the Protect Document button on the Developer tab. (If a menu appears instead of the task pane, click Restrict Formatting and Editing on the menu to display the task pane.)
2. Place a check mark in the 'Limit formatting to a selection of styles' check box in the Formatting restrictions area.
3. Click the Settings link and then select the types of formatting you want to allow.
4. Click the OK button.
5. Click the Yes, Start Enforcing Protection button, enter a password if desired, and then click the OK button.

To Set Editing Restrictions to Tracked Changes or Comments

If you wanted to restrict users from editing a document, you would perform the following steps.

1. Click the Protect Document button on the Developer tab. (If a menu appears instead of the task pane, click Restrict Formatting and Editing on the menu to display the task pane.)

2. Place a check mark in the 'Allow only this type of editing in the document' check box in the Editing restrictions area, click the box arrow, and then click Tracked changes or Comments.

3. Click the Yes, Start Enforcing Protection button, enter a password if desired, and then click the OK button.

To Hide the Developer Tab

You are finished with the commands on the Developer tab. Thus, the following steps hide the Developer tab from the Ribbon.

1 Click the Office Button and then click the Word Options button on the Office Button menu.

2 If necessary, click Popular in the left pane.

3 If it is selected, remove the check mark in the Show Developer tab in the Ribbon check box.

4 Click the OK button to remove the Developer tab from the Ribbon.

To Save the Template Again

The online form template for this project now is complete. Thus, you should save it and quit Word.

1 Save the template with the same file name, Universal Travel.

2 Quit Word.

Working with an Online Form

When you create a template, you use the Open command on the Office Button menu to open the template so that you can modify it. After you have created a template, you then can make it available to users. Users do not open templates with the Open command in Word. Instead, a user displays a new Word document that is based on the template, which means the title bar displays the default file name, Document1 (or a similar name) rather than the template name. When Word displays a document that is based on a template, the document window contains any text and formatting associated with the template. Word provides a variety of templates such as those for memos, letters, fax cover sheets, and resumes. If a user accesses a memo template, Word displays the contents of a basic memo in a new document window.

BTW

Protected Documents
If you open an existing form that has been protected, Word will not allow you to modify the form's appearance until you unprotect it. To unprotect a document, click the Protect Document button on the Developer tab (if a menu appears instead of the task pane, click Restrict Formatting and Editing on the menu to display the task pane), click the Stop Protection button in the Restrict Formatting and Editing task pane, and then close the Restrict Formatting and Editing task pane. If the form has been protected with a password, you will be asked to enter the password when you attempt to unprotect the document.

To Use Windows Explorer to Display a New Document That Is Based on a Template

When you save the template to a USB flash drive, as instructed earlier in this chapter, a user can display a new document that is based on the template through Windows Explorer. This allows the user to work with a new document instead of risking the chance of altering the original template. The following steps display a new Word document that is based on the Universal Travel template.

- Click the Start button on the Windows Vista taskbar to display the Start menu (Figure 8–71).

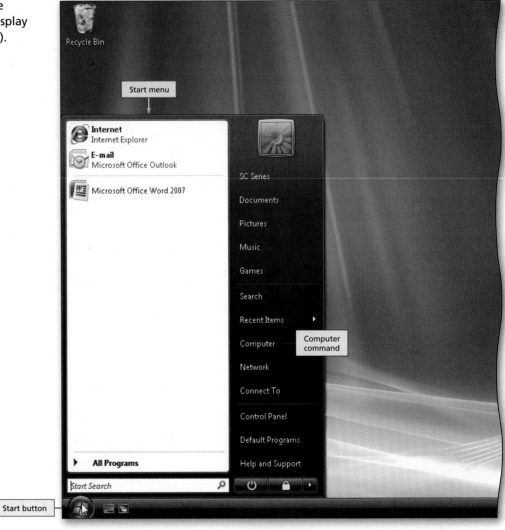

Figure 8–71

2

- Click Computer on the Start menu to display the Explorer window.

- When the Explorer window opens, if necessary, locate your USB flash drive.

- Click the Universal Travel file to select it (Figure 8–72).

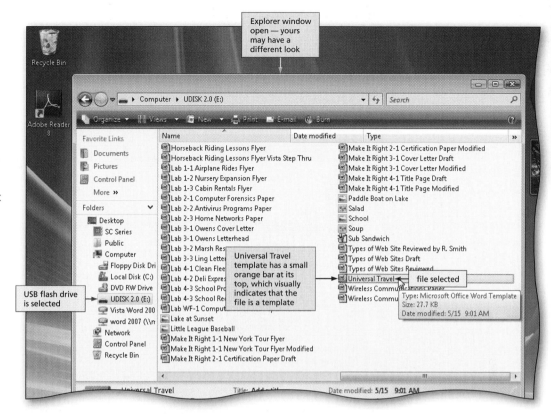

Figure 8–72

3

- Double-click the Universal Travel file in the Explorer window, which starts Word and displays a new document window that is based on the contents of the Universal Travel template (Figure 8–73).

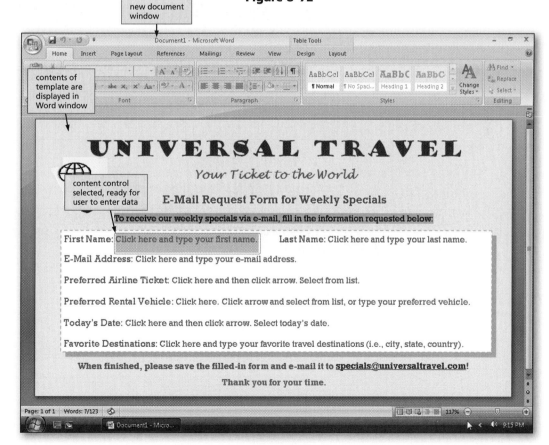

Figure 8–73

To Fill In a Form and Save It

The next step is to enter data in the form. To advance from one content control to the next, a user can click the content control or press the TAB key. To move to a previous content control, a user can click it or press SHIFT+TAB. The following steps fill in the Universal Travel form.

1

- With the First Name content control selected, type Howard and then press the TAB key.

- Type Blasdel in the Last Name content control and then press the TAB key.

- Type blasdel@worldlink .net in the E-Mail Address content control.

- Press the TAB key to select the Preferred Airline Ticket content control and then click its arrow to display the list of choices (shown in Figure 8–1b on page WD 571).

- Click Business in the list and then press the TAB key.

- Type Convertible in the Preferred Rental Vehicle content control and then press the TAB key.

- Click the Today's Date arrow to display the calendar (Figure 8–74).

2

- Click May 29, 2008 in the calendar and then press the TAB key.

- Type Orlando, Florida, and Paris, France in the Favorite Destinations content control to complete the entries in the form (Figure 8–75).

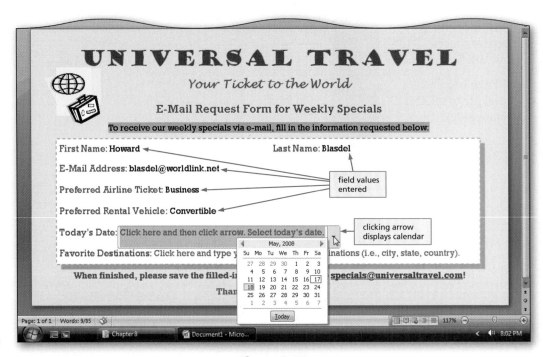

Figure 8–74

Figure 8–75

3

- Click the Save button on the Quick Access Toolbar and then save the file on your USB flash drive with the file name, Blasdel E-Mail Request Form.

Q&A

Can I print the form?

You can print the document as you print any other document. Keep in mind, however, that the colors used were designed for viewing online. Thus, different color schemes would have been selected if the form had been designed for a printout.

Working with Templates

If you want to modify the template, open it by clicking the Open command on the Office Button menu, clicking the template name, and then clicking the Open button in the dialog box. Then, you must **unprotect the form** by clicking the Protect Document button on the Developer tab and then clicking the Stop Protection button in the Restrict Formatting and Editing task pane. (If a menu appears instead of the task pane when you click the Protect Document button, click Restrict Formatting and Editing on the menu to display the task pane.)

When you created the template in this chapter, you saved it on a USB flash drive. In environments other than an academic setting, you would not save the template on a USB flash drive. Instead, you would save it in the Templates folder, which is the folder Word initially displays in the Save As dialog box for a template file type (shown in Figure 8–3 on page WD 574). When you save a template in the Templates folder, you can locate the template by clicking the Office Button, clicking New, and then clicking My templates, which displays the template in the New dialog box (Figure 8–76).

BTW

Conserving Ink and Toner
You can instruct Word to print draft quality documents to conserve ink or toner by clicking the Office Button, clicking the Word Options button, clicking Advanced in the left pane of the Word Options dialog box, scrolling to the Print area, placing a check mark in the 'Use draft quality' check box, and then clicking the OK button. Click the Office Button, point to Print, and then click Quick Print.

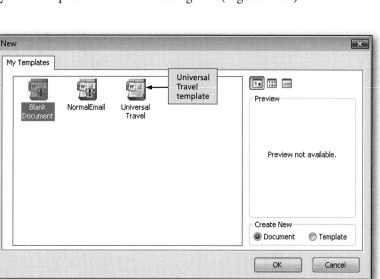

Figure 8–76

To Quit Word

The final steps are to quit Word and close Windows Explorer.

1 Quit Word.

2 If Windows Explorer is still open, close the window.

Chapter Summary

In this chapter, you have learned how to create an online form. Topics covered included saving a document as a template, changing paper size, inserting content controls, editing placeholder text, changing properties of content controls, using the Format Painter, and protecting a form. The items listed below include all the new Word skills you have learned in this chapter.

1. Save a Document as a Template (WD 574)
2. Change Paper Size (WD 577)
3. Adjust the Contrast of a Graphic (WD 584)
4. Highlight Text (WD 586)
5. Show the Developer Tab (WD 588)
6. Insert a Borderless Table in a Form (WD 589)
7. Show Gridlines (WD 592)
8. Insert a Plain Text Content Control (WD 593)
9. Edit Placeholder Text (WD 594)
10. Change the Properties of a Plain Text Content Control (WD 595)
11. Hide Gridlines (WD 599)
12. Insert a Drop-Down List Content Control (WD 601)
13. Change the Properties of a Drop-Down List Content Control (WD 602)
14. Insert a Combo Box Content Control (WD 604)
15. Change the Properties of a Combo Box Content Control (WD 605)
16. Insert a Date Content Control (WD 606)
17. Change the Properties of a Date Content Control (WD 607)
18. Insert a Rich Text Content Control (WD 608)
19. Change the Properties of a Rich Text Content Control (WD 609)
20. Use the Format Painter Button (WD 611)
21. Draw a Rectangle (WD 613)
22. Send a Graphic Behind Text (WD 614)
23. Apply a Shape Style (WD 616)
24. Add a Shadow to a Shape (WD 617)
25. Customize a Theme Color and Save It with a New Theme Name (WD 618)
26. Protect a Form (WD 620)
27. Set Formatting Restrictions (WD 622)
28. Set Editing Restrictions to Tracked Changes or Comments (WD 623)
29. Hide the Developer Tab (WD 623)
30. Use Windows Explorer to Display a New Document That Is Based on a Template (WD 624)
31. Fill In a Form and Save It (WD 626)

 If you have a SAM user profile, you may have access to hands-on instruction, practice, and assessment. Log in to your SAM account (http://sam2007.course.com) to launch any assigned training activities or exams that relate to the skills covered in this chapter.

BTW

Quick Reference
For a table that lists how to complete the tasks covered in this book using the mouse, Ribbon, shortcut menu, and keyboard, see the Quick Reference Summary at the back of this book, or visit the Word 2007 Quick Reference Web page (scsite.com/wd2007/qr).

Learn It Online

Test your knowledge of chapter content and key terms.

Instructions: To complete the Learn It Online exercises, start your browser, click the Address bar, and then enter the Web address `scsite.com/wd2007/learn`. When the Word 2007 Learn It Online page is displayed, click the link for the exercise you want to complete and then read the instructions.

Chapter Reinforcement TF, MC, and SA
A series of true/false, multiple choice, and short answer questions that test your knowledge of the chapter content.

Flash Cards
An interactive learning environment where you identify chapter key terms associated with displayed definitions.

Practice Test
A series of multiple choice questions that test your knowledge of chapter content and key terms.

Who Wants To Be a Computer Genius?
An interactive game that challenges your knowledge of chapter content in the style of a television quiz show.

Wheel of Terms
An interactive game that challenges your knowledge of chapter key terms in the style of the television show *Wheel of Fortune*.

Crossword Puzzle Challenge
A crossword puzzle that challenges your knowledge of key terms presented in the chapter.

Apply Your Knowledge

Reinforce the skills and apply the concepts you learned in this chapter.

Filling In an Online Form
Instructions: In this assignment, you access a template through Windows Explorer. The template contains an online form. You are to fill in the form, save it, and print it. The template is located on the Data Files for Students. See the inside back cover of this book for instructions on downloading the Data Files for Students, or contact your instructor for information about accessing the required files.

Perform the following tasks:
1. Start Windows Explorer. In the Explorer window, select the USB flash drive. Double-click the Apply 8-1 That Pool Place template in Windows Explorer.
2. When Word displays a new document based on the Apply 8-1 That Pool Place template, if necessary, hide formatting marks and change the zoom to page width. Your screen should look like Figure 8–77 on the next page.
3. With the First Name content control selected, type Celaine and then press the TAB key.
4. With the Last Name content control selected, type Raam and then press the TAB key.
5. Click the Today's Date content control arrow, click May 29, 2008 in the calendar and then press the TAB key.
6. With the E-Mail Address content control selected, type cr@linkworld.net and then press the TAB key.
7. Click the Pool Size content control arrow and then review the list. Press the ESCAPE key because none of these choices meets your criteria. Type 7,000 gallons as the pool size and then press the TAB key.
8. Click the Type of Pool content control arrow and then click Liner in the list.

Continued >

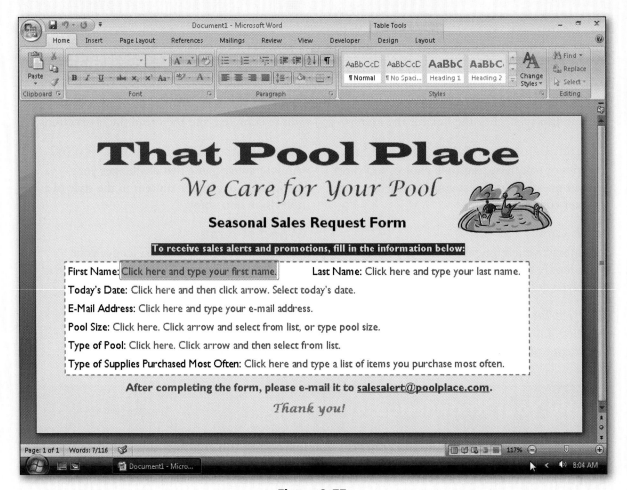

Figure 8–77

9. Click the Type of Supplies Purchased Most Often content control and then type `chlorine and water test kits` as the supplies.

10. Save the file with the name Apply 8-1 Raam Form. Print the form. Close the document.

11. Open the Apply 8-1 That Pool Place template from the Data Files for Students.

12. Unprotect the Apply 8-1 That Pool Place template.

13. Save the template with a new name, Apply 8-1 That Pool Place Modified.

14. Change the Today's Date content control to the format M/d/yyyy (i.e., 5/20/2008).

15. Adjust the contrast of the graphic to +30 %.

16. Protect the modified template.

17. Save the modified template.

18. Print the modified template.

Extend Your Knowledge

Extend the skills you learned in this chapter and experiment with new skills. You may need to use Help to complete the assignment.

Working with Picture Content Controls, Text Boxes, Shadows, Themes, and Passwords

Instructions: Start Word. Open the document, Extend 8-1 Pampered Pals Draft, from the Data Files for Students. See the inside back cover of this book for instructions on downloading the Data Files for Students, or contact your instructor for information about accessing the required files.

You will add a pattern fill effect to the page color, add a picture content control in a text box and format the text box, rotate graphics, change the highlight color, change the shadow color, nudge the shadow, change theme colors, reset theme colors, save a modified theme, and protect a form with a password.

Perform the following tasks:

1. Use Help to review and expand your knowledge about these topics: fill effects, picture content controls, text boxes, rotating graphics, shadows, changing theme colors, and protecting forms with passwords.

2. Add a pattern fill effect, of your choice, to the page color.

3. Add a simple text box to the empty space in the bottom-right corner of the data entry area. Resize the text box so that it fits completely in the data entry area.

4. In the text box, type the label, Pet Photo:, and then below the label, insert a picture content control. Resize the picture content control so that it fits in the text box (Figure 8–78). Remove the border from the text box.

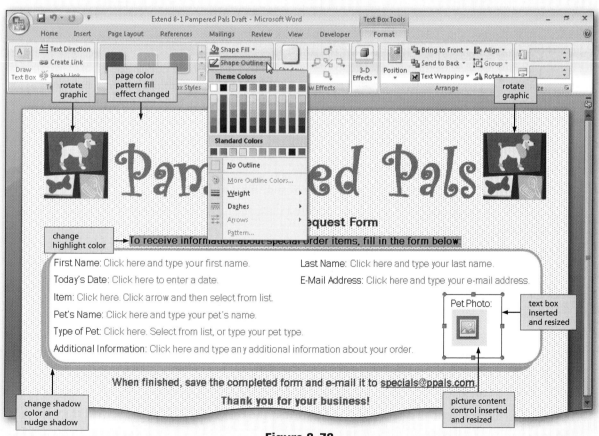

Figure 8–78

Continued >

Extend Your Knowledge *continued*

5. Rotate the graphics at the top of the form so that the dogs are angled instead of horizontal. If necessary, move the rotated graphics so that they do not cover text in the form title.

6. Change the highlight color of the third line of text to a color other than Gray-25%. If necessary, change the text color so that you can read the text in the new highlight color.

7. Change the color of the shadow on the rectangle to a color other than the default.

8. Nudge the shadow up, down, left, and/or right so that it looks different from the default shadow.

9. Change the theme colors for Text/Background - Dark 1 and Accent 3. Reset the theme colors.

10. Change the theme colors for Accent 1 and Hyperlink. Save the modified theme colors.

11. Make any necessary formatting changes to the form.

12. Protect the form with a password.

13. Change the document properties as specified by your instructor.

14. Save the revised document with a new file name.

15. Test the form. When filling in the form, use the picture called Dog on the Data Files for Students for the picture content control.

16. Submit the online form in the format specified by your instructor.

Make It Right

Analyze a document and correct all errors and/or improve the design.

Formatting an Online Form

Instructions: Start Word. Open the document, Make It Right 8-1 Party Tunes Draft, from the Data Files for Students. See the inside back cover of this book for instructions on downloading the Data Files for Students, or contact your instructor for information about accessing the required files.

The document is an online form whose elements are not formatted (Figure 8–79). You are to change the graphic's wrapping style; change the page color; change fonts, font sizes, and font colors; change the graphic's contrast; remove the table border; edit placeholder text; change content control properties; use the Format Painter; draw a rectangle and format it; and protect the form.

Perform the following tasks:

1. Change the graphic's wrapping style to In Front of Text.

2. Change the page color to a color of your choice (other than white).

3. Change the font, font size, and font color for the first three lines and last two lines of text. Center the five lines.

4. Change the graphic's contrast and move the graphic to an appropriate location on the form.

5. Remove the border from the 2 × 1 table that surrounds the First Name and Last Name content controls. Show table gridlines.

6. Edit all placeholder text so that each content control contains meaningful instructions.

7. For each content control, change the properties as follows: add a title and set the locking so that the content control cannot be deleted.

8. Change the format of the First Name: label. Use the Format Painter to copy the formatting to all other labels in the data entry area of the form.

9. Draw a rectangle around the data entry area. Format the rectangle so that it is behind the text. Add a shape style and a shadow to the rectangle.

10. Hide table gridlines. Protect the form.

11. Change the document properties as specified by your instructor.

12. Save the revised document with a new file name and then submit it in the format specified by your instructor.

13. Save the revised document with a new file name. Test the form.

14. Submit the online form in the format specified by your instructor.

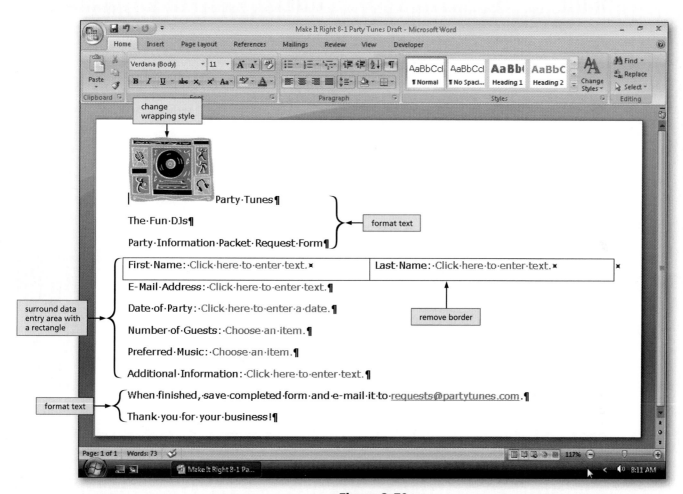

Figure 8–79

In the Lab

Design and/or create a document using the guidelines, concepts, and skills presented in this chapter. Labs are listed in order of increasing difficulty.

Lab 1: Creating an Online Form

Problem: You work as a part-time assistant at Andrew County Public Library. Your supervisor has asked you to prepare the event notification request form shown in Figure 8–80.

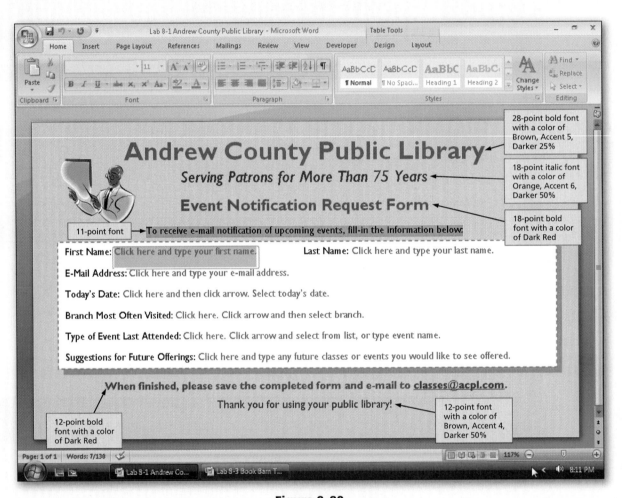

Figure 8–80

Perform the following tasks:

1. Save a blank document as a template, called Lab 8-1 Andrew County Public Library, for the online form.

2. If necessary, change the view to page width.

3. Change the paper size to a height of 8.5 inches and a width of 4.75 inches.

4. Change the margins as follows: top — 0.25", bottom — 0", left — 0.5", and right — 0.5".

5. Change the theme fonts to Origin. Change the theme colors to Trek.

6. Change the page color to Light Yellow, Background 2, Darker 10%.

7. Enter and format the company name, business tag line, and form title as shown in Figure 8–80 (or with similar fonts). Insert the clip art image (which is installed by default with Word). Change the wrapping style of the graphic to In Front of Text. If necessary, resize the graphic and move to the location shown.

8. Enter the instructions above the data entry area and highlight the line Gray-25%.

9. In the data entry area, enter the labels as shown in Figure 8–80 and the content controls as follows: First Name, Last Name, and E-Mail Address are plain text content controls. Today's Date is a date content control. Branch Most Often Visited is a drop-down list content control with these choices: River Fork, Eakins, Main, and Manning. Type of Event Last Attended is a combo box content control with these choices: Computer Class, Author Lecture, Book Discussion, Children's Program, and Craft/Hobby Class. Suggestions for Future Offerings is a rich text content control.

10. Edit the placeholder text of all content controls to match Figure 8–80. Change the properties of the content controls so that each contains a title and all have locking set so that the content control cannot be deleted.

11. Enter the two lines below the data entry area as shown in Figure 8–80.

12. Adjust spacing above and below paragraphs as necessary so that all contents fit on a single screen.

13. Draw a rectangle around the data entry area. Change the shape style of the rectangle to Dashed Outline - Accent 5. Apply Shadow Style 4 to the rectangle.

14. Protect the form.

15. Save the form again and submit it in the format specified by your instructor.

16. Access the template through Windows Explorer. Fill in the form using personal data and submit it in the format specified by your instructor.

In the Lab

Lab 2: Creating an Online Form with Clip Art from the Web

Problem: You work part-time for Entrée Express, a company that delivers meals to the customer's door. Your supervisor has asked you to prepare the online weekly menu request form shown in Figure 8–81.

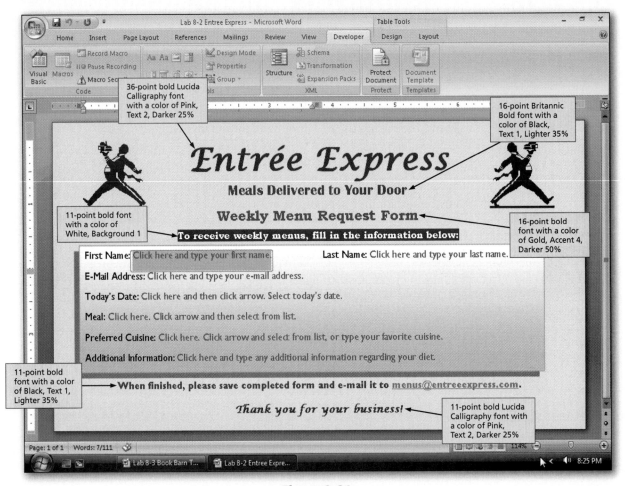

Figure 8–81

Perform the following tasks:

1. Save a blank document as a template, called Lab 8-2 Entree Express, for the online form.
2. If necessary, change the view to page width.
3. Change the paper size to a height of 8.5 inches and a width of 4.75 inches.
4. Change the margins as follows: top — 0.25", bottom — 0", left — 0.5", and right — 0.5".
5. Change the theme fonts to Origin. Change the theme colors to Opulent.
6. Change the page color to Orange, Accent 6, Lighter 80%.
7. Enter and format the company name, business tag line, and form title as shown in Figure 8–81 (or with similar fonts). Locate a clip art image on the Web similar to the one in the figure (or insert the image on the Data Files for Students) and insert it twice. Change the wrapping style of the graphics to In Front of Text. If necessary, resize the graphics. Move the graphics to the locations shown. Flip the graphic on the right.
8. Enter the instructions above the data entry area and highlight the line violet.

9. In the data entry area, enter the labels as shown in Figure 8–81 and the content controls as follows: First Name, Last Name, and E-Mail Address are plain text content controls. Today's Date is a date content control. Meal is a drop-down list content control with these choices: Breakfast, Lunch, and Dinner. Preferred Cuisine is a combo box content control with these choices: American, Asian, French, Italian, Mexican, Southwestern, and Vegetarian. Additional Information is a rich text content control.

10. Edit the placeholder text of all content controls to match Figure 8–81. Change the properties of the content controls so that each contains a title and all have locking set so that the content control cannot be deleted.

11. Enter the two lines below the data entry area as shown in Figure 8–81.

12. Adjust spacing above and below paragraphs as necessary so that all contents fit on the screen.

13. Change the theme color for the hyperlink color to Light Yellow, Hyperlink, Darker 50%.

14. Draw a rectangle around the data entry area. Change the shape style of the rectangle to Linear Up Gradient - Accent 5. Apply Shadow Style 3 to the rectangle.

15. Protect the form.

16. Save the form again and submit it in the format specified by your instructor.

17. Access the template through Windows Explorer. Fill in the form using personal data and submit it in the format specified by your instructor.

In the Lab

Lab 3: Creating an Online Form with Clip Art from the Web and a Texture Fill Effect

Problem: You work part-time for the Book Barn, a bookshop that specializes in rare and out-of-print books. Your supervisor has asked you to prepare an e-mail request form.

Perform the following tasks:

1. Save a blank document as a template, called Lab 8-3 Book Barn, for the online form.

2. If necessary, change the view to page width.

3. Change the paper size to a height of 8.5 inches and a width of 4.75 inches.

4. Change the margins as follows: top — 0.25", bottom — 0", left — 0.5", and right — 0.5".

5. Change the theme fonts to Office. Change the theme colors to Aspect.

6. Change the page color to Tan, Background 2, Darker 10%.

7. Enter and format the company name, business tag line, and form title as shown in Figure 8–82 on the next page (or with similar fonts). Locate a clip art image on the Web similar to the one in the figure. Change the wrapping style of the graphic to In Front of Text. If necessary, resize the graphic and move it to the location shown.

8. Enter the instructions above the data entry area and highlight the line dark yellow.

9. In the data entry area, enter the labels as shown in Figure 8–82 and the content controls as follows: First Name, Last Name, and E-Mail Address are plain text content controls. Today's Date is a date content control. Genre is a combo box content control with these choices: Mystery, Science Fiction, Romance, Historical, Juvenile, and Nonfiction. Second Choice If Written Book Is Unavailable is a drop-down list content control with these choices: Audio Book and DVD/VHS Movie. Particular Items Sought is a rich text content control.

10. Edit the placeholder text of all content controls to match Figure 8–82. Change the properties of the content controls so that each contains a title and all have locking specified so that the content control cannot be deleted.

Continued >

In the Lab *continued*

11. Enter the two lines below the data entry area as shown in Figure 8–82.

12. Change the font size and color of the E-Mail Address: label as shown in Figure 8–82. Use the Format Painter to copy the format from this label to the remaining labels in the data entry area of the form.

13. Adjust spacing above and below paragraphs as necessary so that all contents fit on the screen.

14. Draw a rectangle around the data entry area. Change the shape style of the rectangle to Compound Outline - Accent 2. Add the Parchment texture fill effect to the rectangle. Apply Shadow Style 4 to the rectangle. Color the shadow Red, Accent 2.

15. Protect the form.

16. Save the form again and submit it in the format specified by your instructor.

17. Access the template through Windows Explorer. Fill in the form using personal data and submit it in the format specified by your instructor.

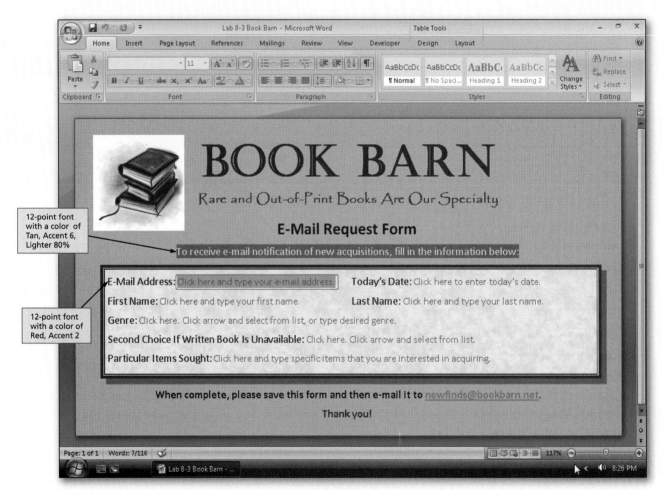

Figure 8–82

Cases and Places

Apply your creative thinking and problem solving skills to design and implement a solution.

• Easier   •• More Difficult

• 1: Create an Online Form for an Auto Dealership

Your boss at Cool Ride Auto Sales, a new and used car dealership, recently decided to explore online auto sales. He has asked you to create an online form that customers can complete when they have an inquiry about purchasing a car. Create a template that contains the business name (Cool Ride Auto Sales), the business tag line (Quality Cars – Guaranteed!), and appropriate clip art. The third line should have the text, Auto Search Form. The fourth line should be highlighted and should read: To receive information, fill in the information requested below:. The data entry area should contain two plain text content controls on the first line placed within a table: First Name and Last Name. The second line should contain a plain text content control with the label, E-Mail Address. The third line should contain a drop-down list content control with the label, Price Range. The choices for this drop-down list are as follows: < $5,000; $5,000 – $10,000; $10,000 – $20,000; $20,000 – $30,000; and > $30,000. The fourth line should contain a combo box content control with the label, Desired Style. The choices for this content control are Sedan, SUV, Van/Minivan, Truck, Sports Car, and Luxury. The fifth line should contain a date content control with the label, Today's Date. The sixth line in the data entry area should have a rich text content control with the label, Additional Information. Below the data entry area, add this message: Save this form and e-mail to deals@coolrides.com. On the last line, include the text: Thank you for your time. Use meaningful instructional text for all content controls. (For example, the instructional text for the First Name text box content control could be as follows: Click here and then type your first name.) Draw a rectangle around the data entry area of the form. Add a shadow to the rectangle. Protect the form and test it.

•• 2: Create an Online Form for a Real Estate Office

You work part-time for your neighbor's real estate office. She has asked you to design a template for an online information form that prospective buyers can complete to receive information about new listings that might interest them. The top of the form should have the name of the real estate office (Richards Realty), with the tag line: Great homes at great prices. The third line should be: New Listing Alert Request Form. The fourth line should read: For information about new listings, fill in the information below. Be sure to highlight this line so that it stands out. Include appropriate clip art, and add plain text content controls for buyer's first name, last name, and e-mail address. Add a drop-down list content control with the label, Type of House. The choices for this content control should include the following: Condo, Ranch, Two-Story, Split-Level. Use a combo box content control with the label, Price Range. The choices should include the following: $100,000 – $150,000; $150,000 – $200,000; $200,000 – $300,000; and > $300,000. Include a date content control so that form users can enter the current date and a rich text content control where they can provide additional information about their home search. Use meaningful instructional text for all content controls. Draw a rectangle with a shadow around the data entry area. Protect the form and test it.

•• 3: Create an Online Form for a Property Management Agency

As a part-time assistant at Sunshine Rentals, you have been assigned the project of designing an online form that clients can access via the Web in order to inquire about rental properties in Florida. Include the company name and appropriate clip art, as well as the tag line: We Cover All of Florida! The third line should read: Rental Request Form. The fourth line should be highlighted and should read: Complete the form below to receive rental information. Include plain text content controls for all pertinent information, such as first name, last name, and e-mail address. Add a drop-down list content

Continued >

Cases and Places *continued*

control for general location (North, South, East, West, Central, and Island). Use a combo box content control for type of unit (Condo, House, Hotel/Motel, and Cabin). Provide a plain text content control for number of guests and a date content control for the date. Include another combo box content control labeled, Desired Amenities, with these choices: Pool, Kitchen, Pets Allowed, Kitchen, Beachside, Beach Access, Wheelchair Access. Use meaningful instructional text for all content controls. Draw a rectangle with a shadow around the data entry area. Protect the form and test it.

•• 4: Create an Online Form for Your Future Business

Make It Personal

Most people, at some point, wish they owned their own business, or at least worked for themselves rather than someone else. Considering your major and/or your job skills and experience, what type of business would you open if you could? With this choice in mind, design an online form that would help facilitate your business. The form could gather information from customers or disperse information to them. Use the techniques and skills you learned in this chapter to design the form. Include appropriate clip art, a company name and tag line, and other appropriate elements. Add content controls to the form as necessary. Use meaningful instructional text for all content controls. When the form is complete, protect it and test it.

•• 5: Create an Online Form for Your School

Working Together

For this assignment, you will form a team to investigate a campus organization, club, or facility that could benefit from using an online form. For example, a fitness facility might benefit from an online form that alerts members to open court times or special events. The library might find it easier if it could inform patrons of new books and other publications and materials as they become available. A club or organization might use an online form to gather information about members' interests or inform members of upcoming events or meetings. Once you have made your choice, as a team, choose a title, clip art, and tag line. Decide on the overall design of the form, as well as the fonts, colors, and other visual elements. Each member then should design an area of the form. First, determine what information is required for the form to be effective and helpful. Then, decide which choices to include in the various content controls you include. Be sure to include at least one of each of the following content controls: plain text, combo box, drop-down list, rich text box, building block, and photo. Use the techniques and skills you learned in this chapter to format and design the form so that it is attractive and easy to use.

9 Enhancing an Online Form and Working with Macros, Document Security, and XML

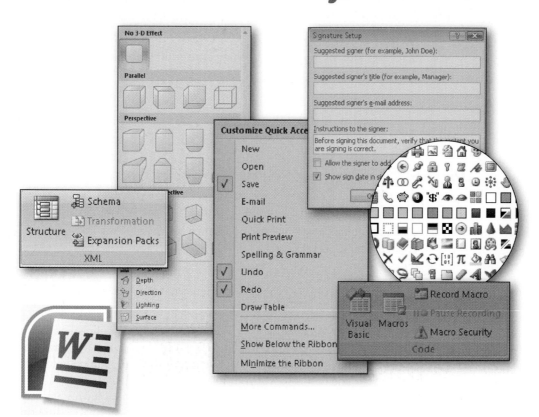

Objectives

You will have mastered the material in this chapter when you can:

- Unprotect a document
- Specify macro settings
- Use fill effects
- Convert a table to text
- Add a 3-D effect to a shape
- Rotate a graphic
- Insert and edit a field
- Record and execute a macro

- Customize the Quick Access Toolbar
- Edit a macro's VBA code
- Save a document with a password
- Use the Document Inspector
- Add a signature line or a digital signature
- Work with XML

9 | Enhancing an Online Form and Working with Macros, Document Security, and XML

Introduction

Word provides many tools that allow you to improve the appearance, functionality, and security of your documents, as well as provide formats for sharing document data with other programs. This chapter discusses tools used to perform the following tasks:

- Enhance the look of graphics and shapes with fill effects and 3-D effects.
- Automate a series of tasks with a macro.
- Secure a document with digital signatures, passwords, and other settings.
- Use XML formats if data will be shared with other programs.

Project — Online Form Revised

This chapter is divided into three separate projects:

1. The first improves the visual appearance of and adds macros to the online form created in Chapter 8.
2. The second incorporates security in a document.
3. The third uses XML so that a document's data can be shared and re-used by other programs.

The first project in this chapter uses Word to produce the online form shown in Figure 9–1a. This project begins with the Universal Travel online form created in Chapter 8. Thus, you will need the online form template created in Chapter 8 to complete this project. (If you did not create the template, see your instructor for a copy.)

This project modifies the fonts and font colors of the text in the Universal Travel online form and enhances the contents of the form to include a texture fill effect, a 3-D effect, and a picture fill effect. The graphic in the form is rotated, and the date automatically displays the computer date, instead of requiring the user to enter the date.

This form also includes macros to automate tasks. A **macro** is a set of commands and instructions grouped together to allow a user to accomplish a task automatically. One macro allows the user to hide the Developer tab by pressing a shortcut key or clicking a button on the Quick Access Toolbar. Another macro specifies how the form is displayed initially on a user's Word screen. As shown in Figure 9–1b, when a document contains macros, Word may generate security warnings that allow you to enable or disable macros. If you are sure the macros are from a trusted source and free of viruses, then enable the macros. Otherwise, disable them to protect your computer from potentially harmful viruses or other malicious software.

The second and third projects are presented when they are discussed later in the chapter.

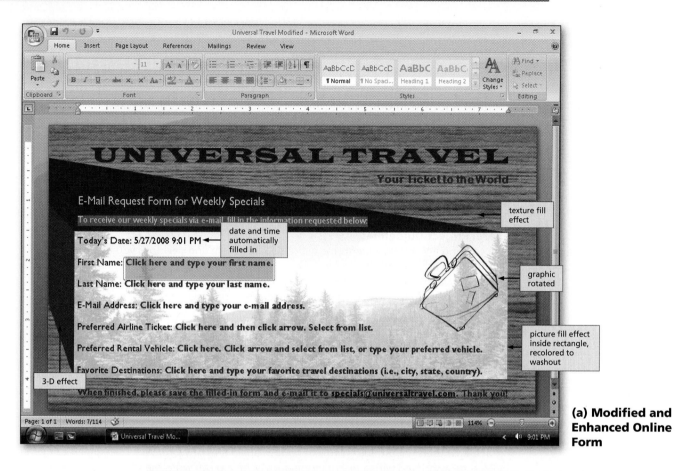

(a) Modified and Enhanced Online Form

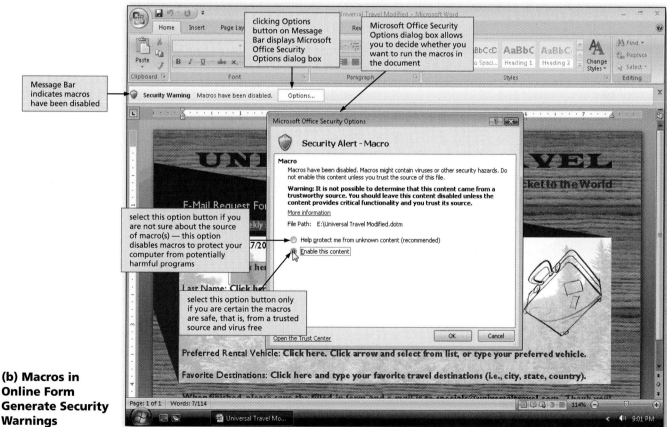

(b) Macros in Online Form Generate Security Warnings

Figure 9–1

Overview

As you read through this chapter, you will learn how to create the online form shown in Figure 9–1 on the previous page, make a document more secure, and prepare a document data for use in other programs by performing these general tasks:

- Enhance the look of an online form.
- Add macros to automate tasks.
- Incorporate security in a document.
- Use XML.

Plan
Ahead

General Project Guidelines

When creating a Word document, the actions you perform and decisions you make will affect the appearance and characteristics of the finished document. As you enhance an online form, such as the project shown in Figure 9–1, add macros, incorporate security, and use XML, you should follow these general guidelines:

1. **Save the form to be modified as a macro-enabled template.** If you plan to include macros in a template for a form, be sure to save the template as a macro-enabled template. Basic Word templates cannot store macros.

2. **Enhance the visual appeal of a form.** Use colors and images that complement one another. Draw the user's attention to important sections. Arrange data entry fields in logical groups on the form and in an order that users would expect.

3. **Add macros to automate tasks.** In Word, a macro consists of VBA code. **VBA**, which stands for **Visual Basic for Applications**, is a powerful programming language included with Word that allows users to customize and extend the capabilities of Word. Word can generate the VBA code associated with a macro automatically, or you can write the VBA code yourself. To add macros, you do not need a computer programming background. To write VBA code, however, you should be familiar with computer programming.

4. **Incorporate security in a document.** Word provides several tools that allow you to secure your documents. For example, you can add a digital signature, insert a signature line, mark the document as final, save the document with a password, and customize Word settings.

5. **Determine how the form data will be analyzed.** If the data entered in the form will be analyzed by a program outside of Word, create the data entry fields so that the entries are stored in a format, such as XML, that can be shared with other programs.

When necessary, more specific details concerning the above guidelines are presented at appropriate points in the chapter. The chapter also will identify the actions performed and decisions made regarding these guidelines during the creation of the documents in this chapter.

To Start Word

If you are using a computer to step through the project in this chapter and you want your screens to match the figures in this book, you should change your computer's resolution to 1024 × 768. For information about how to change a computer's resolution, read Appendix D.

The following steps start Word and verify Word settings.

1 Start Word.

2 If the Word window is not maximized, click its Maximize button.

3 If the Print Layout button on the status bar is not selected, click it so that Word is in Print Layout view.

4 If the rulers are displayed, click the View Ruler button on the vertical scroll bar because you will not use the rulers to perform tasks in this project.

5 If the edges of the page do not extend to the edge of the document window, click View on the Ribbon and then click Page Width on the View tab to zoom page width.

To Save a Macro-Enabled Template

The first project in this chapter contains macros. To provide added security to templates, a basic Word template does not contain macros. Word instead provides a specific type of template, called a **macro-enabled template**, in which you can store macros. Thus, the first step in this chapter is to open the Universal Travel template created in Chapter 8 and to save it as a macro-enabled template. (If you did not create the template, see your instructor for a copy.) The following steps open an existing Word template from a USB flash drive and then save it with a new name as a Word macro-enabled template.

1

- Open the template named Universal Travel from the USB flash drive.

2

- Click the Office Button and then click Save As on the Office Button menu to display the Save As dialog box.

- Type `Universal Travel Modified` in the File name text box to change the file name.

- Click the Save as type box arrow and then click Word Macro-Enabled Template in the list to change the file type (Figure 9–2).

3

- Click the Save button in the Save As dialog box to save the file called Universal Travel Modified as a macro-enabled template on the USB flash drive.

Q&A

How does Word differentiate between a Word template and a Word macro-enabled template?

A Word template has an extension of .dotx, whereas a Word macro-enabled template has an extension of .dotm. Also, the icon for a macro-enabled template contains an exclamation point.

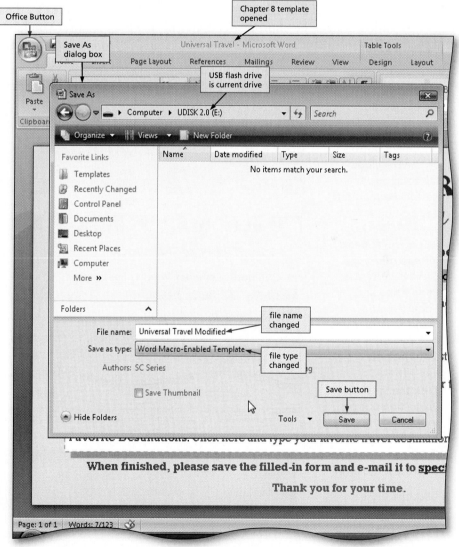

Figure 9–2

Macro-Enabled Documents

The steps on the previous page showed how to create a macro-enabled template. If you wanted to create a macro-enabled document, you would click the Office Button, click Save As, click the Save as type box arrow, click Word Macro-Enabled Document, and then click the Save button.

To Show the Developer Tab

Many of the tasks you will perform in this chapter use commands on the Developer tab. Thus, the following steps show the Developer tab on the Ribbon.

 Click the Office Button and then click the Word Options button on the Office Button menu.

2 If necessary, click Popular in the left pane of the Word Options dialog box.

3 If it is not selected, place a check mark in the Show Developer tab in the Ribbon check box.

4 Click the OK button to show the Developer tab on the Ribbon.

To Unprotect a Document

The Universal Travel Modified template is protected. Recall that Chapter 8 showed how to protect a form so that users could enter data only in designated areas, specifically, the content controls. Before this form can be modified, it must be unprotected. Later in this project, after you have completed the modifications, you will protect the document again. The following steps unprotect a document.

1

- Display the Developer tab.

- Click the Protect Document button on the Developer tab to display the Restrict Formatting and Editing task pane (Figure 9–3). (If a menu appears instead of the task pane, click Restrict Formatting and Editing on the menu to display the task pane.)

2

- Click the Stop Protection button in the Restrict Formatting and Editing task pane to unprotect the form.

- Click the Close button in the Restrict Formatting and Editing task pane to close the task pane.

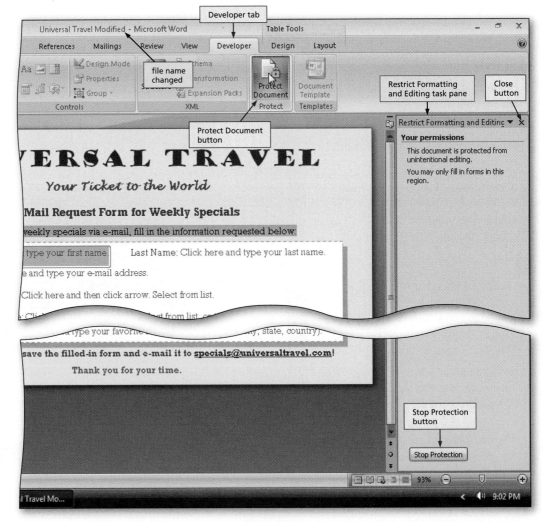

Figure 9–3

Word Macro Settings

A **computer virus** is a type of malicious software, or malware, which is a potentially damaging computer program that affects, or infects, a computer negatively by altering the way the computer works without the user's knowledge or permission. Currently, more than 180,000 known viruses and other malicious programs exist. The increased use of networks, the Internet, and e-mail has accelerated the spread of computer viruses and other malicious programs.

To combat this evil, most computer users run **antivirus programs** that search for viruses and other malware and destroy the malicious programs before they ever have a chance to infect the computer. Macros are a known carrier of viruses and other malware. For this reason, you can specify a macro setting in Word to reduce the chance your computer will be infected with a macro virus. These macro settings allow you to enable or disable macros. An **enabled macro** is a macro that Word will execute, and a **disabled macro** is a macro that is unavailable to Word.

As shown in Figure 9–1b on page WD 643, you can instruct Word to display a security warning if it opens a document that contains a macro(s). If you are confident of the source (author) of the document and macros, enable the macros. If you are uncertain about the reliability of the source of the document and macros, then disable the macros.

BTW

Macro Viruses
A macro virus is a type of computer virus that is stored in a macro within a file, template, or add-in. For the best protection against macro viruses, purchase and install antivirus software.

To Specify Macro Settings in Word

This project shows how to create macros. When you open the online form in this chapter, you want the macros enabled. At the same time, your computer should be protected from potentially harmful macros. Thus, you will specify a macro setting that allows you to enable or disable the macros each time you open this project or any document that contains a macro from an unknown source. The following steps specify macro settings.

1

• Click the Macro Security button on the Developer tab to display the Trust Center dialog box.

• If it is not selected already, click the 'Disable all macros with notification' option button, which causes Word to alert you when a document contains a macro so that you can decide whether to enable or disable the macro (Figure 9–4).

2

• Click the OK button.

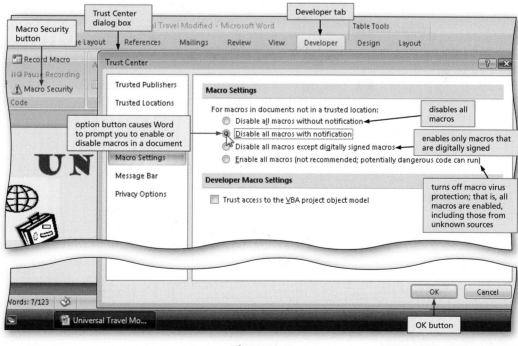

Figure 9–4

Other Ways

1. Click Office Button, click Word Options button, click Trust Center in left pane, select desired setting, click OK button

Enhancing a Form

The look of this form in this chapter is enhanced from the one in Chapter 8 by performing these steps:

1. Delete the current clip art image, and change the color scheme and font set.
2. Apply a texture fill effect for the page color.
3. Change the fonts, colors, and alignments of the first four lines of text.
4. Convert the 2 × 1 table containing the First Name and Last Name content controls to text so that each of the content controls is on a separate line.
5. Combine the last two lines of text and change their colors.
6. Add a 3-D effect to the rectangle shape.
7. Fill the rectangle with a picture.
8. Insert a new clip art image and rotate it.
9. Delete the date content control and replace it with a date field.
10. Modify the style of the placeholder text.

The following pages apply these changes to the form.

To Delete a Graphic and Change Theme Colors and Fonts

The online form in this chapter has a different clip art image and uses the Module color scheme and Solstice font set. The following steps delete the current clip art image and change the theme colors and the theme fonts.

1 Click the clip art image of the luggage to select it and then press the DELETE key to delete the clip art image.

2 Display the Home tab. Click the Change Styles button on the Home tab, point to Colors on the Change Styles menu, and then select Module in the Colors gallery to change the document theme colors to Module.

3 Click the Change Styles button on the Home tab, point to Fonts on the Change Styles menu, and then select Solstice in the Fonts gallery to change the document theme fonts to Solstice.

To Save a New Theme

In the previous steps, you modified the color scheme and font set. So that you can use this same combination of color scheme and font set again in the future, you save these new settings with a theme name. The next steps save the current theme settings with a new theme name.

1

- Display the Page Layout tab.

- Click the Themes button on the Page Layout tab to display the Themes gallery (Figure 9–5).

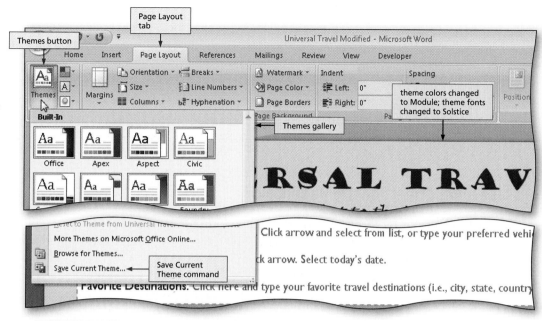

Figure 9–5

2

- Click Save Current Theme in the Themes gallery to display the Save Current Theme dialog box.

- Type Universal Travel Modified in the File name text box as the custom theme name (Figure 9–6).

3

- Click the Save button to add the theme to the Themes gallery as a custom theme.

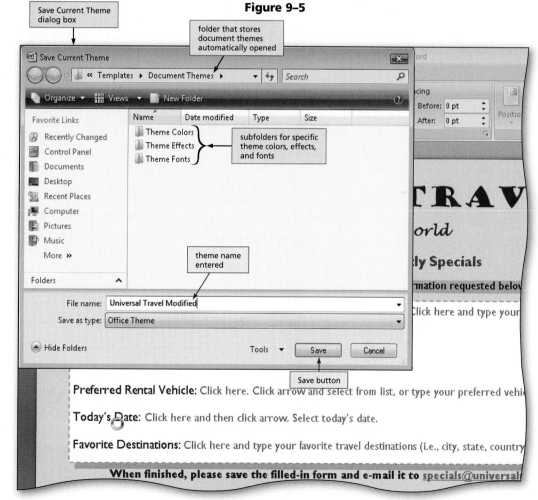

Figure 9–6

BTW

Restore Theme Templates
If you want to reset the theme template to the default, you would click the Themes button on the Page Layout tab and then click Reset to Theme from Template in the Themes gallery.

TO SET A THEME AS A DEFAULT

The current default theme is the Office theme, which means that new documents are based on this theme. If you wanted to change the default on which new documents are based, you would perform the following steps.

1. Select the theme you want to be the default theme, or select the color scheme, font set, and theme effects you would like to use as the default.

2. Click the Change Styles button on the Home tab and then click Set as Default, which uses the current settings for the new default.

To Use a Fill Effect for the Page Color

Instead of a color for the page color, this online form uses a texture for the page color. Word provides a gallery of 24 predefined textures you can apply to a page. These textures resemble various wallpaper patterns. The following steps change the page color to a texture fill effect.

- Click the Page Color button on the Page Layout tab to display the Page Color gallery (Figure 9–7).

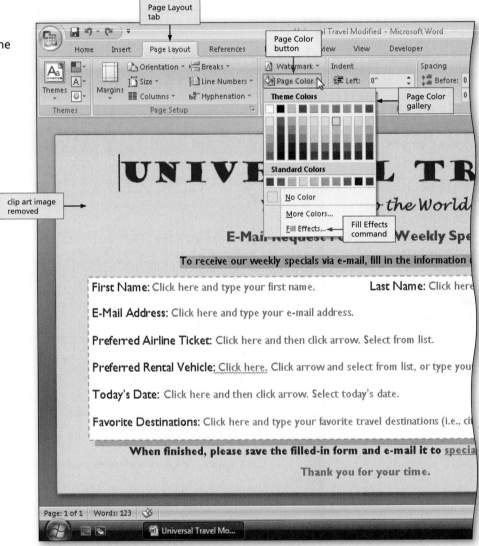

Figure 9–7

2

- Click Fill Effects in the Page Color gallery to display the Fill Effects dialog box.

- Click the Texture tab in the dialog box to display the Texture sheet.

- Scroll to the bottom of the Texture gallery and then click Oak to select the Oak texture (Figure 9–8).

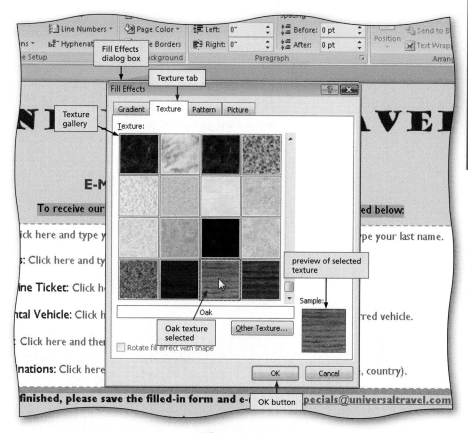

Figure 9–8

3

- Click the OK button to use the Oak texture as the page color in the document (Figure 9–9).

Q&A

How would I remove a texture page color?

You would click the Page Color button on the Page Layout tab and then click No Color in the Page Color gallery.

Figure 9–9

To Format Text

The next step in modifying the online form for this project is to change the formats of the company name, business tag line, form name, and form instructions.

1 Select the first line of text, UNIVERSAL TRAVEL, and then change its font to Wide Latin. Right-align the line of text.

2 Select the second line of text, which contains the business tag line: Your Ticket to the World. Change its font to Arial Rounded MT Bold. Change its color to Green, Accent 4, Darker 50%. Right-align the line of text.

3 Select the third line of text, which contains the form name, E-Mail Request Form for Weekly Specials. Remove the bold format from the text. Change its color to Gold, Accent 1, Lighter 40%. Left-align the line of text.

4 Select the fourth line of text, which are the user instructions that currently are highlighted gray. Change the highlight color to Dark Yellow. Change the font color to Gray-25%, Background 2. Left-align the line of text (Figure 9–10).

Figure 9–10

To Change the Properties of a Plain Text Content Control

In this online form, the First Name and Last Name content controls are on separate lines. In Chapter 8, you selected the 'Content control cannot be deleted' check box in the Content Control Properties dialog box so that users accidentally could not delete the content control while filling in the form. This selected check box, however, prevents you from moving a content control. Thus, the following steps change the locking properties of the First Name and Last Name content controls so that you can rearrange them.

1 Display the Developer tab.

2 Click the First Name content control to select it.

3 Click the Control Properties button on the Developer tab to display the Content Control Properties dialog box.

4 Remove the check mark from the 'Content control cannot be deleted' check box (Figure 9–11).

5 Click the OK button to assign the modified properties to the content control.

6 Click the Last Name content control to select it and then click the Control Properties button on the Developer tab to display the Content Control Properties dialog box.

7 Remove the check mark from the 'Content control cannot be deleted' check box, and then click the OK button to assign the modified properties to the content control.

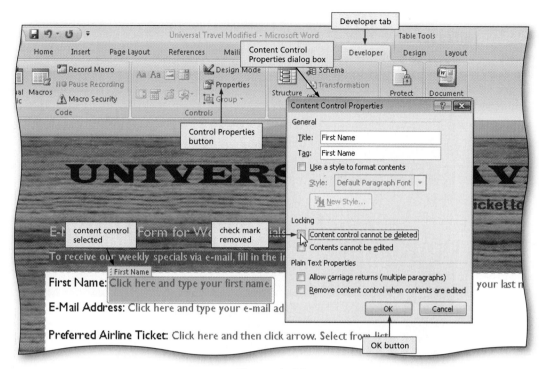

Figure 9–11

To Convert a Table to Text

The First Name and Last Name content controls currently are in a 2 × 1 table. In this project, these content controls are on separate lines, one below the other. That is, they are not in a table. The following steps convert the table to regular text, placing a paragraph break at the location of the second column.

1

- Position the insertion point somewhere in the table.

- Display the Layout tab.

- Click the Convert to Text button on the Layout tab to display the Convert Table To Text dialog box.

- In the 'Separate text with' area, click Paragraph marks, which will place a paragraph mark at the location of each new column in the table (Figure 9–12).

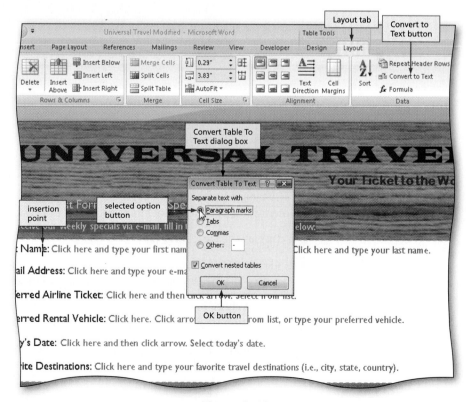

Figure 9–12

● Click the OK button to convert the table to text, separating each column with a paragraph mark (Figure 9–13).

Q & A

Why did the Last Name content control move below the First Name content control?

The 'Separate text with' area controls how the table is converted to text. The Paragraph marks setting converts each column in the table to a line of text below the previous line. The Tabs setting places a tab character where each column was located, and the Commas setting places a comma where each column was located.

● Click anywhere to remove the selection from the text.

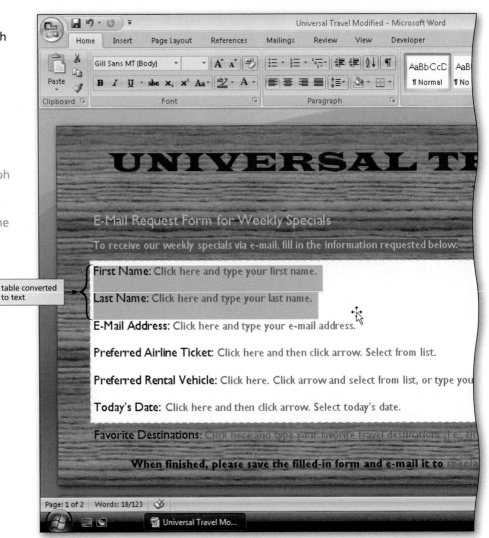

Figure 9–13

To Change the Properties of a Plain Text Content Control

You are finished moving the First Name and Last Name content controls. The following steps reset the locking properties of these content controls.

1 Display the Developer tab.

2 Click the First Name content control to select it and then click the Control Properties button on the Developer tab to display the Content Control Properties dialog box.

3 Place a check mark in the 'Content control cannot be deleted' check box and then click the OK button to assign the modified properties to the content control.

4 Repeat Steps 2 and 3 for the Last Name content control.

To Resize the Rectangle Shape

With the First Name and Last Name content controls on separate lines, the rectangle outline in the data entry area now is too short. The following steps extend the rectangle shape downward so that it surrounds the entire data entry area.

1 If necessary, click the rectangle shape to select it.

2 Position the mouse pointer on the bottom-middle sizing handle of the rectangle shape.

3 Drag the bottom-middle sizing handle downward so that the shape includes the Favorite Destinations content control (Figure 9–14).

4 Release the mouse button.

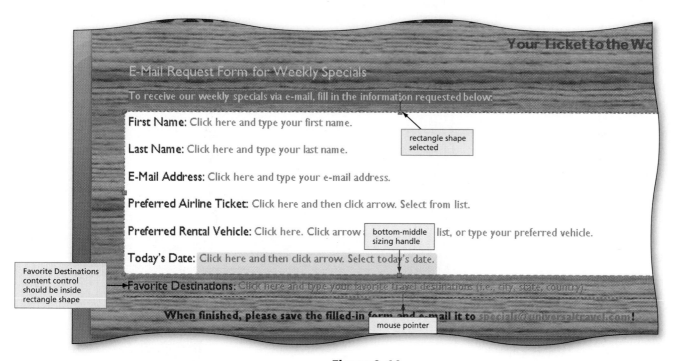

Figure 9–14

To Modify and Format Text

Because the First Name and Last Name content controls are on separate lines, the last line of the online form now spills onto a second page. So that the form fits on a single page, you delete the last line of the form and place a thank-you message at the end of the new last line. The following steps modify and format text below the data entry area of the form.

1 Scroll to display the second page of the online form and then delete the line of text on this page. If necessary, press the BACKSPACE key as many times as required to delete the page entirely. Scroll to display page one in the document window.

2 Change the exclamation point at the end of the last line to a period, press the SPACEBAR, and then type Thank You!

3 Select the line and change its font color to Green, Accent 4, Darker 50%. Click anywhere to remove the selection from the text (Figure 9–15 on the next page).

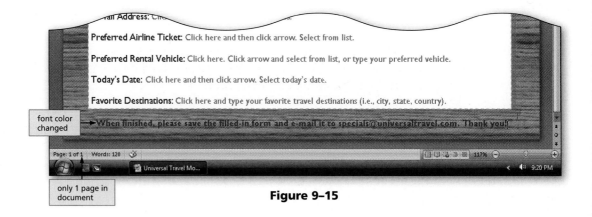

Figure 9–15

To Modify a Style Using the Styles Task Pane

When the font color of the line below the data entry area changed, the hyperlink color also changed. In this project, the hyperlink should be a dark red color (similar to the company name) so that it is noticeable. The Hyperlink style is not in the Styles gallery. To modify a style that is not in the Styles gallery, you can use the Styles task pane. The following steps modify the Hyperlink style using the Styles task pane.

- If necessary, scroll to display the entire form in the window.
- Select the hyperlink in the form.
- Display the Home tab.
- Click the Styles Dialog Box Launcher to display the Styles task pane.
- Click Hyperlink in the list of styles in the task pane and then click the Hyperlink box arrow to display the Hyperlink menu (Figure 9–16).

Q&A

What if the style I want to modify is not in the list?

Click the Manage Styles button at the bottom of the task pane, locate the style, and then click the Modify button in the dialog box.

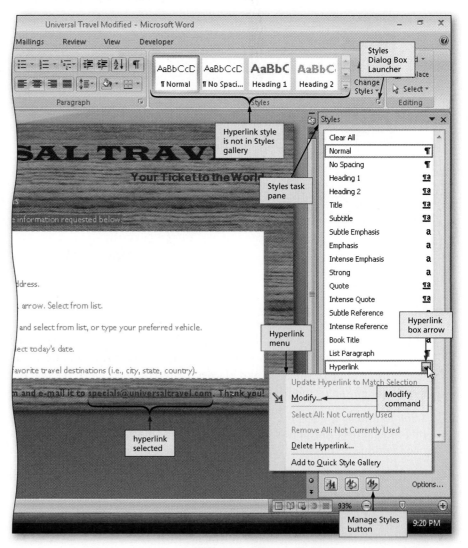

Figure 9–16

2

- Click Modify on the Hyperlink menu to display the Modify Style dialog box.

- Click the Bold button in the dialog box.

- Click the Font Color box arrow to display the Font Color gallery (Figure 9–17).

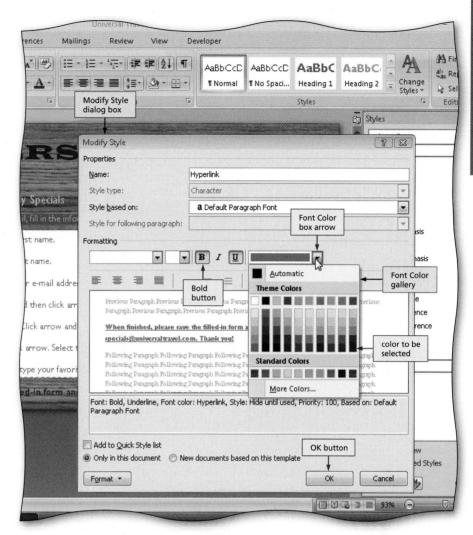

Figure 9–17

3

- Click Red, Accent 6, Darker 50% as the new hyperlink color.

- Click the OK button. Close the Styles task pane.

- Click outside the selected text to remove the selection (Figure 9–18).

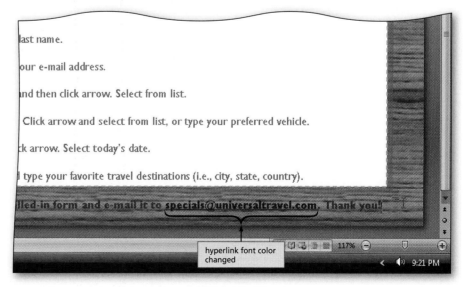

Figure 9–18

To Add a 3-D Effect to a Shape

To give the data entry area of the form more depth, this online form has a 3-D effect added to the rectangle shape. A shape can have either a 3-D effect or a shadow effect. Thus, when you add the 3-D effect, the shadow effect will disappear. The following steps add a 3-D effect to the rectangle shape.

1

- Click the rectangle shape to select it.

- Display the Format tab.

- Click the 3-D Effects button on the Format tab to display the 3-D Effects gallery.

2

- Point to 3-D Style 9 in the 3-D Effects gallery to display a live preview of that 3-D effect applied to the rectangle shape in the document (Figure 9–19).

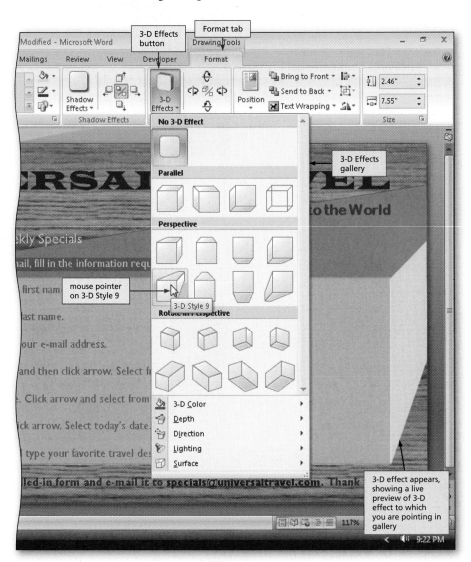

Figure 9–19

 Experiment

- Point to various effects in the 3-D Effects gallery and watch the 3-D effect change on the rectangle shape.

3

- Click 3-D Style 9 in the 3-D Effects gallery to apply the selected 3-D effect to the rectangle shape.

Q&A

How would I remove a 3-D effect?

Click the 3-D Effects button on the Format tab and then click No 3-D Effect.

To Change the Direction of a 3-D Effect

The 3-D effect that you just added to the rectangle angles toward the top-right of the form. In this project, the 3-D effect should angle toward the top-left. The following steps change the direction of the 3-D effect.

1

- With the rectangle shape still selected, click the 3-D Effects button on the Format tab to display the 3-D Effects gallery.

- Point to Direction in the 3-D Effects gallery to display the Direction gallery.

- Point to Top Left in the Direction gallery to display a live preview of that direction applied to the 3-D effect in the document (Figure 9–20).

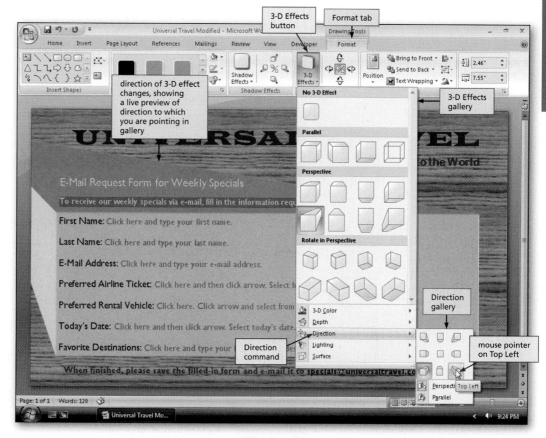

Figure 9–20

 Experiment

- Point to various directions in the Direction gallery and watch the direction of the 3-D effect change.

2

- Click Top Left in the Direction gallery to apply the selected direction to the 3-D effect.

BTW

Certification
The Microsoft Certified Application Specialist (MCAS) program provides an opportunity for you to obtain a valuable industry credential — proof that you have the Word 2007 skills required by employers. For more information see Appendix G or visit the Word 2007 Certification Web page (scsite.com/ wd2007/cert).

To Change the Color of a 3-D Effect

The 3-D color in this project is dark green. The following steps change the 3-D color.

- With the rectangle shape still selected, click the 3-D Effects button on the Format tab to display the 3-D Effects gallery.

- Point to 3-D Color in the 3-D Effects gallery to display the 3-D Color gallery.

- Point to Green, Accent 4, Darker 50% in the 3-D Color gallery to display a live preview of that 3-D color in the document (Figure 9–21).

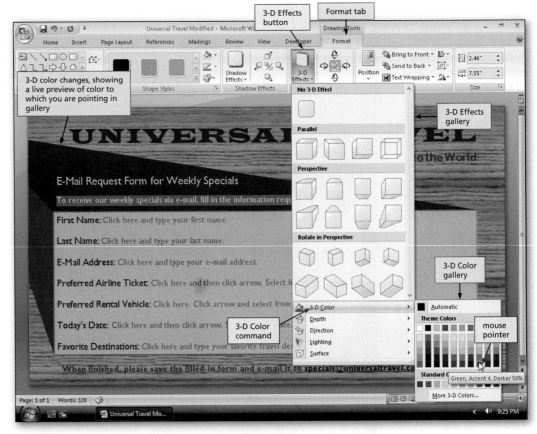

Figure 9–21

Experiment
- Point to various colors in the 3-D Color gallery and watch the 3-D color change.

2
- Click Green, Accent 4, Darker 50% in the 3-D Color gallery to apply the selected 3-D color.

To Fill a Shape with a Picture

The rectangle in this online form contains a picture of pine trees on a mountainside. The picture, called Trees, was taken with a digital camera and is located on the Data Files for Students. See the inside back cover of this book for instructions on downloading the Data Files for Students, or contact your instructor for information about accessing the required files. The next steps fill a shape with a picture.

1

- With the rectangle shape still selected, click the Shape Fill button arrow on the Format tab to display the Shape Fill gallery (Figure 9–22).

My Shape Fill gallery did not display. Why not?

You clicked the Shape Fill button instead of the Shape Fill button arrow. Repeat Step 1.

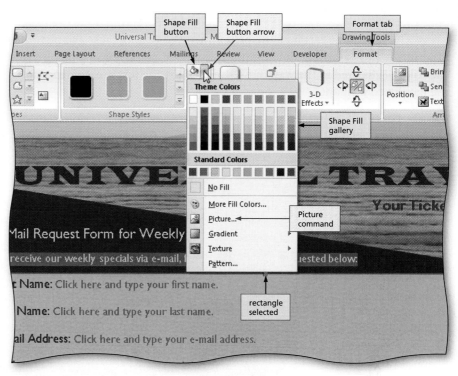

Figure 9–22

2

- Click Picture in the Shape Fill gallery to display the Select Picture dialog box.

- With your USB flash drive connected to one of the computer's USB ports, locate and then click the file called Trees on the USB flash drive to select the file.

- Click the Insert button in the dialog box to fill the rectangle shape with the picture (Figure 9–23).

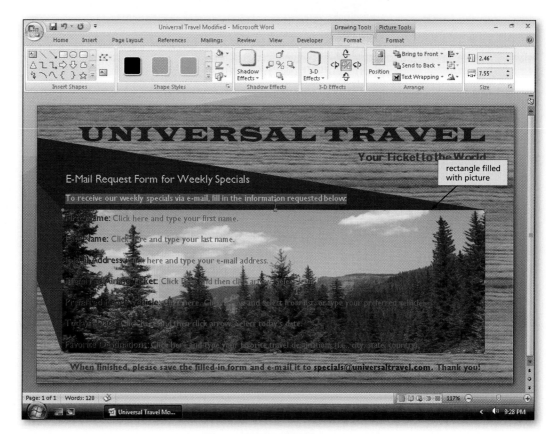

Figure 9–23

To Change the Color of a Picture

The text in the rectangle shape is difficult to read because the picture just inserted is too colorful. You can experiment with adjusting the brightness, contrast, and color of a picture so that the text is readable. In this project, the color is changed to the washout setting so that the text is easier to read. The following steps change the color of the picture to washout.

- Display the Picture Tools Format tab.

- With the rectangle shape still selected, click the Recolor button on the Picture Tools Format tab to display the Recolor gallery.

- Point to Washout in the Recolor gallery to display a live preview of the Washout color applied to the picture (Figure 9–24).

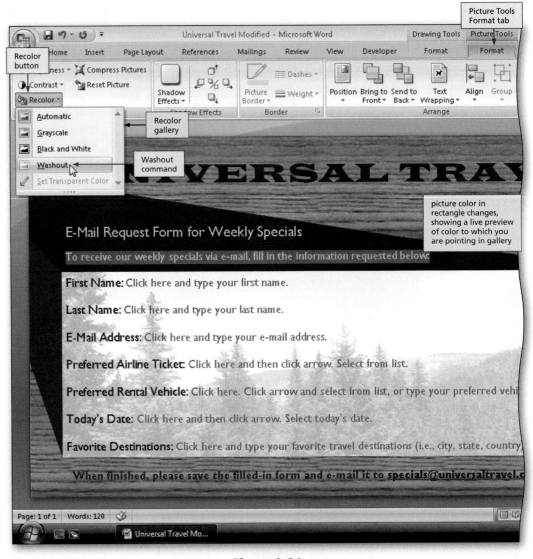

Figure 9–24

 Experiment

- Point to various colors in the Recolor gallery and watch the picture color change.

❷
- Click Washout in the Recolor gallery to apply the Washout color to the picture.

To Insert Clip Art from the Web

The next step is to insert a luggage image from the Web in the form.

Note: The following steps assume your computer is connected to the Internet. If it is not, go directly to the shaded steps below that are titled To Insert a Graphic File from the Data Files for Students.

1 Display the Insert tab. Click the Clip Art button on the Insert tab to display the Clip Art task pane.

2 In the Clip Art task pane, type luggage in the Search for text box.

3 Click the Go button to display a list of clips that match the description, luggage.

4 Scroll to and then click the luggage clip art that matches the one in Figure 9–25 on the next page.

5 Close the Clip Art task pane.

To Insert a Graphic File from the Data Files for Students

If you do not have access to the Internet, you can insert the clip art file in the Word document from the Data Files for Students. See the inside back cover of this book for instructions on downloading the Data Files for Students, or contact your instructor for information about accessing the required files. Only perform these steps if you were not able to insert the luggage clip art from the Web in the steps at the top of this page.

1 Display the Insert tab. Click the Insert Picture from File button on the Insert tab to display the Insert Picture dialog box.

2 With your USB flash drive connected to one of the computer's USB ports, locate and then click the file called Luggage on the USB flash drive to select the file.

3 Click the Insert button in the dialog box to insert the picture at the location of the insertion point in the document.

To Scale the Graphic, Change Its Wrapping Style, and Move It

Because the graphic's original size is too large, you will scale it to 70 percent of its original size. Then, you will change its wrapping so that the picture can be positioned in front of the text. Finally, you will move the graphic to its correct location.

1 With the graphic still selected, click the Size Dialog Box Launcher on the Picture Tools Format tab to display the Size dialog box.

2 Change the values in the Height and Width text boxes in the Scale area to 70%.

3 Close the Size dialog box.

4 Click the Text Wrapping button on the Format tab to display the Text Wrapping menu.

5 Click In Front of Text on the Text Wrapping menu to change the graphic from inline to floating with In Front of Text wrapping.

6 Point inside the selected graphic, and when the mouse pointer has a four-headed arrow attached to it, drag the graphic to the location shown in Figure 9–25.

To Rotate a Graphic

The image of the luggage in this form is angled to the left more. In Word, you can rotate a floating graphic. The following steps rotate a graphic.

1
- Position the mouse pointer on the graphic's rotate handle (Figure 9–25).

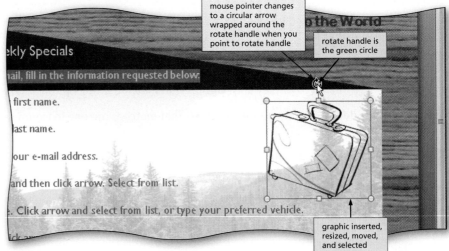

Figure 9–25

2
- Drag the rotate handle leftward and downward to rotate the graphic as shown in Figure 9–26.

Q&A Can I drag the rotate handle in any direction?

You can drag the rotate handle clockwise or counter-clockwise.

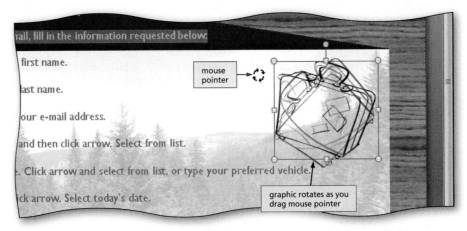

Figure 9–26

3
- Release the mouse button to position the graphic in the location where you dragged the rotate handle (Figure 9–27). (You may need to rotate the graphic a few times to position it in the desired location.)

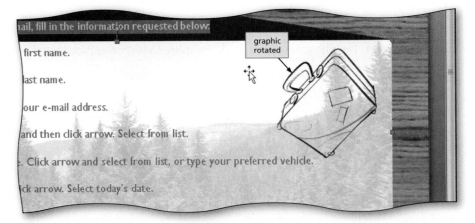

Figure 9–27

To Change the Properties of a Date Content Control

In this online form, instead of the user entering the current date, the system date will be filled in automatically by Word. Thus, the Today's Date content control is not needed and can be deleted. To delete the content control, you first will need to remove the check mark from the 'Content control cannot be deleted' check box in the Content Control Properties dialog box. The following steps change the locking properties of the Today's Date content control and then delete the content control.

1 Display the Developer tab.

2 Click the Today's Date content control to select it.

3 Click the Control Properties button on the Developer tab to display the Content Control Properties dialog box.

4 Remove the check mark from the 'Content control cannot be deleted' check box (Figure 9–28).

5 Click the OK button to assign the modified properties to the content control.

6 Click the Today's Date content control to select it again and then press the DELETE key to delete it.

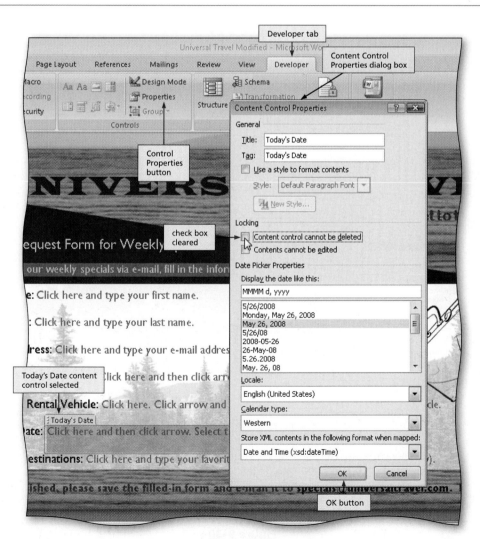

Figure 9–28

To Insert a Date Field

The next step is to instruct Word to display the current date and time at the location of the insertion point. The current date and time is a field. Recall that a field is a set of codes that instructs Word to perform a certain action. The following steps insert the date and time as a field in the form at the location of the insertion point.

- Display the Insert tab.

- With the insertion point positioned as shown in Figure 9–29, click the Quick Parts button on the Insert tab to display the Quick Parts menu.

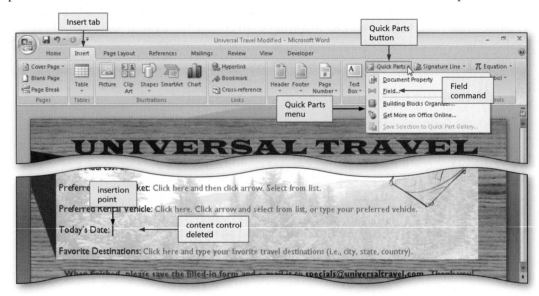

Figure 9–29

- Click Field on the Quick Parts menu to display the Field dialog box.

- Scroll through the Field names list and then click Date, which displays the Date formats list in the Field properties area.

- Click the format, 5/26/2008 9:35:34 PM, in the Date formats list — your date and time will differ (Figure 9–30).

Figure 9–30

❸

- Click the OK button to insert the current date and time at the location of the insertion point (Figure 9–31).

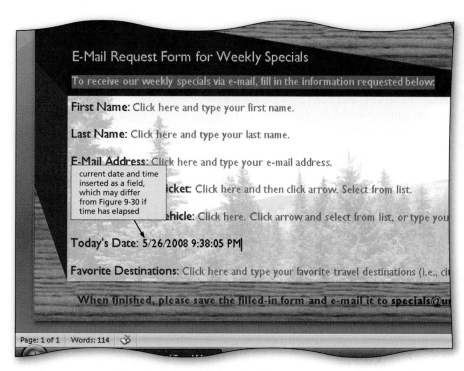

Figure 9–31

To Edit a Field

When looking at the date and time in the form, you decide not to include the seconds in the time. That is, you want just the hours and minutes. Thus, following steps edit the field.

❶

- Right-click the date field to display a shortcut menu (Figure 9–32).

Figure 9–32

- Click Edit Field on the shortcut menu to display the Field dialog box.

- If necessary, scroll through the Field names list and then click Date, which displays the Date formats list in the Field properties area.

- Select the desired date format, in this case, 5/26/2008 9:38 PM (Figure 9–33).

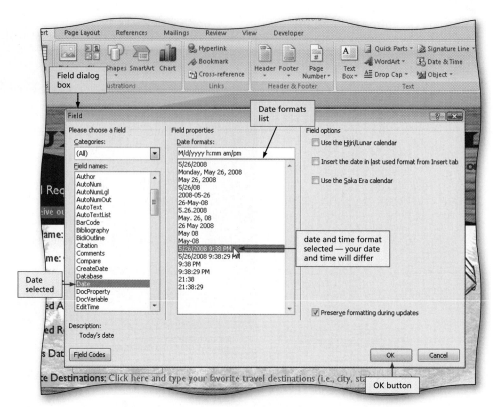

Figure 9–33

- Click the OK button to insert the edited current date and time at the location of the insertion point (Figure 9–34).

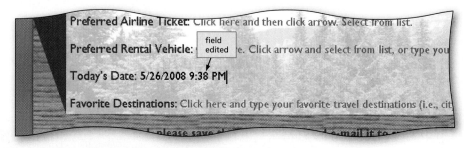

Figure 9–34

To Move Text

Because the user no longer enters data in the date field, the date field is not in a logical location. Typically, all content controls are placed together. In this online form, the current date is positioned at the top of the data entry area. The following steps move the date so that it is above the First Name content control.

1. Select the entire date line.

2. Use drag-and-drop editing to move the selection so that it is positioned just above the First Name content control.

3. If the graphic also moves when you move the text, drag the graphic to the correct location.

To Modify a Style Using the Manage Styles Button

The font color of placeholder text, such as 'Click here and type your first name.', is a little too light. In this online form, the placeholder text is dark green and bold. The Placeholder Text style is not in the Styles gallery, nor is it in the Styles task pane — because it is hidden. When you cannot locate a style you wish to update, you can display all possible styles through the Manage Styles button. The following steps modify the hidden Placeholder Text style.

①

- Display the Home tab.

- Click the Styles Dialog Box Launcher on the Home tab to display the Styles task pane (Figure 9–35).

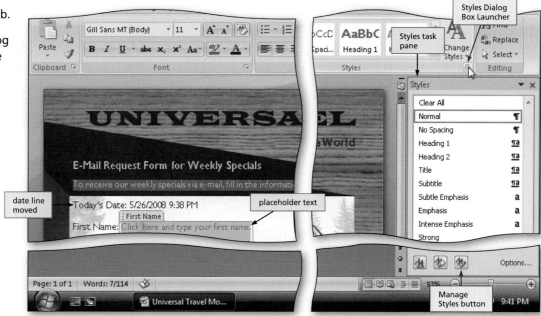

Figure 9–35

②

- Click the Manage Styles button in the Styles task pane to display the Manage Styles dialog box.

- Click the Sort order box arrow and then click Alphabetical so that the styles are listed in alphabetical order.

- Scroll through the list of styles and select the one you wish to modify, Placeholder Text, in this case, and then click the Modify button to display the Modify Style dialog box.

- Click the Bold button in the dialog box.

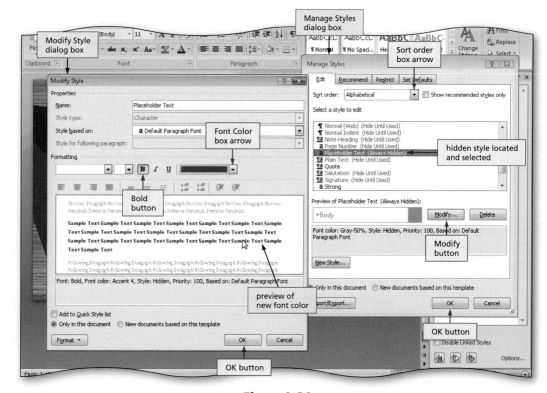

Figure 9–36

- Click the Font Color box arrow and then click Green, Accent 4, Darker 50% as the new placeholder text color (Figure 9–36).

3

• Click the OK button in each open dialog box. Close the Styles task pane.

• If necessary, click outside the selected text to remove the selection (Figure 9–37).

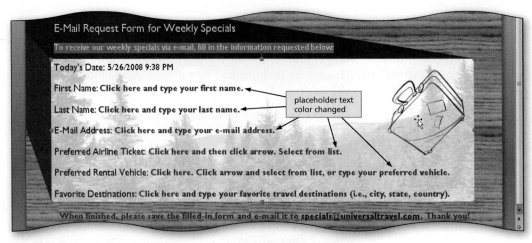

E-Mail Request Form for Weekly Specials

To receive our weekly specials via e-mail, fill in the information requested below.

Today's Date: 5/26/2008 9:38 PM

First Name: Click here and type your first name.

Last Name: Click here and type your last name.

placeholder text color changed

E-Mail Address: Click here and type your e-mail address.

Preferred Airline Ticket: Click here and then click arrow. Select from list.

Preferred Rental Vehicle: Click here. Click arrow and select from list, or type your preferred vehicle.

Favorite Destinations: Click here and type your favorite travel destinations (i.e., city, state, country).

When finished, please save the filled-in form and e-mail it to specials@universaltravel.com. Thank you!

Figure 9–37

To Save a Template Again

The enhancements to the appearance of the online form are complete. You have performed many tasks since the last save and should save the template again.

1 Save the template again with the same file name, Universal Travel Modified.

Using a Macro to Automate a Task

A **macro** consists of a series of Word commands or instructions that are grouped together as a single command. This single command is a convenient way to automate a difficult or lengthy task. Macros often are used to simplify formatting or editing activities, to combine multiple commands into a single command, or to select an option in a dialog box using a shortcut key.

To create a macro, you can use the macro recorder or the Visual Basic Editor. With the macro recorder, Word generates the VBA instructions associated with the macro automatically as you perform actions in Word. If you wanted to write the VBA instructions yourself, you would use the Visual Basic Editor. This chapter uses the macro recorder to create a macro and the Visual Basic Editor to modify it.

The **macro recorder** creates a macro based on a series of actions you perform while the macro recorder is recording. The macro recorder is similar to a video camera: after you start the macro recorder, it records all actions you perform while working in a document and stops recording when you stop the macro recorder. To record a macro, you follow this sequence of steps:

1. Start the macro recorder and specify options about the macro.

2. Execute the actions you want recorded.

3. Stop the macro recorder.

After you record a macro, you can execute the macro, or play it, any time you want to perform the same set of actions.

To Record a Macro and Assign It a Shortcut Key

Before sending this online form to users, you want to hide the Developer tab because it contains commands that the users do not need. To simplify this task, the macro in this project hides the Developer tab. In Word, you can assign a shortcut key to a macro so that you can execute the macro by pressing the shortcut key instead of using a dialog box to execute it. The following steps record a macro that hides the Developer tab; the macro is assigned the shortcut key, ALT+D.

- Display the Developer tab.

- Click the Record Macro button on the Developer tab to display the Record Macro dialog box.

- Type HideDeveloperTab in the Macro name text box.

- Click the 'Store macro in' box arrow and then click Documents Based On Universal Travel Modified.

- In the Description text box, type this sentence (Figure 9–38): Hides the Developer tab.

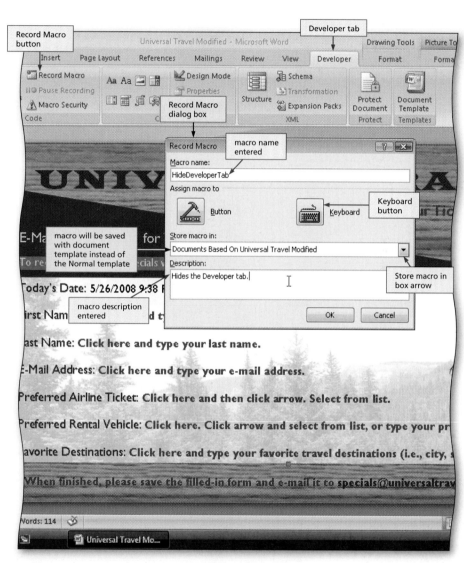

Figure 9–38

Q&A Do I have to name a macro?

If you do not enter a name for the macro, Word assigns a default name. Macro names can be up to 255 characters in length and can contain only numbers, letters, and the underscore character. A macro name cannot contain spaces or other punctuation.

Q&A What is the difference between storing a macro with the document template versus the Normal template?

Macros saved in the Normal template are available to all future documents; macros saved with the document template are available only with a document based on the template.

2

- Click the Keyboard button to display the Customize Keyboard dialog box.

- Press ALT+D to display the characters ALT+D in the 'Press new shortcut key' text box (Figure 9–39).

Q&A

Can I type the letters in the shortcut key (ALT+D) in the text box?

Although typing the letters places them in the text box, the shortcut key is valid only if you press the shortcut key combination itself.

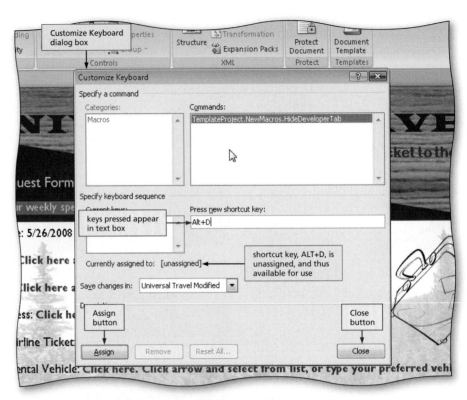

Figure 9–39

3

- Click the Assign button to assign the shortcut key, ALT+D, to the macro named HideDeveloperTab.

- Click the Close button, which closes the dialog box, places a Macro Recording button on the status bar, and starts the macro recorder (Figure 9–40).

Q&A

How do I record the macro?

While the macro recorder is running, any action you perform in Word will be part of the macro — until you stop or pause the macro.

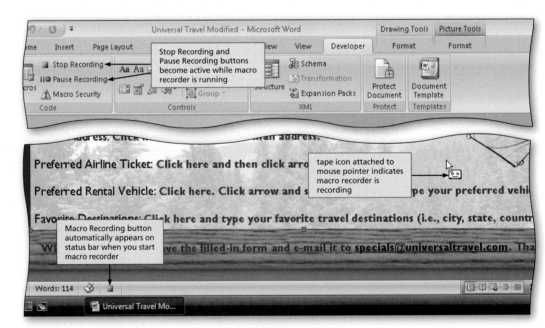

Figure 9–40

Q&A

What is the purpose of the Pause Recording button?

If, while recording a macro, you want to perform some actions that should not be part of the macro, click the Pause Recording button to suspend the macro recorder. The Pause Recording button changes to a Resume Recorder button that you click when you want to continue recording.

4

- Click the Office Button to display the Office Button menu (Figure 9–41).

Q&A

What happened to the tape icon?

While recording a macro, the tape icon might disappear from the mouse pointer when the mouse pointer is in a menu, on the Ribbon, or in a dialog box.

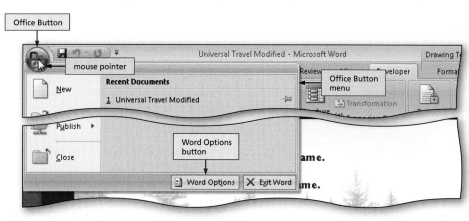

Figure 9–41

5

- Click the Word Options button on the Office Button menu to display the Word Options dialog box.

- If necessary, click Popular in the left pane.

- Remove the check mark from the Show Developer tab in the Ribbon check box (Figure 9–42).

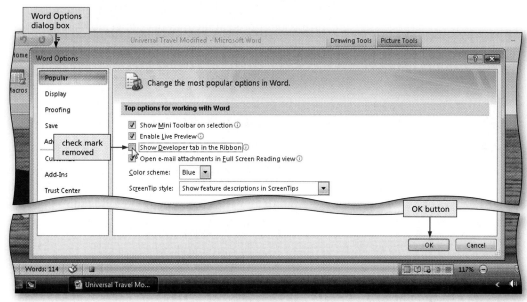

Figure 9–42

6

- Click the OK button to remove the Developer tab from the Ribbon (Figure 9–43).

7

- Click the Macro Recording button on the status bar to turn off the macro recorder, that is, to stop recording actions you perform in Word.

Q&A

What if I made a mistake while recording the macro?

Delete the macro and record it again. To delete a macro, click the View Macros button on the Developer tab, select the macro name in the list, click the Delete button, and then click the Yes button.

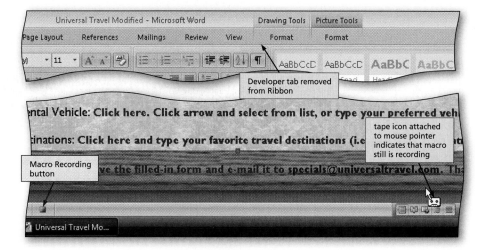

Figure 9–43

Other Ways

1. Click Macro Recording button on status bar

BTW

Running Macros
You can run a macro by clicking the View Macros button on the Developer tab or by pressing ALT+F8 to display the Macros dialog box, selecting the macro name in the list, and then clicking the Run button in the dialog box.

To Run a Macro

The next step is to execute, or run, the macro to ensure that it works. Recall that this macro hides the Developer tab, which means you must be sure the Developer tab shows on the Ribbon before running the macro. Because you created a shortcut key for the macro in this project, the following steps show the Developer tab so that you can run the HideDeveloperTab macro using the shortcut key, ALT+D.

1 Click the Office Button and then click the Word Options button on the Office Button menu. If necessary, click Popular in the left pane of the Word Options dialog box.

2 If it is not selected, place a check mark in the Show Developer tab in the Ribbon check box.

3 Click the OK button to show the Developer tab on the Ribbon.

4 With the Developer tab showing on the Ribbon, press ALT+D, which causes Word to perform the instructions stored in the HideDeveloperTab macro, that is, to hide the Developer tab on the Ribbon.

To Add a Macro as a Button to the Quick Access Toolbar

Word allows you to add buttons to and delete buttons from the Quick Access Toolbar, as shown in Appendix E on pages APP 27 through APP 32. You also can assign a command, such as a macro, to a button on the Quick Access Toolbar. This project shows how to create a button for the HideDeveloperTab macro so that instead of pressing the shortcut keys, you can click the button to hide the Developer tab. The following steps assign the HideDeveloperTab macro to a new button on the Quick Access Toolbar.

1

• Click the Customize Quick Access Toolbar button on the Quick Access Toolbar to display the Customize Quick Access Toolbar menu (Figure 9–44).

Q&A

What happens if I click the commands listed on the Customize Quick Access Toolbar menu?

If the command does not have a check mark beside it and you click it, Word places the command on the Quick Access Toolbar. If the command has a check mark beside it and you click it, Word removes the command from the Quick Access Toolbar.

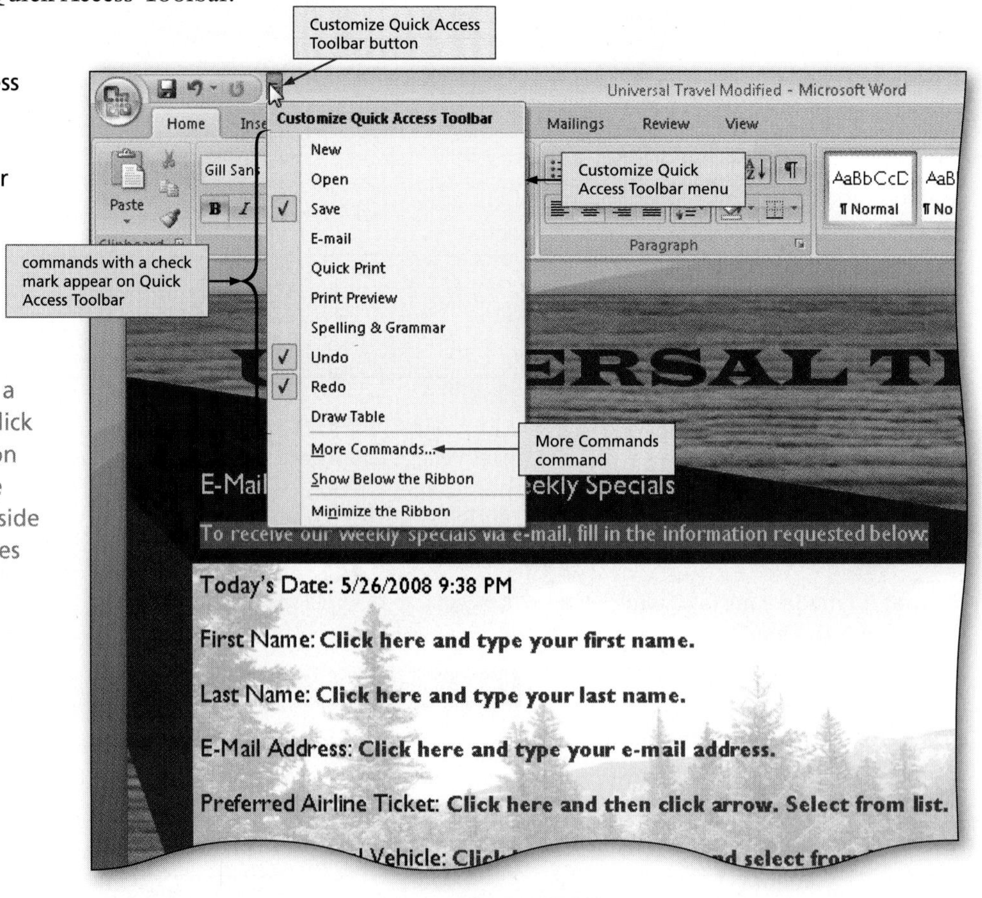

Figure 9–44

2

- Click More Commands on the Customize Quick Access Toolbar menu to display the Word Options dialog box with Customize selected in the left pane (Figure 9–45).

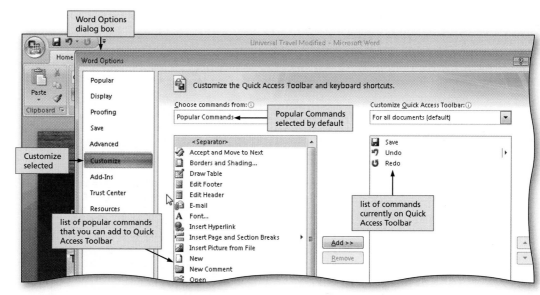

Figure 9–45

3

- Click the 'Choose commands from' box arrow to display a list of categories of commands (Figure 9–46).

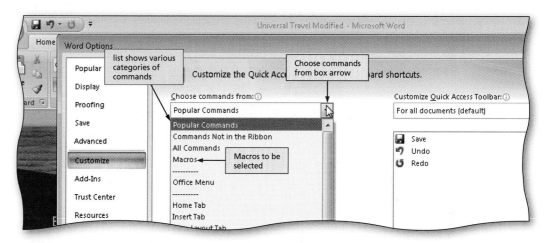

Figure 9–46

4

- Click Macros in the list to display the macro in this document (Figure 9–47).

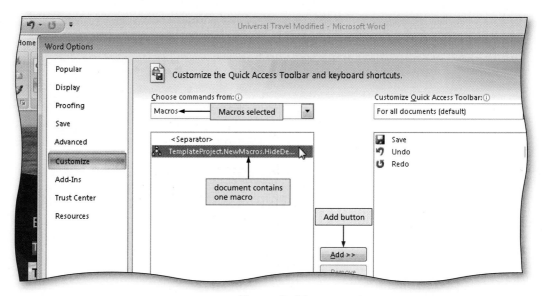

Figure 9–47

- If necessary, click the macro to select it.

- Click the Add button to display the selected macro in the Customize Quick Access Toolbar list.

- Click the Modify button to display the Modify Button dialog box.

- Change the name in the Display name text box to Hide Developer Tab, which will be the text that appears in the ScreenTip for the button.

- Scroll through the list of symbols and click the eraser icon as the new face for the button (Figure 9–48).

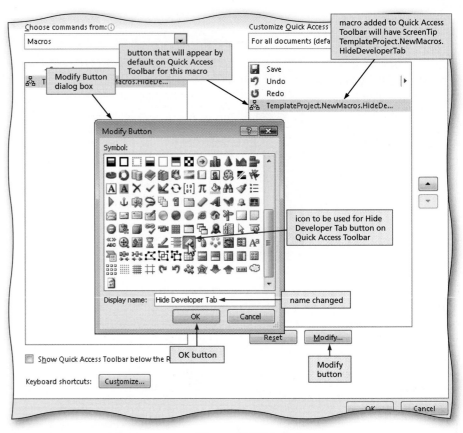

Figure 9–48

- Click the OK button in the Modify Button dialog box to change the button characteristics in the Customize Quick Access Toolbar list (Figure 9–49).

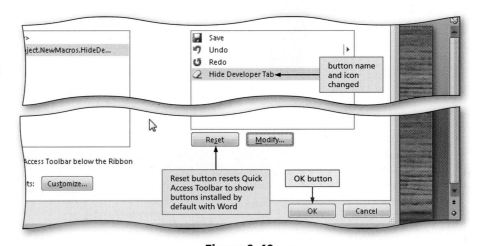

Figure 9–49

- Click the OK button to add the button to the Quick Access Toolbar (Figure 9–50).

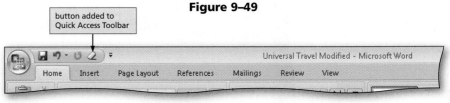

Figure 9–50

Other Ways

1. Right-click Quick Access Toolbar, click Customize Quick Access Toolbar on shortcut menu

To Run the Macro by Clicking the Button on the Quick Access Toolbar

The next step is to execute, or run, the macro again to ensure that it works — by clicking the button on the Quick Access Toolbar. Recall that this macro hides the Developer tab, which means you must be sure the Developer tab shows on the Ribbon before clicking the button. The following steps show the Developer tab so that you can test the macro by clicking the button that is assigned to the Quick Access Toolbar.

BTW

Quick Access Toolbar
You can add any object (button, box, etc.) on the Ribbon to the Quick Access Toolbar by right-clicking the object and then clicking Add to Quick Access Toolbar.

1 Click the Office Button and then click the Word Options button on the Office Button menu. If necessary, click Popular in the left pane of the Word Options dialog box.

2 If it is not selected, place a check mark in the Show Developer tab in the Ribbon check box.

3 Click the OK button to show the Developer tab on the Ribbon.

4 With the Developer tab showing on the Ribbon, point to the Hide Developer Tab button on the Quick Access Toolbar to ensure the ScreenTip displays correctly (Figure 9–51).

5 Click the Hide Developer Tab button on the Quick Access Toolbar, which causes Word to perform the instructions stored in the HideDeveloperTab macro, that is, to hide the Developer tab on the Ribbon.

Figure 9–51

To Delete a Button from a Toolbar

If you no longer plan to use a button on the Quick Access Toolbar, you can delete it. The following steps delete the Hide Developer Tab button from the Quick Access Toolbar.

1
- Right-click the button to be deleted from the Quick Access Toolbar, in this case the Hide Developer Tab button, to display a shortcut menu (Figure 9–52).

Figure 9–52

2
- Click Remove from Quick Access Toolbar on the shortcut menu to remove the button from the Quick Access Toolbar.

To Rename a Macro

If you wanted to rename a macro, you would perform the following steps.

1. Click the View Macros button on the Developer tab to display the Macros dialog box.

2. Click the Organizer button to display the Organizer dialog box.

3. Click the macro to rename and then click the Rename button.

4. Enter the new macro name in the New name text box and then click the OK button to rename the macro.

5. Close the Organizer dialog box.

To Delete a Macro

If you wanted to delete a macro, you would perform the following steps.

1. Click the View Macros button on the Developer tab to display the Macros dialog box.

2. Click the Delete button and then click the Yes button.

3. Close the Macros dialog box.

Automatic Macros

The previous section showed how to create a macro, assign it a unique name (HideDeveloperTab) and a shortcut key, and then on the Quick Access Toolbar, add a button that executes the macro. This section creates an **automatic macro**, which is a macro that executes automatically when a certain event occurs. Word has five prenamed automatic macros. Table 9–1 lists the name and function of these automatic macros.

The automatic macro you choose depends on when you want certain actions to occur. In this project, when a user creates a new Word document that is based on the Universal Travel Modified template, you want to be sure that the zoom is set to page width. Thus, the AutoNew automatic macro is used in this online form.

Table 9–1 Automatic Macros	
Macro Name	**Event That Causes Macro to Run**
AutoClose	Closing a document that contains the macro
AutoExec	Starting Word
AutoExit	Quitting Word
AutoNew	Creating a new document based on a template that contains the macro
AutoOpen	Opening a document that contains the macro

To Create an Automatic Macro

The online form in this chapter is displayed properly when the zoom is set to page width. Thus, you will record the steps to zoom to page width in the AutoNew macro. The following steps create an AutoNew macro, using the macro recorder.

- Show the Developer tab on the Ribbon and then display the Developer tab.

- Click the Record Macro button on the Developer tab to display the Record Macro dialog box.

- Type AutoNew in the Macro name text box.

- Click the 'Store macro in' box arrow and then click Documents Based On Universal Travel Modified.

- In the Description text box, type this sentence (Figure 9–53): Specifies how the form initially is displayed.

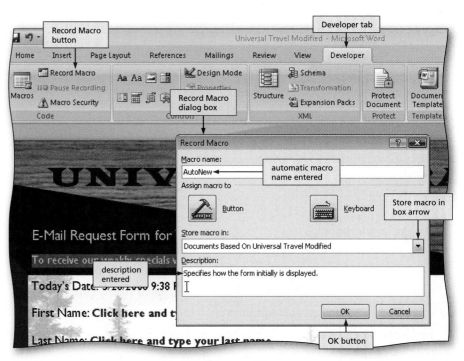

Figure 9–53

2

- Click the OK button to close the Record Macro dialog box and start the macro recorder.

- Display the View tab.

- Click the Page Width button on the View tab to zoom page width (Figure 9–54).

3

- Click the Macro Recording button on the status bar to turn off the macro recorder, that is, stop recording actions you perform in Word.

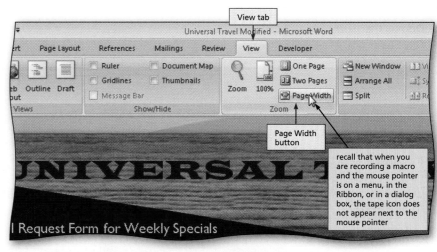

Figure 9–54

Q&A

How do I test an automatic macro?

Activate the event that causes the macro to execute. For example, the AutoNew macro runs whenever you create a new Word document that is based on the template.

To Run the AutoNew Macro

The next step is to execute, or run, the AutoNew macro to ensure that it works. To run the AutoNew macro, you need to create a new Word document that is based on the Universal Travel Modified template. This macro contains instructions to zoom page width. To verify that the macro works as intended, you will change the zoom to 100% before testing the macro.

1 Use the Zoom Out button on the status bar to change the zoom to 100%.

2 Save the template with the same name, Universal Travel Modified.

3 Click the Start button on the Windows Vista taskbar to display the Start menu. Click Computer on the Start menu to display the Explorer window.

4 Locate your USB flash drive in the Explorer window and then double-click the file named Universal Travel Modified to display a new document window that is based on the contents of the Universal Travel Modified template, which should be zoomed to page width as shown in Figure 9–1a on page WD 643.

5 Close the new document that displays the form in the Word window. Click the No button when Word asks if you want to save the changes to the new document.

6 Change the zoom back to page width.

BTW

Automatic Macros
A document can contain only one AutoClose macro, one AutoNew macro, and one AutoOpen macro. The AutoExec and AutoExit macros, however, are not stored with the document; instead, they must be stored in the Normal template. Thus, only one AutoExec macro and only one AutoExit macro can exist for all Word documents.

To Edit a Macro's VBA Code

In addition to zooming page width when the online form displays in new document window, you would like to be sure that the Developer tab is hidden and the formatting marks are hidden. As mentioned earlier, a macro consists of VBA instructions. To edit a recorded macro, you use the Visual Basic Editor.

The steps on the next page use the Visual Basic Editor to add VBA instructions to the AutoNew macro. These steps are designed to show the basic composition of a VBA procedure and illustrate the power of VBA code statements.

❶

- Display the Developer tab.

- Click the View Macros button on the Developer tab to display the Macros dialog box.

- If necessary, select the macro to be edited, in this case, AutoNew (Figure 9–55).

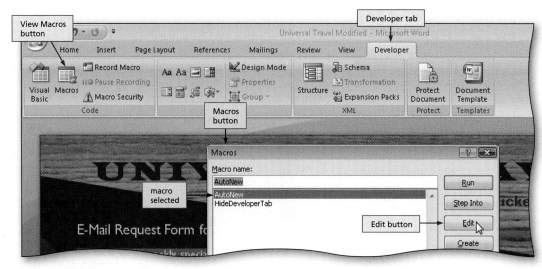

Figure 9–55

❷

- Click the Edit button to start the Visual Basic Editor and display the VBA code for the AutoNew macro in the Code window — your screen may appear differently depending on previous Visual Basic Editor settings (Figure 9–56).

Q&A

What if the Code window does not appear in the Visual Basic Editor?

In the Visual Basic Editor, click View on the menu bar and then click Code. If it still does not appear and you are in a network environment, this feature may be disabled for some users.

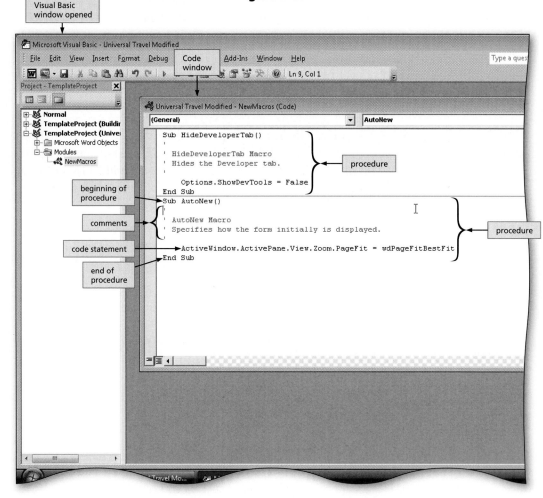

Figure 9–56

Q&A

What are the lines of text (instructions) in the Code window?

The named set of instructions associated with a macro is called a **procedure**. It is this set of instructions — beginning with the words Sub and continuing sequentially to the line with the words End Sub — that executes when you run the macro. The instructions within a procedure are called **code statements**.

- Position the insertion point at the end of the second-to-last line in the AutoNew macro and then press the ENTER key to insert a blank line for a new code statement.

- On a single line, type Options .ShowDevTools = False and then press the ENTER key, which enters the VBA code statement that hides the Developer tab.

What are the lists that appear in the Visual Basic Editor as I enter code statements?

The lists present valid statement elements to assist you with entering code statements. Ignore them because they are beyond the scope of this chapter.

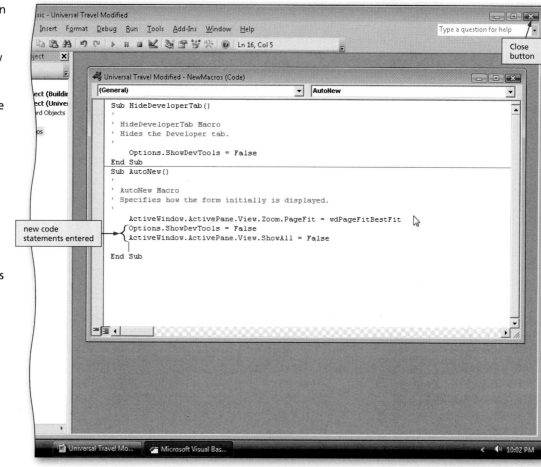

Figure 9–57

- On a single line, type ActiveWindow.ActivePane.View.ShowAll = False and then press the ENTER key, which enters the VBA code statement that turns off formatting marks (Figure 9–57).

- Click the Close button on the right edge of the Microsoft Visual Basic window title bar.

To Run the AutoNew Macro

The next step is to execute, or run, the AutoNew macro again to ensure that it works. To be sure the macro works as intended, you first will display the formatting marks and ensure the Developer tab is on the Ribbon. The AutoNew macro should hide the formatting marks and hide the Developer tab.

1. Display the Home tab. If necessary, click the Show/Hide ¶ button on the Home tab to display formatting marks.

2. Ensure the Developer tab appears on the Ribbon.

3. Save the template with the same name, Universal Travel Modified.

4 Click the Start button on the Windows Vista taskbar to display the Start menu and then click Computer on the Start menu to display the Explorer window.

5 Locate your USB flash drive in the Explorer window and then double-click the file named Universal Travel Modified to display a new document window that is based on the contents of the Universal Travel Modified template, which should be zoomed to page width as shown in Figure 9–1a on page WD 643.

6 Close the new document that displays the form in the Word window. Click the No button when Word asks if you want to save the changes to the new document.

7 Close the Explorer window.

8 In the Word window, hide formatting marks on the screen.

VBA

VBA
VBA includes many more statements than those presented in this project. You may need a background in computer programming if you plan to write VBA code instructions in macros you develop and if the VBA code instructions are beyond those instructions presented in this project.

As shown in the steps on pages WD 680 and WD 681, a VBA procedure begins with a Sub statement and ends with an End Sub statement. The Sub statement is followed by the name of the procedure, which is the macro name (AutoNew). The parentheses following the macro name in the Sub statement are required. They indicate that arguments can be passed from one procedure to another. Passing arguments is beyond the scope of this chapter, but the parentheses still are required. The End Sub statement signifies the end of the procedure and returns control to Word.

Comments often are added to a procedure to help you remember the purpose of the macro and its code statements at a later date. Comments begin with an apostrophe (') and appear in green in the Code window. The macro recorder, for example, placed four comment lines below the Sub statement. These comments display the name of the macro and its description, as entered in the Record Macro dialog box. Comments have no effect on the execution of a procedure; they simply provide information about the procedure, such as its name and description, to the developer of the macro.

For clarity, code statement lines are indented four spaces. Table 9–2 explains the function of each element of a code statement.

Table 9–2 Elements of a Code Statement

Code Statements

Element	Definition	Examples
Keyword	Recognized by Visual Basic as part of its programming language. Keywords appear in blue in the Code window.	Sub End Sub
Variable	An item whose value can be modified during program execution.	ActiveWindow.ActivePane.View.Zoom.PageFit
Constant	An item whose value remains unchanged during program execution.	False
Operator	A symbol that indicates a specific action.	=

To Protect a Form

You now are finished enhancing the online form and adding macros to it. The following steps protect the online form so that users are restricted to entering data only in content controls.

1 Show the Developer tab and then display the Developer tab.

2 Click the Protect Document button on the Developer tab to display the Restrict Formatting and Editing task pane. (If a menu appears instead of the task pane, click Restrict Formatting and Editing on the menu to display the task pane.)

3 In the Editing restrictions area, if necessary, place a check mark in the 'Allow only this type of editing in the document' check box and then click its box arrow and select 'Filling in forms' in the list.

4 In the Start enforcement area, click the Yes, Start Enforcing Protection button and then click the OK button in the dialog box to protect the document without a password.

5 Close the Restrict Formatting and Editing task pane.

To Run the Compatibility Checker

Assume you have considered saving this template in the Word 97-2003 format so that it can be opened by users with earlier versions of Microsoft Word. Before saving a document or template in an earlier format, however, you want to ensure that all of its elements (such as fields, building blocks, and content controls) are compatible (will work with) earlier versions of Word. The following steps run the compatibility checker.

1
- Click the Office Button and then point to Prepare to display the Prepare submenu (Figure 9–58).

Figure 9–58

- Click Run Compatibility Checker on the Prepare submenu to display the Microsoft Office Word Compatibility Checker dialog box, which shows any content that may not be supported by earlier versions of Word (Figure 9–59).

- Analyze the results of the compatibility checker: Because the compatibility checker indicated that content controls are not supported in earlier versions of Word, you will not save the template in the Word 97-2003 format.

- Click the OK button in the dialog box.

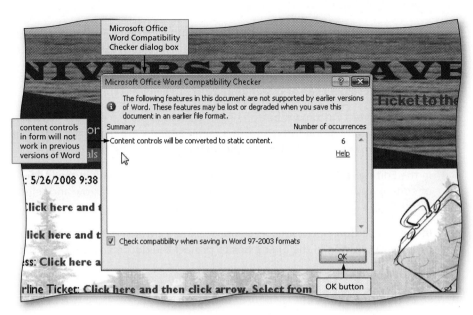

Figure 9–59

To Save the Document Again and Close the Template

You now are finished with the first project in this chapter, enhancing the online form and adding macros to it. Thus, you will save it a final time and close it. You will leave Word running for the next project in the chapter.

1 Save the template again with the same name, Universal Travel Modified.

2 Click the Office Button and then click Close on the Office Button menu to close the template and leave Word running.

Incorporating Security and Functionality in a Document

The project for this section of the chapter is a business letter that incorporates both security and functionality because you intend to share the letter with others. For example, you may want to e-mail a document to others for their review, signature, or information and ensure that the document cannot be modified. When preparing documents to be shared, you might want to consider several modifications to the document:

1. Save a document with a password.
2. Save frequently used data as building blocks.
3. Remove personal information, hidden text, and other nonessential content.
4. Add a signature line and/or digital signature.
5. Save the document as an XPS file.

The following pages apply these modifications to a letter.

> **Save a document with a password.**
> To keep unauthorized users from accessing files, save the file with a password and keep your password confidential. Choose a password that is easy to remember and that no one can guess. Do not use any part of your first or last name, your spouse's or child's name, telephone number, street address, license plate number, Social Security number, birthday, and so on. Be sure your password is at least six characters long, and if possible, use a mixture of numbers and letters.

To Save a Document with a Password

The first step in this project is to open the document, Best Business Solutions Draft, from the Data Files for Students. See the inside back cover of this book for instructions on downloading the Data Files for Students, or contact your instructor for information about accessing the required files. Then, you will save the document with a new file name and with a password. Saving the file with a password protects unauthorized users from altering the contents of a file. The following steps save a file with a password.

- Open the file called Best Business Solutions Draft from the Data Files for Students.

🔎 **Experiment**

- Scroll through the letter to familiarize yourself with its contents.

❷

- Click the Office Button and then click Save As to display the Save As dialog box.

- Type Best Business Solutions Modified as the new file name.

- Click the Tools button in the dialog box to display the Tools menu (Figure 9–60).

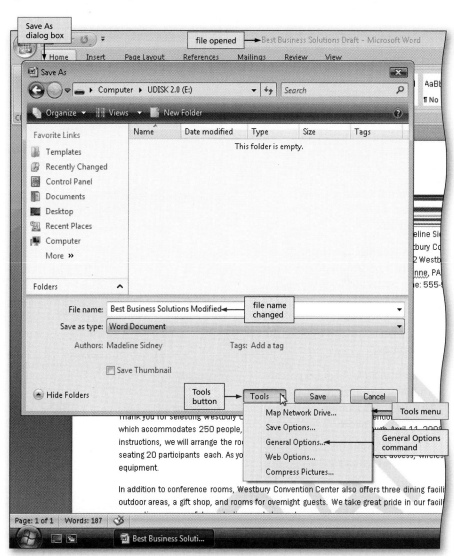

Figure 9–60

3

- Click General Options on the Tools menu to display the General Options dialog box.

- In the 'Password to modify' text box, type computer as the password (Figure 9–61).

Why do dots appear in the text box instead of the word, computer?

Many programs display a series of dots instead of the actual characters so that others cannot see your password as you type it.

Is the word, computer, a good password?

For purposes of this project, the password was designed to be easy to remember. In real-world settings, you should choose more secure passwords.

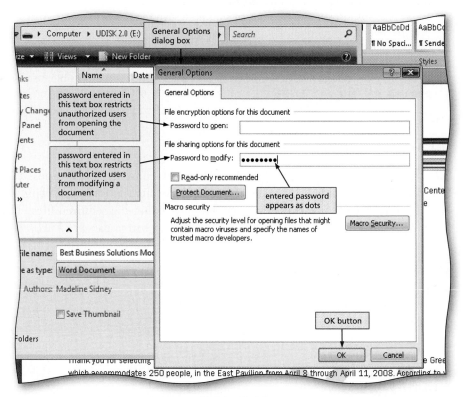

Figure 9–61

4

- Click the OK button, which displays a Confirm Password dialog box.

- In the 'Reenter password to modify' text box, type computer as the password (Figure 9–62).

5

- Click the OK button to close the dialog box.

- When the Save As dialog box is visible again, click its Save button to save the document with the entered password.

What if I forget my password?

Do not forget your password because you will not be able to modify the document without it.

When will the password be requested?

When the document is opened, a Password dialog box will appear that requests the password.

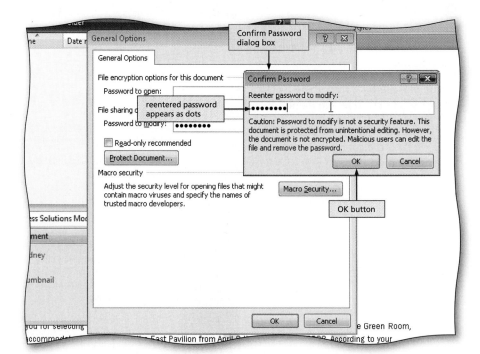

Figure 9–62

To Create a Building Block

Recall that if you use the same text or graphic frequently, you can store the text or graphic in a **building block** and then use the stored building block entry in the open document, as well as in future documents. Because the company contact information in this letter may be needed again in future documents, you create a building block for this information. The following steps create a building block.

1 Select the text to be a building block, in this case, the five lines in the inside address.

2 Display the Insert tab. Click the Quick Parts button on the Insert tab to display the Quick Parts menu.

3 Click Save Selection to Quick Part Gallery on the Quick Parts menu to display the Create New Building Block dialog box.

4 Type Best Business Solutions in the Name text box (Figure 9–63).

5 Click the OK button to store the building block entry in the Quick Parts gallery and close the dialog box. If Word displays another dialog box, click the Yes button.

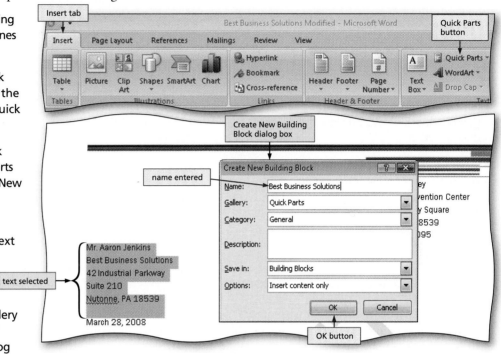

Figure 9–63

To Modify a Building Block

When you save a building block in the Quick Parts gallery, it appears when you click the Quick Parts button on the Insert tab. When you point to the building block in the Quick Parts gallery, the ScreenTip displays the building block name. If you want to display more information when the user points to the building block, you can include a description as an Enhanced ScreenTip. The following steps modify a building block to include a description.

1
• Click the Quick Parts button on the Insert tab to display the Quick Parts gallery.

Experiment
• Point to the Best Business Solutions building block in the Quick Parts gallery to display the ScreenTip.

2
• Right-click the Best Business Solutions building block to display a shortcut menu (Figure 9–64).

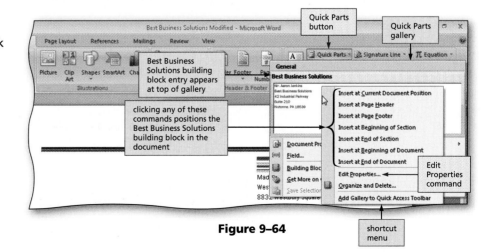

Figure 9–64

- Click Edit Properties on the shortcut menu to display the Modify Building Block dialog box, which is filled in with information related to the Best Business Solutions building block.

- Type `Conference Room Reservation` in the Description text box (Figure 9–65).

- Click the OK button to store the building block entry and close the dialog box.

- Click the Yes button when asked if you want to redefine the building block entry.

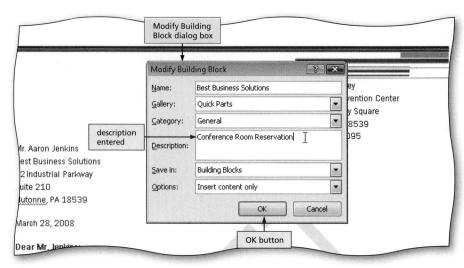

Figure 9–65

To Use the Document Inspector

Before sharing a document with others, you should proofread it to be sure it is free from spelling and grammar errors. When sending an electronic file, you also want to check the content of the information that may be stored with the document. Word includes a Document Inspector that checks a document for content you might not want to share with others such as comments, tracked changes, annotations, personal information, and data formatted as hidden text. The following steps use the Document Inspector to remove personal information and other similar content from a document.

- Click the Office Button and then point to Prepare on the Office Button menu (Figure 9–66).

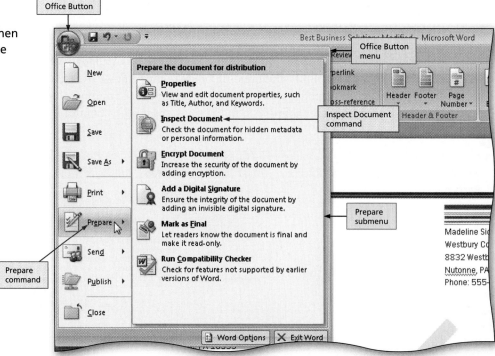

Figure 9–66

2

- Click Inspect Document on the Prepare submenu to display the Document Inspector dialog box.

- Review the list of items in the Document Inspector dialog box and, if necessary, place a check mark for content you may want to remove; in this case, select all items in the list (Figure 9–67).

Q&A

What is an annotation?

If you have a Tablet PC, you can enter ink annotations (handwriting) in a comment in the document.

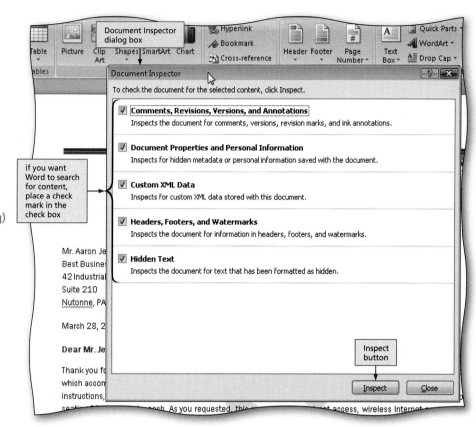

Figure 9–67

3

- Click the Inspect button so that Word searches for content that you selected and displays the search results in the dialog box (Figure 9–68).

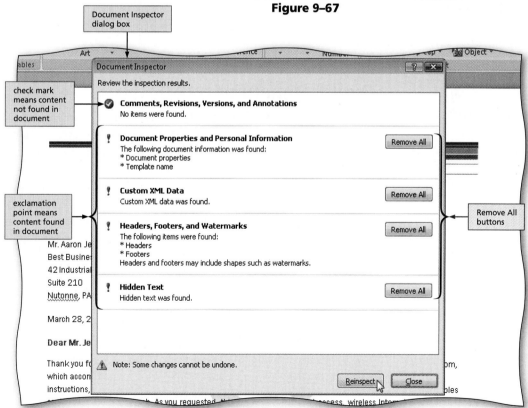

Figure 9–68

4

- Review the inspection results and determine which content you want to remove from the document.

- Click the first Remove All button to remove document properties and personal information.

- Click the next Remove All button to remove XML data.

- Click the next Remove All button to remove headers, footers, and watermarks.

- Click the next Remove All button to remove hidden text (Figure 9–69).

Q&A What if the document contained an ink annotation?

The inspection would have located it, and you would have clicked the Remove All button to remove the ink annotation.

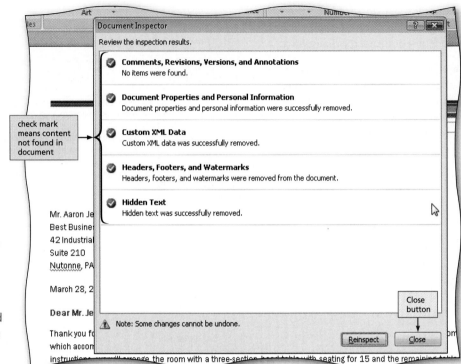

Figure 9–69

5

- Click the Close button to close the dialog box.

Digital Signatures

Some users attach a **digital signature** to a document to verify its authenticity. A digital signature is an electronic, encrypted, and secure stamp of authentication on a document. This signature confirms that the file originated from the signer (file creator) and that it has not been altered.

A digital signature references a digital certificate. A **digital certificate** is an attachment to a file, macro project, or e-mail message that vouches for its authenticity, provides secure encryption, or supplies a verifiable signature. Many users who receive online forms enable the macros based on whether they are digitally signed by a developer on the user's list of trusted sources.

You can obtain a digital certificate from a commercial certification authority or from your network administrator, or you can create a digital signature yourself. A digital certificate you create yourself is not issued by a formal certification authority. Documents using such a certificate are referred to as self-signed documents. Certificates you create yourself are considered unauthenticated and still will generate a warning when opened at certain security levels. Many users, however, consider self-signed documents safer to open than those with no certificates at all.

Once a digital signature is added, the document becomes a read-only document, which means that modifications cannot be made to it. Thus, you only should create a digital signature when the document is final. In Word, you can add two types of digital signatures to a document: (1) a signature line or (2) an invisible digital signature. The following sections address each of these types of digital signatures.

To Add a Signature Line to a Document

A digital signature line, which resembles a printed signature placeholder, allows a recipient of the electronic file to type a signature, include an image of his or her signature, or write a signature using the ink feature on a Tablet PC. Digital signature lines enable organizations to use paperless methods of obtaining signatures on official documents such as contracts. The following steps add a digital signature line to a document.

- Position the insertion point at the location for the digital signature, in this case, at the very bottom of the document.

- Click the Signature Line button on the Insert tab to display the Signature Setup dialog box.

- If a dialog box appears about signature services, click its OK button.

- Type the name of the person who should sign the document, Aaron Jenkins, in this case.

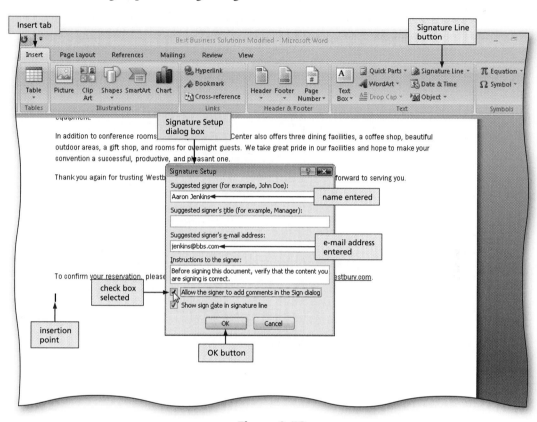

Figure 9–70

- If available, type the signer's e-mail address, jenkins@bbs.com, in this case.

- Place a checkmark in the 'Allow the signer to add comments in the Sign dialog' check box so that the recipient can add a message back to you (Figure 9–70).

- Click the OK button to insert a signature line in the document at the location of the insertion point (Figure 9–71).

How does a recipient insert his or her digital signature?

When the recipient opens the document, a Message Bar appears that contains a View Signatures button. The recipient can click the View Signatures button to display the Signatures task pane, click the requested signature box arrow, and then click Sign in the menu (or double-click the signature line in the document) to display a dialog box that the recipient then completes.

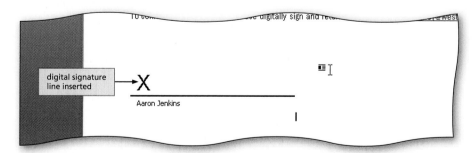

Figure 9–71

To Add an Invisible Digital Signature to a Document

An invisible digital signature does not appear as a tangible signature in the document. If the status bar displays a Signatures button, the document has an invisible digital signature. The following steps add an invisible digital signature to a document.

1

- Click the Office Button and then point to Prepare to display the Prepare submenu (Figure 9–72).

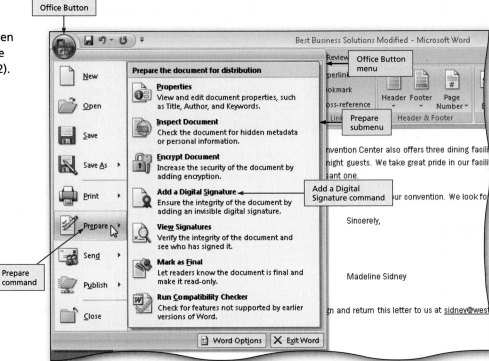

Figure 9–72

2

- Click Add a Digital Signature on the Prepare submenu to display the Sign dialog box.

- If a dialog box about signature services appears, click its OK button.

Q&A

What if a dialog box appears indicating I need a digital ID?

If necessary, select the 'Get your own digital ID' option button, click the OK button, and then follow the on-screen instructions.

- In the 'Purpose for signing this document' text box, type Verify its authenticity. (Figure 9–73).

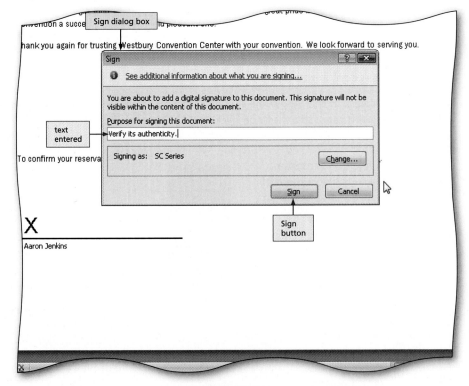

Figure 9–73

3

- Click the Sign button to add the digital signature, show the Signatures button on the status bar, and display the Signatures task pane, which lists all current digital signatures in the document — your list may differ (Figure 9–74).

- If a dialog box appears indicating the signature has been saved successfully, click its OK button.

4

- Click the Close button on the Signatures task pane.

Q&A

How can I view the digital signatures in a document?

Click the Signatures button on the status bar or click the Office Button, point to Prepare, and then click View Signatures.

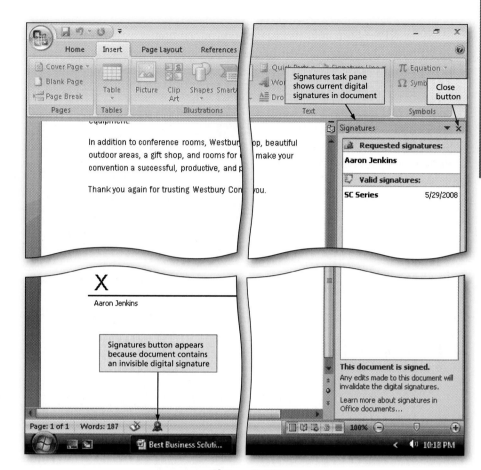

Figure 9–74

XPS

XPS, which stands for XML Paper Specification, is a file format developed by Microsoft that shows all elements of a printed document as an electronic image. Like the PDF format, users can view a XPS document without the software that created the original document. Thus, the XPS format enables users easily to share documents with others. Windows Vista has built-in capability to view, navigate, and print an XPS file; for other operating systems, users can download a viewer.

Microsoft provides a free add-in utility that enables you to convert a Word document to an XPS format. To check if the utility has been downloaded to your computer, click the Office Button menu and then point to Save As. If your Save As submenu contains the PDF or XPS command, then the add-in utility has been installed. If your Save As submenu contains the 'Find add-ins for other file formats' command, then the add-in utility has not been installed. To download the add-in utility, click 'Find add-ins for other file formats' on the Save As submenu to display the 'Enable support for other file formats, such as PDF and XPS' Help window. Scroll through the Help window and then click the Microsoft Save as PDF or XPS Add-in for 2007 Microsoft Office Programs, which displays a Web page at Microsoft's site. Follow the instructions at that Web page to download and install this add-in utility.

With the XPS add-in utility installed on your computer, you can save your documents as XPS files or e-mail the document to others as a XPS file.

To Save a Document in an XPS Format

If the XPS add-in utility is installed on your computer, you can save the document displayed in the Word window as an XPS file. The original Word document remains intact — Word creates a copy of the file in an XPS format. The following steps save an XPS version of the current document.

1
- Click the Office Button and then point to Save As on the Office Button menu to display the Save As submenu (Figure 9–75).

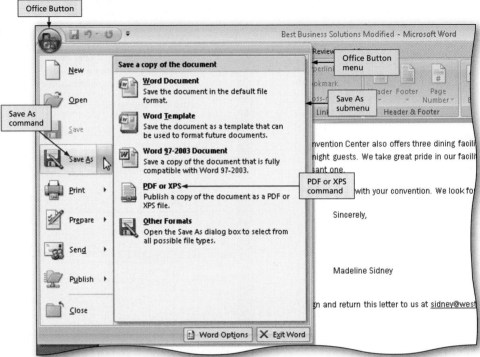

Figure 9–75

2
- Click PDF or XPS on the Save As submenu to display the Publish as PDF or XPS dialog box.

Q&A What if the PDF or XPS command is not on my Save As submenu?

The XPS add-in utility has not been installed on your computer. See the discussion on the previous page for information about installing the XPS add-in utility.

- If necessary, click the 'Save as type' box arrow and then click XPS Document.

- If necessary, place a check mark in the 'Open file after publishing' check box, so that you can see the XPS document that Word creates (Figure 9–76).

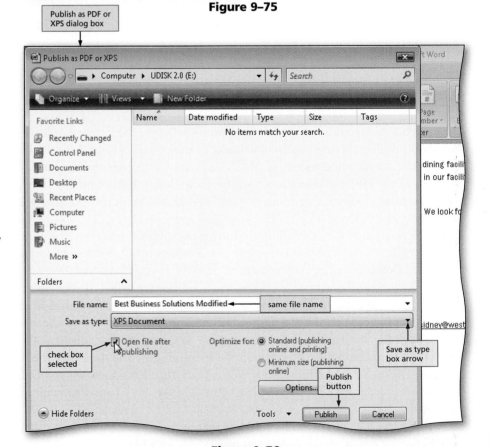

Figure 9–76

- Click the Publish button, which creates an XPS file of the current document, starts your default XPS viewer program, and displays the XPS file in the viewer window, which in this case is Internet Explorer (Figure 9–77).

- Click the Close button to close the XPS file and exit the viewer.

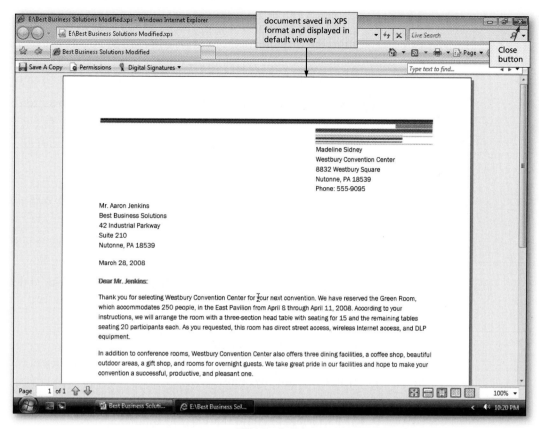

Figure 9–77

To Customize How Word Opens E-Mail Attachments

When a user e-mails you a Word document as an attachment, Word displays the document in Full Screen Reading view. This view is designed to increase the readability and legibility of an on-screen document. Full Screen Reading view, however, does not represent how the document will look when it is printed. For this reason, many users prefer working in Print Layout view to read documents. To exit Full Screen Reading view, click the Close button in the upper-right corner of the screen. As an alternative, you can instruct Word not to use Full Screen Reading view when opening e-mail attachments. The following steps customize how Word opens e-mail attachments.

1. Click the Office Button and then click the Word Options button to display the Word Options dialog box. If necessary, click Popular in the left pane.

2. Remove the check mark from the 'Open e-mail attachments in Full Screen Reading view' check box.

3. Click the OK button.

To Close the Document

You now are finished with the second project in this chapter, incorporating security and functionality in a document. Earlier when you attached a digital signature, Word automatically saved the document, which is why the Save button is dimmed. The following step closes the document and leaves Word running for the next project in the chapter.

 Click the Office Button and then click Close on the Office Button menu to close the document and leave Word running.

To Set a Default Save Location

If you wanted to change the default location that Word uses when it saves a document, you would perform the following steps.

1. Click the Office Button and then click the Word Options button.
2. Click Save in the left pane of the Word Options dialog box.
3. In the 'Default file location' text box, type the new desired default save location.
4. Click the OK button.

To Mark a Document as Final

If you wanted to mark a document as final so that users could not edit it, you would perform the following steps.

1. Click the Office Button and then point to Prepare.
2. Click Mark as Final on the Prepare submenu.
3. Click the OK button.

Working with XML

The final project in this chapter converts an online form to the XML format so that the data in the form can be shared with other programs. XML is a popular format for structuring data, which allows the data to be reused and shared. **XML**, which stands for eXtensible Markup Language, is a language used to encapsulate data and a description of the data in a single text file, the **XML file**. XML uses **tags** to describe data items. Each data item is called an **element**. Businesses often create standard XML file layouts and tags to describe commonly used types of data.

In Word, you have three options for structuring an XML document:

1. Save a file in a default XML format, in which Word parses up the document into individual components that can be used by other programs.
2. Incorporate content controls in a template, which can interact directly with programs stored on central sites such as a SharePoint Server.
3. Specifically identify sections of the document as XML elements. This feature is available only in the stand-alone version of Microsoft Office Word 2007 and in Microsoft Office Professional 2007.

This project guides you through the first and third options. Chapter 8 presented the second option. If you are stepping through this project on a computer, you must have the stand-alone version of Microsoft Office Word 2007 or Microsoft Office Professional 2007 to perform the steps related to option 3.

To Save a Document in the Default XML Format

The first step in this project is to open the document, That Pool Place - No Schema Attached, from the Data Files for Students. See the inside back cover of this book for instructions on downloading the Data Files for Students, or contact your instructor for information about accessing the required files. Then, you will save the document in the XML format. The following steps save a file in the XML format.

- Open the file called That Pool Place - No Schema Attached from the Data Files for Students.

- Click the Office Button and then click Save As to display the Save As dialog box.

- Click the 'Save as type' box arrow and then click Word XML Document in the list (Figure 9–78).

- Click the Save button to save the template as an XML document.

Q&A How can I identify an XML document?

XML documents typically have an .xml extension.

Figure 9–78

To Close the Document

You now are finished saving a file in the default XML format. The following step closes the document and leaves Word running for the next steps in the chapter.

1 Click the Office Button and then click Close on the Office Button menu to close the document and leave Word running.

To Attach a Schema File

An **XML schema** is a special type of XML file that describes the layout of elements in other XML files. Word users typically do not create XML schema files. Computer programmers or other technical personnel create an XML schema file and provide it to Word users. XML schema files, often simply called schema files, usually have an extension of .xsd.

The schema file to be used in this project is on the Data Files for Students. See the inside back cover of this book for instructions on downloading the Data Files for Students, or contact your instructor for information about accessing the required files. The steps on the next page attach a schema to a file.

1

- Open the file called That Pool Place from the Data Files for Students.

- Use the Save As command to save the file with the new name, That Pool Place - Schema Attached.

2

- Display the Developer tab.

- Click the Schema button on the Developer tab to display the Templates and Add-ins dialog box (Figure 9–79).

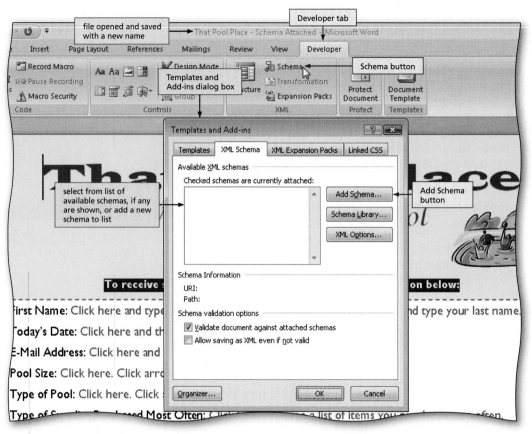

Figure 9–79

3

- Click the Add Schema button to display the Add Schema dialog box.

- Locate the file called That Pool Place.xsd on the Data Files for Students.

- Click That Pool Place.xsd in the list of schema files (Figure 9–80).

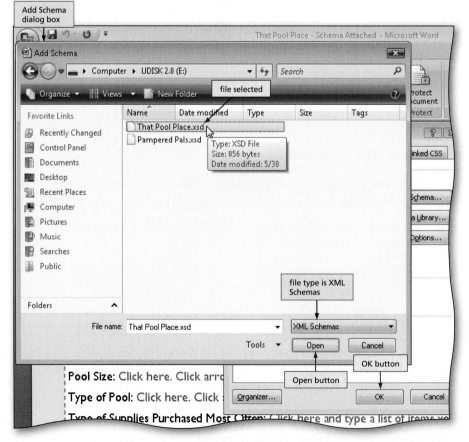

Figure 9–80

4

- Click the Open button in the Add Schema dialog box to display the Schema Settings dialog box.

- Type urn:form-schema-1 in the URI text box, and then type That Pool Place in the Alias text box (Figure 9–81).

Q&A

What is a URI and an alias?

Word uses the URI, also called a **namespace**, to refer to the schema. Because these names are difficult to remember, you can define a namespace alias. In a setting outside of an academic environment, a computer administrator would provide you with the appropriate namespace entry.

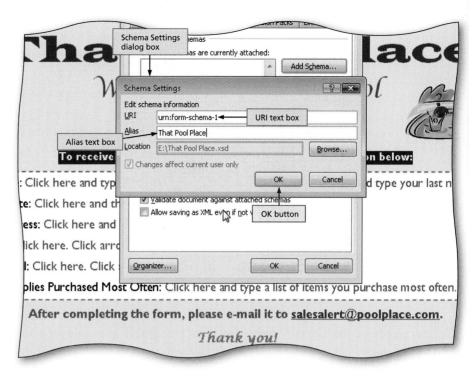

Figure 9–81

5

- Click the OK button to add the schema to the Schema Library and then add the namespace alias to the list of available schemas in the XML Schema sheet in the Templates and Add-ins dialog box.

- If necessary, place a check mark in the That Pool Place check box (Figure 9–82).

6

- Click the OK button, which causes Word to attach the selected schema to the open document and display the XML Structure task pane in the Word window.

Figure 9–82

To Delete a Schema from the Schema Library

To delete a schema from a document, you would remove the check mark from the schema name in the XML Schema sheet in the Templates and Add-ins dialog box (Figure 9–82 on the previous page). If you wanted to delete a schema altogether from the Schema Library, you would do the following.

1. Click the Schema button on the Developer tab to display the Templates and Add-ins dialog box.

2. Click the Schema Library button to display the Schema Library dialog box.

3. Click the schema you want to delete in the 'Select a schema' list and then click the Delete Schema button.

4. When Word displays a dialog box asking if you are sure you wish to delete the schema, click the Yes button.

5. Click the OK button and then click the Cancel button.

To Add a Parent and Child XML Element

After a schema has been attached to a document, the next step is to add XML elements to the document. XML elements are data items whose value often changes. The online form in this project has eight XML elements: First Name, Last Name, Today's Date, E-Mail Address, Pool Size, Type of Pool, Type of Supplies Purchased Most Often, and the entire online form itself. The first step is to add the entire online form XML element, called the **parent element**, to the document and then add the elements subordinate to the parent, called the **child elements**.

The following steps add XML elements to the document, which is called tagging the text. First, you select the item to be tagged and then you add the desired XML element to apply the tag.

1

- Position the insertion point at the top of the document.

- In the 'Choose an element to apply to your current selection' list in the XML Structure task pane, double-click ThatPoolPlace{That Pool Place} to display the 'Apply to entire document' dialog box (Figure 9–83).

Figure 9–83

2

- Click the Apply to Entire Document button to place start and end tags on the entire document, that is, to tag the parent element.

- Be sure the 'Show XML tags in the document' check box contains a check mark (Figure 9–84).

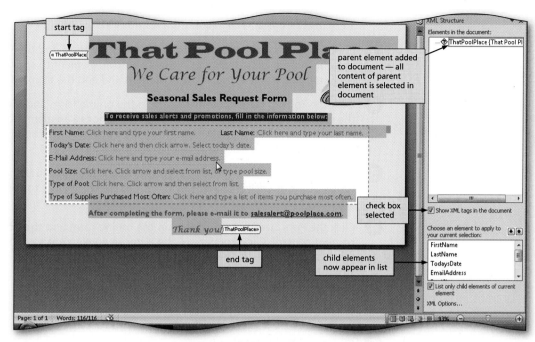

Figure 9–84

3

- Click the First Name content control in the online form and then click its label to select the content control.

What if the item to select is not a content control?

Drag through the item you want to assign to the child element.

- Click FirstName in the 'Choose an element to apply to your current selection' list, which places start and end tags on the text selected in the document and moves the selected child element below the

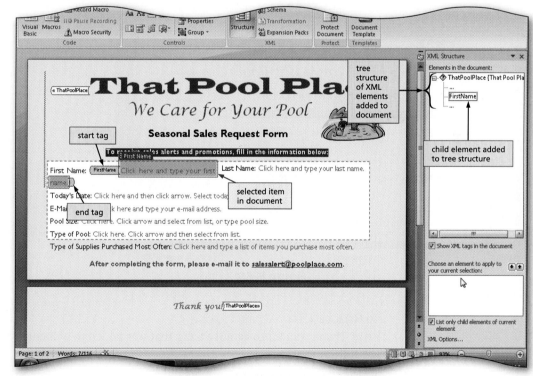

Figure 9–85

parent element in the 'Elements in the document' list in the task pane (Figure 9–85).

To Add XML Elements

The next steps add the remaining child XML elements to the XML tree structure.

1 Click the Last Name content control in the online form and then click its label to select the content control. Click LastName in the 'Choose an element to apply to your current selection' list to tag the text selected in the document and add the element to the XML tree structure.

2 Click the Today's Date content control in the online form and then click its label to select the content control. Click TodaysDate in the 'Choose an element to apply to your current selection' list to tag the text selected in the document and add the element to the XML tree structure.

3 Click the E-Mail Address content control in the online form and then click its label to select the content control. Click EmailAddress in the 'Choose an element to apply to your current selection' list to tag the text selected in the document and add the element to the XML tree structure.

4 Click the Pool Size content control in the online form and then click its label to select the content control. Click PoolSize in the 'Choose an element to apply to your current selection' list to tag the text selected in the document and add the element to the XML tree structure.

5 Click the Type of Pool content control in the online form and then click its label to select the content control. Click TypeOfPool in the 'Choose an element to apply to your current selection' list to tag the text selected in the document and add the element to the XML tree structure.

6 Click the Type of Supplies Purchased Most Often content control in the online form and then click its label to select the content control. Click TypeOfSupplies in the 'Choose an element to apply to your current selection' list to tag the text selected in the document and add the element to the XML tree structure.

7 Click anywhere to remove the selection from the text (Figure 9-86).

8 Remove the check mark from the 'Show XML tags in the document' check box so that the tags no longer appear in the document window.

Figure 9–86

To Remove a Tag

If you wanted to remove a tag that was added to a document, you would perform the following steps.

1. Right-click the start or end tag and then click Remove tag on the shortcut menu — which instructs Word to remove both the start and end tag.

   or

2. Right-click the element name in the XML Structure task pane and then click Remove tag on the shortcut menu.

To Save a Document in the Default XML Format

The next step in this project is to save the XML document.

1 Click the Office Button and then click Save As to display the Save As dialog box.

2 Click the 'Save as type' box arrow and then click Word XML Document in the list.

3 Click the Save button to save the template as an XML document. Close the XML Structure task pane.

To Set Exceptions to Editing Restrictions

When users open an online form, you want them to be able to edit only the placeholder text. You can use the Restrict Formatting and Editing task pane to allow editing in just certain areas of the document, a procedure called adding users excepted from restrictions. The following steps set exceptions to editing restrictions.

1
• Click the Protect Document button on the Developer tab to display the Restrict Formatting and Editing task pane.

2
• If necessary, place a check mark in the 'Allow only this type of editing in the document' check box and then change the associated text box to No changes (Read only), which instructs Word to prevent any editing to the document.

• Click the First Name placeholder text. Press and hold the CTRL key while clicking the rest of the placeholder text in the online form.

• Place a check mark in the Everyone check box in the Exceptions (optional) area, which instructs Word that the selected text can be edited — the rest of the form will be read only (Figure 9–87).

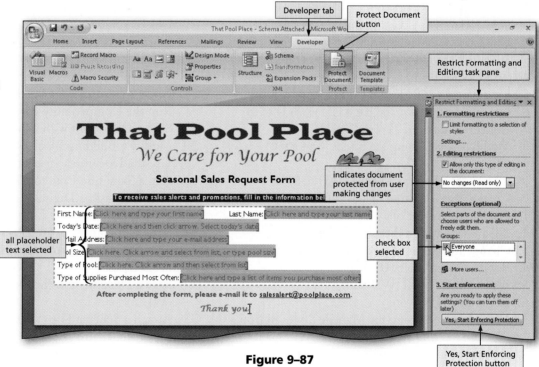

Figure 9–87

3
• Click the Yes, Start Enforcing Protection button in the Restrict Formatting and Editing task pane.

• Click the OK button in the Start Enforcing Protection dialog box.

• Close the Restrict Formatting and Editing task pane.

BTW

Quick Reference
For a table that lists how to complete the tasks covered in this book using the mouse, Ribbon, shortcut menu, and keyboard, see the Quick Reference Summary at the back of this book, or visit the Word 2007 Quick Reference Web page (scsite.com/wd2007/qr).

To Save an XML Document as a Template and Quit Word

The next step is to save the document as a template with a new name so that a user can open a new document window based on the template and then quit Word.

1 Click the Office Button and then click Save As to display the Save As dialog box.

2 Change the file name to That Pool Place Modified - Schema Attached.

3 Click the 'Save as type' box arrow and then click Word Template in the list.

4 Click the Save button to save the template so that users can create new documents based on the template.

5 Click the Close button on the Word title bar.

Chapter Summary

In this chapter, you learned how to enhance the look of graphics and shapes with fill effects and 3-D effects; automate a series of tasks with a macro; secure a document with digital signatures, passwords, and other settings; and use XML for data that will be shared with other programs. The items listed below include all the new Word skills you have learned in this chapter.

1. Save a Macro-Enabled Template (WD 645)
2. Unprotect a Document (WD 646)
3. Specify Macro Settings in Word (WD 647)
4. Save a New Theme (WD 648)
5. Set a Theme as a Default (WD 650)
6. Use a Fill Effect for the Page Color (WD 650)
7. Convert a Table to Text (WD 653)
8. Modify a Style Using the Styles Task Pane (WD 656)
9. Add a 3-D Effect to a Shape (WD 658)
10. Change the Direction of a 3-D Effect (WD 659)
11. Change the Color of a 3-D Effect (WD 660)
12. Fill a Shape with a Picture (WD 660)
13. Change the Color of a Picture (WD 662)
14. Rotate a Graphic (WD 664)
15. Insert a Date Field (WD 666)
16. Edit a Field (WD 667)
17. Modify a Style Using the Manage Styles Button (WD 669)
18. Record a Macro and Assign It a Shortcut Key (WD 671)
19. Run a Macro (WD 674)
20. Add a Macro as a Button to the Quick Access Toolbar (WD 674)
21. Delete a Button from a Toolbar (WD 677)
22. Rename a Macro (WD 677)
23. Delete a Macro (WD 678)
24. Create an Automatic Macro (WD 678)
25. Edit a Macro's VBA Code (WD 679)
26. Run the Compatibility Checker (WD 683)
27. Save a Document with a Password (WD 685)
28. Modify a Building Block (WD 687)
29. Use the Document Inspector (WD 688)
30. Add a Signature Line to a Document (WD 691)
31. Add an Invisible Digital Signature to a Document (WD 692)
32. Save a Document in an XPS Format (WD 694)
33. Customize How Word Opens E-Mail Attachments (WD 695)
34. Save a Document in the Default XML Format (WD 697)
35. Attach a Schema File (WD 697)
36. Delete a Schema from the Schema Library (WD 700)
37. Add a Parent and Child XML Element (WD 700)
38. Remove a Tag (WD 702)
39. Set Exceptions to Editing Restrictions (WD 703)

If you have a SAM user profile, you may have access to hands-on instruction, practice, and assessment. Log in to your SAM account (http://sam2007.course.com) to launch any assigned training activities or exams that relate to the skills covered in this chapter.

Learn It Online

Test your knowledge of chapter content and key terms.

Instructions: To complete the Learn It Online exercises, start your browser, click the Address bar, and then enter the Web address scsite.com/wd2007/learn. When the Word 2007 Learn It Online page is displayed, click the link for the exercise you want to complete and then read the instructions.

Chapter Reinforcement TF, MC, and SA

A series of true/false, multiple choice, and short answer questions that test your knowledge of the chapter content.

Flash Cards

An interactive learning environment where you identify chapter key terms associated with displayed definitions.

Practice Test

A series of multiple choice questions that test your knowledge of chapter content and key terms.

Who Wants To Be a Computer Genius?

An interactive game that challenges your knowledge of chapter content in the style of a television quiz show.

Wheel of Terms

An interactive game that challenges your knowledge of chapter key terms in the style of the television show *Wheel of Fortune*.

Crossword Puzzle Challenge

A crossword puzzle that challenges your knowledge of key terms presented in the chapter.

Apply Your Knowledge

Reinforce the skills and apply the concepts you learned in this chapter.

Working with XML

Instructions: Start Word. Open the document, Apply 9-1 Pampered Pals Draft, from the Data Files for Students. See the inside back cover of this book for instructions on downloading the Data Files for Students, or contact your instructor for information about accessing the required files.

In this assignment, you attach an XML schema file, add XML elements to a template (Figure 9–88), save a file as an XML file, set exceptions to editing restrictions, and save an XML document as a template.

Figure 9–88

Continued >

Apply Your Knowledge *continued*

Perform the following tasks:

1. Unprotect the template.

2. Save the template in the default XML format using the file name Apply 9-1 Pampered Pals - No Schema Attached.

3. Attach the XML schema file called Pampered Pals.xsd to the Pampered Pals template. Use urn:form-schema-2 as the URI and Pampered Pals as the alias. The schema file is on the Data Files for Students. See the inside back cover of this book for instructions on downloading the Data Files for Students, or contact your instructor for information about accessing the required files.

4. Add the parent element, PamperedPals, to the template.

5. Add all the child elements to the template — one for each data entry field.

6. Save the document as an XML document using the file name, Apply 9-1 Pampered Pals - Schema Attached.

7. Set exceptions to editing restrictions so that all users can edit only the placeholder text in the document. Protect the document without a password.

8. Save the XML document as a template using the name, Apply 9-1 Pampered Pals Modified - Schema Attached.

9. Submit the files in the format specified by your instructor.

Extend Your Knowledge

Extend the skills you learned in this chapter and experiment with new skills. You may need to use Help to complete the assignment.

Working with Document Security

Instructions: Start Word. Open the document, Extend 9-1 Innovative Products Letter Draft, from the Data Files for Students. See the inside back cover of this book for instructions on downloading the Data Files for Students, or contact your instructor for information about accessing the required files.

You will create your own digital ID, add an invisible digital signature to a document, add a digital signature line, save the document as an XPS file, and encrypt the document.

Perform the following tasks:

1. Use Help to review and expand your knowledge about these topics: creating a digital ID, invisible digital signatures, signature lines, XPS files, and document encryption.

2. Create your own digital ID.

3. Add a digital signature line to the document. Use your personal information in the signature line.

4. Add an invisible digital signature to the document.

5. Save the document as an XPS file. View and print the XPS file. Familiarize yourself with the buttons and commands in the XPS viewer (Figure 9–89). Close the XPS file.

6. Encrypt the document. Be sure to use a password you will remember.

7. Save the document with a new file name. Then, close the document and re-open it. Enter the password when prompted.

8. View the signatures in the document.

9. Sign the document; that is, enter your digital signature (type it or select an image).

10. Save the document again. Change the document properties as specified by your instructor. Submit the document in the format specified by your instructor.

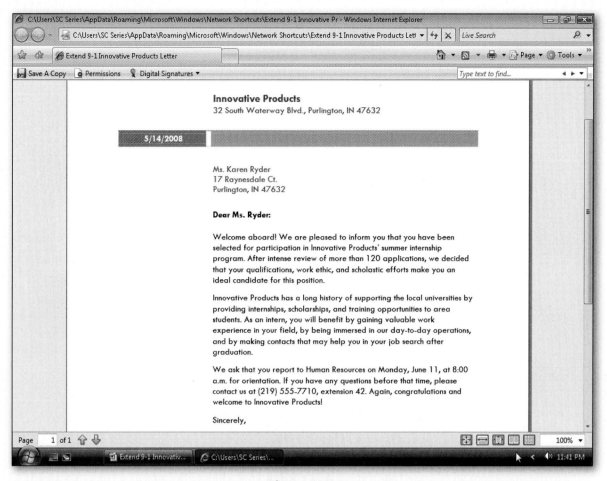

Figure 9–89

Make It Right

Analyze a document and correct all errors and/or improve the design.

Formatting an Online Form

Instructions: Start Word. Open the document, Make It Right 9-1 Parent Athletic Association Letter Draft, from the Data Files for Students. See the inside back cover of this book for instructions on downloading the Data Files for Students, or contact your instructor for information about accessing the required files.

The document is a letter that requires finishing touches before sending (Figure 9–90 on the next page). You are to add and edit a building block, change the font set and save the modified theme, run the compatibility checker, save the document with a password, use the Document Inspector, and disable Full Screen Reading view for e-mail attachments.

Perform the following tasks:
1. Add a building block for the contact information (inside address). Save it to the Quick Parts gallery. Use the name, Nicholas Blake. Do not enter a description.

2. Edit the building block for Nicholas Blake to include this description: Athlete of the Year.

3. Change the font set to one of your choice. Save the modified theme with the name PAA. If approved by your instructor, set the modified theme as the default.

4. Run the compatibility checker to determine if this document can be saved in the Word 97-2003 format. Add a comment to the document indicating the results of the compatibility checker.

Continued >

Make It Right *continued*

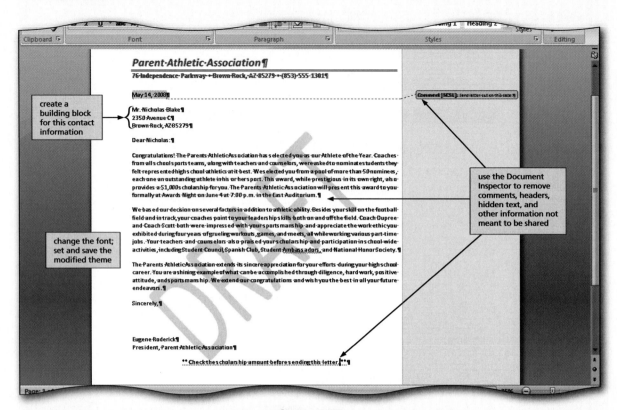

Figure 9–90

5. Save the document with a new name and a password of your choice. Be sure to select a password you will remember.

6. Use the Document Inspector to determine the types of personal information and other hidden content that is in the document. What are the results? Remove the comments, document properties, headers, footers, and hidden text.

7. Change the document properties as specified by your instructor. Save the document again.

8. E-mail a copy of the document to yourself.

9. Disable the open e-mail attachments in Full Screen Reading view setting.

10. Open the e-mail attachment.

11. Submit the document in the format specified by your instructor.

In the Lab

Design and/or create a document using the guidelines, concepts, and skills presented in this chapter. Labs are listed in order of increasing difficulty.

Lab 1: Enhancing the Graphics and Shapes of an Online Form

Problem: You created the online form shown in Figure 8-80 on page WD 634 for Andrew County Public Library. Your supervisor has asked you to change the form's appearance. You modify the form so that it looks like the one shown in Figure 9–91.

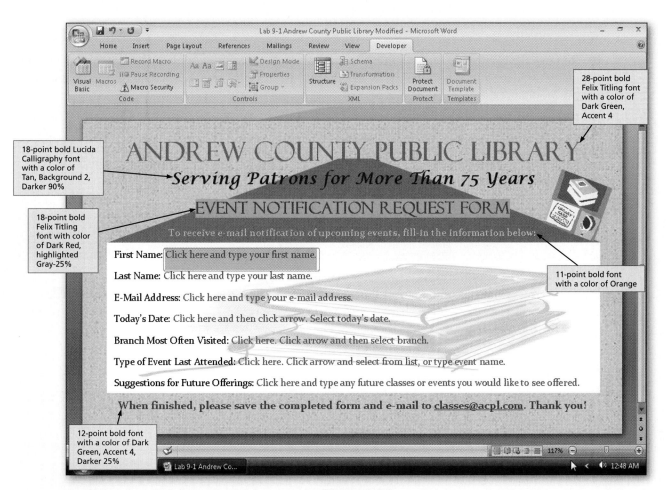

Figure 9–91

Perform the following tasks:

1. Open the template called Lab 8-1 Andrew County Public Library that you created in Lab 1 of Chapter 8. Save the template with a new file name of Lab 9-1 Andrew County Public Library Modified. If you did not complete the lab in Chapter 8, see your instructor for a copy.

2. Use the Recycled paper fill effect for the page color.

3. Change the color scheme to Aspect. Change the font set to Flow.

4. Edit the last two lines so that the text fits on a single line as shown in Figure 9–91.

5. Modify the formats of the company name, business tag line, form title, user instruction, and thank you lines as shown in Figure 9–91 (or with similar fonts).

6. Convert the table to text for the 2 × 1 table containing the First Name and Last Name content controls. Extend the rectangle to cover the entire data entry area.

7. Add the 3-D Style 10 to the rectangle shape. Change the 3-D color to Orange, Accent 1, Lighter 80%.

8. Modify the style of the placeholder text to the color Orange, Accent 1, Darker 25%.

9. Use the picture fill effect to place a picture in the rectangle shape. Use the picture called Books from the Data Files for Students. See the inside back cover of this book for instructions on downloading the Data Files for Students, or contact your instructor for information about accessing the required files.

10. Change the color of the picture in the rectangle to washout.

Continued >

In the Lab *continued*

11. Remove the current clip art and insert the one shown in the figure (or a similar image). Format the image as floating In Front of Text. Resize the clip art. Recolor it to Accent color 4 Light. Rotate the graphic as shown in the figure.

12. Protect the form.

13. Save the form again and submit it in the format specified by your instructor.

14. Access the template through Windows Explorer. Fill in the form and submit the filled-in form in the format specified by your instructor.

In the Lab

Lab 2: Adding a Field and Macros to an Online Form

Problem: You created the online form shown in Figure 8-81 on page WD 636 for Entrée Express. Your supervisor has asked you to change the form's appearance, add a field, and add some macros. You modify the form so that it looks like the one shown in Figure 9–92.

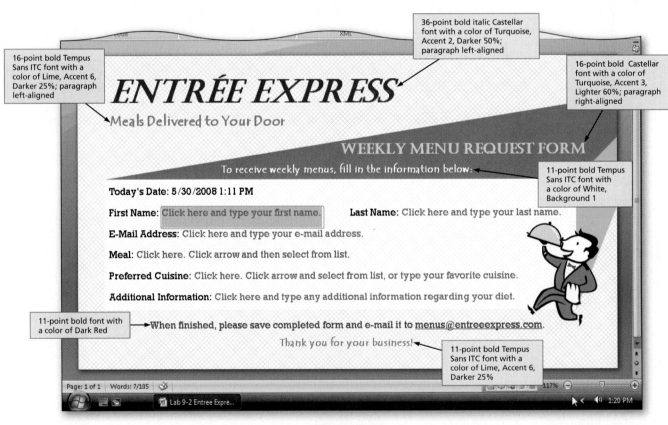

Figure 9–92

Perform the following tasks:

1. Open the template called Lab 8-2 Entree Express that you created in Lab 2 of Chapter 8. Save the template as a macro-enabled template with a new file name of Lab 9-2 Entree Express Modified. If you did not complete the lab in Chapter 8, see your instructor for a copy.

2. Change the color scheme to Flow. Change the font set to Foundry.

3. Use the page color Turquoise, Accent 3, Lighter 60%. Apply the Outlined diamond pattern fill effect to the page color.

4. Modify the formats of the company name, business tag line, form title, user instruction, and thank you lines as shown in Figure 9–92 (or with similar fonts).

5. Remove the Today's Date content control. Insert a date field from Quick Parts in the format 5/31/2008.

6. Edit the date field so that it displays the date and time in the format of 5/31/2008 1:10 PM. Move the date line to the top of the data entry form.

7. Add the 3-D Style 9 to the rectangle shape. Change the 3-D color to Dark Teal, Text 2, Lighter 80%. Change the pattern inside the rectangle to 90%.

8. Remove the current clip art and insert the one shown in the figure (or a similar image). Format the image as floating In Front of Text. Resize the clip art. Rotate the graphic as shown in the figure.

9. Record a macro that hides the Developer tab. Assign it the shortcut key, ALT+D. Run the macro to test it.

10. Create an automatic macro called AutoNew using the macro recorder. The macro should change the view to page width.

11. Protect the form.

12. Save the form again and submit it in the format specified by your instructor.

13. Access the template through Windows Explorer. Fill in the form and submit the filled-in form in the format specified by your instructor.

In the Lab

Lab 3: Enhancing the Look of an Online Form and Adding Macros to It

Problem: You created the online form shown in Figure 8-82 on page WD 638 for the Book Barn. Your supervisor has asked you to change the form's appearance, add a field, and add some macros. You modify the form so that it looks like the one shown in Figure 9–93.

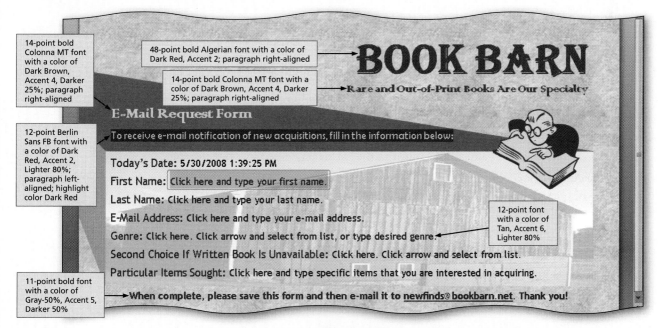

Figure 9–93

Continued >

In the Lab *continued*

Perform the following tasks:

1. Open the template called Lab 8-3 Book Barn that you created in Lab 3 of Chapter 8. Save the template as a macro-enabled template with a new file name of Lab 9-3 Book Barn Modified. If you did not complete the lab in Chapter 8, see your instructor for a copy.

2. Use the Stationery paper fill effect for the page color.

3. Change the color scheme to Equity. Change the font set to Opulent.

4. Edit the last two lines so that the form fits on a single line as shown in Figure 9–93 on the previous page.

5. Modify the formats of the company name, business tag line, form title, user instruction, and thank you lines as shown in Figure 9–93 (or with similar fonts).

6. Convert the two tables in the data entry area to text. Extend the rectangle to cover the entire data entry area.

7. Remove the Today's Date content control. Insert a date field from Quick Parts in the format 5/31/2008 1:39:25 PM.

8. Add the 3-D Style 9 to the rectangle shape. Change the direction to Top Left. Change the 3-D color to Tan, Background 2, Darker 10%.

9. Modify the style of the placeholder text to the color Brown, Accent 6, Darker 50%.

10. Use the picture fill effect to place a picture in the rectangle shape. Use the picture called Barn from the Data Files for Students. See the inside back cover of this book for instructions on downloading the Data Files for Students, or contact your instructor for information about accessing the required files.

11. Change the color of the picture in the rectangle to washout.

12. Remove the current clip art and insert the one shown in the figure (or a similar image). Format the image as floating In Front of Text. Resize the clip art. Rotate the graphic as shown in the figure.

13. Record a macro that hides the Developer tab. Assign it the shortcut key, ALT+D. Run the macro to test it.

14. Add a button to the Quick Access Toolbar for the macro created in Step 13. Test the button and then delete the button.

15. Create an automatic macro called AutoNew using the macro recorder. The macro should change the view to page width.

16. Edit the macro so that it also hides the Developer tab and hides formatting marks.

17. Protect the form.

18. Save the form again and submit it in the format specified by your instructor.

19. Access the template through Windows Explorer. Fill in the form and submit the filled-in form in the format specified by your instructor.

Cases and Places

Apply your creative thinking and problem solving skills to design and implement a solution.

• EASIER   •• MORE DIFFICULT

• 1: Modify an Online Form for an Auto Dealership

You created the online form for Cool Ride Auto Sales that was defined in Cases and Places Assignment 1 in Chapter 8 on page WD 639. Your boss was pleased with the results and by the response from customers. You and your boss, however, believe the form can be improved by enhancing its appearance. Make the following modifications to the form: Change the company name, slogan, and title to a different font and color; change the page color to a texture or fill pattern; change the highlight; and change the font and color of the last line. Add a 3-D effect to the rectangle; if necessary, resize the rectangle to include all text. In the rectangle, add a suitable picture fill effect and recolor it using the Washout effect. If necessary, delete the last line on the form so that the entire form's contents fit on one page. Delete the existing clip art, replace it with new clip art, and then rotate it. Use the concepts and techniques presented in this chapter to modify the online form.

•• 2: Modify an Online Form for a Real Estate Office

You created the online form for Richards Realty that was defined in Cases and Places Assignment 2 in Chapter 8 on page WD 639. Your neighbor was pleased with the results, but now she wants you to make a few modifications to the form you created. Make the following modifications to the form: change the company name, slogan, and title to a different font and color; change the page color to a texture or fill pattern; and change the font and color of the last line. Add a 3-D effect to the rectangle; if necessary, resize the rectangle to include all text. Change the direction and color of the 3-D effect. In the rectangle, add a suitable picture fill effect and recolor it using the Washout effect. If necessary, delete the last line on the form so that the entire form's contents fit on one page. Delete the existing clip art, replace it with new clip art, and then rotate it. Use the concepts and techniques presented in this chapter to modify the online form. When finished, mark the document as final.

•• 3: Modify an Online Form for a Property Management Agency

You created the online form for Sunshine Rentals that was defined in Cases and Places Assignment 3 in Chapter 8 on page WD 639. Your boss has asked you to change the form's appearance by changing its clip art, fonts and font color, and page color. He has decided that the slogan should be changed to: We've Got Florida Covered. He wants you to add a picture as fill and a 3-D effect to the rectangle, and resize it so that it contains all data entry area text. In addition, delete the date content control and insert a date field in its place. Then, move the date content control to the top of the form. Specify the appropriate macro security level. Add a macro to the form and assign it to a button on the Quick Access Toolbar. Then, add an AutoNew macro that controls how the form initially is displayed on the screen. Use the concepts and techniques presented in this chapter to modify the online form.

•• 4: Create an Online Form for Your Future Business

Make It Personal

You created the online form that was defined in Cases and Places Assignment 4 in Chapter 8 on page WD 640. Now you have decided to make a few embellishments and improvements to your form. Use the concepts and techniques you learned in this chapter to modify the form. Set your USB flash drive

Continued >

Cases and Places *continued*

as the default save location. At a minimum, you should change all fonts, font colors, and clip art; use a pattern or texture fill effect for the page; move the date content control to the top of the form and change it to a date field that includes date and time; and add a 3-D effect to the data entry area. When finished, mark the document as final.

• • 5: Create an Online Form for Your School

Working Together

You created the online form that was defined in Cases and Places Assignment 5 in Chapter 8 on page WD 640. Now your team has decided to make a few embellishments and improvements to your form. Use the concepts and techniques you learned in this chapter to modify the form. At a minimum, you should change all fonts, font colors, and clip art; use a pattern or texture fill effect for the page; move the date content control to the top of the form and change it to a date field that includes date and time; and add a 3-D effect to the data entry area. Add three macros to the form and assign each to a button on the Quick Access Toolbar. Then, add an AutoNew macro that controls how the form initially is displayed on the screen. Assign each team member a section of the form to modify. Then, as a team, determine which changes look best in the new form and implement the changes.

Blogging Feature

Creating a Blog Post

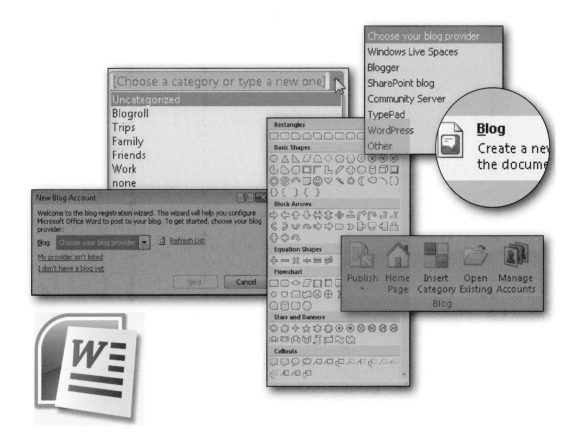

Objectives

You will have mastered the material in this feature when you can:

- Create a new blog post
- Crop a picture
- Change the shape of a picture
- Insert a blog category
- Display the Web page associated with your blog
- Publish a blog post

Blogging Feature Introduction

A **blog**, short for **Weblog**, is an informal Web site consisting of date- or time-stamped articles, or **posts**, in a diary or journal format, usually listed in reverse chronological order. Blogs reflect the interests, opinions, and personalities of the author, called the **blogger**, and sometimes of the site visitors as well.

Project — Blog Post

Blogs have become an important means of worldwide communication. Businesses create blogs to communicate with employees, customers, and vendors. Teachers create blogs to collaborate with other teachers and students, and home users create blogs to share aspects of their personal life with family, friends, and others.

The project in this feature creates a blog post and then publishes it to a registered blog account at WordPress.com, which is a blogging service on the Web. Figure 1a shows the blog Web page with just one post; Figure 1b shows a new blog post created in Word and published to a Web site; Figure 1c shows the updated blog Web page, which shows the new post published at the top of the Web page.

Overview

As you read through this feature, you will learn how to create the blog post shown in Figure 1b and then publish it by performing these general tasks:

- Create the blog post.
- Publish the blog post.

Plan Ahead

> **General Project Guidelines**
>
> When creating a blog post, the actions you perform and decisions you make will affect the appearance and characteristics of the finished document. As you create a blog post, such as the project shown in Figure 1, you should follow these general guidelines:
>
> 1. **Create a blog account on the Web.** Many Web sites exist that allow users to set up a blog free or for a fee. Blogging services that work with Word 2007 include Blogger, Community Server, SharePoint blog, TypePad, and WordPress.com. For illustration purposes in this feature, a free blog account was created at WordPress.com.
>
> 2. **Register your blog account in Word.** Before you can use Word to publish a blog post, you must register your blog account in Word. This step establishes a connection between Word and your blog account. The first time you create a new blog post, Word will ask if you want to register a blog account. You can click the Register Later button if you want to learn how to create a blog post without registering a blog account.
>
> 3. **Create a blog post.** Use Word to enter the text and any graphics in your blog post. Some blogging services accept graphics directly from a Word blog post. Others require that you use a picture hosting service to store pictures you use in a blog post.
>
> 4. **Publish a blog post.** When you publish a blog post, the blog post in the Word document is copied to your account at the blogging service. Once the post is published, it appears at the top of the blog Web page. You may need to click the Refresh button in the browser window to display the new post.

(a) Blog Web Page Before New Posting

**(b) Blog Post Created in Word
and Published to Web Site**

**(c) Blog Web Site
with New Posting**

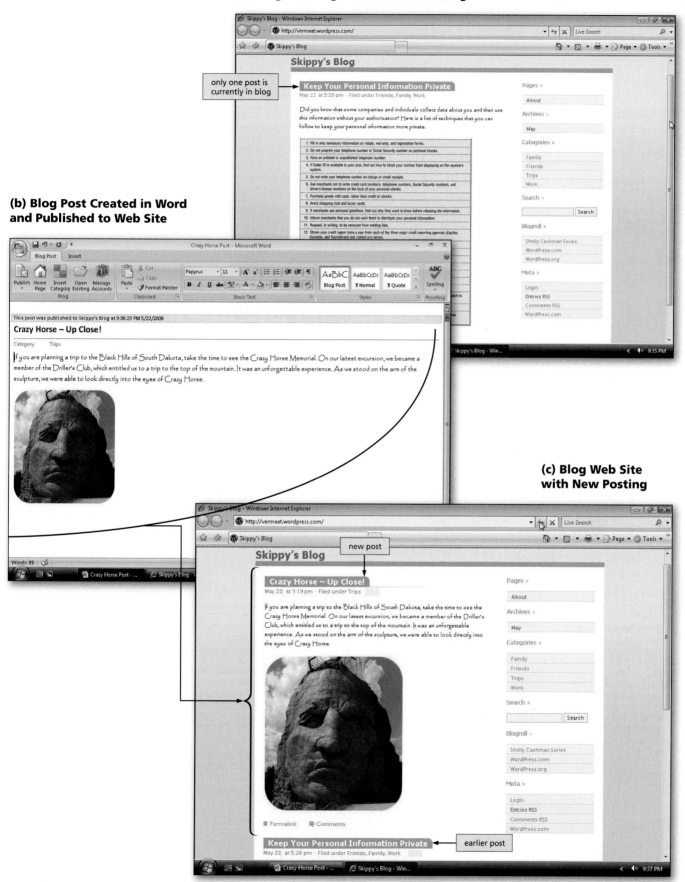

Figure 1

Creating the Blog Post

The blog post in this feature contains a title (Crazy Horse - Up Close!) above a paragraph of text, which is followed by a picture. To create the blog post in this feature, you will follow these general steps:

1. Start Word and create a new blank document for your blog post.
2. Enter the text in the blog post and then format the text.
3. Insert the picture in the blog post and then format the picture.

To Create a Blank Word Document for a Blog Post

The following steps create a blog post based on the current document. Because the current document is blank, the new blog post also will be blank. The following steps create a new blank Word document for a blog post.

1

- Start Word.

2

- With a blank document in the Word window, click the Office Button and then point to Publish on the Office Button menu to display the Publish submenu (Figure 2).

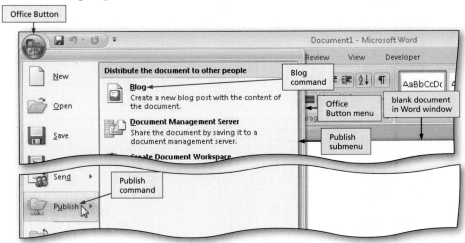

Figure 2

3

- Click Blog on the Publish submenu to display a new blank document for your blog post (Figure 3).

Q&A What if a Register a Blog Account dialog box appears?

Click the Register Later button to skip the registration process at this time. Or, if you have a blog account, you can click the Register Now button and follow the instructions to register your account.

Figure 3

Q&A Why did the Ribbon change?

When creating a blog post, the Ribbon in Word changes to display only the tools required to create and publish a blog post.

Other Ways

1. Click Office Button, click New, click New blog post, click Create button

To Enter Text

The next step is to enter the blog post title and paragraph of text in the blog post.

1 Click the Enter Post Title Here content control and then type Crazy Horse - Up Close! as the title.

2 Position the insertion point below the blue horizontal line and then type this paragraph of text

title entered	
paragraph entered	

Crazy Horse – Up Close!

If you are planning a trip to the Black Hills of South Dakota, take the time to see the Crazy Horse Memorial. On our latest excursion, we became a member of the Driller's Club, which entitled us to a trip to the top of the mountain. It was an unforgettable experience. As we stood on the arm of the sculpture, we were able to look directly into the eyes of Crazy Horse.

insertion point

Figure 4

(Figure 4): If you are planning a trip to the Black Hills of South Dakota, take the time to see the Crazy Horse Memorial. On our latest excursion, we became a member of the Driller's Club, which entitled us to a trip to the top of the mountain. It was an unforgettable experience. As we stood on the arm of the sculpture, we were able to look directly into the eyes of Crazy Horse.

To Format Text and Create a New Style Based on the Formatted Text

The paragraph of text below the title in this blog post is formatted with the Papyrus font. Thus, you will change the format of the paragraph of text. Because you want future posts to use the same font, you will create a Quick Style based on the new formats. The following steps select and format the paragraph and then create a Quick Style based on the formats in the selected paragraph.

1 Triple-click the paragraph below the title to select it. Use the Font box arrow on the Blog Post tab to change the font of the selected text to Papyrus.

2 Right-click the selected paragraph to display a shortcut menu. Point to Styles on the shortcut menu to display the Styles submenu (Figure 5).

3 Click Save Selection as a New Quick Style on the Styles submenu to display the Create New Style from Formatting dialog box.

4 Type Blog Post in the Name text box. Click the OK button to create the new Quick Style and add it to the Styles gallery.

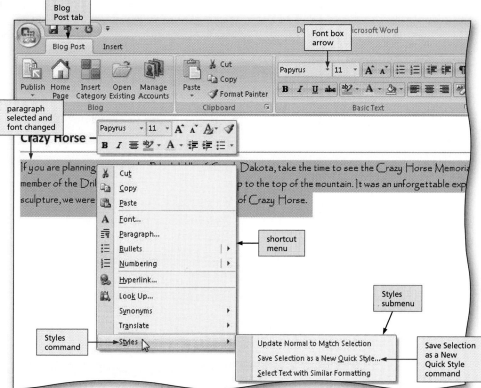

Figure 5

BTW

Certification
The Microsoft Certified Application Specialist (MCAS) program provides an opportunity for you to obtain a valuable industry credential — proof that you have the Word 2007 skills required by employers. For more information see Appendix G or visit the Word 2007 Certification Web page (scsite.com/wd2007/cert).

To Insert a Picture

The next step in creating the blog post is to insert a picture of the Crazy Horse Memorial below the paragraph of text. The picture, which was taken with a digital camera, is available on the Data Files for Students. See the inside back cover of this book for instructions on downloading the Data Files for Students, or contact your instructor for information about accessing the required files. The following steps insert a picture from the USB flash drive.

1 Position the insertion point at the end of the paragraph of text and then press the ENTER key.

2 Display the Insert tab.

3 Click the Insert Picture from File button on the Insert tab to display the Insert Picture dialog box.

4 With your USB flash drive connected to one of the computer's USB ports, locate and then click the file called Crazy Horse on the USB flash drive to select the file (Figure 6).

5 Click the Insert button in the dialog box to insert the picture at the location of the insertion point in the document.

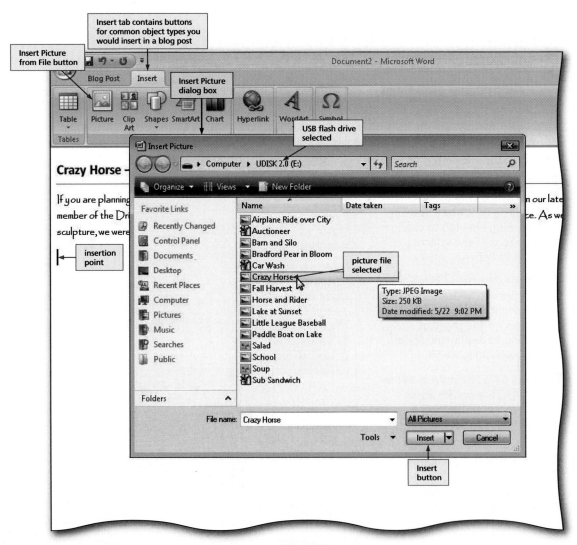

Figure 6

To Crop a Graphic

The next step is to format the picture just inserted. Currently, the image of Crazy Horse's head is not centered in the picture. To make the focal point of the picture centered, you would like to remove a section of the left edge and also the top edge from the picture. Word allows you to **crop**, or remove edges from, a graphic. The following steps crop a picture.

- Click the Crop button on the Format tab, which changes the graphic's sizing handles to cropping handles and also attaches a cropping image to the mouse pointer.

- Position the mouse pointer on the middle-left cropping handle so that it looks like a sideways letter T (Figure 7).

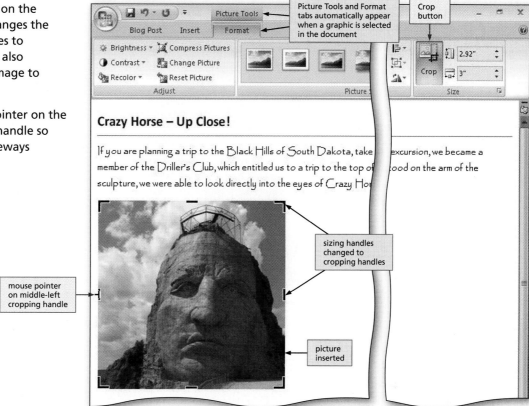

Figure 7

- Drag the middle-left cropping handle rightward to the location of the mouse pointer shown in Figure 8.

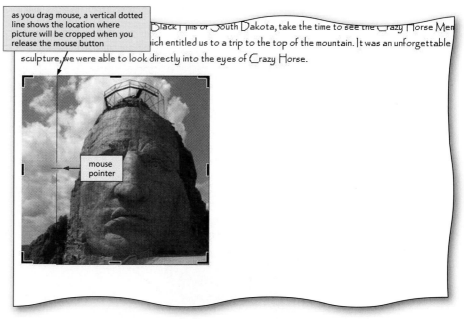

Figure 8

● Release the mouse button to crop the graphic to the location shown in Figure 8 on the previous page.

● Position the mouse pointer on the middle-top cropping handle so that it looks like an upside-down letter T and then drag the cropping handle downward to the location of the mouse pointer shown in Figure 9.

● Release the mouse button to crop the graphic to the location shown in Figure 9.

● Click the Crop button on the Format tab to deactivate the cropping tool, which changes the cropping handles on the graphic back to sizing handles.

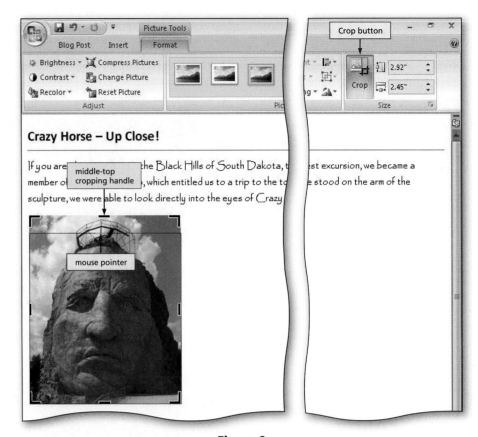

Figure 9

Other Ways
1. With graphic selected, click Size Dialog Box Launcher on Format tab, enter values in Crop from text boxes, click Close button

To Change a Picture Shape

The picture in the blog post currently has a rectangle shape. In this feature, the picture is the shape of a rounded rectangle. Thus, the following steps change the shape of the picture.

● With the picture selected, click the Picture Shape button on the Format tab to display the Picture Shape gallery (Figure 10).

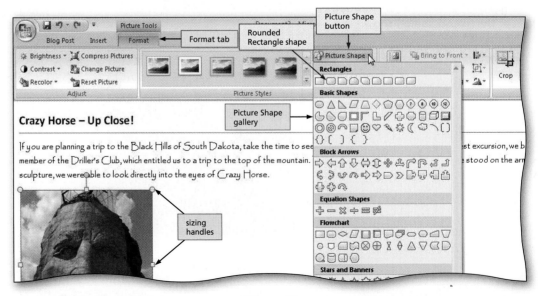

Figure 10

- Click Rounded Rectangle in the Picture Shape gallery to apply the rounded rectangle shape to the selected picture.

- Click outside of the picture to remove the selection from the picture (Figure 11).

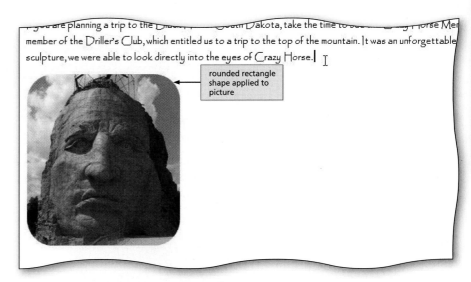

If you are planning a trip to the Black Hills of South Dakota, take the time to see the Crazy Horse Mer member of the Driller's Club, which entitled us to a trip to the top of the mountain. It was an unforgettable sculpture, we were able to look directly into the eyes of Crazy Horse.

rounded rectangle shape applied to picture

Figure 11

To Insert a Category

In this feature, the blog post is associated with the Trips category. This category already has been created in the blog account that was registered with Word. The following steps associate this blog post with the Trips category in the registered blog account.

Note: If you have not registered a blog account, you will not be able to perform the following steps.

1

- Display the Blog Post tab.

- Click the Insert Category button on the Blog Post tab to insert the Category drop-down list content control in the blog post (Figure 12).

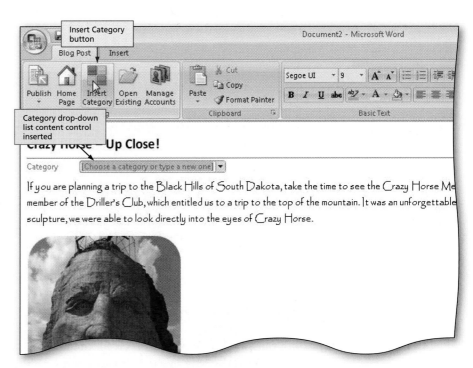

Insert Category button

Document2 - Microsoft Word

Blog Post | Insert

Publish | Home Page | Insert Category | Open Existing | Manage Accounts | Paste | Cut | Copy | Format Painter | Segoe UI | 9 | A A | B I U abe ab A

Clipboard | Basic Text

Category drop-down list content control inserted

Crazy Horse — Up Close!

Category [Choose a category or type a new one] ▼

If you are planning a trip to the Black Hills of South Dakota, take the time to see the Crazy Horse Me member of the Driller's Club, which entitled us to a trip to the top of the mountain. It was an unforgettable sculpture, we were able to look directly into the eyes of Crazy Horse.

Figure 12

2

- Click the 'Choose a category or type a new one' box arrow to display a list of categories associated with the registered blog account (Figure 13).

Q&A

What if I do not have anything in the list?

Either your blog account is not registered or your account does not have any categories. In this case, skip Step 3.

3

- Click Trips in the list, so that this blog post is categorized in the Trips category when you publish the blog post.

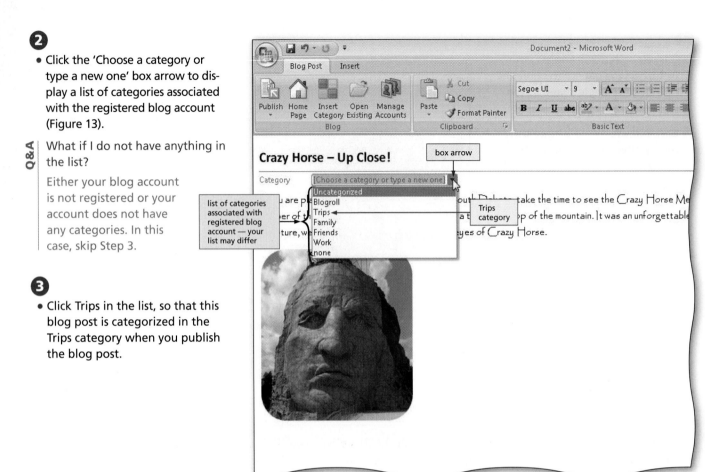

Figure 13

To Save a Document

You are finished entering and formatting the content of the blog post. The next step is to save the blog post.

1 With a USB flash drive connected to one of the computer's USB ports, click the Save button on the Quick Access Toolbar to display the Save As dialog box.

2 Type `Crazy Horse Post` in the File name text box to change the file name.

3 Select your USB flash drive as the save location.

4 Click the Save button in the Save As dialog box to save the document on the USB flash drive with the file name, Crazy Horse Post.

Publishing the Blog Post

With the blog post created and saved, the next step is to publish it. The next series of steps displays the blog Web page associated with the registered account, publishes the blog post, and then redisplays the updated blog Web page. If you do not have a registered account, you will not be able to perform these steps on a computer.

To Display a Blog Web Page in a Web Browser Window

Before publishing the blog post, you want to verify the correct blog account is associated with Word. The following steps display the current blog account's Web page in a browser window.

1

- Position the mouse pointer on the Home Page button on the Blog Post tab (Figure 14).

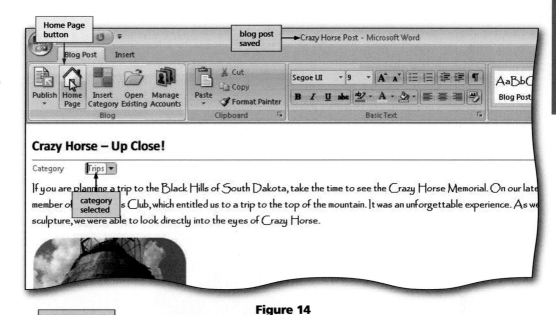

Figure 14

2

- Click the Home Page button on the Blog Post tab, which starts the default browser (Internet Explorer, in this case) and displays the Web page associated with the registered blog account in the browser window (Figure 15).

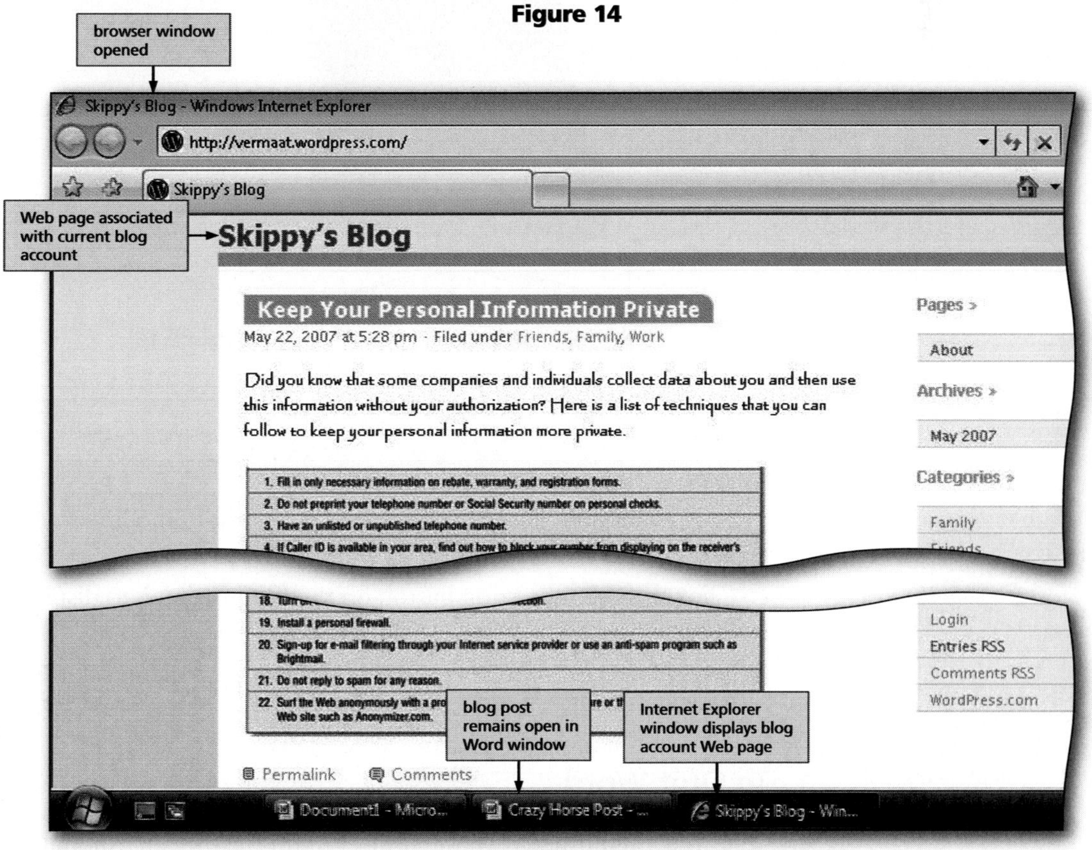

Q&A

What if the wrong Web page is displayed?

You may have multiple blog accounts registered with Word. To select a different blog account registered with Word, switch back to Word, click the Manage Accounts button on the Blog Post tab, click the desired account in the Blog Accounts dialog box, and then click the Close button. Then, repeat Steps 1 and 2.

Figure 15

To Publish a Blog Post

The final step in this feature is to publish the blog post, so that it appears at the top of the Web page associated with this blog account. The following steps publish the blog post.

- Click the Crazy Horse Post - Microsoft Word program button on the taskbar to redisplay the Word window.

- Click the Publish button on the Blog Post tab, which causes Word to display a brief message that it is contacting the blog provider and then display a message on the screen that the post was published (Figure 16).

- To view the newly published post, click the Home Page button on the Blog Post tab again (Figure 1c on page WD 717). You may need to click the Refresh button in your browser window to display the most current Web page contents.

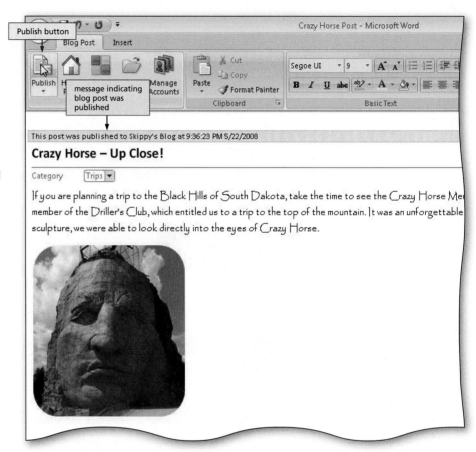

Figure 16

To Open an Existing Blog Post

If you wanted to open an existing blog post to modify or view it in Word, you would perform the following steps.

1. Click the Open Existing button on the Blog Post tab to display the Open Existing Post dialog box.

2. Select the title of the post you wish to open and then click the OK button.

BTW

Quick Reference
For a table that lists how to complete the tasks covered in this book using the mouse, Ribbon, shortcut menu, and keyboard, see the Quick Reference Summary at the back of this book, or visit the Word 2007 Quick Reference Web page (scsite.com/wd2007/qr).

To Quit Word

You are finished with the project in this feature and should quit Word and close your browser window.

1. Quit Word.

2. Close your browser window.

Feature Summary

In this feature, you have learned how to create a new blog post, crop a picture, change the shape of a picture, and publish a blog post. The items listed below include all the new Word skills you have learned in this feature.

1. Create a Blank Word Document for a Blog Post (WD 718)
2. Crop a Graphic (WD 721)
3. Change a Picture Shape (WD 722)
4. Insert a Category (WD 723)
5. Display a Blog Web Page in a Web Browser Window (WD 725)
6. Publish a Blog Post (WD 726)
7. Open an Existing Blog Post (WD 726)

 If you have a SAM user profile, you may have access to hands-on instruction, practice, and assessment. Log in to your SAM account (http://sam2007.course.com) to launch any assigned training activities or exams that relate to the skills covered in this feature.

In the Lab

Design and/or create a document using the guidelines, concepts, and skills presented in this chapter. Labs are listed in order of increasing difficulty.

Lab 1: Creating a Blog Post from Supplied Data

Problem: Your assignment is to use Word to create the blog post that is shown on the Web page in Figure 1a on page WD 717.

Instructions:
1. Start Word and create a new blank document for a blog post.
2. Type Keep Your Personal Information Private as the blog title.
3. Type the following as the paragraph of text below the blue line in the blog post document:
   Did you know that some companies and individuals collect data about you and then use this information without your authorization? Here is a list of techniques that you can follow to keep your personal information more private.
4. Format the blog post paragraph entered in Step 3 to the Papyrus font. Create a new style called Blog Post that is based on the paragraph with the modified font.
5. Below the paragraph entered in Step 3, insert the graphic called Privacy Tips, which is located on the Data Files for Students. See the inside back cover of this book for instructions on downloading the Data Files for Students, or contact your instructor for information about accessing the required files.
6. Resize the graphic to 50 percent of its original size.
7. Remove the title from the top of the image by cropping the top of the image.
8. Save the blog post with the name Lab BF-1 Privacy. Submit the blog post in the format specified by your instructor.
9. If you have permission and your instructor requests it, create a blog account on the Web. Register your blog account in Word. Display the blog account's Web page in a browser window. Use Word to publish the blog post created in these steps to your Web blog account. Display the updated blog Web page in a browser window. Submit the blog Web page in a format requested by your instructor.

In the Lab

Lab 2: Creating Your Own Blog Post

Problem: In this assignment, you are to create a blog post that presents your interests, opinions, or personality.

Instructions:

1. Decide on an issue, idea, or opinion about a topic that you would like to share on a blog.

2. Start Word and create a new blank blog post document.

3. Enter an appropriate blog title for your blog. Enter at least 250 words in text below the title that presents your discussion.

4. Format the blog post paragraph entered in Step 3 by changing the font, and font size if desired, to one of your choice. Create a new style called Blog Post that is based on the paragraph with the modified font.

5. Below the paragraph entered in Step 3, insert an appropriate graphic. The graphic may be a table, picture, clip art image, SmartArt, or chart. Resize the graphic, if necessary. Crop the graphic, if necessary.

6. Save the blog post with a name that appropriately reflects its content. Submit the blog post in the format specified by your instructor.

7. If you have permission and your instructor requests it, create a blog account on the Web. Register your blog account in Word. Display the blog account's Web page in a browser window. Use Word to publish the blog post created in these steps to your Web blog account. Display the updated blog Web page in a browser window. Submit the blog Web page in a format requested by your instructor.

7 Using Macros and Visual Basic for Applications (VBA) with Excel

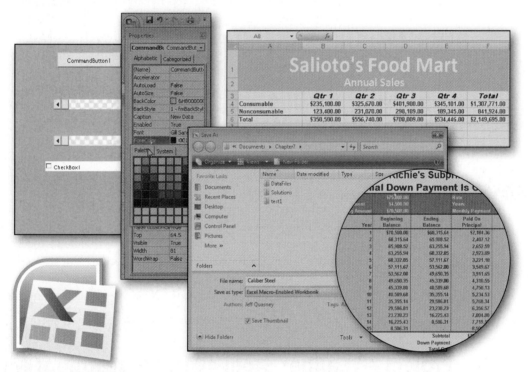

Objectives

You will have mastered the material in this chapter when you can:

- Use passwords to assign protected and unprotected status to a worksheet

- Use the macro recorder to create a macro

- Execute a macro and view and print code for a macro

- Understand Visual Basic for Applications (VBA) code and explain event-driven programs

- Customize the Quick Access Toolbar by adding a button

- Add controls, such as command buttons, scroll bars, check boxes, and spin buttons to a worksheet

- Assign properties to controls

- Use VBA to write a procedure to automate data entry into a worksheet

- Understand Do-While and If-Then-Else statements

- Review a digital signature on a workbook

7 | Using Macros and Visual Basic for Applications (VBA) with Excel

Introduction

Before a computer can take an action and produce a desired result, it must have a step-by-step description of the task to be accomplished. The step-by-step description is a series of precise instructions called a **procedure**. **Program** and **code** are other names for a procedure. The process of writing a procedure is called **computer programming**. Every Excel command and Ribbon button has a corresponding procedure that the computer will execute, or carry out the step-by-step instructions, when you click the command or button. In a Windows Vista environment, the instructions associated with a task are executed when an event takes place, such as clicking a button, clicking a command, dragging a scroll box, or right-clicking a screen element.

Because Excel does not have a command or button for every possible worksheet task, Microsoft has included a powerful programming language called Visual Basic for Applications. **Visual Basic for Applications (VBA)** is a programming language that allows you to customize and extend the capabilities of Excel. You can create a macro to group together commonly used combinations of tasks, which then can be reused later. In this chapter, you will learn how to create macros using a code generator called a **macro recorder**. A **macro** is a procedure composed of VBA code. It is called a macro, rather than a procedure, because it is created using the macro recorder. You also will learn how to add buttons to the Quick Access Toolbar and then associate these with macros. Finally, you will learn the basics of VBA, including creating a user interface, setting the properties, and writing the code.

Project — Caliber Steel 401(k) Investment Model Worksheet

The project in the chapter follows proper design guidelines and uses Excel to create the worksheets shown in Figure 7–1 and Figure 7–2. Caliber Steel provides a 401(k) retirement savings plan to its employees. A 401(k) plan is a retirement savings plan that allows employees to invest pretax dollars through payroll deductions. To help recruit employees and show the benefit of the plan, the human resources department uses an investment model workbook to demonstrate how the plan works. The department requires that the workbook be automated with an easy-to-use interface that steps the user through the entry of data.

The 401(k) investment model workbook in this chapter is created according to the following three phases:

Phase 1 — Use the macro recorder to create a macro that prints the worksheet in portrait orientation using the Fit to option. Assign the macro to a button on the Quick Access Toolbar (Figure 7–1a), so a user can execute the macro by clicking the button.

Phase 2 — Create a New Data button on the worksheet as shown in Figure 7–1a, assign the button properties, and write an associated procedure (Figure 7–1b) that steps the user through entering the required data.

Phase 3 — Create an area on the worksheet called the Personalization Center (Figure 7–2) that allows the user to enter his or her name and annual salary using a button and the remaining data using scroll bars, a check box, and spin buttons. Verify that the annual salary entered is positive.

Figure 7–3 illustrates the requirements document for the Caliber Steel 401(k) Investment Model worksheet. It includes the needs, source of data, summary of calculations, and other facts about its development. The requirements document indicates that the development of the worksheet should be done in three phases, as outlined above.

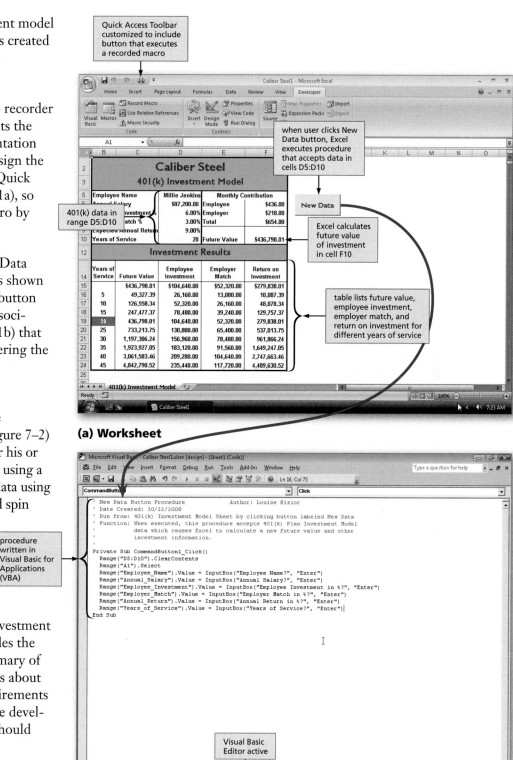

(a) Worksheet

(b) Visual Basic for Applications

Figure 7–1

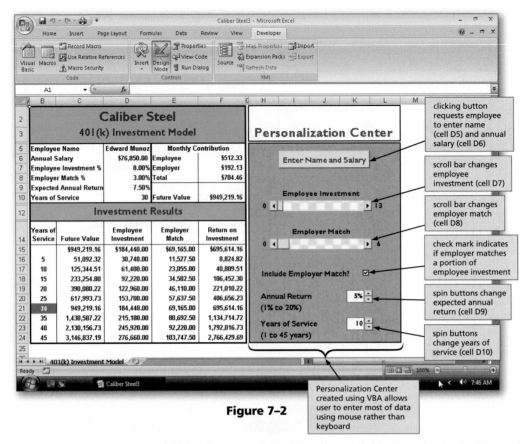

Figure 7–2

REQUEST FOR NEW WORKBOOK

Date Submitted:	October 14, 2008
Submitted By:	Louise Kizior
Worksheet Title:	Caliber Steel 401(k) Investment Model
Needs:	Implement an easy-to-use interface for the client's 401(k) investment model workbook according to the following three phases: Phase 1 — Create a macro using the macro recorder that prints the worksheet in portrait orientation using the Fit to option. Assign the macro to a button on the Quick Access Toolbar (Figure 7-1a) so the user can execute the macro by clicking the button. Phase 2 — Create a button on the worksheet as shown in Figure 7-1a, assign the button properties, and write an associated procedure (Figure 7-1b) that steps the user through entering the required data in the range D5:D10. Phase 3 — Create an area on the worksheet called Personalization Center (Figure 7-2) that allows the user to enter his or her name and annual salary using a button and the remaining data using scroll bars, a check box, and spin buttons. Verify that the annual salary entered is positive.
Source of Data:	The workbook currently used by Caliber Steel is shown in Figure 7-1a, without the button on the worksheet and the button on the toolbar. The workbook is available with the Data Files for Students with the file name Caliber Steel.
Calculations:	None.
Web Requirements:	None.

Approvals

Approval Status:	X	Approved
		Rejected
Approved By:	Susan Paulsom	
Date:	October 21, 2008	
Assigned To:	J. Quasney, Spreadsheet Specialist	

Figure 7–3

Overview

As you read this chapter, you will learn how to modify the existing Caliber Steel workbook as shown in Figure 7–1 and Figure 7–2 by performing these general tasks:

- Use passwords to protect and unprotect a worksheet
- Use the macro recorder to create a macro
- Execute a macro, view and print code for a macro, and assign a macro to a button on the Quick Access Toolbar
- Add controls to a worksheet and assign properties to the controls
- Use VBA to write a procedure to automate data entry into a worksheet
- Test and validate incoming data

General Project Decisions

Plan
Ahead

While working with an Excel worksheet, you need to make several decisions that will determine the appearance and characteristics of the finished worksheet. As you update an existing worksheet to meet the requirements shown in Figure 7–3, you should follow these general guidelines:

1. Ascertain the steps needed to create a macro. A macro is created by performing a set of steps and recording the steps as they are performed. The steps and order of the steps should be determined and rehearsed before creating the macro.

2. Create the user interface. In this chapter, two separate user interfaces are created that automate the entry of the employee's investment model data. Excel provides several types of controls, such as buttons, text boxes, and spin buttons, that you can use in a user interface. Which controls you use for each task is determined by the type of data the control is used to enter.

3. Determine properties for controls in the user interface. Each type of control includes a different set of properties that you set as you design the user interface. For example, the size, color, and shape of a button are all properties of the button. The properties that you set give meaning and limitations to the user regarding the control's use.

4. Establish the Visual Basic code needed for each control. When a user interacts with a control, such as clicking a button, Visual Basic code that is associated with that action is executed. Which actions will require a response from Visual Basic code? What should that response from the Visual Basic code be? For example, what precise actions should occur on a worksheet when a button is clicked? As a worksheet developer, you design and write the Visual Basic code.

5. Evaluate the completed user interface through testing. The final step in creating a user interface is to test it in order to prove that the interface behaves as designed and as a user expects.

In addition, using a sketch of the worksheet can help you visualize its design. Figure 7–4 shows a sketch of the Personalization Center described in Phase 3 in the requirements document, to provide a visual representation of the more complex aspects of the requirements. The sketch for the Phase 3 Personalization Center includes labels, scroll bars, a check box, and spin buttons, so that the user can enter data using the mouse, rather than the keyboard.

The sketch in Figure 7–4 indicates the cells that change as the user interacts with the controls in the Personalization Center. For example, as the user moves the Employee Investment scroll bar, the value in cell D7 changes.

When necessary, more specific details concerning the above guidelines are presented at appropriate points in the chapter. The chapter also will identify the actions you perform and decisions made regarding these guidelines during the modification of the worksheet shown in Figure 7–1 on page EX 531 and Figure 7–2 on page EX 532.

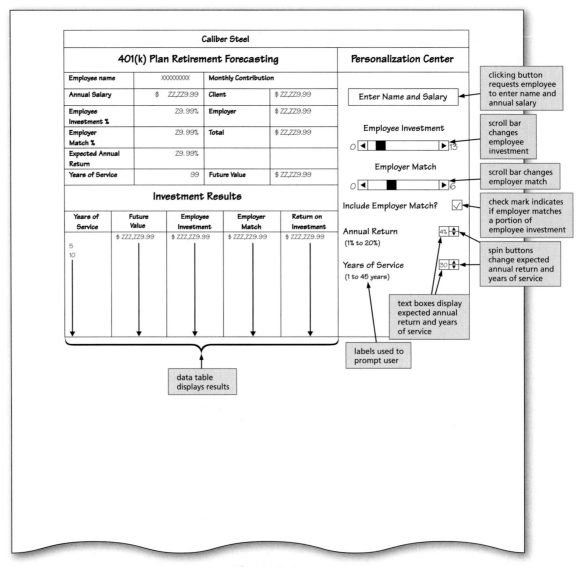

Figure 7–4

Opening Workbooks
Macros are an easy place for computer virus programmers to hide computer viruses. For this reason, Microsoft Office Excel 2007 displays a warning whenever you open a workbook that contains a macro. The dialog box requires that you choose to enable or disable the attached macro before it will open the workbook. If you disable the macro and the macro contains a virus, it cannot damage your system. You should enable macros only if you trust the author who created the workbook with the macro.

With a good understanding of the requirements document, an understanding of the necessary decisions, and a sketch of the worksheet, the next step is to use Excel to open the existing Caliber Steel Investment Model workbook.

To Start Excel and Open a Workbook

If you are using a computer to step through the project in this chapter and you want your screen to match the figures in this book, you should change your computer's resolution to 1024 × 768. For information about how to change a computer's resolution, see page APP 21 in Appendix E.

The following steps start Excel and open the workbook Caliber Steel from the Data Files for Students.

1 Start Excel.

2 Open the file Caliber from the Data Files for Students and then save the workbook using the file name, Caliber Steel.

3 If the Excel window is not maximized, double-click its title bar to maximize it.

4 If the worksheet window in Excel is not maximized, click the Maximize button next to the Close button on its title bar to maximize the worksheet within Excel (Figure 7–5).

Q&A

What does the worksheet contain?

As shown in Figure 7–5, the 401(k) Investment Model worksheet in the Caliber Steel workbook is divided into two parts. The top part contains the data (range D5:D10) and the results (range F6:F10). The bottom part of the worksheet is a data table that organizes the results of four formulas in the range C15:F24 — future value (column C), employee investment (column D), employer match (column E), and return on investment (column F) — based on the years of service in column B. In the data table, the return on investment (column F) is the future value less the sum of the employee and employer investments.

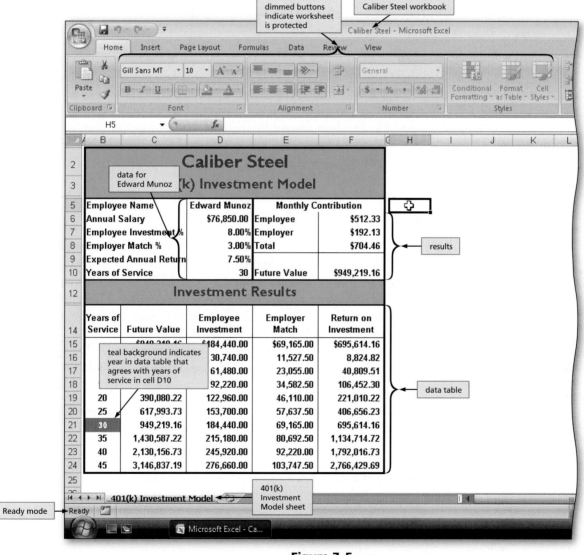

Figure 7–5

BTW

Gaining Confidence in a Workbook
Some Excel commands provide additional ways to uncover details of workbooks created by another author. For example, the Page Setup Dialog Box Launcher on the Page Layout tab on the ribbon and the Print Preview command can tell you if the author used any unusual settings. To list the macros in the workbook, click the Developer tab on the Ribbon and then click the Macros button on the Ribbon.

Learning More about a Workbook Created by Someone Else

When you modify a workbook created by someone else, such as the Caliber Steel workbook, you should learn as much as you can about the workbook before you modify it. You can learn more about a workbook by doing the following:

1. Press CTRL+ACCENT MARK (`) to display the formulas version to gain an understanding of what formulas and functions are used in the worksheet and which cells are referenced by the formulas and functions.

2. Use Range Finder or the auditing commands to show which cells are referenced in formulas and functions. You double-click a cell with a formula or function to activate Range Finder.

3. Check which cells are locked and which cells are unlocked. Usually all cells in a workbook are locked, except for those in which you enter data. For example, on the 401(k) Investment Model worksheet, only the cells in the range D5:D10 are unlocked.

4. Enter sample data and verify the results.

The worksheet shown in Figure 7–5 is protected. When buttons are dimmed even when Excel is in Ready mode, then the worksheet is protected. In this case, the cells in the range D5:D10 are unlocked so users can enter data, but the rest of the cells in the worksheet are protected and, therefore, cannot be changed. Later in this project, the worksheet will be unprotected so that changes can be made to it. Additionally, each cell in the range D5:D10 is assigned a cell name associated with the labels in the range B5:B10.

BTW

401(k) Plans
Most employers who make contributions to 401(k) or similar plans require an employee to be vested before the employer matching contributions are granted to the employee. Usually a company requires three to five years of continuous employment before an employee is completely vested. Virtually all 401(k) plans, however, can be transferred from one employer to another.

To Enter Data in a Selected Range of Cells

To illustrate the entry of sample data, the following steps enter the sample data: Employee Name (cell D5) — Ali Kunar; Annual Salary (cell D6) — $68,400.00; Employee Investment % (cell D7) — 9.00%; Employer Match % (cell D8) — 6.00%; Expected Annual Return (cell D9) — 8.00%; and Years of Service (cell D10) — 25. Before entering the data, selecting the range D5:D10 automatically makes the next cell in the range the active one when you complete a cell entry by pressing the ENTER key.

The following steps enter the sample data in the selected range D5:D10. As each cell is selected, view the Name box in order to understand the cell name that is assigned to each cell.

1 Select the range D5:D10. In cell D5, type `Ali Kunar` as the employee name and then press the ENTER key.

2 In cell D6, type `68400` as the annual salary and then press the ENTER key.

3 In cell D7, type `9%` as the employee investment percentage and then press the ENTER key.

4 In cell D8, type `6%` as the employer match percentage and then press the ENTER key.

5 In cell D9, type `8%` as the annual return and then press the ENTER key.

6 In cell D10, type `25` as the years of service and then press the ENTER key to display the new future value of $813,127.57 in cell F10 (Figure 7–6).

7 Click cell H5 to remove the selection from the range D5:D10. You may have to scroll down the worksheet to refresh the pointer in the range B16:B24.

Q&A What do the results of the calculation mean?

As shown in Figure 7–6, if Ali Kunar earns $68,400 a year and invests 9% of his income a year in the 401(k) plan, then his investment will be worth $813,127.57 in 25 years. If he works an additional 10 years, then Ali's investment will be worth an astonishing $1,961,269.52, as shown in cell C22. These future values assume the annual return on the investment will be 8%. They also assume that Ali will never get a raise, which means the investment could be worth significantly more if he does get raises, because he is investing a percentage of his income, rather than a fixed amount.

Q&A Why does the pointer not match the years of service?

Due to an error in some versions of Excel, you must scroll the worksheet down until the pointer is no longer displayed and then scroll back to update the pointer.

BTW

Benefits of 401(k) Investment Plans
Outside of winning the lottery or receiving a large inheritance, a retirement savings plan, such as a 401(k) plan, is the easiest way for a person on a fixed income to legally become a millionaire at some point in his or her lifetime. A significant benefit of the plan is that participants usually do not pay taxes on the money that they invest into the plan. After you start drawing funds from the plan, you are required to pay taxes on what you withdraw. Plans usually have penalties for withdrawing funds before you are 59 years old. For example, you may pay a 10 percent penalty on withdrawals made before you are 59 years old.

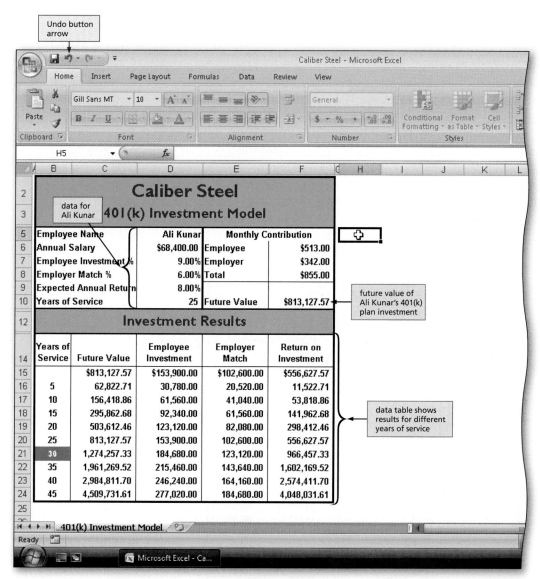

Figure 7–6

To Undo a Group of Entries Using the Undo Button

The following steps undo the cell entries to change the data in the range D5:D10 back to its original values.

1 Click the Undo button arrow on the Quick Access Toolbar (Figure 7–6).

2 When the Undo list appears, drag from the top down through Ali Kunar and then release the left mouse button to change the range D5:D10 back to its original values. Click cell H5. You may have to scroll down the worksheet to refresh the pointer in the range B16:B24.

Other Ways

1. Press ALT+2, drag through actions to undo

To Unprotect a Password-Protected Worksheet

The 401(k) Investment Model worksheet in the Caliber Steel workbook is protected. When a worksheet is protected, users cannot change data in locked cells or modify the worksheet in any manner. Thus, before modifying the worksheet in the three phases, you must unprotect it. To unprotect the worksheet, you will need to enter the password assigned when it first was protected. A **password** ensures that users cannot unprotect the worksheet simply by clicking the Unprotect button. The password for the 401(k) Investment Model worksheet is caliber.

In Excel, a password, such as caliber, can contain any combination of letters, numerals, spaces, and symbols; it also can be up to 15 characters long. Passwords are case sensitive, so if you vary the capitalization when you assign the password, you must use the same capitalization later when entering the password to unprotect the worksheet.

The following steps unprotect the password-protected worksheet.

1

• Click the Review tab on the Ribbon (Figure 7–7).

Q&A

What other protection is available for a workbook or worksheet?

The Review tab on the Ribbon shown in Figure 7–7 also has a Protect Workbook button. Protecting a workbook, instead of a worksheet, protects the structure and windows of the workbook, but not individual worksheets. Protecting the structure of a workbook means that users cannot add, delete, move, hide, unhide, or rename sheets. Protecting a workbook's windows means users cannot move, resize, hide, unhide, or close the workbook's windows.

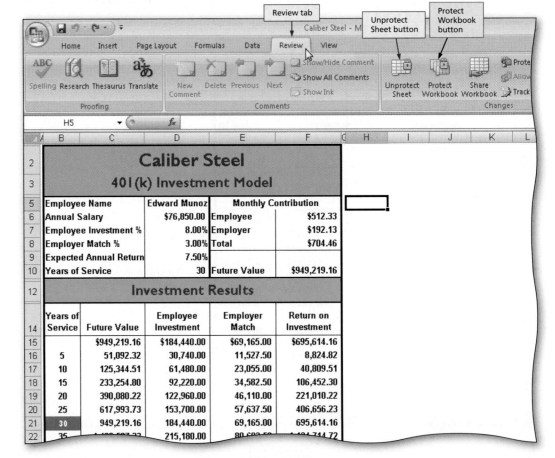

Figure 7–7

- Click the Unprotect Sheet button to display the Unprotect Sheet dialog box.

- When the Unprotect Sheet dialog box appears, type caliber in the Password text box (Figure 7–8).

- Click the OK button to unprotect the 401(k) Investment Model worksheet.

Q&A

Can I work with the entire worksheet now?

Yes. With the worksheet unprotected, you can modify the contents of cells regardless of whether they are locked or unlocked. If you decide to password-protect a worksheet, make sure you write down the password and keep it in a secure place. If you lose the password, you cannot open or gain access to the password-protected worksheet.

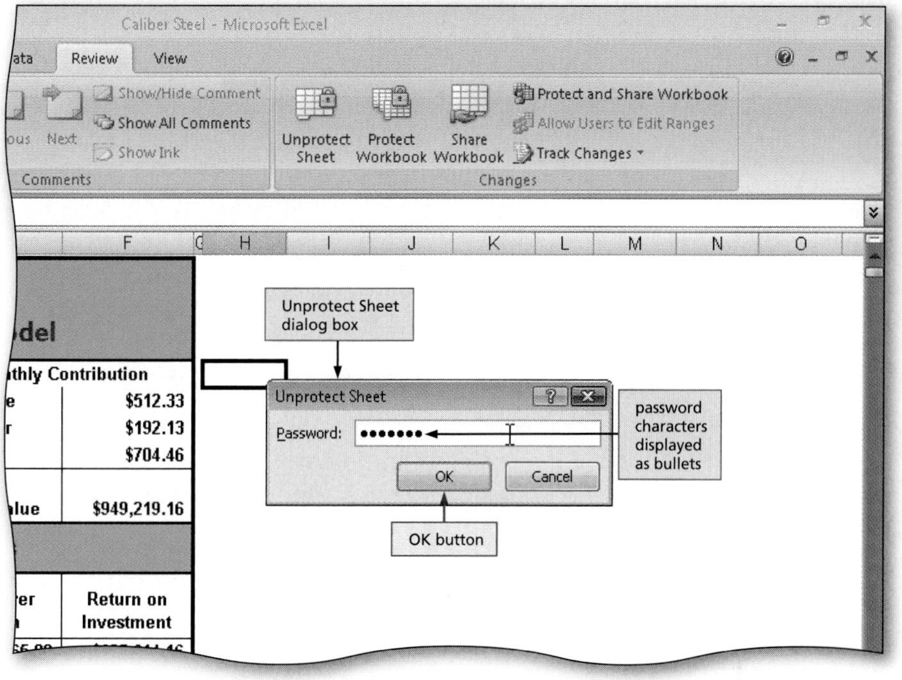

Figure 7–8

Other Ways

1. Press ALT+R, PS

Phase 1 — Recording a Macro and Assigning It to a Toolbar Button and Menu Command

The first phase of this project creates a macro to automate printing the worksheet in portrait orientation using the Fit to option. Recall that the Fit to option ensures that the worksheet will fit on one printed page. The orientation for the printout currently is set to landscape in the Caliber Steel workbook. The planned macro will (1) change the orientation from landscape to portrait and use the Fit to option to ensure the printout fits on one page; (2) print the worksheet; and (3) reset the print settings back to their original settings.

The purpose of this macro is to give users the option of printing the worksheet in landscape orientation by clicking the Print button on the Office Button menu or executing the macro to print the worksheet in portrait orientation. After the macro is created, it will be assigned to a button on the Quick Access Toolbar.

Excel includes a macro recorder that creates a macro automatically based on a series of actions you perform while it is recording. As with a video recorder, the macro recorder records everything you do to a workbook over time. The macro recorder can be turned on, during which time it records your activities, and then turned off to stop the recording. After the macro is recorded, it can be played back, or executed, as often as you want.

Three steps must be taken in preparation for working with macros in Excel. The Developer tab on the Ribbon includes commands used to work with macros. By default, the Developer tab does not appear in Excel, it must be made available by selecting an option in the Excel Options dialog box. Second, a security setting in Excel must be modified to allow macros to be enabled whenever you use Excel. Finally, Excel requires a workbook that includes macros to be saved as an Excel Macro-Enabled Workbook file type.

BTW

Undoing Several Actions
To undo recent actions one at a time, click the Undo button on the quick Access Toolbar. To undo several actions at once, click the Undo button arrow and select an action from the list. Excel will undo the selected action, as well as all the actions above it.

To Display the Developer Tab, Enable Macros, and Save a Workbook as a Macro-Enabled Workbook

The following steps display the Developer tab on the Ribbon, enable macros, and save the workbook as a macro-enabled workbook.

1

- Click the Office Button to display the Office Button menu and then the Excel Options button to display the Excel Options dialog box.

- Click the Show Developer tab in the Ribbon check box (Figure 7–9).

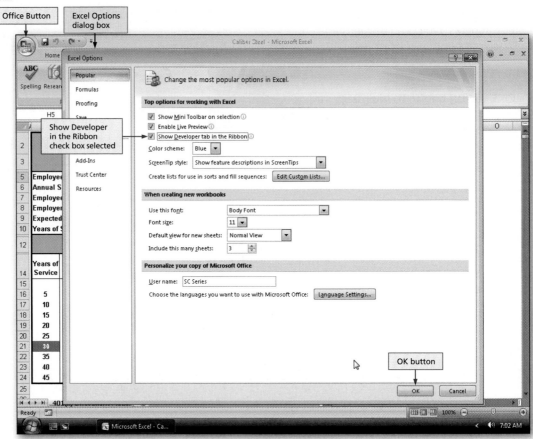

Figure 7–9

2

- Click the OK button in the Excel Options dialog box to display the Developer tab on the Ribbon.

- Click the Developer tab (Figure 7–10).

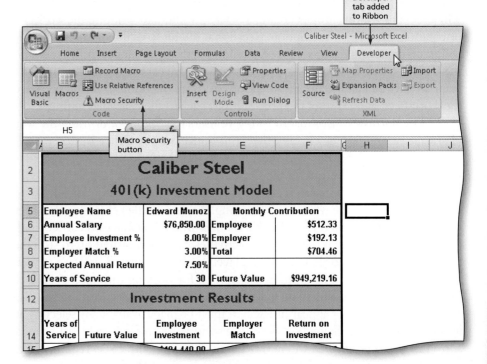

Figure 7–10

- Click the Macro Security button on the Ribbon to display the Trust Center dialog box.

- When the Trust Center dialog box appears, click the 'Enable all macros' option button to select it (Figure 7–11).

- Click the OK button to close the Macro Security dialog box.

- Click the Office Button and then click Save As to display the Save As dialog box.

- When the Save As dialog box appears, click the 'Save as type' box arrow and then click Excel Macro-Enabled Workbook in the 'Save as type' list (Figure 7–12).

- Click the Save button in the Save As dialog box to save the workbook as an Excel Macro-Enabled Workbook file type.

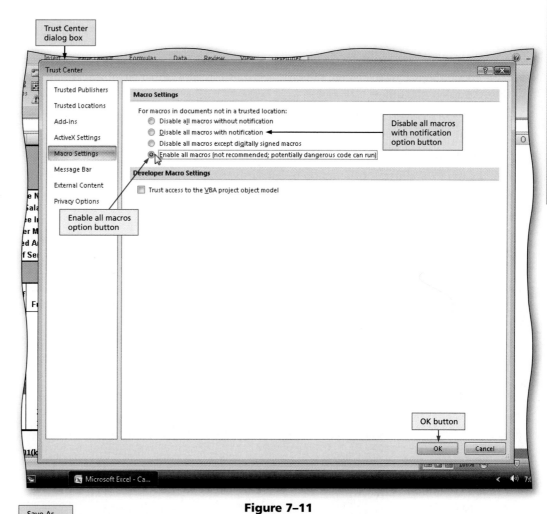

Figure 7–11

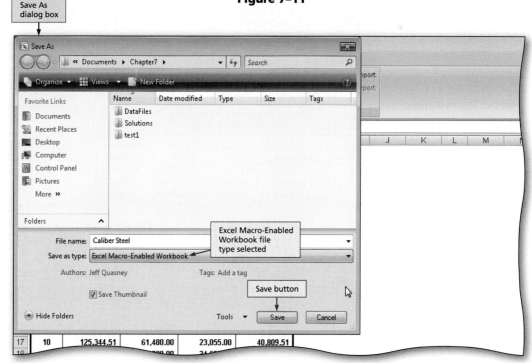

Figure 7–12

To Record a Macro to Print the Worksheet in Portrait Orientation Using the Fit to Option

To create the macro to change the print settings for the Caliber Steel workbook, turn on the macro recorder and then complete the following tasks.

1. If necessary, switch from landscape orientation to portrait orientation and from 100% normal size printing to Fit to one page.

2. Print the worksheet.

3. Switch from portrait orientation to landscape orientation and from Fit to one page to 100% normal size printing.

4. Stop the macro recorder.

With the macro recorder, you actually step through the task as you create the macro. Therefore, you see exactly what the macro will do before you use it.

When you first create the macro, you must name it. The name is used later to reference the macro when you want to execute it. Executing a macro causes Excel to step through all of the recorded steps. The macro name in this project is PrintPortrait. A **macro name** can be up to 255 characters long; it can contain numbers, letters, and underscores, but it cannot contain spaces and other punctuation.

The following steps record the PrintPortrait macro to print the worksheet in portrait orientation using the Fit to option.

- If necessary, click the Developer tab on the Ribbon.

- Click the Record Macro button on the Ribbon to display the Record Macro dialog box.

- When the Record Macro dialog box appears, type `PrintPortrait` in the Macro name text box.

- Type `r` in the Shortcut key text box to set the shortcut key for the macro to CTRL+R.

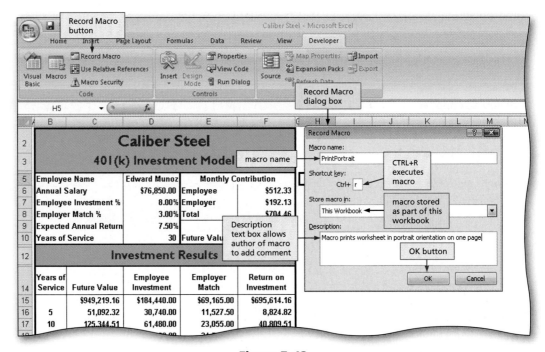

Figure 7–13

- Make sure the 'Store macro in' box displays This Workbook and then type `Macro prints worksheet in portrait orientation on one page` in the Description text box (Figure 7–13).

Q&A

Where can I store macros?

In the Record Macro dialog box, you can select the location to store the macro in the 'Store macro in' box. If you want a macro to be available to use in any workbook whenever you use Microsoft Excel, select Personal Macro Workbook in the 'Store macro in' list. This selection causes the macro to be stored in the **Personal Macro Workbook**, which is part of Excel. If you click New Workbook in the 'Store macro in' list, then Excel stores the macro in a new workbook. Most macros created with the macro recorder are workbook-specific and thus are stored in the active workbook. Selecting This Workbook in the 'Store macro in' list, as was done in the steps above, stores the macro in the active workbook.

• Click the OK button to begin recording the macro and cause the Record Macro button to become the Stop Recording button (Figure 7–14).

Q&A

How do I go about recording the macro?

Any task you perform in Excel will be part of the macro. When you are finished recording the macro, clicking the Stop Recording button on the Ribbon or on the status bar ends the recording.

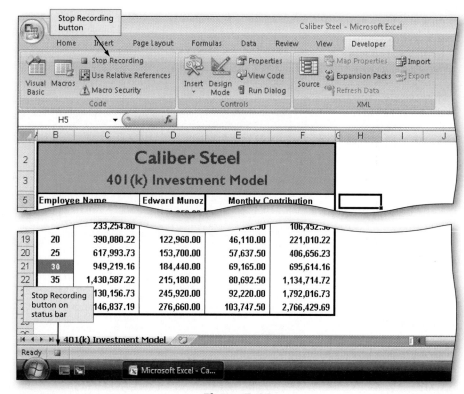

Figure 7–14

• Click the Page Layout tab on the Ribbon.

• Click the Page Setup Dialog Box Launcher to display the Page Setup dialog box.

• When the Page Setup dialog box displays, click the Page tab. If necessary, click Portrait in the Orientation area, and then click Fit to in the Scaling area (Figure 7–15).

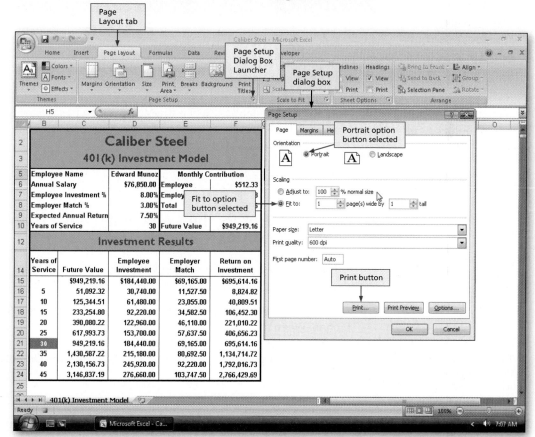

• Click the Print button in the Page Setup dialog box.

• When the Print dialog box displays, click the OK button to print the worksheet.

Figure 7–15

6

- Click the Page Setup Dialog Box Launcher to display the Page Setup dialog box.

- If necessary, when the Page Setup dialog box displays, click the Page tab; click Landscape in the Orientation area; click Adjust to in the Scaling area; and then, if necessary, type 100 in the % normal size box (Figure 7–16).

7

- Click the OK button to close the Page Setup dialog box (Figure 7–15).

- Click the Developer tab on the Ribbon and then click the Stop Recording button to stop recording the worksheet activities.

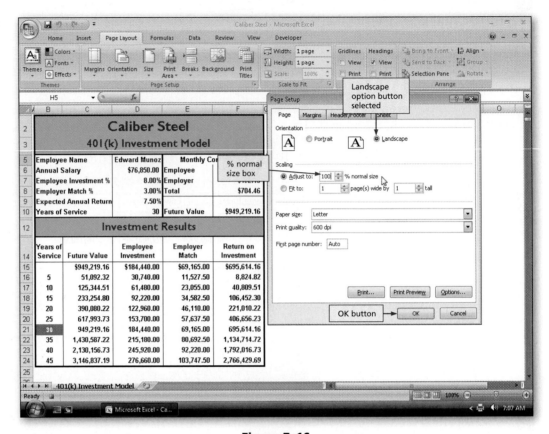

Figure 7–16

What if I make a mistake while recording the macro?

If you recorded the wrong actions, delete the macro and record it again. You delete a macro by clicking the Developer tab and then clicking the Macros button on the Ribbon. When the Macro dialog box is displayed, click the name of the macro (PrintPortrait) and then click the Delete button. Finally, record the macro again.

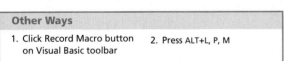

Other Ways

1. Click Record Macro button on Visual Basic toolbar	2. Press ALT+L, P, M

Password Protection
Excel offers three basic levels of password protection: (1) file level when you save it to disk; (2) workbook level, so the window cannot be modified; and (3) worksheet level, so locked cells cannot be changed. The first level is available through the Save As command on the Office Button menu. The second and third levels are available through the Protect Sheet and Protect Workbook buttons on the Review tab on the Ribbon.

To Password-Protect the Worksheet, Save the Workbook, and Close the Workbook

The following steps protect the 401(k) Investment Model worksheet, save the workbook using the file name Caliber Steel1, and then close the workbook.

1 Click the Review tab on the Ribbon, and then click the Protect Sheet button on the Ribbon. When the Protect Sheet dialog box appears, type caliber in the 'Password to unprotect sheet' text box and then click the OK button. When the Confirm Password dialog box is displayed, type caliber and then click the OK button.

2 Click the Office Button and then click Save As. When the Save As dialog box is displayed, type Caliber Steel1 in the File name text box. Make sure UDISK (E:) displays in the Save in box and then click the Save button in the Save As dialog box.

3 Click the workbook's Close button on the right side of its menu bar to close the workbook and leave Excel active.

To Set the Macro Security Level to Medium

A **computer virus** is a potentially damaging computer program designed to affect, or infect, your computer negatively by altering the way it works without your knowledge or permission. The increased use of networks, the Internet, and e-mail have accelerated the spread of computer viruses.

To combat this menace, most computer users run antivirus programs that search for viruses and destroy them before they ever have a chance to infect the computer. Macros are known carriers of viruses, because of the ease with which a person can add programming code to macros. Excel provides four levels of protection from macro viruses: Disable all macros without notification, Disable all macros with notification, Disable all macros except digitally signed macros, and Enable all macros. By default, the macro security level is set to Disable all macros with notification, meaning that only macros from trusted sources can be used. Trusted sources are discussed later in this project. The following steps set the level of protection to Disable all macros with notification.

1
- Click the Developer tab on the Ribbon.
- Click the Macro Security button on the Ribbon to display the Trust Center dialog box.

2
- Click the 'Disable all macros with notification' option button (Figure 7–17).

3
- Click the OK button in the Trust Center dialog box to close it.

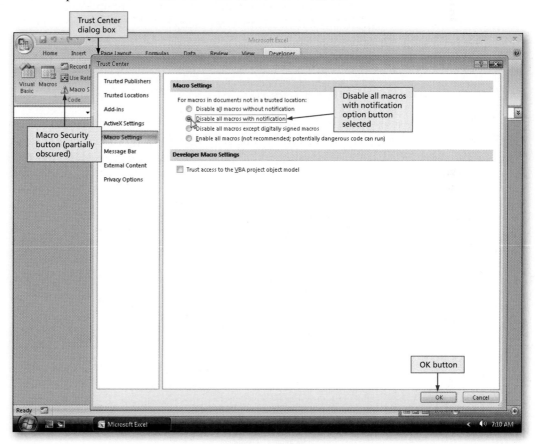

Figure 7–17

Other Ways
1. Click Office Button, Excel Options, click Trust Center
2. Press ALT+T, M, S

BTW

Macros and Protected Worksheets
A macro cannot modify a protect worksheet unless you explicitly tell the macro to unprotect the worksheet. Excel displays an error message if you execute a macro that attempts to modify a protected worksheet. If you want to modify a protected worksheet using a macro, have the macro unprotect the worksheet at the beginning, and then have the macro protect the worksheet at the end.

More About Macro Security

Each time you open a workbook with an associated macro and the macro security level is set to 'Disable all macros with notification', Excel displays a Security Warning box and an Options button immediately below the Ribbon alerting you that a macro is attached. Clicking the Options button displays the Microsoft Office Security Options dialog box. Table 7–1 summarizes the option buttons and links from which users can select to continue the process of opening a workbook with macros.

Table 7–1 Option Buttons and Links in the Microsoft Office Security Options Dialog Box When Opening a Workbook with Macros	
Buttons and Links	**Description**
Help protect me from unknown content	Macros are unavailable to the user
Enable this content	Macros are available to the user to execute
More Information	Opens the Excel Help window and displays information on viruses and workbook macros
Open the Trust Center	Displays the Trust Center dialog box

If you are confident of the source (author) of the workbook and macros, click the 'Enable this content' option button. If you are uncertain about the reliability of the source of the workbook and macros, then click the 'Help protect me from unknown content' option button. For more information on this topic, click the More Information link.

To Open a Workbook with a Macro and Execute the Macro

The following steps open the Caliber Steel1 workbook to illustrate the Microsoft Excel dialog box that is displayed when a workbook contains a macro. The steps then show how to execute the recorded macro PrintPortrait by using the shortcut key CTRL+R. Recall that the shortcut key was established in Step 1 of the set of steps that begin on page EX 542.

1
- With Excel active, open the Caliber Steel1 workbook.

- Click the Options button in the Security Warning box to display the Microsoft Office Security Options dialog box (Figure 7–18).

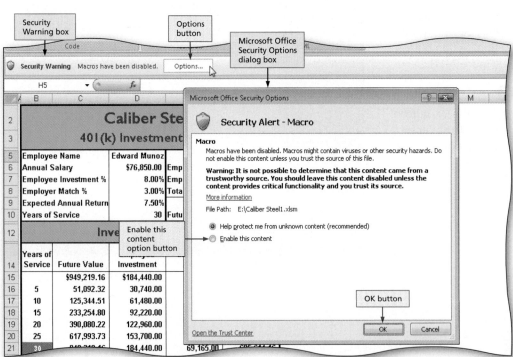

Figure 7–18

2

- Click the 'Enable this content' option button to select it.

- Click the OK button.

- When the Caliber Steel1 workbook opens, press CTRL+R to run the macro and print the worksheet (Figure 7–19).

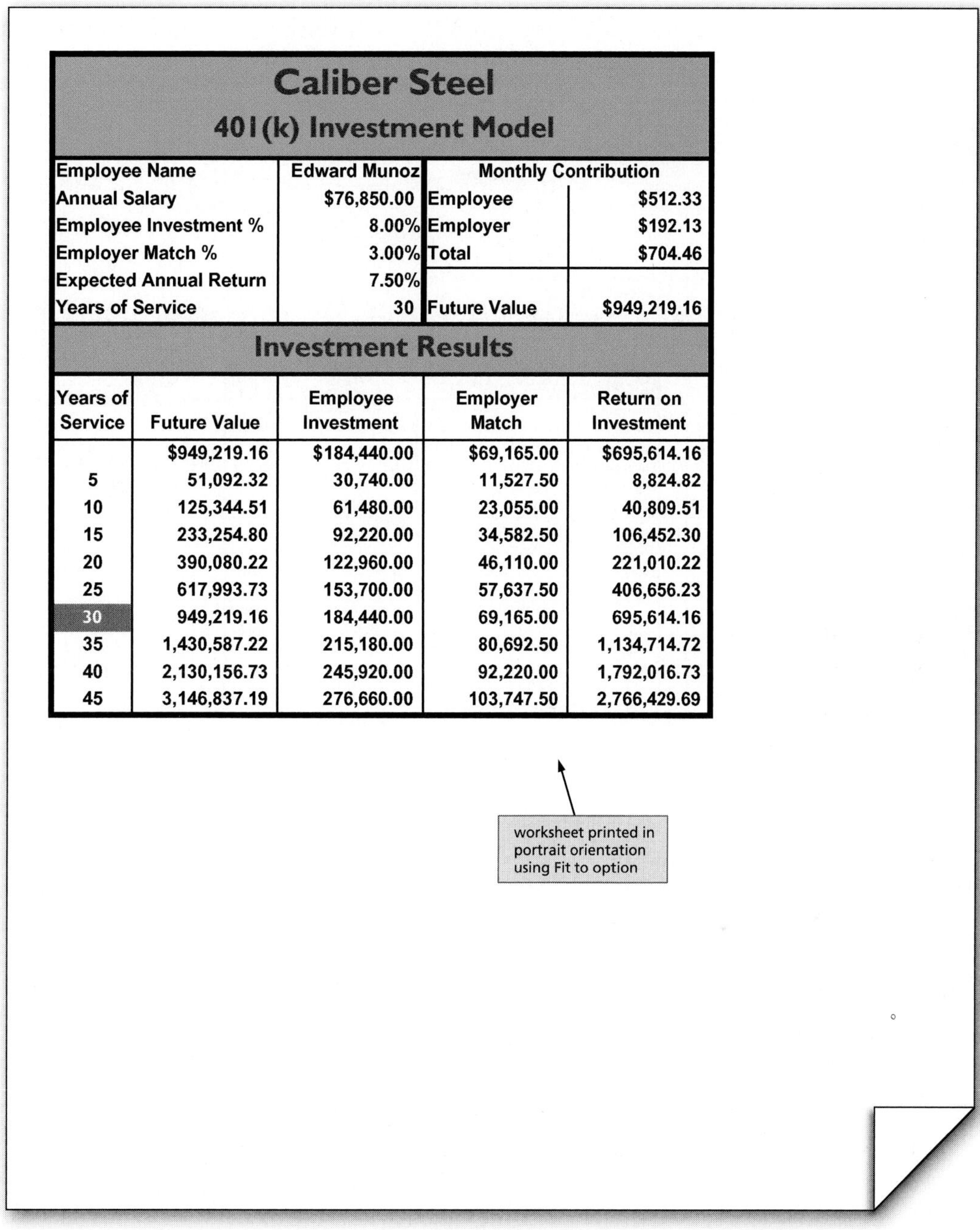

Caliber Steel
401(k) Investment Model

Employee Name	Edward Munoz	Monthly Contribution	
Annual Salary	$76,850.00	Employee	$512.33
Employee Investment %	8.00%	Employer	$192.13
Employer Match %	3.00%	Total	$704.46
Expected Annual Return	7.50%		
Years of Service	30	Future Value	$949,219.16

Investment Results

Years of Service	Future Value	Employee Investment	Employer Match	Return on Investment
	$949,219.16	$184,440.00	$69,165.00	$695,614.16
5	51,092.32	30,740.00	11,527.50	8,824.82
10	125,344.51	61,480.00	23,055.00	40,809.51
15	233,254.80	92,220.00	34,582.50	106,452.30
20	390,080.22	122,960.00	46,110.00	221,010.22
25	617,993.73	153,700.00	57,637.50	406,656.23
30	949,219.16	184,440.00	69,165.00	695,614.16
35	1,430,587.22	215,180.00	80,692.50	1,134,714.72
40	2,130,156.73	245,920.00	92,220.00	1,792,016.73
45	3,146,837.19	276,660.00	103,747.50	2,766,429.69

worksheet printed in portrait orientation using Fit to option

Figure 7–19

Other Ways

1. Click Run Macro button on Visual Basic toolbar
2. On Developer tab, click Macros button, double-click macro name
3. Press ALT+F8, double-click macro name
4. Press ALT+L, P, M

To View and Print a Macro's VBA Code

As described earlier, a macro is comprised of VBA code, which is created automatically by the macro recorder. You can view and print the VBA code through the **Visual Basic Editor**. The Visual Basic Editor is used by all Office applications to enter, modify, and view VBA code. The following steps view and print the PrintPortrait macro's VBA code.

1

- Click the Developer tab on the Ribbon.

- Click the Macros button on the Ribbon to display the Macro dialog box (Figure 7–20).

- If necessary, when the Macro dialog box is displayed, click PrintPortrait in the Macro name list.

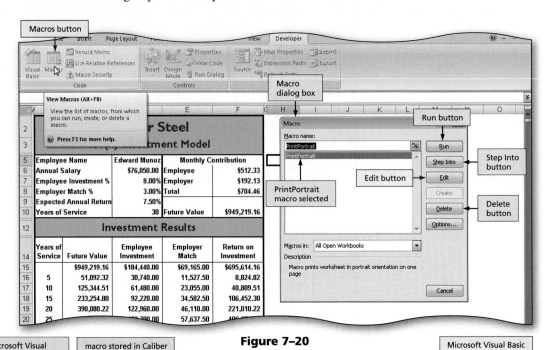

Figure 7–20

2

- Click the Edit button to start the Microsoft Visual Basic Editor (Figure 7–21).

 What is shown in the Microsoft Visual Basic Editor?

Figure 7–21 shows the instructions, beginning with line 1 and continuing sequentially to the last line, that are executed when you run the PrintPortrait macro. By scrolling through the VBA code, you can see that the macro recorder generates a lot of instructions. In this case, 109 lines of code are generated to print the worksheet in portrait orientation using the Fit to option. The instructions in the VBA code execute when you run the macro. Your screen may appear differently depending on how it appeared the last time the Microsoft Visual Basic Editor was activated.

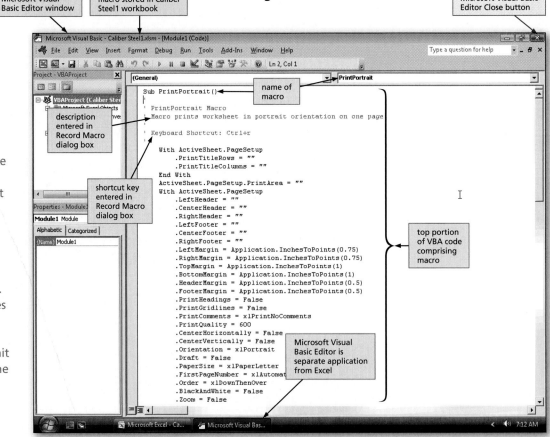

Figure 7–21

3

- Use the scroll bar to scroll through the VBA code.

- When you are finished, click File on the menu bar (Figure 7–22).

4

- Click Print.

- When the Print - VBAProject dialog box is displayed, click the OK button to print the macro code.

5

- Click the Microsoft Visual Basic Editor Close button on the right side of the title bar.

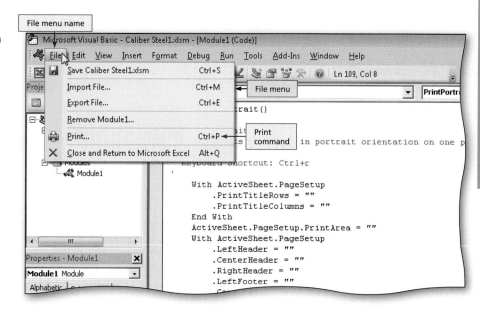

Figure 7–22

Other Ways		
1. Click Visual Basic button on Developer tab	2. Right-click the worksheet tab, click View Code on shortcut menu	3. Press ALT+L, V, click Edit

To Add a Button to the Quick Access Toolbar, Assign the Button a Macro, and Use the Button

You can add as many buttons as you want to the Quick Access Toolbar. You add commands that you use commonly to the Quick Access Toolbar. You also can select an icon for the commands you add. The following steps add a button to the Quick Access Toolbar, change the button image, assign the PrintPortrait macro to the button, and use the button to print the worksheet.

1

- Right-click anywhere on the Quick Access Toolbar to display the shortcut menu (Figure 7–23).

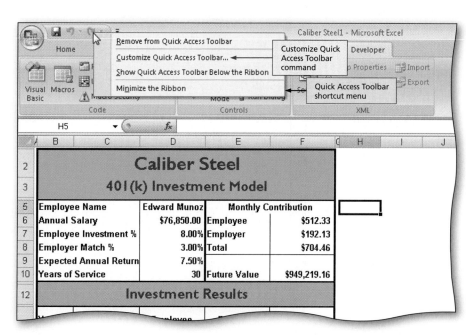

Figure 7–23

- Click the Customize Quick Access Toolbar command on the shortcut menu to display the Customize the Quick Access Toolbar page of the Excel Options dialog box.

- Click the 'Choose commands from' box arrow (Figure 7–24).

- Click Macros in the 'Choose commands from' list to display a list of macros.

- If necessary, click the PrintPortait macro to select it.

- Click the Add button to add the PrintPortrait macro to the Customize Quick Access Toolbar list (Figure 7–25).

Q&A

How can I delete the buttons that I add to the Quick Access Toolbar?

You can reset the Quick Access Toolbar to its installation default by clicking the Reset button on the Customize Quick Access Toolbar page of the Excel Options dialog box. If you share a computer with others, you should reset the Quick Access Toolbar before you quit Excel.

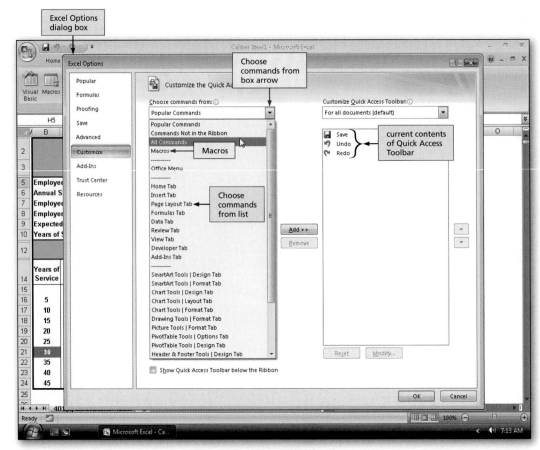

Figure 7–24

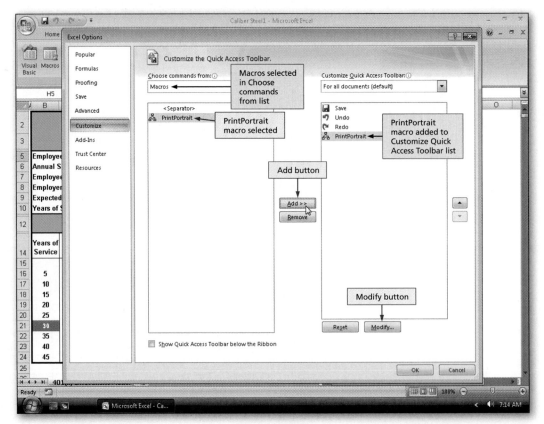

Figure 7–25

4

- Click the Modify button to display the Modify Button dialog box.

- Click the printer icon (column 5, row 2) in the Symbol list (Figure 7–26).

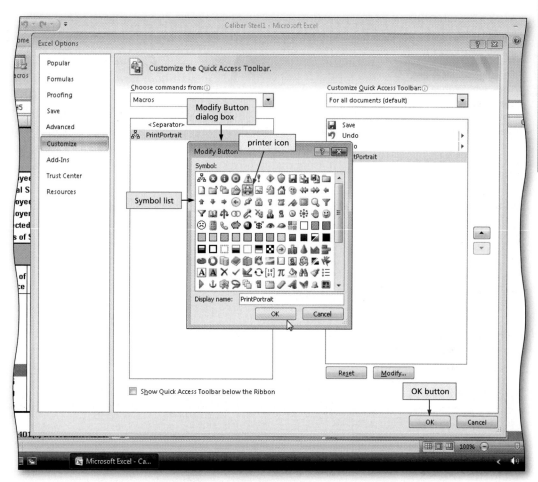

Figure 7–26

5

- Click the OK button to assign the printer icon to the new command and to close the Modify Button dialog box.

- Click the OK button in the Excel Options dialog box to close it.

- Point to the PrintPortrait button on the Quick Access Toolbar to display the ScreenTip for the button (Figure 7–27).

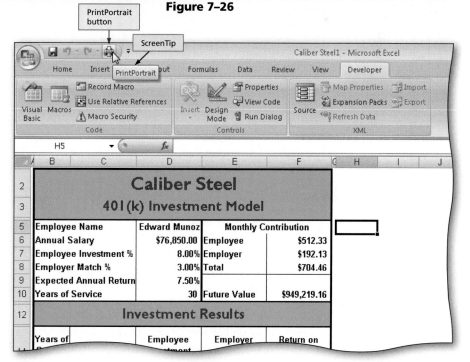

Figure 7–27

BTW

Visual Basic for Applications
All of the applications in the Microsoft Office System 2007 (Word, Excel, Access, PowerPoint, and Outlook) use Visual Basic for Applications. Thus, what you learn in this chapter applies to the other applications as well. Today, Visual Basic for Applications is one of the most widely used Windows applications programming languages.

Phase 2 — Creating a Procedure to Automate the 401(k) Investment Model Data Entry

Earlier in this chapter, on page EX 536, sample data for Ali Kunar was entered to test the formulas and verify the calculation of new future value information. A novice user, however, might not know what cells to select or how much 401(k) investment model data is required to obtain the desired results. To facilitate entering the 401(k) investment model data, Phase 2 calls for creating a Command Button control (Figure 7–28a) and an associated procedure (Figure 7–28b) that steps the user through entering data in the range D5:D10 using dialog boxes.

(a) Worksheet with New Data Command Button

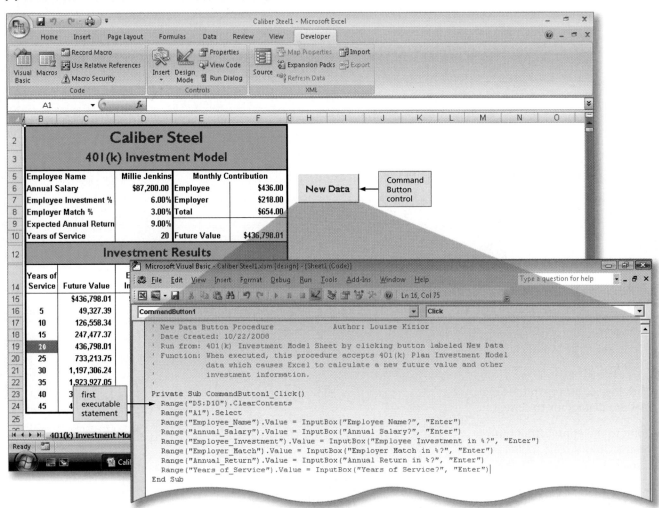

(b) Procedure Associated with New Data Command Button

Figure 7–28

A Command Button control is different from a toolbar button in that it is an object you draw on the worksheet. In this chapter, after a user triggers the event by clicking the New Data Command Button control, the instructions in the associated procedure guide the user through entering the required 401(k) plan data in the range D5:D10. The Command Button control also serves as the user interface. The user interface can be as simple as a button or as complex as a series of windows that accept data and display results. The **user interface**, together with the procedure, is called an **application**.

If you step through the procedure (Figure 7–28b) beginning at the line just below Private Sub CommandButton1_Click(), you can see how a procedure methodically steps the user through entering the data in the range D5:D10. Cell names that have been assigned to the cells in the range are used in the code to make the code more readable.

1. The first line clears the range D5:D10.

2. The second line selects cell A1.

3. Lines 3 through 8 accept data for the cells in the range D5:D10 using the cell name, one cell at a time. Recall from the earlier review of the workbook that the cell names in the range D5:D10 are as follows: D5 is named Employee_Name; D6 is named Annual_Salary; D7 is named Employee_Investment; D8 is named Employer_Match; D9 is named Annual_Return; and D10 is named Years_of_Service.

Visual Basic applications are built using the three-step process shown in Figure 7–29: (1) create the user interface; (2) set the properties; and (3) write the VBA code. Before you can create the user interface, the 401(k) Investment Model worksheet in the Caliber Steel1 workbook must be unprotected. The following steps unprotect the worksheet.

BTW

Macros form Earlier Excel Versions
Some earlier versions of Excel use a language called XLM, rather than VBA, for their macros. Excel 2007 supports both languages. That is, you can execute macros created using XLM as well as those created using VBA. Excel 2007, however, will not allow you to create macros in XLM.

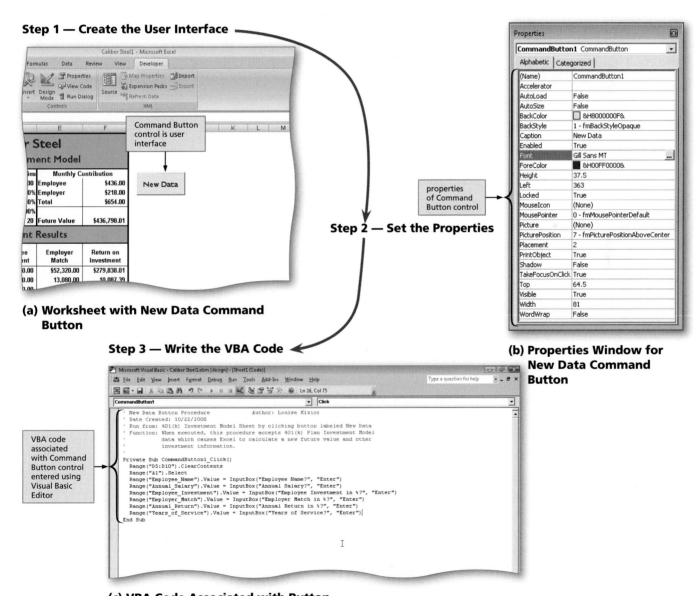

Step 1 — Create the User Interface

(a) Worksheet with New Data Command Button

Step 2 — Set the Properties

(b) Properties Window for New Data Command Button

Step 3 — Write the VBA Code

(c) VBA Code Associated with Button

VBA code associated with Command Button control entered using Visual Basic Editor

Figure 7–29

To Unprotect a Password-Protected Worksheet

1 With the Caliber Steel1 workbook open, click the Review tab on the Ribbon, and then click the Unprotect Sheet button on the Ribbon.

2 When the Unprotect Sheet dialog box appears, type `caliber` as the password and then click the OK button to unprotect the worksheet.

Plan Ahead

Step 1 — Create the user interface.
The most common way to execute a procedure in Excel is to create a Command Button control. To create the control, click the Command Button button in the Controls gallery on the Developer tab on the Ribbon. Next, you use the mouse to locate and size the control in the same way you locate and size an embedded chart. You then can assign properties and the procedure to the Command Button control while Excel is in Design mode.

BTW

Design Mode
If Excel is in Run mode and you click any control button in the Controls Gallery, Excel immediately switches to Design mode.

Two modes of Visual Basic for Applications exist within Excel: Design mode and Run mode. **Design mode** allows you to resize controls, assign properties to controls, and enter VBA code. **Run mode** means that all controls are active and thus cannot be changed. If you click a control in Run mode, it triggers the event, and Excel executes the procedure associated with the control.

To Add a Command Button Control to the Worksheet

The following steps add a Command Button control to the worksheet.

1
- Click the Developer tab on the Ribbon.

- Click the Insert button on the Ribbon to display the Controls gallery (Figure 7–30).

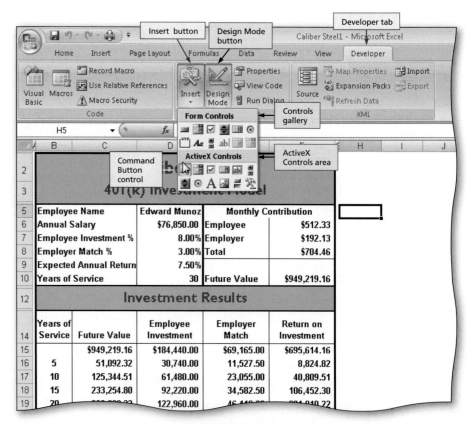

Figure 7–30

2

- Click the Command Button button in the ActiveX area of the Controls gallery (column 1, row 1 of ActiveX area) to switch to Design mode.

- Move the mouse pointer (a crosshair) to the upper-left corner of cell H5.

- Drag the mouse pointer so the rectangle defining the button area appears as shown in Figure 7–31 and hold.

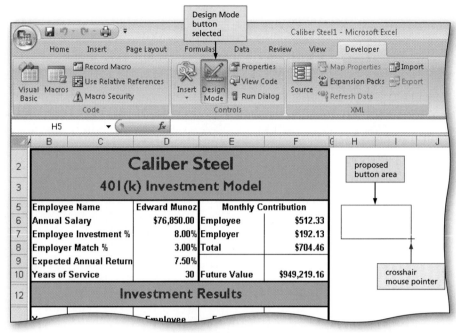

Figure 7–31

3

- Release the left mouse button to add the Command Button control with the default caption CommandButton1 (Figure 7–32).

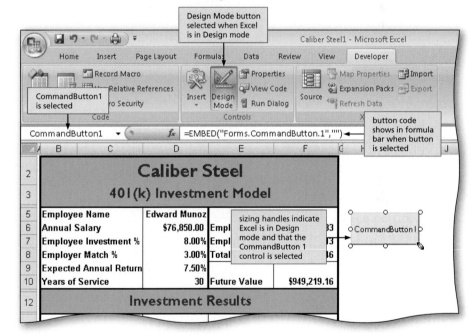

Figure 7–32

Other Ways

1. Click Design Mode button on Developer tab

Step 2 — Determine properties for controls in the user interface.

As shown in the Properties window in Figure 7–29b on page EX 553, a Command Button control has 25 different **properties**, such as caption (the words on the face of the button), background color, foreground color, height, width, and font. After you add a Command Button control to a worksheet, you can change any one of the 25 properties to improve the control's appearance and modify how it works. For the 401(k) Investment Model, the control's caption should read New Data to reflect the purpose of the button. The color of the caption's font should be changed to a color that is consistent with the worksheet.

Plan Ahead

To Set the Command Button Control Properties

The following steps change the Command Button control's caption, the font size of the caption, and the color of the caption.

- With the Command Button control selected and Excel in Design mode, click the Properties button on the Ribbon to open the Properties window for the Command Button control.

- If necessary, when the Properties window opens, click the Alphabetic tab, click Caption in the Properties list, and then type New Data as the caption.

- Click ForeColor in the Properties list, click the ForeColor arrow, and then click the Palette tab (Figure 7–33).

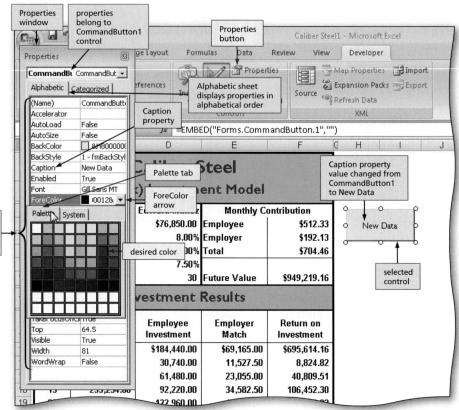

Figure 7–33

- Click blue (column 7, row 3) on the ForeColor palette.

- Click Font in the Properties list and then click the Font button.

- When the Font dialog box appears, click Bold in the Font style list and 12 in the Size list (Figure 7–34).

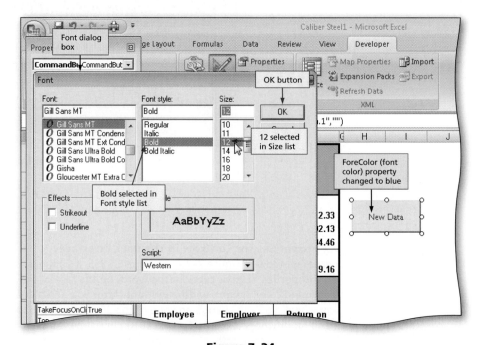

Figure 7–34

• Click the OK button to display the Command Button control. If necessary, drag the lower-right corner of the Properties window to make all of the properties display in the window (Figure 7–35).

Q&A

How should I use the Properties window?

The Properties window (Figure 7–35) includes two sheets: Alphabetic and Categorized. The Alphabetic sheet displays the properties in alphabetical order by property name. The Categorized sheet displays the properties in categories, such as appearance, behavior, font, and miscellaneous. Depending on the application, you can modify any one of the Command Button control properties shown in Figure 7–35, much like the previous steps changed the Caption, ForeColor, and Font properties.

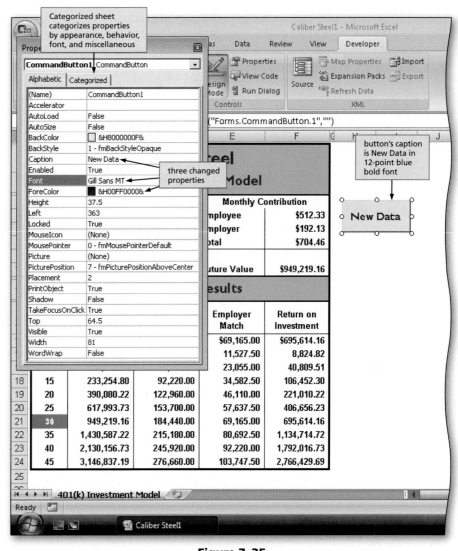

Figure 7–35

Other Ways

1. In Design mode, right-click control, click Properties on shortcut menu

---

Step 3 — Establish the Visual Basic code needed for each control.
The next step is to write and then enter the procedure that will execute when the user clicks the New Data button.

When you trigger the event that executes a procedure, such as clicking a button, Excel steps through the Visual Basic statements one at a time, beginning at the top of the procedure. Thus, when you plan a procedure, remember that the order in which you place the statements in the procedure is important because the order determines the sequence of execution. An **event-driven program** includes procedures that execute when the specific actions taken by the user or other events occur.

After you know what you want the procedure to accomplish, write the VBA code on paper, creating a table similar to Table 7–2. Then, before entering the procedure into the computer, test it by putting yourself in the position of Excel and stepping through the instructions one at a time. As you do so, think about how the procedure affects the worksheet. Testing a procedure before entering it is called **desk checking** and is an important part of the development process.

(continued)

Plan Ahead

BTW

Improving Productivity
If you find yourself entering the same series of Excel commands over and over, you can use the macro recorder or VBA to complete the steps automatically. This can improve your productivity by eliminating routine tasks and simplifying complex tasks.

Plan Ahead

(continued)

Adding comments before a procedure will help you remember its purpose at a later date or help somebody else understand its purpose. In Table 7–2, the first seven lines are comments. **Comments** begin with the word Rem (short for Remark) or an apostrophe ('). In a procedure, comments contain overall documentation and are placed before the procedure, above the Sub statement. Comments have no effect on the execution of a procedure; they simply provide information about the procedure, such as name, creation date, and function. Comments also can be placed in between lines of code or at the end of a line of code as long as the comment begins with an apostrophe (').

Table 7–2 New Data Button Procedure

Line	Statement
1	' New Data Button Procedure Author: Louise Kizior
2	' Date Created: 10/22/2008
3	' Run from: 401(k) Investment Model Sheet by clicking button labeled New Data
4	' Function: When executed, this procedure accepts 401(k) Plan Investment Model
5	' data which causes Excel to calculate a new future value and other
6	' investment information.
7	'
8	Private Sub CommandButton1_Click()
9	Range("D5:D10").ClearContents
10	Range("A1").Select
11	Range("Employee_Name").Value = InputBox("Employee Name?", "Enter")
12	Range("Annual_Salary").Value = InputBox("Annual Salary?", "Enter")
13	Range("Employee_Investment").Value = InputBox("Employee Investment in %?", "Enter")
14	Range("Employer_Match").Value = InputBox("Employer Match in %?", "Enter")
15	Range("Annual_Return").Value = InputBox("Annual Return in %?", "Enter")
16	Range("Years_of_Service").Value = InputBox("Years of Service?", "Enter")
17	End Sub

BTW

The Microsoft Visual Basic Editor Window
If the window displaying the VBA code appears different from the one shown in Figure 7–37 on page 560, double-click the Code window's title bar to maximize the window. If the Project window or Properties window displays on the left side of the Microsoft Visual Basic Editor window, click its Close button.

About the Command Button Control Code

A procedure begins with a Sub statement and ends with an End Sub statement (lines 8 and 17 in Table 7–2). The **Sub statement** includes the keyword Private or Public followed by the name of the procedure, which Excel determines from the name of the control (in this case, CommandButton1) and the event that causes the procedure to execute (in this case, Click). **Private** means that the procedure can be executed only from this workbook. **Public** means that it can be executed from other workbooks or programs. The name of the Command Button control procedure is CommandButton1_Click().

The parentheses following the keyword Click in the Sub statement in line 8 are required. They indicate that arguments can be passed from one procedure to another. Passing arguments is beyond the scope of this chapter, but the parentheses still are required. The **End Sub statement** in line 17 signifies the end of the procedure and returns Excel to Ready mode.

The first executable statement in Table 7–2 is line 9, which clears the cells in the range D5:D10. Line 10 selects cell A1 to remove clutter from the screen. One at a time, lines 11 through 16 accept data from the user and assign the data to the cells in the range D5:D10. Each cell in the range D5:D10 is assigned a cell name. The code uses the cell name to make the code more readable. Each one of the six statements handles one cell.

To the right of the equal sign in lines 11 through 16 is the InputBox function. A **function** returns a value to the program. In this case, the **InputBox function** displays a dialog box and returns the value entered by the user. For example, in line 11, the InputBox function displays a dialog box with the message, "Employee Name?" When the user responds and enters a name, the InputBox function returns the value entered to the program and assigns it to the cell named Employee_Name, which is cell D5.

BTW

Entering VBA Comments
If a horizontal line displays between the comment and Sub Statement, press the ENTER key after the last comment to begin a new line. Then press the DELETE key to delete the horizontal line.

To Enter the New Data Button Procedure Using the Visual Basic Editor

To enter a procedure, you use the Visual Basic Editor. To activate the Visual Basic Editor, Excel must be in Design mode. To activate the Visual Basic Editor, select a control to switch Excel to Design mode and then click the View Code button on the Ribbon.

The **Visual Basic Editor** is a full-screen editor, which allows you to enter a procedure by typing the lines of VBA code as if you were using word processing software. At the end of each line, you press the ENTER key or use the DOWN ARROW key to move to the next line. If you make a mistake in a statement, you can use the arrow keys and the DELETE or BACKSPACE key to correct it. You also can move the insertion point to previous lines to make corrections.

The following steps activate the Visual Basic Editor and create the procedure for the New Data button.

1

• With the New Data button selected and Excel in Design mode, point to the View Code button on the Ribbon (Figure 7–36).

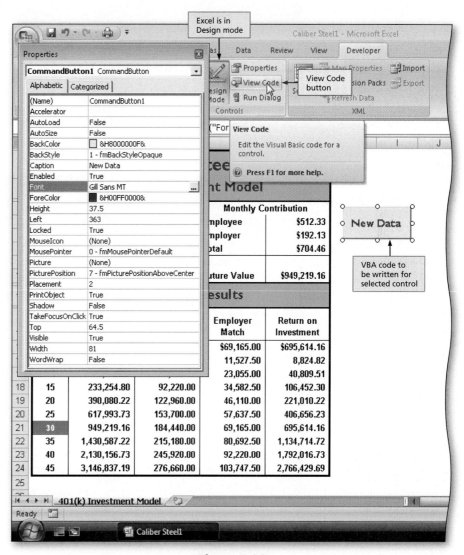

Figure 7–36

2

- Click the View Code button on the Ribbon to start the Microsoft Visual Basic Editor.

- When the Microsoft Visual Basic Editor starts, if the Project Explorer window appears on the left, click its Close button.

- If necessary, double-click the title bar to maximize the Microsoft Visual Basic Editor window.

- If necessary, double-click the title bar of the Microsoft Visual Basic window to maximize it (Figure 7–37).

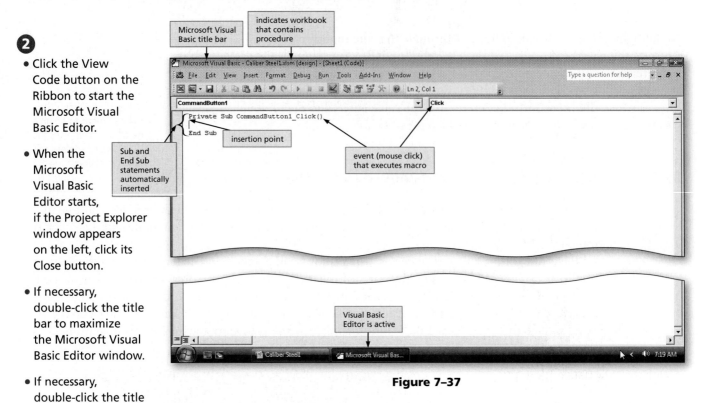

Figure 7–37

 Why is there already code in the Microsoft Visual Basic Editor window?

The Visual Basic Editor automatically inserts the Sub and End Sub statements and positions the insertion point between the two statements.

3

- Click to the left of the letter P in the word Private on the first line and press the ENTER key to add a blank line before the Sub statement.

- Move the insertion point to the blank line and then type the seven comment statements (lines 1 through 7) in Table 7–2 on page EX 558. Make sure you enter an apostrophe (') at the beginning of each comment line.

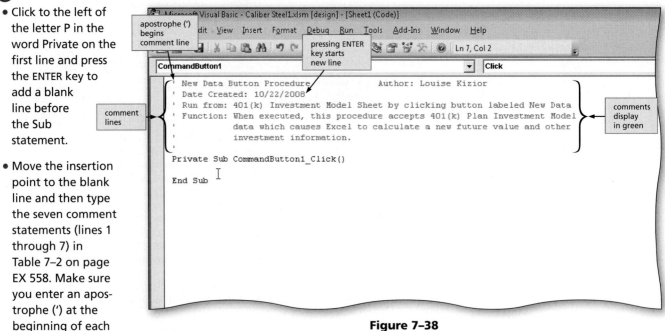

Figure 7–38

- Press the ENTER key to start a new line (Figure 7–38).

Why does the code appear in different colors?

Excel automatically displays the comment lines in green. Keywords, such as Private and Sub, appear in blue. Other code appears with a black font color.

4

- Position the insertion point on the blank line between the Sub and End Sub statements.

- Enter lines 9 through 16 in Table 7–2. For clarity, indent all lines between the Sub statement and End Sub statement by three spaces (Figure 7–39).

How should I exit the Visual Basic Editor and return to Excel?

Excel provides two ways to return control from the Visual Basic Editor to the worksheet. The Close button on the title bar (Figure 7–39) closes the Visual Basic Editor and returns control to the worksheet. The View Microsoft Excel button on the Standard toolbar (Figure 7–39) also returns control to Excel, but only minimizes the Visual Basic Editor window. If you plan to switch between Excel and the Visual Basic Editor, then use the View Microsoft Excel button; if you want to close the Visual Basic Editor and return to Excel, use the Close button.

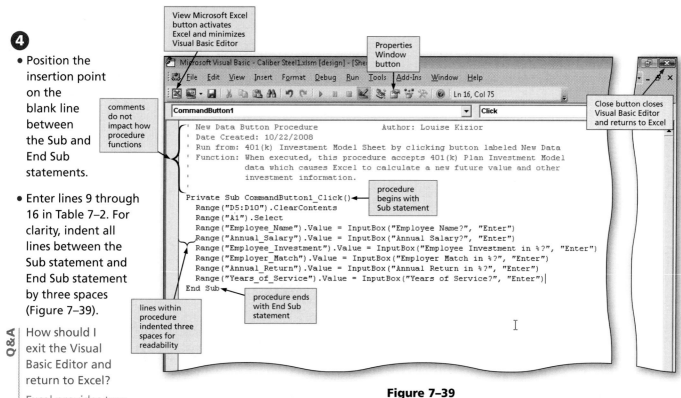

Figure 7–39

5

- Click the Close button on the right side of the Microsoft Visual Basic title bar to return to the worksheet.

- Click the Close button on the right side of the Properties window (Figure 7–40).

6

- Click the Design Mode button on the Ribbon to return to Run mode.

What is the result of clicking the Design Mode button?

Excel returns to Run mode, which means if you click the New Data button, Excel will execute the associated procedure.

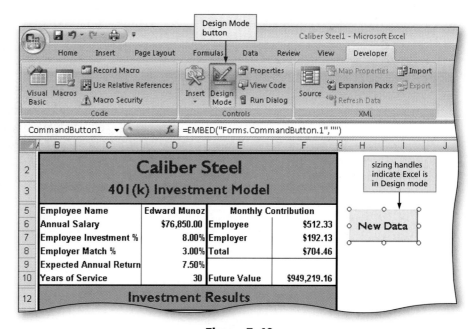

Figure 7–40

Other Ways
1. Click Visual Basic button on Ribbon   2. In Design mode, right-click control, click View Code on shortcut menu

BTW

Printing the VBA Code
To print the VBA code while the Visual Basic Editor is active, click File on the menu bar and then click Print.

More About Visual Basic for Applications

Visual Basic for Applications includes many more statements than those presented here. Even this simple procedure, however, should help you understand the basic composition of a Visual Basic statement. For example, each of the statements within the procedure shown in Figure 7–39 includes a period. The entry on the left side of the period tells Excel which object you want to affect. An **object** can be a cell, a range, a chart, a worksheet, a workbook, a button, or any other control you create on a worksheet. Objects also can be other applications in Windows or parts of other applications. The entry on the right side of the period tells Excel what you want to do to the object. You can place a method or property on the right side of the period. For example, the statement

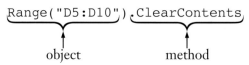

clears the range D5:D10. You use a method, such as ClearContents, to change an object's behavior. In this case, the method ClearContents is changing the behavior of the range by clearing its contents.

You previously were shown how to change an object's properties using the Properties window (Figure 7–33 on page EX 556). The following example shows that you also can change an object's properties during execution of a procedure. The object in this case is a Command Button control.

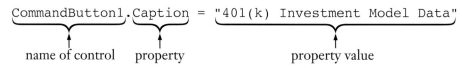

This statement changes the value of the Caption property of the button to 401(k) Investment Model Data during execution of the procedure.

As shown in Figure 7–39, the second statement in the procedure,

```
Range("A1").Select
```

selects cell A1, which, in effect, hides the heavy border that surrounds the active cell. Several of the statements in the procedure also include equal signs. An equal sign instructs Excel to make an assignment to a cell. For example, when executed as part of the procedure

```
Range("Employee_Name").Value = InputBox("Employee Name?",
    "Enter")
```

the equal sign instructs Excel to display a dialog box called Enter with the prompt message, Employee Name?. The statement then assigns the value entered by the user in response to the dialog box to cell D5, which is named Employee_Name. Thus, the first argument in the InputBox function is the message that should be displayed to the user, and the second argument identifies the title to be displayed in the dialog box's title bar.

A message box often is used to display informative messages to a user. A message box is a type of dialog box that does not provide an input area for the user, but allows the user only to click one or more buttons. The **MsgBox function** is used to display a message. For example, when executed as part of the procedure

```
Result = MsgBox("You must enter a value between 1 and
    10,000.", , "Input Error")
```

the MsgBox function displays a dialog box with Input Error on the title bar and the message, You must enter a value between 1 and 10,000., in the dialog box. By default, the dialog box includes only an OK button. In this example, the second parameter between the message and dialog box title does not include any values to list the buttons that the

BTW

Running Procedures
Always save a workbook before you execute a procedure in case something unexpected occurs. This is especially true when testing a procedure.

BTW

Message Box Buttons
By setting the second parameter of the MsgBox function, you can change the buttons that display in the message box. VBA includes several shortcuts for specifying the buttons. For example, vbAbortRetryIgnore displays Abort, Retry, and Ignore buttons in the message box. Other shortcuts include vbOK-Cancel, vbRetryCancel, vbYesNo, and vbYesNoCancel.

dialog box should display; the dialog box thus includes only an OK button. After the user clicks the OK button, a value indicating that the user clicked the OK button is assigned to the Result variable in the code above.

To Enter 401(k) Investment Model Data Using the New Data Button

Before attempting to enter data using the New Data button, be sure you exit Design mode and return Excel to Run mode, as illustrated in Step 6 in the previous set of steps. The following steps enter 401(k) Investment Model data as follows: Employee Name (cell D5) — Millie Jenkins; Annual Salary (cell D6) — $87,200.00; Employee Investment % (cell D7) — 6.00%; Employer Match % (cell D8) — 3.00%; Expected Annual Return (cell D9) — 9.00%; and Years of Service (cell D10) — 20.

- Click the New Data button.

- When Excel displays the first Enter dialog box with the prompt message, Employee Name?, type Millie Jenkins in the text box (Figure 7–41).

Q&A

What happens when I click the New Data button?

Excel clears the range D5:D10 and then selects cell A1. Next, it displays the Enter dialog box shown in Figure 7–41.

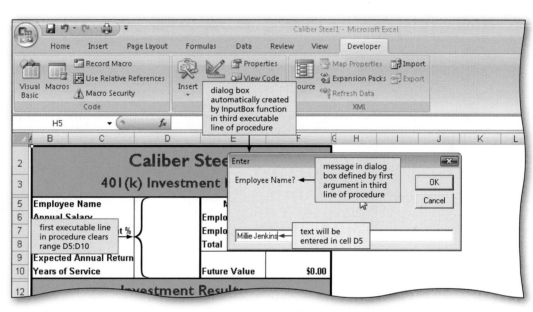

Figure 7–41

- Click the OK button or press the ENTER key.

- When Excel displays the next Enter dialog box with the prompt message, Annual Salary?, type 87200 in the text box (Figure 7–42).

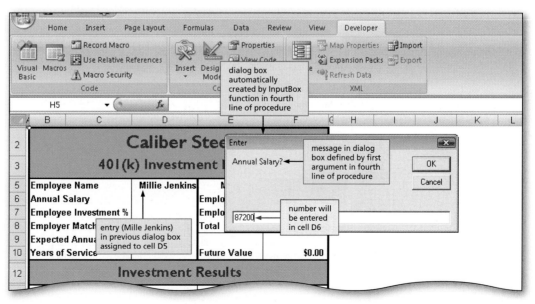

Figure 7–42

3

- Click the OK button.

- When Excel displays the next Enter dialog box with the prompt message, Employee Investment in %?, type 6% in the text box, making certain to type the percent (%) sign (Figure 7–43).

Q&A

What happens when I click the OK button?

Excel assigns the value $87,200.00 to cell D6, applying the formatting assigned to cell D6 to the value. Excel then displays the third Enter dialog box as shown in Figure 7–43.

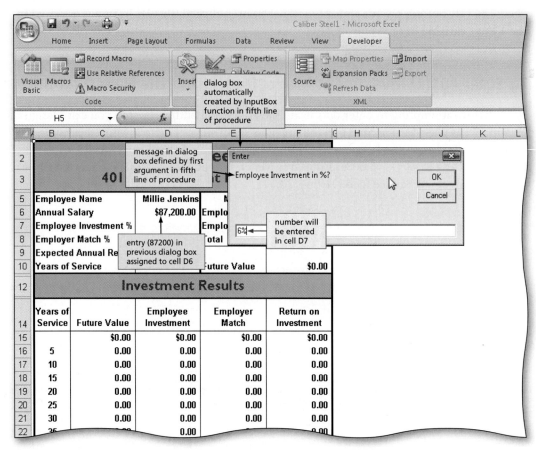

Figure 7–43

4

- Click the OK button.

- When Excel displays the next Enter dialog box with the prompt message, Employer Match in %?, type 3% in the text box (Figure 7–44).

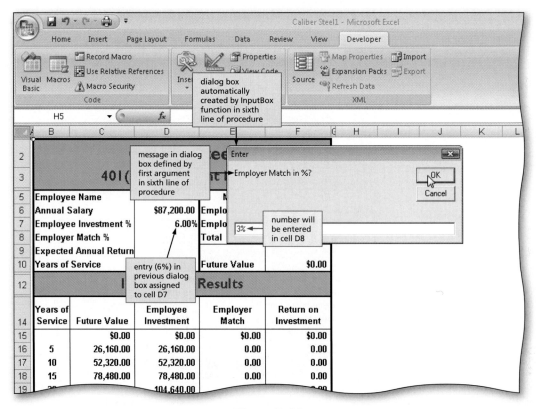

Figure 7–44

5

- Click the OK button.

- When Excel displays the next Enter dialog box with the prompt message, Annual Return in %?, type 9% in the text box (Figure 7–45).

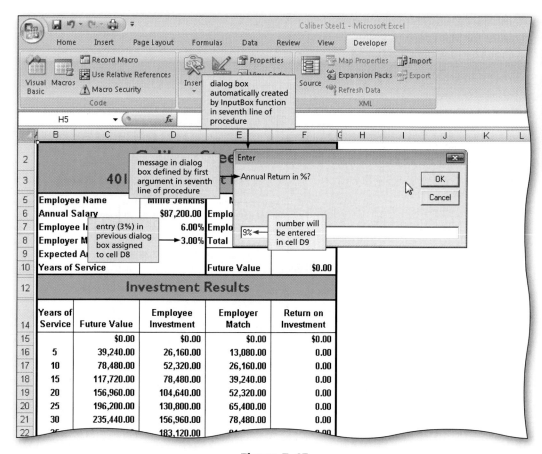

Figure 7–45

6

- Click the OK button to assign 9.00% to cell D9.

- When Excel displays the next Enter dialog box with the prompt message, Years of Service?, type 20 in the text box (Figure 7–46).

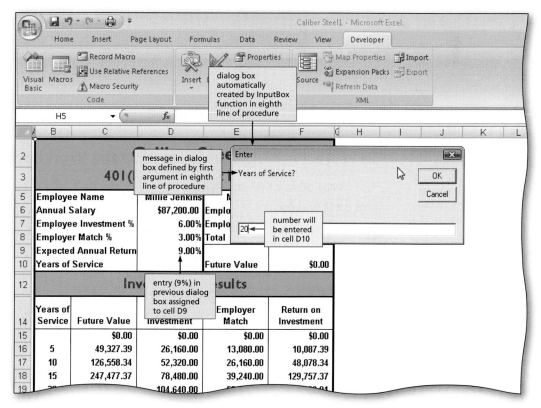

Figure 7–46

7
- Click the OK button to display the results for Millie Jenkins in the range F6:F10 (Figure 7–47).

Q&A

What is the result on the worksheet?

Figure 7–47 shows that the future value of Millie Jenkins' investment of $436.00 per month (cell F6) for 20 years is $436,798.01 (cell C19 and F10). After 20 years of monthly contributions, Millie Jenkins's total 401(k) plan investment will be $104,640.00 (cell D19) and the total employer match will be $52,320.00 (cell E19).

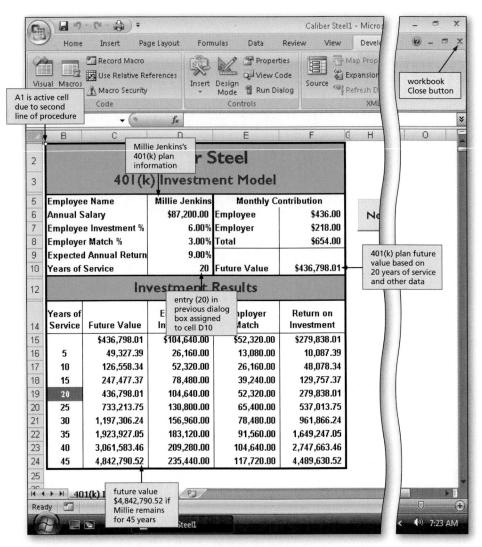

Figure 7–47

BTW
Data Validation
The VBA code entered in Step 4 on page EX 561 does not check the incoming data to make sure it is reasonable. For example, if a user enters a negative value for the Years of Service in Step 6 on the previous page, Excel will calculate an incorrect Future Value. In the next phase of this chapter, you will learn how to write VBA code that will ensure that unreasonable numbers are rejected. See the VBA code in Figure 7–79 on page EX 593 for an example.

To Protect a Worksheet and Save the Workbook

With Phase 2 of this chapter complete, the final step is to protect the worksheet and save the workbook.

1 Click the Review tab on the Ribbon, and then click the Protect Sheet button on the Ribbon.

2 When the Protect Sheet dialog box appears, type caliber in the 'Password to unprotect sheet' text box and then click the OK button. When the Confirm Password dialog box appears, type caliber and then click the OK button.

3 Click the Office Button and then click Save As on the Office Button menu. When the Save As dialog box is displayed, type Caliber Steel2 in the File name text box. Make sure UDISK 2.0 (E:) displays in the Address bar and then click the Save button.

4 Click the Close button on the right side of the title bar to close the Caliber Steel2 workbook.

Phase 3 — Creating a Personalization Center to Automate the 401(k) Investment Model Data Entry

The final phase of this chapter requires that more controls are added to the worksheet to automate the 401(k) Investment Model data entry. In Phase 2, clicking the New Data button triggered Excel to display a series of input dialog boxes. This phase uses input dialog boxes only for the employee name and annual salary. The remaining data (employee investment, employer match, annual return, and years of service) is entered using scroll bars, a check box, and spin buttons to help reduce input errors that can be caused by mistyped data.

Figure 7–48 shows how the Personalization Center will look when complete. When you click the Enter Name and Salary button, Excel displays input dialog boxes to accept the employee name for cell D5 and the annual salary for cell D6.

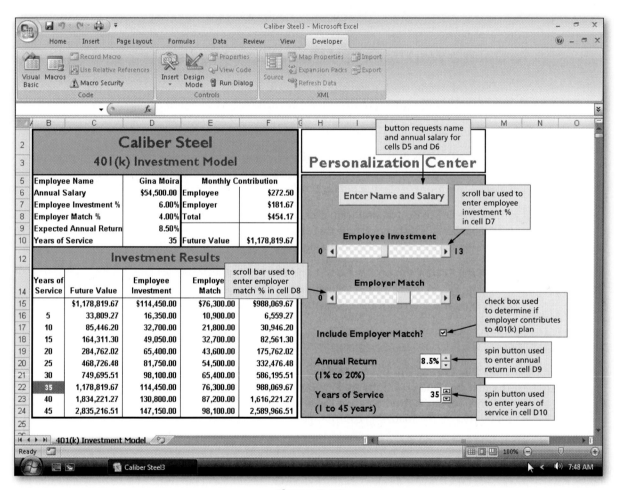

Figure 7–48

The Employee Investment scroll bar immediately below the Enter Name and Salary button allows you to set the employee investment percentage in cell D7. Recall that a scroll bar is made up of three separate elements that you can click or drag — the **scroll arrows** on each side that you can click; the **scroll box** between the scroll arrows that you can drag; and the clickable **scroll bar** that extends from one scroll arrow to the other.

The Employee Investment scroll bar has a minimum value of 0% and a maximum value of 13%. If you click one of its scroll arrows, the employee investment percent in cell D7 increases or decreases by 0.5%, depending on which scroll arrow you click. If you click the scroll bar on either side of the scroll box, the employee investment percent in cell D7 increases or decreases by 1%. Finally, you can drag the scroll box to the right or left to increase or decrease the employee investment percentage in cell D7.

The Employer Match scroll bar works the same way, except that the scroll bar runs from 0% to 6% and the employer match changes by 0.25% when you click a scroll arrow.

The Include Employer Match? check box in the middle of the Personalization Center in Figure 7–48 determines if the Employer Match scroll bar is enabled or disabled. If the check mark is present, then the scroll bar above the check box is enabled. If the check mark is removed, then cell D8 is set equal to 0% and the scroll bar is disabled.

The Annual Return spin button in the lower portion of the Personalization Center increases or decreases the expected annual return in cell D9 by 0.25% each time you click a spin button arrow. A **spin button** has two spin button arrows, one to increment and one to decrement the value in the cell with which it is associated. The Years of Service spin button in the lower portion of the Personalization Center increases or decreases the years of service in cell D10 by one each time you click a spin button arrow.

To Open a Workbook and Unprotect a Worksheet

The following steps open the workbook Caliber Steel1, save it using the file name Caliber Steel3, and unprotect the 401(k) Investment Model worksheet.

1 Open the Caliber Steel1 workbook saved in Phase 1 of this chapter.

2 Click the Options button in the Security Warning box. When the Microsoft Office Security Options dialog box appears, click the 'Enable this content' option button and then click the OK button to close the dialog box.

3 Click the Office Button and then click Save As on the Office Button menu. When the Save As dialog box is displayed, type Caliber Steel3 in the File name text box and then click the Save button in the Save As dialog box.

4 Click the Review tab on the Ribbon and then click the Unprotect Sheet button on the Ribbon. When the Unprotect Sheet dialog box appears, type caliber in the Password text box, and then click the OK button to unprotect the worksheet.

Plan Ahead

Step 1 — Create the user interface.
The first step is to create the Personalization Center user interface shown in Figure 7–48 on the previous page. After creating the gray background for the Personalization Center in the range H5:L24, the following controls must be added:

1. One Command Button control

2. Two Scroll Bar controls

3. One Check Box control

4. Two Spin Button controls

5. Label controls to identify controls and display data

When you first create a user interface, you position the controls as close as you can to their final location on the screen, and then you finalize the locations of the controls, after setting the properties.

Figure 7–49 shows the Controls gallery and where the above referenced controls can be found in the gallery.

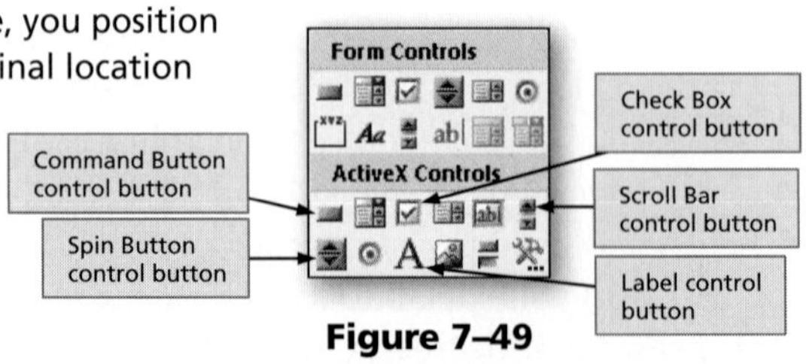

BTW

More Controls
The bottom-right button shown in Figure 7-49 is the More Controls button. If you click this button, nearly 200 additional controls, are available to incorporate in a user interface. The controls will vary depending on the software that is installed on your computer.

Figure 7–49

To Add Controls to a User Interface

The following steps create the controls, but make no attempt to position them exactly in the locations shown in Figure 7–48.

- Select the range H5:L24.

- Click the Fill Color button arrow on the Home tab on the Ribbon and then click White, Background 1, Darker 25% (column 1, row 4) on the Fill Color palette.

- Click the Borders button arrow on the Ribbon and then click Thick Box Border on the Borders palette.

- Click the Developer tab on the Ribbon.

- Click the Insert button on the Ribbon, click the Command Button button in the ActiveX area in the Controls gallery, and then drag the mouse pointer so the control displays as shown in Figure 7–50.

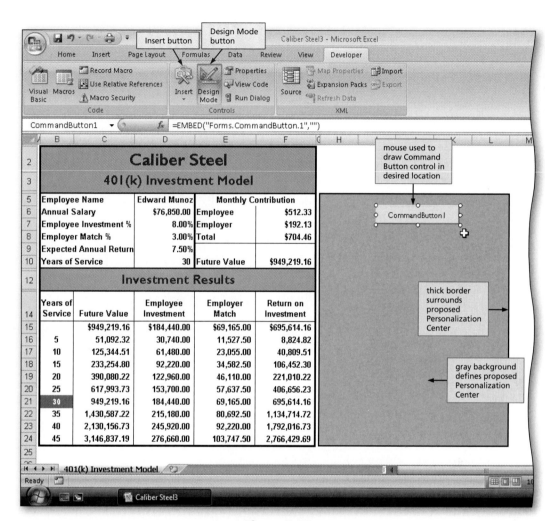

Figure 7–50

2

- Click the Insert button on the Ribbon, click the Scroll Bar button in the ActiveX area in the Controls gallery, and then move the mouse pointer to approximately the left of cell I12.

- Drag the mouse pointer so the Scroll Bar control displays as shown in Figure 7–51.

Q&A

What if I need to delete a control that I added?

If you want to delete a control, select the control while in Design mode and then press the DELETE key. If you want to resize a control, select the control while in Design mode and then drag its sizing handles. If you want to reposition a control, select the control while in Design mode and then drag it to its new location.

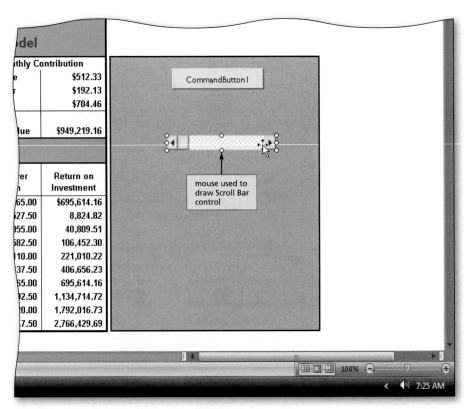

Figure 7–51

3

- Point to the Scroll Bar control.

- Hold down the CTRL key and drag a copy of the Scroll Bar control to the location shown in Figure 7–52. It is important that you release the left mouse button before you release the CTRL key.

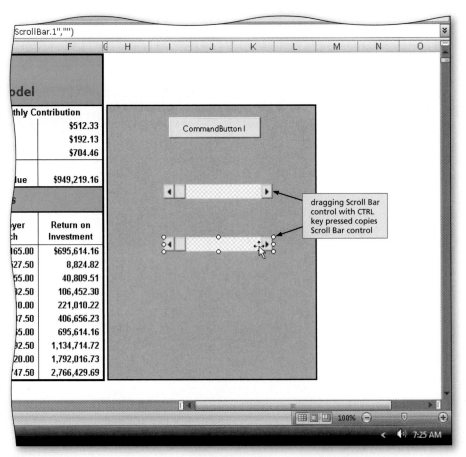

Figure 7–52

• Click the Insert button on the Ribbon, click the Check Box button in the ActiveX area in the Controls gallery, and then move the mouse pointer to the upper-left corner of the location of the Check Box control as shown in Figure 7–53.

• Drag the mouse pointer so the rectangle defining the Check Box control area displays with the word CheckBox1 showing.

Q&A

Why does the check box not seem to be the right size?

The check box will be resized after its caption is changed later in this chapter.

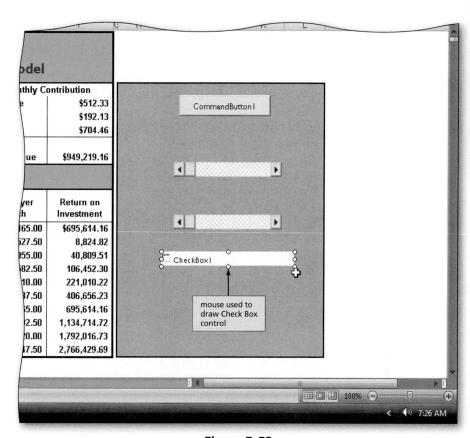

Figure 7–53

• Click the Insert button on the Ribbon, click the Spin Button button in the ActiveX area in the Controls gallery, and then move the mouse pointer to the upper-left corner of the location of the Spin Button control shown in Figure 7–48 on page 567.

• Drag the mouse pointer so the rectangle defining the Spin Button control area displays as shown in Figure 7–54.

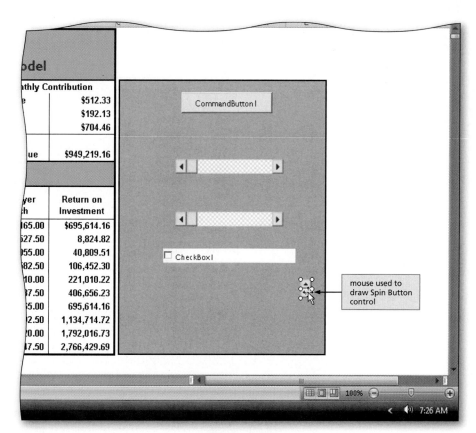

Figure 7–54

6

- Point to the Spin Button control in the Personalization Center.

- Hold down the CTRL key and drag a copy of the Spin Button control to the second location shown in Figure 7–55. It is important that you release the left mouse button before you release the CTRL key.

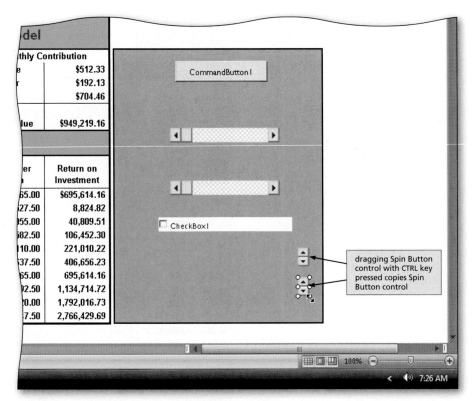

Figure 7–55

7

- Click the Insert button on the Ribbon, click the Label button in the ActiveX area in the Controls gallery, and then move the mouse pointer to the left of the first Scroll Bar control below the CommandButton1 button.

- Drag the mouse pointer so the rectangle defining the Label control displays as shown in Figure 7–56.

Q&A

What is the purpose of this particular Label control?

This Label control is used to indicate the lowest value (zero) on the scroll bar.

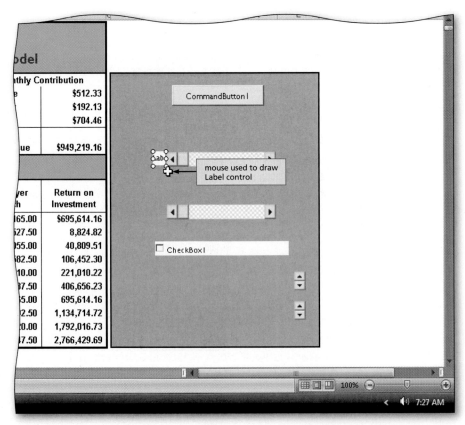

Figure 7–56

- Point to the Label control.

- Hold down the CTRL key and then drag a copy of the Label control created in Step 7 to the center of cell J3. While holding down the CTRL key, drag the newly copied Label control to the next location where a Label control is required.

- Continue in this fashion until you have a total of 11 Label controls as shown in Figure 7–57.

Q&A

What appears on the added Label controls?

When you create a Label control, a caption automatically is associated with it. The Caption property for the first Label control is Label1. For the next Label control you create, the Caption property is Label2, and so on. Because of the size of the Label controls in Figure 7–57, only two characters of the caption, La, appear in the Personalization Center.

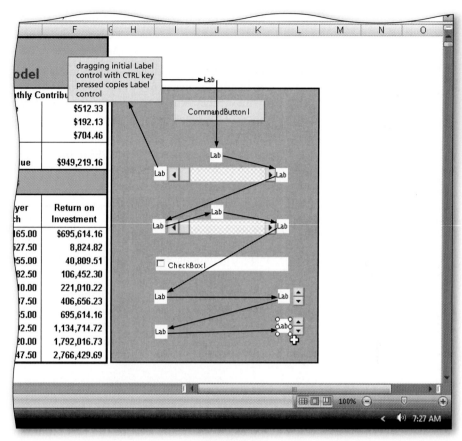

Figure 7–57

Other Ways

1. Select control, click Copy button on Home tab on Ribbon, click Paste button on Home tab on Ribbon

2. Right-click control, click Copy on shortcut menu, click Paste on shortcut menu

3. Select control, press CTRL+C to copy, press CTRL+V to paste

---

Step 2 — Determine properties for controls in the user interface.

Plan Ahead

The next step is to set the properties for the 17 controls that make up the user interface. The 17 controls best can be seen by referring to Figure 7–57 and counting the button, labels, scroll bars, check box, and spin buttons. The properties will be set as follows:

1. **Constant Labels and Check Box** — Set the BackColor property of the Label controls that identify other controls and the Check Box control to gray, so they match the gray background of the user interface. Set the Font property to bold. Set the Caption property and Text Align property for each Label control that identifies another control. As needed, resize the Label controls so the entire caption shows. For the Label control used for the Personalization Center title, change the Caption property to Personalization Center and set the Font property to 20-point bold.

2. **Command Button** — Change the Caption property to Enter Name and Salary and set the ForeColor property to blue. Change the Font property to 12-point bold and resize the Command Button control so the entire caption shows.

3. **Employee Investment Scroll Bar** — Change the Name property to scrEmployeeInvest, the SmallChange property to 50 (0.5%), the LargeChange property to 100 (1%), the Min property to 0 (0%), and the Max property to 1300 (13%).

(continued)

**Plan
Ahead**

(continued)

4. **Employer Match Scroll Bar** — Change the Name property to scrEmployerMatch, the SmallChange property to 25 (0.25%), the LargeChange property to 100 (1%), the Min property to 0 (0%), and the Max property to 600 (6%).

5. **Employer Match Check Box** — Change the Name property to chkEmployerMatch and the Caption property to Include Employer Match?. Change the SpecialEffect property to fmButtonEffectFlat and change the TextAlign property to fmAlignLeft. Set the Value property to True. Resize the check box so the entire caption shows.

6. **Annual Return Spin Button** — Change the Name property to spnAnnualReturn, the SmallChange property to 25 (0.25%), the Min property to 0 (0%), and the Max property to 2000 (20%).

7. **Years of Service Spin Button** — Change the Name property to spnYearsofService, the SmallChange property to 1, the Min property to 1, and the Max property to 45.

8. **Annual Return Label** — Change the Name property to lblAnnualReturn, the Caption property to 5%, the BackColor property to white, the TextAlign property to 1 - fmTextAlignRight, and the BorderStyle property to 1 - fmBorderStyleSingle. Resize the Label control so the entire caption shows.

9. **Years of Service Label** — Change the Name property to lblYearsofService, the Caption property to 10, the BackColor property to white, the TextAlign property to 1 - fmTextAlignRight, and the BorderStyle property to 1 - fmBorderStyleSingle. Resize the Label control so the entire caption shows.

BTW

The Max Property
One of the more difficult concepts to understand about scroll bars is why the Max property is set to such a large number (600 for the Employer Match Check Box), when the maximum value of the scroll bar is only 6% (.06). The two reasons are (1) the Max property can be set equal to only a whole number; and (2) the large number allows you to assign reasonable increments to the SmallChange and LargeChange properties of the scroll bar.

Preparing to Set Properties

Excel automatically assigns the first Command Button control the name CommandButton1. If you create a second Command Button control, Excel will call it CommandButton2, and so on. In the controls just listed, some will have their Name property changed as indicated, while others will not. Usually, you do not change the Name property of Label controls that identify other controls in the user interface. On the other hand, controls that are referenced in the VBA code should be given names that help you recall the control. Table 7–3 summarizes the controls whose Name properties will be changed because they will be referenced in the VBA code.

Table 7–3 Referenced Controls and Their Names	
Control	**Name**
Employee Investment Scroll Bar	scrEmployeeInvest
Employer Match Scroll Bar	scrEmployerMatch
Employer Match Check Box	chkEmployerMatch
Annual Return Spin Button	spnAnnualReturn
Years of Service Spin Button	spnYearsofService
Annual Return Label	lblAnnualReturn
Years of Service Label	lblYearsofService

BTW

Determining Properties
It is best to have all of your properties determined before you sit down at the computer. Using a grid, or graph paper, is often the best way to lay out a screen by hand and set properties such as height, width, and location. Other properties should be determined in this manner as well. Often, this design is detailed in a formal document called a functional specification, which is reviewed and approved by users of the finished worksheet.

The name of a control, such as scrEmployeeInvest, must begin with a letter; cannot exceed 255 characters; and cannot include a space, period, exclamation point, or the characters @, &, $, or #. You should develop a naming convention of your own and then use it consistently to name controls. In this book, the first three characters of the name identify the type of control. For example, scr stands for scroll bar, chk stands for check box, and spn stands for spin button. Following the three characters are words that identify what the control is controlling. In this case, scrEmployeeInvest is a scroll bar controlling the Employee Investment % value in cell D7. You also must make sure that each control in a workbook uses a unique name, because Excel does not allow the use of duplicate names.

To Set Properties of the Label Controls and Check Box Control

When you create a Label control, it has a white background. If the Label control identifies another control and the value remains constant, the background color must be changed so it matches the user interface background. If the Label control is going to display a value that varies, the background is left white. The following steps use the SHIFT key to select all the Label controls and the Check Box control, except the title Label control, so that the BackColor property can be changed for all selected items at one time. The Font property of the selected controls also is changed to Bold. After the BackColor and Font properties are changed, each Label control is selected and the Caption and Text Align properties are set.

1

- With Excel in Design mode, click the Label control in the top-right of the user interface.

- Hold down the SHIFT key and then one at a time click the Check Box control and all Label controls except the title Label control, as shown on the right side of Figure 7–58.

- Release the SHIFT key.

- Click the Properties button on the Ribbon.

- When the Properties window opens, click BackColor; if necessary, click the BackColor box arrow; and then click the Palette tab (Figure 7–58).

Q&A

Why do there seem to be fewer properties in the Property window?

Every control has its own set of properties, although many controls share common properties, such as BackColor, Caption, and ForeColor. When you select multiple controls, Excel displays only those properties that are common to the controls selected.

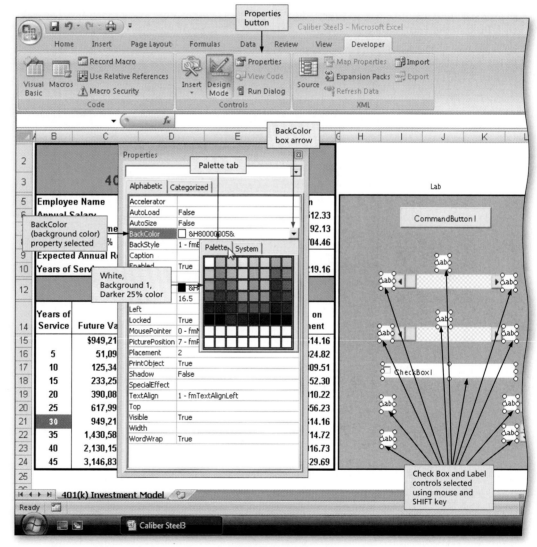

Figure 7–58

● Click the White, Background 1, Darker 25% (column 1, row 3) color on the BackColor palette to add a gray background to the selected controls.

● Click Font in the Properties window and then click the Font button.

● When the Font dialog box appears, click Bold in the Font style list and click 12 in the Size list (Figure 7–59).

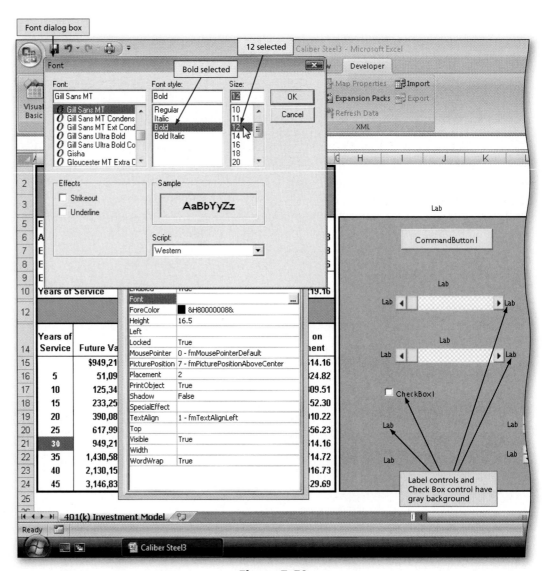

Figure 7–59

- Click the OK button.

- Click anywhere in the Personalization Center area to deselect the Label controls and Check Box control.

- Click the Label control to the left of the first (Employee Investment) Scroll Bar control.

- Click Caption in the Properties window and then type 0 as the caption.

- Click TextAlign in the Properties window, click the TextAlign box arrow, and then click 2 – fmTextAlignCenter (Figure 7–60).

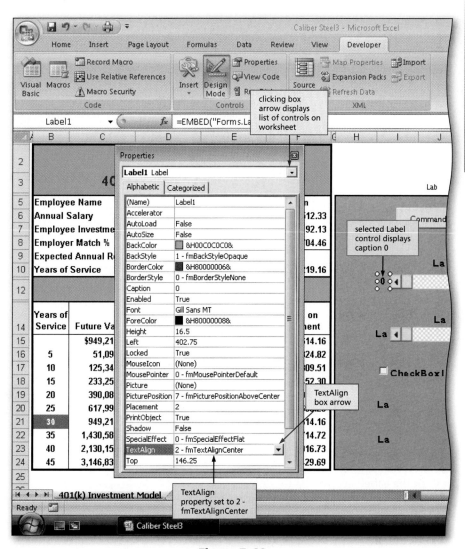

Figure 7–60

- Click the Label control to the right of the first Scroll Bar control.

- Click Caption in the Properties window and then type 13 as the caption.

- Click TextAlign in the Properties window, click the TextAlign box arrow, and then click 2 - fmTextAlignCenter.

5

- If necessary, resize the Label control so the caption 13 is visible (Figure 7–61).

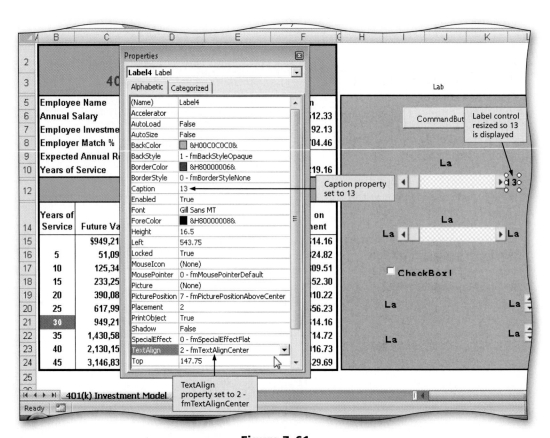

Figure 7–61

6

- Click the Label control above the first Scroll Bar control.

- Click Caption in the Properties window and then type Employee Investment as the caption.

- Click TextAlign in the Properties window, click the TextAlign box arrow, and then click 2 - fmTextAlignCenter.

- Resize the Label control so the caption Employee Investment is visible (Figure 7–62).

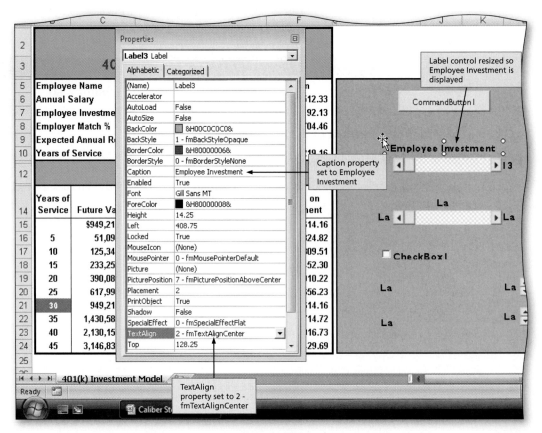

Figure 7–62

- Click the Label control to the left of the second Scroll Bar control.

- Click Caption in the Properties window and then type 0 as the caption.

- Click TextAlign in the Properties window, click the TextAlign box arrow, and then click 2 - fmTextAlignCenter.

- Click the Label control on the right side of the second Scroll Bar control.

- Click Caption in the Properties window and then type 6 as the caption.

- Click TextAlign in the Properties window, click the TextAlign box arrow, and then click 2 - fmTextAlignCenter (Figure 7–63).

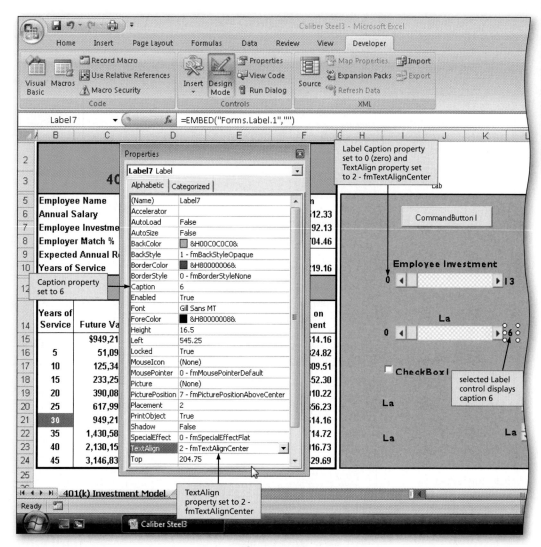

Figure 7–63

8
- Click the Label control above the Personalization Center area.

- Click Caption in the Properties window and then type Personalization Center as the caption.

- Click TextAlign in the Properties window, click the TextAlign box arrow, and then click 2 - fmTextAlignCenter.

- Change the font style to 18-point, bold, and red.

9
- Resize the Label control so the entire caption shows.
- Select the range H2:L3.
- Click the Home tab on the Ribbon. Click the Borders button arrow on the Ribbon and then click Thick Box Border in the Borders gallery.
- Click the Developer tab on the Ribbon (Figure 7–64).

10
- Click the Label control directly above the second Scroll Bar.
- Click Caption in the Properties window and then type `Employer Match` as the caption.
- Click TextAlign in the Properties window, click the TextAlign box arrow, and then click 2 - fmTextAlignCenter.
- Resize the Label control so the entire caption shows.
- Click the Label control to the far left of the top Spin Button control.
- Click Caption in the Properties window and then type `Annual Return (1% to 20%)` as the caption.
- Click TextAlign in the Properties window, click the TextAlign box arrow, and then, if necessary, click 1 - fmTextAlignLeft.
- Resize the Label control so the entire caption shows (Figure 7–65).

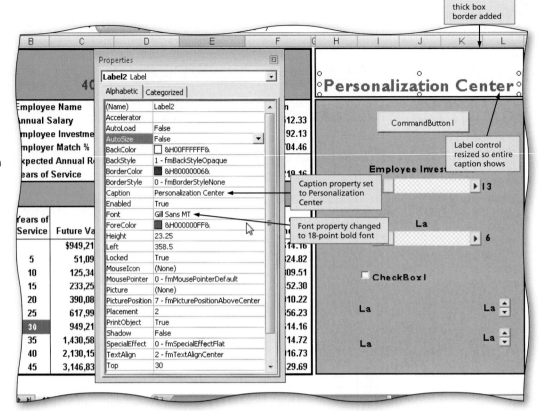

Figure 7–64

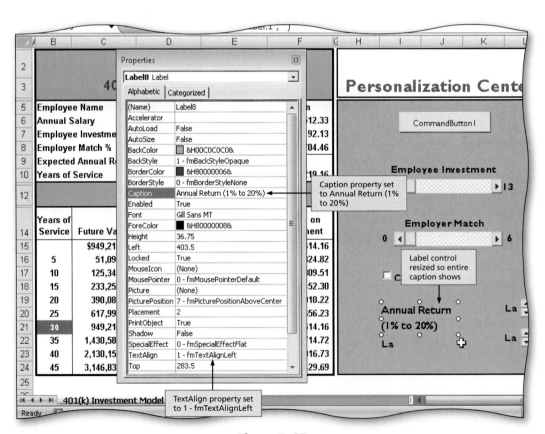

Figure 7–65

- Click the Label control to the far left of the second Spin Button control.

- Click Caption in the Properties window and then type Years of Service (1 to 45 years) as the caption.

- Click TextAlign in the Properties window, click the TextAlign box arrow, and then click 1 - fmTextAlignLeft.

- Resize the Label control so the entire caption shows (Figure 7–66).

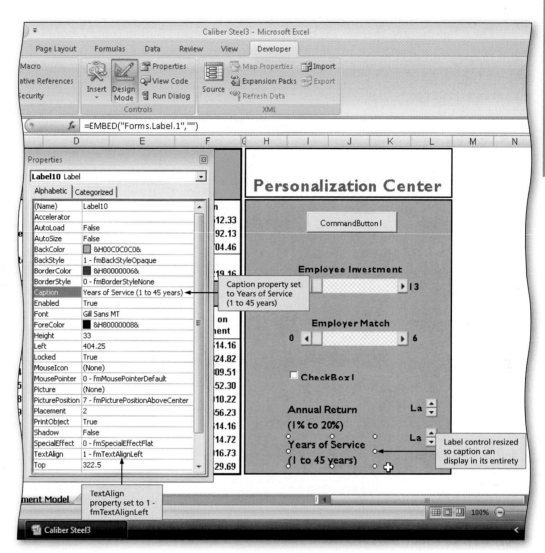

Figure 7–66

To Set the Command Button Control Properties

The following step changes the caption on the Command Button control from CommandButton1 to Enter Name and Salary and resizes it so the entire caption shows on the button.

- With Excel in Design mode, click the Command Button control in the Personalization Center.

- Click Caption in the Properties window and then type `Enter Name and Salary` as the caption.

- Click ForeColor, click the ForeColor box arrow, and then click the Palette tab.

- Click red (row 4, column 2) on the ForeColor palette.

- Click Font in the Properties window and then click the Font button.

- When the Font dialog box appears, click Bold in the Font style list, click 12 in the Size list, and then click the OK button.

- Resize the Command Button control so that the entire caption shows (Figure 7–67).

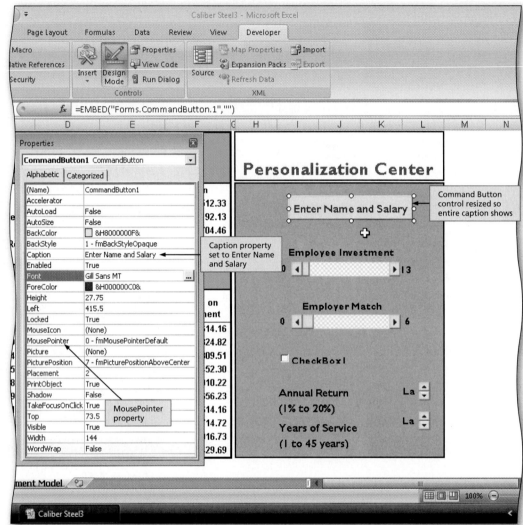

Figure 7–67

Q&A   Can I experiment with some of the other properties in the Property window?

Yes. As you can see from the Properties window shown in Figure 7–67, a Command Button control has many different properties. One that may interest you that is not used in this chapter is the MousePointer property. If you click MousePointer in the Properties window and then click the MousePointer box arrow, several mouse pointer shapes are listed, including hourglass, I-beam, arrow, and crosshair, and others with which you are familiar from your experiences in Excel. If you change the MousePointer property, the mouse pointer will change to the selected mouse pointer shape when you point to the button.

To Set the Employee Investment Scroll Bar Control Properties

The next step is to set the properties of the Employee Investment Scroll Bar control. The function of this Scroll Bar control is to assign cell D7 a value. When you use a control, such as a Scroll Bar, you must set the Min and Max properties. The **Min property** is the minimum value the control can register. The **Max property** is the maximum value the control can register. You also have to set the SmallChange and LargeChange values. The **SmallChange property** is the value by which the control will change each time you click the scroll arrow. The **LargeChange property** is the value by which the control will change each time you click the scroll bar.

You can assign only whole numbers for these four properties. This increases the complexity of the VBA code, because the value the user selects using the scroll bar is assigned to cell D7, which must be assigned a percentage as a decimal number. Thus, to assign cell D7 the maximum value 0.13 (13%), the Scroll Bar control actually must have a Maximum property of 1300. Later in the VBA code, this value is divided by 10,000 to assign cell D7 a value of 0.13.

The following step sets the properties of the Employee Investment Scroll Bar control.

- With Excel in Design mode, click the Employee Investment Scroll Bar control.

- Click (Name) in the Properties window and then type scrEmployeeInvest as the name.

- If necessary, change the LargeChange property to 100, the Max property to 1300, the Min property to 0, and the SmallChange property to 50 (Figure 7–68).

Q&A

Do I need to determine the exact distance in pixels that the scroll button on the scroll bar will move?

No. Excel automatically will determine how far to move the scroll button on the scroll bar when you click the scroll button (small change) and when you click the scroll boxes (large change) from the four numeric values entered in Step 1.

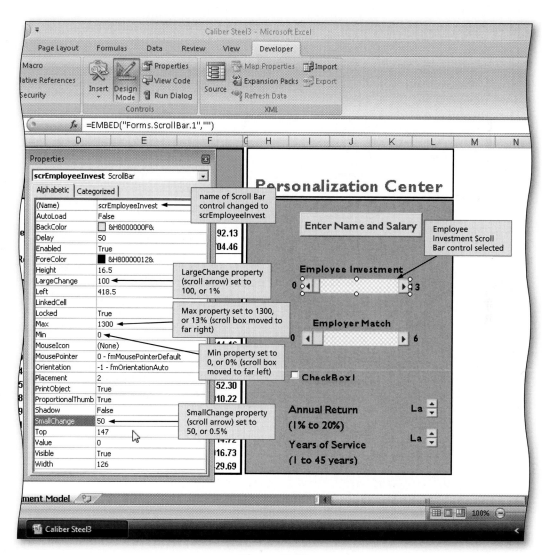

Figure 7–68

To Set the Employer Match Scroll Bar Control Properties

The next step sets the properties of the Employer Match Scroll Bar control. The property settings are similar to those assigned to the Employee Investment Scroll Bar control. After the VBA code is written, the Employer Match Scroll Bar control will assign a value to cell D8.

- With Excel in Design mode, click the Employer Match Scroll Bar control.

- Click (Name) in the Properties window and then type scrEmployerMatch as the name.

- Change the LargeChange property to 100, the Max property to 600, the Min property to 0, and the SmallChange property to 25 (Figure 7–69).

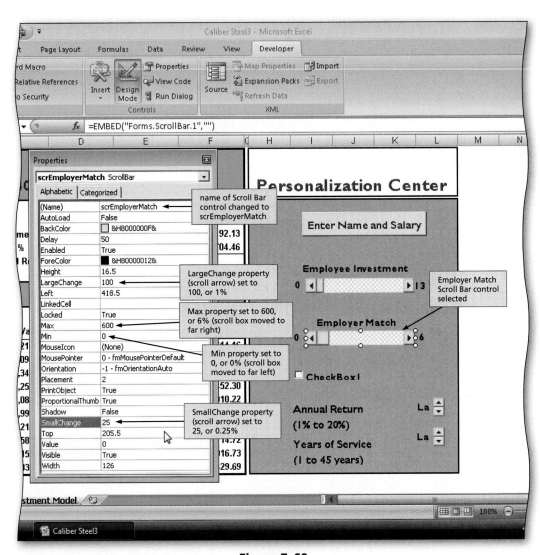

Figure 7–69

To Set the Check Box Control Properties

The Employer Match Check Box control enables or disables the Employer Match Scroll Bar control. In Run mode, if the Employer Match check box contains a check mark, then the Employer Match scroll bar is enabled and can be used to change the value in cell D8. If the check box is empty, then the Employer Match scroll bar is disabled. The VBA code will enable or disable the Employer Match scroll bar based on the check box status. The following step sets the properties of the Check Box control.

- With Excel in Design mode, click the Check Box control.

- Click (Name) in the Properties window and then type `chkEmployerMatch` as the name.

- Click Alignment in the Properties window and then click 0 - fmAlignmentLeft.

- Click Caption in the Properties window and then type `Include Employer Match?` as the caption.

- Click SpecialEffect, click the box arrow in the Properties window, and then click 0 - fmButtonEffectFlat.

- Click Value in the Properties window and then type `True` as the value.

- Resize the Check Box control so the entire caption shows (Figure 7–70).

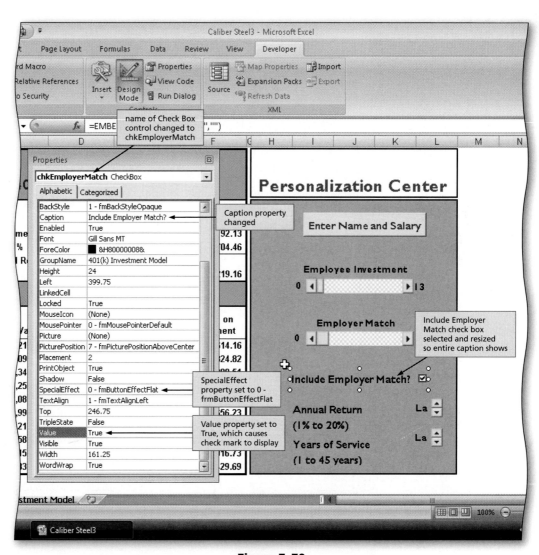

Figure 7–70

Q&A

What is the result of setting the Value property to True?

Setting the Value property to True inserts a check mark in the Include Employer Match check box. The check box thus will contain a check mark by default.

To Set Properties for the Annual Return and Years of Service Spin Button Controls

The Annual Return Spin Button control increments or decrements the value in cell D9 by 0.25%. The Years of Service Spin Button control increments or decrements the value in cell D10 by one. With a Spin Button control, the up arrow increases the value and the down arrow decreases the value. The Label controls to the left of the Spin Button controls (Figure 7–71) indicate the values to be assigned to the associated cells. The Min, Max, and SmallChange properties must be set. The SmallChange property indicates the change each time you click an arrow.

The following steps set the properties for the Annual Return and Years of Service Spin Button controls.

1

- With Excel in Design mode, click the Annual Return Spin Button control.

- Click (Name) in the Properties window and then type spnAnnualReturn as the name.

- If necessary, change the Max property to 2500, the Min property to 0, and the SmallChange property to 25 (Figure 7–71).

Q&A

How will the Annual Return spin button work?

The least value the Annual Return spin button can be set to is 0 (0%). The greatest value is 2500 (25%). After the VBA code is written, each time you click a button, the Expected Annual Return value in cell D9 will change by 0.25%. At this point in this phase of the chapter, no rela-

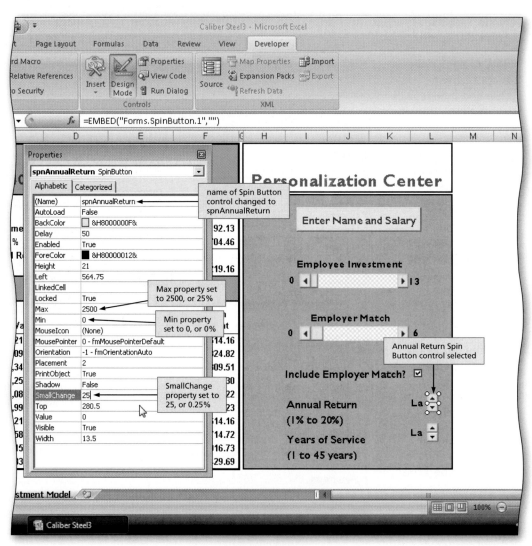

Figure 7–71

tionship exists between the Annual Return spin button and the Expected Annual Return value in cell D9. This relationship will be established later in the VBA code. A similar relationship will be established between the Years of Service spin button and the Years of Service value in cell D10.

2

- Click the Years of Service Spin Button control.

- Click (Name) in the Properties window and then type `spnYearsofService` as the name.

- Change the Max property to 45, the Min property to 1, and the SmallChange property to 1 (Figure 7–72).

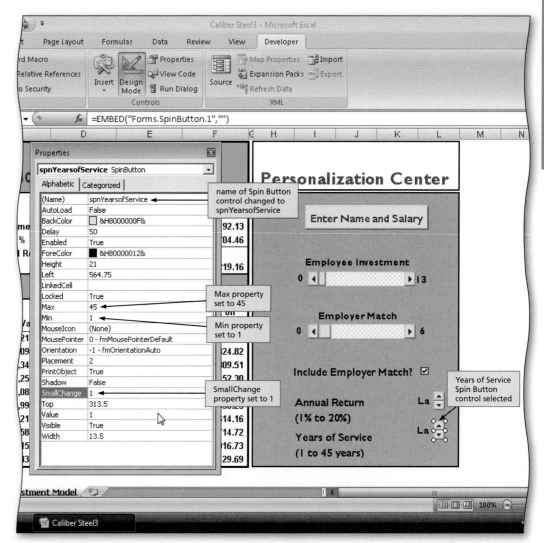

Figure 7–72

To Set the Variable Label Control Properties

The Label controls to the left of the two Spin Button controls (Figure 7–48 on page EX 567) are variable and will change to display the values of their respective Spin Button controls. Thus, when you select a value by clicking the Annual Return spin button, the new value will appear in the Label control next to the Annual Return spin button as well as in cell D9. The following steps set the Name property, Caption property, and TextAlign property for the two variable Label controls to the left of the Spin Button controls.

- With Excel in Design mode, click the Label control to the left of the Annual Return Spin Button control.

- Click (Name) in the Properties window and then type `lblAnnualReturn` as the name.

- Click Caption in the Properties window and then type 5% as the caption.

- Change the BorderStyle property to 1 - fmBorderStyleSingle.

- Change the BackColor property to white.

- Change the TextAlign property to 3 - fmTextAlignRight.

- Resize the Label control as shown in Figure 7–73.

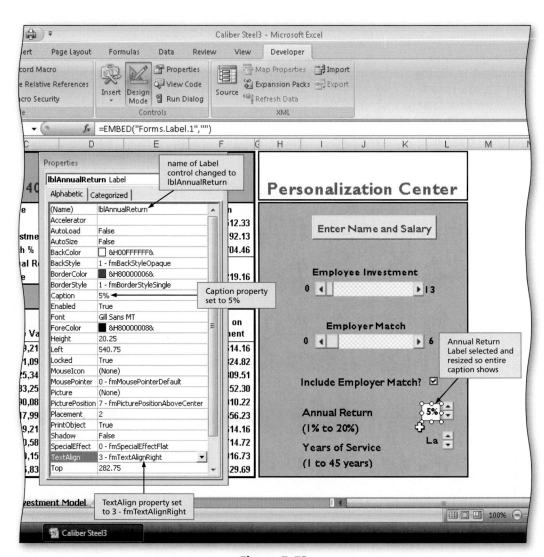

Figure 7–73

2

- Click the Label control to the left of the Years of Service Spin Button control.

- Click (Name) in the Properties window and then type `lblYearsofService` as the name.

- Click Caption in the Properties window and then type 10 as the caption.

- Change the BorderStyle property to 1 - fmBorderStyleSingle.

- Change the BackColor property to white.

- Change the TextAlign property to 3 - fmTextAlignRight.

- Resize the Label control as shown in Figure 7–74.

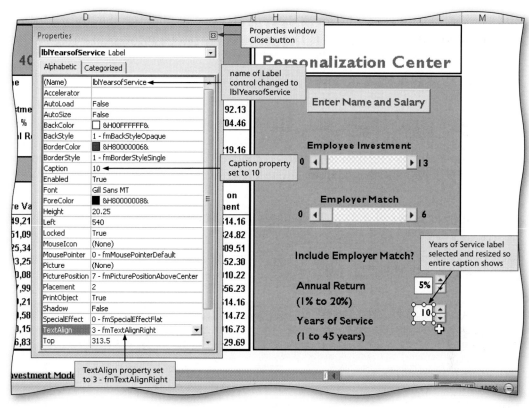

Figure 7–74

3

- Click the Close button on the right side of the Properties window title bar (Figure 7–75).

How will these Label controls be used?

Later, in the VBA code, the Label controls will be set equal to the corresponding Spin Button controls through the use of the names. For example, the VBA statement lblAnnualReturn = spnAnnualReturn.Value

/ 10000 & "%" assigns the value of the Annual Return Spin Button control divided by 10000 to its corresponding Label control. The & "%" appends a percent sign to the number that appears in the Label control.

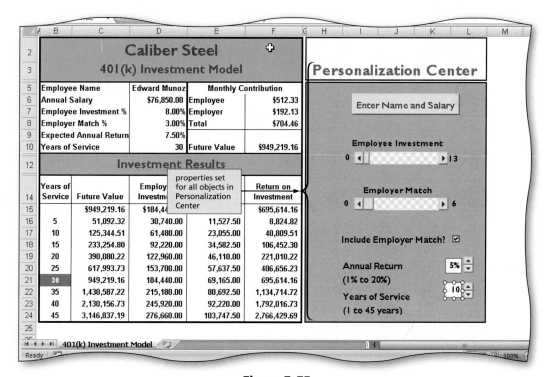

Figure 7–75

To Resize and Reposition the Controls in the Personalization Center

After setting the properties for all the controls, you can fine-tune the size and location of the controls in the Personalization Center. With Excel in Design mode, you have three ways to reposition a control:

1. Drag the control to its new location.

2. Select the control and use the arrow keys to reposition it.

3. Select the control and set the control's Top and Left properties in the Properties window.

To use the third technique, you need to know the distance the control is from the top of row 1 (column headings) and the far left of column A (row headings) in points. Recall that a point is equal to 1/72 of an inch. Thus, if the Top property of a control is 216, then the control is 3 inches (216/72) from the top of the window.

With Excel in Design mode, you also can resize a control in two ways:

1. Drag the sizing handles.

2. Select the control and set the control's Height and Width properties in the Properties window.

As with the Top and Left properties, the Height and Width properties are measured in points. Table 7–4 lists the exact point values for the Top, Left, Height, and Width properties of each of the controls in the Personalization Center.

The following steps resize and reposition the controls in the Personalization Center using the values in Table 7–4.

Table 7–4 Exact Locations of Controls in Personalization Center				
Control	**Top**	**Left**	**Height**	**Width**
Enter Name and Salary Command Button	71.25	402.75	27.75	144
Personalization Center Label	30	358.5	23.25	229.5
Employee Investment Label	128.25	401.25	14.25	136.5
Employee Investment Scroll Bar	147	387	16.5	162
Employee Investment 0 Label	147	372	16.5	15
Employee Investment 13 Label	147	552.75	16.5	15
Employer Match Label	186.75	401.25	14.25	136.5
Employer Match Scroll Bar	205.5	387	16.5	162
Employer Match 0 Label	205.5	372	16.5	15
Employer Match 6 Label	205.5	552.75	16.5	15
Employer Match Check Box	246.75	372	24	173.25
Annual Return Label	284.25	372	36.75	88.5
Annual Return Spin Button	284.25	536.25	20.25	13.5
Annual Return value Label	284.25	508.5	20.25	28.5
Years of Service Label	326.25	372	35.25	101.25
Years of Service Spin Button	326.25	536.25	20.25	13.5
Years of Service value Label	326.25	508.5	20.25	28.5

- Click the Properties button on the Ribbon.

- If necessary, drag the Properties window to the left side of the Excel window.

- Click the Enter Name and Salary Command Button control.

- Change its Top, Left, Height, and Width properties to those listed in Table 7–4 to display the Enter Name and Salary Command Button as shown in Figure 7–76.

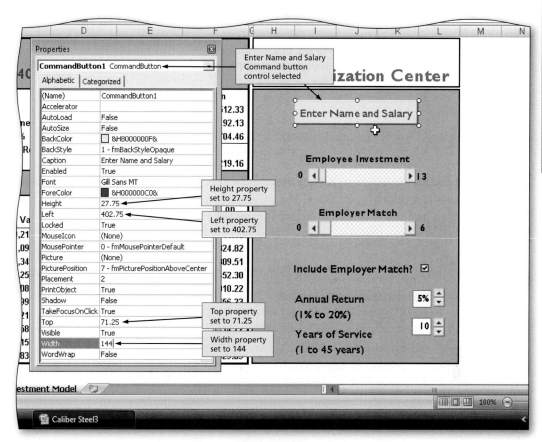

Figure 7–76

- One at a time, select the controls in the Personalization Center and change their Top, Left, Height, and Width properties to those listed in Table 7–4.

- Close the Properties window and then deselect the Years of Service (1 to 45 years) label by clicking cell A1 (Figure 7–77).

3

- Click the Save button on the Quick Access Toolbar to save the workbook using the file name, Caliber Steel3.

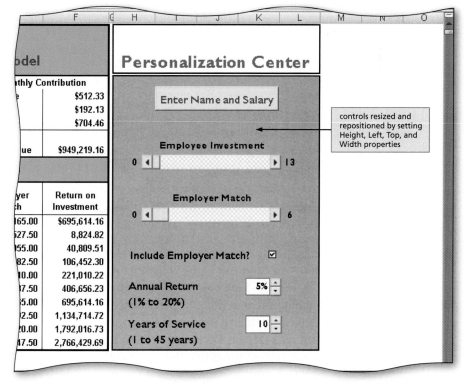

Figure 7–77

> **Step 3 — Write the code.**
> The next step is to write a procedure for each of the following six controls: (1) Enter Name and Salary Command Button; (2) Employee Investment Scroll Bar; (3) Include Employer Match Check Box; (4) Employer Match Scroll Bar; (5) Annual Return Spin Button; and (6) Years of Service Spin Button. The design decisions and explanation for each procedure will be explained before the code is entered.

To Enter the Enter Name and Salary Button Procedure

In Run mode, the function of the Enter Name and Salary button is to accept the employee name and annual salary. It also assigns values to the Scroll Bar controls and Spin Button controls, which in turn resets the values in the range D7:D10. The Enter Name and Salary Button procedure is shown in Table 7–5.

Table 7–5 Enter Name and Salary Button Procedure

Line	Statement
1	' Name and Salary Button Procedure Author: Louise Kizior
2	' Date Created: 10/21/2008
3	' Run from: 401(k) Investment Model Sheet by clicking button
4	' labeled Enter Name and Salary
5	' Function: This procedure initializes the scroll bars and spin buttons,
6	' clears the range D5:D6, selects cell A1, accepts the Employee
7	' name (cell D5) and annual salary (cell D6), and validates the
8	' annual salary before assigning it to cell D6, named Annual_Salary.
9	'
10	Private Sub CommandButton1_Click()
11	scrEmployeeInvest = 100
12	scrEmployerMatch = 0
13	spnAnnualReturn = 500
14	spnYearsofService = 10
15	Range("D5:D6").ClearContents
16	Range("A1").Select
17	Range("Employee_Name").Value = InputBox("Employee Name?", "Enter")
18	AnnualSalary = InputBox("Annual Salary?", "Enter")
19	Do While AnnualSalary <= 0
20	AnnualSalary = InputBox("Annual salary must be > zero.", "Please Re-enter")
21	Loop
22	Range("Annual_Salary").Value = AnnualSalary
23	End Sub

Lines 1 through 9 in Table 7–5 are comments and have no bearing on the execution of this procedure. Comments help you remember the function of a procedure. Lines 10 and 23 identify the beginning and end of the procedure. Lines 11 through 14 initialize the Scroll Bar controls and Spin Button controls by assigning values to their names. Line 15 clears cells D5 and D6 in preparation to receive the employee name and annual salary. Line 16 selects cell A1 so the heavy border surrounding the active cell does not clutter the screen.

Line 17 accepts the employee name and assigns it to cell D5, which is named Employee_Name. Lines 18 through 22 accept and validate the annual salary to ensure it is greater than zero. The annual salary is accepted in line 18. Line 19 is called a **Do-While statement**. It tests to see if the annual salary accepted in line 18 is less than or equal to zero. If the annual salary is less than or equal to zero, line 20 displays an error message and requests that the user re-enter the annual salary. The **Loop statement** in line 21 transfers control back to the corresponding Do-While statement in line 19, which tests the annual salary again. The VBA code in lines 19 through 21 is called a **loop**.

If the variable, Annual Salary, is determined to be greater than zero in line 19, then the Do-While statement in line 19 transfers control to line 22, which assigns the value of AnnualSalary to cell D6, which is named Annual_Salary. Line 23 halts execution of the procedure and returns Excel to Ready mode.

The variable, AnnualSalary, first was used in line 18. A **variable** is a location in the computer's memory whose value can change as the program executes. You create variables in VBA code as you need them. In this case, a variable is needed to hold the value accepted from the user in lines 18 and 20. Variable names follow the same rules as control names (see page EX 574).

The following steps enter the Enter Name and Salary Button procedure shown in Table 7–5.

1

- With Excel in Design mode, click the View Code button on the Ribbon (Figure 7–36 on page EX 559).

- Click the Object box arrow at the top of the window and then click CommandButton1 in the alphabetical list (Figure 7–78).

What does the Visual Basic Editor display when the CommandButton1 control is selected?

When the CommandButton1 control is selected in the Object list, the Visual Basic Editor displays the Sub and End Sub statements for the procedure and positions the insertion point between the two statements.

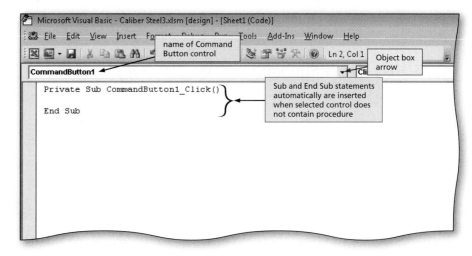

Figure 7–78

2

- Click before the P in Private and then press the ENTER key. Enter the lines 1 through 9 in Table 7–5. Click the blank line between the Sub and End Sub statements. Enter lines 11 through 22 in Table 7–5 (Figure 7–79) being sure to indent each line of code by three spaces for readability.

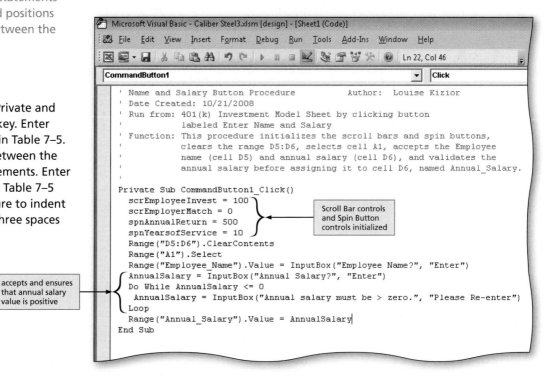

Figure 7–79

To Enter the Employee Investment Scroll Bar Procedure

The Employee Investment Scroll Bar procedure assigns the value of the scroll bar to cell D7, which is named Employee_Investment. The procedure is shown in Table 7–6.

Line	Statement
	Table 7–6 Employee Investment Scroll Bar Procedure
1	' Employee Investment Scroll Bar Procedure Author: Louise Kizior
2	' Date Created: 10/21/2008
3	' Run from: 401(k) Investment Model Sheet by clicking the
4	' scroll bar labeled Employee Investment
5	' Function: This procedure assigns the value of the Employee Investment scroll
6	' bar to cell D7, named Employee_Investment.
7	'
8	Private Sub scrEmployeeInvest_Change()
9	Range("Employee_Investment").Value = scrEmployeeInvest.Value / 10000
10	End Sub

The first seven lines in Table 7–6 are comments. Lines 8 and 10 define the beginning and end of the procedure. Line 9 assigns the value of the Scroll Bar control (scrEmployeeInvest) divided by 10000 to cell D7, which is named Employee_Investment. Recall that the scroll bar was assigned a Max property of 1300, which is equivalent to 130,000%. Thus, the value of scrEmployeeInvest must be divided by 10000 to assign the correct percentage value to cell D7, named Employee_Investment. The following steps enter the Employee Investment Scroll Bar procedure shown in Table 7–6.

1
- With the Visual Basic Editor active, click the Object box arrow at the top of the window and then click scrEmployeeInvest.

2
- Enter the VBA code shown in Table 7–6 (Figure 7–80).

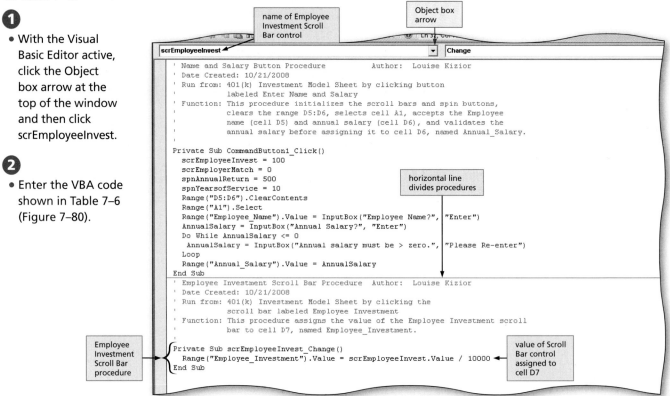

Figure 7–80

To Enter the Employer Match Check Box Procedure

As with the other procedures, the Employer Match Check Box procedure executes only when the check box is checked. If the check box is checked, then the Value property of the check box (chkEmployerMatch) is set to True. If the check box is unchecked, then the Value property of the check box is set to False. Adding a check mark or removing a check mark triggers the event that executes the Employer Match Check Box procedure shown in Table 7–7.

Line	Statement
Table 7–7 Employer Match Check Box Procedure	
1	' Employer Match Check Box Procedure Author: Louise Kizior
2	' Date Created: 10/21/2008
3	' Run from: 401(k) Investment Model Sheet by clicking check box
4	' labeled Employer Match
5	' Function: This procedure assigns the value of the Employer Match scroll bar
6	' or 0 (zero) to cell D8, which is named Employer_Match.
7	'
8	Private Sub chkEmployerMatch_Click()
9	If chkEmployerMatch.Value = True Then
10	Range("Employer_Match").Value = scrEmployerMatch.Value / 10000
11	Else
12	scrEmployerMatch = 0
13	Range("Employer_Match").Value = 0
14	End If
15	End Sub

In Table 7–7, lines 1 through 7 are comments. Lines 8 and 15 define the beginning and end of the procedure. Lines 9 through 14 include an If-Then-Else statement. An **If-Then-Else statement** represents a two-way decision with action specified for each of the two alternatives. The computer never executes both the true and false alternatives; it selects one or the other.

If the logical test (chkEmployerMatch = True) is true in line 9 of Table 7–7, then line 10 is executed and cell D8, named Employer_Match, is set equal to scrEmployerMatch divided by 10000 — that is, the value selected on the Employer Match scroll bar divided by 10000. If the logical test is false, then lines 12 and 13 are executed. Line 12 sets the scroll box to zero percent (0%), and line 13 sets cell D8, named Employer_Match, equal to zero percent (0%). The following steps enter the code for the Employer Match Check Box procedure.

- With the Visual Basic Editor active, click the Object box arrow at the top of the window and then click chkEmployerMatch.

- Enter the VBA code shown in Table 7–7 (Figure 7–81).

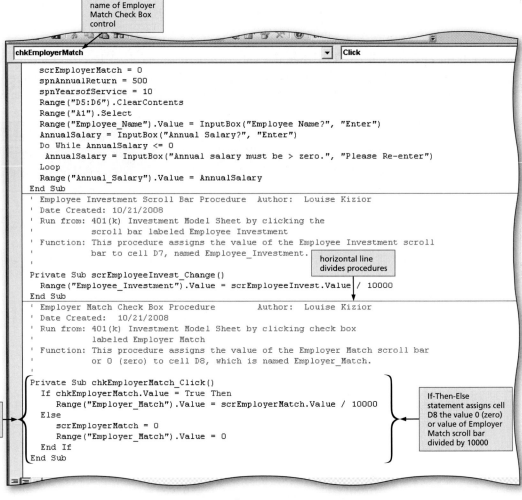

Figure 7–81

To Enter the Employer Match Scroll Bar Procedure

The Employer Match Scroll Bar procedure executes whenever you use the Scroll Bar control above the Employer Match Check Box control. The Employer Match Scroll Bar control is active only when the Employer Match Check Box control is checked. The Employer Match Scroll Bar procedure assigns the value of scrEmployerMatch to cell D8, named Employer_Match. The Employer Match Scroll Bar procedure is shown in Table 7–8.

Line	Statement
	Table 7–8 Employer Match Scroll Bar Procedure
1	' Employer Match Scroll Bar Procedure Author: Louise Kizior
2	' Date Created: 10/21/2008
3	' Run from: 401(k) Investment Model Sheet by clicking the
4	'scroll bar labeled Employer Match
5	' Function: This procedure assigns the value of the Employer Match scroll bar
6	' to cell D8, named Employer_Match.
7	'
8	Private Sub scrEmployerMatch_Change()
9	If chkEmployerMatch.Value = True Then

Table 7–8 Employer Match Scroll Bar Procedure *(continued)*	
Line	**Statement**
10	Range("Employer_Match").Value = scrEmployerMatch.Value / 10000
11	End If
12	End Sub

Lines 9 through 11 in Table 7–8 are an If-Then statement. Line 10 in the If-Then statement assigns the value of the scroll bar (scrEmployerMatch) divided by 10,000 to cell D8, which is named Employer_Match. This statement, however, is executed only if the logical test in line 9 (chkEmployerMatch =True) is true. Thus, the Employer Match Check Box control determines whether the Employer Match Scroll Bar control is active. The following steps enter the code.

• With the Visual Basic Editor active, click the Object box arrow at the top of the window and then click scrEmployerMatch.

• Enter the VBA code shown in Table 7–8 (Figure 7–82).

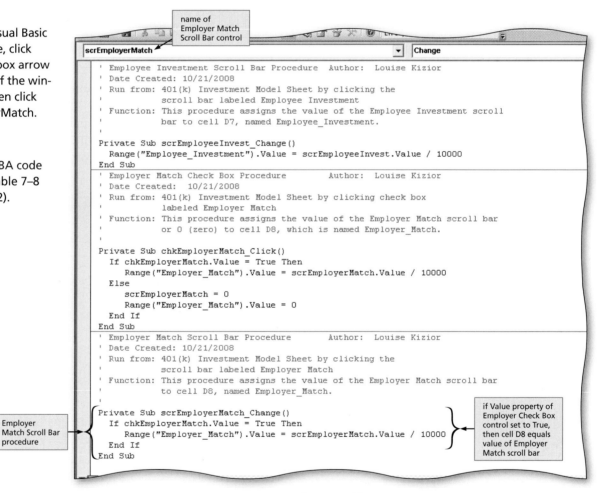

Figure 7–82

To Enter the Annual Return Spin Button Procedure

The Annual Return Spin Button procedure executes whenever you click one of the buttons on the Annual Return Spin Button control. The procedure determines the percent value assigned to cell D9, named Annual_Return, and to the corresponding Annual Return Label control. Recall that you set the SmallChange property of the Annual Return Spin Button control to 25, which, when divided by 10000, equals 0.25%. The Annual Return Spin Button Control procedure is shown in Table 7–9.

Line	Statement
	Table 7–9 Annual Return Spin Button Procedure
1	' Annual Return Spin Button Procedure Author: Louise Kizior
2	' Date Created: 10/21/2008
3	' Run from: 401(k) Investment Model Sheet by clicking the spin
4	' button labeled Annual Return
5	' Function: This procedure assigns the value of the Annual Return spin button
6	' to cell D9, named Annual_Return.
7	'
8	Private Sub spnAnnualReturn_Change()
9	lblAnnualReturn = spnAnnualReturn.Value / 100 & "%"
10	Range("Annual_Return").Value = spnAnnualReturn.Value / 10000
11	End Sub

In Table 7–9, line 9 uses the names of the two controls to assign the value of the Annual Return Spin Button control to the Annual Return Label control. In this case, spnAnnualReturn is divided by 100, because a percent should appear as a whole number in the Label control. The & "%" at the end of line 9 appends a percent sign to the value. Line 10 assigns the value of spnAnnualReturn divided by 10,000 to cell D9, which has a cell name of Annual_Return. The following steps enter the code for the Annual Return Spin Button procedure.

- With the Visual Basic Editor active, click the Object box arrow at the top of the window and then click spnAnnualReturn.

- Enter the VBA code shown in Table 7–9 (Figure 7–83).

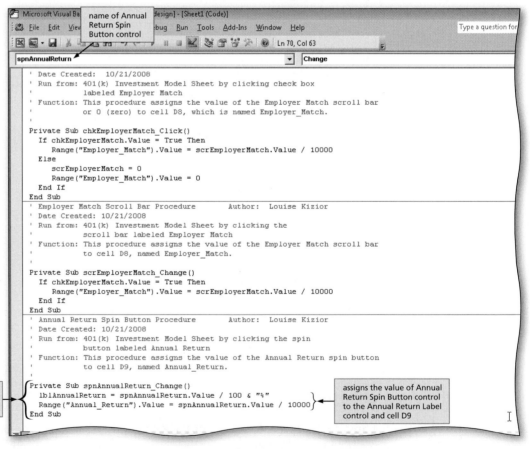

Figure 7–83

To Enter the Years of Service Spin Button Procedure

The Years of Service Spin Button procedure executes whenever you click one of the buttons on the Years of Service Spin Button control. The procedure determines the value assigned to cell D10, named Years_of_Service, and to the corresponding Years of Service Label control. The Years of Service Spin Button procedure is shown in Table 7–10.

Table 7–10 Years of Service Spin Button Procedure	
Line	**Statement**
1	' Years of Service Spin Button Procedure Author: Louise Kizior
2	' Date Created: 10/21/2008
3	' Run from: 401(k) Investment Model Sheet by clicking the spin
4	' button labeled Years of Service
5	' Function: This procedure assigns the value of the Years of Service spin
6	' button to cell D10, named Years_of_Service.
7	'
8	Private Sub spnYearsofService_Change()
9	lblYearsofService = spnYearsofService
10	Range("Years_of_Service").Value = spnYearsofService
11	End Sub

In Table 7–10, line 9 assigns spnYearsofService (the value of the Years of Service Spin Button control) to the corresponding Years of Service Label control. Line 10 assigns the value of spnYearsofService to cell D10, which has a cell name of Years_of_Service. The following steps enter the code for the Years of Service Spin Button procedure.

1

- With the Visual Basic Editor active, click the Object box arrow at the top of the window and then click spnYearsofService.

2

- Enter the VBA code shown in Table 7–10 (Figure 7–84).

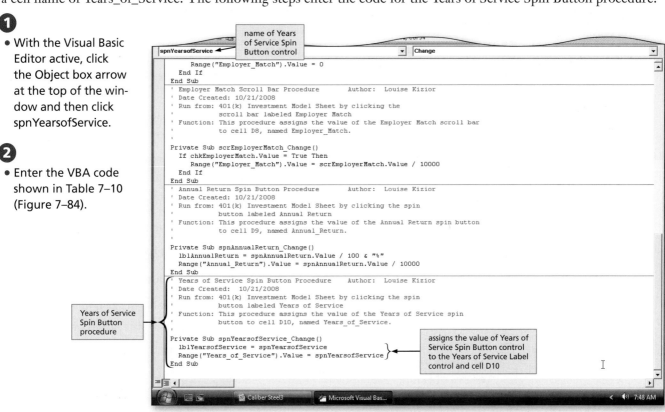

Figure 7–84

BTW

The Visual Basic Editor
When you open the Visual Basic Editor, the same windows display that displayed when you closed it the last time.

To Close the Visual Basic Editor, Protect the Worksheet, and Save the Workbook

The VBA code is complete. The following steps close the Visual Basic Editor, quit Design mode, protect the worksheet, and save the workbook. Before closing the Visual Basic Editor, you should verify your code by comparing it with Figures 7–78 through 7–84 on pages EX 593 through EX 599.

1 Click the Close button on the right side of the Visual Basic Editor title bar.

2 When the Excel window is visible, click the Design Mode button on the Ribbon to exit Design mode.

3 Click the Review tab on the Ribbon and then click the Protect Sheet button on the Ribbon. When Excel displays the Protect Sheet dialog box, type caliber in the 'Password to unprotect sheet' text box. Verify the password when prompted and then click the OK button.

4 Click the Save button on the Quick Access Toolbar to save the workbook using the file name, Caliber Steel3.

BTW

Debugging VBA Code
The Visual Basic Editor allows you to locate the source of errors in your code through the use of the Debug menu. You can set a breakpoint in your code that will cause Excel to stop executing your code at a certain point. At that time, Excel shows the current executing code in the editor. You can point at variables in your code to make sure they are set correctly. Or you can step through your code line by line to make sure the code is getting executed in the expected order. Click Microsoft Visual Basic Help on the Help menu in the Visual Basic Editor window for more information about debugging.

To Test the Controls in the Personalization Center

The final step is to test the controls in the Personalization Center. To test the controls, use the following data: Employee Name — Gina Moira (cell D5); Annual Salary (cell D6) — $54,500.00; Employee Investment % (cell D7) — 6.00%; Employer Match % (cell D8) — 4.00%; Expected Annual Return (cell D9) — 8.5%; and Years of Service (cell D10) — 35.

1 Click the Enter Name and Salary button in the Personalization Center.

2 When Excel displays the Enter dialog box with the prompt message, Employee Name?, type Gina Moira as the employee name.

3 When Excel displays the Enter dialog box with the prompt message, Annual Salary?, type the negative number –54500 as the annual salary.

4 When Excel displays the Enter dialog box with the prompt message, Annual salary must be > zero, type 54500 as the annual salary.

5 Use the Employee Investment scroll bar to change the value in cell D7 to 6%.

6 Click the Include Employer Match check box if it does not have a check mark.

7 Use the Employer Match scroll bar to change the value in cell D8 to 4%.

8 Click the Annual Return spin button arrows to change the value in cell D9 to 8.5%.

9 Click the Years of Service spin button arrows to change the value in cell D10 to 35.

Q&A What is the result of interacting with the user interface to enter the 401(k) investment model data?

The future value of Gina Moira's 401(k) Plan investment is $1,178,819.67 as shown in cell F10 of Figure 7–85. If she changes her years of service to 45 years, the 401(k) Plan investment is worth $2,589,966.51 (cell C24). Both future value amounts assume she will never get a raise.

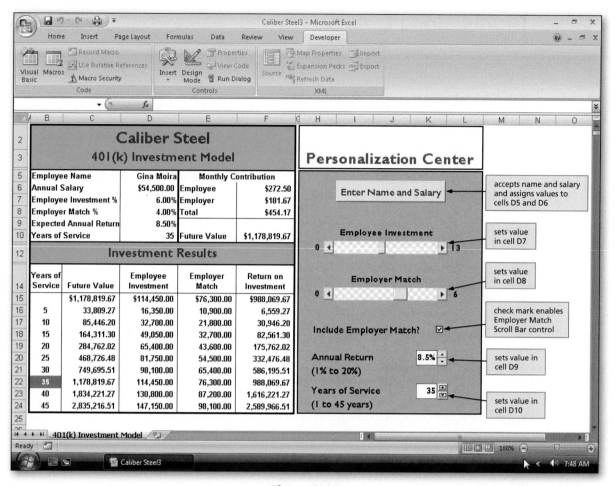

Figure 7–85

To Reset the Quick Access Toolbar and Ribbon and Quit Excel

The following steps reset the Quick Access Toolbar in order to remove the PrintPortrait button, remove the Developer tab from the Ribbon, and quit Excel.

1 Right-click anywhere on the Quick Access Toolbar and then click Customize Quick Access Toolbar on the shortcut menu.

2 When the Excel Options dialog box appears, click the Reset button and then click the OK button in the Reset Customizations dialog box. Click the OK button to close the Excel Options dialog box.

3 Click the Office Button and then click the Excel Options button on the Office Button menu.

4 Click the 'Show Developer tab in the Ribbon' check box to remove the check mark and then click the OK button to close the Excel Options dialog box.

5 Click the Close button on the right side of the title bar.

6 If the Microsoft Office Excel dialog box appears, click the No button.

Digital Signatures

BTW

Quick Reference
For a table that lists how to complete the tasks covered in this book using the mouse, Ribbon, shortcut menu, and keyboard, see the Quick Reference Summary at the back of this book, or visit the Excel 2007 Quick Reference Web page (scsite.com/ex2007/qr).

Some users prefer to attach a digital signature to verify the authenticity of a document. A **digital signature** is an electronic, encrypted, and secure stamp of authentication on a document. This signature confirms that the file originated from the signer (file developer) and that it has not been altered.

A digital signature may be visible or invisible. In either case, the digital signature references a digital certificate. A **digital certificate** is an attachment to a file or e-mail message that vouches for its authenticity, provides secure encryption, or supplies a verifiable signature. Many users who receive files enable the macros based on whether they are digitally signed by a developer on the user's list of trusted sources.

You can obtain a digital certificate from a commercial **certificate authority**, from your network administrator, or you can create a digital signature yourself. A digital certificate you create yourself is not issued by a formal certification authority. Thus, signed macros using such a certificate are referred to as **self-signed projects**. Certificates you create yourself are considered unauthenticated and still will generate a warning when opened if the security level is set to very high, high, or medium. Many users, however, consider self-signed projects safer to open than those with no certificates at all.

To Add a Digital Signature to a Workbook

After adding a digital signature, Excel will display the digital signature whenever the document is opened. The following steps add a visible digital signature to an Excel workbook.

1 Click the Insert tab on the Ribbon and then click the Signature Line button on the Ribbon. If the Microsoft Office Excel dialog box appears, click the OK button.

2 When the Signature Setup dialog box appears, type your name in the Suggested signer text box and then click the OK button.

3 When Excel adds the signature box to the workbook, right-click anywhere in the signature box and then click Sign on the shortcut menu.

4 When the Sign dialog box appears, type your name in the signature box or click the Select Image link to select a file that contains an image of your signature.

5 Click the OK button to digitally sign the document.

Q&A

How can I obtain a digital certificate?

If you do not have any digital certificates on your computer when you click the Sign command in Step 3, you will be prompted in the Microsoft Office Excel dialog box to obtain or create a new digital certificate (Figure 7–86). You can choose to create a certificate online with a service provider recommended by Microsoft by clicking the Signature Services from the Office Marketplace button. By doing so, other users can authenticate the signature on your workbooks because the certificate is available online. This alternative, however, may require payment. You also can click the Create your own Digital ID button to create a digital certificate that is valid only on your computer, but is free of charge.

BTW

Excel Help
The best way to become familiar with Excel Help is to use it. Appendix C includes detailed information about Excel Help and exercises that will help you gain confidence in using it.

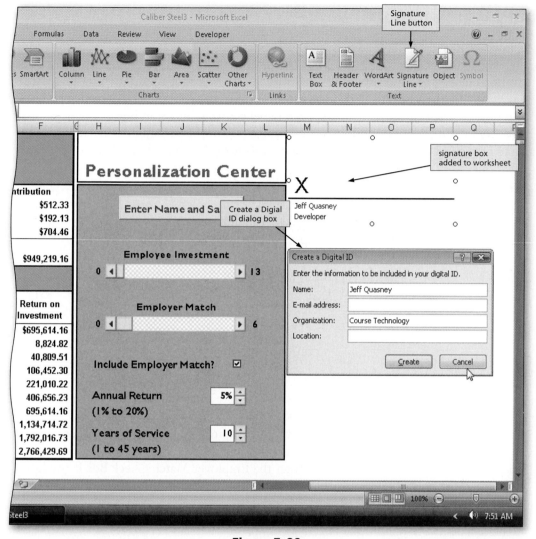

Figure 7–86

To Review a Digital Signature on a Workbook

A **file digital signature** is a digital signature that is displayed when you e-mail a document from Excel. Excel will display the digital signature whenever the document is opened. When you open a digitally signed document, Excel displays a message announcing the signature on the status bar while the file opens. After the file is opened, Excel displays a certification icon on the status bar. You can click the icon to find out who digitally signed the document. The word, (Signed), also appears on the title bar in parentheses, indicating the document is signed digitally. The following steps show how to review a digital signature on a workbook.

1. Click the Office Button and then click Prepare on the Office Button menu.

2. Click View Signature on the Prepare submenu.

3. Select a name from the Valid signature list in the signature pane and then click the button arrow next to the name. When the shortcut menu appears, click Signature Details.

4. When you are finished reviewing the certificate, click the OK button in the Signature Details dialog box.

BTW

Certification
The Microsoft Certified Application Specialist (MCAS) program provides an opportunity for you to obtain a valuable industry credential – proof that you have the Excel 2007 skills required by employers. For more information, see Appendix G or visit the Excel 2007 Certification Web page (scsite.com/ ex2007/cert).

Chapter Summary

In this chapter, you learned how to unprotect and protect a worksheet and workbook using a password. In Phase 1, you learned how to record a macro and assign it to a button on the Quick Access Toolbar. In Phase 2, you learned how to create a Command Button control, assign it properties, and write Visual Basic for Applications (VBA) code that executes when you click the button. In Phase 3, you learned how to create a user interface made up of a Command Button control, Scroll Bar controls, a Check Box control, Label controls, and Spin Button controls, set properties for those controls using the Properties window, write VBA code that included looping and decision-making, and add and review a digital signature on a workbook. The items listed below include all the new Excel skills you have learned in this chapter.

1. Enter Data in a Selected Range of Cells (536)
2. Undo a Group of Entries Using the Undo Button (EX 538)
3. Unprotect a Password-Protected Worksheet (EX 538)
4. Display the Developer Tab, Enable Macros, and Save a Workbook as a Macro-Enabled Workbook (EX 540)
5. Record a Macro to Print the Worksheet in Portrait Orientation Using the Fit to Option (EX 542)
6. Password-Protect the Worksheet, Save the Workbook, and Close the Workbook (EX 544)
7. Set Macro Security to Medium (EX 545)
8. Open a Workbook with a Macro and Execute the Macro (EX 546)
9. View and Print a Macro's VBA Code (EX 548)
10. Add a Button to the Quick Access Toolbar, Assign the Button a Macro, and Use the Button (EX 549)
11. Add a Command Button Control to the Worksheet (EX 554)
12. Set the Command Button Control Properties (EX 556)
13. Enter the New Data Button Procedure Using the Visual Basic Editor (EX 559)
14. Enter 401(k) Investment Model Data Using the New Data Button (EX 563)
15. Protect a Worksheet and Save the Workbook (EX 566)
16. Add Controls to a User Interface (EX 569)
17. Set Properties of the Label Controls and Check Box Control (EX 575)

18. Set the Command Button Control Properties (EX 582)
19. Set the Employee Investment Scroll Bar Control Properties (EX 583)
20. Set the Employer Match Scroll Bar Control Properties (EX 584)
21. Set the Check Box Control Properties (EX 585)
22. Set Properties for the Annual Return and Years of Service Spin Button Controls (EX 586)
23. Set the Variable Label Control Properties (EX 588)
24. Resize and Reposition the Controls in the Personalization Center (EX 590)
25. Enter the Enter Name and Salary Button Procedure (EX 592)
26. Enter the Employee Investment Scroll Bar Procedure (EX 594)
27. Enter the Employer Match Check Box Procedure (EX 595)
28. Enter the Employer Match Scroll Bar Procedure (EX 596)
29. Enter the Annual Return Spin Button Procedure (EX 597)
30. Enter the Years of Service Spin Button Procedure (EX 599)
31. Close the Visual Basic Editor, Protect the Worksheet, and Save the Workbook (EX 600)
32. Test the Controls in the Personalization Center (EX 600)
33. Add a Digital Signature to a Workbook (EX 602)
34. Review a Digital Signature on a Workbook (EX 603)

 If you have a SAM user profile, you may have access to hands-on instruction, practice, and assessment. Log in to your SAM account (http://sam2007.course.com) to launch any assigned training activities or exams that relate to the skills covered in this chapter.

Learn It Online

Learn It Online is a series of online student exercises that test your knowledge of chapter content and key terms.

Instructions: To complete the Learn It Online exercises, start your browser, click the Address bar, and then enter the Web address scsite.com/ex2007/learn. When the Excel 2007 Learn It Online page is displayed, click the link for the exercise you want to complete and then read the instructions.

Chapter Reinforcement TF, MC, and SA
A series of true/false, multiple choice, and short answer questions that test your knowledge of the chapter content.

Flash Cards
An interactive learning environment where you identify chapter key terms associated with displayed definitions.

Practice Test
A series of multiple choice questions that test your knowledge of chapter content and key terms.

Who Wants To Be a Computer Genius?
An interactive game that challenges your knowledge of chapter content in the style of a television quiz show.

Wheel of Terms
An interactive game that challenges your knowledge of chapter key terms in the style of the television show *Wheel of Fortune*.

Crossword Puzzle Challenge
A crossword puzzle that challenges your knowledge of key terms presented in the chapter.

Apply Your Knowledge

Reinforce the skills and apply the concepts you learned in this chapter.

Creating a Macro and Assigning It to a Button
Instructions: Perform the steps below to enable macros, open a workbook, create a macro to print a section of the worksheet, assign the macro to a button on the Quick Access Toolbar, execute the macro, and then disable macros.

1. Start Excel. If the Developer tab does not display on the Ribbon, click the Office Button, click the Excel Options button, and then click the 'Show Developer tab in the Ribbon' check box.

2. To enable macros, click the Macro Security button on the Developer tab on the Ribbon. When the Trust Center dialog box is displayed, click the 'Enable all macros' option and then click the OK button.

Continued >

Apply Your Knowledge *continued*

3. Open the workbook Apply 7-1 Salioto's Food Mart (Figure 7–87) from the Data Files for Students and then save the workbook using the file name, Apply 7-1 Salioto's Food Mart Complete as an Excel Macro-Enabled Workbook file type. See the inside back cover of this book for instructions for downloading the Data Files for Students or see your instructor for information on accessing the files required in this book.

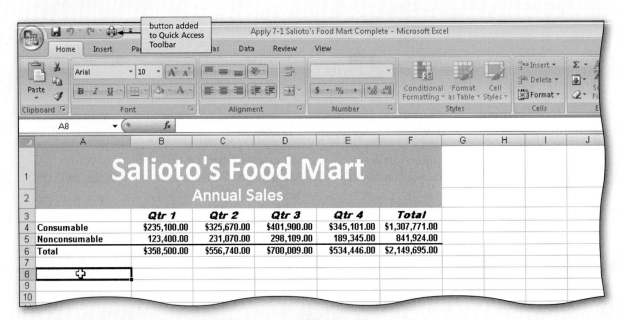

Figure 7–87

4. Unprotect the worksheet. Type `sheltered` as the password.

5. Change the document properties as specified by your instructor. Add a worksheet header with your name, course number, and other information requested by your instructor.

6. Create a macro that prints the range A3:F5 by doing the following:

   a. Click the Record Macro button on the Developer tab on the Ribbon.

   b. When the Record Macro dialog box appears, name the macro PrintRangeA3toF5, assign the shortcut key CTRL+N, store the macro in this workbook, enter your name in the Description box, and then click the OK button to start the macro recording process.

   c. Select the range A3:F5, click the Office Button, and then click Print. When the Print dialog box appears, click the Selection option in the Print what area, click the OK button, and then click the Stop Recording button on the Developer tab on the Ribbon.

7. Click the Macros button on the Developer tab on the Ribbon to display the Macro dialog box. Run the PrintRangeA3toF5 macro to print the range A3:F5. Click the Macros button again, select the PrintRangeA3toF5 macro, and then click the Edit button. When the Visual Basic Editor displays the macro, click File on the menu bar and then click Print.

8. Right-click the Quick Access Toolbar and then click Customize Quick Access Toolbar. When the Excel Options dialog box is displayed, click the 'Choose commands from' box arrow and choose Macros. Click PrintRangeA3toF5 and then click the Add button. Click the Modify button, choose the printer icon (column 5, row 2), click the OK button to close the Modify Button dialog box, and then click the OK button to close the Excel Options dialog box.

9. Run the macro as follows: (a) click the PrintRangeA3toF5 button on the Quick Access Toolbar; and (b) press CTRL+SHIFT+N.

10. To disable macros, click the Macro Security button on the Developer tab on the Ribbon. When the Trust Center dialog box is displayed, click 'Disable all macros with notification' and then click the OK button.

11. Protect the worksheet using the password, sheltered.

12. Right-click the Quick Access Toolbar and then click Customize Quick Access Toolbar. Remove the PrintRangeA3toF5 button and then click the OK button.

13. Save the workbook and then quit Excel.

14. Submit the assignment as specified by your instructor.

Extend Your Knowledge

Extend the skills you learned in this chapter and experiment with new skills. You may need to use Help to complete the assignment.

Creating and Using a Custom Function

Instructions: Use VBA to create and then use a custom function (Figure 7–88a) that determines the commission in column C (Figure 7–88b) to pay the salespersons based on the logic shown in Table 7–11.

Table 7–11 Commission Based Upon Sales	
Sales	Commission
Sales <= 50,000,000	0.01 * Sales
50,000,000 < Sales <= 100,000,000	0.02 * Sales
Sales > 100,000,000	0.03 * Sales

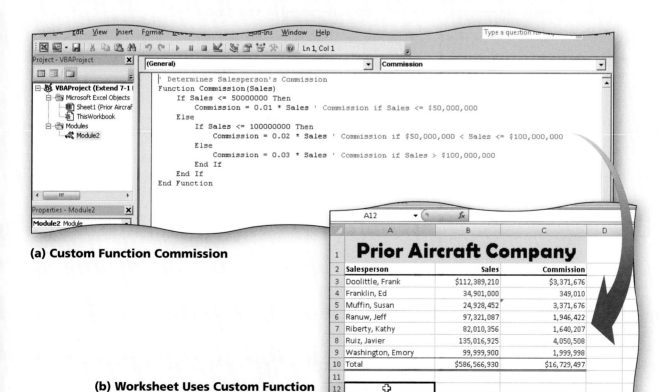

(a) Custom Function Commission

(b) Worksheet Uses Custom Function Commission in Column C

Figure 7–88

Continued >

Extend Your Knowledge *continued*

Perform the following tasks:

1. Start Excel. If the Developer tab does not display on the Ribbon, click the Office Button, click the Excel Options button, and then click the 'Show Developer tab in the Ribbon' check box.

2. To enable macros, click the Macro Security button on the Developer tab on the Ribbon. When the Trust Center dialog box is displayed, click 'Enable all macros' and then click the OK button.

3. Open the workbook Extend 7-1 Prior Aircraft Company from the Data Files for Students and then save the workbook using the file name, Extend 7-1 Prior Aircraft Company Complete as an Excel Macro-Enabled Workbook file type. See the inside back cover of this book for instructions for downloading the Data Files for Students or see your instructor for information on accessing the files required in this book.

4. Click the Developer tab on the Ribbon and then click the Visual Basic button. Click Module on the Insert menu. Enter the custom function Commission shown in Figure 7–88a. Carefully review the code to understand how this custom function reflects the logic in Table 7–11. Close the Visual Basic Editor.

5. Enter =Commission(B3) in cell C3 of the worksheet. The argument, cell B3 ($112,389,210), replaces the variable Sales in the custom function in Figure 7–88a and the custom function returns a value ($3,371,676) to cell C3.

6. Copy cell C3 to the range C4:C9 by copying cell C3 to the Clipboard, selecting the range C4:C9, and then using the Formulas command on the Paste menu to complete the copy (Figure 7–88b).

7. To disable macros, click the Macro Security button on the Developer tab on the Ribbon. When the Trust Center dialog box is displayed, click 'Disable all macros with notification' and then click the OK button.

8. Change the document properties as specified by your instructor. Add a worksheet header with your name, course number, and other information requested by your instructor.

9. Print both the worksheet and VBA custom function code. Print the formulas version of the worksheet.

10. Save the workbook and then quit Excel.

11. Submit the assignment as specified by your instructor.

Make It Right

Analyze a workbook and correct all errors and/or improve the design.

1 Changing Properties and Correcting Visual Basic Code

Instructions: Start Excel. If the Developer tab does not display on the Ribbon, click the Office Button, click the Excel Options button, and then click the 'Show Developer tab in the Ribbon' check box. To enable macros, click the Macro Security button on the Developer tab on the Ribbon. When the Trust Center dialog box is displayed, click 'Enable all macros' and then click the OK button.

Do the following:

1. Open the Make It Right 7-1 Loan Calculator workbook from the Data Files for Students and then save the workbook using the file name, Make It Right 7-1 Loan Calculator Complete as an Excel Macro-Enabled Workbook type file. See the inside back cover of this book for instructions for downloading the Data Files for Students or see your instructor for information on accessing the files required in this book. Click the Design Mode button on the Developer tab on the Ribbon.

2. Change the caption of the button to New Loan. Change the foreground color of the button to Green (Figure 7–89a) and move the button from column B to column C.

3. Click the View Code button on the Ribbon and make the following adjustments to the procedure shown in Figure 7–89b:

   a. Add comments before the first line of code. Include a procedure title, your name, date, and the purpose of the procedure.

   b. Select cell E12 while the data is entered.

   c. Change the variable Price (lines 5 through 9 and line 15 of Figure 7–89b) to LoanAmount and accept a loan amount between 1000 and 92000 inclusive. Also adjust the error message.

   d. Accept an interest rate between 2.5% and 13.5% inclusive.

   e. Select cell B13 before exiting the procedure.

4. Click the View Microsoft Excel button on the Standard toolbar to exit Microsoft Visual Basic and return to Excel.

5. Click the Design Mode button on the Developer tab on the Ribbon to exit Design mode.

6. Click the New Loan button and enter the following loan data: Loan Amount = $55,000; Down Payment = $4,500; Interest Rate = 10.75%; Years = 8. The monthly payment in cell C7 should equal $786.48. Enter additional data that tests the limits of acceptable loan data.

7. To disable macros, click the Macro Security button on the Developer tab on the Ribbon. When the Trust Center dialog box is displayed, click 'Disable all macros with notification' and then click the OK button.

8. Change the document properties as specified by your instructor. Add a worksheet header with your name, course number, and other information requested by your instructor.

9. Print both the worksheet and Visual Basic code.

10. Save the workbook and then quit Excel.

11. Submit the assignment as specified by your instructor.

Continued >

Make It Right *continued*

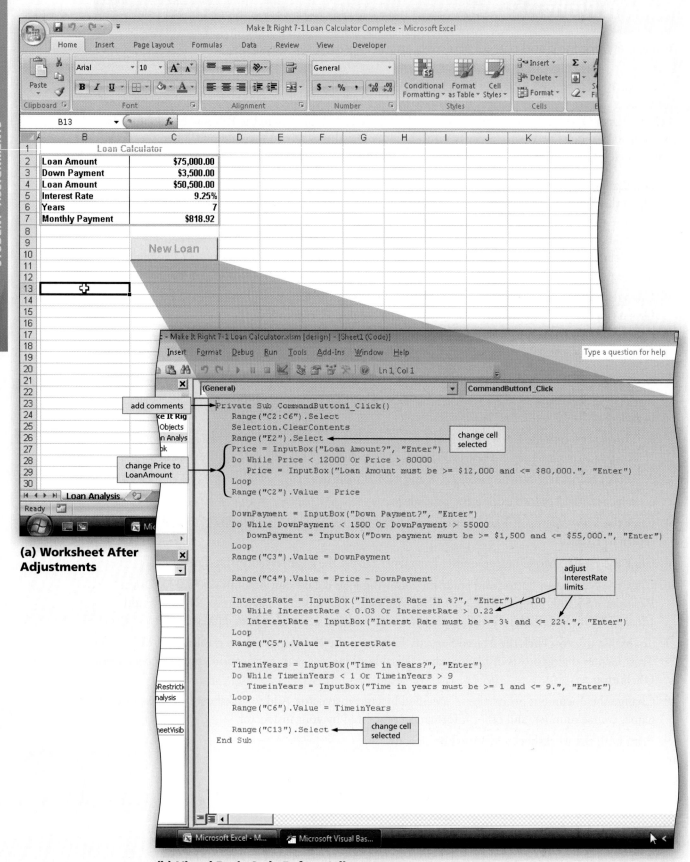

(a) Worksheet After Adjustments

(b) Visual Basic Code Before Adjustments

Figure 7–89

In the Lab

Create a workbook using the guidelines, concepts, and skills presented in this chapter. Labs are listed in order of increasing difficulty.

Lab 1: Automating a Financing Worksheet

Problem: Richie's Subprime provides financing for customers who lack the usual down payments for a loan. The chief financial officer, Richard Bill, has asked you to automate the entry of financing data into a worksheet that computes the monthly payment and total cost of a loan.

Part 1 Instructions: Perform the following tasks.

1. Start Excel. If the Developer tab does not display on the Ribbon, click the Office Button, click the Excel Options button, and then click the 'Show Developer tab in the Ribbon' check box.

2. To enable macros, click the Macro Security button on the Developer tab on the Ribbon. When the Trust Center dialog box is displayed, click 'Enable all macros' and then click the OK button.

3. Open the Lab 7-1 Richie's Subprime workbook from the Data Files for Students and then save the workbook using the file name, Lab 7-1 Part 1 Richie's Subprime as an Excel Macro-Enabled Workbook file type. See the inside back cover of this book for instructions for downloading the Data Files for Students or see your instructor for information on accessing the files required in this book.

4. Unprotect the worksheet using the password, smoak.

5. Click the Developer tab on the Ribbon. Click the Insert button and then click Command Button (column 1, row 1) in the ActiveX Controls area. Draw the button at the top of column F as shown in Figure 7–90.

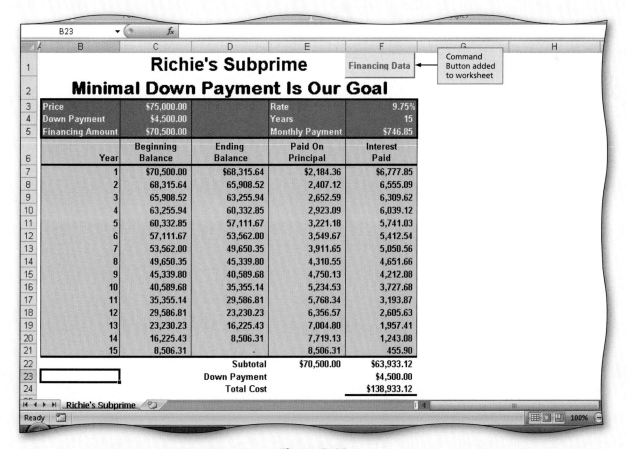

Figure 7–90

In the Lab *continued*

6. With the Command Button control selected, click the Properties button on the Ribbon. If necessary, change the following properties: (a) Caption = Financing Data; (b) Font = Bold; and (c) PrintObject = False. Close the Properties window.

7. With the Command Button control selected, click the View Code button on the Ribbon. Enter the procedure shown in Figure 7–91. Check your code carefully.

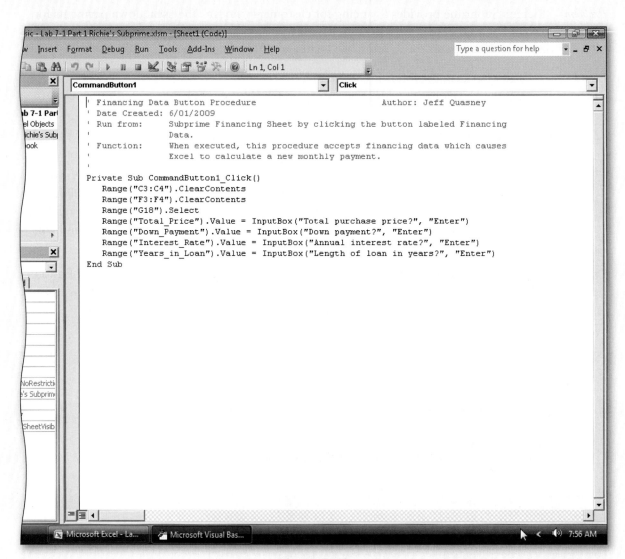

Figure 7–91

8. Close the Visual Basic Editor window. Click the Design Mode button on the Ribbon to return to the workbook.

9. Change the document properties as specified by your instructor. Add a worksheet header with your name, course number, and other information requested by your instructor.

10. Use the newly created button to determine the monthly payment for the following financing data and then print the worksheet for each data set: (a) Total Price Paid = $45,000; Down Payment = $3,500; Rate = 8.75%; and Years = 6; (b) Total Price Paid = $25,500; Down Payment = $4,000; Rate = 15.75%; and Years = 11. The Monthly Payment for (a) is $742.92 and for (b) is $343.65.

11. Print the worksheet and then print the Visual Basic code.

12. To disable macros, click the Macro Security button on the Developer tab on the Ribbon. When the Trust Center dialog box is displayed, click 'Disable all macros with notification' and then click the OK button.

13. Protect the worksheet using the password, smoak. Save the workbook and then quit Excel.

14. Submit the assignment as specified by your instructor.

Instructions Part 2: Perform the following tasks to add a macro to the workbook and add a button to the Quick Access Toolbar that executes the macro:

1. Start Excel. If the Developer tab does not display on the Ribbon, click the Office Button, click the Excel Options button, and then click the 'Show Developer tab in the Ribbon' check box. To enable macros, click the Macro Security button on the Developer tab on the Ribbon. When the Trust Center dialog box is displayed, click 'Enable all macros' and then click the OK button.

2. Open the workbook Lab 7-1 Part 1 Richie's Subprime and then save the workbook using the file name Lab 7-1 Part 2 Richie's Subprime as an Excel Macro-Enabled Workbook file type.

3. Unprotect the worksheet using the password, smoak.

4. Create a macro that prints the formulas version of the worksheet by doing the following:

   a. Click the Record Macro button on the Developer tab on the Ribbon. When the Record Macro dialog box appears, name the macro PrintFormulasVersion, assign the shortcut key CTRL+V, add your name in the Description box, and store the macro in this workbook. Click the OK button to start the macro recording process.

   b. Press CTRL+ACCENT mark (`); click the Page Layout tab on the Ribbon; click the Scale to Fit button arrow on the Ribbon; when the Page Setup dialog box appears, click Landscape in the Orientation area; click Fit to in the Scaling area; click the Print button in the Page Setup dialog box; click the OK button in the Print dialog box; press CTRL+ACCENT mark (`); click the Scale to Fit Dialog Box Launcher on the Ribbon; click Portrait in the Orientation area; in the Scaling area, click Adjust to and type 100 in the Adjust to box; click the OK button; and click the Stop Recording button on the Developer tab on the Ribbon.

5. Click the Macros button on the Ribbon to display the Macro dialog box. Run the PrintFormulasVersion macro. Display the Macro dialog box a second time. Select the PrintFormulasVersion macro and then click the Edit button. When the Visual Basic Editor displays the macro, click File on the menu bar and then click Print. Click the View Microsoft Excel button on the Standard toolbar.

Continued >

In the Lab *continued*

6. Right-click the Quick Access Toolbar and then click Customize Quick Access Toolbar. When the Excel Options dialog box is displayed, click the 'Choose commands from' box arrow and choose Macros. Click PrintFormulasVersion, click the Add button, and then click the OK button. The PrintFormulasVersion button should appear on the Quick Access Toolbar as shown in Figure 7–92.

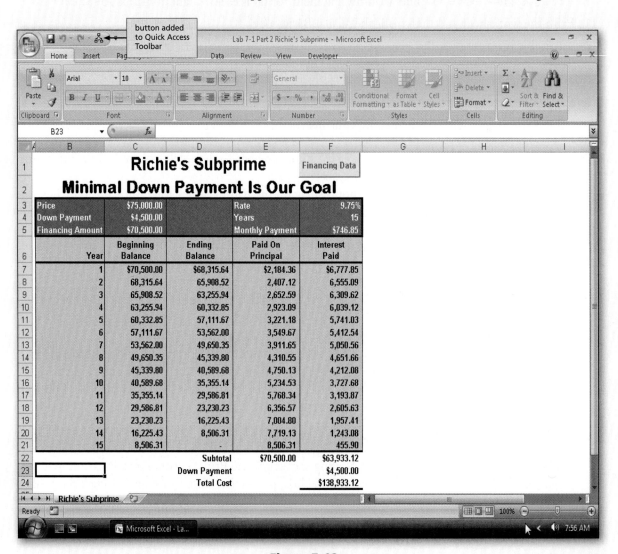

Figure 7–92

7. Run the macro as follows: (a) click the PrintFormulasVersion button on the Quick Access Toolbar; and (b) press CTRL+SHIFT+V.

8. Right-click the Quick Access Toolbar and then click Customize Quick Access Toolbar. Remove the PrintFormulasVersion button and then click the OK button.

9. To disable macros, click the Macro Security button on the Developer tab on the Ribbon. When the Trust Center dialog box is displayed, click 'Disable all macros with notification' and then click the OK button.

10. Protect the worksheet using the password, smoak. Save the workbook and then quit Excel.

11. Submit the assignment as specified by your instructor.

In the Lab

Lab 2: Automating a Projected Income Workbook

Problem: You work in the planning department of Riley, Inc., a small manufacturer. Your manager needs a workbook (Figure 7–93) to be automated to make it easier for her analysts to use. Because you are taking an advanced Excel course that includes Visual Basic for Applications, she has asked you to design a user interface to automate the data entry in cells D4 (Units Sold); D5 (Price per Unit); D14 (Material Cost per Unit); and D16 (Manufacturing Cost per Unit). All other cells in the worksheet use formulas.

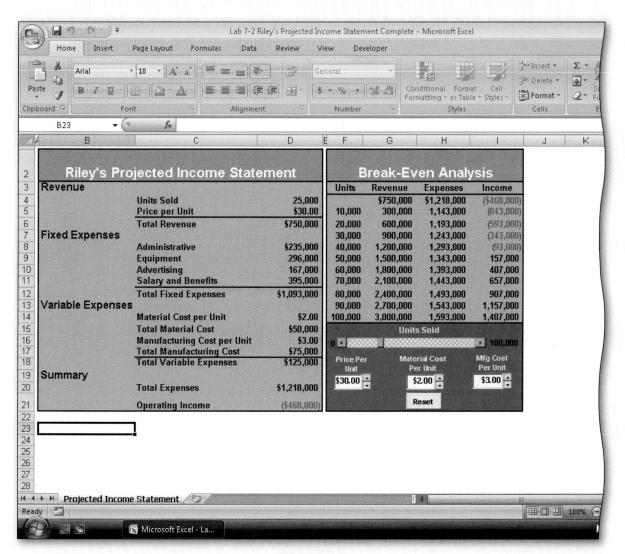

Figure 7–93

Instructions: Start Excel. If the Developer tab does not display on the Ribbon, click the Office Button, click the Excel Options button, and then click the 'Show Developer tab in the Ribbon' check box. To enable macros, click the Macro Security button on the Developer tab on the Ribbon. When the Trust Center dialog box is displayed, click 'Enable all macros' and then click the OK button. Do the following:

1. Open the Lab 7-2 Riley's Projected Income Statement workbook from the Data Files for Students and then save the workbook using the file name, Lab 7-2 Riley's Projected Income Statement Complete as an Excel Macro-Enabled Workbook file type. See the inside back cover of this book for instructions for downloading the Data Files for Students or see your instructor for information on accessing the files required in this book.

Continued >

2. Unprotect the worksheet using the password, breakeven.

3. Draw a thick box border (column 1, row 8 in the Borders gallery) around the range F15:I21 and color the background Black, Text 1, Lighter 50% (column 2, row 2 on the Fill Color palette).

4. Use the concepts and techniques developed in this project to add the 14 controls shown in the lower-right corner of Figure 7–93. The Units Sold scroll bar should assign a value to cell D4. The Price Per Unit spin button should assign a value to cell D5. The Material Cost Per Unit spin button should assign a value to cell D14. The Mfg Cost Per Unit spin button should assign a value to cell D16.

5. Modify the properties of the 14 controls as described in Table 7–12. Save the workbook.

6. Enter the Reset Button procedure, which sets the Units Sold scroll bar (scrUnitsSold) to 25000; the Price Per Unit spin button (spnPrice) to 3000; the Material Cost Per Unit spin button (spnMaterialCost) to 200; and the Mfg Cost Per Unit spin button (spnMfgCost) to 300. It also should select cell A1.

7. The Units Sold Scroll Bar procedure should assign the value of the scroll bar (scrUnitsSold) to cell D4, which is named Units_Sold. For example:

```
Range("Units_Sold ").Value = scrUnitsSold.Value
```

8. Enter the Price Per Unit Spin Button procedure, which assigns the value of spnPrice / 100, formatted to the Currency style, to the Price Per Unit Spin Button Label control. It also should assign the value of spnPrice / 100 to cell D5, which is named Price_per_Unit. For example:

```
lblPrice = Format$(spnPrice.Value / 100, "currency")
Range("Price_per_Unit ").Value = spnPrice.Value / 100
```

The Format$ function in the first line formats the result that will be displayed in the Price Per Unit Spin Button Label control to include a floating dollar sign and two decimal positions to the right of the decimal. The value assigned to cell D5 will display in the same format because the cell was formatted to the Currency style as part of the normal worksheet formatting.

9. Enter the Material Cost Per Unit Spin Button procedure, which assigns the value of spnMaterialCost / 100, formatted to the Currency style, to the Material Cost Per Unit Spin Button Label control. It also should assign the value of spnMaterialCost / 100 to cell D14, which is named Materials_Cost_per_Unit. For example:

```
lblMaterialCost = Format$(spnMaterialCost.Value / 100, "currency")
Range("Material_Cost_per_Unit ").Value = spnMaterialCost.Value / 100
```

10. Enter the Mfg Cost Per Unit Spin Button procedure, which assigns the value of the spnMfgCost / 100, formatted to the Currency style, to the Mfg Cost Per Unit Spin Button Label control. It also should assign the value of spnMfgCost / 100 to cell D16, which is named Manufacturing_Cost_per_Unit. For example:

```
lblMfgCost = Format$(spnMfgCost.Value / 100, "currency")
Range("Manufacturing_Cost_per_Unit ").Value = spnMfgCost.Value / 100
```

11. Close the Microsoft Visual Basic window. Click the Design Mode button on the Developer tab on the Ribbon.

12. Change the document properties as specified by your instructor. Add a worksheet header with your name, course number, and other information requested by your instructor.

13. Protect the worksheet using the password, breakeven.

14. Use the newly designed user interface to determine the operating income for the following projections and then print the worksheet for each data set: (a) Units Sold = 75,000; Price per Unit = $25.00; Material Cost per Unit = $2.50; and Manufacturing Cost per Unit = $3.70; (b) Units Sold = 34,000; Price per Unit = $42.00; Material Cost per Unit = $13.50; and Manufacturing Cost per Unit = $8.30. The Operating Income in cell D21 for (a) is $317,000 and for (b) is ($406,200).

15. Print the worksheet. Print the procedure. Save the workbook.

16. To disable macros, click the Macro Security button on the Developer tab on the Ribbon. When the Trust Center dialog box is displayed, click 'Disable all macros with notification' and then click the OK button. Quit Excel.

17. Submit the assignment as specified by your instructor.

Table 7–12 Controls and Their Properties

Control	Name	Caption	Font	Text Align	Word Wrap	Special Effect	Max	Min	Small Chg/ Large Chg	Back Color
0 Label		0	White, 10-point bold	Center						Gray
Units Sold Label		Units Sold	White,10-point bold	Center						Gray
100,000 Label		100,000	White,10-point bold	Center						Gray
Units Sold Scroll Bar	scrUnitsSold						100000	0	100/1000	
Price Per Unit Label		Price Per Unit	White,8-point bold	Center	True					Gray
Price Per Unit Spin Button	spnPrice						9999	0	10	
Price Per Unit Spin Button Label	lblPrice	$30.00	10-point bold	Right		Sunken				
Material Cost Per Unit Label		Material Cost Per Unit	White,8-point bold	Center	True					Gray
Material Cost Per Unit Spin Button	spnMaterial Cost						9999	0	10	
Material Cost Per Unit Spin Button Label	lblMaterial Cost	$2.00	10-point bold	Right		Sunken				
Mfg Cost Per Unit Label		Mfg Cost Per Unit	White,8-point bold	Center	True					Gray
Mfg Cost Per Unit Spin Button	spnMfgCost						9999	0	10	
Mfg Cost Per Unit Spin Button Label	lblMfgCost	$3.00	10-point bold	Right		Sunken				
Reset Button	btnReset	Reset	Black,8-point bold							Inactive Border

In the Lab

Lab 3: Automating a Forecast Workbook

Problem: As a summer intern at Hank's Handheld Mobile Devices, you have been asked to use your Visual Basic for Applications skills to automate the Forecast workbook as shown in Figure 7–94. The objective is to simplify data entry for the company's financial analysts. This worksheet projects financial information for a five-year period based on the previous year's sales and additional data. The user interface on the right side of the screen accepts the assumptions in the range I18:I22. The numbers in the range B5:F18 are based on these assumptions.

The user interface in the range H2:I16 has two command buttons, one spin button, and three scroll bars. The Reset Assumptions command button resets the assumptions as follows: (a) cell I18 = 2,000; (b) cell I19 = $500.00; (c) I20 = 15%; (d) I21 = 3%; and (e) I22 = 50%. The Devices Sold in 2008 Command Button accepts and ensures the units sold figure in 2008 is greater than zero and then assigns it to cell I18. The Unit Cost spin button changes the unit cost in cell I19. The Annual Sales Growth scroll bar changes the annual sales growth in cell I20. The Annual Price Decrease scroll bar changes the annual price decrease in cell I21. The Margin scroll bar changes the margin in cell I22.

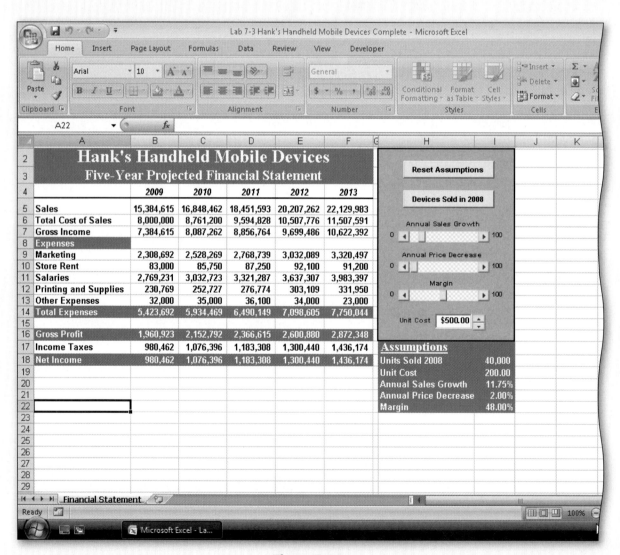

Figure 7–94

Instructions: Start Excel. If the Developer tab does not display on the Ribbon, click the Office Button, click the Excel Options button, and then click the 'Show Developer tab in the Ribbon' check box. To enable macros, click the Macro Security button on the Developer tab on the Ribbon. When the Trust Center dialog box is displayed, click 'Enable all macros' and then click the OK button. Complete the following tasks:

1. Open the Lab 7-3 Hank's Handheld Mobile Devices from the Data Files for Students and then save the workbook using the file name, Lab 7-3 Hank's Handheld Mobile Devices Complete as an Excel Macro-Enabled Workbook file type. See the inside back cover of this book for instructions for downloading the Data Files for Students or see your instructor for information on accessing the files required in this book.

2. Unprotect the Financial Statement worksheet using the password, mobile.

3. Set the background color of the range H2:I16 to White, Background 1 Darker 25% (column 1, row 4 on the Fill Color palette). Draw a thick box border around the range H2:I16.

4. Click the Design Mode button on the Developer tab on the Ribbon. Use the concepts and techniques developed in this project to add the 17 controls shown in Figure 7–94. The controls' properties are described in Table 7-13.

5. One at a time, click the buttons, scroll bars, and spin button listed below and enter the corresponding procedures. Click the View Code button on the Developer tab on the Ribbon to display the Visual Basic window after selecting a button, scroll bar, or spin button. Click the View Microsoft Excel button on the Standard toolbar to display the workbook after you finish entering a procedure.

   a. Enter the Reset Assumptions Button procedure, which resets the assumptions as follows:

   ```
   Range("I18").Value = 2000
   spnUnitCost = 50000
   scrAnnualSalesGrowth = 1500
   scrAnnualPriceDecrease = 300
   scrMargin = 5000
   Range("A22").Select
   ```

   b. Enter the Devices Sold in 2008 Button procedure, which accepts and validates the number of devices sold in 2008 in cell I18 as follows:

   ```
   DevicesSold = InputBox("Devices Sold in 2008?", "Enter")
   Do While DevicesSold <= 0
     DevicesSold = InputBox("Devices Sold in 2008 must be > zero.",
   "Please Reenter")
   Loop
   Range("I18").Value = DevicesSold
   ```

   c. Enter the Unit Cost Spin Button procedure, which enters the unit cost in the Unit Cost Spin Button Label control and in cell I19 as follows:

   ```
   lblUnitCost = Format$(spnUnitCost.Value / 100, "currency")
   Range("I19").Value = spnUnitCost.Value / 100
   ```

   The Format$ function in the first line formats the result that will be displayed in the Unit Cost Spin Button Label control to include a floating dollar sign and two decimal positions to the right of the decimal.

Continued >

In the Lab *continued*

    d. Enter the Annual Sales Growth Scroll Bar procedure, which changes the annual sales growth in cell I20 as follows:

```
Range("I20").Value = scrAnnualSalesGrowth.Value / 10000
```

    e. Enter the Annual Price Decrease Scroll Bar procedure and the Margin Scroll Bar procedure. These procedures work in a fashion similar to the procedure for the Annual Sales Growth scroll bar, except that they assign values to cells I21 and I22, respectively.

6. Click the Design Mode button on the Developer tab on the Ribbon to turn off Design mode.

7. Use the newly designed interface to determine the five-year projections based on the following assumptions and then print the worksheet for each data set: (a) Devices Sold in 2008 = 4,750; Unit Cost = $207.00; Annual Sales Growth = 17%; Annual Price Decrease = 5%; and Margin = 57%; (b) Devices Sold in 2008 = 5,600; Unit Cost = $325.00; Annual Sales Growth = 9%; Annual Price Decrease = 3%; and Margin = 44%. The Net Income for the year 2013 in cell F18 for (a) is $335,032 and for (b) is $135,317.

Table 7–13 Controls and Their Properties

Control	Name	Caption	Back Color	Font	Text Align	Special Effect	Max	Min	Small Chg	Large Chg
Reset Assumptions Button	btnReset	Reset Assumptions		8-point bold						
Devices Sold in 2008 Button	btnDevicesSold	Devices Sold in 2008		8-point bold						
Unit Cost Label	Unit Cost		Gray	8-point bold	Right					
Unit Cost Spin Button	spnUnitCost						100000	0	100	
Unit Cost Spin Button Label	lblUnitCost	$500.00		10-point bold	Right	Sunken				
All three 0 Labels		0	Gray	8-point bold	Center					
All three 100 Labels		100	Gray	8-point bold	Center					
Annual Sales Growth Label		Annual Sales Growth	Gray	8-point bold	Center					
Annual Sales Growth Scroll Bar	scrAnnualSalesGrowth						10000	0	25	100
Annual Price Decrease Label		Annual Price Decrease	Gray	8-point bold	Center					
Annual Price Decrease Scroll Bar	scrAnnualPriceDecrease						10000	0	25	100
Margin Label		Margin	Gray	8-point bold	Center					
Margin Scroll Bar	scrMargin						10000	0	25	100

8. Change the document properties as specified by your instructor. Add a worksheet header with your name, course number, and other information requested by your instructor.

9. Print the worksheet and the procedures.

10. Protect the worksheet using the password, mobile. Save the workbook.

11. To disable macros, click the Macro Security button on the Developer tab on the Ribbon. When the Trust Center dialog box is displayed, click 'Disable all macros with notification' and then click the OK button. Quit Excel.

12. Submit the assignment as specified by your instructor.

Cases and Places

Apply your creative thinking and problem solving skills to design and implement a solution.

• Easier •• More Difficult

• 1: Adding a Macro to a Workbook

Open the workbook Case 7-1 Jack's Fish & Chips from the Data Files for Students and then save the workbook using the file name, Case 7-1 Jack's Fish & Chips Complete. See the inside back cover of this book for instructions for downloading the Data Files for Students or see your instructor for information on accessing the files required in this book. Create a macro that prints the formulas version of the Forecast worksheet in landscape orientation using the Fit to option. Make sure that the macro resets the Page Setup options before terminating. Execute the macro. Print the worksheet and macro. Save the workbook. Submit the assignment as specified by your instructor.

• 2: Automating Data Entry in a Forecast Workbook

Open the workbook Case 7-2 Jack's Fish & Chips from the Data Files for Students and then save the workbook using the file name, Case 7-2 Jack's Fish & Chips Complete. See the inside back cover of this book for instructions for downloading the Data Files for Students or see your instructor for information on accessing the files required in this book. Create a Command Button control next to the Assumptions box. Change the Command Button control's caption to Assumptions. Write a procedure for the Command Button control that accepts data for each of the five assumptions in the range B23:B27. When finished accepting the data, the procedure should display a message indicating that all of the data was accepted. Use the MsgBox function to display the message. Print the Forecast worksheet. Print the Command Button control procedure. Use the Assumptions button to enter the following data sets and then print the worksheet for each data set: (a) Food = 38%; Travel = 12%; Salaries = 35%; Storage = 2%; Marketing = 5%; (b) Food = 46%; Travel = 9%; Salaries = 27%; Storage = 6%; Marketing = 3%. The Total Net Income in cell E18 for (a) is $244,922.64 and for (b) is $275,537.97. Save the workbook. Submit the assignment as specified by your instructor.

• 3: Creating a Well-Balanced User Interface

Open the workbook Case 7-3 Jack's Fish & Chips from the Data Files for Students and then save the workbook using the file name, Case 7-3 Jack's Fish & Chips Complete. See the inside back cover of this book for instructions for downloading the Data Files for Students or see your instructor for information on accessing the files required in this book. Create a well-balanced user interface made up of a Reset button and five scroll bars, one for each of the cells in the range B21:B25. Have the Reset button set the five assumptions to 38%, 7%, 37%, 4%, and 6%, respectively. The scroll bars should range from 0% to 100% and increment by 0.25% (scroll arrows) and 1% (scroll bars). Use the titles in the Assumptions box in the range A23:A27 for the names of the scroll bars. Print the worksheet and the Reset button control procedure. Use the interface to enter the data specified in Cases and Places Exercise 2 above. Save the workbook. Submit the assignment as specified by your instructor.

•• 4: Validating Incoming Data

Make It Personal

Consider the next auto that you wish to purchase and determine possible models, their current sales prices including tax, and other information regarding the financing of an auto loan. Open the workbook Case 7-4 My Loan Calculator from the Data Files for Students and then save the workbook using the file name, Case 7-4 My Loan Calculator Complete. See the inside back cover of this book for instructions for downloading the Data Files for Students or see your instructor for information on accessing the files required in this book. Add a New Auto Loan button that accepts the values in the cells C3, C4, C5, C7, and C8. The procedure associated with the New Auto Loan button on the worksheet should validate the price, down payment, interest rate, and years as follows: (a) the price must be between $12,000 and $80,000 inclusive; (b) the down payment must be between $1,500 and $55,000 inclusive; (c) the interest rate must be between 3% and 22% inclusive; and (d) the years must be between 1 and 9 inclusive. Print the procedure. Create and enter two sets of valid test data based on your personal preference for an auto and your financial information. Print the worksheet for each set. Save the workbook. Submit the assignment as specified by your instructor.

•• 5: Creating a User Interface and Validating Incoming Data

Working Together

Open the workbook Case 7-5 My Loan Calculator from the Data Files for Students and then save the workbook using the file name, Case 7-5 My Loan Calculator Complete. See the inside back cover of this book for instructions for downloading the Data Files for Students or see your instructor for information on accessing the files required in this book. Each member should design on paper a well-balanced user interface that allows input for the values in the cells C3, C4, C5, C7, and C8. Use at least one text box control, at least one scroll bar control, and at least one spin button control. Use the same validation rules as detailed in Cases and Places Exercise 4. Include a text box control that is labeled as the Maximum Requested Monthly Payment. As a group, choose the best features of each design and proceed to create the interface. After creating the user interface in Excel, write the code for the controls. At the end of each procedure that you create for the controls, include a check that determines if the Monthly Payment in cell C9 is greater than the Maximum Requested Monthly Payment. If so, set the font color in the cell to red by using the Visual Basic statement, `Range("C9").Font.Color = RGB(255, 0, 0)`, in the VBA code. If the value in C9 is less than or equal to the Maximum Requested Monthly Payment, then set the color in cell C9 to black by using the Visual Basic statement, `Range("C9").Font.Color = RGB(0, 0, 0)`, in the VBA code. The value of cell C9 must be compared with a numeric value. Use the syntax, `CDBL(txtMaxPayment.Value)`, to make the Maximum Requested Monthly Payment a numeric value. Save the workbook. Submit the assignment as specified by your instructor.

8 Formula Auditing, Data Validation, and Complex Problem Solving

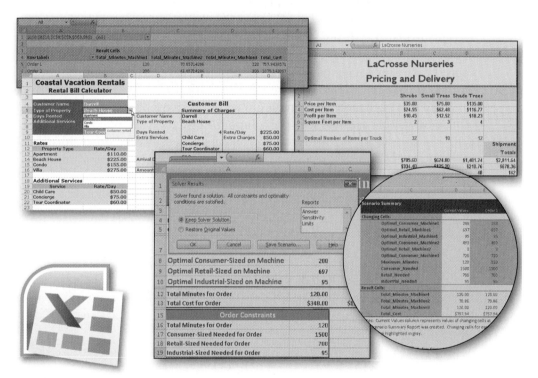

Objectives

You will have mastered the material in this chapter when you can:

- Use formula auditing techniques to analyze a worksheet

- Trace precedents and dependents

- Add data validation rules to cells

- Use trial and error to solve a problem on a worksheet

- Use goal seeking to solve a problem

- Circle invalid data on a worksheet

- Use Excel's Solver to solve a complex problem

- Password-protect a workbook file

- Use Excel's Scenario Manager to record and save different sets of what-if assumptions

- Create a Scenario Summary of scenarios

- Create a Scenario PivotTable

- Save a workbook for use in a previous version of Excel

8 | Formula Auditing, Data Validation, and Complex Problem Solving

Introduction

This chapter introduces you to formula auditing a worksheet, data validation, and solving complex problems. **Formula auditing** allows you to check both the cells being referenced in a formula and the formulas that reference those cells. Formula auditing a worksheet is especially helpful when you want to learn more about a workbook created by someone else or you want to verify the formulas in a newly created workbook.

Data validation allows you to define cells in such a way that only certain values are accepted. This feature, introduced in Chapter 5, also lets Excel display a prompt message when the user selects the cell and an error message if the user attempts to enter a value outside of a valid range that you define. Another powerful data validation feature in Excel allows you to circle invalid data entered in a worksheet cell to indicate an error.

In some situations, the simplest way to solve a problem is to keep trying different data until you are satisfied with the solution. This process is called **trial and error**. Often, you can use trial and error to solve a problem on your own. In other situations, a complex problem might have many possible solutions, meaning that the best way to solve the problem is to use a computer.

Excel provides you with tools to solve such problems. One of these tools is **Solver**, which allows you to specify up to 200 different cells that can be adjusted to find a solution to a problem. Solver also lets you place constraints on the values entered in a cell. A **constraint** is a limitation on the possible values that a cell can contain. After you define the constraints and instruct Solver about the solution you are seeking, it will try many possible solutions until it finds the best one.

Project — Perfected Packaging Order Optimization Worksheet

The majority of this chapter introduces you to solving complex problems that involve changing the values entered in cells to arrive at a solution, while abiding by constraints imposed on the values. The worksheet in Figure 8–1a on page EX 628 is used by Perfected Packaging to decide how to best allocate the work for a customer job among three different packaging machines.

Perfected Packaging obtains bulk-quantities of items from a customer and then repackages the items in one of three package sizes: consumer-sized, retail-sized, and industrial-sized. Each machine packages items at a different rate per minute and operates at a different cost per minute. Figure 8–1a shows the details of the customer order requirements for the project in this chapter. Columns B, C, and D each refer to one of the three machines currently used to package items in bags. The row titles in rows 4 and 5 refer to known information about each machine, including its speed, based on bags per minute, and operating cost per minute. Rows 8 through 10 represent the optimal number of each bag type that each machine should fill for a particular order. The empty cells in these rows reflect the fact that some of the machines cannot fill certain types of bags. For example, cell C10 is empty because Machine 2 cannot fill industrial-sized bags. Rows 12 and 13 show total minutes and total cost per machine for each order. The values in these rows change as the numbers of each bag size are updated in rows 8 through 10.

After you enter the number of each bag size for each machine, Excel determines the results of the suggested order scheduling in column E. The objective is to minimize the total cost for the order (cell E13) while producing the required number of bags within a certain time frame. All the machines are run at the same time for a particular job. The constraints for the current order under consideration are entered in the range B16:B19.

In Figure 8–1b and 8–1d on the next page, Solver has modified the values of cells in the range B8:D10 to find the best combination of bags to fill on each machine to minimize cost and meet the requirements for two different customer orders: Order 1 and Order 2, respectively. When Solver finishes solving a problem, you can instruct it to create an Answer Report. An **Answer Report** (Figures 8–1c and 8–1e on page EX 628) shows the answer that Solver found, the values that Solver manipulated to find the answer, and the constraints that were used to solve the problem.

Excel's **Scenario Manager** is a what-if analysis tool that allows you to record and save different sets of what-if assumptions used to forecast the outcome of a worksheet model. This chapter shows you how to use Scenario Manager to manage the two different sets of Solver data for Orders 1 and 2. Scenario Manager also allows you to create reports that summarize the scenarios on your worksheet. Figure 8–1f on page EX 629 shows a Scenario Summary and Scenario PivotTable that concisely report the differences in the two order scenarios shown in Figures 8–1b and 8–1d.

BTW

Constraints
The constraints of a problem are the rules that you must follow to solve that problem. You even may add constraints to cells that are not referenced in the formulas you are solving. Solver will modify these types of cells to meet the constraints, but they will not affect the solution. For example, you can change row or column headers or worksheet headers to better explain to the user the results of a Solver solution.

BTW

The Solver Add-In
If you do not have Solver installed on your computer, see your instructor about obtaining the Microsoft Office System 2007 CD-ROMs. To install the Solver Add-In, use the Excel Options button on the Office Button menu, click Add-ins, click the Go button, check the Solver option box, and then follow the instructions.

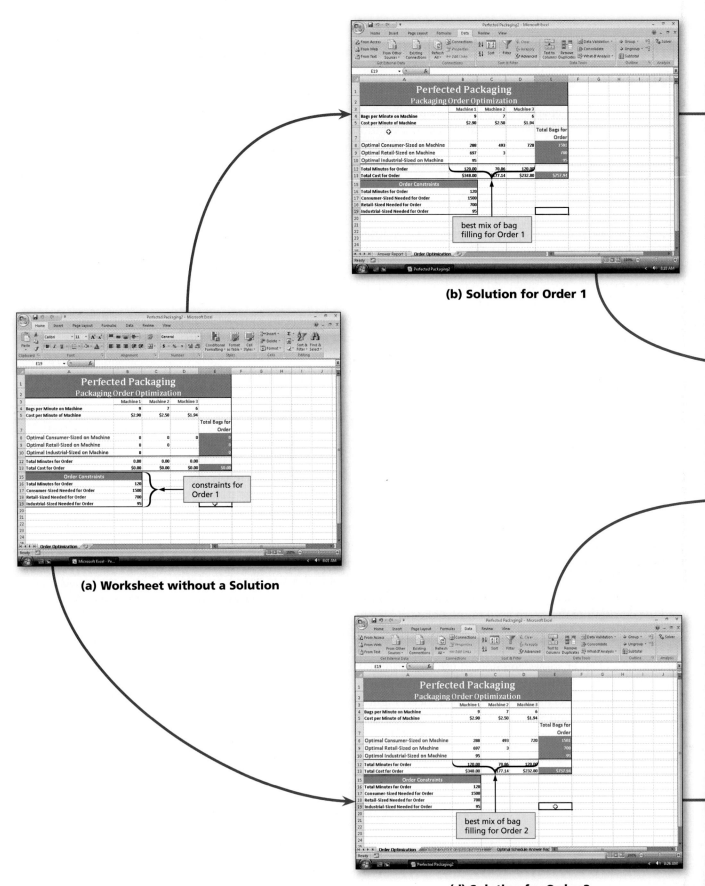

(b) Solution for Order 1

(a) Worksheet without a Solution

(d) Solution for Order 2

Figure 8–1

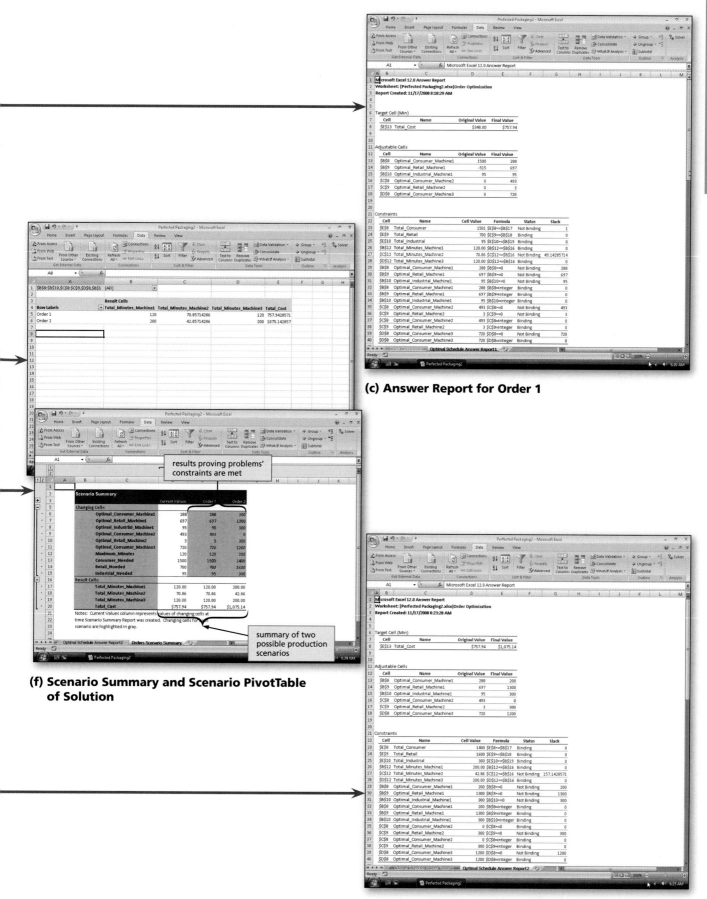

(c) Answer Report for Order 1

(f) Scenario Summary and Scenario PivotTable of Solution

(e) Answer Report for Order 2

Figure 8–2 illustrates the requirements document for the Perfected Packaging Order Optimization worksheet. It includes the needs, source of data, data for two scenarios, and other facts about its development.

REQUEST FOR NEW WORKBOOK

Date Submitted:	November 10, 2008
Submitted By:	Nancy Heneghan
Worksheet Title:	Packaging Order Optimization
Needs:	Perfected Packaging needs to schedule a customer order that requires packaging at least 1,500 consumer-sized bags, 700 retail-sized bags, and 95 industrial-sized bags. The order can take no more than 120 minutes to complete on the company's three packaging machines. You are to determine the optimal use of the company's three machines in order to meet the order number for each item, while minimizing the cost to fulfill the order. Reports need to be generated that indicate that the production and time constraints have been met. In addition, a second order for a different customer must be analyzed and compared with the first order so the company can decide which job to schedule first. The second order requires 1,400 consumer-sized bags, 1,600 retail-sized bags, and 300 industrial-sized bags. The job must take no longer than 200 minutes. Finally, the workbook should be made available in Excel 97-2003 format for use by those that use previous versions of Excel. The workbook should be finalized by removing any private data from the workbook.
Source of Data:	The workbook shown in Figure 8-1a is available with the Data Files for Students with the file name, Perfected Packaging.
Calculations:	Analyze the Perfected Packaging Order optimization worksheet to understand the calculations involved in the worksheet.
Web Requirements:	None.

Approvals

Approval Status:	X	Approved
		Rejected
Approved By:	Myles Bromund	
Date:	November 17, 2008	
Assigned To:	J. Quasney, Spreadsheet Specialist	

Figure 8–2

Overview

As you read this chapter, you will learn how to modify the existing workbook as shown in Figure 8–1 by performing these general tasks:

- Use formula auditing techniques to analyze a worksheet
- Add data validation rules to cells
- Use Solver to solve a complex problem and produce reports to summarize the solution
- Use Scenario Manager to record and save two different customer orders and use reports to compare the scenarios
- Save a workbook for use in a previous version of Excel
- Prepare a workbook for distribution

General Project Decisions
While working with an Excel worksheet, you need to make several decisions that will determine the appearance and characteristics of the finished worksheet. As you update an existing worksheet to meet the requirements shown in Figure 8–2, you should follow these general guidelines:

1. **Analyze the formulas in the workbook to learn about the workbook.** Excel provides several commands to use when analyzing, or auditing, a workbook. Tracing precedents and dependents allows you quickly to learn how cells in a worksheet are related.

2. **Establish data validation rules for changing cells.** Data validation commands in Excel allow you to place rules on cells that restrict a user to entering only particular values in cells. For example, the requirements document in Figure 8–2 implies that cells in the ranges B8:B10 and C8:C9, and cell D8 must be nonnegative whole numbers. Data validation rules should be applied to those cells to restrict a user from entering invalid data.

3. **Propose strategies for solving a complex problem.** Excel provides many methods for solving complex problems. Strategies should be tested from the least complex method to the most complex method.

4. **Consider which cells in the worksheet constitute a scenario.** An Excel scenario needs to recall only the values in those cells that change, or have an impact on, the solution. In essence, a scenario recalls cell values that serve as input data for the problem solved by a worksheet.

5. **Evaluate the steps to take in finalizing a workbook.** Before sending a workbook to colleagues and co-workers, several steps should be taken to ensure that the workbook is finalized and saved in a proper format. The steps you take to perform this task depend on several factors that are discussed later in this chapter.

When necessary, more specific details concerning the above guidelines are presented at appropriate points in the chapter. The chapter also will identify the actions you perform and decisions made regarding these guidelines during the modification of the worksheets shown in Figure 8–1 on page EX 628.

With a good understanding of the requirements document and an understanding of the necessary decisions, the next step is to use Excel to learn about the existing worksheet and solve the problem.

To Start Excel and Open a Workbook

If you are using a computer to step through the project in this chapter and you want your screen to match the figures in this book, you should change your computer's resolution to 1024 × 768. For information about how to change a computer's resolution, see page 21 in Appendix E.

The following steps start Excel and open the workbook Perfected Packaging from the Data Files for Students.

1 Start Excel.

2 Open the file Perfected Packaging from the Data Files for Students and then save the workbook using the file name, Perfected Packaging2.

3 If the Excel window is not maximized, double-click its title bar to maximize it.

4 If the worksheet window in Excel is not maximized, click the Maximize button next to the Close button on its title bar to maximize the worksheet within Excel (Figure 8–3).

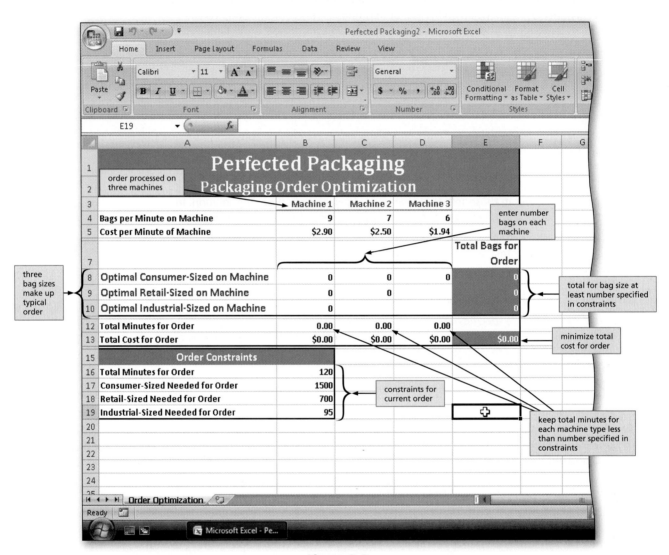

Figure 8–3

About the Order Optimization Worksheet

The Order Optimization worksheet shown in Figure 8–3 provides information for three replication machines and three bag sizes. Rows 4 and 5 show the operating speed and operating cost for each of the three machines. The range B8:D10 contains the optimal combination of bag sizes filled on each machine for a particular order, which is the information that needs to be determined in this chapter. The empty cells — cells C10, D9, and D10 — indicate that a particular machine cannot fill a certain size bag. Rows 12 and 13 show the total minutes and cost for each machine, based on the optimal values listed in the range B8:D10. As cells in the range B8:D10 change, the values in the range B12:D13 are updated. Finally, the total cost for the order is calculated and shown in cell E13. The goals of the project in this chapter are (1) to keep the total number of bags filled for the order (range E8:E10) equal to or greater than the order constraints in the range B16:B19 and (2) to minimize the total order cost in cell E13 without using each machine more than the number of minutes shown in cell B16.

The current worksheet displays order constraints for Order 1 in the range B16:B19. As outlined in the requirements document in Figure 8–2 on page EX 630, a second order for a different customer must be analyzed and compared with the first order so the company can decide which job to schedule first. The information in the range B16:B19 thus will be modified later in the chapter to reflect the order constraints for Order 2, so that it can be compared with Order 1.

Formula Auditing

The term, formula auditing, refers to the practice of proving the correctness of a worksheet. Formula auditing is useful both for analyzing a complex worksheet and for finding the source of errors that may occur in your worksheet. The Formula Auditing group on the Formulas tab on the Ribbon supplies several tools that you can use to analyze the formulas in a worksheet. Excel also provides visual auditing tools that display cues to help you understand the worksheet. These cues take the form of tracer arrows and circles around worksheet cells. **Tracer arrows** are blue arrows that point from cell to cell and let you know what cells are referenced in a formula in a particular cell. Tracer arrows appear in red when one of the referenced cells contains an error.

To Trace Precedents

The Formula Auditing group on the Formulas tab on the Ribbon contains buttons that allow you to trace the details of a formula or locate the source of errors in a worksheet. A formula that relies on other cells for a computation is said to have precedents. A **precedent** is a cell that is referenced in a formula. For example, if you assign cell A5 the formula =A1+A2, then cells A1 and A2 are precedents of cell A5. Tracing precedent cells shows you how a particular cell is calculated. Often a precedent cell has precedents itself. For instance, in the previous example, if you assign cell A1 the formula =B1+B2, then cell A1, which is a precedent of cell A5, also has precedents. Excel allows you to trace the precedents of a cell by clicking the Trace Precedents button in the Formula Auditing group on the Formulas tab on the Ribbon. You can audit only one cell at a time, however; that is, Excel does not allow you to audit ranges. The following steps show how to trace the precedent cells for cell E13, which displays the total cost for an order.

1

- Click the Formulas tab on the Ribbon.

- Click cell E13 and then click the Trace Precedents button on the Ribbon to draw an arrow across the range B13:E13.

2

- Click the Trace Precedents button two more times to draw arrows indicating precedents of cells B13:D13 and the precedents of B12:D12 (Figure 8–4).

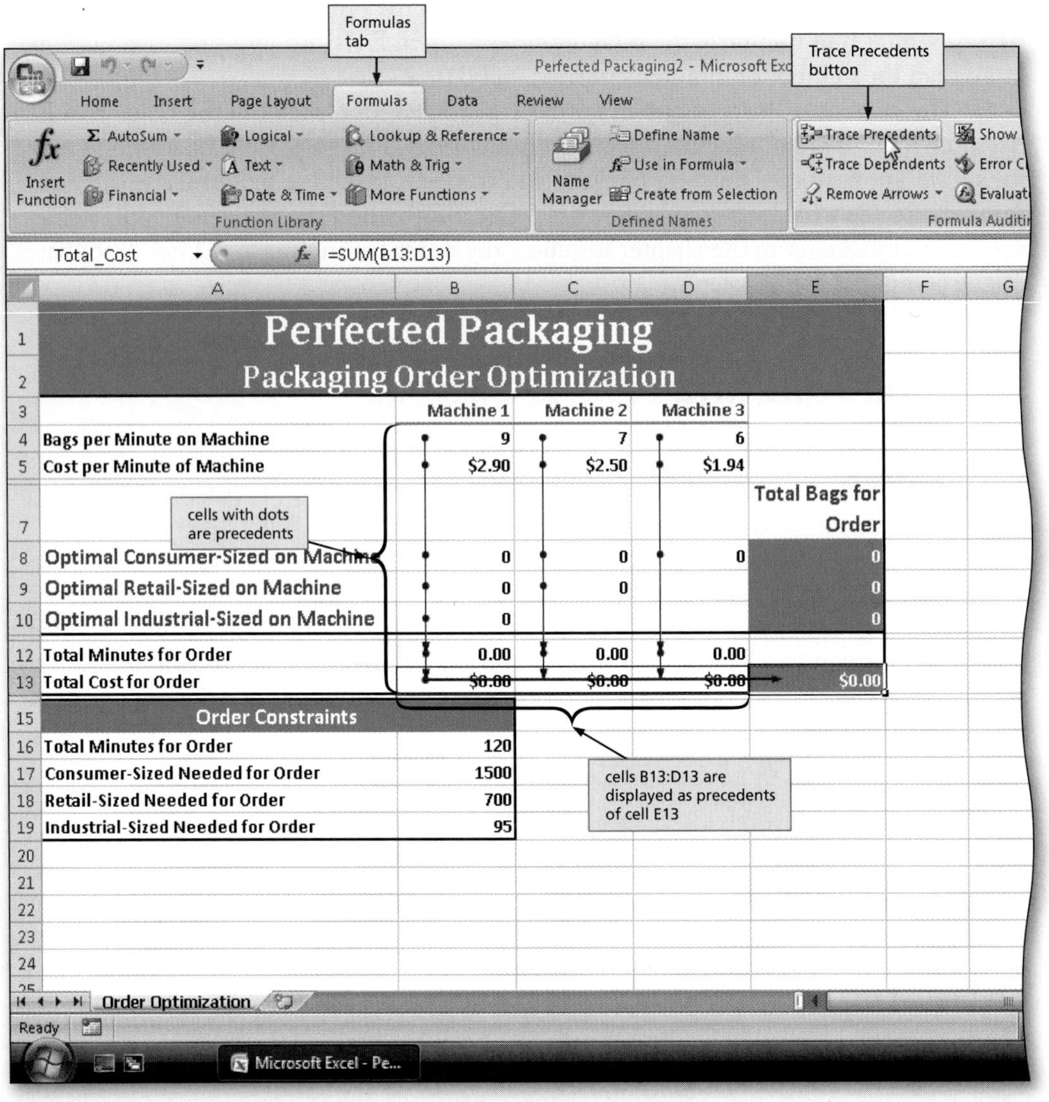

Q&A

What is the meaning of the precedent arrows?

The arrows in Figure 8–4 have arrowheads on cells that are·traced and dots on cells that are direct precedents of the cells with arrowheads. For example, cells B13 through D13 are precedents of cell E13. Cell B13, which is assigned the formula =B12*B5, has

Figure 8–4

precedents in cells B5 and B12. As you click the Trace Precedents button, you visually can follow the levels of precedents through the worksheet. A heavier blue line through a range of cells indicates that all cells in the range are precedents. For example, in Figure 8–4, the heavier blue line through the range B9:B10 indicates that these cells are precedents of cell B13, along with cell B4 and B8, which contain blue dots.

Other Ways
1. Press ALT+M, P

To Remove the Precedent Arrows

After understanding the precedents of a particular cell, you can remove the precedent arrows one level at a time, as shown in the following steps.

1

• Click the Remove All Arrows button arrow to display the Remove All Arrows menu and then point to the Remove Precedent Arrows command on the Remove All Arrows menu (Figure 8–5).

2

• Click Remove Precedent Arrows to remove precedent arrows from the range B4:D12.

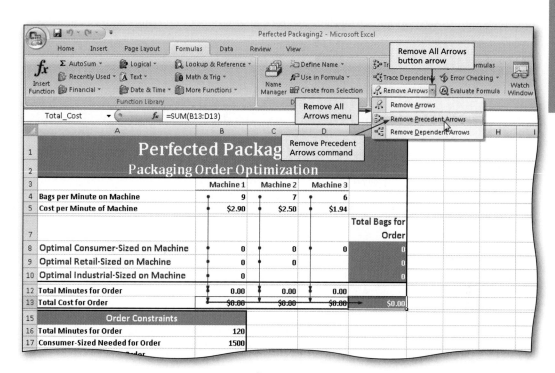

Figure 8–5

3

• Repeat Steps 1 and 2 to remove the remaining precedent arrows from the range B13:D13 (Figure 8–6).

Q&A Why should I trace precedents?

By using the Trace Precedents button and Remove Precedent Arrows command, you slowly can begin to see the structure of the worksheet that is hidden in the formulas within the cells. By doing more analysis, you can assure yourself that you understand the worksheet and that it contains no errors.

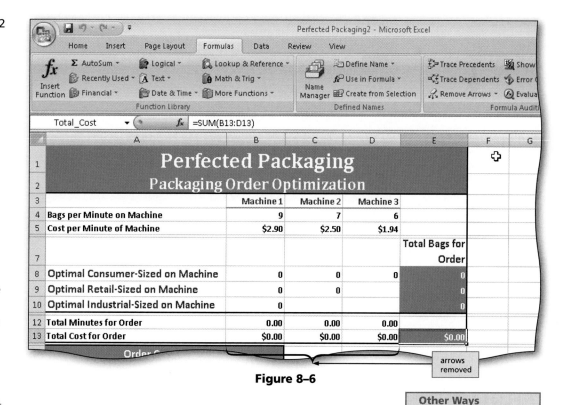

Figure 8–6

Other Ways

1. Press ALT+M, A, P

To Trace Dependents

A cell is a **dependent** if it is referenced in a formula in another cell. Often, it is useful to find out where a cell is used to perform calculations in a worksheet. In other words, you can discover which cells in the worksheet use the cell in question. Excel allows you to trace the dependent cells by clicking the Trace Dependents button in the Formula Auditing group. The following steps trace the dependents of cell B8, which shows the optimal number of bags to fill on Machine 1.

- Click cell B8 and then click the Trace Dependents button on the Ribbon to draw arrows to dependent cells E8 and B12.

- Click the Trace Dependents button two more times to draw arrows indicating the remaining dependents of cell B8 (Figure 8–7).

Q&A

What is the meaning of the dependent arrows?

Figure 8–7 indicates that cells E8 and B12 depend on cell B8. Subsequently, the cells B13 and E13 depend on those cells. As indicated by the dependent arrows, before any results can be computed in cells B13 and E13, cell B8 must have a value.

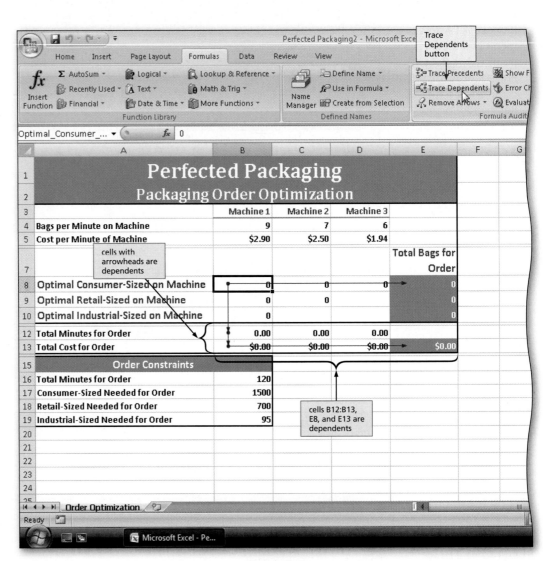

Figure 8–7

Other Ways

1. Press ALT+M, D

To Remove the Dependent Arrows

When you have finished auditing the worksheet with formula auditing, the easiest way to clear all of the precedent or dependent arrows is to use the Remove All Arrows button on the Ribbon, as shown in the following step.

1

• Click the Remove All Arrows button on the Ribbon to remove all of the dependent arrows (Figure 8–8).

Q&A

What if a cell depends on or is a precedent of a cell in another worksheet or workbook?

Sometimes, a cell has precedents or dependents on other worksheets or in other workbooks. In this case, Excel draws a dashed arrow to an icon of a work-sheet to indicate that the precedent or dependent cell is outside of the current worksheet. If the workbook that contains the precedent or dependent is open and you click the dashed arrow, Excel displays the Go To dialog box that allows you to navigate to that cell.

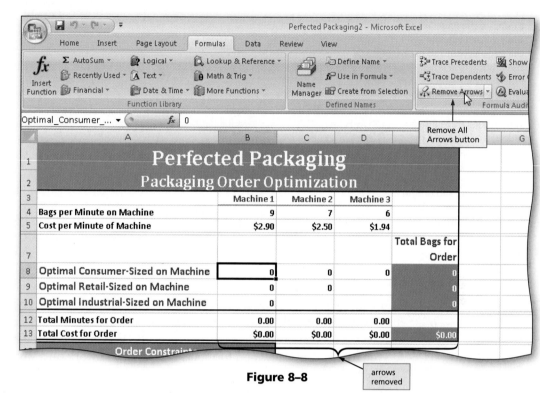

Figure 8–8

Other Ways

1. Press ALT+M, A, D

Buttons in the Formula Auditing Group

Figure 8–9 shows the buttons in the Formula Auditing group on the Formulas tab on the Ribbon. Table 8–1 summarizes the functions of the buttons in the Formula Auditing group.

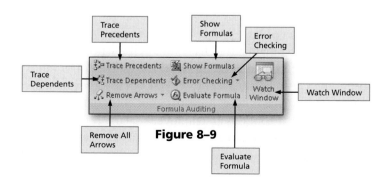

Figure 8–9

BTW

Tracing Precedents and Dependents
When no more levels of precedents are available on the worksheet, Excel will beep if you try to trace another level. If you double-click a tracer arrow, the cell at the end of the arrow will be selected. This is useful on complex worksheets where the destination of an arrow may not be easy to ascertain.

BTW

Gaining Confidence in a Workbook
Some Excel commands provide additional ways to uncover details of workbooks created by another author. For example, the Page Setup Dialog Box Launcher on the Page Layout tab on the Ribbon, the Print Preview command on the Office Button menu, and the Excel Options button on the Office Button menu can tell you if the author used any unusual settings. To list the macros in the workbook, click the Developer tab on the Ribbon and then click the Macros button on the Ribbon.

Validation Circles
Validation circles display in red to indicate that these cells contain error values. Excel will display a maximum of 256 invalid data circles at a time.

Goal Seeking
Goal seeking is a methodology in which you know what value you want a formula in a cell to produce, but you do not know the value to place in a cell that is involved in the formula. You can goal seek by changing the value in a cell that is used indirectly in the formula.

Table 8–1 Summary of Buttons in the Formula Auditing Group

Name	Function
Error Checking	Checks the entire worksheet for errors. The Trace Error command on the Error Checking menu is used when the active cell contains an error value. It draws tracer arrows to the cells that may be causing the error value to appear. The Circular References command on the Error Checking menu draws circles around the cells that contain values outside of the limits defined through the Validation command on the Data menu.
Trace Precedents	Draws tracer arrows from the cells that affect the formula in the current cell.
Remove All Arrows	Removes all tracer arrows from the active worksheet.
Trace Dependents	Draws tracer arrows to the cells that use the current cell in their formula.
Show Formulas	Shows the formulas view of the active worksheet (CTRL+ ').
Watch Window	Opens a window that displays the values and formulas in cells that you select to monitor.
Evaluate Formula	Allows you to debug complex formulas by monitoring a formula step by step.

The Error Checking button will search the current worksheet for any errors and then display the Error Checking dialog box to help you take corrective action. You then can trace the source of the error. If you see an error in a cell — including #DIV/0!, #NAME?, #NA, #NULL!, #NUM!, #REF!, and #VALUE! — select the cell, click the Error Checking button arrow, and then click the Trace Error command on the Error Checking menu to display red tracer arrows that point to the precedent cells. You then can inspect the precedent cells to see if you can determine the cause of the error and correct it.

The Watch Window button opens the Watch Window. The Watch Window allows you to monitor values and formulas in cells as you work on a worksheet. The Evaluate Formula button displays the Evaluate Formula dialog box, which allows you to debug or understand complex formulas in a worksheet, much in the manner that programmers debug source code.

Data Validation, Trial and Error, and Goal Seek

Often, it is necessary to limit the values that should be placed in a particular cell. Excel allows you to place limitations on the values of cells by using data validation. Data validation restricts the values that a user can enter into a cell. Excel allows you to determine the restrictions placed on data entered into a cell, set an input message that the user will see when selecting the cell, and set an error message to display if the user violates the restrictions placed on the cell. By implementing these features, you reduce the likelihood of data entry errors by giving the user as much information as possible about how to use the worksheet properly.

One important aspect of Excel's data validation is that the rules apply only when the user enters data into the cell manually. That is, if a cell is calculated by a formula or set in a way other than direct input by the user, Excel does not check the validation rules.

When using the Custom validation type, you can use a formula that evaluates to either true or false. If the value is false, users may not enter data in the cell. Suppose, for example, you have a cell that contains an employee's salary. If the salary is zero, which indicates the employee no longer is with the company, you may want to prohibit a user from entering a percentage in another cell that contains the employee's raise for the year.

To Add Data Validation to Cells

Recall from the requirements document for this chapter on page EX 630 that the number of bags filled must be nonnegative whole numbers. By examining the worksheet, you can see that cells in the ranges B8:B10, C8:C9, and D8 must have these restrictions. Data validation is added to cells by using the Data Validation button on the Data tab on the Ribbon.

The following steps add data validation to cells in the ranges B8:B10, C8:C9, and D8.

1

- Select the range B8:B10.

- While holding down the CTRL key, select the range C8:C9.

- While holding down the CTRL key, select the cell D8.

- Click the Data tab on the Ribbon (Figure 8–10).

Figure 8–10

2

- Click the Data Validation button on the Ribbon to display the Data Validation dialog box.

- When Excel displays the Data Validation dialog box, click the Allow box arrow and then click Whole number in the Allow list.

- Click the Data box arrow and then click 'greater than or equal to' in the Data list.

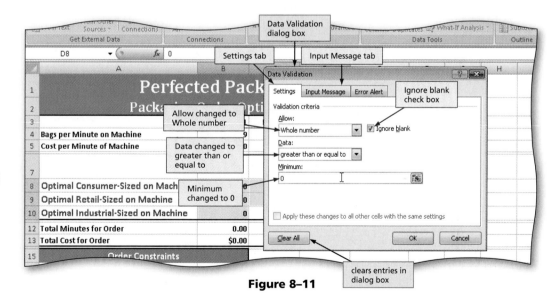

Figure 8–11

- Type 0 in the Minimum box (Figure 8–11).

 Q&A

What is the purpose of the Ignore blank check box?

The Ignore blank check box should be cleared if you want to require that the user enter data in the cell. By leaving the Ignore blank check box selected, Excel allows the user to select the cell and then deselect the cell with no data being entered.

- Click the Input Message tab and then type Bags to Fill in the Title text box.

- Type Enter the number of bags to fill on the machine. The number must be a whole number that is greater than or equal to zero. in the Input message box (Figure 8–12).

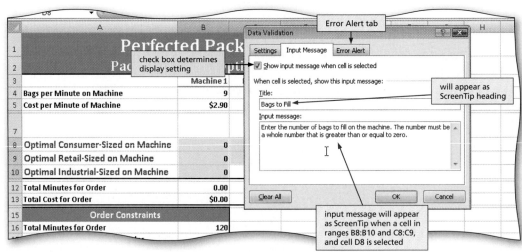

Figure 8–12

Q&A How else can I validate data?

Excel allows several types of validation to be set in the Validation criteria area shown in Figure 8–11. Each selection in the Validation criteria area changes the type of value that Excel allows a user to enter in the cell. In the Allow list, the Any value selection allows you to enter any value, but still allows you to specify an input message for the cell. The Whole number, Decimal, Date, and Time selections permit only values of those types to be entered in the cell. The List selection allows you to specify a range that contains a list of valid values for the cell. The Text length selection allows only a certain length of text string to be entered in the cell. The Custom selection allows you to specify a formula that validates the data entered by the user.

- Click the Error Alert tab and then type Input Error in the Title text box.

- Type You must enter a whole number that is greater than or equal to zero. in the Error message box (Figure 8–13).

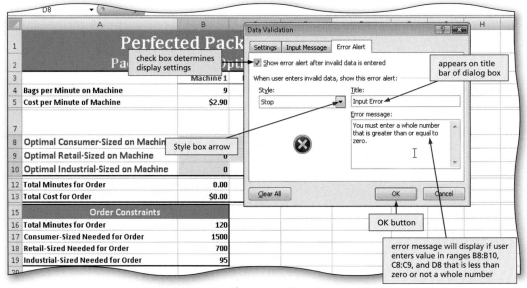

Figure 8–13

5

- Click the OK button.

- Click cell E21.

Q&A What is the result of the new data validation rules?

If a user selects one of the cells in the ranges B8:B10, C8:C9, or D8, then Excel displays the input message defined in Figure 8–12. If the user enters a value that either is less than zero or is not a whole number in cells in the ranges B8:B10, C8:C9, and D8, then Excel displays the error message defined in Figure 8–13 and forces the user to change the value to a valid number before deselecting the cell.

Other Ways
1. Press ALT+A, V, V

To Open the Watch Window and Add Cell Watches

As previously discussed, the Watch Window allows you to monitor the values and formulas in cells as you work on a worksheet. You add cells to the Watch Window using the Add Watch button on the Watch Window toolbar. The Watch Window continues to show the values of watched cells even as you navigate the worksheet and the cells are no longer in view on the screen. Similarly, if you change the view to another worksheet or workbook, the Watch Window allows you to continue to monitor the cell values.

The Watch Window displays six columns of information for each cell: the workbook that contains the cell (Book), the worksheet that contains the cell (Sheet), the cell name (Name), the cell reference (Cell), the current value in the cell (Value), and the formula for the cell (Formula). The following steps open the Watch Window and add cell watches to cells in the range E8:E10 and cell E13.

- Click the Formulas tab on the Ribbon.

- Click the Watch Window button on the Ribbon to open the Watch Window (Figure 8–14).

Figure 8–14

- Click the Add Watch button on the Watch Window toolbar to display the Add Watch dialog box (Figure 8–15).

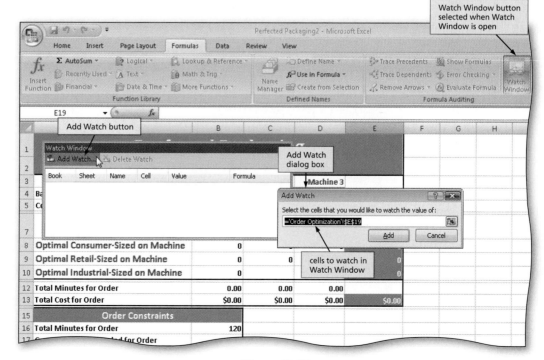

Figure 8–15

- If necessary, move the Add Watch dialog box so that rows 8 through 10 of column E are not hidden.

- Select the range E8:E10.

- Hold down the CTRL key and then click cell E13 (Figure 8–16).

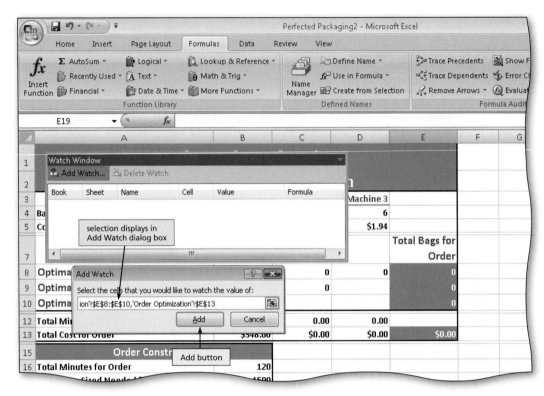

Figure 8–16

4

- Click the Add button in the Add Watch dialog box.

- If necessary, expand the Name column to view the cell names in the third column and information about the four watched cells (Figure 8–17).

Q&A

How should I use the Watch Window?

You continue to display the Watch Window while you make adjustments to the structure of a worksheet or while you modify other values in the worksheet. To remove a watch, select the watched cell in the Watch Window and then click the Delete Watch button on the Watch Window toolbar.

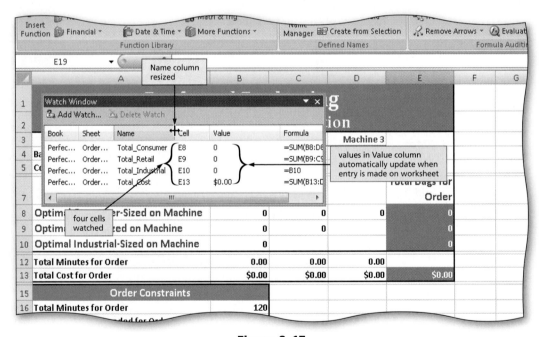

Figure 8–17

Other Ways

1. ALT+M, W

To Use Trial and Error to Attempt to Solve a Complex Problem

**Plan
Ahead**

Propose strategies for solving a complex problem.

When considering an approach to a complex problem in Excel, start with the least complex method of attempting to solve the problem. In general, the following methods can be useful in the order shown:

1. Use trial and error to modify the input, or changing, values in the worksheet. Use a common sense approach and keep in mind the range of acceptable answers to your problem. For example, the number of bags filled by a machine in this chapter should not be a negative number.

2. Use Excel's Goal Seek feature to have Excel automatically modify a cell's value in a worksheet in an attempt to reach a certain goal in a dependent cell.

3. Use Excel's Solver feature to provide Excel with all of the known rules, or constraints, of your problem as well as the goal you are seeking. Allow Solver to attempt as many different solutions to your problem as possible.

As previously discussed, trial and error refers to the practice of adjusting cells in a worksheet manually to try to find a solution to a problem. In the Order Optimization worksheet, you could adjust cells in the ranges B8:B10, C8:C9, and D8 until the criteria for the order are met. Because many combinations of possible values exist, you could try keeping one or two of the values constant while adjusting the others.

Trial and error is more than just guessing. Because you understand the constraints on the problem and the goals, you can use logic to make subsequent trials better than the previous ones. For example, if you increase the number of bags filled on Machine 1 by 500 and it causes the total minutes for Machine 1 to exceed 120 minutes, you instead may try to increase the number of bags filled by 100 to see if that keeps the total minutes within the 120-minute constraint.

The following steps illustrate the process of using trial and error to attempt to solve a complex problem.

- If necessary, resize the Watch Window so that only the cell watches appear as shown in Figure 8–18.

- Click cell B8 and type 82.5 as the number of retail-sized bags to fill on Machine 1 and then press the ENTER key (Figure 8–18).

Q&A What is the result of entering 82.5 in cell B8?

Excel displays the Input Error dialog box because 82.5 is not a whole number and thus is not a valid entry in this cell. The Bags to Fill ScreenTip is displayed because cell B8 is selected. The Watch Window displays the updated values of the watched cells as Excel changes the values in the cells.

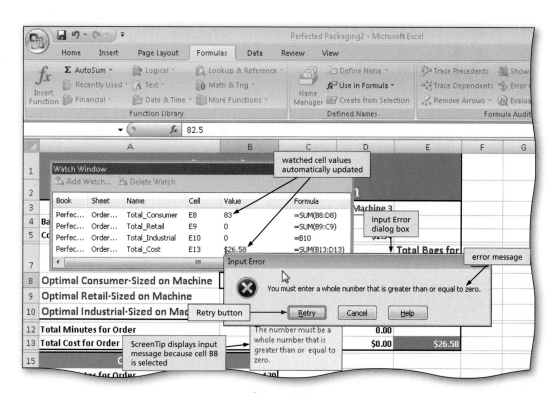

Figure 8–18

2

- Click the Retry button.

- Type 700 as the number of retail-sized bags to fill on Machine 1 in cell B9.

- Click cell B10 and type 95 as the number of industrial-sized bags to fill on Machine 1.

- Click cell D8 and type 1500 as the number of consumer-sized bags to fill on Machine 3 and then press the ENTER key to display the new values and update the totals in the range B12:D13 and column E (Figure 8–19).

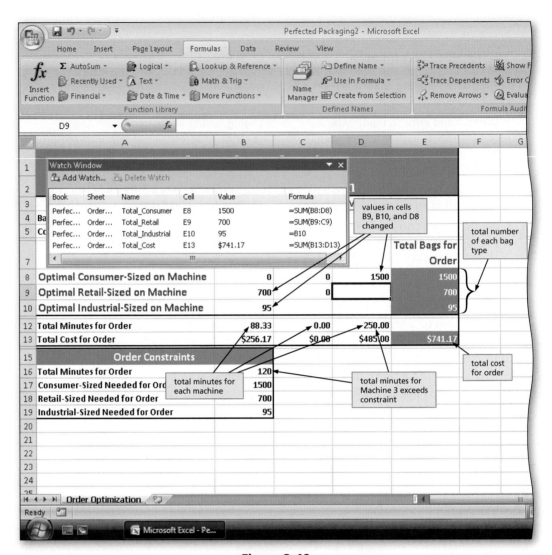

Figure 8–19

3

- Click cell B8 and type 1500 as the number of consumer-sized bags to fill on Machine 1.

- Click cell D8, type 0 as the number of consumer-sized bags to fill on Machine 3, and then press the ENTER key. Select cell E19 (Figure 8–20).

Q&A

What are some problems with using trail and error?

While trial and error can be used on simple problems, it has many limitations when used to solve complex problems. The Order Optimization worksheet has six cells (B8, B9, B10, C8, C9, and D8) that can be adjusted to solve the problem. Because each

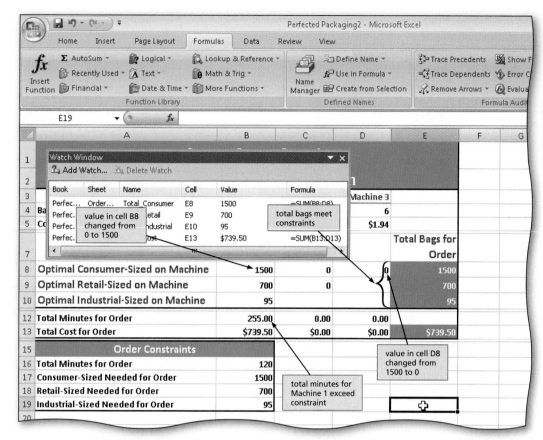

Figure 8–20

cell can contain a value greater than or equal to zero, you could try many different combinations of values that result in the proper minutes and number of bags to fill in the order. Using trial and error, it is difficult to determine if the total order cost has been minimized.

To Use the Goal Seek Command to Attempt to Solve a Complex Problem

If you know the result you want a formula to produce, you can use goal seeking to determine the value of a cell on which a formula depends. Goal seeking takes trial and error one step further by automatically changing the value of a cell until a single criterion is met in another cell. In this case, suppose you suspect that by varying the number of retail-sized bags filled on Machine 1, you can achieve the goal of 120 minutes for the order on Machine 1. In doing this, you hope that the other constraints of the problem also are satisfied.

The following steps show how Goal Seek can be used to alter the number of retail-sized bags filled on Machine 1 to keep the total minutes used on Machine 1 at less than or equal to 120 minutes.

- Click the Data tab on the Ribbon and then click the What-If Analysis button on the Ribbon to display the What-If Analysis menu (Figure 8–21).

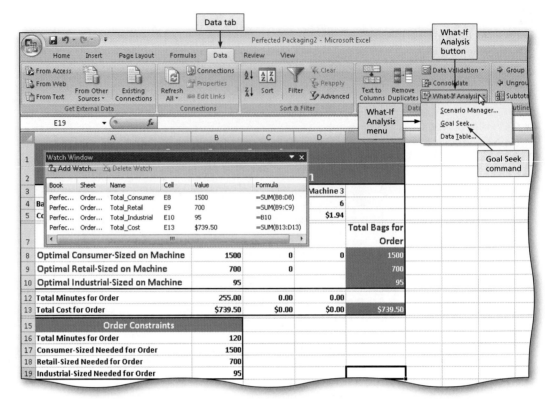

Figure 8–21

- Click Goal Seek to display the Goal Seek dialog box.

- Type B12 in the Set cell text box.

- Click the To value text box.

- Type 120 and then click the 'By changing cell' text box.

- Click cell B9 on the worksheet.

- If necessary, move the Goal Seek dialog box (Figure 8–22).

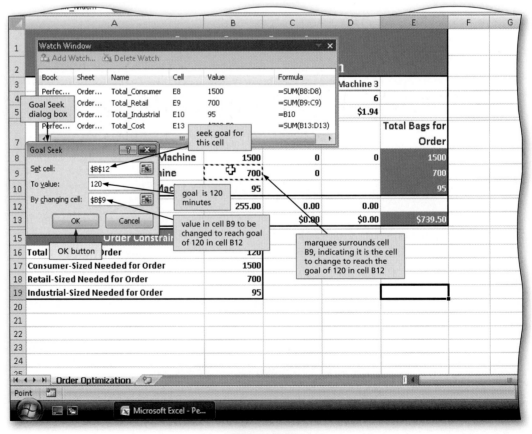

Figure 8–22

4
- Click the OK button to seek the goal of 120 minutes in cell B12 (Figure 8–23).

5
- Click the OK button to close the Goal Seek Status dialog box and display the updated worksheet.

- Click cell E19 to deselect cell B12.

Q&A

What are some problems with using goal seeking?

Goal seeking assumes you can change the value of only one cell referenced directly or indirectly to reach a desired goal. In this example, to change the total number of minutes used on Machine 1 to 120 minutes, the number of retail-sized bags to fill on Machine 1 is changed to –515. While mathematically correct, the solution contradicts the order constraints as stated in the requirements document and is illogical (the company cannot fill a negative number of bags).

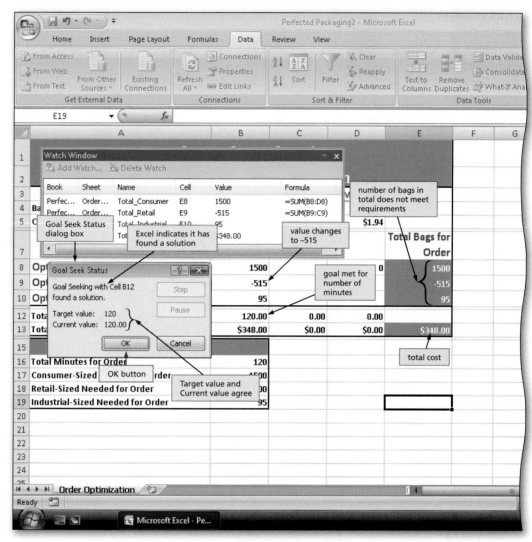

Figure 8–23

Other Ways

1. Press ALT+A, W, G

To Circle Invalid Data and Clear Validation Circles

The situation resulting from using Goal Seek on the Order Optimization worksheet illustrates the fact that the data validation rules of the cell apply only when a user types a value directly into the cell. Because some techniques, such as Goal Seek, can violate data validation rules, it is good practice to ensure periodically that the values of cells in a worksheet are following data validation rules. The Circle Invalid Data command on the Data Validation menu places a red validation circle around any cells containing values that violate the data validation rules. The following steps circle the invalid data on the Order Optimization worksheet and then clear the validation circles.

1

- Click the Data Validation button arrow on the Ribbon to display the Data Validation menu.

- Click Circle Invalid Data on the Data Validation menu to place a red validation circle around cell B9 (Figure 8–24).

Q&A

Has the problem been solved?

No. At this point, the total minutes for Machine 1 are within order constraints, but the total retail-sized bags needed for the order are not met. Even if all order constraints were met, you still have no way of knowing whether the goal to minimize cost (cell E13) has been achieved. The requirements state that total cost be minimized while satisfying the number of bags filled and minutes limitations of the order. Surely, other combinations of filling bags on machines satisfy the order requirements while producing a lower total cost.

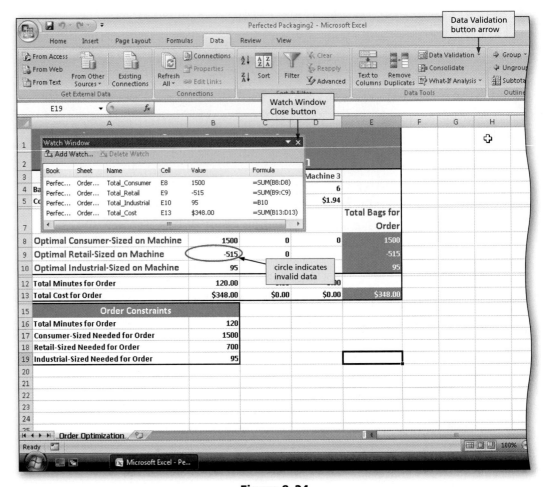

Figure 8–24

2

- Click the Data Validation button arrow on the Ribbon to display the Data Validation menu.

- Click Clear Validation Circles on the Data Validation menu to clear the red validation circles.

- If necessary, select cell E19.

- Click the Close button on the Watch Window title bar to close the Watch Window.

Other Ways
1. ALT+A, V, I

Using Solver to Solve Complex Problems

Solver allows you to solve complex problems where a number of variables can be changed in a worksheet in order to meet a goal in a particular cell. As previously noted, goal seeking allows you to change only one cell, while trial and error requires too much uncertainty and time to solve complex problems adequately.

Solver uses a technique called linear programming to solve problems. **Linear programming** is a complex mathematical process used to solve problems that include multiple variables and the minimizing or maximizing of result values. Solver essentially tries as many possible combinations of solutions as it can. On each attempt to solve the problem, Solver checks to see if it has found a solution.

Figure 8–25a shows the result of using Solver on the Order Optimization worksheet. Cells in the ranges B8:B10, C8:C9, and D8 are called the changing cells. **Changing cells**, or **adjustable cells**, are the cells modified by Solver to solve the problem. The total cost in cell E13 serves as the **target cell**, which means that Solver will attempt to meet some criteria (lowest cost) in this cell by varying the changing cells. Constraints are the requirements that have been placed on certain values in the problem. For example, the total number of consumer-sized bags should be greater than or equal to 1500 (cell B17), and the total number of minutes required by each machine should not exceed 120 minutes (cell B16).

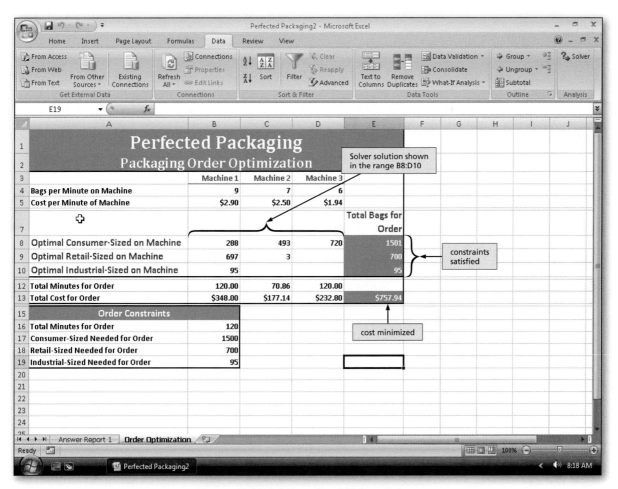

Figure 8–25 (a) Result of Using Solver

Figure 8–25b shows a Solver Answer Report. As previously discussed, an Answer Report is a worksheet that shows the results of a Solver calculation in a concise format, showing the answer that Solver found, the values that Solver manipulated to find the answer, and the constraints that were used to solve the problem. The report satisfies the requirement to document the results of the order optimization, as shown in Figure 8–2 on page EX 630.

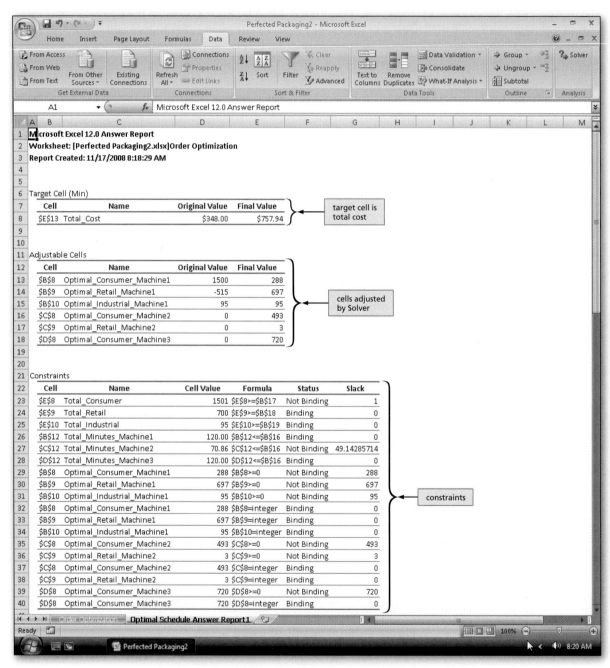

Figure 8–25 (b) Solver Answer Report

To Use Solver to Find the Optimal Solution to a Complex Problem

The Data tab on the Ribbon includes the Solver button, which starts Solver.

Note: If the Solver button does not appear on the Data tab, then you must use the Add-Ins page in the Excel Options dialog box to add it.

The cell that is the target for Solver is cell E13, which contains the total cost for the order. The goal is to minimize the value in that cell. The cells that can be changed by Solver to accomplish this goal are cells in the ranges B8:B10, C8:C9, and D8, which contain the number of bags to fill on each machine. The constraints are summarized in Table 8–2.

Table 8–2 Constraints for Solver		
Cell or Range	**Operator**	**Constraint**
B8:B10	>=	0
B8:B10	int	
E8	>=	B17
C8:C9	>=	0
C8:C9	int	
D8	>=	0
D8	int	
E9	>=	B18
E10	>=	B19
B12	<=	B16
C12	<=	B16
D12	<=	B16

The following steps show how to use Solver to find the optimal solution to solve the Order Optimization worksheet within the given constraints.

- If necessary, click the Data tab on the Ribbon (Figure 8–26).

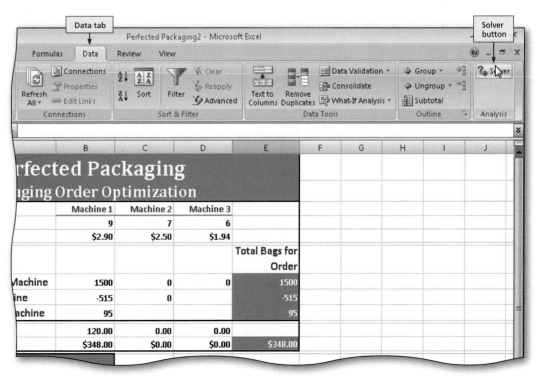

Figure 8–26

2

- Click the Solver button on the Ribbon to display the Solver Parameters dialog box.

- When Excel displays the Solver Parameters dialog box, click cell E13 to set the target cell to the name of cell E13, Total_Cost.

- Click Min in the Equal To area.

- Click the Collapse Dialog button in the By Changing Cells area to minimize the Solver Parameters dialog box.

- Click the By Changing Cells box and then select the range B8:B10.

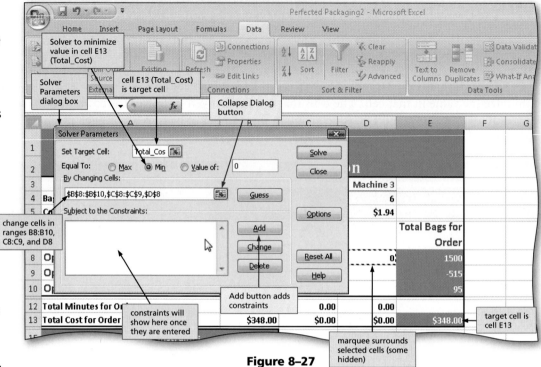

Figure 8–27

- Hold down the CTRL key and then select the ranges C8:C9 and D8.

- Click the Expand Dialog button on the right side of the minimized Solver Parameters dialog box to maximize it (Figure 8–27).

3

- Click the Add button to display the Add Constraint dialog box.

- If necessary, move the Add Constraint dialog box so that the range B8:B10 is visible.

- Select the range B8:B10 to set the value of the Cell Reference box.

- Click the middle box arrow and then select >= in the list.

- Type 0 in the Constraint box (Figure 8–28) to set the constraint on the cells in the range B8:B10 to be greater than or equal to 0.

Q&A

How is the Constraint box used?

When adding constraints, as shown in Figure 8–28, Solver allows you to enter a cell reference followed by an operator. If the

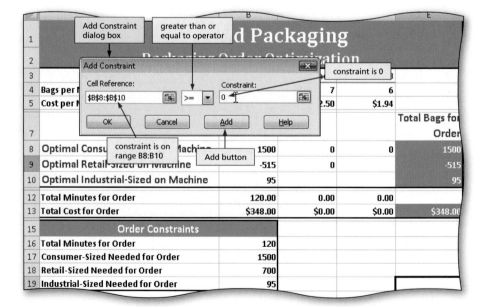

Figure 8–28

operator is <=, >=, or =, then you enter the constraint value in the Constraint box. The constraint can be a value or a cell reference. Other valid operators are **int**, for an integer value, or **bin**, for cells that contain only one of two values, such as yes/no or true/false.

4

- Click the Add button.

- Select the range B8:B10 to set the value of the Cell Reference box.

- Click the middle box arrow and then select int in the list to set a constraint on the cells in the range B8:B10 to be assigned only integer values (Figure 8–29).

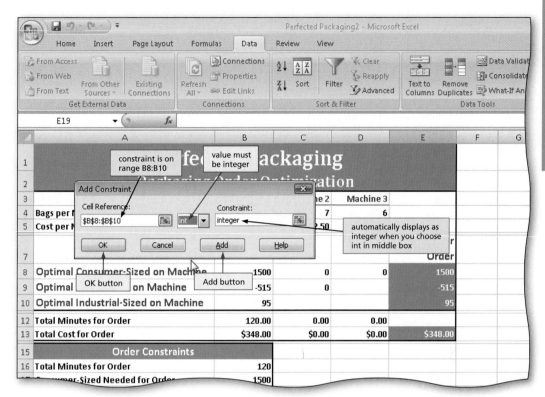

Figure 8–29

5

- Click the Add button.

- Click cell E8 to set the value of the Cell Reference box.

- Click the middle box arrow and then select >= in the list.

- Click the Constraint box and then click cell B17 to add a constraint to cell E8 indicating that its value must be greater than or equal to the value in cell B17 (Figure 8–30).

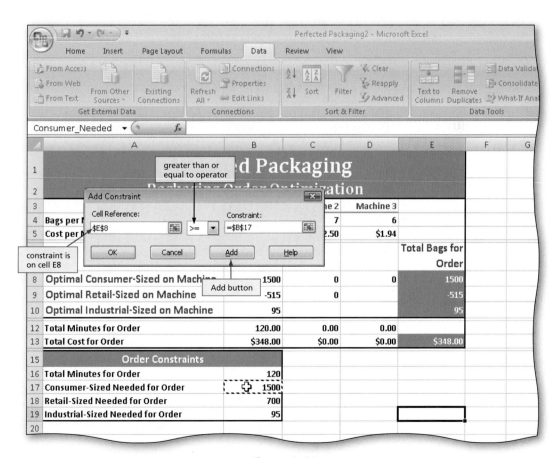

Figure 8–30

6

- Click the Add button.

- Enter the remaining constraints shown in Table 8–2 on page EX 651, beginning with the constraints for the range C8:C9.

- When finished with the final constraint, click the OK button in the Add Constraint dialog box to close it (Figure 8–31).

What is the purpose of the Guess button?

Rather than selecting the ranges B8:B10, C8:C9, and D8 as the changing cells in Step 2, clicking the

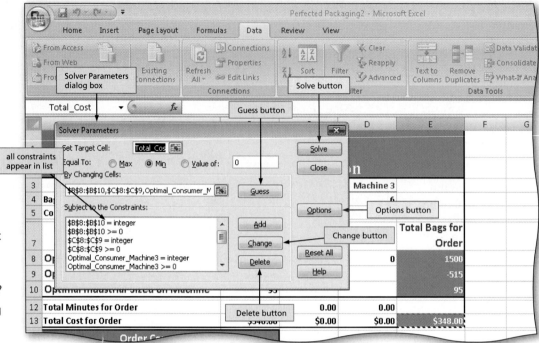

Figure 8–31

Guess button in the Solver Parameters dialog box (Figure 8–31) instructs Solver to try to determine which cells affect the target cell. The button works in much the same way as the Trace Precedents button on the Formulas tab on the Ribbon. Solver searches the formula in the target cell to determine which cells are precedents of the target cell and then automatically adds these cells to the By Changing Cells box. The Guess button is not always accurate, however, which then requires you to change the cells selected by Solver.

7

- Click the Options button.

- When Excel displays the Solver Options dialog box, click Assume Linear Model (Figure 8–32).

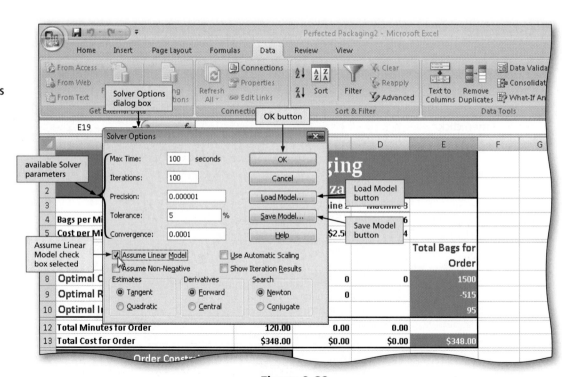

Figure 8–32

8

- Click the OK button.

- Click the Solve button in the Solver Parameters dialog box to display the Solver Results dialog box, indicating that Solver found a solution to the problem (Figure 8–33).

Q&A

Why does the answer found for cell E8 exceed the limit of 1,500 consumer-sized bags?

The limitations placed on Solver allowed for a small degree in error (Figure 8–32 on page EX 654). If no degree of error or uncertainly is allowed, then Solver may never find an exact solution. Spreadsheet specialists, therefore, often allow Solver some degree of error, and the default values shown in Figure 8–32 reflect the need to allow for some error. If this degree of uncertainty was not allowed, Solver might take an extremely long time to find a solution.

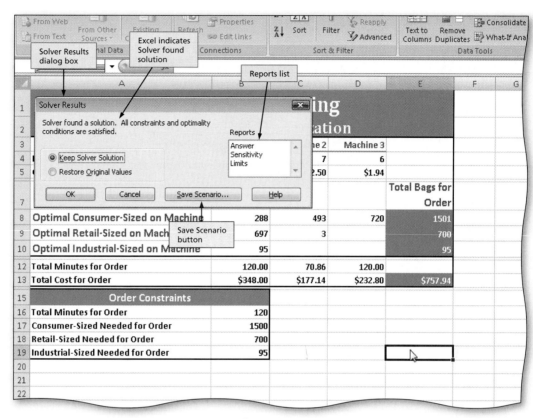

Figure 8–33

9

- Click Answer in the Reports list (Figure 8–34).

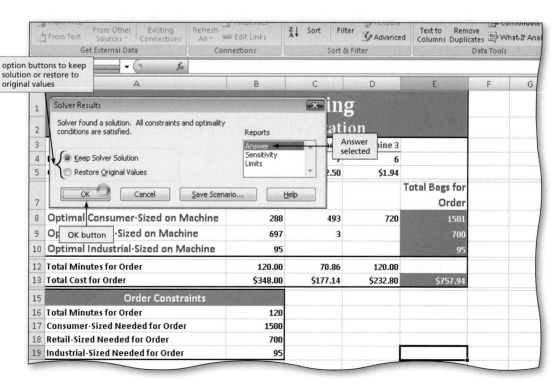

Figure 8–34

10

- Click the OK button to display the values found by Solver and the newly recalculated totals (Figure 8–35).

Q&A

What is the result of using Solver?

Figure 8–35 shows that all of the constraints in the problem have been satisfied. The cost for the order is $757.94, which is the only solution thus far that both meets the constraints and minimizes cost.

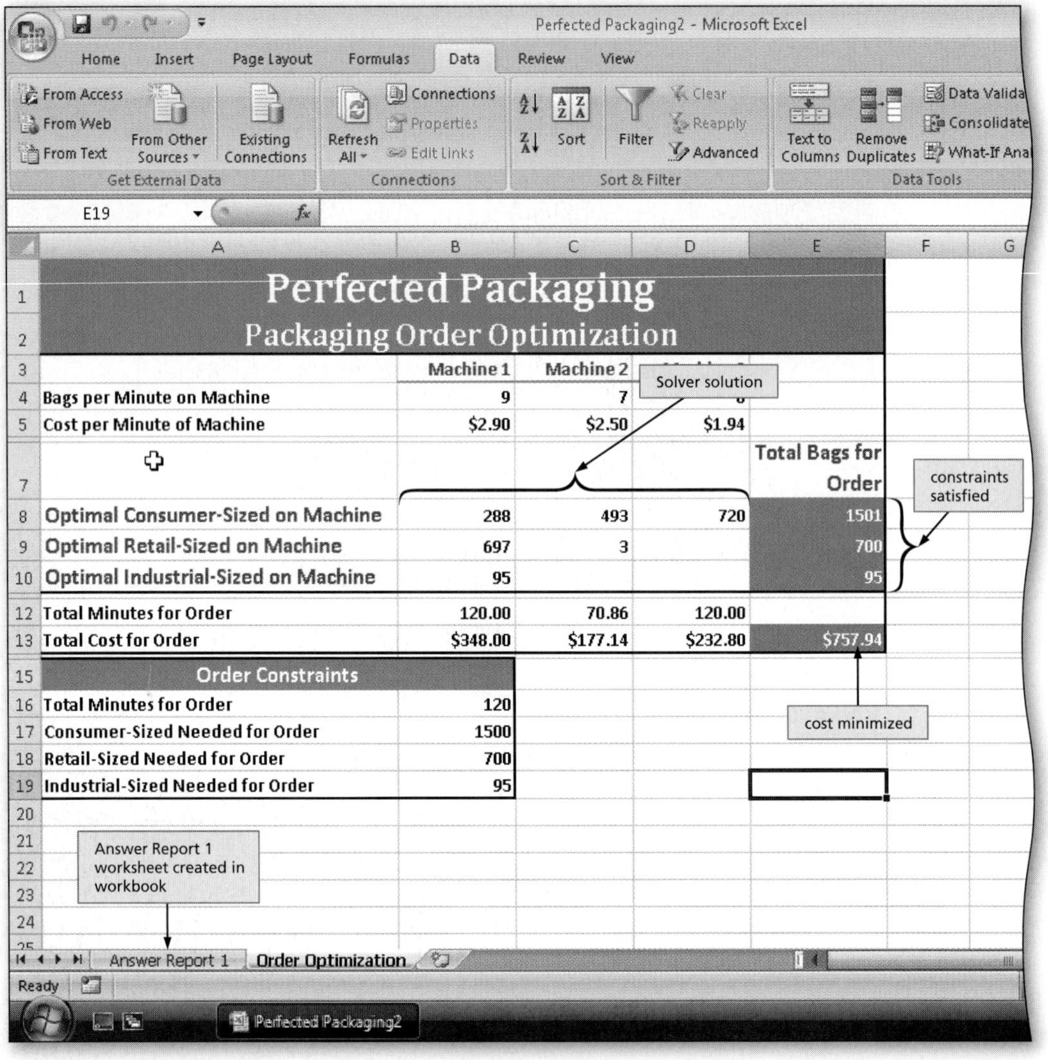

Figure 8–35

Other Ways

1. Press ALT+A, Y, 2

BTW

Solver Models
A model is a collection of the data in the target cell, changing cells, and constraints. When you save a model, Excel does not save the solution itself. The solution can be saved separately by using the Save Scenario button in the Solver Results dialog box shown in Figure 8–34 on page EX 655. When you save a model, the data is saved in an area you select in a worksheet. You should note carefully where you save a model, because Excel does not label or mark the model in any way.

Working with Solver Options

The Solver Options dialog box in Figure 8–32 contains several technical parameters that allow you to configure the inner workings of Solver. Many of these parameters are beyond the scope of this discussion. Usually, you already have the information for a problem that lets you determine which parameters you need to vary to determine a solution. Table 8–3 shows the meaning of some of the more commonly used Solver parameters.

Table 8–3 Commonly Used Solver Parameters in the Solver Options Dialog Box

Parameter	Meaning
Max Time	The total time that Solver should spend trying different solutions, expressed in seconds.
Iterations	The number of different combinations of possible answer values that Solver should try.
Tolerance	Instructs Solver how close it must come to the target value in order to consider the problem to be solved. For example, if the target value is 100 and the Tolerance is 5%, then 95 is an acceptable answer.
Assume Linear Model	If selected, assume that this problem is linear in nature. That is, the changing values have a proportional effect on the value of the target cell.
Assume Nonnegative	If selected, for all changing cells that do not have constraints on them, Solver should keep these numbers positive.

Excel automatically saves the most recently used Solver parameters and options. Excel also allows you to save the current target cell, changing cells, constraint values, and option values for Solver, so that you can try using new values and then reuse the previous values. To do so, clicking the Save Model button and Load Model button in the Solver Options dialog box (Figure 8–32 on page EX 654) allows you to save the values and then reuse them in the future. The Save Model button saves the target cell, changing cells, constraint values, and all of the option values in the Solver Options dialog box to a range of cells that you specify when you click the Save Model button. When you click the Load Model button, Excel prompts you to select the range where you previously saved a model. By saving models, you can tweak the Solver parameters and options without remembering or writing down the values you have tried.

The Save Scenario button shown in Figure 8–33 on page EX 655 allows you to save a Solver solution in a separate area in your workbook. Scenarios are discussed in detail later in this chapter.

When using Solver, three other issues must be kept in mind. First, some problems do not have solutions. The constraints may be constructed in such a way that an answer that satisfies all of the constraints cannot be found. Second, sometimes multiple answers solve the same problem. Solver does not indicate when this is the case, and you will have to use your own judgment to determine if this is the case. As long as you are confident that you have given Solver all of the constraints for a problem, however, all answers should be equally valid. Finally, Solver may require more time or iterations to solve the problem if it fails to find a solution.

To View the Solver Answer Report for Order 1

As shown in Figure 8–35, Solver automatically creates an Answer Report on a separate worksheet after it finds a solution. The Solver Answer Report summarizes the problem that you have presented to Solver. It shows the original and final values of the target cell along with the original and final values of the changing cells (adjustable cells) that Solver adjusted to find the answer. Additionally, it lists all of the constraints that you imposed on Solver.

The Answer Report documents that a particular problem has been solved correctly. Because it lists all of the relevant information in a concise format, you can use the Answer Report to make certain that you have entered all of the constraints and allowed Solver to vary all the cells necessary to solve the problem. You also can use the report to reconstruct the Solver model in the future.

The following steps view the Solver Answer Report.

1

- Click the Answer Report 1 tab at the bottom of the Excel window to display the Solver Answer Report (Figure 8–36).

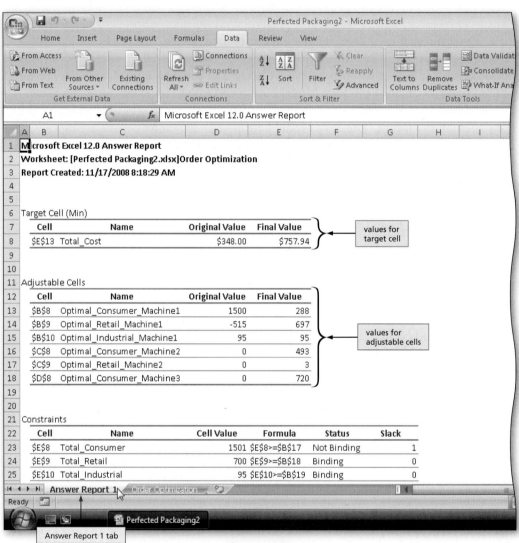

Figure 8–36

2

- Drag the Answer Report 1 tab to the right of the Order Optimization tab.

- Double-click the Answer Report 1 tab and type `Optimal Schedule Answer Report1` as the worksheet name.

- Click cell A1. Right-click the Optimal Schedule Answer Report1 tab and then point to Tab Color on the shortcut menu.

- Click Dark Teal, Text 2 (column 4, row 1).

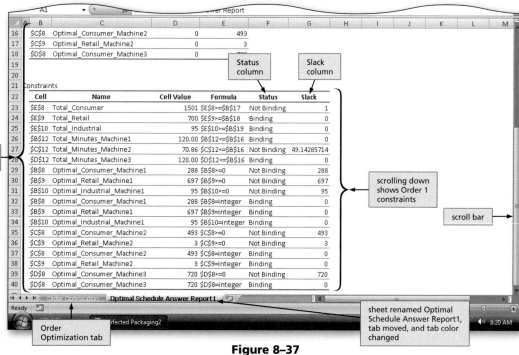

Figure 8–37

- Scroll down to view the remaining cells of the Answer Report (Figure 8–37).

Q&A

What is shown in the Answer Report?

Figure 8–37 shows additional information about the constraints that you placed on the problem and how the constraints were used to solve the problem. Column F, the **Status column**, indicates whether the constraint was binding or not. A constraint that is **binding** is one that limited the final solution in some way. For example, the total number of retail-sized bags filled in cell E9 is binding because the solution found the minimum number required by the constraints, which is 700 bags. No fewer bags could be filled given the constraints. A constraint that is **not binding** is one that was not a limiting factor in the solution that Solver provided.

Saving the Workbook with Passwords

Excel allows you to protect your data at the worksheet level, workbook level, and file level. At the worksheet level, you protect cells. At the workbook level, you protect the Excel window. Both of these levels of protection are available on the Review tab on the Ribbon as described in Chapter 7. The highest level of protection is file protection. **File protection** lets you assign a workbook one password for users who are allowed to view the workbook and a second password for users who are permitted to modify the workbook. Recall that, in Excel, a password is case sensitive and can be up to 15 characters long.

File protection is performed when Excel saves a workbook. Even though you are the workbook creator, you will be prompted for the passwords when you open the workbook later. The following steps save the workbook with passwords to enable file protection.

BTW

File Protection
Once you have protected your workbook with a password, it is important to write the password down or memorize it for future reference. Once you have saved the file with a password, it always will be a password-protected file; no way exists to bypass the requirement for a password.

To Save the Workbook with Passwords

1

- Click the Order Optimization tab at the bottom of the window.

- Click the Office Button and then click Save As.

- Click the Tools button in the Save As dialog box (Figure 8–38).

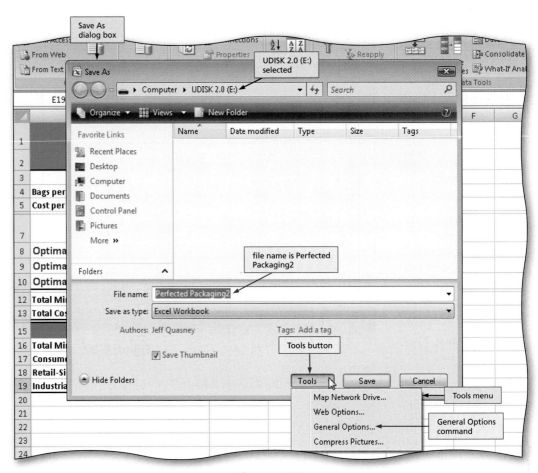

Figure 8–38

2

- Click General Options on the Tools menu to display the General Options dialog box.

- Type `mincost` in the 'Password to open' text box.

- Type `mincost` in the 'Password to modify' text box (Figure 8–39).

Why does Excel display bullets for the password?

Excel displays bullets in place of the password, mincost, in both instances, so that no one is able to see the password you typed.

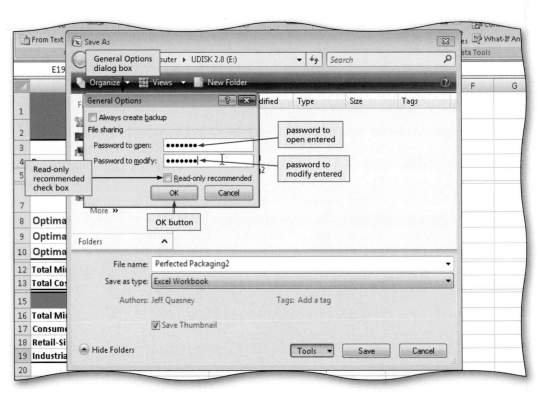

Figure 8–39

- Click the OK button.

- When Excel displays the Confirm Password dialog box, type `mincost` in the 'Reenter password to proceed' text box (Figure 8–40).

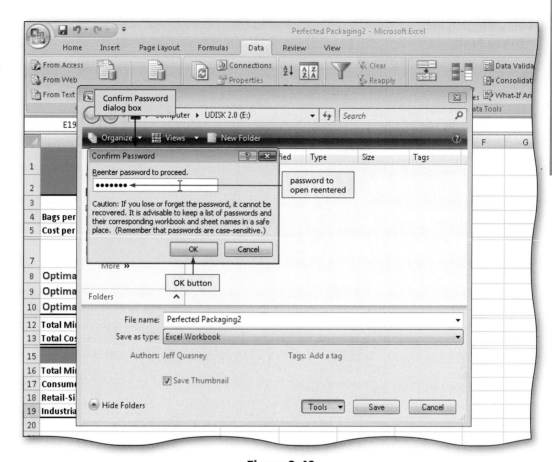

Figure 8–40

- Click the OK button.

- When Excel displays the Confirm Password dialog box, type `mincost` in the 'Reenter password to modify' text box (Figure 8–41).

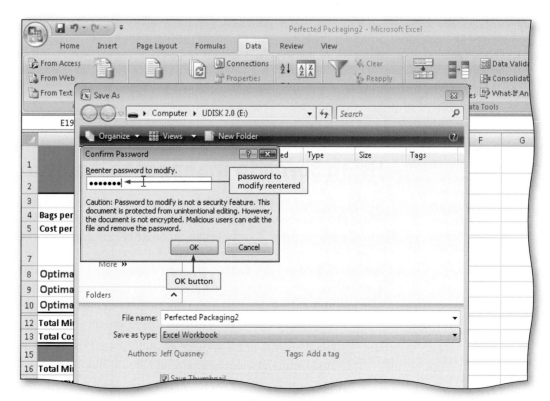

Figure 8–41

• Click the OK button (Figure 8–42).

• Click the Save button in the Save As dialog box to save the file to the UDISK 2.0 (E:) drive with the file name, Perfected Packaging2. If the Microsoft Office Excel dialog box appears, click the OK button to close it.

Q&A

What is the result of using file protection?

When a user opens the workbook, Excel will prompt for a password to open the workbook. If the user enters the correct password, Excel prompts for the password to modify the work-book. At this point, the user can enter the correct password or choose to open the

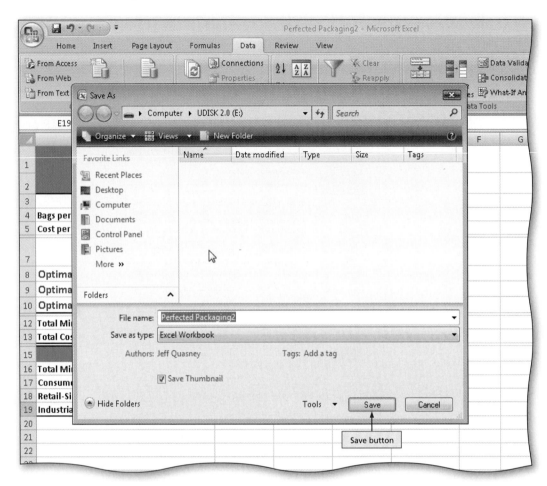

Figure 8–42

workbook as read-only, meaning that the user can view the contents of the workbook, but cannot modify it. The Read-only recommended check box shown in Figure 8–39 allows you to notify users who open your workbook that it is best to open the workbook as read-only.

Using Scenario Manager to Analyze Data

Excel's Scenario Manager allows you to record and save different sets of what-if assumptions (data values) called scenarios. In this chapter, each different order being analyzed can be considered a scenario. For example, an order requiring a maximum of 120 minutes to replicate 1,500 consumer-sized bags, 700 retail-sized bags, and 95 industrial-sized bags makes up a scenario for Order 1. Also, an order requiring a maximum of 200 minutes to replicate 1,400 consumer-sized bags, 1,600 retail-sized bags, and 300 industrial-sized bags makes up a scenario for Order 2. Each set of values in these examples represents a what-if assumption.

The primary uses of Scenario Manager are to:

1. Create different scenarios with multiple sets of changing cells
2. Build summary worksheets that contain the different scenarios
3. View the results of each scenario on your worksheet

Consider which cells in the worksheet constitute a scenario.

When considering which cells to save in a scenario, you should plan to save as few cells in a scenario as possible. You can first rule out cells with the following three characteristics:

1. Cells that contain sheet title, row heading, or column heading text. These cells will not change among various scenarios that you consider in your worksheet.

2. Cells that include formulas. These cells are considered to be result, or output, cells.

3. Cells that have constant values among various scenarios. For example, in the Order Optimization worksheet, the bags per minute that each machine can fill remains constant for the scenarios that should be considered according to the requirements document in Figure 8–2 on page EX 630.

   You should include cells that are considered to be input cells for your problem. Consider which cells change among the different situations that you want to consider and which cells contribute to the result you want to obtain. The requirements document in Figure 8–2 states that order constraints change for each order. Cells in the range B16:B19 are, therefore, changing cells for each scenario. Earlier in this chapter, trial and error and goal seeking were used to change cells in the ranges B8:B10, C8:C9, and D8. These are input cells that cause the results, or output, of the problem to change. The cells B8:B10, C8:C9, and D8, therefore, are changing cells for each scenario.

The next section in this chapter shows how to use Scenario Manager for each of the three uses listed above. After you create the scenarios, you can instruct Excel to build the summary worksheets, including a Scenario Summary worksheet and a Scenario PivotTable worksheet.

To Save the Current Data as a Scenario

The current data on the worksheet consists of Order 1 constraints and contains the values that correctly solve one problem presented by the first order. These values can be saved as a scenario that can be accessed later or compared side by side with other scenarios. The following steps save the current data for the Order 1 scenario using the Scenario Manager dialog box.

- With the Data tab active, click the What-If Analysis button on the Ribbon (Figure 8–43).

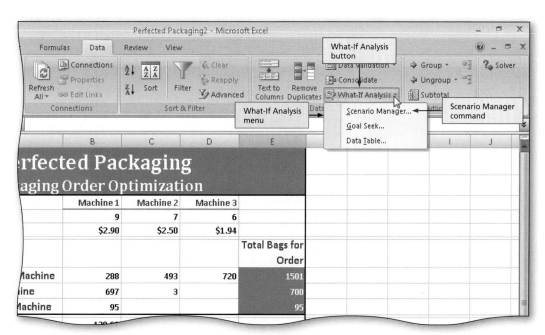

Figure 8–43

2

- Click Scenario Manager on the What-If Analysis menu to display the Scenario Manager dialog box, which indicates that no scenarios are defined (Figure 8–44).

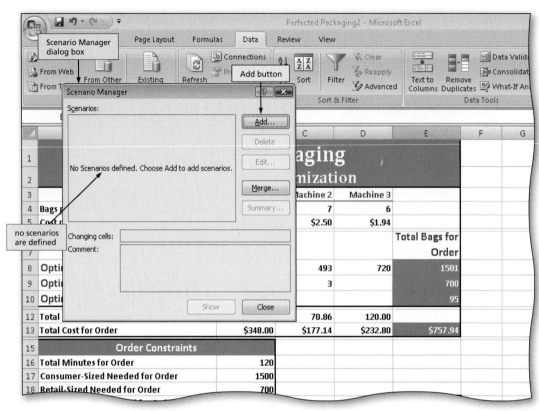

Figure 8–44

3

- Click the Add button.

- When Excel displays the Add Scenario dialog box, type Order 1 in the Scenario name text box (Figure 8–45).

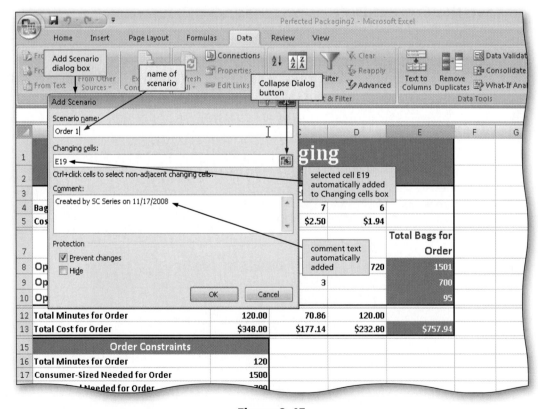

Figure 8–45

4

- Click the Collapse Dialog button.

- When Excel displays the Add Scenario - Changing cells dialog box, select the range B8:B10, hold down the CTRL key, and then select the ranges C8:C9, D8, and B16:B19.

- Release the CTRL key to display a marquee around the selected cells and assign the cells to the Changing cells text box (Figure 8–46).

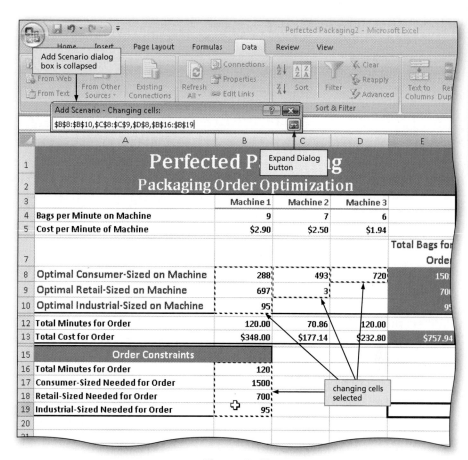

Figure 8–46

5

- Click the Expand Dialog button to change the Add Scenario dialog box to the Edit Scenario dialog box (Figure 8–47).

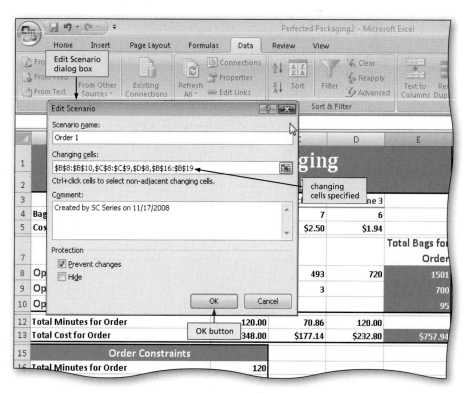

Figure 8–47

6

- Click the OK button (Figure 8–48).

Q&A

What does Excel display in the list?

The selected cell names appear in a numbered list with their current values (Figure 8–48). Because names were assigned to these cells when the work-sheet was created, the cell names, rather than cell references, appear in the numbered list.

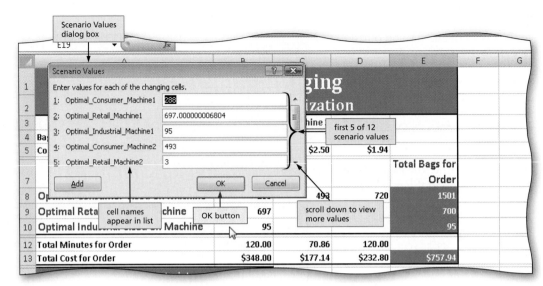

Figure 8–48

Q&A

What can I do with the scenario?

After the scenario has been saved, you can recall it at any time using Scenario Manager. In Figure 8–48, the values of the changing cells in the Scenario Values dialog box are defaulted to the current values in the worksheet. By changing the text boxes next to the cell names, you can save the scenario using values different than the current values.

7

- Click the OK button to display the Order 1 scenario in the Scenarios list (Figure 8–49).

8

- Click the Close button in the Scenario Manager dialog box.

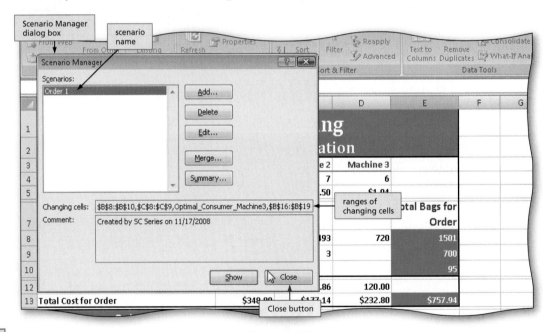

Figure 8–49

Other Ways

1. Press ALT+A, W, S

To Add the Data for a New Scenario

After the Order 1 scenario is saved, you can enter the data for the Order 2 scenario directly in the worksheet and then use Solver to solve the Order 2 scenario (Figure 8–50a) in the same way that you solved the Order 1 scenario. The same constraints apply for both scenarios, so Solver does not require you to reenter all of the con-straints. The Answer Report (Figure 8–50b) meets the requirement that you create supporting documentation for your answer. After solving the Order 2 scenario, you should save the scenario, just as you saved the Order 1 scenario.

(a) Results of Using Solver with Second Order

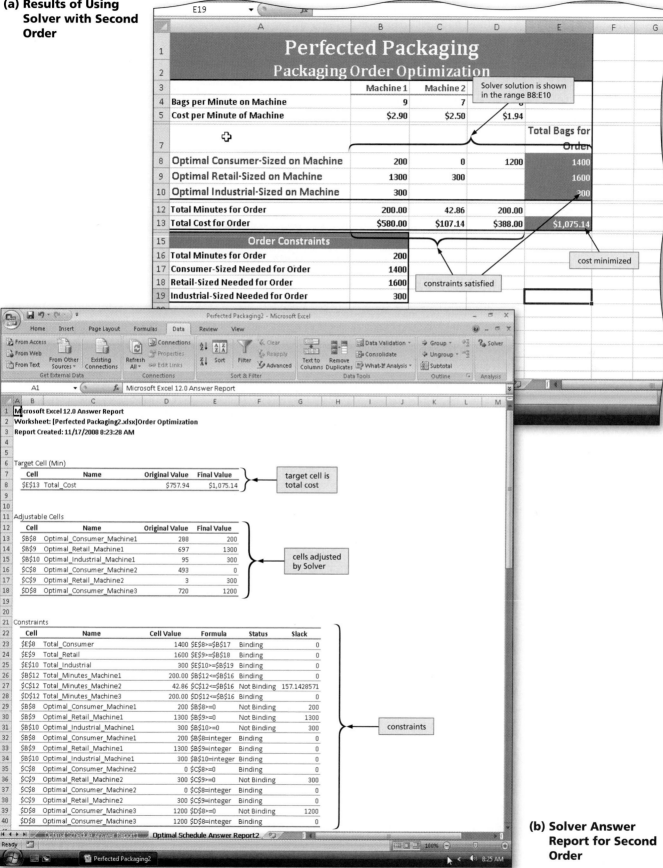

(b) Solver Answer Report for Second Order

Figure 8–50

The order constraints for Order 2 are that the order must be completed within 200 minutes and include 1,400 consumer-sized bags, 1,600 retail-sized bags, and 300 industrial-sized bags. These values must be entered into the appropriate cells before you can use Solver.

The following step adds the data for a new scenario.

1

- Click cell B16 and type 200 as the maximum minutes for the order.

- Click cell B17 and type 1400 as the number of consumer-sized bags.

- Click cell B18 and type 1600 as the number of retail-sized bags.

- Click cell B19, type 300 as the number of industrial-sized bags, and then click cell E19 (Figure 8–51).

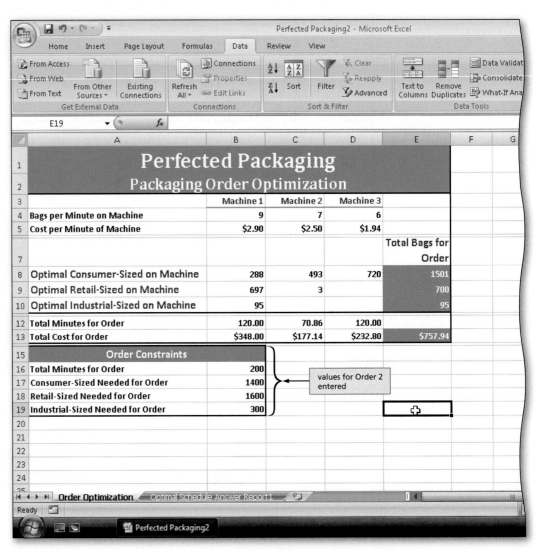

Figure 8–51

BTW

New Scenarios
When you are beginning to create scenarios in a worksheet, a few guidelines can help in organizing the data. First, create a base scenario that contains the original values of the worksheet. Second, name the cells that will be changing cells and result cells, as was done in the worksheet in this project. Finally, if you plan to save different types of scenarios in a worksheet (that is, different changing cells), use a naming convention for the scenarios that will help you remember which scenario contains which set of changing cells.

To Use Solver to Find a New Solution

Next, Solver must be used to find a new solution to determine the optimal combination of bags and machines that satisfies the constraints and minimizes cost for Order 2.

As was true of the Order 1 scenario, the Order 2 scenario must be solved before saving it as a scenario. Figure 8–51 shows that the total number of bags for the order in the range E8:E10 does not satisfy order constraints for Order 2. It is unknown whether a possible solution to the problem even exists. Solver must be used to make this determination, as shown in the following steps.

- Click the Solver button on the Data tab on the Ribbon to display the Solver Parameters dialog box with the target cell, changing cells, and constraints used with Order 1 (Figure 8–52).

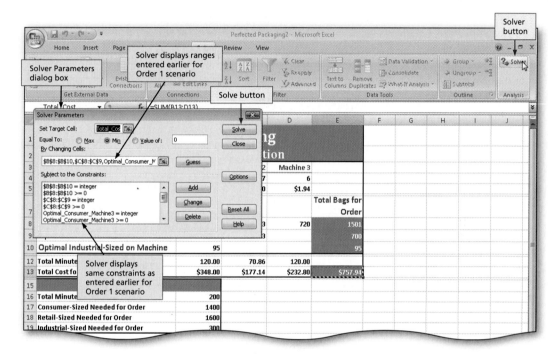

Figure 8–52

- Click the Solve button to solve the problem using Solver.

- Click Answer in the Reports list (Figure 8–53).

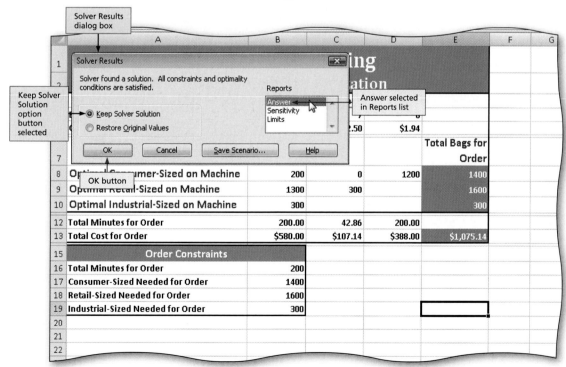

Figure 8–53

3

- Click the OK button to display the values found by Solver (Figure 8–54).

Q&A

What did Solver accomplish?

As shown in Figure 8–54, Solver found a solution that satisfies all of the constraints and minimizes cost. With Order 1, the order breakdown was 288 consumer-sized bags, 697 retail-sized bags, and 95 industrial-sized bags on Machine 1; 493 consumer-sized bags and 3 retail-sized bags on Machine 2; and 720 consumer-sized bags on Machine 3 (Figure 8–35 on page EX 656). With Order 2, the order breakdown is 200 consumer-sized bags, 1300 retail-sized bags, and 300 industrial-sized bags on Machine 1;

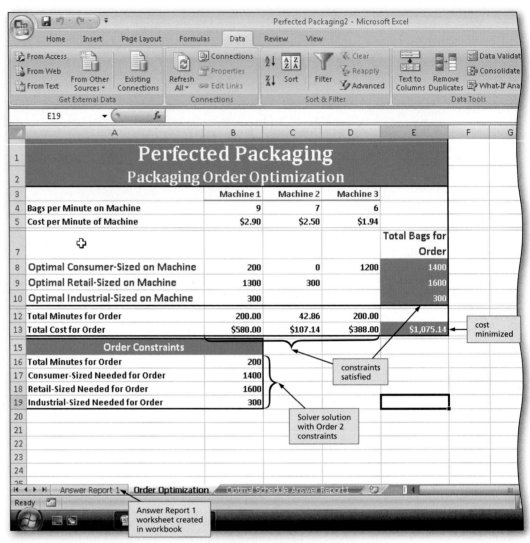

Figure 8–54

300 retail-sized bags on Machine 2; and 1200 consumer-sized bags on Machine 3 (Figure 8–54). The cost for Order 1 was $757.94. The cost for Order 2 is $1,075.14.

Other Ways
1. Press ALT+A, Y, 2

To View the Solver Answer Report for Order 2

The next step is to view the Answer Report for the Order 2 solution that will be presented to the company's management.

- Click the Answer Report 1 tab at the bottom of the Excel window (Figure 8–55).

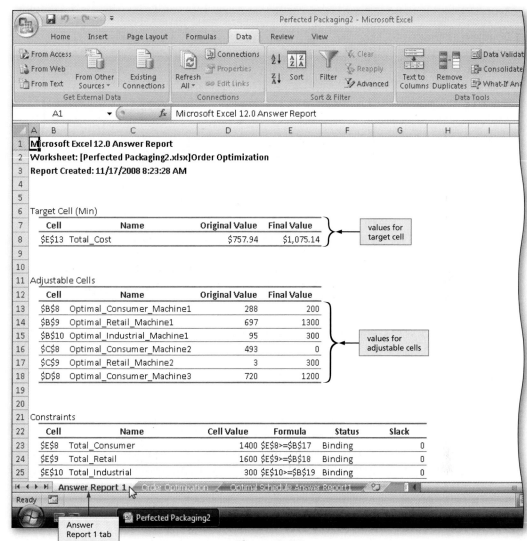

Figure 8–55

- Drag the Answer Report 1 tab to the right of the Optimal Schedule Answer Report1 tab.

- Double-click the Answer Report 1 tab and type Optimal Schedule Answer Report2 as the worksheet name.

- Click cell A1.

- Right-click the Optimal Schedule Answer Report2 tab and then point to Tab Color on the shortcut menu.

- Click Bright Green, Accent 4 (column 8, row 1).

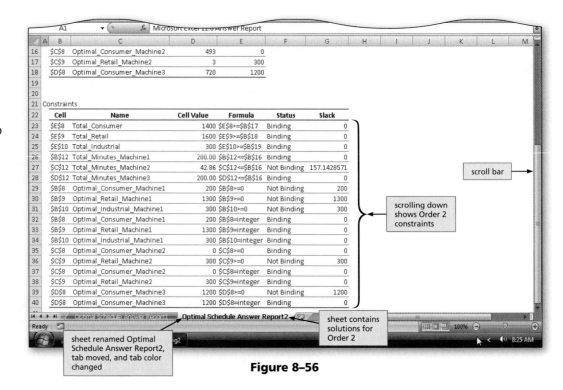

Figure 8–56

- Scroll down to view the remaining cells of the Order 2 Answer Report (Figure 8–56).

To Save the Second Solver Solution as a Scenario

The power of Scenario Manager becomes evident when you begin adding scenarios to your worksheet. Multiple scenarios can be compared side by side. Using multiple scenarios on the same worksheet also saves time by reusing the work that you did to create the initial worksheet.

The following steps save the second Solver solution as a scenario.

1

- Click the Order Optimization tab at the bottom of the window.

- Click the What-If Analysis button on the Ribbon (Figure 8–57).

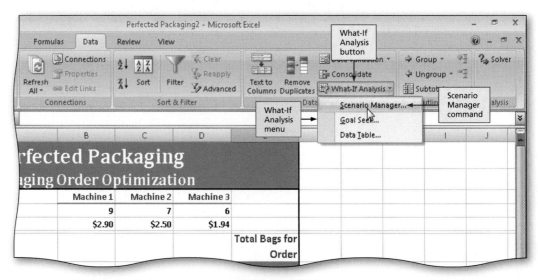

Figure 8–57

2

- Click Scenario Manager on the What-If Analysis menu to display the Scenario Manager dialog box (Figure 8–58).

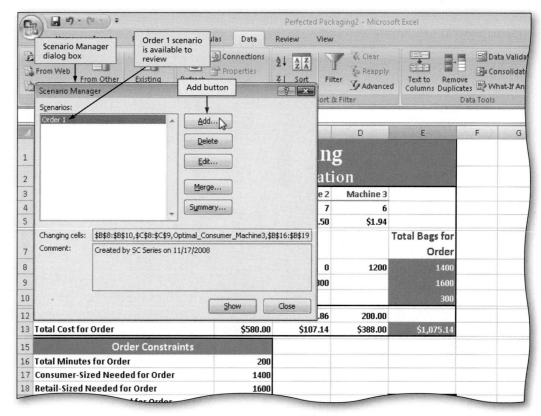

Figure 8–58

3

- Click the Add button.

- Type Order 2 in the Scenario name text box (Figure 8–59).

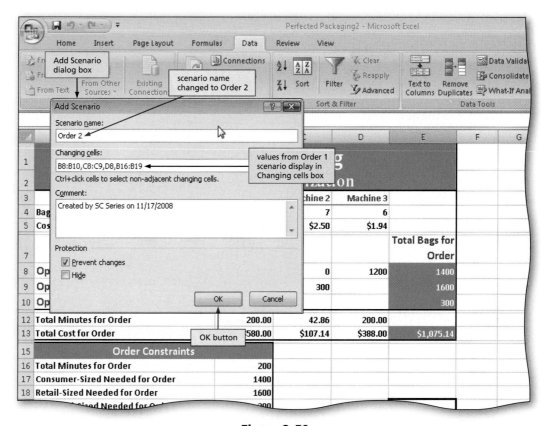

Figure 8–59

4

- Click the OK button to display the Scenario Values dialog box with the current values from the worksheet (Figure 8–60).

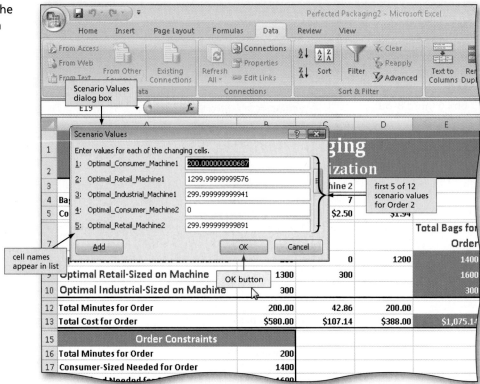

Figure 8–60

5

- Click the OK button to display Order 2 along with Order 1 in the Scenarios list (Figure 8–61).

6

- Click the Close button.

Q&A

How can I use the new Order 2 scenario?

The Order 2 scenario now can be recalled using Scenario Manager. Figure 8–60 shows the list of changing cells for the scenario. Instead of entering the data in the worksheet, you simply could enter values here to add new scenarios. Because Solver is needed to find a solution to the Order 2 scenario, however, the values were entered on the worksheet first.

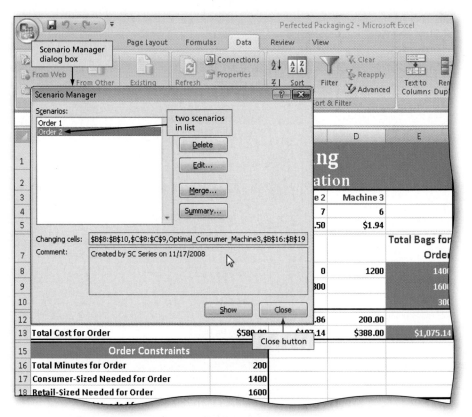

Figure 8–61

To Show a Saved Scenario

After a scenario is saved, you use the Show button in the Scenario Manager dialog box to view the scenario. The following steps show how to show the Order 1 scenario created earlier in the chapter.

- Click the What-If Analysis button on the Ribbon (Figure 8–62).

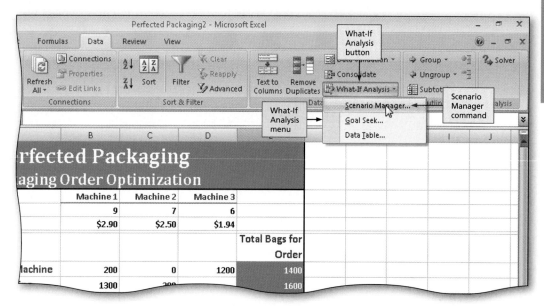

Figure 8–62

2

- Click Scenario Manager on the What-If Analysis menu.

- If necessary, in the Scenario Manager dialog box, select Order 1 in the Scenarios list (Figure 8–63).

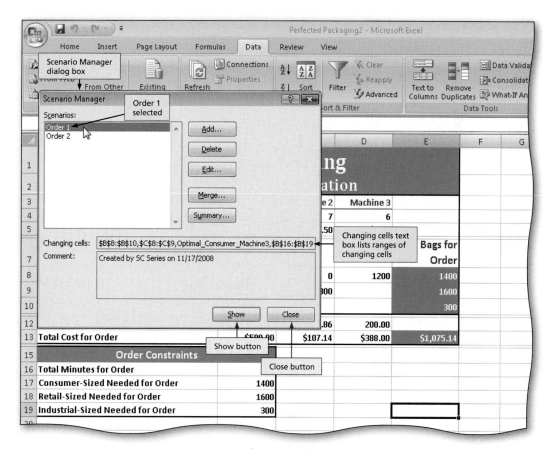

Figure 8–63

3

- Click the Show button and then click the Close button to display the data for the Order 1 scenario in the worksheet (Figure 8–64).

Q&A What can I do to view the worksheet with the previous data?

You can undo showing the Order 1 scenario results by clicking the Undo button on the Quick Access Toolbar. If desired, you then can click the Redo button on the Quick Access Toolbar to show the Order 1 scenario results again. If you had several saved scenarios, you could view each one and then use the Undo and Redo buttons to switch between them.

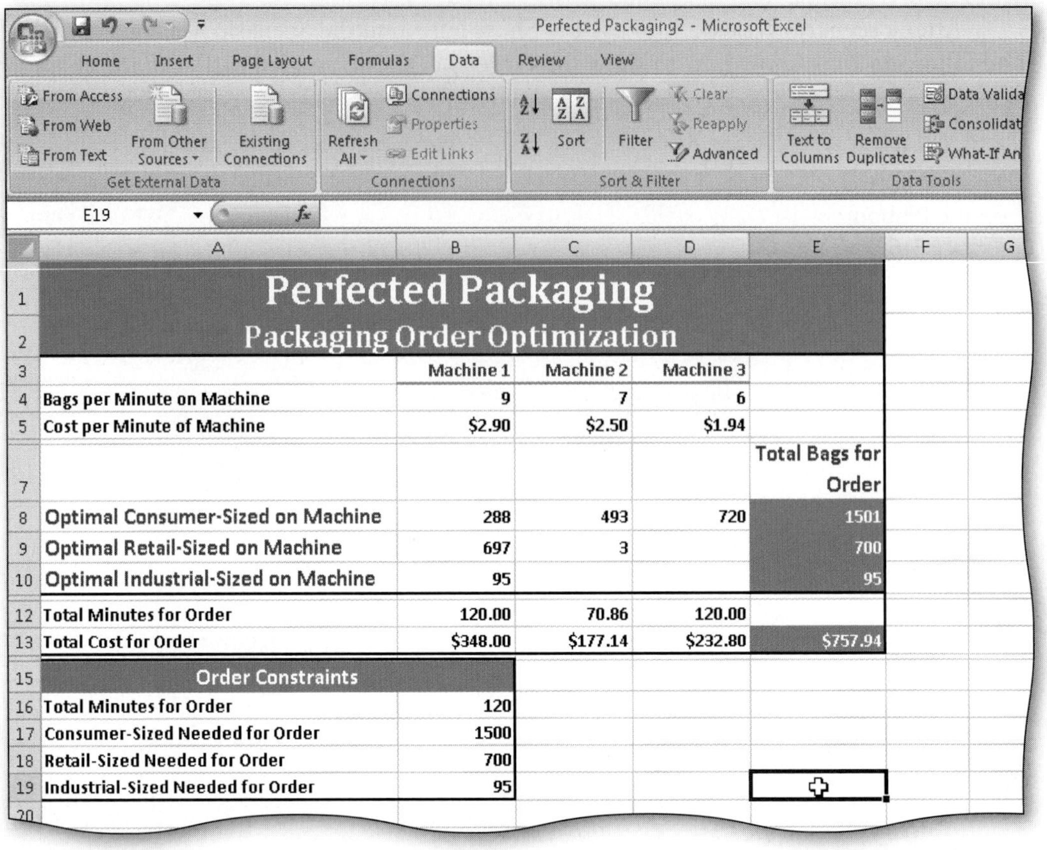

Figure 8–64

Other Ways

1. Press ALT+A, W, S, double-click scenario name

Summarizing Scenarios

This section creates a Scenario Summary worksheet and a Scenario PivotTable worksheet. These concise reports allow you to view and manipulate several what-if situations to assist in decision-making. The **Scenario Summary worksheet** generated by the Scenario Manager actually is an outlined worksheet (Figure 8–65a) that you can print and manipulate just like any other worksheet. As you learned in Chapter 5, an outlined worksheet is one that contains symbols (buttons) that allow you to collapse and expand rows and columns.

The **Scenario PivotTable worksheet** (Figure 8–65b) generated by the Scenario Manager also is a worksheet that you can print and manipulate like other worksheets. A **PivotTable** is a table that summarizes large amounts of information and can be manipulated to show the data from different points of view. The Scenario PivotTable worksheet allows you to compare the results of scenarios.

BTW **Showing Scenarios** You can add a list of scenarios to the Quick Access Toolbar by using the More Commands command on the Customize Quick Access Toolbar menu. Click the Customize Quick Access Toolbar button and then click More Commands. Add the Scenarios command in the 'Choose commands from' list and then close the Excel Options dialog box. You then can switch quickly between scenarios on your worksheet.

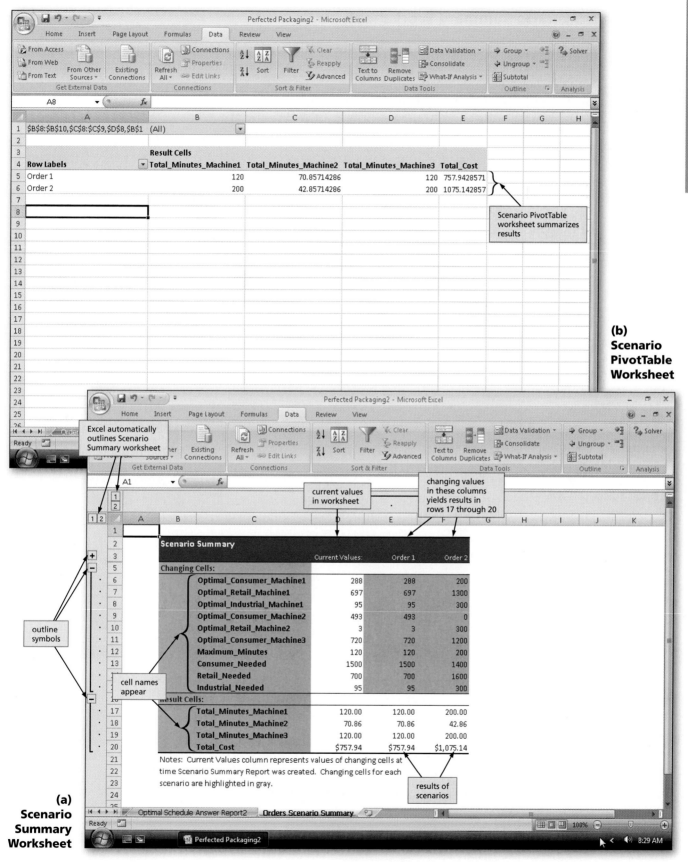

Figure 8–65

To Create a Scenario Summary Worksheet

The Scenario Summary worksheet in Figure 8–65a shows the total hours for each machine and total cost for the current worksheet values and the Order 1 and 2 scenarios. The optimal number of bags to fill on each machine calculated by Solver is shown for both orders.

The following steps create a Scenario Summary worksheet.

- Click the What-If Analysis button on the Ribbon (Figure 8–66).

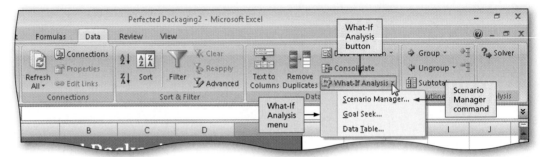

Figure 8–66

- Click Scenario Manager on the What-If Analysis menu to display the Scenario Manager dialog box.

- If necessary, in the Scenario Manager dialog box, select Order 1 (Figure 8–67).

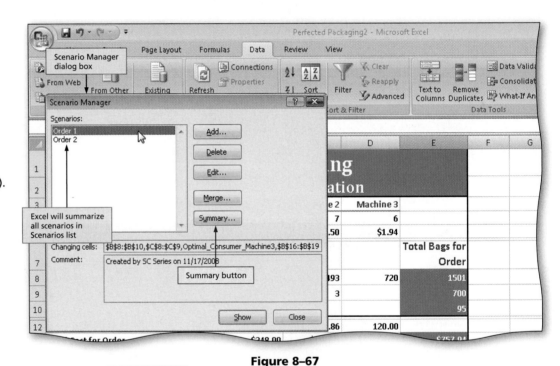

Figure 8–67

❸

- Click the Summary button to display the Scenario Summary dialog box (Figure 8–68).

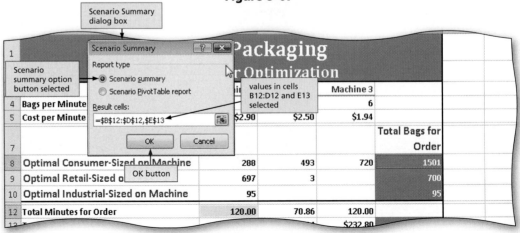

Figure 8–68

4

- Click the OK button.

- When Excel displays the Scenario Summary, double-click the Scenario Summary tab, type `Orders Scenario Summary` as the new worksheet name, and then press the ENTER key.

- Right-click the Orders Scenario Summary tab and then point to Tab Color on the shortcut menu.

- Click Black, Text 1, Lighter 50% (column 2, row 2).

- Drag the Orders Scenario Summary tab to the right of the Optimal Schedule Answer Report2 tab (Figure 8–69).

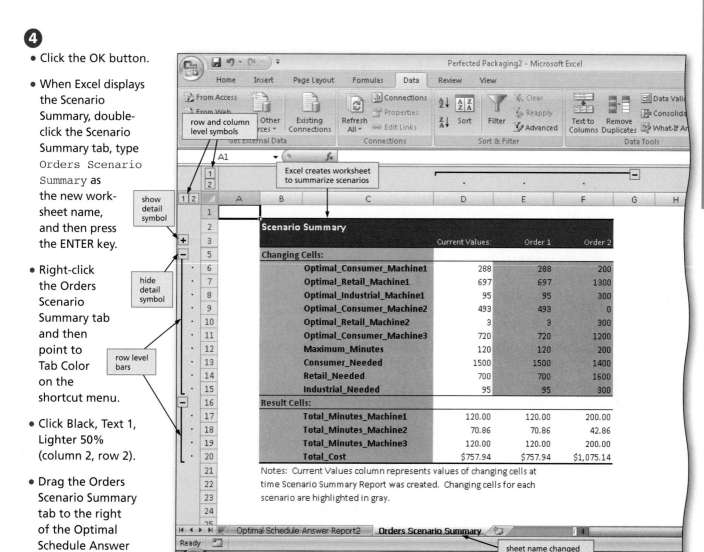

Figure 8–69

Q&A | What is shown in the Orders Scenario Summary worksheet?

Column D in the Scenario Summary worksheet in Figure 8–69 shows the results of the current values in the Order Optimization worksheet, which is the Order 1 scenario; columns E and F show the results of the two scenarios. The Scenario Summary worksheet makes it easier to compare the results of the scenarios.

Other Ways

1. Press ALT+A, W, S, ALT+U, press ENTER key

Working with an Outlined Worksheet

As shown in Figure 8–69, Excel automatically outlines the Scenario Summary worksheet. The outline symbols appear above and to the left of the worksheet. As discussed in Chapter 5, you can click the outline symbols to expand or collapse the rows and columns in a worksheet. For example, if you click the show detail symbol, Excel displays additional rows or columns that are summarized on the displayed row or column.

BTW | **Outlined Worksheets**
You can outline any worksheet by using the Auto Outline command on the Group submenu that appears when you click the Group button arrow on the Data tab on the Ribbon.

If you click a hide detail symbol, Excel hides any detail rows that extend through the length of the corresponding row level bar or column level bar. You also can expand or collapse a worksheet by clicking the row level symbol or column level symbol above and to the left of row title 1.

An outline is especially useful when working with large worksheets. To remove an outline, click the Ungroup button arrow on the Data tab on the Ribbon and then click Clear Outline.

To Create a Scenario PivotTable Worksheet

Excel also can generate a Scenario PivotTable worksheet to help analyze and compare the results of multiple scenarios. A Scenario PivotTable worksheet gives you the ability to summarize the scenario data and then rotate the table's row and column titles to obtain different views of the summarized data. The Scenario PivotTable worksheet to be created in this chapter is shown in Figure 8–65b on page EX 677. The table summarizes the Order 1 and Order 2 scenarios and shows the result cells for the two scenarios for easy comparison.

PivotTables are powerful data analysis tools because they allow you to view the data in various ways by interchanging or pairing the row and column fields by dragging the buttons located on cells A4 and B1 as shown in Figure 8–65b. The process of rotating the field values around the data fields will be discussed in the next chapter.

The following steps create the Scenario PivotTable worksheet shown in Figure 8–65b.

- Scroll to the Order Optimization tab and then click the Order Optimization tab at the bottom of the window.

- Click the What-If Analysis button on the Ribbon and then click Scenario Manager to display the Scenario Manager dialog box (Figure 8–70).

- If necessary, when Excel displays the Scenario Manager dialog box, select Order 1.

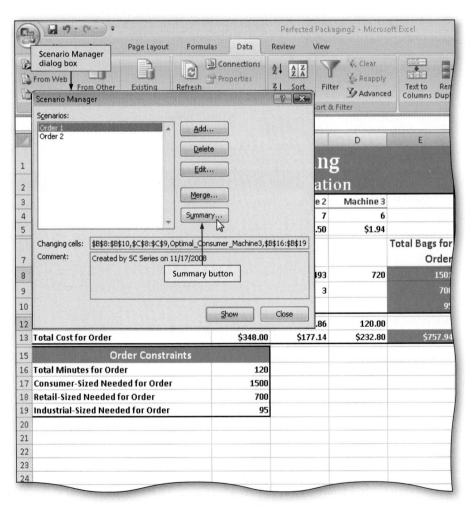

Figure 8–70

2

- Click the Summary button to display the Scenario Summary dialog box.

- In the Scenario Summary dialog box, click Scenario PivotTable report in the Report type area (Figure 8–71).

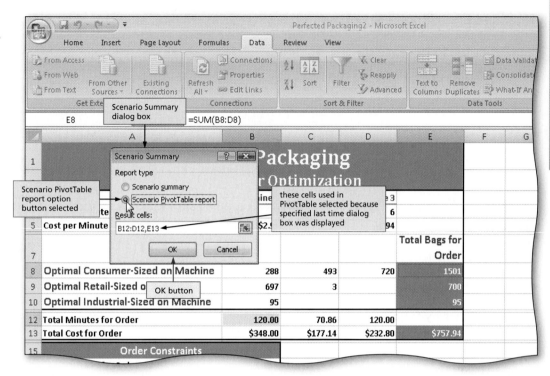

Figure 8–71

3

- Click the OK button (Figure 8–72).

Q&A

What if my worksheet appears differently than that shown in Figure 8–72?

Excel displays the Scenario PivotTable worksheet with the cell references of the changing values in column A (Figure 8–72). Excel may display the worksheet differently; you also may have to resize the column width of column A if it appears too large. In addition, the worksheet may have cell names instead of cell references in cell A1.

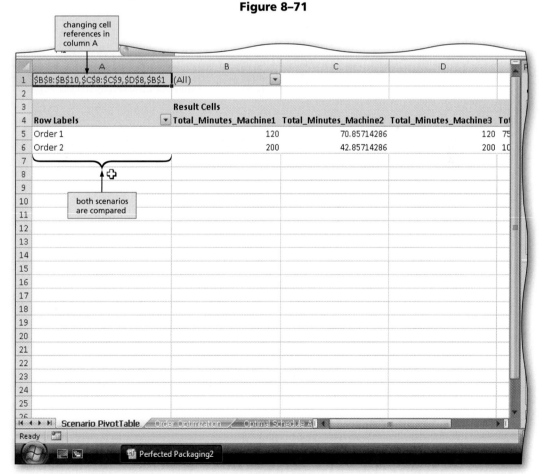

Figure 8–72

4

- Double-click the Scenario PivotTable tab and type `Order Scenario PivotTable` as the worksheet name.

- Click cell A8.

- Right-click the Order Scenario PivotTable tab and then point to Tab Color on the shortcut menu.

- Click Lime, Accent 6 (column 10, row 1).

- Drag the tab to the right of the Orders Scenario Summary tab (Figure 8–73).

How can I use the PivotTable?

After the PivotTable is created, you can treat it like any other worksheet. Thus, you can print or chart a PivotTable. If you update the data in one of the scenarios, click the Refresh All button on the Data tab on the Ribbon to update the PivotTable. If you show a scenario and merely change values on the scenario worksheet, it is not the same as changing the scenario. If you want to change the data in a scenario, you must use Scenario Manager.

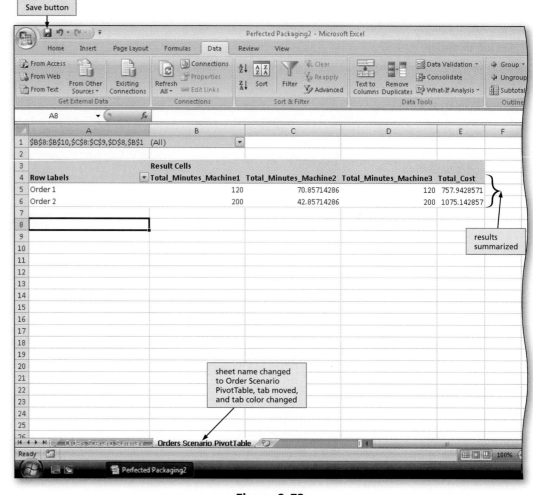

Figure 8–73

5

- Click the Save button on the Quick Access Toolbar to save the workbook using the file name, Perfected Packaging2.

Other Ways

1. Press ALT+A, W, S, ALT+U, ALT+P, press ENTER key

Preparing a Workbook for Distribution

Excel provides several methods to protect your privacy and/or data that you may not want to share with others. Before distributing your workbook to others, you should consider what type of hidden information may be in your document. In previous chapters, you have learned to hide rows and columns, protect cells, protect worksheets, and protect workbooks. Other types of information may be hidden in a workbook. Excel provides a tool, the Document Inspector, to inspect and report such information. You then easily can remove the hidden information or choose to leave the information in the document.

BTW

Scenario PivotTables

A Scenario PivotTable is a powerful analysis tool for comparing the results of scenarios when the differences and causes of the differences among scenarios are not completely obvious. You can compare scenarios side by side, perform sorts and filters on the values of the result cells, and rotate rows and columns of the table to gain a different perspective on the results.

When distributing a workbook, you also should consider whether the intended recipients have the most recent version of Excel. If this is not the case, Excel allows you to save a workbook for use in previous versions of Excel, such as Excel 97-2003. When you save a workbook in the Excel 97-2003 Workbook file format, Excel will invoke the Compatibility Checker, which notifies you if any of the content of your workbook cannot be saved in that format. Additionally, the Compatibility Checker will inform you if any content will not appear the same, such as cell or chart formatting.

BTW

Quick Reference
For a table that lists how to complete the tasks covered in this book using the mouse, Ribbon, shortcut menu, and keyboard, see the Quick Reference Summary at the back of this book, or visit the Excel 2007 Quick Reference Web page (scsite.com/ex2007/qr).

To Inspect a Document for Hidden and Personal Information

The Document Inspector should be used before sharing a workbook publicly or when you believe that you may have left extraneous information in hidden rows and columns, hidden worksheets, document properties, headers and footers, or worksheet comments.

The following steps inspect the Perfected Packaging2 workbook for hidden and personal information.

1

- Click the Order Optimization tab at the bottom of the Excel window.

- Click the Office Button and then point to the Prepare command on the Office Button menu (Figure 8–74).

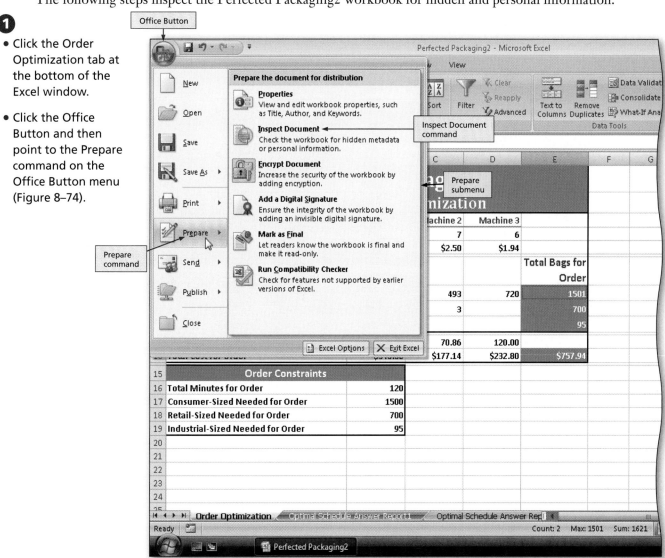

Figure 8–74

● Click Inspect
Document on
the Prepare sub-
menu to display
the Document
Inspector dialog box
(Figure 8–75).

Q&A

What is shown in the
Document Inspector
dialog box?

The Document
Inspector dialog box
allows you to choose
which types of
content to inspect.
Unless you are
comfortable with
some items not
being checked,
you typically should
leave all of the
items selected. In
Figure 8–75, the
Document Inspector
will search the docu-
ment properties,
which may contain
your name. You
purposefully want
your name or other
personal informa-
tion in the document
properties, so you
may remove the
check mark from the
Document Properties and Personal Information check box.

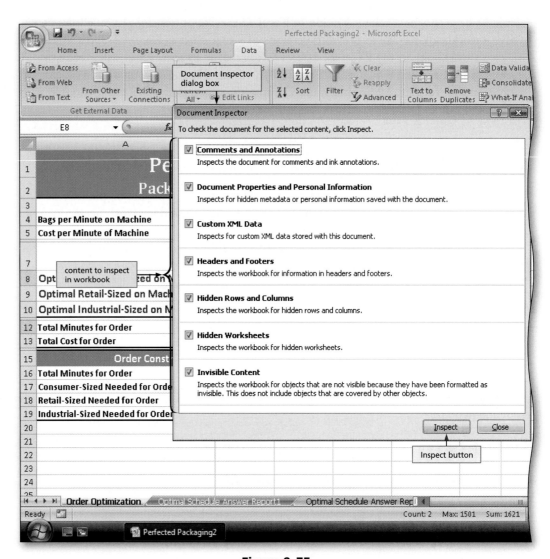

Figure 8–75

3

- Click the Inspect button in the Document Inspector dialog box to run the Document Inspector (Figure 8–76).

Q&A What did the Document Inspector find?

The Document Inspector found document properties, comments in the scenarios created in this chapter, a hidden row in the Scenario PivotTable, and two hidden worksheets. The Remove All button in the dialog box allows you quickly to remove the items found. In many instances, you may want to take notes of the results and then investigate and remedy each one separately. In the Perfected Packaging2 workbook, all of these items found by the Document Inspector are expected and do not need to be remedied.

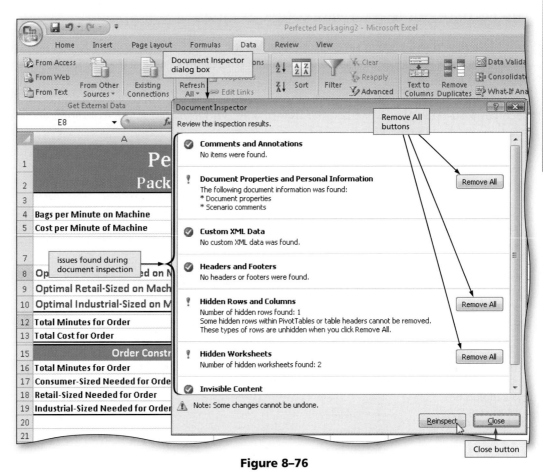

Figure 8–76

4

- Click the Close button in the Document Inspector dialog box.

Other Ways
1. Press ALT+F, E, I

Information Rights Management

Information Rights Management (IRM) is a feature of Excel that allows you to restrict access to workbooks. IRM allows you to restrict who can view, modify, print, forward, and copy a workbook. The types of restrictions include a variety of options. For example, expiration dates for reading or modifying a workbook are available. Before using IRM, your computer first must be configured with IRM, as should the computers of anyone attempting to use a document that includes IRM features.

When IRM is installed properly on your computer, the Prepare submenu on the Office Button menu includes the Restrict Permission command. When you click the Restrict Permission command, the Permission dialog box is displayed. The Permission dialog box allows you to set the level of access to your workbook. You can determine who can read and who can change your workbook by selecting users from your address book. You also can select specific users and assign varying levels of permissions to different users of your workbook. For more information about IRM, search Excel Help for Information Rights Management.

BTW

Excel Help
The best way to become familiar with Excel Help is to use it. Appendix C includes detailed information about Excel Help and exercises that will help you gain confidence in using it.

To Check Compatibility and Save a Workbook Using the Excel 97-2003 Workbook File Format and Mark a Workbook as Final

Often, you will need to save a workbook for use in previous versions of Excel. Because each version of Excel includes varying features, you should determine if the features you use in your workbook are compatible with earlier versions of Excel.

Before sharing a workbook with others, you can mark the workbook as being final. By doing so, the workbook becomes read-only. Also, when another user of your workbook opens the workbook, he or she will be notified that you have marked the workbook as final.

The following steps check the compatibility of the workbook while saving the workbook in the Excel 97-2003 Workbook file format.

1
- Click the Office Button and then click the Save As button arrow on the Office Button menu to display the Save As submenu.
- Click Excel 97-2003 Workbook on the Save As submenu to display the Save As dialog box (Figure 8–77).

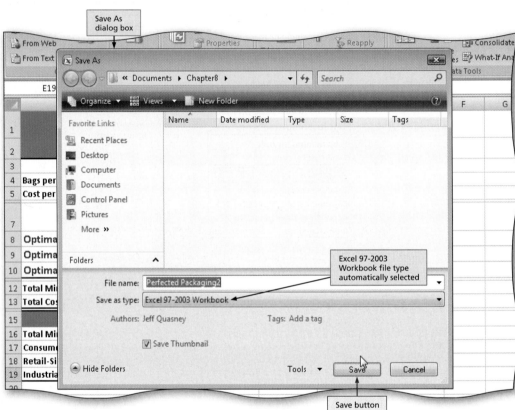

Figure 8–77

2
- Click the Save button in the Save As dialog box to display the Microsoft Office Excel dialog box (Figure 8–78).

Q&A

What is the meaning of the message in the Microsoft Office Excel dialog box?

The message notifies you that a better choice of file format may be the Office Open XML file format. Because this format is not compatible with Excel 2003, it is not a good choice of file format for the Perfected Packaging2 workbook.

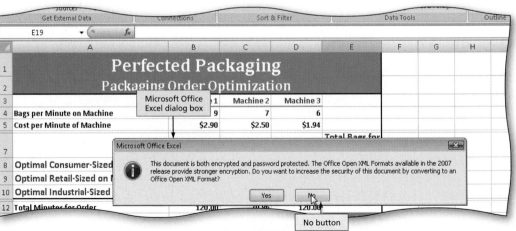

Figure 8–78

3

- Click the No button in the Microsoft Office Excel dialog box to display the Microsoft Office Excel - Compatibility Checker dialog box (Figure 8–79).

What is shown in the Microsoft Office Excel - Compatibility Checker dialog box?

The Summary column of the list of issues shows that both the PivotTable and the style used to format the PivotTable are not compatible with previous versions of Excel. While the workbook still will be saved in the Excel 97-2003 file format, the Orders Scenario PivotTable will not be available.

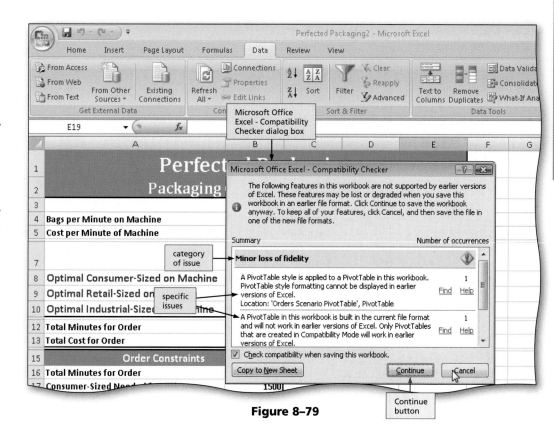

Figure 8–79

4

- Click the Continue button in the Microsoft Office Excel - Compatibility Checker dialog box to save the workbook in the Excel 97-2003 Workbook file format.

5

- Click the Office Button, point to the Prepare command on the Office Button menu, and then point to the Mark as Final command on the Prepare submenu (Figure 8–80).

Figure 8–80

- Click Mark as Final to display the Microsoft Excel dialog box (Figure 8–81).

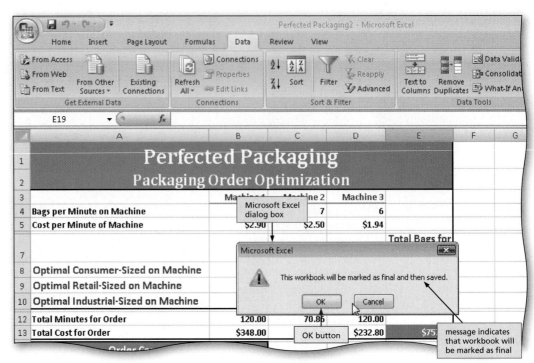

Figure 8–81

- Click the OK button and then click the OK button if the Compatibility Checker dialog box is displayed to display the Microsoft Office Excel dialog box (Figure 8–82).

- Click the OK button to close the Microsoft Office Excel dialog box.

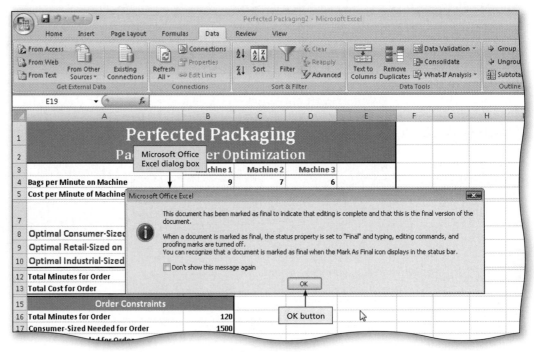

Figure 8–82

Other Ways

1. Press ALT+F, A, A, select type in 'Save as type' box, ALT+S

To Quit Excel

The following steps quit Excel.

1 Click the Close button on the right side of the title bar.

2 If Excel displays a Microsoft Office Excel dialog box, click the No button.

BTW

Certification
The Microsoft Certified Application Specialist (MCAS) program provides an opportunity for you to obtain a valuable industry credential – proof that you have the Excel 2007 skills required by employers. For more information, see Appendix G or visit the Excel 2007 Certification Web page (scsite.com/ex2007/cert).

Chapter Summary

In this chapter, you learned how to use a number of techniques to solve problems using Excel, including using trial and error, goal seeking, and Solver; analyze a worksheet using formula auditing techniques; use data validation on cells and inform a user about the validation rules; manage different problems on the same worksheet using Scenario Manager and then summarize the results of the scenarios with a Scenario Summary worksheet and a Scenario PivotTable worksheet; save a workbook file with passwords; prepare a workbook for distribution; and save a workbook for use in a previous version of Excel. The items listed below include all the new Excel skills you have learned in this chapter.

1. Trace Precedents (EX 633)
2. Remove the Precedent Arrows (EX 635)
3. Trace Dependents (EX 636)
4. Remove the Dependent Arrows (EX 637)
5. Add Data Validation to Cells (EX 639)
6. Open the Watch Window and Add Cell Watches (EX 641)
7. Use Trial and Error to Attempt to Solve a Complex Problem (EX 643)
8. Use the Goal Seek Command to Attempt to Solve a Complex Problem (EX 645)
9. Circle Invalid Data and Clear Validation Circles (EX 647)
10. Use Solver to Find the Optimal Solution to a Complex Problem (EX 651)
11. View the Solver Answer Report for Order 1 (EX 658)
12. Save the Workbook with Passwords (EX 660)
13. Save the Current Data as a Scenario (EX 663)
14. Add the Data for a New Scenario (EX 666)
15. Use Solver to Find a New Solution (EX 669)
16. View the Solver Answer Report for Order 2 (EX 671)
17. Save the Second Solver Solution as a Scenario (EX 672)
18. Show a Saved Scenario (EX 675)
19. Create a Scenario Summary Worksheet (EX 678)
20. Create a Scenario PivotTable Worksheet (EX 680)
21. Inspect a Document for Hidden and Personal Information (EX 683)
22. Check Compatibility and Save a Workbook Using the Excel 97-2003 Workbook File Format and Mark a Workbook as Final (EX 686)

If you have a SAM user profile, you may have access to hands-on instruction, practice, and assessment. Log in to your SAM account (http://sam2007.course.com) to launch any assigned training activities or exams that relate to the skills covered in this chapter.

Learn It Online

Learn It Online is a series of online student exercises that test your knowledge of chapter content and key terms.

Instructions: To complete the Learn It Online exercises, start your browser, click the Address bar, and then enter the Web address scsite.com/ex2007/learn. When the Excel 2007 Learn It Online page is displayed, click the link for the exercise you want to complete and then read the instructions.

Chapter Reinforcement TF, MC, and SA
A series of true/false, multiple choice, and short answer questions that test your knowledge of the chapter content.

Flash Cards
An interactive learning environment where you identify chapter key terms associated with displayed definitions.

Practice Test
A series of multiple choice questions that test your knowledge of chapter content and key terms.

Who Wants To Be a Computer Genius?
An interactive game that challenges your knowledge of chapter content in the style of a television quiz show.

Wheel of Terms
An interactive game that challenges your knowledge of chapter key terms in the style of the television show *Wheel of Fortune*.

Crossword Puzzle Challenge
A crossword puzzle that challenges your knowledge of key terms presented in the chapter.

Apply Your Knowledge

Reinforce the skills and apply the concepts you learned in this chapter.

Determining the Product Mix for a Shipment
Instructions: LaCrosse Nurseries ships truck loads of shrubs and trees to landscape companies. Follow the steps below to use trial and error and then Solver to find the optimal product mix that should be shipped on a truck that can hold 144 square feet of shrubs and trees based on current product costs and prices. The products available for shipment include shrubs, small trees, and shade trees. The company has up to 32 shrubs, 24 small trees, and 12 shade trees available for delivery at one time. Total profit must be maximized for the shipment.

1. Start Excel, open the workbook Apply 8–1 LaCrosse Nurseries from the Data Files for Students, and then save the workbook using the file name, Apply 8–1 LaCrosse Nurseries Complete.

2. Using trial and error, enter values in cells B8, C8, and D8 to try to solve the problem.

3. Use Solver to find a solution to the problem so that the total profit on the shipment (cell E11) is maximized. Allow Solver to change cells B8, C8, and D8. The total square feet of the items should not exceed 144 square feet. The results in B8, C8, and D8 should be integer values. Add constraints to Solver to constrain the number of shrubs, small trees, and shade trees as noted above. Use the Assume Linear Model option in Solver.

4. Instruct Solver to create the Answer Report for your solution. Solver should find the answer as shown in Figure 8–83.

5. Trace precedents for cell E12 by clicking the Trace Precedents button on the Formulas tab on the Ribbon three times. Remove the precedent arrows. Trace dependents for cell B8 by clicking the Trace Dependents button on the Formulas tab on the Ribbon three times. Remove the dependent arrows.

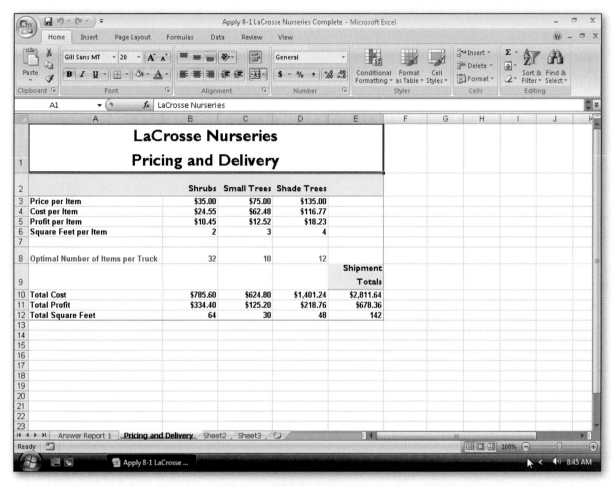

Figure 8–83

6. Use the Watch Window to monitor cells E10:E12. Change values in the range B8:D8 and view changes in the Watch Window. Close the Watch Window. Use the Undo button on the Quick Access Toolbar to change the values in the range B8:D8 to their original values.

7. Change the document properties as specified by your instructor. Add a worksheet header to the original worksheet with your name, course number, and other information requested by your instructor.

8. Save the workbook. Print the worksheet and the Answer Report 1 worksheet. Submit the assignment as specified by your instructor.

Extend Your Knowledge

Extend the skills you learned in this chapter and experiment with new skills. You may need to use Help to complete the assignment.

Creating Data Validation Rules

Instructions: Start Excel. Open the workbook Extend 8–1 Coastal Rentals Calculator from the Data Files for Students and then save the workbook using the file name Extend 8–1 Coastal Rentals Calculator Complete (Figure 8–84). You have been asked to create data validation rules in an Excel worksheet that calculates rental charges for Coastal Rentals, a company that manages vacation rental properties in Florida and the south Atlantic coast of the United States. Coastal Rentals offers four types of rental properties and rents each type at a different daily rate for a maximum of one week. They also provide services such as child care for an additional daily rate and offer a 10% discount for customers who rent properties in the summer.

Perform the following tasks.

1. In cell B4 on the Bill Calculator worksheet, enter a data validation rule that allows users to enter any value. Use `Customer Name` as the input message title and `Enter the customer's first name.` as the input message. Because entering the first name is not required, an error alert is not necessary. Remove the check mark from the 'Show error alert after invalid data is entered' check box.

2. In cell B5, enter a data validation rule that requires users to select a property type from a list. Allow users to select the data from a list of property types, which is contained in the range A13:A16. Do not allow users to leave cell B5 blank. Use `Property Type` as the input message title and `Select the type of property the customer rented.` as the input message. Because entering the property type is required, choose a Stop style of error alert. Use `Invalid Property Type` as the error alert title and `Select Apartment, Beach House, Condo, or Villa from the list.` as the error message.

3. In cell B6, enter a data validation rule that requires users to enter a whole number from 1 to 7 for the number of days the customer rented a property. Do not allow users to leave cell B6 blank. Use `Days Rented` as the input message title and enter an input message that reminds users to enter the number of nights the customer stayed at the property. Choose an appropriate style of error alert. Use `Invalid Entry` as the error alert title and enter an error message that instructs users to enter a number from 1 to 7.

4. In cell B7, enter another data validation rule that allows users to select a valid entry from a list of additional services, which are included in cells A20:A22. These are optional services, so you can allow users to leave cell B7 blank. For the input message, use an appropriate title and display text that reminds users to enter the first additional service the customer used. Choose a style of error alert considering that if users enter a service, they must select one of the three services in the list. Enter an appropriate error alert title and an error message that instructs users to select a service from the list.

5. In cell B8, enter a data validation rule that uses the custom formula `=AND(B8<>B7,B8<>B9)` as its validation criteria to verify that the value entered in cell B8 is not the same as the value in cell B7 or B9. For the input message, use an appropriate title and display text that reminds users to enter the second service the customer used. Choose a style of error alert considering that if users enter a second service, they must enter one of the three services not already entered. Enter an appropriate error alert title and an error message.

6. In cell B9, enter a data validation rule that uses a custom formula similar to the one you entered for cell B8. This formula, however, should verify that the value entered in cell B9 is not the same as the value in cell B7 or B8. For the input message, use an appropriate title and display text that reminds users to enter the third service the customer used. Choose an appropriate style of error, error alert title, and error message.

7. In cell E14, enter a data validation rule that displays an informational message when users enter a date between 5/28/2010 and 9/2/2010. For the input message, use an appropriate title and display text that reminds users to enter the date the customer arrived. Choose the appropriate style of error alert, error alert title, and error message that reminds users the summer discount applies only from 5/28/10 to 9/2/10.

8. Test the data validation rules by entering the following values in the specified cells. If an error message appears, click the Retry button or the Cancel button and then enter valid data.

   B4: Darrell

   B5: Room

   B6: 24

   B7: Child Care

   B8: Tour Coordinator

   B9: Maid Service

   E14: 10/1/2010

9. Change the document properties as specified by your instructor. Change the worksheet header with your name, course number, and other information requested by your instructor.

10. Submit the assignment as specified by your instructor.

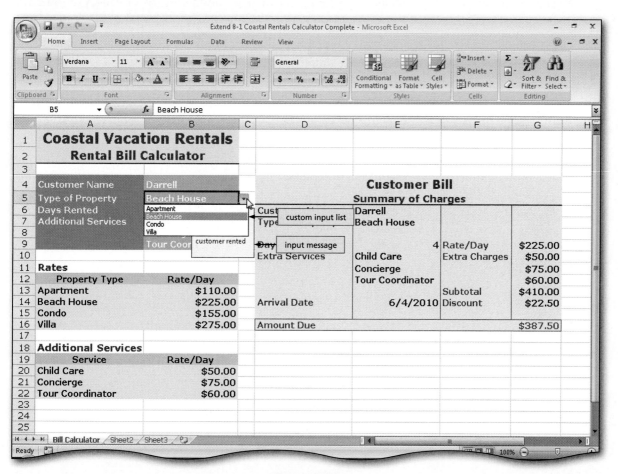

Figure 8–84

Make It Right

Analyze a workbook and correct all errors and/or improve the design.

1 Correcting Solver Parameters and Options

Instructions: Start Excel. Open the workbook Make It Right 8–1 H&D Financial and then save the workbook using the file name, Make It Right 8–1 H&D Financial Complete. The workbook is used to forecast retirement savings over 30 years. In the situation shown in Figure 8–85, suppose a client has $24,500 to start saving for retirement, and that she wants to contribute to a retirement account for 30 years. She estimates that from year 1 to year 20, she will earn 10% interest on the money in the account. After that, she will earn 5%. After her initial deposit in year 1, she will deposit $500 in year 2. Each subsequent year she plans to increase her contribution by $500. Starting in year 26, she will withdraw $100,000 per year. The workbook uses Solver to determine how much she must save each year, starting with year 1.

Correct the following problems with formulas, solver parameters, and solver options as shown in Figure 8–85.

1. The formula for the ending balance in column F does not properly include the annual return on investment listed in column E or any withdrawals. Update the formula in the column to correctly include the return and the withdrawals.

2. Click the Solver button on the Data tab on the Ribbon to view the solver parameters for the worksheet.

3. The solver target is set to maximize the first annual contribution in cell C3. The value should be minimized rather than maximized. The changing cells should be set to change cell C3, rather than F3.

4. The constraints set for Solver include two constraints that are not necessary for cells A32 and E32. Delete these two constraints.

5. The constraint on cell F32 is incorrect. The value in this cell should be greater than or equal to $1,000,000.

6. Click the Options button in the Solver Parameters dialog box to display the Solver Options dialog box. Make sure that the Assume Linear Model check box is selected. Click the OK button to close the Solver Options dialog box. Click the Solve button in the Solver Parameters dialog box to run Solver. Create an answer report.

7. Change the document properties as specified by your instructor. Add a worksheet header with your name, course number, and other information requested by your instructor.

8. Print the worksheet, save the workbook, and then quit Excel.

9. Submit the assignment as specified by your instructor.

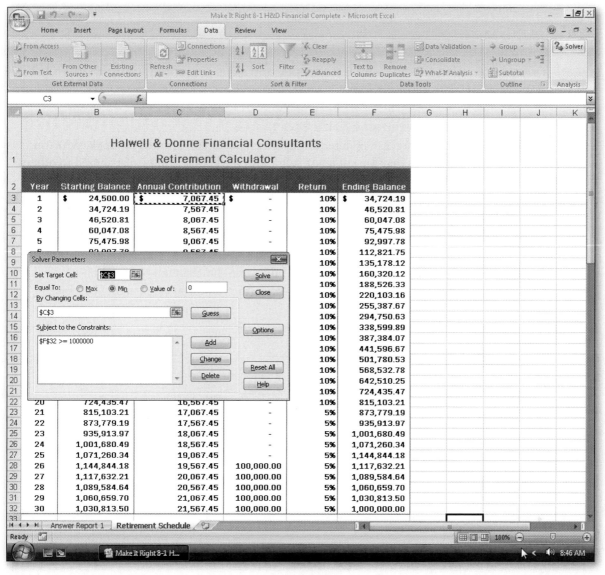

Figure 8–85

Continued >

In the Lab

Create a workbook using the guidelines, concepts, and skills presented in this chapter. Labs are listed in order of increasing difficulty.

Lab 1: Using Goal Seek to Determine Sales Goals

Problem: You have been given the task of determining how your small business can make $500 on each of three types of sports caps that the company sells. The workbook is to be distributed to others, including some managers who have an older version of Excel.

Instructions: Start Excel and perform the following tasks.
1. Open the Lab 8–1 Forrest Specialty Sports Caps workbook from the Data Files for Students and then save the workbook using the file name, Lab 8–1 Forrest Specialty Sports Complete.
2. Select cell B5 and then click the What-If Analysis button on the Data tab on the Ribbon. Click Goal Seek on the What-If Analysis menu. Set cell B5 to the value 500 by changing cell B4.

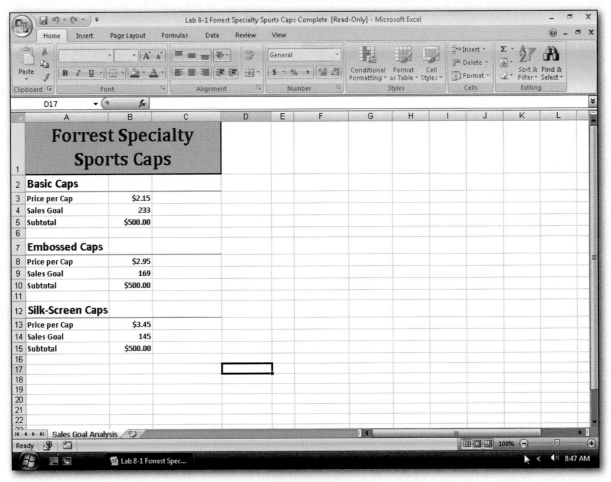

Figure 8–86

3. Use Goal Seek on cells B10 and B15 to seek a sales goal of 500 for each of the other types of caps by changing cell B9 and B14 respectively as shown in Figure 8–86.

4. Use the Inspect Document command on the Prepare submenu of the Office Button menu to find any personal data or hidden columns or rows that are included with the workbook. Note that columns D and E are hidden. Use the Remove All buttons in the Document Inspector dialog box to remove the items.

5. Use the Compatibility Checker command on the Prepare submenu of the Office Button menu and note any potential problems that the workbook may have if it is saved using an earlier file format. Save the workbook with the file name, Lab 8–1 Forrest Specialty Sports Caps Complete, using the Excel 97 - 2003 Workbook format.

6. Change the document properties as specified by your instructor. Add a worksheet header with your name, course number, and other information requested by your instructor.

7. Use the Mark as Final command on the Prepare menu of the Office Button menu to mark the document as final and save it.

8. Quit Excel. Submit the assignment as specified by your instructor.

In the Lab

Lab 2: Finding the Optimal Production Mix

Problem: Witte Lawn Equipment produces four types of lawn mowers in its factory. Each type of mower requires a different amount of labor input and a different amount of materials to produce a single mower. As the production manager, your job is to determine the best mix of mowers to produce based on the amount of available labor and materials for a given week. The company should produce no more than 20 electric and power lawn mowers in a week due to a high level of inventory. Due to contractual obligations with a distributor, the company must produce at least 16 self-propelled mowers each week. Overall, the company does not want to produce more than 65 of any type of mower in a week.

Instructions: Start Excel and perform the following tasks.

1. Open the workbook Lab 8–2 Witte Lawn Equipment from the Data Files for Students and then save the workbook using the file name, Lab 8–2 Witte Lawn Equipment Complete.

2. Use Solver to determine the mix of products that maximizes the number of units produced in the week. The total amount of labor hours available in the first week of March is 6,200 hours, and $75,000 worth of materials is available. Use the Assume Linear Model option in Solver. Instruct Solver to create an Answer Report if it can find a solution to the problem. Figure 8–87a shows the values Solver should find.

3. Save the scenario as March Week 1. The changing cells are B8:E8. Rename the Answer Report containing the scenario as March Week 1.

4. Change the worksheet header to include your name, course number, and other information requested by your instructor. Print the Mower Production Planning worksheet and the March Week 1 worksheet.

5. The company president thinks the assumptions about the number of labor hours needed to produce the mowers is not correct. The new assumptions are that Electric Lawn Mowers take 32 labor hours to produce, Power Lawn Mowers take 40 labor hours to produce, Riding Garden Tractors take 55 labor hours to produce, and Riding Lawn Tractors take 68 labor hours to produce. Enter these new values in the Mower Production Planning worksheet.

6. Use Solver to find a solution to the problem of maximizing the number of units produced in one week, based on the new labor assumptions. Instruct Solver to create an Answer Report if it can find a solution to the problem. Solver should report that the optimal number of units of

Continued >

In the Lab *continued*

Electric Lawn Mowers is 20, of Power Lawn Tractors is 20, of Riding Garden Tractors is 65, and of Riding Lawn Tractors is 17.

7. Save the scenario as March Week 2. Rename the worksheet containing the second scenario as March Week 2.

8. Change the March Week 2 worksheet header to include your name, course number, and other information requested by your instructor. Print the Mower Production Planning worksheet and the March Week 2 worksheet.

9. Create a Scenario Summary (Figure 8–87b) showing the two scenarios you saved in Scenario Manager. Change the Scenario Summary worksheet header to include your name, course number, and other information requested by your instructor. Print the Scenario Summary worksheet. Delete Sheet2 and Sheet3.

10. Change the document properties as specified by your instructor. Save the workbook.

11. Submit the assignment as specified by your instructor.

(a) Answer Report

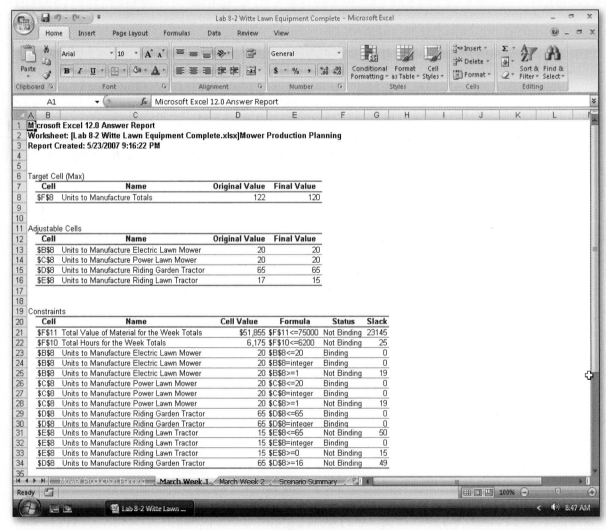

Figure 8–87

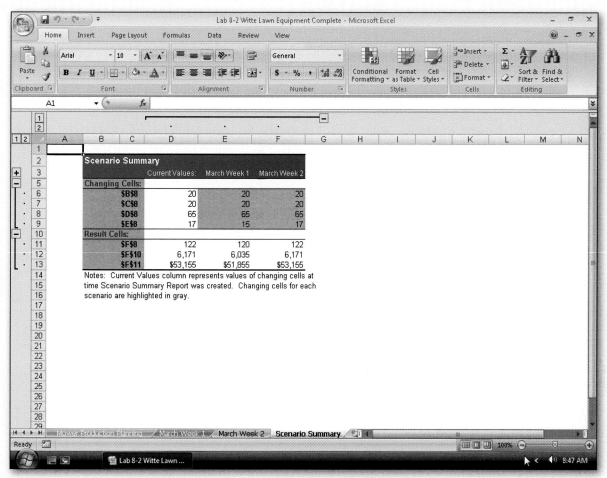

(b) Scenario Summary

Figure 8–87 (continued)

In the Lab

Lab 3: Creating and Comparing Scenarios

Problem: The owners of Upside Recreation, a retailer of bicycles, would like to determine the impact of a request by the sales team that their commissions be raised from 4% to 6%. To accommodate the potential increase, the owners need to increase the markup at which they sell bicycles. Currently, the markup is 10%. When the owners increase price, they feel that they will sell fewer bicycles. Create and compare three scenarios for the new commission rate and projected bicycle sales based on three different potential price markups.

Instructions: Start Excel and perform the following tasks.

1. Open the Lab 8–3 Upside Recreation workbook from the Data Files for Students and then save the workbook using the file name, Lab 8–3 Upside Recreation Complete.

2. Create three new scenarios with the changing cells as cells B3, B5, and B8. The first scenario, Markup 11, Bikes 78 should include bicycles sold as 78, markup as 11%, and the proposed commission rate of 6%. The second scenario, Markup 12, Bikes 75 should include bicycles sold as 75, markup as 12%, and the proposed commission rate of 6%. The third scenario, Markup 13, Bikes 70 should include bicycles sold as 70, markup as 13%, and the proposed commission rate of 6%.

3. Create a Scenario PivotTable report (Figure 8–88a) showing the three scenarios that you have saved in Scenario Manager. The result cells are B6, B7, and B9.

Continued >

In the Lab *continued*

4. Create a Scenario Summary (Figure 8–88b) showing the three scenarios that you have saved in Scenario Manager. The result cells are B6, B7, and B9.

5. Change the document properties as specified by your instructor. Add a worksheet header with your name, course number, and other information requested by your instructor.

6. Save the workbook with the password, lab8–3. Print the Scenario Summary and Scenario PivotTable report. Quit Excel. Submit the assignment as specified by your instructor.

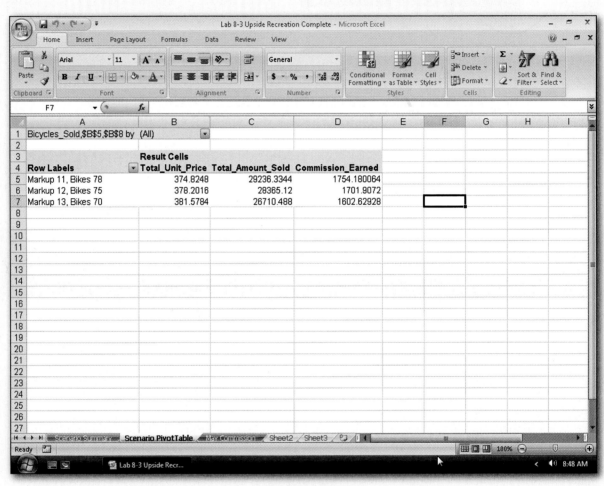

(a)
Scenario
PivotTable

Figure 8–88

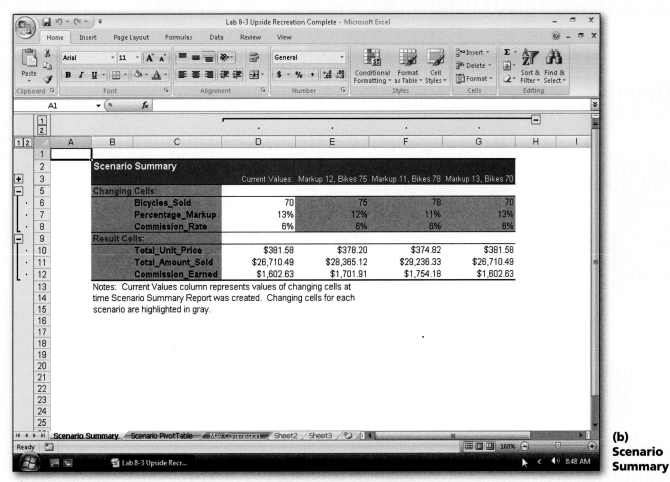

Figure 8–88 *(continued)*

(b) Scenario Summary

Cases and Places

The difficulty of these case studies varies: • are the least difficult and •• are more difficult. The last exercise is a group exercise.

• 1: Using Solver to Find the Most Profitable Product Mix

Island Beverages sells beverages in single cans, 6-packs, and 12-packs. They are expanding to a new grocery store chain where they have purchased 46 feet of shelf space, and they want to be certain the most profitable combination of products is placed on the shelves. They want no more than 45 single cans, 25 6-packs, and 25 12-packs. Table 8–4 shows the three types of items, their profitability per item, and how much shelf space each item requires. Create a worksheet with the necessary information and use Solver to determine the most profitable combination of items to place on the shelves. Create an Answer Report that shows that the constraints have been met. Print the worksheet and Answer Report.

Table 8–4 Island Beverages Item Information		
Item Type	**Profit per Item**	**Square Feet per Item**
Single cans	$0.06	0.1
6-packs	$0.46	1
12-packs	$0.84	2

• 2: Using Formula Auditing and Goal Seeking

Open the workbook Case 8–2 Northwest Storage from the Data Files for Students and then save the workbook using the file name, Case 8–2 Northwest Storage Complete. Use formula auditing to learn about the worksheet. Trace two levels of precedents for cell B22, the Total Rental Revenue. Print the worksheet with the arrows and submit it to your instructor. Use goal seeking to determine the number of rental units the company needs to meet their sales goal for each building. The company wants to generate $2,000 per month for the two types of small units and $2,500 per month for the two types of large units. Save the workbook. Note that the number of units for each unit type is not an integer value. Prepare an explanation of this fact and submit the explanation to your instructor.

•• 3: Creating Scenarios for a Car Loan

Open the workbook Case 8–3 Car Loan from the Data Files for Students and then save the workbook using the file name, Case 8–3 Car Loan Complete. Create three scenarios based on three different loan assumptions outlined in Table 8–5. Create a Scenario Summary that summarizes the cells C9, C10, F5, G5, and H5. Print the Scenario Summary worksheet.

Table 8–5 Personal Car Loan Scenarios			
Assumption	**Scenario 1**	**Scenario 2**	**Scenario 3**
Car	Toyota Corolla	Volkswagon Jetta	Honda Civic
Price	$20,600	$21,750	$18,459
Down payment	$1,100	$1,250	$800
Interest rate	9.00%	9.85%	8.15%
Years	4	5	5

•• 4: Meeting a Personal Financial Goal

Make It Personal

Consider a personal situation for which you want to save money. For example, you might want a vacation, new car, or a semester abroad. Create a monthly budget to track your expenses and remaining balance. Then develop scenarios to answer questions such as "What if I increase the amount that I save each month? Can I afford to take a trip this summer?" or "If I cut my fuel costs by biking to class, can I upgrade my car when I graduate?"

Create a worksheet that lists your monthly expenses, such as rent, food, phone bill, credit cards, fuel, and clothes. Calculate your total expenses, and subtract them from your monthly income to determine how much you have to save at the end of each month.

Determine the amount you need to save each month to reach your goal, and then develop at least three scenarios. For example, in one scenario you could reduce the amount of money you spend on fuel, clothes, and food each month. In another scenario, you could increase your monthly income, such as by working more hours at a part-time job. A third scenario could combine assumptions by reducing one or two expenses and increasing income slightly. Create the scenarios, and then produce a Scenario Summary report to examine the results.

•• 5: Optimizing the Nutritional Value of a Meal

Working Together

As a group, use Excel to help you create a menu for people who visit the Meals To Go location and create nutritious meals from scratch. Your challenge is to maximize the profile for the customers, while basing the menu on certain nutritional requirements. Open the workbook Case 8–5 Meals on the Go from the Data Files for Students and then save the workbook using the file name, Case 8–5 Meals on the Go Complete. Use Excel to find the optimal servings mix to comprise a meal with no more than 1,800 calories and 45 grams of fat. The meal must include at least one serving of each item and not more than four. Maximize profit for the Meals to Go business based on product costs and selling prices, while meeting the meal constraints. Use three methods to attempt to solve the problem: trial and error, goal seeking, and Solver. Discuss how each approach went about finding an optimal solution and present your findings.

9 Importing Data, Working with PivotCharts, PivotTables, and Trendlines

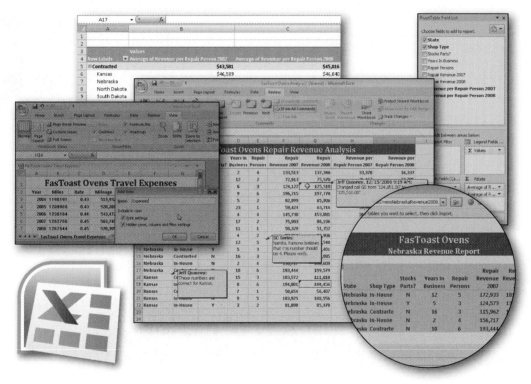

Objectives

You will have mastered the material in this chapter when you can:

- Import data from a text file, an Access database, a Web page, and a Word Document

- Transpose data while pasting it

- Convert text to columns

- Replicate formulas

- Explain sharing and collaboration techniques

- Insert, edit, and delete a comment

- Track changes and share a workbook

- Accept and reject tracked changes made to a workbook

- Analyze worksheet data using a PivotTable and a PivotChart

- Compare and merge shared workbooks

- Analyze worksheet data using a trendline

- Save a custom view of a worksheet and format a worksheet background

9 | Importing Data, Working with PivotCharts, PivotTables, and Trendlines

Introduction

In today's diverse business environment, the ability to use and analyze data from a wide variety of sources is a necessity. In this chapter, you will learn how to **import**, or bring, data from various external sources into an Excel worksheet and then analyze that data. Excel allows you to import data from a number of types of sources, including text files, Web pages, tables in databases, data stored in Word documents, and XML files. In this chapter, you also will learn how to create new types of tables and charts, such as PivotTables, PivotCharts, and trendlines, which allow you to represent and analyze data visually.

Other techniques introduced in this chapter apply to issues of multiple users of the same workbook, including sharing, tracking changes, and comments. To allow several people to view and make changes to a workbook at the same time, a user can **share** the workbook. Excel also has the capability to **track changes** to a workbook by marking who changed what data, in which cell, and when. **Comments**, or descriptions, which do not regularly appear as part of the worksheet data, can be added to the workbook to alert the recipients to special instructions and then later can be edited or deleted. Workbooks that have been saved and copied to others also can be compared and merged. **Comparing** workbooks allows users to view and scroll worksheets side by side and visually search the worksheets for differences. **Merging** allows users to bring together copies of workbooks that others have worked on independently. You also will learn how to save a **custom view** of a worksheet, which enables each user to view the worksheet in a familiar manner, even if other users alter the appearance or layout of a worksheet.

Project — FasToast Ovens Repairs Revenue Analysis

FasToast Ovens provides sandwich-toasting ovens to fast food restaurants. The company provides repair services in four states. Each state includes a central office and several locations from which repair technicians are dispatched. The repair locations are either company-owned or contracted to other companies. The company owner has requested that the repair revenue for the last two years be compared among the four states. One of the states provides the requested data in text format (Figure 9–1a on page EX 708) rather than in an Excel workbook. To make use of that data in Excel, the data must be imported, before it can be formatted and manipulated. The same is true of other formats in which the offices in various states store data, such as Microsoft Access tables (Figure 9–1b on page EX 708), Web pages (Figure 9–1c on page EX 708), or Word documents (Figure 9–1d on page EX 708). Excel provides the tools necessary to import and manipulate the data from these sources into a worksheet (Figure 9–1f on page EX 709).

PivotTables, PivotCharts, and trendlines provide additional methods to manipulate and visualize data. A **PivotTable** (Figure 9–1g on page EX 709) is an interactive view of worksheet data that gives users the ability to summarize the data and then rotate the table's row and column titles to show different views of the summarized data.

A **PivotChart** (Figure 9–1h on page EX 709) is an interactive chart that provides the user with ways to analyze data visually by varying the fields and categories to present different graphical views. For example, if FasToast Ovens wanted to view a pie chart showing percentages of repair revenue from each state, a PivotChart could show that percentage using any field, such as total revenue for a year or total revenue for offices that stock parts. Excel creates and associates a PivotTable with every PivotChart. A **trendline** (Figure 9–1i on page EX 709) is a visual way to show how some particular data is changing over time. Excel can overlay a trendline on any chart, including a PivotChart. Using PivotTables, PivotCharts, and trendlines, an inexperienced user with little knowledge of formulas, functions, and ranges can complete powerful what-if analyses of a set of data.

BTW

External Data
Imported data that maintains a refreshable link to its external source is called external data. When you use external data, your worksheet will update whenever a change is made to the original file and the data in the worksheet is refreshed. You can choose when and how the data is refreshed.

BTW

Importing Data
If your system contains only a minimum installation of Excel, the first time you use one of the import features, Excel may attempt to install MSQuery. MSQuery is the supplemental application included in Microsoft Office 2007 that is used to retrieve data from external data sources. If Excel attempts to install MSQuery, follow the prompts to complete the installation.

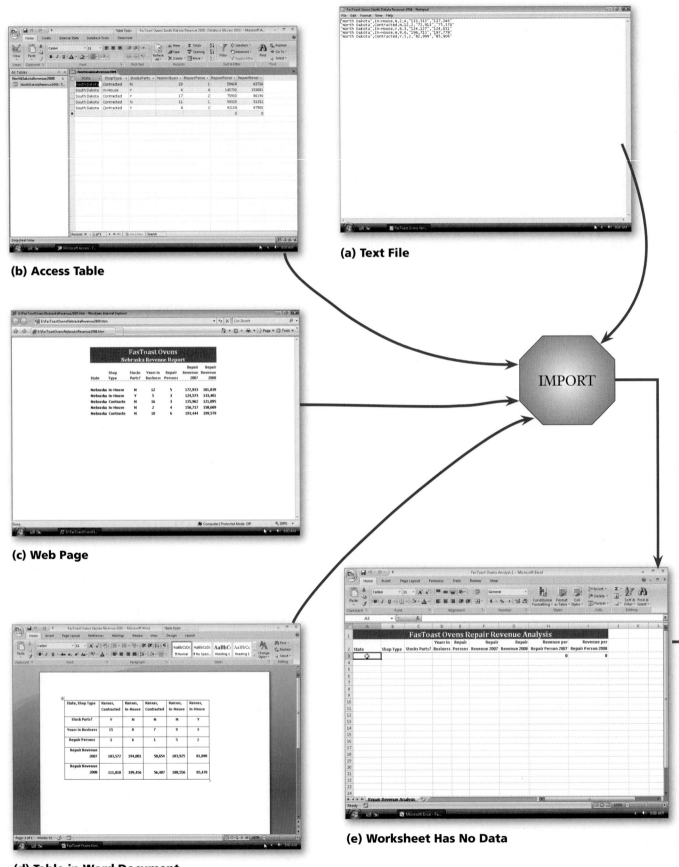

(a) Text File

(b) Access Table

(c) Web Page

(d) Table in Word Document

(e) Worksheet Has No Data

Figure 9–1

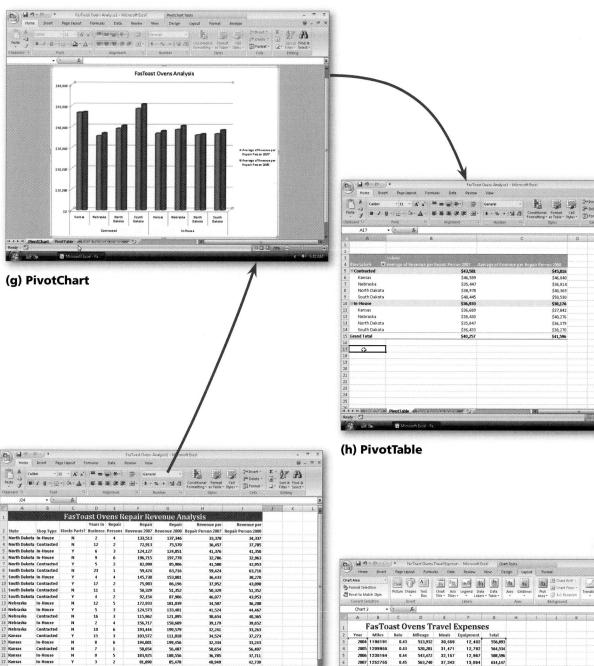

(g) PivotChart

(h) PivotTable

(f) Data Imported into Worksheet

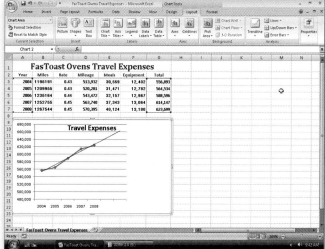

(i) Trendline on Chart

Figure 9–2 illustrates the requirements document for the FasToast Ovens Repair Revenue Analysis worksheet. It includes the needs, source of data, calculations, and other facts about the worksheet's development.

REQUEST FOR NEW WORKBOOK

Date Submitted:	December 9, 2008
Submitted By:	Namita Aziz
Worksheet Title:	FasToast Ovens Sales Analysis
Needs:	Import data from the four states in which FasToast Ovens operates (Figures 9-1a, 9-1b, 9-1c, and 9-1d on page EX XXX) into a worksheet containing headings and formulas, but no data (Figure 9-1e on page EX XXX). After the data is imported, the formulas in cells H3 and I3 must be copied to each row of data (Figure 9-1f on page EX XXX). After the import is complete, the data in the worksheet requires verification by the main office's management team and then the regional sales managers. Create a PivotTable (Figure 9-1g on page EX XXX) and a PivotChart (Figure 9-1h on page EX XXX) to allow interactive views of the data in the worksheet.
Source of Data:	The four state sales managers for FasToast Ovens will submit data from their respective states via a text file (North Dakota), an Access database (South Dakota), a Web page (Nebraska), and a Word Document (Kansas).
Calculations:	The formulas used to calculate the revenue per repair person in 2007 and 2008 are in cells H3 and I3 of the worksheet (Figure 9-1e). The formulas divide revenue amounts for each year by the number of repair persons for a particular office each year. After importing the data, the formulas need to be copied down for all rows of data.
Special Requirements:	Before creating the PivotTable and PivotChart, share the workbook with the main office management, coordinate changes, and route the workbook with the imported data (Figure 9-1f) to the four state sales managers for verification; and then accept the tracked changes. Create a PivotTable (Figure 9-1g) and PivotChart (Figure 9-1h) that analyze sales based on several combinations of fields in the data to make comparisons about effective sales strategies.

Approvals

Approval Status:	X	Approved
		Rejected
Approved By:	Ramone Wallace	
Date:	December 16, 2008	
Assigned To:	J. Quasney, Spreadsheet Specialist	

Figure 9–2

Overview

As you read this chapter, you will learn how to modify the existing workbook as shown in Figure 9–1 by performing these general tasks:

- Import data to an Excel worksheet from a text file, an Access database, a Web page, and a Word document
- Insert, edit, and delete comments

- Track changes and share a workbook
- Analyze worksheet data using a PivotTable and a PivotChart
- Analyze worksheet data using a trendline
- Compare and merge shared workbooks

Plan
Ahead

General Project Decisions

While working with an Excel worksheet, you need to make several decisions that will determine the appearance and characteristics of the finished worksheet. As you update an existing worksheet to meet the requirements shown in Figure 9–2, you should follow these general guidelines:

1. **Analyze the existing workbook and the formats of the data to be imported.** You should have a good understanding of the layout of the data you want to import and how each data element will be arranged in the worksheet. In some cases, the data will need to be transposed, meaning that the rows and columns need to be switched. In other cases, you may need to further manipulate the data once it is in Excel.

2. **Evaluate the various options Excel provides for collaboration.** Excel provides several methods to work with others on a workbook. In some cases, you may send the workbook to a group of people all at once and then consolidate their changes and suggestions. In other cases, you may want to send a workbook to one person at a time and allow each person to add to the changes and suggestions that others have made.

3. **Visualize your workbook in various PivotTable and PivotChart layouts.** PivotTables and PivotCharts provide a great deal of flexibility in how data is summarized. You should consider the types of comparisons and summary functions that you may want to make. Often, sketches of a few ideas will help you in planning effective PivotTables and PivotCharts.

4. **Identify the trend or trends to analyze with a trendline.** Consider what trend you are looking to analyze. You typically analyze a trend in data over a period of time. Consider which data to analyze and which time frame to consider. You also should consider if the trendline should forecast the trend into the future and how far into the future the forecast would be reasonable.

5. **Gather workbooks to be merged and then assess any differences in the workbooks that are in disagreement.** In the case of the FasToast Ovens expense worksheets noted in the requirements document (Figure 9–2 on page EX 710), several people will be sending changes to a workbook. Before merging the workbooks, ensure that you have all of the workbooks from the individuals. When merging the workbooks, conflicts in changes to cells may arise, at which point you must make decisions to resolve the conflicts.

When necessary, more specific details concerning the above guidelines are presented at appropriate points in the chapter. The chapter also will identify the actions you perform and decisions made regarding these guidelines during the modification of the worksheet shown in Figure 9–1 on pages EX 708–709.

BTW

Importing External Data
Excel assigns a name to each external data range. You can view these names by clicking the Name box arrow in the formula bar. External data ranges from text files are named with the text file name. External data ranges from databases are named with the name of the query. External data ranges from Web queries are named with the name of the Web page from which the data was retrieved.

With a good understanding of the requirements document and an understanding of the necessary decisions, the next step is to use Excel to learn about the existing worksheet and solve the problem.

To Start Excel and Open a Workbook

If you are using a computer to step through the project in this chapter and you want your screen to match the figures in this book, you should change your computer's resolution to 1024 × 768. For information about how to change a computer's resolution, see page 21 in Appendix E.

The following steps start Excel and open the workbook FasToast Ovens Analysis from the Data Files for Students.

1 Start Excel.

2 Open the file FasToast Ovens Analysis from the Data Files for Students and then save the workbook using the file name, FasToast Ovens Analysis1. h

3 If the Excel window is not maximized, double-click its title bar to maximize it.

4 If the worksheet window in Excel is not maximized, click the Maximize button next to the Close button on its title bar to maximize the worksheet within Excel (Figure 9–3).

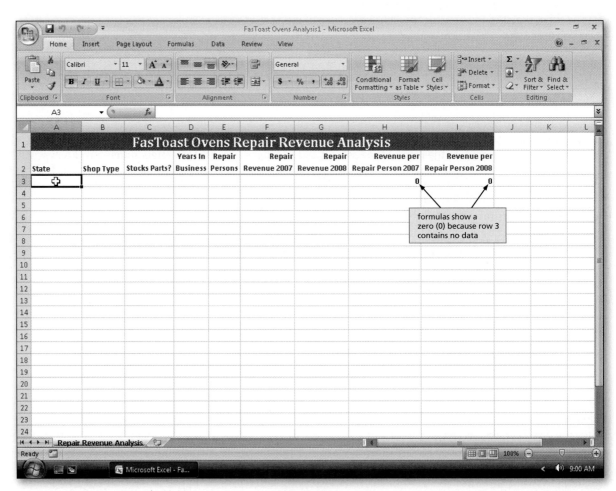

Figure 9–3

About the FasToast Ovens Repair Revenue Analysis Worksheet

As shown in Figure 9–3, columns A through I have been resized and formatted so the imported data will be readable. Table 9–1 shows a description of each data field in the FasToast Ovens Repair Revenue Analysis workbook.

Table 9–1 FasToast Ovens Repair Revenue Analysis Data Fields	
Name Of Field	**Data Description**
State	Name of the state in which office is located
Shop Type	Indicates whether the sales location is an In-House location or Contracted (outside) location
Stock Parts?	Indicates whether the location keeps replacement parts in stock
Years In Business	Number of years the sales office has been in operation
Repair Persons	Number of repair persons based in the office
Repair Revenue 2007	Total revenue from warranties and repairs for this office in 2007
Repair Revenue 2008	Total revenue from warranties and repairs for this office in 2008
Revenue per Repair Person 2007	Average total revenue per repair person for this office in 2007 (2007 Revenue / Repair Persons)
Revenue per Repair Person 2008	Average total revenue per repair person for this office in 2008 (2008 Revenue / Repair Persons)

When data is imported into a formatted worksheet, Excel formats the incoming data using the formats assigned to the cells as best it can.

Importing Files

Data may be sent from a variety of sources and in a range of formats. Even though many users keep data in databases such as Microsoft Access, it is common to receive text files with fields of data separated by commas, especially from mainframe computer users. In addition, with the increasing popularity of the World Wide Web, more companies are creating HTML files and posting data on the Web as a Web page. Word documents, especially those including tables of data, often are used in business as a source of data for workbooks. XML also is a very popular format for data exchange. Excel allows you to import data made available in many formats, including text files, Access tables, Web pages, Word documents, and XML files. Importing data into Excel can create a refreshable link that can be used to update data whenever the original file changes.

To Import Data from a Text File into a Worksheet

A **text file** contains electronic data created with little or no formatting. Many software applications, including Excel, offer an option to import data from a text file, also called an ASCII text file. **ASCII** stands for the American Standard Code for Information Interchange.

In text files, commas, tabs, or other characters often separate the fields. Alternately, the text file may have fields of equal length in columnar format. Each record usually exists on a separate line. A **delimited file** contains data fields separated by a selected character, such as a comma. A **fixed width file** contains data fields of equal length with spaces between the fields. In the case of a fixed width file, a special character need not separate the data fields. During the import process, Excel provides a preview to help identify the type of text file being imported.

BTW

Opening a Text File in Excel
If you open a text file, such as FasToast Ovens North Dakota Revenue 2008.txt, in Excel, the Text Import Wizard will start automatically. You then can make the same choices shown in the following set of steps to import the data from the text file. To open a text file in Excel, you must choose Text Files or All Files in the 'Files of type' box in the Open dialog box.

BTW

Dragging and Dropping a Text File
You also can drag a text file to Excel. Simply drag the file name or the icon from its location to a blank worksheet. You then can format the data easily using the Text to Columns button on the Data tab on the Ribbon. The data does not maintain a refreshable link to the text file.

The following steps import a comma-delimited text file into the FasToast Ovens Analysis1 workbook using the **Text Import Wizard**. The text file on the Data Files for Students contains data about repair revenue for North Dakota for 2007 and 2008 (Figure 9–1a on page EX 708).

❶

- With the Repair Revenue Analysis worksheet active, if necessary, select cell A3.

- Click the Data tab on the Ribbon (Figure 9–4).

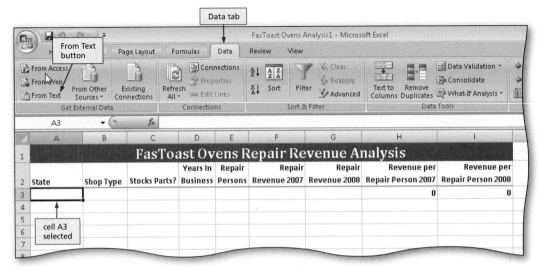

Figure 9–4

❷

- Click the From Text button on the Ribbon to display the Import Text File dialog box. If you have more than one Excel add-in installed, such as Solver, the From Text button may appear on a submenu that is displayed when you click the Get External Data button. The Get External Data group on the Ribbon may be collapsed to a single Get External Data button.

- When Excel displays the Import Text File dialog box, select UDISK 2.0 (E:) in the Address bar to display the text files on drive E (Figure 9–5).

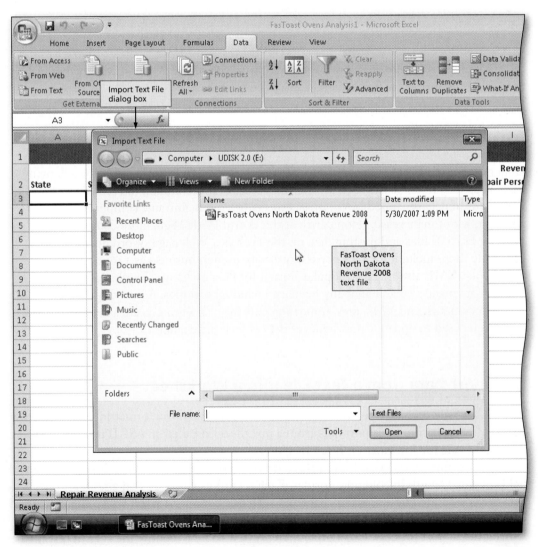

Figure 9–5

❸

- Double-click the file name, FasToast Ovens North Dakota Revenue 2008, to display the Text Import Wizard - Step 1 of 3 dialog box (Figure 9–6).

What is the purpose of the Text Import Wizard?

The Text Import Wizard provides step-by-step instruction on importing data from a text file into an Excel worksheet. The Preview box shows that the text file contains one record per line and the fields are separated by commas. The Delimited option button is selected in the 'Original data type' area.

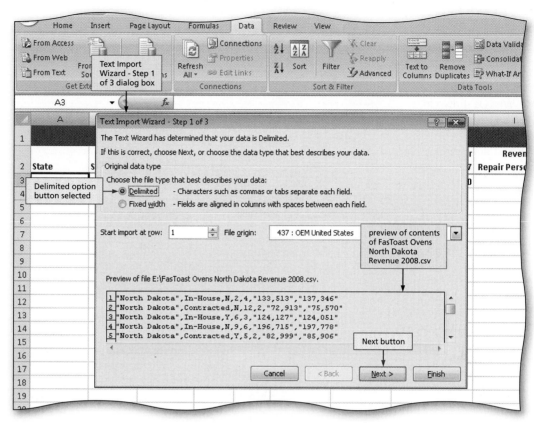

Figure 9–6

❹

- Click the Next button to display the Text Import Wizard - Step 2 of 3 dialog box.

- When Excel displays the Text Import Wizard - Step 2 of 3 dialog box, click Comma in the Delimiters area to display the data fields correctly in the Data preview area.

- Click Tab in the Delimiters area to clear the check box (Figure 9–7).

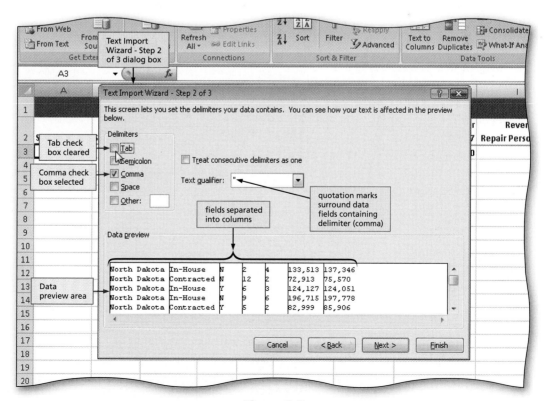

Figure 9–7

5

- Click the Next button to display the Text Import Wizard - Step 3 of 3 dialog box (Figure 9–8).

Q&A

What is shown in the Text Import Wizard - Step 3 of 3 dialog box?

Step 3 allows the format of each column of data to be selected. General is the default selection. The Data preview area shows the data separated based on the comma delimiter. The commas in the last two columns of numbers in the Data preview area (Figure 9–8) are not considered to be delimiters because each of these data values was surrounded by quotation marks in the text file.

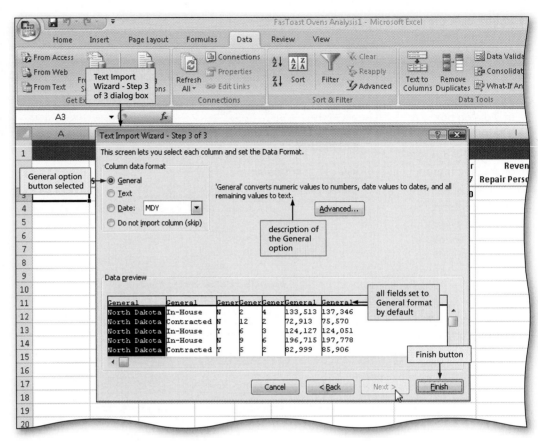

Figure 9–8

6

- Click the Finish button to display the Import Data dialog box (Figure 9–9).

Q&A

What is the purpose of the Import Data dialog box?

The Import Data dialog box provides options to define where the data is placed on the worksheet, and also provides a way to tailor the data before importing it. Data will be imported beginning at cell A3 of the existing worksheet. A marquee surrounds cell A3. By default, the cell that is active when the text import is performed will become the upper-left cell of the imported range. To import the data to a different location, change the location in the Import Data dialog box.

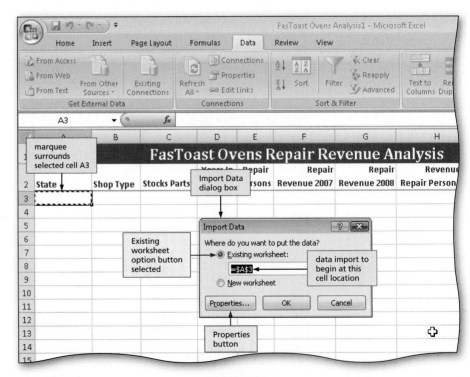

Figure 9–9

7
- Click the Properties button.

- When Excel displays the External Data Range Properties dialog box, click 'Adjust column width' in the 'Data formatting and layout' area to clear the check box (Figure 9–10).

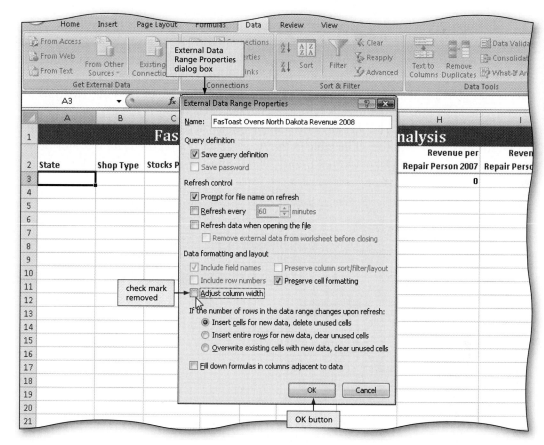

Figure 9–10

8
- Click the OK button.

- When Excel displays the Import Data dialog box, click the OK button to import the data from the text file into the worksheet beginning at cell A3 (Figure 9–11).

What if the data in the text file is changed?

After the text file is imported, Excel can **refresh**, or update, the data whenever the original text file changes, using the Refresh All button on the Data tab on the Ribbon.

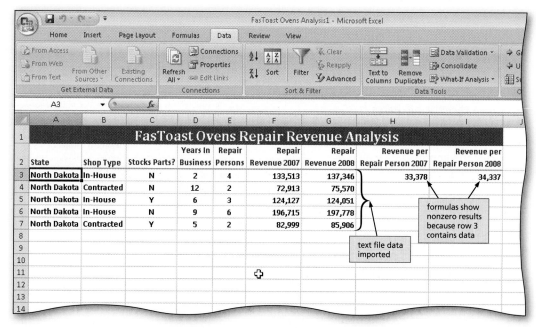

Figure 9–11

Other Ways

1. Press ALT+A, F, T

To Import Data from an Access Table into a Worksheet

To import data from an Access database, the first step is to make a query of the data. A **query** is a way to qualify the data to import by specifying a matching condition or asking a question of a database. For example, a query can identify only those records that pass a certain test, such as records containing numeric fields greater than a specific amount or records containing text fields matching a specific value. When Excel imports a database table, the data is placed in a table. A table format is not desirable for the Repair Revenue Analysis worksheet, so the table must be converted to a range and the cells reformatted after Excel imports the data.

The following steps import an entire table from an Access database into a table and then reformat the data to match the existing worksheet. The table in the Access database on the Data Files for Students contains data about repair revenue in South Dakota for 2007 and 2008 (Figure 9–1b on page EX 708).

- Select cell A8.

- With the Data tab active, click the From Access button on the Ribbon to display the Select Data Source dialog box.

- When Excel displays the Select Data Source dialog box, select UDISK 2.0 (E:) in the Address bar to display the Access database files on drive E (Figure 9–12).

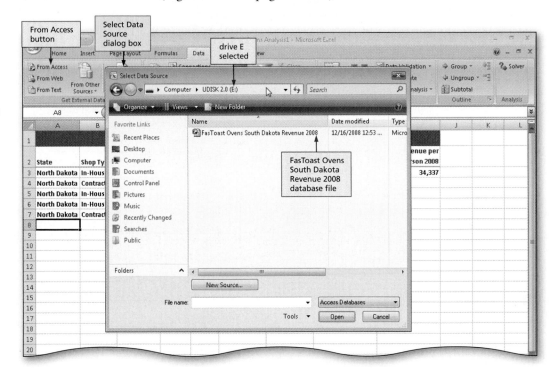

Figure 9–12

- Double-click the file name, FasToast Ovens South Dakota Revenue 2008 in the Name list to display the Import Data dialog box (Figure 9–13).

Q&A What is shown in the Import Data dialog box?

The Import Data dialog box allows you to choose whether to import the data into a table, a PivotTable Report, or a PivotChart and associated PivotTable Report. You also can choose to import the data to an existing worksheet or a new worksheet.

Q&A What if the database contained more than one table?

If more than one table is in the database, then Excel allows you to choose which table to import.

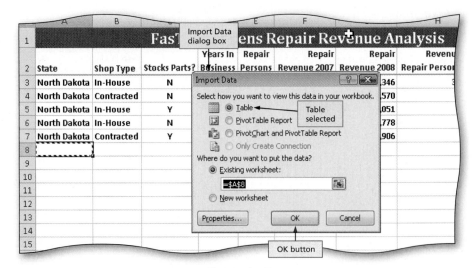

Figure 9–13

3

- Click the OK button to import the data in the database to a table in the range A8:G13 (Figure 9–14).

Q&A

What happened to the layout of the worksheet when Excel imported the data?

Excel created a table with the data in the only table in the database. The names of the fields in the Access database show in row 8. The table is formatted with the default table style for the worksheet's theme. Excel also changed the widths of the columns in the worksheet.

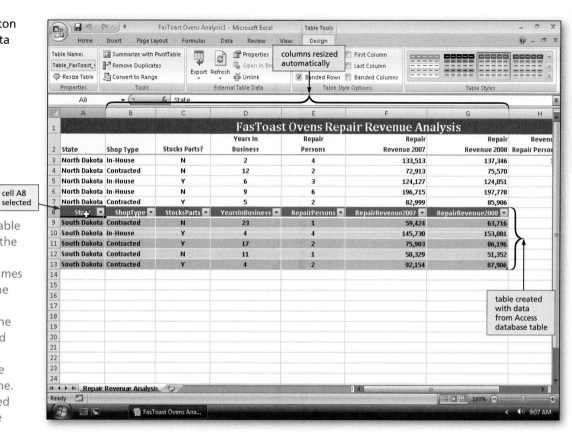

Figure 9–14

Q&A

What should be done to format the worksheet?

The table in the range A8:G13 must be converted to a range. When the table is converted to a range, the cells in each column in the converted range should be formatted to match the data in the cells that were imported for North Dakota. The column widths must be adjusted to best fit. The table headers in row 8 should be deleted by deleting the entire row.

4

- Right-click cell A8 and then point to the Table on the shortcut menu.

- Click Convert to Range.

- When Excel displays the Microsoft Office Excel dialog box, click the OK button to convert the table to a range (Figure 9–15).

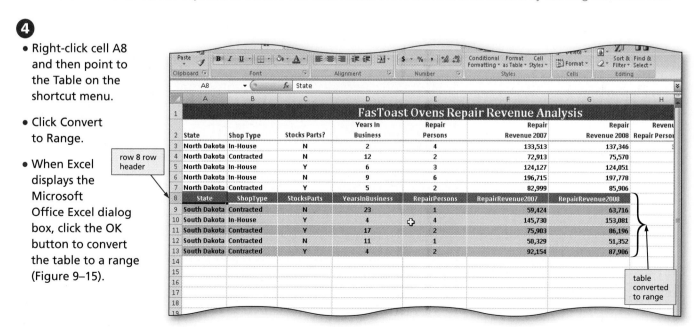

Figure 9–15

5

- Right-click the row heading for row 8 to display the shortcut menu.

- Click Delete on the shortcut menu to delete row 8 (Figure 9–16).

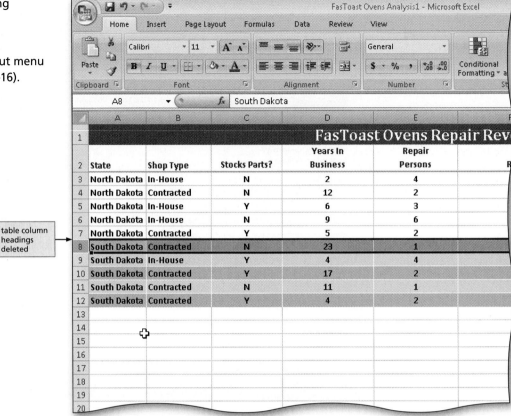

table column headings deleted

Figure 9–16

6

- Drag through the column headings of column A through G in the column heading area to select the columns.

- Double-click the column separator in the column headings area between columns A and B to change the widths of each column to best fit (Figure 9–17).

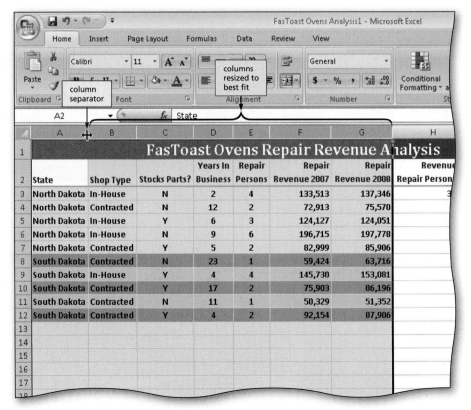

Figure 9–17

7

- If necessary, click the Home tab on the Ribbon and then select the range A7:G7.

- Click the Format Painter button on the Ribbon and then drag though the range A8:G12 to copy the formats of the selected range to the range A8:G12.

- Select cell A13 (Figure 9–18).

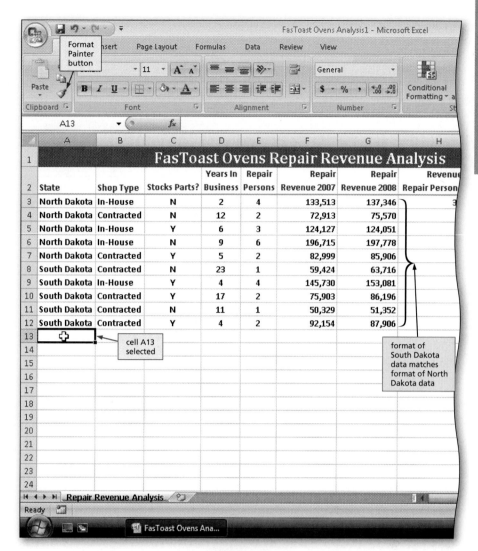

Figure 9–18

Other Ways

1. Press ALT+A, F, A

To Import Data from a Web Page into a Worksheet

A Web page uses a file format called HTML. **HTML** stands for **Hypertext Markup Language**, which is a language that Web browsers can interpret. Excel can import data from a Web page into preformatted areas of the worksheet using a Web query. The Web Query dialog box includes options to specify which parts of the Web page to import and how much of the HTML formatting to keep.

The following steps create a new Web query and import data from a Web page into a worksheet. Performing these steps does not require being connected to the Internet, because the Web page (Figure 9–1c on page EX 708) is available on the Data Files for Students.

1

- With cell A13 selected, click the Data tab on the Ribbon.

- Click the From Web button on the Ribbon to display the New Web Query dialog box.

- When Excel displays the New Web Query dialog box, type e:\ FasToastOvensNebr askaRevenue2008. htm in the Address bar and then click the Go button to display the Web page in the preview area (Figure 9–19).

Q&A

Why does file:/// appear at the beginning of the address in the Address bar?

Excel appends file:/// to the beginning of the address to indicate that the address points to a file saved on disk.

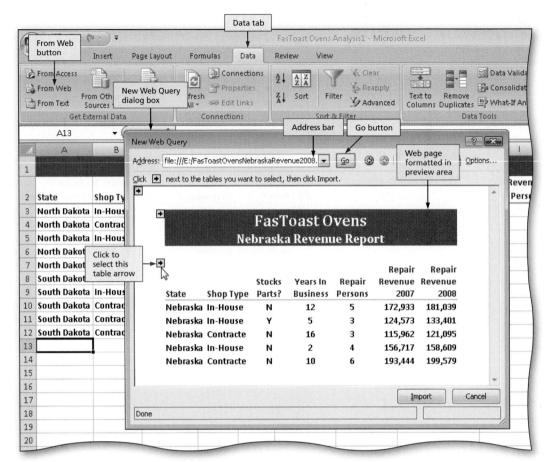

Figure 9–19

2

- Click the 'Click to select this table' arrow to select the HTML table containing the Nebraska repair revenue report (Figure 9–20).

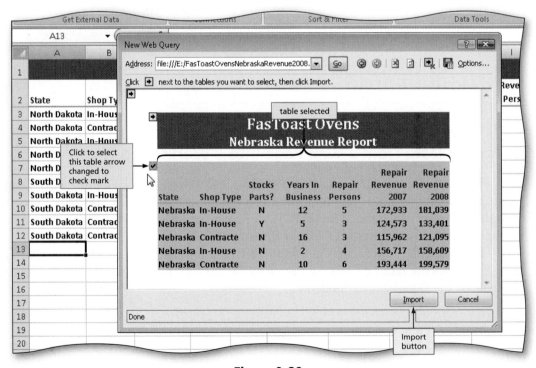

Figure 9–20

3

- Click the Import button to display the Import Data dialog box and display a marquee around cell A13 (Figure 9–21).

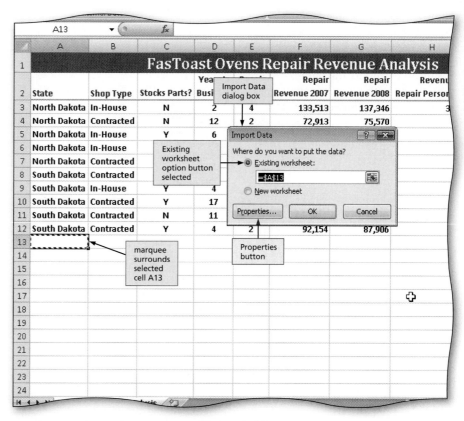

Figure 9–21

4

- Click the Properties button to display the External Data Range Properties dialog box.

- When Excel displays the External Data Range Properties dialog box, click 'Adjust column width' in the 'Data formatting and layout' area to clear the check box (Figure 9–22).

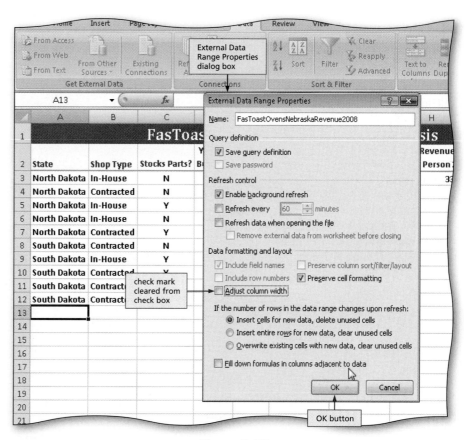

Figure 9–22

5

- Click the OK button.

- When Excel displays the Import Data dialog box, click the OK button to import the data from the Web page into the worksheet beginning at cell A13 (Figure 9–23).

Q&A

Why is the data imported starting at cell A13?

By default, the cell that is active when the Web query is performed will become the upper-left cell of the imported range. To import the data to a different location, change the location in the Import Data dialog box.

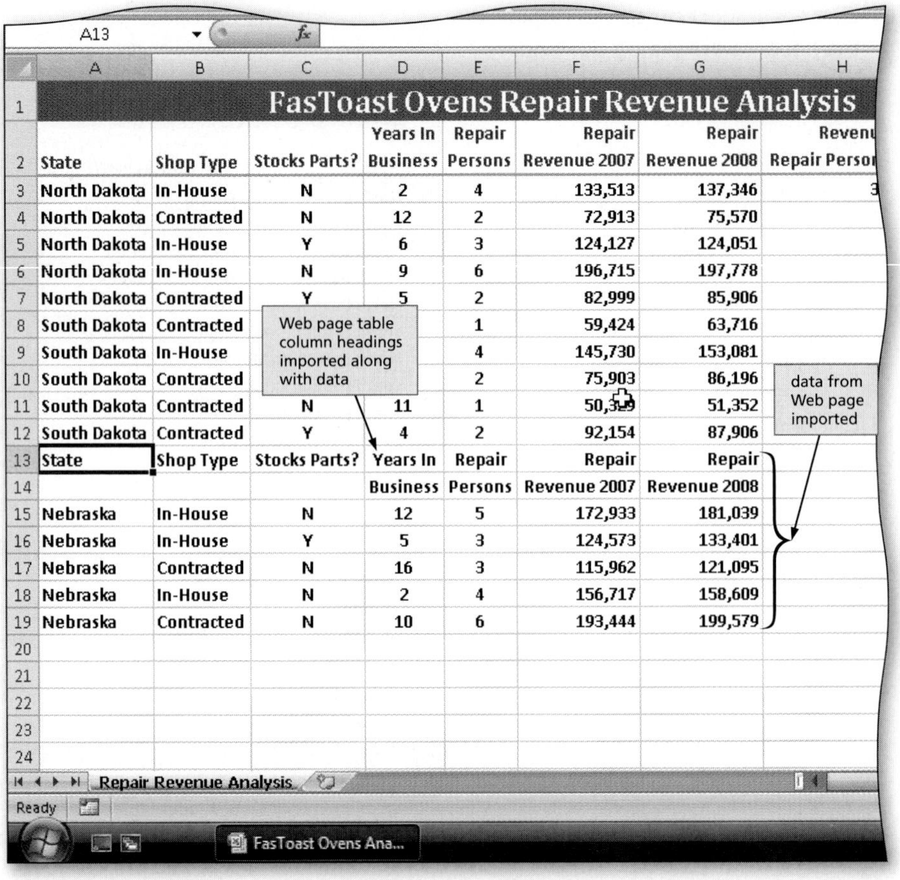

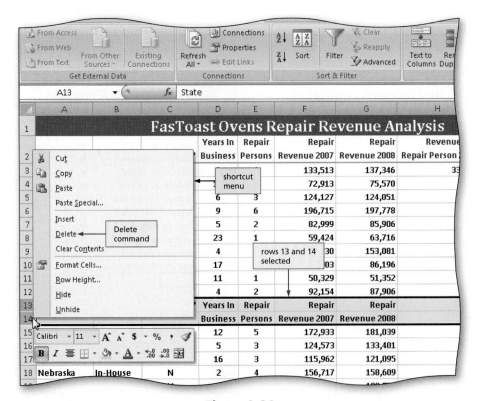

Figure 9–23

6

- Drag through the row 13 and 14 row headings and then right-click to display the shortcut menu (Figure 9–24).

Q&A

Why are the column headings repeated in row 13?

Because the column headings appeared in the Web page, they are imported with the other data and are displayed in rows 13 and 14. The extra column headings must be deleted from the imported Web page table.

Figure 9–24

❼

- Click Delete on the shortcut menu to delete rows 13 and 14, which contained the column headings from the Web Page (Figure 9–25).

Q&A

Why should I use a Web query instead of copying and pasting from a Web page?

Using a Web query has advantages over other methods of importing data from a Web page. For example, copying data from Web pages to the Office Clipboard and then pasting it into Excel does not maintain all of the Web page formatting. In addition, copying just the desired data from a Web page can be tedious. Finally, copying and pasting does not create a link to the Web page for future updating.

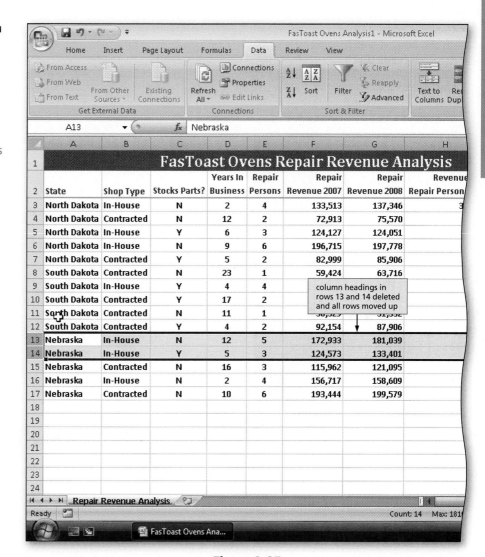

Figure 9–25

Other Ways
1. Press ALT+A, F, W

To Copy and Transpose Data from a Word Document to a Worksheet

A Word document often contains data stored in a table. You can use the Office Clipboard and copy and paste commands to copy the data in the table to an Excel worksheet. On some occasions, imported data requires a great deal of manipulation once you import the data into Excel. For example, the imported data may be easier to work with if the rows and columns were switched, or **transposed**. In other situations, you may find that an imported column of data should be split into two columns.

The Word document that contains the Kansas repair revenue analysis data (Figure 9–1d on page EX 708) includes a table in which the rows and columns are switched when compared with the Repair Revenue Analysis worksheet. The second column of data also includes data for both the state name and the shop type. The steps on the next page copy and transpose the data from the Word document to the Repair Revenue Analysis worksheet.

- Click the Home tab on the Ribbon and then select cell A24.

- Start Word and then open the Word document named, FasToast Ovens Kansas Revenue 2008, from the Data Files for Students.

- In Word, if necessary, click the Home tab on the Ribbon.

- Drag through all of the cells in the second through last columns in the table in the Word document and then click the Copy button on the Ribbon to copy the contents of the table to the Office Clipboard (Figure 9–26).

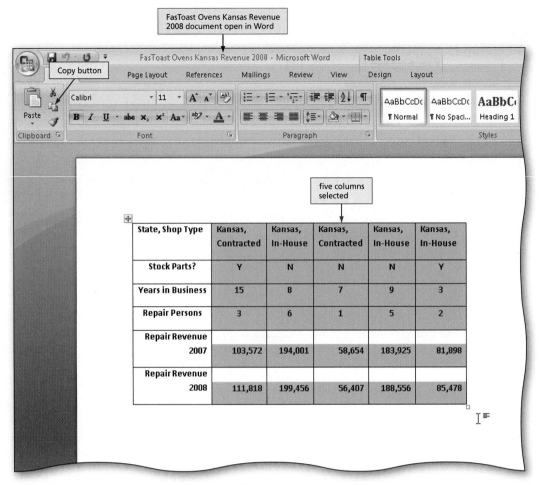

Figure 9–26

- Quit Word and, if necessary, click the FasToast Ovens Analysis1 workbook taskbar button to make it active.

- Click the Paste button arrow on the Ribbon to display the Paste menu (Figure 9–27).

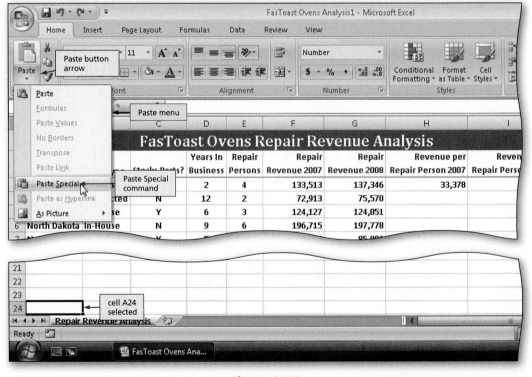

Figure 9–27

3

- Click Paste Special on the Paste menu to display the Paste Special dialog box.

- When the Paste Special dialog box appears, click Text in the As list (Figure 9–28).

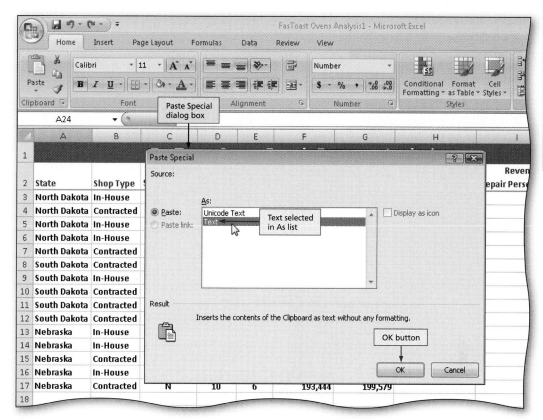

Figure 9–28

4

- Click the OK button in the Paste Special dialog box to paste the contents of the Office Clipboard to the range A24:E29 (Figure 9–29).

Why is the data pasted to the range A24:E29?

Excel's Transpose command requires that the source of the transposed data be different from the destination. In this case the source is the range A24:E29 and the destination will be the range A18:E22.

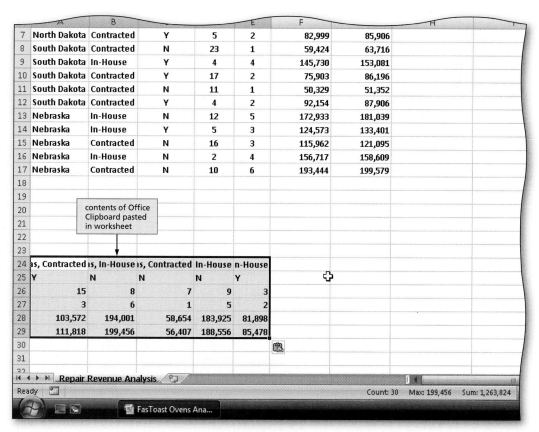

Figure 9–29

- Select the range A24:E29 and then click the Copy button on the Ribbon.

- Select cell A18.

- Click the Paste button arrow on the Ribbon and then point to Transpose on the Paste menu (Figure 9–30).

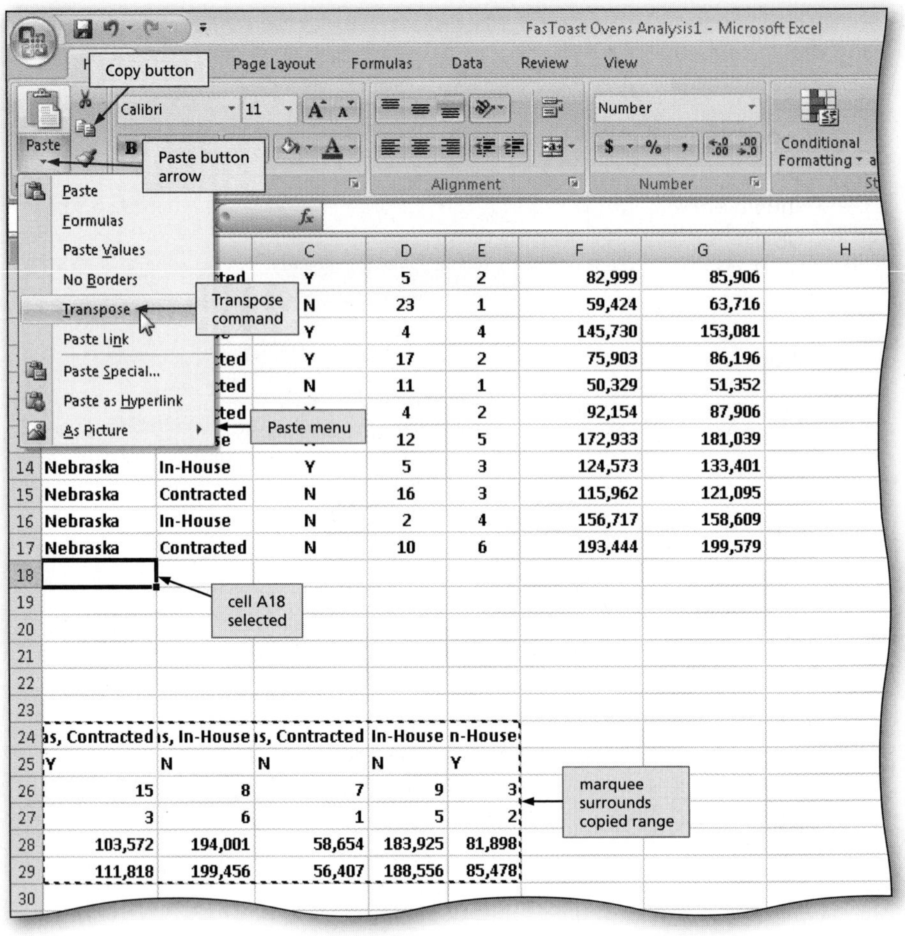

	A	B	C	D	E	F	G	H
			Y	5	2	82,999	85,906	
			N	23	1	59,424	63,716	
			Y	4	4	145,730	153,081	
		cted	Y	17	2	75,903	86,196	
		cted	N	11	1	50,329	51,352	
		cted		4	2	92,154	87,906	
				12	5	172,933	181,039	
14	Nebraska	In-House	Y	5	3	124,573	133,401	
15	Nebraska	Contracted	N	16	3	115,962	121,095	
16	Nebraska	In-House	N	2	4	156,717	158,609	
17	Nebraska	Contracted	N	10	6	193,444	199,579	
18								
19								
20								
21								
22								
23								
24	as, Contracted	s, In-House	s, Contracted	In-House	n-House			
25	Y	N	N	N	Y			
26	15	8	7	9	3			
27	3	6	1	5	2			
28	103,572	194,001	58,654	183,925	81,898			
29	111,818	199,456	56,407	188,556	85,478			
30								

Copy button

Paste button arrow

Transpose command

Paste menu

cell A18 selected

marquee surrounds copied range

Figure 9–30

- Click Transpose on the Paste menu to transpose and paste the copied cells to a range beginning with cell A18 (Figure 9–31).

Q&A

What happens when the range is copied and transposed?

When the range is transposed, the first row of the selected range becomes the first column of the destination range, and so on. For example, row 14 (A24:E24) in the source range becomes column A (A18:A22) in the destination range.

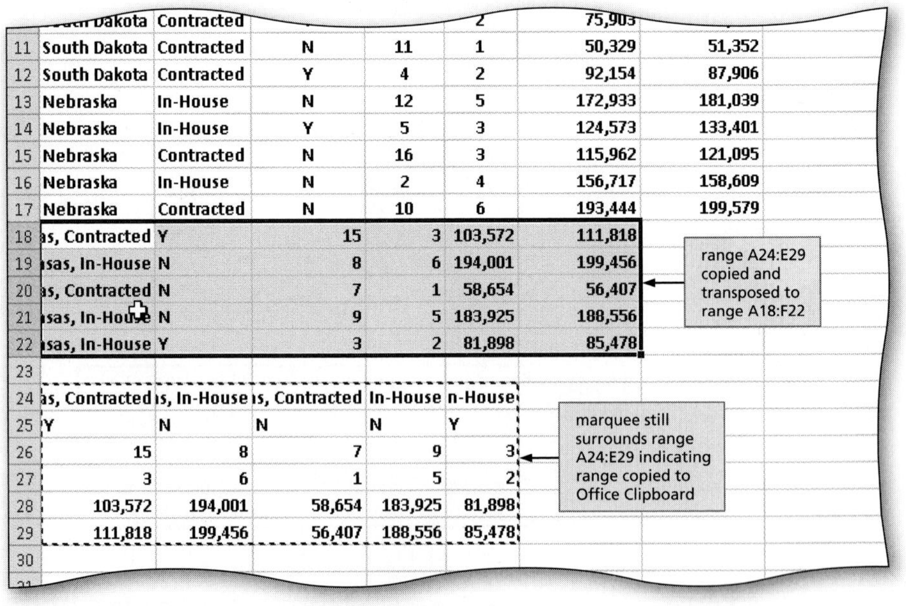

	A	B	C	D	E	F	G
10	South Dakota	Contracted			2	75,903	
11	South Dakota	Contracted	N	11	1	50,329	51,352
12	South Dakota	Contracted	Y	4	2	92,154	87,906
13	Nebraska	In-House	N	12	5	172,933	181,039
14	Nebraska	In-House	Y	5	3	124,573	133,401
15	Nebraska	Contracted	N	16	3	115,962	121,095
16	Nebraska	In-House	N	2	4	156,717	158,609
17	Nebraska	Contracted	N	10	6	193,444	199,579
18	as, Contracted	Y		15	3	103,572	111,818
19	sas, In-House	N		8	6	194,001	199,456
20	as, Contracted	N		7	1	58,654	56,407
21	sas, In-House	N		9	5	183,925	188,556
22	sas, In-House	Y		3	2	81,898	85,478
23							
24	as, Contracted	s, In-House	s, Contracted	In-House	n-House		
25	Y	N	N	N	Y		
26	15	8	7	9	3		
27	3	6	1	5	2		
28	103,572	194,001	58,654	183,925	81,898		
29	111,818	199,456	56,407	188,556	85,478		
30							

range A24:E29 copied and transposed to range A18:F22

marquee still surrounds range A24:E29 indicating range copied to Office Clipboard

Figure 9–31

Other Ways

1. Press ALT+H, V, T

To Convert Text to Columns

As stated earlier and shown in Figure 9–31, column A of the imported Kansas data includes both the state and shop type. The data must be separated using Excel's Convert Text to Columns command so that the shop type information is in column B. Before doing so, the source range for the data (A24:E29) should be deleted because it no longer is needed. Also, the cells in the range B18:F22 must be shifted one column to the right to accommodate the shop type data.

The following steps clear the range A24:E29, move the range B18:F22 one column to the right, and move the shop type data in column A to column B.

1

- If necessary, click the Home tab on the Ribbon.

- Select the range A24:E29 and press the DELETE key to delete the range.

- Select the range B18:F22 and then click the Cut button on the Ribbon to copy the range to the Office Clipboard (Figure 9–32).

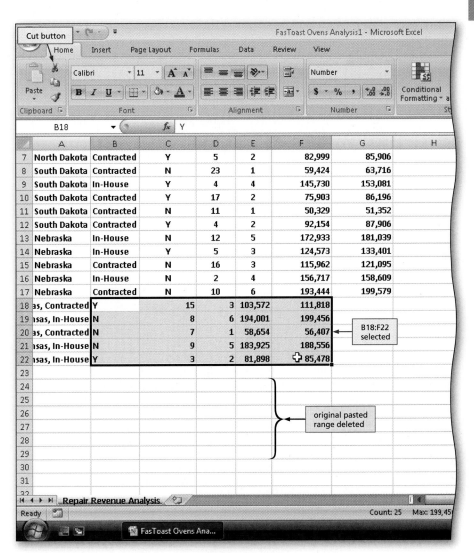

Figure 9–32

- Select cell C18 and then click the Paste button on the Ribbon (Figure 9–33).

Q&A

Why does the range B18:F22 need to be cut and pasted to the new range?

The data in the range A18:A22 contains the shop type information that needs to be placed in the range B18:B22. Moving the range B18:F22 one column to the right will accommodate the shop type information.

Figure 9–33

- Select the range C17:G17 and then click the Format Painter button on the Ribbon.

- Select the range C18:G22 to copy the formats in range C17:G17 down to the corresponding columns of range C18:G22 (Figure 9–34).

Q&A

What other tasks can be accomplished using the Convert Text to Columns Wizard?

The wizard can be used only when a range that includes a single column is selected. The Convert Text to Columns Wizard is a powerful tool for manipulating text data in columns, such as splitting first and last names into separate columns. Most often, however, you will use the wizard to manipulate imported data. For example, survey data may be imported in one column as a series of Y and N characters, indicating answers to questions on the survey (e.g., YNNYYN). You can split the answers into separate columns by specifying fixed width fields of one character each.

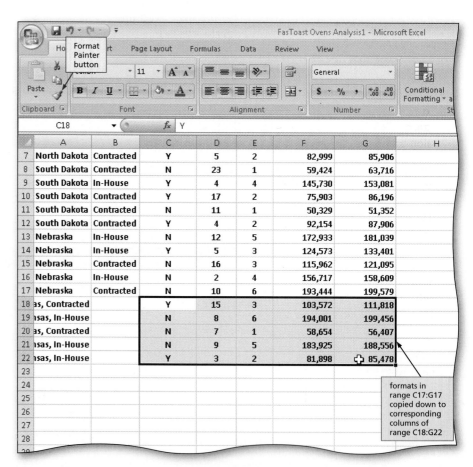

Figure 9–34

- Select the range
  A18:A22 and then
  click the Data tab on
  the Ribbon.

- Click the Text to
  Columns button
  on the Ribbon to
  display the Convert
  Text to Columns
  Wizard - Step 1
  of 3 dialog box
  (Figure 9–35).

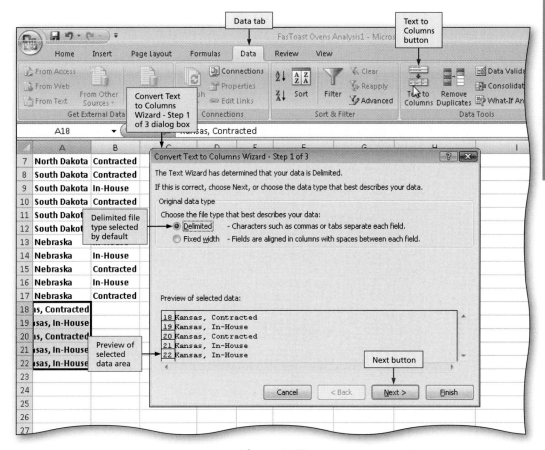

Figure 9–35

❺

- Click the Next
  button to display
  the Convert
  Text to Columns
  Wizard - Step 2 of 3
  dialog box.

- When Excel displays
  the Convert
  Text to Columns
  Wizard - Step 2
  of 3 dialog box,
  click Comma in the
  Delimiters area to
  display the data
  fields correctly in the
  Data preview area.

- Click Tab in the
  Delimiters area to
  clear the check box
  (Figure 9–36).

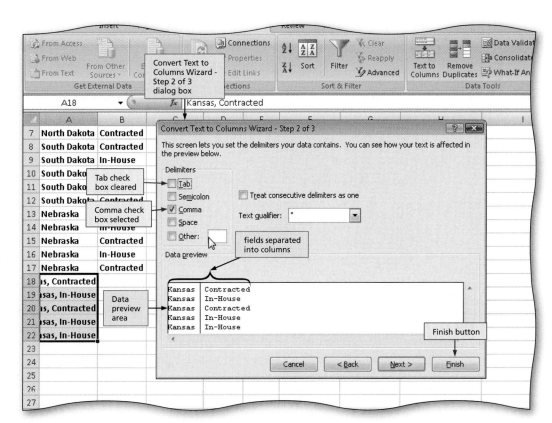

Figure 9–36

6

- Click the Finish button to close the Convert Text to Columns Wizard - Step 2 of 3 dialog box and separate the data in column A to two columns (Figure 9–37).

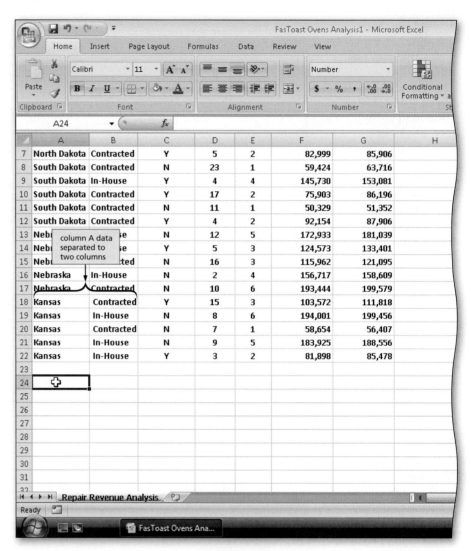

Figure 9–37

Other Ways

1. Press ALT+A, E

Importing XML Data

BTW

Dragging and Dropping an Access File
If you have both Excel and Access open on your desktop, you can drag and drop an entire table or query from Access to Excel. Select the table or query you want to transfer in the database window and drag it to the desired location in the worksheet.

XML is an increasingly popular format for sharing data. **XML** stands for **Extensible Markup Language**, which is a language that is used to encapsulate data and a description of the data in a single text file, or **XML file**. **Tags** are used in XML files to describe data items, which are called **elements**. XML files typically have a file extension of xml. Industry organizations and companies create standard XML file layouts and tags to describe commonly used types of data.

Excel is capable of importing and exporting XML in a variety of layouts, as long as the XML file is described by a schema. A **schema** is a special type of XML file used to describe the layout of data in other XML files. A schema describes what information an XML file should contain, the order in which the elements should appear, the values allowed for each element, and a variety of other information. A schema file typically is sent from a technical source, such as a programmer or a person in a company's information technology department.

Before importing XML data into a worksheet or exporting XML data from a worksheet, the schema file that describes the format of the XML file to import must be added to a workbook. When a schema is added to a workbook, the schema is called an **XML map** in Excel.

With an XML map, an import area can be created on a worksheet by dragging elements from the XML map to cells in a worksheet. When the XML data is imported, it is imported as a table. To attach an XML map to a workbook, you first must display the Developer tab on the Ribbon as described in Chapter 7 on page EX 540. The XML group displays on the Developer tab on the Ribbon. Click the Source button on the Ribbon to display the XML Source task pane. Click the XML Maps button and then click the Add button. You then can navigate to the location of the schema file that was provided to you and drag and drop XML elements to your worksheet to create the XML map. When your XML map is complete, click the Import button on the Developer tab to begin the process of importing an XML file. After importing the XML data, you often may need to convert the table to a range because, as stated earlier, XML data always is imported as a table.

BTW

XML
XML can describe any type of data. Banks use it to transfer financial information among various systems, and graphic artists use it to share multimedia data. The versatility of XML is matched by its simplicity. XML also is being used to make queries over the Web using a common set of rules available to any user. For example, a user can send an XML query to a travel Web site and receive the current information for a specific flight in XML format.

To Replicate Formulas

The workbook opened at the beginning of this project contained a worksheet title, headings for each column, and formulas in cells H3 and I3 to calculate the revenue per repair person for 2007 and 2008. The formulas must be copied, or replicated, through row 22 to complete the calculations for the remaining rows in the worksheet. Some spreadsheet specialists refer to copying formulas as **replication**. This technique of replicating the formulas after completing the import is necessary because the total number of records to be imported usually is unknown. The following steps use the fill handle to replicate the formulas.

1

- Select the range H3:I3 (Figure 9–38).

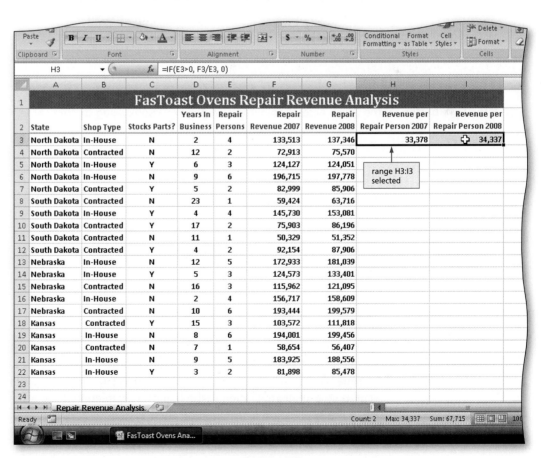

Figure 9–38

2

- Drag the fill handle down through row 22 to copy the two formulas to the range H4:I22 and display the new values for the Revenue per Repair Person 2007 and Revenue per Repair Person 2008 columns (Figure 9–39).

Q&A

What if I just want to copy formulas rather than replicating?

Recall that copying, or replicating, a formula, causes Excel to adjust the cell references so the new formulas contain references corresponding to the new locations. Excel then performs calculations using the appropriate values. To create an exact copy without replication, hold down the CTRL key while dragging the fill handle. Holding down the SHIFT key while dragging the fill handle inserts new cells, rather than overwriting existing data.

H3   =IF(E3>0, F3/E3, 0)

	State	Shop Type	Stocks Parts?	Years In Business	Repair Persons	Repair Revenue 2007	Repair Revenue 2008	Revenue per Repair Person 2007	Revenue per Repair Person 2008
1									
2									
3	North Dakota	In-House	N	2	4	133,513	137,346	33,378	34,337
4	North Dakota	Contracted	N	12	2	72,913	75,570	36,457	37,785
5	North Dakota	In-House	Y	6	3	124,127	124,051	41,376	41,350
6	North Dakota	In-House	N	9	6	196,715	197,778	32,786	32,963
7	North Dakota	Contracted	Y	5	2	82,999	85,906	41,500	42,953
8	South Dakota	Contracted	N	23	1	59,424	63,716	59,424	63,716
9	South Dakota	In-House	Y	4	4	145,730	153,081	36,433	38,270
10	South Dakota	Contracted	Y	17	2	75,903	86,196	37,952	43,098
11	South Dakota	Contracted	N	11	1	50,329	51,352	50,329	51,352
12	South Dakota	Contracted	Y	4	2	87,906	87,906	46,077	43,953
13	Nebraska	In-House	N	12	5	181,439	181,439	34,587	36,208
14	Nebraska	In-House	Y	5	3	133,401	133,401	41,524	44,467
15	Nebraska	Contracted	N	16	3	115,962	121,095	38,654	40,365
16	Nebraska	In-House	N	2	4	156,717	158,609	39,179	39,652
17	Nebraska	Contracted	N	10	6	193,444	199,579	32,241	33,263
18	Kansas	Contracted	Y	15	3	103,572	111,818	34,524	37,273
19	Kansas	In-House	N	8	6	194,001	199,456	32,334	33,243
20	Kansas	Contracted	N	7	1	58,654	56,407	58,654	56,407
21	Kansas	In-House	N	9	5	183,925	188,556	36,785	37,711
22	Kansas	In-House	Y	3	2	81,898	85,478	40,949	42,739
23									
24									

formulas in range H3:I3 copied to range H4:I22

Repair Revenue Analysis

Ready   Count: 40   Max: 63,716   Sum: 1,636,245   100%

FasToast Ovens Ana...

Figure 9–39

3

- Click the Save button on the Quick Access Toolbar to save the workbook using the file name, FasToast Ovens Analysis1.

Other Ways

1. Click Copy button on Quick Access Toolbar, click Paste button on Quick Access Toolbar
2. Press CTRL+C, press CTRL+V
3. Click Copy on shortcut menu, click Paste on shortcut menu

BTW

Replicating Formulas
You automatically can replicate a formula when you import data. The External Data Range Properties dialog box includes a check box labeled 'Fill down formulas in column adjacent to data' that you can use to automatically replicate formulas when importing data.

Collaborating and Tracking Changes on a Workbook

The next steps are to share the workbook, insert a comment, and then turn on features to track changes.

If others need to edit a workbook or suggest changes, Excel provides four ways to collaborate. **Collaborating** means working together in cooperation on a document with other Excel users.

The first option is to **distribute** the workbook to others, physically on a disk or through e-mail using the Send command on the Office Button menu. With the Send command, the document can be embedded as part of the e-mail message or the file can be sent as an e-mail attachment, which allows recipients of the e-mail message to open the file if the application is installed on their system.

A second option is to **collaborate** interactively with other people through discussion threads or online meetings. The integration of **SharePoint** with Microsoft Office 2007 allows people at different sites to share and exchange files.

A third option is to collaborate by sharing the workbook. Sharing involves more than simply giving another user a copy of a file; it allows multiple people to work independently on the same workbook at the same time, if they are in a networked environment.

BTW

Removing Duplicate Rows

After importing data, you often may want to remove duplicate rows of data. If your data is formatted as an Excel table, click anywhere on the table and then click the Remove Duplicates button on the Data tab. You then can select the columns in the table that contain duplicate values that you want to eliminate, such as duplicate names.

To Share a Workbook and Collaborate on a Workbook

Sharing can be turned on for a workbook using the Share Workbook button on the Review tab on the Ribbon. When workbook sharing is enabled, a number of Excel features — merging cells, deleting worksheets, changing or removing passwords, using scenarios, creating data tables, modifying macros, using data validation, and creating PivotTables — are disabled for the workbook. See Excel Help for a complete list of features disabled by Excel while a workbook is shared. For this reason, the time when a workbook is shared should be limited; further, sharing should be used only for the purpose of reviewing and modifying the contents of worksheet data.

When a workbook is shared with another user, changes made and saved by the other user are visible only when you attempt to save changes. When Excel recognizes that another user has modified a shared workbook, Excel displays a dialog box indicating that the workbook has been updated with changes saved by other users; you then can review and accept or reject the other user's work. If both you and the other user change the same cell, then Excel displays a Resolve Conflicts dialog box when the workbook is saved. The dialog box lists the conflicting changes and provides options to choose which change to accept in the workbook.

The following steps turn on sharing for the FasToast Ovens Analysis1 workbook and then show collaboration with another user to make changes to the workbook.

1
- Click the Review tab on the Ribbon (Figure 9–40).

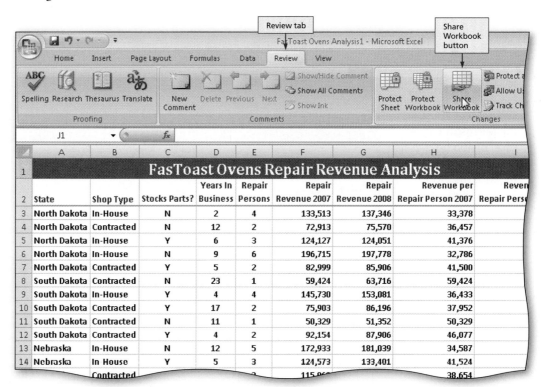

Figure 9–40

2

- Click the Share Workbook button on the Ribbon to display the Share Workbook dialog box.

- When Excel displays the Share Workbook dialog box, click 'Allow changes by more than one user at the same time' (Figure 9–41).

What is shown in the Share Workbook dialog box?

The 'Allow changes by more than one user at the same time' check box is selected, indicating that the workbook should be shared. The 'Who has this workbook open now' list in the Share Workbook dialog box lists all users who currently have a copy of the workbook open.

3

- Click the OK button.

- When Excel displays the Microsoft Office Excel dialog box, click the OK button to place the workbook in share mode (Figure 9–42).

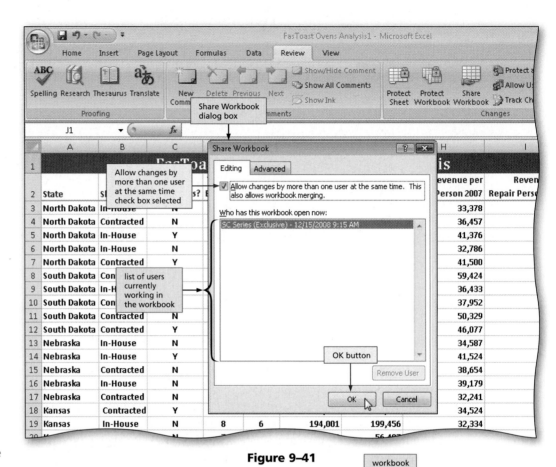

Figure 9–41

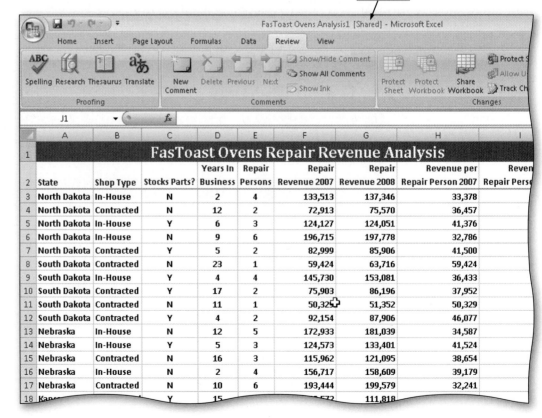

Figure 9–42

4

- If possible, have a classmate open a second copy of the workbook.

- With a second copy of the workbook open, click the Share Workbook button on the Review tab on the Ribbon to display the Share Workbook dialog box, which lists all users who currently have the workbook open (Figure 9–43).

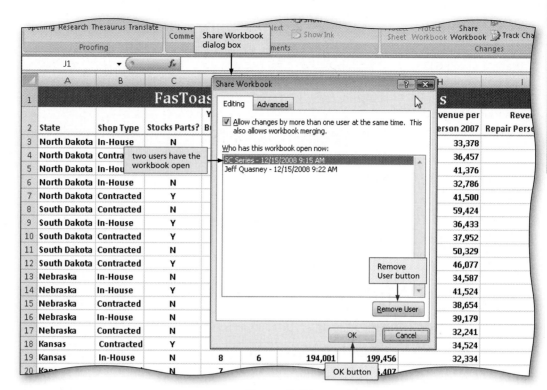

Figure 9–43

5

- Click the OK button.

- Ask the second workbook user to select G13, enter 183,540 as the new value, and then save the workbook.

- Click the Save button on the Quick Access Toolbar to display the Microsoft Office Excel dialog box indicating that the workbook has been updated with changes saved by another user (Figure 9–44).

Q&A

Must I save the workbook before I am notified of another user's changes?

Yes. As shown in Figure 9–44, until the workbook is saved, Excel provides no indication that another user has changed the shared workbook. To prohibit another user from saving additional updates to the workbook, click the user name in the Share Workbook dialog box and then click the Remove User button.

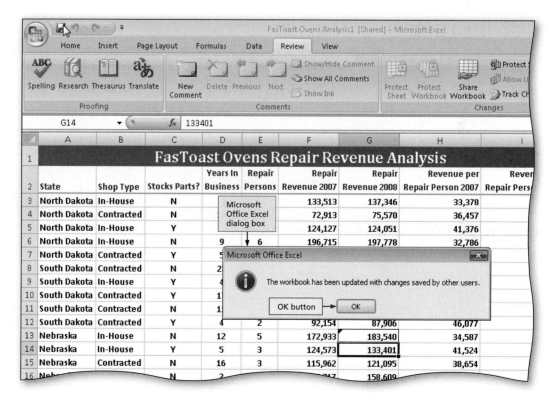

Figure 9–44

- Click the OK button.

- Point to the blue triangle in cell G13 to display the comment indicating the other user's changes (Figure 9–45).

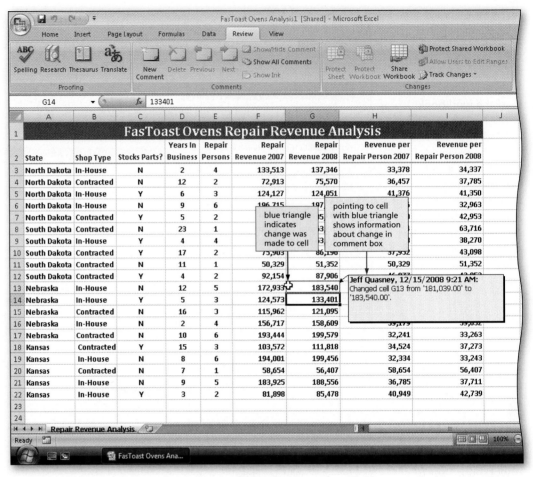

Figure 9–45

7

- Ask the second user of the workbook to close the workbook.

- Click the Review tab on the Ribbon and then click the Share Workbook button on the Ribbon to display the Share Workbook dialog box.

- When Excel displays the Share Workbook dialog box, click 'Allow changes by more than one user at the same time' to clear the check box (Figure 9–46).

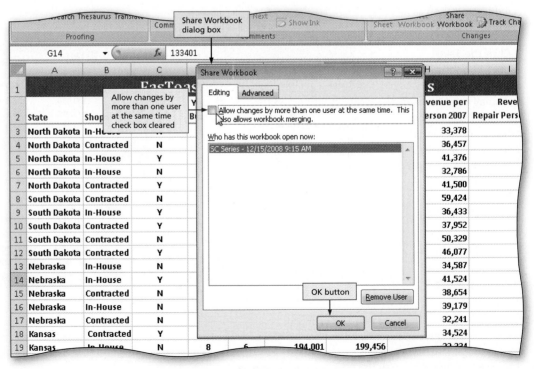

Figure 9–46

- Click the OK button to stop sharing the workbook (Figure 9–47).

- If Excel displays the Microsoft Office Excel dialog box, click the Yes button.

Figure 9–47

Other Ways
1. Press ALT+R, W

To Insert a Comment

Comments are used to describe the function of a cell, a range, a sheet, or an entire workbook or to clarify entries that otherwise might be difficult to understand. Multiple users reviewing the workbook often use comments to communicate suggestions, tips, and other messages. The following steps insert a comment to indicate that the worksheet may contain an incorrect number of repair persons for one of the Nebraska offices.

1
- Right-click cell E13 to display the shortcut menu (Figure 9–48).

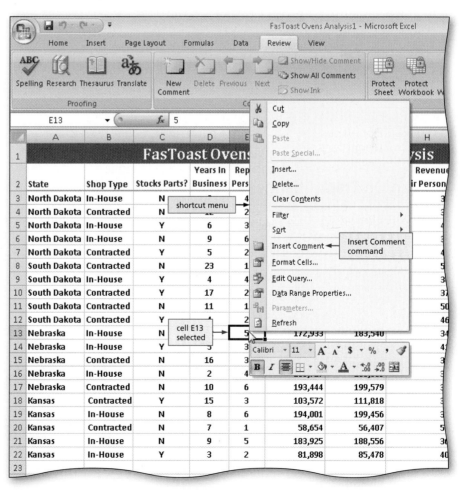

Figure 9–48

- Click Insert Comment on the shortcut menu to open a comment box next to the selected cell and display a comment indicator in the cell.

- When Excel displays the comment box, enter the comment as shown in Figure 9–49.

3

- Click anywhere outside the comment box to close the comment box and display a red comment indicator in cell E13.

- Click the Save button on the Quick Access Toolbar.

Q&A

Can I print comments?

Yes. To print the comments where they appear on the worksheet, click Show All Comments on the Review tab on the Ribbon, move and resize the comments as necessary, and then print the worksheet. To print the comments at the end of the worksheet, click the Page Setup Dialog Box Launcher on the Page Layout tab on the Ribbon. When Excel displays the Page Setup dialog box, click the Sheet tab, click the Comments box arrow, and then click 'At end of sheet' in the Comments list. Click the OK button and then print the worksheet.

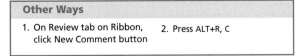

Figure 9–49

Other Ways

1. On Review tab on Ribbon, click New Comment button
2. Press ALT+R, C

To Turn On Track Changes

With the first two types of collaboration in particular, distributing and using SharePoint to keep track of the changes that others make to a workbook is important. Tracking changes means that Excel, through the Track Changes command, will display the edited cells with a comment indicating who made the change, when the change was made, and what the original value was of the cell that was changed. Tracking and sharing work together. If either tracking or sharing is enabled, Excel enables the other by default. The following steps turn on track changes.

1

- If necessary, click the Review tab on the Ribbon and then click the Track Changes button on the Ribbon to display the Track Changes menu (Figure 9–50).

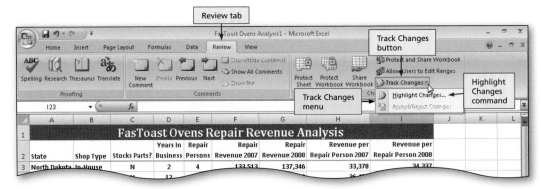

Figure 9–50

2

- Click Highlight Changes on the Track Changes menu to display the Highlight Changes dialog box.

- When Excel displays the Highlight Changes dialog box, click 'Track changes while editing'.

- If necessary, click all of the check boxes in the 'Highlight which changes' area to clear them (Figure 9–51).

Q&A

What is the purpose of clearing the check marks?

Clicking the 'Track changes while editing' check box enables track changes and shares the workbook. The When, Who, and Where check boxes and list boxes play no role when track changes first is enabled.

3

- Click the OK button.

- When Excel displays the Microsoft Office Excel dialog box, click the OK button to save the workbook (Figure 9–52).

4

- Close the workbook.

Q&A

What is the change history and how can it be protected?

Excel keeps a **change history** with each shared workbook. In the case of a shared workbook in which changes should be tracked, Excel provides a way for users to make data entry changes, but does not allow them to modify the change history. To protect the change history associated with a shared workbook, click the Review tab on the Ribbon and then click the Protect Shared Workbook button on the Ribbon. When Excel displays the Protect Shared Workbook dialog box, click 'Sharing with track changes' to select it and then click the OK button. After a shared workbook is protected, no one can unprotect or change it, except the owner.

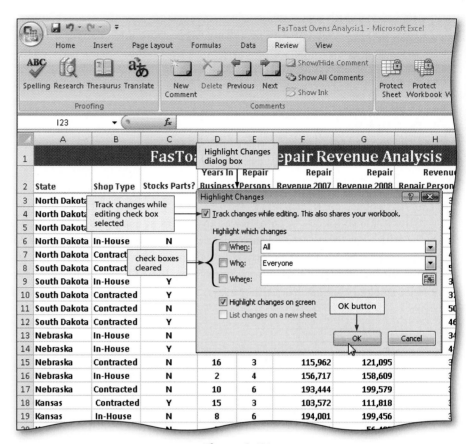

Figure 9–51

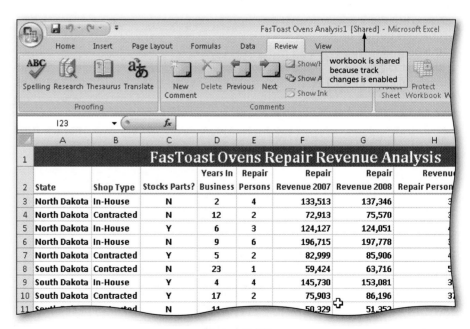

Figure 9–52

Other Ways
1. Press ALT+R, G, H

BTW

Selecting External Data
If you want to view which part of your spreadsheet is imported, or if you want to format or delete an external data range, click the arrow next to the Name box in the formula bar, and then click the external data range name.

Reviewing Tracked Changes

Instead of writing suggestions and changes on a printed draft copy and sending it to the person in charge of a workbook, Excel's track changes feature allows users to enter suggested changes directly in the workbook. The owner of the workbook then looks through each change and makes a decision about whether or not to accept it.

To Open a Workbook and Review Tracked Changes

After a workbook has been reviewed by others, it usually is returned to the owner. Because track changes was enabled for the FasToast Ovens Analysis1 workbook, the file will be returned with other users' changes, corrections, and comments. The owner of the workbook then can review those changes and make decisions about whether or not to accept the changes. A workbook named FasToast Ovens Analysis2 is saved on the Data Files for Students, and it includes tracked changes from other users. The following steps use this workbook to illustrate reviewing tracked changes.

- With Excel active, open the file, FasToast Ovens Analysis2, from the Data Files for Students.

- Click the Review Tab on the Ribbon and then click the Track Changes button on the Ribbon to display the Track Changes menu (Figure 9–53).

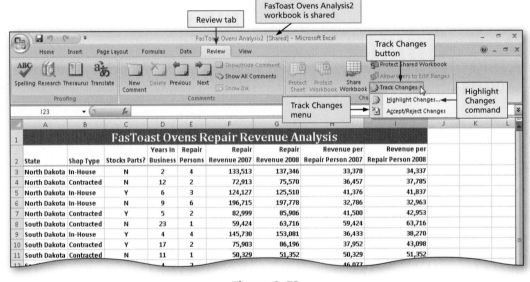

Figure 9–53

- Click Highlight Changes on the Track Changes menu.

- When Excel displays the Highlight Changes dialog box, click When to clear the check box (Figure 9–54).

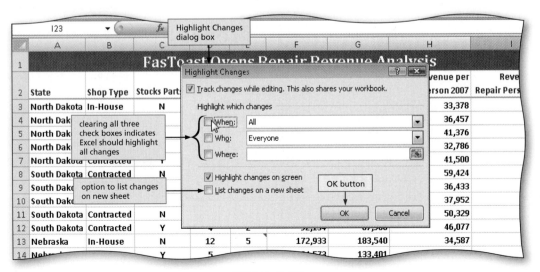

Figure 9–54

3

- Click the OK button.

- Click the Show All Comments button on the Ribbon to display all comments.

- Point to the blue triangle in cell G5 to display the comment box with information about the change made to the cell G5 (Figure 9–55).

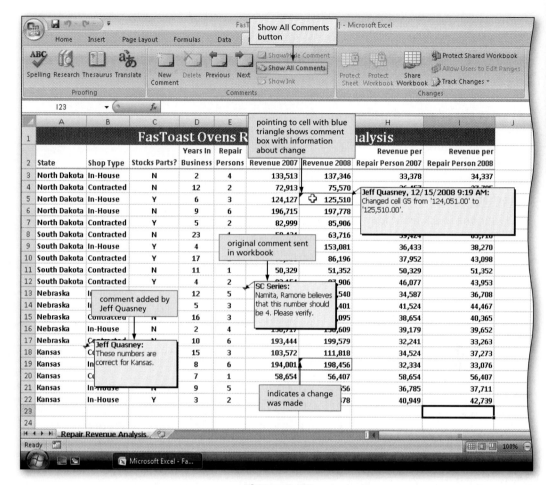

Figure 9–55

4

- Click the Track Changes button on the Ribbon to display the Track Changes menu (Figure 9–56).

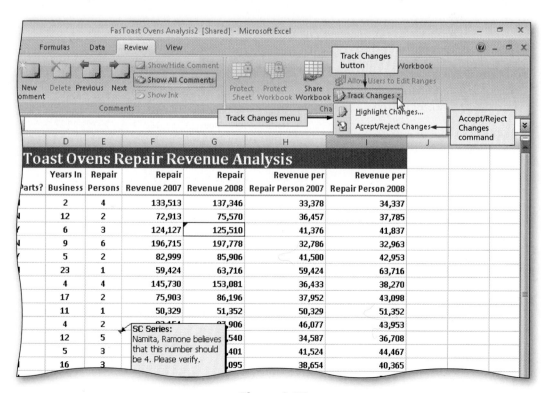

Figure 9–56

5

- Click Accept/Reject Changes on the Track Changes menu.

- If necessary, when Excel displays the Select Changes to Accept or Reject dialog box, click all check boxes to clear them, indicating that all changes in the change history file should be reviewed (Figure 9–57).

What is the purpose of clearing the check mark?

Clearing the check mark from the When check box indicates that all changes in the change history should be available for review. Excel can track three categories of changes in the change history. The When check box allows you to specify the time from which you wish to review changes. The Who check box allows you to specify individual users from whom to review changes. The Where check box allows you to specify a range of cells to check for changes.

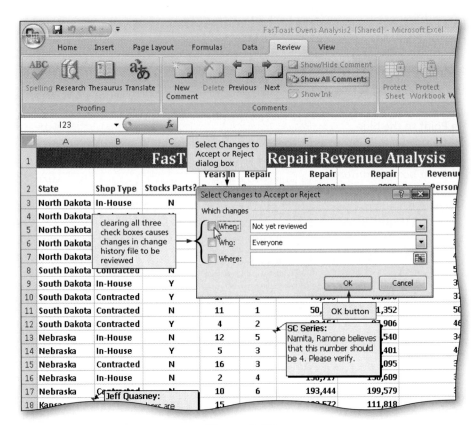

Figure 9–57

6

- Click the OK button to display the first tracked change (Figure 9–58).

7

- Click the Accept button.

- As Excel displays each change in the Accept or Reject Changes dialog box, click the Accept button.

- Right-click cell A18 and then click Delete Comment on the shortcut menu.

- Right-click cell E13 and then click Delete Comment on the shortcut menu.

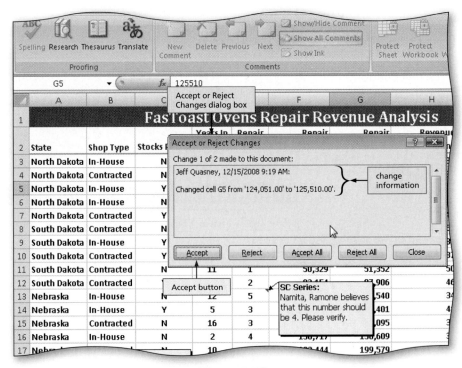

Figure 9–58

Other Ways

1. Press ALT+R, G, C

To Save the Workbook with a New File Name

1 Click the Office Button then click Save As on the Office Button menu.

2 When Excel displays the Save As dialog box, type `FasToast Ovens Analysis3` in the File name text box.

3 Click the Save button in the Save As dialog box to save the workbook with the new file name.

To Turn Off Track Changes

As previously discussed, when workbook sharing is enabled, Excel denies access to a number of features, including creating PivotTables. The following steps turn off track changes, which also automatically turns off sharing and saves the workbook as an exclusive workbook. An **exclusive workbook** is a workbook that is not shared and can be opened only by a single user.

1 Click the Track Changes button on the Ribbon, and then click Highlight Changes on the Track Changes menu.

2 When Excel displays the Highlight Changes dialog box, click Track Changes while editing to clear the check box.

3 Click the OK button.

4 When Excel displays the Microsoft Office Excel dialog box asking if the workbook should be made exclusive, click the Yes button.

Q&A

What happens when track changes is disabled?

When track changes is disabled, sharing is disabled as well. At the same time, Excel erases the change history. The workbook automatically is resaved as an exclusive workbook, which is not shared and can be opened only by a single user.

Creating and Formatting PivotTables and PivotCharts

A PivotTable is an interactive view of worksheet data that gives users the ability to summarize data in the database and then rotate the table's row and column titles to show different views of the summarized data. After a PivotTable is created, it can be used to view different levels of detail, reorganize the layout of the chart by dragging its fields, or show and hide items in lists. While a PivotTable usually is created on a separate worksheet in the workbook containing the data to be analyzed, a PivotTable also can be created on the same worksheet as the data.

A PivotChart is an interactive chart used to analyze data graphically by varying the fields and categories to present different views. When a PivotChart is created, Excel automatically creates and associates a PivotTable with the PivotChart.

BTW

Resolving Shared Workbook Conflicts
When you save a shared workbook, Excel may notify you that one or more of your changes conflict with changes made by another user. The Resolve Conflicts dialog box displays the conflicting information and allows you to click the Accept Mine button or the Accept Other button to resolve the conflict. You also can choose to accept all of your changes or all of the other user's changes. Finally, you can choose to always accept your changes and never see the Resolve Conflicts dialog box.

BTW

Shared Workbook Change History
Shared workbooks usually are current, active spreadsheets. Excel maintains a preset change history of 30 days. If you want more time to keep track of changes, you may change the number of days. For example, when you turn on the change history but are not sure exactly when the merge will take place, you can preserve the change history by setting a large number of days to maintain the change history, up to the maximum of 32,767 days.

BTW

Tracking Changes with Passwords
If you want to make sure others will not turn off the change history or reduce the number of days in the history, you can protect a shared workbook with a password. On the Review tab on the Ribbon, click the Protect and Share Workbook button. Passwords may be added only if the workbook is unshared at the time of protection.

The PivotTable required for this project is shown in Figure 9–59. It summarizes the data in the Repair Revenue Analysis worksheet to show the average of revenue per repair person in 2007 and 2008 for each state by shop type (Contracted or In-House). The interactive button in cell A4 allows the user to filter the table by shop type. Columns B and C show the values for the average of revenue per repair person in 2007 and 2008.

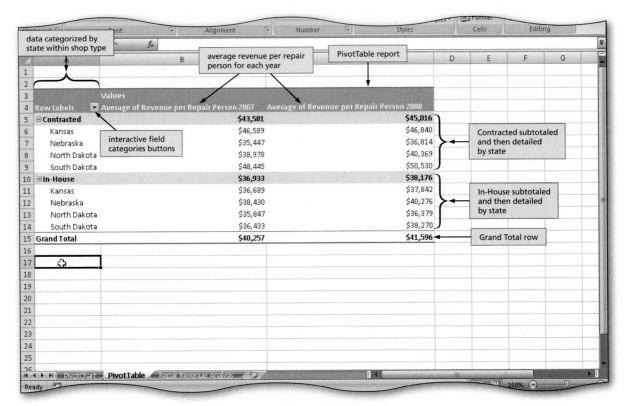

Figure 9–59

To Create a PivotTable

The following steps begin to create the PivotTable shown in Figure 9–59 using the Create PivotTable dialog box.

1

- Select cell A3 and then click the Insert tab on the Ribbon.

- Click the PivotTable button arrow on the Ribbon to display the PivotTable menu (Figure 9–60).

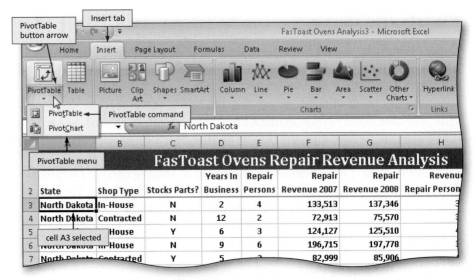

Figure 9–60

2

- Click PivotTable to display the Create PivotTable dialog box (Figure 9–61).

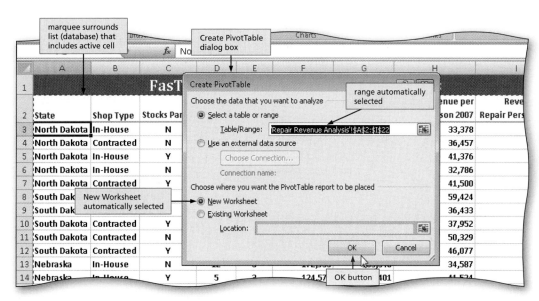

Figure 9–61

3

- Click the OK button to create the PivotTable on a new worksheet and display the PivotTable Field List pane (Figure 9–62).

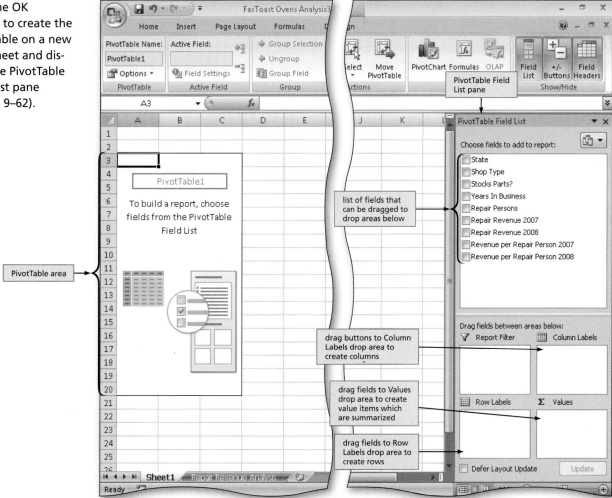

Figure 9–62

Other Ways

1. Press ALT+N, V, T

To Add Data to the PivotTable

The next step in creating the PivotTable as shown in Figure 9–59 on page EX 746 is to add data by dragging four fields from the 'Choose fields to add to report' list to the 'Drag fields between area below' areas: two for the table columns and two for the table rows. As shown in Figure 9–59, the rows show states within shop types. The columns include the two data fields, Revenue per Repair Person 2007 and Revenue per Repair Person 2008. The following step adds data to the PivotTable.

1

- Drag the Shop Type field from the 'Choose fields to add to report' list to the Row Labels area to add the Shop Type field to the PivotTable.

- Drag the State field from the 'Choose fields to add to report' list below the Shop Type button in the Row Labels area to add the State field to the PivotTable.

- Drag the Revenue per Repair Person 2007 field to the Values area to add the field to column B of the PivotTable.

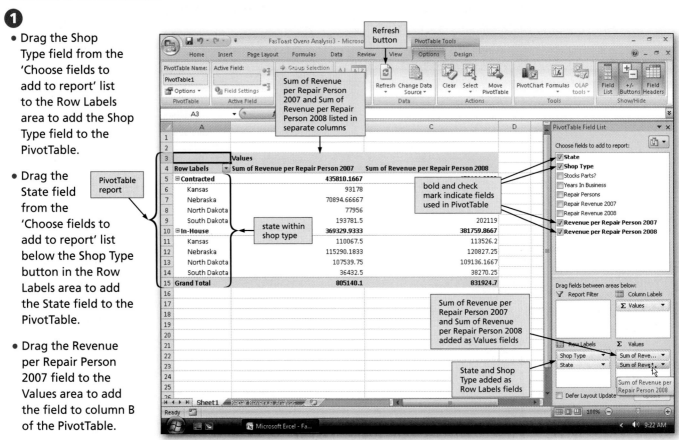

- Drag the Revenue per Repair Person 2008 field to the Values area to add the field to column C of the PivotTable (Figure 9–63).

Figure 9–63

Q&A

What is shown by the PivotTable?

Excel displays the Shop Type and State fields as Row Labels in the PivotTable. Revenue per Repair Person 2007 and 2008 are totaled for each state within shop type.

More About PivotTables

The information in PivotTables is not linked directly to worksheet cells, which means that when data changes in the worksheet cell, the table is not updated automatically. The PivotTable Tools Options contextual tab on the Ribbon contains a Refresh button (Figure 9–63) to update data when it changes on the worksheet. PivotTables can be based on several different types of data, including Excel lists and databases, multiple data ranges to be consolidated, and external sources, such as Microsoft Access databases.

To Change the View of a PivotTable

With regular tables or lists, one table or list must be created for each view of the data summary. With a PivotTable, a single table can be created and summaries can be viewed several ways just by using the mouse. The PivotTable provides a powerful interactive summarization of data with the visual appeal and benefits of a table.

The FasToast Ovens Analysis PivotTable currently shows the sum of revenue per repair person for each year within state within shop type (Figure 9–63). The data can be viewed in many other ways, however, such as just looking at one year's worth of information. To compare the data in different combinations, use the interactive buttons in the Row Labels area and Value area in the PivotTable Field List pane.

Because the Nebraska and South Dakota shops have similar marketing strategies, viewing the data and comparing only these two states, rather than all four, might be beneficial. While moving the two data ranges next to each other in the worksheet would be tedious, using the interactive AutoFilter button in cell A4 makes it easy to choose which categories to show.

The following steps interact with the PivotTable categories and series of data to change the view of the PivotTable.

- Drag the Shop Type button in the Row Labels area below the State button to group revenue by shop type, rather than by state (Figure 9–64).

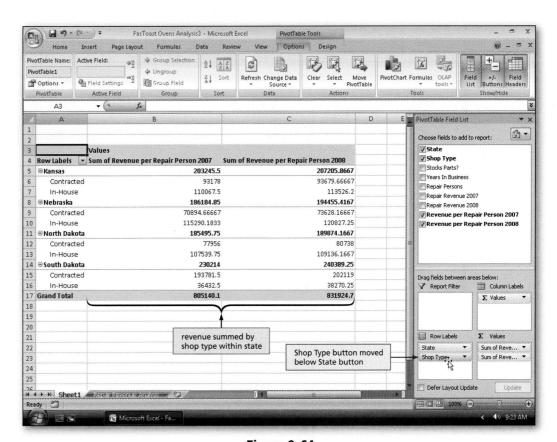

Figure 9–64

2

• Click the Sum of Revenue per Repair Person 2007 button arrow in the Values area to display the shortcut menu (Figure 9–65).

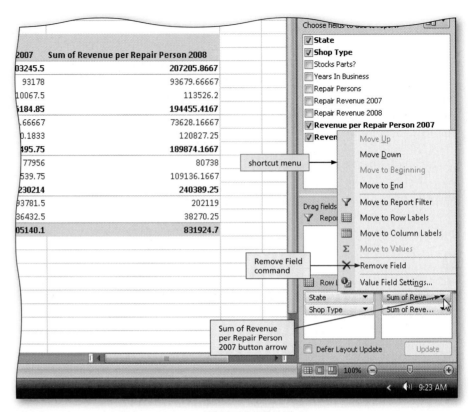

Figure 9–65

3

• Click Remove Field on the shortcut menu to remove Sum of Revenue per Repair Person 2007 from the PivotTable (Figure 9–66).

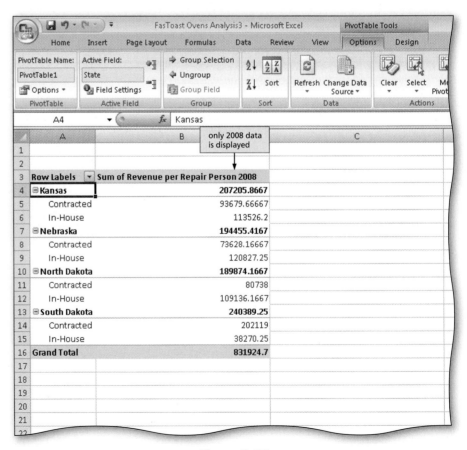

Figure 9–66

4

- Click the Undo button on the Quick Access Toolbar to undo the removal of Sum of Revenue per Repair Person 2007 column from the PivotTable.

- Click the Row Labels AutoFilter button in cell A4 to display the Row Labels AutoFilter menu.

- When Excel displays the Row Labels AutoFilter menu, click the check boxes for Kansas and North Dakota to clear them (Figure 9–67).

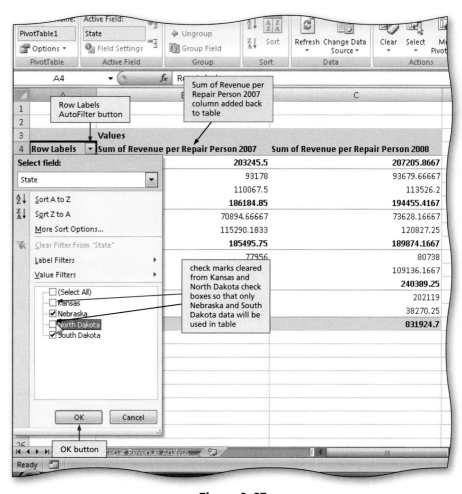

Figure 9–67

5

- Click the OK button to display only the Nebraska and South Dakota data in the PivotTable (Figure 9–68).

6

- Click the Undo button on the Quick Access Toolbar to display the data for all states.

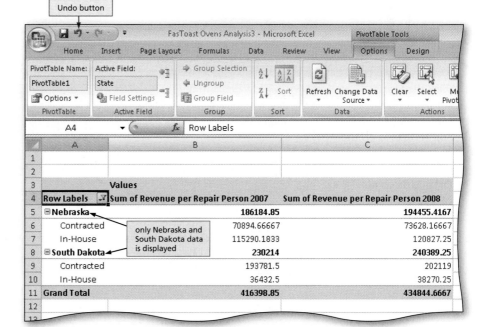

Figure 9–68

Other Ways

1. To remove data, click check box next to checked fields in PivotTable Field List

To Filter a PivotTable Using a Page Field

In a PivotTable, row and column fields can be rotated around the data fields by dragging the buttons to different areas at the bottom of the PivotTable Field List pane. For example, if you drag the State button to the Report Filter area, the view of the PivotTable changes. The State button then can be used to select specific states for which to view total sales. The use of this technique is known as filtering.

The following steps add a page field to change the view of the PivotTable and then filter the PivotTable using the page field.

- Drag the State button in the Row Labels area to the Report Filter area in the PivotTable Field List pane to create a new page field in the PivotTable (Figure 9–69).

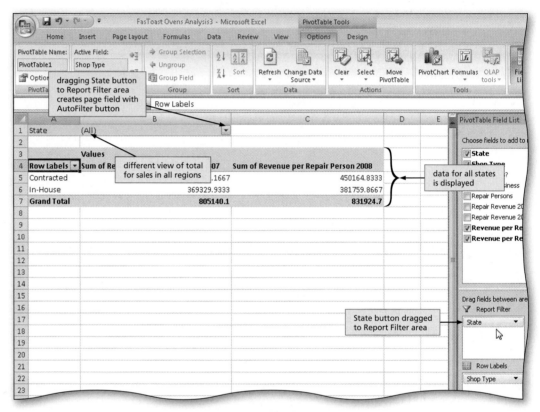

Figure 9–69

- Click the State AutoFilter button in cell B1, click South Dakota on the AutoFilter menu, and then click the OK button to display totals for South Dakota (Figure 9–70).

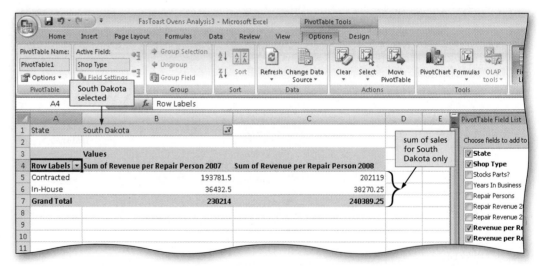

Figure 9–70

To Format a PivotTable

Once created, a PivotTable should be formatted to use colors and borders that enhance the data. To assist in formatting a PivotTable, Excel includes PivotTable styles that are used and appear similarly to Table styles. Different colors, patterns, alignments, fonts, and borders can be selected to apply to the entire PivotTable. Any of the wide range of Excel's normal formats to individual cells also can be applied. You also can format the numeric values in a PivotTable by specifying a format for an entire column. For the FasToast Ovens Analysis PivotTable, the values should be formatted with the Currency style and no decimal places. The following steps format a PivotTable.

- Double-click the Sheet1 tab.

- Type PivotTable and then press the ENTER key.

- Select cell A4, right-click the PivotTable tab, and then point to Tab Color on the shortcut menu.

- Click Olive Green, Accent 3 (column 7, row 1) in the Theme Color area.

- If necessary, select a cell in the PivotTable and then click the Design tab on the Ribbon.

- Click the PivotTable Styles More button to display the PivotTable Styles gallery.

- Point to the Pivot Style Medium 11 PivotTable style in the PivotTable Styles gallery to view a preview of the style in the PivotTable (Figure 9–71).

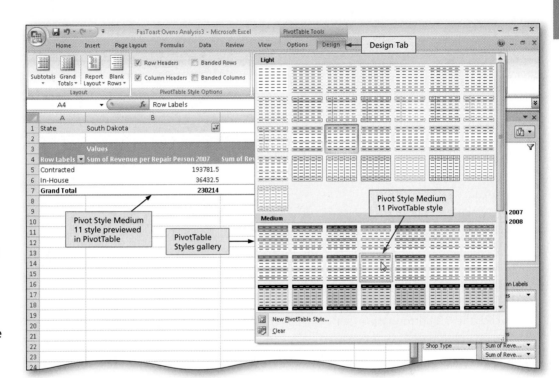

Figure 9–71

- Click the Pivot Style Medium 11 PivotTable style to apply the style to the PivotTable (Figure 9–72).

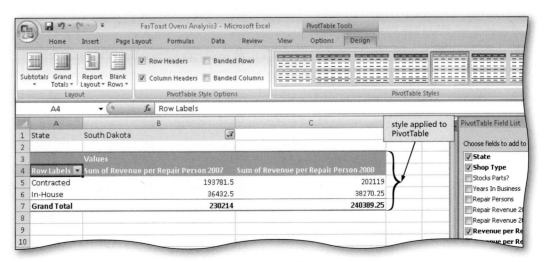

Figure 9–72

- Right-click anywhere in cell B4 to display the shortcut menu (Figure 9–73).

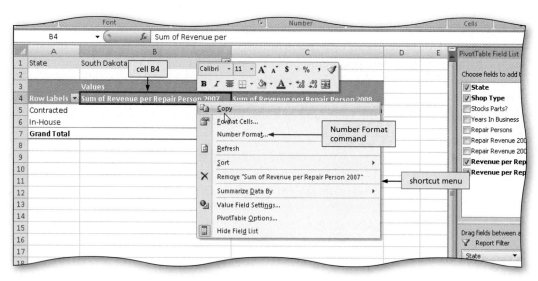

Figure 9–73

- Click Number Format on the shortcut menu to display the Format Cells dialog box.

- When Excel displays the Format Cells dialog box, if necessary, click Currency in the Category list, type 0 in the Decimal places box, and then click the OK button.

- Right-click anywhere in cell C4 to display the shortcut menu.

- Click Number Format on the shortcut menu to display the Format Cells dialog box.

- When Excel displays the Format Cells dialog box, click Currency in the Category list, type 0 in the Decimal places box, and then click the OK button to format the numeric values in the PivotTable with the Currency style (Figure 9–74).

- Select cell A9 to deselect the worksheet.

- Click the Save button on the Quick Access toolbar to save the workbook.

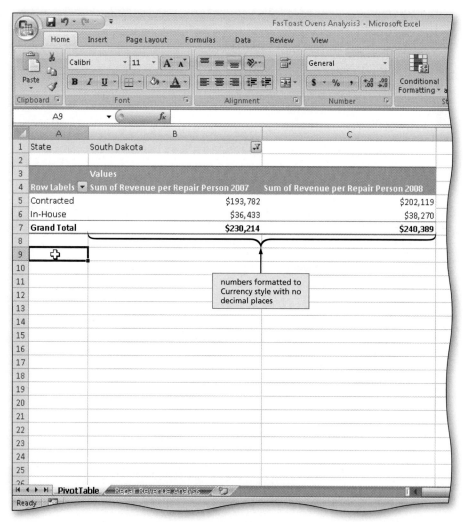

Figure 9–74

Other Ways

1. Press ALT+JY, S

To Switch Summary Functions in a PivotTable

Excel allows users to change the way the data fields are summarized on a PivotTable, add new fields to the analysis, or rotate the row and column fields. The PivotTable in the FasToast Ovens Analysis3 workbook illustrates the sum of the revenue per repair persons. The results, however, may be skewed because different offices in each state have a different mix of in-house and contracted shops. An average might be a better way to compare the revenue. The following steps show how to switch summary functions in a PivotTable.

 1

- Select cell B4 and then drag the State button in the Report Filter area above the Shop Type button in the Row Labels area.

- Right-click cell B4 to display the shortcut menu.

- Point to Summarize Data By on the shortcut menu (Figure 9–75).

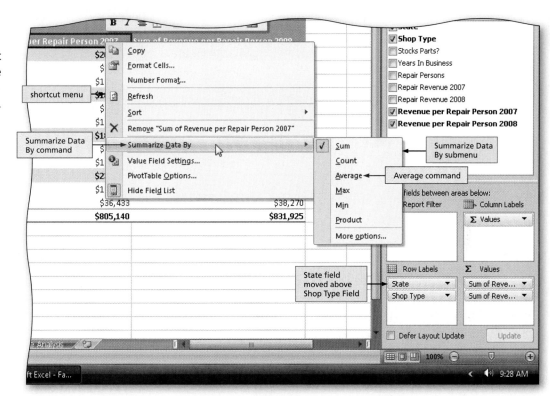

Figure 9–75

 2

- Click Average on the Summarize Data By submenu to change the numbers in column B from sums to averages.

- Right-click cell C4 to display the shortcut menu.

- Point to Summarize Data By on the shortcut menu.

- Click Average on the Summarize Data By submenu to change the numbers in column C from sums to averages.

- Click cell A19 to deselect the PivotTable and close the PivotTable Field List (Figure 9–76).

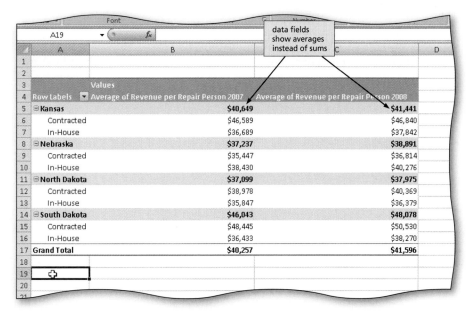

Figure 9–76

BTW

PivotTables
The PivotTable is one of the most powerful analytical tools available in Excel. PivotTables are used to show the relationships among the data in a list or a database. These tables allow you to use drag and drop to examine the data from different views.

Summary Functions for PivotCharts and PivotTables

Table 9–2 lists the summary functions Excel provides for analysis of data in PivotCharts and PivotTables. As shown in the previous steps, these functions can be selected by pointing to the Summarize Data By command on the shortcut menu and then clicking the function on the submenu. The last five summary functions can be accessed by clicking More options on the Summarize Data By submenu.

Table 9–2 Summary Functions for PivotChart and PivotTable Data Analysis	
Summary Function	**Description**
Sum	Sum values; this is the default function for numeric source data
Count	The number of items
Average	The average of the values
Max	The largest value
Min	The smallest value
Product	The product of the values
Count Nums	The number of rows that contain numeric data
StdDev	An estimate of the standard deviation of all of the data to be summarized
StdDevp	The standard deviation of all of the data to be summarized
Var	An estimate of the variance of all of the data to be summarized
Varp	The variance of the data to be summarized

To Create a PivotChart, Change the PivotChart Type, and Format the Chart

Excel provides two ways to create a PivotChart: (1) selecting the PivotChart command on the PivotTable menu as shown in Figure 9–60 on page EX 746 or (2) clicking the PivotChart button on the Options tab on the Ribbon while viewing a PivotTable.

Excel provides many ways to format PivotCharts. Most of the steps in formatting a PivotChart, such as choosing a chart type, showing category or axis labels, and inserting titles, are performed in the same way as for regular charts.

The default chart type for a PivotChart is a Clustered Column chart. PivotCharts can be any chart type except XY (Scatter), Stock, or Bubble. The following steps create the FasToast Ovens Repair Revenue Analysis PivotChart as a Clustered Cylinder chart that shows the two-year data side by side. A title also is added to the chart.

1

- Select cell A4.

- Click the Options tab on the Ribbon and then click the PivotChart button on the Ribbon to display the Insert Chart dialog box.

- Click Clustered Cylinder (column 1, row 2) in the 'Column chart type' gallery (Figure 9–77).

Figure 9–77

2

- Click the OK button to add the chart to the PivotTable worksheet.

- With the chart selected, click the Move Chart button on the Ribbon to display the Move Chart dialog box.

- When Excel displays the Move chart dialog box, click New sheet to select it and then type PivotChart in the New sheet text box (Figure 9–78).

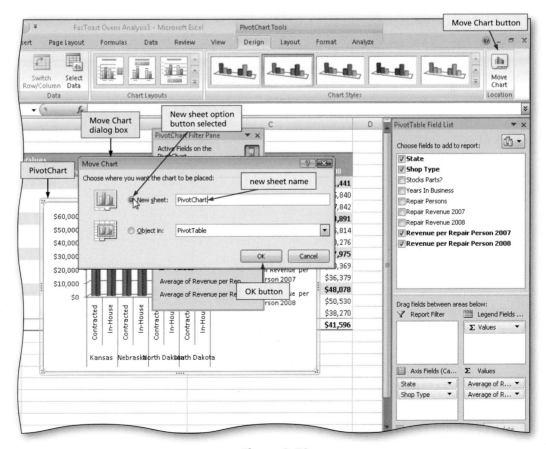

Figure 9–78

- Click the OK button.

- Right-click the PivotChart tab and then point to Tab Color on the shortcut menu.

- Click Purple, Accent 4 (column 8, row1) to change the color of the PivotChart sheet tab.

- Click the Layout tab on the Ribbon and then click the Chart Title button on the Ribbon to display the Chart Title menu.

- Point to Above Chart on the Chart Title menu (Figure 9–79).

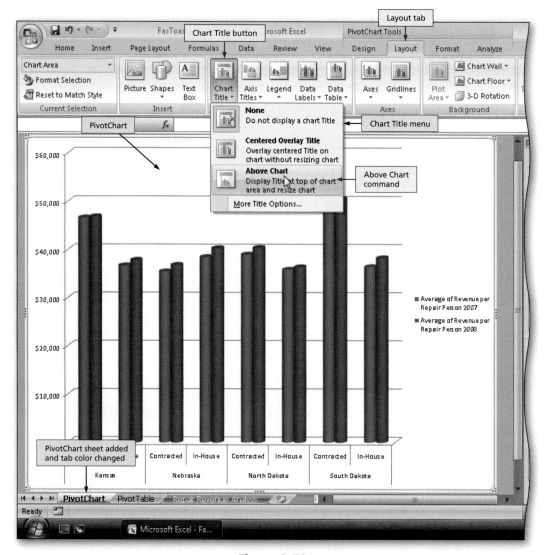

Figure 9–79

- Click Above Chart on the Chart Title menu.

- When the title is placed above the chart, select the title text. Type FasToast Ovens Analysis and then click anywhere on the chart to add the title to the chart (Figure 9–80).

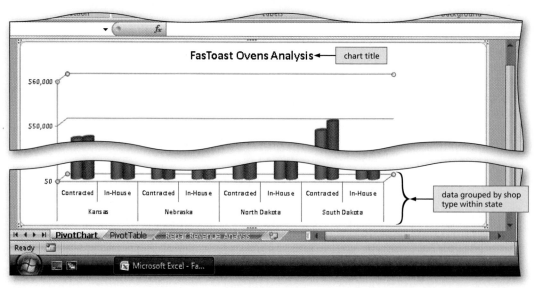

Figure 9–80

To Change the View of a PivotChart

When the PivotTable was created, the PivotTable and PivotChart Wizard also provided the option of creating a PivotChart with a PivotTable. A PivotChart cannot exist in Excel without an associated PivotTable. Excel automatically keeps a PivotTable and its associated PivotChart in synchronization, so that changes made to one are reflected in the other. The following steps change the view of the PivotChart and then show how the change in the PivotChart causes a corresponding change in the view of the associated PivotTable.

1

• Drag the Shop Type button in the Row Labels above the State button to group the data by state within shop type (Figure 9–81).

2

• Click the PivotTable sheet tab (Figure 9–82).

Q&A

What happens when the view of the PivotChart changes?

When the position of a field in a PivotChart or PivotTable is changed, the corresponding field in the other changes automatically. **Row fields** in a PivotTable correspond to category (x-axis) fields in a PivotChart, while **column fields** in a PivotTable correspond to series (y-axis) fields in charts. Further, if the data on the Repair Revenue Analysis worksheet is updated, clicking the Refresh button on the Options tab on the Ribbon updates the corresponding PivotTable and PivotChart.

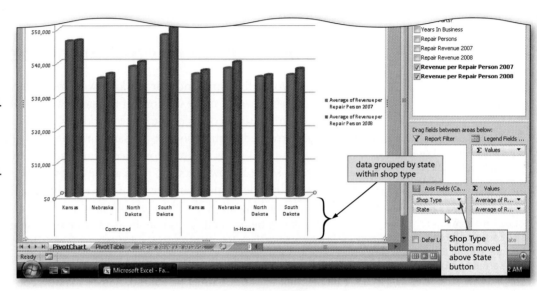

Figure 9–81

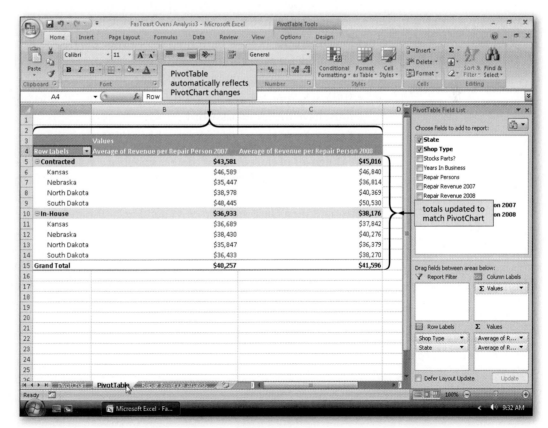

Figure 9–82

To Close the Workbook

The FasToast Ovens Analysis3 workbook is complete. The following steps close the FasToast Ovens Analysis3 workbook.

1 Click the workbook Close button.

2 When Excel displays the Microsoft Office Excel dialog box, click the Yes button.

Comparing and Merging Workbooks

Excel includes two useful commands for working with multiple versions of a workbook, including comparing two or more versions of the same workbook. Excel provides the capability to open multiple copies of the same workbook and move through the workbooks in a synchronized manner so that the same area of each workbook is always in view. For example, as a user scrolls down a worksheet, Excel automatically updates the view of the second worksheet to show the same rows as the first worksheet. This functionality allows for a side-by-side, visual comparison of two workbooks.

Instead of tracking all of the changes to a single copy of a workbook, copies of the same workbook can be merged. This may be necessary because multiple users are entering data or because new data has come from a different source. To merge the changes from one workbook into another, both workbooks must satisfy the following requirements:

- The original workbook must be shared, before making copies, and each workbook must be a copy of the same workbook.
- When copies of the workbook are made, track changes or sharing must be enabled, so that the change history of the workbook is kept.
- The Share Workbook button on the Review tab on the Ribbon displays a dialog box with a tab for recording the number of days to record the change history. Shared workbooks must be merged within that time period.
- If the workbooks have been assigned passwords, all workbooks involved in the merge must have the same password.
- Each copy of the workbook must have a different file name.

When all of the copies of the workbook are available on your hard disk or USB drive, open the copy of the shared workbook into which to merge changes from another workbook file. Next, add the Compare and Merge Workbooks button to the Quick Access Toolbar and then click the button. When Excel displays the Select Files to Merge Into Current Workbook dialog box, select a workbook or workbooks to merge. When Excel merges the workbooks, both data and comments are merged, so that if comments are recorded, they appear one after another in a given cell's comment box. If Excel cannot merge the two workbooks, information from one workbook still can be incorporated into the other by copying and pasting the information from one workbook to another.

BTW

Sorting PivotTable and PivotChart Data
You can sort the data in a PivotTable or PivotChart in a number of ways. Excel allows items to be sorted in ascending or descending order, to be sorted by a particular data value, or to be sorted in a custom order. You also can turn off sorting. After Excel sorts a PivotTable or PivotChart, some formatting on the PivotChart may be lost. See Excel Help for more information about sorting PivotTables and PivotCharts.

BTW

Merging
If you are not sure of the time period that will elapse before you merge workbooks that you send out for changes, set a large number of days for keeping the change history. You can set the number of days to be as large as 32,767 days.

To Compare Workbooks

FasToast Ovens maintains historical travel expense information in a workbook that has been shared and copied to two other members of the staff for review. The FasToast Ovens Travel Expenses workbook also contains a chart that shows total expenses over the past five years. Because two different users — Maura and Stanley — modified the separate workbooks, the workbooks must be merged. Before merging the workbooks, the workbooks should be compared visually to note the changes. The following steps open the FasToast Ovens Travel Expenses and FasToast Ovens Travel Expenses Maura workbooks and compare the workbooks side by side.

- Open the file, FasToast Ovens Travel Expenses, from the Data Files for Students.

- Open the file, FasToast Ovens Travel Expenses Maura, from the Data Files for Students.

- Click the View tab on the Ribbon (Figure 9–83).

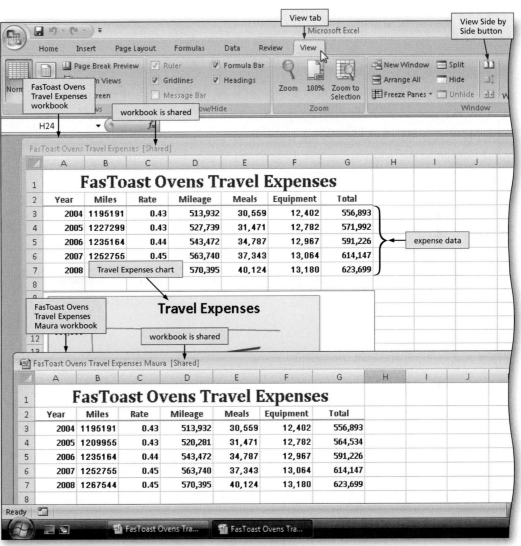

Figure 9–83

• Click the View Side by Side button on the Ribbon to display the workbooks side by side. Depending on how previous Excel windows were arranged on your computer, the workbooks may appear next to each other left-to-right.

• Use the scroll bar in the top window to scroll the FasToast Ovens Travel Expenses Maura worksheet (Figure 9–84).

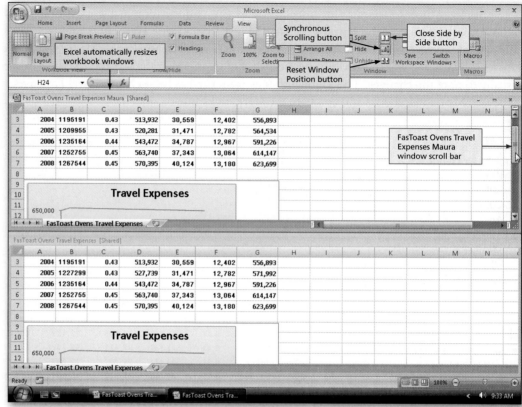

Figure 9–84

• Click the View Side by Side button on the Ribbon again.

• Click the workbook Close Window button to close the FasToast Ovens Travel Expenses Maura workbook.

• If Excel displays the Microsoft Office Excel dialog box, click the No button.

• If necessary, click the Maximize button in the FasToast Ovens Travel Expenses window.

Q&A

What happens when I scroll the workbook?

Because the Synchronous Scrolling button is selected, both workbooks scroll at the same time so that you can make a visual comparison of the workbooks.

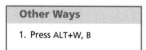

Other Ways

1. Press ALT+W, B

To Merge Workbooks

The next step is to merge the two workbooks changed by Maura and Stanley into the original FasToast Ovens Travel Expenses workbook. All three of the workbooks are shared. The following steps merge the workbooks containing changes from the other members of the staff with the original workbook, FasToast Ovens Travel Expenses.

- Click the Customize Quick Access Toolbar button arrow next to the Quick Access Toolbar and then click More Commands on the Customize Quick Access Toolbar menu.

- When the Excel Options dialog box appears, select All Commands in the 'Choose commands from' list.

- Scroll to the Compare and Merge Workbooks command in the list on the left and then select it.

- Click the Add button to add the Compare and Merge Workbooks button to the list on the right side of the dialog box (Figure 9–85).

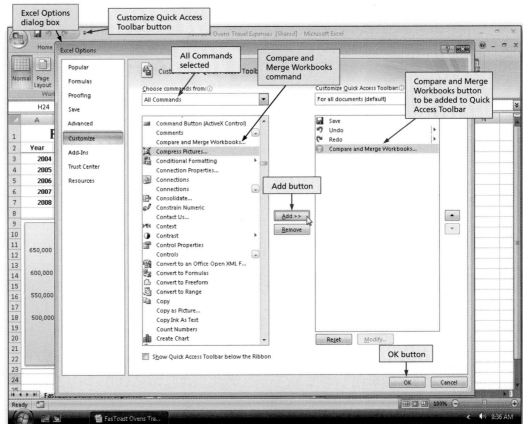

Figure 9–85

- Click the OK button to add the Compare and Merge Workbooks button to the Quick Access Toolbar.

- Click the Compare and Merge Workbooks button on the Quick Access Toolbar to display the Select Files to Merge Into Current Workbook dialog box.

- Select UDISK 2.0 (E:) in the Address bar.

- Click FasToast Ovens Travel Expenses Stanley, hold down the SHIFT key, and then click FasToast Ovens Travel Expenses Maura to select both files (Figure 9–86).

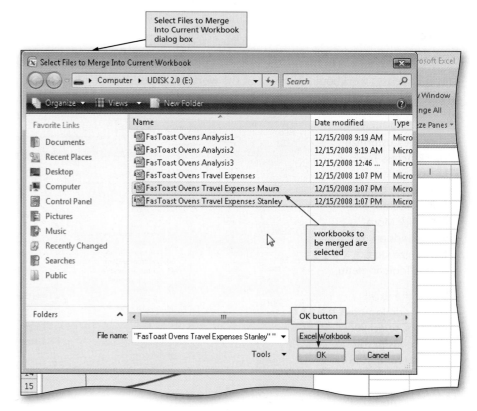

Figure 9–86

- Click the OK button to merge the workbooks (Figure 9–87).

Q&A

What is result of the merge?

The workbooks have been merged, and the FasToast Ovens Travel Expenses worksheet reflects the changes from Maura and Stanley. Excel also updated the Total Expenses historical chart. If Stanley and Maura had changed a common cell with different values, Excel would have displayed a prompt, asking which change to keep in the merged workbook.

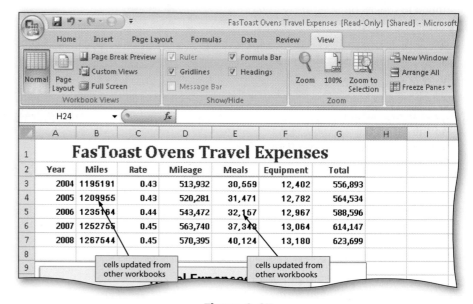

Figure 9–87

To Turn Off Workbook Sharing and Save the Workbook

The next step is to turn off workbook sharing so that the chart can be manipulated.

1. Click the Review tab on the Ribbon and then click the Share Workbook button on the Ribbon.

2. When Excel displays the Share Workbook dialog box, click 'Allow changes by more than one user at the same time' to clear the check box.

3 Click the OK button.

4 If Excel displays the Microsoft Office Excel dialog box, click the Yes button.

5 Click the Save button on the Quick Access Toolbar.

Adding a Trendline to a Chart

A trendline is used on certain Excel charts to show the general tendency of how data in a chart is changing. Trendlines are calculated automatically and overlaid onto charts using the Trendline menu. Excel allows trendlines to be added to several types of charts, including Unstacked 2-D Area, Bar, Column, Line, Stock, XY (Scatter), and Bubble charts.

Trendlines become valuable when they are used to project data beyond the values of a data set. This process is called forecasting. **Forecasting** helps predict data values that are outside of a data set. For example, if a data set is for a 10-year period and the data shows a trend in that 10-year period, Excel can predict values beyond that period or estimate what the values may have been before that period.

BTW

Quick Reference
For a table that lists how to complete the tasks covered in this book using the mouse, Ribbon, shortcut menu, and keyboard, see the Quick Reference Summary at the back of this book, or visit the Excel 2007 Quick Reference Web page (scsite.com/ex2007/qr).

BTW

The R-squared Value
The R-squared value of a trendline can tell you how accurate the projection may be. Trendlines are most reliable when their R-squared values are at or near 1. When you create a trendline, Excel automatically calculates the R-squared value. You then can display this value on your chart.

To Add a Trendline to a Chart

The following steps add a trendline to the Total Expenses chart and predict the total expenses two years beyond the data set in the FasToast Ovens Travel Expenses worksheet.

1

• Select the chart by clicking the shaded area within the chart.

• Click the Design tab on the Ribbon.

• Click the Change Chart Type button on the Ribbon to display the Change Chart Type dialog box.

• Click the Line with Markers chart type in the Change Chart Type dialog box (Figure 9–88).

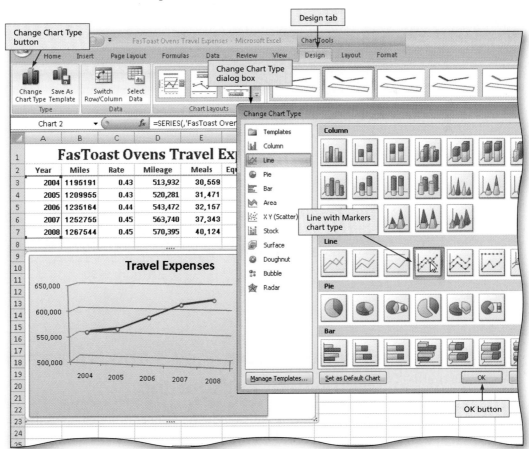

Figure 9–88

- Click the OK button to change the Travel Expenses chart to a line with markers chart.

- With the chart selected, click the Layout tab on the Ribbon.

- Click the Trendline button on the Ribbon to display the Trendline menu (Figure 9–89).

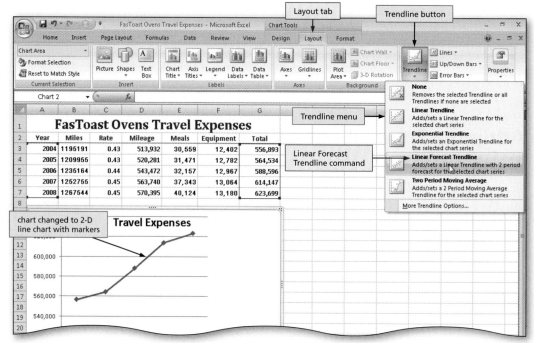

Figure 9–89

❸

- Click Linear Forecast Trendline to add a trendline to the chart with a 2-period forecast (Figure 9–90).

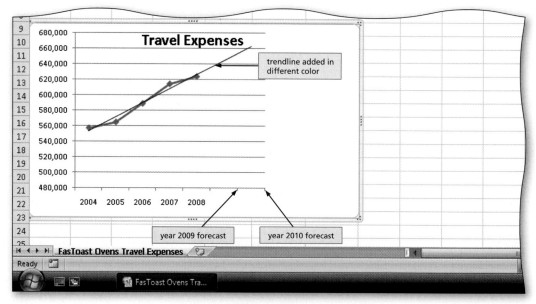

Figure 9–90

Other Ways

1. ALT+JA, N

BTW

Excel Help
The best way to become familiar with Excel Help is to use it. Appendix C includes detailed information about Excel Help and exercises that will help you gain confidence in using it.

Saving Custom Views and Formatting a Worksheet Background

After a workbook functions in the manner in which it was designed, final touches can be added to the worksheets in the workbook to make them more attractive and usable to users of the workbook. Custom views allow certain layout and printing characteristics of a workbook to be saved and then used later. **Worksheet backgrounds** allow an image to be specified for use as a watermark behind the data in cells of a worksheet.

To Save a Custom View of a Workbook

When a custom view of a workbook is saved, Excel stores information about the window size of the workbook and print settings that have been applied to the workbook at the time it is saved. Because of this, the workbook thus should be changed to have the desired layout and print settings before saving a custom view of a workbook. Each custom view that is created includes a name. The Custom Views button on the View tab on the Ribbon is used to save, delete, and show custom views. When a user saves a view, Excel also stores the name of the current worksheet. When a user shows a view by clicking the Show button in the Custom Views dialog box, Excel switches to the worksheet that was active in the workbook when the workbook view was saved.

The following steps create and save a custom view of the FasToast Ovens Travel Expenses workbook.

- Resize the FasToast Ovens Travel Expenses workbook window as shown in Figure 9–91.

- Click the View tab on the Ribbon (Figure 9–91).

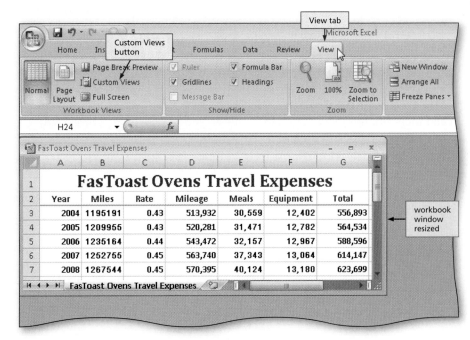

Figure 9–91

- Click the Custom Views button on the Ribbon to display the Custom Views dialog box (Figure 9–92).

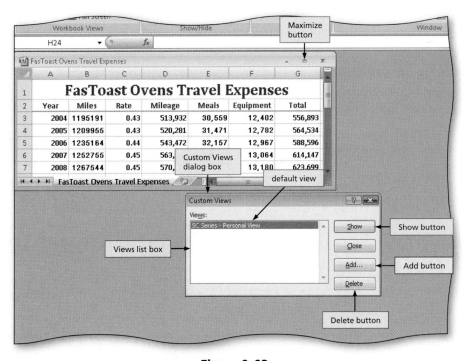

Figure 9–92

- Click the Add button to display the Add View dialog box.

- Type Expenses in the Name text box (Figure 9–93).

- Click the OK button.

- Click the Maximize button on the FasToast Ovens Travel Expenses workbook title bar.

- Click the Custom Views button on the Ribbon to display the Custom Views dialog box.

- Click Expenses in the Views list and then click the Show button to resize the workbook to the size saved in the Expenses view.

Q&A

Can I delete a view?

Yes. To delete views, use the Delete button in the Custom Views dialog box as shown in Figure 9–92 on the previous page.

Figure 9–93

Other Ways

1. Press ALT+W, C

To Format a Worksheet Background

In addition to adding color to the background of cells or ranges, Excel also allows an image to be used as a worksheet background. Worksheet backgrounds provide a more interesting look to a worksheet, allowing for a corporate logo or other identifying image to serve as the background for an entire worksheet.

The following steps add an image as a worksheet background to the FasToast Ovens Travel Expenses worksheet.

- Click the Maximize button on the FasToast Ovens Travel Expenses workbook title bar.

- Click the Page Layout tab on the Ribbon (Figure 9–94).

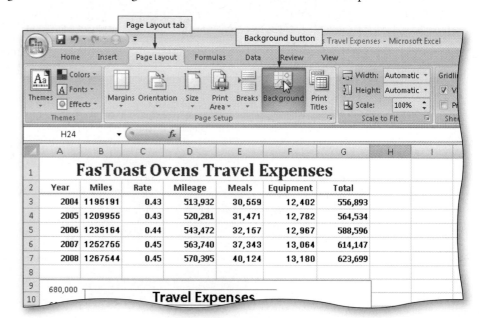

Figure 9–94

2

- Click the Background button on the Ribbon to display the Sheet Background dialog box.

- If necessary, select UDISK 2.0 (E:) in the Address bar.

- Click the file name, FasToast Travel (Figure 9–95).

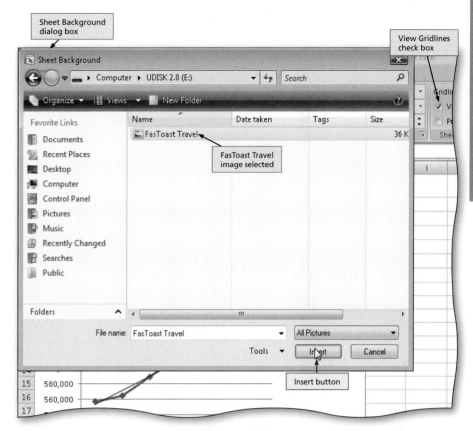

Figure 9–95

3

- Click the Insert button to display the image as the worksheet background.

- Click the View Gridlines check box on the Ribbon to turn off gridlines (Figure 9–96).

Q&A

Why does the image repeat?

When a background is added, the image is **tiled**, or repeated, over the length and width of the worksheet. Figure 9–96 demonstrates that image backgrounds sometimes make the worksheet less readable; this fact should be taken into account. Finally, worksheet backgrounds do not print when all or a portion of the worksheet is printed.

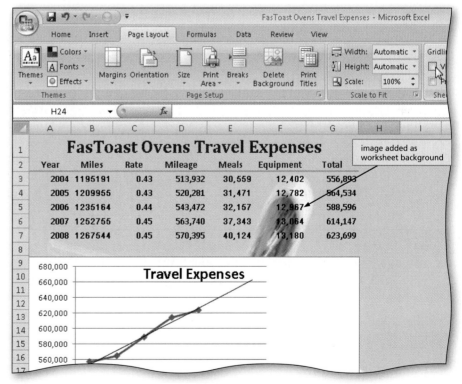

Figure 9–96

Other Ways

1. Press ALT+P, G

BTW

Certification
The Microsoft Certified Application Specialist (MCAS) program provides an opportunity for you to obtain a valuable industry credential – proof that you have the Excel 2007 skills required by employers. For more information, see Appendix G or visit the Excel 2007 Certification Web page (scsite.com/ex2007/cert).

To Quit Excel

The following steps quit Excel.

1 Remove the Compare and Merge Workbooks button from the Quick Access Toolbar.

2 Click the Close button on the right side of the title bar.

3 If Excel displays the Microsoft Office Excel dialog box, click the No button.

Chapter Summary

In this chapter, you learned how to import data in different formats into a worksheet, track changes, create visual representations of the data in a worksheet, share a workbook and track changes, create interactive PivotTables and PivotCharts, compare and merge workbooks and how to create a trendline on a chart. The items listed below include all the new Excel skills you have learned in this chapter.

1. Import Data from a Text File into a Worksheet (EX 713)
2. Import Data from an Access Table into a Worksheet (EX 718)
3. Import Data from a Web Page into a Worksheet (EX 721)
4. Copy and Transpose Data from a Word Document to a Worksheet (EX 725)
5. Convert Text to Columns (EX 729)
6. Replicate Formulas (EX 733)
7. Share a Workbook and Collaborate on a Workbook (EX 735)
8. Insert a Comment (EX 739)
9. Turn On Track Changes (EX 740)
10. Open a Workbook and Review Tracked Changes (EX 742)
11. Turn Off Track Changes (EX 745)
12. Create a PivotTable (EX 746)
13. Add Data to the PivotTable (EX 748)
14. Change the View of a PivotTable (EX 749)
15. Filter a PivotTable Using a Page Field (EX 752)
16. Format a PivotTable (EX 753)
17. Switch Summary Functions in a PivotTable (EX 755)
18. Create a PivotChart, Change the PivotChart Type, and Format the Chart (EX 756)
19. Change the View of a PivotChart (EX 759)
20. Compare Workbooks (EX 761)
21. Merge Workbooks (EX 763)
22. Turn Off Workbook Sharing and Save the Workbook (EX 764)
23. Add a Trendline to a Chart (EX 765)
24. Save a Custom View of a Workbook (EX 767)
25. Format a Worksheet Background (EX 768)

If you have a SAM user profile, you may have access to hands-on instruction, practice, and assessment. Log in to your SAM account (http://sam2007.course.com) to launch any assigned training activities or exams that relate to the skills covered in this chapter.

Learn It Online

Learn It Online is a series of online student exercises that test your knowledge of chapter content and key terms.

Instructions: To complete the Learn It Online exercises, start your browser, click the Address bar, and then enter the Web address scsite.com/ex2007/learn. When the Excel 2007 Learn It Online page is displayed, click the link for the exercise you want to complete and then read the instructions.

Chapter Reinforcement TF, MC, and SA

A series of true/false, multiple choice, and short answer questions that test your knowledge of the chapter content.

Flash Cards

An interactive learning environment where you identify chapter key terms associated with displayed definitions.

Practice Test

A series of multiple choice questions that test your knowledge of chapter content and key terms.

Who Wants To Be a Computer Genius?

An interactive game that challenges your knowledge of chapter content in the style of a television quiz show.

Wheel of Terms

An interactive game that challenges your knowledge of chapter key terms in the style of the television show *Wheel of Fortune*.

Crossword Puzzle Challenge

A crossword puzzle that challenges your knowledge of key terms presented in the chapter.

Apply Your Knowledge

Reinforce the skills and apply the concepts you learned in this chapter.

Merging Workbooks and Creating a Trendline

Instructions: Start Excel. Open the workbook Apply 9-1 Purity Systems from the Data Files for Students and then save the workbook using the file name, Apply 9-1 Purity Systems Complete. See the inside back cover of this book for instructions for downloading the Data Files for Students or see your instructor for information on accessing the files required in this book.

Perform the following tasks.

1. Review the FilterPro Room Air Purifier worksheet, which contains expense information for manufacturing one of Purity Systems' products (Figure 9–97 on the next page), as well as a graph of the total expenses from each month. The workbook is shared.

2. If necessary, add the Compare and Merge Workbooks button to the Quick Access Toolbar. Use the Compare and Merge Workbooks command to merge the workbooks Apply 9-1 Purity Systems South and Apply 9-1 Purity Systems West into the Apply 9-1 Purity Systems Complete workbook. The values in the range B3:G12 should appear as shown in Figure 9–97.

Continued >

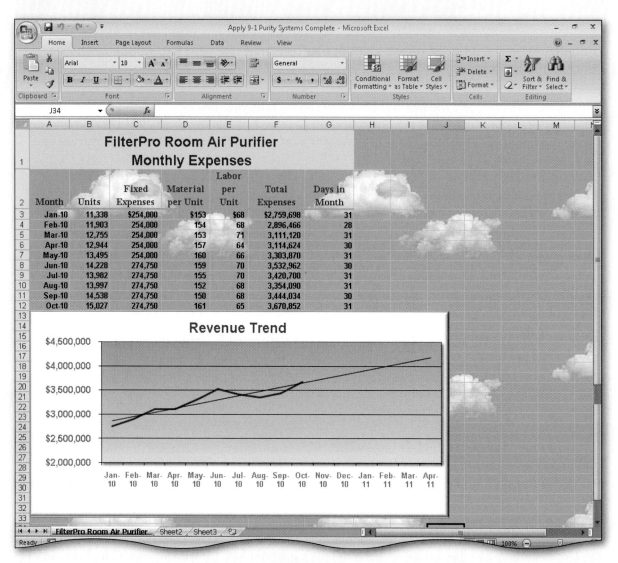

Figure 9–97

3. Turn off sharing so that the workbook is exclusive.

4. Click the Page Layout tab on the Ribbon and then click the Fonts button in the Themes group. Select the Office font style in the Fonts gallery. Save the style changes as a new theme named Purity.

5. On the Page Layout tab, click the Margins button in the Page Setup group, and then click Narrow to change the margin setting to Narrow.

6. Change the document properties as specified by your instructor. Change the worksheet header to include your name, course number, and other information requested by your instructor.

7. Print the FilterPro Room Air Purifier worksheet in landscape orientation.

8. Add a linear trendline to the chart on the worksheet. Forecast the total expenses two months forward. Print the worksheet.

9. Display the Format Trendline dialog box by right-clicking the trendline and then clicking Format Trendline on the shortcut menu. You also can click the Chart Tools Layout tab on the Ribbon, click the Trendline button in the Analysis group, and then click More Trendline Options to display the Format Trendline dialog box. Click Trendline Options in the Format Trendline dialog box and forecast five months forward. Print the worksheet.

10. Display the Format Trendline dialog box again. Click Trendline Options and use a custom trendline name of Forecasted Expenses. Forecast six months forward. Resize the chart if necessary so all the dates on the horizontal axis appear on two lines.

11. Resize the worksheet window so that the chart with the trendline is the only part of the worksheet that appears. Save this view of the worksheet as a view named Trendline View. Maximize the Excel worksheet window, and then add a background image to the worksheet, using the file Apply 9-1 Purity Systems.jpg from the Data Files for Students as the background image.

12. Save the workbook and then print the worksheet.

13. Submit the assignment as specified by your instructor.

Extend Your Knowledge

Extend the skills you learned in this chapter and experiment with new skills. You may need to use Help to complete the assignment.

Setting Criteria to Analyze Data

Instructions: Start Excel. Open the workbook Extend 9-1 Mariner Cruises from the Data Files for Students and then save the workbook using the file name, Extend 9-1 Mariner Cruises Complete. See the inside back cover of this book for instructions for downloading the Data Files for Students or see your instructor for information on accessing the files required in this book. You have been asked to analyze the March sales for Mariner Cruises, who record the cruises they sell each month in an Excel worksheet (Figure 9–98).

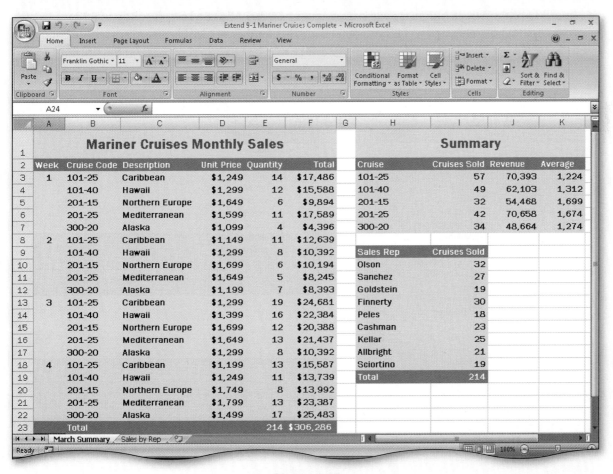

Figure 9–98

Continued >

Extend Your Knowledge *continued*

Mariner Cruises offers five types of cruises, and the price of each cruise varies by the week. For this reason, the March Summary worksheet lists the five cruises sold each week, the price of the cruise that week, the quantity of cruises sold, and the total revenue generated by each cruise that week. The Sales by Rep worksheet lists each cruise sold and the code for the sales rep who handled the sales (Figure 9–99).

To complete the summary information on the March Summary worksheet, you need to use two types of functions: conditional functions (AVERAGEIF, COUNTIF, and SUMIF) and text functions (LOWER, PROPER, SUBSTITUTE, and UPPER).

You use the three conditional functions — AVERAGEIF, COUNTIF, and SUMIF — in similar ways to average, count, or sum values in a range based on a single criteria. For example, in a product list that contains the name of each product your company sells and the corresponding price, you can use the COUNTIF function to calculate how many products sell for more than $100. In a sales list, you can use the SUMIF function to total the sales of a particular product, or use the AVERAGEIF function to calculate the average sale for products sold to a particular customer.

The UPPER, LOWER, and PROPER text functions let you change the case of text, such as from uppercase to lowercase, to make the text easier to read. The SUBSTITUTE function substitutes new text for old, such as substituting “Price” for “Cost.”

Perform the following tasks.

1. Review the March Summary and Sales by Rep worksheets by clicking the appropriate tabs.
2. Select cell F3 on the Sales by Rep worksheet, and then import the tab-delimited text file, Extend 9-1 Mariner Cruises.txt, from the Data Files for Students. Resize columns as necessary to display all the data.
3. In cell I3 of the March Summary worksheet, enter `=COUNTIF('Sales by Rep'!B$3:B$216,'March Summary'!H3)` to determine the number of Caribbean cruises (cruise code 101-25) sold in March. Copy the formula in cell I3 to cells I4:I7 (Figure 9–98 on the previous page).

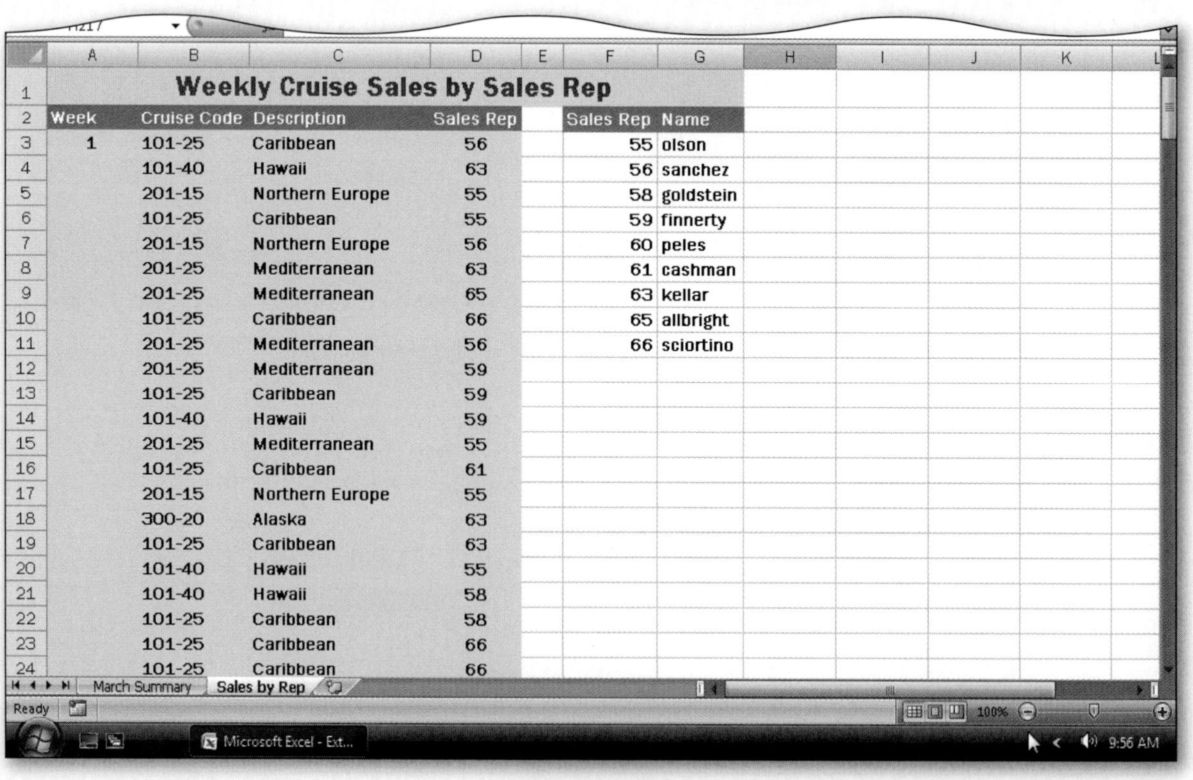

Week	Cruise Code	Description	Sales Rep		Sales Rep	Name
1	101-25	Caribbean	56		55	olson
	101-40	Hawaii	63		56	sanchez
	201-15	Northern Europe	55		58	goldstein
	101-25	Caribbean	55		59	finnerty
	201-15	Northern Europe	56		60	peles
	201-25	Mediterranean	63		61	cashman
	201-25	Mediterranean	65		63	kellar
	101-25	Caribbean	66		65	allbright
	201-25	Mediterranean	56		66	sciortino
	201-25	Mediterranean	59			
	101-25	Caribbean	59			
	101-40	Hawaii	59			
	201-25	Mediterranean	55			
	101-25	Caribbean	61			
	201-15	Northern Europe	55			
	300-20	Alaska	63			
	101-25	Caribbean	63			
	101-40	Hawaii	55			
	101-40	Hawaii	58			
	101-25	Caribbean	58			
	101-25	Caribbean	66			
	101-25	Caribbean	66			

Figure 9–99

4. In cell J3, insert a formula that uses the SUMIF function to determine the total sales of Caribbean cruises in March. All of the data you need is contained on the March Summary worksheet. Use absolute or relative cell references as necessary so you can copy the formula to other cells in column J. Copy the formula in cell J3 to cells J4:J7.

5. In cell K3, insert a formula that uses the AVERAGEIF function to determine the average unit price of Caribbean cruises in March. All of the data you need is contained on the March Summary worksheet. Use absolute or relative cell references as necessary so you can copy the formula to other cells in column K. Copy the formula in cell K3 to cells K4:K7. Format as necessary to preserve the appearance of the worksheet (Figure 9–98 on page EX 773).

6. In cell H10, insert a formula that uses a text function to display the names of the sales reps using the appropriate case for proper names. The names of the sales reps are listed on the Sales by Rep worksheet. Use absolute or relative cell references as necessary so you can copy the formula to other cells in column H. Copy the formula in cell H10 to cells H11:H18.

7. In cell I10, insert a formula that uses the COUNTIF function to determine the total number of cruises sold by each sales rep. All of the data you need is included on the Sales by Rep worksheet. (Hint: In the formula, refer to each sales rep by their number.) Use absolute or relative cell references as necessary so you can copy the formula to other cells in column I. Copy the formula in cell I10 to cells I11:I18. Format as necessary to preserve the appearance of the worksheet.

8. In cell E23, insert a formula that calculates the total number of cruises sold.

9. Type Total in cell H19. In cell I19, insert a formula that calculates the total number of cruises sold. Verify that the result in cell I19 is the same as in cell E23. Format cells H19:I19 to match the format of cell E23.

10. Change the document properties as specified by your instructor. Change the worksheet header to include your name, course number, and other information requested by your instructor.

11. Change the print orientation to landscape and then print the worksheet. Print the formulas version of the worksheet. Save the workbook.

12. Submit the assignment as specified by your instructor.

Make It Right

Analyze a workbook and correct all errors and/or improve the design.

PivotTables and PivotCharts

Instructions: Start Excel. Open the workbook Make It Right 9-1 Pacific Restaurant Supply from the Data Files for Students and then save the workbook using the file name, Make It Right 9-1 Pacific Restaurant Supply Complete. See the inside back cover of this book for instructions for downloading the Data Files for Students or see your instructor for information on accessing the files required in this book. Click the PivotTable and PivotChart tab. Correct the PivotTable and PivotChart so that they appear as shown in Figure 9–100 on the next page.

Continued >

Make It Right *continued*

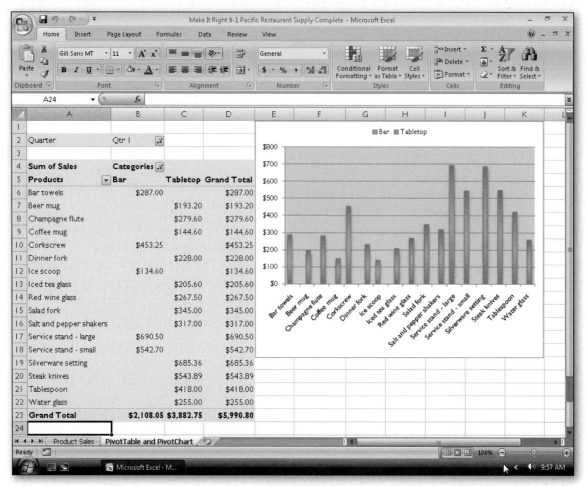

Figure 9–100

1. On the PivotTable and PivotChart worksheet, add all of the fields to the PivotTable. Use the Quarter field as the Report Filter. Use the Category field as the Column Labels, the Product field as the Row Labels, and the Sum of Sales as the Values.

2. Apply the Pivot Style Light 16 style to the PivotTable.

3. Change the contents of cell A5 to Products and change the contents of cell B4 to Categories.

4. Filter the PivotTable to show bar and tabletop product sales data for the first quarter only.

5. Move and resize the PivotChart so it covers cells F1:K13.

6. Change the background color of the range A6:D22 to the Orange, Accent 2, Lighter 80% fill color.

7. Format all the sales values, including the grand totals, as Currency values with a dollar sign and two decimal places.

8. Change the chart style of the PivotChart to Style 18.

9. Format the values in the vertical axis so they appear as Currency values with a dollar sign and no decimal places. Format the background of the plot area to display a solid fill in Dark Green, Text 2, Lighter 80% fill. Display the legend at the top of the chart.

10. Resize the chart as shown in Figure 9–100.

11. Change the document properties as specified by your instructor. Change the PivotTable and PivotChart worksheet header to include your name, course number, and other information requested by your instructor.

12. Change the print orientation to landscape, and then print the PivotTable and PivotChart worksheet. Save the workbook.

13. Submit the assignment as specified by your instructor.

In the Lab

Create a workbook using the guidelines, concepts, and skills presented in this chapter. Labs are listed in order of increasing difficulty.

Lab 1: Importing Data into an Excel Worksheet

Problem: You work as an assistant to a building contractor that has offices in three parts of the state. You are starting to consolidate information about the clients, projects, billable hours, and other hours employees work at each office. You asked each office manager to send you this billing information, but each data set is in a different format. The Center office manager sent a text file with fields separated by commas. The North office manager, who uses an Access database to maintain data, queried the database to create a table to send to you. The East office manager provided the data in a Word table.

Instructions: Create the worksheet shown in Figure 9–101 using the techniques learned in this chapter and following the instructions on the next page.

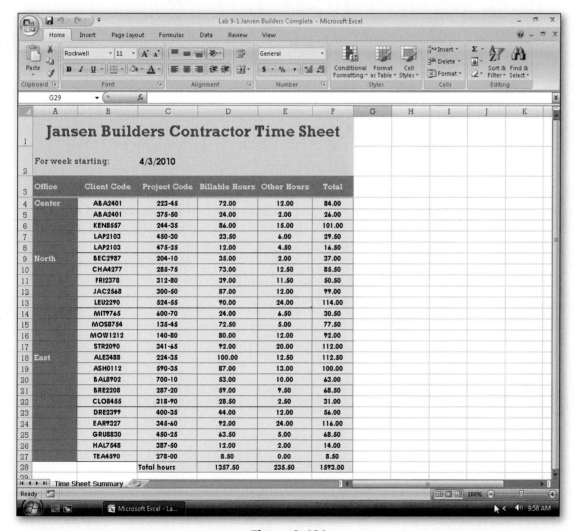

Figure 9–101

In the Lab *continued*

1. Open the workbook Lab 9-1 Jansen Builders from the Data Files for Students and then save the workbook using the file name, Lab 9-1 Jansen Builders Complete. See the inside back cover of this book for instructions for downloading the Data Files for Students or see your instructor for information on accessing the files required in this book.

2. Select cell A4, and then enter the text Center. Select cell A9, and then enter the text North. Select cell A18, and then enter the text East.

3. Select cell B4. Import the comma-delimited text file, Lab 9-1 Center, from the Data Files for Students. In the Text Import Wizard - Step 2 of 3 dialog box, click the Comma check box to select it and then click Tab to clear the check box; otherwise accept the default settings. In the Import Data dialog box, click the Properties button. In the External Data Range Properties dialog box, click 'Adjust the column width' to clear the check box. Import the text data to cell B4 of the existing worksheet.

4. Select cell B9. Import the Access database file, Lab 9-1 North, from the Data Files for Students. Choose to view the data as a table, and insert the data starting in cell B9 in the existing workbook. Accept all of the default settings to import the data. Right-click any cell in the table, point to Table, and then click Convert to Range. Click the OK button to permanently remove the connection to the query. Delete row 9.

5. Start Microsoft Office Word, and then open the Word file, Lab 9-1 East, from the Data Files for Students. Copy all of the data in the table. Switch to Excel. Select cell B18, and then using the Paste Special command, paste the data only into the Time Sheet Summary worksheet. Close Word. Adjust the column widths as necessary to display all of the data.

6. Select cell F4 and then enter the formula =D4+E4. Copy the formula to cells F5:F27.

7. In cells D28, E28, and F28, enter formulas to calculate the total billable hours, total other hours, and total hours.

8. Change the document properties as specified by your instructor. Change the worksheet header to include your name, course number, and other information requested by your instructor.

9. Print the worksheet, and then save the workbook.

10. Delete Sheet2 and Sheet3.

11. Export the Time Sheet Summary worksheet to a tab-delimited text file by clicking the Office Button, pointing to Save As, and then clicking Other Formats. When Excel displays the Save As dialog box, select Text (Tab delimited) in the 'Save as type' list and then click the Save button. If Excel displays one or more Microsoft Office Excel dialog boxes, click the Yes button. Open the text file using Notepad and then print the text file. Quit Notepad.

12. Submit the assignment as specified by your instructor.

In the Lab

Lab 2: Routing Workbooks, Tracking Changes, and Inserting Comments

Problem: This problem requires collaboration with two other classmates. Make sure that you can send e-mail to other classmates before completing this exercise.

You work as an assistant for a professor who is in charge of several sections of the school's Economics 101 class. The professor has asked you to verify the grades for students before she submits them to the registrar. To do so, you must ask the graduate students who teach each section to review the grades that are in the current Economics 101 Fall 2010 worksheet (Figure 9–102).

Instructions: Start Excel and perform the following tasks.

1. Open the workbook Lab 9-2 Economics 101 from the Data Files for Students and then save the workbook using the file name, Lab 9-2 Economics 101 Complete. See the inside back cover of this book for instructions for downloading the Data Files for Students or see your instructor for information on accessing the files required in this book.

2. Add a comment to cell E10 as shown in Figure 9–102.

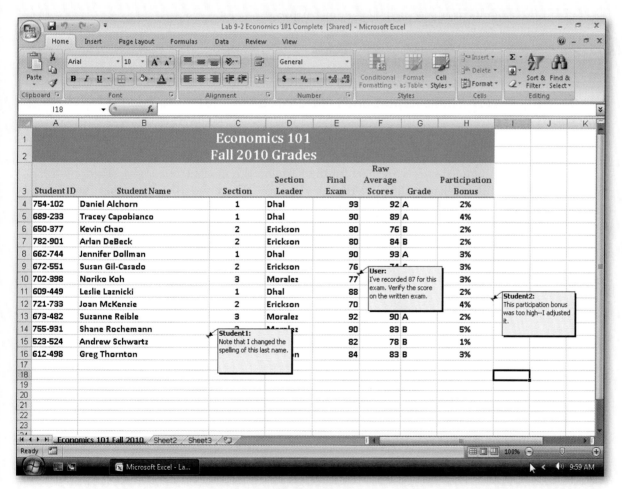

Figure 9–102

3. Track changes to the workbook. Click the Review tab on the Ribbon, click Track Changes in the Changes group, and then click Highlight Changes on the Track Changes submenu. Click the 'Track changes while editing' check box and then clear the three check boxes in the 'Highlight which changes' area.

Continued >

In the Lab *continued*

4. Send the workbook to two classmates by clicking the Office Button, pointing to Send, and then clicking E-mail on the Send submenu. Select the e-mail addresses of two classmates and enter `Economics 101 Grade Verification` in the Subject text box. Enter appropriate message text in the Message text box, requesting that each classmate add comments to at least one cell and change the contents of two cells. Click the Send button.

5. Ask a classmate to send the workbook to you as well. When you receive the e-mail, print it. Add a comment to at least one cell and change the contents of at least two cells before sending the workbook to the next recipient.

6. When you receive your workbook back after it has been sent to all recipients, click the Review tab on the Ribbon, click the Track Changes button on the Ribbon, and then click Accept/Reject Changes on the Track Changes menu. Reject one change and accept all the others.

7. In the Comments group on the Review tab, click the Show All Comments button.

8. Change the document properties as specified by your instructor. Change the worksheet header to include your name, course number, and other information requested by your instructor. Print the worksheet in landscape orientation. Save the workbook.

9. Submit the assignment as specified by your instructor.

In the Lab

Lab 3: Creating a PivotTable Report and PivotChart Report for an Annual Sales Workbook

Problem: You work for the Farmers Wholesale Cooperative and help the financial director prepare and analyze revenue and expenses. He has asked you to create two PivotTables and corresponding PivotCharts from the annual sales worksheet for the Farmers Wholesale Cooperative (Figure 9–103a). One PivotTable and PivotChart summarize the sales by farm (Figure 9–103b). The other PivotTable and PivotChart summarize the dairy sales by month for the top dairy producer (Figure 9–103c).

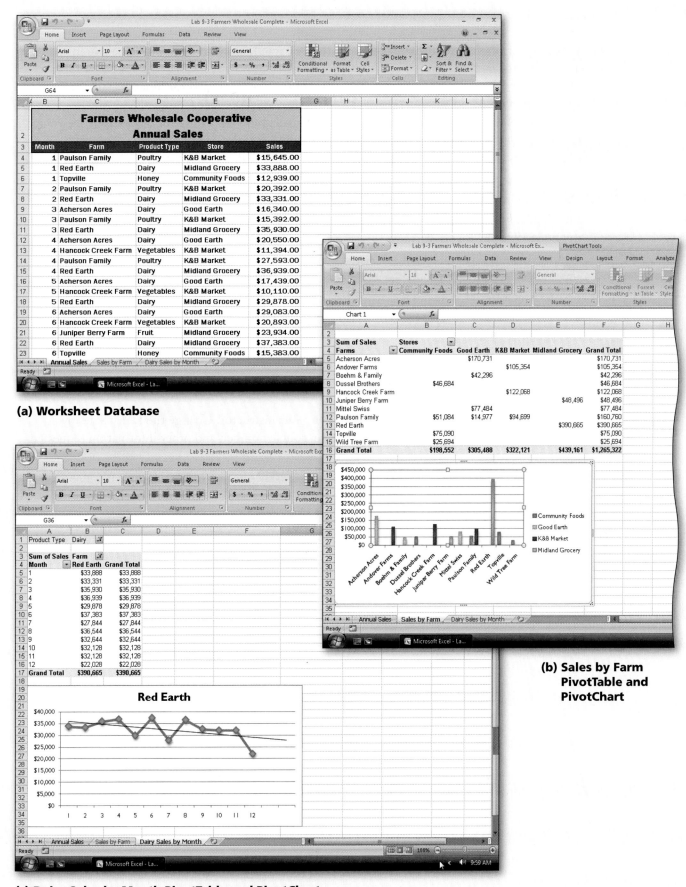

(a) Worksheet Database

**(b) Sales by Farm
PivotTable and
PivotChart**

(c) Dairy Sales by Month PivotTable and PivotChart

Figure 9–103

Continued >

In the Lab *continued*

Instructions: Perform the following tasks to create the PivotTables and PivotCharts shown in Figure 9–103b and 9–103c.

1. Open the workbook Lab 9-3 Farmers Wholesale from the Data Files for Students and then save the workbook using the file name, Lab 9-3 Farmers Wholesale Complete. See the inside back cover of this book for instructions for downloading the Data Files for Students or see your instructor for information on accessing the files required in this book.

2. Create the PivotTable and associated PivotChart shown in Figure 9–103b in a separate sheet in the workbook. Name the worksheet Sales by Farm.

3. Change cell A4 to Farms and cell B3 to Stores. Apply the Pivot Style Light 16 style to the PivotTable. Format the values as Currency values with a dollar sign and no decimal places. Apply the Style 19 to the PivotChart.

4. Create a second PivotTable and associated PivotChart as shown in Figure 9–103c in a separate sheet in the workbook. Name the worksheet Dairy Sales by Month.

5. Change cell A4 to Month and cell B3 to Farm. Apply the Pivot Style Light 16 style to the PivotTable. Format the values as Currency values with a dollar sign and no decimal places. Turn off the legend for the chart.

6. Filter the product type by Dairy. Filter the farm to Red Earth.

7. Change the chart type to Line and then add a linear Trendline that forecasts the trend for two more months.

8. Change the document properties as specified by your instructor. Change the Dairy Sales by Month worksheet header to include your name, course number, and other information requested by your instructor.

9. Print the worksheet. Change the Sales by Farm worksheet header to include your name, course number, and other information requested by your instructor. Print the worksheet, and then save the workbook.

10. Submit the assignment as specified by your instructor.

Cases and Places

Apply your creative thinking and problem solving skills to design and implement a solution.

• EASIER   •• MORE DIFFICULT

• 1: Merging Workbooks and Reviewing Changes

Northwest College has several targeted fundraising drives, in addition to their regular annual fundraising event. During one of these targeted fundraising drives at the college, a computer used for updating information had a hard drive failure. After reconstructing the latest donation records from paper receipts, you have been asked to compare the two worksheets containing reconstructed data against the master worksheet to ensure that all information has been updated.

Open the workbook Case 9-1 Northwest College from the Data Files for Students and then save the workbook as Case 9-1 Northwest College Complete. See the inside back cover of this book for instructions for downloading the Data Files for Students or see your instructor for information on accessing the files required in this book. Review the Donations worksheet, which lists donations made to the Friends of Northwest College fund. Merge the workbooks Case 9-1 Northwest College Fundraising and Case 9-1 Northwest College Director into the Case 9-1 Northwest College Complete workbook. Highlight and review the changes the Director and Fundraiser made to the workbook. Accept all the changes and then turn off sharing so that the workbook is exclusive. In cell D16, insert the label Subtotal. In cell E16, calculate the sum of the donations made to date. Format the label and results using the Total cell style. Use Print Preview to view the worksheet, and then click the Page Setup button to display the Page Setup dialog box. Click the Margins tab, and then click the Horizontally and Vertically check boxes to center the worksheet on the page. Print the worksheet and save the workbook. Submit the assignment as specified by your instructor.

• 2: Importing Data and Formatting and Filtering a Table

Open the workbook Case 9-2 City Sports from the Data Files for Students and then save the workbook using the file name, Case 9-2 City Sports Complete. See the inside back cover of this book for instructions for downloading the Data Files for Students or see your instructor for information on accessing the files required in this book. Import the Sales table in the Case 9-2 City Sports Sales Access database as a table starting in cell A2. Insert spaces in the column headings of the imported table to separate text into words. Copy the data (not the headings) from the table contained in the Case 9-2 City Sports Word document, and paste it in the table in the Sales Analysis worksheet, beginning in the row immediately following the data imported from Access. Extend the table to include the range G2:H27. Copy formulas as necessary to complete the calculations for Sales by Rep 2008 and Sales by Rep 2009. Format the entire table using the Table Style Light 2 style. Filter the table to show sales only from Ohio and Indiana. Format the background of the worksheet by adding the graphic Case 9-2 City Sports.jpg as the worksheet background. Print the worksheet in landscape orientation and save the workbook. Submit the assignment as specified by your instructor.

•• 3: Creating a PivotTable, PivotChart, and Custom View

Aspen Packaging has been tracking targeted vs. actual hours for two business years, in an effort to better understand and control their labor costs. They are particularly interested in whether or not there are patterns by position or shift. You have been asked to create a chart and table that will allow the managers at Aspen Packaging to better evaluate what is happening. Open the Case 9-3 Aspen Packaging workbook from the Data Files for Students and then save the workbook using the file name, Case 9-3 Aspen Packaging Complete. See the inside back cover of this book for instructions for downloading the Data Files for Students or see your instructor for information on accessing the files required in this book.

Continued >

Cases and Places *continued*

Create a PivotTable that includes the fields in the areas shown in Table 9–3. Format the PivotTable. Apply the cell style 40% Accent5 to the report filter labels, the column headings, and the grand total row. Apply the cell style 20% Accent5 to the row labels and values. Change column and row labels as necessary to reflect field names. Create a PivotChart. Choose similar fill colors and styles for the chart elements. Change the sheet name containing the PivotTable and PivotChart to Employee Hours Evaluation. Create a custom view named Hours by Position Chart for the workbook that displays only the PivotChart. Print the worksheet in landscape orientation and save the workbook. Submit the assignment as specified by your instructor.

Table 9–3 PivotTable Fields and Areas

Report Filter	Column Labels	Row Labels	Values
Shift	Values	Position	Sum of Hours 2009
			Sum of Target Hours 2009
			Sum of Hours 2010
			Sum of Target Hours 2010

•• 4: Collaborating on a Health Worksheet

Make It Personal

Design a worksheet that tracks and analyzes an aspect of your health, such as an exercise tracker, fitness chart, nutrition log, or health record. Include at least five columns of information, such as date and various measurements (weight and height, for example). Include at least three calculations such as your body mass index (BMI), estimated body fat, and estimated lean body weight. Record at least one week (or seven rows) of data. Create a PivotTable and PivotChart that compares at least three pieces of data. Exchange your workbook with a partner. Review the workbook you receive and consider how to improve the workbook. Track changes as you revise the data or formulas, if necessary. Insert at least three comments to offer suggestions. Return the workbook to its author. When you receive your reviewed workbook, consider the suggestions your partner made and apply those changes that you feel will improve the workbook. Do not delete your partner's comments. Print the worksheets and save the workbook. Submit the assignment as specified by your instructor.

•• 5: Importing and Analyzing Sales Data

Working Together

Open a blank workbook and then save the workbook using the file name, Case 9-5 Edgeway Electronics. Import the data from the Sales table in the Case 9-5 Edgeway Electronics database to a table starting in cell A2 of a blank worksheet. See the inside back cover of this book for instructions for downloading the Data Files for Students or see your instructor for information on accessing the files required in this book. Work with your group to add a title to the worksheet, change the name on the sheet tab, and format the worksheet. Add at least one calculation to the worksheet. Continue working as a group to create a PivotTable and PivotChart that analyzes the sales data in a meaningful way. Save the workbook and then share it so that each person in the group has a shared copy. Be sure to allow changes by more than one user. Keep the original workbook separate from the ones distributed to members of the group. In the original copy of the workbook, change the document properties as specified by your instructor. Change the headers of all the worksheets to include your name, course number, and other information requested by your instructor. Each person in the group should make at least one change to the workbook. (Hint: as a group, you may decide to split up the table content for changes in a meaningful way, such as assigning each person a region, a year, or a product). Compare and merge the workbooks into the original workbook. Print the worksheets and save the workbook. Submit the assignment as specified by your instructor.

Collaboration Feature

Using SharePoint and Excel Services

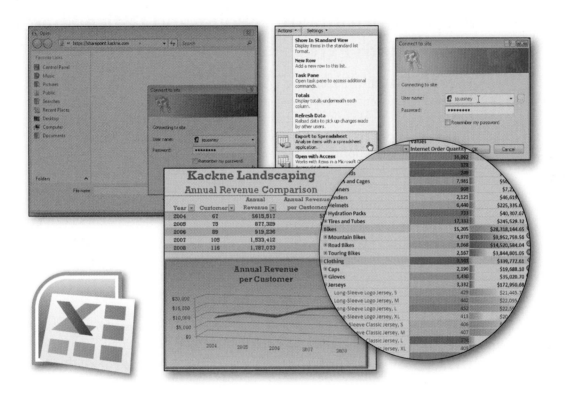

Objectives

You will have mastered the material in this Collaboration feature when you can:

- Describe the relationships among SharePoint Services, Office SharePoint Server, and Excel Services

- Save an Excel table to a SharePoint Services list

- Use a SharePoint Services list in an Excel worksheet

- Save a workbook to an Office SharePoint Server site

- Open a workbook in a Web browser from an Office SharePoint Server site

- Describe when and why Excel Services can benefit the users of a workbook

Collaboration Feature Introduction

Excel allows you to share data with others using SharePoint Services. See page APP 7 in Appendix B for more information regarding collaboration and SharePoint Services. You can import, export, and link data to a SharePoint Services Web site. The data will reside as a workbook file or as a list on the Web site. When an Excel table is saved as a SharePoint Services list, then other applications can use the data. For example, an Access user can import the data from a SharePoint Services list into an Access database table. A **SharePoint list** is similar to an Excel table in that it includes column headings and users can add, delete, and modify rows of data.

Project — Using SharePoint and Office SharePoint Server with Excel

Figure 1a shows the Annual Revenue Comparison worksheet for Kackne Landscaping. Kackne Landscaping provides residential landscaping services and has experienced growth over the past several years. The company owners wish to understand how the growing number of customers affects how much revenue each customer generates. The owners want to share this information on the company's SharePoint Services Web site in two ways. First, they would like the table in the worksheet shared as a SharePoint list (Figure 1b) so that the data can be reused by other applications, such as Access. Second, they would like the entire workbook saved to the SharePoint Services Web site so that other users can open the workbook from the Web site.

Office SharePoint Server is an add-on program for SharePoint Services. Office SharePoint Server includes Excel Services. When the Office SharePoint Server is used along with SharePoint Services, Excel users benefit from a number of additional features. For example, a workbook can be saved to an Office SharePoint Server Web site and then used in a Web browser (Figure 1c). Users of the workbook do not need to have Excel installed on their computers. Instead, they interact with the workbook through their Web browsers. This Collaboration feature discusses Office SharePoint Server, although the steps required to use Office SharePoint Server is beyond the scope of this book.

Excel Collaboration Feature

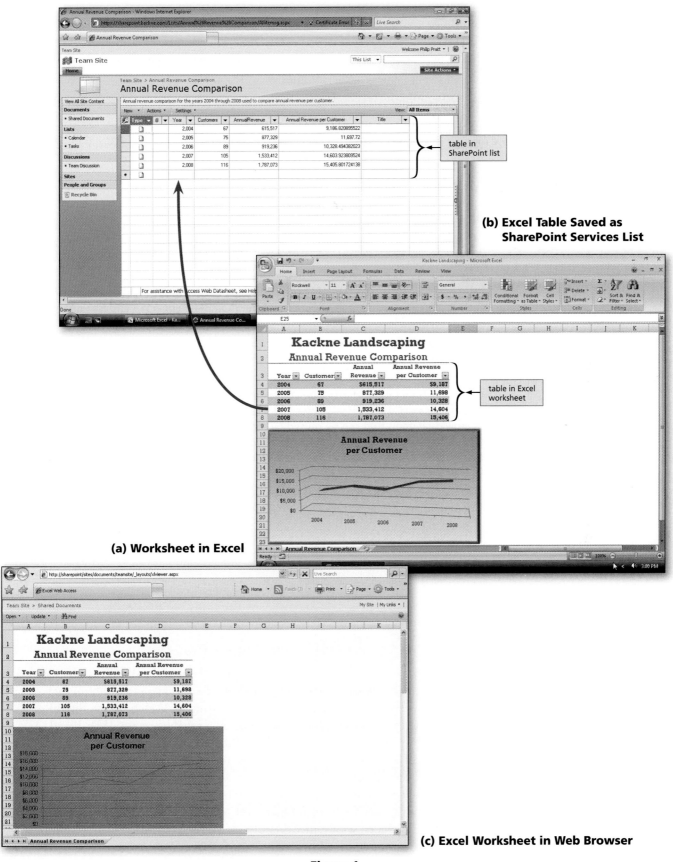

(b) Excel Table Saved as SharePoint Services List

(a) Worksheet in Excel

(c) Excel Worksheet in Web Browser

Figure 1

Overview

As you read through this feature, you will learn how to create and work with SharePoint and Excel Services by performing the following tasks:

- Save an Excel table as a SharePoint list
- Use a SharePoint Services list in an Excel worksheet
- Save a workbook to an Office SharePoint Server site
- Open a workbook in a Web browser from an Office SharePoint Server site

Plan
Ahead

General Project Decisions

1. **Choose workbooks and parts of worksheets to publish.** At the worksheet, range, or cell level, you can decide which parts of a workbook will be visible to and which parts can be modified by other users. Just as when choosing which range or cells to protect, you always should err on the side of caution and start with publishing as little as possible.

2. **Determine access rights for other users.** SharePoint Services allows you to specify which users have specific rights to a published workbook. You can specify that groups of users, such as managers, can modify financial information, while only warehouse workers are allowed to modify information about inventory.

3. **Evaluate which calculations are better performed on a server.** Excel Services allows you to have worksheet calculations performed on a server. For complex calculations, this often is the better choice.

4. **Determine how tables, charts, PivotTables, PivotCharts, and other data will be used by other users.** Excel Services allows you to publish objects such as tables and charts as individual items that can be reused by others. For example, another user can reuse a published PivotTable on a Web page, as opposed to an entire worksheet containing the PivotTable, and maintain the high level of interactivity that Excel users expect when working with PivotTables.

When necessary, more specific details concerning the above guidelines are presented at appropriate points in the feature.

BTW

Excel Services
The features of Excel Services are only available for workbooks saved using the Office Excel 2007 document type. Excel Services is part of Microsoft Offices SharePoint Server 2007, which is an add-in product for Microsoft SharePoint Services.

Note: To work with Excel Services, you need access to a SharePoint Web site that is running Office SharePoint Server 2007 and Excel Services.

SharePoint Services

Excel allows you to share tables and workbooks with others using Windows SharePoint Services and Office SharePoint Server 2007. SharePoint Services is a program that runs on a Windows server and is accessed by users through a Web browser. SharePoint Services allows team members to share documents in a reliable, secure Web-based environment. Access rights can be strictly applied to shared documents. To access a SharePoint Services Web site, you need a user name and password, as well as a Web address (URL) for the Web site.

Office SharePoint Server 2007 is a program that extends the capabilities of SharePoint Services to offer more tools for users of Office 2007 programs, such as Excel. Excel Services is a program that is included with Office SharePoint Server 2007 and provides additional capabilities for those using Excel with a SharePoint Services Web site.

Creating a SharePoint List

Any Excel table can be exported to a SharePoint list on a SharePoint Services Web site using the Export Table to SharePoint List command on the Export menu on the Design tab on the Ribbon (Figure 2). The table first must be selected.

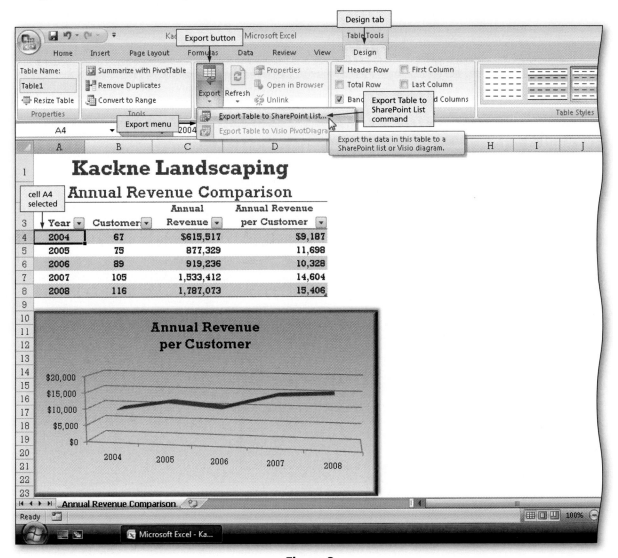

Figure 2

You must know the Web address (URL) of the SharePoint Services Web site (Figure 3), your user name, and your password. After exporting the list, you then can use your Web browser to access the list, change access permissions for the list, and move or edit the list.

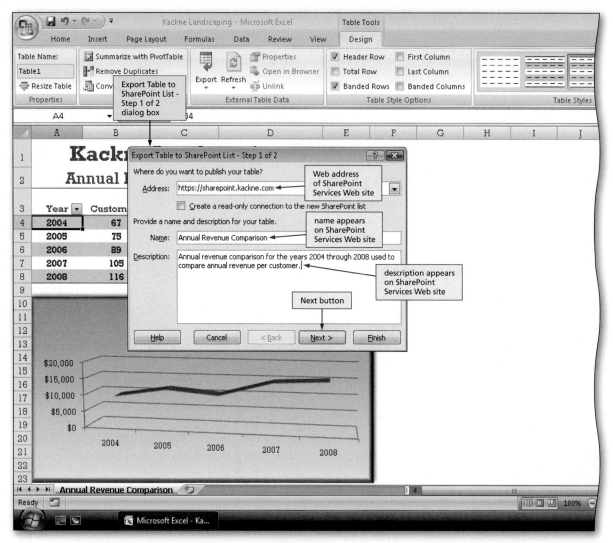

Figure 3

BTW

Exporting an Excel Table
Once a table is exported to the SharePoint list, other users can update the list within the SharePoint site and their changes will be reflected in your Excel worksheet. If you do not wish to see other users' changes in your Excel table, export the table without a connection to the SharePoint list.

TO CREATE A SHAREPOINT LIST BY EXPORTING AN EXCEL TABLE

The following steps create a SharePoint list from the Kackne Landscaping workbook by exporting an Excel table.

1. With cell A4 selected, click the Design tab on the Ribbon and then click the Export button on the Ribbon to display the Export menu (Figure 2).

2. Click Export Table to SharePoint List to display the Export Table to SharePoint List – Step 1 of 2 dialog box.

3. Enter the Web address (URL) of the SharePoint Services Web site in the Address bar. Enter a name and description of the table in the Name text box and Description text box (Figure 3).

4. Click the Next button to display the Export Table to SharePoint List – Step 2 of 2 dialog box. Enter your user name and password and then click the OK button to export the table to a SharePoint list.

Excel Collaboration Feature

Viewing and Using a SharePoint List

After the SharePoint list is created, you can view the list in SharePoint (Figure 4) by selecting it from the list of available lists for your SharePoint team. Figure 4 shows that the numbers in the Year, AnnualRevenue, and Annual Revenue per Customer columns are not formatted as they were in the Excel table. SharePoint Services converts all of the numbers to a common number format when you export a table to a SharePoint list. Years, therefore, appear with thousand separators. You can modify the formatting, or data type, of each column in the list by clicking the Settings button and then clicking the List Settings command on the Settings menu.

BTW

Creating a SharePoint List by Importing an Excel Table
You can create a SharePoint list by using the Import Spreadsheet command from within a SharePoint Web site. You will be prompted for the location of a workbook and then you can select a table, a named range, or enter a range of cell from which to create the list.

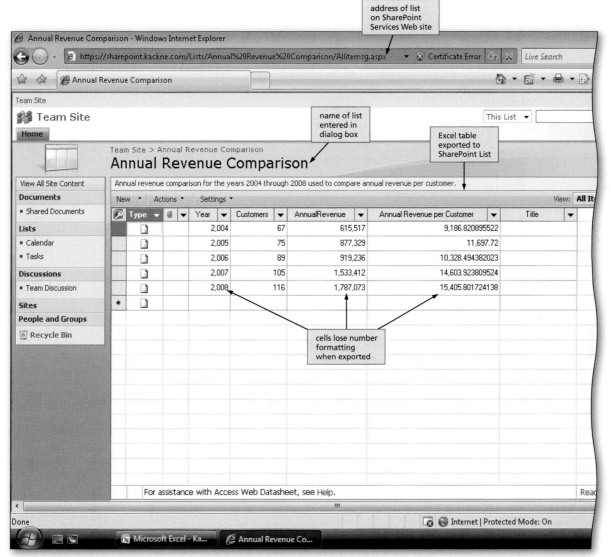

Figure 4

BTW

Unlinking an Excel Table from a SharePoint List
To unlink a table from a SharePoint list, select the table in Excel and then click the Design tab on the Ribbon. Click Unlink in the External Data group on the Ribbon. Once the table is unlinked, the connection cannot be restored.

You can add new items to the list by clicking the New button and then clicking New Item on the New menu. You can click the button arrows next to each column heading in the list to sort and filter the list. For example, you could click the Year button arrow and then click Largest on Top to sort the list in descending order by Year.

If you want to use a SharePoint list in an Excel worksheet, you first must export the list to an Excel worksheet by clicking the Export to Spreadsheet command on the Actions menu (Figure 5). SharePoint then prompts you for a location to save the exported worksheet and then opens a new workbook in Excel. You can choose to import the list into a Table, PivotTable, or PivotChart and PivotTable Report. You then can use the worksheet like any other worksheet or copy and paste the exported list to another worksheet.

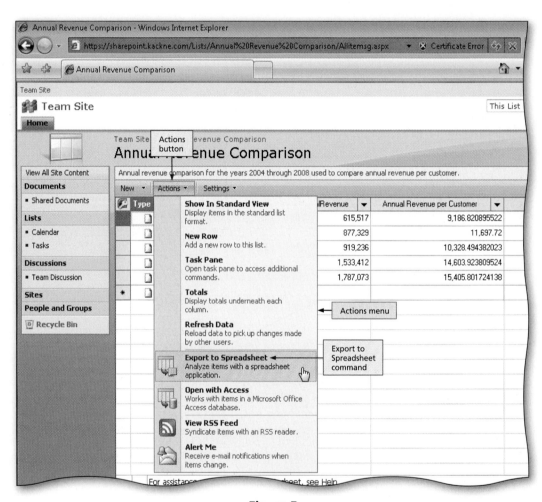

Figure 5

BTW

The Document Management Task Pane
Depending on how your SharePoint Web site is configured, you may be able to use the Document Management task pane in Excel to obtain more information about a workbook stored on a SharePoint Web site. If the site is configured properly, click the Office Button, click Server, and then click Document Management Information to view the Document Management task pane.

Saving a Workbook to a SharePoint Services Web Site

Any workbook can be saved to a SharePoint Services Web site. You save a workbook to a SharePoint Services Web site in order to share the workbook with colleagues. After a workbook is shared, you can use your Web browser to change access permissions for the workbook and move the workbook to another location on the SharePoint Services Web site. To share a workbook on a SharePoint Services Web site, you must have a user name and password and permissions to save workbooks to the site. To save a workbook to a SharePoint Services Web site, display the Save As dialog box and then type the Web address of the Web site in the Address bar (Figure 6).

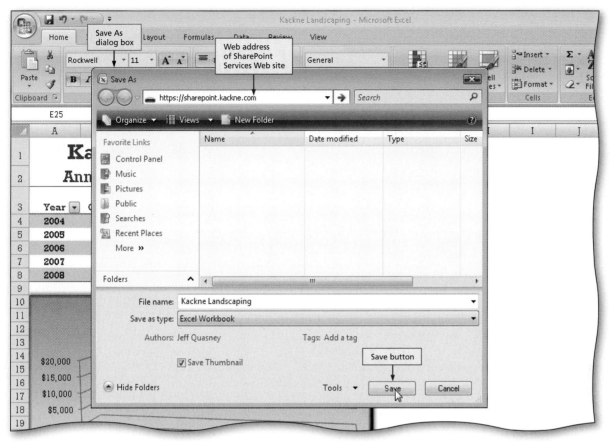

Figure 6

After clicking the Save button in the Save As dialog box, Excel then prompts you for your user name and password for the Web site (Figure 7). After you click the OK button in the Connect to dialog box, Excel saves the workbook to the SharePoint Services Web site.

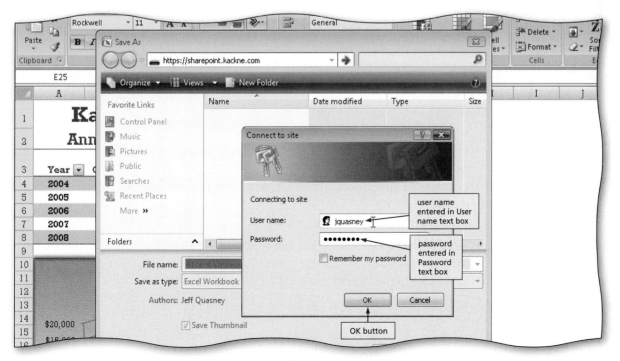

Figure 7

After you save the workbook to the Web site, a Web browser can be used to access the workbook on the Web site (Figure 8). In SharePoint, you can edit the workbook properties, such as the name and description, change permissions, and open the workbook in Excel. You also can set alerts so that you are notified by e-mail when another team member modifies the workbook.

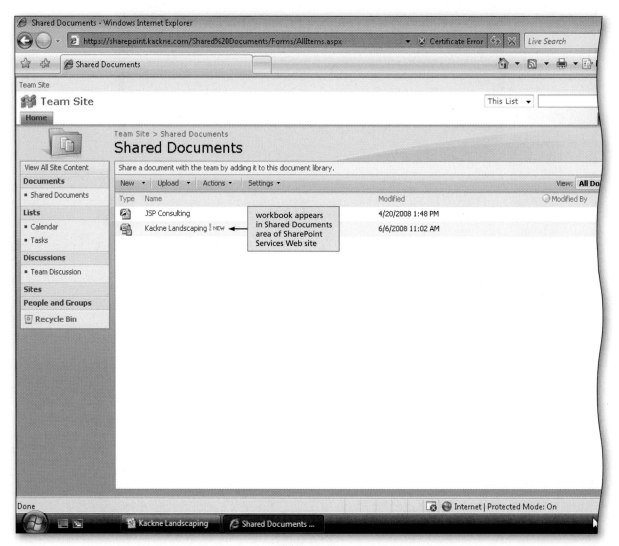

Figure 8

TO SAVE A WORKBOOK TO A SHAREPOINT SERVICES WEB SITE
The following steps save a workbook to a SharePoint Services Web site.

1. With the workbook open, click the Office Button and then click Save As on the Office Button menu.
2. Type the SharePoint Services Web address in the Address bar (Figure 6 on the previous page) and then click the Save button in the Save As dialog box.
3. Enter your user name and password and then click the OK button in the Connect to dialog box to save the workbook to the Web site.

Opening a Workbook from a SharePoint Services Web Site

You can open a workbook saved on a SharePoint Services Web site from a Web browser (Figure 8) or from Excel by using the Open command on the Office Button menu. When you attempt to open a workbook stored on a SharePoint Services Web site using the Open dialog box, Excel prompts you for your user name and password (Figure 9).

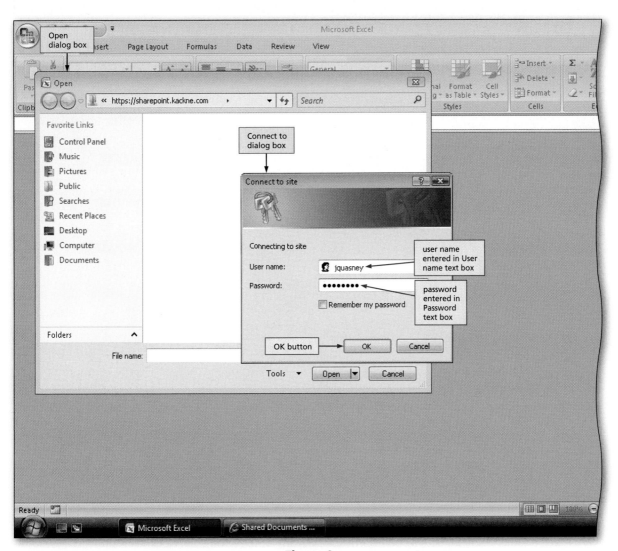

Figure 9

If you enter the correct user name and password, then Excel displays the shared documents in the SharePoint Services Web site in the Open dialog box as shown in Figure 10.

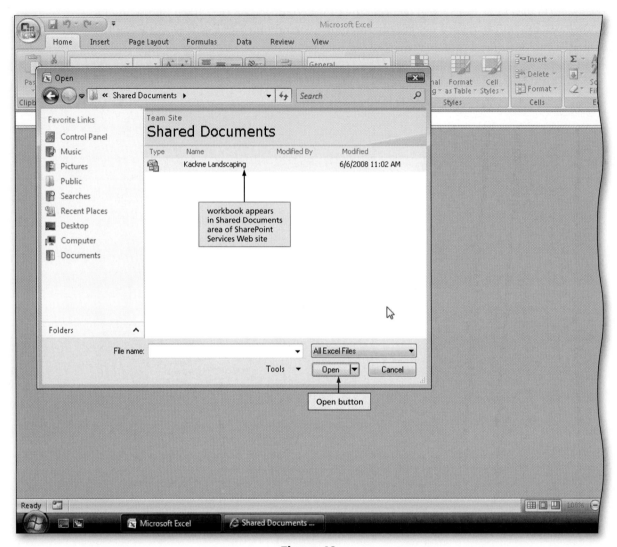

Figure 10

BTW

Quick Reference
For a table that lists how to complete the tasks covered in this book using the mouse, Ribbon, shortcut menu, and keyboard, see the Quick Reference Summary at the back of this book, or visit the Excel 2007 Quick Reference Web page (scsite.com/ex2007/qr).

TO OPEN A WORKBOOK FROM A SHAREPOINT SERVICES WEB SITE

The following steps open a workbook from a SharePoint Services Web site.

1. With Excel running, click the Office Button and then click Open on the Office Button menu to display the Open dialog box.

2. Enter the Web address (URL) of the SharePoint Services Web site in the Address bar and then press the ENTER key to display the Connect to dialog box.

3. Enter your user name and password and then click the OK button in the Connect to dialog box to display the shared documents from the Web site in the Open dialog box.

4. Select the workbook and then click the Open button to open the workbook.

Working with Excel Services

Excel Services is a part of the Office SharePoint Server 2007 program and provides additional capabilities for users of Excel who use SharePoint Services Web sites. Using Excel Services, you can view and interact with workbooks using a Web browser instead of using Excel. A user does not need Excel installed on a personal computer in order to work with a workbook. You also can publish parts of worksheets or use others' published worksheet parts in your own worksheet.

Choosing to Work with Excel Services

You may choose to work with Excel Services for a variety of reasons. Three of the main reasons for choosing to work with Excel Services are listed below.

1. Integrity and ease of use: Your organization takes a one-version-of-the-truth approach to workbook management. This means that within the organization, any critical workbook is stored and managed in exactly one location, such as a SharePoint Services Web site. Using Excel Services, all users can view and modify the workbook from exactly one location on the server using a common interface, a Web browser. Such a tightly controlled system results in everyone having confidence that they are working with the correct version of a workbook.

2. Performance: You may have a very large workbook that includes intensive calculations or requires complex business analysis. In such a case, Excel services allows you to separate your data from the calculations. You can store your workbook on your USB flash drive, yet have the intense calculations performed on a very fast server that is running Excel Services. A calculation that may take hours for a personal computer to perform sometimes can be performed in minutes on a high-end server running Excel Services.

3. Sharing: The combination of the above two reasons provides a good basis to allow Excel Services to manage all of your critical workbooks. Because Excel Services is part of SharePoint Services, an organization gains the capability to properly share workbooks. For example, when a workbook is properly shared, SharePoint Services does not allow two users to make changes to the workbook at the same time. Users check out workbooks, make changes, and then check in the workbooks.

Capabilities of Excel Services

Three major capabilities of Excel Services are listed below:

1. Save as a Web page: The ability to work with a worksheet in a browser means that a worksheet user does not need to have Excel installed. Customers, mobile workers such as sales persons, and suppliers all can work with the same version of the worksheet in a common user environment. Figure 11 on the next page shows an Excel worksheet in a browser. The user has full control of the worksheet in the browser.

2. Sharing formulas and functions: Organizations often maintain complex Excel formulas and functions that are critical to the organization. For example, a sales department may have a complex formula for setting prices of their products and services each day. If the formula changes, then all of the workbooks that use the formula typically need to be updated as well. Using Excel Services, such a formula could reside in one location on the SharePoint Services server. All workbooks, even those stored on personal computers, would reference the centrally stored formula instead of including the formula itself in the workbook.

3. Web Parts: Parts of worksheets, such as ranges, formulas, tables, charts, PivotTables, and PivotCharts, can be saved to Excel Services as a Web Part. Other users or developers of Web pages and other programs can then reuse these Web Parts to create new Web pages and programs. For example, the company's current stock price can be charted and displayed automatically on the company's Web page in real time.

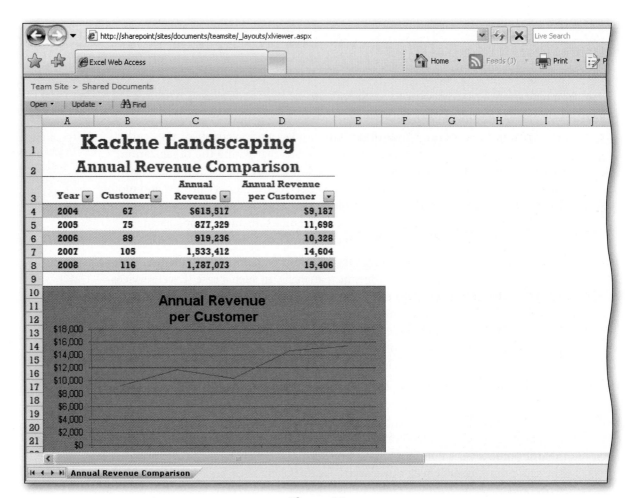

Figure 11

When working with an Excel workbook in a browser, some capabilities and features are not available as they are in Excel. VBA and macros will not function with Excel Services. Inserted pictures, shapes, SmartArt, and WordArt also will not work with Excel Services. Some 3-D charting features will not display with Excel Services, and some 3-D chart types will not function, such as 3-D surface charts, wireframe 3-D surface charts, contour surface charts, and wireframe contour surface charts. See Excel Help for a complete list of supported and unsupported functionality when working with Excel Services.

Feature Summary

This Collaboration feature introduced you to publishing Excel tables and workbooks to SharePoint Services Web sites, working with SharePoint Services, and using Office SharePoint Server and Excel Services. The items listed below include all the new Office 2007 skills you have learned in this Collaboration feature.

1. Create a SharePoint List by Exporting an Excel Table (EX 790)
2. Save a Workbook to a SharePoint Services Web Site (EX 794)
3. Open a Workbook from a SharePoint Services Web Site (EX 796)

In the Lab

Modify a workbook using the guidelines, concepts, and skills presented in this graphics feature. Labs are listed in order of increasing difficulty.

Lab 1: Saving a Worksheet to a SharePoint Services Web Site

Problem: As an accounting intern for Maury's Mobiles, a retailer of mobile devices and services, you have been asked to make the monthly sales report available on the company's SharePoint Services Web site.

Instructions: Start Excel and then open the file Lab CF-1 Maury's Mobiles from the Data Files for Students. Perform the following tasks:

1. Save the workbook to a SharePoint Services Web site with the file name, Maurys Mobiles Monthly Sales.
2. Format the range A3:D12 as a table and then save the table as a SharePoint list to the same SharePoint Services Web site.
3. Display the SharePoint Web site in your browser, navigate to the list, and then view the list in your browser. Print the Web page.
4. Using the button arrow next to the Representative column header, select only those records in the list for the representative named Sun. Print the Web page.
5. Display the SharePoint Web site in your browser and navigate to the workbook in your Documents folder. Print the Web page. Open the workbook from the Web site in Excel.
6. Close the workbook. Submit the assignment as specified by your instructor.

In the Lab

Lab 2: Saving a Table as a SharePoint List

Problem: As the student assistant for the Technical Writing 203 course, you have been asked to make this quarter's final student grades available on the department's SharePoint Services Web site.

Instructions: Start Excel and then open the file Lab CF-2 Technical Writing from the Data Files for Students. Perform the following tasks:

1. Save the workbook to a SharePoint Services Web site named, Technical Writing 203 - Final Student Grades.
2. Format the range A3:E11 as a table and then save the table as a SharePoint list to the same SharePoint Services Web site.
3. Display the SharePoint Web site in your browser, navigate to the list, and then view the list in your browser. Print the Web page.

Continued >

In the Lab *continued*

4. Using the button arrow next to the Grade column header, select only those records in the list for those receiving a grade of C. Print the Web page.

5. Display the SharePoint Web site in your browser and navigate to the workbook in your Documents folder. Print the Web page. Open the workbook from the Web site in Excel.

6. Close the workbook. Submit the assignment as specified by your instructor.

7 | Advanced Report Techniques

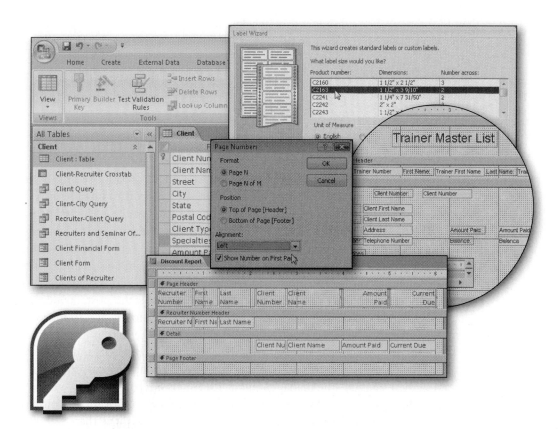

Objectives

You will have mastered the material in this project when you can:

- Change a caption
- Create queries for reports
- Create reports in Design view
- Add fields and text boxes to a report
- Format controls
- Group and ungroup controls

- Update multiple controls
- Add and modify a subreport
- Modify section properties
- Add a title, page number, and date
- Add totals and subtotals
- Create and print mailing labels

7 | Advanced Report Techniques

Introduction

In this chapter, you will create two reports in Design view. Both reports feature grouping and sorting. The first report contains a subreport, which is a report that is contained in another report. The subreport contains data from a query that is related to data in the main report. The second report uses aggregate functions to calculate subtotals and grand totals. It also uses a function to calculate a value where the calculation will vary from record to record depending on whether a given criterion is true. Finally, the steps in the chapter produce mailing labels.

Project — Advanced Report Techniques

The management at JSP Recruiters wants a master list of recruiters. This list should be available as an Access report. For each recruiter, the report is to include full details for all the clients assigned to the recruiter. In addition, for each of these clients for whom seminars currently are scheduled, the report should list the specific seminars being offered to the client. The actual report is shown in Figure 7–1a. The report is organized by recruiter. For each recruiter, the report lists the number, first name, and last name. Following the recruiter number and name, the report lists data for each client served by that recruiter. The client data includes the number, name, address, city, state, postal code, client type, specialties needed, amount paid, current due, and total amount. It also includes any seminars currently being offered to the client. For each seminar, it lists the number, description, total hours the seminar requires, hours already spent, and hours remaining.

Many organizations offer discounts as a way of rewarding current clients and attracting new clients. The management at JSP is considering offering a discount on the Current Due amount to its current clients. The exact amount of the discount depends on how much the client already has paid. If the amount paid is more than $20,000, the discount will be 4 percent of the current due amount. If the amount paid is $20,000 or less, then the discount will be 2 percent of the current due amount. To assist in determining the discount, JSP needs a report like the one shown in Figure 7–1b. The report groups clients by recruiter. It includes subtotals and grand totals of both the Amount Paid and Current Due fields. Finally, it shows the discount amount, which is calculated by multiplying the current due amount by .04 (4 percent) for those clients for whom the amount paid is more than $20,000 and by .02 (2 percent) for all others.

The management also wants to be able to produce mailing labels for their clients. These labels must align correctly with the particular labels they have purchased and must be sorted by postal code (Figure 7–1c).

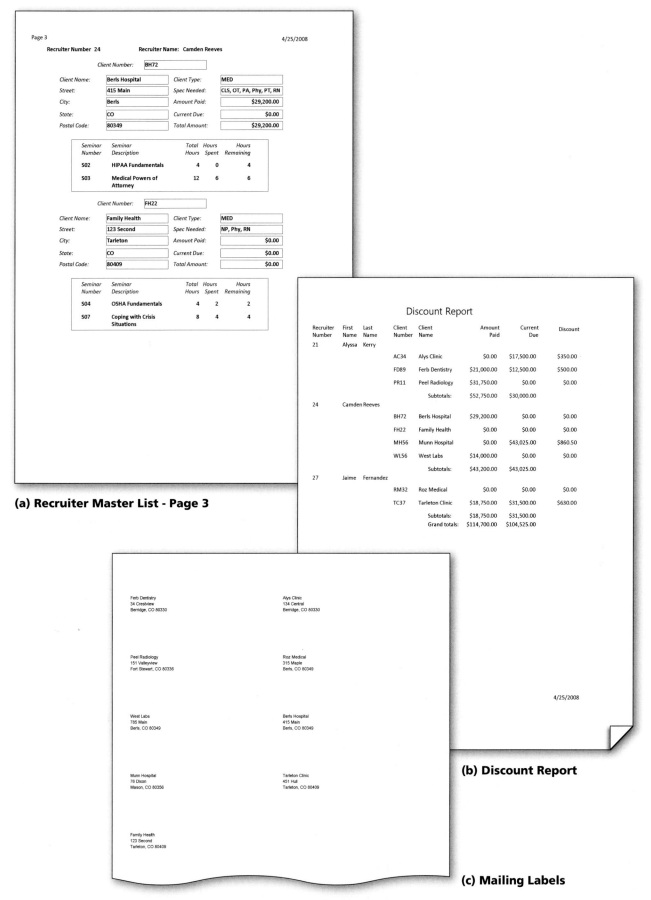

(a) Recruiter Master List - Page 3

(b) Discount Report

(c) Mailing Labels

Figure 7–1

Overview

As you read through this chapter, you will learn how to create the reports and labels by performing these general tasks:

- Change a caption and create queries for a report.
- Create a report, specify grouping and sorting, and add fields and text boxes to the report.
- Add a subreport to the report.
- Create a second report, specify grouping and sorting, and add fields and text boxes to the report.
- Add totals and subtotals to the report, and add a text box that uses a function.
- Create mailing labels.

Plan Ahead

Report Design Guidelines

1. **Determine the intended audience and purpose of the report.** Who will use the report? How will they use it? What data do they need? What level of detail do they need?

2. **Determine the source of data for the report.** Is all the data found in a single table or does it come from multiple related tables? Is the data found in a query? Do you need to create multiple reports for a query where the criterion for a field changes? If so, use a parameter query and enter the criterion when you run the report. If the data comes from multiple related tables, you may wish to create a query and use the query as a source of data.

3. **Determine the fields that belong on the report.** What data items are needed by the user of the report?

4. **Determine the organization of the report.** In what order should the fields appear? How should they be arranged? Should the records in the report be grouped in some way? Should the report contain any subreports?

5. **Determine any calculations required for the report.** Should the report contain totals or subtotals? Are there any special calculations? For example, the Recruiter Master List contains a Total Amount field that is calculated by adding the contents of the Amount Paid field and the Current Due field. The Discount Report contains a Discount field, which is calculated by multiplying the amount in the Current Due field by 4 percent if the amount in the Amount Paid field is greater than $20,000 and by 2 percent otherwise.

6. **Determine the format and style of the report.** What information should be in the report heading? Do you want a title and date, for example? Do you want a logo? What should be in the body of the report? What should the style be? In other words, what visual characteristics should the various portions of the report have? Does the organization have specific style requirements for reports?

7. **For mailing labels, determine the contents, order, and type of label.** What fields should appear on the label and how should they be arranged? Is there a certain order (for example, by postal code) in which the labels should be printed? Who is the manufacturer and what is the style number for the labels? What are the dimensions for each label and how many labels print across a page?

When necessary, more specific details concerning the above decisions and/or actions are presented at appropriate positions within the chapter. The chapter also will identify the use of these guidelines in the design of the reports and labels such as the ones shown in Figure 7–1 on the previous page.

Starting Access

If you are using a computer to step through the project in this chapter and you want your screen to match the figures in this book, you should change your screen's resolution to 1024 × 768. For information about how to change a computer's resolution, read Appendix E.

To Start Access

The following steps, which assume Windows Vista is running, start Access.

Note: If you are using Windows XP, refer to Appendix F for alternate steps.

1 Click the Start button on the Windows Vista taskbar to display the Start menu.

2 Click All Programs at the bottom of the left pane on the Start menu to display the All Programs list, and then click Microsoft Office on the All Programs list to display the Microsoft Office list.

3 Click Microsoft Office Access 2007 on the Microsoft Office list to start Access and display the Getting Started with Microsoft Office Access window.

4 If the Access window is not maximized, click the Maximize button on its title bar to maximize the window.

To Open a Database

In Chapter 1, you created your database on a USB flash drive using the file name, JSP Recruiters. There are two ways to open the file containing your database. If the file you created appears in the Recent Documents list, you could click it to open the file. If not, you can use the More button to open the file. The following steps use the More button to open the JSP Recruiters database from the USB flash drive.

Note: If you are using Windows XP, refer to Appendix F for alternate steps.

1 With your USB flash drive connected to one of the computer's USB ports, click the More button to display the Open dialog box.

2 If the Folders list is displayed below the Folders button, click the Folders button to remove the Folders list.

3 If necessary, click Computers in the Favorite Links section and then double-click UDISK 2.0 (E:) to select the USB flash drive, Drive E in this case as the new open location. (Your drive letter might be different.)

4 Click JSP Recruiters to select the file name.

5 Click the Open button to open the database.

6 If a Security Warning appears, click the Options button to display the Microsoft Office Security Options dialog box.

7 With the option button to enable the content selected, click the OK button to enable the content.

Creating Reports in Design View

You do not have to use the wizard when you create a report. You simply can create the report in Design view. In the previous reports you created, you used the wizard to create an initial report, and then used Layout view to modify the design the wizard created. You also can use Design view to modify a report created by the wizard. If you do not use the wizard before moving to Design view, the design will be empty. It then is up to you to place all the fields in the desired locations. It also is up to you to specify any sorting or grouping that is required.

Whether you use the wizard or simply use Design view, you must decide the table or query on which the report is to be based. If the report is to be based on a query, you first must create the query, unless, of course, it already exists.

To Change a Caption

Normally, the field name will appear as the label for a field on a form or report and as the column name in Datasheet view. If you would rather have a different name appear, you can change the field's caption to the desired name. Because JSP wants to shorten Specialties Needed to Spec Needed on reports and forms, the following steps change the caption of the Specialties Needed field to Spec Needed.

- Open the Client table in Design view.

- Click the row selector for the Specialties Needed field to select the field.

- Click the Caption property box and then type Spec Needed as the new caption (Figure 7–2).

- Click the Save button on the Quick Access Toolbar to save the change.

- Close the Client table.

Q&A

Will the column heading for the field change when the table is displayed in Datasheet view?

Yes. When the table appears in Datasheet view and when any query results appear in Datasheet view, the column heading will show the changed caption.

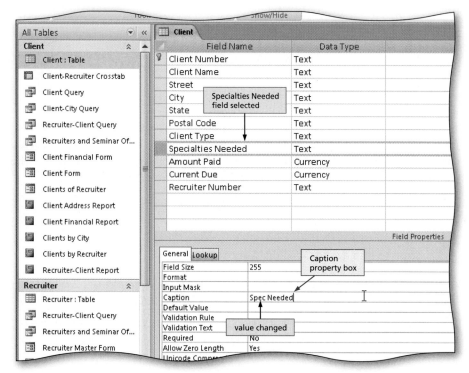

Figure 7–2

To Create a Query for the Report

The analysis of JSP requirements for the reports shows that it would be convenient to use two queries for the report. These queries do not yet exist. The first query relates recruiters and clients and the second query relates seminars and seminar offerings. The following steps create the Recruiters and Clients query.

1 Hide the Navigation Pane, click Create on the Ribbon to display the Create tab, and then click the Query Design button on the Create tab to create a new query.

2 Click the Recruiter table, click the Add button, click the Client table, click the Add button, and then click the Close button to close the Show Table dialog box.

3 Double-click the Recruiter Number, First Name, and Last Name fields from the Recruiter table. Double-click the Client Number, Client Name, Street, City, State, Postal Code, Client Type, Specialties Needed, Amount Paid, and Current Due fields from the Client table to add the fields to the design grid.

4 View the query results and scroll through the fields to make sure you have included all the necessary fields. If you have omitted a field, return to Design view and add it.

5 Click the Save button on the Quick Access Toolbar to save the query, type `Recruiters and Clients` as the name of the query, and then click the OK button.

6 Close the query.

To Create an Additional Query for the Report

JSP Recruiters needs to include the number of hours that remain in a seminar offering in the Recruiter Master List shown in Figure 7–1a on page AC 459. The following steps create the Seminar Offerings and Seminars query that includes a calculated field for hours remaining.

1

• Click Create on the Ribbon to display the Create tab and then click the Query Design button on the Create tab to create a new query.

• Click the Seminar table, click the Add button, click the Seminar Offerings table, click the Add button, and then click the Close button to close the Show Table dialog box.

• Double-click the Client Number and Seminar Number fields from the Seminar Offerings table. Double-click the Seminar Description field from the Seminar table. Double-click the Total Hours and Hours Spent fields from the Seminar Offerings table to add the fields to the design grid.

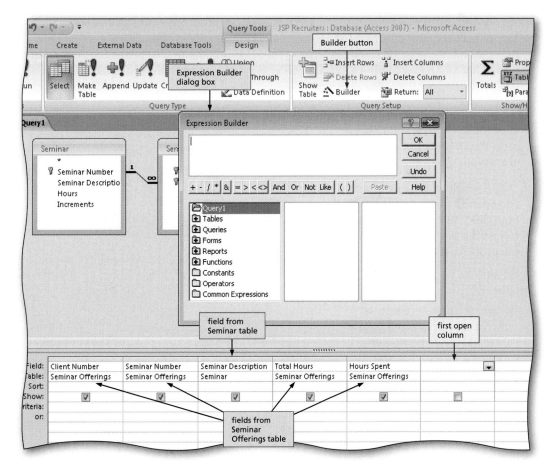

Figure 7–3

• Click the first open column in the design grid to select it.

• Click the Builder button on the Design tab to display the Expression Builder dialog box (Figure 7–3).

2

- Double-click Tables to display a list of tables, and then click the Seminar Offerings table to select it.

- Click the Total Hours field to select it and then click the Paste button to paste it into the expression.

- Click the minus sign to add it to the expression.

- Click the Hours Spent field to select it and then click the Paste button to paste it into the expression (Figure 7–4).

Q&A Why are the fields preceded by a table name and an exclamation point?

This notation qualifies the field, that is, it indicates to which table the field belongs.

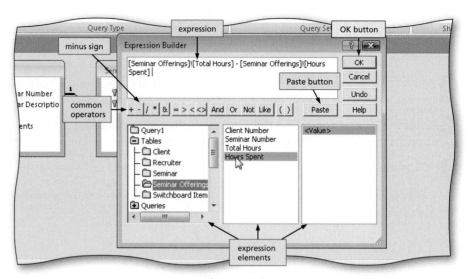

Figure 7–4

Q&A Could I type the expression instead of using the Expression Builder?

Yes. You could type it directly into the design grid. You also could right-click the column and click Zoom to allow you to type the expression in the Zoom dialog box. Finally, you could use the Expression Builder, but simply type the expression rather than clicking any buttons. Use whichever method you find most convenient.

3

- Click the OK button and then press the ENTER key to enter the expression.

- Click the field in the grid in which you entered the expression and then click the Property Sheet button on the Design tab to display the property sheet.

Q&A What if the wrong property sheet appears?

You either did not click in the right location or you have not yet completed entering the expression. The easiest way to ensure you have done both is to click any other column in the grid and then click the column with the expression.

- Click the Caption property box and type Hours Remaining as the caption (Figure 7–5).

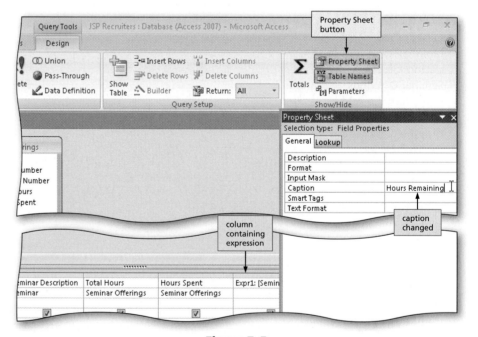

Figure 7–5

4

- Close the property sheet and then view the results of the query (Figure 7–6).

5

- Verify that your query results match those in the figure. If not, return to Design view and make the necessary corrections.

- Click the Save button, type `Seminar Offerings and Seminars` as the name of the query, and then click the OK button to save the query.

- Close the query.

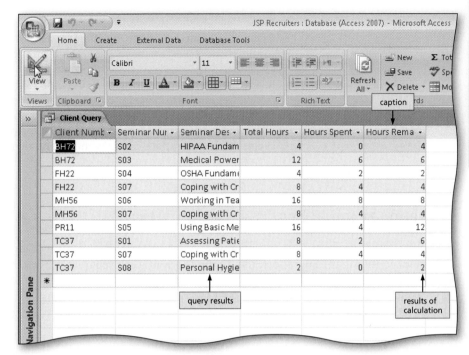

Figure 7–6

	Plan Ahead
Determine the fields that belong on the report.	

1. **Examine the requirements for the report in general to determine the tables.** Do the requirements only relate to data in a single table, or does the data come from multiple tables? How are the tables related? Is the data in a query or could a query be created that contains some or all of the fields necessary for the report?

2. **Examine the specific requirements for the report to determine the fields necessary.** Look for all the data items that are specified for the report. Each should correspond to a field in a table or be able to be computed from a field in a table. This information gives you the list of fields.

3. **Determine the order of the fields.** Examine the requirements to determine the order in which the fields should appear. Be logical and consistent in your ordering. For example, in an address, the city should come before the state and the state should come before the postal code unless there is some compelling reason for another order.

	Plan Ahead
Determine the organization of the report.	

1. **Determine sort order.** Is there a special order in which the records should appear?

2. **Determine grouping.** Should the records be grouped in some fashion? If so, what should appear before the records in a group? If, for example, clients are grouped by recruiter number, the number of the recruiter should probably appear before the group. Should the recruiter name also appear? What should appear after the group? For example, are there some fields for which subtotals should be calculated? If so, the subtotals would come after the group.

(continued)

Plan Ahead

(continued)

3. **Determine whether to include a subreport.** Rather than grouping, you may choose to include a subreport as in the Recruiter Master List. The data concerning seminar offerings for the client could have been presented by grouping the seminar offerings data by client number. The headings currently in the subreport would have appeared in the group header. Instead, it is presented in a subreport. Subreports, which are reports in their own right, offer more flexibility in formatting than group headers and footers. More importantly in the Recruiter Master List, some clients do not have any seminar offerings. If this information were presented using grouping, the group header still will appear for these clients. With a subreport, clients who have no seminar offerings do not appear.

To Create an Initial Report in Design View

Creating the report shown in Figure 7–1a on page AC 459 from scratch involves creating the initial report in Design view, adding the subreport, modifying the subreport separately from the main report, and then making the final modifications to the main report.

When you want to create a report from scratch, you use Report Design rather than Report Wizard. The Report Wizard is suitable for simple, customized reports. With Report Design, you can make advanced design changes, such as adding subreports. The following steps create the initial version of the Recruiter Master List and select the **record source** for the report, that is the table or query that will furnish the data for the report. The steps then specify sorting and grouping for the report.

- Click Create on the Ribbon to display the Create tab.

- Click the Report Design button on the Create tab to create a report in Design view.

- Ensure the selector for the entire report, the box in the upper-left corner of the report, is selected.

- Click the Property Sheet button on the Design tab to display a property sheet.

- With the All tab selected, click the Record Source property box arrow to display the list of available tables and queries (Figure 7–7).

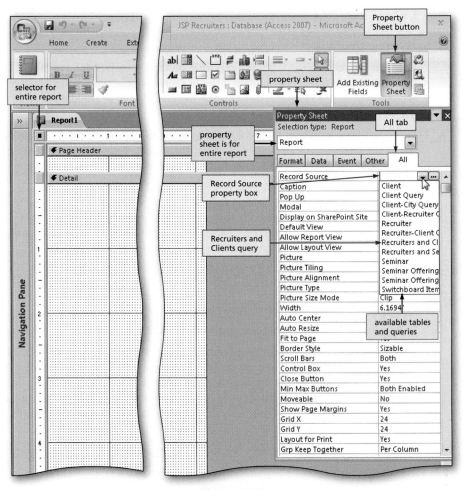

Figure 7–7

2

- Click the Recruiters and Clients query to select the query as the record source for the report.

I only see portions of names and some are similar. How can I be sure I selected the correct query?

Click the Record Source property in the property sheet to produce an insertion point and then repeatedly press the RIGHT ARROW key to move through the letters in the name. You also can expand the property sheet by pointing to the right or left edge of the sheet and dragging.

- Close the property sheet by clicking the Property Sheet button on the Design tab.

- Click the Group & Sort button to display the Group, Sort, and Total pane (Figure 7–8).

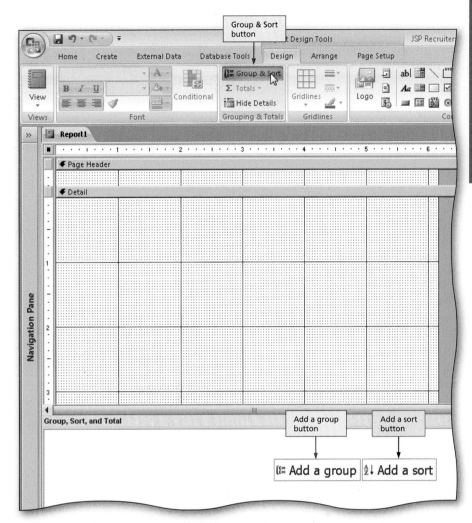

Figure 7–8

3

- Click the 'Add a group' button to display the list of available fields for grouping (Figure 7–9).

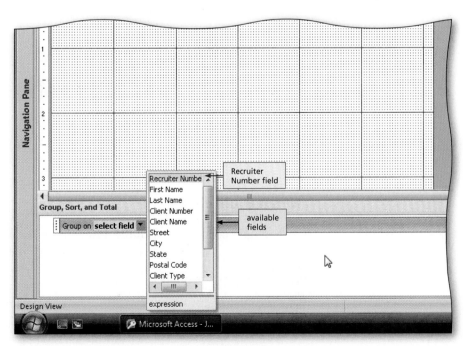

Figure 7–9

- Click the Recruiter Number field to group by Recruiter Number (Figure 7–10).

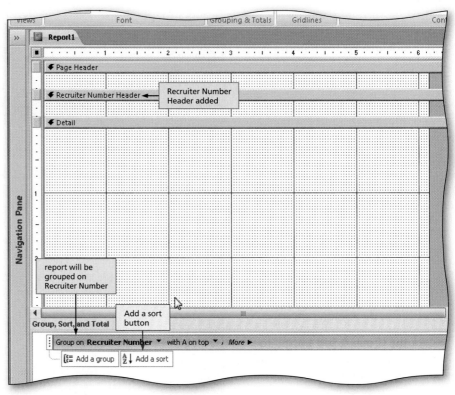

Figure 7–10

- Click the 'Add a sort' button to display the list of available fields for sorting (Figure 7–11).

- Click the Client Number field to sort by Client Number.

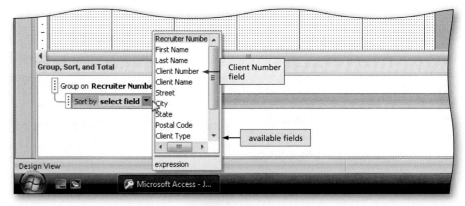

Figure 7–11

To Save the Report

Before proceeding with the next steps in the modification of the report, it is a good idea to save your work. The following steps save the report as Recruiter Master List.

1 Click the Save button.

2 Type `Recruiter Master List` as the report name.

3 Click the OK button.

Understanding Report Sections

As you create the report in Design view, you will place controls into sections on the form. There are three types of controls: bound controls, unbound controls, and calculated controls. **Bound controls** are used to display data that comes from fields in the database, such as the client number and name. **Unbound controls** are not associated with data from the database and are used to display such things as the report's title. Finally, **calculated controls** are used to display data that is calculated from other data, such as a total.

When you place a control, you will need to decide in which section to place the control. To do so, you must understand the purpose of each of the sections. The contents of the **Report Header section** print once at the beginning of the report. This section often contains a title. The contents of the **Report Footer section** print once at the end of the report. This section might contain grand totals of some of the items on the report. The contents of the **Page Header section** print once at the top of each page and often contain the column headings. The contents of the **Page Footer section** print once at the bottom of each page and may contain a date and a page number. The contents of the **Detail section** print once for each record in the table or query.

When the data in a report is grouped, there are two additional possible sections. The contents of the **Group Header section** are printed before the records in a particular group, and the contents of the **Group Footer section** are printed after the group. In the Discount Report (Figure 7–1b on page AC 459), for example, which is grouped by Recruiter Number, the Group Header section contains the recruiter number and name and the Group Footer section contains subtotals of Amount Paid and Current Due.

To Add Fields to the Report

When you have determined the fields that are necessary for the report, you need to add them. You can add the fields to the report by dragging them from the field list to the appropriate position on the report. The following steps add the fields to the report.

1

- Click the Add Existing Fields button on the Design tab to add a field list.

- Drag the Recruiter Number field to the approximate position shown in Figure 7–12.

Q&A

My field list does not look like the one in the figure. It has several tables listed and at the bottom it has Show only fields in the current record source. Yours has Show all tables. What should I do?

Click the 'Show only fields in the current record source' link. Your field list then should match the one in the figure.

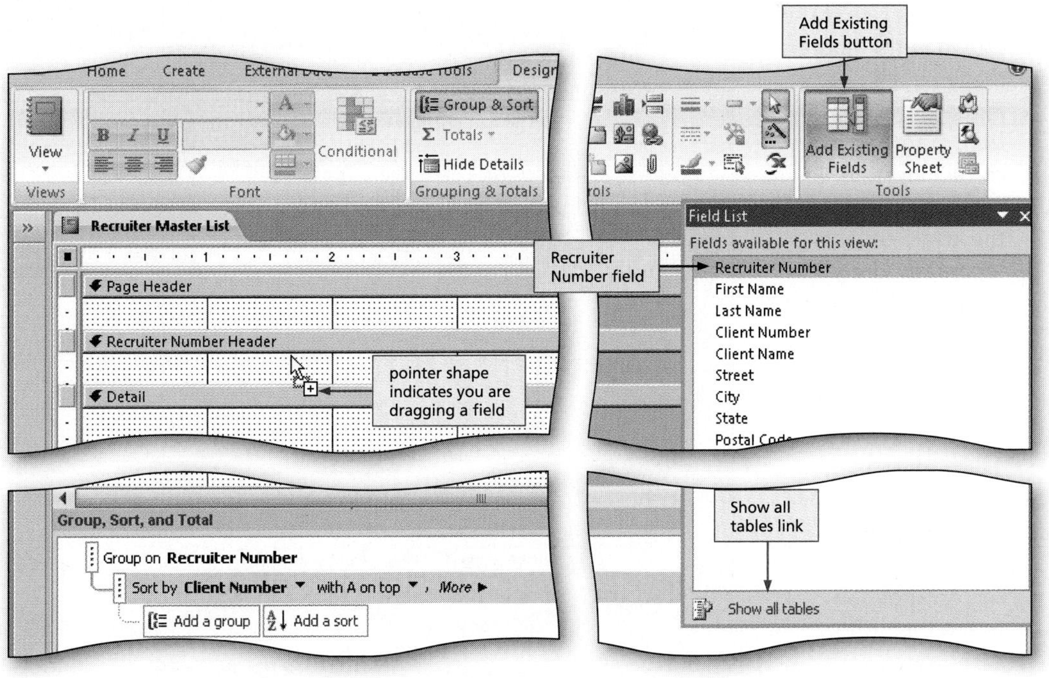

Figure 7–12

2

- Release the left mouse button to place the field (Figure 7–13).

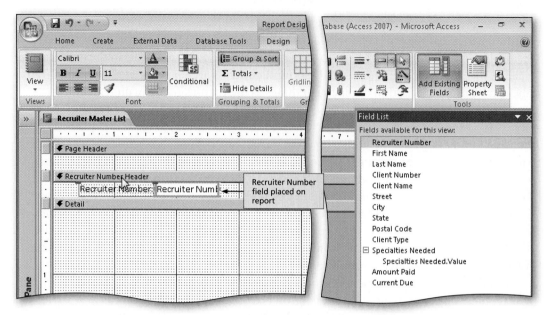

Figure 7–13

3

- Place the remaining fields in the positions shown in Figure 7–14.

- Click Arrange on the Ribbon to display the Arrange tab.

- Adjust the positions of the labels to those shown in the figure. If any field is not in the correct position, drag it to its correct location. To move the control or the attached label separately, drag the large handle in the upper-left corner of the control or label.

Experiment

- Select more than one control and then experiment with buttons on the Arrange tab to see their effect. After trying each one, click the Undo button on the Quick Access Toolbar to undo the change.

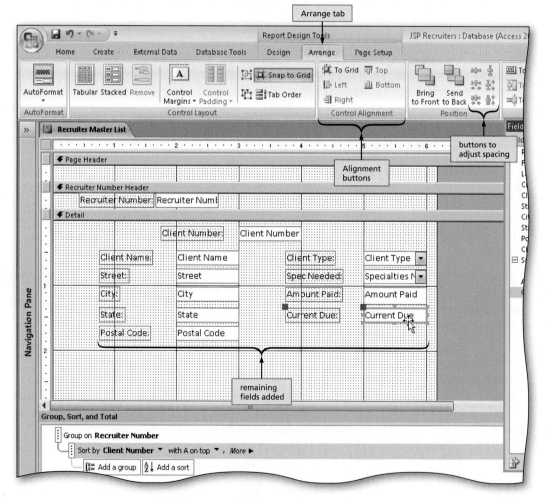

Figure 7–14

- Click Design on the Ribbon to display the Design tab.

- Remove the field list by clicking the Add Existing Fields button.

- Remove the Group, Sort, and Total pane by clicking the Group & Sort button on the Design tab.

Aligning Controls Using the Arrange Tab

When working on a report in Design view, you can make changes to the alignment of the controls in your report by using the Arrange tab, which is shown in Figure 7–14. Table 7–1 shows the groups that contain buttons relevant to aligning controls along with a description of the use of the buttons in the group.

Table 7–1 Arrange Tab

Group	Description
Control Alignment	Click To Grid button to align upper-left corner of selected object to closest grid location. With multiple controls selected, click Left to align left edge of selected controls with left edge of leftmost control. Click Right to align right edge of selected controls with right edge of rightmost control. Click Top to align top edge of selected controls with top edge of topmost control. Click Bottom to align bottom edge of selected controls with bottom edge of bottommost control.
Position	Bring to Front or Send to Back is only relevant when two controls overlap. If so, Bring to Front will bring the selected control in front of other overlapping controls and Send to Back will place it behind other controls. The other controls in the group affect the spacing between controls. The buttons in the first row are Make Horizontal Spacing Equal and Make Vertical Spacing Equal. Both of these require at least three controls to be selected. Clicking the button will equalize the horizontal or vertical spacing between the controls. The buttons in the second row are Increase Horizontal Spacing and Increase Vertical Spacing. Clicking these buttons will increase the horizontal or vertical spacing between selected controls by one grid unit. The buttons in the third row are Decrease Horizontal Spacing and Decrease Vertical Spacing. Clicking these buttons will decrease the horizontal or vertical spacing between selected controls by one grid unit.
Size	The To Fit button sizes a control to best fit the data within it and the To Grid button sizes a control to the closest gridlines. The remaining controls require multiple controls be selected. To Tallest sizes the height of the selected controls to the height of the tallest control. To Widest sizes the width of the selected controls to the width of the widest control. To Shortest sizes the height of the selected controls to the height of the shortest control. To Narrowest sizes the width of the selected controls to the width of the narrowest control.
Show/Hide	The buttons in this group show or hide some component of a report. The first button in the first row shows or hides the grid. The second shows or hides the Report Header and Report Footer. The first button in the second row shows or hides the ruler. The second shows or hides the Page Header and Page Footer.

To Add Text Boxes

You can place a text box on a report or form by using the Text Box tool in the Controls group on the Design tab. The text box consists of a control that is initially unbound and an attached label. When you enter an expression in the text box, it becomes a calculated control. If the expression is just a single field (for example, =[Amount Paid]), it would be a bound control. Expressions also can be arithmetic operations, for example, calculating the sum of amount paid and current due. Many times, you need to **concatenate**, or combine, two or more text data items into a single expression; the process is called **concatenation**. To concatenate strings, you use the **ampersand (&)** operator. The process of converting an unbound control to a bound control is called **binding**.

The following steps add text boxes and create calculated controls.

1

• Click the Text Box tool on the Design tab and move the pointer to the approximate position shown in Figure 7–15.

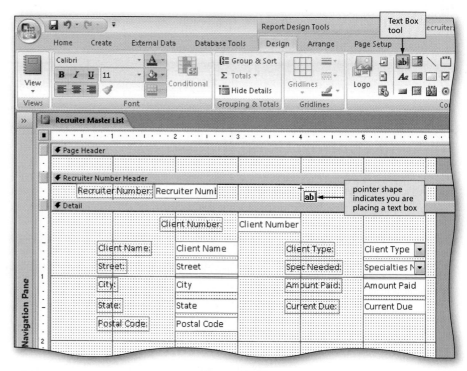

Figure 7–15

2

• Click the position shown in Figure 7–15 to place a text box on the report (Figure 7–16).

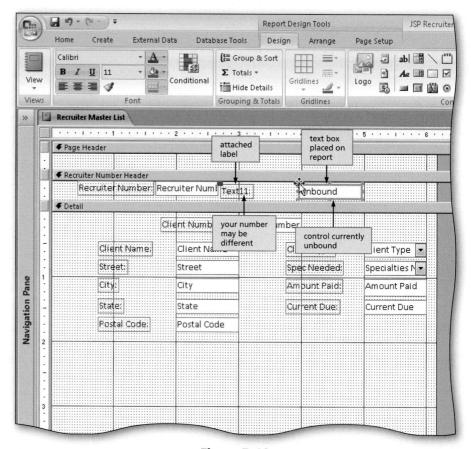

Figure 7–16

3

- Click in the text box to produce an insertion point (Figure 7–17).

Q&A I inadvertently clicked somewhere else so the text box was no longer selected. When I clicked the text box a second time it was selected, but there was no insertion point. What should I do?

Simply click another time.

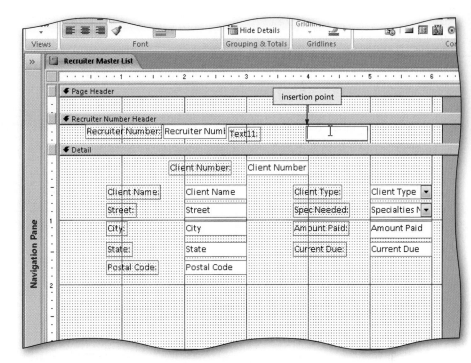

Figure 7–17

4

- Type =[First Name] &' '&[Last Name] as the entry in the text box.

Q&A What is the result of the expression I just entered?

The expression will display the first name of the recruiter followed by a space and then the last name of the recruiter. Any extra spaces at the end of the first name will be removed.

Q&A Could I use the Expression Builder instead of typing the expression?

Yes. Click the Property Sheet button and then click the Build button, which contains three dots, next to the Control Source property.

Q&A Do I need to use single quotes (')?

You also could use double quotes (").

- Click in the attached label to produce an insertion point (Figure 7–18).

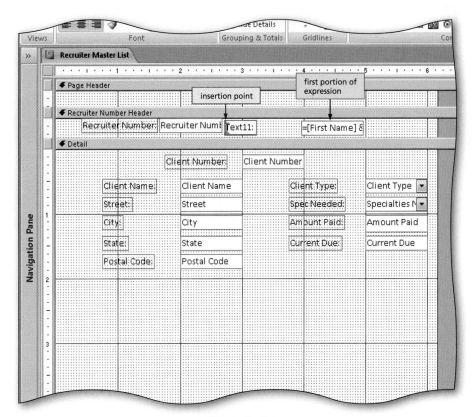

Figure 7–18

5

- Use the BACKSPACE or DELETE key to erase the current entry in the label except for the colon and then type `Recruiter Name` prior to the colon as the new entry (Figure 7–19).

- Click outside the label to deselect it and then drag the label to the position shown in the figure by dragging the Move handle in the upper-left corner of the label.

 I inadvertently erased the colon. What should I do?

Just type a colon after the Recruiter Name.

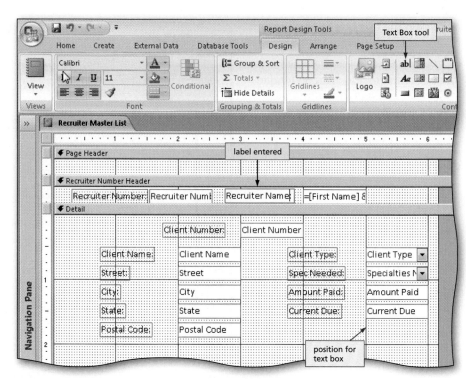

Figure 7–19

6

- Use the techniques in Steps 1 to 5 to place a text box in the position indicated in Figure 7–20. Type `=[Amount Paid]+[Current Due]` as the expression in the text box, drag the label to the position shown in the figure, erase the contents of the label other than the colon and type `Total Amount` in the label.

 My label is not in the correct position. What should I do?

Click outside the label to deselect it, click the label, and then drag it to the desired position.

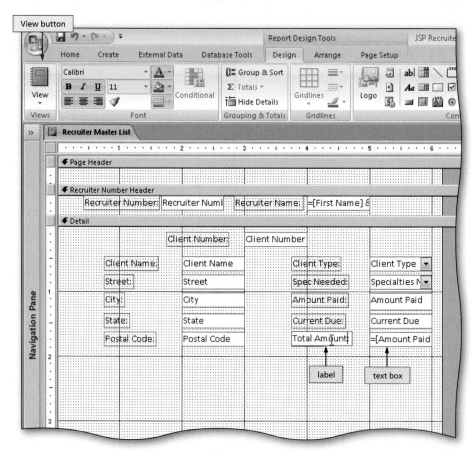

Figure 7–20

To View the Report

As you are working on a report in Design view, it is useful to periodically view the report to gauge how it will look containing data. One way to do so is to use Print Preview. The following steps view the report in Print Preview.

- Click the View button arrow to produce the View button menu.

- Click Print Preview on the View button menu to view the report in Print Preview (Figure 7–21).

Q&A

What would happen if I clicked the View button instead of the View button arrow?

The icon on the View button is the icon for Report View, so you would view the results in Report view. This is another useful way to view a report, but compared to Print Preview, Report View does not give as accurate a picture of how the final printed report will look.

Q&A

The total amount does not appear as currency and the Specialties Needed field does not display all the values. How can I fix these issues?

You will see how to fix these issues in the next sections.

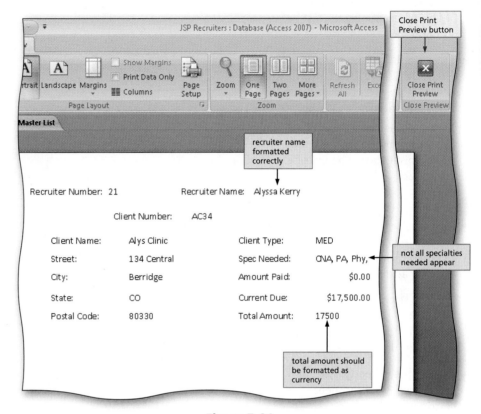

Figure 7–21

2

- Click the Close Print Preview button on the Print Preview tab to return to Design view.

To Format a Control

When you add a calculated control, you often need to format the control. You can use a control's property sheet and change the value in the appropriate property. If a property does not appear in the property sheet, you have two choices. You can click the tab on which the property is located. For example, if it is a control related to data, you would click the Data tab to show only data-related properties. Many people, however, prefer to click the All tab, which shows all properties, and then simply scroll through the properties, if necessary, until locating the appropriate property. The following steps change the format of the Total Amount by changing the value of the Format property and the Decimal Places property.

1

• Click the control containing the expression for Total Amount to select it and then click the Property Sheet button on the Design tab to display the property sheet.

• If necessary, click the All tab (Figure 7–22).

 **Experiment**

• Click the other tabs to see the types of properties on each tab. When finished, once again click the All tab.

2

• Click the Format property box, click the arrow that appears, and then click Currency to select Currency as the format.

• Click the Decimal Places property box, click the arrow that appears, and then click 2 to select 2 as the number of decimal places.

• Remove the property sheet by clicking the Property Sheet button.

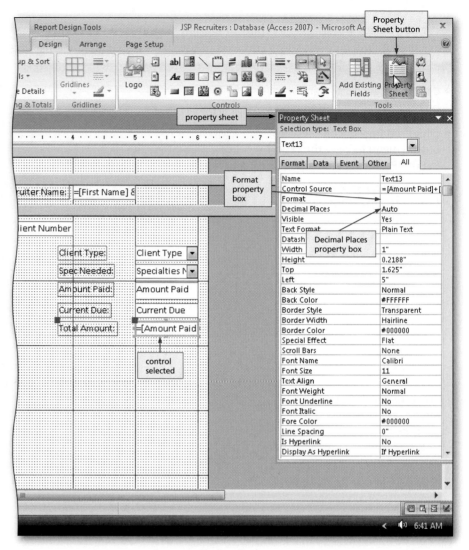

Figure 7–22

To Group Controls

If there is a collection of controls that you frequently will want to modify in the same way, you can simplify the process of selecting all the controls by grouping them. Once they are grouped, selecting any control in the group automatically selects all of the controls in the group. You then can make the desired change and it will affect all the controls.

The following step groups the controls within the Detail section.

1

- Click the Client Number control to select it.

Q&A Do I click the white space or the label?

I The white space.

- While holding the SHIFT key down, click all the other controls in the Detail section to select them.

Q&A Does it matter in which order I select the other controls?

No. It is only important that you ultimately select all the controls.

- Release the SHIFT key.

- Click Arrange on the Ribbon to display the Arrange tab.

- Click the Group button on the Arrange tab to group the controls (Figure 7–23).

Q&A What if I make a mistake and group the wrong collection of controls?

Click the Ungroup button to ungroup the controls, select the collection you want, and then click the Group button.

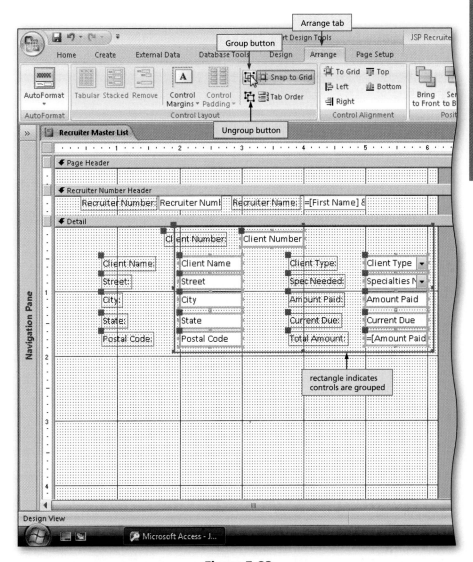

Figure 7–23

To Ungroup Controls

If you no longer need to simultaneously modify all the controls you have placed in a group, you can ungroup the controls. To do so, you would use the following steps.

1. Click any of the controls in a group to select the entire group.

2. Click Arrange on the Ribbon to display the Arrange tab.

3. Click the Ungroup button on the Arrange tab to ungroup the controls.

To Update Grouped Controls

To update grouped controls, click any control in the group to select the entire group. Any change you then make affects all controls in the group. The following steps bold the controls in the group, resize them, and then change the border style.

- If necessary, click any one of the grouped controls to select the group.

- Click Design on the Ribbon to display the Design tab.

- Click the Bold button on the Design tab to bold all the controls in the group (Figure 7–24).

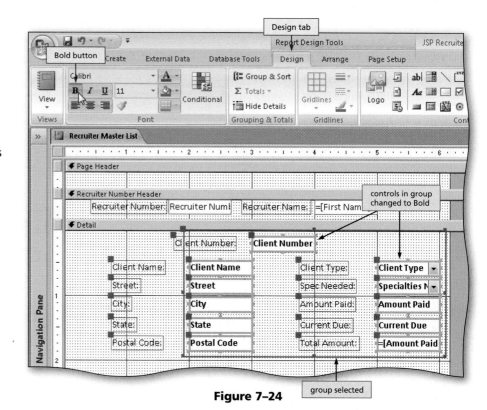

Figure 7–24

- Drag the right sizing handle of the Specialties Needed field to the approximate position shown in Figure 7–25 to resize all the controls in the group.

Q&A

What if I only want to change one control in the group?

Double-click the control to select just the one control and not the entire group. You then can make any change you wish to that one control.

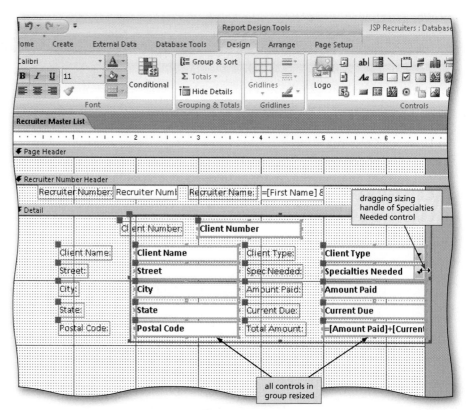

Figure 7–25

3

- Click the Property Sheet button on the Design tab to display the property sheet for the grouped controls.

- With the All tab selected, click the Border Style property box to display an arrow and then click the arrow to display the list of available border styles (Figure 7–26).

4

- Click Solid to change the border styles for all the controls in the group to Solid.

Experiment

- Try the other border styles to see their effect. When finished, once again select Solid as the border style.

- Close the property sheet.

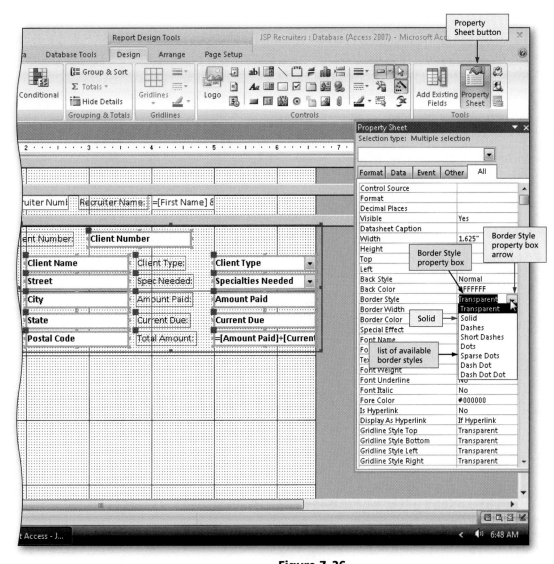

Figure 7–26

To Update Multiple Controls that Are Not Grouped

To update multiple controls that are not grouped together, you must select all the controls. To do so, click one of the controls and then hold the SHIFT key down while selecting the others. The following steps italicize all the labels in the Detail section and then bold all the controls and labels in the Recruiter Number Header section.

- Click the label for the Client Number control to select it.

- While holding the SHIFT key down, click the labels for all the other controls in the Detail section to select them.

- Release the SHIFT key.

- Click the Italic button to italicize the labels (Figure 7–27).

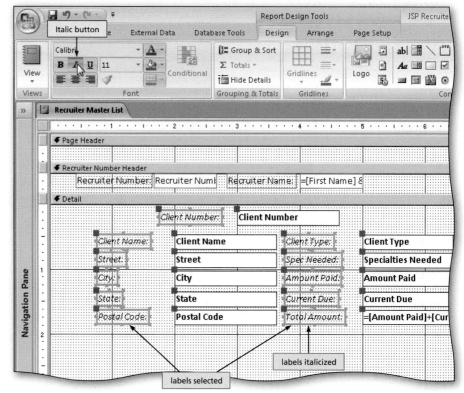

Figure 7–27

- Click in the vertical ruler to the left of the Recruiter Number Header section to select all the controls in the section.

Q&A What exactly is selected when I click in the vertical ruler?

If you picture a horizontal line through the point you clicked, any control that intersects that horizontal line would be selected.

- Click the Bold button on the Design tab to bold all the selected controls (Figure 7–28).

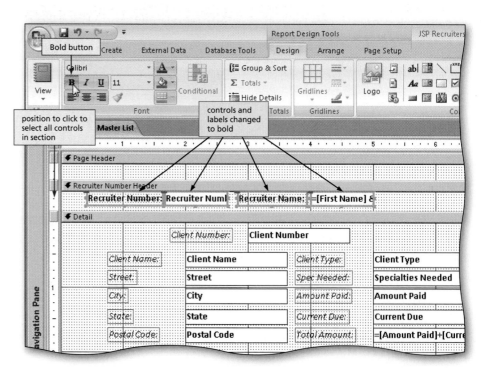

Figure 7–28

3

- Click outside the selected controls to deselect them. Click the control containing the expression for the recruiter's name to select it.

Q&A

Why do I have to deselect the controls and then select one of them a second time?

If you do not do so, any action you take would apply to all the selected controls rather than just the one you want.

- Drag the right sizing handle of the selected control to the approximate position shown in Figure 7–29.

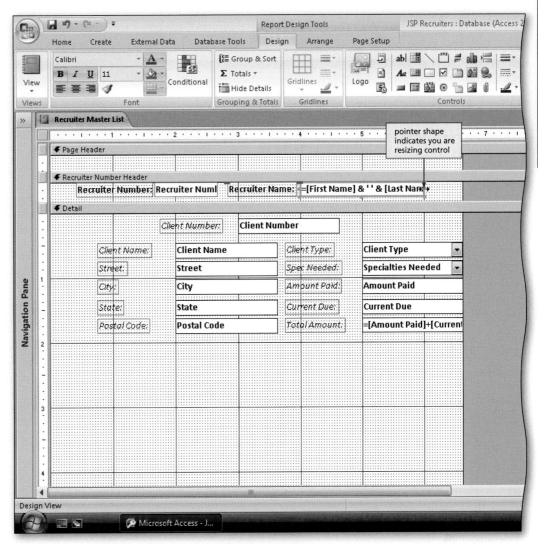

Figure 7–29

Undoing and Saving

Remember that if you make a mistake, you often can correct it by clicking the Undo button on the Quick Access Toolbar. Clicking the Undo button will reverse your most recent change. You also can click the Undo button more than once to reverse multiple changes.

You should save your work frequently. That way, if you have problems that the Undo button will not fix, you can close the report without saving it and open it again. The report will be in exactly the state it was in at the time you saved it.

To Add a Subreport

To add a subreport to a report, you use the Subform/Subreport tool on the Design tab. Provided the Use Control Wizards button is selected, a wizard will guide you through the process of adding the subreport. The following steps add a subreport.

- Click the Use Control Wizards button, click the Subform/ Subreport tool, and then move the pointer, which has changed to a plus sign with a subreport, to the approximate position shown in Figure 7–30.

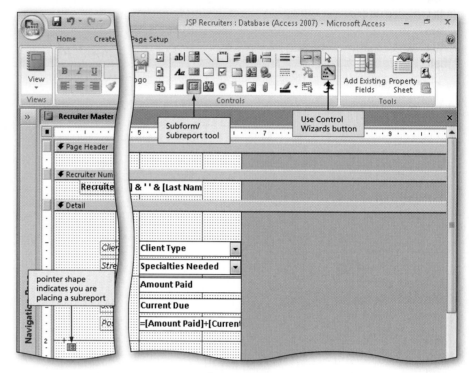

Figure 7–30

- Click the position shown in Figure 7–30 to place the subreport and display the SubReport Wizard dialog box. Be sure the 'Use existing Tables and Queries' option button is selected (Figure 7–31).

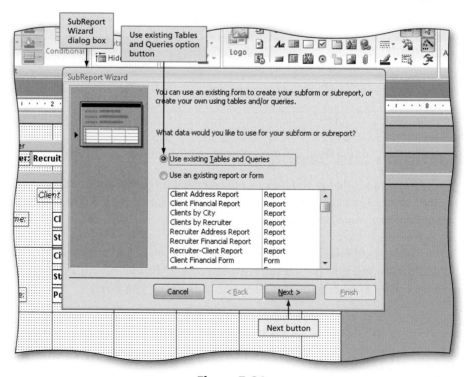

Figure 7–31

③

- Click the Next button.
- Click the Tables/Queries box arrow.
- Scroll down until Query: Seminar Offerings and Seminars is visible, click Query: Seminar Offerings and Seminars, and then click the Add All Fields button to select all the fields in the query (Figure 7–32).

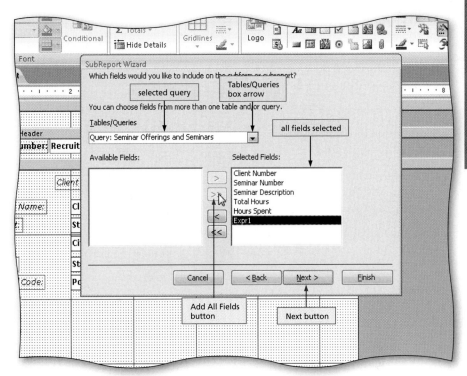

Figure 7–32

④

- Click the Next button and then ensure the 'Choose from a list' option button is selected (Figure 7–33).

 Q&A What is the purpose of this dialog box?

You use this dialog box to indicate the fields that link the main report (referred to as "report") to the subreport (referred to as "subreport"). If the fields have the same name, as they often will, you can simply select Choose from a list and then accept the selection Access already has made.

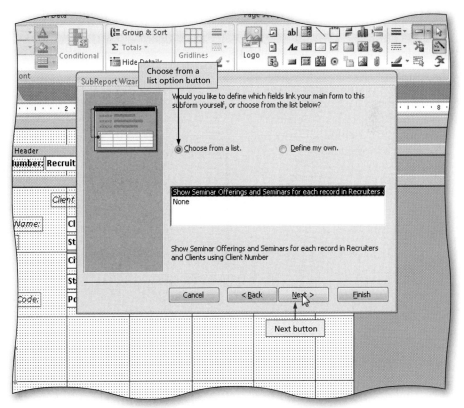

Figure 7–33

- Click the Next button, type
  `Seminar Offerings by Client`
  as the name of the subreport, and
  then click the Finish button to add
  the subreport (Figure 7–34).

- Click outside the subreport to
  deselect the subreport.

- Click the Save button on the
  Quick Access Toolbar to save your
  changes.

- Close the Recruiter Master List
  report.

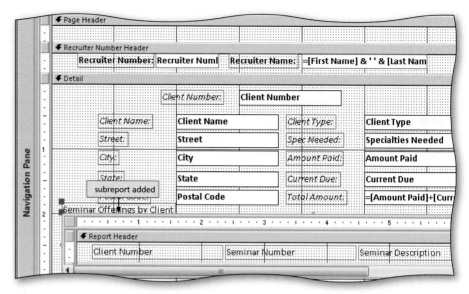

Figure 7–34

To Open the Subreport in Design View

The subreport appears as a separate report in the Navigation Pane. It can be modified just like any other report. The following steps open the subreport in Design view.

- Show the Navigation Pane,
  scroll down so that the Seminar
  Offerings by Client report appears,
  and then right-click the Seminar
  Offerings by Client report to
  produce a shortcut menu
  (Figure 7–35).

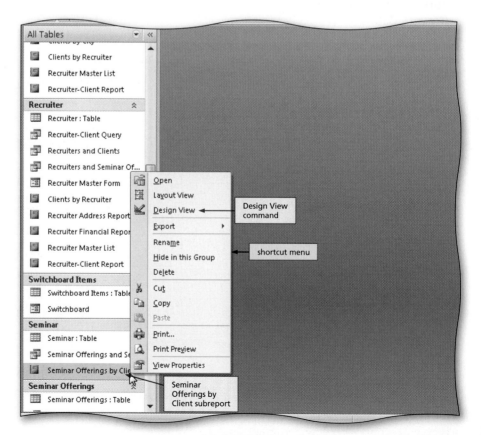

Figure 7–35

2

- Click Design View on the shortcut menu to open the subreport in Design view.

- Hide the Navigation Pane.

- Click the Client Number control in the Detail section to select the control (Figure 7–36).

Q&A
My screen does not look the same as yours. My headings have a blue background. How can I remove the background?

Click the ruler to the left of the Report Header section to select all the controls in the section. Click the Fill/Back Color arrow and then click Transparent.

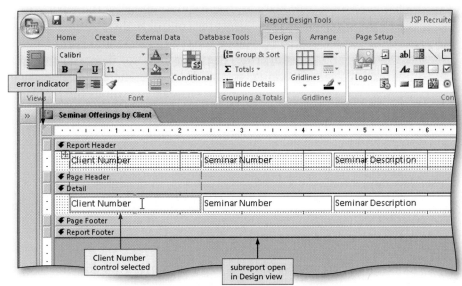

Figure 7–36

Print Layout Issues

The green triangular symbol in the upper-left corner of the report is an error indicator. Pointing to it displays an Error Checking Options button. Clicking the Error Checking Options button produces the Error Checking Options menu, as shown in Figure 7–37.

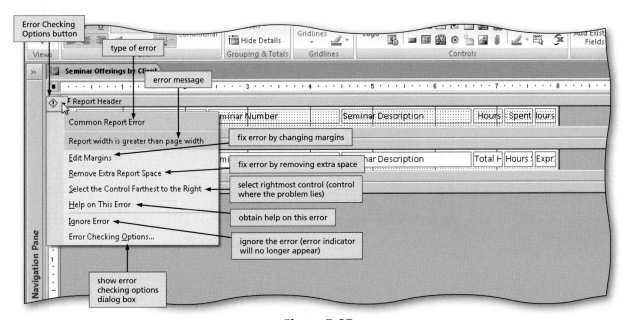

Figure 7–37

The first line in the menu is simply a statement of the type of error that occurred, and the second is a description of the specific error, in this case, the fact that the report width is greater than the page width, a situation that could lead to data not appearing where you expect it to as well as the printing of some blank pages.

BTW

Subreports
A main report can contain more than one subreport. If the main report is based on a table or query, each subreport must contain information related to the information in the main report. If the main report is not based on a table or query, it simply serves as a container for the subreports, which then have no restrictions on the information they contain.

The next three lines provide alternatives for addressing the error. You could change the margins to allow more space for the report. You could remove some extra space. You could select the control farthest to the right and move it. The next line gives more detailed help on the error. The Ignore Error command instructs Access to not consider this an error. The error indicator then would disappear. The final line displays the Error Checking Options dialog box where you can make other changes.

Later in this chapter, you will fix the problem by changing the width of the report, so you do not need to take any action at this time.

To Modify the Controls in the Subreport

Because the client number appears in the main report, it does not need to be duplicated in the subreport. Also, the column headers in the subreport should extend over two lines, as shown in Figure 7–1a on page AC 459. The following step modifies the subreport by deleting the Client Number control and revising the column headings.

- With the Client Number control selected, press the DELETE key to delete the control.

- Change the labels in the Report Header section to match those shown in Figure 7–38. To extend a heading over two lines, click prior to the second word to produce an insertion point and then press SHIFT+ENTER to move the second word to a second line.

- Change the sizes of the controls to match those in the figure by selecting the controls and dragging the sizing handles.

- Use the alignment buttons on the Design tab to change the alignment to Center or Right as necessary to match the labels in the figure.

Q&A Why does Expr1 appear in the Detail section under the Hours Remaining label?

Expr1 indicates that Hours Remaining is a calculated control.

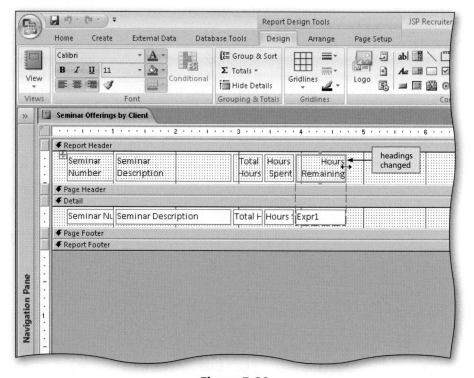

Figure 7–38

Experiment

- There is currently a space between the two names in the labels. To delete the space, click immediately after the first word to produce an insertion point and then press the DELETE key. Try the various alignments (left, right, and center) before removing the space. Remove the space and try the various alignments again to see if the removal of the space makes any difference. When finished, make sure your labels look like the one in the figure.

To Change the Can Grow Property

Some of the seminar descriptions are too long to fit in the available space. This problem can be addressed in several ways.

1. Move the controls to allow more space in between controls. Then, drag the appropriate handles on the controls that need to be expanded to enlarge them.

2. Use the Font Size property to select a smaller font size. This will allow more data to fit in the same space.

3. Use the Can Grow property. By changing the value of this property from No to Yes, the data can be spread over two lines, thus allowing all the data to print. Access will split data at natural break points, such as commas, spaces, and hyphens.

The third approach is the easiest to use and also produces a very readable report. The following step changes the Can Grow property for the Seminar Description field.

- Click the Seminar Description control to select it.

- Click the Property Sheet button on the Design tab to display the property sheet.

- With the All tab selected, scroll down until the Can Grow property appears, click the Can Grow property box arrow to display the list of possible values for the Can Grow property (Figure 7–39).

- Click Yes in the list.

- Close the property sheet.

Q&A What is the effect of the Can Shrink property?

If the Can Shrink property is set to Yes, Access will remove blank lines that occur when the field is empty.

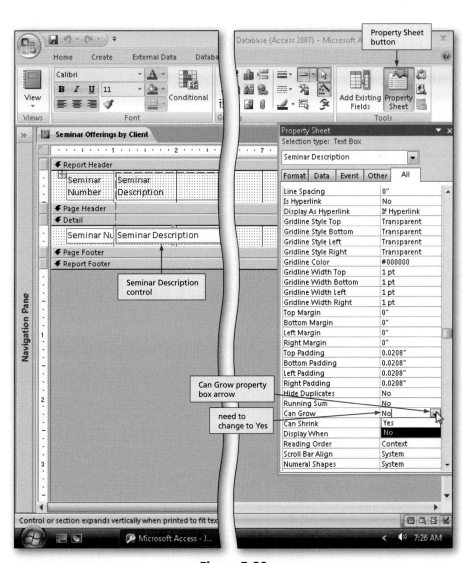

Figure 7–39

To Change the Appearance of the Controls in the Subreport

The following steps change the appearance of the controls in the subreport.

- Drag the right boundary of the subreport to the approximate position shown in Figure 7–40.

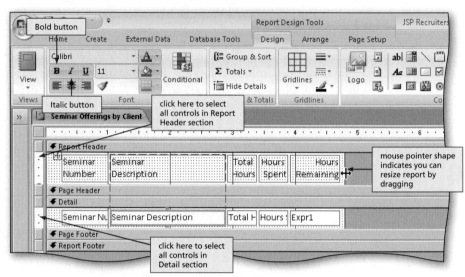

- Click the ruler to the left of the controls in the Detail section to select the controls, and then click the Bold button on the Design tab to bold the controls.

- Click the ruler to the left of the labels in the Report Header section to select the labels, and then click the Italic button on the Design tab to italicize the controls.

- Click the Save button on the Quick Access Toolbar to save the changes.

- Close the Seminar Offerings by Client subreport.

Figure 7–40

To Resize the Subreport and the Report

The following steps resize the subreport control in the main report and then resize the main report.

- Show the Navigation Pane.

- Open the Recruiter Master List in Design view.

- Click the subreport and then drag the right sizing handle to change the size to the approximate size shown in Figure 7–41, and then drag the subreport to the approximate position shown in the figure.

- Drag the right boundary of the report to the approximate position shown in the figure.

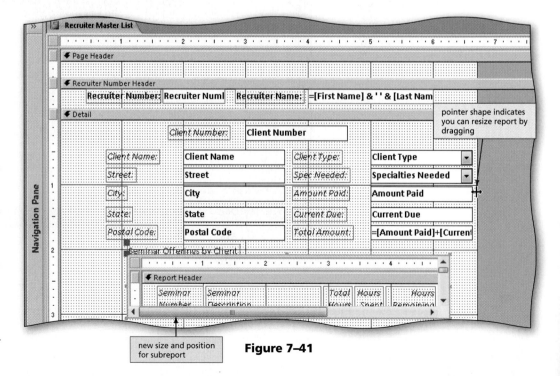

Figure 7–41

2

- Scroll down so that the lower boundary of the Detail section appears and then drag the lower boundary of the section to the approximate position shown in Figure 7–42.

Q&A

I scrolled down to see the lower boundary of the Detail section and the controls are no longer on the screen. What is the easiest way to drag the boundary when the position to which I want to drag it is not visible?

You don't need to see the location to drag to it. As you get close to the top of the visible portion of the screen, Access automatically will scroll. You might find it easier, however to drag it near the top of the visible portion of the report, use the scroll bar to scroll up, and then drag some more. You might have to scroll a couple of times.

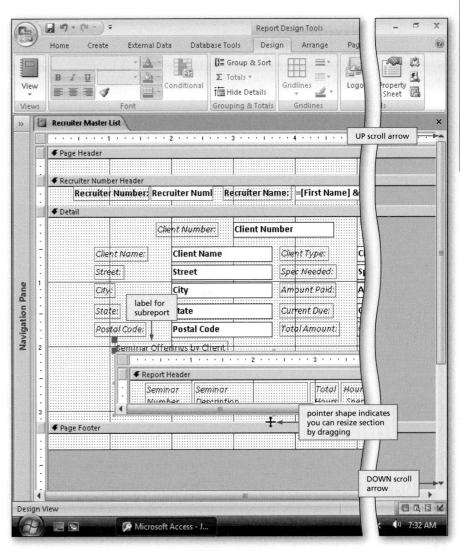

Figure 7–42

To Modify Section Properties

The following step first deletes the label for the subreport and then makes two modifications to the Recruiter Number Header section. The first modification, which causes the contents of the group header section to appear at the top of each page, changes the Repeat Section property to Yes. Without this change, the recruiter number and name only would appear at the beginning of the group of clients of that recruiter. If the list of clients occupies more than one page, it would not be apparent on subsequent pages which recruiter is associated with those clients. The second modification changes the Force New Page property to Before Section, causing each section to begin at the top of a page.

- Click the label for the subreport (the label that reads Seminar Offerings by Client), and then press the DELETE key to delete the label.

- Click the Recruiter Number Header bar to select the header and then click the Property Sheet button on the Design tab to display the property sheet.

- With the All tab selected, click the Repeat Section property box, click the arrow that appears, and then click Yes to cause the contents of the group header to appear at the top of each page.

- Click the Force New Page property box, click the arrow that appears, and then click Before Section to cause a new group to begin at the top of the next page (Figure 7–43).

- Close the property sheet.

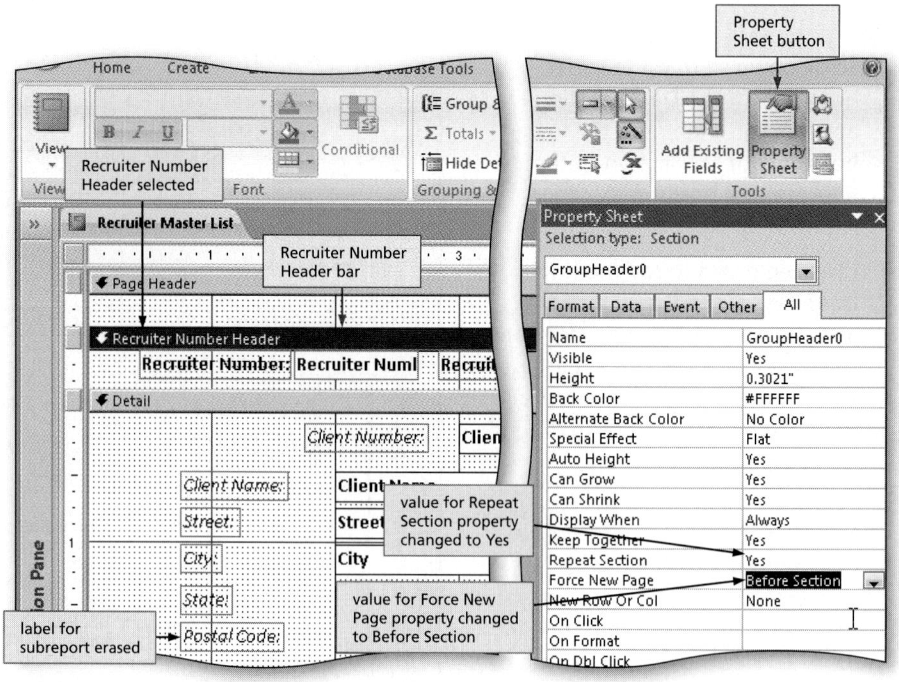

Figure 7–43

To Add a Title, Page Number, and Date

You can add a title, a page number, and a date to a report using the Title button, the Insert Page Number button, and the Date & Time button respectively. The buttons are found on the Design tab. The following steps add a title, page number, and date to the Recruiter Master List report.

- Click the Title button on the Design tab to add a title and then drag the title to the middle of the Report Header section.

Q&A

The title is the same as the name of the report object. Can I change the report title without changing the name of the report object in the database?

Yes. The report title is a label and you can change it using any of the techniques that we used for changing column headings and other labels.

- Click the Insert Page Number button on the Design tab to display the Page Numbers dialog box.

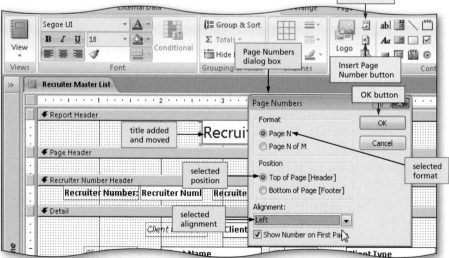

Figure 7–44

- Be sure Page N and Top of Page [Header] option buttons are selected and then, if necessary, click the Alignment arrow and select Left (Figure 7–44).

- Click the OK button to add the page number.

- Click the Date & Time button on the Design tab to display the Date and Time dialog box.

- Click the option button for the third date format and click the Include Time check box to remove the check mark (Figure 7–45).

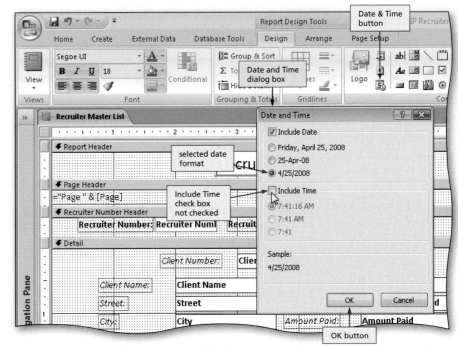

Figure 7–45

- Click the OK button to add the date to the Report Header.

- Drag the Date control to the position shown in Figure 7–46.

- Drag the boundary of the report to the position shown in the figure.

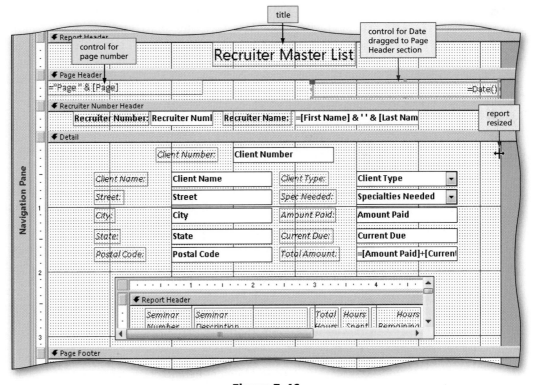

Figure 7–46

To Save and Close the Report

The following steps save the final report and then close the report.

1 Click the Save button on the Quick Access Toolbar to save the report.

2 Close the report by clicking the Close 'Recruiter Master List' button.

To Print the Report

The following steps print the Recruiter Master List report.

1 Show the Navigation Pane, ensure the Recruiter Master List report is selected, and then click the Office Button to display the Microsoft Office Button menu.

2 Point to Print on the Office Button menu and then click Quick Print on the Print submenu to print the report.

To Create a Second Report

JSP Recruiters also would like a report that groups clients by recruiter. The report should include subtotals and grand totals. Finally, it should show the discount amount for each client. The discount amount is based on the current due amount. Clients who owe more than $20,000 will receive a 4 percent discount and clients who owe $20,000 or less will receive a 2 percent discount. The following steps create the Discount Report, select the record source, and specify grouping and sorting options.

1 Hide the Navigation Pane.

2 Click Create on the Ribbon to display the Create tab and then click the Report Design button on the Ribbon to create a report in Design view.

3 Ensure the selector for the entire report, which is the box in the upper-left corner of the report, is selected and then click the Property Sheet button on the Design tab to display a property sheet.

4 With the All tab selected, click the Record Source property box, click the arrow that appears, and then click the Recruiters and Clients query to select the query as the record source for the report.

5 Close the property sheet by clicking the Property Sheet button on the Design tab.

6 Click the Group & Sort button to display the Group, Sort, and Total pane.

7 Click the 'Add a group' button to display the list of available fields for grouping and then click the Recruiter Number field to group by Recruiter Number.

8 Click the 'Add a sort' button to display the list of available fields for sorting, and then click the Client Number field to sort by Client Number.

9 Remove the Group, Sort, and Total pane by clicking the Group & Sort button on the Design tab.

To Add a Field to the Report

As with the previous report, you can add a field to the report by dragging the field from the field list. You can drag an attached label separately from the control to which it is attached by dragging the Move handle in its upper-left corner. This technique does not work, however, if you want to drag the attached label to a different section from the control's section. If you want the label to be in a different section, you must select the label, cut the label, select the section to which you want to move the label, and then paste the label. You then can move the label to the desired location.

The following steps add the Recruiter Number field to the Recruiter Number Header section and then move the label to the Page Header Section.

1

- Click the Add Existing Fields button on the Design tab to add a field list.

- If necessary, click the 'Show only fields in the current record source' link at the bottom of the field list to display only those fields in the Recruiters and Clients query (Figure 7–47).

Why does the text on the button in Figure 7–47 display Show all tables?

The button text changes based on what appears in the Field List pane. If only the fields from the current record source appear, then the button text is Show all tables. If you click the button, all tables in the database will appear in the Field List pane and the button text will display 'Show only fields in the current record source'.

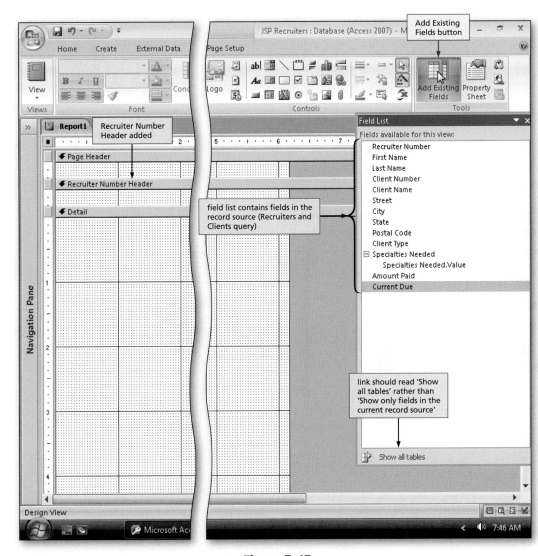

Figure 7–47

2

- Drag the Recruiter Number field to the approximate position shown in Figure 7–48.

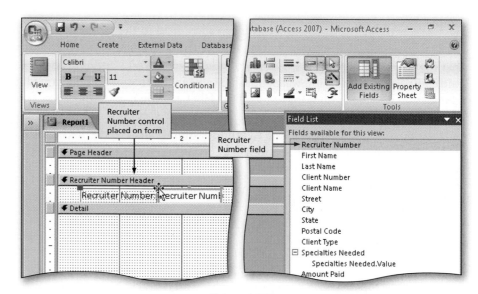

Figure 7–48

3

- Click the label for the Recruiter Number control to select it (Figure 7–49).

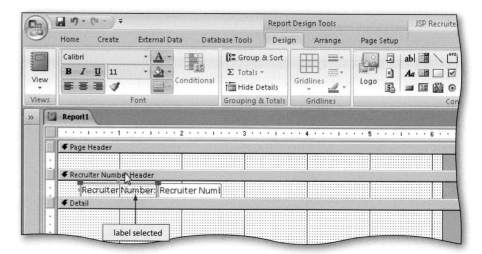

Figure 7–49

4

- Click Home on the Ribbon to display the Home tab.

- Click the Cut button on the Home tab to cut the label.

- Click the Page Header bar to select the page header (Figure 7–50).

Q&A

Do I have to click the bar or could I click somewhere else within the section?

You also could click within the section. Clicking the bar is usually safer, however. If you click in a section intending to select the section, but click within one of the controls in the section, you will select the control rather than the section. Clicking the bar always selects the section.

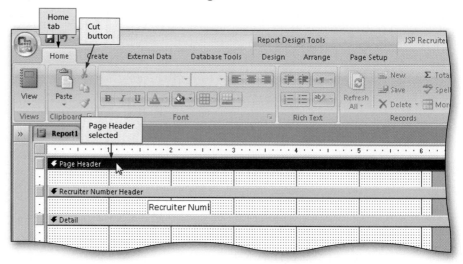

Figure 7–50

5

• Click the Paste button on the Home tab to paste the label in the Page Header section (Figure 7–51).

Q&A When would I want to click the Paste button arrow rather than just the button?

Clicking the arrow displays the Paste button menu, which includes the Paste command and two additional commands. Paste Special allows you to paste data into different formats. Paste Append, which is available if you have cut or copied a record, allows you to paste the record to a table with a similar structure. If you want the simple Paste command, you can just click the button.

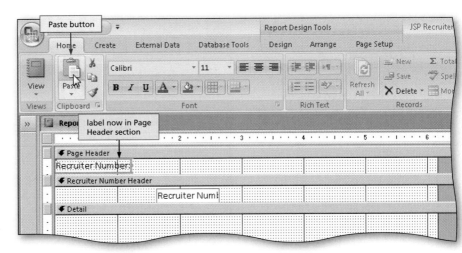

Figure 7–51

6

• Click in the label in front of the word, Number, to produce an insertion point.

• Press SHIFT+ENTER to move the word, Number, to a second line.

• Erase the colon following the word, Number.

To Add the Remaining Fields

The following steps add the remaining fields by dragging them into the Detail section. They next save the report, move the labels into the Page Header section, and move the controls containing the fields to the appropriate locations.

1

• Resize and move the Recruiter Number control to the approximate size and position shown in Figure 7–52.

• Resize the Recruiter Number label to the size shown in the figure.

• Drag the First Name, Last Name, Client Number, Client Name, Amount Paid, and Current Due fields into the Detail section, as shown in the figure.

Q&A Why drag them to the positions shown in the figure? That is not where they go. Could I drag them all at once?

Dragging them gets them onto the report, where you now can move the controls and labels individually to the desired locations. You can drag multiple fields by selecting the first field, holding down the SHIFT key and then selecting other adjacent fields. To select fields that are not adjacent to each other use the CTRL key. How you choose to select fields and drag them onto the report is a matter of personal preference.

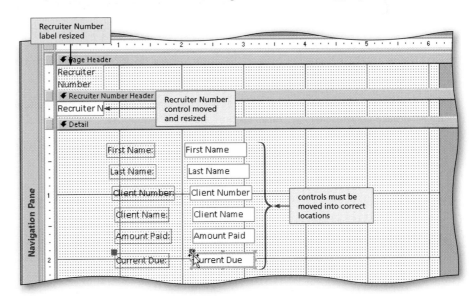

Figure 7–52

2

- Close the field list.

- Click the Save button on the Quick Access toolbar, type `Discount Report` as the report name, and click the OK button to save the report.

Q&A Why save it at this point?

You do not have to save it at this point. Because you are about to move several labels between sections, however, saving it here gives you a convenient point from which to restart if you have problems.

- One at a time, cut each of the labels, paste the label into the Page Header section, resize, reformat, delete the colon, and move the labels to the approximate positions shown in Figure 7–53.

Q&A When I paste the label, it always places it at the left edge, superimposing the Recruiter Number control. Can I change where Access places it?

Unfortunately, when you paste to a different section, Access places the control at the left edge. You will need to drag each control to its proper location after pasting it into the Page Header section.

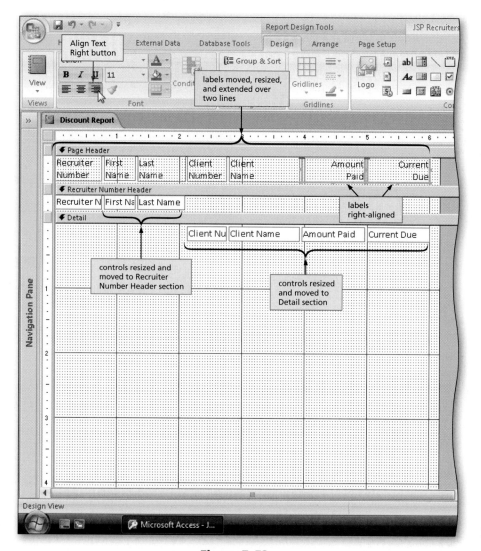

Figure 7–53

- One at a time, resize and move the First Name and Last Name controls to the approximate positions in the Recruiter Number Header section shown in the figure.

- One at a time, resize and move the Client Number, Client Name, Amount Paid, and Current Due controls to the approximate positions in the Detail section shown in the figure.

- Select both the Amount Paid and Current Due labels and click Home on the Ribbon to display the Home tab.

- Click the Align Text Right button on the Design tab to align the headings to the right, as shown in the figure.

To Resize the Detail Section

The following step resizes the detail section of the Discount Report to remove most of the extra space below the controls in the section.

1 Scroll down so that the lower boundary of the Detail section appears and then drag the lower boundary of the section to a position just slightly below the controls in the section.

Q&A

I scrolled down to see the lower boundary of the Detail section and the controls are no longer on the screen. What is the easiest way to drag the boundary when the position to which I want to drag it is not visible?

You don't need to see the location to drag to it. As you get close to the top of the visible portion of the screen, Access automatically will scroll. You might find it easier, however to drag it near the top of the visible portion of the report, use the scroll bar to scroll up, and then drag some more. You might have to scroll a couple of times.

Plan Ahead

Determine any calculations required for the report.

1. **Determine whether to include calculations in the group and report footers.** Should the report contain subtotals? Should the report contain grand totals? Are there other statistics that should be calculated (for example, averages)?

2. **Determine whether any special calculations are required.** Are there any special calculations? What are they? What fields are involved and how are they to be combined? Are any of the calculations conditional, that is, does the calculation depend on whether a certain criterion is true or false?

Totals and Subtotals

To add totals or other statistics to a footer, add a text box. You can use any of the aggregate functions: COUNT, SUM, AVG (average), MAX (largest value), MIN (smallest value), STDEV (standard deviation), VAR (variance), FIRST, and LAST. To use a function, type an equal (=) sign, followed by the function name. You then include a set of parentheses containing the item for which you want to perform the calculation. If the item name contains spaces, such as Amount Paid, you must enclose it in square brackets. For example, to calculate the sum of the amount paid values, the expression would be =SUM([Amount Paid]). Calculated controls that contain aggregate functions also are called aggregate fields.

Access will perform the calculation for the appropriate collection of records. If you enter this expression in the Recruiter Number Footer section, Access only will calculate the total for clients with the given recruiter; that is, it will calculate the appropriate subtotal. If you enter the expression in the Report Footer section, Access will calculate the total for all clients.

To Add Totals and Subtotals

An analysis of requirements at JSP indicated that the Discount Report should contain subtotals and grand totals of amounts paid and current due. The following steps first display the Recruiter Number Footer section and then add the total of amount paid and current due to both the Recruiter Number Footer section and the Report Footer section. The steps label the totals in the Recruiter Number Footer section as subtotals and the totals in the Report Footer section as grand totals. The steps also change the format of the new controls to currency and the number of decimal places to 2.

- Click the Group & Sort
  button on the Design tab to
  display the Group, Sort, and
  Total pane (Figure 7–54).

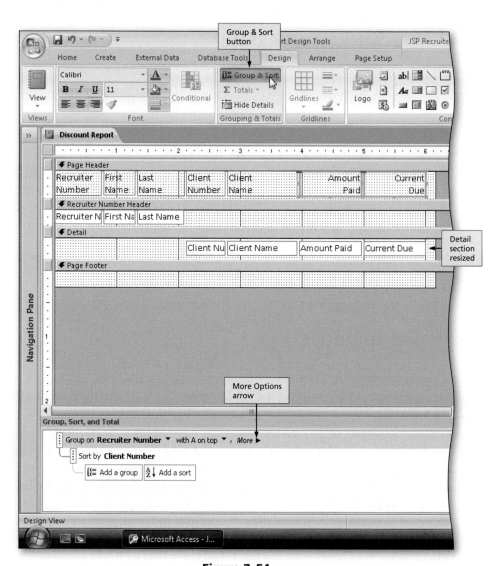

Figure 7–54

- Click Group on Recruiter Number and then click the More Options arrow to display additional options.

- Click the 'without a footer section' arrow to display the available options (Figure 7-55).

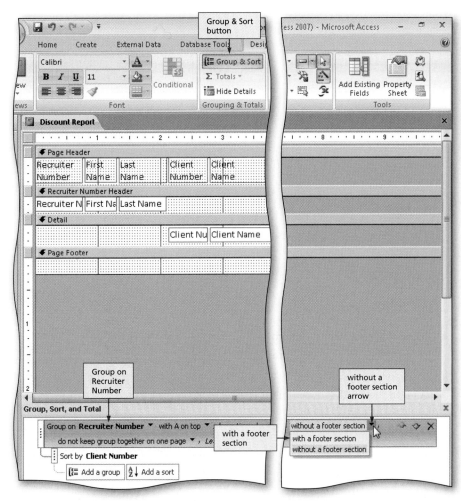

Figure 7–55

3

- Click 'with a footer section' to add a footer.

- Close the Group, Sort, and Total pane by clicking the Group & Sort button on the Design tab.

- Click the Text Box tool on the Design tab, and then point to the position shown in Figure 7–56.

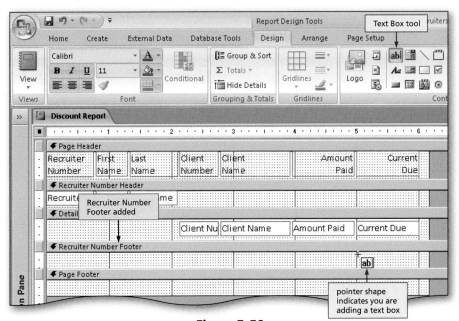

Figure 7–56

● Click the position shown in Figure 7–56 on the previous page to place a text box (Figure 7–57).

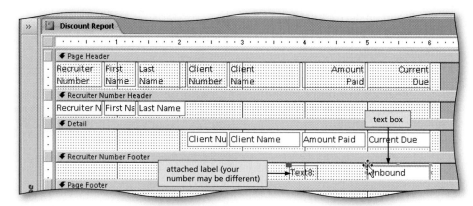

Figure 7–57

● Type =Sum([Current Due]) in the control, and then press the ENTER key.

● Click the label to select it.

● Click the label a second time to produce an insertion point.

● Use the DELETE or BACKSPACE key to delete the Text8 (your number might be different). Do not delete the colon.

● Type Subtotals as the label.

● Click outside the label to deselect it.

● Resize and align the Current Due controls in the Detail section and the Recruiter Number footer section as shown in Figure 7–58.

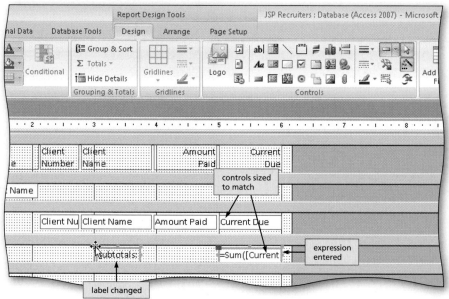

Figure 7–58

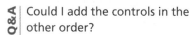

● Click the Text Box tool on the Design tab, and then click in the Recruiter Number Footer just to the left of the control for the sum of Current Due to place another text box.

● Click the text box to produce an insertion point, type =Sum ([Amount Paid]) in the control, and then press the ENTER key to enter the expression (Figure 7–59).

Q&A

Could I add the controls in the other order?

Yes. The only problem is that the label of the second control overlaps the first control. Adding the controls in the order shown in the steps cuts down on the overlap. It is not a major difference, however.

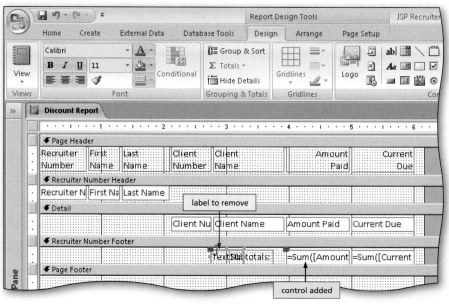

Figure 7–59

7

- Click the label to select it, and then press the DELETE key to delete the label.

I inadvertently deleted the other control rather than the label. What should I do?

The first thing to try is to click the Undo button on the Quick Access Toolbar to reverse your deletion. You then can delete the correct control. If that does not work for you, you simply can delete the remaining control or controls in the section and start these steps over.

- Click the control for the sum of Amount Paid to select it and then hold the SHIFT key down and click the control for the sum of Current Due to select both controls.

- Click the Property Sheet button on the Design tab to display the property sheet.

- Change the format to Currency and the number of decimal places to 2 (Figure 7–60).

- Close the property sheet.

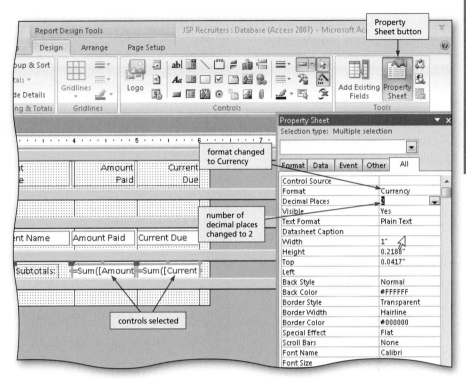

Figure 7–60

8

- Click Arrange on the Ribbon to display the Arrange tab.

- Click the Report Header/Footer button to display the Report Footer section (Figure 7–61).

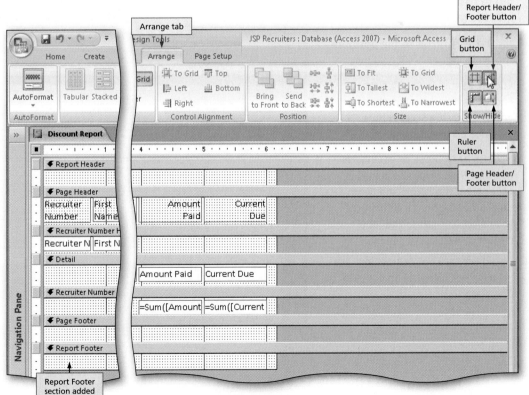

Figure 7–61

9

- Click the ruler in the Recruiter Number Footer to the left of the controls in the section to select the controls.

- Click Home on the Ribbon to display the Home tab.

- Click the Copy button on the Home tab to copy the selected controls to the clipboard (Figure 7–62).

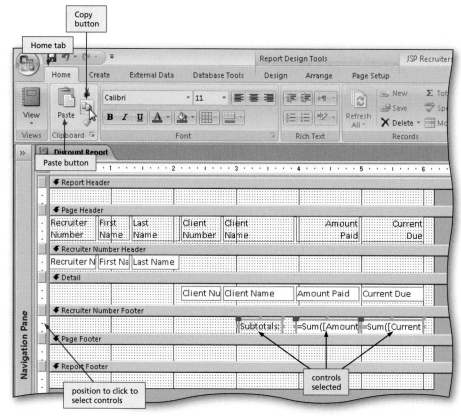

Figure 7–62

10

- Click the Report Footer bar to select the footer and then click the Paste button on the Home tab to paste a copy of the controls into the report footer.

- Move the controls to the positions shown in Figure 7–63.

- Click the label in the Report Footer section to select the label and then click a second time to produce an insertion point.

- Use the BACKSPACE or DELETE key to erase the current contents other than the colon and then type Grand totals in front of the colon to change the label (Figure 7–63).

Q&A

Could I enter the controls just as I did earlier rather than copying and pasting?

Yes. Copying and pasting is a little simpler, but it is a matter of personal preference.

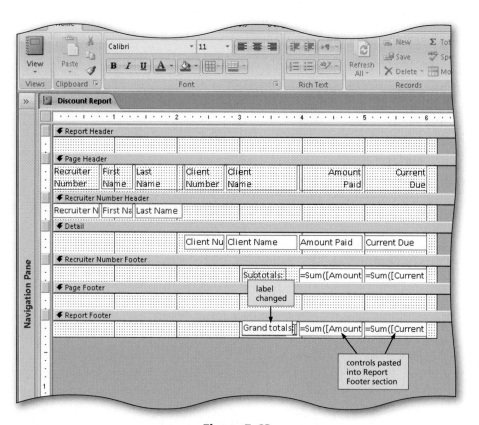

Figure 7–63

To View the Report

The following steps view the report in Print Preview.

1 Click the View button arrow on the Home tab to display the View button menu.

2 Click Print Preview on the View button menu to view the report in Print Preview (Figure 7–64).

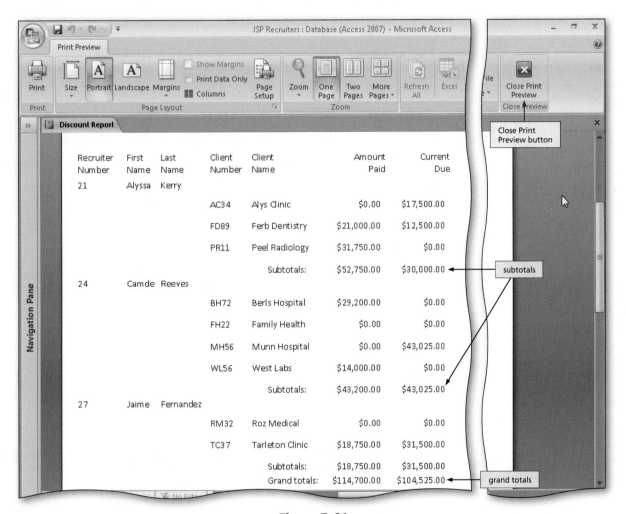

Figure 7–64

To Assign a Conditional Value

The JSP requirements for this report also involved a conditional value related to the amount of a client's discount. To assign a conditional value, you will use the **IIF function**. The IIF function consists of the letters IIF followed by three items, called **arguments**, in parentheses. The first argument is a criterion; the second and third arguments are expressions. If the criterion is true, the function assigns the value of the expression in the second argument. If the criterion is false, the function assigns the value of the expression in the third argument. The IIF function you will use is IIF([Amount Paid]>20000, .04*[Current Due], .02*[Current Due]). If the amount paid is greater than $20,000, the value assigned would be .04*[Current Due]; that is, 4 percent of the current due amount. If the amount paid is not greater than $20,000, the value assigned would be .02*[Current Due]; that is, 2 percent of the current due amount.

The following steps add a text box and then use the Expression Builder to enter the appropriate IIF function in the text box. The steps then change the format of the text box. The steps modify and move the label for the text box. The steps add a title, page number, and date, and then change the size of the report.

1

- Click the Close Print Preview button arrow on the Print Preview tab to return to Design view.

- If necessary, click Design on the Ribbon to display the Design tab.

- Click the Text Box tool on the Design tab and point to the approximate position shown in Figure 7–65.

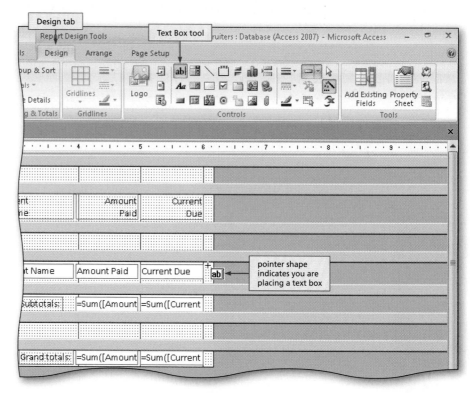

Figure 7–65

2

- Click the position shown in Figure 7–65 to place a text box.

- Click the attached label to select it and then press the DELETE key to delete the attached label.

- Click the text box to select it and then click the Property Sheet button on the Design tab to display a property sheet.

- Click the Control Source property to select it (Figure 7–66).

Q&A

Why did I choose Control Source not Record Source?

You use Record Source to select the source of the records in a report, usually a table or a query. You use the Control Source property to specify the source of data for the control. This allows you to bind an expression or field to a control.

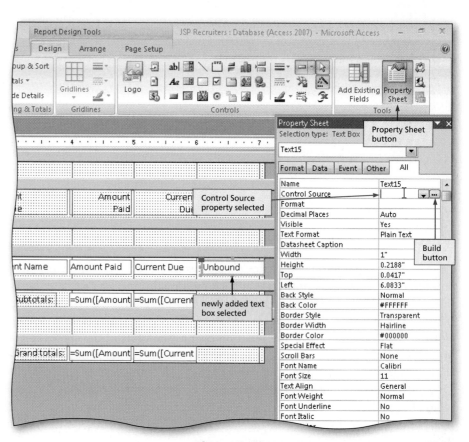

Figure 7–66

3

- Click the Build button to display the Expression Builder dialog box.

- Double-click Functions in the first column to display the function subfolders.

- Click Built-In Functions in the first column to display the various function categories in the second column.

- Scroll down in the second column so that Program Flow appears, and then click Program Flow to display the available program flow functions in the third column.

- Click IIF in the third column to select the IIF function and then click the Paste button (Figure 7–67).

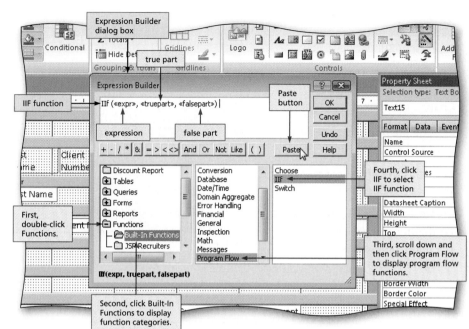

Figure 7–67

Q&A Do I have to select Program Flow? Couldn't I just scroll down to IIF?

You do not have to select Program Flow. You indeed could scroll down to IIF. You will have to scroll through a large number of functions in order to get to IIF, however.

4

- Click the <expr> argument to select it and type [Amount Paid]>20000 as the expression.

- Click the <truepart> argument and type .04*[Current Due] as the true part.

- Click the <falsepart> argument and type .02*[Current Due] as the false part (Figure 7–68).

Q&A Are there other ways I could enter the expression?

Yes. You could just type the whole expression. On the other hand, you could select the function just as in these steps and when entering each argument you could select the fields from the list of fields and click the desired operators.

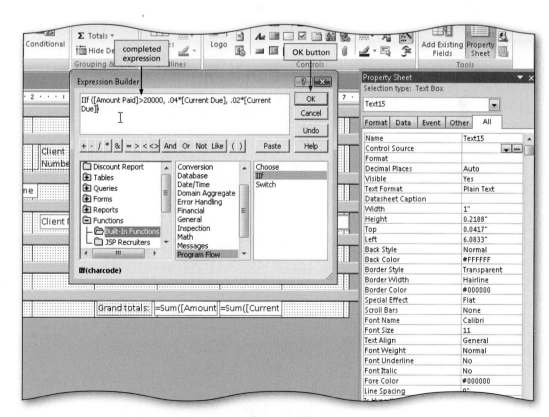

Figure 7–68

5

- Click the OK button in the Expression Builder dialog box to specify the expression as the control source for the text box.

- Change the format to Currency.

- Change the number of decimal places to 2.

- Close the property sheet by clicking the Property Sheet button.

- Click the Label (Form Control) tool on the Design tab and point to the approximate position shown in Figure 7–69.

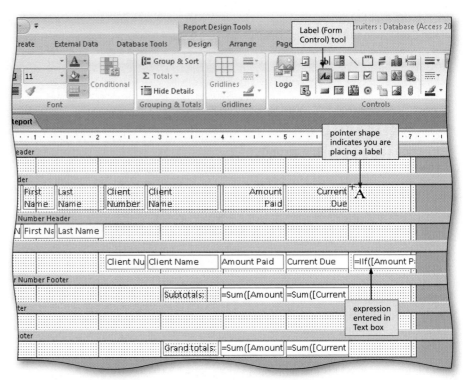

Figure 7–69

6

- Press and hold the left mouse button, drag the pointer to the approximate position for the lower-right corner of the label shown in Figure 7–70, and then release the left mouse button to place the label.

Q&A

I made the label the wrong size. What should I do?

With the label selected, drag the sizing handles to resize the label as needed. Drag the control in a position away from the sizing handles if you need to move the label.

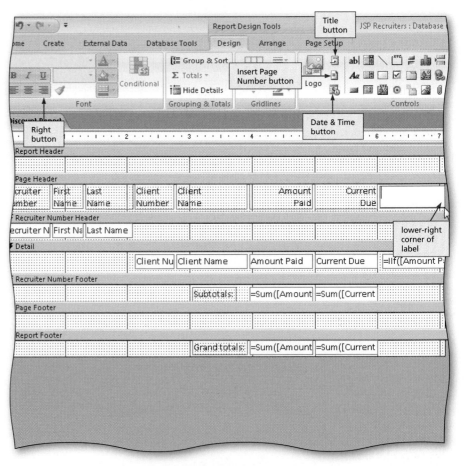

Figure 7–70

7

- Type `Discount` to enter the name of the label.

- Click outside the label to deselect the label and then click the label to select it once more.

- Click the Align Text Right button on the Design tab to right-align the text within the label.

- Move or resize the label as necessary so that it aligns with the new text box and with the other controls in the Page Header section.

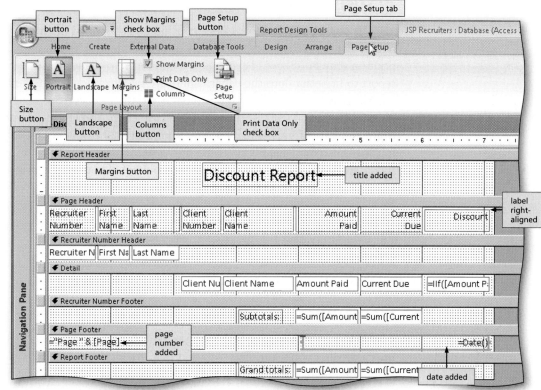

Figure 7–71

- Using the techniques on Pages AC 490 and AC 491, add a title, page number, and date at the positions shown in Figure 7–71.

- Resize the Report Header section to the approximate size shown in the figure by dragging its lower edge.

- If necessary, drag the right boundary of the report to the position shown in the figure.

- Click Page Setup on the Ribbon to display the Page Setup tab as shown in the figure.

Obtaining Help on Functions

There are many functions available in Access for a variety of purposes. To see the list of functions, use the Expression Builder. Double-click Functions in the first column and then click Built-In Functions. You then can scroll through the entire list of functions in the third column. Alternatively, you can click a function category in the second column, in which case the third column only will contain the functions in that category. To obtain detailed help on a function, highlight the function in the third column and click the Help button. The Help presented will show the syntax of the function, that is, the specific rule for how you must type the function and any arguments. It will give you general comments on the function as well as examples illustrating the use of the function.

BTW

Changing the Date Format
To change the format used to display the date, right-click the date control and then click Properties on the short-cut menu. You then can select a format for the date and/or the time by changing the value for the Format property.

To Change the Report Margins

If you look at the horizontal ruler in Figure 7–71 on the previous page, you will notice that the report width is slightly over seven inches. Because the report probably will print on standard 8 ½ × 11 paper, it is a good idea to reduce the margins. This will allow the report to fit better onto the paper. There are two ways to change the margins. You can click the Margins button on the Page Setup tab and then select from some predefined options: Normal (right and left margins of .35"), Wide (right and left margins of .75"), and Narrow (right and left margins of .25"). If you want more control, you can click the Page Setup button to display the Page Setup dialog box. You then can specify your own margins, change the orientation, and also specify multiple columns if you want a multi-column report.

The following steps use the Margins button to select Narrow margins.

1 Click the Margins button on the Page Setup tab.

2 If necessary, click Narrow to specify the Narrow margin option.

Fine-Tuning a Report

When you have finished a report, you should review it to make sure the layout is precisely what you want. You may find that not all the data in a particular column appears as you intended. For example, in Figure 7–64 on page AC 503, the final n in the name Camden does not appear. To correct such a problem you could increase the size of the control by selecting the control and dragging the appropriate sizing handle. You may realize you need an additional control, which you could add by using the appropriate tool in the Controls group or by dragging a field from the field list.

In both cases, you have a potential problem. You may not have the room to increase the size or to add an additional control. If the control is part of a control layout as you had when you modified earlier reports in Layout view, you can resize controls or add new fields, and the remaining fields automatically adjust for the change. In Design view with individual controls, you must make any necessary adjustments yourself.

To Make Room for Resizing or Additional Controls

To make room for resizing a control or for adding additional controls, you would use the following steps.

1. Select all controls to the right of the control you wish to resize or the position where you wish to add another control.

2. Drag any of the selected controls to the right to make room for the change.

To Save and Close the Report

The following steps save the final report and then close the report.

1 Click the Save button on the Quick Access Toolbar to save the report.

2 Close the report by clicking the Close 'Discount Report' button.

To Print the Report

The following steps print the Discount Report.

1 Show the Navigation Pane, ensure that Discount Report is selected, and then click the Office Button to display the Microsoft Office Button menu.

2 Point to Print on the Office Button menu and then click Quick Print on the Print submenu to print the report.

Mailing Labels

Organizations need to send invoices and other correspondence to clients on a regular basis. Using preprinted mailing labels eliminates much of the manual labor involved in preparing materials to be sent through the mail system. To print mailing labels, you create a special type of report. When this report prints, the data will appear on the mailing labels aligned correctly and in the order you specify.

BTW

Customizing Mailing Labels
Once you create mailing labels, you can customize them just as you can customize other reports. In Design view, you can add a picture to the label, change the font size, adjust the spacing between controls, or make any other desired changes.

To Create Labels

In Access, labels are a special type of report. Therefore, you create labels just as you create reports. The Label Wizard assists you in the process. Using the wizard, you can specify the type and dimensions of the label, the font used for the label, and the content of the label. The following steps create the labels.

1

- Show the Navigation Pane and select the Client table.

- Click Create on the Ribbon to display the Create tab.

- Click the Labels button on the Ribbon to display the Label Wizard dialog box.

- Ensure that English is selected as the Unit of Measure and that Avery is selected in the "Filter by manufacturer" box.

- Click C2163 in the Product number list (Figure 7–72).

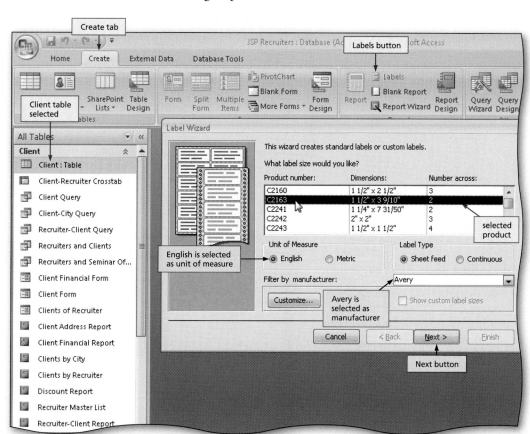

Figure 7–72

- Click the Next button (Figure 7–73).

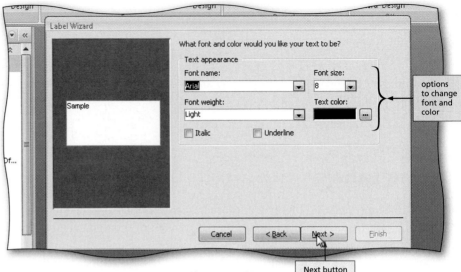

Figure 7–73

- Click the Next button to accept the default font and color settings.

- Click the Client Name field and then click the Add Field button (Figure 7–74).

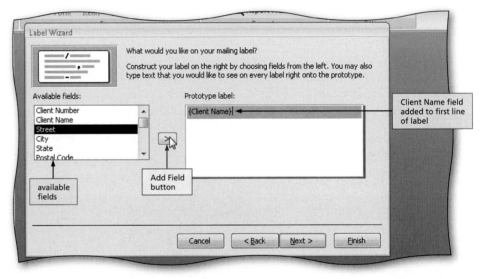

Figure 7–74

- Click the second line in the label, and then add the Street field.

- Click the third line of the label.

- Add the City field, type , (a comma), press the SPACEBAR, add the State field, press the SPACEBAR, and then add the Postal Code field (Figure 7–75).

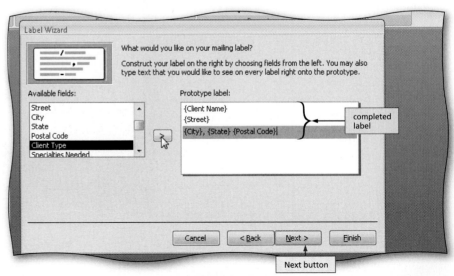

Figure 7–75

5

- Because the label now is complete, click the Next button.

- Select the Postal Code field as the field to sort by, and then click the Add Field button (Figure 7–76).

Q&A Why am I sorting by postal code?

When you need to do a bulk mailing, that is, mail a large number of items using a special mail rate, mail organizations require that the mail be sorted in postal code order.

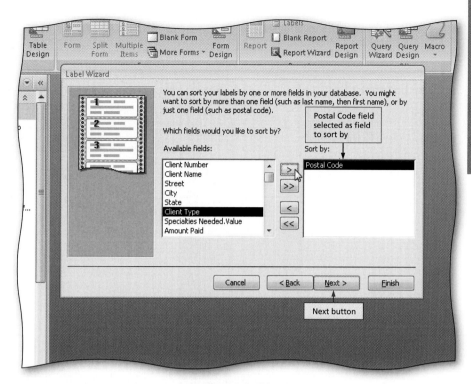

Figure 7–76

6

- Click the Next button.

- Ensure the name for the report (that is, the labels) is Labels Client (Figure 7–77).

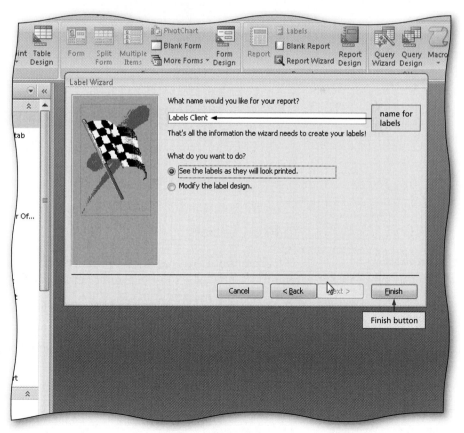

Figure 7–77

7
- Click the Finish button to complete the labels (Figure 7–78).

8
- Close the Labels Client report.

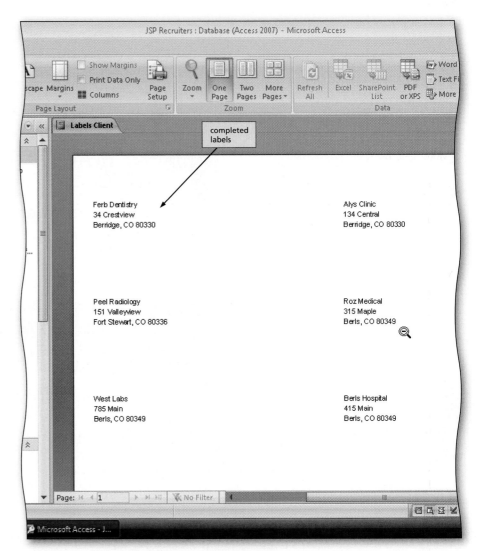

Figure 7–78

To Print Labels

You print labels just as you print a report. The only difference is that you would want to load the labels in the printer before printing. The following steps print the labels.

1 Show the Navigation Pane and ensure the Labels Client report is selected and then click the Office Button to display the Microsoft Office menu.

2 Point to Print on the Office Button menu and then click Quick Print on the Print submenu to print the report.

Q&A I want to load the correct number of labels. How do I know how many pages of labels will print?

If you are unsure how many pages of labels will print, open the labels in Print Preview first. Use the Navigation buttons in the status bar of the Print Preview window to determine how many pages of labels will print.

To Quit Access

BTW

Quick Reference
For a table that lists how to complete the tasks covered in this book using the mouse, Ribbon, shortcut menu, and keyboard, see the Quick Reference Summary at the back of this book, or visit the Access 2007 Quick Reference Web page (scsite.com/ac2007/qr).

You saved all your changes and are ready to quit Access. The following step quits Access.

 Click the Close button on the right side of the Access title bar to quit Access.

Chapter Summary

In this chapter you have learned to change captions; create queries for a report; create reports in Design view; add fields and text boxes to a report; format controls; group and ungroup controls; update multiple controls; add and modify a subreport; modify section properties; add a title, page number, and date; add totals and subtotals; use a function in a text box; and create and print mailing labels. The following list includes all the new Access skills you have learned in this chapter.

1. Change a Caption (AC 462)
2. Create a Query for the Report (AC 462)
3. Create an Additional Query for the Report (AC 463)
4. Create an Initial Report in Design View (AC 466)
5. Add Fields to the Report (AC 469)
6. Add Text Boxes (AC 471)
7. View the Report (AC 475)
8. Format a Control (AC 475)
9. Group Controls (AC 476)
10. Ungroup Controls (AC 477)
11. Update Grouped Controls (AC 478)
12. Update Multiple Controls that are not Grouped (AC 480)
13. Add a Subreport (AC 482)
14. Open the Subreport in Design View (AC 484)
15. Modify the Controls in the Subreport (AC 486)
16. Change the Can Grow Property (AC 487)
17. Change the Appearance of the Controls in the Subreport (AC 488)
18. Resize the Subreport and the Report (AC 488)
19. Modify Section Properties (AC 489)
20. Add a Title, Page Number, and Date (AC 490)
21. Create a Second Report (AC 492)
22. Add a Field to the Report (AC 493)
23. Add the Remaining Fields (AC 495)
24. Resize the Detail Section (AC 497)
25. Add Totals and Subtotals (AC 498)
26. Assign a Conditional Value (AC 503)
27. Change the Report Margins (AC 508)
28. Make Room for Resizing or Additional Controls (AC 508)
29. Create Labels (AC 509)
30. Print Labels (AC 512)

 If you have a SAM user profile, you may have access to hands-on instruction, practice, and assessment. Log in to your SAM account (http://sam2007.course.com) to launch any assigned training activities or exams that relate to the skills covered in this chapter.

Learn It Online

Test your knowledge of chapter content and key terms.

Instructions: To complete the Learn It Online exercises, start your browser, click the Address bar, and then enter the Web address `scsite.com/ac2007/learn`. When the Access 2007 Learn It Online page is displayed, click the link for the exercise you want to complete and then read the instructions.

Chapter Reinforcement TF, MC, and SA
A series of true/false, multiple choice, and short answer questions that test your knowledge of the chapter content.

Flash Cards
An interactive learning environment where you identify chapter key terms associated with displayed definitions.

Practice Test
A series of multiple choice questions that test your knowledge of chapter content and key terms.

Who Wants To Be a Computer Genius?
An interactive game that challenges your knowledge of chapter content in the style of a television quiz show.

Wheel of Terms
An interactive game that challenges your knowledge of chapter key terms in the style of the television show *Wheel of Fortune*.

Crossword Puzzle Challenge
A crossword puzzle that challenges your knowledge of key terms presented in the chapter.

Apply Your Knowledge

Reinforce the skills and apply the concepts you learned in this chapter.

Creating a Report with a Subreport
Instructions: Start Access. If you are using the Microsoft Office Access 2007 Comprehensive text, open The Bike Delivers database that you used in Chapter 6. Otherwise, see your instructor for information on accessing the files required in this book.

Perform the following tasks:
1. Create a query that joins the Courier and Customer tables. Include the Courier Number, First Name, and Last Name fields from the Courier table. Include all fields except the courier number from the Customer table. Save the query as Couriers and Customers.

2. Create a query that joins the Weekly Services and Services Offered tables. Include the Customer Number, Service Code from the Weekly Services table, Service Date, Service Time, and Service Fee. Save the query as Weekly Services and Descriptions.

3. Create the report shown in Figure 7–79. The report uses the two queries that you created in steps 1 and 2. Use the name, Courier Master List, for the report. The report is in the same style as the Recruiter Master List shown in Figure 7–1a on page AC 459.

4. Submit the revised database in the format specified by your instructor.

Courier Master List

Page 1   4/25/2008

Courier Number   102   **Courier Name: Chou Dang**

Customer Number: | AS36 |

Customer Name: | Asterman Ind. | Telephone Number: | 555-2050 |

Street: | 200 Bard | Balance: | $185.00 |

Service Code	Service Description	Service Date	Service Time	Service Fee
01	Medical Supplies Delivery	4/7/2008	9:30 AM	$10.00
01	Medical Supplies Delivery	4/7/2008	1:15 PM	$10.00

Customer Number: | CJ16 |

Customer Name: | CJ Gallery | Telephone Number: | 555-1304 |

Street: | 277 Fordham | Balance: | $195.00 |

Service Code	Service Description	Service Date	Service Time	Service Fee
02	Post Office Pick-up or Delivery	4/9/2008	3:30 PM	$7.00
04	Document Delivery	4/9/2008	11:00 AM	$6.50

Customer Number: | ME71 |

Customer Name: | Mentor Group | Telephone Number: | 555-4110 |

Street: | 543 Fleming | Balance: | $138.00 |

Service Code	Service Description	Service Date	Service Time	Service Fee
04	Document Delivery	4/11/2008	10:00 AM	$6.50

Figure 7–79

Extend Your Knowledge

Extend the skills you learned in this chapter and experiment with new skills. You may need to use Help to complete the assignment.

Modifying Reports

Instructions: Copy the JSP Recruiters database and rename the database to your last name. For example, if your last name is Smith, then name the database Smith Recruiters. Start Access and open the database that you copied and renamed.

Perform the following tasks:

1. Open the Recruiter Master List in Design view. Add your name to the report footer. Your name should appear at the left.

2. Change the report title from Recruiter Master List to Recruiter/Seminar Master List. Change the font color to red and underline the title.

3. Open the Discount Report in Design view. Calculate the average, maximum, and minimum aggregate statistics for both the amount paid and current due columns. These statistics should be displayed in the report footer. Include an appropriate label for the statistics.

4. Submit the revised database in the format specified by your instructor.

Make It Right

Analyze a database and correct all errors and/or improve the design.

Correcting Form Design Errors

Instructions: Start Access. Open the InPerson Fitness database. See the inside back cover of this book for instructions on downloading the Data Files for Students, or contact your instructor for more information about accessing the required files.

The InPerson Fitness database contains data about an organization that does personal fitness training in an individual's home. The owner of the company has created the report shown in Figure 7–80, but there are a few problems. She really wanted to concatenate the first and last name of the trainer. The title of the report should appear in the report header, not in the page header. She wants to know the total amount for each client. Finally, she would like to add page numbers and a date to the report.

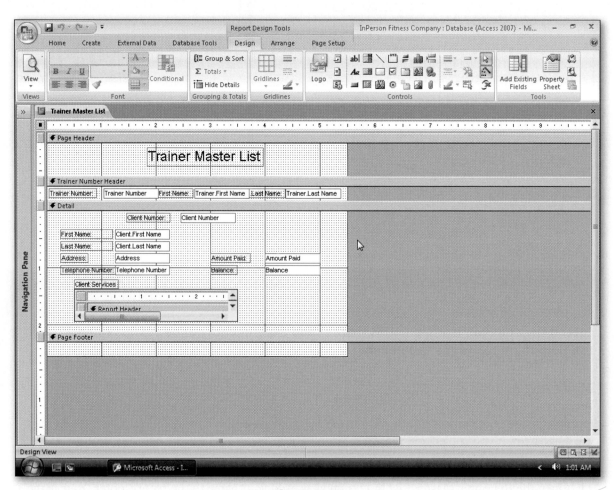

Figure 7–80

Correct these errors and submit the revised database in the format specified by your instructor.

In the Lab

Design, create, modify, and/or use a database following the guidelines, concepts, and skills presented in this chapter. Labs are listed in order of increasing difficulty.

Lab 1: Creating Reports and Mailing Labels for the JMS TechWizards Database

Problem: JMS TechWizards needs a report that displays technician information as well as information about client accounts. The company would like to show its appreciation to current clients by discounting the amount clients currently owe. JMS also needs mailing labels for its clients.

Instructions: If you are using the Microsoft Office Access 2007 Comprehensive text, open the JMS TechWizards database that you used in Chapter 6. Otherwise, see the inside back cover of this book for instructions on downloading the Data Files for Students, or contact your instructor for more information about accessing the required files.

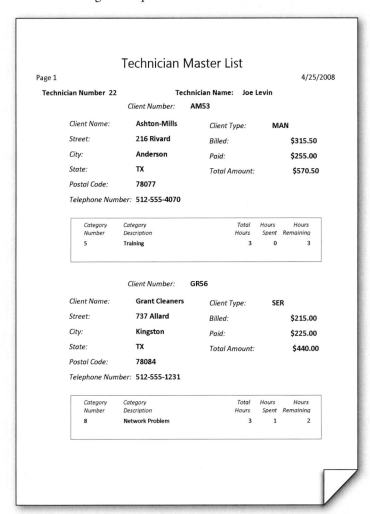

Figure 7–81

Perform the following tasks:

1. Create a query that includes the technician number, first name and last name from the Technician table and all the fields from the Client table except technician number. Name the query, Technicians and Clients.

2. Create a query that joins the Category and the Work Orders tables. Include the client number, category number, category description, total hours, and hours spent. Create a calculated field that subtracts hours spent from total hours. Use Hours Remaining as the caption for the field. Name the query, Categories and Work Orders.

3. Create the report shown in Figure 7–81. The report uses the Technicians and Clients query as the basis for the main report and the Categories and Work Orders query as the basis for the subreport. Use the name, Technician Master List, for the report. The report is similar in style to the Recruiter Master List shown in Figure 7–1a on page AC 459.

4. Create mailing labels for the Technician table. Use Avery labels C2163 and format the label with first and last name on the first line, street on the second line, and city, state, and postal code on the third line. There is a comma and a space after city and a space between state and postal code. Sort the labels by postal code.

5. Submit the revised database in the format specified by your instructor.

In the Lab

Lab 2: Creating Reports for the Hockey Fan Zone Database

Problem: The management of the Hockey Fan Zone store needs a report that displays supplier information as well information about items and the order status of items. The company also is considering an in-store sale and would like a report that shows the regular selling price as well as the sale price of all items.

Instructions: If you are using the Microsoft Office Access 2007 Comprehensive text, open the Hockey Fan Zone database that you used in Chapter 6. Otherwise, see the inside back cover of this book for instructions on downloading the Data Files for Students, or contact your instructor for more information about accessing the required files.

Perform the following tasks:

1. Create the report shown in Figure 7–82. The report uses the Supplier-Item Query that previously was created as the basis for the main report and the Reorder table as the basis for the subreport. Use the name, Supplier Master Report, for the report. The report is the same style as that demonstrated in the project. Use conditional formatting to display the on hand value in red for all items with fewer than 10 items on hand.

2. Open the Supplier-Item Query in Design view and add the Selling Price field to the query. Save the query.

3. Create the report shown in Figure 7–83. The report uses the Supplier-Item Query and calculates the sale amount for each item. Items with a selling price greater than $15.00 have a 10 percent discount and 5 percent otherwise. Note that the report shows the sale price, not the discount. The report is similar to the Discount Report shown in Figure 7–1b on page AC 459. However, there are no group subtotals or report totals. Use the name, Item Discount Report.

4. Submit the revised database in the format specified by your instructor.

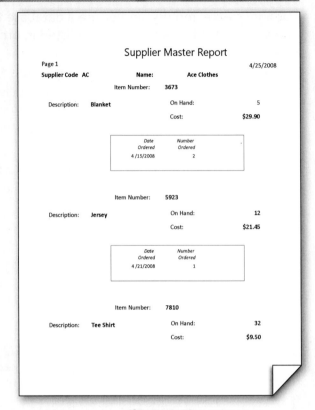

Figure 7–82

Item Discount Report

Supplier Code	Supplier Name	Item Number	Description	Cost	Selling Price	Sale Price
AC	Ace Clothes					
		3673	Blanket	$29.90	$34.00	$30.60
		5923	Jersey	$21.45	$24.75	$22.28
		7810	Tee Shirt	$9.50	$14.95	$14.20
LG	Logo Goods					
		3663	Ball Cap	$11.15	$18.95	$17.06
		4563	Earrings	$4.50	$7.00	$6.65
		7550	Sweatshirt	$19.90	$22.95	$20.66
		7930	Visor	$11.95	$17.00	$15.30
MN	Mary's Novelti					
		3683	Bumper Sticker	$0.95	$1.50	$1.43
		6078	Key Chain	$3.00	$5.00	$4.75
		6189	Koozies	$2.00	$4.00	$3.80
		6343	Note Cube	$5.75	$8.00	$7.60

Figure 7–83

In the Lab

Lab 3: Creating Reports for the Ada Beauty Supply Database

Problem: Ada Beauty Supply needs a report that displays sales rep information as well as information about customers and any open orders that the customer has. The company also needs mailing labels for its sales reps.

Instructions: If you are using the Microsoft Office Access 2007 Comprehensive text, open the Ada Beauty Supply database that you used in Chapter 6. Otherwise, see the inside back cover of this book for instructions on downloading the Data Files for Students, or contact your instructor for more information about accessing the required files. Submit the revised database in the format specified by your instructor.

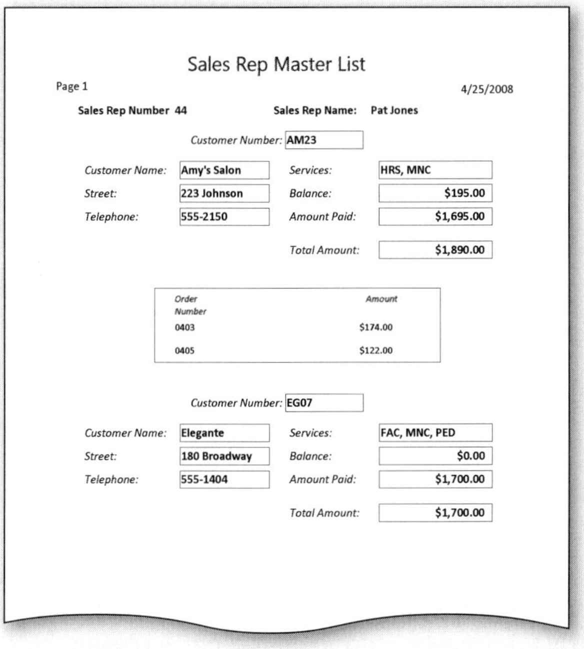

Figure 7–84

Instructions Part 1:   In the Customer table, change the caption for the Services Offered field to Services. Create a query that includes the sales rep number, first name, and last name from the Sales Rep table and all fields from the Customer table except the sales rep number. Use the name, Reps and Customers, for the query.

Instructions Part 2:   Create the report shown in Figure 7–84. The report is similar in style to the Recruiter Master List shown in Figure 7–1a on page AC 459.

Instructions Part 3:   Create mailing labels for the Sales Rep table. Use Avery labels C2163 and format the label with first and last name on the first line, street on the second line, and city, state, and postal code on the third line. There is a comma and a space after city and a space between state and postal code. Use a font size of 10 and a font weight of semi-bold. Sort the labels by postal code.

Cases and Places

Apply your creative thinking and problem solving skills to design and implement a solution.

• EASIER   •• MORE DIFFICULT

• 1: Creating Reports for the Second Hand Goods Database

If you are using the Microsoft Office Access 2007 Comprehensive text, open the Second Hand Goods database that you used in Chapter 6. Otherwise, see the inside back cover of this book for instructions on downloading the Data Files for Students, or contact your instructor for more information about accessing the required files. Create a report that is similar in style to the Discount Report shown in Figure 7–1b on page AC 459. Group the report by seller code and include the seller's first name and last name. The detail section should include the item number, description, date posted, and price. Create a calculated control, Sale Price, that displays the sale price (not the discount) for all items. Items that have a price of $10.00 or more will have a 5 percent discount. Items that have a price of less than $10.00 will have a 3 percent discount. Name the report Item Sale Report. Select your own fonts for the report. Filter the report to find all items that have a price less than $10. Print the filtered report and

Continued >

Cases and Places *continued*

then remove the filter. Submit the revised database and the printed filtered report in the format specified by your instructor.

• 2: Creating Reports and Mailing Labels for the BeachCondo Rentals Database

If you are using the Microsoft Office Access 2007 Comprehensive text, open the BeachCondo Rentals database that you used in Chapter 6. Otherwise, see the inside back cover of this book for instructions on downloading the Data Files for Students, or contact your instructor for more information about accessing the required files. Create a report that is similar in style to the Recruiter Master List shown in Figure 7–1a on page AC 459. You will need two queries for the report. The first query should include the owner code, owner first and last name, unit number, and weekly rate. The second query should include the renter number, renter first and last name, unit number, start date, and length. Group the report by owner and display the unit number and weekly rate in the detail section. Include a subreport with information about the current rentals using the second query. Create mailing labels for the Owner table. Submit the revised database in the format specified by your instructor.

•• 3: Creating Reports for the Restaurant Database

If you are using the Microsoft Office Access 2007 Comprehensive text, open the restaurant database that you used in Chapter 6. Otherwise, see the inside back cover of this book for instructions on downloading the Data Files for Students, or contact your instructor for more information about accessing the required files. Using the Plan Ahead guidelines presented in this chapter, determine what additional reports you need for your database. For example, you want to prepare listings of restaurants for conference attendees. These listings are really reports. How should the reports be organized? What data should appear in the reports? Are subreports needed? Do you want to create listings grouped by food type, by distance from the university, or by cost?

•• 4: Creating Reports for Your Contacts Database

Make It Personal

If you are using the Microsoft Office Access 2007 Comprehensive text, open the Contacts database that you used in Chapter 6. Otherwise, see the inside back cover of this book for instructions on downloading the Data Files for Students, or contact your instructor for more information about accessing the required files. Using the Plan Ahead guidelines presented in this chapter, determine what additional reports you need for your database. Do these reports require subreports? For example, if you have contacted several individuals at the same company, you may want to display the names of the individuals in a subreport. Concatenate the first and last names of the individuals to give the report a professional appearance.

•• 5: Understanding Reports

Working Together

Copy the JSP Recruiters database and rename the database to your team name. For example if your team is FabFour, then name the database FabFour Recruiters. As a team, design an appropriate company letterhead for the Recruiter Master List and the Discount Report. Try different fonts and incorporate a picture or clip art. Modify the report header sections in both reports to accommodate the letterhead. Add a label to the page footer section that includes the names of the team members.

8 | Advanced Form Techniques

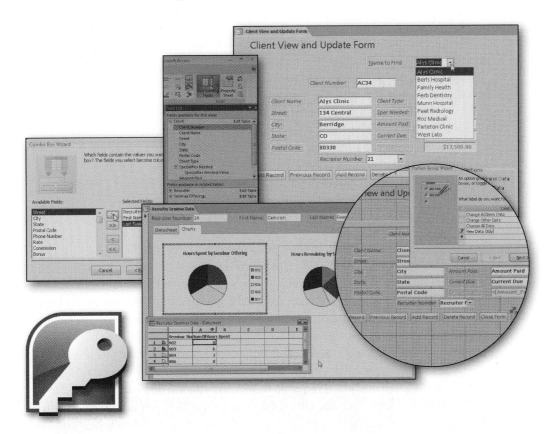

Objectives

You will have mastered the material in this project when you can:

- Create a form in Design view
- Add a calculated field
- Add combo boxes that include selection lists and search boxes
- Format and resize controls
- Add command buttons to a form
- Modify buttons and combo boxes
- Add an option group and create a macro for the option group

- Use tab controls to create a multipage form
- Add and modify a subform
- Insert charts
- Modify a chart type
- Format a chart

8 | Advanced Form Techniques

Introduction

This chapter creates two new forms. The first form contains two combo boxes, one for selecting data from a related table and one for finding a record on the form. It also contains command buttons to accomplish various tasks as well as an **option group**, a rectangle containing a collection of option buttons. For the command buttons and the option group to function correctly, you will create macros. In addition to the actions, the macro for the option group also contains conditions.

You also will create a **multipage form**, a form that contains more than one page of information. The form contains a tab control that allows you access two different pages. Clicking the first tab displays a page containing a subform. Clicking the second tab displays a page containing two charts.

Project — Advanced Form Techniques

JSP Recruiters wants two additional forms to use with its Client and Recruiters tables. The first form, Client View and Update Form (Figure 8–1a), contains the fields in the Client table as well as the Total Amount, which is the sum of the amount paid and the current due. Because users should not update the total amount, it appears dim on the form. Users cannot tab to it, nor will clicking it have any effect. The form has several command buttons: Next Record, Previous Record, Add Record, Delete Record, and Close Form. Clicking any of these buttons causes the action indicated on the button to take place.

In the lower-right corner of the form is an option group called Form Options. Users can click one of the options to indicate the portion of the form they wish to be able to update. If they click the Change Address Data option button, for example, they would be able to update the client number, the client name, the street, the city, the state, and the postal code, but no other data related to the client. All other fields would be dim, just like Total Amount. This restriction prevents users from inadvertently changing something they should not change.

The form also contains a combo box for the Recruiter Number field that assists users in selecting the correct recruiter (Figure 8–1b).

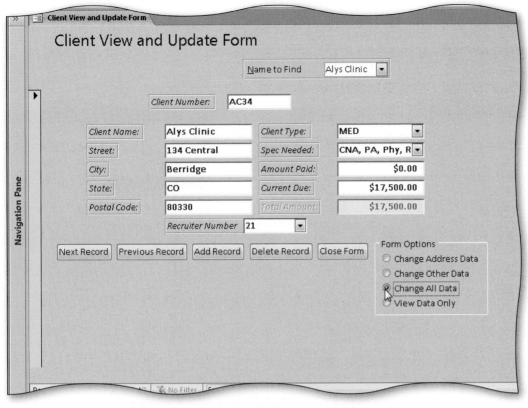

Figure 8–1a Form with Total Amount dimmed

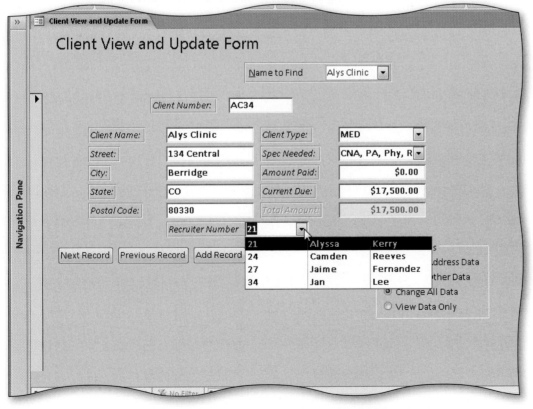

Figure 8–1b Using combo box control for Recruiter Number

To assist users in finding a client when they know the client's name, the form also includes a combo box they can use for this purpose (Figure 8–1c). After clicking the arrow, the user simply can click the client they wish to find and Access will locate the client (Figure 8–1d) and display that client's data in the form.

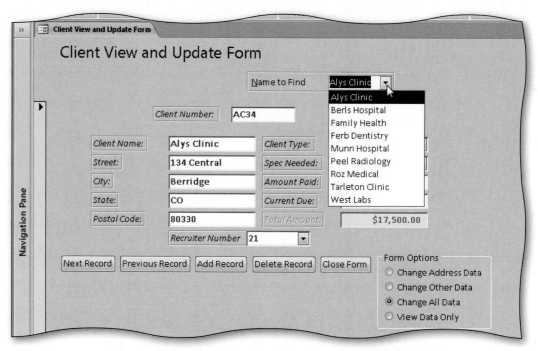

Figure 8–1c Using combo box to search for Client Name

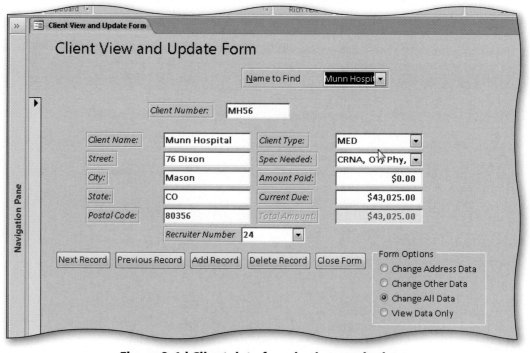

Figure 8–1d Client data found using combo box

For the second new form, JSP Recruiters needs a multipage form that lists the number and name of recruiters. Selecting the first tab, the one labeled Datasheet, displays a subform listing information about the seminar offerings for clients of the recruiter (Figure 8–2a).

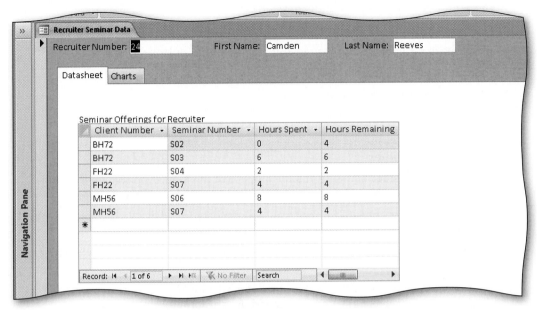

Figure 8–2a

Selecting the other tab, the one labeled Charts, displays two charts that illustrate the total hours spent and hours remaining by the recruiter for the various seminars (Figure 8–2b). In both charts, the slices of the pie represent the various seminars. They are color-coded and the legend at the bottom indicates the meaning of the various colors. The size of the pie gives a visual representation of the portion of the hours spent or hours remaining by the recruiter for that particular seminar. The chart also includes specific percentages. If you look at the bottom (light blue) slice in the Hours Spent by Seminar Offering, for example, you see that the color indicates it represents seminar S06. It represents 34 percent of the total. Thus, for all the hours already spent on the various seminar offerings by recruiter 24, 34 percent have been spent on seminar S06.

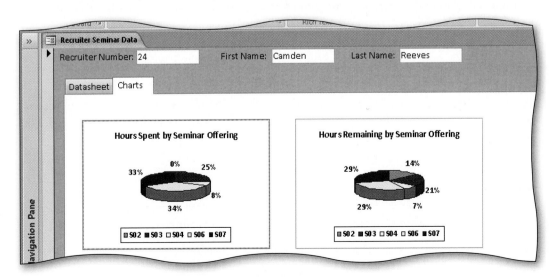

Figure 8–2b

Overview

As you read through this chapter, you will learn how to create the forms by performing these general tasks:

- Create a form with a calculated field, a combo box for finding records in a related table, and a combo box for finding a record.
- Add command buttons and an option group to the form.
- Create macros for the option group and for one of the buttons.
- Create a form with a tab control.
- Add a subform to one of the tabbed pages.
- Add charts to the other tabbed page.

Plan Ahead

Form Design Guidelines

1. **Determine the intended audience and the purpose of the form.** Who will use the form? How will they use it? What data do they need? What level of detail do they need?

2. **Determine the source of data for the form.** Is all the data found in a single table, or does it come from multiple related tables? Which table or tables contain the data?

3. **Determine the fields that belong on the form.** What data items are needed by the user of the form?

4. **Determine any calculations required for the form.** Should the form contain any special calculations? For example, the Client View and Update Form contains a Total Amount field that is calculated by adding the contents of the Amount Paid field and the Current Due field.

5. **Determine the organization of the form along with any additional items that should be on the form.** In what order should the fields appear? How should they be arranged? Should the form contain a subform? Should the form contain a chart? Should the form contain command buttons to assist the user in performing various functions? Should the form contain a combo box to assist the user in searching for a record?

6. **Determine the format and style of the form.** What should be in the form heading? Do you want a title, for example? Do you want a logo? What should be in the body of the form? What should the style be? In other words, what visual characteristics should the various portions of the form have?

When necessary, more specific details concerning the above decisions and/or actions are presented at appropriate points in the chapter. The chapter also will identify the use of these guidelines in the design of the forms such as the ones shown in Figure 8–1 on pages AC 523 and AC 524.

Starting Access

If you are using a computer to step through the project in this chapter and you want your screen to match the figures in this book, you should change your screen's resolution to 1024 × 768. For information about how to change a computer's resolution, read Appendix E.

To Start Access

The following steps, which assume Windows Vista is running, start Access.

Note: If you are using Windows XP, see Appendix F for alternate steps.

1 Click the Start button on the Windows Vista taskbar to display the Start menu.

2 Click All Programs at the bottom of the left pane on the Start menu to display the All Programs list and then click Microsoft Office on the All Programs list to display the Microsoft Office list.

3 Click Microsoft Office Access 2007 on the Microsoft Office list to start Access and display the Getting Started with Microsoft Office Access window.

4 If the Access window is not maximized, click the Maximize button on its title bar to maximize the window.

To Open a Database

In Chapter 1, you created your database on a USB flash drive using the file name, JSP Recruiters. There are two ways to open the file containing your database. If the file you created appears in the Recent Documents list, you could click it to open the file. If not, you can use the More button to open the file. The following steps use the More button to open the JSP Recruiters database from the USB flash drive.

Note: If you are using Windows XP, see Appendix F for alternate steps.

1 With your USB flash drive connected to one of the computer's USB ports, click the More button to display the Open dialog box.

2 If the Folders list is displayed below the Folders button, click the Folders button to remove the Folders list.

3 If necessary, click Computers in the Favorite Links section and then double-click UDISK 2.0 (E:) to select the USB flash drive, Drive E in this case, as the new open location. (Your drive letter might be different.)

4 Click JSP Recruiters to select the file name.

5 Click the Open button to open the database.

6 If a Security Warning appears, click the Options button to display the Microsoft Office Security Options dialog box.

7 With the option button to enable the content selected, click the OK button to enable the content.

Plan Ahead

Determine the fields that belong on the form.

1. **Examine the requirements for the form in general to determine the tables.** Do the requirements only relate to data in a single table, or does the data come from multiple tables? How are the tables related?

2. **Examine the specific requirements for the form to determine the fields necessary.** Look for all the data items that are specified for the form. Each should correspond to a field in a table or be able to be computed from a field in a table. This information gives you the list of fields.

3. **Determine whether there are any special calculations required.** Are there any special calculations? What are they? What fields are involved and how are they to be combined?

> **Determine the organization of the form.**
>
> 1. **Determine the order of the fields.** Examine the requirements to determine the order in which the fields should appear. Be logical and consistent in your ordering. For example, in an address, the city should come before the state and the state should come before the postal code, unless there is some compelling reason for another order.
>
> 2. **Determine whether to include a subform.** If the fields for the form come from exactly two tables and there is a one-to-many relationship between the two tables and if the form is based on the "one" table, you often will place the data for the "many" table in a subform. If there are multiple tables involved, you may be able to create a query on which you can base the subform.
>
> 3. **Determine whether to include a chart.** Do you want to represent data in a visual manner? If so, you can include a chart. If you do decide to use a chart, which type of chart would best represent the data? If you want to represent total amounts, for example, a bar chart may be appropriate. If, instead, you want to represent portions of the whole, a pie chart may be better.

> **Determine any additional items that should be on the form.**
>
> 1. **Determine whether the form should include any combo boxes.** A combo box is a combination of a text box, where users can type data, and a list box, where users can click an arrow to display a list. Would a combo box improve the functionality of the form? Is there a place where it would be convenient for users to enter data by selecting the data from a list, either a list of predefined items or a list of values from a related table? If users need to search for records, you may wish to include a combo box to assist in the process.
>
> 2. **Determine whether the form should include any command buttons.** Can you make certain actions more convenient for users by including command buttons? Buttons can carry out record navigation actions (for example, go to the next record), record operation actions (for example, add a record), form operation actions (for example, close a form), report operation actions (for example, print a report), an application action (for example, quit application), and some miscellaneous actions (for example, run a macro).
>
> 3. **Determine whether the form should contain any option groups.** If users are to select from a list of predefined choices, you can consider adding an option group. If, for example, there are different ways users might choose to interact with the form, you could include an option group. In the Client View and Update Form, for example, there is an option group in which users can select the portion of the form they will be able to update.
>
> 4. **Determine whether the form should contain a tab control.** If the form contains more information than conveniently will fit on the screen at a time, consider adding a tab control. With a tab control, you can organize the information within a collection of tabbed pages. To access any of the tabbed pages, users need only click the corresponding tab.

Creating a Form with Combo Boxes, Command Buttons, and Option Groups

After planning a form, you may decide that you need to use features such as combo boxes, command buttons, and option groups. You can include such items while modifying the form in Design view. Selecting the Use Control Wizards button on the Design tab activates a wizard that will assist you in the process.

To Create a Form in Design View

You can create a form using several different form tools, such as the Form Wizard and the Split Form. Creating a form in Design view gives you the most flexibility in laying out the form. You will be presented with a blank design on which to place objects. The following steps create a form in Design view.

- Click Create on the Ribbon to display the Create tab.

- Click Form Design on the Create tab to create a new form in Design view.

- Hide the Navigation Pane.

- Click the Property Sheet button on the Design tab to display a property sheet.

- With the All tab selected, click the Record Source property, click the arrow, and then click the Client table to select the Client table as the record source.

- Click the Save button on the Quick Access Toolbar, then type `Client Master Form` as the form name (Figure 8–3).

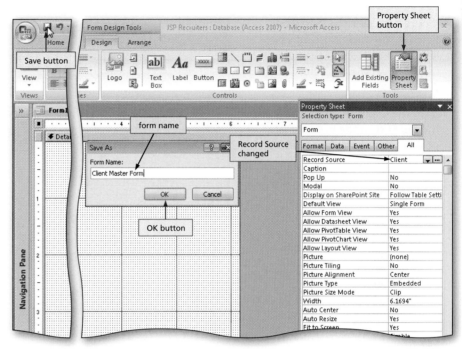

Figure 8–3

- Click the OK button to save the form.

- Click the Caption property in the property sheet, and then type `Client View and Update Form` as the new caption.

- Close the property sheet by clicking the Property Sheet button on the Design tab.

- Click the Add Existing Fields button to display the Field List (Figure 8–4).

Why doesn't the name on the tab change to the new caption, Client View and Update Form?

The name on the tab will change to the new caption in Form view. In Design view, you still see the name of the form.

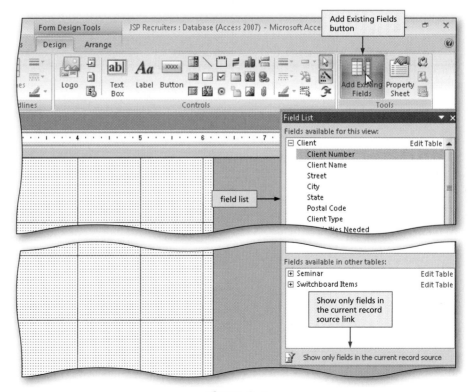

Figure 8–4

To Add Fields to the Form Design

After deciding the fields to add to the Client View and Update Form, you can place them on the form by dragging the fields from the field list to the desired position. The following steps place all the fields except the Recruiter Number field on the form.

- If necessary, click the 'Show only fields in the current record source' link at the bottom of the field list to show only the fields in the Client table.

- Drag the Client Number field from the field list to the approximate position shown in Figure 8–5.

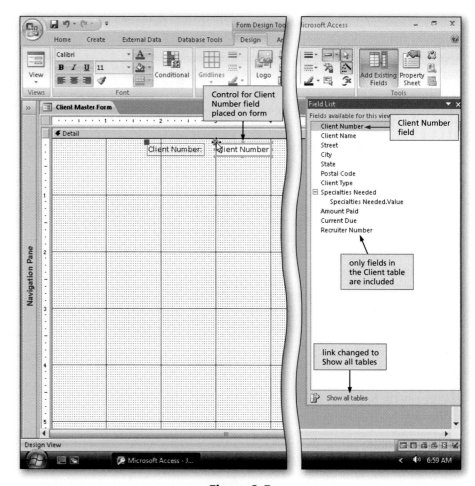

Figure 8–5

- Click the Client Name field in the field list.

- While holding the SHIFT key down, click the Postal Code field in the field list to select multiple fields (Figure 8–6).

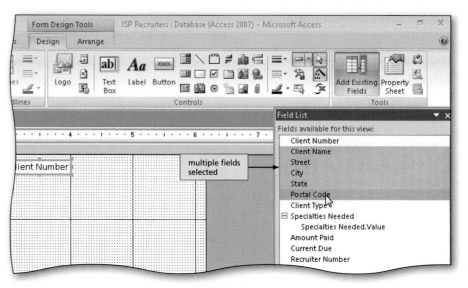

Figure 8–6

- Drag the selected fields to the approximate position shown in Figure 8–7.

- Select the Client Type through Current Due fields and then drag the selected fields to the approximate position shown in the figure.

- If controls for any of the fields are not aligned properly, align them by dragging them to the desired location or by using the alignment buttons on the Arrange tab.

- Close the field list.

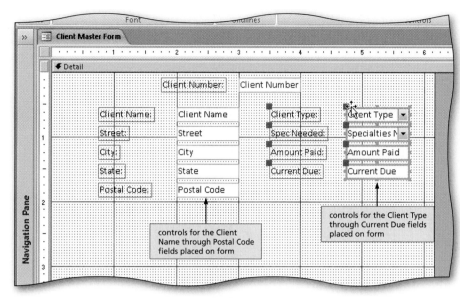

Figure 8–7

To Add a Calculated Field to the Form

If you have determined that a calculated field is appropriate for a form, you can create one by using the Text Box tool in the Controls group on the Design tab. Place the text box on the form, and then indicate the contents of the field.

The following steps add the Total Amount field to the form. The total amount is calculated by adding the contents of the Amount Paid field and the contents of the Current Due field.

1

- Click the Text Box tool in the Controls group on the Design tab, and then move the mouse pointer, which has changed shape to a small plus symbol accompanied by a text box, to the position shown in Figure 8–8.

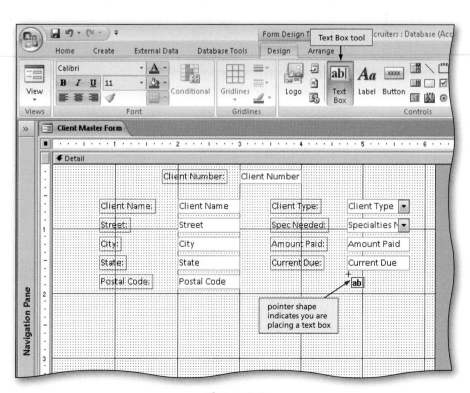

Figure 8–8

2

- Click the position shown in Figure 8–8 on the previous page to place a text box.

- Click inside the text box and type `=[Amount Paid]+[Current Due]` as the expression in the text box.

- Click the attached label (the box that contains the word, Text) twice, once to select it and a second time to produce an insertion point.

- Use the DELETE key or the BACKSPACE key to delete the current entry.

- Type `Total Amount:` as the new entry (Figure 8–9).

Q&A

Could I use the expression builder instead to create the calculation?

Yes. Click the field, click the Property Sheet button on the Design tab, and then click the Build button (the three dots). You then can use the expression builder to create the expression. Use whichever method you find most convenient.

3

- Ensure that the newly added text box aligns properly with the other controls as shown in Figure 8–9.

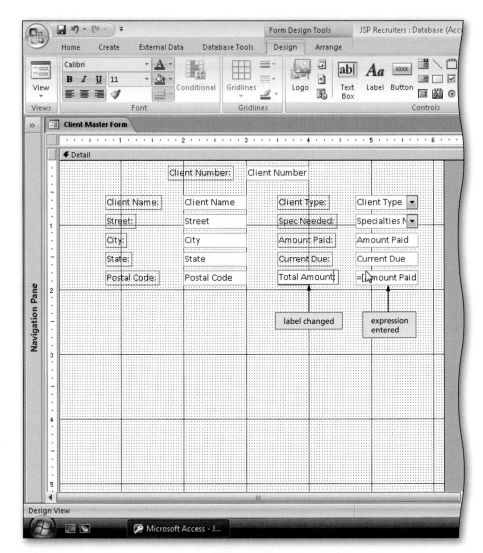

Figure 8–9

To Change the Format of a Field

Access automatically formats fields from the database appropriately because it knows their data types. Usually, you will find the formats assigned by Access to be acceptable. For calculated fields, such as Total Amount, however, Access just assigns a general number format. The value will not appear automatically with two decimal places and a dollar sign.

To change to another format, such as Currency, which displays the number with a dollar sign and two decimal places, use the field's property sheet to change the Format property. The following steps change the format for the Total Amount field to Currency.

- Click the control for the Total Amount field (the box containing the expression), and then click the Property Sheet button to display the property sheet.

- With the All tab selected, click the Format property, click the Format property box arrow to produce a list of available formats, and then select Currency.

- Click the Decimal Places property, click the Decimal Places property box arrow, and then select 2 (Figure 8–10).

- Close the property sheet by clicking the Property Sheet button on the Design tab.

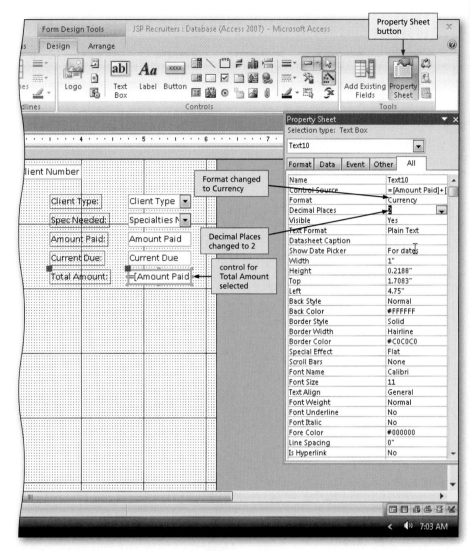

Figure 8–10

Combo Boxes

When entering a recruiter number, the value must match the number of a recruiter currently in the Recruiter table. To assist the users in entering this data, the form will contain a combo box. A **combo box** combines the properties of a **text box**, a box into which you can type an entry, and a **list box**, a box you can use to display a list. With a combo box, the user either can enter the data or click the combo box arrow to display a list of possible values and then select an item from the list.

To Add a Combo Box that Selects Values from a Related Table

If you have determined that a combo box that selects values from a related table would be useful on your form, you can add the combo box to a form using the Combo Box tool in the Controls group on the Design tab. If the Use Control Wizards button in the Controls group on the Design tab is selected, you can use a wizard to guide you through the process of creating the combo box. The following steps place a combo box that selects values from a related table for the Recruiter Number field on the form.

- With the Use Control Wizards button in the Controls group on the Design tab selected, click the Combo Box (Form Control) tool in the Controls group, and then move the mouse pointer, whose shape has changed to a small plus symbol accompanied by a combo box, to the position shown in Figure 8–11.

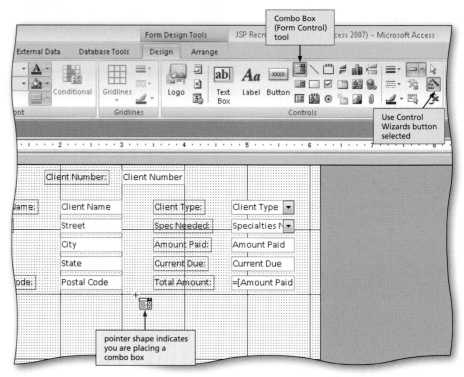

Figure 8–11

- Click the position shown in Figure 8–11 to place a combo box.

- If necessary, in the Combo Box Wizard dialog box, click the 'I want the combo box to look up the values in a table or query.' option button (Figure 8–12).

Q&A

What is the purpose of the other options?

Use the second option if you want to type a list from which the user will choose. Use the third option if you want to use the combo box to search for a record.

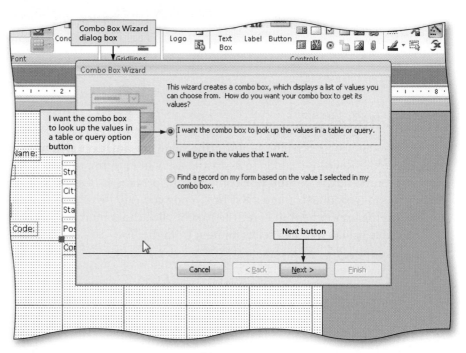

Figure 8–12

3

- Click the Next button and then, with the Tables option button selected, click Table: Recruiter to specify that the combo box values will come from the Recruiter table (Figure 8–13).

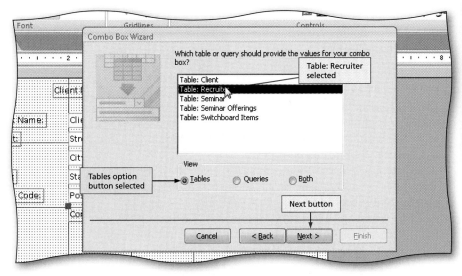

Figure 8–13

4

- Click the Next button to display the next Combo Box Wizard screen.
- Click the Add Field button to add the Recruiter Number as a field in the combo box.
- Click the First Name field and then click the Add Field button.
- Click the Last Name field and then click the Add Field button (Figure 8–14).

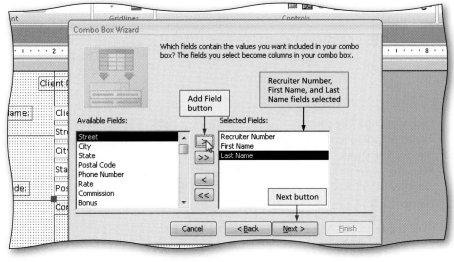

Figure 8–14

5

- Click the Next button to display the next Combo Box Wizard screen.
- Click the arrow in the first text box, and then select the Recruiter Number field (Figure 8–15).

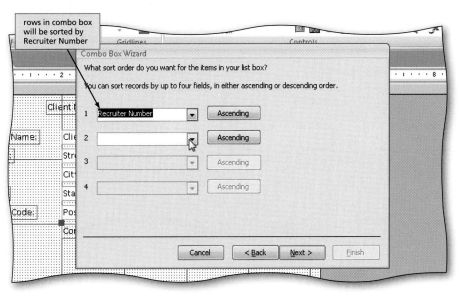

Figure 8–15

6

- Click the Next button to display the next Combo Box Wizard screen (Figure 8–16).

Q&A

What is the key column? Do I want to hide it?

The key column would be the Recruiter Number, the column that identifies both a first name and a last name. Because the purpose of this combo box is to update recruiter numbers, you certainly do not want them hidden.

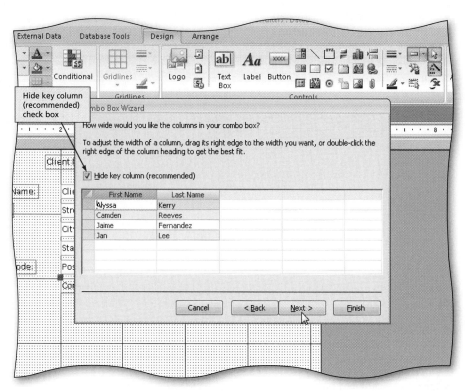

Figure 8–16

7

- Click the 'Hide key column (recommended)' check box to remove the check mark so that the Recruiter Number field will appear along with the First Name and Last Name fields.

- Click the Next button to display the next Combo Box Wizard screen (Figure 8–17).

Q&A

Do I need to make any changes here?

No. The Recruiter Number field, which is the field you want to store, already is selected.

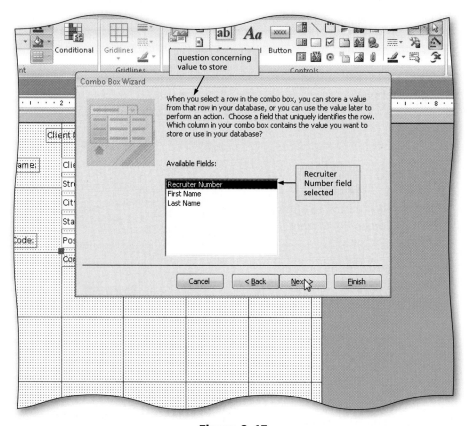

Figure 8–17

- Click the Next button to display the next Combo Box Wizard screen.

- Click the 'Store that value in this field:' option button.

- Because you want to store the value in the Recruiter Number field, click the 'Store that value in this field:' box arrow, and then click Recruiter Number (Figure 8–18).

- Click the Next button to display the next Combo Box Wizard screen.

- Be sure `Recruiter Number` is entered as the label for the combo box, and then click the Finish button to place the combo box.

Q&A Could I change the label to something else?

Yes. If you think something else would be better, you could change it.

- Save your changes to the form.

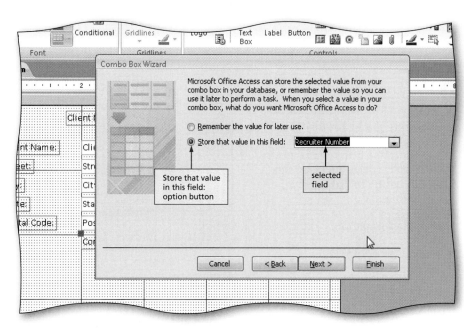

Figure 8–18

To Change the Background Color

You can use the Fill/Back Color button on the Design tab to change the background color of a form. The following steps change the background color of the form to Light Gray 2.

- Click anywhere in the Detail section but outside all the controls to select the section.

- Click the Fill/Back Color button arrow on the Design tab to display a color palette (Figure 8–19).

- Click the Light Gray 2 color, the first color in the third row under Standard Colors, to change the background color.

Experiment

- Try other colors to see their effect. When finished, once again select the Light Gray 2 color.

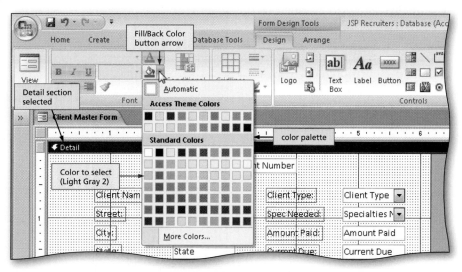

Figure 8–19

To Format a Control

You can use buttons on the Design tab to format a control in a variety of ways. You have even more control over the types of changes you can make, however, if you use the property sheet. The following steps make a variety of changes to the format of the Client Number control.

- Click the Client Number control (the white space, not the label) to select it.
- Click the Property Sheet button on the Design tab to display the property sheet.
- Click the Format tab.
- Change the Font Weight to Semi-bold.
- Change the Special Effect to Sunken.
- Close the Property Sheet by clicking the Property Sheet button.
- Click the Font color arrow on the Design tab to display a color palette (Figure 8–20).

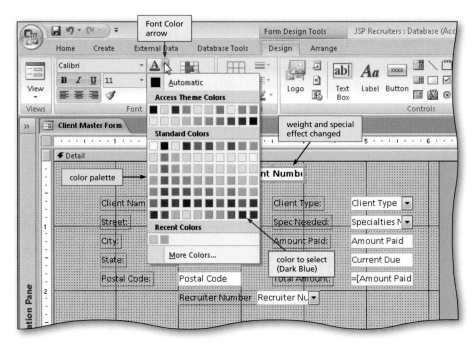

Figure 8–20

2

- Click the Dark Blue color (the second color from the right in the bottom row) to select it as the font color.
- Click the label for the Client Number field to select it.
- Click the Italic button on the Design tab to italicize the label.
- Click the Property Sheet button on the Design tab to display a property sheet.
- Change the Special Effect to Etched (Figure 8–21).
- Close the property sheet.

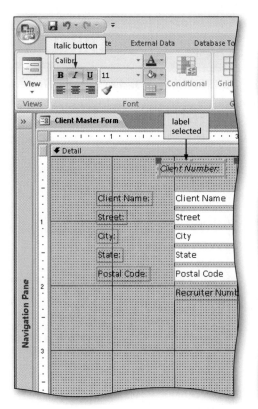
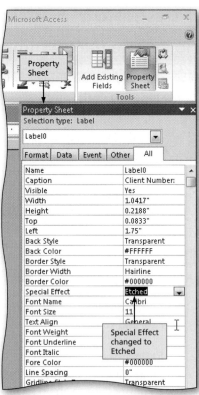

Figure 8–21

To Use the Format Painter

Once you have formatted a control and its label the way you want, you can format other controls in exactly the same way by using the format painter. To do so, click the control whose format you want to copy, click the Format Painter button on the Design tab and then click the other control. If you want to copy the format to more than one other control, double-click the Format Painter button instead of simply clicking the button, then click each of the controls that you want to change. The following steps copy the formatting of the Client Number control and label to the other controls.

- With the Client Number control selected, double-click the Format Painter button on the Design tab.

- Point to the Client Name control (Figure 8–22).

- Click the Client Name control to assign it the same formatting as the Client Number control.

- Click all the other controls on the form to assign them the same formatting.

- Click the Format Painter button to prevent further format copying.

Q&A Should I always click the Format Painter button when I have finished copying the formatting?

If you double-clicked the Format Painter button to enable you to copy the formatting to multiple controls, you need to click the Format Painter button again to turn off the copying. If you simply clicked the Format Painter button to enable you to copy the formatting to a single control, you do not need to click the button again. As soon as you copy the formatting to the single control, the copying will be turned off.

Q&A Does the order in which I click the other controls matter?

No. The only thing that is important is that you ultimately click all the controls whose formatting you want to assign.

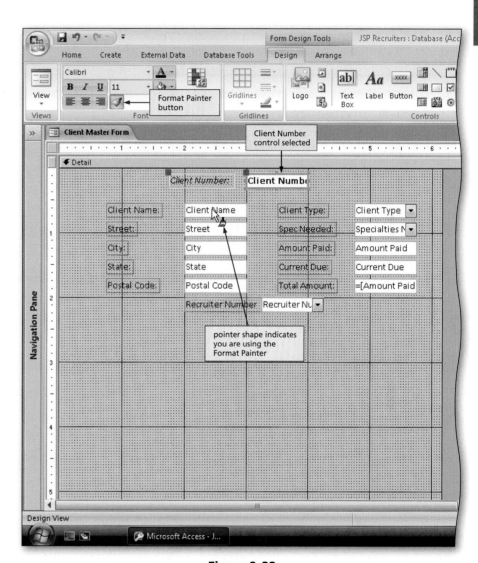

Figure 8–22

To Resize Multiple Controls

You can resize multiple controls at the same time by selecting all the controls to be resized before dragging a sizing handle. The following step resizes multiple controls.

- Click the Client Name control to select it.

- While holding the SHIFT key down, click the Street, City, State, Postal Code, Client Type, Specialties Needed, Amount Paid, Current Due, and Total Amount controls to select them.

- Drag the right sizing handle of any of the selected controls to resize the controls to the approximate size shown in Figure 8–23.

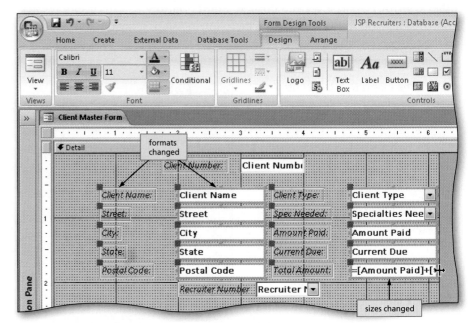

Figure 8–23

To Add a Title and Expand the Form Header Section

The form you are creating has a title, Client Master Form. The following step adds the title to the form.

- Click the Title button on the Design tab to add a Form Header section and to add a control for the title to the Form Header section (Figure 8–24).

Q&A Why is the title Client View and Update Form rather than Client Master Form?

If you have changed the caption, the title will use the new value of the Caption property.

Q&A Could I add the Form Header section before adding the title? If I do, what happens when I add the title?

Access will place the title in the Form Header section that you already added.

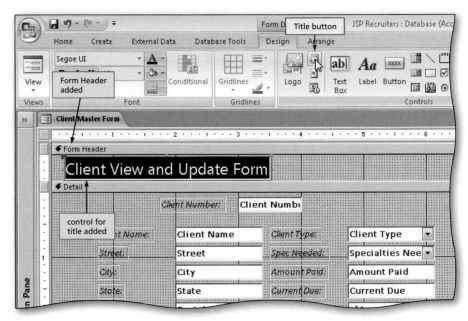

Figure 8–24

2

• Drag the lower boundary of the Form Header section down to the approximate position shown in Figure 8–25.

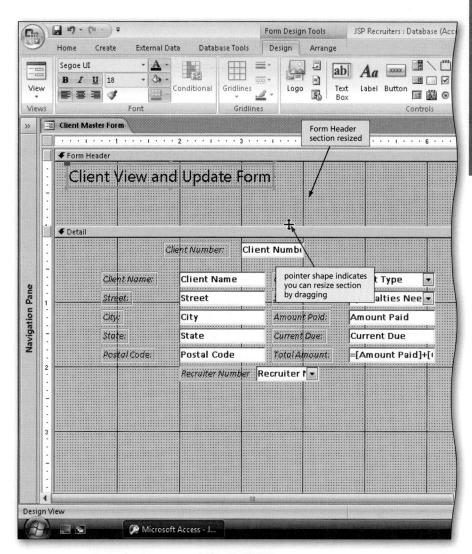

Figure 8–25

To Add Command Buttons to a Form

You may find that you can improve the functionality of your form by adding command buttons. To add command buttons, you use the Use Control Wizards button and Button (Form Control) tool in the Controls group on the Design tab. When using the series of Command Button Wizard dialog boxes, you provide the action that should be taken when the button is clicked. Several categories of actions are available.

In the Record Navigation category, you will select the Go To Next Record action for one of the buttons. From the same category, you will select the Go To Previous Record action for another. Other buttons will use the Add New Record and the Delete Record actions from the Record Operations category. The Close Form button will use the Close Form action from the Form Operations category.

The following steps add command buttons to move to the next record, move to the previous record, add a record, delete a record, and close the form.

1

- Make sure the Use Control Wizards button is selected.

- Click the Button (Form Control) tool and move the mouse pointer to the approximate position shown in Figure 8–26.

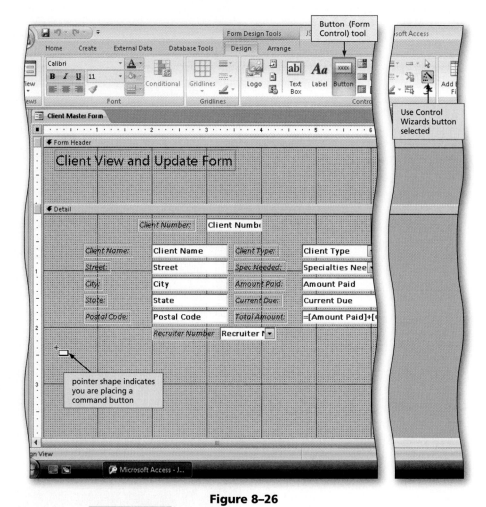

Figure 8–26

2

- Click the position shown in Figure 8–26 to display the Command Button Wizard dialog box.

- With Record Navigation selected in the Categories box, click Go To Next Record in the Actions box (Figure 8–27).

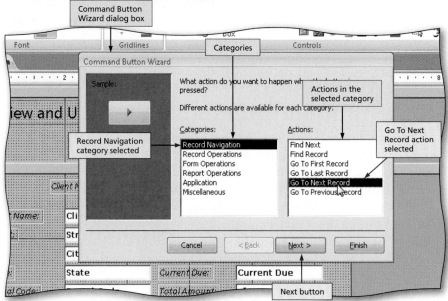

Figure 8–27

3

- Click the Next button to display the next Command Button Wizard screen (Figure 8–28).

What is the purpose of these option buttons?

Choose the first option button to place text on the button. You then can specify the text to be included or accept the default choice. Choose the second option button to place a picture on the button. You then can select a picture.

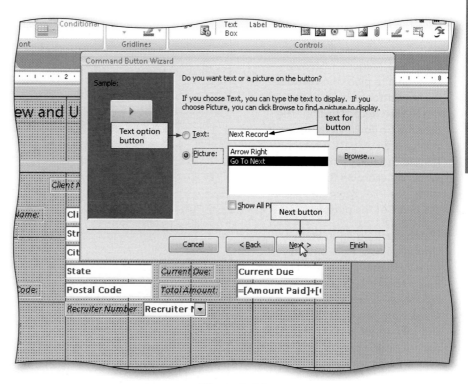

Figure 8–28

4

- Click the Text option button.

- Because Next Record is the desired text and does not need to be changed, click the Next button.

- Type Next Record as the name of the button (Figure 8–29).

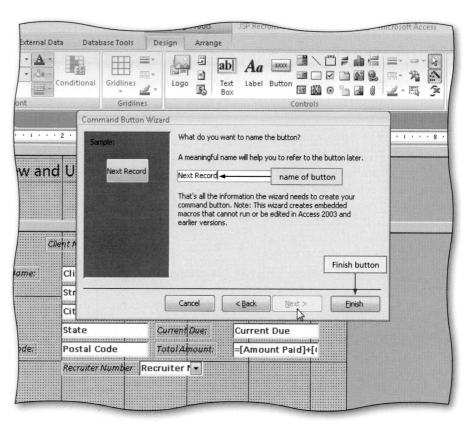

Figure 8–29

5

- Click the Finish button to finish specifying the button.

- Use the techniques in Steps 1 through 4 to place the Previous Record button directly to the right of the Next Record button. The action is Go To Previous Record in the Record Navigation category. Choose the Text option button and Previous Record on the button, and then type `Previous Record` as the name of the button.

- Use the techniques in Steps 1 through 4 to place a button directly to the right of the Previous Record button. The action is Add New Record in the Record Operations category. Choose the Text option button and Add Record on the button, and then type `Add Record` as the name of the button.

- Use the techniques in Steps 1 through 4 to place the Delete Record and Close Form buttons in the positions shown in Figure 8–30. For the Delete Record button, the category is Record Operations and the action is Delete Record. For the Close Form button, the category is Form Operations and the action is Close Form.

Q&A

My buttons are not aligned like yours are. What should I do?

If your buttons are not aligned properly, you can drag them to the correct positions. You also can use the Arrange tab.

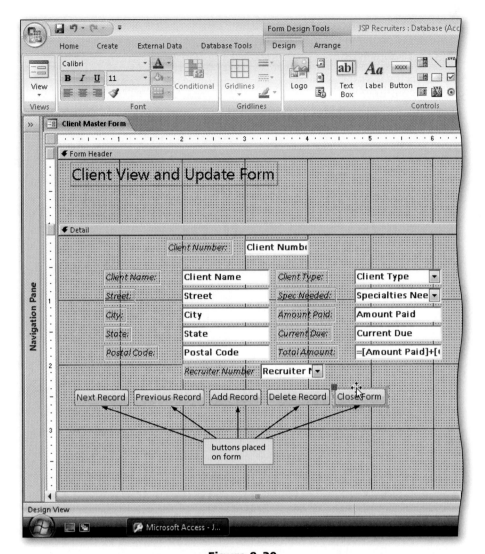

Figure 8–30

To Add a Combo Box that Is Used to Find a Record

Although you can use the Ribbon to locate records on a form, it may be more convenient to use a combo box. You could type the client's name directly into the box. Alternatively, you can click the Name to Find box arrow, and Access displays a list of client names. To select a name from the list, simply click the name.

To create a combo box, use the Combo Box tool in the Controls group on the Design tab. The Combo Box Wizard then will guide you through the steps of adding the combo box. The following steps show how to place a combo box for names on the form.

1

- With the Use Control Wizards button selected, click the Combo Box (Form Control) tool and then move the mouse pointer, whose shape has changed to a small plus sign with a combo box, to the position shown in Figure 8–31.

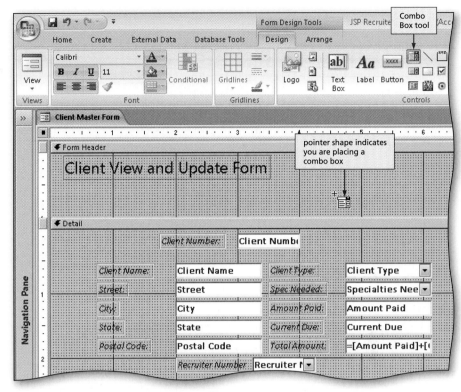

Figure 8–31

2

- Click the position shown in Figure 8–31 to display the Combo Box Wizard.

- Click the 'Find a record on my form based on the value I selected in my combo box.' option button.

- Click the Next button, click the Client Name field, and then click the Add Field button to select the Client Name field for the combo box (Figure 8–32).

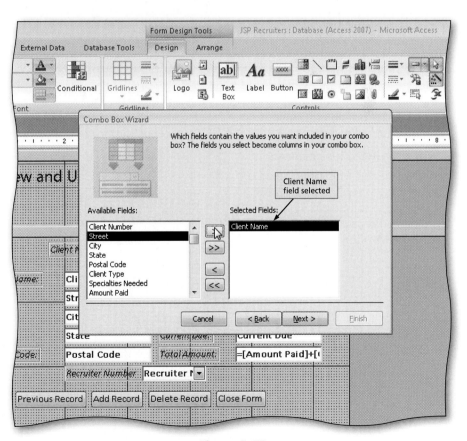

Figure 8–32

• Click the Next button.

• Drag the right boundary of the column heading to the approximate size shown in Figure 8–33.

Q&A

Can I also resize the column to best fit the data by double-clicking the right boundary of the column heading?

Yes.

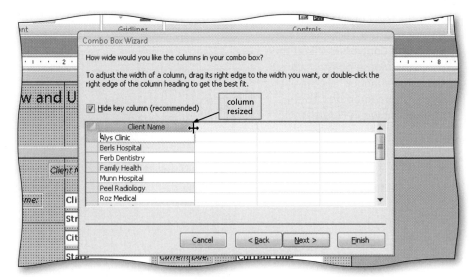

Figure 8–33

• Click the Next button, and then type `&Name to Find` as the label for the combo box.

Q&A

What is the purpose of the ampersand in front of the letter, N?

The ampersand (&) in front of the letter N indicates that users can select the combo box by pressing ALT+N.

• Click the Finish button. Position the control and label in the approximate position shown in Figure 8–34.

Q&A

Why is the letter, N, underlined?

The underlined N in Name indicates that you can press ALT+N to select the combo box. It is underlined because you preceded the letter N with the ampersand.

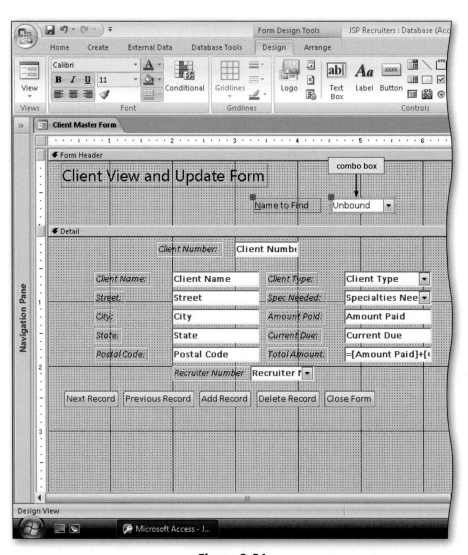

Figure 8–34

To Place a Rectangle

To emphasize the special nature of the combo box, you can place a rectangle around it as a visual cue. The following steps use the Rectangle tool to place a rectangle.

- Click the Rectangle tool in the Controls group on the Design tab, point to the upper-left corner of the rectangle in Figure 8–35, press the left mouse button, drag the pointer to the lower-right corner of the rectangle, and then release the left mouse button to place the rectangle.

- Click the Property Sheet button on the Design tab to display the property sheet for the rectangle.

- Change the value of the Special Effect property to Etched.

- Make sure the value of the Back Style property is Transparent, so the combo box will appear within the rectangle.

Q&A

What if the value is not Transparent?

If the value is not Transparent, the rectangle would cover the combo box completely and the combo box would not be visible.

- Close the property sheet.

- Save and then close the form.

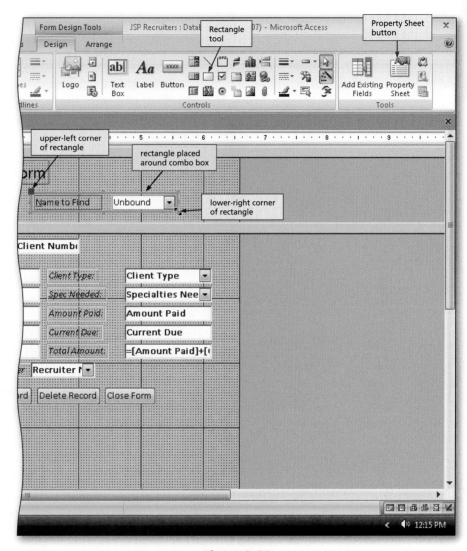

Figure 8–35

To Open a Form

Once you have created the form, you can use it at any time by opening it. The following step opens the Client Master Form.

- Show the Navigation Pane. Right-click the Client Master Form to display the shortcut menu.

- Click Open on the shortcut menu to open the form (Figure 8–36).

- Hide the Navigation Pane.

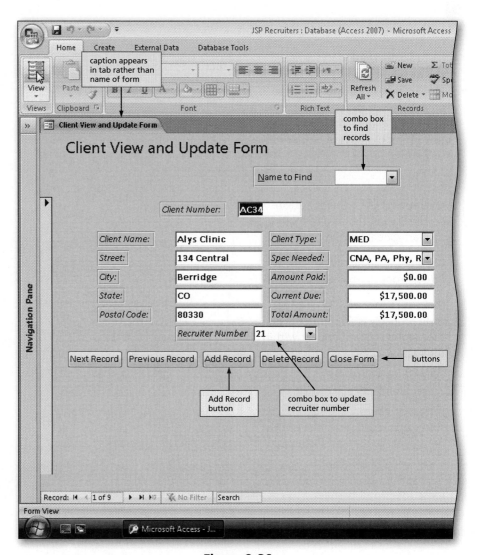

Figure 8–36

Using the Buttons

To move around on the form, you can use the buttons to perform the actions you specify. To move to the next record, click the Next Record button. Click the Previous Record button to move to the previous record. Clicking the Delete Record button will delete the record currently on the screen. You will get a message requesting that you verify the deletion before the record actually is deleted. Clicking the Close Form button will remove the form from the screen.

To Use the Add Record Button

Clicking the Add Record button will clear the contents of the form so you can add a new record. The following step uses the Add Record button.

• Click the Add Record button (Figure 8–37).

Q&A There is no insertion point in the Client Number field. How would I begin entering a new record?

To begin entering a record, you would have to click the Client Number field before you can start typing.

Q&A Why does MED appear in the Client Type field?

The value MED is the default value assigned to the Client Type field.

Experiment

• Try each of the other buttons to see their effect. Do not delete any records. After clicking the Close Form button, open the form once again.

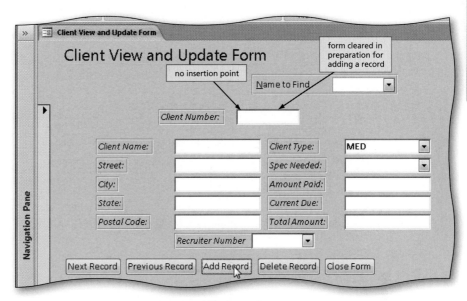

Figure 8–37

To Use the Combo Box

Using the combo box, you can search for a client in two ways. First, you can click the combo box arrow to display a list of client names, and then select the name from the list by clicking it. Alternatively, you can begin typing the name. As you type, Access will display automatically the name that begins with the letters you have typed. Once the correct name is displayed, select the name by pressing the TAB key. Regardless of the method you use, the data for the selected client appears on the form once the selection is made.

The following steps first locate the client whose name is Munn Hospital, and then use the Next Record button to move to the next client.

• Click the Name to Find box arrow to display a list of client names (Figure 8–38).

Q&A The list is not in alphabetical order, because Ferb Dentistry is before Family Health. Wouldn't it be easier to use if the list was in alphabetical order?

Yes. You will change the combo box later so that the names appear in alphabetical order.

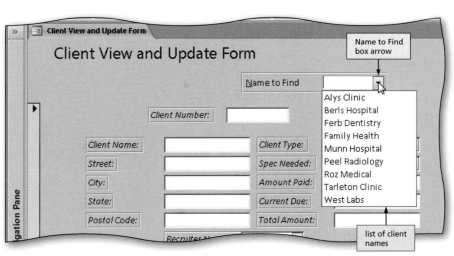

Figure 8–38

2

• Click Munn Hospital to display the data for Munn Hospital in the form (Figure 8–39).

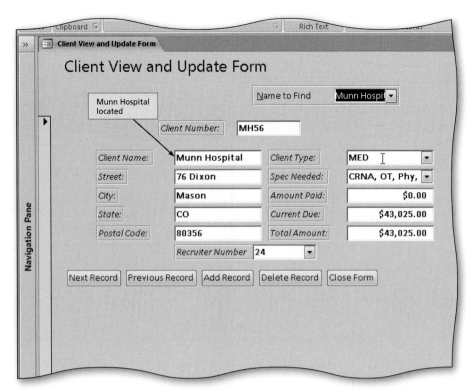

Figure 8–39

3

• Click the Next Record button to display the next record (Figure 8–40).

 Q&A
Why does the combo box still contain Munn Hospital, rather than Peel Radiology?

This is a problem with the combo box. You will address this issue later.

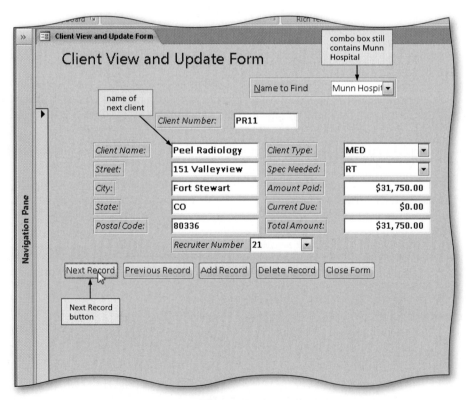

Figure 8–40

Issues with the Add Record Button

Although clicking the Add Record button does erase the contents of the form in preparation for adding a new record, there is a problem with it. After clicking the Add Record button there should be an insertion point in the control for the first field, the Client Number field, but there is not. To display an insertion point automatically when you click the Add Record button, you need to change the focus. A control is said to have the **focus** when it becomes active; that is, when it becomes able to receive user input through mouse or keyboard actions. At any point in time, only one item on the form has the focus. In addition to adding a new record, clicking the Add Record button needs to update the focus to the Client Number field.

Issues with the Combo Box

The combo box has the following issues. First, if you examine the list of names in Figure 8–38 on page AC 549, you will see that they are not in alphabetical order (Ferb Dentistry comes before Family Health). Second, when you move to a record without using the combo box, the name in the combo box does not change to reflect the name of the client currently on the screen. Third, one way to change the focus from one field to another is to press the TAB key. As you repeatedly press the TAB key, the focus should move through all the fields on the form. It should not move to the combo box, however, because that does not represent a field to be updated.

BTW

Focus
A visual way exists to determine which object on the screen has the focus. If a field has the focus, an insertion point will appear in the field. If a button has the focus, a small rectangle will appear inside the button.

BTW

VBA
Visual Basic for Applications (VBA) is a programming language that can be used with Access. As with other programming languages, programs in VBA consist of code; that is, a collection of statements, also called commands, which are instructions that will cause actions to take place when the program executes. VBA is included with all of the Microsoft Office applications.

To Modify the Add Record Button

To correct the problem with the Add Record button not displaying an insertion point, you will update a macro that is associated with the clicking of the button. You need to add an action to the macro that will move the focus to the control for the Client Number field. The appropriate action is GoToControl and the argument is the name of the control.

When creating macros, it is desirable for control names not to contain spaces. If you are programming in VBA (Visual Basic for Applications), it is a requirement. There are a variety of approaches you can use for changing the names so that they don't contain spaces. The one you will use is to insert an underscore (_) in place of the space. For example, you will change Client Number to Client_Number.

The following steps first change the name of the controls to remove spaces. They then modify the macro that is associated with the clicking of the Add Record button by adding an action that will change the focus to the control for the Client Number field.

1

- Click the View button arrow and then click Design View to return to Design view.

- Click the control for the Client Number field (the white space, not the label), and then click the Property Sheet button to display the property sheet.

- If necessary, click the All tab. Ensure the Name property is selected, click immediately following the word Client, press the DELETE key to delete the space, and then type an underscore (_) to change the name to Client_Number (Figure 8–41).

Q&A Could I just erase the old name and type Client_Number?

Yes. Use whichever method you find most convenient.

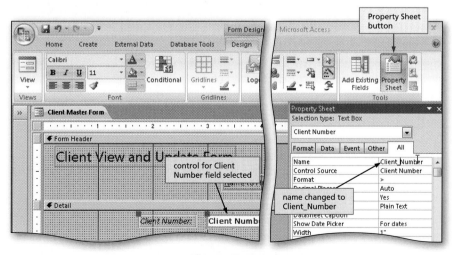

Figure 8–41

2

- Click the control for the Client Name field to display its property sheet and then change the name to Client_Name.

- Using the same technique, change the name for the controls for the Postal Code, Client Type, Specialties Needed, Amount Paid, Current Due, and Recruiter Number fields by replacing the space with an underscore (_).

- Close the property sheet and then right-click the Add Record button to display a shortcut menu (Figure 8–42).

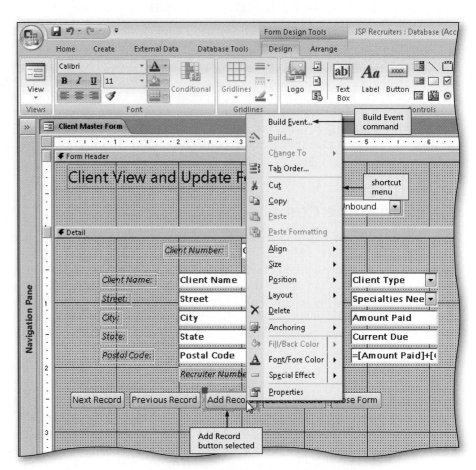

Figure 8–42

3

- Click Build Event on the shortcut menu to display the macro associated with the On Click event (Figure 8–43).

Q&A What is the purpose of the three actions currently in the macro?

The first command indicates that if there is an error, Access should proceed to the next action in the macro rather than immediately stopping the macro. The second action causes Access to go to the record indicated by the values in the arguments. The value New indicates that it is to go to a new record. Because the final action has a condition, it only will be executed if the condition is true, that is, the error code contains a value other than 0. In that case, the MsgBox action will display a description of the error.

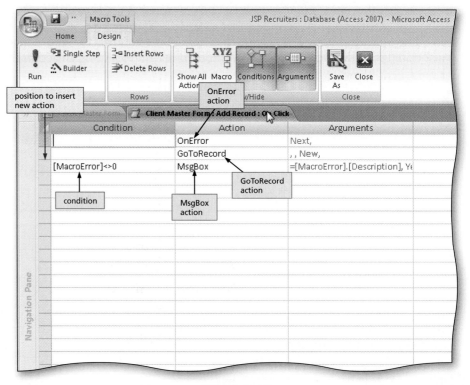

Figure 8–43

4

- Click the row selector for the third row, the row that contains a criterion, and then press the INSERT key to insert a new row.

- Click the Action column on the newly inserted row, click the arrow, and select the GoToControl action to indicate that the focus will move to another control.

- Type Client_Number as the Control Name argument (Figure 8–44).

Q&A

What is the effect of the GoToControl action?

When Access executes this action, the focus will move to the control indicated in the Control Name argument, in this case, the Client_Number control.

5

- Click the Save button on the Quick Access Toolbar to save your changes.

- Click the Close button on the Design tab to close the macro and return to the form design.

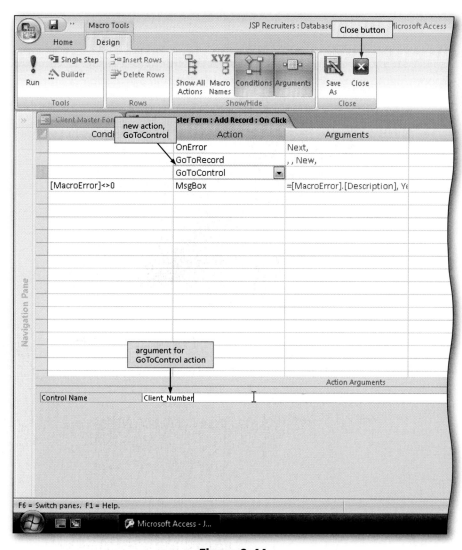

Figure 8–44

BTW

Events
Events are actions that have happened or are happening at the present time. An event can be caused by a user action. For example, one of the events associated with a button on a form is clicking the button. The corresponding event property is On Click. If you associate VBA code with the On Click event property, that code will execute whenever you click the button. Using properties associated with events, you can tell Access to run a macro, call a Visual Basic function, or run an event procedure in response to an event.

To Modify the Combo Box

You need to take special action to correct the issues with the combo box. To ensure the data is sorted in the correct order, you need to modify the query that Access has created for the combo box so the data is sorted by client name. You also need to modify the VBA (Visual Basic for Applications) code associated with what is termed the On Current event property of the entire form. The modification to the On Current event property will ensure that the combo box is kept current with the rest of the form; that is, it contains the name of the client whose number currently appears in the Client Number field. The following steps modify the query and then the code associated with the On Current event property appropriately. The final step changes the Tab Stop property for the combo box from Yes to No.

- Click the Name to Find combo box (the white space, not the label), and then click the Property Sheet button.

- Change the name to Name_to_Find.

- Scroll down in the property sheet so that the Row Source property appears, click the Row Source property, and then click the Build button (the three dots) to display the Query Builder.

- Click the Sort row in the Client Name field, click the box arrow that appears, and then click Ascending to change the order (Figure 8–45).

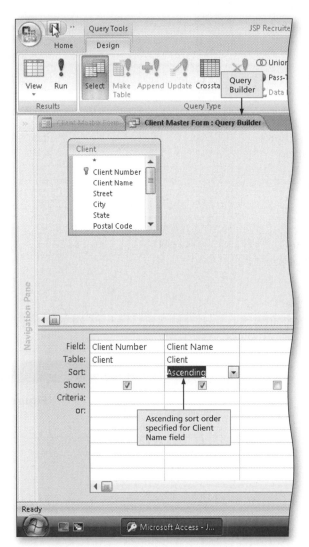
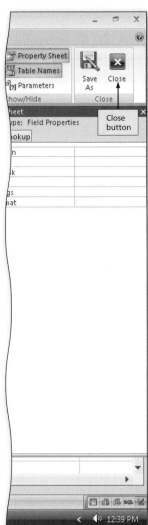

Figure 8–45

2

- Click the Save button to save your changes.

- Close the Query Builder window by clicking the Close button on the Design tab.

- Close the property sheet.

- Click the form selector (the box in the upper-left corner of the form) to select the form.

- Click the Property Sheet button on the Design tab, scroll down until the On Current property appears, and then click the On Current property.

- Click the Build button (the three dots) to display the Choose Builder dialog box (Figure 8–46).

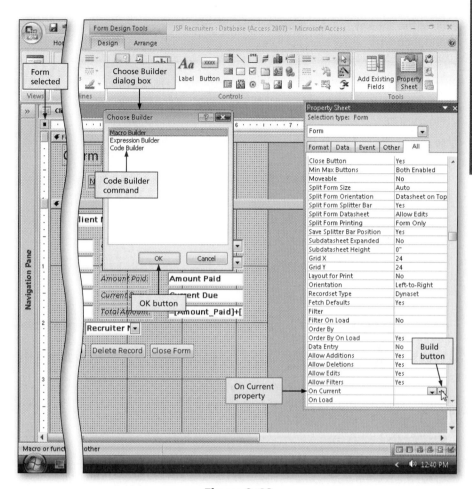

Figure 8–46

3

- Click Code Builder in the Choose Builder dialog box, and then click the OK button to display the VBA code generated for the form (Figure 8–47).

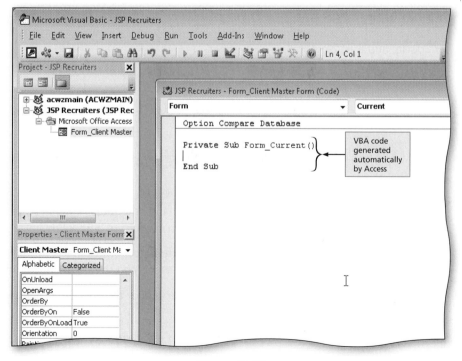

Figure 8–47

4

- Press the TAB key and then type `Name_to_Find = Client_Number ' Update the combo box` as shown in Figure 8–48.

Q&A

How would I construct a command like this in my own form?

Begin with the name you assigned to the combo box followed by an equal sign and then the name of the control containing the primary key of the table. The portion of the statement following the apostrophe is a comment, describing the purpose of the command. You simply could type the same thing that you see in this command.

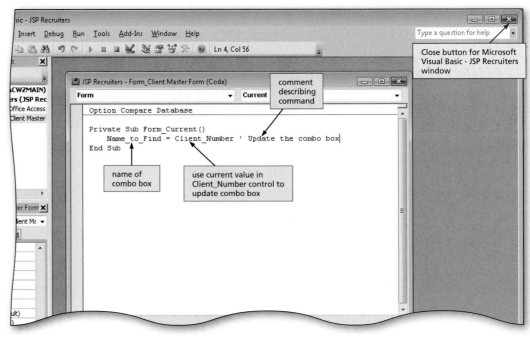

Figure 8–48

5

- Click the Close button for the Microsoft Visual Basic - JSP Recruiters - window, and then close the Form property sheet.

- Click the Name to Find combo box and then click the Property Sheet button.

- Scroll down until the Tab Stop property appears, click the Tab Stop property, and then click the Tab Stop property box arrow.

- Click No, and then close the property sheet.

- Save your changes.

To Change the Enabled Property

In the form in Figure 8–1 on pages AC 523 and AC 524 , the Total Amount field is dimmed, indicating that you cannot change the value in the field. To dim the field, you need to change the field's Enabled property from Yes to No. The following steps change the Enabled property.

1 Click the Total Amount field (the white space, not the label), click the Property Sheet button to display the property sheet, and then scroll down until the Enabled Property appears.

2 Click the Enabled property, click the Enabled property arrow, and then click No to change the value from Yes to No.

3 Close the property sheet and then save your changes.

Using the Modified Form

The problems with the Add Record button and the combo box now are corrected and the Total Amount field is dimmed. When you click the Add Record button, an insertion point appears in the Client Number field (Figure 8–49a). When you click the Name to Find box arrow, the list of names is in alphabetical order (Figure 8–49b). After using the Name to Find box to find a client (Figure 8–49c on page AC 558) and clicking the Next button, the Name to Find box is updated with the correct client name (Figure 8–49d on page AC 558).

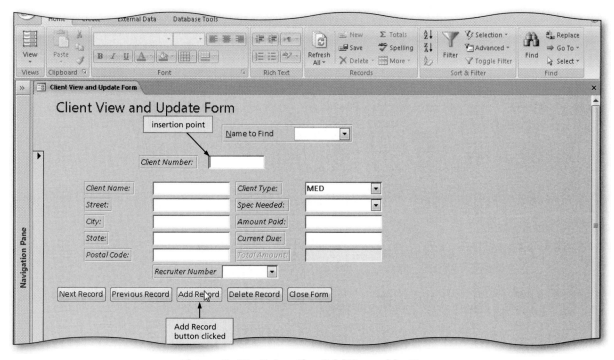

Figure 8–49a Using the Add Record button

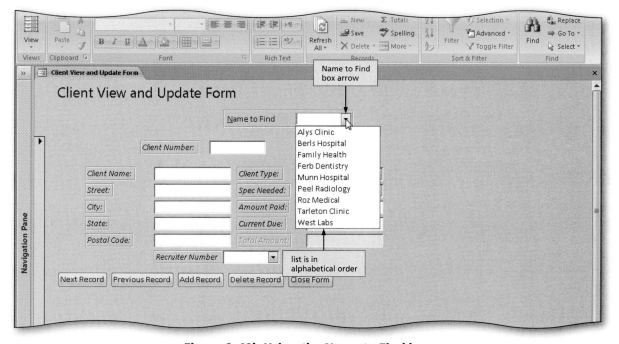

Figure 8–49b Using the Name to Find box

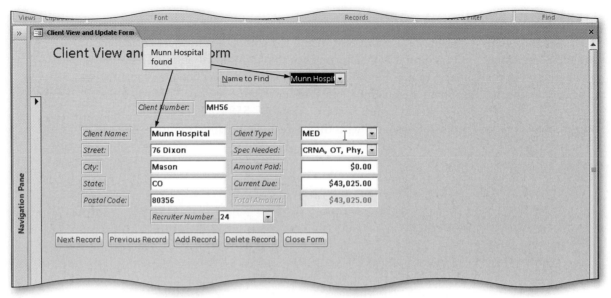

Figure 8–49c Results of using the Name to Find box

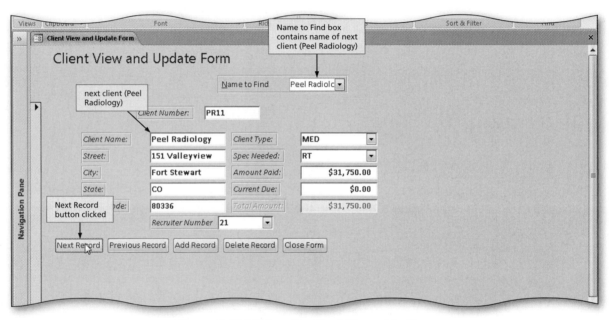

Figure 8–49d Using the Next Record button

To Add an Option Group

You may decide to allow users to make a selection from some predefined options by including an option group. An **option group** is a rectangle containing a collection of option buttons. To select an option, you simply click the corresponding option button. The form you are creating contains an option group called Form Options. In this group, you select an option button to indicate the portion of the form that should be enabled for update.

The following steps use the Option Group tool to create the Form Options option group.

1

- With the Use Control Wizards button selected, click the Option Group tool in the Controls group on the Design tab and then move the pointer to the approximate position shown in Figure 8–50.

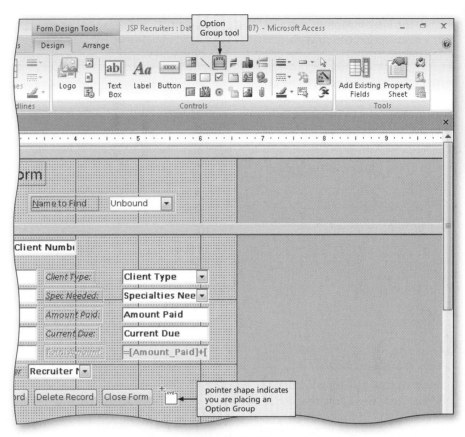

Figure 8–50

2

- Click the position shown in Figure 8–50 to place an option group and start the Option Group Wizard.

- Type Change Address Data in the first row of label names and press the DOWN ARROW key.

- Type Change Other Data in the second row of label names and press the DOWN ARROW key.

- Type Change All Data in the third row of label names and press the DOWN ARROW key.

- Type View Data Only in the fourth row of label names (Figure 8–51).

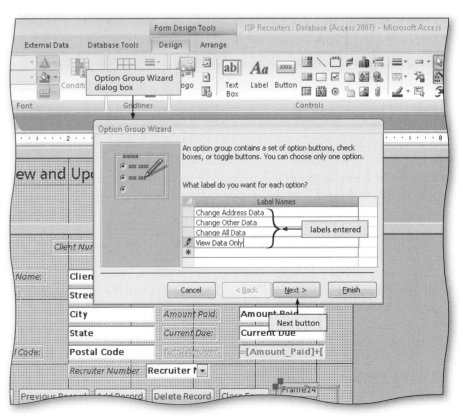

Figure 8–51

3

- Click the Next button to move to the next Option Group Wizard screen.

- With the 'Yes, the default choice is' option button selected, click the arrow and select View Data Only as the default choice (Figure 8–52).

Q&A What is the effect of specifying one of the options as the default choice?

The default choice is the one that initially will be selected when you open the form.

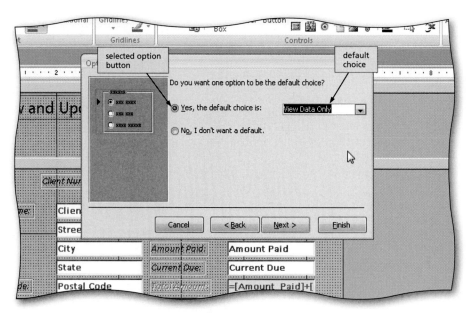

Figure 8–52

4

- Click the Next button to move to the next Option Group Wizard screen and then verify that the values assigned to the labels match those shown in Figure 8–53.

Q&A How do I use the values that I have assigned?

You can use them in macros or VBA. You will use them in a macro later in this chapter.

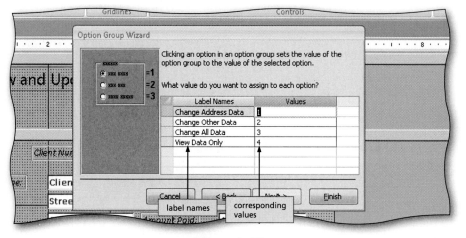

Figure 8–53

5

- Click the Next button to move to the next Option Group Wizard screen and then ensure that the 'Save the value for later use.' option button is selected.

Q&A What is the alternative?
You could store the value in a field.

- Click the Next button to move to the next Option Group Wizard screen and then ensure that the 'Option buttons' option button and the Etched option button are selected.

Q&A What are the alternatives?
Rather than option buttons, you could choose Check boxes or Toggle buttons. Rather than Etched, you could select Flat, Raised, Shadowed, or Sunken.

- Click the Next button to move to the next Option Group Wizard screen, type Form Options as the caption, and then click the Finish button.

To Create a Macro for the Option Group

In order to take appropriate action when the user clicks an option button in the option group, you will create a macro. The macro will set the Enabled property of the controls on the form to the appropriate value. Those controls that should be enabled, that is, those controls the user should be able to update will have the Enabled value set to 1; the rest will have the value set to 0.

Because the specific actions to be taken depend on the option button the user selects, the macro will contain conditions. There will be four conditions: one to test if the user selected option 1, one to test if the user selected option 2, one for option 3, and one for option 4. The expression that contains this number is [Forms]![Client Master Form]![Form_Options]. Because this expression is fairly lengthy, the macro will begin by setting a temporary variable, Optno (short for option number), to this expression. This simply means that Optno is a named location in computer memory. This location can contain a value, in this case the option number on the form. In each of the conditions, you then can use Optno rather than the full expression.

The following steps begin creating the macro and add an action to set the temporary variable to the desired value.

1

- With the option group selected, click the Property Sheet button on the Design tab to display a property sheet.

- Change the name to Form_Options.

- Click the After Update property.

- Click the Build button to display the Choose Builder dialog box (Figure 8–54).

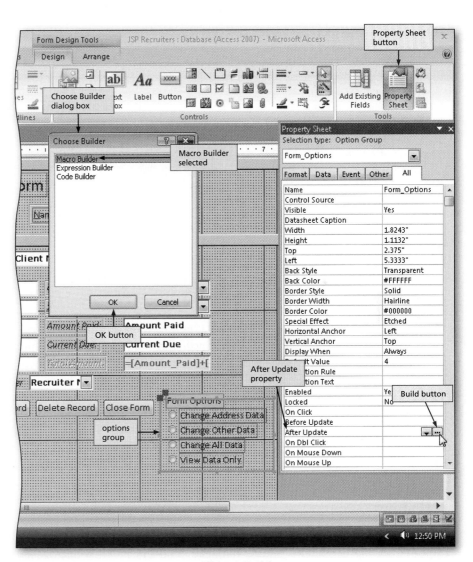

Figure 8–54

2

- With Macro Builder selected in the Choose Builder dialog box, click the OK button to create a macro.

- Click the Conditions button, if necessary, to display the Condition column.

- Select SetTempVar as the action on the first row.

- Enter `Optno` as the value for the Name argument.

- Enter `[Forms]![Client Master Form]![Form_Options]` as the value for the Expression argument (Figure 8–55).

Q&A

What does this expression mean?

The first part indicates that the value is found in a control on a form. The second part indicates that it is the Client Master Form. The final part indicates that it is the control called Form_Options on the Client Master Form. The end result is that the temporary variable Optno will be set to the value of the Form_Options control.

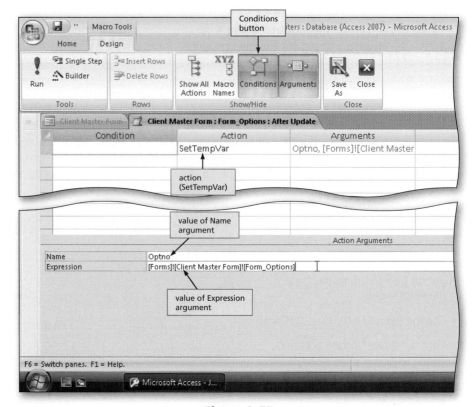

Figure 8–55

Macro for Options Group

The macro contains four conditions. The first is [TempVars]![Optno]=1, which simply means the value in the temporary variable Optno is equal to 1. In other words, the user selected the first option button. The actions associated with this condition are all SetProperty. The arguments will be the name of the control (for example, Client_Number), the property to be set (Enabled), and the value (1 for enabled, 0 for not enabled). For option 1, the Client_Number, Client_Name, Street, City, State, and Postal_Code should all have the value of the Enabled property set to 1; the remaining controls should have the value set to 0. If more than one action is associated with the same condition, the condition column for all actions other than the first should contain three periods (...).

The conditions and actions for options 2, 3, and 4 are similar. The only difference is which controls have their enabled property set to 1. For option 2, the Client_Number, Client_Name, Client_Type, Specialties_Needed, Amount_Paid, Current_Due, and Recruiter_Number should all have the value of the Enabled property set to 1; the remaining controls should have the value set to 0. For option 3, all controls should have their Enabled property set to 1 and for option 4, all controls should have their Enabled property set to 0. Because the temporary variable, Optno, is not needed once the actions in this macro have been performed, the final action removes this temporary variable.

Table 8–1 shows the macro for the option group.

Table 8–1 Macro for After Update Property of the Option Group

Condition	Action	Arguments
	SetTempVar	Name: Optno Expression: [Forms]![Client Master Form]![Form_Options]
[TempVars]![Optno]=1	SetProperty	Control Name: Client_Number Property: Enabled Value: 1
...	SetProperty	Control Name: Client_Name Property: Enabled Value: 1
...	SetProperty	Control Name: Street Property: Enabled Value: 1
...	SetProperty	Control Name: City Property: Enabled Value: 1
...	SetProperty	Control Name: State Property: Enabled Value: 1
...	SetProperty	Control Name: Postal_Code Property: Enabled Value: 1
...	SetProperty	Control Name: Client_Type Property: Enabled Value: 0
...	SetProperty	Control Name: Specialties_Needed Property: Enabled Value: 0
...	SetProperty	Control Name: Amount_Paid Property: Enabled Value: 0
...	SetProperty	Control Name: Current_Due Property: Enabled Value: 0
...	SetProperty	Control Name: Recruiter_Number Property: Enabled Value: 0
[TempVars]![Optno]=2	SetProperty	Control Name: Client_Number Property: Enabled Value: 1
...	SetProperty	Control Name: Client_Name Property: Enabled Value: 1
...	SetProperty	Control Name: Street Property: Enabled Value: 0
...	SetProperty	Control Name: City Property: Enabled Value: 0
...	SetProperty	Control Name: State Property: Enabled Value: 0
...	SetProperty	Control Name: Postal_Code Property: Enabled Value: 0

Table 8–1 Macro for After Update Property of the Option Group (*continued*)

Condition	Action	Arguments
...	SetProperty	Control Name: Client_Type Property: Enabled Value: 1
...	SetProperty	Control Name: Specialties_Needed Property: Enabled Value: 1
...	SetProperty	Control Name: Amount_Paid Property: Enabled Value: 1
...	SetProperty	Control Name: Current_Due Property: Enabled Value: 1
...	SetProperty	Control Name: Recruiter_Number Property: Enabled Value: 1
[TempVars]![Optno]=3	SetProperty	Control Name: Client_Number Property: Enabled Value: 1
...	SetProperty	Control Name: Client_Name Property: Enabled Value: 1
...	SetProperty	Control Name: Street Property: Enabled Value: 1
...	SetProperty	Control Name: City Property: Enabled Value: 1
...	SetProperty	Control Name: State Property: Enabled Value: 1
...	SetProperty	Control Name: Postal_Code Property: Enabled Value: 1
...	SetProperty	Control Name: Client_Type Property: Enabled Value: 1
...	SetProperty	Control Name: Specialties_Needed Property: Enabled Value: 1
...	SetProperty	Control Name: Amount_Paid Property: Enabled Value: 1
...	SetProperty	Control Name: Current_Due Property: Enabled Value: 1
...	SetProperty	Control Name: Recruiter_Number Property: Enabled Value: 1
[TempVars]![Optno]=4	SetProperty	Control Name: Client_Number Property: Enabled Value: 0
...	SetProperty	Control Name: Client_Name Property: Enabled Value: 0

Table 8–1 Macro for After Update Property of the Option Group (*continued*)

Condition	Action	Arguments
...	SetProperty	Control Name: Street Property: Enabled Value: 0
...	SetProperty	Control Name: City Property: Enabled Value: 0
...	SetProperty	Control Name: State Property: Enabled Value: 0
...	SetProperty	Control Name: Postal_Code Property: Enabled Value: 0
...	SetProperty	Control Name: Client_Type Property: Enabled Value: 0
...	SetProperty	Control Name: Specialties_Needed Property: Enabled Value: 0
...	SetProperty	Control Name: Amount_Paid Property: Enabled Value: 0
...	SetProperty	Control Name: Current_Due Property: Enabled Value: 0
...	SetProperty	Control Name: Recruiter_Number Property: Enabled Value: 0
	RemoveTempVar	Name: Optno

To Add Actions to the Macro

The following steps add the remaining conditions and actions to the macro.

1

- Add the condition and actions associated with option number 1 and specify the arguments for the actions (Figure 8–56).

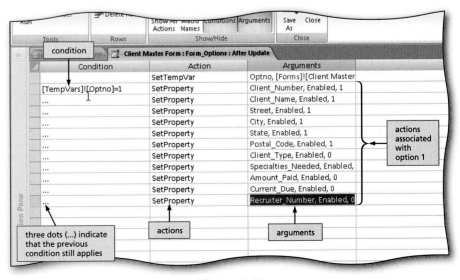

Figure 8–56

2

- Add the conditions and actions associated with options 2, 3, and 4 and specify the arguments for the actions.

Q&A

Do I have to type all these actions? They seem to be very similar to the ones associated with option 1.

You can copy and paste the actions for option 1. (Click the row selector for the row with the condition and then click the final action in the list while holding the SHIFT key down to select the actions. Click the Home tab, click the Copy button, click the row selector for the first empty row, and then click the Paste button.) You then can change the number in the condition to the appropriate option number and then make the appropriate changes to the Enabled argument on the new rows.

- Add the RemoveTempVar action and argument as shown in Figure 8–57.

Q&A

Do I need to remove the temporary variable?

Technically, no. In fact, if you plan to use this temporary variable in another macro and wanted it to retain the value you assigned in this macro, you definitely would not remove it. If you don't plan to use it elsewhere, it is a good idea to remove it, however.

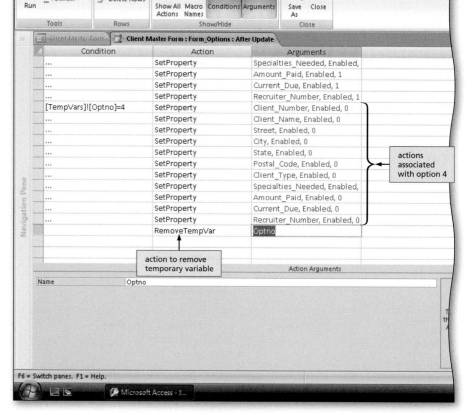

Figure 8–57

3

- Click the Save button to save the macro.
- Click the Close button on the Design tab to close the macro and return to the form.

To Create a Macro for the On Load Property of the Form

There are occasions where there is some special action to be taken when a form first loads into memory. For example, when this form loads, you want to ensure that the correct fields are enabled. In particular, because the View Data Only option is the one that initially is selected, the enabled property for all controls initially should be set to 0. Such an action would be included in a macro that is to be executed when the Form Load event occurs. The macro should set the enabled property for all controls to 0. The following steps create the required macro.

- Click the form selector (the box in the upper-left corner of the form) to select the form.

- If necessary, click the Property Sheet button on the Design tab, scroll down until the On Load property appears, and then click the On Load property.

- Click the Build button (the three dots) to display the Choose Builder dialog box.

- With Macro Builder selected in the Choose Builder dialog box, click the OK button to create a macro.

- Click the Conditions button, if necessary, to remove the Condition column.

- Enter the actions and arguments shown in Figure 8–58.

- Save the changes to the macro.

- Click the Close button on the Design tab to close the macro and return to the form.

- Close the property sheet.

- Save and then close the form.

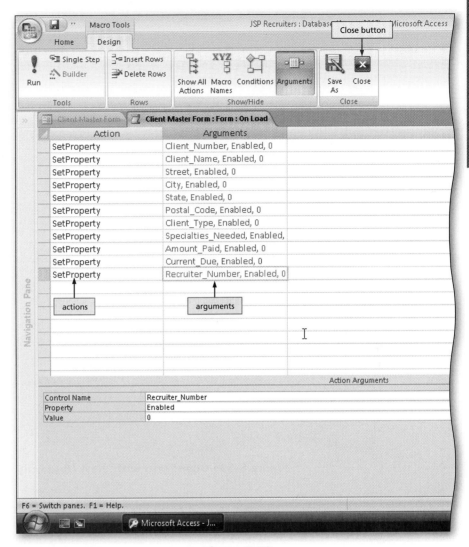

Figure 8–58

Using the Option Group

When you first open the form, the View Data Only option button will be selected (Figure 8–59a on the following page) and none of the controls will be enabled; they all will be dimmed. If you click the Change Address Data option button (Figure 8–59b on the following page), the Client Number, Client Name, Street, City, State, and Postal Code controls will be enabled. The rest will be dimmed. If you click the Change Other Data option button (Figure 8–59c on page AC 569), the Client Number, Client Name, Client Type, Specialties Needed, Amount Paid, Current Due, and Recruiter Number controls will be enabled. Finally, if you click the Change All Data option button (Figure 8–59d on page AC 569), all controls are enabled except the Total Amount control, which cannot be updated.

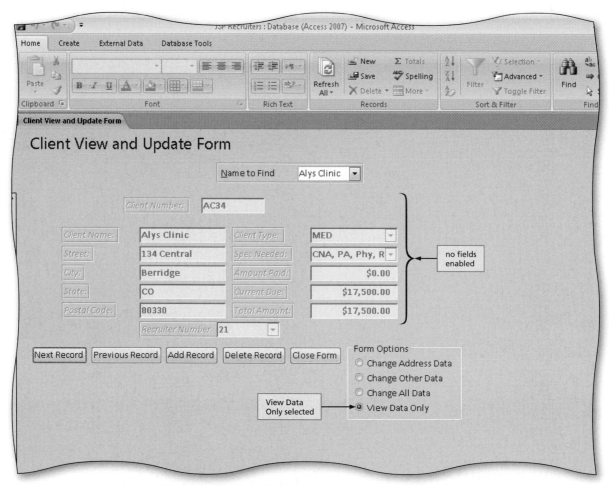

Figure 8–59a Open form with View Data Only option button default

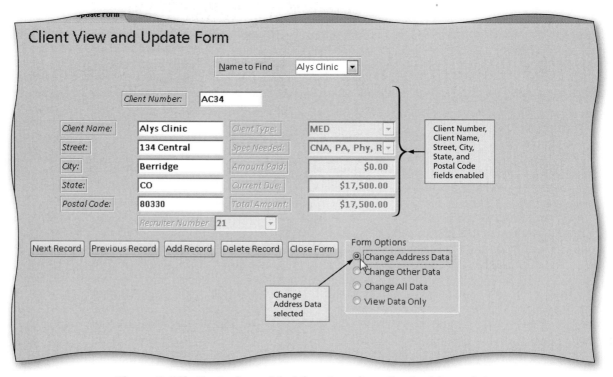

Figure 8–59b Controls enabled for changing client address data

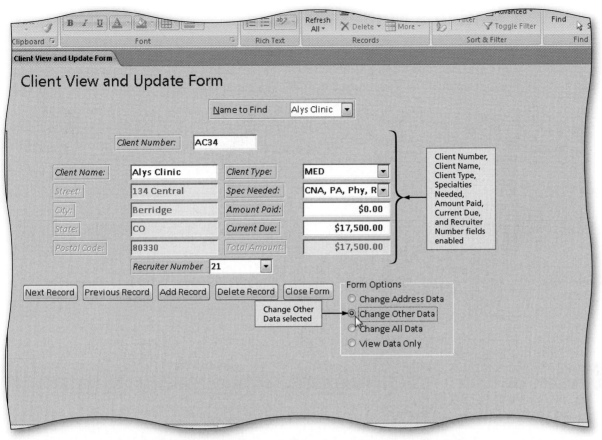

Figure 8–59c Controls enabled for changing other client data

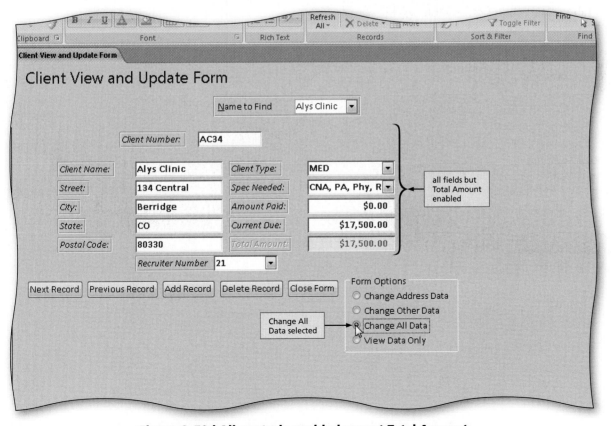

Figure 8–59d All controls enabled except Total Amount

Creating a Multipage Form

If you have determined that you have more data than will fit conveniently on one screen, you can create a **multipage form**, a form that includes more than a single page. There are two ways to create a multipage form. You can insert a page break at the desired location. An alternative that produces a nice-looking and easy-to-use multipage form is to insert a tab control. Once you have done so, users can change from one page to another by clicking the desired tab.

To Create a Form

The following steps create a form in Design view. The form will include two tabs, one that displays a datasheet and another that displays two charts.

- If necessary, hide the Navigation Pane.

- Click Create on the Ribbon to display the Create tab.

- Click Form Design on the Create tab to create a new form in Design view.

- Click the Property Sheet button on the Design tab to display a property sheet.

- With the All tab selected, click the Record Source property, click the arrow that appears, and then click the Recruiter table to select the Recruiter table as the row source.

- Close the property sheet.

- Click the Add Existing Fields button to display a field list, drag the Recruiter Number, First Name, and Last Name fields to the approximate positions shown in Figure 8–60.

- Move the attached labels for the First Name and Last Name fields to the positions shown in the figure by dragging their move handles.

- Close the field list by clicking the Add Existing Fields button a second time.

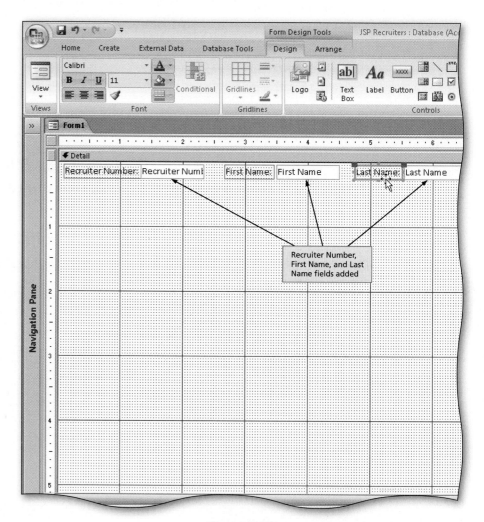

Figure 8–60

To Use Tab Controls to Create a Multipage Form

To use tabs on a form, you need to insert a tab control. The following steps insert a tab control with two tabs — Datasheet and Charts. Users will be able to click the Datasheet tab in the completed form to view seminar offerings in Datasheet view. Clicking the Charts tab will display two charts representing the same seminar data.

- Click the Tab Control tool and move the mouse pointer to the approximate location shown in Figure 8–61.

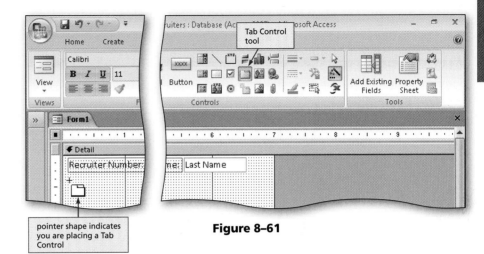

Figure 8–61

- Click the position shown in Figure 8–61 to place a tab control on the form.

- Click the leftmost tab and then click the Property Sheet button on the Design tab to display a property sheet.

- Change the value for the Name property to `Datasheet` (Figure 8–62).

- Click the second tab without closing the property sheet.

- Change the value for the Name property to `Charts`.

- Close the property sheet.

- Save the form using the name, Recruiter Seminar Data.

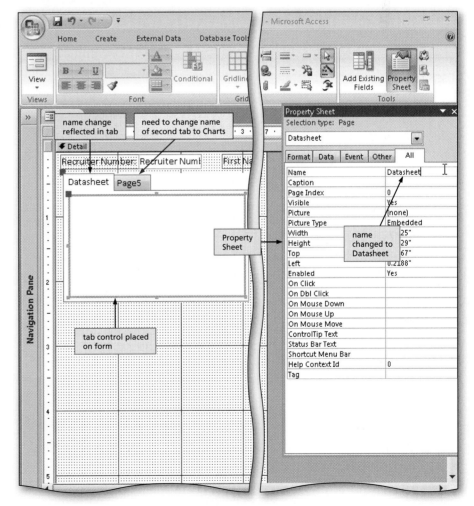

Figure 8–62

To Add a Subform

To add a subform to a form, you use the Subform/Subreport tool in the Controls group on the Design tab. If the Use Control Wizards button is selected, a wizard will guide you through the process of adding the subform. The following steps place a subform on the Datasheet tab.

- Resize the tab control to the approximate size shown in Figure 8–63 by dragging the appropriate sizing handles.

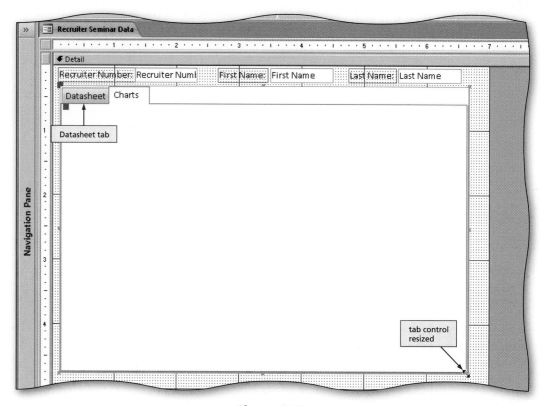

Figure 8–63

- Click the Datasheet tab.

- With the Use Control Wizards button selected, click the Subform/Subreport tool in the Controls group on the Design tab, and then move the mouse pointer to the approximate position shown in Figure 8–64.

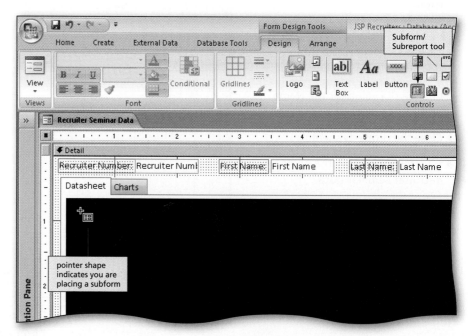

Figure 8–64

● Click the position shown in Figure 8–64 to open the SubForm Wizard.

● Be sure the 'Use existing Tables and Queries' option button is selected.

● Click the Next button to display the next SubForm Wizard screen.

● Click the Tables/Queries box arrow and then click the Recruiters and Seminar Offerings query.

● Click the Add All Fields button (Figure 8–65).

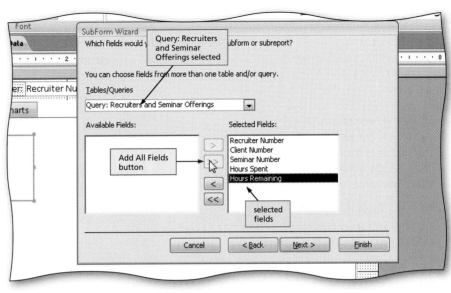

Figure 8–65

● Click the Next button.

● Be sure the 'Choose from a list' option button is selected.

● Click the Next button.

● Type Seminar Offerings for Recruiter as the name of the subform and then click the Finish button to complete the creation of the subform (Figure 8–66).

⑤

● Save and then close the Recruiter Seminar Data form.

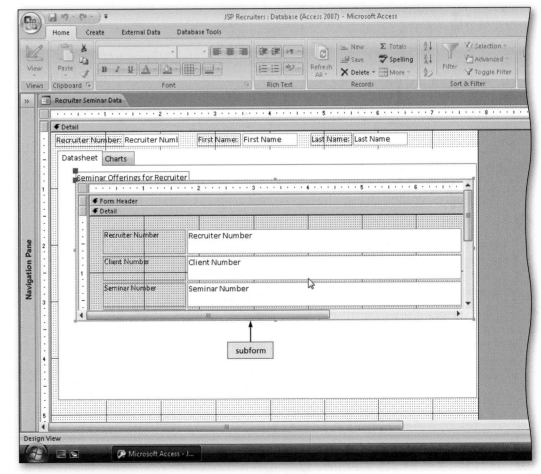

Figure 8–66

To Modify a Subform

The next task is to modify the subform. The Recruiter Number field needed to be in the subform because it is used to link the data in the subform to the data in the main form. It is not supposed to appear in the form, however. In addition, the remaining columns need to be resized to appropriate sizes. The following steps illustrate how to first remove the Recruiter Number field and then convert to Datasheet view to resize the remaining columns.

- Show the Navigation Pane, right-click the Seminar Offerings for Recruiter form, and then click Design View on the shortcut menu.

- Click the Recruiter Number control, and then press the DELETE key to delete the control.

- Click the View button to view the subform in Datasheet view.

- Resize each column to best fit the data by double-clicking the right boundary of the column's field selector (Figure 8–67).

- Save the subform and then close it.

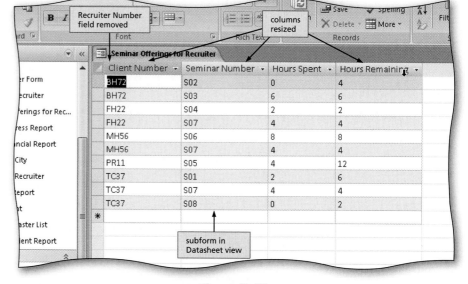

Figure 8–67

To Change the Background Color

The following steps change the background color of the form to Light Gray 2.

- If necessary, show the Navigation Pane, right-click Recruiter Seminar Data, and then click Design View on the shortcut menu.

- Hide the Navigation Pane.

- Click anywhere in the Detail section but outside all the controls to select the section.

- Click the Fill/Back Color button arrow on the Design tab to display a color palette (Figure 8–68).

- Click the Light Gray 2 color, the first color in the third row under Standard Colors, to change the background color.

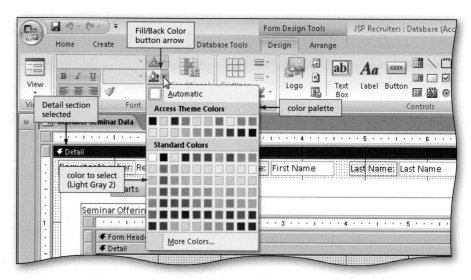

Figure 8–68

To Resize the Subform

The following step resizes the subform to the size shown in Figure 8–2a on page AC 525.

1

- Resize the subform to the size shown in Figure 8–69 by dragging the right sizing handle.

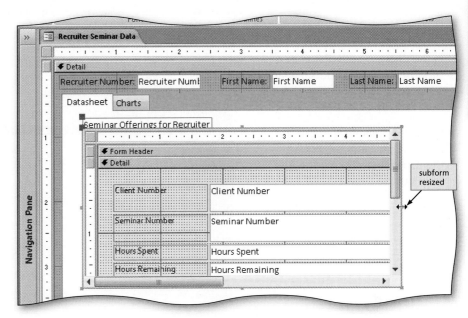

Figure 8–69

To Insert Charts

You may decide that you want to represent data visually in a table or query. If so, you can create a chart. To insert a chart, use the Insert Chart tool on the Design tab. The Chart Wizard then will ask you to indicate the fields to be included on the chart and the type of chart you wish to insert. The following steps insert a chart.

1

- Click the Charts tab and then click the Insert Chart tool in the Controls group on the Design tab.

- Move the pointer to the approximate position shown in Figure 8–70.

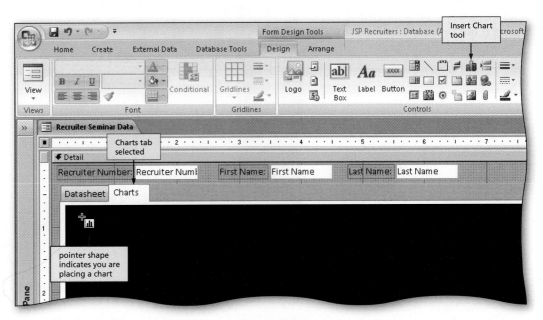

Figure 8–70

- Click the position shown in Figure 8–70 on the previous page to display the Chart Wizard dialog box.

- Click the Queries option button in the Chart Wizard dialog box, click the Recruiters and Seminar Offerings query, and then click the Next button.

- Select the Seminar Number and Hours Spent fields by clicking them and then clicking the Add Field button (Figure 8–71).

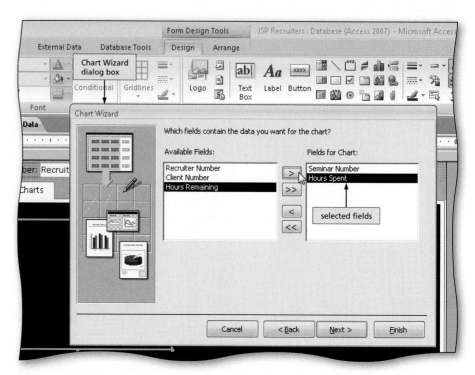

Figure 8–71

- Click the Next button.

- Click the Pie chart, the chart in the lower-left corner (Figure 8–72).

Experiment

- Click the other chart types and read the description of each chart type in the lower-right corner of the Chart Wizard dialog box. When finished, click the Pie chart in the lower-left corner.

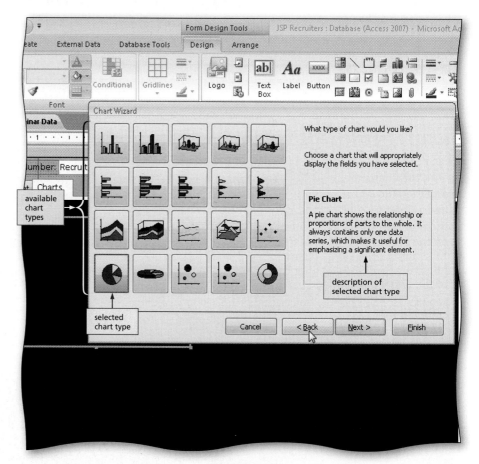

Figure 8–72

4

- Click the Next button (Figure 8–73).

Q&A What do the chart fields mean?

The field under the chart represents the data that will be summarized by slices of the pie. The other field is used to indicate the series. In this example, the field for the series is the seminar number and the sizes of the slices of the pie will represent the sum of the number of hours spent. You can change these by dragging the fields to the desired locations.

Q&A These fields make sense for a pie chart. What if I selected a different chart type?

The items on this screen will be relevant to the particular chart type you select. Just as with the pie chart, the correct fields often will be selected automatically. If not, you can drag the fields to the correct locations.

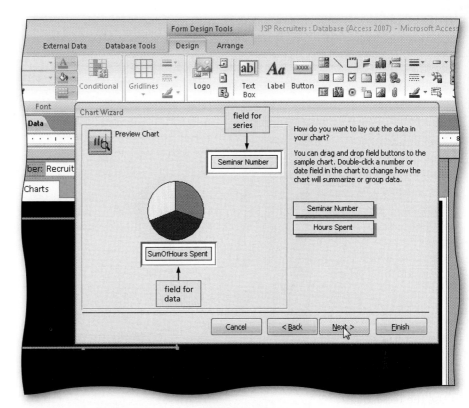

Figure 8–73

5

- Click the Next button (Figure 8–74).

Q&A The Recruiter Number field does not appear in my chart. Can I still use it to link the form and the chart?

Yes. Even though the Recruiter Number does not appear, it still is included in the query on which the chart is based. In fact, it is essential that it is included so that you can link the document (that is, the form) and the chart. Linking the document and the chart ensures that the chart will reflect accurately the data for the correct recruiter, that is, the recruiter who currently appears in the form.

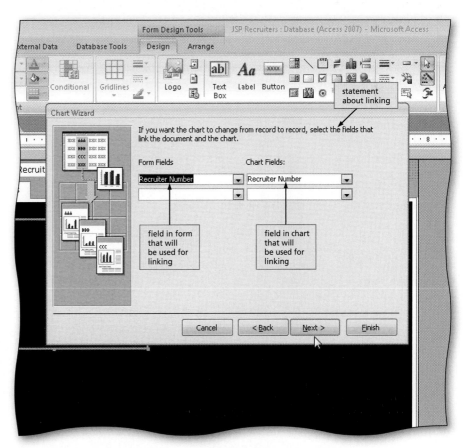

Figure 8–74

6

- Click the Next button, type Hours Spent by Seminar Offering as the title, and then click the Finish button (Figure 8–75).

The data does not look right. What's wrong and what do I need to do to fix it?

The data in the chart is fictitious. The data simply represents the general way the chart will look. When you view the actual form, the data represented in the chart should be correct.

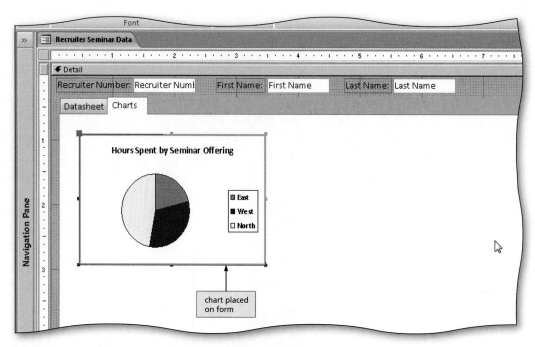

Figure 8–75

7

- Use the techniques shown in Steps 1 through 6 to add a second chart at the position shown in Figure 8–76. In this chart, select Hours Remaining instead of Hours Spent and type Hours Remaining by Seminar Offering as the title of the chart instead of Hours Spent by Seminar Offering.

8

- Save your changes.
- Close the form.

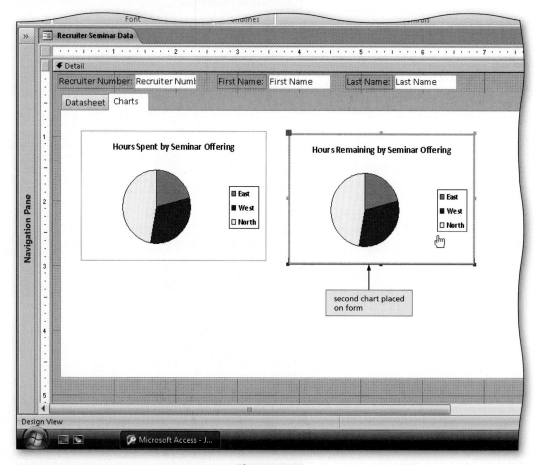

Figure 8–76

To Use the Form

You use this form just like the other forms you have created and used. To move from one tabbed page to another, simply click the desired tab. The corresponding page then will appear. The following steps use the form to view the seminar data.

1

- Show the Navigation Pane, open the Recruiter Seminar Data form in Form view, and hide the Navigation Pane.

- With the Datasheet tab selected, click the Next Record button at the bottom of the form to move to the second record in the Recruiter table (Figure 8–77).

Q&A What is the purpose of the navigation buttons in the subform?

These navigation buttons allow you to move within the records in the subform, that is, within the seminar offerings for the recruiter whose number and name appear at the top of the form.

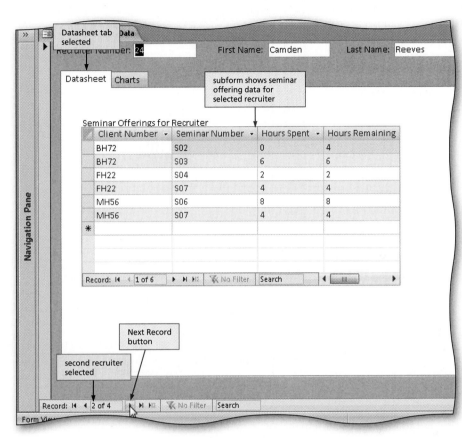

Figure 8–77

2

- Click the Charts tab to display the charts (Figure 8–78).

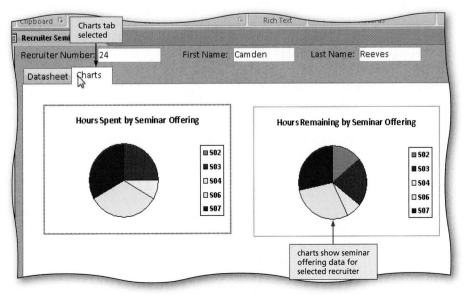

Figure 8–78

To Modify a Chart Type

When you first create a chart you specify the chart type. You later can change the type by editing the chart and selecting the Chart Type command. The following steps change the chart type.

1

• Right-click the Hours Spent by Seminar Offering chart to display a shortcut menu.

Q&A Does it matter where I right-click?

You should right-click within the rectangle but outside any of the items within the rectangle, in other words, in the white space.

Q&A My shortcut menu is very different. What should I do?

Click the View button arrow and then click Form View to ensure that you are viewing the form in Form view and then try again.

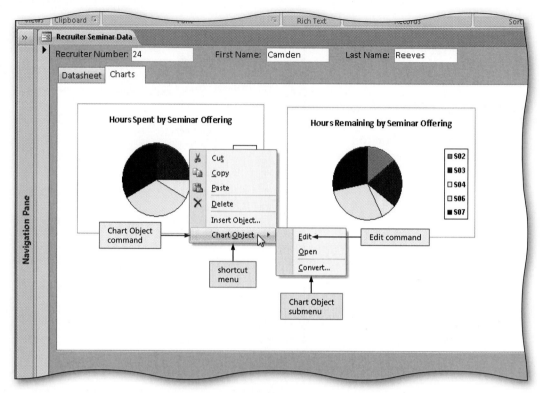

Figure 8–79

• Point to Chart Object on the shortcut menu to display the Chart Object submenu (Figure 8–79).

2

• Click Edit on the Chart Object sub-menu to edit the chart and display the underlying chart data in datasheet view (Figure 8–80).

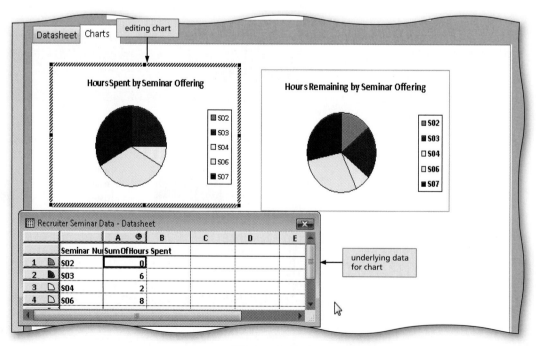

Figure 8–80

3

- Right-click the chart to display the shortcut menu for editing the chart (Figure 8–81).

 Does it matter where I right-click?

You should right-click within the rectangle but outside any of the items within the rectangle, in other words, in the white space.

 What types of changes can I make if I select Format Chart Area?

You can change such things as border style, color, fill effects, and fonts.

 How do I make other changes?

By clicking Chart Options on the shortcut menu, you can change titles, legends, and labels. For 3-D charts, by clicking 3-D View on the shortcut menu, you can change the elevation and rotation of the chart. You also can format specific items on the chart, as you will see in the next section.

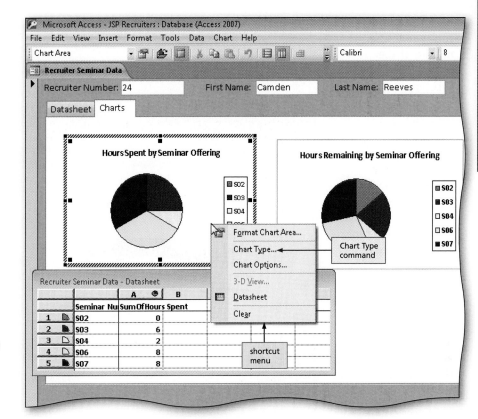

Figure 8–81

4

- Click the Chart Type command on the shortcut menu to display the Chart Type dialog box (Figure 8–82).

 What is the relationship between the Chart type and the Chart sub-type?

You can think of Chart types as categories of charts. There are column charts, bar charts, line charts, and so on. Once you have selected a category, the chart sub-types are those charts in that category. If you have selected the Pie chart category, for example, the charts within the category are the ones shown in the list of chart sub-types in Figure 8–82.

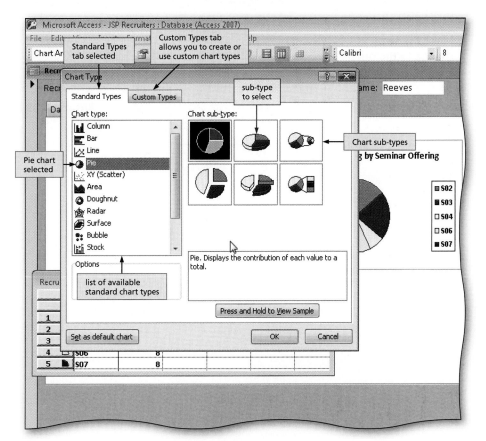

Figure 8–82

5

- Click the chart sub-type in the middle of the first row of chart sub-types to select it as the chart sub-type.

🔎 **Experiment**

- Click each of the chart types and examine the chart sub-types associated with that chart type. When finished, select Pie as the chart type and the sub-type in the middle of the first row as the chart sub-type.

- Click the OK button to change the chart sub-type.

- Click outside the chart and the datasheet to deselect the chart.

- Make the same change to the other chart (Figure 8–83).

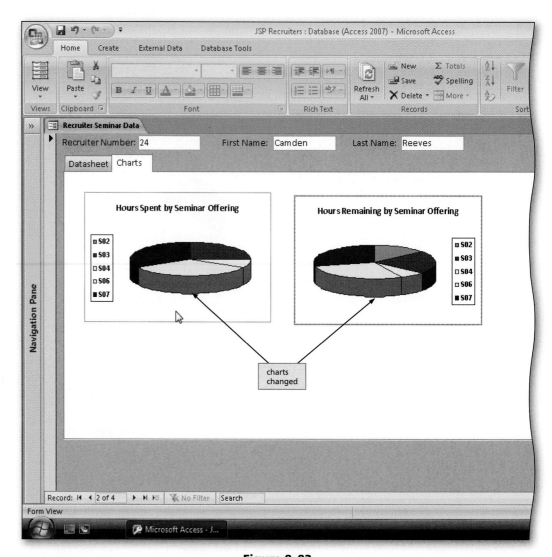

Figure 8–83

To Format a Chart

You can change the border style, color, fill effects, and fonts by using the Format Chart Area command. You can change titles, legends, and labels by using the Chart Options command. You also can format specific portions of a chart by right-clicking the portion you wish to format and then clicking the appropriate command on the shortcut menu. The following steps use this technique to move the legend so that it is at the bottom of the chart and then include percentages in the chart.

- Right-click the Hours Spent by Seminar Offering chart to display a shortcut menu, point to Chart Object on the shortcut menu to display the Chart Object submenu, and then click Edit on the Chart Object submenu.

- Right-click the legend to display a shortcut menu, and then click Format Legend on the shortcut menu to display the Format Legend dialog box.

- Click the Placement tab (Figure 8–84).

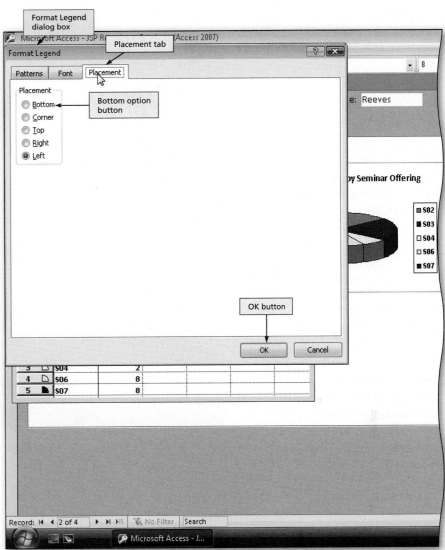

Figure 8–84

2

- Click the Bottom option button to specify that the legend should appear at the bottom of the chart.

What other types of changes can I make in this dialog box?

Click the patterns tab to change such things as border style, color, and fill effects. Click the Font tab to change the font and/or font characteristics.

- Click the OK button to place the legend at the location you selected.

- Right-click the pie chart to display a shortcut menu, and then click Format Data Series on the shortcut menu to display the Format Data Series dialog box.

- Click the Data Labels tab.

- Click the Percentage check box to specify that percentages are to be included (Figure 8–85).

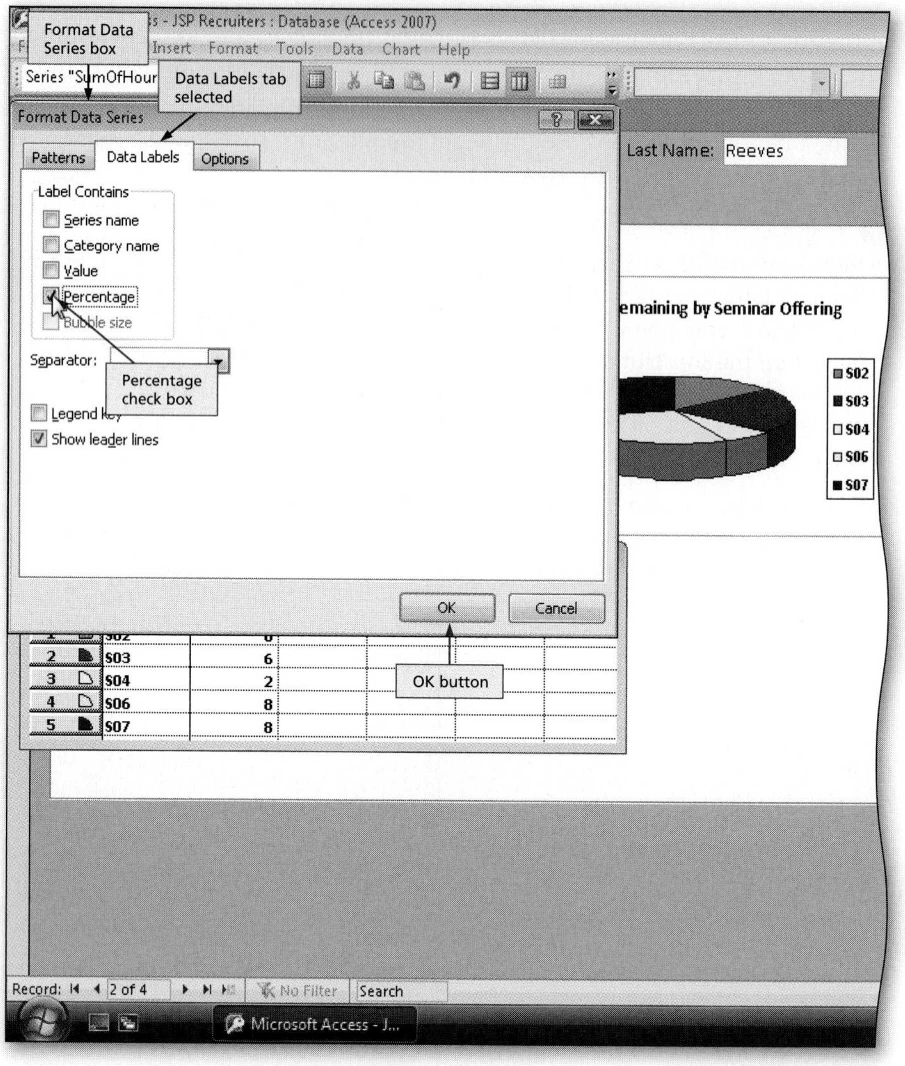

I see a Patterns tab just as with the legend, but how would I use the Options tab? Also, does the fact these are check boxes rather than option buttons mean that I can select more than one?

Use the Options tab to indicate whether the color is to vary by slice and also to specify the angle of the first slice in the pie. Because these are check boxes, you can select as many as you wish. Selecting too many can clutter the chart, however.

These options make sense for a pie chart, but what about other chart types?

The options that you see will vary from one chart type to another. They will be relevant for the selected chart type.

Figure 8–85

3

- Click the OK button to include percentages on the chart (Figure 8–86).

4

- Click outside the chart and the datasheet to deselect the chart.

- Make the same changes to the other chart.

- Save and then close the form.

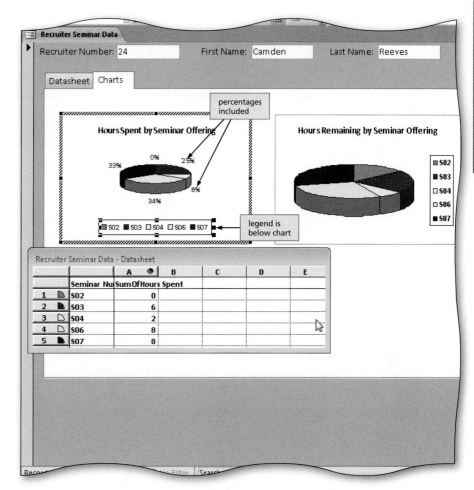

Figure 8–86

Using Other Tools in the Controls Group

You have used several tools within the Controls group on the Design tab. There are additional tools available (Figure 8–87) to customize a form's controls.

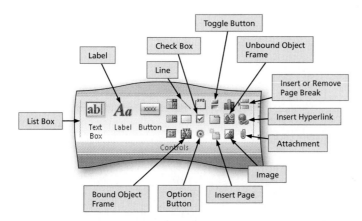

Figure 8–87

A list of the additional tools and a description of their respective uses appears in Table 8–2.

Table 8–2 Additional Tools in the Controls Group

Tool	Description
Label	Create a label, a box containing text that cannot be edited and is independent of other controls, such as a title.
List Box	Create a list box, a box that allows the user to select from a list of options.
Line	Draw a line on a form or report.
Bound Object Frame	Insert an OLE object (for example, a graph, picture, sound file, or video) that is contained in a field in a table within the database.
Check Box	Insert a check box. With a check box, a user can make multiple Yes/No selections.
Option Button	Insert an option button. With an option button, a user can make a single Yes/No selection from among a collection of at least two choices.
Toggle Button	Add a toggle button. With a toggle button, a user can make a Yes/No selection by clicking the button. The button either appears to be pressed (for Yes) or not pressed (for No).
Insert Page	Insert an additional page into a tab control.
Unbound Object Frame	Insert an OLE object (for example, a graph, picture, sound file, or video) that is not contained in a field in a table within the database.
Image	Insert a frame into which you can insert a graphic. The graphic will be the same for all records.
Insert or Remove Page Break	Insert or remove a physical page break (typically in a report).
Insert Hyperlink	Insert a hyperlink to an existing file, Web page, database object, or e-mail address.
Attachment	Insert an Attachment field.

To Quit Access

You saved all your changes and are ready to quit Access. The following step quits Access.

1 Click the Close button on the right side of the Access title bar to quit Access.

Chapter Summary

In this chapter you have learned to add a calculated field to a form; add a combo box that selects from a related table as well as a combo box that is used to find records on a form; format controls and use the format painter; add command buttons to a form; modify a button and a combo box; add and modify an option group; create macros with conditions as well as modify properties using a macro; use a tab control to create a multipage form; add and modify a subform; insert charts; change chart types; and format charts. The following list includes all the new Access skills you have learned in this chapter.

1. Create a Form in Design View (AC 529)
2. Add Fields to the Form Design (AC 530)
3. Add a Calculated Field to the Form (AC 531)
4. Change the Format of a Field (AC 532)
5. Add a Combo Box that Selects Values from a Related Table (AC 534)
6. Change the Background Color (AC 537)
7. Format a Control (AC 538)
8. Use the Format Painter (AC 539)
9. Resize Multiple Controls (AC 540)
10. Add a Title and Expand the Form Header Section (AC 540)
11. Add Command Buttons to a Form (AC 541)
12. Add a Combo Box that is Used to Find a Record (AC 544)
13. Place a Rectangle (AC 547)
14. Open a Form (AC 548)
15. Use the Add Record Button (AC 549)
16. Use the Combo Box (AC 549)
17. Modify the Add Record Button (AC 551)
18. Modify the Combo Box (AC 554)
19. Change the Enabled Property (AC 556)
20. Add an Option Group (AC 558)
21. Create a Macro for the Option Group (AC 561)
22. Add Actions to the Macro (AC 565)
23. Create a Macro for the On Load Property of the Form (AC 566)
24. Use Tab Controls to Create a Multipage Form (AC 571)
25. Add a Subform (AC 572)
26. Modify a Subform (AC 574)
27. Change the Background Color (AC 574)
28. Resize the Subform (AC 575)
29. Insert Charts (AC 575)
30. Use the Form (AC 579)
31. Modify a Chart Type (AC 580)
32. Format a Chart (AC 583)

 If you have a SAM user profile, you may have access to hands-on instruction, practice, and assessment. Log in to your SAM account (http://sam2007.course.com) to launch any assigned training activities or exams that relate to the skills covered in this chapter.

Learn It Online

Test your knowledge of chapter content and key terms.

Instructions: To complete the Learn It Online exercises, start your browser, click the Address bar, and then enter the Web address scsite.com/ac2007/learn. When the Access 2007 Learn It Online page is displayed, click the link for the exercise you want to complete and then read the instructions.

Chapter Reinforcement TF, MC, and SA
A series of true/false, multiple choice, and short answer questions that test your knowledge of the chapter content.

Flash Cards
An interactive learning environment where you identify chapter key terms associated with displayed definitions.

Practice Test
A series of multiple choice questions that test your knowledge of chapter content and key terms.

Who Wants To Be a Computer Genius?
An interactive game that challenges your knowledge of chapter content in the style of a television quiz show.

Wheel of Terms
An interactive game that challenges your knowledge of chapter key terms in the style of the television show *Wheel of Fortune*.

Crossword Puzzle Challenge
A crossword puzzle that challenges your knowledge of key terms presented in the chapter.

Apply Your Knowledge

Reinforce the skills and apply the concepts you learned in this chapter.

Creating a Multipage Form for The Bike Delivers Database
Instructions: Start Access. If you are using the Microsoft Office Access 2007 Comprehensive text, open The Bike Delivers database that you used in Chapter 7. Otherwise, see your instructor for information on accessing the files required in this book.

Perform the following tasks:
1. Open the Couriers and Services query in Design view. Sort the query in ascending order by Courier Number, Customer Number, and Service Code. Save the changes to the query.
2. Create the Courier Service Data form shown in Figure 8–88. The Datasheet tab displays a subform listing information about services for clients of the courier (Figure 8–88a). Data for the subform is based on the Couriers and Services query. Data for the Charts tab also is based on the Couriers and Services query (Figure 8–88b).

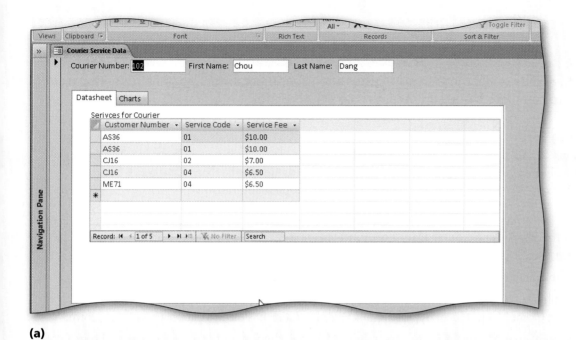

(a)

(b)

Figure 8–88

3. Submit the revised database in the format specified by your instructor.

Extend Your Knowledge

Extend the skills you learned in this chapter and experiment with new skills. You may need to use Help to complete the assignment.

Modifying Forms

Instructions: Copy the JSP Recruiters database and rename the database to Chapter 8_last name Recruiters. For example, if your last name is Smith, then name the database Chapter 8_Smith Recruiters. Start Access and open the database that you copied and renamed.

Perform the following tasks:

1. Open the Recruiter Seminar Data Form in Design view. Add a title to the form and insert the current date in the form header.
2. Add a third tab control to the form. Name the tab control, Clients.
3. Add a subform to the Clients tab control. The Client table is the basis of the subform. Display the Client Number, Client Name, Client Type, Amount Paid, and Current Due in a datasheet on the subform.
4. Open the Client Master Form in Design view. Change the font color for the command button text to Dark Red. Change the label for the option group to Dark Red.
5. Open the Client Financial Form in Design view and change the foreground color of the Client Number field to red.
6. Submit the revised database in the format specified by your instructor.

Make It Right

Analyze a database and correct all errors and/or improve the design.

Correcting Form Design Errors

Instructions: Start Access. Open the YourHouse Fitness Company database. See the inside back cover of this book for instructions on downloading the Data Files for Students, or contact your instructor for more information about accessing the required files.

The YourHouse Fitness Company database contains data about an organization that does personal fitness training in an individual's home. The owner of the company has created the form shown in Figure 8–89, but there are a few problems. Total Amount is a calculated control, but there is a problem with the expression entered for the control. Also, the calculated control should be dimmed. The name in the Name to Find combo box should change when the Next Record navigation button is clicked. Finally, she would like to place a rectangle around the Name to Find combo box and apply the raised special effect.

Correct these errors and submit the revised database in the format specified by your instructor.

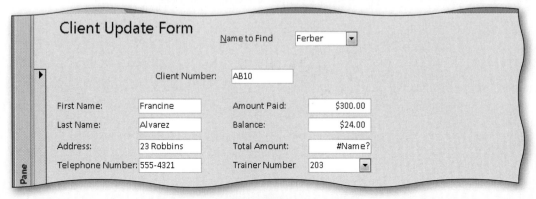

Figure 8–89

In the Lab

Design, create, modify, and/or use a database following the guidelines, concepts, and skills presented in this chapter. Labs are listed in order of increasing difficulty.

Lab 1: Applying Advanced Form Techniques to the JMS TechWizards Database

Problem: JMS TechWizards needs a form for the Client table that will allow users to update data in the table. JMS also needs a form to display work order data for technicians.

Instructions: If you are using the Microsoft Office Access 2007 Comprehensive text, open the JMS TechWizards database that you used in Chapter 7. Otherwise, see the inside back cover of this book for instructions on downloading the Data Files for Students, or contact your instructor for more information about accessing the required files.

Perform the following tasks:

1. Open the Technicians and Work Orders query and sort the query by Technician Number, Client Number, and Category Number. Save the changes to the query.

2. Create the form shown in Figure 8–90. Total Amount is a calculated control and is the sum of the Billed and Paid amounts. Users should not be able to update the Total Amount control. The form includes command buttons, a combo box for the Technician Number field, and a combo box to search for clients by name. Be sure to sort the client names in ascending order, place a rectangle around the combo box, and update the combo box. The user should not be able to tab to the combo box. When the Add Record button is clicked, the insertion point should be in the Client Number field. The form is similar in style to the form shown in Figure 8–1a on page AC 523.

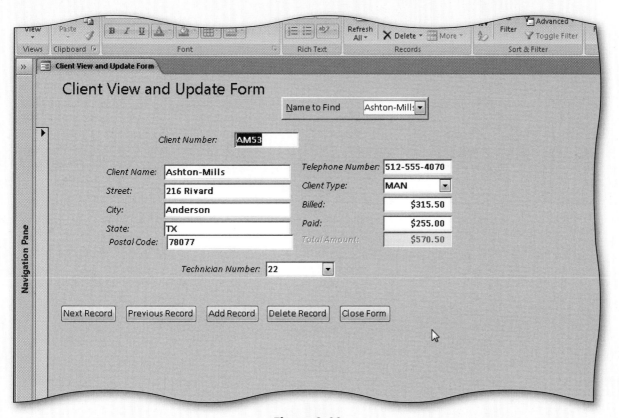

Figure 8–90

Continued >

3. Create the form shown in Figure 8–91. The subform that appears in the Datasheet tab uses the Technicians and Work Orders query (Figure 8–91a). The charts that appear in the Charts tab use the same query and the exploded pie subchart (Figure 8–91b).

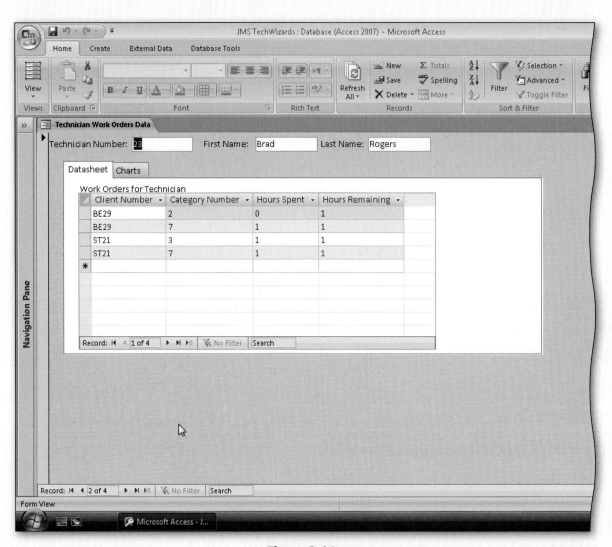

Figure 8–91a

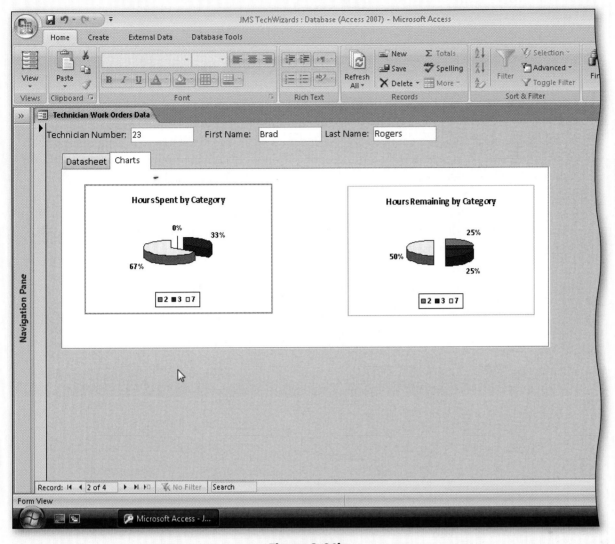

Figure 8–91b

4. Submit the revised database in the format specified by your instructor.

In the Lab

Lab 2: Applying Advanced Form Techniques to the Hockey Fan Zone Database

Problem: The management of the Hockey Fan Zone store needs a form that displays item information. The form should display the total cost of items on hand. It also should include command buttons to perform common operations, a combo box to search for items by description, and an option group that allows different views of the Item table. The company also needs a form that displays supplier information as well as items on order and all items associated with a supplier.

Instructions: If you are using the Microsoft Office Access 2007 Comprehensive text, open the Hockey Fan Zone database that you used in Chapter 7. Otherwise, see the inside back cover of this book for instructions on downloading the Data Files for Students, or contact your instructor for more information about accessing the required files.

Continued >

In the Lab *continued*

Perform the following tasks:

1. Create the Item View and Update Form shown in Figure 8–92. Total Cost is a calculated control and is the result of multiplying On Hand by Cost. Users should not be able to update the Total Cost control. The form includes command buttons, a combo box for the Supplier Code field, and a combo box to search for items by description. Be sure to sort the descriptions in ascending order, place a rectangle around the combo box, and update the combo box. The user should not be able to tab to the combo box. When the Add Record button is clicked, the insertion point should be in the Item Number field. If the user clicks the Change Item Description Data option, they should be able to change only the item number, description, and item type. If the user clicks the Change Other Data option, they should be able to change all data except description and item type. When the form first opens, the View Data Only option should apply. The form is similar in style to that shown in Figure 8–1a on page AC 523.

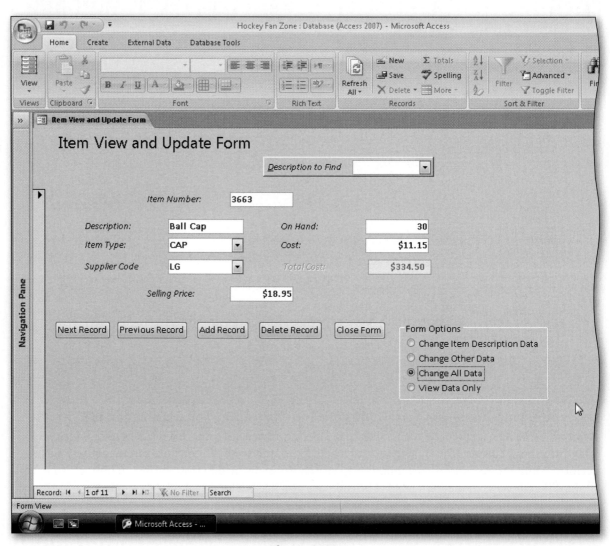

Figure 8–92

2. Open the Supplier and Number of Items query in Design view and add the Description and Date Ordered fields to the query. Sort the query by Item Number and Date Ordered. Save the query.

3. Create the Supplier Master Data form shown in Figure 8–93. The On Order tab (Figure 8–93a) uses the Supplier and Number of Items query for the subform. The Items tab uses the Item table for the subform. Note that the labels for Supplier Code and Supplier Name have been changed and that there is a title on the form. The form's title is bold. Use red as the font for the labels and dark blue as the font for the text boxes. You can use the Format Painter to copy formatting for text boxes and labels.

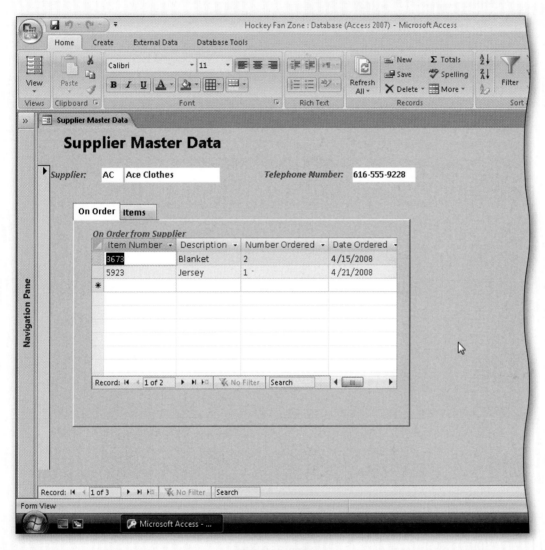

Figure 8–93a

Continued >

In the Lab *continued*

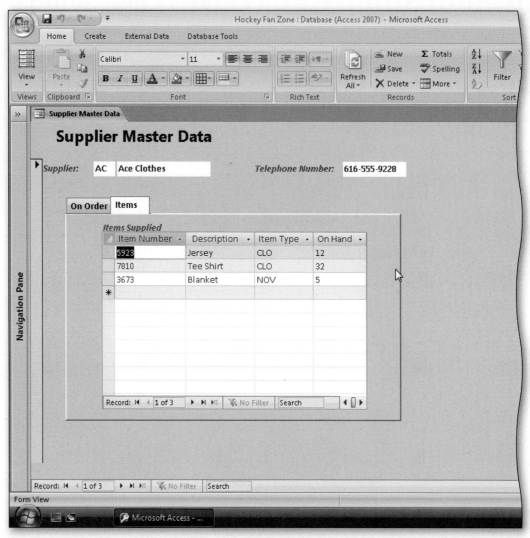

Figure 8–93b

4. Submit the revised database in the format specified by your instructor.

In the Lab

Lab 3: Applying Advanced Form Techniques to the Ada Beauty Supply Database

Problem: Ada Beauty Supply needs a form that displays customer information. The form should display a calculated control that sums the Balance and Amount Paid fields. It also should include a combo box to search for customers by name and an option group that allows different views of the Customer table. The company also needs a form that displays sales rep information as well as open orders for customers.

Instructions: If you are using the Microsoft Office Access 2007 Comprehensive text, open the Ada Beauty Supply database that you used in Chapter 7. Otherwise, see the inside back cover of this book for instructions on downloading the Data Files for Students, or contact your instructor for more information about accessing the required files. Submit the revised database in the format specified by your instructor.

Instructions Part 1:   Create the Customer View and Update Form shown in Figure 8–94.

Instructions Part 2:   Create a query that joins the Sales Rep, Customer, and Open Orders tables. Include the sales rep number, customer number, customer name, order number, and amount in the query. Sort the query by sales rep number, customer number, and order numbers. Save the query as Sales Reps and Orders.

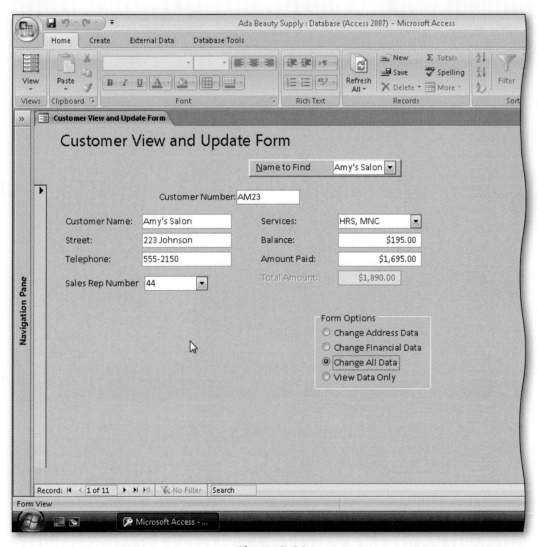

Figure 8–94

Continued >

In the Lab *continued*

Instructions Part 3: Create the Sales Rep Data form shown in Figure 8–95. This form uses the query you created in Part 2. The Chart tab has only one chart that displays the customer number and the total amount of open orders for the customer. The chart uses a 3D column chart style.

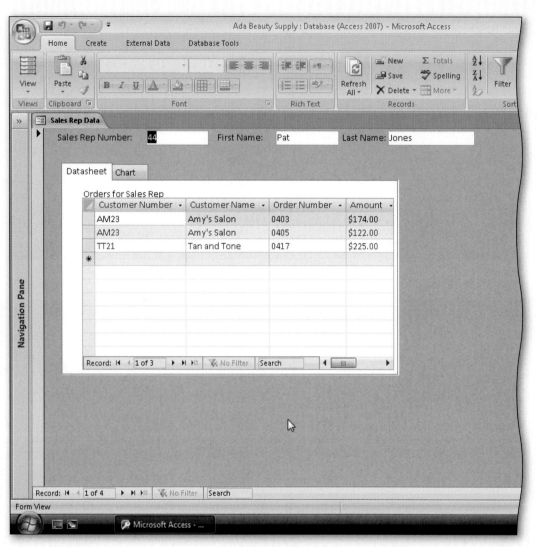

Figure 8–95

Cases and Places

Apply your creative thinking and problem-solving skills to design and implement a solution.

• EASIER   •• MORE DIFFICULT

• 1: Applying Advanced Form Techniques to the Second Hand Goods Database

If you are using the Microsoft Office Access 2007 Comprehensive text, open the Second Hand Goods database that you used in Chapter 7. Otherwise, see the inside back cover of this book for instructions on downloading the Data Files for Students, or contact your instructor for more information about accessing the required files. Modify the Item Update Form that you created previously to include command buttons to move to the next record, move to the previous record, add a record, and delete a record. Delete the seller data that appears on the form and re-add this information as a combo box. When users add a record, the insertion point should be in the item number field. Sort the records in order by Description. Print the form for the record that now appears as the first record. Apply a filter to the form to find only those items that are in Excellent condition. Write the item numbers of the filtered records on the form that you printed. Submit the printed form and the revised database in the format specified by your instructor.

• 2: Applying Advanced Form Techniques to the BeachCondo Rentals Database

If you are using the Microsoft Office Access 2007 Comprehensive text, open the BeachCondo Rentals database that you used in Chapter 7. Otherwise, see the inside back cover of this book for instructions on downloading the Data Files for Students, or contact your instructor for more information about accessing the required files. Modify the Owner Master Form that you created previously to include command buttons to move to the next record, move to the previous record, find a record, and close the form. Use pictures instead of text on the command buttons. Submit the revised database in the format specified by your instructor.

•• 3: Applying Advanced Form Techniques to the Restaurant Database

If you are using the Microsoft Office Access 2007 Comprehensive text, open the restaurant database that you used in Chapter 7. Otherwise, see the inside back cover of this book for instructions on downloading the Data Files for Students, or contact your instructor for more information about accessing the required files. Using the Plan Ahead guidelines presented in this chapter, determine what additional forms you need for your database. Also, determine if you need to make any changes to existing forms. For example, if attendees are using your forms, you want to make them as easy to use as possible. Combo boxes and command buttons may be useful. Should attendees be allowed to change any data? If not, perhaps, you should set certain fields to view only. What data should appear on the forms? Are multipage forms needed? Modify the database as appropriate and submit the revised database in the format specified by your instructor.

Continued >

Cases and Places *continued*

•• 4: Applying Advanced Form Techniques to Your Contacts Database

Make It Personal

If you are using the Microsoft Office Access 2007 Comprehensive text, open the contacts database that you used in Chapter 7. Otherwise, see the inside back cover of this book for instructions on downloading the Data Files for Students, or contact your instructor for more information about accessing the required files. Review the current forms you have in your Contacts database. Could any forms be enhanced by the addition of command buttons? Would a combo box to search for contacts be beneficial? Do you need a multipage form? Modify the forms as necessary. Submit the revised database in the format specified by your instructor.

•• 5: Understanding Forms

Working Together

As a team, choose one of the In the Lab databases. Then, copy and rename the database. Research the purpose of the tools listed in Table 8–2 on page AC 586. Modify the Client Master Form by adding lines and adding a picture. Modify the Recruiter Seminar Data form by adding command buttons. Place pictures instead of text on the command buttons. Submit the revised database in the format specified by your instructor.

9 Administering a Database System

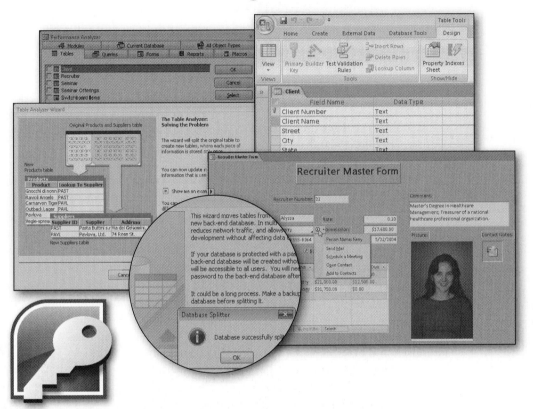

Objectives

You will have mastered the material in this project when you can:

- Convert a database to and from earlier versions of Access

- Use the Table Analyzer, Performance Analyzer, and Documenter

- Create custom categories and groups in the Navigation Pane

- Use table and database properties

- Use field properties to create a custom input mask and to allow zero length

- Create indexes

- Enable and use automatic error checking

- Create and use smart tags

- Select a startup form

- Encrypt a database and set a password

- Understand and use digital certificates

- Understand the purpose and use of options within the Trust Center

- Lock a database

- Split a database

9 | Administering a Database System

Introduction

Administering a database system is an important activity that has many facets. These activities go far beyond the simple updating of a database. They include activities to improve the usability, accessibility, security, and efficiency of the database.

Project — Administering a Database System

BTW

Security
Security is the prevention of unauthorized access to a database. Within an organization, the database administrator determines the types of access individual users can have to the database. Various government rules and regulations, such as Sarbannes-Oxley (SOX) and the Health Insurance Portability and Accountability Act (HIPAA) require database administrators to have strict security procedures in place to protect data from unauthorized access.

JSP Recruiters realizes the importance of database administration, that is, the importance of administering its database system properly. Management realizes that doing so encompasses a wide variety of activities (Figure 9–1). Database administration can include conversion of an Access 2007 database to an earlier version. Database administration usually includes such activities as analyzing tables for potential problems, analyzing performance to see if changes are warranted to make the system perform more efficiently, and documenting the various objects in the database. It can include creating custom categories and groups in the Navigation Pane as well as changing table and database properties. It also can include the use of field properties in such tasks as creating a custom input mask and allowing zero length strings. It can include the creation of indexes to speed up retrieval. The inclusion of automatic error checking and smart tags in tables, queries, forms, and reports is part of the administration of a database system. Securing the database through the use of passwords and encryption also are database administration tasks, as is the selection of a startup form. Understanding the purpose of digital certificates and the trust center is critical to the database administration function. Another important area of database administration is the protection of the database. This protection includes locking the database through the creation of an ACCDE file to prevent unauthorized changes from being made to the VBA source code or to the design of forms and reports. Splitting the database into a front-end and a back-end database is another way to protect the functionality and efficiency of a database.

- Convert a database to an earlier version of Access
- Use the Table Analyzer
- Use the Performance Analyzer
- Use the Documenter
- Enable error checking
- Create a custom input mask
- Specify and use smart tags
- Import and link SharePoint Services lists
- Set startup options
- Set a password
- Encode a database
- Create and use a replica
- Set macro security level
- Synchronize a Design Master and a replica
- Split a database
- Create an MDE file
- Specify user-level security

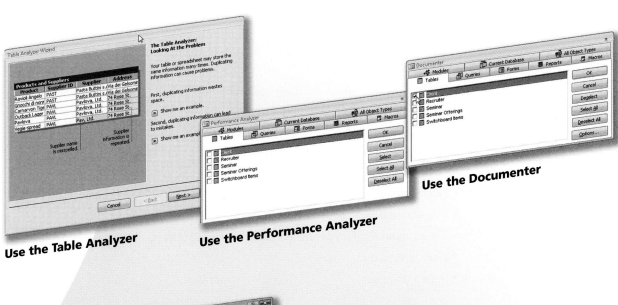

Use the Table Analyzer

Use the Performance Analyzer

Use the Documenter

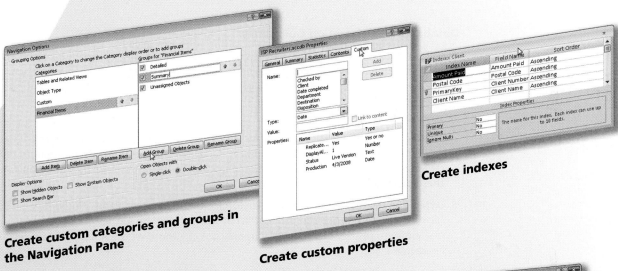

Create custom categories and groups in
the Navigation Pane

Create custom properties

Create indexes

Enable error checking

Specify and use smart tags

Encrypt a database
and set a password

Figure 9–1

Overview

As you read this chapter, you will learn how to administer a database by performing these general tasks:

- Learn how to convert databases to and from earlier versions of Access as well as how to use tools for analyzing and documenting Access databases.
- Create custom categories and groups in the Navigation Pane.
- Use table, database, and field properties.
- Create indexes.
- Learn how to use automatic error checking.
- Use smart tags.
- Understand digital certificates and the Trust Center.
- Lock a database.
- Split a database.

Plan Ahead

Database Administration Guidelines

1. **Determine whether a database needs to be converted to or from an earlier version.** Do users of a previous version of Access need to be able to use the database? If so, you will need to be sure the database does not contain any features that would prevent it from being converted. Is there a database that was created in an earlier version of Access that you would like to use in Access 2007?

2. **Determine when to analyze and/or document the database.** Once you create a database you should use the table and performance analyzers to determine if any changes to the structure are warranted. You also should document the database. You should perform these tasks whenever you change the structure.

3. **Determine the most useful way to customize the Navigation Pane.** Would it be helpful to have custom categories and groups? What items should be in the groups? Would it be helpful to restrict the items that appear to only those whose names contain certain characters?

4. **Determine any table-wide validation rules.** Are there any validation rules that involve more than a single field? For example, a validation rule that states that the hours spent cannot exceed the total hours would involve both the Hours Spent and the Total Hours fields.

5. **Determine any custom database properties.** Are there properties that would be helpful in documenting the database that are not included in the list of database properties you can use? If so, you can add custom properties.

6. **Determine indexes.** Examine retrieval and sorting requirements to determine possible indexes. Indexes can make both retrieval and sorting more efficient.

7. **Determine whether a startup form is appropriate.** Is there a form that should be displayed automatically whenever a user opens the database? If the database includes a switchboard, the switchboard is usually a good candidate for such a form.

8. **Determine whether the database should be encrypted.** Encrypting a database is an excellent security feature. If there are any potential security issues, you should strongly consider encryption. As part of the process, you also will set a password.

9. **Determine whether the database should be locked.** Should users be able to change the design of forms, reports, and/or VBA code? If not, you should lock the database to prevent such changes.

(continued)

Plan
Ahead

(continued)

10. **Determine whether the database should be split.** Would it be preferable to have the database split into a back-end database, which contains only the table data, and a front-end database, which contains other objects, such as queries, forms, and reports? If so, you should split the database.

When necessary, more specific details concerning the above decisions and/or actions are presented at appropriate points in the chapter. The chapter also will identify the use of these guidelines in the administration of a database.

Starting Access

If you are using a computer to step through the project in this chapter and you want your screen to match the figures in this book, you should change your screen's resolution to 1024×768. For information about how to change a computer's resolution, read Appendix E.

To Start Access

The following steps, which assume Windows Vista is running, start Access.

Note: If you are using Windows XP, see Appendix F for alternate steps.

1 Click the Start button on the Windows Vista taskbar to display the Start menu.

2 Click All Programs at the bottom of the left pane on the Start menu to display the All Programs list, and then click Microsoft Office on the All Programs list to display the Microsoft Office list.

3 Click Microsoft Office Access 2007 on the Microsoft Office list to start Access and display the Getting Started with Microsoft Office Access window.

4 If the Access window is not maximized, click the Maximize button on its title bar to maximize the window.

To Open a Database

In Chapter 1, you created your database on a USB flash drive using the file name, JSP Recruiters. There are two ways to open the file containing your database. If the file you created appears in the Recent Documents list, you could click it to open the file. If not, you can use the More button to open the file. The following steps use the More button to open the JSP Recruiters database from the USB flash drive.

Note: If you are using Windows XP, see Appendix F for alternate steps.

1 With your USB flash drive connected to one of the computer's USB ports, click the More button to display the Open dialog box.

2 If the Folders list is displayed below the Folders button, click the Folders button to remove the Folders list.

3 If necessary, click Computers in the Favorite Links section and then double-click UDISK 2.0 (E:) to select the USB flash drive, Drive E in this case, as the new open location. (Your drive letter might be different.)

4 Click JSP Recruiters to select the file name.

5 Click the Open button to open the database.

6 If a Security Warning appears, click the Options button to display the Microsoft Office Security Options dialog box.

7 With the option button to enable the content selected, click the OK button to enable the content.

Converting Databases

There are occasions when you may need to convert from one version of Access to another. For example, an employee in a different location may have an earlier version of Access. Perhaps, you have a database created in an earlier version of Access that you want to use in Access 2007. You can convert from an Access 2007 database to earlier versions. You also can convert from earlier versions to Access 2007.

TO CONVERT AN ACCESS 2007 DATABASE TO AN EARLIER VERSION

To convert an Access 2007 database to an earlier version, the database cannot contain any features that are specific to Access 2007. These include attachments, multivalued fields, offline data, or links to external files not supported in earlier versions of Access. If the database does contain any of these features, Access will not allow you to convert to an earlier version. Provided the database does not contain such features, you can convert the database by pointing to the Save As command on the Microsoft Office Button menu (Figure 9–2). You then can choose the appropriate format.

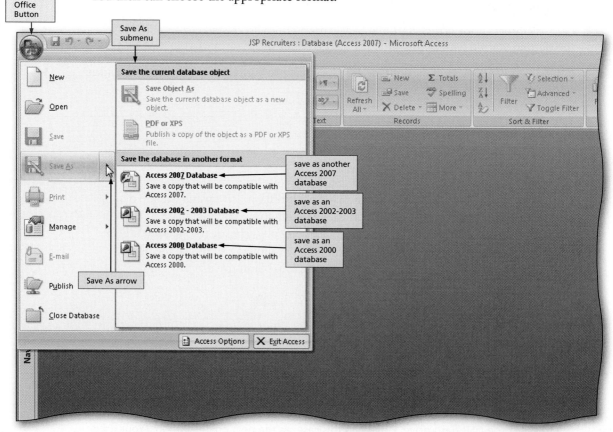

Figure 9–2

Specifically, to convert an Access 2007 database to an earlier version, you would use the following steps.

1. With the database to be converted open, click the Microsoft Office Button to display the Microsoft Office Button menu.

2. Point to the Save As arrow to display the Save As submenu.

3. Click the desired format.

4. Type the name you want for the converted database, select a location, and click the Save button.

TO CONVERT AN ACCESS 2000 OR ACCESS 2002-2003 DATABASE TO ACCESS 2007

To convert an Access 2000 or Access 2002-2003 database to an Access 2007 database, you open the database. Initially, the database is open in compatibility mode, where new features that cannot easily be displayed or converted are disabled. In this mode, the database remains in its original format. If you want to convert it, you use the Convert command on the Microsoft Office Button menu. Once the database is converted, the disabled features will be enabled. You will no longer be able to share the database with users of Access 2000 or Access 2002-2003, however.

Specifically, to convert an Access 2000 or 2002-2003 database to Access 2007, you would use the following steps.

1. With the database to be converted open, click the Microsoft Office Button to display the Microsoft Office Button menu.

2. Click Convert on the Microsoft Office Button menu.

3. Type the name you want for the converted database, select a location, and click the Save button.

BTW

Opening Earlier Versions of Access
You can open a database having an Access 2000 or Access 2002-2003 file format directly, without converting the database to Access 2007. When you open a database that has an Access 2000 or Access 2002-2003 file format, the file format appears in parentheses following the database file name in the title bar.

Microsoft Access Tools

Microsoft Access has a variety of tools that are useful in analyzing databases. These include tools to analyze table structures, to analyze performance, and to create detailed documentation.

To Use the Table Analyzer

Access contains three tools that allow you to analyze the design and performance of your database. The Table Analyzer can analyze tables while looking for potential redundancy. The Performance Analyzer can analyze performance and check for ways to make queries, reports, or forms more efficient. Then, the tool will make suggestions for possible changes. The Database Documenter produces detailed documentation describing the structure and content of the various tables, queries, forms, reports, and other objects in the database.

The Table Analyzer examines tables for **redundancy**, which is duplicated data. If redundancy is found, the Table Analyzer will suggest ways to split the table to eliminate the redundancy. The following steps illustrate how to use the Table Analyzer.

- If necessary, hide the Navigation Pane.

- Click Database Tools on the Ribbon to display the Database Tools tab (Figure 9–3).

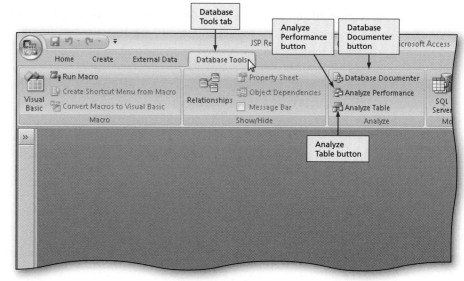

Figure 9–3

- Click the Analyze Table button on the Database Tools tab to display the Table Analyzer Wizard dialog box (Figure 9–4).

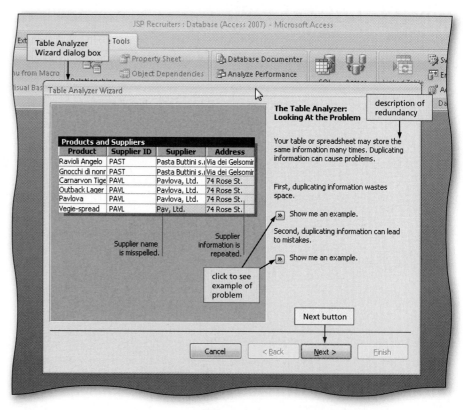

Figure 9–4

3

• Click the Next button to display the next Table Analyzer Wizard screen (Figure 9–5).

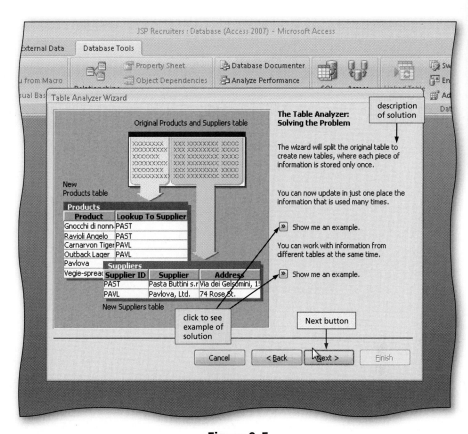

Figure 9–5

4

• Click the Next button to display the next Table Analyzer Wizard screen.

• Make sure the Client table is selected (Figure 9–6).

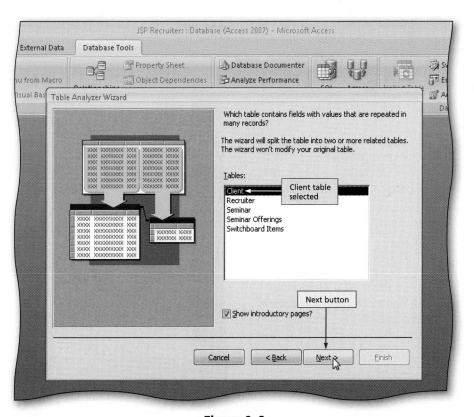

Figure 9–6

5

- Click the Next button.

- Be sure the 'Yes, let the wizard decide.' option button is selected (Figure 9–7).

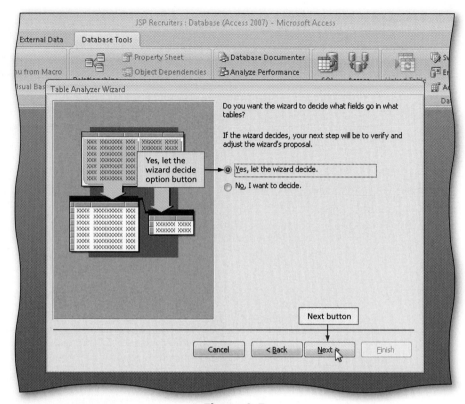

Figure 9–7

6

- Click the Next button to run the analysis (Figure 9–8).

Q&A I can't see all the fields in the field lists on the right. What can I do?

You either can resize the field lists or use the scroll bar to see the other fields.

Q&A I don't really want to put the state in a different table, even though I realize that states are duplicated. Do I have to follow this advice?

Certainly not. This is only a suggestion.

7

- Because the type of duplication identified by the analyzer does not pose a problem, click the Cancel button.

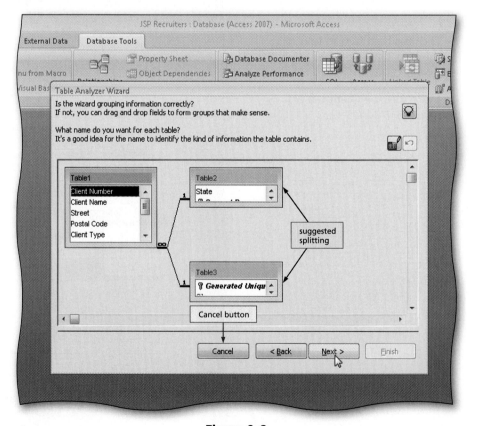

Figure 9–8

To Use the Performance Analyzer

The Performance Analyzer will examine the tables, queries, reports, forms, and other objects in your system, looking for changes that would improve the efficiency of database operations. This could include changes to the way data is stored, as well as changes to the indexes created for the system (you will learn about indexes later in this chapter). Once it has finished, it will make recommendations concerning possible changes. The following steps use the Performance Analyzer.

1

- Click the Analyze Performance button on the Database Tools tab to display the Performance Analyzer dialog box.

- If necessary, click the Tables tab (Figure 9–9).

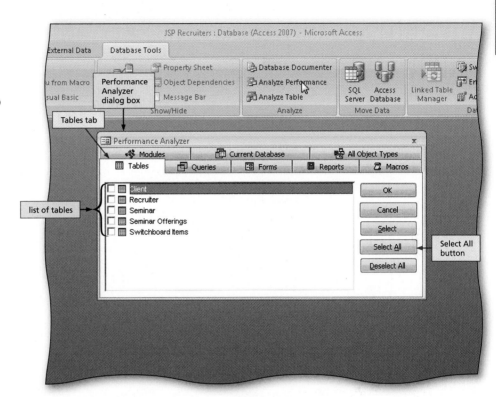

Figure 9–9

2

- Click the Select All button to select all tables.

- Click the OK button to display the results (Figure 9–10).

 What do the results mean?

Access has no changes to suggest. If it did, you could decide whether to follow the suggestions.

3

- Click the OK button to finish working with the Performance Analyzer.

Figure 9–10

To Use the Documenter

The Documenter allows you to produce detailed documentation of the various tables, queries, forms, reports, and other objects in your database. Figure 9–11 shows a portion of the documentation of the Client table. The complete documentation is much lengthier than the one shown in the figure. In the actual documentation, all fields would display as much information as the Client Number field. In the sample documentation shown in the figure, only those items of interest are shown for the other fields.

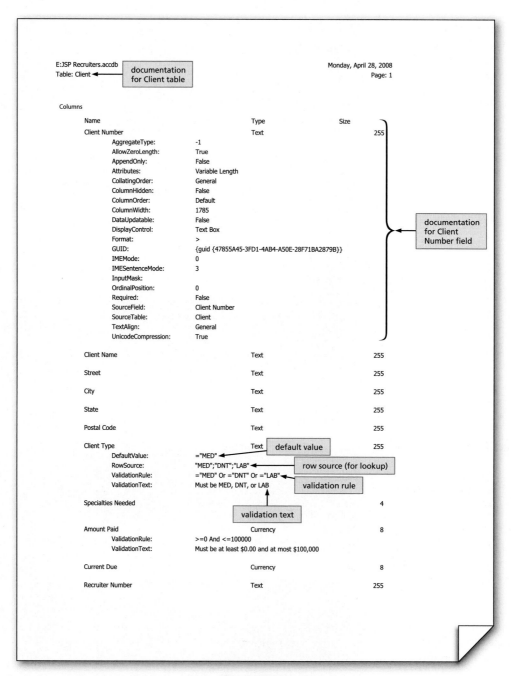

Figure 9–11

Notice that the documentation of the Client Type field contains the default value and the row source associated with the Lookup information for the field. The documentation for both the Client Type and Amount Paid fields contains validation rules and validation text.

The following steps use the Documenter to produce documentation for the Client table.

1

- Click the Database Documenter button on the Database Tools tab to display the Documenter dialog box.

- If necessary, click the Tables tab and then click the Client check box (Figure 9–12).

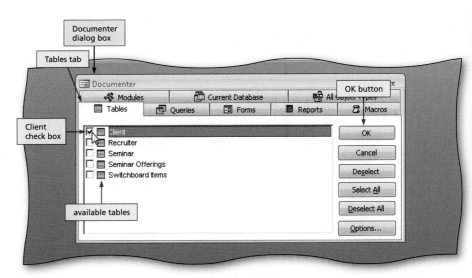

Figure 9–12

2

- Click the OK button to produce a preview of the documentation (Figure 9–13).

Q&A

What can I do with this documentation?

You could print it by clicking the Print button. You could create a PDF or XPS file containing the documentation by clicking the PDF or XPS button and following the directions. You could create a file that is accessible from Word by clicking the Word button and following the directions. You may need to use this documentation later if you make changes to the database.

- Click the Close Print Preview button to close the preview of the documentation.

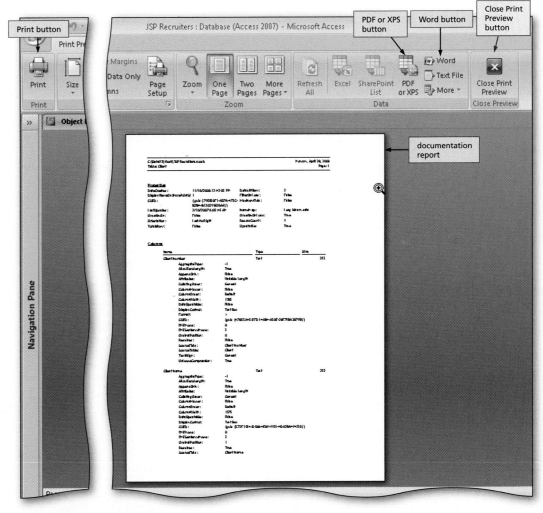

Figure 9–13

Experiment

- Try other options within the Documenter to see the effect of your choice on the documentation produced. Each time, close the preview of the documentation.

BTW

Database Documenter
The Options button in the Documenter dialog box allows you to further specify what to include for each table and for each field in a table.

Navigation Pane

You already have seen how to customize the Navigation Pane by selecting the category and the filter. You also can create custom categories and groups that you can use to categorize the items in the database in ways that are most useful to you. In addition, you can use the Search Bar to restrict the items that appear in the Navigation Pane to only those that have the collection of characters you specify in their names.

Plan Ahead

> **Determine the most useful way to customize the Navigation Pane.**
> Determine the customization of the Navigation Pane that would be most helpful to your users. The types of issues to consider are the following:
>
> 1. Is there a new category that would be useful?
>
> 2. If so, are there new groups that would be useful to include in the new category?
>
> 3. If you have created a new category and a new group, which items should be included in one of the new groups and which should be left uncategorized?

To Create Custom Categories and Groups

You can create custom categories in the Navigation Pane. You also can add custom groups to the categories. The following steps create a custom category called Financial Items. They then add two custom groups, Detailed and Summary, to the Financial Items category.

- Show the Navigation Pane.

- Right-click the Navigation Pane title bar to display a shortcut menu (Figure 9–14).

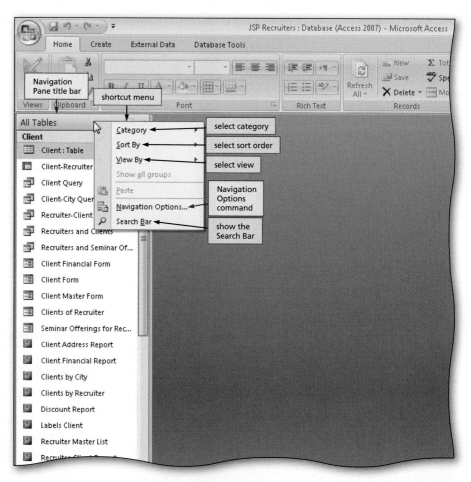

Figure 9–14

2

- Click the Navigation Options command on the shortcut menu to display the Navigation Options dialog box (Figure 9–15).

Q&A What else could I do with the shortcut menu?

You could select a category, select sort order, or select how to view the items within the Navigation Pane.

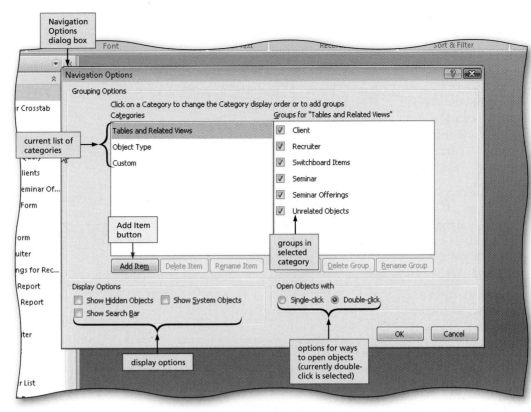

Figure 9–15

3

- Click the Add Item button to add a new category (Figure 9–16).

Q&A Could I use the Custom category?

Yes. It is a good idea to reserve that category by creating your own new category, however.

Q&A If I made a mistake in creating a new category, how can I fix it?

Select the category that is incorrect. If the name is wrong, click the Rename Item button and change the name appropriately. If you do not want the category, click the Delete Item button to delete the category and then click the OK button.

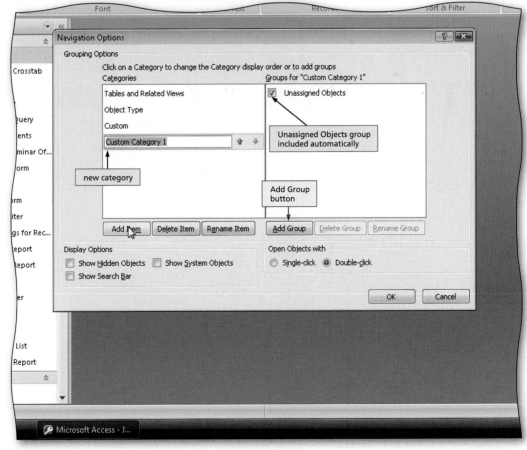

Figure 9–16

4

- Type Financial Items as the name of the category.

- Click the Add Group button to add a group, and then type Detailed as the name of the group.

- Click the Add Group button to add a group, and then type Summary as the name of the group (Figure 9–17).

Q&A

I added the groups in the wrong order. How can I change the order?

Select the group that is in the wrong position. Click the UP or DOWN arrows to move the group to the correct location.

5

- Click the OK button to create the new category and groups.

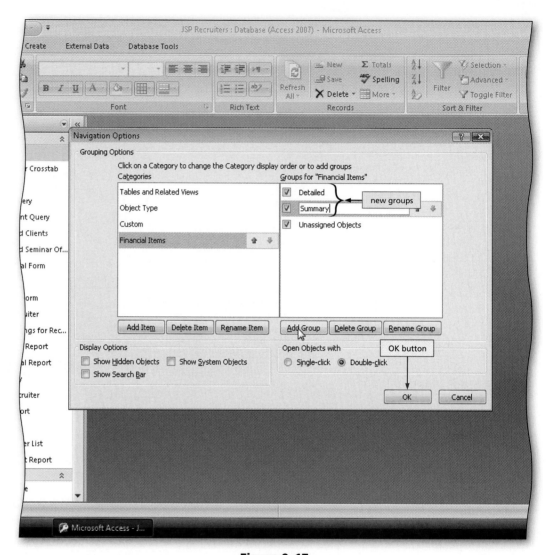

Figure 9–17

To Add Items to Groups

Once you have created new groups, you can add existing items to the new groups. The following steps add items to the Summary and Detailed groups in the Financial Items category.

- Click the Navigation Pane arrow to produce the Navigation Pane menu (Figure 9–18).

Q&A Do I have to click the arrow?

No. If you prefer, you can click anywhere in the title bar for the Navigation Pane. Clicking arrows is a good habit, however, because there are many situations where you must click the arrow.

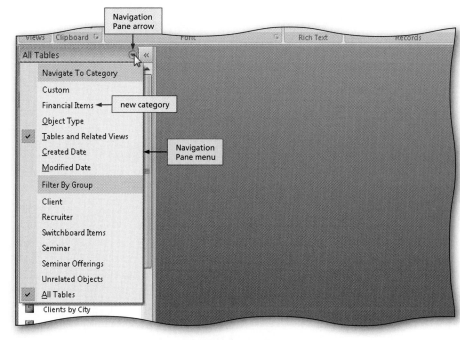

Figure 9–18

2

- Click the Financial Items category to display the groups within the category.

- Right-click Client-Recruiter Crosstab to display the shortcut menu.

- Point to the 'Add to group' command on the shortcut menu to display the list of available groups (Figure 9–19).

Q&A I didn't create an Unassigned Objects group. Where did it come from?

Access creates the Unassigned Objects group automatically. Until you add an object to one of the groups you created, it will be in the Unassigned Objects group.

Q&A What is the purpose of the New Group on the submenu?

You can create a new group using this submenu. This is an alternative to using the Navigation Options dialog box. Use whichever approach you find most convenient.

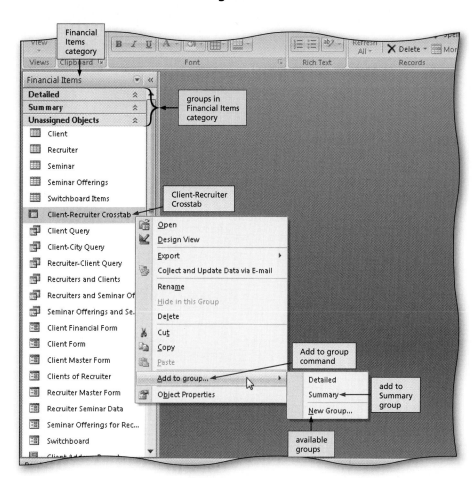

Figure 9–19

3

- Click Summary to add the Client-Recruiter Crosstab to the Summary group.

- Using the same technique, add the items shown in Figure 9–20 to the Detailed and Summary groups.

Why do all the items in the Detailed and Summary groups have the link symbol in front of them?

You actually don't add an object to your group. Rather, you create a link to the object. In practice, you don't have to worry about this. The process for opening an object in one of your custom groups remains the same.

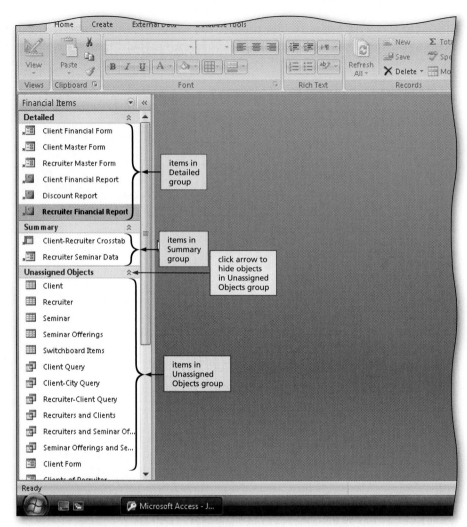

Figure 9–20

4

- Click the arrow in the Unassigned Objects bar to hide the unassigned objects (Figure 9–21).

Do I have to click the arrow?

No. Just as with the Navigation Pane, you can click anywhere in the Unassigned Objects bar.

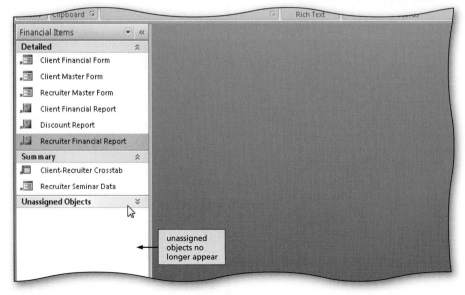

Figure 9–21

To Use the Search Bar

You can reduce the number of items that appear in the Navigation Pane by hiding some of the groups. An alternative method for reducing the number of items that appear is to display only those names that contain a certain collection of characters. To do so, you use the Search Bar. The following steps use the Search Bar to display only those items whose names contain the letters, Sem.

- Return the Navigation Pane to its default state by selecting Tables and Related Views as the category and All Tables as the filter.

- Right-click the Navigation Pane title bar to display a shortcut menu.

- Click Search Bar on the shortcut menu to display the Search Bar.

- Type Sem in the Search Bar to display only items containing Sem (Figure 9–22).

Experiment

- Try other combinations of letters in the search bar to see their effect.

2

- Right-click the Navigation Pane title bar to display a shortcut menu.

- Click Search Bar on the shortcut menu to remove the Search Bar.

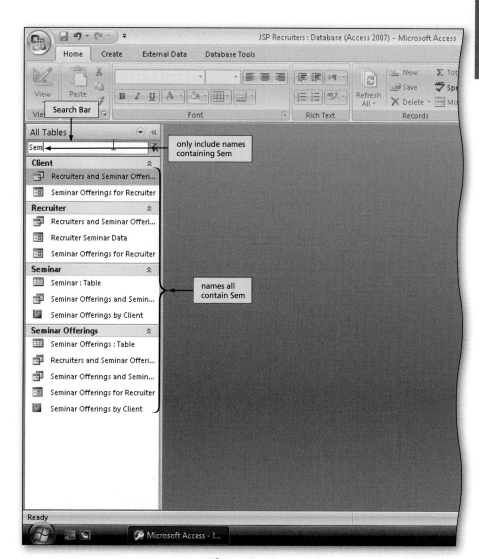

Figure 9–22

Table and Database Properties

You can assign properties to tables. For example, you could assign a validation rule and validation text to an entire table. You also can assign properties to the database, typically for documentation purposes.

To Create a Validation Rule for a Table

Many validation rules apply to individual fields within a table. Some, however, apply to more than one field. For example, in the Seminar Offerings table, you may want to require that the hours spent must be less than or equal to the total hours. This rule involves two fields, Hours Spent and Total Hours. To create a validation rule that involves two or more fields, you need to create the rule for the table using the table's Validation Rule property. The following steps create the appropriate validation rule for the Seminar Offerings table.

- Open the Seminar Offerings table in Design view and hide the Navigation Pane.

- Click the Property Sheet button on the Design tab to display the table's property sheet.

- Click the Validation Rule property and type [Hours Spent]<=[Total Hours] as the validation rule.

- Click the Validation Text property and type Hours spent cannot exceed total hours as the validation text (Figure 9–23).

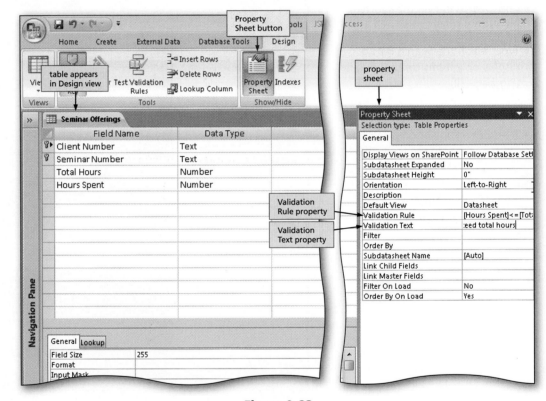

Figure 9–23

Q&A
Could I use the expression builder to create the validation rule?

Yes. Use whichever method you find the most convenient.

❷

- Close the property sheet.

- Click the Save button on the Quick Access Toolbar to save the validation rule and the validation text.

- When asked if you want to test existing data, click the No button.

- Close the Seminar Offerings table.

Effect of the Validation Rule

With this validation rule in place, an attempt to add or change a record on which the hours spent was greater than the total hours would produce the error message shown in Figure 9–24.

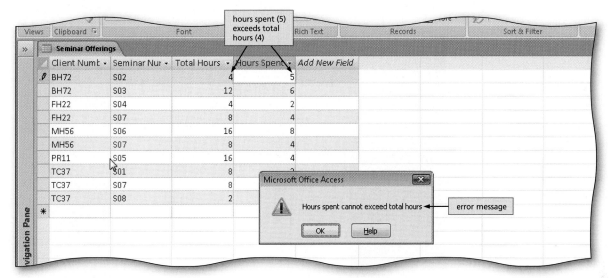

Figure 9–24

To Create Custom Properties

Custom properties are a collection of properties that you can choose from to supplement the general database property categories included in the property sheet. You can use custom properties to further document your database. If you have needs that go beyond the custom properties, you can create your own original or unique properties. The following steps **populate** the Status custom property, that is, they set a value for the property. In this case, they set the Status property to "Live Version," indicating this is the live version of the database. If the database were still in a test environment, the property would be set to "Test Version." The steps also create and populate a new property called Production that represents the date the database was placed into production.

1

- Click the Microsoft Office Button to display the Microsoft Office Button menu.

- Point to the Manage arrow to display a submenu (Figure 9–25).

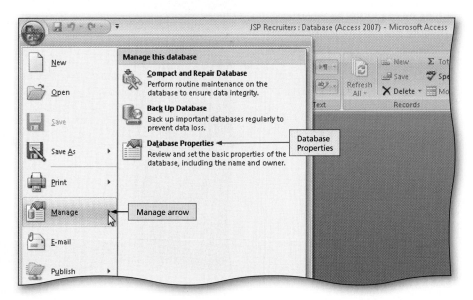

Figure 9–25

- Click Database Properties to display the JSP Recruiters.accdb Properties dialog box.

- Click the Custom tab.

- Scroll down in the Name list so that Status appears, and then click Status.

- Ensure that the Type is Text.

Q&A What if it is not?

Click the Type arrow and then click Text.

- Click the Value box and type Live Version as the value (Figure 9–26).

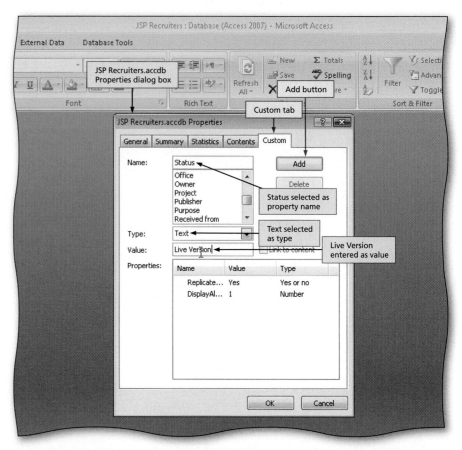

Figure 9–26

- Click the Add button to add the property.

- Type Production in the Name box.

- Select Date as the Type.

- Type 04/03/2008 as the value (Figure 9–27) to indicate that the database went into production on April 3, 2008.

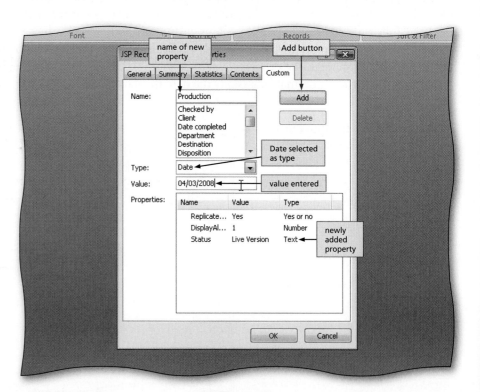

Figure 9–27

4

- Click the Add button to add the property (Figure 9–28).

Q&A What if I add a property that I decide I don't want?

You can delete it. To do so, click the property you no longer want and then click the Delete button.

5

- Click the OK button to close the JSP Recruiters.accdb Properties dialog box.

Q&A How do I view these properties in the future?

The same way you created them. Click the Microsoft Office Button, point to Manage, and then click Database Properties. Click the desired tab to see the properties you want.

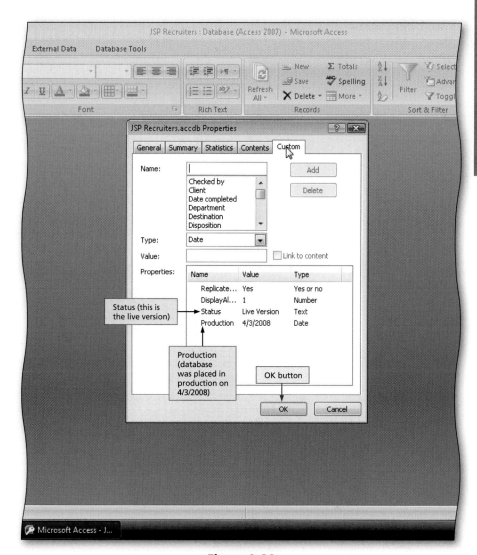

Figure 9–28

Special Field Properties

There are a variety of field properties available. Two special field properties, the Custom Input Mask property and the Allow Zero Length property, are described in this section.

Custom Input Masks

A way to prevent users from entering data that does not have a certain format is to use an input mask. You already may have used the Input Mask Wizard to create an input mask. Using the wizard, you can select the input mask that meets your needs from a list. This often is the best way to create the input mask.

If the input mask you need to create is not similar to any in the list, you can create a custom input mask by entering the appropriate characters as the value for the Input Mask property. In doing so, you use the symbols from Table 9–1.

Table 9–1 Input Mask Symbols		
Symbol	**Type Of Data Accepted**	**Data Entry Optional**
0	Digits (0 through 9) without plus (+) or minus (-) sign. Positions left blank appear as zeros.	No
9	Digits (0 through 9) without plus (+) or minus (-) sign. Positions left blank appear as spaces.	Yes
#	Digits (0 through 9) with plus (+) or minus (-) sign. Positions left blank appear as spaces.	Yes
L	Letters (A through Z).	No
?	Letters (A through Z).	Yes
A	Letters (A through Z) or digits (0 through 9).	No
a	Letters (A through Z) or digits (0 through 9).	Yes
&	Any character or a space.	No
C	Any character or a space.	Yes
<	Converts any letter entered to lowercase.	Does not apply
>	Converts any letter entered to uppercase.	Does not apply
!	Characters typed in the input mask fill it from left to right.	Does not apply
\	Character following the slash is treated as a literal in the input mask.	Does not apply

For example, to indicate that client numbers must consist of two letters followed by two numbers, you would enter LL99. The Ls in the first two positions indicate that the first two positions must be letters. Using L instead of a question mark indicates that the users must enter these letters; that is, they are not optional. With the question mark, they could leave these positions blank. The 9s in the last two positions indicate that the users must enter digits (0 through 9). Using 9 instead of 0 indicates that they could leave these positions blank; that is, they are optional. Finally, to ensure that any letters entered are converted to uppercase, you would use the > symbol at the beginning of the input mask. The complete mask would be >LL99.

To Create a Custom Input Mask

The following step creates a custom input mask for the Client Number field.

1

- Open the Client table in Design view and hide the Navigation Pane.

- With the Client Number field selected, click the Input Mask property, and then type >LL99 as the value (Figure 9–29).

Q&A What is the difference between the Format property and the Input Mask property?

The Format property ensures that data is displayed consistently, for example, always in uppercase. The Input Mask property controls how data is entered.

Q&A What is the effect of this input mask?

From this point on, anyone entering a client number will be restricted to letters in the first two positions and numeric digits in the last two. Further, any letters entered in the first two positions will be converted to uppercase.

Q&A In Figure 9–29, the Client Number field has both a custom input mask and a format. Is this a problem?

Technically, you do not need both. When the same field has both an input mask and a format, the format takes precedence. Because the format specified for the Client Number field is the same as the input mask (uppercase), it will not affect the data.

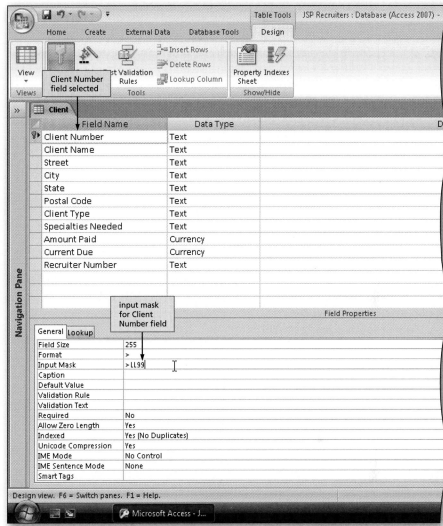

Figure 9–29

To Allow Zero Length

You can use zero-length strings to distinguish data that does not exist from data that is unknown. For example, in the Recruiter table, you may want to set the Required property for the Comment field to Yes, so that users cannot forget to enter a comment. If you do forget to enter a comment, Access will display an error message and not let you add the record. If, on the other hand, you find a certain recruiter for whom no comment is appropriate, you can enter a zero-length string ("") and Access will accept the record without giving you an error message. A **zero-length string** is a string whose length is zero. To enter a zero-length string you type two quotation marks with no spaces in between (""). If you enter a zero-length string into a Text or Memo field whose Required property is set to Yes, Access will not report an error, because entering a zero-length string is not the same as leaving the field blank.

If you want to ensure that data is entered in the field and that a zero-length string is not appropriate, you can set the Required property to Yes and the Allow Zero Length property to No. The following steps set the Allow Zero Length property for the Client Name field to No. (The Required property already has been set to Yes.)

- Click the row selector for the Client Name field to select the field.

- Click the Allow Zero Length property and then click the arrow that appears to display a menu.

- Click No in the menu to change the value of the Allow Zero Length property from Yes to No (Figure 9–30).

Q&A

Could I just type the word, No?

Yes. In fact, you could type the letter N and Access would complete the word No. Use whichever technique you prefer.

- Save your changes and click the No button when asked if you want to test existing data.

- Close the table.

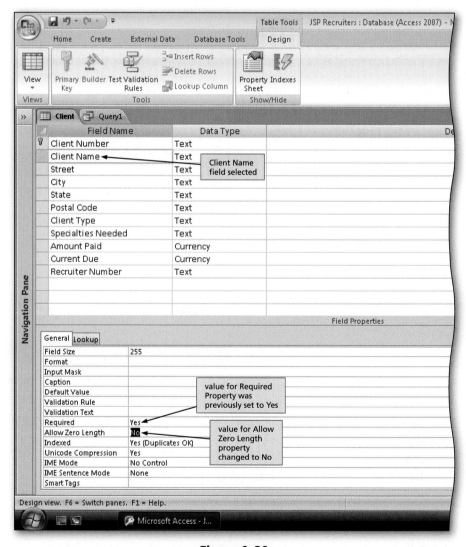

Figure 9–30

Effect of Allowing Zero Length

If the value for the Allow Zero Length property is set to No, an attempt to enter a zero length string ("") will result in an error message (Figure 9–31).

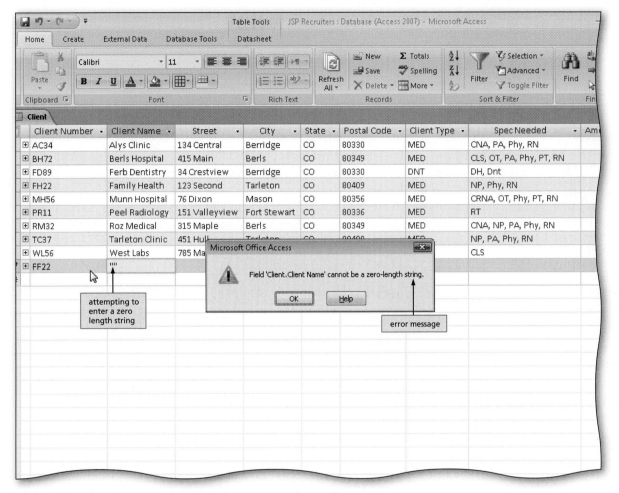

Figure 9–31

Creating and Using Indexes

You already are familiar with the concept of an index. The index in the back of a book contains important words or phrases together with a list of pages on which the given words or phrases can be found. An **index** for a table is similar. An index is created based on a field or combination of fields. An index on the Client Name field, for example, would enable Access to rapidly locate a record that contains a particular client name. In this case, the items of interest are client names instead of keywords or phrases, as is the case in the back of this book. The field or fields on which the index is built is called the **index key**. Thus, in the index on client names, the Client Name field is the index key.

Each name occurs in the index along with the number of the record on which the corresponding client is located. Further, the names appear in the index in alphabetical order, so Access could use this index to rapidly produce a list of clients alphabetized by client name.

Indexes make the process of retrieving records very fast and efficient. (With relatively small tables, the increased efficiency associated with indexes will not be as apparent as in larger tables. In practice, it is common to encounter tables with thousands, tens of thousands,

BTW

Define and Modify Multi-Field Primary Keys
When you define a multi-field primary key (a primary key that includes more than one field), you should examine carefully the length and data type of the fields that participate in the primary key. For example, in the Seminar Offerings table, both the Client Number and the Seminar Number participate in the primary key. Both fields have a data type of Text and a length of 255. You should be certain that this data type and length match the Client Number field in the Client table and the Seminar Number field in the Seminar table. If either field that participates in the primary key does not match, then you can modify the data type and/or length in Design view.

or even hundreds of thousands of records. In such cases, the increase in efficiency provided by indexes is dramatic. In fact, without indexes, many operations in such databases simply would not be practical. They would take too long to complete.)

Another benefit of indexes is that they provide an efficient way to order records. That is, if the records are to appear in a certain order, Access can use an index instead of physically having to rearrange the records in the database. Physically rearranging the records in a different order can be a very time-consuming process.

To gain the benefits of an index, you first must create one. Access automatically creates an index on the primary key as well as on some other special fields. If, as is the case with both the Client and Recruiter tables, a table contains a field called Postal Code, for example, Access will create an index for it automatically. You must create any other indexes you determine would be useful, indicating the field or fields on which the index is to be built.

Although the index key usually will be a single field, it can be a combination of fields. For example, you might want to sort records by amount paid within client type. In other words, the records are ordered by a combination of fields: Client Type and Amount Paid. An index can be used for this purpose by using a combination of fields for the index key. In this case, you must assign a name to the index. It is a good idea to assign a name that represents the combination of fields. For example, an index whose key is the combination of the Client Type and Amount Paid fields might be called TypePaid.

How Access Uses Indexes

Access creates an index whenever you request that it do so. It takes care of all the work in setting up and maintaining the index. In addition, Access will use the index automatically.

If you request that data be sorted in a particular order and Access determines that an index is available that it can use to make the process efficient, it will do so. If no index is available, it still will sort the data in the order you requested; it will just take longer than with the index.

Similarly, if you request that Access locate a particular record that has a certain value in a particular field, Access will use an index if an appropriate one exists. If not, it will have to examine each record until it finds the one you want.

In both cases, the added efficiency provided by an index will not be readily apparent in tables that have only a few records. As you add more records to your tables, however, the difference can be dramatic. Even with only 50 to 100 records, you will notice a difference. You can imagine how dramatic the difference would be in a table with 50,000 records.

Plan Ahead

Determine indexes.
An index improves efficiency for sorting and finding records. On the other hand, indexes occupy space on your disk. They also require Access to do extra work. Access must keep up-to-date all the indexes that have been created. Thus, both advantages and disadvantages exist to using indexes. Consequently, the decision as to which indexes to create is an important one. The following guidelines should help you in this process.

Create an index on a field (or combination of fields) if one or more of the following conditions are present:

1. The field is the primary key of the table (Access creates this index automatically).

2. The field is the foreign key in a relationship you have created.

3. You frequently will need your data to be sorted on the field.

4. You frequently will need to locate a record based on a value in this field.

(continued)

(continued)

Because Access handles 1 automatically, you only need to concern yourself about 2, 3, and 4. If you think you will need to see client data arranged in order of current due amounts, for example, you should create an index on the Current Due field. If you think you will need to see the data arranged by amount paid within client type, you should create an index on the combination of the Client Type field and the Amount Paid field. Similarly, if you think you will need to find a client given the client's name, you should create an index on the Client Name field.

Plan Ahead

To Create a Single-Field Index

A **single-field index** is an index whose key is a single field. If you need to frequently locate clients by name, you would create a single-field index. The index key would be the Client Name field. In creating an index, you need to indicate whether to allow duplicates in the index key; that is, two records that have the same value. For example, in the index for the Client Name field, if duplicates are not allowed, Access would not allow the addition of a client whose name is the same as the name of a client already in the database. In the index for the Client Name field, duplicates will be allowed. The following steps create a single-field index.

- Open the Client table in Design view and hide the Navigation Pane.

- Select the Client Name field.

- Click the Indexed property box in the Field Properties pane to select the property.

- Click the down arrow that appears to display the Indexed list (Figure 9–32).

- If necessary, click the Yes (Duplicates OK) value in the list to specify that duplicates are to be allowed.

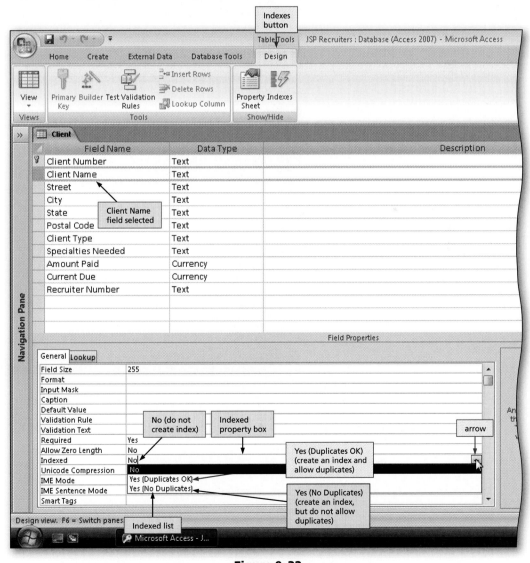

Figure 9–32

To Create a Multiple-Field Index

Creating **multiple-field indexes**, that is, indexes whose key is a combination of fields, involves a different process from creating single-field indexes. To create multiple-field indexes, you will use the Indexes button, enter a name for the index, and then enter the combination of fields that make up the index key. Assuming there is a need to sort records on the combination of Client Type and Amount Paid, you would create a multiple-field index whose key is the combination of the Client Type field and the Amount Paid field. The following steps create this multiple-field index and assign it the name TypePaid.

- Click the Indexes button on the Design tab to display the Indexes: Client dialog box (Figure 9–33).

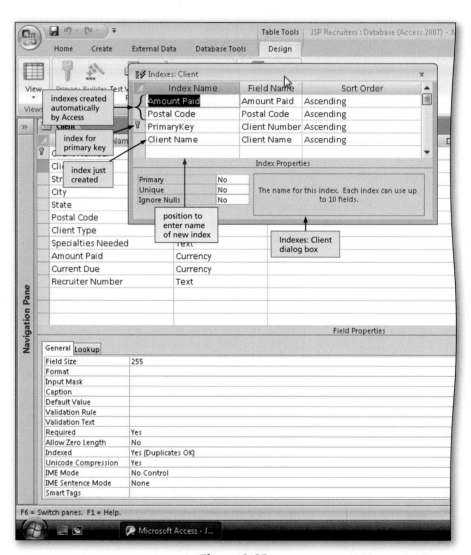

Figure 9–33

2

- Click the blank row (the row following Client Name) in the Index Name column in the Indexes: Client dialog box to select the position to enter the name of the new index.

- Type `TypePaid` as the index name, and then press the TAB key.

- Click the down arrow in the Field Name column to produce a list of fields in the Client table and then select Client Type to enter the first of the two fields for the index.

- Press the TAB key three times to move to the Field Name column on the following row.

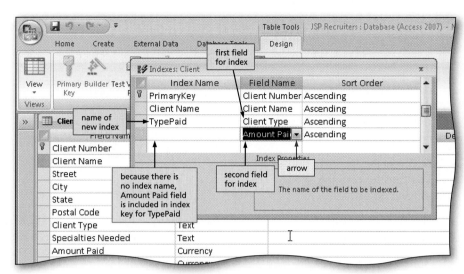

Figure 9–34

- Select the Amount Paid field in the same manner as the Client Type field (Figure 9–34).

3

- Close the Indexes: Client dialog box by clicking its Close button.

- Click the Save button to save your changes.

- Close the Client table.

Automatic Error Checking

Access automatically can check for several types of errors in forms and reports. When Access detects an error, it warns you about the existence of the error and provides you with options for correcting it. The types of errors that Access can detect and correct are shown in Table 9–2.

Table 9–2 Types of Errors	
Data Type	**Description**
Unassociated label and control	A label and control are selected that are not associated with each other.
New unassociated labels	A newly added label is not associated with any other control.
Keyboard shortcut errors	A shortcut key is invalid. This can happen because an unassociated label has a shortcut key, there are duplicate shortcut keys assigned, or a blank space is assigned as a shortcut key.
Invalid control properties	A control property is invalid. For example, the property can contain invalid characters.
Common report errors	The report has invalid sorting or grouping specifications or the report is wider than the page size.

To Enable Error Checking

For automatic error checking to take place, it must be enabled. The following steps ensure that error checking is enabled.

- Click the Microsoft Office Button and then click Access Options to display the Access Options dialog box.

- Click Object Designers to display the options for creating and modifying objects.

- Scroll down so that the Error Checking section appears.

- Be sure the Enable error checking box is checked (Figure 9–35).

Q&A

What is the purpose of the other check boxes in the section?

All the other check boxes are checked, indicating that Access will perform all the various types of automatic error checking that are possible. If there were a particular type of error checking that you would prefer to skip, you would remove its check mark before clicking the OK button.

- Click the OK button to close the Access Options dialog box.

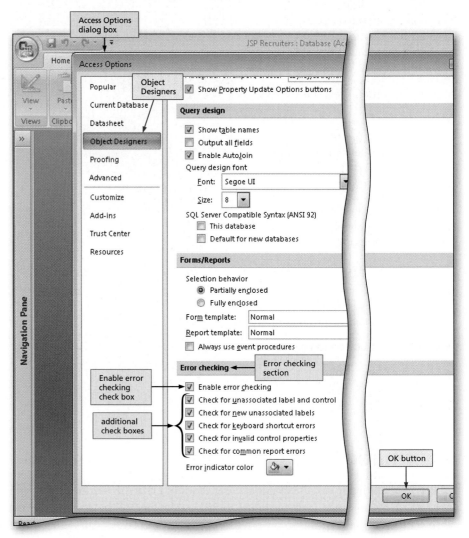

Figure 9–35

Error Indication

If an error occurs, a small triangle called an **error indicator** appears in the appropriate field or control. In Figure 9–36, the label for Recruiter Number in the Client View and Update Form is changed to include an ampersand (&) before the letter N. This will make the letter N a keyboard shortcut for this control, which is a problem because the letter N already is a shortcut for Name to Find.

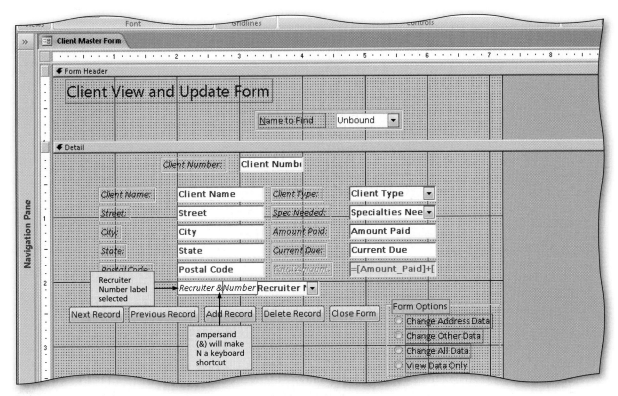

Figure 9–36

Once the change is complete, an error indicator appears in both controls in which the letter N is the keyboard shortcut, as shown in Figure 9–37.

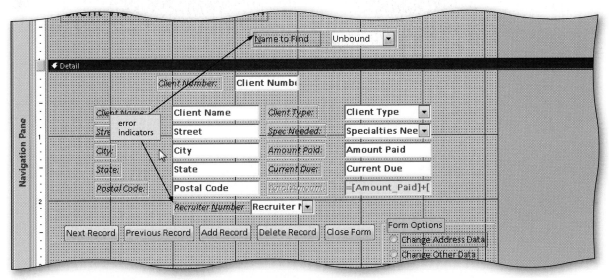

Figure 9–37

Selecting a control containing an error indicator displays an Error Checking Options button. In Figure 9–38, the Error Checking Options button appears next to the Recruiter Number label, which currently is selected.

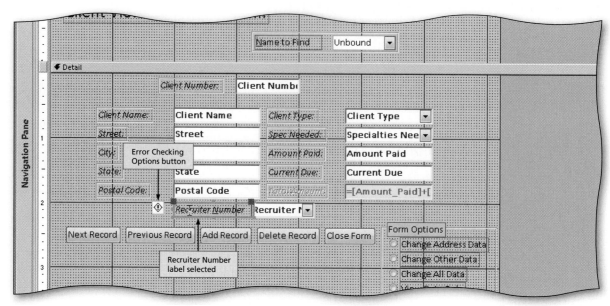

Figure 9–38

Clicking the Error Checking Options button produces the Error Checking Options menu, as shown in Figure 9–39. The first line in the menu is simply a statement of the type of error that occurred, and the second is a description of the specific error. The Change Caption command gives a submenu of the captions that can be changed. The Edit Caption Property command allows you to change the caption directly and is the simplest way to correct this error. The Help on This Error command gives help on the specific error that occurred. You can choose to ignore the error by using the Ignore Error command. The final command, Error Checking Options, allows you to change the same error checking options shown in Figure 9–35 on page AC 632.

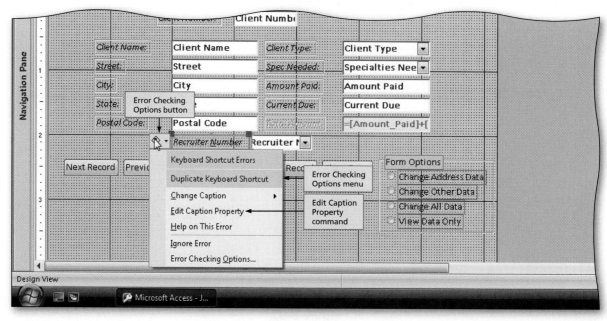

Figure 9–39

The simplest way to fix the keyboard shortcut error is to edit the caption property. Clicking the Edit Caption Property command produces a property sheet with the Caption property highlighted (Figure 9–40). You then can change the Caption property to make another letter the shortcut key. For example, you could make the letter R the shortcut key by typing &Recruiter Number as the entry.

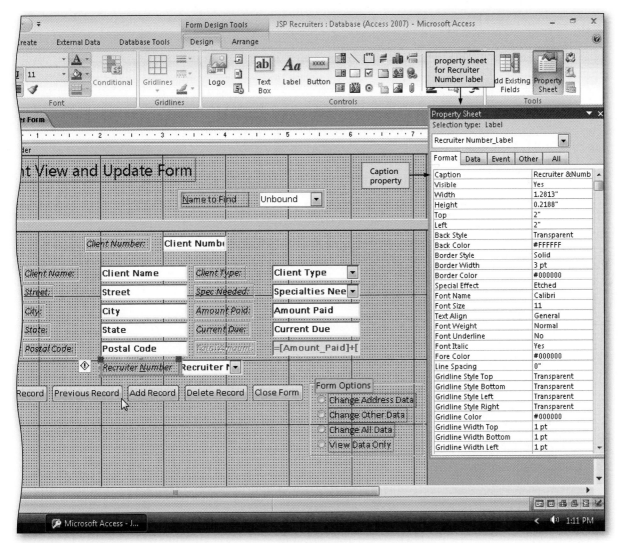

Figure 9–40

Smart Tags

In Access, a **smart tag** is a button that appears in a table, query, form, or report that assists users in accomplishing various tasks, including connecting to the Web. Smart tags are available in other Office applications as well. You can assign smart tags to fields in tables and queries. You also can assign smart tags to controls in forms and reports. For example, adding a smart tag to a name field provides quick access to commands related to names, such as sending mail or scheduling a meeting.

To Add a Smart Tag to a Field in a Table

You use the Smart Tag property for a field to add a smart tag to the field. The following steps add a smart tag to the Last Name field in the Recruiter table.

- Open the Recruiter table in Design view and hide the Navigation Pane.

- Click the row selector for the Last Name field.

- Click the Smart Tags text box to select it (Figure 9–41).

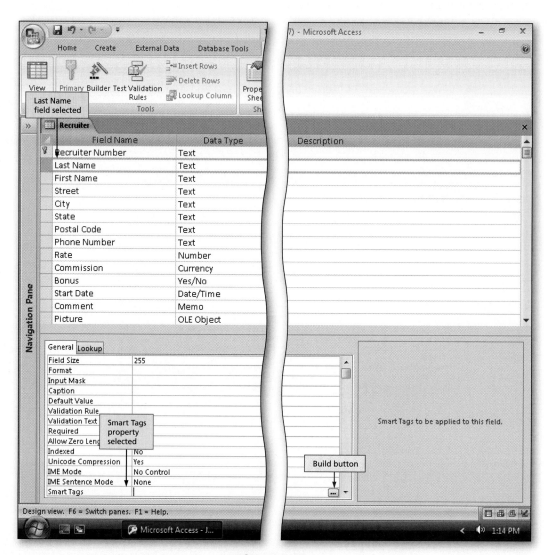

Figure 9–41

2

- Click the Build button.
- Click the check box for the Person Name smart tag (Figure 9–42).

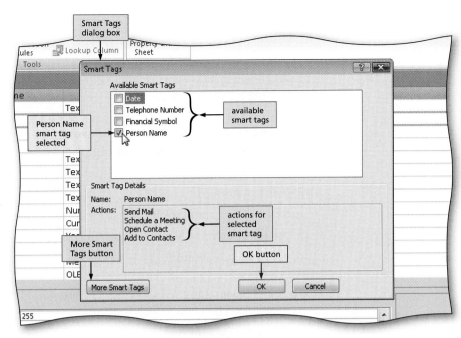

Figure 9–42

3

- Click the OK button to add the smart tag (Figure 9–43).

Q&A Do I have to type that long expression in the Smart Tags box?

No. Access creates it for you automatically.

4

- Save your changes.
- Close the table.

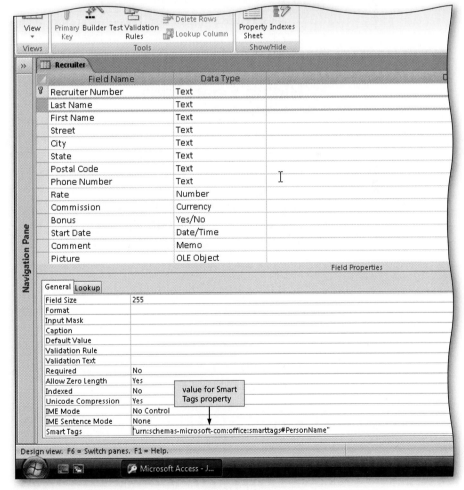

Figure 9–43

Showing Smart Tags

In addition to assigning smart tags, you need to take special action to be sure that the smart tags appear. There actually are two options you have to address. One option concerns smart tags appearing in forms and reports. The other concerns smart tags appearing in tables and queries.

To Show Smart Tags in Forms and Reports

1. Click the Microsoft Office Button.
2. Click Access Options.
3. Click Advanced.
4. If necessary, scroll to the Display section.
5. Be sure the Show Smart Tags on Forms and Reports check box is checked.
6. Click the OK button.

To Show Smart Tags in Tables and Queries

1. Click the Microsoft Office Button.
2. Click Access Options.
3. Click Advanced.
4. If necessary, scroll to the Display section.
5. Be sure the Show Smart Tags on Datasheets check box is checked.
6. Click the OK button.

Hiding Smart Tags

Just as you need to take special action to be sure that smart tags appear, you also need to take special action to hide the smart tags, that is, to be sure that the smart tags do not appear. Again there are two options you have to address. One concerns forms and reports. The other concerns tables and queries.

To Hide Smart Tags in Forms and Reports

1. Click the Microsoft Office Button.
2. Click Access Options.
3. Click Advanced.
4. If necessary, scroll to the Display section.
5. Be sure the Show Smart Tags on Forms and Reports check box is not checked.
6. Click the OK button.

To Hide Smart Tags in Tables and Queries

1. Click the Microsoft Office Button.
2. Click Access Options.
3. Click Advanced.
4. If necessary, scroll to the Display section.
5. Be sure the Show Smart Tags on Datasheets check box is not checked.
6. Click the OK button.

Using the Smart Tag in the Table

After you have created a smart tag for a field in a table, it will appear in the field whenever you view the table. In Figure 9–44, for example, the small triangles indicate smart tags.

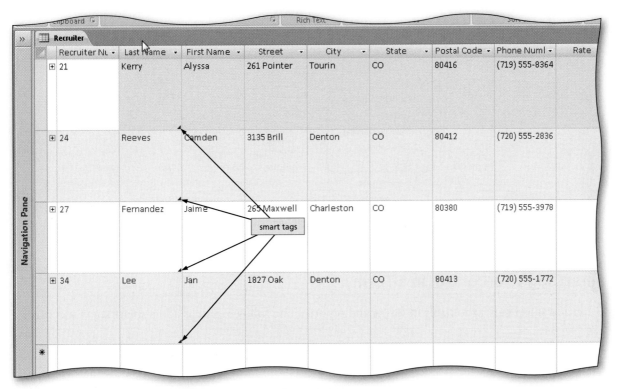

Figure 9–44

When you click a field containing a smart tag, the Smart Tag Actions button appears. In Figure 9–45, the Smart Tag Actions button for the last name Kerry appears next to the field.

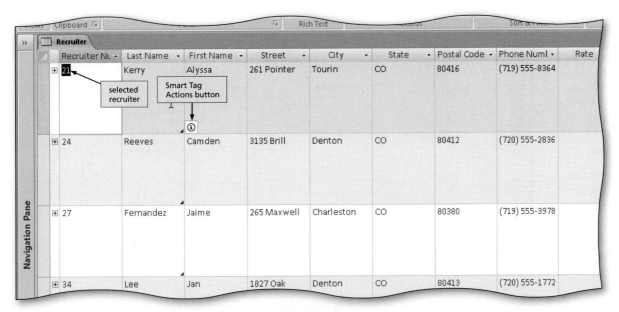

Figure 9–45

Clicking the Smart Tag Actions button produces a menu of possible actions (Figure 9–46). You can click an action on this menu to take the corresponding action.

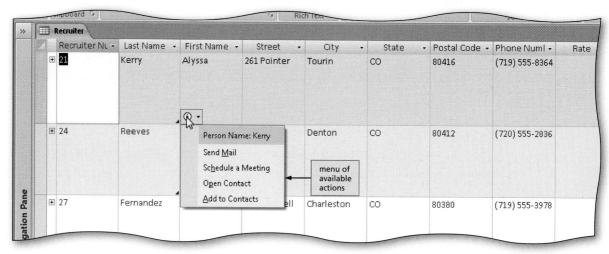

Figure 9–46

To Add a Smart Tag to a Control in a Form

You also can add smart tags to controls in forms and reports. The following steps add a smart tag to a control in a form.

1

- Open the Recruiter Master Form in Design view and hide the Navigation Pane.

- If a field list appears, close the field list by clicking the Add Existing Fields button on the Design tab.

- Click the Last Name control to select it.

- Click the Property Sheet button on the Design tab to display a property sheet.

- Be sure the All tab is selected. Scroll down until the Smart Tags property appears, and then click the Smart Tags property (Figure 9–47).

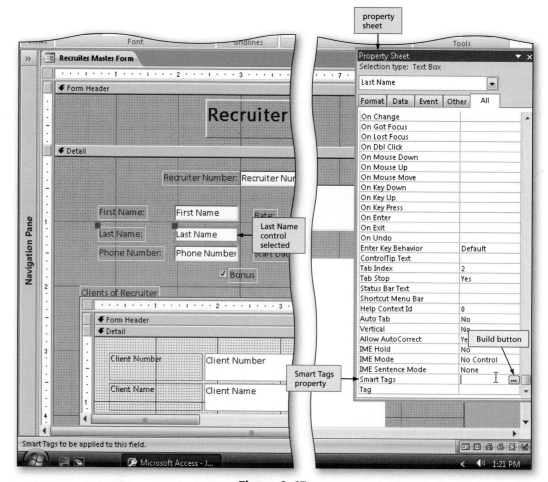

Figure 9–47

2

- Click the Build button to display the Smart Tags dialog box.

- Click the check box for the Person Name smart tag (Figure 9–48).

3

- Click the OK button to add the smart tag to the control.

- Close the property sheet.

- Save your changes.

- Close the form.

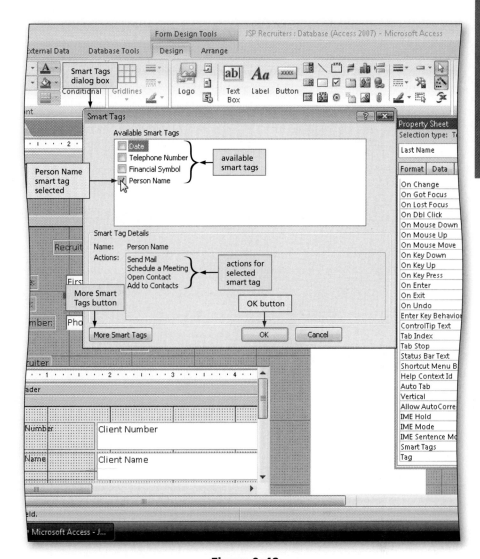

Figure 9–48

Using the Smart Tag in the Form

Once you have created a smart tag for a control in a form, it will appear whenever you view the form, as shown in Figure 9–49.

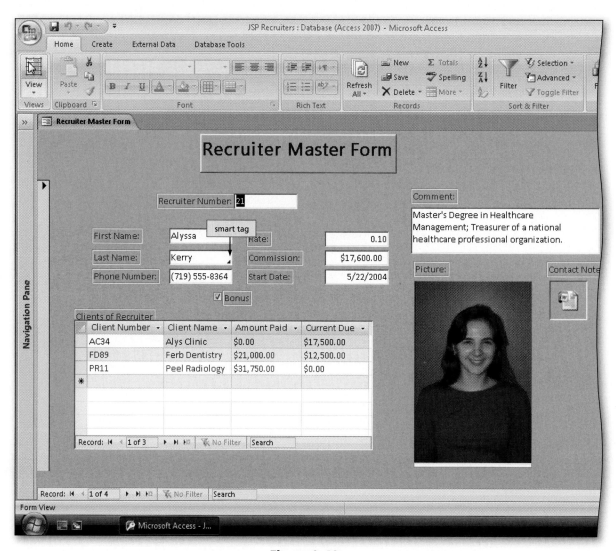

Figure 9–49

When you click a field containing a smart tag, the Smart Tag Actions button will appear. In Figure 9–50, the Smart Tag Actions button for the Last Name control appears next to the control.

Figure 9–50

Clicking the Smart Tag Actions button produces a menu of possible actions (Figure 9–51). You can click an action on this menu to take the corresponding action.

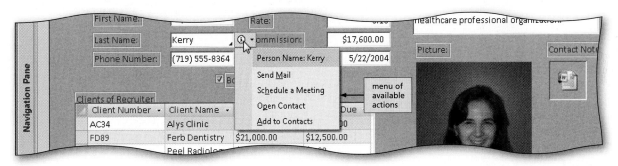

Figure 9–51

Additional Smart Tags

To use other smart tags created by Microsoft or by other companies, click the More Smart Tags button (shown in Figure 9–48 on page AC 641), and then search the Web for the desired smart tag.

Database Options

You can configure the way users will interact with the database by changing database options. Database options are settings that affect how the database appears or functions. For example, you can select a form to display automatically when the database is opened. You also can hide the Navigation Pane. You already have been hiding the Navigation Pane by clicking the Shutter Bar Open/Close Button. Technically, that action closes the Navigation

Pane but leaves the shutter bar on the screen. You then can show the Navigation Pane by clicking the button a second time. You also can completely hide the Navigation Pane, which removes the shutter bar. To make either of these changes, you will click Current Database in the Access Options dialog box and then select the appropriate options.

To Select a Startup Form

If the database includes a switchboard, it is common to select the switchboard as the startup form — that is, the form that appears when a user opens the database. The following steps ensure that the switchboard appears automatically when the JSP Recruiters database is opened.

- Click the Microsoft Office Button and then click Access Options to display the Access Options dialog box.

- Click Current Database to select the options for the current database.

- Click the Display Form box arrow to display the list of available forms (Figure 9–52).

2

- Click Switchboard and then click the OK button to select the switchboard as the form that will automatically be displayed whenever the database is opened.

- Click the OK button when Access displays a message indicating that you must close and reopen the database for the change to take effect.

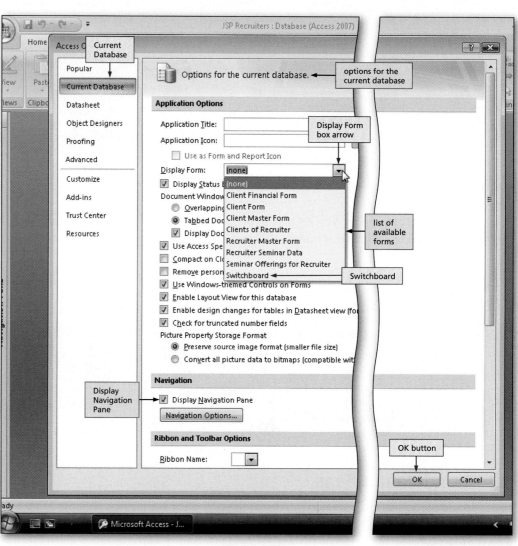

Figure 9–52

Opening a Database with a Startup Form

Whenever you open a database with a startup form, Access automatically displays the startup form. If you have selected the switchboard as the startup form, as in the previous set of steps, the switchboard would be displayed without requiring any special action on the user's part (Figure 9–53).

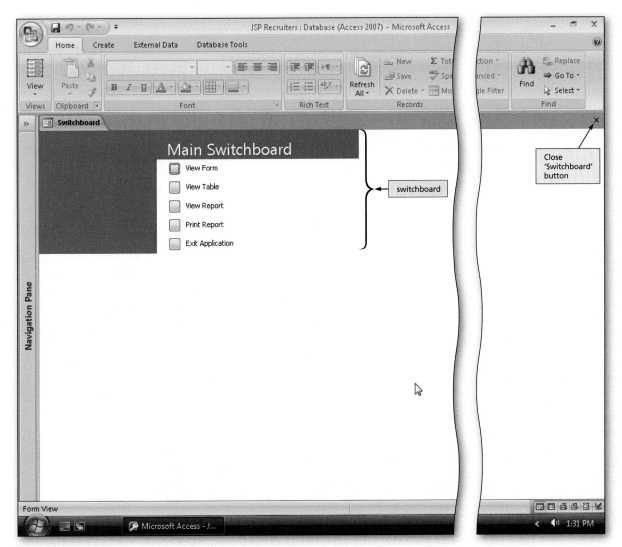

Figure 9–53

You then could use the switchboard by clicking the various buttons in the switchboard. If you click Exit Application, the database will be closed. If you want to exit the switchboard but leave the database open, click the Close 'Switchboard' button.

To Completely Hide the Navigation Pane

Normally, simply hiding the Navigation Pane by closing it is desirable. The shutter bar remains on the screen so you easily can open the Navigation Pane whenever you need it. If you want to completely hide the Navigation Pane, that is, remove the shutter bar from the screen, you would use the following steps. Notice that it is necessary to close and then reopen the database for this change to take effect.

1. Click the Microsoft Office Button and then click Access Options to display the Access Options dialog box.

2. Click Current Database to select the options for the current database.

3. Click the Display Navigation Pane check box (see Figure 9–52 on page AC 644) to remove the check mark.

4. Close and then reopen the database.

To Show the Navigation Pane when it has been Hidden

If you have completely hidden the Navigation Pane, you cannot show it by clicking the Shutter Bar Open/Close Button; that button is no longer on the screen. Instead, you would use the following steps. Just like when you completely hid the Navigation Pane, you will need to close and then reopen the database for the change to take effect.

1. Click the Microsoft Office Button and then click Access Options to display the Access Options dialog box.

2. Click Current Database to select the options for the current database.

3. Click the Display Navigation Pane check box (see Figure 9–52 on page AC 644) to add a check mark.

4. Close and then reopen the database.

BTW

Passwords
Passwords should be eight or more characters in length. The longer the length of the password and the more random the characters, the more difficult it is for someone to determine. Use a combination of uppercase and lowercase letters as well as numbers and special symbols when you create a password.

Encrypting a Database

Encrypting refers to the storing of the data in the database in an encoded (encrypted) format. Any time a user stores or modifies data in the encrypted database, the database management system (DBMS) will encode the data before actually updating the database. Before a legitimate user retrieves the data using the DBMS, the data will be decoded. The whole encrypting process is transparent to a legitimate user; that is, he or she is not even aware it is happening. If an unauthorized user attempts to bypass all the controls of the DBMS and get to the database through a utility program or a word processor, however, he or she will be able to see only the encoded, and unreadable, version of the data. In Access, you encrypt a database and set a password as part of the same operation.

Note: Once you have encrypted a database and set a password, you MUST remember the password to access your database. As a precaution, it is a good idea for you to make a backup copy of your database and store it in a secure location before performing this operation. That way, if you forget your password, you still can use the backup copy.

To Open a Database in Exclusive Mode

To encrypt a database and set a password, the database must be open in exclusive mode, that is, no other user can access the database in any way. The following steps open the Camashaly database in exclusive mode in preparation for setting a password.

1 Close the open database by clicking the Microsoft Office Button and then clicking Close Database on the Microsoft Office Button menu.

2 With your USB flash drive connected to one of the computer's USB ports, click the More button to display the Open dialog box.

3 If the Folders list is displayed below the Folders button, click the Folders button to remove the Folders list.

4 If necessary, click Computer in the Favorite Links section and then double-click UDISK 2.0 (E:) to select the USB flash drive, Drive E in this case, as the new open location. (Your drive letter might be different.)

⑤ Click Camashaly to select the file name.

⑥ Click the Open button arrow to display the Open button menu (Figure 9–54).

⑦ Click Open Exclusive to open the database in exclusive mode.

◁ Q&A

What is the purpose of the other modes?

The mode you use affects how you and other users interact with the database. The first option, Open, opens the database in a mode that allows it to be shared by other users. The second, Open Read-Only, allows you to read the data in the database, but not update the database. Other users can both read and update. The fourth, Open Exclusive Read-Only allows you to read but not update. Other users also can read the data, but they cannot perform updates.

⑧ If a Security Warning appears, click the Options button to display the Microsoft Office Security Options dialog box.

⑨ With the option button to enable the content selected, click the OK button to enable the content.

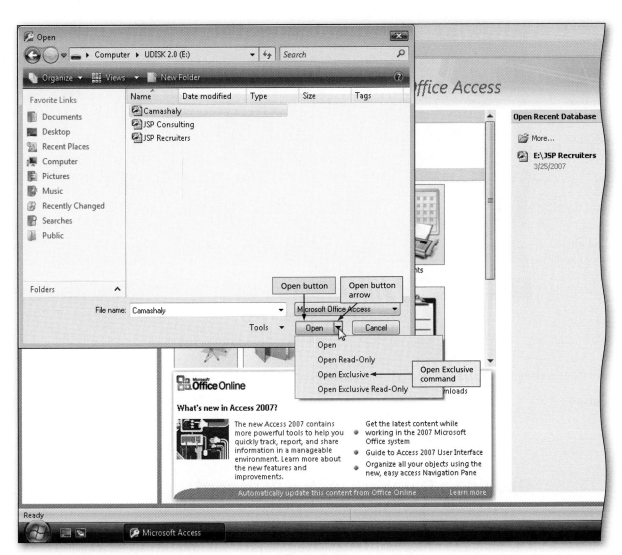

Figure 9–54

To Encrypt a Database with a Password

With the database open in exclusive mode, the following steps encrypt the database with a password. Be sure to remember the password that you type. You will use it again in the next sections.

- Click Database Tools on the Ribbon to display the Database Tools tab.

- Click the Encrypt with Password button on the Database Tools tab to display the Set Database Password dialog box.

- Type a password in the Password text box in the Set Database Password dialog box.

- Press the TAB key and then type your password again in the Verify text box (Figure 9–55).

Q&A | Are passwords case sensitive?

Yes.

Q&A | What if I forget my password?

You will not be able to open your database. You would have to use the backup copy you made of your database.

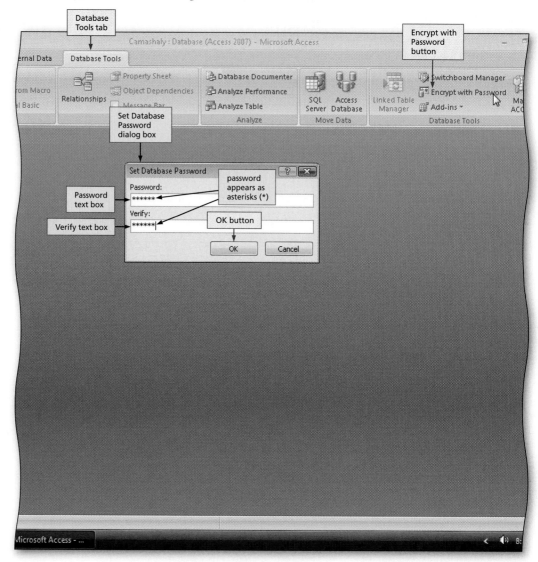

Figure 9–55

- Click the OK button to encrypt the database and set the password.

- Close the database.

Opening a Database with a Password

When you open a database that has a password, you will be prompted to enter your password in the Password Required dialog box. Once you have done so, click the OK button. Assuming yo u have entered your password correctly, Access then will open the database.

To Decrypt the Database and Remove the Password

If you no longer feel the encryption and the password are necessary, you can decrypt the database and remove the password. The following steps accomplish this task.

- Open the Camashaly database in exclusive mode (see the steps on page AC 647), entering your password when requested. If necessary, enable the content.

- Click Database Tools on the Ribbon to display the Database Tools tab.

- Click the Decrypt Database button on the Ribbon to display the Unset Database Password dialog box (Figure 9–56).

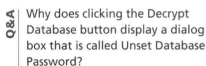 Why does clicking the Decrypt Database button display a dialog box that is called Unset Database Password?

The use of passwords and encryption are part of the same process, as the button you clicked earlier, Encrypt with Password, indicates. The same is true for decryption, even though the word, Password, does not appear on the button.

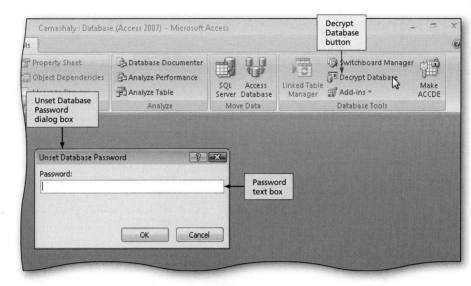

Figure 9–56

- Type the password in the Password dialog box.

- Click the OK button to remove the password and decrypt the database.

- Close the Camashaly database.

Q&A What is the effect of this change?

Users no longer will need to enter a password when they open the database.

Digital Certificates

When you have created your database, you can convey to others that your database can be trusted by adding a **digital signature**, a stamp of authentication, which is contained within a **digital certificate**. To do so, you package and sign your database. You then can send the resulting package to others. The signature confirms that no one has tampered with the database. If the users trust the author, they then can enable the content of the database with confidence.

Note: Do not complete the following section (pages AC 650 through 653) unless your instructor tells you to do so. Even if you are not completing the section, however, you should read it to make sure you understand the process. The steps create a database called JSP Recruiters New, which is used later in the chapter. If you do not complete the steps, you should use the Back Up Database command on the Manage submenu of the Microsoft Office Button menu to create the JSP Recruiters New database.

To Create a Self-Signed Certificate

To use a verified, authenticated digital certificate, you must obtain one from a trusted Microsoft partner certification authority (CA). If you don't have such a certificate you can create your own digital certificate, known as a **self-signed certificate**. In the process, you are creating a certificate that can be used for personal macros only on the machine on which they were created. The following steps create a self-signed certificate.

- Open the JSP Recruiters database and close the switchboard. If necessary, enable the content.

- Click the Start button on the Windows Vista taskbar to display the Start menu.

- Click All Programs at the bottom of the left pane on the Start menu to display the All Programs list and then click Microsoft Office on the All Programs list to display the Microsoft Office list.

- Click Microsoft Office Tools on the Microsoft Office list to display the Microsoft Office Tools list.

- Click Digital Certificate for VBA Projects to display the Create Digital Certificate dialog box.

- Type your name in the 'Your certificate's name' text box (Figure 9–57).

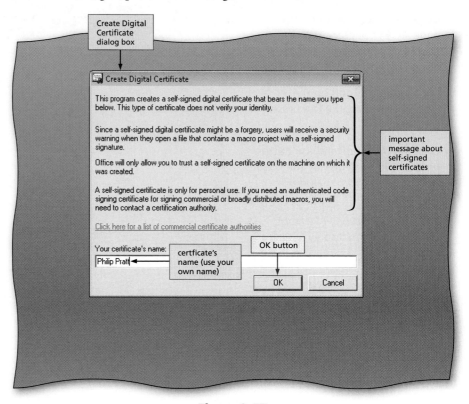

Figure 9–57

- Click the OK button to create the certificate (Figure 9–58).

- Click the OK button in the SelfCert Success message box to close the message box.

Q&A

Do I have to do this from within Access?

No. The digital certificate steps occur in a separate program.

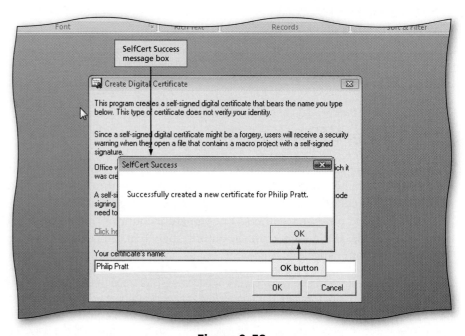

Figure 9–58

To Package and Sign a Database

You can package, digitally sign, and distribute an Access database with a single operation. Access will save the result in the Access Deployment file format (.accdc). Other users then can extract the database from the package and use it. The following steps package and sign the JSP Recruiters database, using the self-signed certificate you created earlier.

- Click the Microsoft Office Button to display the Microsoft Office Button menu.

- Point to the Publish arrow to display the Publish submenu (Figure 9–59).

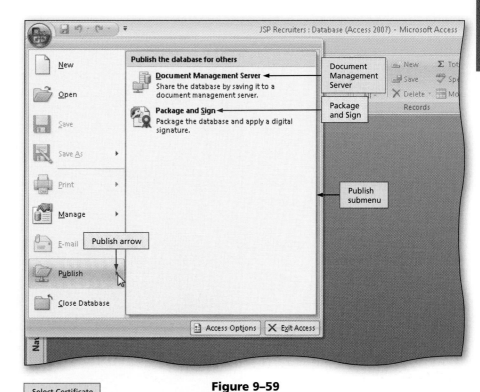

Figure 9–59

- Click Package and Sign to display the Select Certificate dialog box (Figure 9–60).

Q&A What can I do with this dialog box?

You can select a certificate or view details of the selected certificate.

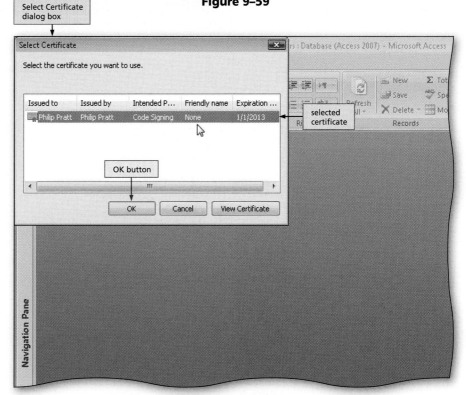

Figure 9–60

3

- With the desired certificate selected, click the OK button.

- Select the location where you will save the certificate, and enter a name for the signed package (Figure 9–61).

Q&A

Did I need to select Microsoft Office Access Signed Package as the Save as type?

No. Access should do this for you automatically. If for some reason Microsoft Office Access Signed Package was not selected, you could select it yourself by clicking the arrow and then clicking the signed package in the list.

4

- Click the Create button to package and sign the database.

- If the switchboard opens, close it by clicking its Close button.

- Close the existing database by clicking the Microsoft Office button and then clicking Close Database.

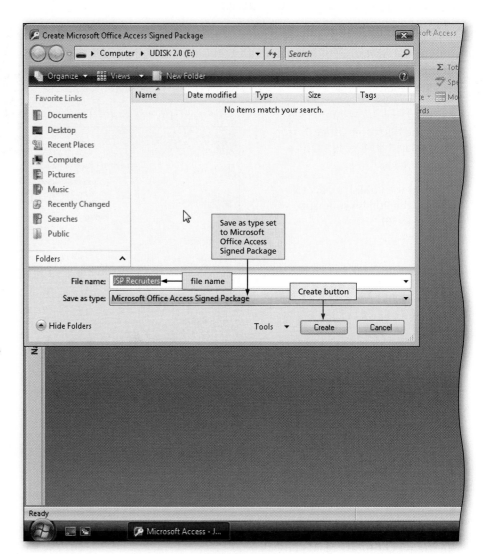

Figure 9–61

BTW

Packaging
Packaging places the database in an Access Deployment (.accdc) file, signs the package, and then places the code-signed package at a location on the user's computer that you determine. Users then can extract the database from the package and work directly in the database (not in the package file).

To Open a Signed Package

The following steps open the signed package you just created and then extract the JSP Recruiters database from the package, giving it the name, JSP Recruiters New.

- From the Getting Started with Microsoft Office Access screen, click the More button to display the Open dialog box.

- Select the location for the package and then change the file type by clicking the 'Files of type' box arrow and selecting Microsoft Office Access Signed Packages.

- Ensure the package you wish to open is selected (Figure 9–62).

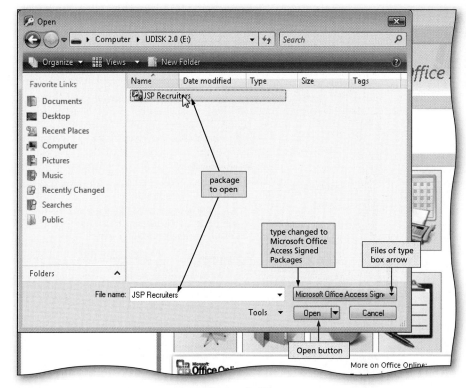

Figure 9–62

- Click the Open button to open the package and, if there is a security concern detected, to display the Microsoft Office Access Security Notice dialog box (Figure 9–63).

- Click the Open button to display the Extract Database To dialog box.

- Select your USB drive as the location and change the database name to JSP Recruiters New.

- Click the OK button to extract the database.

- Because you will not be using this database, close the database and reopen the JSP Recruiters database.

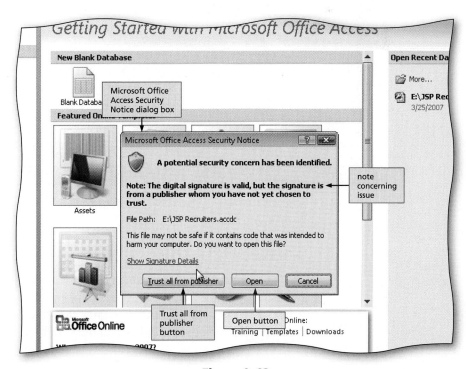

Figure 9–63

The Trust Center

The Trust Center is a place within Access where you can set security options and also find the latest information on technology related to privacy, safety, and security. To use the Trust Center, you click the Microsoft Office Button and then click Access Options to display the Access Options dialog box. You then click Trust Center to display the Trust Center content (Figure 9–64). You then would click the Trust Center Settings button to display the Trust Center dialog box in which you can make changes in the following categories.

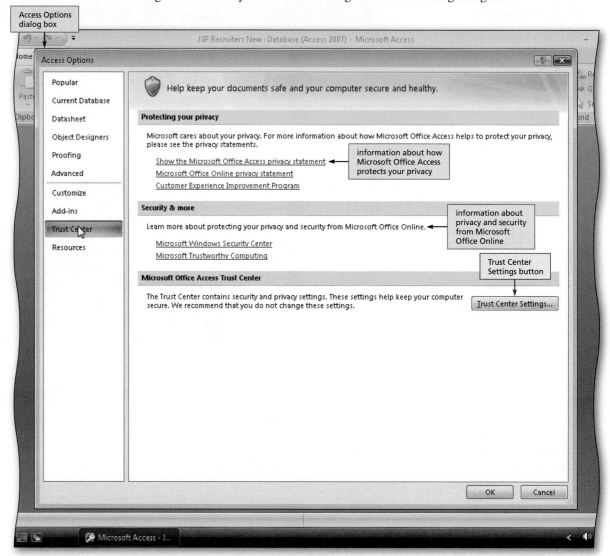

Figure 9–64

Trusted Publishers

Clicking Trusted Publishers in the Trust Center dialog box shows the list of trusted publishers (Figure 9–65). Currently there are none. To view details about a trusted publisher, click the publisher and then click the View button. To remove a trusted publisher from the list, click the publisher and then click the Remove button.

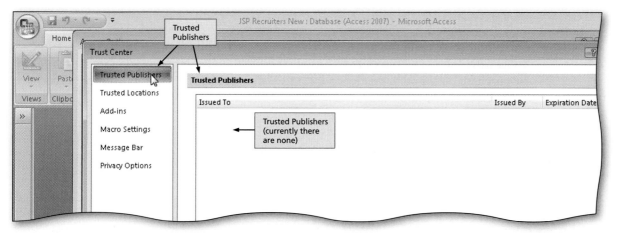

Figure 9–65

Trusted Locations

Clicking Trusted Locations shows the list of trusted locations (Figure 9–66). To add a new location, click the 'Add new location' button. To remove or modify an existing location, click the location and then click the Remove or Modify button.

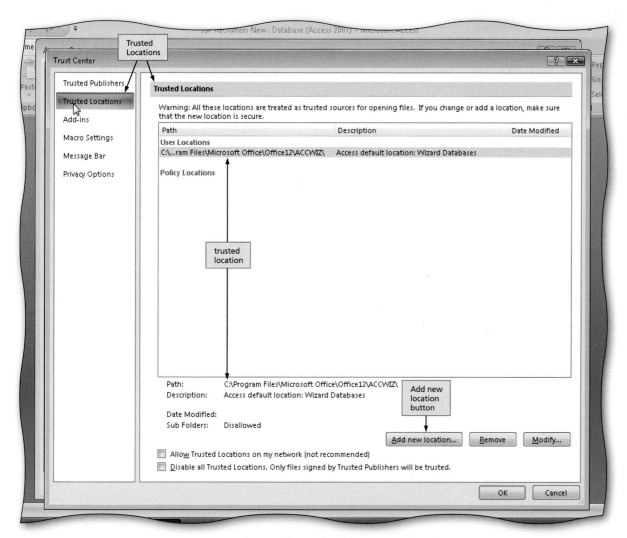

Figure 9–66

Add-Ins

Add-ins are additional programs that you can install and use within Access. Some come with Access and typically are installed using the Access Setup program. Others can be purchased from other vendors. Clicking Add-ins gives you the opportunity to specify restrictions concerning Add-ins (Figure 9–67).

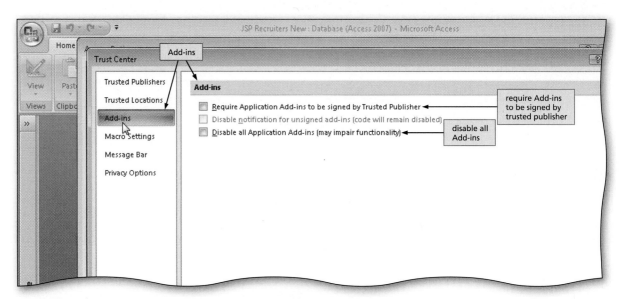

Figure 9–67

Macro Settings

Macros written by others have the potential to harm your computer, for example by spreading a virus. The Trust Center uses special criteria, including valid digital signatures, reputable certificates, and trusted publishers, to ensure a macro is safe. If the Trust Center discovers a macro that potentially is unsafe, it will take appropriate action. The action the Trust Center takes depends on the Macro setting you have selected. Clicking Macro Settings enables you to select or change this setting (Figure 9–68).

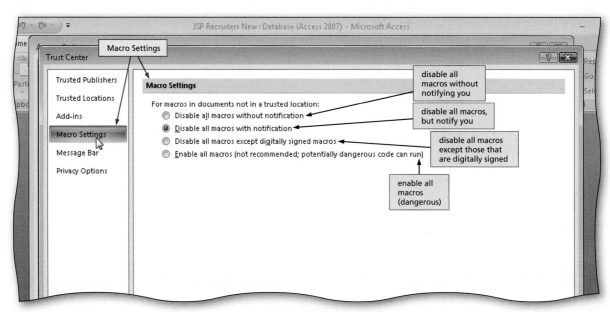

Figure 9–68

Message Bar

Clicking Message Bar lets you choose whether the message bar should appear when content has been blocked (Figure 9–69).

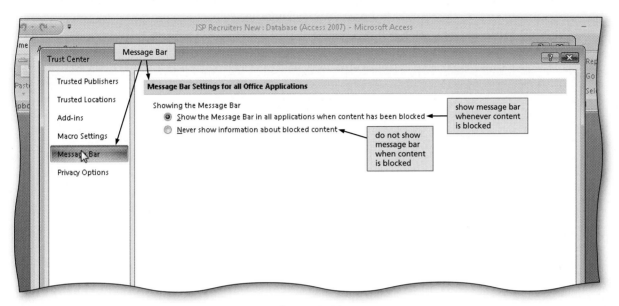

Figure 9–69

Privacy Options

Clicking Privacy Options lets you set security settings to protect your personal privacy (Figure 9–70).

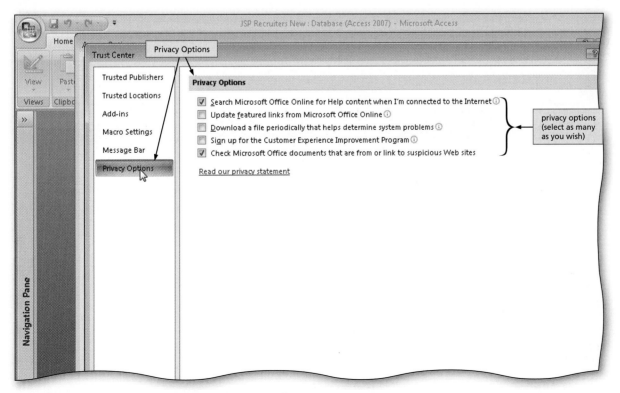

Figure 9–70

Managing Add-Ins

You can manage add-ins by clicking the Microsoft Office Button, clicking Access Options, and then clicking Add-ins (Figure 9–71). You can view details concerning existing add-ins. You also can manage existing add-ins or add new ones by selecting the add-in category in the Manage box and then clicking the Go button to start the Add-in Manager.

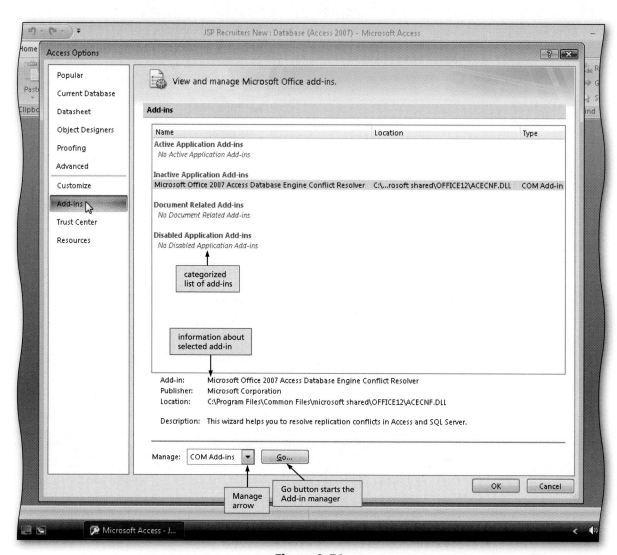

Figure 9–71

You also can start the Add-in Manager by clicking Database Tools on the Ribbon to display the Database Tools tab and then clicking the Add-ins button (Figure 9–72).

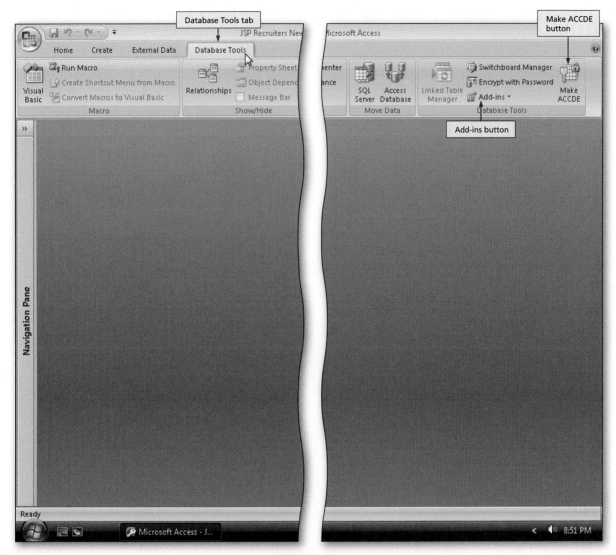

Figure 9–72

Locking a Database

By **locking** a database, you can prevent users from viewing or modifying VBA code in your database or from making changes to the design of forms or reports. When you lock the database, Access changes the file name extension from .accdb to .accde.

TO CREATE A LOCKED DATABASE (ACCDE FILE)
To lock a database, you would use the following steps.
1. With the database to be locked open, click Database Tools on the Ribbon to display the Database Tools tab.
2. Click the Make ACCDE button on the Database Tools tab to display the Save As dialog box.
3. In the Save As dialog box, indicate a location and name for the ACCDE file.
4. Click the Save button in the Save As dialog box to create the file.

Using the Locked Database

You use an ACCDE file just as you use the databases with which you now are familiar with two exceptions. First, you must select ACCDE files in the Files of type box when opening the file. Second, you will not be able to modify any source code or change the design of any forms or reports. If you right-clicked the Client Master Form, for example, you would find that the Design View command on the shortcut menu is dimmed, as are many other commands (Figure 9–73).

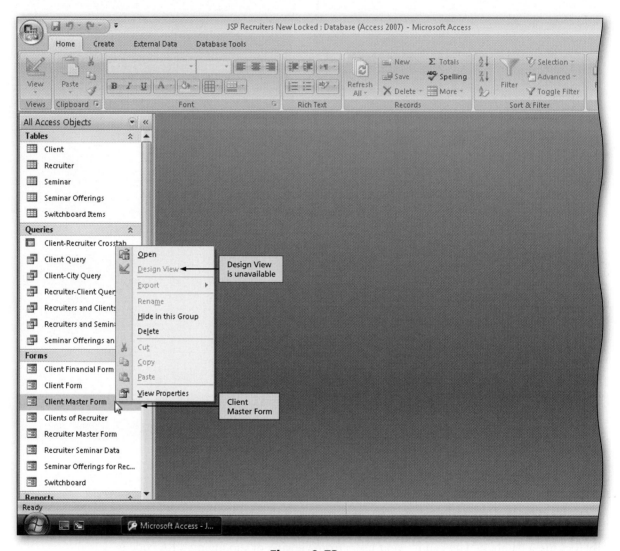

Figure 9–73

It is very important that you save your original database in case you ever need to make changes to VBA code or to the design of a form or report. You cannot use the ACCDE file to make such changes.

Record Locking

You can indicate how records are to be locked when multiple users are using a database at the same time. To do so, click the Microsoft Office Button, click Access Options, and then click Advanced. Scroll down so that the Advanced section appears on the screen (Figure 9–74).

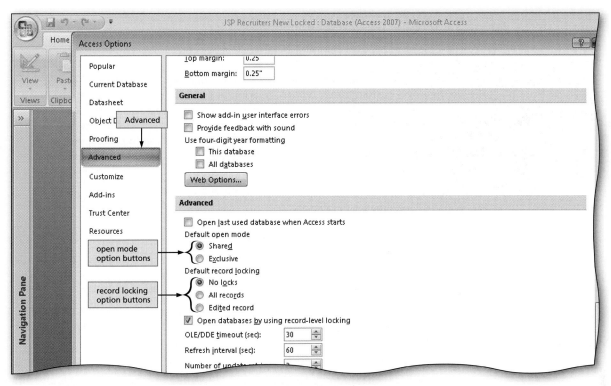

Figure 9–74

If you wanted the default open mode to be exclusive rather than shared, you could click the Exclusive option button. You can select the approach you want for record locking by clicking the appropriate record locking option button. The possible approaches to record locking are shown in Table 9–3.

Table 9–3 Record Locking Approaches	
Locking Type	**Description**
No locks	When you edit a record, Access will not lock the record. Thus, other users also could edit the same record at the same time. When you have finished your changes and attempt to save the record, Access will give you the option of overwriting the other user's changes (not recommended), copying your changes to the clipboard for pasting into a new record, or canceling your changes.
All records	All records will be locked as long as you have the database open. Other users are prevented from editing or locking the records during this time.
Edited record	When you edit a record, Access will lock the record for your use. When other users attempt to edit the same record, they will not be able to do so. Instead, they will see the locked record indicator.

Splitting a Database

You can **split** a database into two databases, one called the **back-end database** that contains only the table data, and another database called the **front-end database** that contains the other objects. While there only would be a single copy of the back-end database, each user could have his or her own copy of the front-end database. Each user would create the desired custom reports, forms, and other objects in his or her own front-end database, thereby not interfering with any other user.

BTW

Quick Reference
For a table that lists how to complete the tasks covered in this book using the mouse, Ribbon, shortcut menu, and keyboard, see the Quick Reference Summary at the back of this book, or visit the Access 2007 Quick Reference Web page (scsite.com/ac2007/qr).

<table>
<tr><td>Plan
Ahead</td><td>**Determine whether the database should be split.**
Should the database be split into a front-end and a back-end? Issues to consider are the following:

1. In many cases, when multiple users share a database, individual users would like to develop their own custom forms, reports, queries, or other objects. If this is the case and each user develops such custom objects, the database can become cluttered and confusing. Many reports, for example, could be developed by different users for different purposes. Further, unless some special action is taken, there is nothing to protect one user's object (for example, a report or form) from being modified by another user. Splitting the database solves this problem.

2. Is there a size issue with the database? Splitting the database into a front-end and a back-end produces smaller databases.</td></tr>
</table>

To Split the Database

When splitting a database, the database to be split must be open. In the process, you will identify a name and location for the back-end database that will be created by the splitter. The following steps show how to split the JSP Recruiters New database (the one you extracted earlier).

- Open the JSP Recruiters New database. If necessary, enable the content and close the Switchboard.

- Click Database Tools on the Ribbon to display the Database Tools tab.

- Click the Access Database button on the Database Tools tab to display the Database Splitter dialog box (Figure 9–75).

The instructions say that I should make a backup copy of my database before splitting it. Should I do that now?

It definitely is a good idea to make a backup copy. Here, because you are using the JSP Recruiters New database rather than the main JSP Recruiters database, it is not necessary. Your JSP Recruiters database still will be intact.

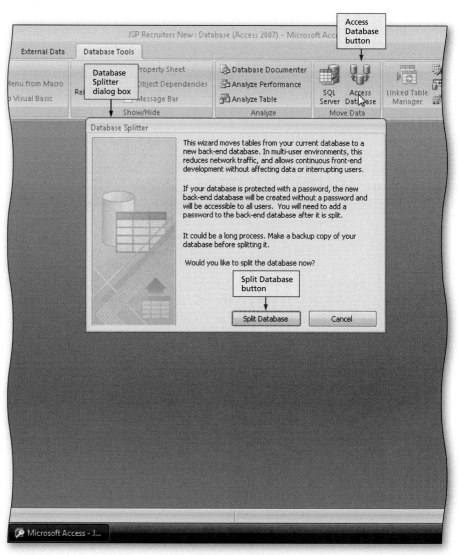

Figure 9–75

2

- Click the Split Database button to display the Create Back-end Database dialog box (Figure 9–76).

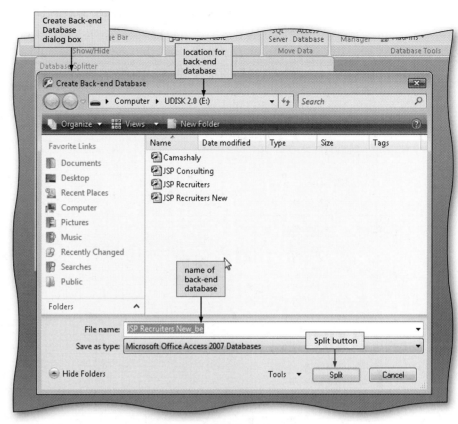

Figure 9–76

3

- Be sure the file name in the Create Back-end Database dialog box that appears is JSP Recruiters New_acc.mdb.

- Select a location for the back-end database, for example, drive E:, and then click the Split button (Figure 9–77).

4

- Click the OK button.

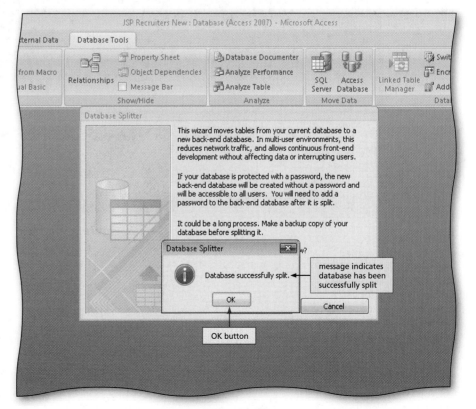

Figure 9–77

The Front-End and Back-End Databases

The database now has been split into separate front-end and back-end databases. The front-end database is the one that you will use. This database contains all the queries, reports, forms, and so on, from the original database. The front-end database only contains links to the tables, however, instead of the tables themselves (Figure 9–78). The back-end database contains the actual tables, but does not contain any other objects.

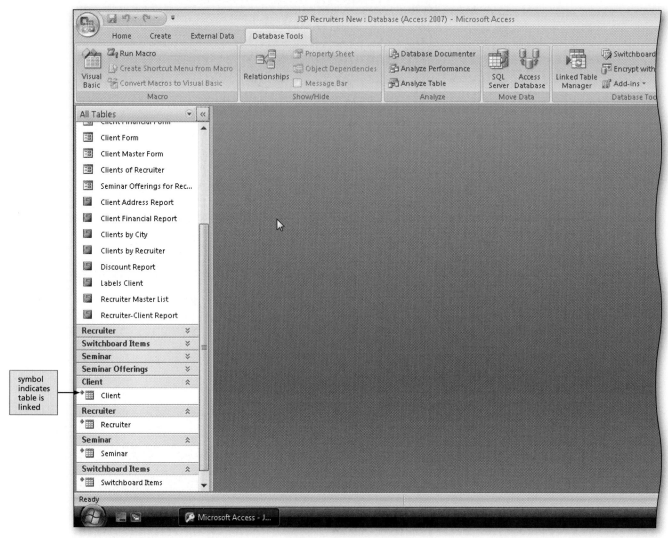

Figure 9–78

BTW

Certification
The Microsoft Certified Application Specialist (MCAS) program provides an opportunity for you to obtain a valuable industry credential — proof that you have the Access 2007 skills required by employers. For more information, see Appendix G or visit the Access 2007 Certification Web page (scsite.com/ac2007/cert).

To Quit Access

You are ready to quit Access. The following step quits Access.

1 Click the Close button on the right side of the Access title bar to quit Access.

Chapter Summary

In this chapter you have learned to convert Access databases to and from earlier versions; use Microsoft Access tools to analyze and document an Access database; add custom categories and groups to the Navigation Pane; use table and database properties; use field properties to create a custom input mask and to allow zero-length strings; create indexes; use automatic error checking; use smart tags; select a startup form; encrypt a database and set a password; use digital certificates; use the Trust Center; lock a database; and split a database. The following list includes all the new Access skills you have learned in this chapter.

1. Convert an Access 2007 Database to an Earlier Version (AC 606)
2. Convert an Access 2000 or Access 2002-2003 Database to Access 2007 (AC 607)
3. Use the Table Analyzer (AC 608)
4. Use the Performance Analyzer (AC 611)
5. Use the Documenter (AC 612)
6. Create Custom Categories and Groups (AC 614)
7. Add Items to Groups (AC 617)
8. Use the Search Bar (AC 619)
9. Create a Validation Rule for a Table (AC 620)
10. Create Custom Properties (AC 621)
11. Create a Custom Input Mask (AC 625)
12. Allow Zero Length (AC 626)
13. Create a Single-Field Index (AC 629)
14. Create a Multiple-Field Index (AC 630)
15. Enable Error Checking (AC 632)
16. Add a Smart Tag to a Field in a Table (AC 636)
17. Show Smart Tags in Forms and Reports (AC 638)
18. Show Smart Tags in Tables and Queries (AC 638)
19. Hide Smart Tags in Forms and Reports (AC 638)
20. Hide Smart Tags in Tables and Queries (AC 638)
21. Add a Smart Tag to a Control in a Form (AC 640)
22. Select a Startup Form (AC 644)
23. Completely Hide the Navigation Pane (AC 645)
24. Show the Navigation Pane when it has been Hidden (AC 646)
25. Open a Database in Exclusive Mode (AC 646)
26. Encrypt a Database with a Password (AC 648)
27. Decrypt the Database and Remove the Password (AC 649)
28. Create a Self-Signed Certificate (AC 650)
29. Package and Sign a Database (AC 651)
30. Open a Signed Package (AC 653)
31. Create a Locked Database (ACCDE File) (AC 659)
32. Split the Database (AC 662)

Learn It Online

Test your knowledge of chapter content and key terms.

Instructions: To complete the Learn It Online exercises, start your browser, click the Address bar, and then enter the Web address scsite.com/ac2007/learn. When the Access 2007 Learn It Online page is displayed, click the link for the exercise you want to complete and then read the instructions.

Chapter Reinforcement TF, MC, and SA
A series of true/false, multiple choice, and short answer questions that test your knowledge of the chapter content.

Flash Cards
An interactive learning environment where you identify chapter key terms associated with displayed definitions.

Practice Test
A series of multiple choice questions that test your knowledge of chapter content and key terms.

Who Wants To Be a Computer Genius?
An interactive game that challenges your knowledge of chapter content in the style of a television quiz show.

Wheel of Terms
An interactive game that challenges your knowledge of chapter key terms in the style of the television show *Wheel of Fortune*.

Crossword Puzzle Challenge
A crossword puzzle that challenges your knowledge of key terms presented in the chapter.

Apply Your Knowledge

Reinforce the skills and apply the concepts you learned in this chapter.

Administering The Bike Delivers Database
Instructions: Start Access. If you are using the Microsoft Office Access 2007 Comprehensive text, open The Bike Delivers database that you used in Chapter 8. Otherwise, see your instructor for information on accessing the files required in this book.

Perform the following tasks:
1. Open the Customer table in Design view and create an index that allows duplicates on the Customer Name field.
2. Create a custom input mask for the Customer Number field. The first two characters of the customer number must be uppercase letters and the last two characters must be digits. No position may be blank.
3. Create a smart tag for the Customer Name field.
4. Save the changes to the Customer table.
5. Populate the Status property for the database with the value, End of Chapter Exercise.
6. Create a custom property with the name Semester. Use Date as the Type and enter the current date as the value.
7. Submit the revised database in the format specified by your instructor.

Extend Your Knowledge

Extend the skills you learned in this chapter and experiment with new skills. You may need to use Help to complete the assignment.

Changing Access Options and Table Properties

Instructions: Copy the JSP Recruiters database and rename the database to Chapter 9_last name Recruiters. For example, if your last name is Smith, then name the database Chapter 9_Smith Recruiters. Start Access and open the database that you copied and renamed.

Perform the following tasks:

1. The switchboard no longer should appear when the database is opened. Change the Access options to ensure that the switchboard does not appear automatically.

2. Change the Navigation options so that the Search Bar always should appear in the Navigation Pane.

3. Open the Seminar table in Design view and create a validation rule that specifies that the value in the Hours field must be greater than or equal to the value in the Increments field.

4. Currently, when you open the Seminar table in Datasheet view, the table is in order by Seminar Number. Change the property for the table so the table is in order by Seminar Description.

5. Change the length of the Seminar Number field in the Seminar table and in the Seminar Offerings table to 20. You will need to delete the relationship between the tables before you can change the length. Re-create the relationship between the Seminar and Seminar Offerings table.

6. In the Integration Feature, you saved the export steps to export the Recruiter-Client Query. Run those saved export steps. Overwrite the existing Excel file.

7. Submit the revised database in the format specified by your instructor.

Make It Right

Analyze a database and correct all errors and/or improve the design.

Correcting Table Design Errors

Instructions: Start Access. Open the Pets and More database. See the inside back cover of this book for instructions on downloading the Data Files for Students, or contact your instructor for more information about accessing the required files.

The Pets and More database contains data about a company that provides a variety of services to pet owners. The owner added the index shown in Figure 9–79 on the next page to the Customer table. The index is to sort records first by City and then by Last Name, but she gets an error message when she tries to save the table change. Create the index correctly.

Continued >

Make It Right *continued*

She also created an input mask for the Customer Number field. The input mask she created is shown in Figure 9–79, however she found that it does not work correctly. It allows a user to input a customer number that does not include letters. The customer number must be two letters followed by two numbers.

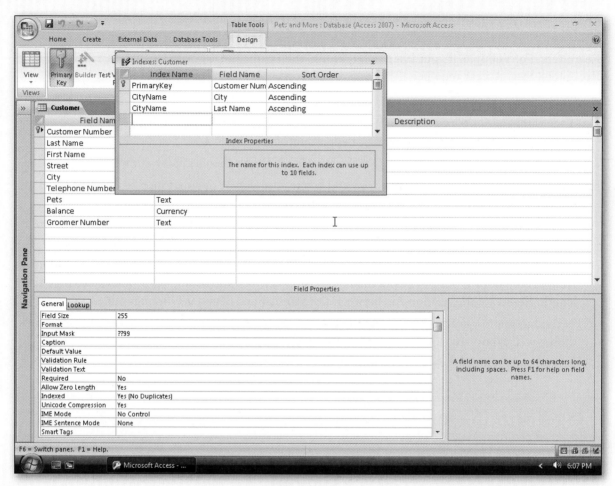

Figure 9–79

Correct these errors and submit the revised database in the format specified by your instructor.

In the Lab

Design, create, modify, and/or use a database following the guidelines, concepts, and skills presented in this chapter. Labs are listed in order of increasing difficulty.

Lab 1: Administering the JMS TechWizards Database

Problem: JMS TechWizards has determined a number of database administration tasks that need to be done. These include creating indexes, setting start up options, creating input masks, creating smart tags, and converting to an earlier version of Access.

Instructions: If you are using the Microsoft Office Access 2007 Comprehensive text, open the JMS TechWizards database that you used in Chapter 8. Otherwise, see the inside back cover of this book for instructions on downloading the Data Files for Students, or contact your instructor for more information about accessing the required files.

Perform the following tasks:

1. Technician Number is a field in both the Client and Technician tables. Create an input mask for the Technician Number field in both tables.

2. Create an index on the Last Name and First Name fields in the Technician table. Name the index, FullName.

3. Open the Client Master Form and create a smart tag for the Client Name field.

4. Select the switchboard as the startup form.

5. Convert the database to an Access 2002-2003 database.

6. Submit the revised database in the format specified by your instructor.

In the Lab

Lab 2: Administering the Hockey Fan Zone Database

Problem: The management of the Hockey Fan Zone store has determined a number of database administration tasks that need to be done. These include creating indexes, setting startup options, creating input masks, creating smart tags, and using table properties.

Instructions: If you are using the Microsoft Office Access 2007 Comprehensive text, open the Hockey Fan Zone database that you used in Chapter 8. Otherwise, see the inside back cover of this book for instructions on downloading the Data Files for Students, or contact your instructor for more information about accessing the required files.

Perform the following tasks:

1. Open the Item table in Design view and create an index on the combination of Item Type and Description. Name the index, TypeDescription.

2. Create a custom input mask for the Item Number field. The values in the field must be four digits in length.

3. Ensure that the cost of an item is less than the selling price of an item.

4. Ensure that the switchboard appears when the database is opened.

5. Open the Supplier table in Design view and create a smart tag for the Supplier Name field.

6. Populate the Status database property with the value, Current Version.

7. Submit the revised database in the format specified by your instructor.

In the Lab

Lab 3: Administering the Ada Beauty Supply Database

Problem: Ada Beauty Supply has determined a number of database administration tasks that need to be done. These include creating indexes, setting startup options, creating input masks, allowing zero-length fields, creating smart tags, and populating database properties.

Instructions: If you are using the Microsoft Office Access 2007 Comprehensive text, open the Ada Beauty Supply database that you used in Chapter 8. Otherwise, see the inside back cover of this book for instructions on downloading the Data Files for Students, or contact your instructor for more information about accessing the required files. Submit the revised database in the format specified by your instructor.

Continued >

In the Lab *continued*

Instructions Part 1: The management of Ada Beauty Supply is concerned that as the database grows, it will take longer to retrieve information on customer names. An index would speed up the retrieval process. The management also feels that an index on the last name and first name of the sales rep would improve efficiency.

Instructions Part 2: The management wants to ensure that the customer number field always contains two uppercase letters followed by two numeric digits. Also, errors are occurring because individuals are entering text instead of numbers in the Postal Code field in the Sales Rep table. In addition, empty strings should not be allowed in the Customer Name field.

Instructions Part 3: Management would like an easy way to select a customer name and send them an e-mail. Management wants to be able to do this from within the Customer table and the Customer Master Form. Management also wants the switchboard to appear when the database is opened.

Instructions Part 4: Management needs to contact all customers with an amount paid greater than $1,000.00. Apply a filter to the Sales Rep-Customer query and print the filtered query results.

Cases and Places

Apply your creative thinking and problem solving skills to design and implement a solution.

● EASIER   ●● MORE DIFFICULT

●1 Administering the Second Hand Goods Database

If you are using the Microsoft Office Access 2007 Comprehensive text, open the Second Hand Goods database that you used in Chapter 8. Otherwise, see the inside back cover of this book for instructions on downloading the Data Files for Students, or contact your instructor for more information about accessing the required files. Perform the following database administration tasks:

    a. Copy the Second Hand Goods database and rename it as Second Hand Furniture.

    b. Split the Second Hand Furniture database into a front-end and a back-end database.

    c. Open the front-end database and open the switchboard form in Design view.

    d. Add a label to the upper-left corner of the form and type your name in the label. Change the font color to white and the font size to 12.

    e. Submit the revised databases in the format specified by your instructor.

●2 Administering the BeachCondo Rentals Database

If you are using the Microsoft Office Access 2007 Comprehensive text, open the BeachCondo Rentals database that you used in Chapter 8. Otherwise, see the inside back cover of this book for instructions on downloading the Data Files for Students, or contact your instructor for more information about accessing the required files. Perform the following database administration tasks:

    a. Use the Database Documenter to produce detailed documentation on the Current Rentals table. Export the documentation to a Word RTF file. Change the name of the file to LastName_ Documentation.rtf where LastName is your last name.

    b. Use the Table Analyzer to analyze the table structure of each table in the database. Open the RTF file that you created in the previous step and report the results of the analysis at the end of the file.

    c. Use the Performance Analyzer to analyze all the tables and queries in the database. Report the results of the analysis in your RTF file.

    d. Customize the Navigation Pane by adding a custom category called Rentals. Then add two custom groups, Potential and Current, to the Rentals category.

    e. Add the Available Rentals report and the Condos by Bedroom report to the Potential group. Add the Current Rentals table and the report that you created in Chapter 7 to the Current category.

    f. Print the relationships for the database.

    g. Submit the RTF file and the revised database in the format specified by your instructor.

●●3 Administering the Restaurant Database

If you are using the Microsoft Office Access 2007 Comprehensive text, open the restaurant database that you used in Chapter 8. Otherwise, see the inside back cover of this book for instructions on downloading the Data Files for Students, or contact your instructor for more information about accessing the required files. Using the Plan Ahead guidelines presented in this chapter, determine what administrative tasks you need to perform on your database. Do you need to customize the Navigation Pane? Do you need to add any indexes, input masks, or smart tags? Are any custom properties needed? Because you probably will have different people using the database, you may want to split the database. Is error checking enabled? Perform the necessary database administration tasks and submit the revised database to your instructor.

Continued >

Cases and Places *continued*

••4 Creating a Digital Certificate for Your Contacts Database

Make It Personal

If you are using the Microsoft Office Access 2007 Comprehensive text, open the contacts database that you used in Chapter 8. Otherwise, see the inside back cover of this book for instructions on downloading the Data Files for Students, or contact your instructor for more information about accessing the required files. If you have your instructor's permission and the ability to create digital certificates, create a digital certificate for your contacts database. Submit the revised database in the format specified by your instructor.

••5 Understand Database Administration Tasks

Working Together

Copy the Hockey Fan Zone database and rename the database to your team name. For each of the database administration tasks listed below, perform the task and record the outcome. Write a short paper that explains what happened when you did these tasks.

    a. Create an earlier version of the database

    b. Encrypt the database and set a password

    c. Create a locked database

    d. Change the macro settings

    e. Change privacy options

    f. Export the AC_History.xlsx file attachment and then detach (remove) the attachment.

Web Feature
Sharing Access Data

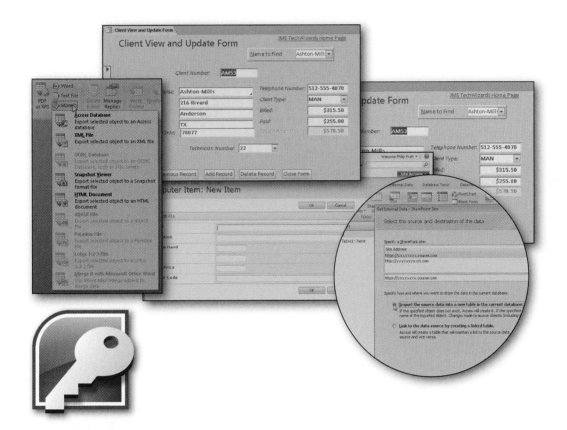

Objectives

You will have mastered the material in this feature when you can:

- Create a SharePoint Services list by exporting an Access table

- Open a SharePoint Services list from within SharePoint

- Import or link a SharePoint Services list to an Access table

- Move a database to SharePoint and share the database

- Insert a hyperlink to a file or Web page

- Export to HTML

Web Feature Introduction

BTW

SharePoint Services
Windows SharePoint offers users the ability to store data on the Web so that access to that data can be shared across a network. It is essentially a storage location that can be accessed collaboratively. No special software is required on the client side. SharePoint Services technology is particularly useful for sharing information across an intranet.

Access users often need to work with their data from a remote location or share database information with colleagues working in another location. You can use the Web for this type of access in one of two ways, either with Windows SharePoint Services or by saving Access objects as HTML files. Using the current version of Windows SharePoint Services 3.0, you can create lists that are like Access tables. Other users with appropriate privileges can access the site and share the lists. Windows SharePoint offers users the ability to store data on the Web so that access to that data can be shared across a network. The other method, saving Access objects as HTML files, lets users view them over the Web in a browser, such as Internet Explorer.

Project — Sharing Access Data

Like other applications, Access allows you to share data with others using SharePoint Services. You can import, export, and link data to a SharePoint Services Web site. The data will reside on the Web site in the form of lists.

A SharePoint Services list is similar to a table in a database. The list is a grid with column headings, which are similar to field names, and data in the columns that match the column headings. Figure 1a shows a list with information about computer items. The first column heading is Item Id, and the items in the column are item ids. The second column heading is Description, and the items in the column are descriptions of products. The data in the list can be imported or linked to a table in an Access database. Figure 1b shows the results of importing the data into a table. Notice that Access has added an additional field, the ID field, which is an AutoNumber field that serves as the primary key.

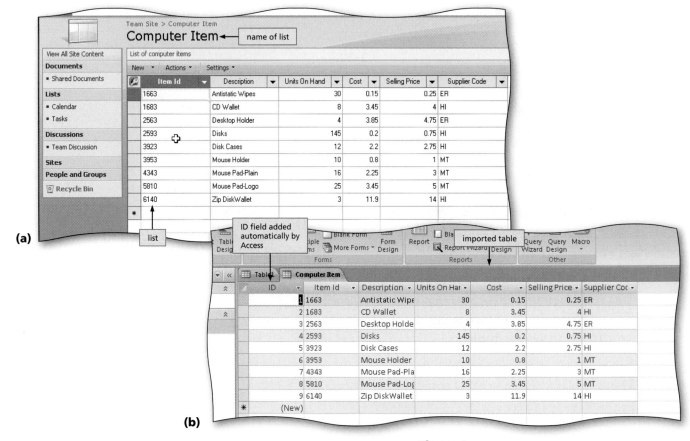

Figure 1

You also can make objects in the database available for viewing by others by exporting the object as an HTML file. Figure 2 shows an HTML version of the Discount Report for JSP Recruiters viewed in a browser. The figure also contains a hyperlink to the JSP Recruiter's Home Page. To display that home page while viewing this data, simply click the link. Unlike the data in SharePoint lists, the HTML versions of objects in the database are static. That is, they do not change when the data in the database changes. If you were to change client data tomorrow and wanted the HTML version to contain the new data, you would need to export the file again, creating an updated version.

Figure 2

Overview

As you read through this feature, you will learn how to perform the following tasks.

- Create a SharePoint list by exporting an Access table.
- Open and use a SharePoint list.
- Import or link a SharePoint list to an Access database.
- Move a database to SharePoint.
- Use a shared database.
- Add a hyperlink to an Access object.
- Export Access data to HTML.

Plan Ahead

> **Guidelines for Sharing Data**
>
> 1. **Determine tables to be shared.** Which tables contain data that should be shared with others over the Internet?
>
> 2. **Determine whether users should import or link SharePoint lists to their Access tables.** If they link the data, any changes they make either in SharePoint or Access will be available to others. If they import the data, the changes only will affect the database on which they are working. For each list and each user, you need to determine whether changes should be immediately available to others.
>
> 3. **Determine whether you should move an entire database to SharePoint.** Should users have access to all the tables in the database? Should they have access to the forms or reports? When they access the database, should they be able to merely view the data (that is, Read-Only mode) or should they be able to change data (that is, Edit mode)?
>
> 4. **Determine whether hyperlinks would be useful in any forms or reports.** Would it be useful to have a hyperlink to move to a Web page? Would it be useful to be able to move to another object in the database or to send e-mail?
>
> 5. **Determine whether any database objects should be exported as HTML.** Exporting the objects as HTML enables them to be viewed over the Internet. They also can be viewed using a Web browser on the local computer. It is important to remember that data that has been exported as HTML does not change when the underlying data in the database changes.
>
> When necessary, more specific details concerning the above decisions and/or actions are presented at appropriate positions within the feature.

Data Access Pages
Microsoft Office Access 2007 does not support Data Access pages. If you want users to access a data entry form over the Web and be able to store the resulting data in Access, you should use Microsoft Windows SharePoint Services 3.0 server. If you open a database created with an earlier version of Access (an .mdb file), and that database contains Data Access pages, you can view the pages in Internet Explorer. However, you cannot take any action with those pages.

SharePoint Services

Access allows you to share data with others using SharePoint Services. You can import, export, and link data to a SharePoint Services site. The data will reside on the Web site in the form of a SharePoint Services list.

Creating a SharePoint Services List

You can create a SharePoint Services list directly on a SharePoint Services site. You also can create one by exporting an Access table or an Excel worksheet. The process for creating one from an Access table is similar to exporting a table to any other format. The only difference is that you would use the SharePoint List button in the Export group on the External Data tab, rather than the Excel, Word, or any of the other buttons (Figure 3).

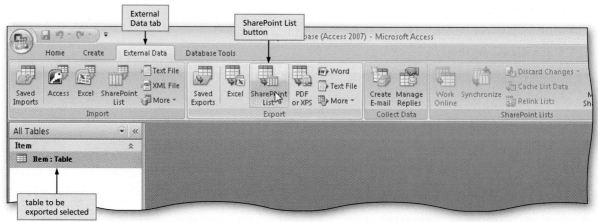

Figure 3

You then would need to identify the site, give a name for the list to be created, and include an optional description of the list (Figure 4).

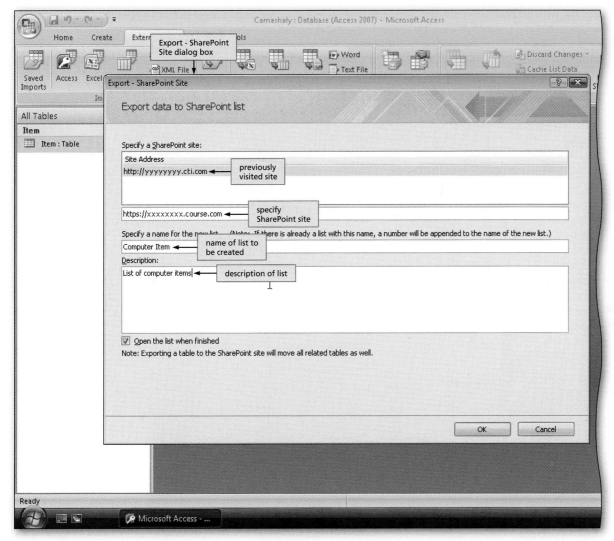

Figure 4

To Create a SharePoint Services List by Exporting an Access Table

To create a SharePoint Services List by exporting an Access table, you would use the following steps.

1. With the table selected within Access, click External Data on the Ribbon to display the External Data tab.

2. Click the SharePoint List button in the Export group on the External Data tab to display the Export - SharePoint Site dialog box.

3. Specify the SharePoint site, specify the name for the list, and, optionally, enter a description of the list.

4. Click the OK button and then enter your user name and password when prompted.

5. Decide whether you want to save the export steps.

Opening a SharePoint Services List

You can use a list directly from the SharePoint site. You can open the list by selecting from the available lists (Figure 5).

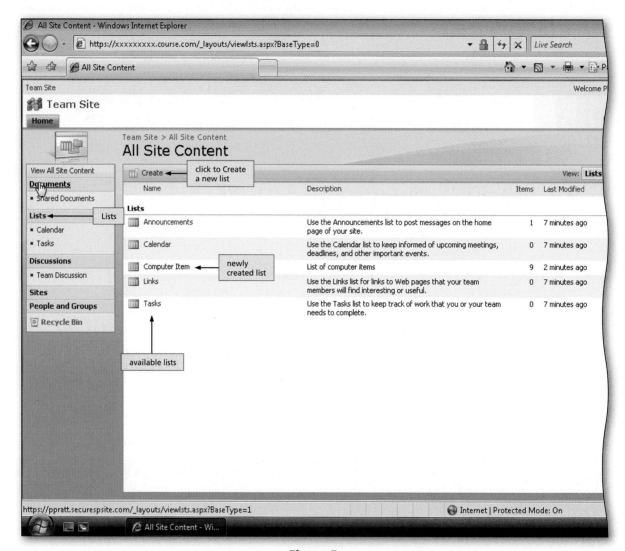

Figure 5

To Open a SharePoint Services List from within SharePoint

To open a list from within SharePoint, you would use the following steps.

1. Enter the SharePoint site, giving your username and password when prompted.
2. Click the Lists link.
3. Click the desired list.

Using a SharePoint Services List

When the list is open, you can view it in Datasheet view, which is very similar to Datasheet view within Access (Figure 6).

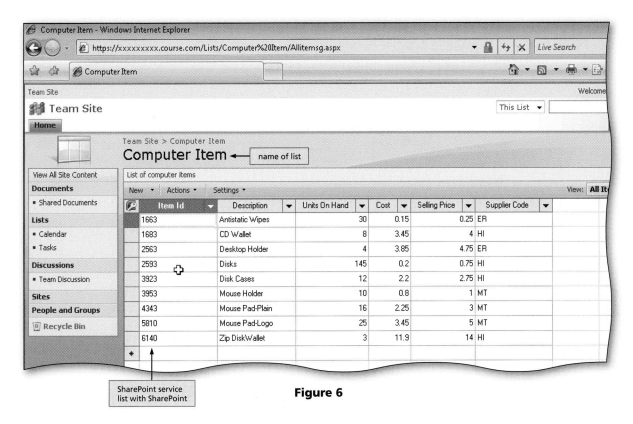

Figure 6

You can filter or sort on a field by clicking the arrow in the column heading for the field (Figure 7). You can click either Sort Ascending or Sort Descending to change the sort order. By clicking a value, only those rows containing that value will appear. By once again clicking Show All you can redisplay all records. If you need more complex filtering, you can click Custom Filter and then specify individual conditions. You also can connect the individual conditions with "and" or "or."

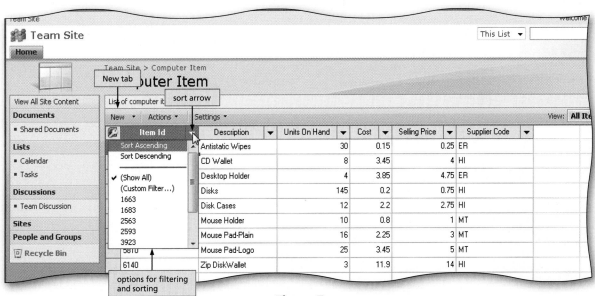

Figure 7

The New tab allows you to add a new row (record) in Form view (Figure 8). You also could add a new row by typing in the blank row at the end of the datasheet.

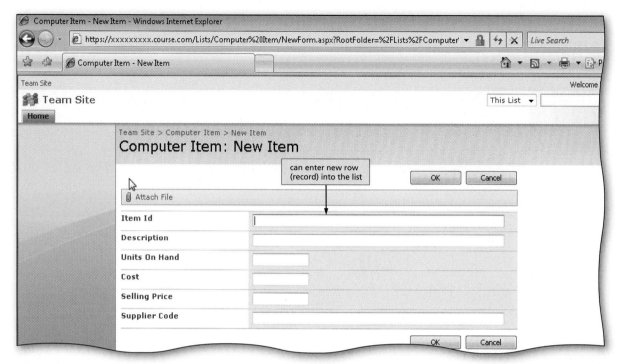

Figure 8

By clicking the Actions arrow, you can display a menu with several useful commands (Figure 9).

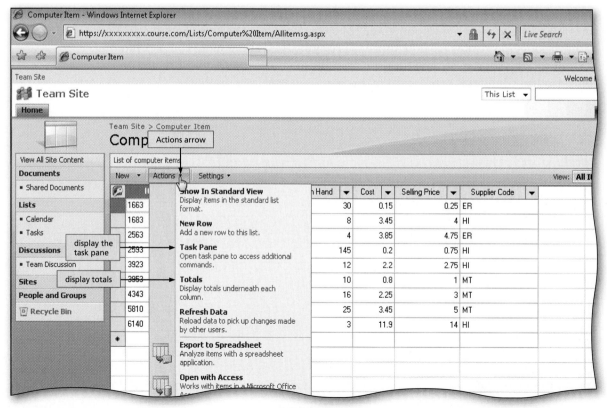

Figure 9

The Task Pane command in the Actions list lets you display a task pane with still additional commands. By clicking the Totals command in the Actions list, you can display totals for numeric fields (Figure 10). Clicking the Settings arrow produces a list of commands that allow you to create a new column, create a view (similar to an Access query), or manage settings for the list.

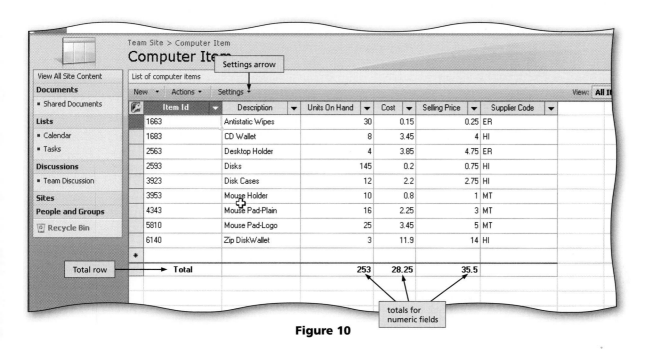

Figure 10

Importing a SharePoint Services List

There are two ways to import a SharePoint Services list to an Access table. You can use the SharePoint Lists button in the Import group on the External Data tab. You also can use the SharePoint Lists button on the Create tab (Figure 11). Clicking Existing SharePoint List on the SharePoint Lists button menu produces the same effect as clicking the SharePoint Lists button in the Import Group. The SharePoint Lists button gives you additional options, because it lists the various SharePoint List templates.

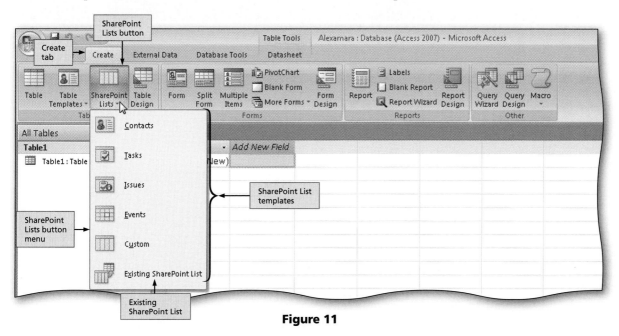

Figure 11

Regardless of which approach you take, Access will display the Get External Data - SharePoint Site dialog box (Figure 12). In this dialog box, you will give the address for the site from which to import, and then select the option button to import the source data into a new table. You also will be prompted to give your user name and password.

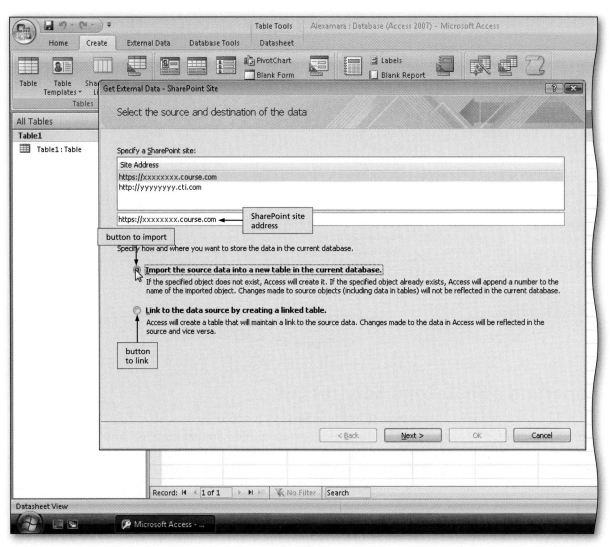

Figure 12

Assuming your user name and password are valid, you will see the available lists from which you can select (Figure 13). You check the list or lists you want to import.

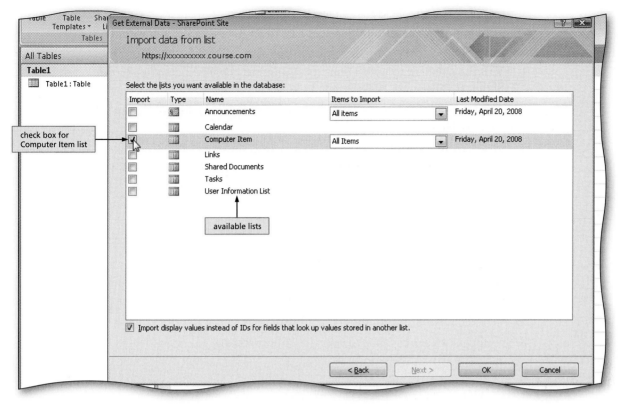

Figure 13

The imported table is shown in Figure 14. The name of the table is Computer Item. Access also has added automatically the ID field, which is an AutoNumber field that functions as the primary key.

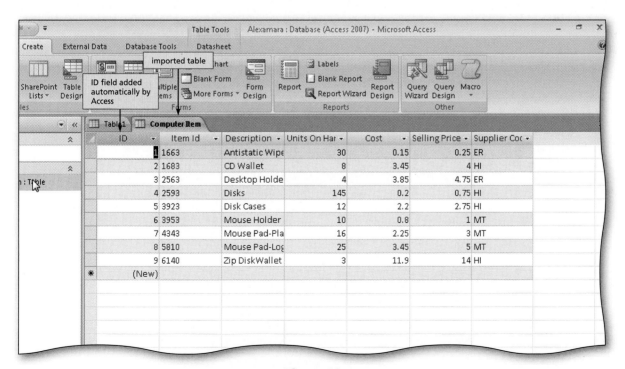

Figure 14

To Import a SharePoint Services List

To import a SharePoint Services List to an Access table, you would use the following steps.

1. With the database to which you wish to import the list open, click Create on the Ribbon to display the Create tab.

2. Click the SharePoint Lists button on the Create tab to display the available SharePoint List templates.

3. Click Existing SharePoint List to display the Get External Data - SharePoint Site dialog box. (Rather than clicking SharePoint Lists on the Create tab, you could have clicked SharePoint List in the Import Group on the External Data tab. In that approach, you would not see the available SharePoint List templates.)

4. Enter the site address for the SharePoint site.

5. Click the 'Import the source data into a new table in the current database' option button.

6. Click the Next button, enter your user name and password when prompted, and then click the check box for the list you want to import (you can click more than one).

7. Click the OK button to import the list.

8. Decide whether you want to save the import steps.

Linking a SharePoint Services List

You also can link a SharePoint Services list to a table in an Access database. The linked table appears in the Navigation Pane preceded by the symbol that indicates it is linked (Figure 15).

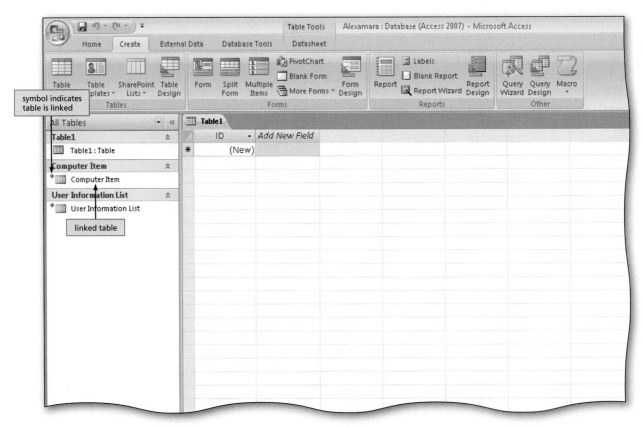

Figure 15

TO LINK A SHAREPOINT SERVICES LIST

To link a SharePoint Services list to an Access table, you would use the following steps.

1. With the database to which you wish to link the list open, click Create on the Ribbon to display the Create tab.

2. Click the SharePoint Lists button on the Create tab to display the available SharePoint List templates.

3. Click Existing SharePoint List to display the Get External Data - SharePoint Site dialog box.

4. Enter the site address for the SharePoint site.

5. Be sure the 'Link to the data source by creating a linked table' option button is selected.

6. Click the Next button, enter your user name and password when prompted, and then click the check box for the list you want to link.

7. Click the OK button to import the list.

8. Decide whether you want to save the import steps.

Using a Linked Table

Because this is a linked table, any change in either the linked table or the list is automatically reflected in the other. In Figure 16, for example, the Units on Hand quantity for Desktop Holder is changed from 4 to 6 in the linked table in Access. Notice that Access automatically has added an Attachments field.

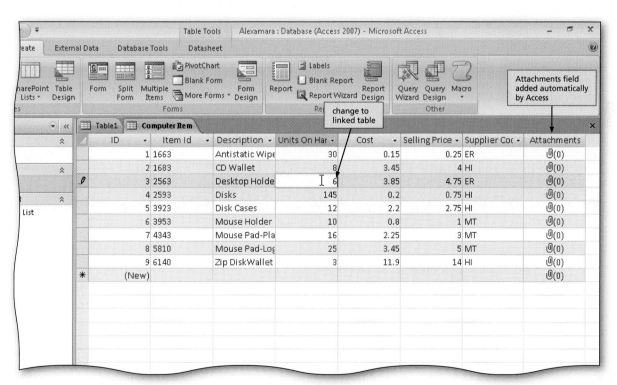

Figure 16

The corresponding SharePoint Services list is shown in Figure 17. The change to the units on hand is reflected in the list. If you already had the SharePoint Services list open when you made the change to the linked table, the change may not immediately be reflected on your screen. You would have needed to click the Action arrow and then click the Refresh Data command.

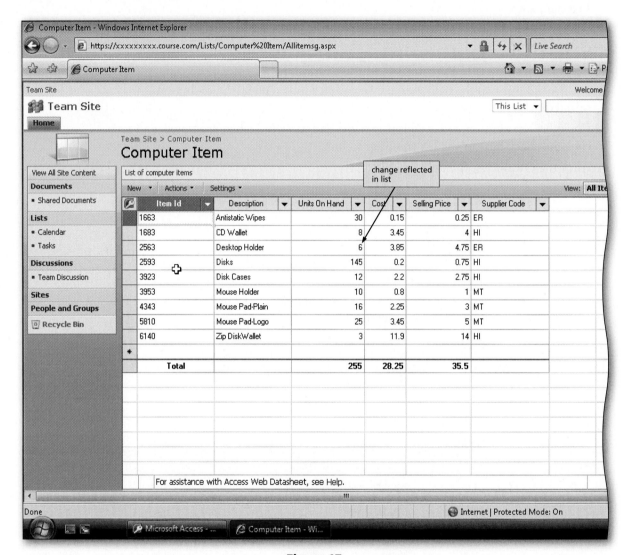

Figure 17

To Move a Database to SharePoint

You can move an entire database to SharePoint. This makes your database available to a wide variety of users. To do so, you click the Move to SharePoint button to start the Move to SharePoint Site Wizard (Figure 18).

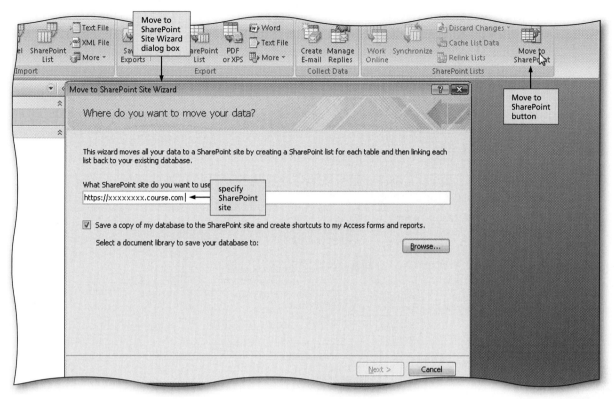

Figure 18

The Wizard will perform the following tasks for you.

1. Create a backup copy of your database so that you can go back to the non-SharePoint version if you need to do so.

2. Create a SharePoint list for every table in the database.

3. Remove the tables from the database and replace them with linked tables, ensuring that all the data is managed by SharePoint.

4. Optionally upload a copy of the database to the SharePoint site so that other users can access your queries, forms, and reports.

To move a database to a SharePoint site, you would use the following steps.

1. With the database to be moved open, click the Move to SharePoint button in the SharePoint Lists group on the External Data tab to start the Move to SharePoint Site Wizard.

2. Enter the address of the SharePoint site, giving your user name and password when requested.

3. If you want to give other users the ability to use your forms and reports, be sure the 'Save a copy of my database to the SharePoint site and create shortcuts to my Access forms and reports' check box is selected.

4. Click the Browse button, select a location for the shared database (for example, the shared document library), and then click the OK button.

5. Click the Next button.

6. If you want to see details concerning issues encountered while moving your data, click the Show Details button.

7. Click the Finish button to complete the movement of the database. If any problems occurred during the movement, a table called Move to SharePoint Site Issues will be created in the database; this table contains details concerning these issues.

To Open a Shared Database

You can open a shared database (one that has been moved to SharePoint) from within SharePoint (Figure 19). In the process, you can determine whether to open the database in Read-Only mode, where you cannot make any changes, or Edit mode, where you can change the data.

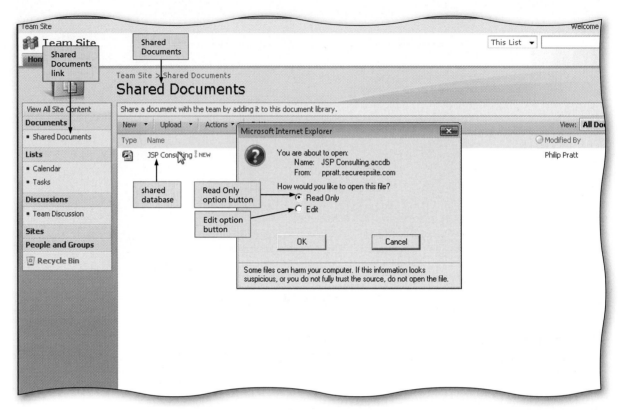

Figure 19

BTW

Working Offline
You can use Microsoft Office Access 2007 to work offline with data that is linked to a list on a Microsoft Windows SharePoint Services 3.0 site. To work offline, open the database that is linked to SharePoint lists, click the External Data tab, and then click Work Offline. To reconnect to the SharePoint server, click Work Online on the External Data tab. To synchronize your data, that is, update the database and lists, click Synchronize on the External Data tab.

To open a shared database, you would use the following steps.

1. Enter the SharePoint Site, giving your user name and password when requested.
2. Select the location of the shared database (for example, Shared Documents).
3. Click the name of the database you wish to open.
4. Select whether you want to open the database in Read-Only mode or in Edit mode.
5. Click the OK button.
6. If you wish to save a local copy, select a location for the local copy.

Update Shared Data

If you open the database in Edit mode, you can make changes to the data and your changes will be sent to the SharePoint server, where they will be available to others. There is a potential problem, however. Another user may be attempting to edit the same record that you are editing. If the other user completes his or her update before you complete yours, you will receive the message shown in Figure 20. You then can choose how you wish to handle the issue.

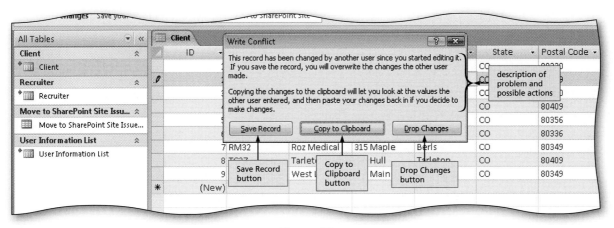

Figure 20

If you click the Save Record button, your changes will be saved. This can be dangerous because the other user's update typically will be lost in the process. If you click the Copy to Clipboard button, the contents of your change will be copied to the clipboard. You then could examine the record to see the effect of the other user's changes. If your changes still are appropriate, you then could paste your changes into the database. Finally, if you click Drop Changes, your changes are abandoned.

Hyperlinks and HTML

In a Web page, a **hyperlink** is an element that you can activate, typically with a click of the mouse, to open another Web document. You can add hyperlinks to forms and reports in an Access database to perform a similar function. The link could be to a Web page, as shown in Figure 21. It also could be to another object in the database or to an e-mail address.

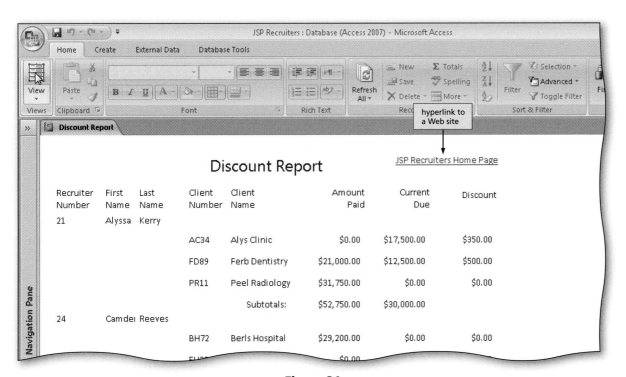

Figure 21

Web pages typically are created using HTML (Hypertext Markup Language). You can create an HTML document from an Access table, query, or report. Such an HTML document can be displayed in a Web browser (Figure 22).

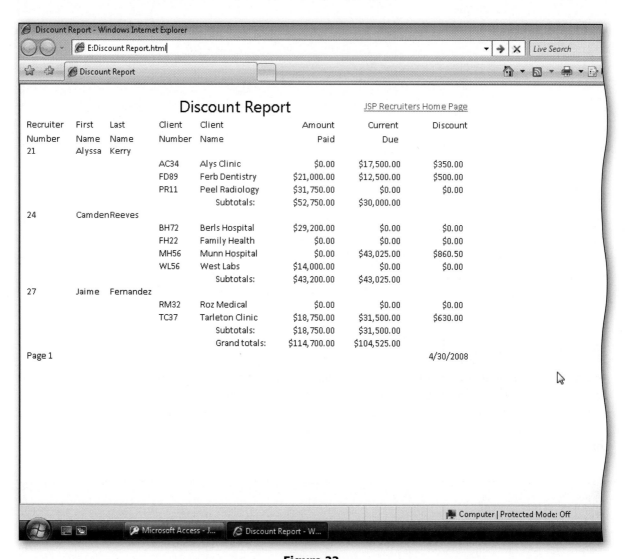

Figure 22

Adding Hyperlinks

To add a hyperlink to a form or report, you use the Insert Hyperlink tool in the Controls group on the Design tab (Figure 23). If the link is to an existing file or Web page, you make sure Existing File or Web Page is selected in the Link to pane, enter the text to display as the link name, and add the address.

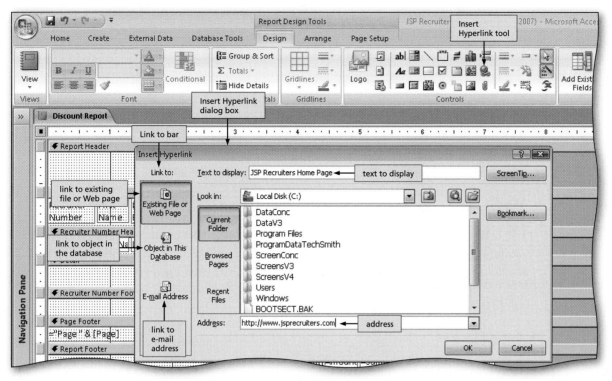

Figure 23

By clicking Object in This Database instead of Existing File or Web Page, you can link to the report, form, or other object. In the process of creating the link, you will identify the specific object to which you wish to link. You can insert a hyperlink with an e-mail address by clicking E-mail Address and then giving the address and, optionally, a subject.

Once you have added the hyperlink, you can drag it to the desired location on the form or report (Figure 24).

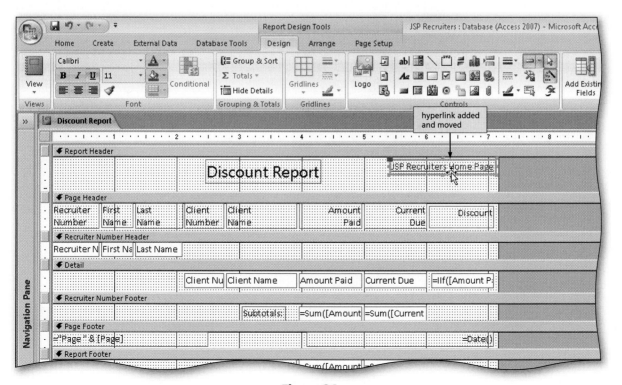

Figure 24

Certification

The Microsoft Certified Application Specialist (MCAS) program provides an opportunity for you to obtain a valuable industry credential — proof that you have the Access 2007 skills required by employers. For more information, see Appendix G or visit the Access 2007 Certification Web page (scsite.com/ac2007/cert).

TO INSERT A HYPERLINK TO A FILE OR WEB PAGE

To insert a hyperlink to a file or Web page, you would use the following steps.

1. With the object to contain the hyperlink open in Design view, click the Insert Hyperlink tool in the Controls group on the Design tab.

2. Type the text to display for the hyperlink.

3. With Existing File or Web Page selected, select the file or type the address.

4. Click the OK button to add the hyperlink.

5. Drag the hyperlink to the desired location.

Exporting to HTML

You can create an HTML version of a table, query, form, or report. This version would be suitable for posting on the Web or for viewing using a Web browser, but cannot be edited by another user. To create an HTML version, you would use the HTML Document command on the More button menu in the Export group on the External Data tab (Figure 25).

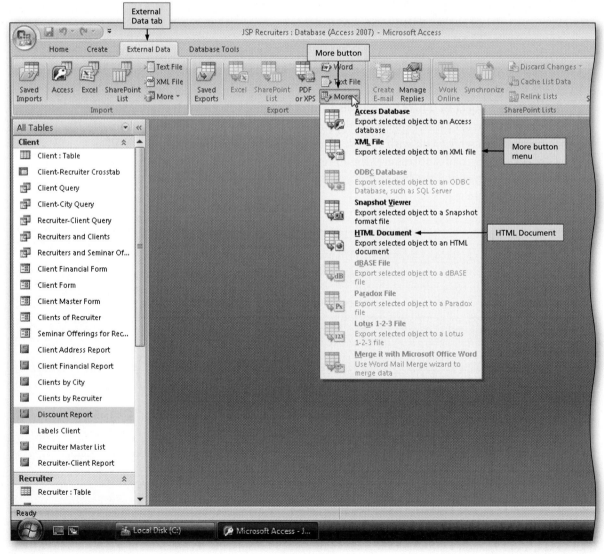

Figure 25

After you have clicked the HTML Document command, you would use the Export - HTML Document dialog box to enter a file name and select a location for the file (Figure 26).

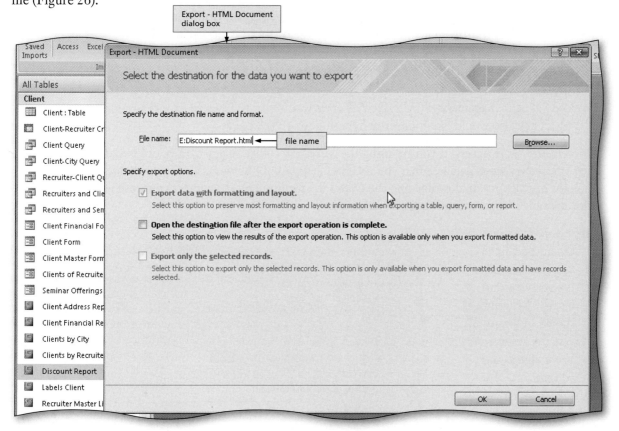

Figure 26

To Export to HTML

To export an object to HTML, you would use the following steps.

1. With the table, query, form, or report to be exported selected in the Navigation Pane, click the More button in the Export group on the External Data tab to display the More menu.

2. Click HTML Document on the More menu.

3. Enter the file name and location for the HTML file to be created and then click the OK button.

4. In the HTML Output Options dialog box, click the OK button.

BTW

Quick Reference
For a table that lists how to complete the tasks covered in this book using the mouse, Ribbon, shortcut menu, and keyboard, see the Quick Reference Summary at the back of this book, or visit the Access 2007 Quick Reference Web page (scsite.com/ac2007/qr).

Feature Summary

In this feature you have learned to share Access data by using SharePoint; create a SharePoint list by exporting an Access table; open and use a SharePoint list; import or link a SharePoint list to an Access database; move a database to SharePoint; use a shared database; add a hyperlink to an Access object; and export Access data to HTML. The following list includes all the new Access skills you have learned in this feature.

1. Create a SharePoint Services List by Exporting an Access Table (AC 677)
2. Open a SharePoint Services List from within SharePoint (AC 678)
3. Import a SharePoint Services List (AC 684)
4. Link a SharePoint Services List (AC 685)
5. Move a Database to SharePoint (AC 686)
6. Open a Shared Database (AC 688)
7. Insert a Hyperlink to a File or Web Page (AC 692)
8. Export to HTML (AC 693)

In the Lab

Design, create, modify, and/or use a database following the guidelines, concepts, and skills presented in this feature. Labs are listed in order of increasing difficulty.

Lab 1: Inserting Hyperlinks into and Exporting HTML Files from the JMS TechWizards Database

Problem: The management of JMS TechWizards would like to learn to export a report and a query to HTML. They also would like to insert a hyperlink to a Web page.

Instructions: Start Access. If you are using the Microsoft Office Access 2007 Comprehensive text, open the JMS TechWizards database that you used in Chapter 9. Otherwise, see the inside back cover of this book for instructions on downloading the Data Files for Students, or contact your instructor for more information about accessing the required files.

Perform the following tasks:

1. Open the Client Master Form in Design view and insert a hyperlink as shown in Figure 27. Use the scsite.com Web page as the address.

2. Export the City-Technician crosstab as an HTML file.

3. Export the Billing Summary Report as an HTML file.

4. Submit the HTML files and the revised database in the format specified by your instructor.

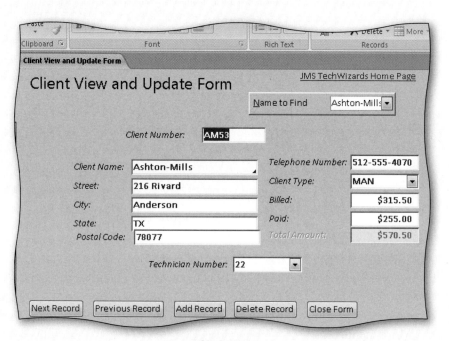

Figure 27

In the Lab

Lab 2: Sharing Data in the Hockey Fan Zone Database

Problem: The management of Hockey Fan Zone would like to learn more about how they might use Windows SharePoint Services to share data.

Instructions: If you are using the Microsoft Office Access 2007 Comprehensive text, use the Hockey Fan Zone database that you used in Chapter 9. Otherwise, see the inside back cover of this book for instructions on downloading the Data Files for Students, or contact your instructor for more information about accessing the required files.

Perform the following tasks:

1. Open Microsoft Office Word, create a new document, and then type your name at the top. List the steps to do the following.

   a. Create a SharePoint Services list by exporting the Supplier table.

   b. Open the Supplier table in SharePoint Services and sort the suppliers in descending order by Last Order Date.

   c. Link the Item table from a SharePoint Services list to a database named FanShare.

   d. Change the cost of ball caps to $10.00.

   e. Import the Supplier table from a SharePoint Services list to a database named FanShare.

2. Submit the Word document in the format specified by your instructor.

3. If you have access to a SharePoint Server, perform the tasks in step 1 and submit the database in the format specified by your instructor.

5 | Reusing a Presentation with Multimedia

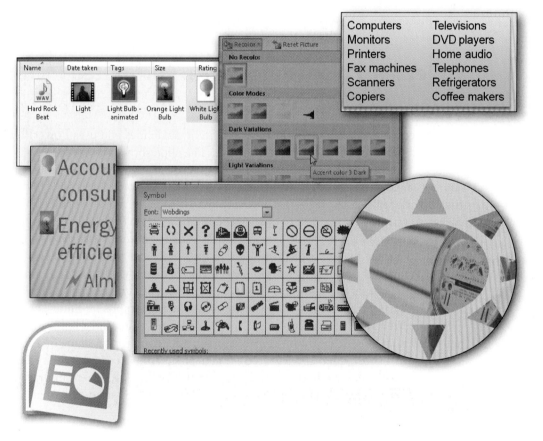

Objectives

You will have mastered the material in this chapter when you can:

- Recolor photographs
- Resize pictures
- Apply a shape to a picture
- Change a bullet character to a picture
- Change a bullet character to a symbol
- Format a bullet size

- Format a bullet color
- Add a movie file and clip
- Add a sound clip
- Create columns in a text box
- Rehearse timings
- Set slide show timings manually

5 | Reusing a Presentation with Multimedia

Introduction

At times you will need to revise a PowerPoint presentation. Changes may include inserting current figures, replacing outdated photographs, and updating visual elements displayed on a slide. Often applying a different theme, changing fonts, and substituting graphical elements give a slide show an entirely new look. Adding multimedia, including sounds, video, and music, can enhance a presentation and help audience members retain the information being presented.

Project — Presentation with Formatted Pictures, Video, and Sounds

The project in this chapter follows visual content guidelines and uses PowerPoint to create the presentation shown in Figure 5–1. The slide show uses several visual and audio elements to introduce the concept that saving electricity is easy to accomplish and necessary in today's world. Using Energy Star appliances, equipment, and light bulbs at home and at work can reduce electricity consumption by as much as 90 percent. The four slides in this presentation use a variety of visual elements to draw the audience into the topic. The speaker's role is to provide specific details of the amount of energy, and, in turn, the amount of money that can be saved by shopping wisely and practicing energy conservation. The presentation begins with upbeat music that should stimulate the audience's interest and help set the mood for energy enlightenment. The electric meter on Slide 1 is colored gold and transformed into a sun shape. The paragraphs on Slide 2 are embellished with formatted graphical bullets in the shape of electric bulbs and a lightning bolt. The power lines on Slide 3 are graphically altered and changed to the shape of a curved arrow. A speaker in a short video clip inserted on that slide shows a compact fluorescent light and describes the cost savings realized by using this bulb. The two-column list on Slide 4 provides a few of the common appliances and office products used daily that can have an Energy Star rating.

Overview

As you read through this chapter, you will learn how to create the presentation shown in Figure 5–1 by performing these general tasks:

- Format pictures by recoloring.
- Add shapes to pictures.
- Add multimedia to a presentation.
- Prepare and print speaker notes.
- Add and adjust slide timings.

(a)

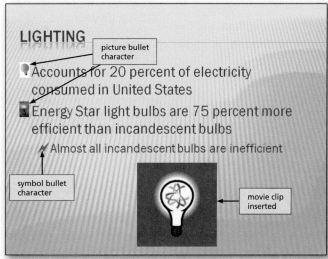
(b)

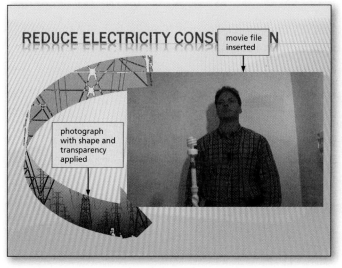
(c)

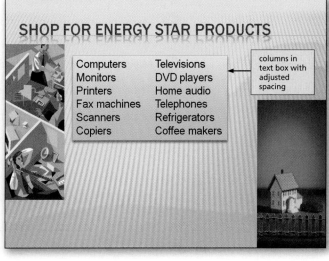
(d)

Figure 5–1

Plan
Ahead

General Project Guidelines

When creating a PowerPoint presentation, the actions you perform and decisions you make will affect the appearance and characteristics of the finished document. As you create a presentation with information graphics, such as the project shown in Figure 5–1, you should follow these general guidelines:

1. **Use multimedia selectively.** Video, music, and sound files can add interest to your presentation. Use these files only when necessary, however, because they draw the audience's attention away from the presenter and toward the slides. Using many multimedia files can be overwhelming.

2. **Coordinate your verbal message with the PowerPoint slides.** Effective speakers take much time to prepare their verbal message that will accompany each slide. They practice their speeches and decide how to integrate the material displayed.

(continued)

Plan
Ahead

> *(continued)*
>
> 3. **Evaluate your presentation.** As soon as you finish your presentation, critique your performance. You will improve your communication skills by eliminating the flaws and accentuating the positives.
>
>   When necessary, more specific details concerning the above guidelines are presented at appropriate points in the chapter. The chapter also will identify the actions you perform and decisions you make regarding these guidelines during the creation of the presentation shown in Figure 5–1.

To Start PowerPoint and Apply a Document Theme

If you are using a computer to step through the project in this chapter and you want your screens to match the figures in this book, you should change your computer's resolution to 1024 × 768. For information about how to change a computer's resolution, read Appendix E.

The following steps start PowerPoint, open a presentation, and apply a document theme and color scheme.

1 Start PowerPoint and then open the presentation, Energy Efficiency, from the Data Files for Students.

2 Maximize the PowerPoint window, if necessary.

3 Apply the Trek document theme.

4 Apply the Metro color scheme.

Formatting Pictures and Text

The slides in your presentation give tips on saving energy. The title slide introduces the topic with a recolored picture in the shape of the sun. The power lines on Slide 3 are transparent and reveal the background. Bullet characters are formed by substituting pictures and symbols for the default bullets. Another visual slide enhancement is to create columns from a list in a text box.

BTW

Creating a Photo Album
The photo album tool allows you to set up a series of photos and captions that can be shown as a stand-alone presentation or inserted into a PowerPoint presentation. To start a photo album, click the Photo Album button on the Insert tab, click the File/Disk button, select a picture, and then click the Insert button. You can use photo editing tools to change the brightness or contrast or to rotate these photos. Click the New Text Box button to include a text slide.

To Recolor a Photograph

To match your document's color scheme or to add interest, you can **recolor** pictures, graphics, and clip art. The Recolor gallery can turn a color picture to pure black and white or grayscale, give it an old-fashioned look by applying a sepia tone, or apply light and dark color variations in such colors as purple, green, pink, and gold. The following steps recolor the Slide 1 electric meter photograph.

1

- Select the Slide 1 electric meter photograph.

- Click Format on the Ribbon under Picture Tools to display the Format tab.

- Click the Recolor button in the Adjust group to display the Recolor gallery (Figure 5–2)

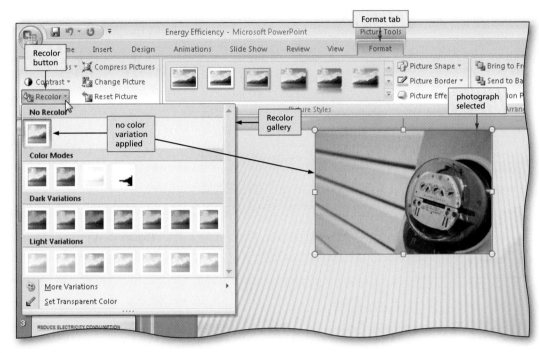

Figure 5–2

2

- Point to Accent color 3 Dark in the Dark Variations area to display a live pre-view of this color (Figure 5–3).

Experiment

- Point to various colors in the Recolor gallery and watch the colors change on the meter photograph.

 Q&A

Are more color variations available?

Yes. If you click More Variations in the Recolor gallery, the Theme Colors palette is displayed. You can select any color shown or click More Colors to choose a Standard or Custom color.

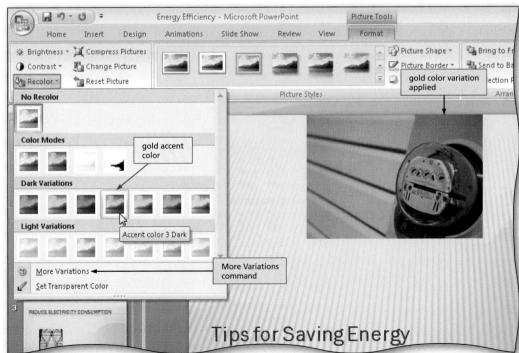

Figure 5–3

3

- Click Accent color 3 Dark to change the color of the electric meter photograph (Figure 5–4).

Q&A

How can I delete this color variation from my picture?

With the picture selected, you would click the Reset Picture button in the Adjust group on the Format tab.

Other Ways

1. Right-click photograph, click Format Picture on shortcut menu, click Picture in left pane, click Recolor button, select color, click Close button

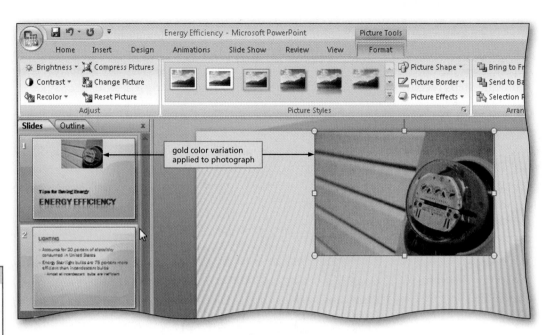

Figure 5–4

To Set a Transparent Color in a Photograph

You can make one color in the picture transparent so that the slide's background is visible through the recolored object. The following steps set a transparent color for the Slide 3 photograph.

1

- Display Slide 3 and then select the power lines photograph.

- Click the Recolor button in the Adjust group on the Format tab to display the Recolor gallery (Figure 5–5).

Figure 5–5

2

- Click Set Transparent Color in the Recolor gallery to display a pen mouse pointer in the document window.

- Position the pen mouse pointer in the black area at the bottom of the photograph where you want to make the color transparent (Figure 5–6).

Q&A Can I point to any black area of the picture?

Yes. Any color on the photograph can become transparent. It is easy to select a particular color when it fills a large area of a graphic.

Figure 5–6

 3

- Click the black area to delete the black lines from the photograph and allow the Trek background to show through the photograph (Figure 5–7).

Q&A Can I also apply a color variation to this photograph?

Yes. You can combine recoloring effects on one picture.

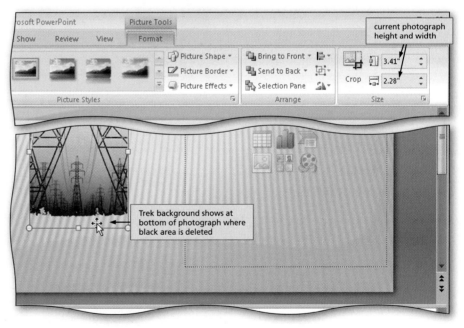

Figure 5–7

To Resize a Picture

Sometimes it is necessary to change the size of photographs and clip art. For example, on Slides 1 and 3, much space appears around the photographs. To make these objects fit onto the slides, you increase their sizes. To change the size of a clip by an exact percentage, enter a height or width in the Shape Height or Shape Width text boxes in the Size area on the Format tab. The steps on the following page describe how to increase the size of the power lines and electric meter photographs.

1

- With the power lines photograph selected and the Format tab displayed, click and hold down the mouse button on the Shape Height box up arrow in the Size group until 6" is displayed (Figure 5–8).

Q&A

Why did the Shape Width value change when I was increasing the height value?

The photograph's **aspect ratio**, or the relationship between the object's height and width, is locked. When you change the value of one measurement, the other measurement changes proportionally so that the image retains its original shape.

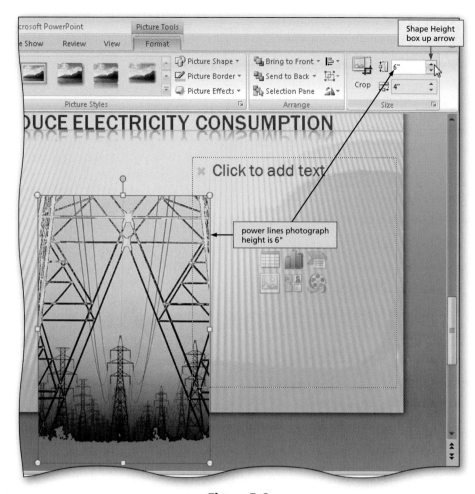

Figure 5–8

2

- Drag the photograph to the location shown in Figure 5–9 (Figure 5–9).

Inserting Visuals into Notes

If you want to see a picture on your printed notes, you can add an image to the Notes pane on an individual slide. You also can insert an image in the Notes Master so that this image will be displayed on all notes pages in a presentation. While you are displaying the Notes Master, you also can change the font style used for all notes and change the look and position of the slide area, notes area, header, footer, page number, and date.

Figure 5–9

- Display Slide 1 and then select the electric meter photograph.

- With the Format tab displayed, click and hold down the mouse button on the Shape Height box up arrow in the Size group until 4" is displayed (Figure 5–10).

Other Ways

1. Right-click photograph, click Size and Position on shortcut menu, click Size tab, click and hold down mouse button on Height box up or down arrow in Scale area until desired size is reached, click OK button

2. Click clip, drag a sizing handle until clip is desired shape and size

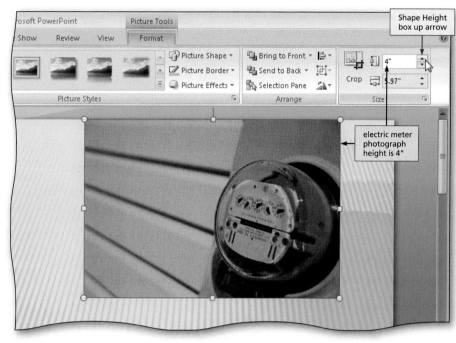

Figure 5–10

To Apply a Shape to a Picture

Adding visual interest to a graphic is possible by applying a shape. Any of the shapes in the Picture Shapes gallery can be inserted in a picture, and the picture then will match this form. Arrows, shapes, stars, and banners often are used to create an appealing slide element. The following steps apply a sun shape to the Slide 1 electric meter photograph and a block arrow shape to the Slide 3 photograph.

- With the electric meter photograph selected on Slide 1 and the Format tab displayed, click the Picture Shape button in the Picture Styles group to display the Picture Shape gallery (Figure 5–11).

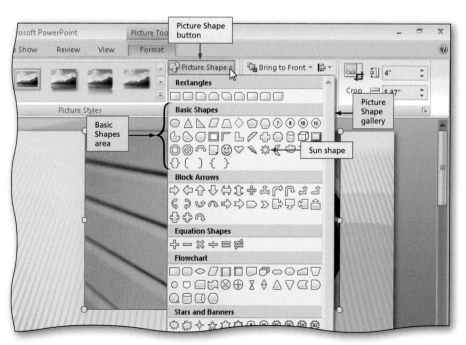

Figure 5–11

2

- Click the Sun shape in the Basic Shapes area (row 3, column 8) to apply this shape to the electric meter photograph (Figure 5–12).

Q&A

Is the live preview feature available for the Picture Shape gallery?

No. To try various shapes, you must click the Reset Picture button in the Adjust area to return the picture to its original format and then repeat Steps 1 and 2 with a different shape.

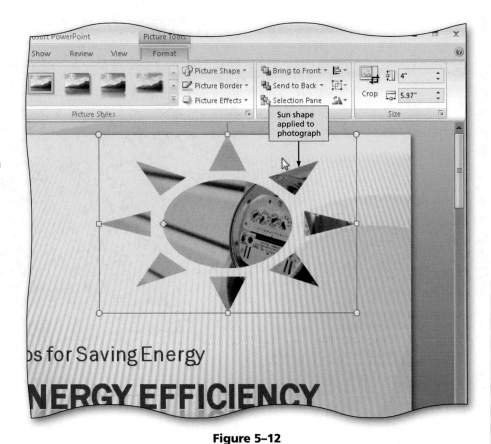

Figure 5–12

3

- Display Slide 3 and then select the power lines photograph.

- Click the Picture Shape button in the Picture Styles group to display the Picture Shape gallery (Figure 5–13).

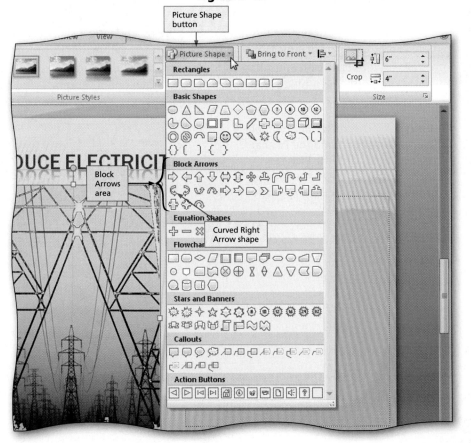

Figure 5–13

4

- Click the Curved Right Arrow shape in the Block Arrows area (row 2, column 1) to apply this shape to the power lines photograph (Figure 5–14).

Q&A Can I move this photograph to a different location on the slide?

Yes. Click the photograph to select it and then drag it to the desired location on the slide.

Q&A How would I resize this photograph?

Select it and then drag a sizing handle to increase or decrease the size.

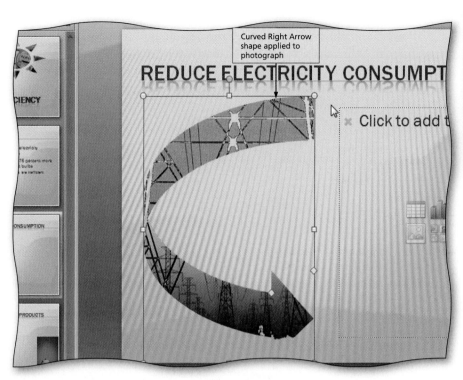

Figure 5–14

Use handouts to organize your speech.

As you develop a lengthy presentation with many visuals, handouts may help you organize your material. Print handouts with the maximum number of slides per page. Use scissors to cut each thumbnail and then place these miniature slide images adjacent to each other on a flat surface. Any type on the thumbnails will be too small to read, so the images will need to work with only the support of the verbal message you provide. You can rearrange these thumbnails as you organize your speech. When you return to your computer, you can rearrange the slides on your screen to match the order of your thumbnail printouts. Begin speaking the actual words you want to incorporate in the body of the talk. This process of glancing at the thumbnails and hearing yourself say the key ideas of the speech is one of the best methods of organizing and preparing for the actual presentation. Ultimately, when you deliver your speech in front of an audience, the images on the slides or on your note cards should be sufficient to remind you of the accompanying verbal message.

Plan Ahead

To Save the Presentation

You formatted photographs by recoloring, resizing, and applying a shape. The next step is to save the presentation.

1 With a USB flash drive connected to one of the computer's USB ports, display the Save As dialog box and type `Energy Savings` in the File name text box to change the file name.

2 Click Computer in the Favorite Links section, and then double-click your USB flash drive in the list of available drives.

3 Save the document with the file name, Energy Savings.

To Change a Bullet Character to a Picture

PowerPoint allows you to change the default appearance of bullets in a slide show. The document themes determine the bullet character. A **bullet character** can be a predefined style, a variety of fonts and characters displayed in the Symbol gallery, or a picture from a file or the Clip Organizer. You may want to change a character to add visual interest and variety. The following steps change the first paragraph bullet character to a light bulb picture with a white background.

- Click Home on the Ribbon, display Slide 2, and then click the first paragraph (Figure 5–15).

Q&A If I want to insert the same bullet character in several paragraphs, can I change all the bullets simultaneously?

Yes. Select all the paragraphs and then perform the steps below.

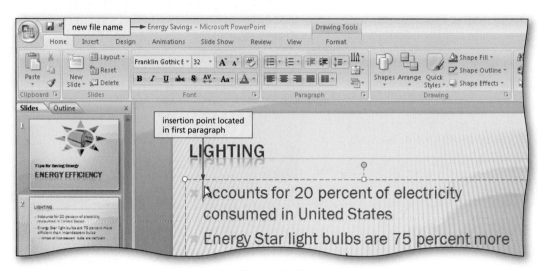

Figure 5–15

- Click the Bullets arrow in the Paragraph group to display the Bullets gallery (Figure 5–16).

Q&A Why is an orange box displayed around the three green x characters?

They are the default first-level bullet characters for the Trek document theme.

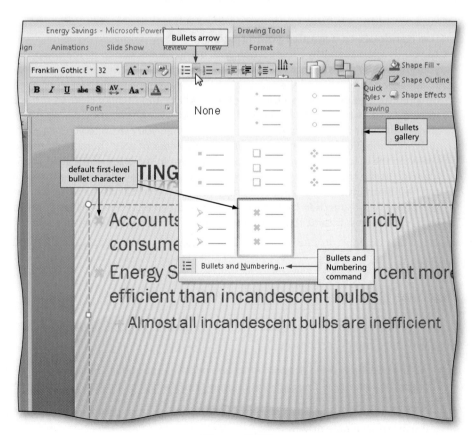

Figure 5–16

- Click Bullets and Numbering to display the Bullets and Numbering dialog box (Figure 5–17).

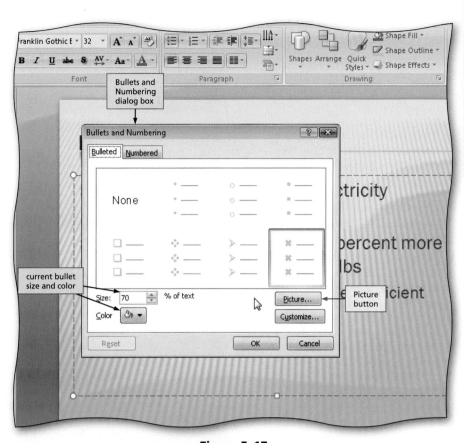

Figure 5–17

4

- Click the Picture button in the Bullets and Numbering dialog box to display the Picture Bullet dialog box (Figure 5–18).

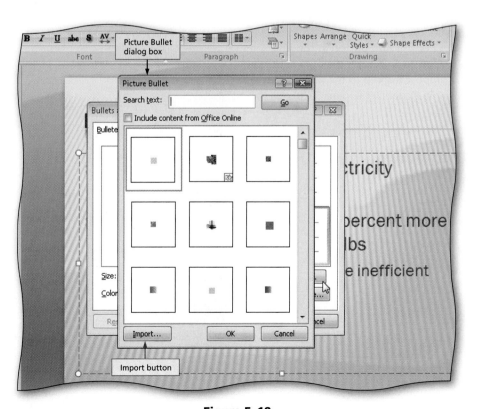

Figure 5–18

5

- With your USB flash drive connected to one of the computer's USB ports, click the Import button in the Picture Bullet dialog box to display the Add Clips to Organizer dialog box.

- If the Folders list is displayed below the Folders button, click the Folders button to collapse the Folders list.

- Click the Previous Locations arrow on the Address bar and then click Computer in the Favorite Links section. Double-click UDISK 2.0 (E:) to select the USB flash drive, Drive E in this case, as the device that contains the picture.

- If necessary, scroll down and then click White Light Bulb to select the file (Figure 5–19).

Figure 5–19

6

- Click the Add button in the Add Clips to Organizer dialog box to import the clip to the Microsoft Clip Organizer (Figure 5–20).

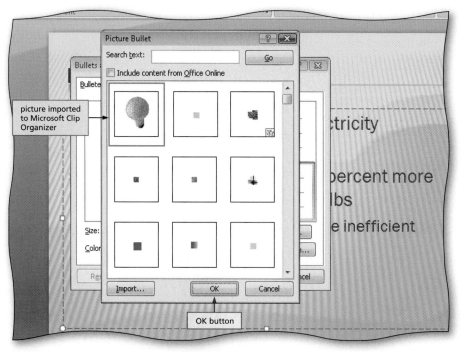

Figure 5–20

7

• Click the OK button in the Picture Bullet dialog box to insert the White Light Bulb picture as the first paragraph bullet character (Figure 5–21).

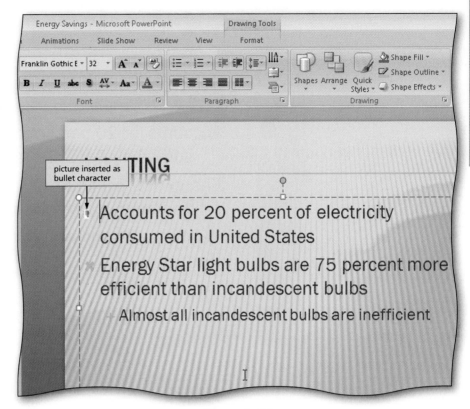

Figure 5–21

Other Ways

1. Right-click paragraph, point to Bullets on shortcut menu, click Bullets and Numbering
2. Select paragraph, click Bullets arrow on Mini toolbar, click Bullets and Numbering

To Change a Second Bullet Character to a Picture

If desired, you can change every bullet in a presentation to a unique character. The Energy Savings presentation has only one slide with bullets, so each bullet on Slide 2 can have a unique look. If your presentation has many bulleted slides, however, you would want to have a consistent look throughout the presentation. This issue will be addressed in Chapter 6 with a discussion of slide masters.

The following steps change the second first-level paragraph bullet character on Slide 2 to a light bulb picture with an orange background.

BTW

Quick Reference
For a table that lists how to complete the tasks covered in this book using the mouse, Ribbon, shortcut menu, and keyboard, see the Quick Reference Summary at the back of this book, or visit the PowerPoint 2007 Quick Reference Web page (scsite.com/ppt2007/qr).

1 Click the second first-level paragraph, which begins with the words Energy Star, click the Bullets arrow in the Paragraph group to display the Bullets gallery, and then click Bullets and Numbering to display the Bullets and Numbering dialog box.

2 Click the Picture button in the Bullets and Numbering dialog box and then click the Import button in the Picture Bullet dialog box.

3 Click Orange Light Bulb to select the file name and then click the Add button in the Add Clips to Organizer dialog box to import the clip to the Microsoft Clip Organizer.

4 Click the OK button in the Picture Bullet dialog box to insert the Orange Light Bulb picture as the second first-level paragraph bullet character (Figure 5–22).

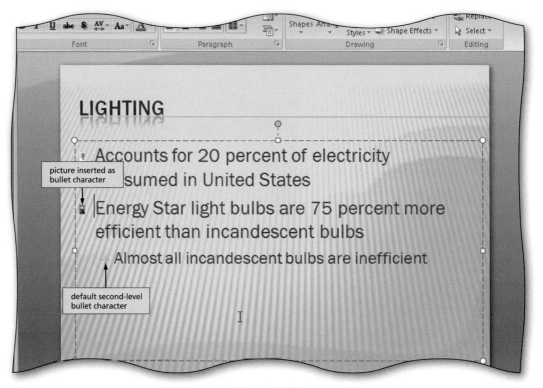

Figure 5–22

To Change a Bullet Character to a Symbol

Picture bullets add a unique quality to your presentations. Another bullet change you can make is to insert a symbol as the character. Symbols are found in several fonts, including Webdings, Wingdings, Wingdings 2, and Wingdings 3. The following steps change the second-level paragraph bullet character on Slide 2 to a lightning bolt symbol in the Webdings font.

- Click the second-level Slide 2 paragraph, which begins with the words Almost all, click the Bullets arrow, and then click Bullets and Numbering (Figure 5–23).

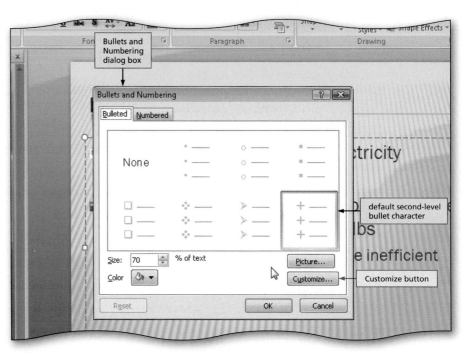

Figure 5–23

2

- Click the Customize button to display the Symbol dialog box.

- Click the Font box arrow in the Symbol dialog box to display the font list (Figure 5–24).

Q&A Why is a plus sign symbol selected?

That character is the default bullet character for the second-level paragraphs in the Trek document theme.

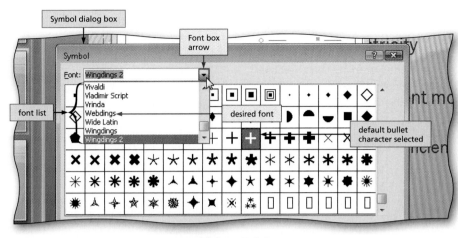

Figure 5–24

3

- Click Webdings in the list and then scroll up to locate the lightning bolt symbol.

- Click the lightning bolt symbol to select it (Figure 5–25).

Q&A Why does my dialog box have more rows of symbols and different fonts from which to choose?

The rows and fonts displayed depend upon how PowerPoint was installed on your system.

Figure 5–25

4

- Click the OK button in the Symbol dialog box to display the Bullets and Numbering dialog box (Figure 5–26).

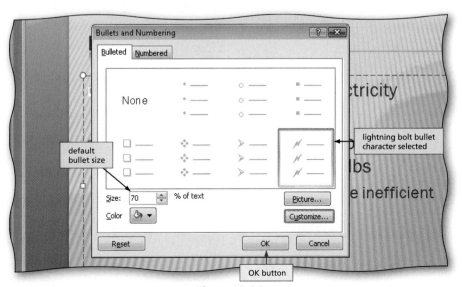

Figure 5–26

- Click the OK button in the Bullets and Numbering dialog box to insert the lightning bolt character as the second-level paragraph bullet (Figure 5–27).

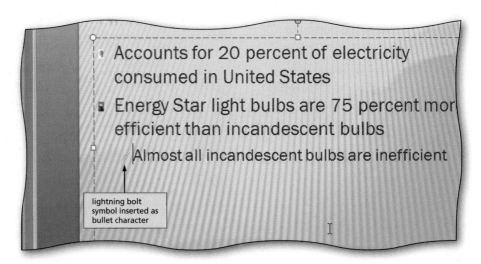

Figure 5–27

To Format a Bullet Size

Bullets have a default size determined by the design theme. **Bullet size** is measured as a percentage of the text size and can range from 25 to 400 percent. The following steps change the White Light Bulb character size.

- Click the first paragraph on Slide 2, click the Bullets arrow, and then click Bullets and Numbering in the Bullets gallery to display the Bullets and Numbering dialog box (Figure 5–28).

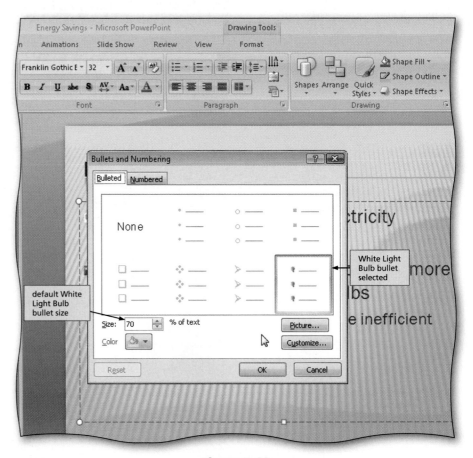

Figure 5–28

• Click and hold down the mouse button on the Size box up arrow until 150 is displayed (Figure 5–29).

Q&A

Can I type a number in the text box instead of clicking the up arrow?

Yes. Double-click the text box and then type the desired percentage.

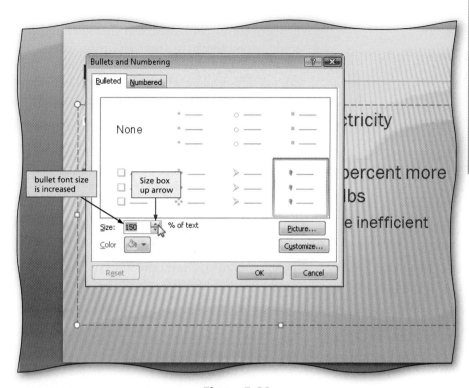

Figure 5–29

❸

• Click the OK button to increase the White Light Bulb bullet size to 150 percent of its original size (Figure 5–30).

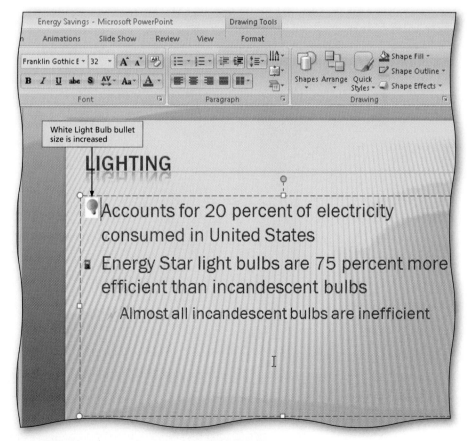

Figure 5–30

To Change the Size of Other Bullet Characters

For consistency, the bullet character in the second first-level paragraph on Slide 2 should have a similar size as that of the first paragraph. In addition, the second-level paragraph's bullet should be somewhat smaller because the paragraph font size is smaller than the first-level paragraph font size. The following steps change the sizes of the Orange Light Bulb and the lightning bolt bullets.

1 Click the second first-level paragraph, which begins with the words Energy Star, click the Bullets arrow, and then click Bullets and Numbering in the Bullets gallery to display the Bullets and Numbering dialog box.

2 Click and hold down the mouse button on the Size box up arrow until 150 is displayed and then click the OK button.

3 Click the second-level paragraph, click the Bullets arrow, and then click Bullets and Numbering in the Bullets gallery.

4 Click and hold down the mouse button on the Size box up arrow until 115 is displayed. Do not click the OK button (Figure 5–31).

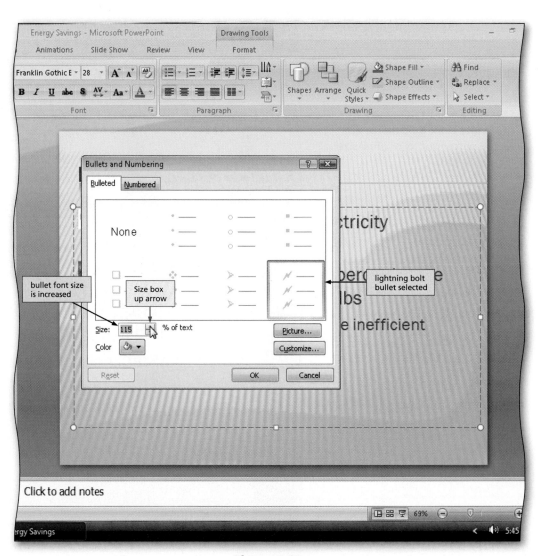

Figure 5–31

To Format a Bullet Color

A default **bullet color** is based on the eight colors in the design theme. Additional standard and custom colors also are available. The following steps change the lightning bolt bullet color from green to red.

1

- With the Bullets and Numbering dialog box displayed, click the Color arrow to display the color palette (Figure 5–32).

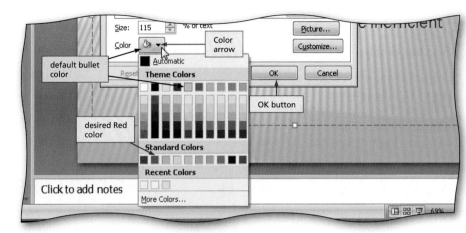

Figure 5–32

2

- Click the color Red in the Standard Colors area to change the bullet color to Red (Figure 5–33).

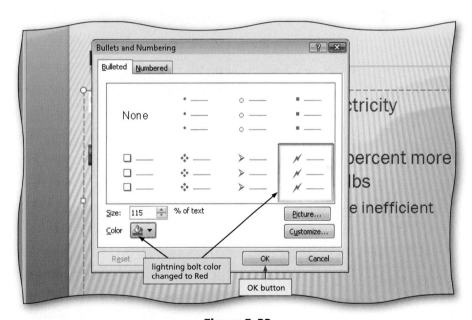

Figure 5–33

3

- Click the OK button to apply the color Red to the lightning bolt bullet (Figure 5–34).

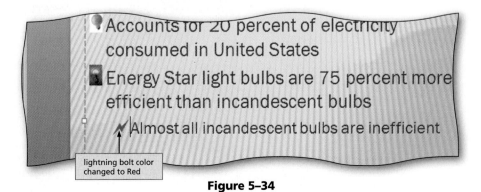

Figure 5–34

To Create Columns in a Text Box

The list of Energy Star products in the Slide 4 text box lacks visual appeal. You can change these items into two, three, or more columns and then adjust the column widths. The following steps change the text box elements into columns and then widen the columns.

- Display Slide 4 and then click the text box to select it.

- With the Home tab displayed, click the Columns button in the Paragraph group to display the Columns menu (Figure 5–35).

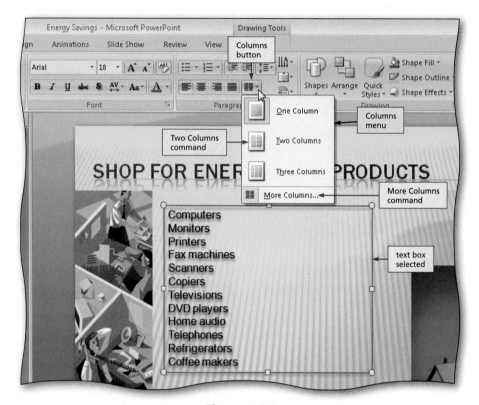

Figure 5–35

- Click Two Columns to create two columns of text.

- Drag the bottom sizing handle up to the location shown in Figure 5–36.

Figure 5–36

To Adjust Column Spacing

The space between the columns in each text box can be increased. The following steps increase the spacing between the columns.

- With the text box selected, click the Columns button, and then click More Columns.

- Click and hold down the mouse button on the Spacing box up arrow in the Columns dialog box until 0.3" is displayed (Figure 5–37).

Q&A Can I type a number in the text box instead of clicking the up arrow?

Yes. Double-click the text box and then type the desired measurement expressed in inches.

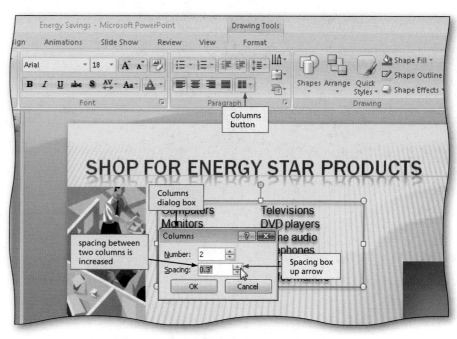

Figure 5–37

- Click the OK button to increase the spacing between the columns (Figure 5–38).

Q&A Can I change the text box back to one column easily?

Yes. Click the Columns button and then click One Column.

Figure 5–38

To Format the Text Box

To add interest to the text box on Slide 4, apply a Quick Style. The following steps apply a green Subtle Effect style to the text box.

1 With the text box selected and the Home tab displayed, click the Quick Styles button in the Drawing group to display the Quick Styles gallery.

2 Click Subtle Effect – Accent 6 (row 4, column 7).

3 Click the Increase Font Size button in the Font group two times to increase the font size to 24 (Figure 5–39).

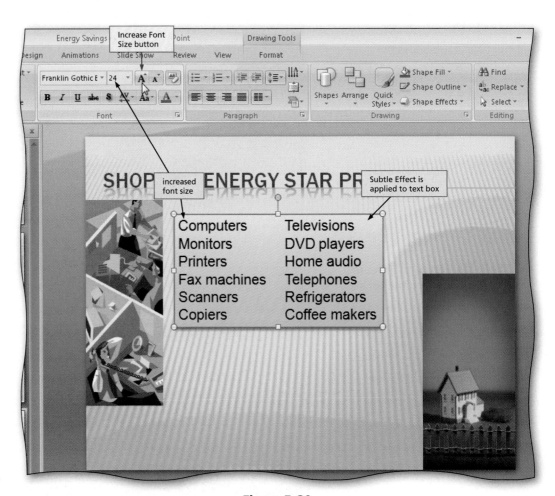

Figure 5–39

Plan Ahead

Use multimedia selectively.
PowerPoint makes it easy to add multimedia to a presentation. Well-produced video clips add value when they help explain a procedure or show movement that cannot be captured in a photograph. Music can help calm or energize an audience, when appropriate. A sound, such as applause when a correct answer is given, can emphasize an action. Before you insert these files on a slide, however, consider whether they really add any value to your overall slide show. If you are adding them just because you can, then you might want to reconsider your decision. Audiences quickly tire of extraneous sounds and movement on slides and will find these media clips annoying. Keep in mind that the audience's attention should focus primarily on the presenter, and extraneous or inappropriate media files may divert their attention, and in turn, decrease the quality of the presentation.

Adding Multimedia to Slides

Multimedia files can enrich a presentation if they are used correctly. Movies files can have two formats: digital video produced with a camera and editing software, and animated GIF (graphics interchange format) file composed of multiple images combined in a single file. Sound files can be from the Microsoft Clip Organizer, files stored on your computer, or an audio track on a CD. To hear the sounds, you need speakers and a sound card on your system.

To Add a Movie File

Slide 3 has an interesting graphic of power lines, which introduce the concept of electricity transmission. A movie clip with a suggestion of how to reduce electricity usage would complement this graphic. A brief video discussing fluorescent light bulbs is available on your Data Files for Students. The following steps add this movie clip to Slide 3.

1

- Display Slide 3. With your USB flash drive connected to one of the computer's USB ports, click the Insert Media Clip button in the content placeholder to display the Insert Movie dialog box.

- If the Folders list is displayed below the Folders button, click the Folders button to collapse the Folders list.

- Click the Previous Locations arrow on the Address bar and then click Computer in the Favorite Links section. Double-click UDISK 2.0 (E:) to select the USB flash drive, Drive E in this case, as the device that contains the picture.

- Click Light to select the file (Figure 5–40).

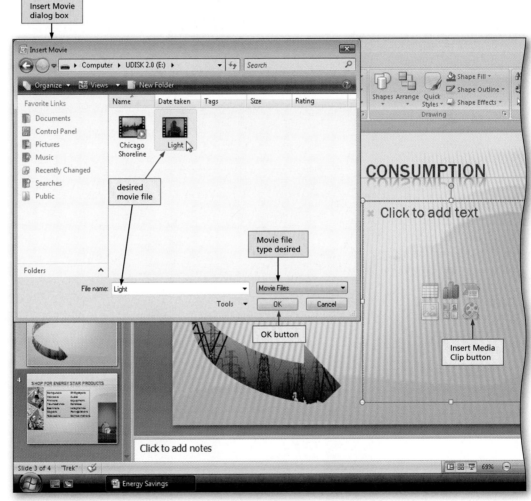

Figure 5–40

What if the movie clip is not on a USB flash drive?

Use the same process, but select the device containing the file in the Favorite Links section.

● Click the OK button
in the dialog box
to insert the movie
clip into Slide 3
(Figure 5–41).

● When the Microsoft
Office PowerPoint
dialog box is dis-
played, click the
Automatically but-
ton to specify the
clip will begin play-
ing when Slide 3 is
displayed during a
slide show.

Q&A

What does the When
Clicked option do?

The movie clip would
begin playing when
a presenter clicks
the slide during the
slide show.

● With the Options
tab displayed, click
and hold down the
mouse button on the
Shape Height box
down arrow in the
Size group until
4" is displayed
(Figure 5–42).

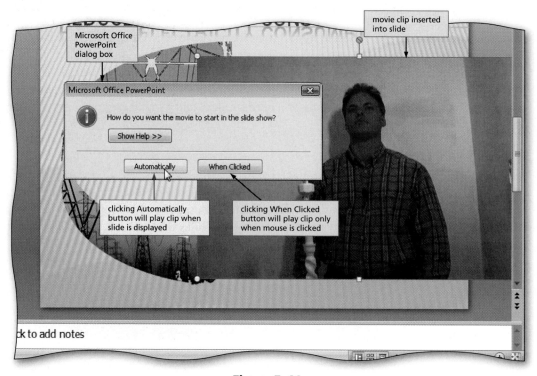

Figure 5–41

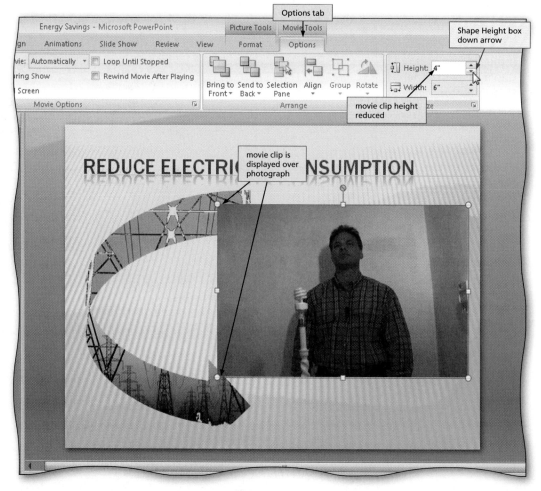

Figure 5–42

5

- Click the Send to Back button in the Arrange group to move the movie clip under the power lines photograph.

- Drag the clip to the location shown in Figure 5–43 (Figure 5–43).

Q&A Can I preview the movie clip?

Yes. Select the clip and then click Options on the Ribbon. The Options tab contains many tools that help control the video presentation. The Preview button will play the video. Other useful buttons allow you to set the movie size precisely, adjust the volume, and replay the clip continually.

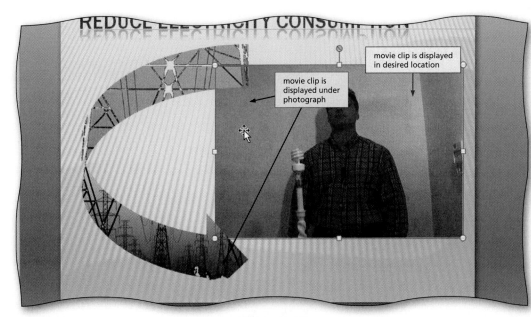

Figure 5–43

Other Ways

1. Click the Movie from File button on Insert tab

To Add a Sound Clip

When the Energy Savings presentation starts, you want a short musical sound clip to play that will add interest and help set an upbeat tempo to the slide show. This clip, Hard Rock Beat, will play for 15 seconds when Slide 1 is displayed. This clip is available on the Microsoft Office Online Clip Art Web site and is on your Data Files for Students. It is a **Windows waveform (wav)** file, which uses a standard format to encode and communicate music and sound between computers, music synthesizers, and instruments. The following steps add the music clip to Slide 1.

1

- Display Slide 1 and then click Insert on the Ribbon to display the Insert tab.

- Click the Sound from File button, which is labeled Sound, in the Media Clips group to display the Insert Sound dialog box (Figure 5–44).

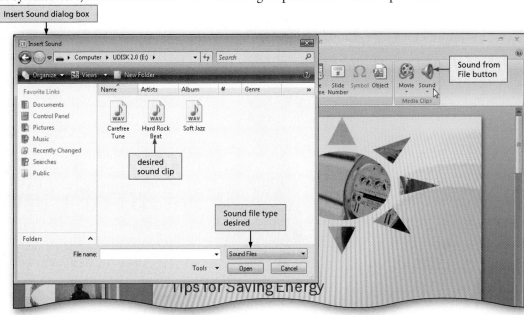

Figure 5–44

2

- With your USB flash drive as the active drive, click Hard Rock Beat to select the file (Figure 5–45).

Q&A

What if the sound clip is not on the USB flash drive?

Use the same process, but select the device containing the file in the Favorite Links section.

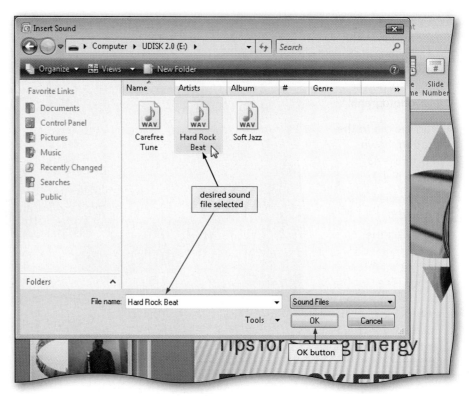

Figure 5–45

3

- Click the OK button in the Insert Sound dialog box to insert the sound clip into Slide 1 (Figure 5–46).

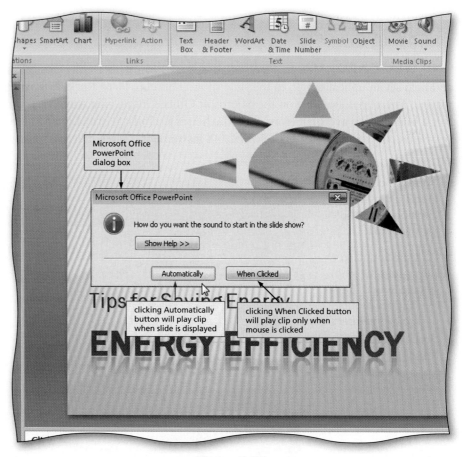

Figure 5–46

4

- When the Microsoft Office PowerPoint dialog box is displayed, click the Automatically button to specify the clip will begin playing when Slide 1 is displayed at the start of the slide show (Figure 5–47).

Q&A Does the When Clicked option function the same way for an audio clip as for a video clip?

Yes. If you were to click the When Clicked button in this dialog box, the music would begin playing only after the presenter clicks Slide 1 during a presentation.

Q&A Why is a speaker icon displayed in the middle of the slide?

The icon indicates a sound file is inserted.

Figure 5–47

5

- Drag the speaker icon off the slide to the lower-right corner of the screen (Figure 5–48).

Q&A Can I hide the speaker icon?

No. You can drag it off the slide because you specified the sound clip will play automatically when Slide 1 is displayed. If you had clicked the When Clicked option, you would need to leave the icon on the slide so that you can click it during a presentation.

Figure 5–48

To Add a Movie Clip

Animated GIF files are commonplace on Web sites. They also are found in PowerPoint presentations when you want to call attention to material on a particular slide. You can insert them into a PowerPoint presentation in the same manner that you insert movie and sound files. They play automatically when the slide is displayed. The following steps add the light bulb movie clip to Slide 2.

1

- Display Slide 2 and then, if necessary, click Insert on the Ribbon to display the Insert tab.

- Click the Insert Picture from File button, labeled Picture, in the Illustrations group to display the Insert Picture dialog box.

- With your USB flash drive as the active drive, click Light Bulb - animated to select the file (Figure 5–49).

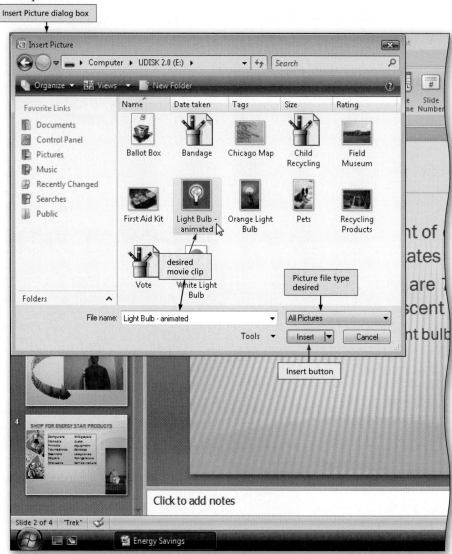

Figure 5–49

2

- Click the Insert button in the Insert Picture dialog box to insert the light bulb movie clip into Slide 2.

- With the Format tab displayed, click and hold down the mouse button on the Shape Height box up arrow in the Size group until 2.5" is displayed.

- Drag the clip to the location shown in Figure 5–50.

Q&A
Why is the animation not showing?
Animated GIF files move only in Slide Show view.

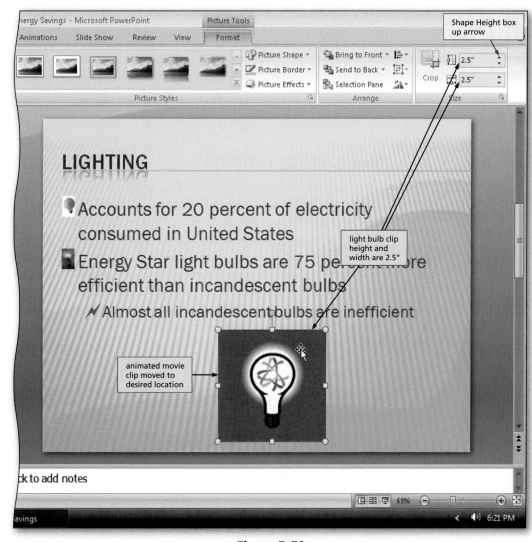

Figure 5–50

Coordinate your verbal message with the PowerPoint slides.

On average, designers spend one hour developing each slide in a presentation. They meticulously decide on effective words and visuals that convey the intended message. Many times, however, they spend so much time developing their presentations that they have insufficient time to rehearse their verbal message.

It is important, therefore, that you allocate time to practice coordinating your PowerPoint presentation with your speech. You should not need to read any material on the screen while presenting. Your notes should contain key phrases, not the exact sentences. Each time you rehearse, your wording should vary slightly because you are elaborating on each major idea.

Stand as you rehearse, preferably in front of a mirror. Speak your words out loud as you envision your audience listening intently to your message. Do not stop if you stumble over some words; just make a note to rework those rough spots later. If possible, record video or audio of your practice session.

Plan
Ahead

Preparing For and Rehearsing Delivery

Polished speakers spend much time preparing their presentations. They memorize their introductions and conclusions, practice in front of a mirror, and test their speech in front of objective colleagues and friends. When they are very familiar with the material, they then practice with the PowerPoint presentation to synchronize the slides with their verbal message. Some speakers set specific timings for each slide to display. Other presenters type notes in the Notes pane as they develop their presentations.

Rehearsing Timings

BTW

Certification
The Microsoft Certified Application Specialist (MCAS) program provides an opportunity for you to obtain a valuable industry credential — proof that you have the PowerPoint 2007 skills required by employers. For more information see Appendix G or visit the PowerPoint 2007 Certification Web page (scsite.com/ppt2007/cert).

In previous slide shows, you clicked to advance from one slide to the next. Because all slide components have been added to the slides in the presentation, you now can set the time each slide is displayed on the screen. You can set these times in two ways. One method is to specify each slide's display time manually. The second method is to use PowerPoint's **rehearsal feature**, which allows you to advance through the slides at your own pace, and the amount of time you view each slide is recorded. You will use the second technique in this chapter and then adjust the last slide's timing manually.

When you begin rehearsing a presentation, the Rehearsal toolbar is displayed. The **Rehearsal toolbar** contains buttons that allow you to start, pause, and repeat viewing the slides in the slide show and to view the times for each slide and the elapsed time. Table 5–1 describes the buttons on the Rehearsal toolbar.

Table 5–1 Rehearsal Toolbar Buttons		
Button	**Button Name**	**Description**
➡	Next	Displays the next slide or next animated element on the slide.
❚❚	Pause	Stops the timer. Click the Next or Pause button to resume timing.
0:00:00	Slide Time	Indicates the length of time a slide has been displayed. You can enter a slide time directly in the Slide Time box.
↺	Repeat	Clears the Slide Time box and resets the timer to 0:00.
0:00:00	Elapsed Time	Indicates slide show total time.

To Rehearse Timings

Table 5–2 indicates the desired timings for the five slides in the Energy Savings presentation. Slide 1 is displayed and the sound clip plays for 15 seconds. Slides 2 and 4 are displayed for 15 seconds. Slide 3 has the video clip, and its length is approximately 10 seconds.

Table 5–2 Slide Rehearsal Timings		
Slide Number	**Display Time**	**Elapsed Time**
1	0:00	0:15
2	0:15	0:30
3	0:10	0:40
4	0:15	0:55

The following steps add slide timings to the slide show.

- Click Slide Show on the Ribbon to display the Slide Show tab (Figure 5–51).

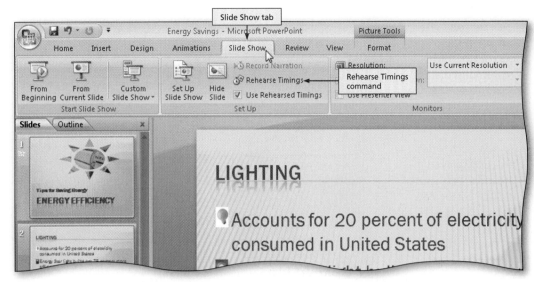

Figure 5–51

- Click the Rehearse Timings command in the Set Up group to start the slide show and the counter (Figure 5–52).

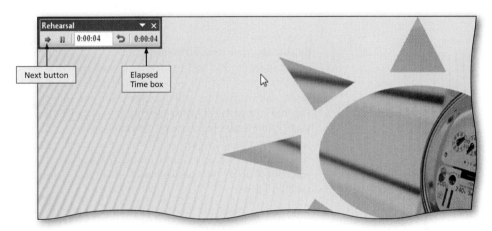

Figure 5–52

③

- When the Elapsed time displays 0:15, click the Next button to display Slide 2.

- When the Elapsed time displays 0:30, click the Next button to display Slide 3.

- When the Elapsed time displays 0:40, click the Next button to display Slide 4.

- When the Elapsed time displays 0:55, click the Next button to display the black slide (Figure 5–53).

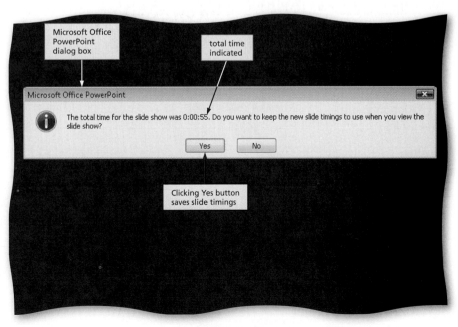

Figure 5–53

- Click the Yes button in the Microsoft Office PowerPoint dialog box to keep the new slide timings with an elapsed time of 0:55.

- Review each slide's timing displayed in the lower-left corner in Slide Sorter view (Figure 5–54).

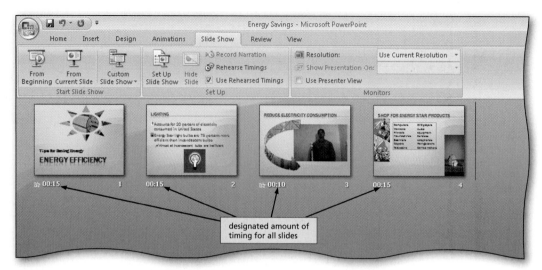

Figure 5–54

Plan Ahead

Evaluate your presentation.
Public speaking is a skill that can improve with practice and evaluation. Immediately after making a presentation, evaluate what aspects worked well and what parts needed improvement. Ask yourself several questions: Did the speech meet the time restrictions? Did I use appropriate gestures? Did I look at my audience? If so, did they seem interested in my message? Did my audience notice my nervousness? Did I follow the intended organizational pattern, or did I forget or ad-lib material? If I were to give the presentation a second time, what qualities would I want to repeat? What aspects would I improve by practicing? If you reflect upon your performance objectively, you will gain confidence and improve your speaking style.

To Adjust Timings Manually

If the slide timings need adjustment, you manually can change the length of time each slide is displayed. In this presentation, you decide to display Slide 4 for 20 seconds instead of 15. The following steps increase the Slide 4 timing.

- Click Animations on the Ribbon to display the Animations tab.

- With Slide 4 selected, click and hold down the Automatically After up arrow in the Transition to This Slide group until 00:20 is displayed (Figure 5–55).

Figure 5–55

To Add Notes

Slides and handouts usually are printed to distribute to audience members. These printouts also are helpful to speakers so they can write notes that will guide them through a presentation. As you create slides, you may find material you want to state verbally and do not want to include on the slide. You can type and format notes in the **Notes pane** as you work in Normal view and then print this information as **notes pages**. Notes pages print with a small image of the slide at the top and the comments below the slide. Charts, tables, and pictures added to the Notes pane also print on these pages. You can make changes to the **Notes Master** if you want to alter the default settings, such as the font or the position of page elements, such as the slide area and notes area.

In this project, comments are added to Slides 2 and 4. After adding comments, you can print a set of speaker notes. The following steps add text to the Notes pane on these slides and then print the notes.

1

- Click the Normal button to display Slide 4 in Normal view.

- Click the Notes pane and then type Energy Star equipment and appliances provide dramatic reductions on electric usage. In general, Energy Star products use less than one-half the electricity that standard products use. (Figure 5–56).

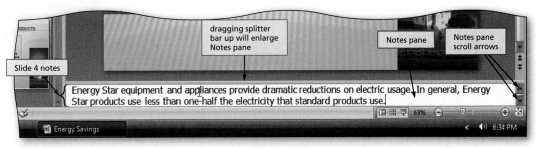

Figure 5–56

Q&A

What if I cannot see all the lines I typed?

You can drag the splitter bar up to enlarge the Notes pane. Clicking the Notes pane scroll arrows allows you to view the entire text.

2

- Display Slide 2, click the Notes pane, and then type CFLs now have brightness and color rendition comparable to incandescent lights. Because of the electrical savings, they pay for themselves during their lifetime of use. (Figure 5–57).

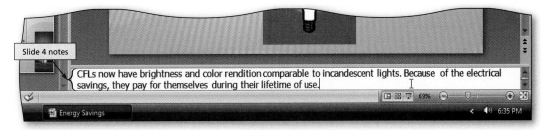

Figure 5–57

To Print Speaker Notes

These notes give additional information that supplements the text on the slides. The following steps print the speaker notes.

1 Click the Office Button, point to Print, and then click Print Preview on the 'Preview and print the document' submenu.

2 Click the Print What arrow in the Page Setup group and then click Notes Pages in the Print What list.

3 Click the Print button in the Print group.

4 Click the OK button in the Print dialog box to print the handouts (Figure 5–58).

5 Click the Close Print Preview button in the Preview group on the Print Preview tab to return to Normal view.

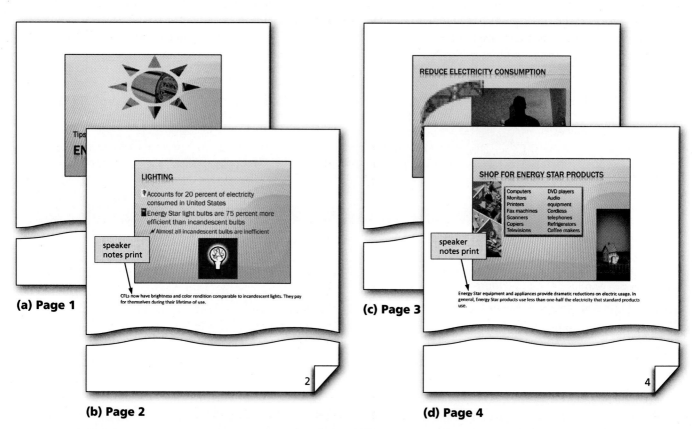

(a) Page 1

(b) Page 2

(c) Page 3

(d) Page 4

Figure 5–58

To Change Document Properties and Save the Presentation

Before saving the presentation again, you want to add your name, class name, and some keywords as document properties. The following steps use the Document Information Panel to change document properties and then save the project.

1 Click the Office Button, point to Prepare, and then click Properties on the 'Prepare the document for distribution' submenu.

2 Type your name as the Author property and your course and section as the Subject properties.

3 Type energy, lighting, energy star as the Keywords property.

4 Close the Document Information Panel.

5 Click the Save button to overwrite the previous Energy Savings file on the USB flash drive.

To Quit PowerPoint

This project is complete. The following steps quit PowerPoint.

1 Click the Close button on the right side of the title bar to quit PowerPoint; or if you have multiple PowerPoint documents open, click the Office Button and then click the Exit PowerPoint button on the Office Button menu to close all open documents and quit PowerPoint.

2 If necessary, click the No button in the Microsoft Office PowerPoint dialog box so that any changes you have made are not saved.

Chapter Summary

In this chapter you have learned how to recolor and resize a picture, apply a shape to a picture, change a bullet character to a picture or a symbol and then change its size and color, create columns and then adjust the width, add multimedia, set slide timings, and then add and print notes. The items listed below include all the new PowerPoint skills you have learned in this chapter.

1. Recolor a Photograph (PPT 333)
2. Set a Transparent Color in a Photograph (PPT 334)
3. Resize a Picture (PPT 335)
4. Apply a Shape to a Picture (PPT 337)
5. Change a Bullet Character to a Picture (PPT 340)
6. Change a Bullet Character to a Symbol (PPT 344)
7. Format a Bullet Size (PPT 346)
8. Format a Bullet Color (PPT 349)
9. Create Columns in a Text Box (PPT 350)
10. Adjust Column Spacing (PPT 351)
11. Add a Movie File (PPT 353)
12. Add a Sound Clip (PPT 355)
13. Add a Movie Clip (PPT 358)
14. Rehearse Timings (PPT 360)
15. Adjust Timings Manually (PPT 362)
16. Add Notes (PPT 363)
17. Print Speaker Notes (PPT 363)

 If you have a SAM user profile, you may have access to hands-on instruction, practice, and assessment. Log in to your SAM account (http://sam2007.course.com) to launch any assigned training activities or exams that relate to the skills covered in this chapter.

Learn It Online

Test your knowledge of chapter content and key terms.

Instructions: To complete the Learn It Online exercises, start your browser, click the Address bar, and then enter the Web address `scsite.com/ppt2007/learn`. When the Office 2007 Learn It Online page is displayed, click the link for the exercise you want to complete and then read the instructions.

Chapter Reinforcement TF, MC, and SA
A series of true/false, multiple choice, and short answer questions that test your knowledge of the chapter content.

Flash Cards
An interactive learning environment where you identify chapter key terms associated with displayed definitions.

Practice Test
A series of multiple choice questions that test your knowledge of chapter content and key terms.

Who Wants To Be a Computer Genius?
An interactive game that challenges your knowledge of chapter content in the style of a television quiz show.

Wheel of Terms
An interactive game that challenges your knowledge of chapter key terms in the style of the television show *Wheel of Fortune*.

Crossword Puzzle Challenge
A crossword puzzle that challenges your knowledge of key terms presented in the chapter.

Apply Your Knowledge

Reinforce the skills and apply the concepts you learned in this chapter.

Resizing and Recoloring a Picture, Applying a Shape to a Picture, Creating Columns, Adding Notes, and Setting Timings
Instructions: Start PowerPoint. Open the presentation, Apply 5-1 Getting a Job, from the Data Files for Students. See the inside back cover of this book for instructions on downloading the Data Files for Students, or contact your instructor for more information about accessing required files.

The four slides in the presentation present information about preparing a resume and cover letter for a job search. The document you open is an unformatted presentation. You are to select a document theme and change the theme colors, recolor the pictures and apply shapes, create columns, and add notes so the slides look like Figure 5–59.

Perform the following tasks:
1. Add the Urban document theme and change the presentation theme colors to Concourse. On Slide 1, change the clip size to 280% and then apply the 7-Point Star shape (row 1, column 6 in the Stars and Banners area). The clip is animated, so it may appear different on your screen than it does in Figure 5–59a. Move the clip so that it is positioned as shown in Figure 5–59a.
2. On Slide 2, change the clip size to 28% and then apply the Multidocument shape (row 1, column 8 in the Flowchart group). Recolor the clip by applying the Accent color 2 Light variation (column 3 in the Light Variations area). Move the clip so that it is positioned as shown in Figure 5–59b.
3. On Slide 3, create two columns in the text box, adjust the column spacing to 0.7", and position the text box as shown in Figure 5–59c. Bold the words Chronological and Functional. Change the clip size to 30%. Move the clip so that it is positioned as shown in Figure 5–59c.

4. On Slide 4, change the clip size to 37% and then recolor the clip by applying the Accent color 2 Light variation (column 3 in the Light Variations area). Move the clip so that it is positioned as shown in Figure 5–59d.

5. Apply the Shape Plus wipe transition (row 6, column 1) to all slides and change the transition speed to Slow.

6. Set the slide timings to 15 seconds for Slide 1 and 10 seconds for the other three slides.

7. On Slide 2, type A resume should include your educational background, work experience, and contact information. Be certain to have someone read your resume to check for clarity and correct spelling and word usage. in the Notes pane.

8. On Slide 4, type Design an attractive letterhead for your cover letter. The paragraphs should give specific examples of your accomplishments in school and on the job. in the Notes pane.

9. Check the spelling, and then display the revised presentation in Slide Sorter view to check for consistency.

10. Use your name in place of Student Name on the title slide. Change the document properties, as specified by your instructor. Save the presentation using the file name, Apply 5-1 Job. Submit the revised document in the format specified by your instructor.

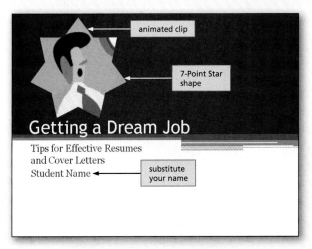

(a)

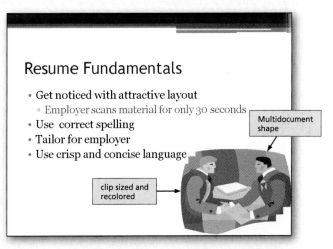

(b)

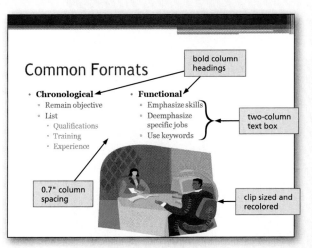

(c)

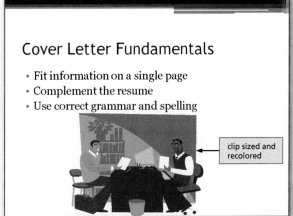

(d)

Figure 5–59

Extend Your Knowledge

Extend the skills you learned in this chapter and experiment with new skills. You may need to use Help to complete the assignment.

Recoloring a Movie File and Changing Bullet Characters

Instructions: Start PowerPoint. Open the presentation, Extend 5-1 Vote, from the Data Files for Students. See the inside back cover of this book for instructions on downloading the Data Files for Students, or contact your instructor for more information about accessing required files.

You will insert, size, and recolor a movie clip and then change both bullet characters (Figure 5–60).

Perform the following tasks:

1. Display the Insert tab, click the Picture button in the Illustrations group, select the Ballot Box file on the Data Files for Students, and then click the Insert button to insert this clip into the slide. Increase the clip size and then apply a variation to recolor the clip.

2. Change the first bullet character to the Vote picture found on the Data File for Students. Change the second bullet character to a symbol of your choice.

3. Increase the size of both bullet characters.

4. Add speaker notes discussing the importance of exercising your right to vote in the election.

5. Insert your name in a footer.

6. Change the document properties, as specified by your instructor. Save the presentation using the file name, Extend 5-1 Revised Vote.

7. Submit the revised document in the format specified by your instructor.

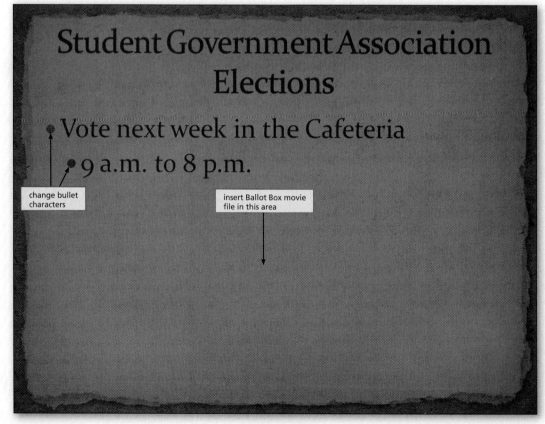

Figure 5–60

Make It Right

Analyze a presentation and correct all errors and/or improve the design.

Modifying Pictures, Bullets, and Timings

Instructions: Start PowerPoint. Open the presentation, Make It Right 5-1 Massage, from the Data Files for Students. See the inside back cover of this book for instructions on downloading the Data Files for Students, or contact your instructor for more information about accessing required files.

Correct the formatting problems and errors in the presentation while keeping in mind the guidelines presented in this chapter (Figure 5–61).

Perform the following tasks:

1. Change the title text color on both sides to a color that complements the slide background. Insert your name in a footer on Slide 2.

2. On Slide 1, replace the picture shape to a shape that shows both people. Increase the size of the picture.

3. On Slide 2, increase the bullet sizes, change the color to a color that complements the slide background, and set a transparent color. Increase the font size of the second body text paragraph so that it complies with the 7 × 7 rule.

4. Delete one of the two clips on Slide 2 because they both portray similar concepts. Recolor the remaining clip, increase the size, and center it between the third body paragraph and the footer.

5. Increase the slide timings, and change the slide transitions to a fade or dissolve.

6. Use the spell checker to correct the misspellings.

7. Change the document properties, as specified by your instructor. Save the presentation using the file name, Make It Right 5-1 Therapy.

8. Submit the revised document in the format specified by your instructor.

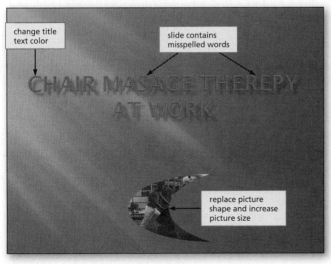

(a)

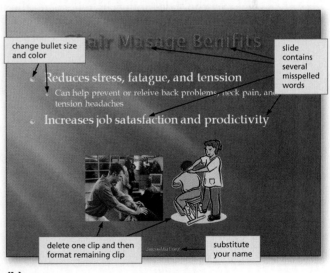

(b)

Figure 5–61

In the Lab

Design and/or create a presentation using the guidelines, concepts, and skills presented in this chapter. Labs 1, 2, and 3 are listed in order of increasing difficulty.

Lab 1: Inserting a Clip, Picture, and Sound

Problem: The "3 Rs" in the waste hierarchy are reduce, reuse, and recycle. Taken together, these three waste management strategies can help minimize garbage and toxic wastes. Children often are enthusiastic participants in the efforts to sort products for recycling and reusing household products. You work several mornings each week at the day care center at your school, and you decide to develop a PowerPoint presentation designed for these children. You begin with a clip of a child recycling newspapers on Slide 1. On the next slide, you insert a picture of three recyclable products: plastic, glass, and paper. You format these objects by resizing, recoloring, and applying a shape. You then enhance the message by adding a sound and transitions to create the slides shown in Figure 5–62 from a blank presentation.

Instructions: Perform the following tasks.

1. Create a new presentation using the Foundry document theme. Apply the Style 7 background style (row 2, column 3). Type the slide title text shown in Figure 5–62a and insert the Child Recycling clip from the Data Files for Students. Increase the clip size to 210% and position the clip as shown in the figure.

2. Insert the Carefree Tune sound clip from the Data Files for Students and have it play automatically when Slide 1 is displayed at the start of the slide show. Drag the speaker icon off the slide to the lower-right corner of the screen.

3. On Slide 2, type the slide title text shown in Figure 5–62b and insert the Recycling Products picture from the Data Files for Students. Resize the picture to 200% and position the picture as shown in the figure. Recolor the picture to Accent color 5 Dark (column 6 in the Dark Variations area). Apply the Plaque shape (row 2, column 9 in the Basic Shapes area) to the picture.

4. Set the slide timings by rehearsing the slide show. Slide 1 should display for 15 seconds and Slide 2 should display for 10 seconds.

5. Apply the Wheel Clockwise, 8 Spokes wipe transition (row 4, column 2) and change the speed to Medium for both slides.

6. Change the document properties, as specified by your instructor. Save the presentation using the file name, Lab 5-1 Recycling.

7. Submit the revised document in the format specified by your instructor.

(a)

(b)

Figure 5–62

In the Lab

Lab 2: Creating a Presentation with Columns and Pictures

Problem: Disasters can occur without warning. In preparation for emergencies, all families should have a first aid kit and an emergency supply kit filled with items that may be needed for survival for at least three days. A separate kit should be prepared for household pets. The supplies should be placed in a sturdy bag or box and checked at least twice a year. You have decided to create the PowerPoint presentation shown in Figures 5–63a through 5–63d to show in your First Aid 101 class.

Instructions: Perform the following tasks.

1. Create a new presentation using the Median document theme and then change the presentation theme colors to Aspect. Using Figure 5–63a as a guide, type the Slide 1 title and subtitle text and replace the presenter's name with your name.

2. Insert the First Aid Kit picture from your Data Files for Students, size the picture to 160%, apply the Cross shape (row 2, column 8 in the Basic Shapes area), and then reposition the picture. Recolor the picture by applying the Accent color 2 Light variation (column 3 in the Light Variations area).

3. Add three slides with the Title and Content slide layout. Format the background with the Stationery texture fill. Type the title text on all slides. Create three columns in Slide 2 and two columns in Slides 3 and 4. Type the supplies in each slide as consecutive bulleted lists. If the AutoFit Layout Options button is displayed, click Stop Fitting Text to This Placeholder to prevent PowerPoint from adjusting the font size.

4. On Slide 4, adjust the column spacing to 1" and then drag the bottom edge of the text box up to divide the columns as shown in Figure 5–63d. Insert the Pets picture from your Data Files for Students, size the picture to 110%, apply the Oval shape (row 1, column 1 in the Basic Shapes area), and then reposition the picture.

5. On Slide 2, select all the text paragraphs and then change the bullet characters to the Bandage picture found on the Data File for Students. Change the bullet size to 80% of text. On Slide 3, change the bullet characters to the ambulance symbol found in the Webdings font (row 5, column 9), change the bullet size to 80% of text, and change the color to Red.

Continued >

In the Lab *continued*

6. Insert the slide number in the footer on all slides except the title slide. Apply the Shape Plus transition (row 6, column 1 in the Wipes category) to all slides. Change the speed to Medium. Check the spelling and correct any errors.

7. Change the document properties, as specified by your instructor. Save the presentation using the file name, Lab 5-2 Supply Kit.

8. Submit the revised document in the format specified by your instructor.

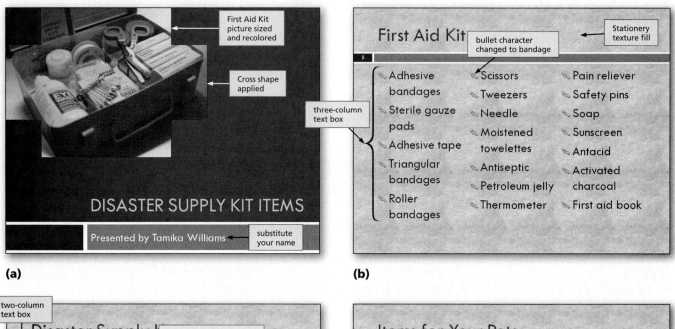

(a)　　　　　　　　　　　　　　　　　　　　　　**(b)**

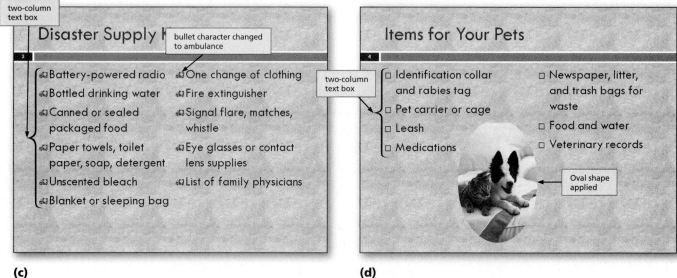

(c)　　　　　　　　　　　　　　　　　　　　　　**(d)**

Figure 5–63

In the Lab

Lab 3: Creating a Presentation with Recolored and Resized Pictures and Bullets, Columns, and a Movie Clip

Problem: This past summer you visited Chicago, and you have decided to begin creating a presentation that showcases the lakefront and attractions. You create the presentation in Figure 5–64 that consists of three slides. Slide 1 contains a resized photograph with a shape, Slide 2 contains a movie clip of the lakeshore, and Slide 3 contains columns and a photograph of the Field Museum of Natural History with a shape.

Instructions: Perform the following tasks.

1. Create a new presentation using the Solstice document theme. Apply the Two Content layout to Slide 2 and the Title and Content layout to Slide 3. Using Figure 5–64, create the three core presentation slides by typing the title and subtitle text.

2. On Slide 1, insert the Chicago Map picture from your Data Files for Students, size the picture to 80%, and then apply the Off-page Connector shape in the Flowchart area. Recolor the picture by applying the Accent color 2 Dark variation (column 3 in the Dark Variations area), and then reposition the picture.

3. On Slide 1, replace the presenter's name with your name. Insert the Soft Jazz sound clip from your Data Files for Students and start it automatically when the slide show begins. Drag the speaker icon off the slide to the lower-right corner of the screen.

4. On Slide 2, insert the Chicago Shoreline movie clip from your Data Files for Students and start it automatically in the slide show. Change the movie clip height to 3.3" and width to 4.4", and then reposition the clip.

5. On Slide 3, create two columns in the text box and adjust the column spacing to 0.1". Insert the Field Museum picture from your Data Files for Students, apply the Rounded Rectangle shape (column 2 in the Rectangles area), size the picture to 35%, and then move it to the bottom edge of the slide centered between the two columns.

6. Change the bullets to the check mark symbol shown in Figure 5–64c (column 13 in the last Wingdings row), change the color to Green, and then increase the size to 110% of text.

7. Rehearse timings for the side show. Have Slide 1 display for 15 seconds, Slide 2 for 10 seconds, and Slide 3 for 20 seconds.

8. On Slide 2, type `Every July 3, millions of people line Chicago's lakefront for an incredible fireworks show. More than 30 food vendors participate in Taste of Chicago, where hungry visitors can sample a wide variety of appetizers, entrees, and desserts.` in the Notes pane.

9. Insert the slide number in Slides 2 and 3. Apply the Wedge transition (row 1, column 5 in the Wipes category) to all slides. Change the speed to Medium. Check the spelling and correct any errors.

10. Click the Slide Sorter view button, view the slides for consistency, and then click the Normal view button.

11. Change the document properties, as specified by your instructor. Save the presentation using the file name, Lab 5-3 Chicago Travels.

12. Submit the revised document in the format specified by your instructor.

Continued >

Cases and Places *continued*

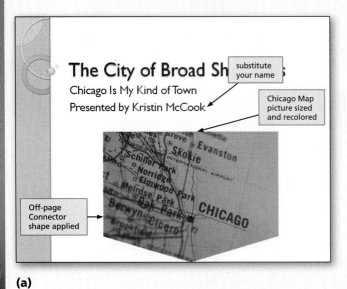

(a)

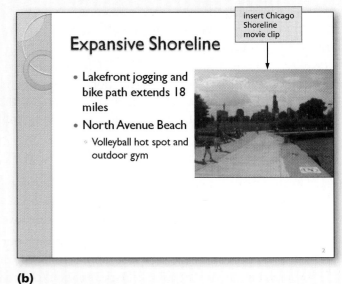

(b)

(c)

Figure 5–64

Cases and Places

Apply your creative thinking and problem solving skills to design and implement a solution.

• EASIER •• MORE DIFFICULT

Note: Remember to use the 7 × 7 rule as you design the presentations: a maximum of seven words on a line and a maximum of seven lines on one slide.

• 1: Design and Create a Words Presentation

Linguists study the origin of words and how they are used. One of their interests is onomatopoeic words, which are words that sound like the noise they describe and often are seen in comic strips. Common onomatopoeic words are shown in Table 5–3.

Another interesting word or phrase is a palindrome, which reads the same backwards and forwards. Some palindromes are shown in Table 5–4.

The ten most common spoken and written words in the English language are shown in Table 5–5.

Using this information, create a presentation with a title slide introducing the topic and two text slides with columns of the onomatopoeic words and palindromes. The fourth slide should include a table with the ten most common English spoken and written words. Include at least one sized and recolored picture with a transparent color. Apply at least three objectives found at the beginning of this chapter to develop the presentation. Add speaker notes in the Notes pane of the slides with the onomatopoeic words and palindromes, giving the definitions of these word types. Apply slide transitions and a footer with your name and the page number on all slides. Be sure to check spelling.

Table 5–3 Onomatopoeic Words		
Bang	Growl	Tap
Boom	Meow	Whack
Clang	Oink	Wham
Cock-a-doodle-doo	Pop	Whizz
Crack	Roar	Whoosh
Crackle	Slam	Woof
Creak	Snap	Zap
Crunch	Splash	Zoom
Gasp		

Table 5–4 Palindromes
A MAN A PLAN A CANAL PANAMA
MADAM I'M ADAM
POOR DAN IS IN A DROOP
ABLE WAS I ERE I SAW ELBA
RATS LIVE ON NO EVIL STAR
HANNAH
ANNA
NOT A TON
ROTOR

• 2: Design and Create a Popular Baby Names Presentation

The Social Security Administration (SSA) tracks popular baby names each year. Visit the SSA Web site (www.ssa.gov/OACT/babynames/) and view the lists of Top 10 male and female names. Scroll down, select one of the four lists (Popular Names by Birth Year, Popularity of a Name, Top 5 names by State, or Top 1000 names by decade), and enter your choice of data, such as your name or your year of birth. Using this information, create a presentation with a title slide introducing the topic and three text slides with columns of the male names, female names, and names from the list of your choice. Include at least one recolored photograph with a transparent color. Rehearse timings for the slide show. Have Slide 1 display

Table 5–5 Ten Most Common English Words	
Spoken	**Written**
the	the
and	of
I	to
to	in
of	and
a	a
you	for
that	was
in	is
it	that

Continued >

Cases and Places *continued*

for 10 seconds and Slides 2, 3, and 4 display for 15 seconds. Apply at least three objectives found at the beginning of this chapter to develop the presentation. Be sure to check spelling.

•• 3: Design and Create a Most Connected Campuses Presentation

College campuses today must provide a variety of technological tools to support learning. Online classes, wireless networking, and computer labs are part of the campus environment. The Princeton Review collects data each year from more than 350 colleges and universities throughout the United States and analyzes the campuses' technologies. Review the latest report (www.forbes.com/connected/) and then create a presentation about America's most connected college campuses. Include one slide with columns showing the ten top schools and another with the methodology used to determine the rankings. Change the bullet characters to the computer monitor symbol in the Webdings font and change the color and default size. Add speaker notes in the Notes pane of two slides. Apply slide transitions and a footer with your name and the slide number on all slides. Be sure to check spelling.

•• 4: Design and Create a Recording Industry Presentation

Make It Personal

The recording industry generates more than $40 billion annually worldwide, according to the Recording Industry Association of America (RIAA). Visit at least one entertainment Web site, such as Yahoo! (http://dir.yahoo.com/Entertainment/Music/) or Information Please (www.infoplease.com/ent. html), and locate information about your favorite musical artist or group. Find a list of the most songs or CDs downloaded or sold, earnings, or concert attendance per year. Use the concepts and techniques presented in this chapter to develop and format a slide show reporting your findings. Include at least two slides with columns of the data you located. Enhance the presentation with at least one resized and recolored photograph with a shape applied. If available, add a sound clip with one of your artist's music. Include hyperlinks to your artist's Web site, and add notes on at least two slides. Be sure to check spelling. Print handouts with speaker notes.

•• 5: Design and Create a Dream Vacation Presentation

Working Together

People save their hard-earned dollars for years in hopes of one day traveling to a dream destination. An African safari, a Hawaiian holiday, and a European vacation top the lists of many students. Decide on a destination, and then have each member of your team call or visit a local travel agency or conduct online research and gather information about airfares during Spring Break, the Christmas holidays, and summer vacation. Also find hotel room rates in economy, moderate, and luxury hotels. Make a list of sightseeing activities and tours. After coordinating the data, create a presentation with pictures that you recolor and resize. Also apply a shape to these pictures. Insert tables with the airfare and hotel information, and then create columns in text boxes listing the sights and activities. Add notes to each of the text slides. Rehearse timings for each slide. As a group, critique each slide. Submit your assignment in the format specified by your instructor.

6 Creating a Self-Running Presentation Containing Animated Shapes

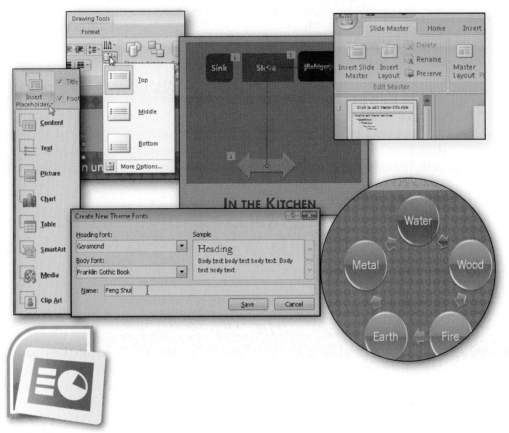

Objectives

You will have mastered the material in this chapter when you can:

- Apply themes to and format backgrounds on slide masters
- Apply Quick Styles to slide masters
- Set text direction and alignment
- Change bullet characters to numbers
- Change paragraph line spacing
- Insert entrance effects

- Change start settings
- Delete slides
- Reuse slides from an existing presentation
- Animate bulleted lists
- Animate SmartArt graphics
- Add and adjust motion paths

6 | Creating a Self-Running Presentation Containing Animated Shapes

Introduction

One method used for disseminating information is a **kiosk**. This freestanding, self-service structure is equipped with computer hardware and software and is used to provide information or reference materials to the public. Some have a touch screen or keyboard that serves as an input device and allows users to select various options to browse through or find specific information. Advanced kiosks allow customers to place orders, make payments, and access the Internet. Many kiosks have multimedia devices for playing sound and video clips.

Kiosks frequently are found in public places, such as shopping centers, hotels, museums, libraries, and airport terminals, where customers or visitors may have questions about community events, local hotels, and rental cars. Military bases have installed kiosks that allow soldiers to conduct personal business and communicate with friends and family back home by sending video clips and photographs. Governments worldwide have installed kiosks that provide Internet access to public services and information.

Project — Presentation with Animated Shapes and Customized Slide Masters

The project in this chapter follows visual content guidelines and uses PowerPoint to create the presentation shown in Figure 6–1. The slide show uses several visual elements to introduce **feng shui**, pronounced "fung shway." This Chinese art of arranging and aligning furniture, objects, and buildings has a goal of creating harmony and balance. It is based on patterns of yin and yang, where an individual's environment has opposite positive and negative, or receptive and active, forces, called chi. The wind (feng) and water (shui) distribute chi throughout the universe, and good health, prosperity, and growth are present when the forces are balanced.

Some interior designers and builders use feng shui principles when designing home and office environments. They position chairs, beds, stairs, doors, and appliances to direct the chi flow throughout the home. The presentation you develop in this chapter illustrates a few of these design concepts. It is developed to run at a kiosk in a local interior decorating store. When the last slide in the presentation is viewed, the slide show will restart at Slide 1. The presentation consists of several animated bulleted lists and an animated SmartArt graphic. The material on the text slides is complemented with three slides inserted from another presentation that illustrates basic feng shui principles in the home. Objects on these slides move to emphasize proper interior design. The presentation is customized with a unique slide master formatted with a yin and yang background graphic, background, placeholder with vertical text, and a Quick Style.

BTW

Arranging Presentation Windows
As you create one presentation, you may want to refer to another presentation and view its slides. PowerPoint allows you to view multiple presentations simultaneously on your monitor. With two or more presentations open, click the Arrange All button in the Window group on the View tab. Clicking the Switch Windows button makes a selected presentation active or current. Clicking the Cascade button overlaps the presentation windows. To close a presentation, click its Close button and then click the Maximize button on the remaining window's title bar.

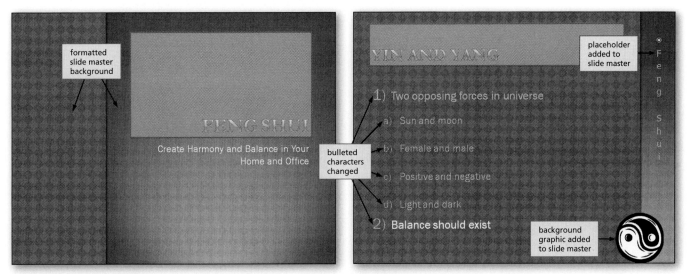

(a) Slide 1 (Title Slide)

(b) Slide 2

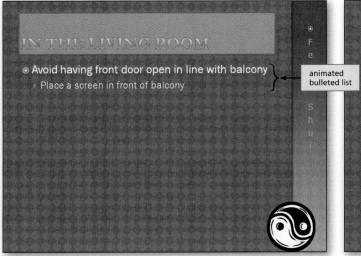

(c) Slide 3

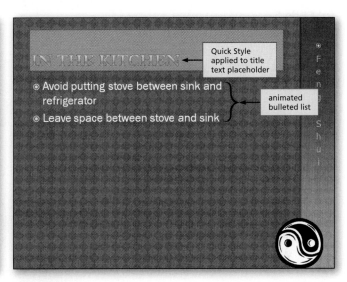

(d) Slide 4

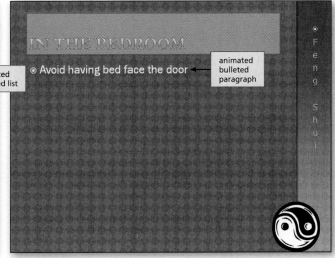

(e) Slide 6

(f) Slide 8

Figure 6–1

Separate Presentation

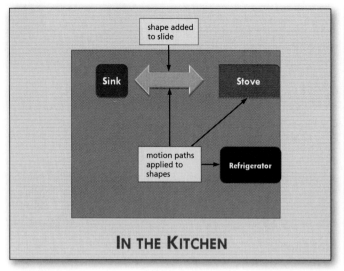

(g) Slide 5

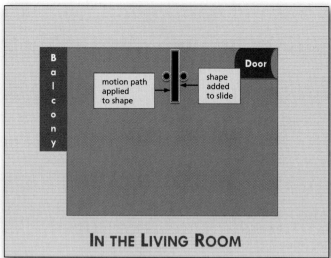

(h) Slide 7

(i) Slide 9

Figure 6–1 (continued)

Overview

As you read through this chapter, you will learn how to create the presentation shown in Figure 6–1 by performing these general tasks:

- Customize slide masters.
- Set text orientation and alignment.
- Create custom animations.
- Insert slides.
- Set slide show options.

Plan Ahead

General Project Guidelines

When creating a PowerPoint presentation, the actions you perform and decisions you make will affect the appearance and characteristics of the finished document. As you create a presentation with information graphics, such as the project shown in Figure 6–1, you should follow these general guidelines:

1. **Plan the slide master.** Using a new slide master gives you the freedom to plan every aspect of the slide. Take care to think about the overall message you are trying to convey before you start to select the elements for this master.

2. **Use animation sparingly.** Prior to using an animation effect, think about why you need it and what effect it will have upon your presentation. Do not use animation merely for the sake of using animation.

3. **Add preset animations to your text and graphics.** PowerPoint has three preset animation effects: Fade, Wipe, and Fly In. Consider using them to save time when developing a presentation.

4. **Give your audience sufficient time to view your slides.** On average, an audience member will spend only eight seconds viewing your slides. When you are setting slide timings, keep this length of time in mind, particularly when the presentation is viewed at a kiosk without a speaker's physical presence.

When necessary, more specific details concerning the above guidelines are presented at appropriate points in the chapter. The chapter also will identify the actions you perform and decisions you make regarding these guidelines during the creation of the presentation shown in Figure 6–1.

To Start PowerPoint, Open a Presentation, and Rename the Presentation

If you are using a computer to step through the project in this chapter and you want your screens to match the figures in this book, you should change your computer's resolution to 1024 × 768. For information about how to change a computer's resolution, read Appendix E.

The following steps start PowerPoint and open a presentation.

1 Start PowerPoint and then open the presentation, Feng Shui, from the Data Files for Students.

2 Maximize the PowerPoint window, if necessary.

3 Type `Revised Feng Shui` in the file name text box in the Save As dialog box.

4 Save the document on your USB flash drive.

BTW

Delivering a Presentation on Two Monitors
Presenter view allows you to run a presentation on one monitor while your audience views the same or another presentation on another monitor. The two monitors allow you to preview your next slide on your monitor, select slides out of sequence to create a customized presentation, display your speaker's notes and use them as a script, view the elapsed time, and black out the screen during the presentation. The icons and buttons in Presenter view are large, so you can navigate easily through the presentation.

Plan Ahead

Plan the slide master.

Using a new slide master gives you the freedom to specify every slide element. Like an artist with a new canvas or a musician with blank sheet music, only your imagination prevents you from creating an appealing master that conveys the overall look of your presentation.

Before you start developing the master, give your overall plan some careful thought. The decisions you make at this point should be reflected on every slide. A presentation can have several master layouts, but you should change these layouts only if you have a compelling need to change. Use the Plan Ahead concepts you have read throughout the chapters in this book to guide your decisions about fonts, colors, backgrounds, art, and other essential slide elements.

Customizing Presentation Masters

BTW

Preserving a Slide Master
Normally an original slide master is deleted when a new design template is selected. To keep the original master as part of your presentation, you can preserve it. To preserve a particular slide master, click the thumbnail and then click the Preserve button in the Edit Master group. An icon in the shape of a pushpin is displayed below the slide number to indicate the master is preserved. If you decide to unpreserve a slide master, select this thumbnail and then click the Preserve button.

PowerPoint has many template files, which have the file extension .potx. Each template file has three masters: slide, handout, and notes. A **slide master** has at least one layout; you have used many of these layouts, such as Two Content and Picture with Caption, to create presentations. A **handout master** designates the placement of text, such as page numbers, on a sheet of paper intended to distribute to audience members. A **notes master** defines the formatting for speaker's notes.

Slide Master

If you select a document theme and want to change one of its components on every slide, you can override that component by changing the slide master. In addition, if you want your presentation to have a unique design, you may want to create a slide master rather than attempt to modify a current document theme. A slide master indicates the size and position of text and object placeholders, font styles, slide backgrounds, transitions, and effects. Any change to the slide master results in changing that component on every slide in the presentation. For example, if you change the second-level bullet on the slide master, each slide with a second-level bullet will display this new bullet.

One presentation can have more than one slide master. You may find two or more slide masters are necessary when your presentation reuses special slide layouts. In this feng shui presentation, for example, some slides will have text explanations, and others will display design concepts. All slides will have a yin yang symbol on the slide master.

To Display the Slide Master

To begin developing a unique design for the feng shui slides, you need to display the slide master so that you can customize the slide components. The following steps display the slide master.

1
• Click View on the Ribbon to display the View tab (Figure 6–2).

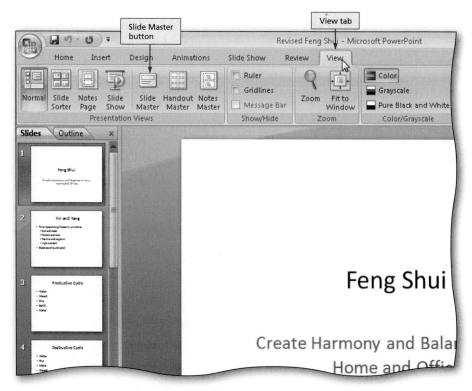

Figure 6–2

2

- Click the Slide Master button in the Presentation Views group to display the slide thumbnails.

- Click the Office Theme slide master (Figure 6–3).

Q&A

What are all the other thumbnails in the left pane below the slide master?

They are all the slide layouts associated with this slide master. You have used many of these layouts in the presentations you have developed for the presentations and exercises in this book.

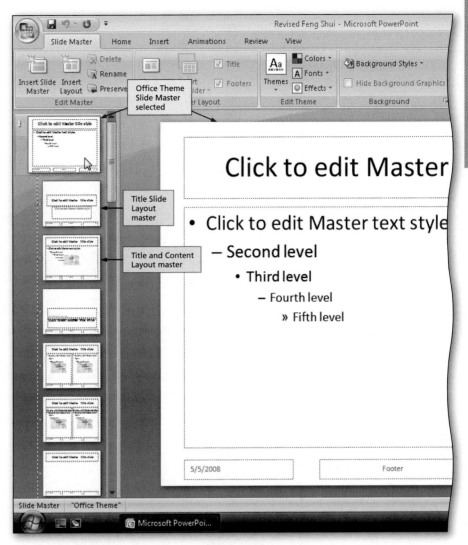

Figure 6–3

To Apply Slide and Font Themes to a Slide Master

You can change the look of an entire presentation by applying formats to the slide master in the same manner that you applied these formats to individual slides. Feng shui methods of balancing chi use natural elements, such as landscapes, crystals, and water, so you want your slides to reflect earthy tones and flowing fonts. The steps on the following page apply a theme and change the font theme.

• With the slide master displayed, click the Themes button in the Edit Theme group on the Slide Master tab to display the Themes gallery (Figure 6–4).

🔍 **Experiment**

• Point to various themes in the Themes gallery and watch the colors and fonts change on the slide master.

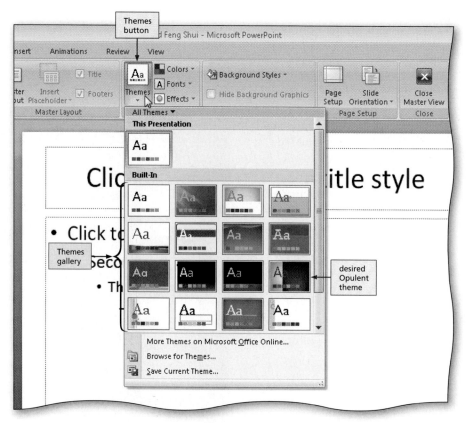

Figure 6–4

• Click the Opulent theme (row 3, column 4) to apply this theme to the slide master.

• Click the Theme Colors button in the Edit Theme group to display the Theme Colors gallery (Figure 6–5).

🔍 **Experiment**

• Point to various themes in the Theme Colors gallery and watch the colors change on the slide master.

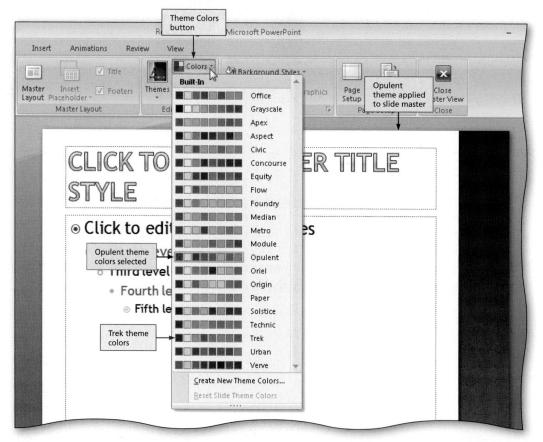

Figure 6–5

3

- Click Trek in the Theme Colors gallery to change the slide master colors to Trek.

- Click the Theme Fonts button in the Edit Theme group to display the Fonts gallery (Figure 6–6).

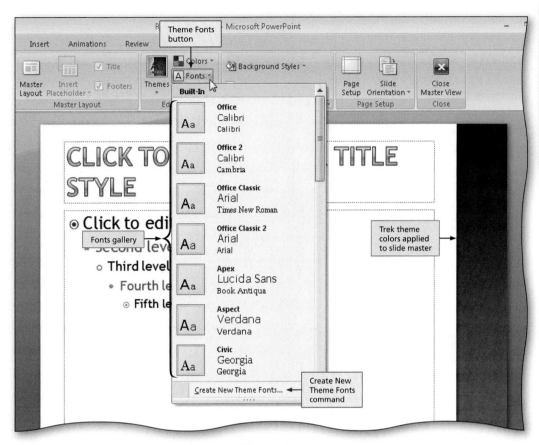

Figure 6–6

4

- Click Create New Theme Fonts in the Fonts gallery to display the Create New Theme Fonts dialog box.

- Click the Heading font arrow and scroll up to display Garamond in the list (Figure 6–7).

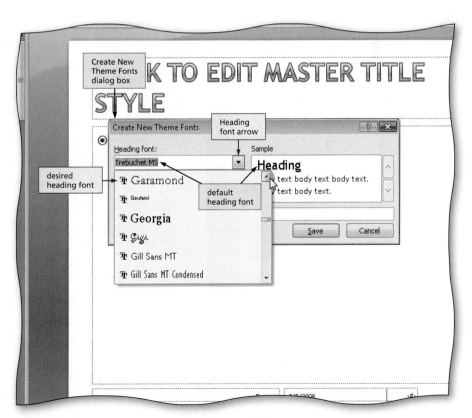

Figure 6–7

- Click Garamond to apply that font as the new heading text font.

- Click the Body font arrow and scroll up to display Franklin Gothic Book in the list (Figure 6–8).

Q&A

What if the Garamond or Franklin Gothic Book fonts are not in my list of fonts?

Select fonts that resemble the fonts shown in Figure 6–8.

Figure 6–8

- Click Franklin Gothic Book to apply that font as the new body text font.

- Select the words, Custom 1, in the Name text box and then type `Feng Shui` to name the new font set (Figure 6–9).

Q&A

Must I name this font set I just created?

No. In the future, however, you easily will recognize this combination in your font set if you want to use it in new presentations. It will display in the Custom area of the Fonts gallery.

7

- Click the Save button in the Create New Theme Fonts dialog box to save this new font set with the name, Feng Shui.

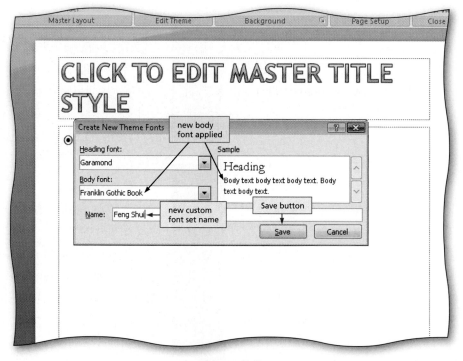

Figure 6–9

To Format a Slide Master Background and Apply a Quick Style

Once you have applied a theme to the slide master and determined the fonts for the presentation, you can further customize the presentation. The following steps format the slide master background and then apply a Quick Style.

1

- Click the title text placeholder to select it.

- Click the Background Styles button in the Background group to display the Background Styles gallery (Figure 6–10).

Experiment

- Point to various styles themes in the Background Styles gallery and watch the backgrounds change on the slide master title text placeholder.

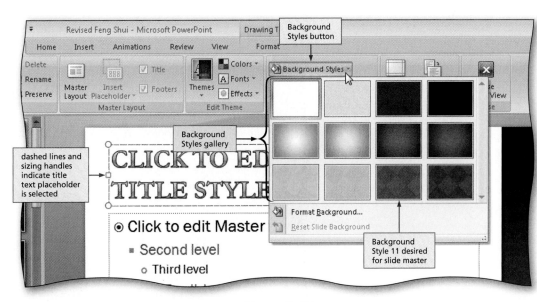

Figure 6–10

2

- Click Background Style 11 (row 3, column 3) to apply this background to the slide master (Figure 6–11).

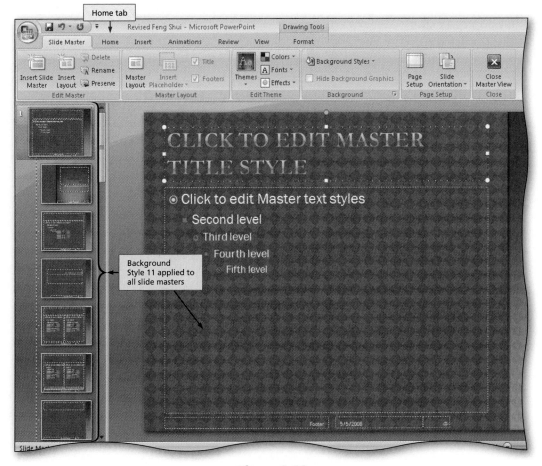

Figure 6–11

3

• Click Home on the Ribbon to display the Home tab. Click the Quick Styles button in the Drawing group to display the Quick Styles gallery (Figure 6–12).

Experiment

• Point to various styles in the Quick Styles gallery and watch the background and borders change on the slide master title text placeholder.

Figure 6–12

4

• Click the Colored Fill – Accent 1 Quick Style (row 2, column 2) to apply the format to the title text placeholder (Figure 6–13).

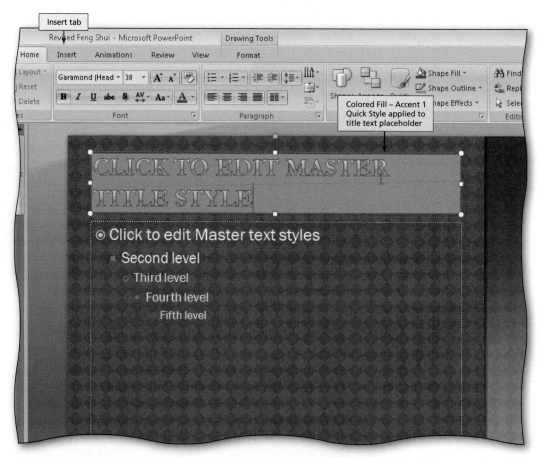

Figure 6–13

To Add a Background Graphic to a Slide Master

The theme, fonts, and background colors are set. The next step is to reinforce one of the basic feng shui concepts: yin and yang. These two opposing forces need a state of balance to keep the universe in harmony and produce chi, energy present in all objects. One technique of emphasizing this constant combination of positive and negative is to place the symbol on every slide. The following steps add the yin and yang symbol to the slide master.

1

- With the slide master displayed, click Insert on the Ribbon and then click the Insert Picture from File button, which is labeled Picture, in the Illustrations group to display the Insert Picture dialog box.

- With your USB flash drive connected to one of the computer's USB ports, select this drive, Drive E in this case, as the device that contains the picture and then click Yin Yang to select the file name (Figure 6–14).

Q&A What if the picture is not on a USB flash drive?

Use the same process, but select the device containing the picture in the Favorite Links section. Another option is to locate this picture or a similar one in the Microsoft Clip Organizer

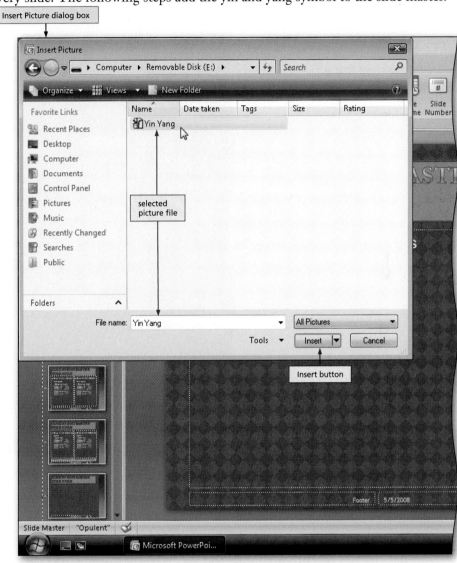

Figure 6–14

BTW

Renaming a Slide Master
PowerPoint names a new slide master, Custom Design. Once all the changes are made to this new master or to another slide master, you may want to rename it with a meaningful name that describes its function or features. To rename the slide master, click the large slide master thumbnail at the top of the left pane and then click the Rename button in the Edit Master group. The new name will be displayed on the status bar.

2

- Click the Insert button in the dialog box to insert the picture into the slide master.

- With the Format tab displayed, click the down arrow in the Size group to change the Shape Height to 1.5".

- Drag the picture to the location shown in Figure 6–15 (Figure 6–15).

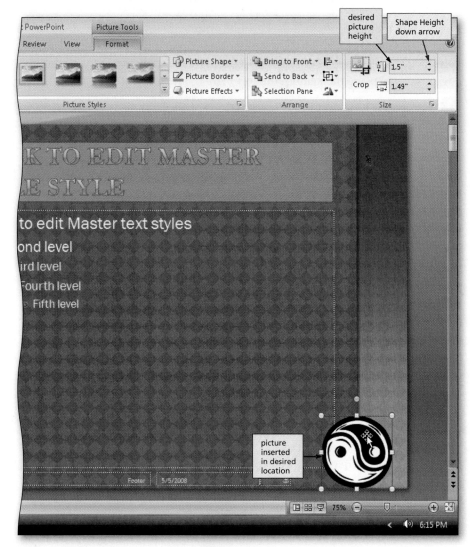

Figure 6–15

BTW

Adding Page Numbers and the Date and Time to a Slide Master
Slide numbers along with the date and time can be displayed anywhere on a slide, not just in the footer. Insert a placeholder and then click either the Slide Number or the Date & Time button in the Text group on the Insert tab. You then can format the date and time by selecting a format in the Available formats list in the Date and Time dialog box. You also can change the default font characteristics in the Font group on the Home tab.

To Insert a Placeholder into Slide Layouts

The words, feng shui, appear on the title slide. To reinforce this concept, you can add these words to every text slide. One efficient method of adding this text is to insert a placeholder, type the words, and, if necessary, format the characters. The following steps insert a placeholder into the Title and Content layout.

- Click the Title and Content Layout thumbnail in the left pane to display this layout.

- With the Slide Master tab displayed, click the Content button arrow, which shows Insert Placeholder on the button, in the Master Layout group to display the placeholder menu (Figure 6–16).

Q&A Can I click the Insert Placeholder button instead of the Insert Placeholder button arrow?

Yes. If you click the Insert Placeholder button, the new placeholder can hold any content, including text, pictures, and tables. If you know the specific kind of content you want to place in the placeholder, it is best to select that placeholder type.

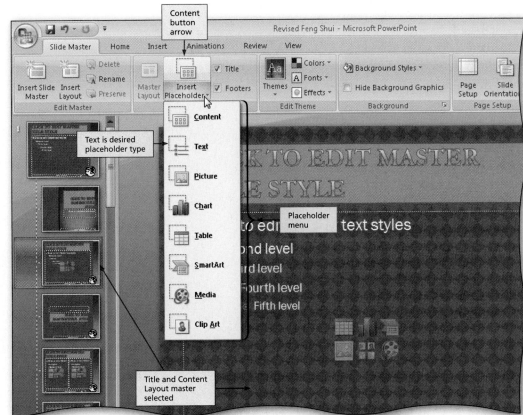

Figure 6–16

- Click Text in the menu to change the mouse pointer to a plus sign shape.

- Position the mouse pointer at the top of the green background in the location shown in Figure 6–17.

❸

- Click to insert the new placeholder into the Title and Content layout.

Figure 6–17

To Add and Format Placeholder Text

Now that the text placeholder is positioned, you can add the desired text and then format the characters. You will need to delete the second-, third-, fourth-, and fifth-level bullets in this placeholder because they are not being used. The following steps add and format the words in the new Title and Content layout placeholder.

1
- Click the new placeholder, press and hold down the CTRL key, and then press the A key to select all the text in the placeholder (Figure 6–18).

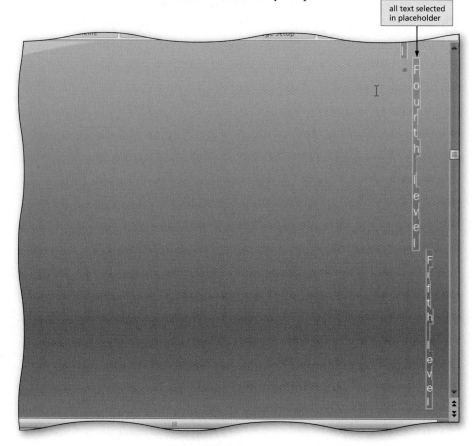

Figure 6–18

2
- Press the DELETE key to delete all the selected text in the placeholder.

- Type Feng Shui in the placeholder.

- Drag the bottom sizing handle down to just above the yin and yang symbol, as shown in Figure 6–19.

Figure 6–19

3

- Click the Home tab and then click the Text Direction button in the Paragraph group to open the Text direction gallery (Figure 6–20)

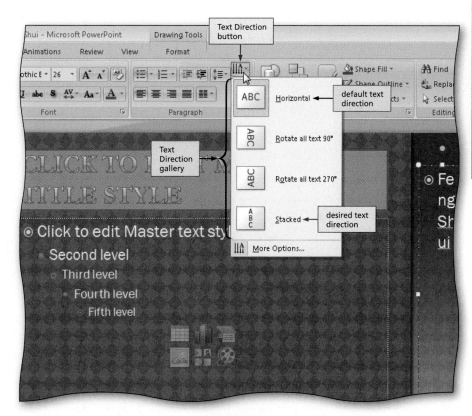

Figure 6–20

4

- Click Stacked to display the text vertically.

- Click the Align Text button in the Paragraph group to display the Align gallery (Figure 6–21).

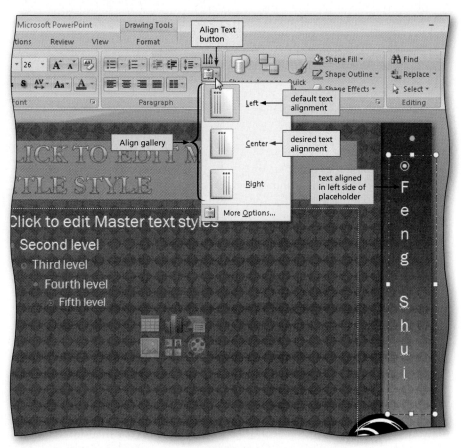

Figure 6–21

5

- Click Center to display the text in the middle of the placeholder.

Q&A

What is the difference between the Center button in the Paragraph group and the Center button in the Align gallery?

The Center button in the Paragraph group positions the text between the top and bottom borders of the placeholder. The Center button in the Align gallery centers the text between the left and right borders.

- If necessary, drag the placeholder to position it as shown in Figure 6–22.

Figure 6–22

6

- Right-click the text to display the Mini toolbar and shortcut menu, click the Font box arrow on the Mini toolbar, and then scroll down and select Tahoma.

- Click the Decrease Font Size button two times to decrease the font size from 26 to 20 point.

- Click the Font Color box arrow and then change the font color to Orange (column 3 in the Standard Colors area) (Figure 6–23).

Figure 6–23

To Copy a Placeholder to the Slide Master

The new formatted placeholder appears only on the Title and Content layout. If you selected any other layout in your presentation, such as Two Content or Title Only, this placeholder would not display. For consistency, this placeholder should appear on all text slides. You are not given the opportunity to insert a placeholder into the slide master, but you can paste a placeholder that you copied from another slide. The following step copies the new placeholder from the Title and Content layout and pastes it into the slide master.

1

- With the Home tab displayed, click the new placeholder border so that it is displayed as a solid blue line.

- Click the Copy button in the Clipboard group to copy the placeholder to the Clipboard (Figure 6–24).

Figure 6–24

2

- Click the Opulent Slide Master thumbnail in the left pane to display the slide master.

- Click the Paste button in the Clipboard group to copy the placeholder from the Clipboard to the slide master (Figure 6–25).

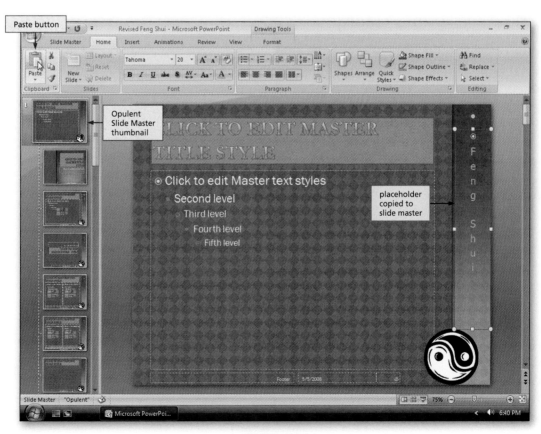

Figure 6–25

To Close Master View

Now that all the changes to the slide master and the Title and Content layout are complete, you can exit Master view and return to Normal view. All slides in the presentation will have the new placeholder, color scheme, fonts, quick style, and yin and yang symbol. The following steps close Master view.

1

• Click Slide Master on the Ribbon to display the Slide Master tab (Figure 6–26).

Figure 6–26

2

• Click the Close Master View button in the Close group to exit Master view and return to Normal view (Figure 6–27).

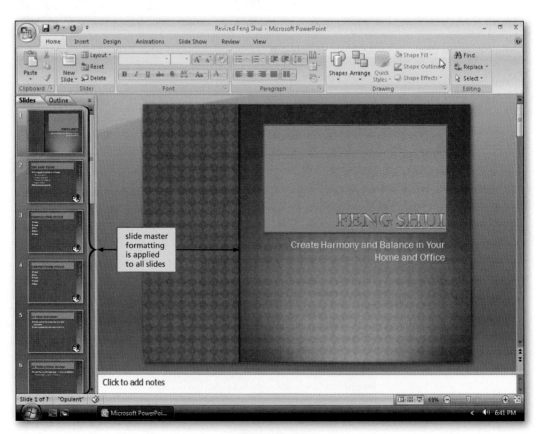

Figure 6–27

Adding and Formatting Numbered Lists

To customize your presentation, you can change the default slide layout bullets to numbers. PowerPoint provides a variety of numbering options, including Arabic and Roman numerals. These numbers can be sized and recolored, and the starting number can be something other than 1 or I. In addition, PowerPoint's numbering options include upper- and lowercase letters.

To Change a First-Level Bullet Character to a Number

PowerPoint allows you to change the default bullets to numbers. The process of changing the bullet characters is similar to the process of changing bullets to symbols. The following steps change the first-level paragraph bullet characters on Slide 2 to numbers.

- Display Slide 2.

- Triple-click the first first-level Slide 2 paragraph, which begins with the words Two opposing forces, to select it.

- Press and hold down the CTRL key and then triple-click the second first-level Slide 2 paragraph, which begins with the word Balance, to select this paragraph (Figure 6–28).

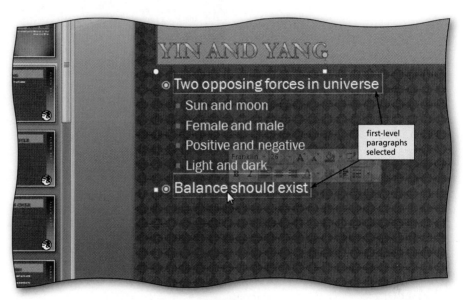

Figure 6–28

- With the Home tab displayed, click the Numbering button arrow to display the Numbering gallery (Figure 6–29).

Experiment

- Point to various numbers in the Numbering gallery and watch the numbers change on Slide 2.

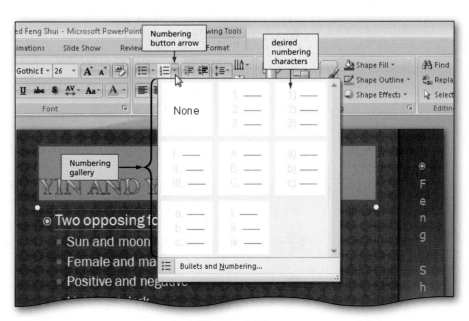

Figure 6–29

3

• Click the 1) 2) 3) numbering option (row 1, column 3) to insert these numbers as the first-level paragraph characters (Figure 6–30).

Q&A How do I change the first number in the list?

Click Bullets and Numbering below the Numbering gallery and then click the up or down arrow in the Start at text box to change the number.

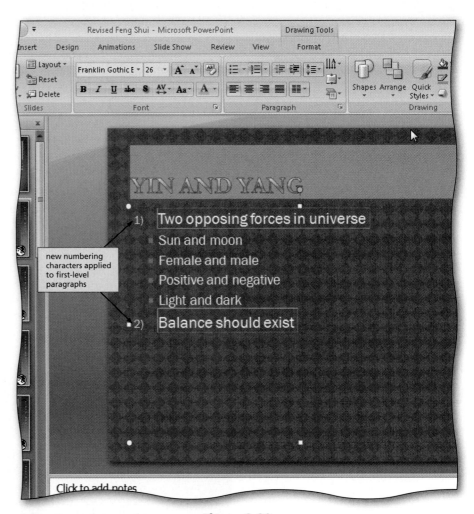

Figure 6–30

To Change a Second-Level Bullet Character to a Number

The second-level square bullets can be changed to a sequence different from the first-level numbers. The following steps change the second-level paragraph bullet characters on Slide 2 to lowercase letters.

1 Triple-click the first second-level Slide 2 paragraph, which begins with the word Sun, to select it.

2 Press and hold down the CTRL key and then triple-click the second second-level Slide 2 paragraph, which begins with the word Female. While holding down the CTRL key, triple-click the third second-level paragraph and the fourth second-level paragraph to select these four paragraphs.

3 With the Home tab displayed, click the Numbering button arrow to display the Numbering gallery.

4 Click the a) b) c) numbering option (row 2, column 3) to insert these letters as the second-level paragraph char acters (Figure 6–31).

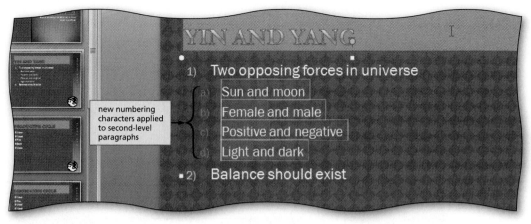

new numbering characters applied to second-level paragraphs

Figure 6–31

To Format a First-Level Numbered List

To add emphasis, you can increase the size of the new numbers and letters inserted in Slide 2. As with bullets, these characters are measured as a percentage of the text size and can range from 25 to 400 percent. The color of these numbers and letters also can change. The original colors are based on the eight colors in the design theme. Additional standard and custom colors are available. The following steps change the size and colors of the first-level numbering characters to 125 percent and Orange, respectively.

1

- Triple-click the first first-level Slide 2 paragraph, press and hold down the CTRL key, and then triple-click the second first-level Slide 2 paragraph to select these paragraphs.

- With the Home tab displayed, click the Numbering button arrow to display the Numbering gallery (Figure 6–32).

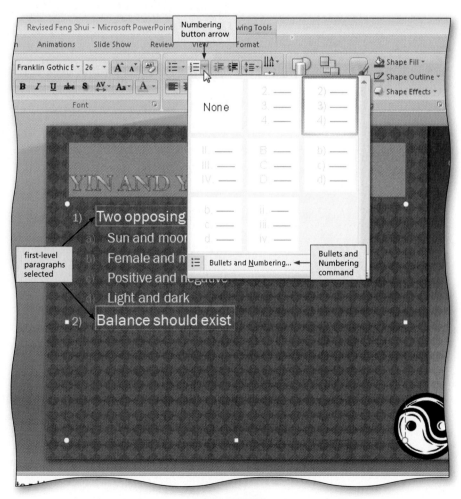

Figure 6–32

- Click Bullets and Numbering to display the Bullets and Numbering dialog box.

- Click the Size box up arrow to change the size to 125%.

Q&A Can I type a number in the text box instead of clicking the up arrow?

Yes. Double-click the text box and then type the desired percentage.

- Click the Color arrow to display the color palette (Figure 6–33).

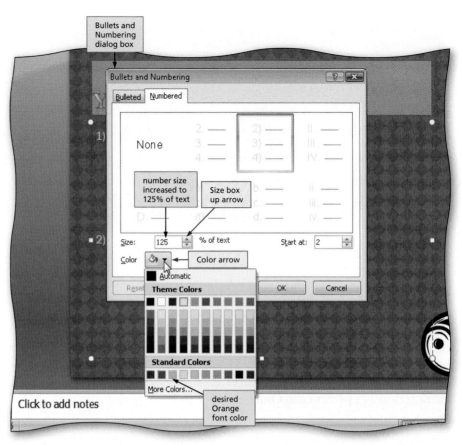

Figure 6–33

- Change the font color to Orange (column 3 in the Standard Colors area) (Figure 6–34).

- Click the OK button to change the font size and color.

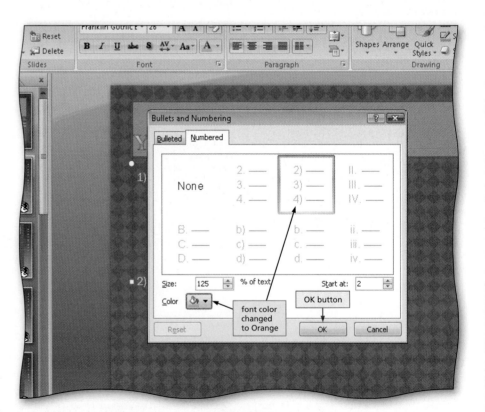

Figure 6–34

To Format a Second-Level Numbered List

For consistency, the letters in the second-level paragraph list on Slide 2 should resemble the numbers in the first-level paragraph list. The font size should be somewhat smaller because the paragraph font size is smaller than the first-level paragraph font size. In addition, the list should be a complementary color. The following steps change the size of the second-level numbered list to 100 percent and the color to Light Green.

1 Select the four second-level paragraphs on Slide 2.

2 Click the Numbering button arrow and then click Bullets and Numbering in the Numbering gallery to display the Bullets and Numbering dialog box.

3 Click the Size box up arrow to change the size to 100%.

4 Click the Color arrow to display the color palette and then click the color Light Green in the Standard Colors area (column 5).

5 Click the OK button to change the font size and letters in the list (Figure 6–35).

Other Ways

1. Right-click paragraph, point to Numbering on shortcut menu, click Bullets and Numbering, click up or down Size arrow until desired size is displayed, click Color button, select color, click OK button

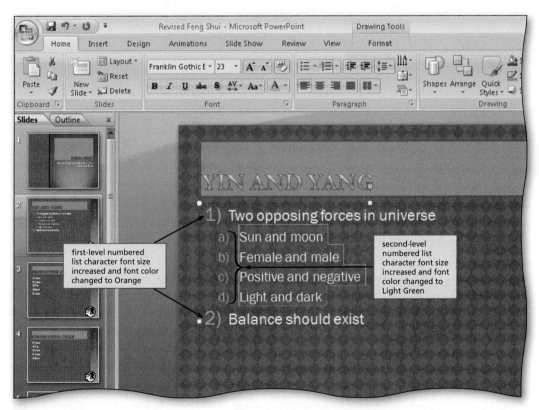

Figure 6–35

To Change the Second-Level Paragraph Line Spacing

The vertical space between paragraphs is called **line spacing**. PowerPoint adjusts the amount of space based on each font size. Default line spacing is 1.0, which is considered single spacing. Other preset options are 1.5, 2.0 (double spacing), 2.5, and 3.0 (triple spacing). You can specify precise line spacing intervals between, before, and after paragraphs in the Indents and Spacing tab of the Paragraph dialog box. The steps on the following page increase the line spacing of the second-level paragraphs from single (1.0) to double (2.0).

- With the Home tab displayed
  and the four second-level Slide 2
  paragraphs selected, click the Line
  Spacing button in the Paragraph
  group (Figure 6–36).

2

- Click 2.0 in the Line Spacing list
  to double space the second-level
  paragraphs.

- Click the content placeholder
  anywhere except the six paragraphs to remove the selection
  from the second-level paragraphs.

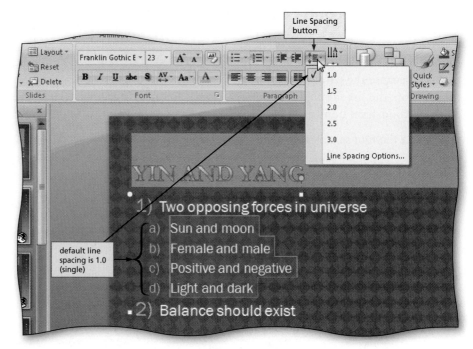

Figure 6–36

Other Ways	
1. Right-click paragraphs, click Paragraph on short-cut menu, on Indents and Spacing tab click Line Spacing box arrow, click Double, click OK button	2. Click Paragraph Dialog Box Launcher, on Indents and Spacing tab click Line Spacing box arrow, click Double, click OK button

To Align Text in a Content Placeholder

The four text paragraphs in the content placeholder on Slide 2 are aligned at the top of the text box. This default setting can be changed easily so that the paragraphs are centered or aligned at the bottom of the placeholder. The following steps center the first- and second-level paragraphs in the content placeholder.

1

- With the Home tab
  displayed and the
  content placeholder
  selected, click the
  Align Text button in
  the Paragraph group
  (Figure 6–37).

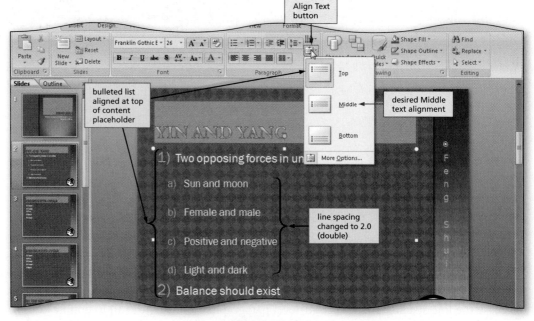

Figure 6–37

2

- Click Middle in the Align Text list to center the paragraphs in the content placeholder (Figure 6–38).

Q&A

What is the difference between centering the paragraphs in the placeholder and centering the text?

Clicking the Align Text button and then clicking Middle moves the paragraphs up or down so that the first and last paragraphs are equal distances from the top and bottom placeholder borders. The Center button, on the other hand, moves the paragraphs left or right so that the first and last words on the longest lines are equal distances from the left and right text box borders.

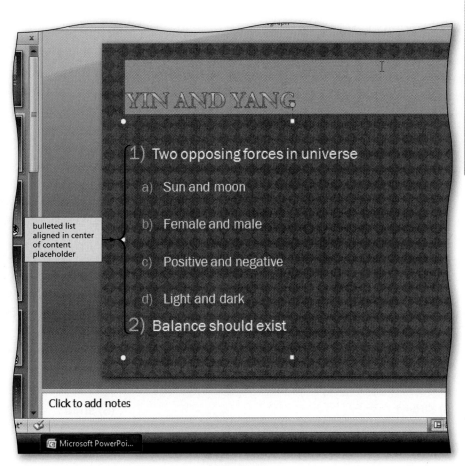

Figure 6–38

Reusing Slides from an Existing Presentation

Occasionally you may want to insert a slide from another presentation into your presentation. PowerPoint offers two methods of obtaining these slides. One way is to open the second presentation and then copy and paste the desired slides. The second method is to use the Reuse Slides task pane to view and then select the desired slides.

SharePoint Servers

In a business environment, PowerPoint presentations may be stored on a centrally located Slide Library that resides on a server running Office SharePoint Server 2007. These slide shows may be shared, reused, and accessed by many individuals who then can copy materials into their individual presentations. The Slide Library functions in much the same manner as your community library, for the SharePoint Server time stamps when an individual has borrowed a particular slide or presentation and then time stamps the slide or presentation when it is returned. If a particular slide in the Library has been updated, anyone who has borrowed that slide is notified that the content has changed. In this manner, people creating PowerPoint presentations can track the changes to presentations, locate the latest versions of slides, and check for slide updates.

BTW

Creating a Document Workspace Site
A SharePoint Server allows coworkers to collaborate efficiently. By creating a Document Workspace site on the server, team members can share and update the same files and keep each other informed about the files' status. Files are stored in a document library, which is a location where team members create, collect, update, and manage files. If a member modifies a file, the team members are notified of the change. The library tracks the file versions so that members can see a history of changes and restore a previous version, if necessary.

To Insert a Slide into a Presentation

The PowerPoint presentation with the file name, Feng Shui Rooms, has room layouts with optimal designs adhering to traditional methods of distributing chi energy. It contains four slides, and you would like to insert three of these slides, shown in Figure 6–39, into your Revised Feng Shui presentation. This Feng Shui Rooms presentation is on your Data Files for Students. See the inside back cover of this book for instructions on downloading the Data Files for Students, or contact your instructor for more information.

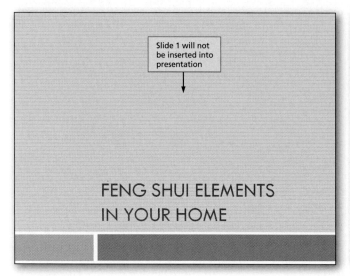

(a) Slide 1

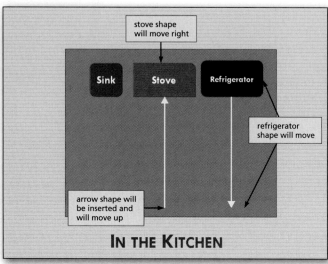

(b) Slide 2

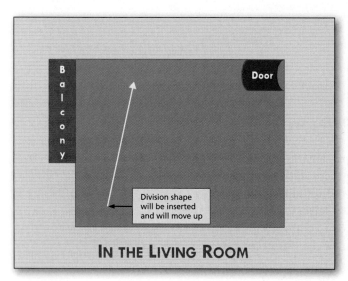

(c) Slide 3

(d) Slide 4

Figure 6–39

The inserted slides will be placed in the presentation directly after Slide 5. They will inherit the styles of the current slide, which is the Feng Shui slide master and layouts, unless the option to keep source formatting is selected. The following steps add these slides to your presentation.

1

- Display Slide 5.

- With the Home tab displayed and your USB flash drive connected to one of the computer's USB ports, click the New Slide button arrow to display the Opulent layout gallery (Figure 6–40).

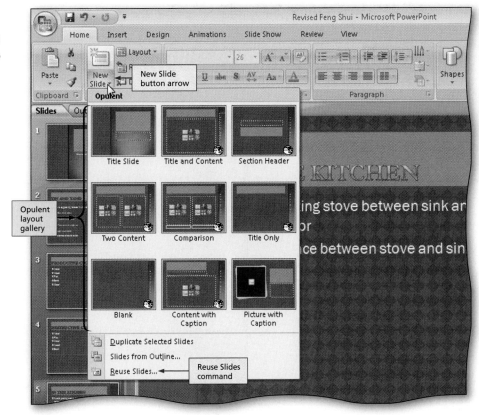

Figure 6–40

2

- Click Reuse Slides in the Opulent layout gallery to display the Reuse Slides task pane.

- Click the Browse button (Figure 6–41).

 What are the two Browse options shown?

If the desired slides are in a Slide Library on an Office SharePoint Server, then you would click Browse Slide Library. The slides you need, however, are on your Data Disk for Students, so you need to click Browse File.

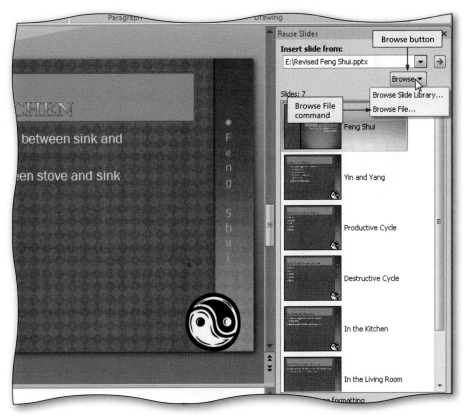

Figure 6–41

- Click Browse File to display the Browse dialog box.

- If necessary, double-click UDISK 2.0 (E:) to select the USB flash drive, Drive E in this case, as the device that contains the Feng Shui Rooms file.

- Click Feng Shui Rooms to select the file (Figure 6–42).

Q&A What if this file is not on a USB flash drive?

Use the same process, but select the device containing the file in the Favorite Links section.

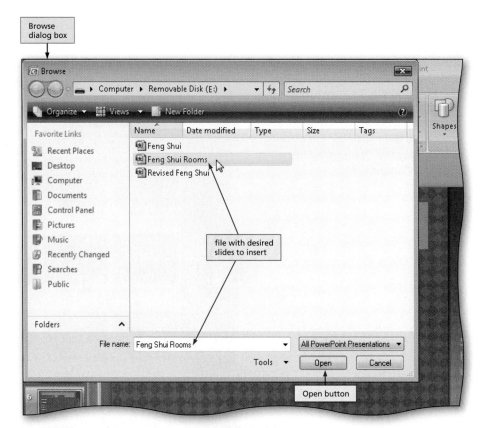

Figure 6–42

- Click the Open button in the dialog box to display thumbnails of the four Feng Shui Rooms slides in the Reuse Slides task pane (Figure 6–43).

Experiment

- Point to each of the thumbnails in the Reuse Slides task pane to see a larger preview of that slide.

Q&A Can I insert all the slides in the presentation in one step instead of selecting each one individually?

Yes. Right-click any thumbnail and then click Insert All Slides.

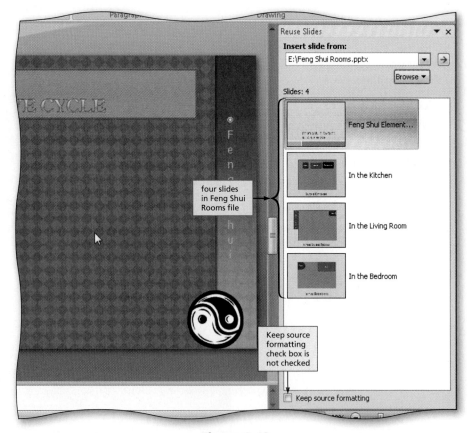

Figure 6–43

5

- Click the 'Keep source formatting' check box at the bottom of the Reuse Slides task pane to preserve the Feng Shui Rooms presentation formatting.

Q&A

What would happen if I did not check this box?

PowerPoint would change the formatting to the characteristics found in the Opulent slide master and layout masters.

- Point to the second slide, In the Kitchen (Figure 6–44).

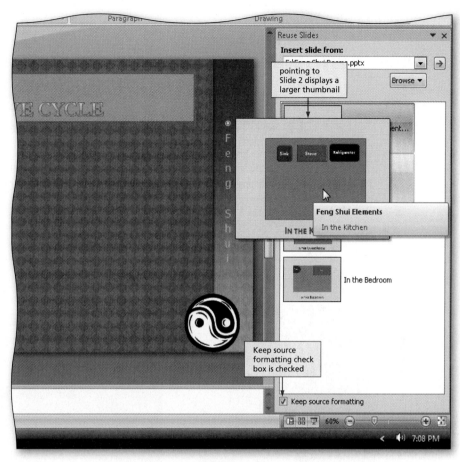

Figure 6–44

6

- Click the In the Kitchen preview to insert this slide into the Revised Feng Shui presentation after Slide 5 (Figure 6–45).

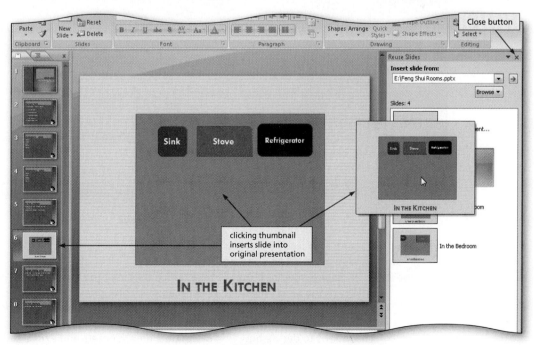

Figure 6–45

To Insert the Remaining Slides into a Presentation

The third and fourth slides in the Feng Shui Rooms presentation can be reused in the Revised Feng Shui presentation. The following steps insert one slide after Slide 7 and another slide as the last slide in the presentation.

1 Display Slide 7 and then point to the third slide in the Reuse Slide task pane, In the Living Room.

2 Click the In the Living Room preview to insert this slide into the Revised Feng Shui presentation after Slide 7.

3 Display Slide 9, point to the fourth slide in the Reuse Slide task pane, In the Bedroom, and then click this preview to insert this slide as the last slide in the Revised Feng Shui presentation.

4 Click the Close button in the Reuse Slides task pane so that it no longer is displayed (Figure 6–46).

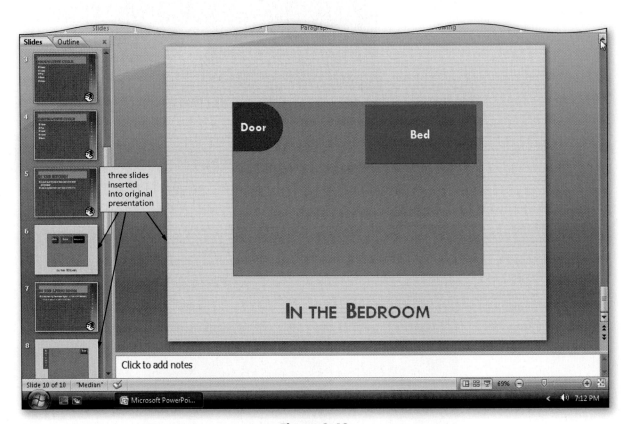

Figure 6–46

Plan Ahead

Use animation sparingly.
Audience members usually take notice the first time an animation is displayed on the screen. When the same animation effect is applied throughout a presentation, the viewers generally become desensitized to the effect unless it is highly unusual or annoying. Resist the urge to use animation effects simply because PowerPoint provides the tools to do so. You have options to decide how text or a slide element enters and exits a slide and how it is displayed once it is present on the slide, but your goal is to use these options wisely. Audiences soon tire of a presentation riddled with abundant animations, which quickly lose their impact.

Using Animations in a Presentation

To add visual interest and clarity to a presentation, you can animate various parts of a presentation, including clips, shapes, text, and other slide elements. **Animation** includes special visual and sound effects applied to text or content. For example, each paragraph on the slide can spin as it is displayed. Individual letters and shapes also can spin or move in a wide variety of motions. You already are familiar with one animation effect: transitions. PowerPoint has a variety of built-in animations that will fade, wipe, or fly-in text and graphics.

Custom Animations

You can create your own **custom animations** to meet your unique needs. Custom animation effects are grouped in categories: entrance, exit, emphasis, and motion paths. **Entrance** effects, as the name implies, determine how the slide element first appears on the slide. **Exit** animations work in the opposite manner as entrance effects: they remove slide elements. **Emphasis** effects modify the text and objects once they are displayed on the screen. For example, letters may darken or increase in font size. The entrance, exit, and emphasis animations are grouped into categories: Basic, Subtle, Moderate, and Exciting. You can set the animation speed to Very Fast, Fast, Medium, Slow, or Very Slow.

If you need to move objects on a slide once they are displayed, you can define a **motion path**. This predefined movement determines where an object will be displayed and then travel. Motion paths are grouped in the Basic, Lines & Curves, and Special categories. You can draw a **custom path** if none of the predefined paths meets your needs.

BTW

Playing Adobe Macromedia Flash Animations
PowerPoint can play an animation created with Adobe Macromedia Flash and saved as a Shockwave file with an .swf extension. The Flash file must be embedded in the presentation, or the ActiveX control named Shockwave Flash Object must be added to the slide and then linked to the Flash file so that it runs using the Adobe Macromedia Flash Player. The Shockwave Flash Object must be registered to your computer. In addition, your computer's security settings must allow ActiveX controls to run.

To Animate a Bulleted List

Used properly, animated text can draw the audience's eyes toward important slide concepts. Slide 2 in this presentation has six paragraphs of text. When you are using PowerPoint to accompany a speech, add animation effects to paragraphs so that you can display only the topic being discussed at a particular time of your speech rather than display the entire slide at once. The following steps insert one entrance effect for these paragraphs.

1

- Display Slide 2 and then click the text placeholder to select it.

- Click Animations on the Ribbon to display the Animations tab.

- Click the Custom Animation button in the Animations group to display the Custom Animation task pane.

- Click the Add Effect button in the Custom Animation task pane to display the Add Effect menu (Figure 6–47).

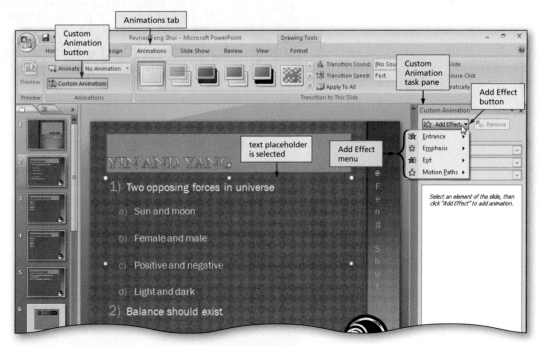

Figure 6–47

• Point to Entrance in the Add Effect menu to display the Entrance effects submenu (Figure 6–48).

Q&A

Why does my list of effects differ from what is shown in Figure 6–48?

The effects in the list are dynamic, so they change based upon whether you have viewed and applied them previously in a presentation.

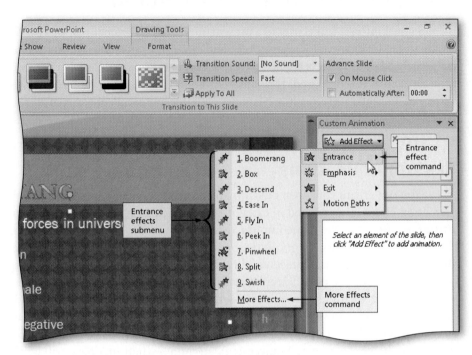

Figure 6–48

• Click More Effects on the Entrance effects submenu to display the Add Entrance Effect dialog box (Figure 6–49).

 **Experiment**

• Click some of the entrance effects in the various categories and watch the effect preview on Slide 2.

Q&A

Can I move the Add Entrance Effect dialog box so that I can see the entrance effects previews in the paragraph?

Yes. Click the dialog box title bar and drag the box to a location where you can view the first bulleted paragraph.

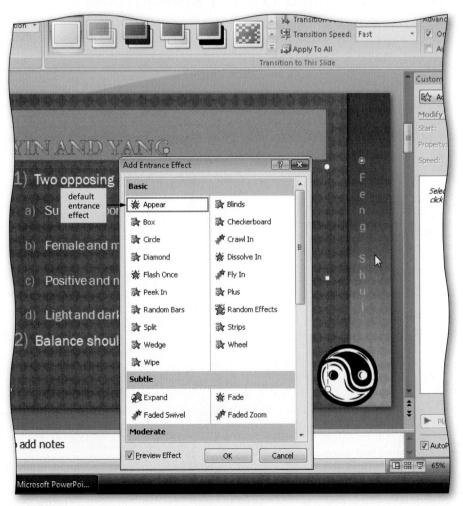

Figure 6–49

4

• Scroll down and then click Ease In in the Moderate category (Figure 6–50).

Q&A Why do I see a preview of the effects when I click their names?

The Preview Effect box is selected. If you do not want to see previews, click the box to deselect it.

5

• Click the OK button to apply the Ease In entrance effect to the paragraphs.

Q&A Why do the numbers 1 and 2 display in boxes on the left side of the paragraphs?

The 1 and 2 are sequence numbers. They indicate the first animation is the first first-level paragraph and the four second-level paragraphs and the second animation is the second first-level paragraph.

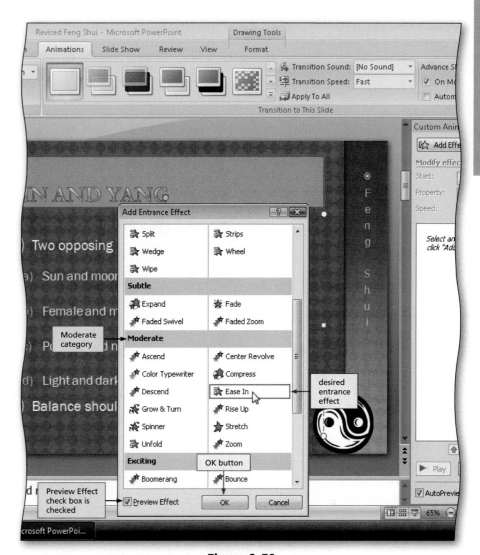

Figure 6–50

To Change Animation Speed and Grouping

Animation can start in one of three ways. The default is On Click, when the slide element is displayed after the user clicks the mouse or presses the SPACEBAR. Another option is With Previous, when the element is displayed simultaneously with whatever item is currently being displayed. The After Previous option specifies that the item will be displayed after a specified interval.

If you want to display a first-level paragraph along with its associated second-level bullets, you would specify that the animation is grouped by first-level paragraphs. If, however, you want the first-level paragraph to display and then pause until you click the mouse or press the SPACEBAR, then you would specify that the animation is grouped by second-level paragraphs. The following steps change the animation speed and group the text by second-level paragraphs.

● Click the Start box arrow in the Custom Animation task pane to display the Start list (Figure 6–51).

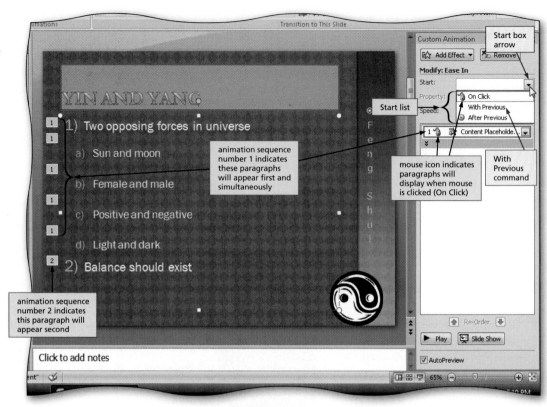

Figure 6–51

② ● Click With Previous to specify the animation will start when the slide is displayed.

Q&A

Why did the sequence numbers change to 0?

All animations will be displayed once the slide appears on the screen. You will not need to click to show each line of bulleted text individually.

● Click the Speed box arrow in the Custom Animation task pane to display the Speed list (Figure 6–52).

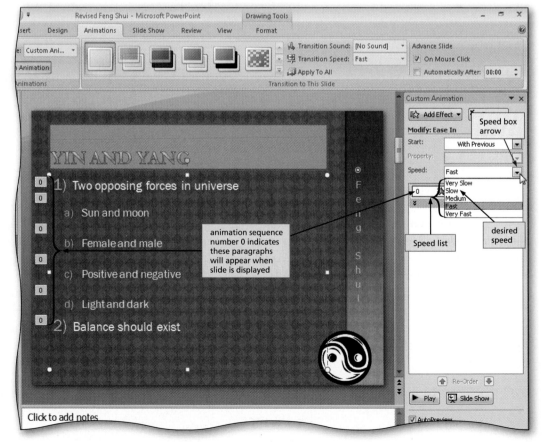

Figure 6–52

- Click Slow in the Speed list to change the display speed.
- Click the Animation Order list arrow to display the Animation Order list (Figure 6–53).

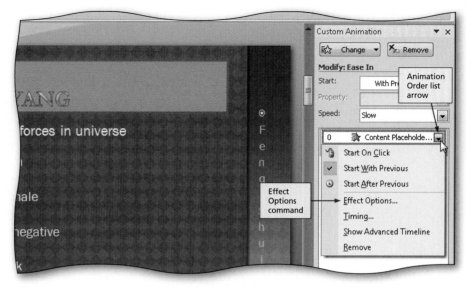

Figure 6–53

- Click Effect Options in the Animation Order list to display the Ease In dialog box.
- Click the Text Animation tab and then click the Group text list arrow (Figure 6–54).

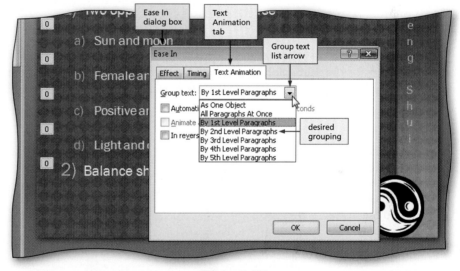

Figure 6–54

- Click By 2nd Level Paragraphs to change the entrance animation grouping (Figure 6–55).

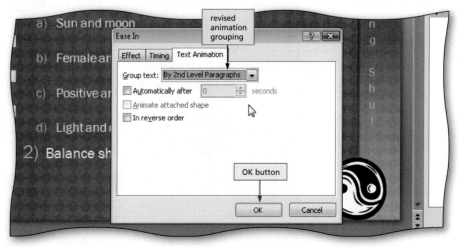

Figure 6–55

6

- Click the OK button to apply this animation (Figure 6–56).

Q&A

How can I change this Ease In effect to another effect?

Click the Change button at the top of the Custom Animation task pane and then select another effect.

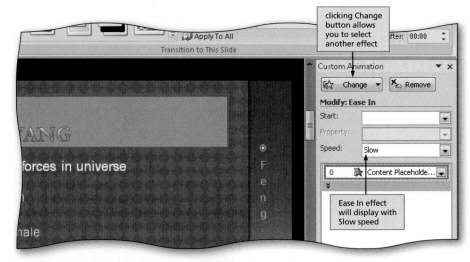

Figure 6–56

To Dim Text after Animation

As each bulleted list item on the slide is displayed, you may desire that the previous paragraph be removed from the screen or the font color be changed. PowerPoint provides several options for you to alter this text by specifying an After Animation effect. The following steps dim each paragraph on Slide 2 by changing the font color to Orange.

1

- With the Custom Animation task pane displayed, click the Animation Order list arrow and then click Effect Options.

- With the Effect tab displayed in the Ease In dialog box, click the After animation list arrow (Figure 6–57).

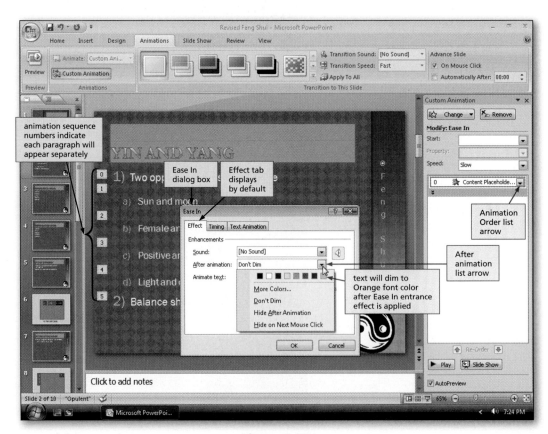

Figure 6–57

2

● Click the color Orange (column 8) in the row of colors to select this color for the dim effect (Figure 6–58).

3

● Click the OK button to apply the dim effect to the Slide 2 bulleted-list paragraphs.

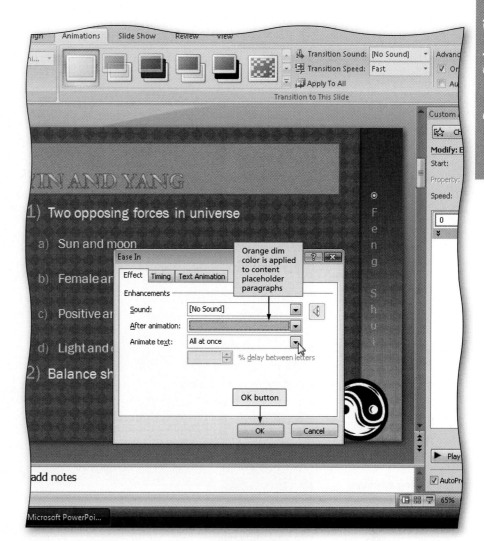

Figure 6–58

To Animate and Dim Text on the Remaining Text Slides

For consistency, you should animate the bulleted-list text on Slides 5, 7, and 9. The following steps apply the Ease In entrance effect and then dim the text on these three slides.

1 With the Custom Animation task pane displayed, display Slide 5 and then click the text placeholder to select it.

2 Click Add Effect, point to Entrance in the Add Effect menu, and then click Ease In in the Entrance effects submenu. Click the OK button to close the Add Entrance Effect dialog box.

3 Click the Start box arrow and then click With Previous. Click the Speed box arrow and then click Slow.

4 Click the Animation Order list arrow, click Effect Options, click the After animation list arrow on the Effect tab in the Ease In dialog box, and then click the color Orange. Click the OK button.

5 Repeat Steps 1 through 4 above for Slides 7 and 9.

6 Click the Close button in the Custom Animation task pane so that it no longer is displayed (Figure 6–59).

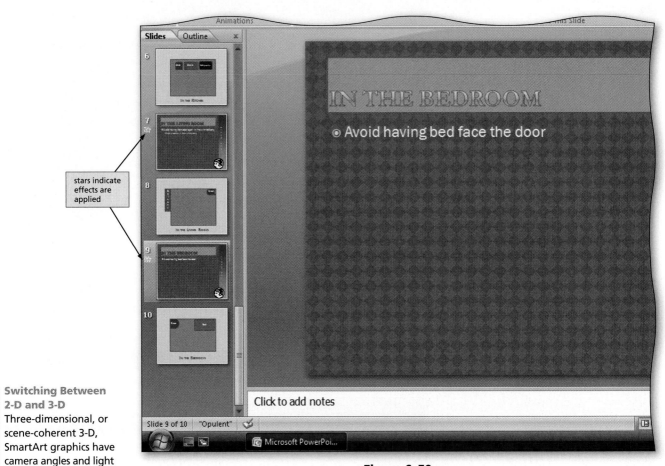

Figure 6–59

BTW

Switching Between 2-D and 3-D
Three-dimensional, or scene-coherent 3-D, SmartArt graphics have camera angles and light settings that affect their orientation, shadow, and perspective. Although you can change the text and formatting of each individual shape, you cannot reposition or resize each object. If you want to make these changes, you need to switch to a two-dimensional scene to unlock the graphic and then move and resize the shapes. To switch to two dimensions, click the Edit in 2-D button in the Shapes group on the Format tab. The 3-D SmartArt style remains applied while you modify the objects. When you click the Edit in 2-D button again, the 3-D SmartArt style reappears.

To Convert Text to a SmartArt Graphic, Apply a SmartArt Style, and Change the Color Variation

One basic feng shui concept is that the universe revolves around the five elements listed on Slide 3: water, wood, fire, earth, and metal. The first element, water, is essential for nourishing trees, which produce wood. This wood fuels fire, and the fire's ashes become part of the earth. Metal is one component of earth. When an individual's world is composed of these elements in this order, then this person is happy and successful. This cycle can be presented effectively as a SmartArt graphic. For further emphasis, you can animate each element on this slide. The following steps covert the Slide 3 text to the Basic Cycle graphic, which is part of the Cycle category, apply a SmartArt style, and then change the color variation.

1 Display Slide 3 and then click Insert on the Ribbon to display the Insert tab.

2 Select the five bulleted list items and then right-click the text to display the shortcut menu. Point to Convert to SmartArt in the shortcut menu and then click the Basic Cycle graphic (row 3, column 2) to apply this shape and convert the text.

3 With the SmartArt graphic selected and the Design tab active, click the More button in the SmartArt Styles group to expand the SmartArt Styles gallery. Click the Polished style (row 1, column 1) in the 3-D category to apply this style to the graphic.

4 Click the Change Colors button in the SmartArt Styles group to display the Change Colors gallery. Click Colorful - Accent Colors (column 1) in the Colorful category to apply this color variation to the graphic (Figure 6–60).

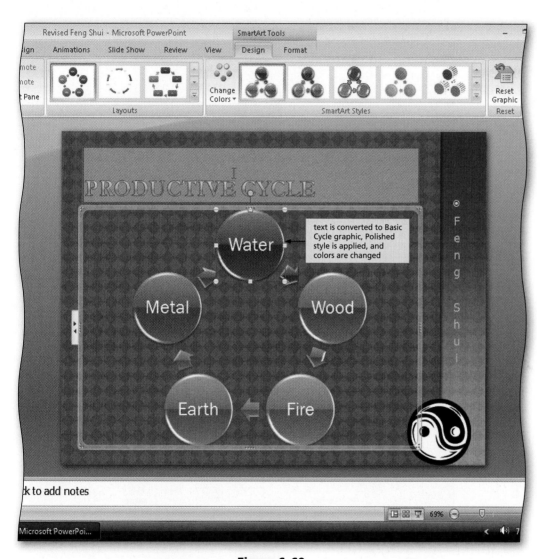

Figure 6–60

Plan Ahead

Add preset animations to your text and graphics.
To animate all text in a placeholder with the same effect, consider using a preset animation. PowerPoint provides three effects – Fade, Wipe, and Fly In – that give your slide show an interesting element. Previous PowerPoint versions contained many more preset animations with plenty of movement and flashy elements. The three included with PowerPoint 2007 are subtle and appealing. They make great additions to your slide show and are easy to apply. They make terrific animation choices.

To Animate a SmartArt Graphic

The bulleted lists on the text slides are animated, and you can build on this effect by adding animation to the Slide 3 SmartArt graphic. You can add a custom animation to each shape in the cycle, but you also can use one of PowerPoint's built-in animations to simplify the animation procedure. The following steps apply the built-in Fly In animation effect to the cycle diagram.

1

- With the SmartArt graphic selected, click Animations on the Ribbon to display the Animations tab.

- Click the Animate button arrow in the Animations group on the Animations tab to display the Animate list (Figure 6–61).

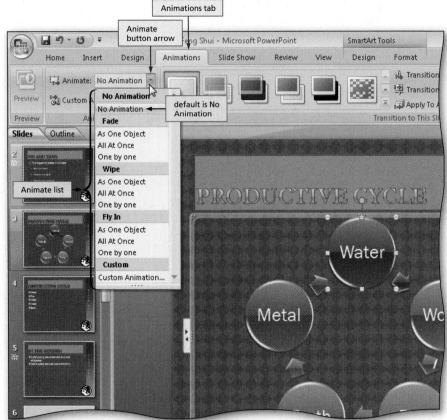

Figure 6–61

2

- Point to One by one in the Fly In category in the Animations list to preview the animation on Slide 3 (Figure 6–62).

Experiment

- Click some of the animations in the various categories and watch the animations preview on Slide 3.

3

- Click One by one in the Fly In category to apply this animation to the SmartArt graphic.

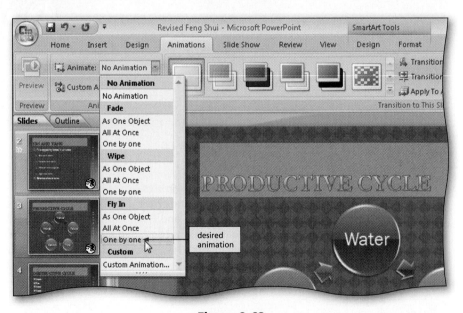

Figure 6–62

To Delete a Slide

Now that you have been working with the slides to illustrate various feng shui concepts, you decide that the Destructive Cycle material on Slide 4 is not necessary. The following steps delete Slide 4 from the presentation.

- Display Slide 4 and then click the Home tab (Figure 6–63).

- Click the Delete button in the Slides group to delete Slide 4.

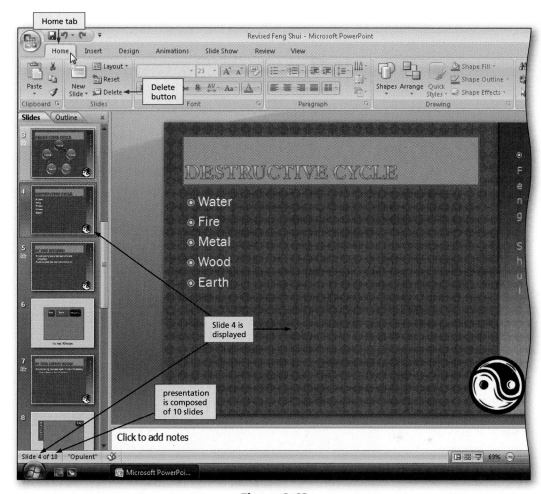

Figure 6–63

Other Ways
1. Right-click Slide 4 thumbnail, click Delete Slide

BTW

Deleting Multiple Slides
In this project you deleted only one slide. You may, however, want to delete multiple slides in a presentation. To select multiple sequential slides, click the first slide you want to delete, press and hold down the SHIFT key, and then click the last slide you want to delete. To select multiple slides that are nonsequential, press and hold down the CTRL key while you click each slide that you want to delete. Then click the Delete button.

To Animate a Shape Using a Motion Path

Slides 5, 7, and 9 contain shapes representing basic elements in three rooms of our homes: the kitchen, living room, and bedroom. Some interior decorators use feng shui principles to arrange these elements and thereby direct the flow of chi energy. The slides in your presentation help illustrate these principles, but they can be enhanced with animation to show audience members how to move appliances and furniture or install a screen so that their homes can benefit from enhanced chi movement.

One of the more effective methods of animating shapes is to use a motion path to predetermine the route the shape will follow. In your presentation, the shapes will move from negative locations to optimal locations on the slides along motion paths. The first bulleted list item on Slide 4 states the feng shui guideline that the stove should not be located between the sink and refrigerator. To solve this problem on Slide 5, you first move the refrigerator and then move the stove to the area where the refrigerator initially was located. The following steps apply a motion path to the Slide 5 refrigerator.

- Display Slide 5 and then click the Animations tab. Click the refrigerator shape to select it.

- Click the Custom Animation button in the Animations group to display the Custom Animation task pane.

- Click the Add Effect button and then point to Motion Paths in the Add Effect menu to display the Motion Paths menu (Figure 6–64).

Q&A Why does my list of motion paths differ from what is shown in Figure 6–64?

As with the entrance effects, the effects in the motion paths list are dynamic; they change based upon whether you have viewed and applied them previously in a presentation.

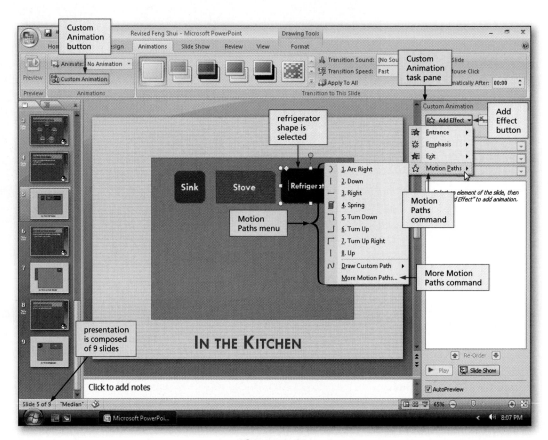

Figure 6–64

2

- Click More Motion Paths in the Motion Paths menu and then click Turn Down in the Lines & Curves category (Figure 6–65).

 Experiment

- Click some of the motion paths in the various categories and watch the refrigerator move on Slide 5.

 Can I move the Add Motion Path dialog box so that I can see the movement on the slide?

Yes. Click the dialog box title bar and drag the box to a location where you can view the refrigerator.

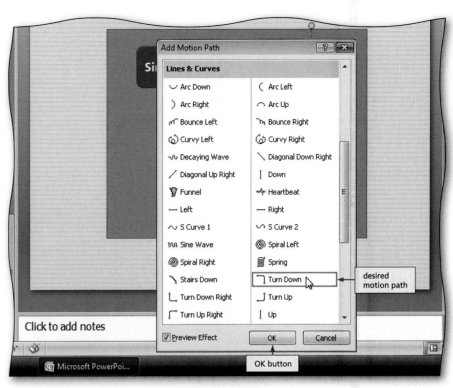

Figure 6–65

3

- Click the OK button to apply the Turn Down motion path to the refrigerator.

- Click the Start arrow in the Custom Animation task pane to display the Start menu (Figure 6–66).

4

- Click With Previous in the Start menu to change the animation from On Click to With Previous.

Q&A Why did the number that was displayed in a box on the left side of the shape change from a 1 to a 0?

The 0 indicates that the animation will play immediately when the slide is displayed. The presenter will not need to click the mouse or press the SPACEBAR to start the animation.

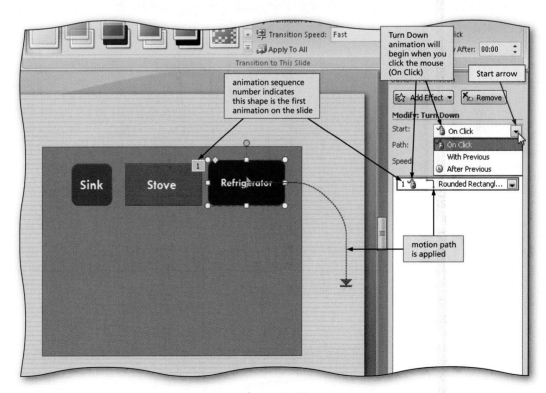

Figure 6–66

To Adjust a Motion Path

The Turn Down motion path moves the refrigerator in the correct direction, but the path is outside the green rectangle representing the kitchen walls. The green triangle in the middle of the refrigerator shape indicates the starting point, and the red triangle along the right side of the slide indicates the stopping point. For the maximum animation effect on the slide, you would like to move the stopping point inside the green rectangle and farther down the slide. The following steps move the stopping point on the Slide 5 refrigerator shape.

- With the refrigerator motion path displayed, click the red stopping point triangle to select the motion path.

- With your cursor displayed as a two-headed arrow, drag the stopping point to the location shown in Figure 6–67.

Q&A My entire motion path moved. How can I move only the red stopping point arrow?

Be certain your cursor is a two-headed arrow and not a four-headed arrow.

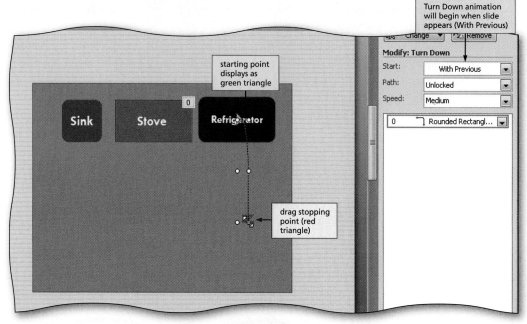

Figure 6–67

❷

- Drag the green starting point to the location shown in Figure 6–68.

- Click the Play button in the Custom Animation task pane to view the refrigerator animation (Figure 6–68).

Q&A My animation is not exactly like the path shown in Figure 6–68. Can I change the path?

Yes. Continue adjusting the starting and stopping points and playing the animation until you are satisfied with the effect.

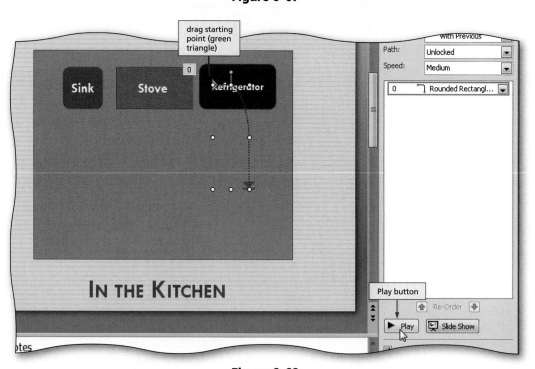

Figure 6–68

To Animate Another Shape

The bulleted text on Slide 4 describes a feng shui principle that sufficient space should exist between the stove and sink. Now that the refrigerator shape is moved on Slide 5, you can animate the stove and move it to the location previously held by the refrigerator. The following steps apply a motion path to the stove to move it to the right.

1 With the Custom Animation task pane displayed, click the stove shape to select it, click the Add Effect button, point to Motion Paths in the Add Effect menu, and then click More Motion Paths in the Motion Paths menu.

2 Click Right in the Lines & Curves category and then click the OK button to apply this motion path to the stove.

3 Click the Start arrow in the Custom Animation task pane to display the Start menu and then click With Previous.

4 Click the Play button in the Custom Animation task pane to view the animations (Figure 6–69).

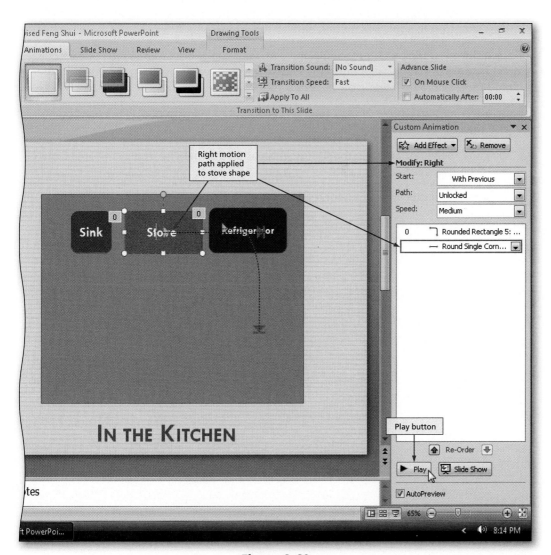

Figure 6–69

To Insert and Format a Shape and Then Apply a Motion Path

The Turn Down motion path moves the refrigerator in the correct direction and the Right motion path moves the stove to the area previously occupied by the refrigerator. To further emphasize this movement, you can add an arrow in the space where the stove originally was placed. The following steps add an arrow symbol, format this shape, and then apply a motion path.

1 Click Insert on the Ribbon to display the Insert tab. Click the Shapes button in the Illustrations group and then click the Left-Right Arrow shape (row 1, column 5 in the Block Arrows area).

2 Click Slide 5 at the bottom edge of the green rectangle. Drag a corner sizing handle so that the arrow shape is approximately the size shown in Figure 6–70 and then move the arrow to the location shown in this figure.

3 Click the Home tab and then click the Shape Quick Styles button in the Drawing group. Click the Intense Effect – Accent 5 Shape Quick Style (row 6, column 6) to apply this format to the arrow.

4 Click the Add Effect button in the Custom Animation task pane, point to Motion Paths, and then click More Motion Paths. Click Up in the Lines & Curves category and then click the OK button to apply this motion path to the arrow.

5 Click the red stopping point triangle and with your cursor displayed as a two-headed arrow, drag the stopping point to the middle of the stove shape. Drag the green starting point triangle to the middle of the arrow, if necessary.

6 Click the Start box arrow in the Custom Animation task pane to display the Start menu and then click With Previous.

7 Click the Speed box arrow in the Custom Animation task pane to display the Speed menu and then click Very Slow.

8 Click the Play button in the Custom Animation task pane to view the animations (Figure 6–70).

BTW

Creating a Custom Show
A custom show allows you to adapt your presentation to various audiences. For example, you can have one show that fits a 20-minute time constraint and a second show on the same topic that fits an hour schedule. The two types of custom shows are basic and hyperlinked. A basic show is a subset of the original presentation and contains selected slides. A hyperlinked show navigates to one or more separate presentations from your main show. To create a basic custom show, click the Custom Slide Show button in the Start Slide Show group on the Slide Show tab and then click Custom Shows. Create a new show and then select the slides you want to include. To create a hyperlinked custom show, follow the steps above to create a basic show and then click the Hyperlink button in the Links group on the Insert tab. Click Place in This Document under Link to and then select either the custom show or a particular slide that you want to view.

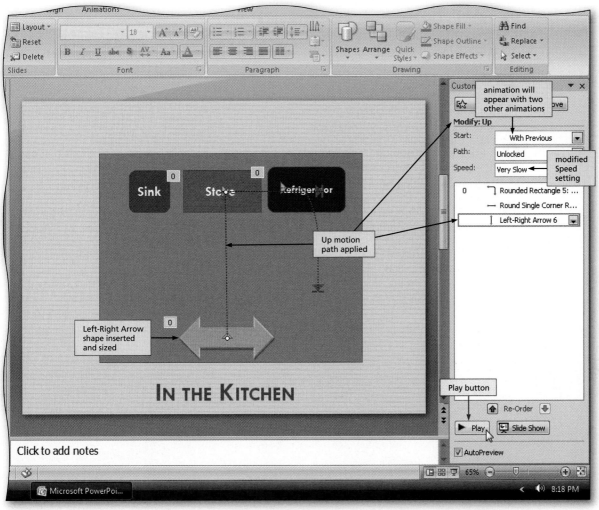

Figure 6–70

To Insert and Format a Second Shape and Then Apply Effects

The feng shui principle on Slide 6 states that a door and a balcony should not directly oppose each other. If they do, the chi energy is likely to enter one side of a room and then quickly exit on the opposite side without having a chance to flow throughout the space. A screen divider placed between the door and balcony will divert the chi. You can represent this concept by adding a rectangle to the room depicted on Slide 7 and then animating this shape. Both of these animations will play automatically in the sequence you specify. The following steps add a rectangle symbol, which is the division sign, format this shape, and then apply both an entrance effect and a motion path.

1 Display Slide 7. Display the Insert tab, click the Shapes button in the Illustrations group, and then click the Division shape (column 4 in the Equation Shapes area).

2 Click Slide 7 at the lower-left corner of the green rectangle. Drag the green rotation handle to the right so that the rectangle displays vertically. Drag a top or bottom sizing handle so that the Division shape is approximately the size shown in Figure 6–71 and then move the shape to the location shown in this figure.

3 Display the Home tab and then click the Shape Quick Styles button in the Drawing group. Click the Light 1 Outline, Colored Fill – Dark 1 Quick Style (row 3, column 1) to apply this format to the shape.

BTW

Translating Text
Bilingual dictionaries can translate words and phrases into different languages. To use this feature, select the text and then click the Translate button on the Review tab. In the Research task pane, click the From list arrow and select the original language and then click the To list arrow and select the translation language. Users are cautioned to have humans check the translation when important or sensitive information is translated because the software translation may not preserve the text's full meaning and tone.

4 Click the Add Effect button in the Custom Animation task pane, point to Entrance, click More Effects, and then click Dissolve In in the Basic category. Click the OK button, click the Start arrow in the Custom Animation task pane to display the Start menu, and then click With Previous.

5 Click the Add Effect button, point to Motion Paths, and then click More Motion Paths. Click Turn Up in the Lines & Curves category and then click the OK button to apply this motion path to the Division shape.

6 Click the red stopping point triangle and then drag the stopping point to the top edge of the green background between the door and the balcony, as shown in Figure 6–71. Drag the green starting point triangle to the middle of the Division shape, if necessary.

7 Click the Start box arrow in the Custom Animation task pane to display the Start menu and then click With Previous. Click the Speed box arrow and change the speed to Slow.

8 Click the Play button in the Custom Animation task pane to view the animations (Figure 6–71).

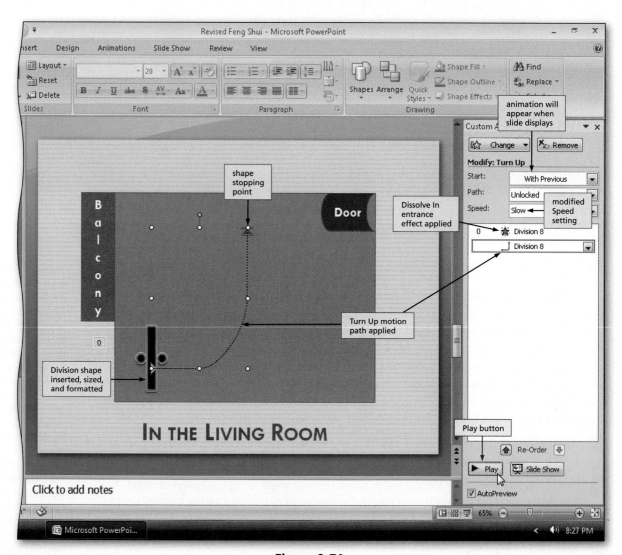

Figure 6–71

To Draw a Custom Motion Path

While PowerPoint supplies a wide variety of motion paths, at times they may not fit the precise animations your presentation requires. In that situation, you can draw a custom path that specifies the unique movement your slide element should make. Slide 8 presents the feng shui concept that the foot of a bed should not face a doorway. To illustrate this principle, you want to move the bed in Slide 9 to a location at the bottom of the slide. No preset motion path presents the exact motion you want to display, so you will draw your own custom path.

Drawing a custom path requires some practice and patience. You click the mouse to begin drawing the line. If you want the line to change direction, such as to curve, you click again. When you have completed drawing the path, you double-click to end the line. The following steps draw a custom motion path.

- With the Custom Animation task pane displayed, display Slide 9. Click the bed shape to select it.

- Click the Add Effect button, point to Motion Paths in the Add Effect menu, and then point to Draw Custom Path in the Motion Paths menu to display the Custom Path menu (Figure 6–72).

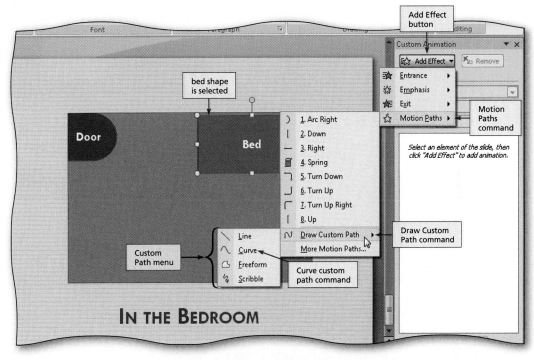

Figure 6–72

- Click Curve in the Custom Path menu.

- Click the bed shape and then move the mouse toward the door shape.

- Click the mouse on the right side of the door shape to indicate where the curve will start (Figure 6–73).

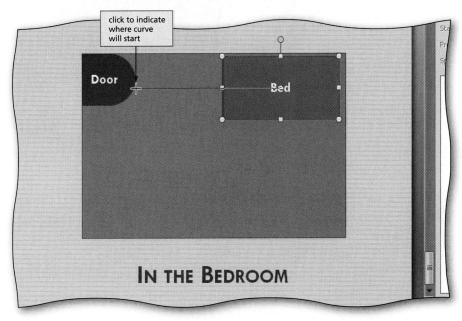

Figure 6–73

- Move the mouse pointer to the location shown in Figure 6–74, which is the ending point of the curve (Figure 6–74).

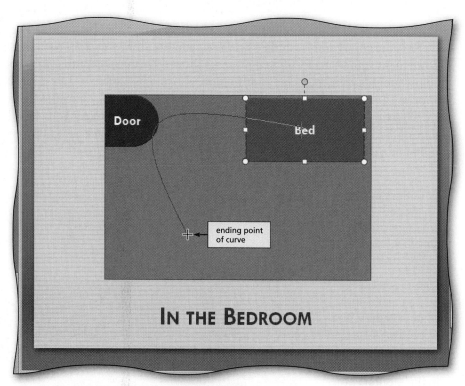

Figure 6–74

- Double-click to indicate the end of the curve.

- Click the Start arrow in the Custom Animation task pane and then click With Previous (Figure 6–75).

Q&A

If my curve is not correct, can I delete it?

Yes. Click the Remove button in the Custom Animation task pane and repeat the steps above.

- Click the Close button in the Custom Animation task pane so that it no longer is displayed.

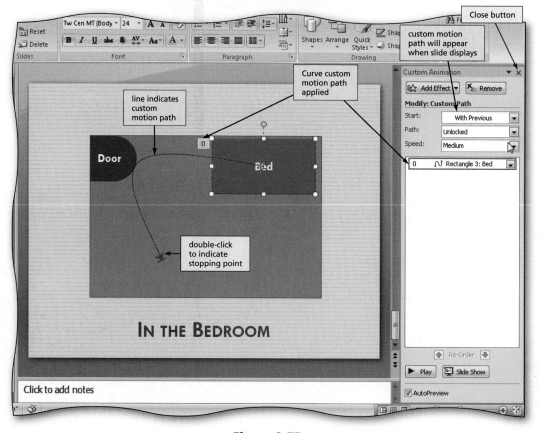

Figure 6–75

To Create a Self-Running Presentation

The feng shui presentation can accompany a speech, but it also can run unattended at furniture stores and home improvement seminars. When the last slide in the presentation is displayed, the slide show **loops**, or restarts, at Slide 1. PowerPoint has the option of running continuously until the user presses the ESC key. The following steps set the slide show to run in this manner.

1

• Click Slide Show on the Ribbon to display the Slide Show tab. Click the Set Up Show button in the Set Up group to display the Set Up Show dialog box (Figure 6–76).

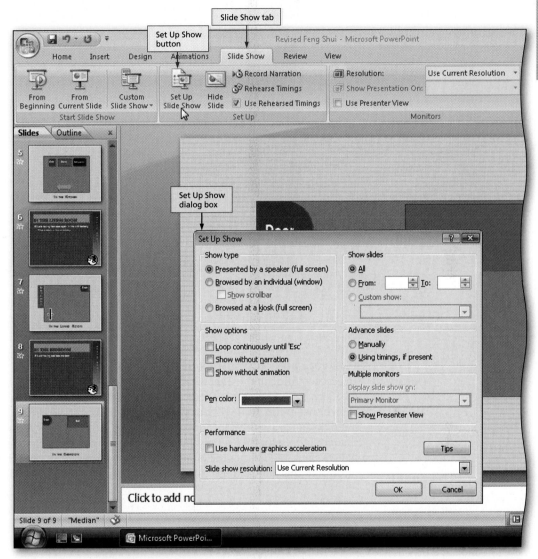

Figure 6–76

Creating a New Default Document Theme

The Office Theme document theme is applied by default. If you want to set another theme as the default, click the More button in the Themes gallery to expand the gallery, right-click the desired theme to set as the default, and then click Set as Default Theme. Every new presentation will use this new theme. You can reset the Office Theme or select another theme to use as the default.

● Click 'Browsed at a kiosk (full screen)' in the Show type area (Figure 6–77).

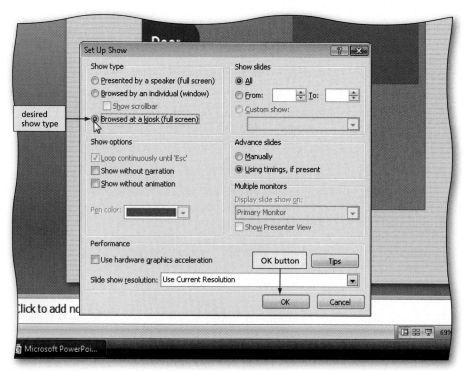

● Click the OK button to apply this show type.

Figure 6–77

Plan
Ahead

Give your audience sufficient time to view a slide.
The presentation in this chapter is designed to run at a kiosk continuously without a speaker's physical presence. Your audience, therefore, must read or view each slide and absorb the information without your help as a narrator. Be certain to give them time to read the slide and grasp the concept you are presenting. They will become frustrated if the slide changes before they have finished viewing and assimilating the material. As you set the slide timings, read each slide aloud and note the amount of time that elapses. Add a few seconds to this time and use this amount for the total time the slide is displayed.

BTW

Participating in the Customer Experience Improvement Program
Microsoft encourages Office users to participate in its Customer Experience Improvement Program in an effort to enhance the software's performance, reliability, and quality. Participants sign up for the program in the Trust Center and agree to allow Microsoft to collect information automatically and anonymously about their computers generally once daily. This information includes error messages, type of hardware, performance, and difficulties running Microsoft software. Users can stop participating at any time.

To Add Slide Timings

You need to determine the length of time each slide should be displayed. Audience members need sufficient time to read the text and watch the animations. Table 6–1 specifies the length of time each slide should be displayed.

Table 6–1 Slide Timings	
Slide Number	**Display Time**
1	00:10
2	00:20
3	00:15
4	00:10
5	00:15
6	00:10

Table 6–1 Slide Timings *(continued)*	
Slide Number	**Display Time**
7	00:15
8	00:10
9	00:15

The following steps add slide timings to the presentation.

1 Display the Animations tab, and then display Slide 1.

2 Use the Automatically After up arrow in the Transition to This Slide group to change the time to 00:10.

3 Repeat Steps 1 and 2 above to set the timing for the remaining slides according to Table 6–1.

4 Click the Slide Sorter view button to review the slide timings (Figure 6–78).

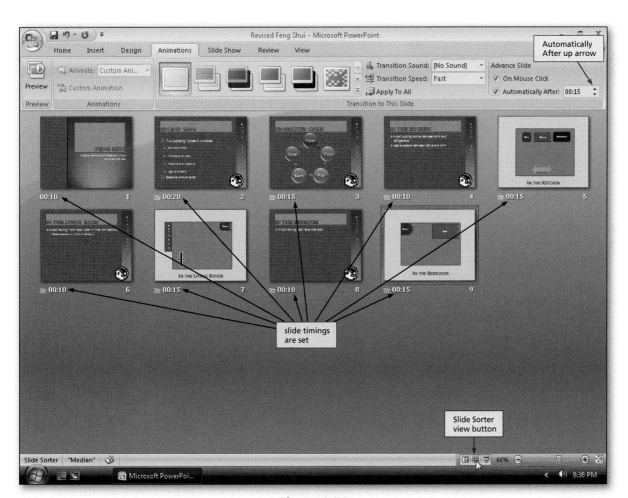

Figure 6–78

Add a Transition between Slides

A final enhancement you will make in this presentation is to apply the Uncover Right transition in the Wipes category to all slides and change the transition speed to Slow. The following steps apply this transition to the presentation.

1 With the Animations tab displayed, click the Normal view button and then expand the Transitions gallery.

2 Click the Uncover Right transition (row 2, column 2) in the Wipes category in the Transitions gallery.

3 Change the Transition Speed to Slow.

4 Apply the transition to all slides in the presentation.

To Run an Animated Slide Show

All changes are complete. You now can view the Revised Feng Shui presentation. The following steps run the presentation.

1 Click Slide 1 in the Slides pane to display the title slide and then click the Slide Show button to display the title slide.

2 As each slide is displayed automatically, review the information.

3 When Slide 1 is displayed again, press the ESC key to stop the presentation.

To Preview and Print Handouts

All changes are complete. You now can create handouts to accompany the slide show. The following steps preview and then print the presentation.

1 Click the Office button, point to Print, and then click Print Preview on the Print submenu.

2 Click the Print What arrow in the Page Setup group and then click Handouts (6 Slides Per Page) in the Print What list.

3 Click the Print button in the Print group.

4 Click the OK button in the Print dialog box to print the handouts (Figure 6–79).

5 Click the Close Print Preview button in the Preview group on the Print Preview tab to return to Normal view.

To Change Document Properties and Save the Presentation

Before saving the presentation again, you want to add your name, class name, and some keywords as document properties. The following steps use the Document Information Panel to change document properties and then save the project.

1 Click the Office Button, point to Prepare, and then click Properties on the 'Prepare the document for distribution' submenu.

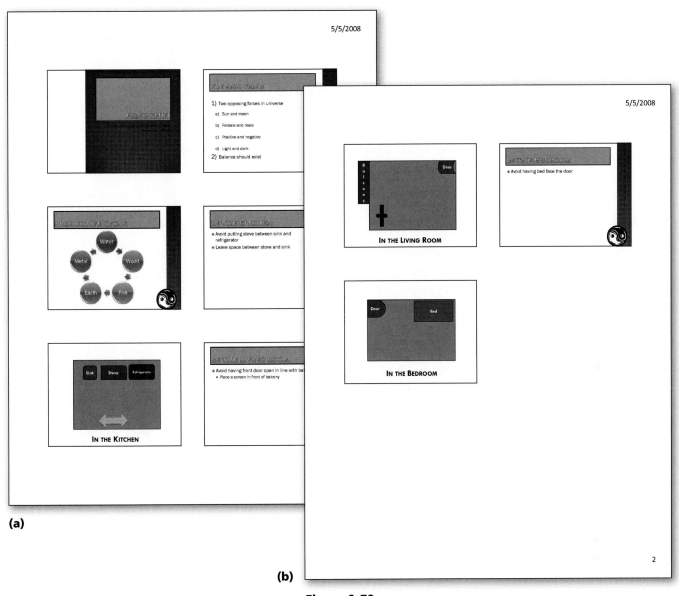

(a)

(b)

Figure 6–79

② Type your name as the Author property and your course and section as the Subject properties.

③ Type `feng shui, chi, Productive Cycle` as the Keywords property.

④ Close the Document Information Panel.

⑤ Click the Save button to overwrite the previous Revised Feng Shui file on the USB flash drive.

To Quit PowerPoint

This project is complete. The following steps quit PowerPoint.

1 Click the Close button on the right side of the title bar to quit PowerPoint; or if you have multiple PowerPoint documents open, click the Office Button and then click the Exit PowerPoint button on the Office Button menu to close all open documents and quit PowerPoint.

2 If necessary, click the No button in the Microsoft Office PowerPoint dialog box so that any changes you have made are not saved.

Chapter Summary

In this chapter you have learned how to format a slide master with a font theme, background, Quick Style, background graphic, and new placeholder. You also changed bullet characters to a numbered list, inserted slides from another presentation, animated a SmartArt graphic, added entrance effects, and created motion paths. The items listed below include all the new PowerPoint skills you have learned in this chapter.

1. Display the Slide Master (PPT 382)
2. Apply Slide and Font Themes to a Slide Master (PPT 383)
3. Format a Slide Master Background and Apply a Quick Style (PPT 387)
4. Add a Background Graphic to a Slide Master (PPT 389)
5. Insert a Placeholder into Slide Layouts (PPT 391)
6. Add and Format Placeholder Text (PPT 392)
7. Copy a Placeholder to the Slide Master (PPT 394)
8. Close Master View (PPT 396)
9. Change a First-Level Bullet Character to a Number (PPT 397)
10. Change a Second-Level Bullet Character to a Number (PPT 398)
11. Format a First-Level Numbered List (PPT 399)
12. Format a Second-Level Numbered List (PPT 401)
13. Change the Second-Level Paragraph Line Spacing (PPT 401)
14. Align Text in a Content Placeholder (PPT 402)
15. Insert a Slide into a Presentation (PPT 404)
16. Insert the Remaining Slides into an Original Presentation (PPT 408)
17. Animate a Bulleted List (PPT 409)
18. Change Animation Speed and Grouping (PPT 411)
19. Dim Text after Animation (PPT 414)
20. Animate and Dim Text on the Remaining Text Slides (PPT 415)
21. Animate a SmartArt Graphic (PPT 418)
22. Delete a Slide (PPT 419)
23. Animate a Shape Using a Motion Path (PPT 420)
24. Adjust a Motion Path (PPT 422)
25. Draw a Custom Motion Path (PPT 427)
26. Create a Self-Running Presentation (PPT 429)

 If you have a SAM user profile, you may have access to hands-on instruction, practice, and assessment. Log in to your SAM account (http://sam2007.course.com) to launch any assigned training activities or exams that relate to the skills covered in this chapter.

Learn It Online

Test your knowledge of chapter content and key terms.

Instructions: To complete the Learn It Online exercises, start your browser, click the Address bar, and then enter the Web address scsite.com/ppt2007/learn. When the Office 2007 Learn It Online page is displayed, click the link for the exercise you want to complete and then read the instructions.

Chapter Reinforcement TF, MC, and SA
A series of true/false, multiple choice, and short answer questions that test your knowledge of the chapter content.

Flash Cards
An interactive learning environment where you identify chapter key terms associated with displayed definitions.

Practice Test
A series of multiple choice questions that test your knowledge of chapter content and key terms.

Who Wants To Be a Computer Genius?
An interactive game that challenges your knowledge of chapter content in the style of a television quiz show.

Wheel of Terms
An interactive game that challenges your knowledge of chapter key terms in the style of the television show *Wheel of Fortune*.

Crossword Puzzle Challenge
A crossword puzzle that challenges your knowledge of key terms presented in the chapter.

Apply Your Knowledge

Reinforce the skills and apply the concepts you learned in this chapter.

Formatting a Slide Master and Applying Entrance and Emphasis Effects
Instructions: Start PowerPoint. Open the presentation, Apply 6-1 Everglades, from the Data Files for Students. See the inside back cover of this book for instructions on downloading the Data Files for Students, or contact your instructor for more information about accessing required files.

The four slides in the presentation present information about endangered wildlife found in the Everglades. The document you open is an unformatted presentation. You are to display the slide master and then apply slide and font themes, format a background, and apply a Quick Style, so the slides look like Figure 6–80.

Perform the following tasks:
1. Display the Slide Master tab and then display the Two Content Layout slide master. Click the Insert Placeholder button in the Master Layout group and insert a text placeholder above the date, footer, and page number placeholders at the bottom of the slide.
2. Type Everglades National Park in this new placeholder, change the font to Baskerville Old Face (or a similar font), change the font size to 24, and then change the font color to Green. Click the Bullets button arrow and then click None to remove the bullet. Align the text in the middle of the placeholder and then center the text.
3. Add the Technic document theme and then change the presentation theme colors to Paper and the theme font to Equity. Exit Master view.
4. Apply the Ease In Entrance effect to the title text on each slide. Change the Start animation from On Click to After Previous and the Speed to Slow. On Slide 1, add the Contrasting Color emphasis effect, change the Start animation to After Previous, and change the Speed to Very Slow.

Continued >

Apply Your Knowledge *continued*

5. Apply the Split Entrance effect to the bulleted lists on Slides 2, 3, and 4. Change the Start animation from On Click to After Previous and the Speed to Slow. Dim the text after animation.

6. Add the Shape Diamond wipe transition (row 5, column 6) to all slides and change the transition speed to Slow.

7. Set the slide timings to 10 seconds for Slide 1 and 15 seconds for the other three slides. Create a self-running presentation to browse at a kiosk. Run the show to check the timings, effects, and transitions.

8. Change the document properties, as specified by your instructor. Save the presentation using the file name, Apply 6-1 Formatted Everglades. Submit the revised document in the format specified by your instructor.

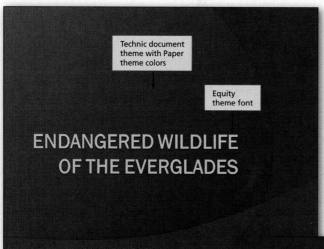

(a)

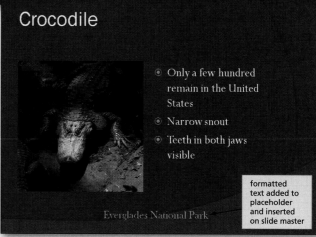

(b)

Figure 6–80

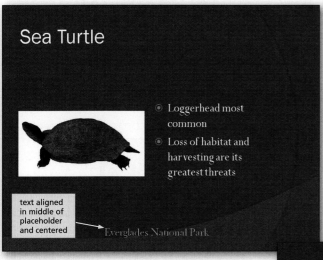

(c)

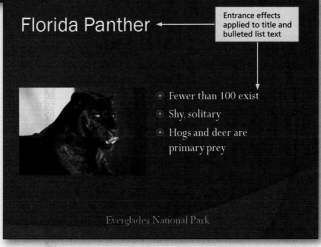

(d)

Figure 6–80 (*continued*)

Extend Your Knowledge

Extend the skills you learned in this chapter and experiment with new skills. You may need to use Help to complete the assignment.

Inserting a Placeholder and Aligning Text

Instructions: Start PowerPoint. Open the presentation, Extend 6-1 Census, from the Data Files for Students. See the inside back cover of this book for instructions on downloading the Data Files for Students, or contact your instructor for more information about accessing required files.

You will insert a placeholder on the left side of the slide and then add text, change the alignment and orientation of the text boxes on the chart bars, and change the animation effect and speed (Figure 6–81).

Perform the following tasks:

1. Display the Slide Master tab and then click the Insert Placeholder button in the Master Layout group. Insert a text placeholder beside the title and text placeholder on the left side of the slide.

2. Select the new placeholder, delete all the default text in this placeholder, type U.S. Census, and then drag the bottom sizing handle down to align with the bottom of the text placeholder. Display the Home tab, click the Text Direction button, and then change the text direction to Stacked. Change the font, the font size, and the font color. Change the text alignment.

Continued >

Extend Your Knowledge *continued*

3. Exit Master view. Change the text direction for each percent label in the 1970, 1980, 1990, and 2000 bars to Stacked and then reduce the font size.

4. Change the Entrance effect for each of the bars from Blinds to another appropriate effect and change the Start animation to After Previous. Select a speed other than Very Fast.

5. Add a background style. Insert your name in a footer along with the date and time updated automatically.

6. Change the document properties, as specified by your instructor. Save the presentation using the file name, Extend 6-1 Revised Census.

7. Submit the revised document in the format specified by your instructor.

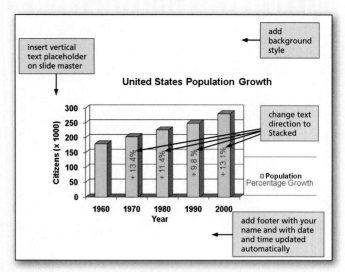

Figure 6–81

Make It Right

Analyze a presentation and correct all errors and/or improve the design.

Formatting a Slide Master Background

Instructions: Start PowerPoint. Open the presentation, Make It Right 6-1 Tents, from the Data Files for Students. See the inside back cover of this book for instructions on downloading the Data Files for Students, or contact your instructor for more information about accessing required files.

The presentation has unsuitable entrance effects applied, small clips, and inconsistent numbering. Correct the formatting problems and errors in the presentation while keeping in mind the guidelines presented in this chapter.

Perform the following tasks:

1. Display the Trek Slide Master. Insert the Tent picture from your Data Files for Students into the slide master, size it, and then position it in the upper-right corner. Insert your name in a footer on all slides.

2. Use the same numbering format on Slides 2, 3, and 4 for the first- and second-level numbered lists.

3. Change the font theme to a theme other than Trek, shown in Figure 6–82.

4. Increase the size of the clips on Slides 2, 3, and 4 so they display prominently on the slides. Insert the Tent picture on Slide 1 and increase its size. Change the entrance effects on the clips on Slides 2, 3, and 4 to one effect in the Moderate category and decrease the speed from Fast.

5. On Slide 2, change the line spacing from 1.0 to another spacing that fits the content placeholder. Also, dim the bulleted list paragraphs after each one is displayed.

6. Change the slide transitions to a fade or dissolve.

7. Set the timings for Slide 1 to 10 seconds and for Slides 2, 3, and 4 to 5 seconds. Create a self-running presentation to browse at a kiosk. Run the show to check the timings, effects, and transitions.

8. Use the spell checker to help correct the misspellings.

9. Change the document properties, as specified by your instructor. Save the presentation using the file name, Make It Right 6-1 Revised Tents.

10. Submit the revised document in the format specified by your instructor.

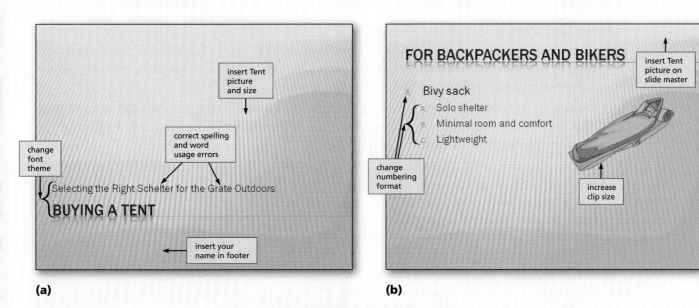

(a)　　　　　　　　　　　　　　　　　　　　(b)

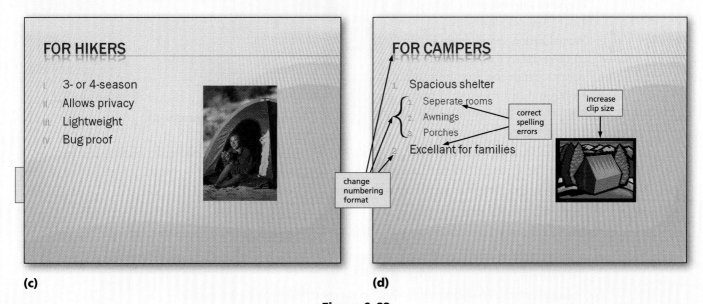

(c)　　　　　　　　　　　　　　　　　　　　(d)

Figure 6–82

In the Lab

Design and/or create a presentation using the guidelines, concepts, and skills presented in this chapter. Labs 1, 2, and 3 are listed in order of increasing difficulty.

Lab 1: Removing, Changing, and Adding Animations

Problem: Abraham Maslow attempted to explain the factors that dictate human behavior. You are studying Maslow's Hierarcy of Needs in your Psychology 101 class and want to develop an animated graphic showing this concept. You create a presentation, which is on your Data Files for Students, and then decide to remove, change, and add animations present in the graphic, which is shown in Figure 6–83.

Instructions: Perform the following tasks:

1. Open the presentation, Lab 6-1 Maslow, from the Data Files for Students. See the inside back cover of this book for instructions on downloading the Data Files for Students, or contact your instructor for more information about accessing required files.

2. Display the Animations tab, click the Custom Animation button in the Animation group, and then click Rectangle 4: Maslow's Hierarchy of Needs in the Animation Order list. Click the Change button to display the Change menu.

3. Point to Emphasis, click More Effects to display the Change Emphasis Effect dialog box, and then select Color Wave in the Subtle category. Change the Start animation from On Click to After Previous and the Speed to Fast.

4. Delete the effect from the Physiological shape. Change the entrance effects for the Safety, Love, Esteem, and Self-Actualization shapes from Fly In to Descend in the Moderate category, change the Start animation from On Click to With Previous, and then change the Speed to Medium for these four hierarchy shapes.

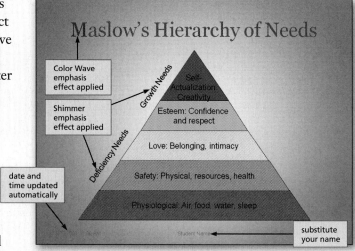

Figure 6–83

5. Add the Shimmer Emphasis Effect in the Moderate category to the two text boxes: Deficiency Needs and Growth Needs. Change the Start animation for both text boxes from On Click to With Previous, and then change the Speed to Slow.

6. Add the Style 9 background style.

7. Insert your name in a footer along with the date and time updated automatically.

8. Change the document properties, as specified by your instructor. Save the presentation using the file name, Lab 6-1 Revised Maslow.

9. Submit the revised document in the format specified by your instructor.

In the Lab

Lab 2: Formatting a Slide Master, Inserting a Slide, Formatting a Numbered List, and Changing SmartArt Animation

Problem: The sources of today's stressors likely come from external factors in our lives and internal reactions while under duress. If we do not release the tension, our bodies react with troubled sleep, back and neck pain, and other health-related problems. You have decided to create the PowerPoint presentation shown in Figures 6-84a through 6-84d to show in your Health 101 class, where you are studying how stress affects our lives.

Instructions: Perform the following tasks:

1. Open the presentation, Lab 6-2 Stress Awareness, from the Data Files for Students. See the inside back cover of this book for instructions on downloading the Data Files for Students, or contact your instructor for more information about accessing required files.

2. Apply the Metro document theme. Display the Slide Master tab and then insert the Stress Photo from the Data Files for Students. Size the photo so that the height is 2" and the width is 1.39". Drag the photo to the upper-right corner of the Metro Slide Master. Copy the resized Stress Photo to the upper-right corner of the Comparison and the Title and Content layouts.

3. Change the presentation theme colors to Solstice. Create a new Theme Font named Stress using Century Gothic for the heading font and Verdana for the body font. Add your name as the Footer text. Close Master view.

4. On Slide 2, change the three bullet characters in each placeholder to the 1. 2. 3. numbering format. Change the numbering color to Red and the size to 100% of text. Change the line spacing to 2.0. Apply the Fade Entrance animation and have the text display All At Once. Dim the text after animation. Move the two pictures to the locations shown in Figure 6–84b.

5. On Slide 3, convert the bulleted list to the Basic Matrix SmartArt style (column 1 in the Matrix category) and apply the Colorful Range – Accent Colors 4 to 5 (column 4 in the Colorful category). Apply the Fade Entrance animation and have the squares display One by one.

6. Delete Slide 4. Insert the one slide in the Stress Graphic file from the Data Files for Students. Do not keep the source formatting. Change the colors to the Colorful Range – Accent Colors 4 to 5.

7. On Slide 1, add the Arc Right motion path to the picture. Change the animation to With Previous and the speed to Slow. Adjust the motion path so that the stopping point is in the area between the title text and the bottom of the slide.

8. On Slide 2, add the Box Entrance effect to both pictures. Change the animation to With Previous, the direction to Out, and the speed to Medium.

9. Apply the Box Out transition (row 3, column 3 in the Wipes category) to all slides. Change the speed to Medium. Check the spelling and correct any errors.

10. Change the document properties, as specified by your instructor. Save the presentation using the file name, Lab 6-2 Revised Stress.

11. Submit the revised document in the format specified by your instructor.

Continued >

In the Lab *continued*

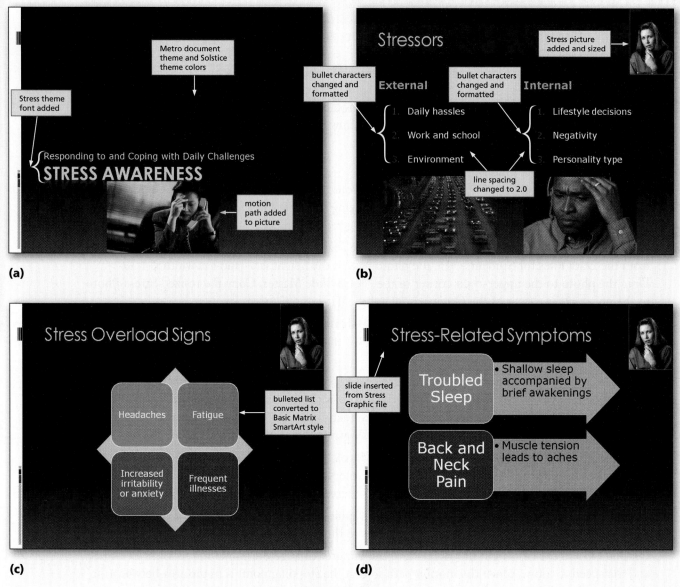

(a)

(b)

(c)

(d)

Figure 6–84

In the Lab

Lab 3: Creating a Presentation with Animation

Problem: Credit card debt has more than doubled among college students. More than 83 percent own at least one credit card, and their average balance is approximately $2,300. You survey the students in your Economics 101 class to gather information about their credit card use and then create the presentation in Figure 6–85. Slide 1 contains a resized photograph with a motion path, and Slides 2 and 3 contain SmartArt graphics with animations.

Instructions: Perform the following tasks:

1. Create a new presentation using the Module document theme. Change the presentation theme colors to Foundry and the theme font to Solstice. Insert the Canvas texture (row 1, column 2 in the Texture gallery) to format the background on all slides. Using Figure 6–85, type the Slide 1 title and subtitle text and the Slides 2 and 3 title text. Apply the Title and Content layout to Slides 2 and 3.

2. On Slide 1, insert the Credit Hands picture from your Data Files for Students and size the picture to 60%. Recolor the picture by applying the Sepia variation (column 2 in the Color Modes area). Add a 10 Point Soft Edges picture effect and then position the picture as shown in Figure 6–85a.

3. On Slide 2, insert the Linear Venn SmartArt graphic (row 8, column 1 in the Relationship gallery). Using Figure 6–85b, type the four lines of text in the graphic. Apply the Inset SmartArt Style (row 1, column 2 in the 3-D category) and then change the color to Colorful – Accent Colors (column 1 in the Colorful category).

4. On Slide 3, insert the Vertical Box List SmartArt graphic (row 1, column 4 in the List gallery). Using Figure 6–85c, type the three lines of text in the graphic. Apply the Metallic Scene SmartArt Style (row 2, column 2 in the 3-D category) and then change the color to Colorful – Accent Colors (column 1 in the Colorful category).

5. On Slide 1, animate the Credit Hands picture by drawing a custom motion path. To draw the path, select the picture, display the Custom Path menu, and then click Scribble. Draw the motion path shown in Figure 6–85a so that the picture moves diagonally downward to the bottom-middle edge of the slide and then diagonally upward to the top-left corner of the slide. Change the Start animation to With Previous and the Speed to Slow.

6. On Slide 2, apply the Fade 'One by one' Entrance animation to the SmartArt graphic. Change the Start animation to With Previous and the speed to Very Slow. Add a Spin Emphasis animation, change the Start animation to After Previous, the Amount to Counterclockwise, and the Speed to Very Slow.

7. On Slide 3, add the Peek In Entrance effect to the SmartArt graphic. Change the Start animation to With Previous, the Direction to From Right, and the speed to Medium. Click the Content Placeholder 5 arrow in the Custom Animation list, click Effect Options, and then click the SmartArt Animation tab in the Peek In dialog box. Click the Group graphic arrow and then click 'One by one'.

8. Set the timings for Slide 1 to 5 seconds and for Slides 2 and 3 to 10 seconds. Create a self-running presentation to browse at a kiosk. Run the show to check the timings, effects, and transitions.

9. Insert the slide number and your name in Slides 2 and 3. Apply the Split Vertical Out transition (row 4, column 6 in the Wipes category) to all slides. Change the speed to Slow. Check the spelling and correct any errors.

10. Click the Slide Sorter view button, view the slides for consistency, and then click the Normal view button. Run the slide show.

11. Change the document properties, as specified by your instructor. Save the presentation using the file name, Lab 6-3 Student Credit.

12. Submit the revised document in the format specified by your instructor.

Continued >

In the Lab *continued*

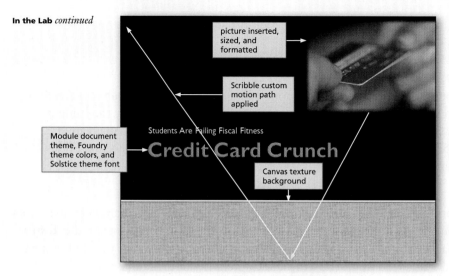

Figure 6–85 (a)

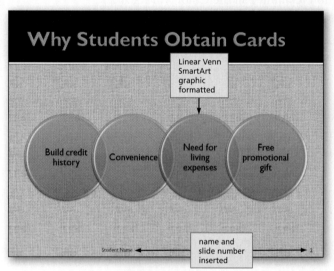

Figure 6–85 (b)

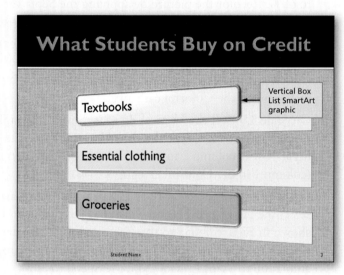

Figure 6–85 (c)

Cases and Places

Apply your creative thinking and problem solving skills to design and implement a solution.

• EASIER   •• MORE DIFFICULT

Note: Remember to use the 7 × 7 rule as you design the presentations: a maximum of seven words on a line and a maximum of seven lines on one slide.

• 1: Design and Create a Health and Wellness Institute Presentation

Your local fitness center is upgrading its services and programs. In turn, it is changing its name from "health club" to "health and wellness institute." New services are listed in Table 6–2.

New programs are listed in Table 6–3.

Create a self-running presentation announcing the name change. Include slides with SmartArt graphics listing the services and programs. Animate the text and the graphics. Apply at least three objectives found at the beginning of this chapter to develop the presentation. Apply slide transitions and a footer with your name and the page number on all slides. Be sure to check spelling.

Table 6–2 Health and Wellness Institute Services
Steam room and saunas
Massage therapy
Aquatic therapy
Café
Pro shop
Playroom
Conference / Meeting rooms

Table 6–3 Health and Wellness Institute Fitness Programs
Sports specific training
Personal training
Walking / running club
Children's activities
Aquatics
Yoga and Pilates
Self defense

• 2: Design and Create a Telemarketing Scams Presentation

Criminals steal money in a variety of ways, and one of the more profitable is through telemarketing schemes. Law enforcement professionals are reporting an increase in complaints about illegal telephone money solicitations. Con artists claiming to represent charities and law enforcement agencies prey upon unsuspecting citizens by stealing credit card numbers from unsuspecting citizens. Common scams are listed in Table 6–4.

People hearing one of the phrases in Table 6–5 should hang up immediately.

The Better Business Bureau Web site (http://bbb.org) and the Federal Trade Commission Web site (http://ftc.gov) include details about identifying and reporting these scams. Visit these sites and review the facts presented. Create a presentation using this information. Begin by displaying the slide master and applying slide and font themes. Format the slide master background and apply a Quick Style. Include one text slide with a bulleted list and two slides with SmartArt graphics listing the scams and pressure phrases. Animate the text and the graphics. Apply at least three objectives found at the beginning of this chapter to develop the presentation. Apply slide transitions and a footer with your name and the page number on all slides. Be sure to check spelling.

Table 6–4 Telemarketing Scams
Prizes / Sweepstakes
Free or discounted travel
Investments with high returns
Telephone slamming
Telephone cramming
Fake charities

Table 6–5 Pressure Phrases
"You have just won…"
"Congratulations! You have won the grand prize…"
"You have been specially selected…"
"You will receive a bonus if you sign up today…."

•• 3: Design and Create a Carbon Monoxide Presentation

Several thousand people suffer accidental carbon monoxide (CO) poisoning each year, and at least 200 of these people die from inhaling this gas. This colorless, odorless, and tasteless gas is called the "silent killer." Furnaces, ovens, clothes dryers, water heaters, and other fuel-burning appliances produce it, and so do fireplaces, barbeque grills, and wood-burning stoves. When the CO is not ventilated properly, home occupants can suffer flu-related symptoms (dizziness, severe headache, nausea, fatigue, and disorientation). CO detectors can help prevent many of these poisonings. Your local fire department chief has asked you to prepare a presentation about CO poisoning. He would like you to include an animated graphic with a safety checklist to help residents protect their homes. Review information about carbon monoxide on the Consumer Product Safety Commission Web site (http://cpsc.gov) and then develop the presentation for the fire chief. Included animated numbered lists with text aligned in the content placeholders. Apply at least three objectives found at the beginning of this chapter to develop the presentation.

Continued >

Cases and Places *continued*

•• 4: Design and Create a U.S. Senate Presentation

Make It Personal

The U.S. Senate Web site (www.senate.gov) has a wealth of information about Senators' biographies, legislation, and the Constitution. Also included is a chart showing the Senate organization. Review the information and then create a presentation about this governmental body. Include an animated chart displaying aspects of this latest Senate organization chart. Also include two slides featuring the two Senators from the state in which you reside; these two slides should have animated numbered lists with text aligned in the content placeholders and also hyperlinks to your Senators' Web sites. Apply slide transitions and a footer with your name and the slide number on all slides. Be sure to check spelling.

•• 5: Design and Create a Digital Camera Presentation

Working Together

Digital cameras offer convenience and fun for amateur and professional photographers alike. Buying this type of camera can be difficult, however, for people who are unfamiliar with the product. Have each member of your team call or visit a local electronics or camera store or conduct online research and gather information about digital single-lens reflex (SLR), slim, and long zoom cameras. Find details about megapixels, optical and digital zoom, scene modes, image stabilization, and storage media. After coordinating the data, create a self-running presentation with animated bulleted lists and pictures. Include an animated SmartArt graphic that can be used as a buying guide. Apply slide and font themes to the slide master, add a background graphic, and copy a placeholder. As a group, critique each slide. Submit your assignment in the format specified by your instructor.

Online Feature

Importing Files from the Microsoft Office Online Web Site

Objectives

You will have mastered the material in this feature when you can:

- Locate and download templates from the Microsoft Office Online Web site

- Save slides as images

- Add images to tables

- Select presentation resolution

- Change presentation orientation

- Write VBA code to create a unique presentation

Online Feature Introduction

The document themes included in Microsoft Office PowerPoint 2007 are visually appealing and present a wide variety of styles and appearances. To give your presentation a unique look, you can search the Microsoft Office Online Web site for additional themes and then download these files. This Web site also includes individual slides that fit a particular purpose, such as a monthly calendar, party invitations, and schedules.

You can customize and extend the capabilities of PowerPoint by using **Visual Basic for Applications** (**VBA**). This powerful programming language allows you to simplify tasks that you repeat frequently, such as updating a PowerPoint presentation with a daily calendar of campus events or featuring the athlete of the week.

Project — Presentation with Imported Templates and VBA

The five slides in the presentation (Figure 1) present information about Arbor Day. J. Sterling Morton started this holiday in 1872 as a day to plant a tree in support of the environment and as a way to emphasize the natural benefits of trees. The presentation has three slides that were imported as templates from the Microsoft Office Online Web site: relationship, hierarchy, and workflow. These templates are modified and then merged with a presentation with a title slide and table. The entire presentation resolution is changed to display favorably on wide-screen monitors, and two slides are saved as images so they easily can be reused in other programs and distributed as a handout.

Another aspect of this chapter is to add VBA code to the presentation so that viewers can be tested on their retention of material presented in the slide show. The inclusion of this programming introduces Visual Basic principles and demonstrates PowerPoint's versatility. One slide displays a question and prompts a user to select one of three answers. A message box displays feedback on whether this choice is correct.

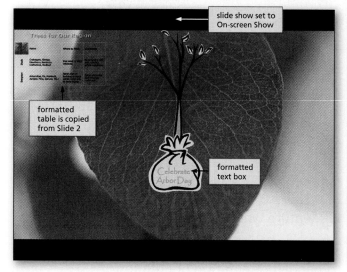

(a)

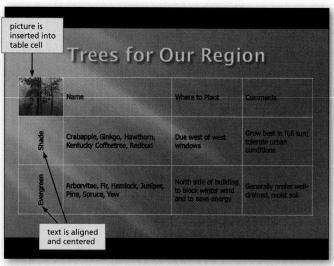

(b)

Figure 1 (continued)

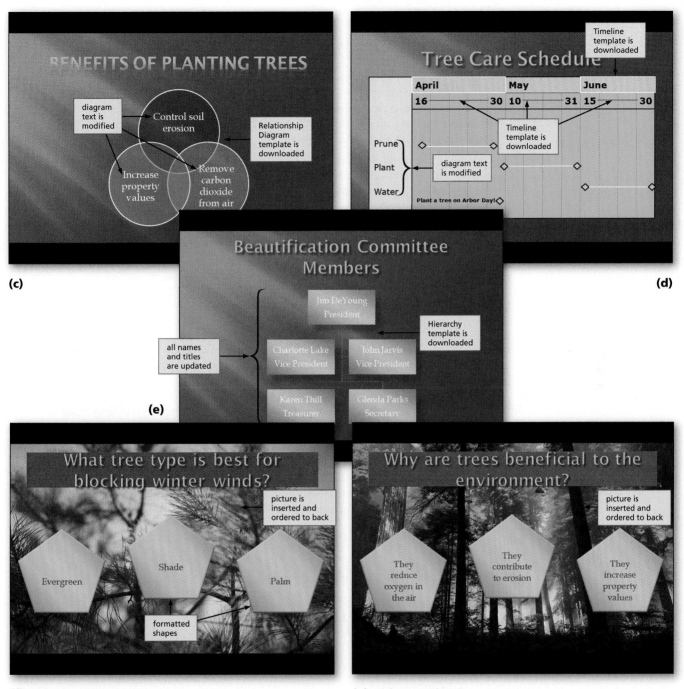

(c)

(d)

(e)

(f) **Quiz question 1**

(g) **Quiz question 2**

Figure 1

Overview

As you read through this feature, you will learn how to create the presentation shown in Figure 1 by performing these general tasks:

- Download SmartArt templates.
- Insert and modify shapes and text boxes.
- Order illustrations and other content.
- Modify tables.
- Write a VBA application.

General Project Guidelines

When creating a PowerPoint presentation, the actions you perform and decisions you make will affect the appearance and characteristics of the finished document. As you create a presentation with templates, such as the project shown in Figure 1, you should follow these general guidelines:

1. **Use a hierarchy chart to depict relationships.** A hierarchy chart is a good tool to help visualize how one concept relates to another. This graphic often is used to show corporate reporting lines and a family's genealogy.

2. **Determine the screen show ratio.** Consider where the presentation will be shown and the type of hardware that will be available. Wide-screen displays are gaining acceptance in the home office and corporate world, but their dimensions present design challenges for the PowerPoint developer.

3. **Desk check the application code before entering it into the Visual Basic Editor.** You can maximize your work time by stepping through your lines of code before you type these instructions on your computer. Viewing the program's structure and working through the instructions helps find errors before they arise during the program execution.

When necessary, more specific details concerning the above guidelines are presented at appropriate points in the feature. The feature also will identify the actions you perform and decisions you make regarding these guidelines during the creation of the presentation shown in Figure 1.

To Start PowerPoint, Open a Presentation, and Rename the Presentation

If you are using a computer to step through the project in this feature and you want your screens to match the figures in this book, you should change your computer's resolution to 1024 × 768. For information about how to change a computer's resolution, read Appendix E. The following steps start PowerPoint and open a presentation.

1 Start PowerPoint and then open the presentation, Arbor Day, from the Data Files for Students.

2 Maximize the PowerPoint window, if necessary.

3 Save the presentation as Arbor Day Revised.

4 Save the document on your USB flash drive.

BTW

Requesting Templates
Microsoft changes the templates based on requests from PowerPoint users and how frequently the templates are downloaded.

Downloading Templates from the Microsoft Office Online Web Site

Designers at Microsoft and other companies have created a wide variety of templates for PowerPoint that are stored on the Microsoft Office Online Web site. They are grouped in useful categories, including Award certificates, Calendars, Diagrams, Invitations, and Schedules. Some of these categories are subdivided into organized groupings. For example, the Presentations category is subdivided into Academic, Business, Design, Healthcare, and other groups. If you cannot locate the templates used in this feature, your instructor can provide the files needed to complete this presentation.

To Locate and Download a Relationship Diagram Template

One template you will use in your presentation is a Relationship diagram, which is a SmartArt graphic. You will locate this template, preview the design, and then **download**, or copy, it to your USB flash drive. Later you will insert it into your Arbor Day Revised presentation. To locate templates, you can type a keyword in the search text box or select a category in the left pane of the New Presentation dialog box. The following steps locate and download the Relationship diagram.

1

• Click the Office Button and then click New to display the New Presentation dialog box.

Q&A

Why do I see slides displaying in the Recently Used Templates area of my screen?

Figure 2 does not show any templates, but some may display on your screen if someone previously down-loaded templates. They remain in this area until you choose to delete them.

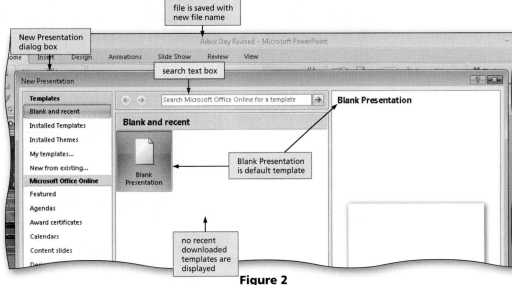

Figure 2

2

• Type relationship in the search text box and then click the Start searching button to search for and display all templates having the keyword, relationship.

Q&A

Can I enter more than one search term in the text box?

Yes. Entering more than one word helps narrow the search results.

• If necessary, click the Relationship diagram thumbnail to display a preview of and infor-mation about this diagram (Figure 3).

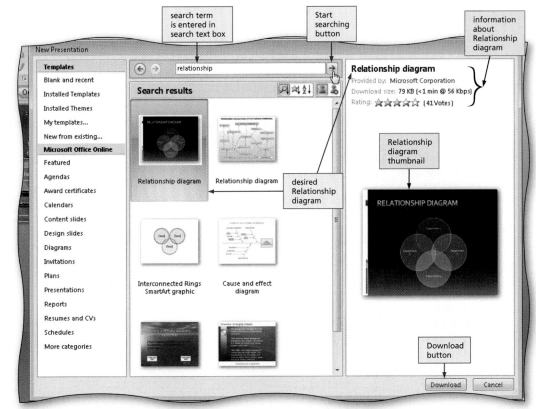

Figure 3

 Experiment

• Click various thumbnails in the Search results area to view a larger thumbnail and information about the template.

③

- With the Relationship diagram pictured in Figure 3 selected, click the Download button to download this template.

- If the Microsoft Office Genuine Advantage dialog box is displayed, click the Continue button to download the template.

- Save the Relationship diagram on your USB flash drive with the file name, Tree Relationship (Figure 4).

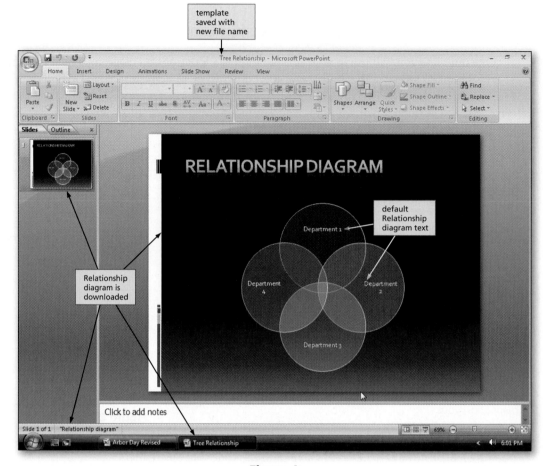

Figure 4

Downloading Templates

Each time you download a template, Microsoft checks your computer to ensure a genuine copy of Microsoft Office is installed. During your first download, Microsoft displays a dialog box informing you that the templates are available only to people with legitimate software. Once Microsoft verifies your software, the check is done without displaying this dialog box. If a nongenuine program is installed, Microsoft will display another dialog box alerting you to which programs are not legitimate, and provide a link to get more information about the steps you can take to make the software legitimate.

To Locate and Download a Timeline Template

You can increase your audience's understanding of when to prepare for and plant trees by using a timeline. The Microsoft Office Online Web site provides a variety of timelines, many of which are categorized in the Schedules group. The following steps locate and download the Three-month timeline template.

① Click the Office Button, click New, and then type `timeline` in the search text box in the New Presentation dialog box.

② Click the Start searching button to search for and display all templates having the keyword, timeline.

③ Click the Three-month timeline thumbnail shown in Figure 5 to select this template (Figure 5).

④ Click the Download button to download this template. If the Microsoft Office Genuine Advantage dialog box is displayed, click the Continue button to download the template.

⑤ Save the Three-month timeline diagram on your USB flash drive with the file name, Planting Timeline.

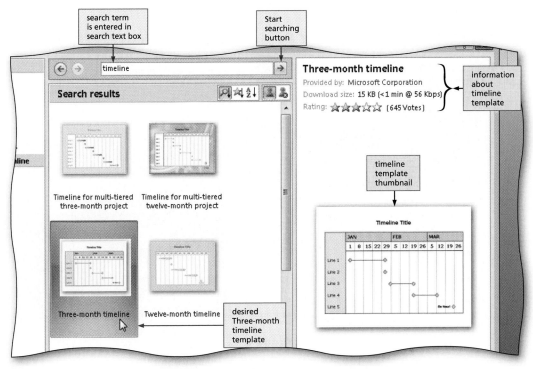

Figure 5

Plan
Ahead

Use a hierarchy chart to depict relationships.
One method of visually showing the structure of people or departments within a organization
is to use a **hierarchy chart**. This type of chart, also called an organization chart, depicts various functions or responsibilities as they relate to a company or organization. Hierarchy charts
are used in a variety of ways to depict relationships. For example, a company uses a hierarchy
chart to describe the relationships between the company's teams. In the engineering and
information sciences fields, organization charts often are used to show a process.

To Locate and Download a Hierarchy Template

Your community has a Beautification Committee. One method of displaying the
Committee structure is to use a hierarchy chart. The following steps locate and download
the Hierarchy diagram template.

1 Display the New Presentation dialog box, type `hierarchy` in the search text box, and
then click the Start searching button to search for and display all templates having the
keyword, hierarchy.

2 If necessary, click the Hierarchy diagram thumbnail shown in Figure 6 to select this template
(Figure 6 on the following page).

3 Click the Download button to download this template. If the Microsoft Office Genuine
Advantage dialog box is displayed, click the Continue button to download the template.

4 Save the Hierarchy diagram on your USB flash drive with the file name, Beautification
Committee.

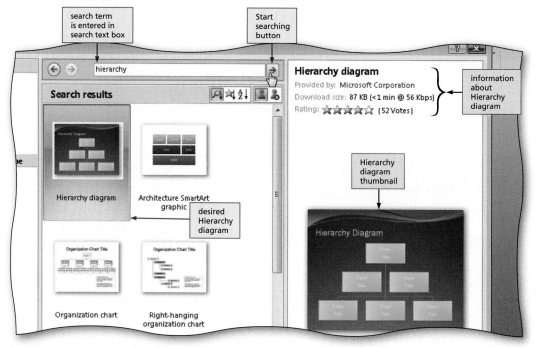

Figure 6

BTW

Deleting Downloaded Templates

If you decide you do not want to use a template you downloaded, you can delete it easily. Right-click a template in the Recently Used Templates area of the New Presentation dialog box and then click Remove template on the shortcut menu. If you want to delete all the templates you downloaded, click 'Remove all recent templates' on the shortcut menu.

Inserting Templates into a Presentation and Modifying Slides

The three downloaded templates are saved on your USB flash drive. You can add them to the Arbor Day Revised presentation and then modify the slide content. To ensure the slides have a consistent look, do not check the Keep source formatting box in the Reuse Slides task pane; the Apex design theme applied to the Arbor Day Revised presentation will then be applied to the newly inserted slides.

To Insert Templates into a Presentation

The three templates you downloaded can be added to the Arbor Day Revised presentation. The following steps insert the templates after Slide 2.

1 Click the Arbor Day Revised button on the Windows Vista taskbar to display this presentation.

2 Display Slide 2. With the Home tab displayed and your USB flash drive connected to one of the computer's USB ports, click the New Slide button arrow and then click Reuse Slides to display the Reuse Slides task pane.

3 Click the Browse button and then click Browse File to display the Browse dialog box. If necessary, double-click UDISK 2.0 (E:) to select the USB flash drive, Drive E in this case, as the device that contains the three templates.

4 Click Tree Relationship in the Browse dialog box to select the file and then click the Open button to display the template in the Reuse Slides dialog box.

5 Click the Tree Relationship preview to insert this slide into the Arbor Day Revised presentation.

6 Repeat Steps 3 through 5 to insert the Planting Timeline and the Beautification Committee templates in the Arbor Day Revised presentation.

7 Click the Close button in the Reuse Slides task pane so that it no longer is displayed (Figure 7).

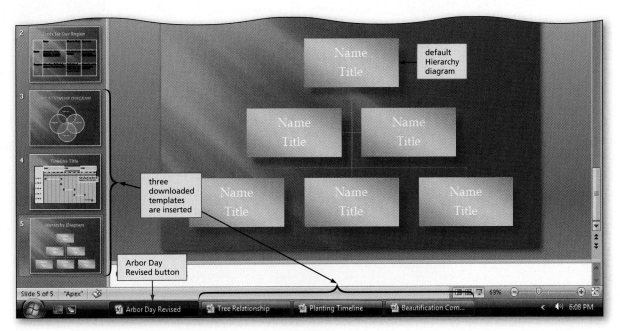

Figure 7

To Set Text Box Margins

The Slide 1 text box appears disconnected from the tree clip. You could reinforce the concept of planting a tree on Arbor Day if you change the margins of this text box and then move the text box on the tan material holding the tree's roots. The following steps set the text box margins.

1

• Display Slide 1, click the text box, and then right-click the text box to display the shortcut menu and the Mini toolbar (Figure 8).

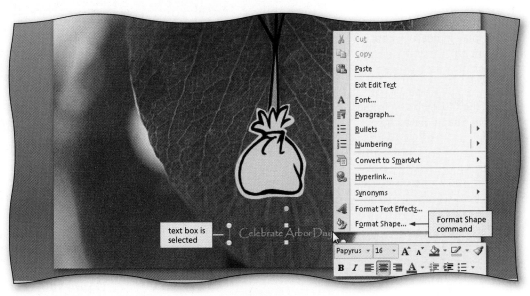

Figure 8

- Click Format Shape on the shortcut menu to display the Format Shape dialog box.

- Click Text Box in the left pane and then click the Left up arrow in the Internal margin area repeatedly until 0.5" is displayed (Figure 9).

Q&A

What are the three Autofit options in the Format Shape dialog box?

By default, PowerPoint changes a shape's size to accommodate text. The three AutoFit options allow you to decide how to use this feature. If you click the Do not Autofit button, automatic resizing is turned off. If you click the 'Shrink text on overflow' button, the font size is reduced to fit within the shape. The 'Reshape shape to fit text' button, which is the default option, increases the size of the shape vertically so that the text fits inside of it.

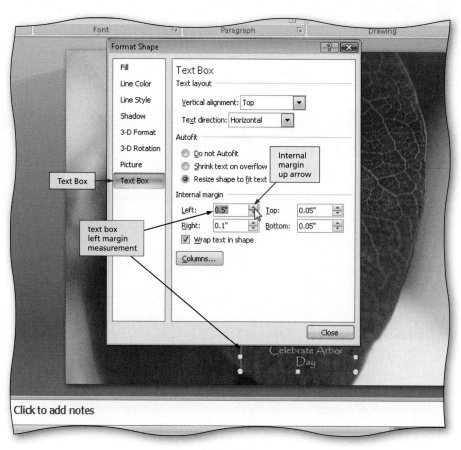

Figure 9

- Click the Right up arrow in the Internal margin area repeatedly until 0.5" is displayed.

- Click the Top down arrow to display a measurement of 0".

- Click the Bottom down arrow to display a measurement of 0" (Figure 10).

4

- Click the Close button in the Format Shape dialog box.

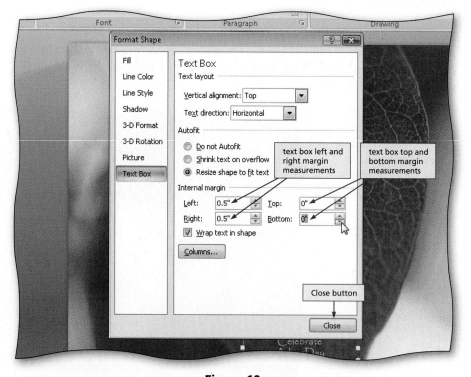

Figure 10

To Order a Text Box on a Slide

The Slide 1 text box now is the proper size to appear with the tree clip. When you drag the text box over the clip, however, it will be positioned behind this clip. You need to change the order of the slide elements so the text box will appear in front of the tree clip. The following steps move the text box and change its order.

1

- Drag the text box to the center of the tan root ball sack in the tree clip.

- Right-click the root ball to display the shortcut menu and then point to Send to Back to display the Send to Back submenu (Figure 11).

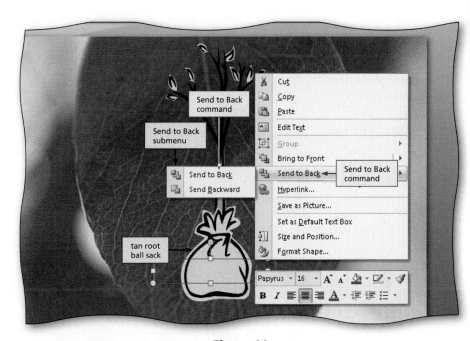

Figure 11

2

- Click Send to Back in the submenu to display the text box on top of the tan area of the tree clip.

- With the Home tab displayed, select the text box and then click the Shape Outline button in the Drawing group to display the Shape Outline gallery (Figure 12).

3

- Click No Outline to remove the border from the text box.

- If necessary, drag the text box to position it in the center of the tan area.

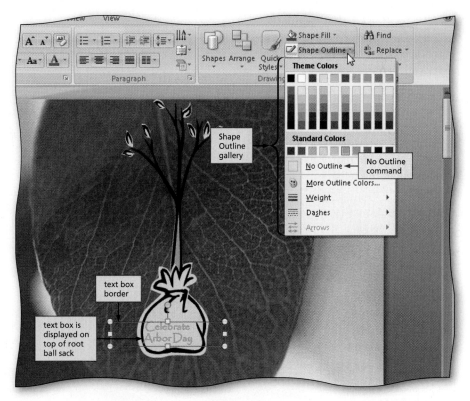

Figure 12

To Change Table Text Alignment

To add visual interest to the table on Slide 2, you change the alignment of each cell. You align table text in a similar manner as centering text in a placeholder. The following steps center the text in each table cell.

- Display Slide 2, click a table cell, and then display the Layout tab.

- Click the Select button in the Table group to display the Select menu (Figure 13).

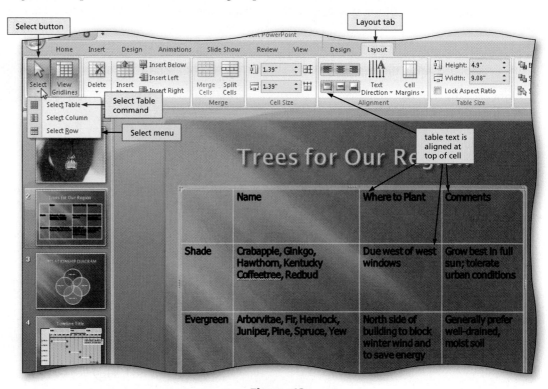

Figure 13

- Click Select Table in the Select menu to select the entire table.

- Click the Center Vertically button in the Alignment group to center the text in the middle of each cell in the table (Figure 14).

Q&A

Must I center all the table cells, or can I center only specific cells?

You can center as many cells as you deem necessary at one time by selecting one or more cells.

Other Ways

1. Right-click selected cells, click Format Shape on shortcut menu, click Text Box, click Vertical alignment arrow

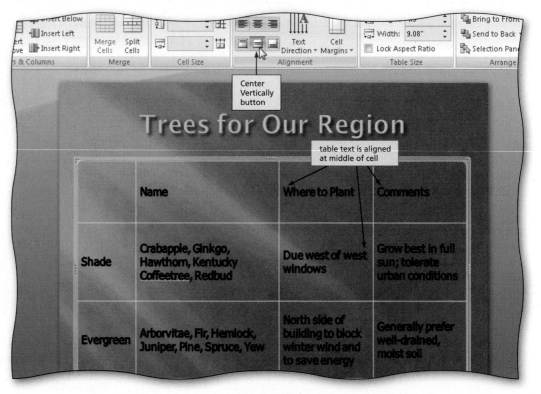

Figure 14

To Change Table Text Orientation

The default orientation of table cells is horizontal. You can change this direction to vertical or stacked, or you can rotate the direction in 90-degree increments. The steps used to align the direction of text in a placeholder are similar to the steps used to align the text in a cell. The following steps rotate the text in two table cells.

1

- With the Layout tab displayed, click the Shade cell and then drag down to select both the Shade and Evergreen table cells.

- Click the Text Direction button in the Alignment group to display the Text Direction gallery (Figure 15).

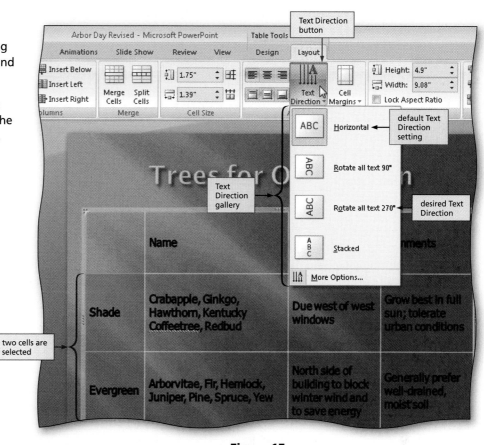

Figure 15

2

- Click 'Rotate all text 270°' to rotate the text in the two cells.

- Click the Center button in the Alignment group to center the Evergreen and Shade text (Figure 16).

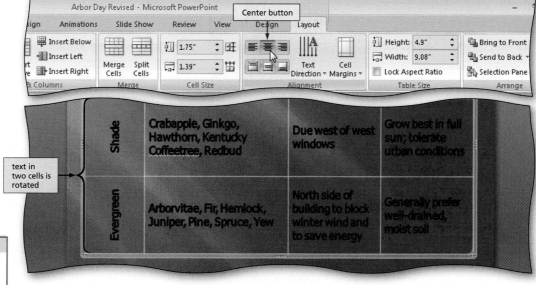

Figure 16

Other Ways

1. Right-click selected cells, click Format Shape on shortcut menu, click Text Box, click Text direction arrow

To Add an Image to a Table

Another table enhancement you can make is to add a picture or clip to a table cell. The following steps add a tree picture to the upper-left table cell.

1

- Right-click the upper-left table cell to display the shortcut menu and Mini toolbar (Figure 17).

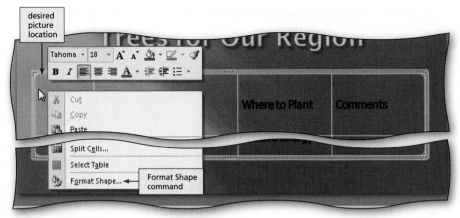

Figure 17

2

- Click Format Shape to display the Format Shape dialog box and then click Picture or texture fill (Figure 18).

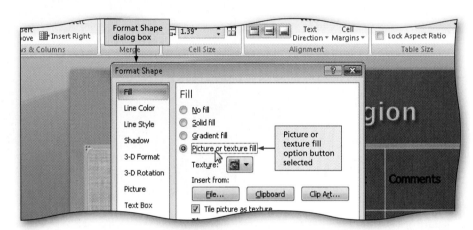

Figure 18

3

- Click the Insert from File button to display the Insert Picture dialog box.

- Select the Foliage picture on the Data Files for Students and then click the Insert button in the Insert Picture dialog box to insert the picture into the table cell (Figure 19).

4

- Click the Close button in the Format Shape dialog box.

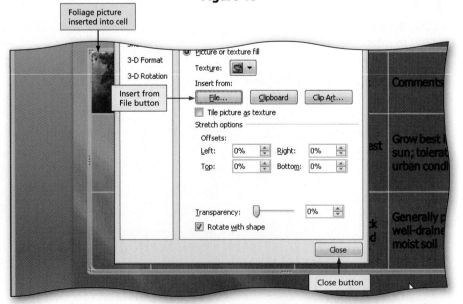

Figure 19

To Enter Text in a Relationship Diagram

The Relationship diagram you downloaded and saved is a SmartArt graphic with default text entered in each of the four circles. You want to change this text to reflect three environmental and social benefits gained by planting trees. If no text is displayed after a bullet in the Text pane, the corresponding shape will not be displayed. The following steps replace the default text in three circles of the Relationship diagram on Slide 3.

1 Display Slide 3 and then click the Relationship diagram to select it and display the Text pane, if necessary, by clicking the Text pane control on the left side of the diagram.

2 Select the Department 1 text in the Text pane and then type `Control soil erosion` in the first bullet line.

3 Select the Department 2 text and then type `Remove carbon dioxide from air` in the second bullet line.

4 Select the Department 3 text and then type `Increase property values` in the third bullet line.

5 Select the Department 4 text and then press the DELETE key to eliminate this shape from the diagram.

6 Select the Relationship Diagram slide title and then type `Benefits of Planting Trees` as the new title text (Figure 20).

BTW

Adjusting AutoRecover Features
PowerPoint creates a recovery file every 10 minutes by default. This feature helps preserve a presentation if a power outage occurs, another program makes your system unstable, or an error occurs in the PowerPoint program. If you want to increase or decrease this length of time, click the Microsoft Office Button and then click the PowerPoint Options button to display the PowerPoint Options dialog box. Click Save in the left pane and then adjust the time in the 'Save AutoRecover information' text box in the Save presentations area.

Other Ways
1. Select text in one shape, type new text

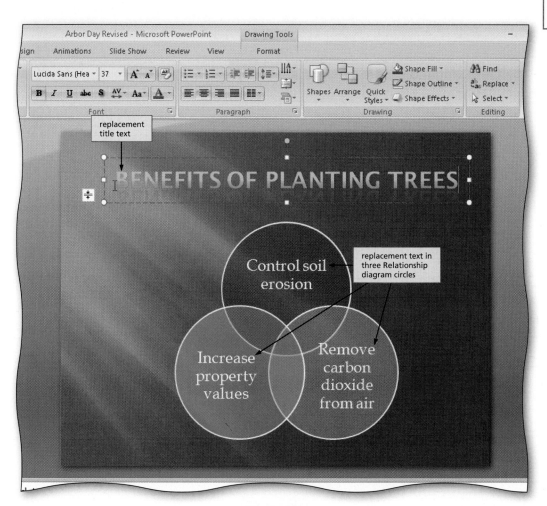

Figure 20

To Zoom a Slide

Slide 5 contains a chart that will display the Beautification Committee members' names and titles. You can decrease or increase the slide size by changing the zoom. When you zoom out, you can view the entire slide and judge its content. When you zoom in, conversely, you can view a small part of the slide and modify the text. The following steps zoom Slide 5.

- Display Slide 5.

 Experiment

- Repeatedly click the Zoom In and Zoom Out button on the status bar and watch the slide size change.

2

- Click the Zoom In button as many times as necessary until the Zoom level button displays 110% on its face (Figure 21).

Q&A

Does changing the zoom affect how the slide prints on a handout?

No. The zoom setting changes only how the slide is displayed on the screen.

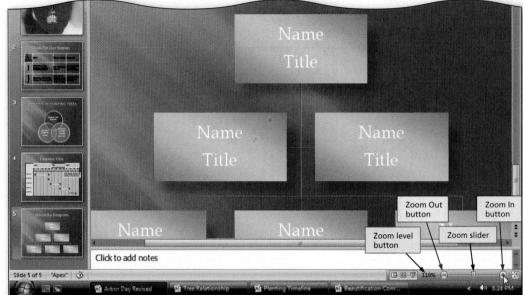

Figure 21

Other Ways

1. Drag Zoom slider on status bar
2. Click Zoom level button on status bar, select desired zoom percent, click OK button
3. Click Zoom button on View tab, select desired zoom percent, click OK button

To Enter Text in a Hierarchy Diagram

The Hierarchy diagram template you downloaded and saved also is a SmartArt graphic. The words Name and Title are the default text entered in each rectangle, and you want to change this text to the Beautification Committee's names and titles, as shown in Figure 22.

As with the Relationship diagram, if no text is displayed after a bullet in the Text pane, the corresponding shape will not be displayed. The following steps replace the default text in the Hierarchy diagram on Slide 5.

1 Click the Hierarchy diagram to select it and display the Text pane.

2 Type `Jim DeYoung` as the first bulleted Name text and type `President` as the new Title text.

3 Continue replacing the default text in the Text pane with the names and titles shown in Figure 22.

4 Type `Beautification Committee Members` as the new Hierarchy Diagram title text (Figure 23).

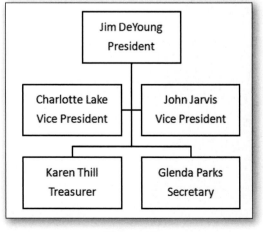

Figure 22

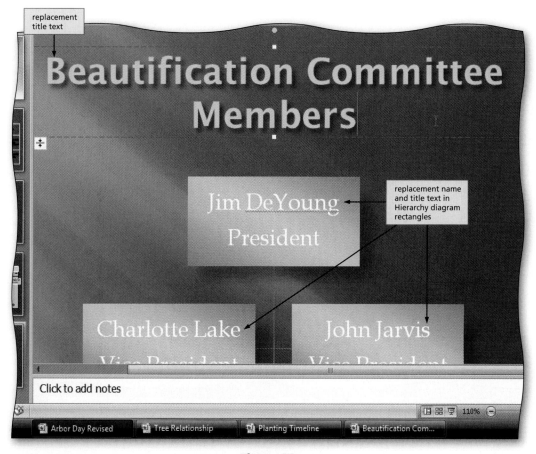

Figure 23

To Modify Timeline Diagram Text

The Timeline diagram template you downloaded and saved is not a SmartArt graphic, so edits will be made directly on this diagram. The modified timeline will show activities that should be performed during the months of April, May, and June. The following steps replace the default text in the Timeline diagram on Slide 4.

1

• Display Slide 4. Click the Zoom Out button as many times as necessary until the Zoom level button displays 80% on its face.

• Select the Timeline Title slide title and then type `Tree Care Schedule` as the new title text.

• Select the first column heading, JAN, and then type `April` as the new column title text (Figure 24).

Figure 24

- Type May as the new second column title and June as the new third column title.

- Select the first row title, Line 1, and then type Prune as the new text (Figure 25).

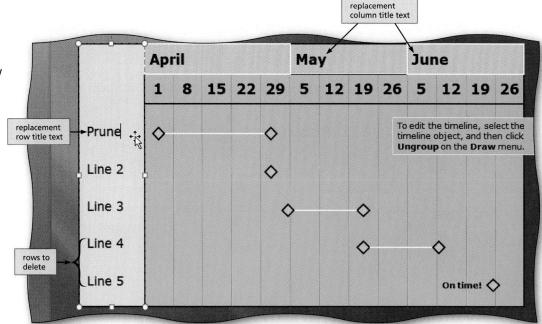

Figure 25

- Type Plant as the new second row title and Water as the new third row title.

- Select the Line 4 and Line 5 row titles and then press the DELETE key to delete this text (Figure 26).

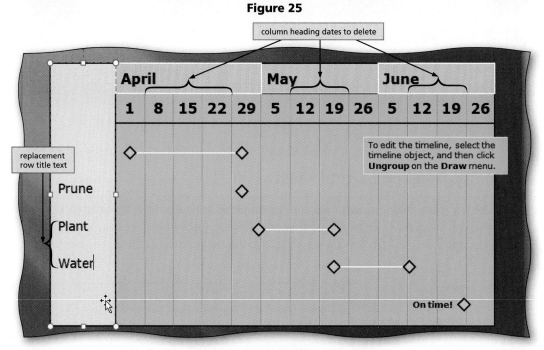

Figure 26

- Select the numbers 8, 15, and 22 under the April heading and then press the DELETE key to delete this text.

- Delete the numbers 12 and 19 under the May and June headings (Figure 27).

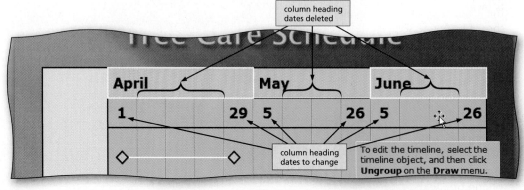

Figure 27

- Change the first April date, 1, to 16 and the second April date, 29, to 30.

- Change the first May date, 5, to 10 and the second May date, 26, to 31.

- Change the first June date, 5, to 15 and the second June date, 26, to 30 (Figure 28).

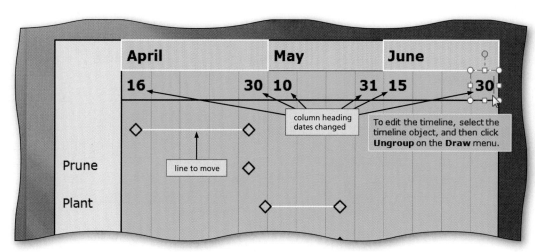

Figure 28

To Modify Timeline Graphics

All the column and row headings and dates are correct. When you deleted the Line 4 and Line 5 row titles, the three remaining row titles were no longer aligned with the timeline graphics. The following steps move the April timeline and the On time! graphic and also delete the edit instruction text box.

- Select the line between the two diamonds under the April heading and drag it down to align with the diamond in the Prune row (Figure 29).

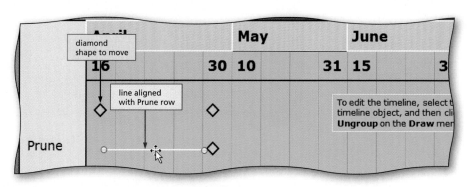

Figure 29

- Select the diamond shape in the April 16 column and drag it down to align with the Prune line, as shown in Figure 30.

- Select the top diamond shape in the April 30 column (Figure 30).

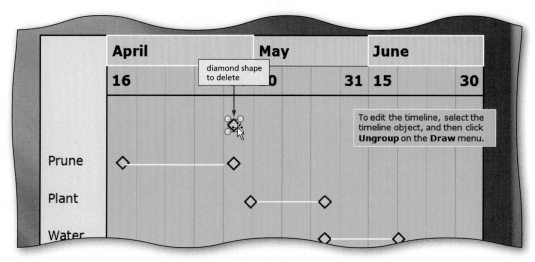

Figure 30

- Press the DELETE key to delete this diamond.

- Click the Edit text box border under the June heading to select this object (Figure 31).

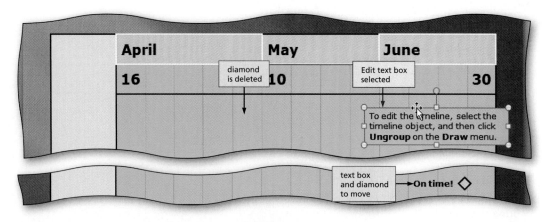

Figure 31

- Press the DELETE key to delete the text box.

- Select the On time! text in the bottom-right corner of the diagram and then type Plant a tree on Arbor Day! as the new text box text.

- Drag this text box and the diamond shape to the left so that they are positioned under the April column heading (Figure 32).

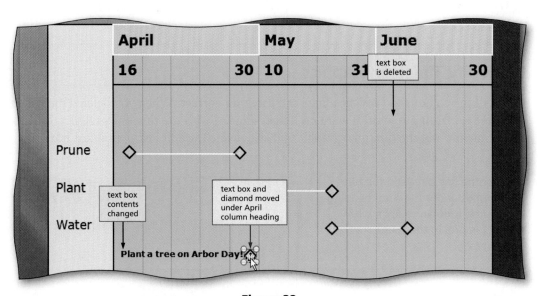

Figure 32

⑤

- Click the Plant right diamond shape and then drag it under the May 31 heading.

- Click the Water right diamond shape and then drag it under the June 30 heading.

- Click the Water left diamond shape and then drag it under the June 15 heading (Figure 33).

Q&A The line connecting the diamonds is not straight. Can I move it?

Yes. Select the shape again and drag it to a new location.

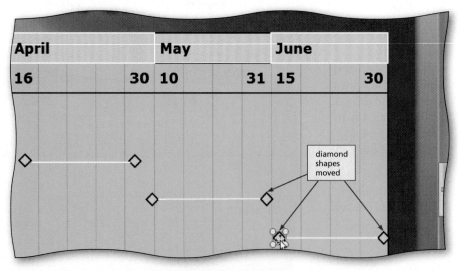

Figure 33

To Add Line Shapes to a Timeline

The three timeline chart elements now are aligned properly under the column headings. The following steps add lines to the column headings.

- Display the Format tab and then click the Line shape in the Insert Shapes gallery (Figure 34).

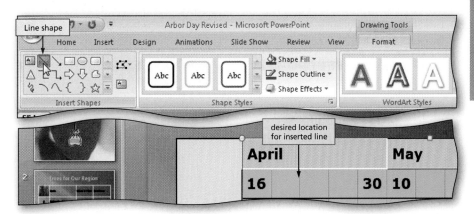

Figure 34

- Position the mouse pointer to the right of the number 16 under the April heading. Click and then drag the line to the left of the number 30 (Figure 35).

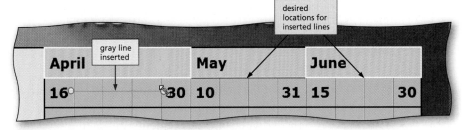

Figure 35

- Repeat Steps 1 and 2 to insert a line between the May 10 and 31 headings and the June 15 and 30 headings.

To Change a Line Shape Color

The default line shape color is gray. To draw attention to the time span between the heading dates, you can change the shape color. The following steps change the line shape color from dark gray to red.

- With the Format tab displayed and June line selected, click the Shape Outline button in the Shape Styles group to display the Shape Outline color palette (Figure 36).

Experiment

- Point to various colors in the Shape Outline gallery and watch the line color change.

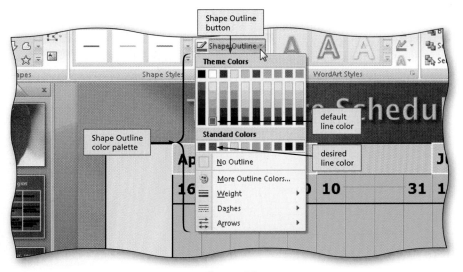

Figure 36

- Click Red (column 2) in the Standard Colors area to apply this color to the line.

- Select the May line and then click the Shape Outline button to apply the Red color to the line.

- Apply the Red color to the April line (Figure 37).

Q&A Can I change the color of these three lines simultaneously?

Yes. If you select all three lines and then click the Shape Outline button, you can select one color for these lines.

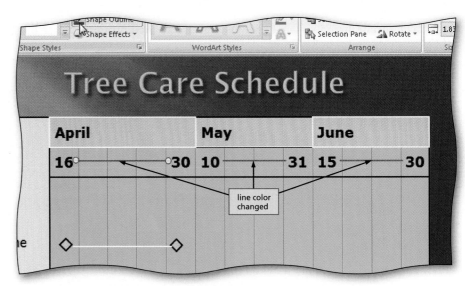

Figure 37

Paste Special

One method of copying a slide object is to copy it to the Clipboard and then use the Paste Special command to insert it on the slide. The **Paste Special** command groups all the individual object elements and then inserts the object as one picture. You specify the type of picture format PowerPoint should use.

To Copy a Formatted Table to the Title Slide

The red leaf picture on Slide 1 is attractive and helps introduce the Arbor Day theme to the audience. You can pique their interest even more by displaying the formatted table and the three templates on this slide. While the text on these objects will be too small to read, its visual nature will give a preview of the concepts that will be explored later in the presentation. The following steps use the Paste Special command to duplicate the table on the title slide.

- Display Slide 2. With the Home tab displayed, click a gray area of the slide other than the table or the title text placeholder and then click the Select button in the Editing group to display the Select menu (Figure 38).

Figure 38

2

- Click Select All in the Select menu and then click the Copy button in the Clipboard group (Figure 39).

Q&A

Can I delete the borders between the table cells?

Yes. When you delete the border, you combine the cell contents. To perform this action, display the Design tab under Table Tools and then click the Eraser button in the Draw Borders group. Click a cell border that you want to delete.

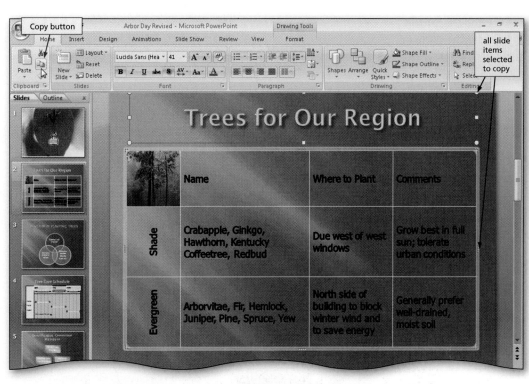

Figure 39

3

- Display Slide 1 and then click the Paste button arrow in the Clipboard group to display the Paste menu (Figure 40).

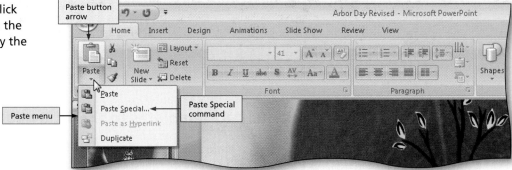

Figure 40

4

- Click Paste Special and then click Picture (PNG) in the Paste Special dialog box to select this picture type (Figure 41).

Q&A

Can I simply paste the table instead of using the Paste Special command?

Yes, and the table would look identical to the one displayed on your screen now. The table would be composed of individual pieces, however, which could be a problem if you inadvertently moved or deleted one of these components.

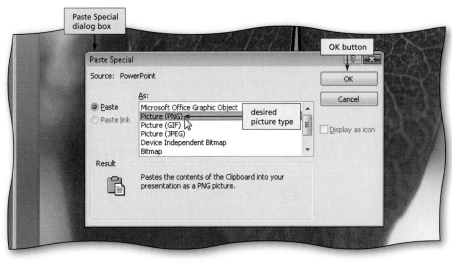

Figure 41

- Click the OK button to paste the table in the title slide.

- Display the Format tab and then click the Shape Height down arrow in the Size group to reduce the table height to 2.0".

- Drag the table to the upper-left corner of the slide, as shown in Figure 42.

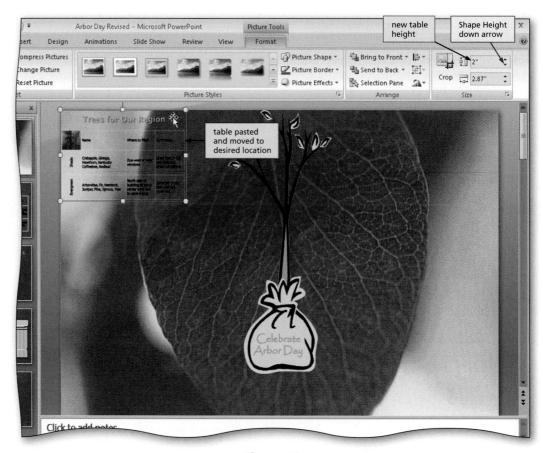

Figure 42

To Copy Formatted Templates to the Title Slide

The tree region table is pasted on Slide 1, and you can copy the three formatted templates to the title slide following the same procedure using the Paste Special command. The following steps copy the formatted Relationship, Hierarchy, and Timelines templates to Slide 1.

1. Display Slide 3. With the Home tab displayed, click a gray area of the slide, click the Select button in the Editing group to display the Select menu, and then click Select All.

2. Click the Copy button in the Clipboard group, display Slide 1, click the Paste button arrow in the Clipboard group, and then click Paste Special in the Paste menu.

3. Click Picture (PNG) in the Paste Special dialog box to select this picture type and then click the OK button to paste the Relationship diagram in the title slide.

4. Size the diagram so its height is 2.0". Drag the diagram to the upper-right corner of the slide.

5. Repeat Steps 1 through 4 for the Hierarchy diagram on Slide 4 and the Timelines diagram on Slide 5. Position these objects as shown in Figure 43.

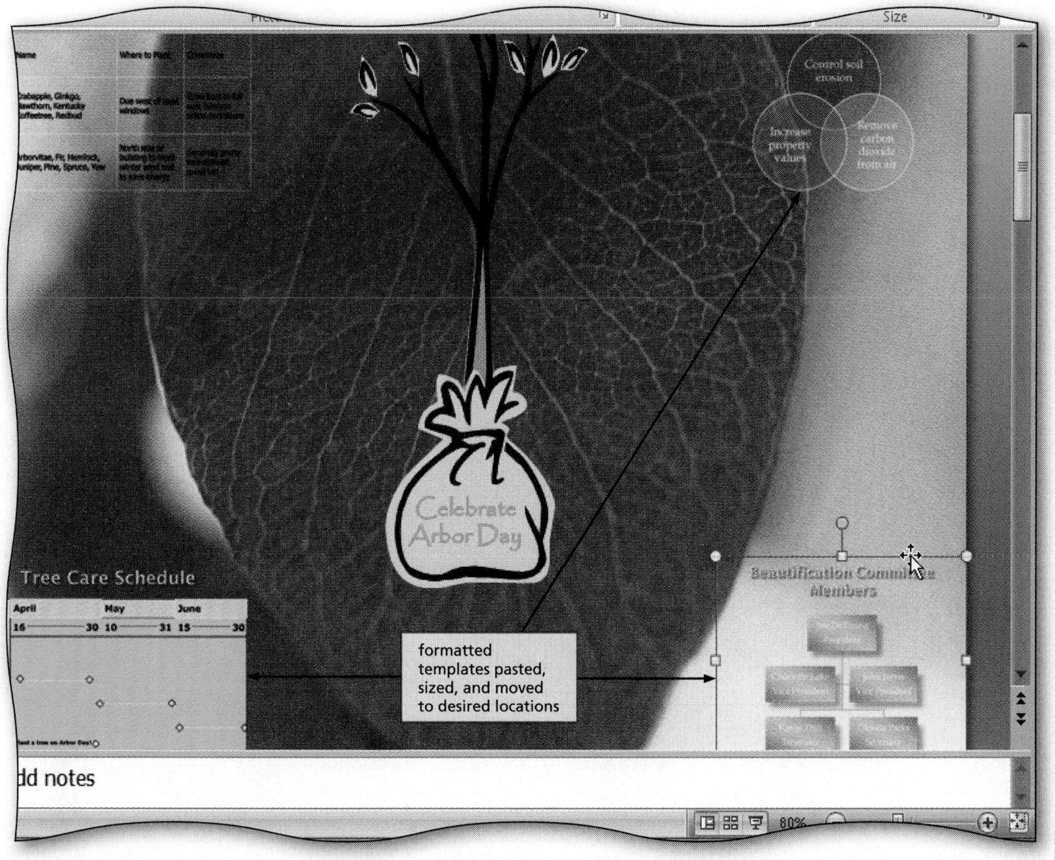

Figure 43

To Animate the Slide 1 Objects

Slide 1 contains many visual elements. Your viewer would be more apt to focus on one aspect of the slide if the objects were displayed one at a time. The following steps apply the Dissolve In entrance effect and a Box exit effect for the objects on the title slide.

1 Click the Zoom Out button as many times as necessary until the Zoom level button displays 70% on its face. Display the Animations tab and then click the Custom Animation button in the Animations group to display the Custom Animation task pane. Select the Trees table object, click the Add Effect button, point to Entrance in the Add Effect menu, and then click More Effects.

2 Click Dissolve In in the Basic category and then click the OK button to close the Add Entrance Effect dialog box.

3 Click the Start box arrow and then click After Previous. Click the Speed box arrow and then click Slow.

4 Click the Add Effect button, point to Exit in the Add Effect menu, and then click More Effects.

5 Click Box in the Basic category and then click the OK button to close the Add Exit Effect dialog box. Change the Speed to Slow.

6 Repeat Steps 1 through 5 above for the Tree Relationship, the Planting Timeline, and the Beautification Committee objects (Figure 44 on the following page).

7 Click the Close button in the Custom Animation task pane so that it no longer is displayed.

BTW

Using the Document Recovery Task Pane
The Document Recover feature can be helpful if PowerPoint or another Microsoft Office program closes abnormally. This feature recovers as many changes as possible that you made after the last time you saved this file. When you restart PowerPoint after it closes unexpectedly, the program may be able to display this file if it can recover all the changes you made. Another possibility may be that PowerPoint displays the Document Recovery task pane and shows a maximum of three versions of your file. In this situation, you can identify which version of the file you want to keep. The most current version is at the top of the list. If you are uncertain which file is the one you want to keep, save all three files using different names and then review each one.

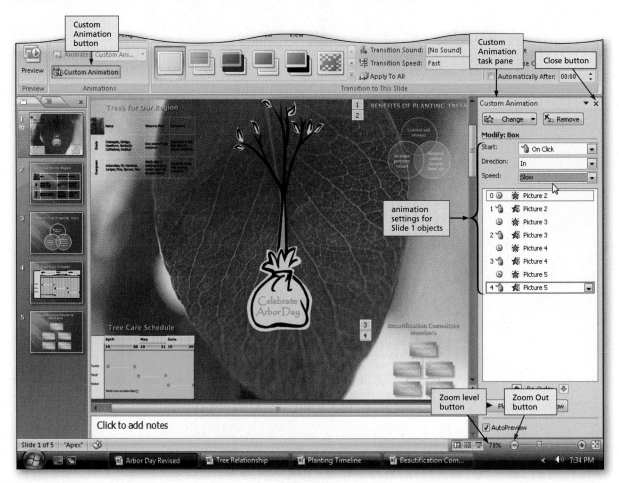

Figure 44

Determine the screen show ratio.

Your presentation can be viewed on one of three different screen sizes. A standard monitor has a ratio of 4:3. Many new wide-screen notebook computers have a 16:10 ratio, and high-definition televisions have displays with a 16:9 ratio. These numbers describe the dimensions of the screen. For example, a display with a 4:3 ratio would be four feet wide if it were 3 feet high. Similarly, a notebook computer screen would be 16 inches wide if it were 10 inches high. While these exact measurements do not fit all displays and screens, the hardware height and width dimensions remain in the same proportion using these ratios.

Changing the default ratio offers many advantages. Audience members perceive a presentation in the wide-screen format as being trendy and new. In addition, the wider screen allows more layout area to display photographs and clips. In rooms with low ceilings, the wide-screen displays mirror the room dimensions and blend with the environment.

Slides created in the 4:3 format and then converted to 16:9 or 16:10 may look distorted, especially if images of people or animals are inserted. You consequently may need to adjust these stretched graphics if they look unnatural. If you present your slide show frequently on computers and screens with varying formats, you may want to save the slide show several times using the different ratios and then open the presentation that best fits the environment where it is being shown.

While the wide screen presents the opportunity to place more text on a slide, resist the urge to add words. Continue to use the 7 × 7 guideline (a maximum of seven lines on a slide and a maximum of seven words on a line).

Setting Slide Size and Slide Show Options and Saving Individual Slides

BTW

Changing the Starting Slide Number
The first slide number is 1 by default. To change this number, click the 'Number slides from' up button in the Page Setup dialog box.

Today's technology presents several options you should consider when developing your presentation. The on-screen show ratio determines the height and width proportions. The screen resolution affects the slides' clarity. In addition, you may want to save an individual slide as an image so it can be imported into another file or easily printed by itself.

To Set Slide Size

By default, PowerPoint sets a slide in a 4:3 ratio, which is the proportion found on a standard monitor. If you know your presentation will be viewed on a wide-screen high-definition television (HDTV) or you are using a wide-screen notebook computer, you can change the slide size to optimize the proportions. The following steps change the default resolution to 16:10, which is the proportion of a notebook computer.

- Display the Design tab and then click the Page Setup button in the Page Setup group to display the Page Setup dialog box.

- Click the 'Slides sized for' arrow to display the size list (Figure 45).

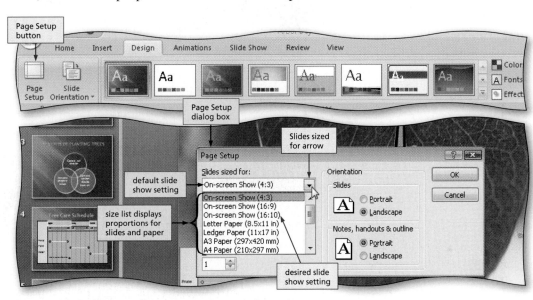

Figure 45

- Click 'On-screen Show (16:10)' to change the slide size setting (Figure 46).

Q&A

Can I also change the default slide orientation from Landscape to Portrait?

Yes, but all slides in the presentation will change to this orientation. You cannot mix Portrait and Landscape orientations in one presentation. If you need to use both orientations during a speech, you can use a hyperlink to seamlessly jump from one slide show in Landscape orientation to another in Portrait orientation.

Figure 46

3

- Click the OK button to change the slide size in the presentation.

To Select Presentation Resolution

As discussed in Appendix E, screen, or presentation, resolution affects the number of pixels that are displayed on your screen. When screen resolution is increased, more information is displayed, but it is decreased in size. Conversely, when screen resolution is decreased, less information is displayed, but that information is increased in size. Throughout this book, the screen resolution has been set to 1024×768. The following steps change the presentation resolution to 800×600.

- Display the Slide Show tab and then click the Set Up Slide Show button in the Set Up group to display the Set Up Show dialog box.

- Click the 'Slide show resolution' arrow in the Performance area to display the resolution list (Figure 47).

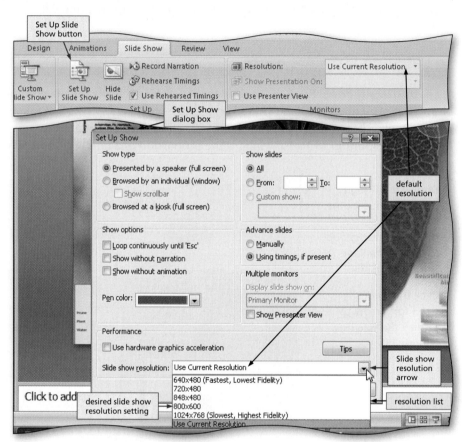

Figure 47

- Click 800 × 600 to change the slide show resolution setting (Figure 48).

- Click the OK button to change the presentation resolution.

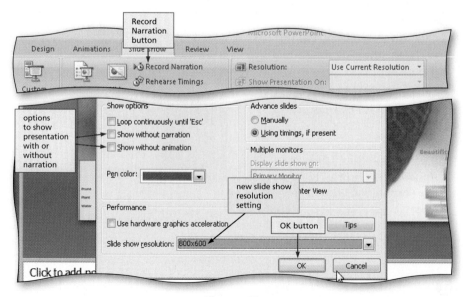

Figure 48

To Record Narration

In special occasions you may want your viewers to hear recorded narration that accompanies slides. If your topic is poetry written by local poets, you may want to hear their voices interpret the poetry that is displayed on slides. You can record narration separately and then add this file to the slide. You also can record narration while the slide show is running. To record this narration, you would perform the following steps.

1. Display the Slide Show tab and then click the Record Narration button in the Set Up group.

2. Click the Set Microphone Level button in the Record Narration dialog box, determine the microphone level, and then click the OK button in the Microphone Check dialog box.

3. Click the Change Quality button in the Record Narration dialog box, click the Name arrow, select the desired recording quality, and then click the OK button in the Sound Selection dialog box.

4. If your narration is lengthy, click the 'Link narrations in' check box to link the narration file to your presentation.

5. If your presentation consists of more than one slide, click Current Slide or First Slide to match the narration with a particular part of the presentation.

6. In Slide Show view, begin speaking into the microphone. When finished, click the black Exit screen.

7. Click the Save button if you want to save the slide timings along with your narration.

To Show a Presentation with or without Narration

If you have recorded narration to accompany your slides, you can choose whether to include this narration when you run your slide show. You would perform the following steps to run the slide show either with or without narration.

1. On the Slide Show tab, click the Set Up Slide Show button in the Set Up group.

2. If you do not want the narration to play, click 'Show without narration' in the Show options area of the Set Up Show dialog box and then click the OK button.

3. If you have chosen to show the presentation without narration and then desire to let audience members hear this recording, click 'Show without narration' to deselect this option in the Set Up Show dialog box and then click the OK button.

To Save a Slide as an Image

Throughout this book you have inserted images into your presentation. The need may arise for you to insert a PowerPoint slide into another file. For example, you may want to insert the information on one slide into a Microsoft Word document. The following steps save Slide 2 as a .jpg image.

- Display Slide 2, click the Office Button, and then point to Save As to display the Save As submenu (Figure 49).

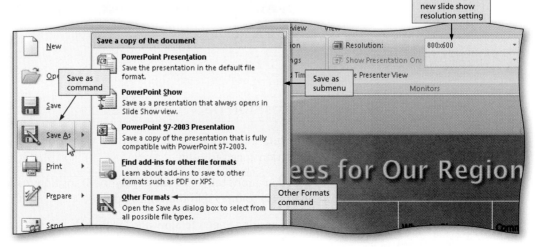

Figure 49

2

- Click Other Formats on the Save As submenu to display the Save As dialog box.
- Type `Regional Trees` in the File name text box and then click the 'Save as type' arrow to display the Save as type list (Figure 50).

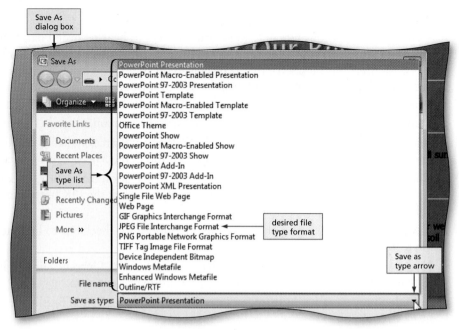

Figure 50

3

- Click JPEG File Interchange Format in the Save as type list to change the file type (Figure 51).

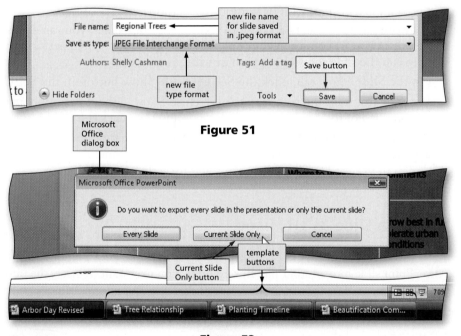

Figure 51

4

- Click the Save button in the Save As dialog box.
- Click the Current Slide Only button in the Microsoft Office PowerPoint dialog box to save only Slide 2 as a file in .jpeg format (Figure 52).

Figure 52

To Add a Transition between Slides

The following steps apply the Uncover Up transition to the presentation and change the transition speed to Slow.

1. Display the Animations tab and then display the Transitions gallery. Click the Uncover Up transition (row 2, column 3) in the Wipes category.
2. Change the Transition Speed to Slow and then apply this transition and speed to all slides.

To Change Document Properties and Save the Presentation

Before saving the presentation again, you want to add your name, class name, and some keywords as document properties. The following steps use the Document Information Panel to change document properties and then save the project.

1 Display the Document Information Panel and then type your name as the Author property.

2 Type your course and section as the Subject property.

3 Type Arbor Day, regional trees, Beautification Committee as the Keywords property.

4 Close the Document Information Panel and then save the presentation on the USB flash drive.

To Close the Downloaded Template Files

The five main slides in your presentation are complete. The three templates you downloaded from the Microsoft Office Online Web site are open, but you will not need to reference them to complete this project. You therefore should close these files. The following steps close the three downloaded templates.

1 Right-click the Tree Relationship button on the Windows Vista taskbar and then click Close.

2 Repeat Step 1 for the Planting Timeline and the Beautification Committee files.

> **Other Ways**
> 1. Click Close button on right side of title bar
> 2. Press ALT+F4

Using Visual Basic for Applications to Create a Quiz

Visual Basic for Applications (VBA) programs can add unique features to your presentation. The fundamentals of VBA will be presented later in this feature when you create an interactive quiz with questions for audience members to answer. Before you learn to write the VBA instructions, however, you first need to create the two slides that will display questions pertaining to the Arbor Day presentation and three possible answers for each question.

To Insert a Slide and then Add and Format a Shape

Three possible answers will display on the slide. To add interest, you can display the text of each answer in a shape. One method for creating these answers is to create one shape, copy it, and then position the shapes on the slide. The following steps insert and format a shape.

1 Insert a new slide at the end of the Arbor Day Revised presentation and apply the Title Only slide layout.

2 With the Home tab displayed, click the Shapes button in the Drawing group and then click the Regular Pentagon shape (row 1, column 8 in the Basic Shapes area).

3 Click Slide 6 anywhere below the title text placeholder to insert the shape and then size the Regular Pentagon shape to a height of 2.5" and a width of 2.7".

4 Apply the Intense Effect – Accent 1 Shape Style (row 6, column 2) to the shape (Figure 53).

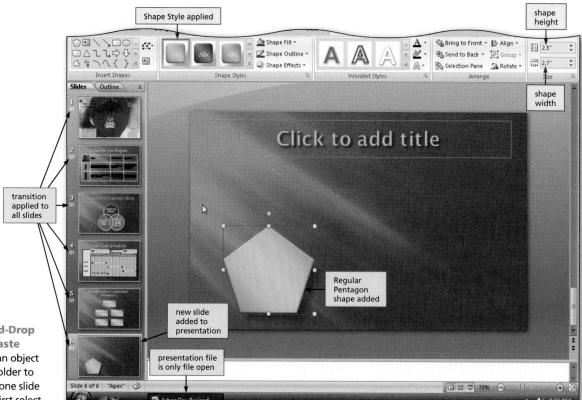

Figure 53

Using Drag-and-Drop and Cut-and-Paste
To move text or an object from one placeholder to another or from one slide to another, you first select the text or object and then use drag-and-drop editing or the cut-and-paste technique to move these characters or items. With **drag-and-drop editing**, you drag the selected item to a new location on the slide or a different slide and then insert, or drop, it there. **Cutting** involves removing the selected item from the document and then placing it on the Clipboard. **Pasting** is the process of copying an item from the Clipboard into the slide at the location of the insertion point.

Cutting Techniques
After selecting the text or object, you can cut your selection using one of three methods: click the Cut button on the Home tab, click the Cut command on the shortcut menu, or press the CTRL+X keys simultaneously.

Copying and Pasting

With one shape inserted and formatted on the slide, the next step is to create two identical objects for the quiz answers. One way to create these shapes is to repeat Steps 2 through 4 on the previous page. Another way is to copy the original shape to the Clipboard and then paste this shape from the Clipboard into the same slide or another slide at the location of the insertion point. The Clipboard holds text or objects temporarily until you copy another object or character. The same procedure of copying and pasting objects works for copying and pasting text from one text box or placeholder to another.

When moving characters or an object from one slide to another, use the Clipboard to cut and paste; when moving these items a short distance, use the drag-and-drop technique for efficiency. The following steps demonstrate copying and pasting.

To Copy a Shape

Now that the shape is formatted, you can copy it twice on the slide. The following steps copy the Regular Pentagon shape.

1 Display the Home tab and then click the Copy button in the Clipboard group.

2 Click the Paste button in the Clipboard group twice to insert two Regular Pentagon shapes on Slide 6 (Figure 54).

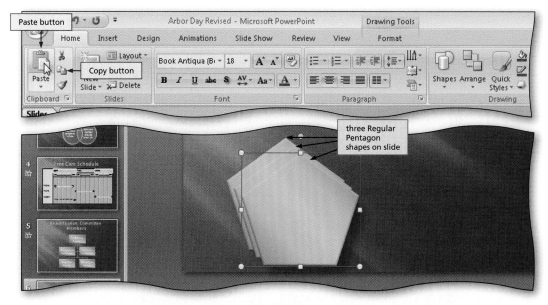

Figure 54

To Display the Gridlines and Align the Shapes

The **grid** is a set of intersecting lines used to align objects on the slide. By default, the **Snap objects to grid** option is active so that objects move to the nearest grid intersection automatically when the object's borders are near the grid lines. The following steps display the gridlines and then move the three shapes to the desired location.

● Right-click Slide 6 anywhere except the title text and shapes to display the short-cut menu (Figure 55).

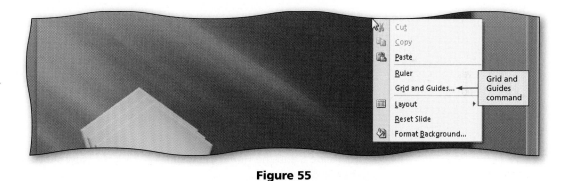

Figure 55

● Click Grid and Guides on the shortcut menu to display the Grid and Guides dialog box and then click the 'Display grid on screen' check box in the Grid settings area (Figure 56).

Q&A

Can I change the spacing of the grid lines?

Yes. Click the Spacing arrow in the Grid and Guides dialog box and then select the desired measurement.

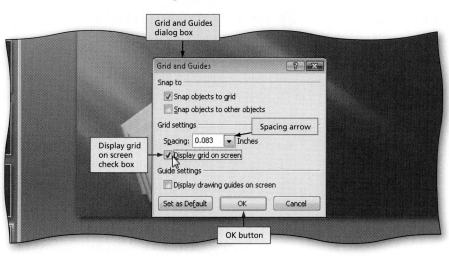

Figure 56

- Click the OK button to display the grids.

- Drag each shape to the locations shown in Figure 57.

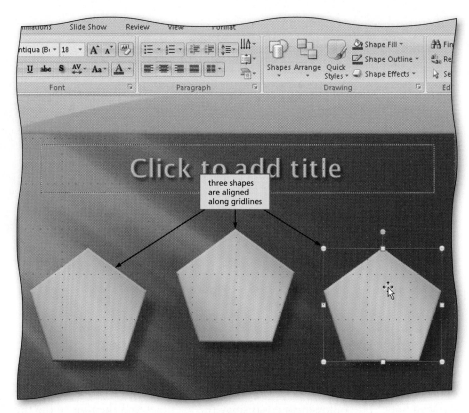

Figure 57

To Duplicate a Slide

Your quiz will have questions on two slides. Now that one slide is formatted, you can duplicate it and then add the questions and answers to both slides. The following steps duplicate Slide 6.

1 With Slide 6 and the Home tab displayed, click the New Slide button arrow to display the Apex layout gallery.

2 Click Duplicate Selected Slides to insert a new Slide 7, which is identical to Slide 6.

To Add Text to Shapes and the Title Text Placeholders

With both quiz slides added to the presentation, you now can type the quiz questions and answers. The following steps add the questions to the title text placeholders and the answers to the Regular Pentagon shapes on Slides 6 and 7.

1 Display Slide 6 and then type `What tree type is best for blocking winter winds?` in the title text placeholder.

2 If necessary, select the title text placeholder, click the Shape Fill button arrow in the Drawing group, and then click Red (column 2 in the Standard Colors area) to add a fill color to the title text placeholder.

3 Select the left Regular Pentagon shape and then type `Evergreen` in the shape.

4 Select the middle shape and then type `Shade` in the shape. Select the right shape and then type `Palm` in the shape.

5 Change the font color of these three answers to Red and the font size to 20 point.

6 Display Slide 7 and then type `Why are trees beneficial to the environment?` in the title text placeholder.

7 Select the title text placeholder, if necessary, and then click the Shape Fill button to add a Red fill color to the title text placeholder.

8 Type `They reduce oxygen in the air` in the left shape, type `They contribute to erosion` in the center shape, and then type `They increase property values` in the right shape.

9 Change the font color of these three answers to Red and the font size to 20 point (Figure 58).

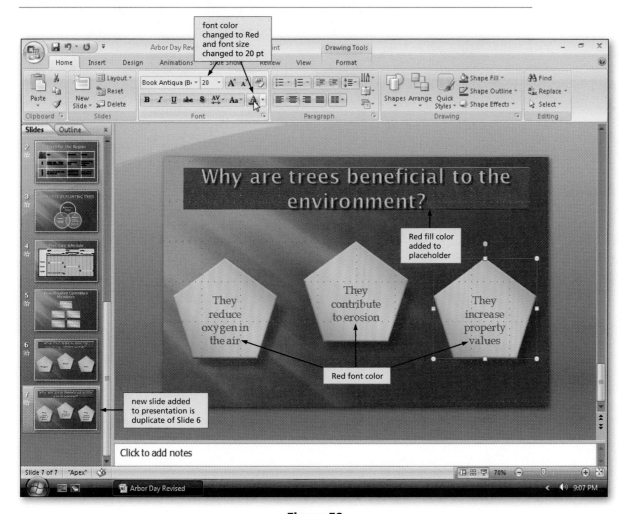

Figure 58

To Insert and Order a Picture on a Slide

Adding pictures of trees on the quiz slides will help add interest. If you insert these pictures now, they will cover the shapes and text you just added. To move these pictures underneath the slide objects, you order the pictures to the back of the slide. The following steps insert photographs and then send them to the back of Slides 6 and 7.

- Display Slide 6, display the Insert tab, and then click the Picture button to display the Insert Picture dialog box.

- Select the Evergreens picture on the Data Files for Students and then click the Insert button in the Insert Picture dialog box to insert the picture on Slide 6.

2

- Drag the Evergreens sizing handles so the picture covers the entire slide.

Q&A

Is it acceptable to use the side sizing handles to change the picture dimensions?

In previous chapters you have used the corner sizing handles to change the picture sizes so the picture stays in proportion. This guideline is important for some picture images, such as people or animals. This Evergreen picture, however, does not look distorted when you drag the side sizing handles outward, so enlarging the photograph in this manner is fine.

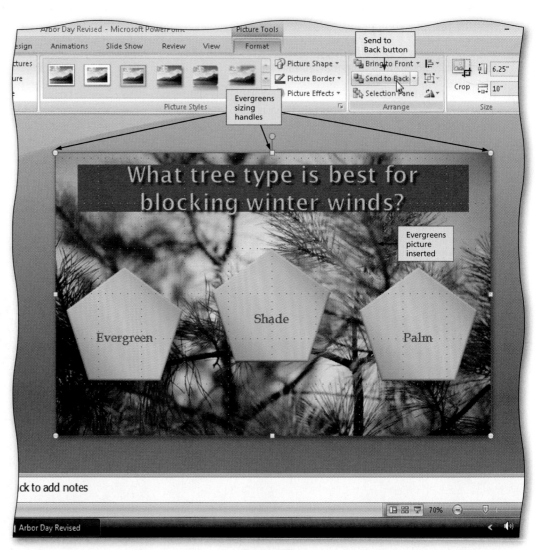

Figure 59

- Click the Send to Back button in the Arrange group to move the Evergreens picture under the Slide 6 content (Figure 59).

3

- Display Slide 7, display the Insert tab, and then insert the Forest picture on the Data Files for Students.

- Drag the Forest sizing handles so the picture covers the entire slide.

- Click the Send to Back button in the Arrange group to move the Forest picture under the Slide 7 content (Figure 60).

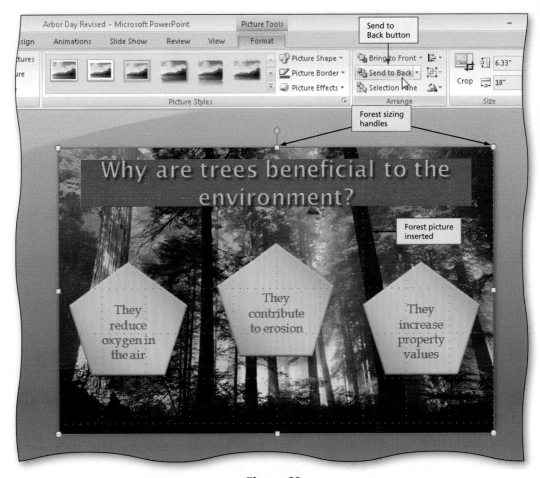

Figure 60

Other Ways

1. Right-click picture, click Send to Back on shortcut menu

To Hide Gridlines

The shapes and text are entered on the two quiz slides and are located in the desired locations. The grid no longer is needed. The following step hides the gridlines.

1 Display the View tab and then click Gridlines.

Other Ways

1. Press SHIFT+F9

Visual Basic Code Elements

The lines of instruction, called code, customize and extend PowerPoint's capabilities. The step-by-step set of instructions is called an **application**. Thus, Microsoft created the name Visual Basic for Applications for its programming language used to customize PowerPoint and other Microsoft Office 2007 programs. PowerPoint and other Office programs use the **Visual Basic Editor** to enter, modify, and view VBA code.

Table 1 shows the VBA code you will use to create a quiz. The lines of code, taken as a whole, are called a **macro**, which is a set of instructions that automates multi-step tasks. This quiz macro contains three procedures, each beginning with a **Sub statement** and ending with an **End Sub statement**. The Sub statement begins with the name of

BTW

Indenting Lines
The indents are only for clarity; in this project they help you recognize the three subroutines. Indent these lines three spaces.

the procedure. In Table 1, lines 10, 13, and 16 give the names of the three procedures: WrongAnswer, CorrectAnswer, and LastCorrect. The parentheses following the procedure names allow the passing of data variables, or arguments, from one procedure to another. Passing arguments is beyond the scope of this project, but the parentheses still are required. Every procedure must end with an End Sub statement; the End Sub statements in lines 12, 15, and 18 signify the end of the three procedures.

Table 1 Create Quiz Procedures	
Line	**VBA Code**
1	' Create Quiz Procedure Author: Shelly Cashman
2	' Date Created: 5/7/08
3	' Function: When the slide is displayed, this procedure accepts data indicating
4	' whether a user has selected a correct or incorrect quiz answer. If the
5	' answer is correct, a message box is displayed indicating the user
6	' entered a correct response. If the answer is incorrect, a message box
7	' is displayed indicating an incorrect answer was chosen. When the
8	' correct answer is selected on the last slide, the procedure ends.
9	'
10	Sub WrongAnswer()
11	MsgBox ("Please select a different answer.")
12	End Sub
13	Sub CorrectAnswer()
14	MsgBox ("You are correct.")
15	End Sub
16	Sub LastCorrect()
17	MsgBox ("You are correct.")
18	End Sub

BTW

Using Comments
Comments contain overall documentation about the procedure and may be placed anywhere in the procedure. Most programmers place comments before the Sub statement. Comments have no effect on the execution of a procedure; they simply provide information about the procedure, such as name, creation date, and function.

The first executable statement in Table 1 is line 10. Adding comments before a procedure will help you remember its purpose at a later date. In Table 1, the first nine lines are comments. **Comments** begin with the word Rem or an apostrophe (').

To enter a procedure, use the Visual Basic Editor. This Editor allows you to type the lines of VBA code as if you were using word-processing software. At the end of a line, press the ENTER key to move to the next line. If you make a mistake in a statement, use the ARROW keys and the DELETE or BACKSPACE keys to correct it. You also can move the insertion point to previous lines to make corrections.

Plan Ahead

Desk check the application code before entering it into the Visual Basic Editor.
PowerPoint steps through the Visual Basic statements one at a time beginning at the top of the procedure. When you a plan a procedure, remember that the order in which you place the statements is important because the order determines the sequence of execution.

Once you know what you want the procedure to do, write the VBA code on paper. Then, before entering the procedure into the computer, test it by putting yourself in the position of PowerPoint and stepping through the instructions one at a time. As you do so, think about how the instructions affect the slide show. Testing a procedure before entering it is called **desk checking**, and it is an important part of the development process.

To Enter the Create Quiz Procedures

Once you have determined the VBA instructions for the quiz, you can enter this code in the Visual Basic Editor. The following steps activate the Editor and create the three quiz procedures.

- Click the Office Button and then click the PowerPoint Options button to display the PowerPoint Options dialog box.

- Click the Show Developer tab in the Ribbon check box (Figure 61).

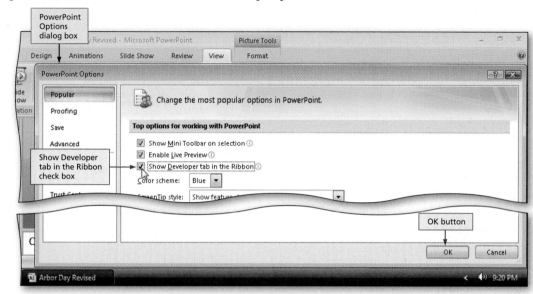

Figure 61

- Click the OK button to close the PowerPoint Options dialog box.

- Click Developer to display the Developer tab (Figure 62).

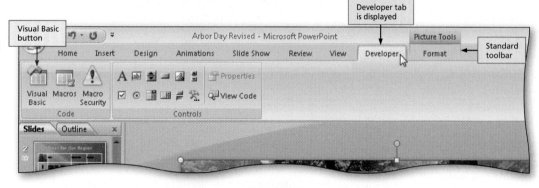

Figure 62

- Click the Visual Basic button in the Code group to open the Microsoft Visual Basic Editor.

- Click the Insert UserForm button arrow on the Standard toolbar to display the Insert UserForm list (Figure 63).

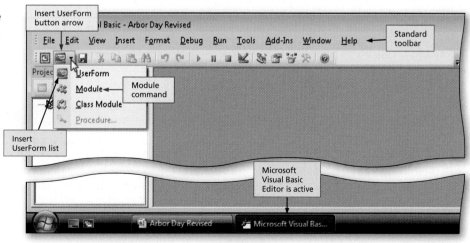

Figure 63

4

- Click Module in the Insert UserForm list to display the Visual Basic Editor.

- If necessary, click the Maximize button in the Arbor Day Revised – [Module1 (Code)] window to maximize the window.

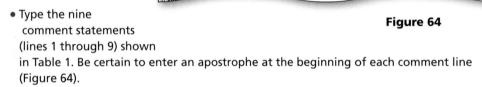

Figure 64

- Type the nine comment statements (lines 1 through 9) shown in Table 1. Be certain to enter an apostrophe at the beginning of each comment line (Figure 64).

Why do these lines display in a green font color?

The green font color indicates these lines are comments.

5

- Press the ENTER key to position the insertion point on the next line.

- Enter lines 10 through 18 shown in Table 1 (Figure 65).

Do I need to type the End Sub statements shown in lines 12, 15, and 18?

No. The Visual Basic Editor displays these lines automatically when you type the Sub statements.

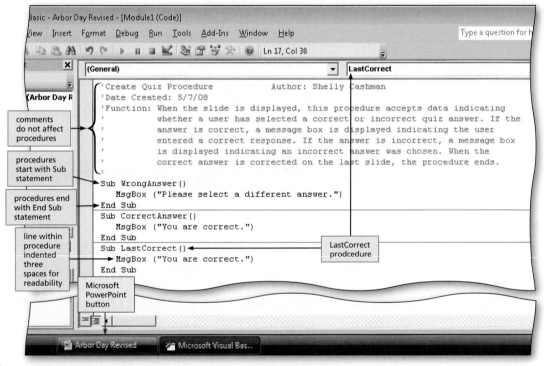

Figure 65

6

- Click the Microsoft PowerPoint button on the Standard toolbar to return to Slide 7.

Why did I leave the Visual Basic Editor open?

At this point you are not absolutely certain your VBA code is correct. If you run the presentation and encounter an error, you easily can view the code by clicking the Microsoft Visual Basic – Arbor Day Revised Macro button that is displayed on the Windows Vista taskbar.

To Assign a Macro to the First Quiz Question Shapes

One of the three shapes on Slide 6 displays the correct answer to the question displayed in the title text placeholder. The other two shapes display incorrect answers. You need to assign the CorrectAnswer macro to the corresponding shape and the WrongAnswer macro to the two corresponding shapes. The following steps assign action settings to the three shapes on Slide 6.

1

- Display Slide 6, click the Evergreen shape anywhere but the text, and then display the Insert tab.

Q&A Should the shape border be a dashed or a solid line?

Solid. If your shape has a dashed line, click the shape again. The solid line ensures that the macro will be assigned to the entire shape.

- Click the Action button in the Links group to display the Action Settings dialog box (Figure 66).

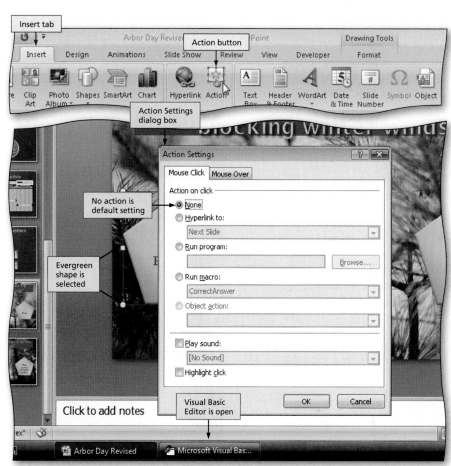

Figure 66

2

- With the Mouse Click tab displayed, click Run macro, and then verify that CorrectAnswer is the macro name displayed in the Run macro box (Figure 67).

Q&A How are the names generated for the macro list?

When you typed the VBA code, you entered the names of three procedures, or macros, followed by parentheses. Those three names are displayed in the macro list.

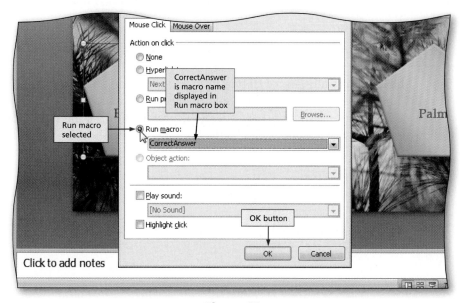

Figure 67

- Click the OK button to apply the CorrectAnswer macro to the Evergreen shape.

- Click the Shade shape anywhere but the text and then, if necessary, display the Insert tab.

- Click the Action button in the Links group, click Run macro in the Action Settings dialog box, click the Run macro arrow, and then click WrongAnswer in the macro list (Figure 68).

- Click the OK button to apply the WrongAnswer macro to the Shade shape.

- Click the Palm shape anywhere but the text, click the Action button in the Links group on the Insert tab, click Run macro, and then select WrongAnswer in the macro list.

- Click the OK button to apply the WrongAnswer macro to the Palm shape.

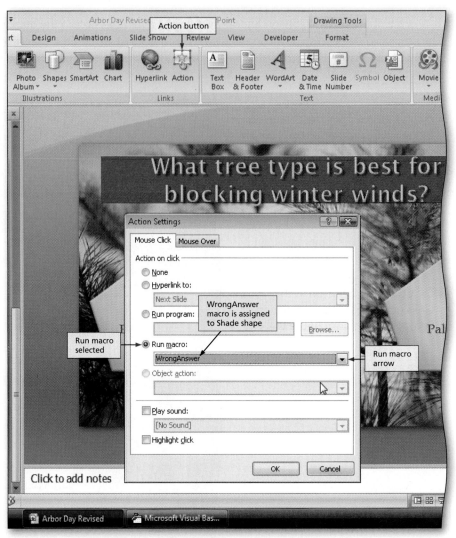

Figure 68

To Assign a Macro to the Final Quiz Question Shapes

The last quiz slide uses a different macro action setting to end the quiz after the user selects the correct answer. The LastCorrect macro will display a message box and then return to the slide show. In this presentation, this last quiz question also is the last slide in the presentation, so the slide show ends when the quiz ends. The following steps assign action settings to the three shapes on Slide 7.

- Display Slide 7. With the Insert tab displayed, click the right shape, which displays the text, They increase property values.

- Display the Action Settings dialog box, click Run macro, and then display the macro list.

- Click LastCorrect to select this macro (Figure 69).

- Click the OK button to apply the LastCorrect macro to the right shape.

- Click the left shape, click the Action button, click Run macro in the Action Settings dialog box, select WrongAnswer in the macro list, and then click the OK button.

- Apply the Wrong Answer macro to the middle shape and then click the OK button.

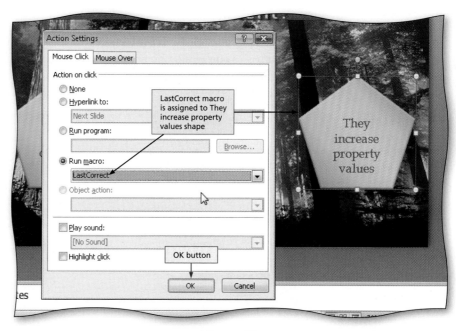

Figure 69

To Save the Presentation with a Macro

By default, PowerPoint will not save this presentation with a macro. You need to save the file as a macro-enabled presentation, which has the .pptm file extension. The following steps save the presentation in this format.

- Display the Save As dialog box, click the Save as type arrow, and then click PowerPoint Macro-Enabled Presentation in the Save as type list.

- Type `Arbor Day Revised Macro` in the File name text box (Figure 70).

- Click the Save button to save the presentation with a macro.

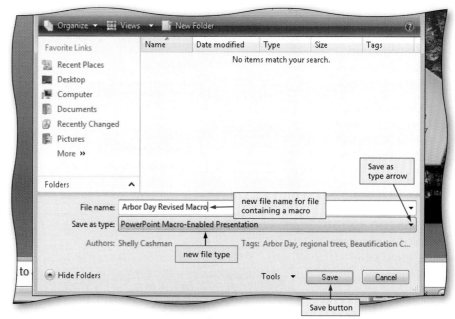

Figure 70

To Test Macro Settings

Unscrupulous people sometimes write macros to damage computer systems or to obtain information illegally. For this reason, Microsoft Office 2007 includes a Trust Center that allows users to determine security levels. In this feature, you should allow all macros to run while you are developing and testing this quiz code. The following steps test the macro level and adjust the setting, if necessary.

- Click the Office Button, click the PowerPoint Options button, and then click the Trust Center link in the left pane (Figure 71).

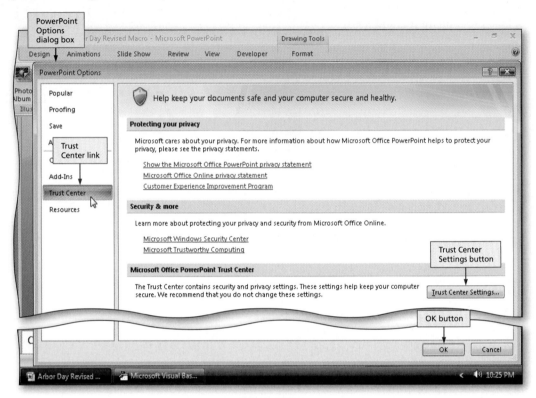

Figure 71

- Click the Trust Center Settings button in the Microsoft Office PowerPoint Trust Center area to view the Macro Settings.

- If is it not already selected, click the 'Enable all macros' option (Figure 72).

- Click the OK button to apply this macro setting and to close the Trust Center dialog box.

- Click the OK button to close the PowerPoint Options dialog box.

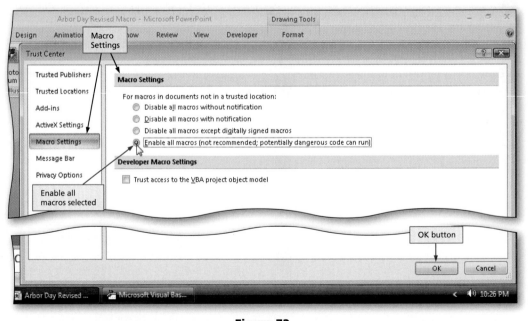

Figure 72

To Run a Slide Show with Macros

Running a slide show that contains a macro is the same as running any other slide show. When a quiz slide is displayed, click one of the shapes to display a message box indicating you have selected a correct or an incorrect answer. The following steps run the Arbor Day Revised Macro presentation.

BTW

Quick Reference
For a table that lists how to complete the tasks covered in this book using the mouse, Ribbon, shortcut menu, and keyboard, see the Quick Reference Summary at the back of this book, or visit the PowerPoint 2007 Quick Reference Web page (scsite.com/ppt2007/qr).

1 Click Slide 1 on the Slides tab. Click the Slide Show button to run the slide show and display Slide 1. Click to display the template images that are pasted on the slide.

2 Display Slides 2, 3, 4, and 5.

3 Display Slide 6. Click a shape with an incorrect answer and view the message box indicating that your choice was wrong. Click the OK button in this message box to close it. Click the other incorrect answer, view the message box, and then click the OK button in this message box.

4 Click the correct answer and view the message box. Click the OK button to close this message box.

5 Display Slide 7. Repeat Steps 3 and 4 to view the message boxes for the incorrect and correct answers. Click the OK button in the message box.

6 Click Slide 7 so that the black slide appears announcing the end of the slide show.

To Preview and Print Handouts

All changes are complete, and the presentation is saved. You now can create handouts to accompany the slide show. The following steps preview and then print the presentation.

1 Use Print Preview to preview the Arbor Day Revised Macro presentation.

2 Click Handouts (4 Slides Per Page) in the Print What list.

3 Click the Page Orientation button in the Page Setup group and then click Landscape in the Orientation list.

4 Click the Options button in the Print group and then Header and Footer in the Options list.

5 Click Header and then type `Celebrate Arbor Day` in the Header text box. Click the Apply to All button in the Header and Footer dialog box.

6 Print the handouts.

7 Close Print Preview and return to Normal view.

BTW

Certification
The Microsoft Certified Application Specialist (MCAS) program provides an opportunity for you to obtain a valuable industry credential – proof that you have the PowerPoint 2007 skills required by employers. For more information see Appendix G or visit the PowerPoint 2007 Certification Web page (scsite.com/ppt2007/cert).

To Reset Settings and Quit PowerPoint

You should reset the options you changed to their defaults. The following steps reset the resolution and slide size and also disable macros.

1 On the Slide Show tab, click the Resolution arrow in the Monitors group. Click Use Current Resolution or the original setting you changed.

2 On the Design tab, click the Page Setup button. Click the 'Slides sized for' arrow and then scroll up and click On-Screen Show (4:3). Click the OK button to close the dialog box.

3 Display the Office Button menu, click the PowerPoint Options button, click Trust Center in the left pane, click the Trust Center Settings button, and then click 'Disable all macros with notification' or the original setting you changed to run the macro in this project.

4 Click the OK button to close the Trust Center dialog box and then click the OK button to close the PowerPoint Options dialog box.

5 Display the Office Button menu and then click the Exit PowerPoint button to close all open documents and quit PowerPoint.

6 If a Microsoft Office PowerPoint dialog box is displayed, click the Yes button to save the changes.

Online Feature Summary

This Online feature introduced you to downloading templates from the Microsoft Online Web site, adding images to tables and changing the alignment of table text, changing presentation orientation and resolution, using Paste Special to copy objects, and writing VBA code. The items listed below include all the new Office 2007 skills you have learned in this Online feature.

1. Locate and Download a Relationship Diagram Template (PPT 451)
2. Locate and Download a Timeline Template (PPT 452)
3. Locate and Download a Hierarchy Template (PPT 453)
4. Insert Templates into a Presentation (PPT 454)
5. Set Text Box Margins (PPT 455)
6. Order a Text Box on a Slide (PPT 457)
7. Change Table Text Alignment (PPT 458)
8. Change Table Text Orientation (PPT 459)
9. Add an Image to a Table (PPT 460)
10. Enter Text in a Relationship Diagram (PPT 461)
11. Zoom a Slide (PPT 462)
12. Enter Text in a Hierarchy Diagram (PPT 462)
13. Modify Timeline Diagram Text (PPT 463)
14. Modify Timeline Graphics (PPT 465)
15. Add Line Shapes to a Timeline (PPT 467)
16. Change a Line Shape Color (PPT 467)
17. Copy a Formatted Table to the Title Slide (PPT 468)
18. Copy Formatted Templates to the Title Slide (PPT 470)
19. Animate the Slide 1 Objects (PPT 471)
20. Set Slide Size (PPT 473)
21. Select Presentation Resolution (PPT 474)
22. Record Narration (PPT 475)
23. Show a Presentation with or without Narration (PPT 475)
24. Save a Slide as an Image (PPT 475)
25. Close the Downloaded Template Files (PPT 477)
26. Display the Gridlines and Align the Shapes (PPT 479)
27. Insert and Order a Picture on a Slide (PPT 482)
28. Hide Gridlines (PPT 483)
29. Enter the Create Quiz Procedures (PPT 485)
30. Assign a Macro to the First Quiz Question Shapes (PPT 487)
31. Assign a Macro to the Final Quiz Question Shapes (PPT 488)
32. Save a Presentation with a Macro (PPT 489)
33. Test Macro Settings (PPT 490)
34. Run a Slide Show with Macros (PPT 491)
35. Reset Settings and Quit PowerPoint (PPT 492)

If you have a SAM user profile, you may have access to hands-on instruction, practice, and assessment. Log in to your SAM account (http://sam2007.course.com) to launch any assigned training activities or exams that relate to the skills covered in this chapter.

In the Lab

Create a presentation using the guidelines, concepts, and skills presented in this feature. Labs 1, 2, and 3 are listed in order of increasing difficulty.

Lab 1: Inserting Photographs in a Table and Adding Narration

Problem: Jim DeYoung, the Beautification Committee president, is planning a series of workshops to teach homeowners how to prune their trees properly. He would like to use a slide during his demonstration that shows an incorrect stem cut and a correct collar cut. He sends you two photographs of these cuts and also records a message describing these cuts. You create the slide shown in Figure 73.

Instructions:

1. Create a new presentation using the Origin document theme and the Title and Table slide layout. Set the slide size to On-screen Show (16:9). Change the slide show resolution to 800 × 600.

2. Type Pruning Techniques in the title text placeholder. Insert the OF-1 Pruning narration file from the Data Files for Students and set the narration to start automatically. Drag the speaker icon to the outer lower-right corner of the slide.

3. Insert a table with three columns and one row. Add the OF-1 Incorrect Prune photograph from the Data Files for Students to the left table cell and the OF-1 Correct Prune photograph from the Data Files for Students to the center table cell.

4. Resize the table by pointing to the sizing handle (the cluster of dots) on the bottom edge. When your mouse pointer becomes a double-headed arrow, click and drag the handle down to the location shown in Figure 73.

5. Use the drag-and-drop technique to move the title text, Pruning Techniques, to the right table cell. Rotate the text direction to 90° and then center the text vertically in the cell. Change the font size to 32.

6. Insert a text box in the left table cell and type Incorrect Stem Cut in the box. Change the font color to Red. Copy this text from the left cell and paste it into the center cell, and then change the word, Correct, to Incorrect. Change the font color to Green. Apply the Subtle Effect – Accent 3 Quick Style (row 4, column 4) to these two text boxes and add an Orange border (shape outline) with a 3 pt line weight.

7. Set the Left and Right text box margins to 0.1" and the Top and Bottom margins to 0.2". Display the gridlines and align the text boxes with the top-left squares.

8. Type Keep Your Tree Healthy as the new title text. Add an Orange (column 3) fill color to the title text placeholder. Insert an Elbow Connector shape (column 4 in the Lines area) to the right of the word, Healthy, and change the color to Green.

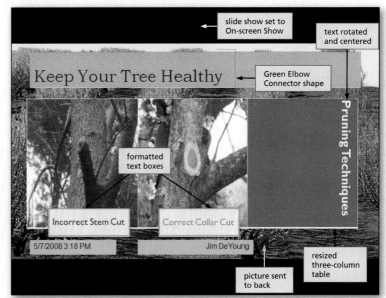

Figure 73

Continued >

In the Lab continued

9. Insert the OF-1 Pear Trees picture and drag the sizing handles to cover the entire slide. Use the Send to Back button to move the picture under the slide content.

10. Display your name and current date and time in the footer. Select each footer placeholder and add a Light Green (column 5) fill color.

11. Change the document properties, as specified by your instructor. Save the presentation using the file name, Lab OF-1 Pruning. Print the slides.

12. Save the slide as a .jpg image with the file name, Lab 0F-1 Pruning Picture.

13. Run the presentation with and without narration.

14. Submit the revised document in the format specified by your instructor. Reset the resolution and slide show settings.

In the Lab

Lab 2: Importing and Modifying a Radical Sports Design Template

Problem: Your local park district is preparing marketing materials for its summer recreational program. You have volunteered to help produce a PowerPoint presentation that will be displayed at the community center. The title slide will be incorporated in the front page of the brochure that will be mailed to all community residents and in print advertisements in the local paper. You create this title slide, which is shown in Figure 74, to show to the Park District marketing director.

Instructions:

1. Start a new presentation. Locate and download the 'Radical sports design template', which is located in the Sports subcategory of the Design slides category on the Microsoft Office Online Web site.

2. Insert the marketing theme, Wheels and Fields, in the title text placeholder and the name of your community along with the words, Parks and Recreation Department, in the subtitle text placeholder. Insert your name in the footer.

3. Insert a two-column table with one row and then insert the OF-2 Skateboard photograph in the left cell and the OF-2 Baseball photograph in the right cell. Both photographs are on your Data Files for Students. Display the Layout tab and then change the table size height to 2.75".

4. Insert a text box with Left and Right margins of 0.5" and Top and Bottom margins of 0.3". Change the Shape Fill color to Red and the Shape Outline color to Yellow. Drag the text box to the right side of the subtitle text placeholder and rotate it to the left, as shown in Figure 74. Then send the text box back so that the subtitle text is displayed on top of this text box.

5. Save the slide as a .jpg image using the file name, Lab OF-2 Summer Brochure. Save the presentation using the file name, Lab OF-2 Radical Sports.

6. Submit the revised document in the format specified by your instructor.

Figure 74

In the Lab

Lab 3: Creating an Interactive Quiz to Reinforce Feng Shui Concepts

Problem: In Chapter 6 you created a presentation illustrating feng shui concepts. You want to see if your message is reaching your audience correctly, so you create a True-False quiz, shown in Figure 75, to test viewers' understanding of this Chinese practice of creating harmony and balance.

Instructions:

1. Open the presentation, Revised Feng Shui, from your USB flash drive. (If you did not complete this presentation, see your instructor for a copy.) Display the slides in Slide Sorter view and then select all slides by clicking Slide 1, pressing and holding down the SHIFT key, and then clicking Slide 9. Click the Advance Slide Automatically After check box in the Transition to This Slide group on the Animations tab to uncheck the box and remove slide timings.

2. Return to Normal view and then add a slide at the end of the presentation. Insert the Isosceles Triangle shape (row 1, column 3 in the Basic Shapes area) in the lower-left side of the slide and size it to a height of 2.5" and a width of 2.9", which is 250% of the original size. Apply the Intense Effect – Accent 1 Shape Style (row 6, column 2) to the shape.

3. Copy the shape to the lower-right side of the slide and apply the Intense Effect – Accent 6 Shape Style (row 6, column 7) to this shape. Change the outline color to Purple. Type True in the left triangle and False in the right triangle. Rotate the True and False text 270° and then change the font color to Dark Blue (column 9) and the font size to 40. Align the text in the left side of the shapes. Rotate the right shape 180° so that it is upside down.

4. Duplicate the slide twice and then type the questions in Table 2 in the title text placeholders.

Table 2 Quiz Questions and Answers		
New Quiz Slide	**Question**	**Answers**
1	The two opposing forces active in the environment are called yin and yang.	True
2	The five elements in the Productive Cycle shape daily life.	True
3	This room illustrates the correct placement of kitchen appliances.	False

5. Click the AutoFit Options button on the left side of the placeholders and then click Stop Fitting Text to This Placeholder to stop PowerPoint from changing the title text font size. On Slide 1, drag the placeholder's bottom sizing handle down to position the entire placeholder on the slide.

6. Display the gridlines and the ruler. Display the Opulent Slide Master and then copy the Yin and Yang symbol to the first quiz slide. Size this symbol to 150% and then align the upper-left corner with the gridline at 2" left of center and 1" above center.

7. Use the Paste Special command to copy the Productive Cycle from Slide 3 to the second quiz slide. Paste the Productive Cycle as a picture with the .png file format. Size the picture to a height of 5.5" and align the upper-left corner with the gridline at 4" left of center and 2" above center.

8. Use the Paste Special command to copy the kitchen diagram from Slide 5 to the third quiz slide and paste it as a picture with the .png file format. Size the picture to a height of 4.7" and align the upper-left corner with the gridline at 4" left of center and 2" above center.

9. Animate the two triangles and the picture on each quiz slide using the settings in Table 3.

10. Hide the gridlines and the ruler. Delete Slides 1 through 9. Open the Microsoft Visual Basic Editor and then enter the procedure to display a slide, accept a True or False answer, and then display a message box giving feedback. Use the code in Table 1 on page PPT 484 as a guide. The quiz should terminate when the user has selected the correct answer on the final quiz slide.

Continued >

STUDENT ASSIGNMENTS

In the Lab *continued*

Table 3 Quiz Objects Animation				
Order	**Object**	**Effect**	**Start Setting**	**Speed**
1	Picture	Entrance Spinner (Moderate category)	After Previous	Medium
2	Left Isosceles Triangle	Entrance Ascend (Moderate category)	After Previous	Slow
3	Right Isosceles Triangle	Entrance Ascend (Moderate category)	With Previous	Slow
4	Picture	Emphasis Blink (Exciting category)	After Previous	Slow
5 (for quiz slides 1 and 2 only)	Picture	Exit Spinner (Moderate category)	After Previous	Medium

11. Assign the macros to the two triangle shapes on each quiz slide.

12. Save the quiz as a macro-enabled presentation using the file name, Lab OF-3 Feng Shui Macro. If necessary, change the Trust Center macro setting to 'Enable all macros'.

13. Submit the revised document in the format specified by your instructor. Reset the macro setting.

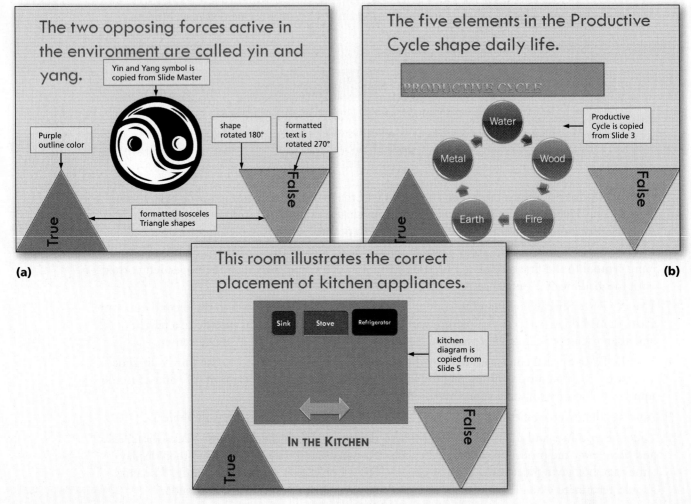

(a)

(b)

Figure 75 (c)

Appendix A
Project Planning Guidelines

Using Project Planning Guidelines

The process of communicating specific information to others is a learned, rational skill. Computers and software, especially Microsoft Office 2007, can help you develop ideas and present detailed information to a particular audience.

Using Microsoft Office 2007, you can create projects such as Word documents, Excel spreadsheets, Access databases, and PowerPoint presentations. Computer hardware and productivity software such as Microsoft Office 2007 minimizes much of the laborious work of drafting and revising projects. Some communicators handwrite ideas in notebooks, others compose directly on the computer, and others have developed unique strategies that work for their own particular thinking and writing styles.

No matter what method you use to plan a project, follow specific guidelines to arrive at a final product that presents information correctly and effectively (Figure A–1). Use some aspects of these guidelines every time you undertake a project, and others as needed in specific instances. For example, in determining content for a project, you may decide that a bar chart communicates trends more effectively than a paragraph of text. If so, you would create this graphical element and insert it in an Excel spreadsheet, a Word document, or a PowerPoint slide.

Determine the Project's Purpose

Begin by clearly defining why you are undertaking this assignment. For example, you may want to track monetary donations collected for your club's fundraising drive. Alternatively, you may be urging students to vote for a particular candidate in the next election. Once you clearly understand the purpose of your task, begin to draft ideas of how best to communicate this information.

Analyze Your Audience

Learn about the people who will read, analyze, or view your work. Where are they employed? What are their educational backgrounds? What are their expectations? What questions do they have?

PROJECT PLANNING GUIDELINES

1. DETERMINE THE PROJECT'S PURPOSE
Why are you undertaking the project?

2. ANALYZE YOUR AUDIENCE
Who are the people who will use your work?

3. GATHER POSSIBLE CONTENT
What information exists, and in what forms?

4. DETERMINE WHAT CONTENT TO PRESENT TO YOUR AUDIENCE
What information will best communicate the project's purpose to your audience?

Figure A–1

Design experts suggest drawing a mental picture of these people or finding photographs of people who fit this profile so that you can develop a project with the audience in mind.

By knowing your audience members, you can tailor a project to meet their interests and needs. You will not present them with information they already possess, and you will not omit the information they need to know.

Example: Your assignment is to raise the profile of your college's nursing program in the community. How much do they know about your college and the nursing curriculum? What are the admission requirements? How many of the applicants admitted complete the program? What percent pass the state Boards?

Gather Possible Content

Rarely are you in a position to develop all the material for a project. Typically, you would begin by gathering existing information that may reside in spreadsheets or databases. Web sites, pamphlets, magazine and newspaper articles, and books could provide insights of how others have approached your topic. Personal interviews often provide perspectives not available by any other means. Consider video and audio clips as potential sources for material that might complement or support the factual data you uncover.

Determine What Content to Present to Your Audience

Experienced designers recommend writing three or four major ideas you want an audience member to remember after reading or viewing your project. It also is helpful to envision your project's endpoint, the key fact you wish to emphasize. All project elements should lead to this ending point.

As you make content decisions, you also need to think about other factors. Presentation of the project content is an important consideration. For example, will your brochure be printed on thick, colored paper or transparencies? Will your PowerPoint presentation be viewed in a classroom with excellent lighting and a bright projector, or will it be viewed on a notebook computer monitor? Determine relevant time factors, such as the length of time to develop the project, how long readers will spend reviewing your project, or the amount of time allocated for your speaking engagement. Your project will need to accommodate all of these constraints.

Decide whether a graph, photograph, or artistic element can express or emphasize a particular concept. The right hemisphere of the brain processes images by attaching an emotion to them, so audience members are more apt to recall these graphics long term rather than just reading text.

As you select content, be mindful of the order in which you plan to present information. Readers and audience members generally remember the first and last pieces of information they see and hear, so you should put the most important information at the top or bottom of the page.

Summary

When creating a project, it is beneficial to follow some basic guidelines from the outset. By taking some time at the beginning of the process to determine the project's purpose, analyze the audience, gather possible content, and determine what content to present to the audience, you can produce a project that is informative, relevant, and effective.

Appendix B

Introduction to Microsoft Office 2007

What Is Microsoft Office 2007?

Microsoft Office 2007 is a collection of the more popular Microsoft application software. It is available in Basic, Home and Student, Standard, Small Business, Professional, Ultimate, Professional Plus, and Enterprise editions. Each edition consists of a group of programs, collectively called a suite. Table B-1 lists the suites and their components. **Microsoft Office Professional Edition 2007** includes these six programs: Microsoft Office Word 2007, Microsoft Office Excel 2007, Microsoft Office Access 2007, Microsoft Office PowerPoint 2007, Microsoft Office Publisher 2007, and Microsoft Office Outlook 2007. The programs in the Office suite allow you to work efficiently, communicate effectively, and improve the appearance of the projects you create.

Table B-1

	Microsoft Office Basic 2007	Microsoft Office Home & Student 2007	Microsoft Office Standard 2007	Microsoft Office Small Business 2007	Microsoft Office Professional 2007	Microsoft Office Ultimate 2007	Microsoft Office Professional Plus 2007	Microsoft Office Enterprise 2007
Microsoft Office Word 2007	✓	✓	✓	✓	✓	✓	✓	✓
Microsoft Office Excel 2007	✓	✓	✓	✓	✓	✓	✓	✓
Microsoft Office Access 2007					✓	✓	✓	✓
Microsoft Office PowerPoint 2007		✓	✓	✓	✓	✓	✓	✓
Microsoft Office Publisher 2007				✓	✓	✓	✓	✓
Microsoft Office Outlook 2007	✓		✓				✓	✓
Microsoft Office OneNote 2007		✓				✓		
Microsoft Office Outlook 2007 with Business Contact Manager				✓	✓	✓		
Microsoft Office InfoPath 2007						✓	✓	✓
Integrated Enterprise Content Management						✓	✓	✓
Electronic Forms						✓	✓	✓
Advanced Information Rights Management and Policy Capabilities						✓	✓	✓
Microsoft Office Communicator 2007							✓	✓
Microsoft Office Groove 2007						✓		✓

Microsoft has bundled additional programs in some versions of Office 2007, in addition to the main group of Office programs. Table B–1 on the previous page lists the components of the various Office suites.

In addition to the Office 2007 programs noted previously, Office 2007 suites can contain other programs. Microsoft Office OneNote 2007 is a digital notebook program that allows you to gather and share various types of media, such as text, graphics, video, audio, and digital handwriting. Microsoft Office InfoPath 2007 is a program that allows you to create and use electronic forms to gather information. Microsoft Office Groove 2007 provides collaborative workspaces in real time. Additional services that are oriented toward the enterprise solution also are available.

Office 2007 and the Internet, World Wide Web, and Intranets

Office 2007 allows you to take advantage of the Internet, the World Wide Web, and intranets. The Microsoft Windows operating system includes a **browser**, which is a program that allows you to locate and view a Web page. The Windows browser is called Internet Explorer.

One method of viewing a Web page is to use the browser to enter the Web address for the Web page. Another method of viewing a Web page is clicking a hyperlink. A **hyperlink** is colored or underlined text or a graphic that, when clicked, connects to another Web page. Hyperlinks placed in Office 2007 documents allow for direct access to a Web site of interest.

An **intranet** is a private network, such as a network used within a company or organization for internal communication. Like the Internet, hyperlinks are used within an intranet to access documents, pages, and other destinations on the intranet. Unlike the Internet, the materials on the network are available only for those who are part of the private network.

Online Collaboration Using Office

Organizations that, in the past, were able to make important information available only to a select few, now can make their information accessible to a wider range of individuals who use programs such as Office 2007 and Internet Explorer. Office 2007 allows colleagues to use the Internet or an intranet as a central location to view documents, manage files, and work together.

Each of the Office 2007 programs makes publishing documents on a Web server as simple as saving a file on a hard disk. Once placed on the Web server, users can view and edit the documents and conduct Web discussions and live online meetings.

Using Microsoft Office 2007

The various Microsoft Office 2007 programs each specialize in a particular task. This section describes the general functions of the more widely used Office 2007 programs, along with how they are used to access the Internet or an intranet.

Microsoft Office Word 2007

Microsoft Office Word 2007 is a full-featured word processing program that allows you to create many types of personal and business documents, including flyers, letters, resumes, business documents, and academic reports.

Word's AutoCorrect, spelling, and grammar features help you proofread documents for errors in spelling and grammar by identifying the errors and offering suggestions for corrections as you type. The live word count feature provides you with a constantly updating word count as you enter and edit text. To assist with creating specific documents, such as a business letter or resume, Word provides templates, which provide a formatted document before you type the text of the document. Quick Styles provide a live preview of styles from the Style gallery, allowing you to preview styles in the document before actually applying them.

Word automates many often-used tasks and provides you with powerful desktop publishing tools to use as you create professional looking brochures, advertisements, and newsletters. SmartArt allows you to insert interpretive graphics based on document content.

Word makes it easier for you to share documents for collaboration. The Send feature opens an e-mail window with the active document attached. The Compare Documents feature allows you easily to identify changes when comparing different document versions.

Word 2007 and the Internet   Word makes it possible to design and publish Web pages on the Internet or an intranet, insert a hyperlink to a Web page in a word processing document, as well as access and search the content of other Web pages.

Microsoft Office Excel 2007

Microsoft Office Excel 2007 is a spreadsheet program that allows you to organize data, complete calculations, graph data, develop professional looking reports, publish organized data to the Web, and access real-time data from Web sites.

In addition to its mathematical functionality, Excel 2007 provides tools for visually comparing data. For instance, when comparing a group of values in cells, you can set cell backgrounds with bars proportional to the value of the data in the cell. You can also set cell backgrounds with full-color backgrounds, or use a color scale to facilitate interpretation of data values.

Excel 2007 provides strong formatting support for tables with the new Style Preview gallery.

Excel 2007 and the Internet   Using Excel 2007, you can create hyperlinks within a worksheet to access other Office documents on the network or on the Internet. Worksheets saved as static, or unchanging Web pages can be viewed using a browser. The person viewing static Web pages cannot change them.

In addition, you can create and run queries that retrieve information from a Web page and insert the information directly into a worksheet.

Microsoft Office Access 2007

Microsoft Office Access 2007 is a comprehensive database management system (DBMS). A **database** is a collection of data organized in a manner that allows access, retrieval, and use of that data. Access 2007 allows you to create a database; add, change, and delete data in the database; sort data in the database; retrieve data from the database; and create forms and reports using the data in the database.

Access 2007 and the Internet   Access 2007 lets you generate reports, which are summaries that show only certain data from the database, based on user requirements.

Microsoft Office PowerPoint 2007

Microsoft Office PowerPoint 2007 is a complete presentation graphics program that allows you to produce professional looking presentations. With PowerPoint 2007, you can create informal presentations using overhead transparencies, electronic presentations using a projection device attached to a personal computer, formal presentations using 35mm slides or a CD, or you can run virtual presentations on the Internet.

PowerPoint 2007 and the Internet   PowerPoint 2007 allows you to publish presentations on the Internet or other networks.

Microsoft Office Publisher 2007

Microsoft Office Publisher 2007 is a desktop publishing program (DTP) that allows you to design and produce professional quality documents (newsletters, flyers, brochures, business cards, Web sites, and so on) that combine text, graphics, and photographs. Desktop publishing software provides a variety of tools, including design templates, graphic manipulation tools, color schemes or libraries, and various page wizards and templates. For large jobs, businesses use desktop publishing software to design publications that are **camera ready**, which means the files are suitable for production by outside commercial printers. Publisher 2007 also allows you to locate commercial printers, service bureaus, and copy shops willing to accept customer files created in Publisher.

Publisher 2007 allows you to design a unique image, or logo, using one of more than 45 master design sets. This, in turn, permits you to use the same design for all your printed documents (letters, business cards, brochures, and advertisements) and Web pages. Publisher includes 70 coordinated color schemes; 30 font schemes; more than 10,000 high-quality clip art images; 1,500 photographs; 1,000 Web-art graphics; 340 animated graphics; and hundreds of unique Design Gallery elements (quotations, sidebars, and so on). If you wish, you also can download additional images from the Microsoft Office Online Web page on the Microsoft Web site.

Publisher 2007 and the Internet   Publisher 2007 allows you easily to create a multipage Web site with custom color schemes, photographic images, animated images, and sounds.

Microsoft Office Outlook 2007

Microsoft Office Outlook 2007 is a powerful communications and scheduling program that helps you communicate with others, keep track of your contacts, and organize your schedule. Outlook 2007 allows you to view a To-Do bar containing tasks and appointments from your Outlook calendar. Outlook 2007 allows you to send and receive electronic mail (e-mail) and permits you to engage in real-time communication with family, friends, or coworkers using instant messaging. Outlook 2007 also provides you with the means to organize your contacts, and you can track e-mail messages, meetings, and notes with a particular contact. Outlook's Calendar, Contacts, Tasks, and Notes components aid in this organization. Contact information is available from the Outlook Calendar, Mail, Contacts, and Task components by accessing the Find a Contact feature. **Personal information management (PIM)** programs such as Outlook provide a way for individuals and workgroups to organize, find, view, and share information easily.

Microsoft Office 2007 Help

At any time while you are using one of the Office programs, you can interact with **Microsoft Office 2007 Help** for that program and display information about any topic associated with the program. Several categories of help are available. In all programs, you can access Help by pressing the F1 key on the keyboard. In Publisher 2007 and Outlook 2007, the Help window can be opened by clicking the Help menu and then selecting Microsoft Office Publisher or Outlook Help command, or by entering search text in the 'Type a question for help' text box in the upper-right corner of the program window. In the other Office programs, clicking the Microsoft Office Help button near the upper-right corner of the program window opens the program Help window.

The Help window in all programs provides several methods for accessing help about a particular topic, and has tools for navigating around Help. Appendix C contains detailed instructions for using Help.

Collaboration and SharePoint

While not part of the Microsoft Office 2007 suites, SharePoint is a Microsoft tool that allows Office 2007 users to share data using collaborative tools that are integrated into the main Office programs. SharePoint consists of Windows SharePoint Services, Office SharePoint Server 2007, and, optionally, Office SharePoint Designer 2007.

Windows SharePoint Services provides the platform for collaboration programs and services. Office SharePoint Server 2007 is built on top of Windows SharePoint Services. The result of these two products is the ability to create SharePoint sites. A SharePoint site is a Web site that provides users with a virtual place for collaborating and communicating with their colleagues while working together on projects, documents, ideas, and information. Each member of a group with access to the SharePoint site has the ability to contribute to the material stored there. The basic building blocks of SharePoint sites are lists and libraries. Lists contain collections of information, such as calendar items, discussion points, contacts, and links. Lists can be edited to add or delete information. Libraries are similar to lists, but include both files and information about files. Types of libraries include document, picture, and forms libraries.

The most basic type of SharePoint site is called a Workspace, which is used primarily for collaboration. Different types of Workspaces can be created using SharePoint to suit different needs. SharePoint provides templates, or outlines of these Workspaces, that can be filled in to create the Workspace. Each of the different types of Workspace templates contain a different collection of lists and libraries, reflecting the purpose of the Workspace. You can create a Document Workspace to facilitate collaboration on documents. A Document Workspace contains a document library for documents and supporting files, a Links list that allows you to maintain relevant resource links for the document, a Tasks list for listing and assigning To-Do items to team members, and other links as needed. Meeting Workspaces allow users to plan and organize a meeting, with components such as Attendees, Agenda, and a Document Library. Social Meeting Workspaces provide a place to plan social events, with lists and libraries such as Attendees, Directions, Image/Logo, Things To Bring, Discussions, and Picture Library. A Decision Meeting Workspace is a Meeting Workspace with a focus on review and decision-making, with lists and libraries such as Objectives, Attendees, Agenda, Document Library, Tasks, and Decisions.

Users also can create a SharePoint site called a WebParts page, which is built from modules called WebParts. WebParts are modular units of information that contain a title bar and content that reflects the type of WebPart. For instance, an image WebPart would contain a title bar and an image. WebParts allow you quickly to create and modify a SharePoint site, and allow for the creation of a unique site that can allow users to access and make changes to information stored on the site.

Large SharePoint sites that include multiple pages can be created using templates as well. Groups needing more refined and targeted sharing options than those available with SharePoint Server 2007 and Windows SharePoint Services can add SharePoint Designer 2007 to create a site that meets their specific needs.

Depending on which components have been selected for inclusion on the site, users can view a team calendar, view links, read announcements, and view and edit group documents and projects. SharePoint sites can be set up so that documents are checked in and out, much like a library, to prevent multiple users from making changes simultaneously. Once a SharePoint site is set up, Office programs are used to perform maintenance of the site. For example, changes in the team calendar are updated using Outlook 2007, and changes that users make in Outlook 2007 are reflected on the SharePoint site. Office 2007 programs include a Publish feature that allows users easily to save file updates to a SharePoint site. Team members can be notified about changes made to material on the site either by e-mail or by a news feed, meaning that users do not have to go to the site to check to see if anything has been updated since they last viewed or worked on it. The search feature in SharePoint allows users quickly to find information on a large site.

Appendix C
Microsoft
Office 2007 Help

Using Microsoft Office Help

This appendix shows how to use Microsoft Office Help. At any time while you are using one of the Microsoft Office 2007 programs, you can use Office Help to display information about all topics associated with the program. To illustrate the use of Office Help, this appendix uses Microsoft Office Word 2007. Help in other Office 2007 programs responds in a similar fashion.

In Office 2007, Help is presented in a window that has Web browser-style navigation buttons. Each Office 2007 program has its own Help home page, which is the starting Help page that is displayed in the Help window. If your computer is connected to the Internet, the contents of the Help page reflect both the local help files installed on the computer and material from Microsoft's Web site. As shown in Figure C–1, two methods for accessing Word's Help are available:

1. Microsoft Office Word Help button near the upper-right corner of the Word window
2. Function key F1 on the keyboard

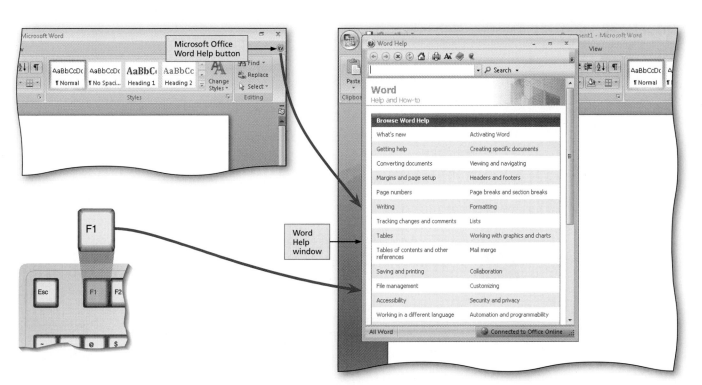

Figure C–1

To Open the Word Help Window

The following steps open the Word Help window and maximize the window.

- Start Microsoft Word, if necessary. Click the Microsoft Office Word Help button near the upper-right corner of the Word window to open the Word Help window (Figure C–2).

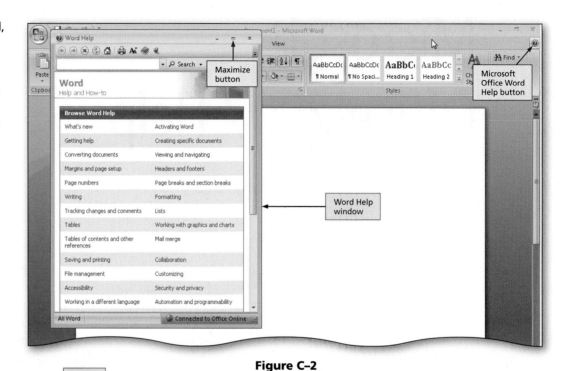

Figure C–2

- Click the Maximize button on the Help title bar to maximize the Help window (Figure C–3).

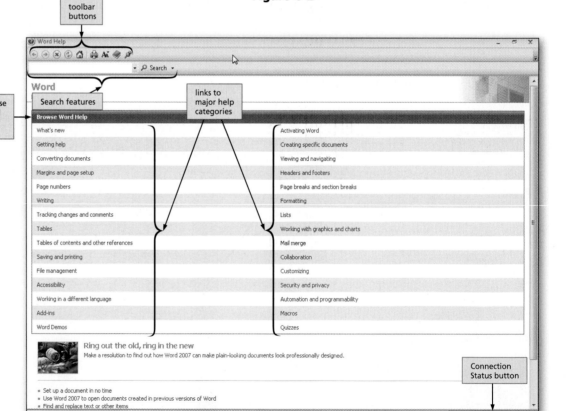

Figure C–3

The Word Help Window

The Word Help window provides several methods for accessing help about a particular topic, and also has tools for navigating around Help. Methods for accessing Help include searching the help content installed with Word, or searching the online Office content maintained by Microsoft.

Figure C–3 shows the main Word Help window. To navigate Help, the Word Help window includes search features that allow you to search on a word or phrase about which you want help; the Connection Status button, which allows you to control where Word Help searches for content; toolbar buttons; and links to major Help categories.

Search Features

You can perform Help searches on words or phrases to find information about any Word feature using the 'Type words to search for' text box and the Search button (Figure C–4a). Click the 'Type words to search for' text box and then click the Search button or press the ENTER key to initiate a search of Word Help.

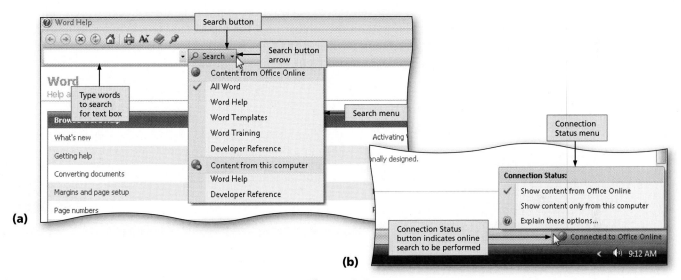

Figure C–4

Word Help offers the user the option of searching the online Help Web pages maintained by Microsoft or the offline Help files placed on your computer when you install Word. You can specify whether Word Help should search online or offline from two places: the Connection Status button on the status bar of the Word Help window, or the Search button arrow on the toolbar. The Connection Status button indicates whether Help currently is set up to work with online or offline information sources. Clicking the Connection Status button provides a menu with commands for selecting online or offline searches (Figure C–4b). The Connection Status menu allows the user to select whether Help searches will return content only from the computer (offline), or content from the computer and from Office Online (online).

Clicking the Search button arrow also provides a menu with commands for an online or offline search (Figure C–4a). These commands determine the source of information that Help searches for during the current Help session only. For example, assume that your preferred search is an offline search because you often do not have Internet access. You would set Connection Status to 'Show content only from this computer'. When you have Internet access, you can select an online search from the Search menu to search Office Online for information for your current search session only. Your search will use the Office Online resources until you quit Help. The next time you start Help, the Connection Status once again will be offline. In addition to setting the source of information that Help searches for during the current Help session, you can use the Search menu to further target the current search to one of four subcategories of online Help: Word Help, Word Templates, Word Training, and Developer Reference. The local search further can target one subcategory, Developer Reference.

In addition to searching for a word or string of text, you can use the links provided on the Browse Word Help area (Figure C–3 on page APP 10) to search for help on a topic. These links direct you to major help categories. From each major category, subcategories are available to further refine your search.

Finally, you can use the Table of Contents for Word Help to search for a topic the same way you would in a hard copy book. The Table of Contents is accessed via a toolbar button.

Toolbar Buttons

You can use toolbar buttons to navigate through the results of your search. The toolbar buttons are located on the toolbar near the top of the Help Window (Figure C–5). The toolbar buttons contain navigation buttons as well as buttons that perform other useful and common tasks in Word Help, such as printing.

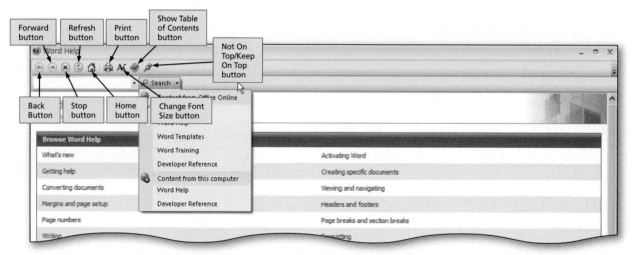

Figure C–5

The Word Help navigation buttons are the Back, Forward, Stop, Refresh, and Home buttons. These five buttons behave like the navigation buttons in a Web browser window. You can use the Back button to go back one window, the Forward button to go forward one window, the Stop button to stop loading the current page, and the Home button to redisplay the Help home page in the Help window. Use the Refresh button to reload the information requested into the Help window from its original source. When getting Help information online, this button provides the most current information from the Microsoft Help Web site.

The buttons located to the right of the navigation buttons — Print, Change Font Size, Show Table of Contents, and Not on Top — provide you with access to useful and common commands. The Print button prints the contents of the open Help window. The Change Font Size button customizes the Help window by increasing or decreasing the size of its text. The Show Table of Contents button opens a pane on the left side of the Help window that shows the Table of Contents for Word Help. You can use the Table of Contents for Word Help to navigate through the contents of Word Help much as you would use the Table of Contents in a book to search for a topic. The Not On Top button is an example of a toggle button, which is a button that can be switched back and forth between two states. It determines how the Word Help window behaves relative to other windows. When clicked, the Not On Top button changes to Keep On Top. In this state, it does not allow other windows from Word or other programs to cover the Word Help window when those windows are the active windows. When in the Not On Top state, the button allows other windows to be opened or moved on top of the Word Help window.

You can customize the size and placement of the Help window. Resize the window using the Maximize and Restore buttons, or by dragging the window to a desired size. Relocate the Help window by dragging the title bar to a new location on the screen.

Searching Word Help

Once the Word Help window is open, several methods exist for navigating Word Help. You can search for help by using any of the three following methods from the Help window:

1. Enter search text in the 'Type words to search for' text box
2. Click the links in the Help window
3. Use the Table of Contents

To Obtain Help Using the Type words to search for Text Box

Assume for the following example that you want to know more about watermarks. The following steps use the 'Type words to search for' text box to obtain useful information about watermarks by entering the word, watermark, as search text. The steps also navigate in the Word Help window.

1

- Type watermark in the 'Type words to search for' text box at the top of the Word Help window.

- Click the Search button arrow to display the Search menu (Figure C–6).

- If it is not selected already, click All Word on the Search menu to select the command. If All Word is already selected, click the Search button arrow again to close the Search menu.

Q&A

Why select All Word on the Search menu?

Selecting All Word on the Search menu ensures that Word Help will search all possible sources for information on your search term. It will produce the most complete search results.

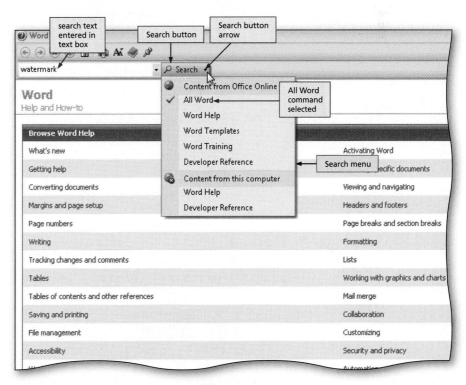

Figure C–6

• Click the Search button to display the search results (Figure C–7).

Why do my results differ?

If you do not have an Internet connection, your results will reflect only the content of the Help files on your computer. When searching for help online, results also can change as material is added, deleted, and updated on the online Help Web pages maintained by Microsoft.

Q&A Why were my search results not very helpful?

When initiating a search, keep in mind to check the spelling of the search text; and to keep your search very specific, with fewer than seven words, to return the most accurate results.

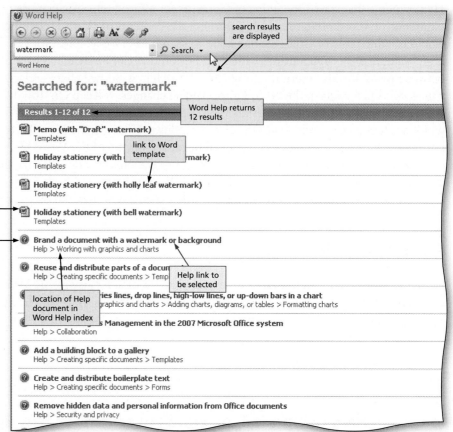

Figure C–7

• Click the 'Brand a document with a watermark or background' link to open the Help document associated with the link in the Help window (Figure C–8).

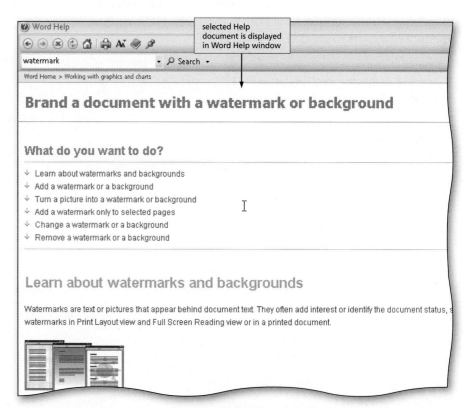

Figure C–8

4

- Click the Home button on the task-bar to clear the search results and redisplay the Word Help home page (Figure C–9).

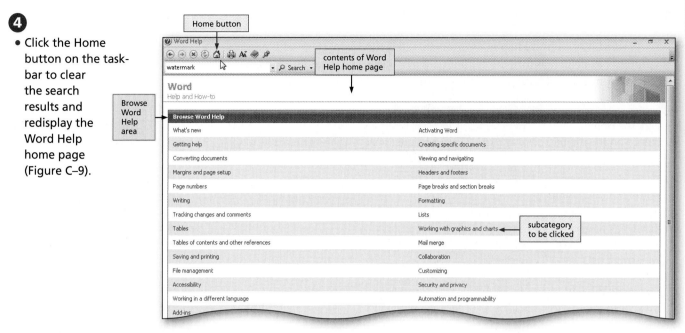

Figure C–9

To Obtain Help Using the Help Links

If your topic of interest is listed in the Browse Word Help area, you can click the link to begin browsing Word Help categories instead of entering search text. You browse Word Help just like you would browse a Web site. If you know in which category to find your Help information, you may wish to use these links. The following steps find the watermark Help information using the category links from the Word Help home page.

1

- Click the 'Working with graphics and charts' link to open the 'Working with graphics and charts' page.

- Click the 'Brand a document with a watermark or background' link to open the Help document associated with the link (Figure C–10).

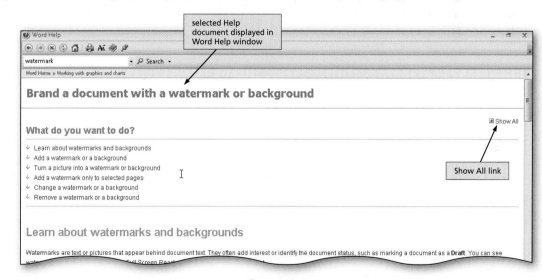

Figure C–10

Q&A What does the Show All link do?

In many Help documents, additional information about terms and features is available by clicking a link in the document to display additional information in the Help document. Clicking the Show All link opens all the links in the Help document that expand to additional text.

To Obtain Help Using the Help Table of Contents

A third way to find Help in Word is through the Help Table of Contents. You can browse through the Table of Contents to display information about a particular topic or to familiarize yourself with Word. The following steps access the watermark Help information by browsing through the Table of Contents.

• Click the Home button on the toolbar.

• Click the Show Table of Contents button on the toolbar to open the Table of Contents pane on the left side of the Help window. If necessary, click the Maximize button on the Help title bar to maximize the window (Figure C–11).

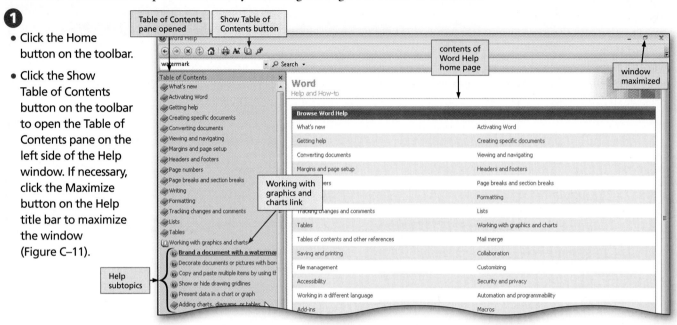

Figure C–11

• Click the 'Working with graphics and charts' link in the Table of Contents pane to view a list of Help subtopics.

• Click the 'Brand a document with a watermark or background' link in the Table of Contents pane to view the selected Help document in the right pane (Figure C–12).

Q&A

How do I remove the Table of Contents pane when I am finished with it?

The Show Table of Contents button acts as a toggle switch. When the Table of Contents pane is visible, the button changes to Hide Table of Contents. Clicking it hides the Table of Contents pane and changes the button to Show Table of Contents.

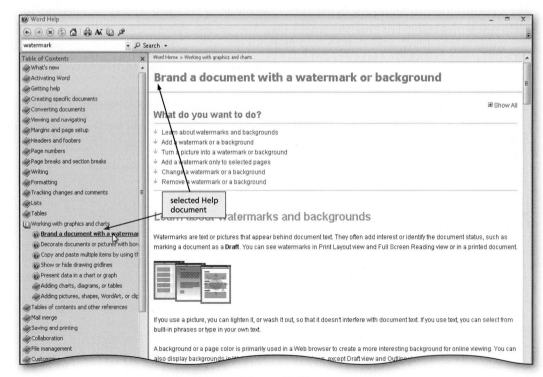

Figure C–12

Obtaining Help while Working in Word

Often you may need help while working on a document without already having the Help window open. For example, you may be unsure about how a particular command works, or you may be presented with a dialog box that you are not sure how to use. Rather than opening the Help window and initiating a search, Word Help provides you with the ability to search directly for help.

Figure C–13 shows one option for obtaining help while working in Word. If you want to learn more about a command, point to the command button and wait for the Enhanced ScreenTip to appear. If the Help icon appears in the Enhanced ScreenTip, press the F1 key while pointing to the command to open the Help window associated with that command.

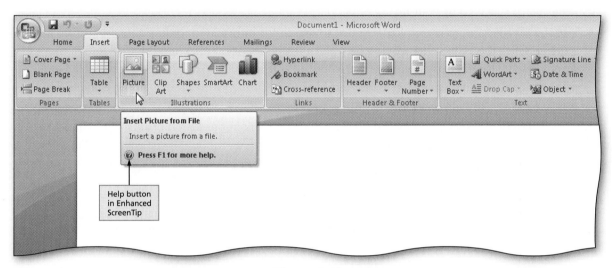

Figure C–13

Figure C–14 shows a dialog box with a Get help button in it. Pressing the F1 key while the dialog box is displayed opens a Help window. The Help window contains help about that dialog box, if available. If no help file is available for that particular dialog box, then the main Help window opens.

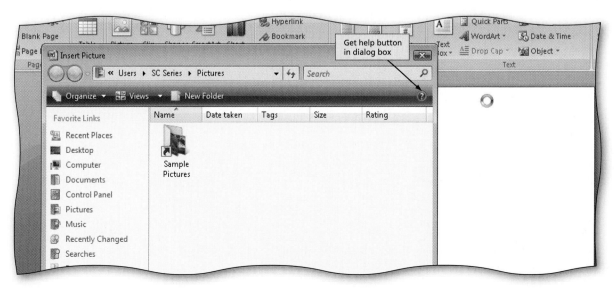

Figure C–14

Use Help

1 Obtaining Help Using Search Text

Instructions: Perform the following tasks using Word Help.

1. Use the 'Type words to search for' text box to obtain help about landscape printing. Use the Connection Status menu to search online help if you have an Internet connection.

2. Click Select page orientation in the list of links in the search results. Double-click the Microsoft Office Word Help window title bar to maximize it. Read and print the information. At the top of the printout, write down the number of links Word Help found.

3. Use the Search menu to search for help offline. Repeat the search from Step 1. At the top of the printout, write down the number of links that Word Help found searching offline. Submit the printouts as specified by your instructor.

4. Use the 'Type words to search for' text box to search for information online about adjusting line spacing. Click the 'Adjust the spacing between a list bullet or number and the text' link in the search results. If necessary, maximize the Microsoft Office 2007 Word Help window. Read and print the contents of the window. Close the Microsoft Office Word Help window. Submit the printouts as specified by your instructor.

5. For each of the following words and phrases, click one link in the search results, click the Show All link, and then print the page: page zoom; date; print preview; Ribbon; word count; and citation. Submit the printouts as specified by your instructor.

2 Expanding on Word Help Basics

Instructions: Use Word Help to better understand its features and answer the questions listed below. Answer the questions on your own paper, or submit the printed Help information as specified by your instructor.

1. Use Help to find out how to customize the Help window. Change the font size to the smallest option and then print the contents of the Microsoft Office Word Help window. Change the font size back to its original setting. Close the window.

2. Press the F1 key. Search for information about tables, restricting the search results to Word Templates. Print the first page of the Search results.

3. Search for information about tables, restricting the search results to Word Help files. Print the first page of the Search results.

4. Use Word Help to find out what happened to the Office Assistant, a feature in the previous version of Word. Print out the Help document that contains the answer.

Appendix D

Publishing Office 2007 Web Pages to a Web Server

With the Office 2007 programs, you use the Save As command on the Office Button menu to save a Web page to a Web server using one of two techniques: Web folders or File Transfer Protocol. A **Web folder** is an Office shortcut to a Web server. **File Transfer Protocol (FTP)** is an Internet standard that allows computers to exchange files with other computers on the Internet.

You should contact your network system administrator or technical support staff at your Internet access provider to determine if their Web server supports Web folders, FTP, or both, and to obtain necessary permissions to access the Web server. If you decide to publish Web pages using a Web folder, you must have the Office Server Extensions (OSE) installed on your computer.

Using Web Folders to Publish Office 2007 Web Pages

When publishing to a Web folder, someone first must create the Web folder before you can save to it. If you are granted permission to create a Web folder, you must obtain the Web address of the Web server, a user name, and possibly a password that allows you to access the Web server. You also must decide on a name for the Web folder. Table D–1 explains how to create a Web folder.

Office 2007 adds the name of the Web folder to the list of current Web folders. You can save to this folder, open files in the folder, rename the folder, or perform any operations you would to a folder on your hard disk. You can use your Office 2007 program or Windows Explorer to access this folder. Table D–2 explains how to save to a Web folder.

Table D–1 Creating a Web Folder
1. Click the Office Button and then click Save As or Open.
2. When the Save As dialog box (or Open dialog box) appears, click the Tools button arrow, and then click Map Network Drive... When the Map Network Drive dialog box is displayed, click the 'Connect to a Web site that you can use to store your documents and pictures' link.
3. When the Add Network Location Wizard dialog box appears, click the Next button. If necessary, click Choose a custom network location. Click the Next button. Click the View examples link, type the Internet or network address, and then click the Next button. Click 'Log on anonymously' to deselect the check box, type your user name in the User name text box, and then click the Next button. Enter the name you want to call this network place and then click the Next button. Click to deselect the 'Open this network location when I click Finish' check box, and then click the Finish button.

Table D–2 Saving to a Web Folder
1. Click the Office Button, click Save As.
2. When the Save As dialog box is displayed, type the Web page file name in the File name text box. Do not press the ENTER key.
3. Click the Save as type box arrow and then click Web Page to select the Web Page format.
4. Click Computer in the Navigation pane.
5. Double-click the Web folder name in the Network Location list.
6. If the Enter Network Password dialog box appears, type the user name and password in the respective text boxes and then click the OK button.
7. Click the Save button in the Save As dialog box.

Using FTP to Publish Office 2007 Web Pages

When publishing a Web page using FTP, you first must add the FTP location to your computer before you can save to it. An FTP location, also called an **FTP site**, is a collection of files that reside on an FTP server. In this case, the FTP server is the Web server.

To add an FTP location, you must obtain the name of the FTP site, which usually is the address (URL) of the FTP server, and a user name and a password that allows you to access the FTP server. You save and open the Web pages on the FTP server using the name of the FTP site. Table D–3 explains how to add an FTP site.

Office 2007 adds the name of the FTP site to the FTP locations list in the Save As and Open dialog boxes. You can open and save files using this list. Table D–4 explains how to save to an FTP location.

Table D–3 Adding an FTP Location
1. Click the Office Button and then click Save As or Open.
2. When the Save As dialog box (or Open dialog box) appears, click the Tools button arrow, and then click Map Network Drive... When the Map Network Drive dialog box is displayed, click the 'Connect to a Web site that you can use to store your documents and pictures' link.
3. When the Add Network Location Wizard dialog box appears, click the Next button. If necessary, click Choose a custom network location. Click the Next button. Click the View examples link, type the Internet or network address, and then click the Next button. If you have a user name for the site, click to deselect 'Log on anonymously' and type your user name in the User name text box, and then click Next. If the site allows anonymous logon, click Next. Type a name for the location, click Next, click to deselect the 'Open this network location when I click Finish' check box, and click Finish. Click the OK button.
4. Close the Save As or the Open dialog box.

Table D–4 Saving to an FTP Location
1. Click the Office Button and then click Save As.
2. When the Save As dialog box is displayed, type the Web page file name in the File name text box. Do not press the ENTER key.
3. Click the Save as type box arrow and then click Web Page to select the Web Page format.
4. Click Computer in the Navigation pane.
5. Double-click the name of the FTP site in the Network Location list.
6. When the FTP Log On dialog box appears, enter your user name and password and then click the OK button.
7. Click the Save button in the Save As dialog box.

Appendix E
Customizing Microsoft Office 2007

This appendix explains how to change the screen resolution in Windows Vista to the resolution used in this book. It also describes how to customize the Word window by changing the Ribbon, Quick Access Toolbar, and the color scheme.

Changing Screen Resolution

Screen resolution indicates the number of pixels (dots) that the computer uses to display the letters, numbers, graphics, and background you see on the screen. When you increase the screen resolution, Windows displays more information on the screen, but the information decreases in size. The reverse also is true: as you decrease the screen resolution, Windows displays less information on the screen, but the information increases in size.

The screen resolution usually is stated as the product of two numbers, such as 1024×768 (pronounced "ten twenty-four by seven sixty-eight"). A 1024×768 screen resolution results in a display of 1,024 distinct pixels on each of 768 lines, or about 786,432 pixels. The figures in this book were created using a screen resolution of 1024×768.

The screen resolutions most commonly used today are 800×600 and 1024×768, although some Office specialists set their computers at a much higher screen resolution, such as 2048×1536.

To Change the Screen Resolution

The following steps change the screen resolution from 1280×1024 to 1024×768. Your computer already may be set to 1024×768 or some other resolution.

- If necessary, minimize all programs so that the Windows Vista desktop appears.

- Right-click the Windows Vista desktop to display the Windows Vista desktop shortcut menu (Figure E–1).

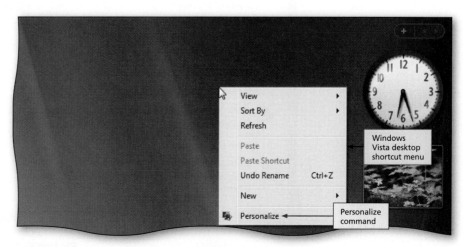

Figure E–1

- Click Personalize on the shortcut menu to open the Personalization window.

- Click Display Settings in the Personalization window to display the Display Settings dialog box (Figure E–2).

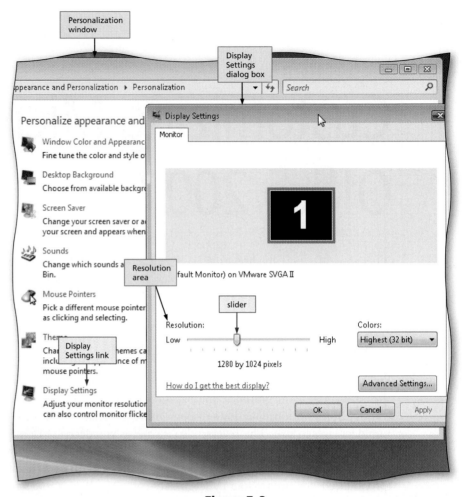

Figure E–2

- Drag the slider in the Resolution area so that the screen resolution changes to 1024 × 768 (Figure E–3).

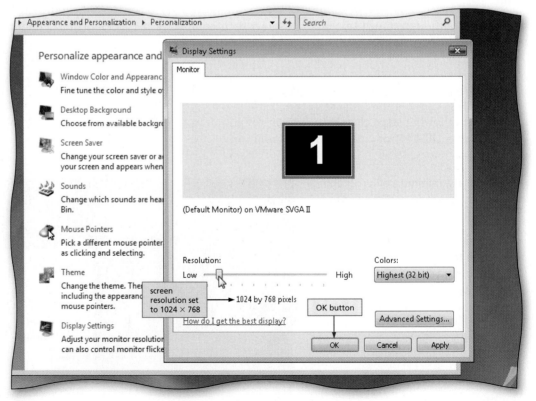

Figure E–3

4

- Click the OK button to change the screen resolution from 1280 × 1024 to 1024 × 768 (Figure E–4).

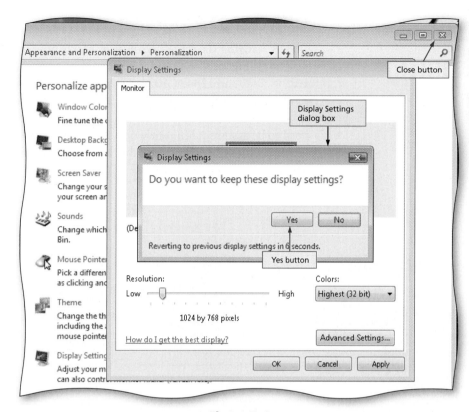

Figure E–4

5

- Click the Yes button in the Display Settings dialog box to accept the new screen resolution (Figure E–5).

Q&A

What if I do not want to change the screen resolution after seeing it applied after I click the OK button?

You either can click the No button in the inner Display Settings dialog box, or wait for the timer to run out, at which point Windows Vista will revert to the original screen resolution.

- Click the Close button to close the Personalization Window.

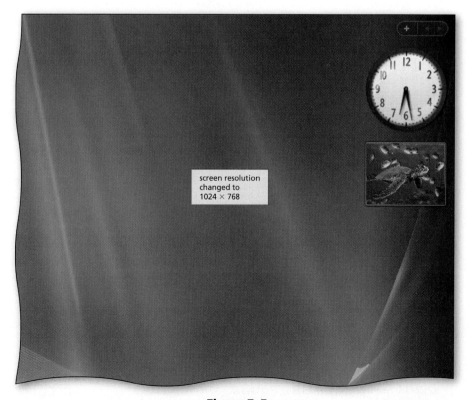

Figure E–5

Screen Resolution and the Appearance of the Ribbon in Office 2007 Programs

Changing the screen resolution affects how the Ribbon appears in Office 2007 programs. Figure E–6 shows the Word Ribbon at the screen resolutions of 800 × 600, 1024 × 768, and 1280 × 1024. All of the same commands are available regardless of screen resolution. Word, however, makes changes to the groups and the buttons within the groups to accommodate the various screen resolutions. The result is that certain commands may need to be accessed differently depending on the resolution chosen. A command that is visible on the Ribbon and available by clicking a button at one resolution may not be visible and may need to be accessed using its group button at a different resolution.

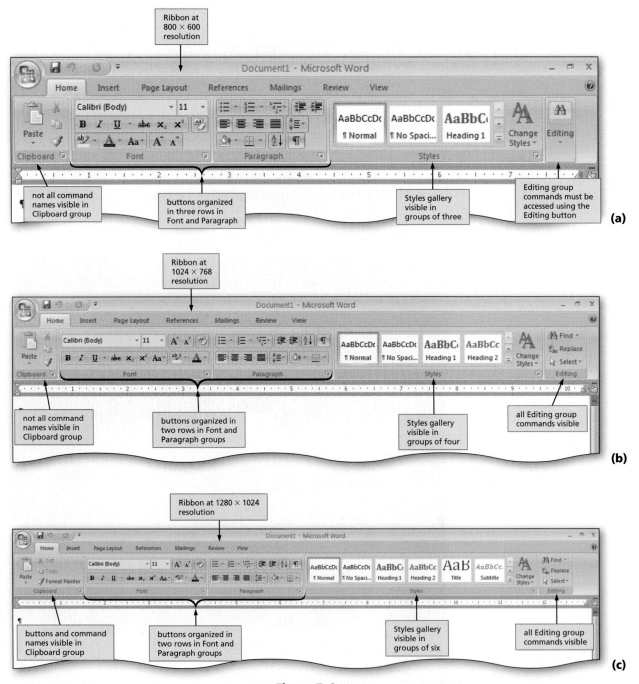

Figure E–6

Comparing the three Ribbons, notice changes in content and layout of the groups and galleries. In some cases, the content of a group is the same in each resolution, but the layout of the group differs. For example, the same buttons appear in the Font and Paragraph groups in the three resolutions, but the layouts differ. The buttons are displayed in three rows at the 800 × 600 resolution, and in two rows in the 1024 × 768 and 1280 × 1024 resolutions. In other cases, the content and layout are the same across the resolution, but the level of detail differs with the resolution. In the Clipboard group, when the resolution increases to 1280 × 1024, the names of all the buttons in the group appear in addition to the buttons themselves. At the lower resolution, only the buttons appear.

Changing resolutions also can result in fewer commands being visible in a group. Comparing the Editing groups, notice that the group at the 800 × 600 resolution consists of an Editing button, while at the higher resolutions, the group has three buttons visible. The commands that are available on the Ribbon at the higher resolutions must be accessed using the Editing button at the 800 × 600 resolution.

Changing resolutions results in different amounts of detail being available at one time in the galleries on the Ribbon. The Styles gallery in the three resolutions presented show different numbers of styles. At 800 × 600, you can scroll through the gallery three styles at a time, at 1024 × 768, you can scroll through the gallery four styles at a time, and at 1280 × 1024, you can scroll through the gallery six styles at a time.

Customizing the Word Window

When working in Word, you may want to make your working area as large as possible. One option is to minimize the Ribbon. You also can modify the characteristics of the Quick Access Toolbar, customizing the toolbar's commands and location to better suit your needs.

To Minimize the Ribbon in Word

The following steps minimize the Ribbon.

- Start Word.

- Maximize the Word window, if necessary.

- Click the Customize Quick Access Toolbar button on the Quick Access Toolbar to display the Customize Quick Access Toolbar menu (Figure E–7).

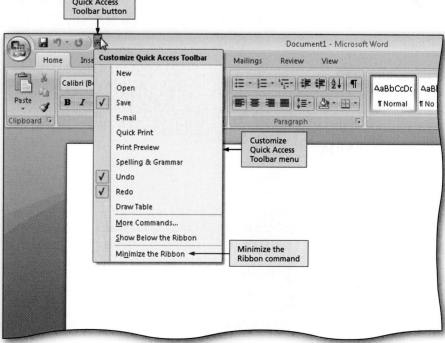

Figure E–7

2

- Click Minimize the Ribbon on the Quick Access Toolbar to reduce the Ribbon display to just the tabs (Figure E–8).

Figure E–8

Other Ways

1. Double-click the active Ribbon tab
2. Press CTRL+F1

Customizing and Resetting the Quick Access Toolbar

The Quick Access Toolbar, located to the right of the Microsoft Office Button by default, provides easy access to some of the more frequently used commands in Word (Figure E–7). By default, the Quick Access Toolbar contains buttons for the Save, Undo, and Redo commands. Customize the Quick Access Toolbar by changing its location in the window and by adding additional buttons to reflect which commands you would like to be able to access easily.

To Change the Location of the Quick Access Toolbar

The following steps move the Quick Access Toolbar to below the Ribbon.

1

- Double-click the Home tab to redisplay the Ribbon.

- Click the Customize Quick Access Toolbar button on the Quick Access Toolbar menu to display the Customize Quick Access Toolbar menu (Figure E–9).

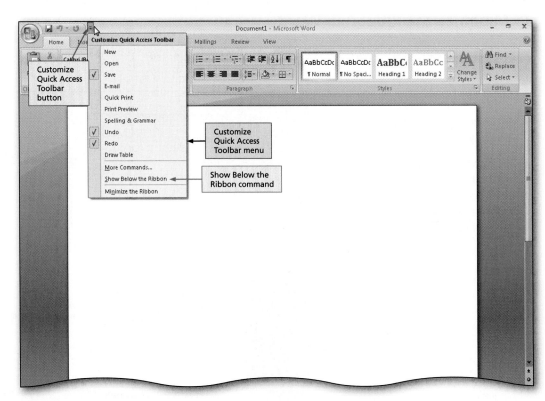

Figure E–9

● Click Show Below the Ribbon on the Quick Access Toolbar menu to move the Quick Access Toolbar below the Ribbon (Figure E–10).

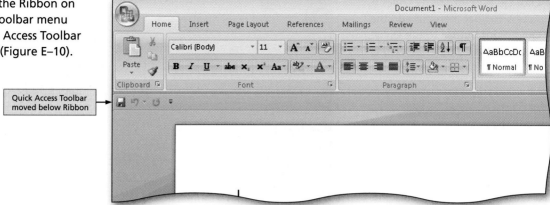

Figure E–10

To Add Commands to the Quick Access Toolbar Using the Customize Quick Access Toolbar Menu

Some of the more commonly added commands are available for selection from the Customize Quick Access Toolbar menu. The following steps add the Quick Print button to the Quick Access Toolbar.

● Click the Customize Quick Access Toolbar button to display the Customize Quick Access Toolbar menu (Figure E–11).

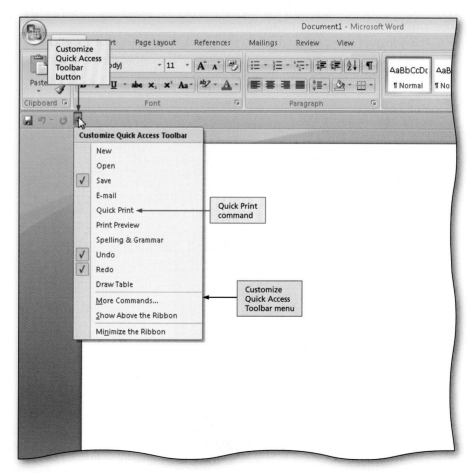

Figure E–11

- Click Quick Print on the Quick Access Toolbar menu to add the Quick Print button to the Quick Access Toolbar (Figure E–12).

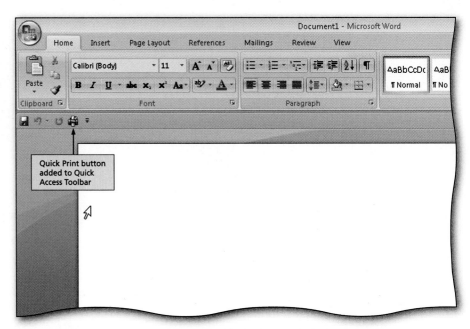

Figure E–12

To Add Commands to the Quick Access Toolbar Using the Shortcut Menu

Commands also can be added to the Quick Access Toolbar from the Ribbon. Adding an existing Ribbon command that you use often to the Quick Access Toolbar makes the command immediately available, regardless of which tab is active.

- Click the Review tab on the Ribbon to make it the active tab.

- Right-click the Spelling & Grammar button on the Review tab to display a shortcut menu (Figure E–13).

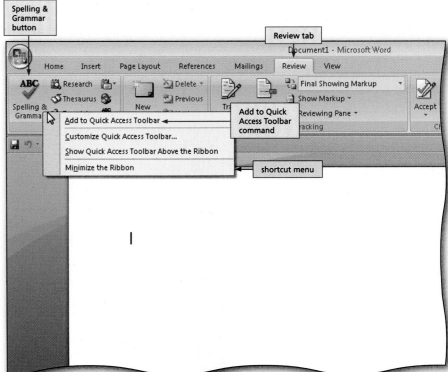

Figure E–13

2

- Click Add to Quick Access Toolbar on the shortcut menu to add the Spelling & Grammar button to the Quick Access Toolbar (Figure E–14).

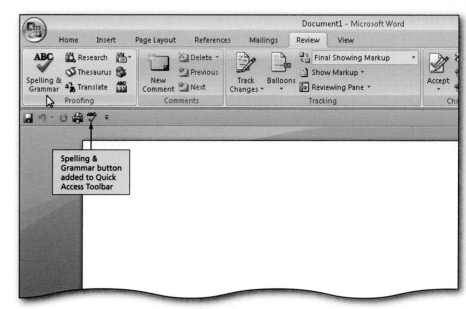

Spelling & Grammar button added to Quick Access Toolbar

Figure E–14

To Add Commands to the Quick Access Toolbar Using Word Options

Some commands do not appear on the Ribbon. They can be added to the Quick Access Toolbar using the Word Options dialog box.

1

- Click the Office Button to display the Office Button menu (Figure E–15).

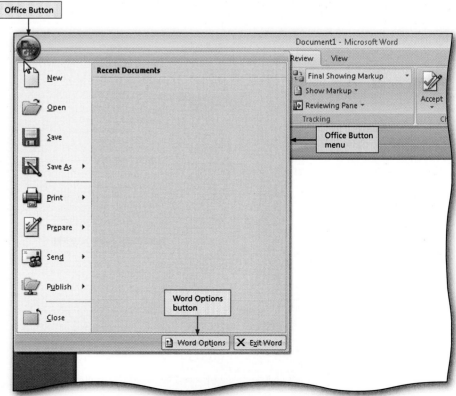

Office Button

Office Button menu

Word Options button

Figure E–15

- Click the Word Options button on the Office Button menu to display the Word Options dialog box (Figure E–16).

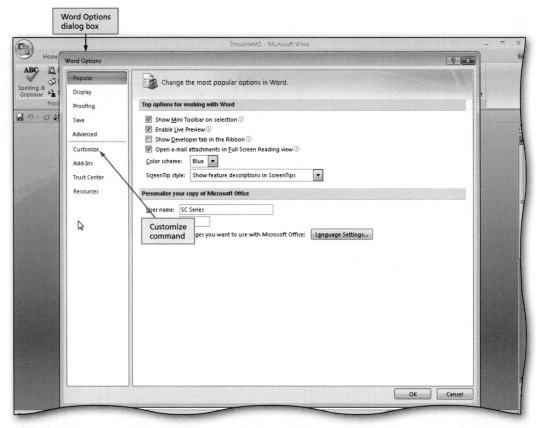

Figure E–16

- Click Customize in the left pane.

- Click 'Choose commands from' box arrow to display the 'Choose commands from' list.

- Click Commands Not in the Ribbon in the 'Choose commands from' list.

- Scroll to display the Web Page Preview command.

- Click Web Page Preview to select it (Figure E–17).

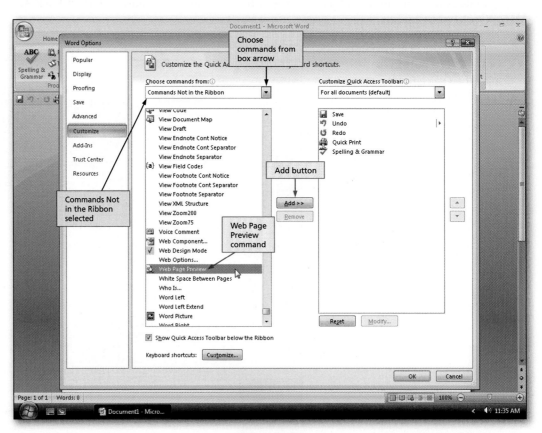

Figure E–17

4

• Click the Add button to add the Web Page Preview button to the list of buttons on the Quick Access Toolbar (Figure E–18).

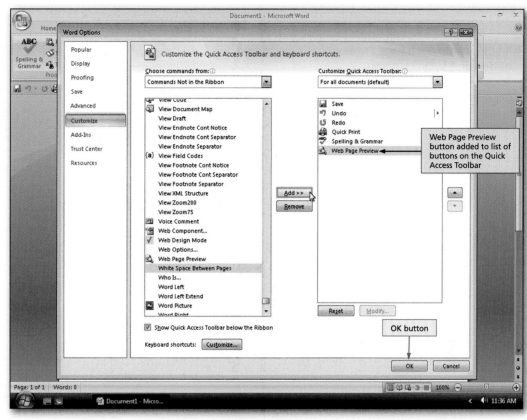

Figure E–18

5

• Click the OK button to add the Web Page Preview button to the Quick Access Toolbar (Figure E–19).

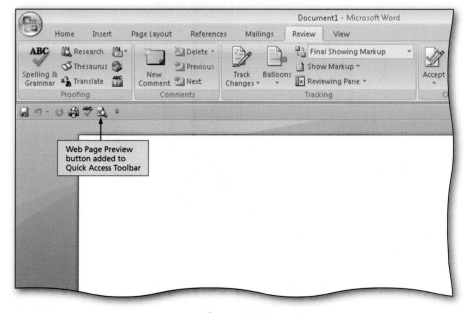

Figure E–19

Other Ways

1. Click Customize Quick Access Toolbar button, click More Commands, select commands to add, click Add button, click OK button

To Remove a Command from the Quick Access Toolbar

- Right-click the Web Page Preview button on the Quick Access Toolbar to display a shortcut menu (Figure E–20).

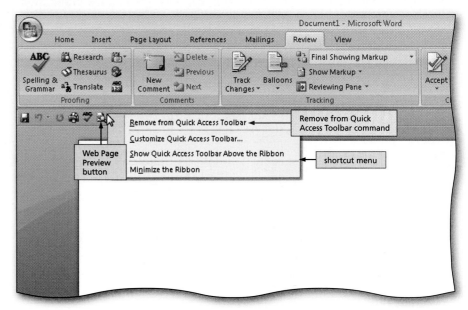

Figure E–20

- Click Remove from Quick Access Toolbar on the shortcut menu to remove the button from the Quick Access Toolbar (Figure E–21).

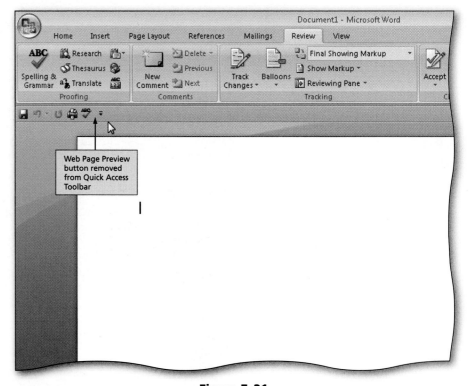

Figure E–21

Other Ways

1. Click Customize Quick Access Toolbar button, click More Commands, click the command you wish to remove in the Customize Quick Access Toolbar list, click Remove button, click OK button

2. If the command appears on the Customize Quick Access Toolbar menu, click the Customize Quick Access Toolbar button, click the command you wish to remove

To Reset the Quick Access Toolbar

1

- Click the Customize Quick Access Toolbar button on the Quick Access Toolbar.

- Click More Commands on the Quick Access Toolbar menu to display the Word Options Dialog box.

- Click the Show Quick Access Toolbar below the Ribbon check box to deselect it (Figure E–22).

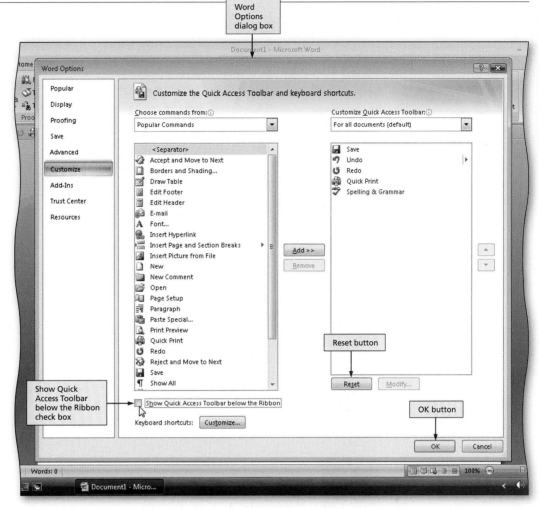

Figure E–22

- Click the Reset button, click the Yes button in the dialog box that appears, and then click the OK button in the Word Options dialog box, to reset the Quick Access Toolbar to its original position to the right of the Office Button, with the original three buttons (Figure E–23).

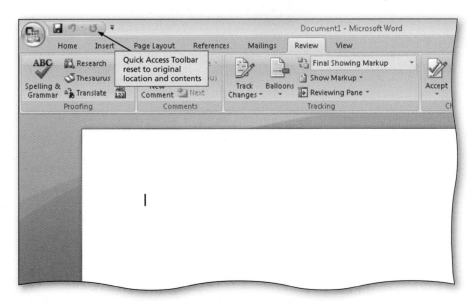

Figure E–23

Changing the Word Color Scheme

The Microsoft Word window can be customized by selecting a color scheme other than the default blue one. Three color schemes are available in Word.

To Change the Word Color Scheme

The following steps change the color scheme.

1

- Click the Office Button to display the Office Button menu.

- Click the Word Options button on the Office Button menu to display the Word Options dialog box.

- If necessary, click Popular in the left pane. Click the Color scheme box arrow to display a list of color schemes (Figure E–24).

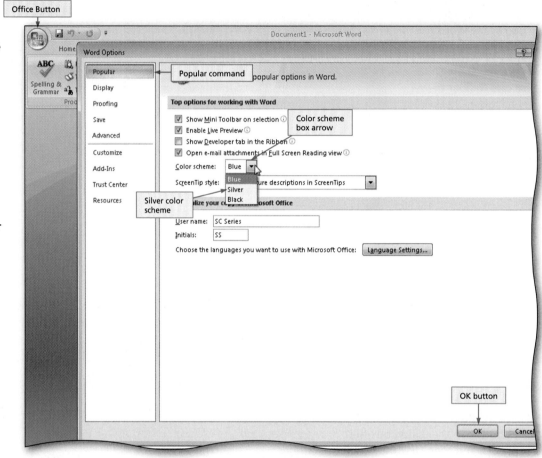

Figure E–24

2

- Click Silver in the list.

- Click the OK button to change the color scheme to silver (Figure E–25).

 Q&A

How do I switch back to the default color scheme?

Follow the steps for changing the Word color scheme, and select Blue from the list of color schemes.

Figure E–25

Appendix F
Steps for the Windows XP User

For the XP User of this Book

For most tasks, no differences exist between using Office 2007 under the Windows Vista operating system and using an Office 2007 program under the Windows XP operating system. With some tasks, however, you will see some differences, or need to complete the tasks using different steps. This appendix shows how to Start an Application, Save a Document, Open a Document, Insert a Picture, and Insert Text from a File while using Microsoft Office under Windows XP. To illustrate these tasks, this appendix uses Microsoft Word. The tasks can be accomplished in other Office programs in a similar fashion.

To Start Word

The following steps, which assume Windows is running, start Word based on a typical installation. You may need to ask your instructor how to start Word for your computer.

1

- Click the Start button on the Windows taskbar to display the Start menu.

- Point to All Programs on the Start menu to display the All Programs submenu.

- Point to Microsoft Office on the All Programs submenu to display the Microsoft Office submenu (Figure F–1).

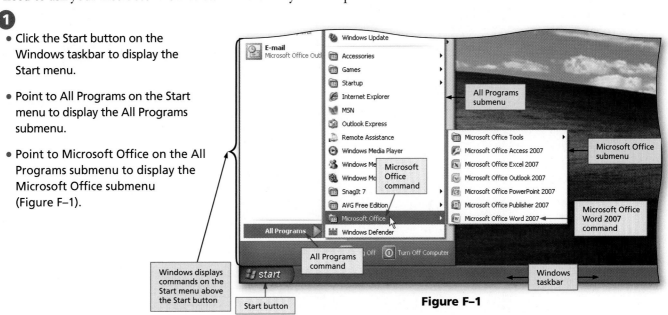

Figure F–1

- Click Microsoft Office Word 2007 to start Word and display a new blank document in the Word window (Figure F–2).

- If the Word window is not maximized, click the Maximize button next to the Close button on its title bar to maximize the window.

- If the Print Layout button is not selected, click it so that your screen layout matches Figure F–2.

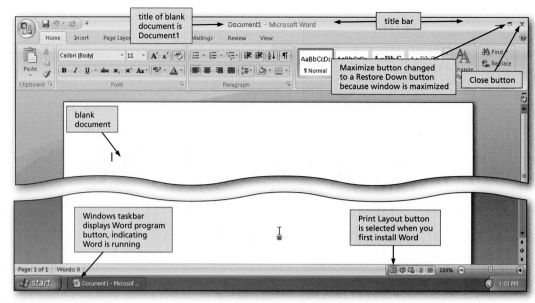

Figure F–2

Other Ways
1. Double-click Word icon on desktop, if one is present
2. Click Microsoft Office Word 2007 on Start menu

To Save a Document

After editing, you should save the document. The following steps save a document on a USB flash drive using the file name, Horseback Riding Lessons Flyer.

- With a USB flash drive connected to one of the computer's USB ports, click the Save button on the Quick Access Toolbar to display the Save As dialog box (Figure F–3).

Q&A

Do I have to save to a USB flash drive?

No. You can save to any device or folder. A **folder** is a specific location on a storage medium. You can save to the default folder or a different folder. You also can create your own folders, which is explained later in this book.

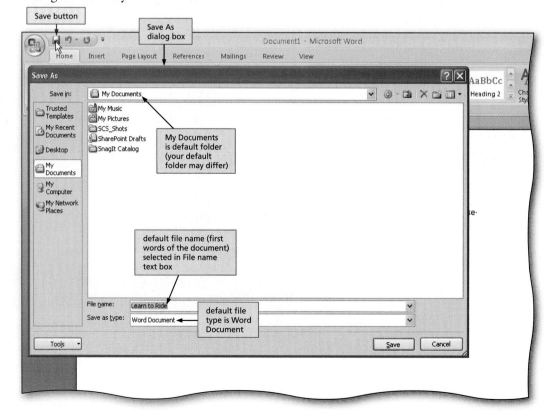

Figure F–3

• Type the name of your file (Horseback Riding Lessons Flyer in this example) in the File name text box to change the file name. Do not press the ENTER key after typing the file name (Figure F–4).

Q&A What characters can I use in a file name?

A file name can have a maximum of 255 characters, including spaces. The only invalid characters are the backslash (\), slash (/), colon (:), asterisk (*), question mark (?), quotation mark ("), less than symbol (<), greater than symbol (>), and vertical bar (|).

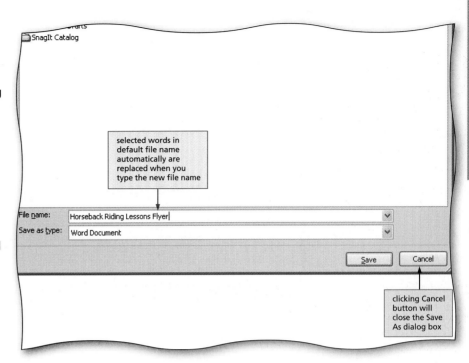

Figure F–4

• Click the Save in box arrow to display a list of available drives and folders (Figure F–5).

Q&A Why is my list of files, folders, and drives arranged and named differently from those shown in the figure?

Your computer's configuration determines how the list of files and folders is displayed and how drives are named. You can change the save location by clicking shortcuts on the **My Places bar**.

Q&A How do I save the file if I am not using a USB flash drive?

Use the same process, but be certain to select your device in the Save in list.

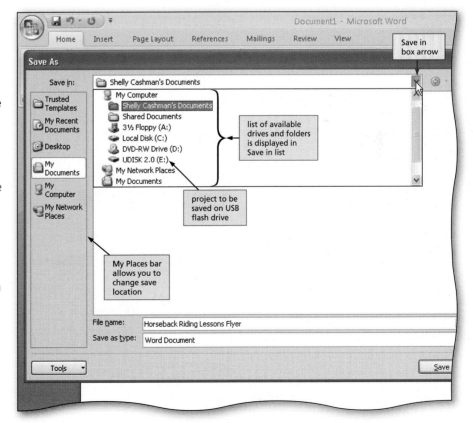

Figure F–5

• Click UDISK 2.0 (E:) in the Save in list to select the USB flash drive, Drive E in this case, as the new save location (Figure F–6).

• Click the Save button to save the document.

Q&A

What if my USB flash drive has a different name or letter?

It is very likely that your USB flash drive will have a different name and drive letter and be connected to a different port. Verify the device in your Save in list is correct.

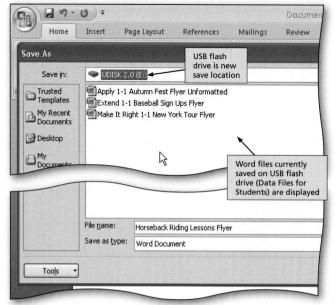
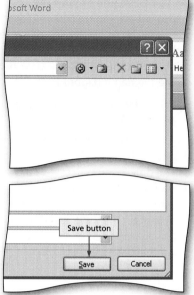

Figure F–6

Other Ways

1. Click Office Button, click Save, type file name, select drive or folder, click Save button

2. Press CTRL+S or press SHIFT+F12, type file name, select drive or folder, click Save button

To Open a Document

The following steps open the Horseback Riding Lessons Flyer file from the USB flash drive.

❶

• With your USB flash drive connected to one of the computer's USB ports, click the Office Button to display the Office Button menu.

• Click Open on the Office Button menu to display the Open dialog box.

• If necessary, click the Look in box arrow and then click UDISK 2.0 (E:) to select the USB flash drive, Drive E in this case, in the Look in list as the new open location.

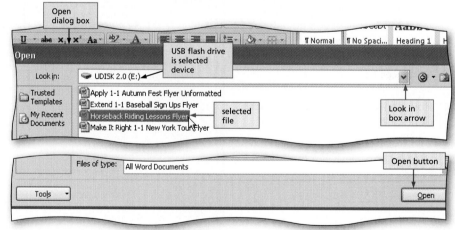

Figure F–7

• Click Horseback Riding Lessons Flyer to select the file name (Figure F–7).

• Click the Open button to open the document.

Q&A

How do I open the file if I am not using a USB flash drive?

Use the same process, but be certain to select your device in the Look in list.

Other Ways

1. Click Office Button, double-click file name in Recent Documents list

2. Press CTRL+O, select file name, press ENTER

To Insert a Picture

The following steps insert a centered picture, which, in this example, is located on a USB flash drive.

1 Position the insertion point where you want the picture to be located. Click Insert on the Ribbon to display the Insert tab. Click the Insert Picture from File button on the Insert tab to display the Insert Picture dialog box.

2 With your USB flash drive connected to one of the computer's USB ports, if necessary, click the Look in box arrow and then click UDISK 2.0 (E:) to select the USB flash drive, Drive E in this case, in the Look in list as the device that contains the picture. Select the file name of the picture file.

3 Click the Insert button in the dialog box to insert the picture at the location of the insertion point in the document.

To Insert Text from a File

The following steps insert text from a file located on the USB flash drive.

1 Click where you want to insert the text. Click Insert on the Ribbon to display the Insert tab. Click the Object button arrow in the Text group to display the Object menu. Click Text from File to display the Insert File dialog box.

2 With your USB flash drive connected to one of the computer's USB ports, if necessary, click the Look in box arrow and then click UDISK 2.0 (E:) to select the USB flash drive, Drive E in this case, in the Look in list as the device that contains the file. Click to select the file name.

3 Click the Insert button in the dialog box to insert the file at the location of the insertion point in the document.

To Create a New Database

The following steps create a database on a USB flash drive.

1 With a USB flash drive connected to one of the computer's USB ports, click Blank Database in the Getting Started with Microsoft Office Access screen to create a new blank database.

2 Type the name of your database in the File Name text box and then click the 'Browse for a location to put your database' button to display the File New Database dialog box.

3 Click the Save in box arrow to display a list of available drives and folders and then click UDISK 2.0 (E:) (your letter may be different) in the Save in list to select the USB flash drive as the new save location.

4 Click the OK button to select the USB flash drive as the location for the database and to return to the Getting Started with Microsoft Office Access screen.

5 Click the Create button to create the database on the USB flash drive with the file name you selected.

To Open a Database

The following steps use the More button to open a database from the USB flash drive.

1 With your USB flash drive connected to one of the computer's USB ports, click the More button to display the Open dialog box.

2 If necessary, click the Look in box arrow and then click UDISK 2.0 (E:) to select the USB flash drive in the Look in list as the new open location. (Your drive letter might be different.)

3 Select the file name. Click the Open button to open the database.

4 If a Security Warning appears, click the Options button to display the Microsoft Office Security Options dialog box. With the option button to enable this content selected, click the OK button to enable the content.

Appendix G
Microsoft Business Certification Program

What Is the Microsoft Business Certification Program?

The Microsoft Business Certification Program enables candidates to show that they have something exceptional to offer – proved expertise in Microsoft Office 2007 programs. The two certification tracks allow candidates to choose how they want to exhibit their skills, either through validating skills within a specific Microsoft product or taking their knowledge to the next level and combining Microsoft programs to show that they can apply multiple skill sets to complete more complex office tasks. Recognized by businesses and schools around the world, more than 3 million certifications have been obtained in more than 100 different countries. The Microsoft Business Certification Program is the only Microsoft-approved certification program of its kind.

What Is the Microsoft Certified Application Specialist Certification?

The Microsoft Certified Application Specialist certification exams focus on validating specific skill sets within each of the Microsoft Office system programs. Candidates can choose which exam(s) they want to take according to which skills they want to validate. The available Application Specialist exams include:

- Using Windows Vista™
- Using Microsoft® Office Word 2007
- Using Microsoft® Office Excel® 2007
- Using Microsoft® Office PowerPoint® 2007
- Using Microsoft® Office Access™ 2007
- Using Microsoft® Office Outlook® 2007

> For more information and details on how Shelly Cashman Series textbooks map to Microsoft Certified Application Specialist certification, visit scsite.com/off2007/cert.

What Is the Microsoft Certified Application Professional Certification?

The Microsoft Certified Application Professional certification exams focus on a candidate's ability to use the 2007 Microsoft® Office system to accomplish industry-agnostic functions, for example Budget Analysis and Forecasting, or Content Management and Collaboration. The available Application Professional exams currently include:

- Organizational Support
- Creating and Managing Presentations
- Content Management and Collaboration
- Budget Analysis and Forecasting

Index

Quick Reference Summary

In the Microsoft Office 2007 programs, you can accomplish a task in a number of ways. The following five tables (one each for Microsoft Office Word 2007, Microsoft Office Excel 2007, Microsoft Office Access 2007, Microsoft Office PowerPoint 2007, and Microsoft Office Outlook 2007) provide a quick reference to each task presented in this textbook. The first column identifies the task. The second column indicates the page number on which the task is discussed in the book. The subsequent four columns list the different ways the task in column one can be carried out.

Table 1 Microsoft Office Word 2007 Quick Reference Summary

Task	Page Number	Mouse	Ribbon	Shortcut Menu	Keyboard Shortcut
1.5 Line Spacing	WD 86		Line spacing button on Home tab	Paragraph | Indents and Spacing tab	CTRL+5
Address, Validate	WD 348		Edit Recipient List button on Mailings tab | Validate addresses link		
AddressBlock Merge Field, Add	WD 357		Address Block button on Mailings tab		
Arrange All Open Documents	WD 435		Arrange All button on View tab		
AutoCorrect Entry, Create	WD 93	Office Button | Word Options button | Proofing | AutoCorrect Options button			
AutoCorrect Options Menu, Display	WD 92	Point to text automatically corrected, point to small blue box, click AutoCorrect Options button			
Background Color, Add	WD 221		Page Color button on Page Layout tab		
Bibliographical List, Create	WD 113		Bibliography button on References tab | Insert Bibliography		
Bibliographical List, Modify Source and Update List	WD 117		Manage Sources button on References tab | select source | Edit button		

Table 1 Microsoft Office Word 2007 Quick Reference Summary (continued)

Task	Page Number	Mouse	Ribbon	Shortcut Menu	Keyboard Shortcut
Bibliography Style, Change	WD 95		Bibliography Style box arrow on References tab		
Blank Page, Insert	WD 535		Blank Page button on Insert tab		
Blog Post, Create Blank Document for	WD 718	Office Button | Publish | Blog			
Blog Post, Insert Category	WD 723		Insert Category button on Blog Post tab		
Blog Post, Open Existing	WD 726		Open Existing button on Blog Post tab		
Blog Post, Publish	WD 726		Publish button on Blog Post tab		
Blog Web Page, Display in Web Browser Window	WD 725		Home Page button on Blog Post tab		
Bold	WD 34	Bold button on Mini toolbar	Bold button on Home tab	Font | Font tab | Bold in Font style list	CTRL+B
Bookmark, Add	WD 551		Bookmark button on Insert tab		
Bookmark, Go To	WD 552	In Bookmark dialog box, click name | Go To button			F5
Border, Paragraph	WD 161, WD 231, WD 396		Border button arrow on Home tab | Borders and Shading		
Building Block, Create	WD 170		Quick Parts button on Insert tab | Save Selection to Quick Part Gallery		ALT+F3
Building Block, Edit Properties	WD 518, WD 687		Quick Parts button on Insert tab | Building Blocks Organizer | select building block | Edit Properties button	Right-click building block on Quick Parts menu | Edit Properties	
Building Block, Insert	WD 172		Quick Parts button on Insert tab | building block name		F3
Building Blocks Organizer	WD 516		Quick Parts button on Insert tab | Building Blocks Organizer		
Bullets, Apply	WD 32	Bullets button on Mini toolbar	Bullets button on Home tab	Bullets	ASTERISK KEY | SPACEBAR
Bullets, Customize	WD 278		Bullets button on the Home tab | Define New Bullet		
Capital Letters	WD 86		Change Case button on Home tab | UPPERCASE	Font	CTRL+SHIFT+A
Caption, Add	WD 509		Insert Caption button on References tab		

Table 1 Microsoft Office Word 2007 Quick Reference Summary *(continued)*

Task	Page Number	Mouse	Ribbon	Shortcut Menu	Keyboard Shortcut
Case of Letters, Change	WD 86		Change Case button on Home tab	Font | Font tab	SHIFT+F3
Center	WD 26	Center button on Mini toolbar	Center button on Home tab	Paragraph | Indents and Spacing tab	CTRL+E
Character Spacing, Modify	WD 240		Font Dialog Box Launcher on Home Tab | Character Spacing tab	Font | Character Spacing tab	
Character Style, Create	WD 276		More button in Styles gallery | Save Selection as New Quick Style	Styles | Save Selection	
Chart Table	WD 269		Object button arrow on Insert tab		
Chart Type, Change	WD 272			Chart Type | Standard Types tab	
Chart, Move Legend	WD 270			Format Legend | Placement tab	
Chart, Resize	WD 271	Drag sizing handle			
Citation Placeholder, Insert	WD 101		Insert Citation button on References tab | Add New Placeholder		
Citation, Insert	WD 547		Mark Citation button on References tab		ALT+SHIFT+I
Citation, Insert and Create Source	WD 96		Insert Citation button on References tab | Add New Source		
Citation, Edit	WD 98	Click citation, Citation Options box arrow | Edit Citation			
Close Document	WD 60	Office Button | Close			
Color Text	WD 152, WD 240	Font Color button arrow on Mini toolbar	Font Color button arrow on Home tab		
Column Break, Insert	WD 420		Insert Page and Section Breaks button on Page Layout tab | Column		
Column Break, Remove	WD 421		Cut button on Home tab		DELETE
Columns, Balance	WD 438		Insert Page and Section Breaks button on Page Layout tab		
Columns, Change Number	WD 410, WD 433		Columns button on Page Layout tab		
Columns, Increase Width	WD 414	Drag column boundaries	Columns button on Page Layout tab | More Columns		
Combine Revisions	WD 502		Compare button on Review tab | Combine on Compare menu		
Comment, Delete One	WD 496		Delete Comment button on Review tab	Right-click comment | Delete Comment	

Table 1 Microsoft Office Word 2007 Quick Reference Summary *(continued)*

Task	Page Number	Mouse	Ribbon	Shortcut Menu	Keyboard Shortcut
Comment, Edit	WD 493	Click balloon, type new text			
Comment, Insert	WD 488		Insert Comment button on Review tab		CTRL+ALT+M
Comments, Balloons Setting, Turn On	WD 488		Balloons button on Review tab | Show Only Comments and Formatting in Balloons		
Comments, Delete All	WD 499		Delete Comment button arrow on Review tab | Delete All Comments in Document		
Compare Documents	WD 500		Compare button on Review tab | Compare on Compare menu		
Compared Documents, Display Original and Revised Documents	WD 500		Show Source Documents button on Review tab		
Compatibility Checker	WD 683	Office Button | Prepare | Run Compatibility Checker			
Compress Pictures	WD 524	Tools button in Save As dialog box | Compress Pictures on Tools menu	Compress Pictures button on Format tab		
Content Control, Change Text	WD 187, WD 534	Triple-click content control, change text			
Content Control, Combo Box, Change Properties	WD 605		Control Properties button on Developer tab		
Content Control, Combo Box, Insert	WD 604		Combo Box button on Developer tab		
Content Control, Date, Change Properties	WD 607		Control Properties button on Developer tab		
Content Control, Date, Insert	WD 606		Date Picker button on Developer tab		
Content Control, Drop-Down List, Change Properties	WD 602		Control Properties button on Developer tab		
Content Control, Drop-Down List, Insert	WD 601		Drop-Down List button on Developer tab		
Content Control, Plain Text, Change Properties	WD 595		Control Properties button on Developer tab		
Content Control, Plain Text, Insert	WD 593		Text button on Developer tab		
Content Control, Rich Text, Change Properties	WD 609		Control Properties button on Developer tab		

Table 1 Microsoft Office Word 2007 Quick Reference Summary *(continued)*

Task	Page Number	Mouse	Ribbon	Shortcut Menu	Keyboard Shortcut
Content Control, Rich Text, Insert	WD 608		Rich Text button on Developer tab		
Copy	WD 189, WD 428		Copy button on Home tab	Copy	CTRL+C
Count Words	WD 107	Word Count indicator on status bar	Word Count button on Review tab		CTRL+SHIFT+G
Cover Page, Insert	WD 533		Cover Page button on Insert tab		
Cross-Reference, Create	WD 511		Cross-reference button on References tab		
Cross-Reference, Update Manually	WD 511			Right-click reference | Update Field	Select reference, F9
Cut	WD 121, WD 257		Cut button on Home tab	Cut	CTRL+X
Data Source, Associate with Main Document	WD 340		Select Recipients button on Mailings tab | Use Existing List		
Data Source, Create	WD 323		Start Mail Merge button on Mailings tab		
Date, Insert	WD 168, WD 330		Insert Date and Time button on Insert tab		
Delete	WD 59				DELETE
Developer Tab, Show	WD 588	Office Button | Word Options button | Popular | Show Developer tab in the Ribbon check box			
Dictionary, Custom, View or Modify Entries	WD 127	Office Button | Word Options button | Proofing | Custom Dictionaries button			
Dictionary, Set Custom	WD 127	Office Button | Word Options button | Proofing | Custom Dictionaries button | select desired dictionary name | Change Default button			
Digital Signature, Add to a Document	WD 692	Office Button | Prepare | Add a Digital Signature			
Document Inspector	WD 688	Office Button | Prepare | Inspect Document			
Document Map	WD 537		Document Map check box on View tab		
Document Properties, Set or View	WD 51	Office Button | Prepare | Properties			
Documents, Switch Between	WD 189	Program button on Windows taskbar	Switch Windows button on View tab		ALT+TAB
Double-Space Text	WD 87		Line spacing button on Home tab	Paragraph | Indents and Spacing	CTRL+2

Table 1 Microsoft Office Word 2007 Quick Reference Summary (continued)

Task	Page Number	Mouse	Ribbon	Shortcut Menu	Keyboard Shortcut
Double-Underline	WD 35		Font Dialog Box Launcher on Home tab	Font | Font tab	CTRL+SHIFT+D
Drawing Canvas, Display Automatically	WD 314	Office Button | Word Options button | Advanced | Editing Options area			
Drawing Canvas, Format	WD 315		Drawing Tools Format tab		
Drawing Canvas, Insert	WD 314		Shapes button on Insert tab | New Drawing Canvas		
Drawing Canvas, Resize	WD 320	Drag a sizing handle	Shape Width and Shape Height text boxes on Format tab	Format Drawing Canvas | Size tab	
Drop Cap	WD 417		Drop Cap button on Insert tab		
Editing Restrictions, Set	WD 623		Protect Document button on Developer tab | set options in task pane		
E-Mail, Customize Opening	WD 695	Office Button | Word Options button | Popular			
E-Mail Document, as Attachment	WD 478	Office Button | Send | E-mail			
E-Mail Document, as PDF Attachment	WD 449	Office Button | Send | E-mail as PDF Attachment			
Envelope, Address and Print	WD 203		Envelopes button on Mailings tab | Envelopes tab | Print button		
Exceptions, Set Editing Restrictions	WD 703		Protect Document button on Developer tab		
Field Codes, Display or Remove	WD 261, WD 331, WD 341			Toggle Field Codes	ALT+F9
Field Codes, Print	WD 342	Office Button | Word Options button | Advanced			
Field, Edit	WD 667			Edit Field	
Field, Insert	WD 666		Quick Parts button on Insert tab		
Field, Lock	WD 345				CTRL+F11
Field, Unlock	WD 345				CTRL+SHIFT+F11
File, Create from Existing File	WD 165	Office Button | New | New from existing			
Fill Effect for Background, Add	WD 222, WD 650		Page Color button on Page Layout tab | Fill Effects | Pattern tab		

Table 1 Microsoft Office Word 2007 Quick Reference Summary *(continued)*

Task	Page Number	Mouse	Ribbon	Shortcut Menu	Keyboard Shortcut
Find Format	WD 274	Select Browse Object button on vertical scroll bar | Find icon	Find button on Home tab		CTRL+F
Find Text	WD 124	Select Browse Object button on vertical scroll bar | Find icon	Find button on Home tab		CTRL+F
Find and Replace Text	WD 123	Select Browse Object button on vertical scroll bar | Find icon | Replace tab	Replace button on Home tab		CTRL+H
First-Line Indent Paragraphs	WD 88	Drag First Line Indent marker on ruler	Paragraph Dialog Box Launcher on Home tab | Indents and Spacing tab	Paragraph | Indents and Spacing tab	TAB
Folder, Create While Saving	WD 321	Save button on Quick Access Toolbar | Create a new, empty folder button			F12
Font, Change	WD 29	Font box arrow on Mini toolbar	Font box arrow on Home tab	Font | Font tab	CTRL+SHIFT+F
Font, Change Case	WD 243		Change Case button on Home tab		SHIFT+F3
Font Settings, Modify Default	WD 242		Font Dialog Box Launcher on Home Tab | Default button | Yes button		
Font Size, Change	WD 28	Font Size box arrow on Mini toolbar	Font Size box arrow on Home tab	Font | Font tab	CTRL+SHIFT+P
Font Size, Decrease	WD 152	Shrink Font button on Mini toolbar	Shrink Font button on Home tab	Font | Font tab	CTRL+SHIFT+<
Font Size, Decrease 1 Point	WD 86			Font | Font tab	CTRL+ [
Font Size, Increase	WD 151	Grow Font button on Mini toolbar	Grow Font button on Home tab		CTRL+SHIFT+>
Font Size, Increase 1 Point	WD 86			Font | Font tab	CTRL+]
Footer, Insert Formatted	WD 261		Footer button on Design tab		
Footnote Reference Mark, Insert	WD 100		Insert Footnote button on References tab		CTRL+ALT+F
Footnote, Delete	WD 106	Delete note reference mark in document window	Cut button Home tab		BACKSPACE | BACKSPACE
Footnote, Edit	WD 106	Double-click note reference mark in document window	Show Notes button on References tab		
Footnote, Move	WD 106	Drag note reference mark in document window	Cut button on Home tab | Paste button on Home tab		

Table 1 Microsoft Office Word 2007 Quick Reference Summary *(continued)*

Task	Page Number	Mouse	Ribbon	Shortcut Menu	Keyboard Shortcut
Footnote Style, Modify	WD 102		Click footnote text | Styles Dialog Box Launcher | Manage Styles button | Modify button	Style | Footnote Text | Modify button	
Format Characters	WD 240		Font Dialog Box Launcher on Home Tab		
Format Painter	WD 611		Format Painter button on Home tab		
Formatting Marks	WD 14, WD 248, WD 515		Show/Hide ¶ button on Home tab		CTRL+SHIFT+*
Formatting Restrictions, Set	WD 622		Protect Document button on Developer tab | set options in task pane		
Formatting, Clear	WD 162		Clear Formatting button on Home tab		CTRL+ SPACEBAR
Go To, Section	WD 258	Page number in document button on status bar	Find button arrow on Home tab | Go To on Find menu		CTRL+G
Graphic, Adjust Brightness	WD 404		Brightness button on Format tab	Format Picture | Picture	
Graphic, Adjust Contrast	WD 584		Contrast button on Format tab	Format Picture | Picture	
Graphic, Crop	WD 721		Crop button on Format tab		
Graphic, Flip	WD 403		Rotate button on Format tab		
Graphic, Format as Floating	WD 402		Text Wrapping button on Format tab	Text Wrapping	
Graphic, Insert	WD 153		Clip Art button on Insert tab		
Graphic, Recolor	WD 156		Recolor button on Format tab	Format Picture | Picture | Recolor button	
Graphic, Resize	WD 46	Drag sizing handle	Format tab in Picture Tools tab or Size Dialog Box Launcher on Format tab	Size | Size tab	
Graphic, Restore	WD 404		Reset Picture button on Format tab		
Graphic, Rotate	WD 664	Drag rotate handle			
Graphic, Send Behind Text	WD 614		Send to Back button on Format tab	Order | Send Behind Text	
Graphic, Set Transparent Color	WD 157		Recolor button on Format tab | Set Transparent Color		
GreetingLine Merge Field, Edit	WD 332			Right-click field | Edit Greeting Line	

Table 1 Microsoft Office Word 2007 Quick Reference Summary *(continued)*					
Task	**Page Number**	**Mouse**	**Ribbon**	**Shortcut Menu**	**Keyboard Shortcut**
Gridlines, Show/Hide	WD 592, WD 599		View Table Gridlines button on Layout tab		
Hanging Indent, Create	WD 116	Drag Hanging Indent marker on ruler	Paragraph Dialog Box Launcher on Home tab	Indents and Spacing tab	Paragraph	Indents and Spacing tab	CTRL+T
Hanging Indent, Remove	WD 86		Paragraph Dialog Box Launcher on Home tab	Indents and Spacing tab	Paragraph	Indents and Spacing tab	CTRL+SHIFT+T
Header & Footer, Close	WD 83	Double-click dimmed document text	Close Header and Footer button on Design tab		
Header, Different for Section	WD 259		Header button on Insert Tab	Edit Header		
Header, Display	WD 80	Double-click dimmed header	Header button on Insert tab	Edit Header		
Header, Distance from Edge	WD 261		Page Setup Dialog Box Launcher on Page Layout tab	Layout tab		
Header, Insert Formatted	WD 260		Header button on Design tab		
Headers, Alternating	WD 548		Header button on Insert tab	Edit Header	Different Odd & Even Pages		
Help	WD 60		Office Word Help button		F1
Hidden Text, Format Text as	WD 366		Font Dialog Box Launcher	Font tab	Font	Font tab	
Hidden Text, Hide/ Show	WD 367		Show/Hide ¶ button on Home tab		CTRL+SHIFT+*
Highlight Text	WD 586		Text Highlight Color button on Home tab		
Hyperlink, Format Text as	WD 220		Insert Hyperlink button on Insert tab	Hyperlink	CTRL+K
Hyperlink, Insert	WD 552		Select text	Insert Hyperlink button on Insert tab		
Hyperlink, Remove	WD 163		Hyperlink button on Insert tab	Remove Link button	Remove Hyperlink	
IF Field, Insert	WD 338		Rules button on Mailings tab		
Indent Paragraph	WD 196, WD 233	Drag Left Indent marker on ruler	Increase Indent button on Home tab	Paragraph	Indents and Spacing sheet	CTRL+M
Index Entry, Delete	WD 546	Display formatting marks, delete entry			
Index Entry, Edit	WD 546	Display formatting marks, change text inside quotation marks			

Table 1 Microsoft Office Word 2007 Quick Reference Summary *(continued)*

Task	Page Number	Mouse	Ribbon	Shortcut Menu	Keyboard Shortcut
Index Entry, Mark	WD 512		Select text | Mark Entry button on References tab		ALT+SHIFT+X
Index, Build	WD 544		Insert Index button on References tab		
Index, Change Format	WD 547		Insert Index button on References tab		
Index, Delete	WD 547	Select index, drag through field code, delete index entry			
Index, Update	WD 546		Update Index button on References tab		Select index, F9
Insert Document in Existing Document	WD 251		Object button arrow on Insert tab		
Insertion Point, Move to Beginning of Document	WD 24	Scroll to top of document, click			CTRL+HOME
Insertion Point, Move to End of Document	WD 25	Scroll to bottom of document, click			CTRL+END
Italicize	WD 36	Italic button on Mini toolbar	Italic button on Home tab	Font | Font tab	CTRL+I
Justify Paragraph	WD 86, WD 411		Justify button on Home tab	Paragraph | Indents and Spacing tab	CTRL+J
Left-Align	WD 86		Align Text Left button on Home tab	Paragraph | Indents and Spacing tab	CTRL+L
Line Break, Enter	WD 194				SHIFT+ENTER
Link Object	WD 469		Copy object | Paste button on Home tab | Paste Special		
Linked Object, Break Links	WD 476	Office Button | Prepare | Edit Links to Files | Break Link button		Linked Object | Links | Break Link button	CTRL+SHIFT+F9
Linked Object, Edit	WD 476	Double-click linked object			
Macro Settings, Specify	WD 647	Office Button | Word Options button | Trust Center	Macro Security button on Developer tab		
Macro, Delete	WD 678		View Macros button on Developer tab | Delete button		
Macro, Edit VBA Code	WD 679		View Macros button on Developer tab | Edit button		
Macro, Pause Recording	WD 672	Pause Recording button on status bar			
Macro, Record	WD 671, WD 678	Macro Recording button on status bar	Record Macro button on Developer tab		
Macro, Rename	WD 677		View Macros button on Developer tab | Organizer button		

Table 1 Microsoft Office Word 2007 Quick Reference Summary *(continued)*

Task	Page Number	Mouse	Ribbon	Shortcut Menu	Keyboard Shortcut
Macro, Run	WD 674		View Macros button on Developer tab | Run button		
Mail Merge Fields, Insert	WD 333		Insert Merge Field button arrow on Mailings tab		
Mail Merge to New Document Window	WD 363		Finish & Merge button on Mailings tab | Edit Individual Documents		
Mail Merge to Printer	WD 344		Finish & Merge button on Mailings tab | Print Documents		
Mail Merge, Directory	WD 358		Start Mail Merge button on Mailings tab		
Mail Merge, Envelopes	WD 356		Start Mail Merge button on Mailings tab		
Mail Merge, Identify Main Document	WD 309		Start Mail Merge button on Mailings tab		
Mail Merge, Mailing Labels	WD 350		Start Mail Merge button on Mailings tab		
Mail Merge, Select Records	WD 345		Edit Recipient List button on Mailings tab		
Mail Merge, Sort Data Records	WD 348		Edit Recipient List button on Mailings tab		
Mail Merged Data, View	WD 349		View Merged Data button on Mailings tab		
Main Document File, Convert	WD 368		Start Mail Merge button on Mailings tab		
Margin, Gutter	WD 550		Margins button on Page Layout tab		
Margins, Change Settings	WD 313, WD 389, WD 579	Drag margin boundary on ruler	Margins button on Page Layout tab		
Markup, Select Next	WD 496		Next Change button on Review tab		
Markups, Change How Document is Displayed	WD 496		Display for Review box arrow on Review tab		
Markups, Display in Balloons	WD 492		Balloons button on Review tab | Show Revisions in Balloons		
Markups, Display Inline	WD 492		Balloons button on Review tab | Show All Revisions Inline		
Markups, Print	WD 495	Office Button | Print | Print | Print what box arrow | Document showing markup			
Markups, Select Items to Display	WD 496		Show Markup button on Review tab		

Table 1 Microsoft Office Word 2007 Quick Reference Summary *(continued)*

Task	Page Number	Mouse	Ribbon	Shortcut Menu	Keyboard Shortcut
Merge Condition, Remove	WD 348		Edit Recipient List button on Mailings tab | Filter link | Clear All button		
Move Selected Text	WD 121	Drag and drop selected text	Cut button on Home tab | Paste button on Home tab	Cut | Paste	CTRL+X, CTRL+V
Multilevel List, Change Levels	WD 336		Increase (Decrease) Indent button on Home tab	Increase Indent or Decrease Indent	TAB, SHIFT+TAB
Multilevel List, Create	WD 335		Multilevel List button on Home tab		
Nonbreaking Space, Insert	WD 171		Symbol button on Insert tab | More Symbols | Special Characters tab		CTRL+SHIFT+SPACEBAR
Numbered List, Enter	WD 519		Numbering button on Home tab		
Numbered List, Format	WD 519		Numbering button arrow on Home tab		
Open Document	WD 56	Office Button | Open			CTRL+O
Outline, Create	WD 525	Outline button on status bar	Outline View on View tab		
Page Border, Add	WD 48		Page Borders button on Page Layout tab		
Page Break, Delete	WD 256		Cut button on Home tab	Cut	CTRL+X, BACKSPACE
Page Break, Manual	WD 112		Page Break button on Insert tab		CTRL+ENTER
Page Number, Insert	WD 82		Insert Page Number button on Design tab		
Page Numbers, Start at Different Number	WD 262		Insert Page Number button on Design tab | Format Page Numbers on Insert Page Number menu		
Page Orientation	WD 362		Page Orientation button on Page Layout tab		
Paper Size, Change	WD 577		Page Size button on Page Layout tab		
Paragraph, Add Space Above	WD 79		Line spacing button on Home tab | Add Space Before (After) Paragraph	Paragraph | Indents and Spacing tab	CTRL+0 (zero)
Paragraph, Decrease Indent	WD 196	Decrease Indent button on Mini toolbar	Decrease Indent button on Home tab	Paragraph | Indents and Spacing tab	CTRL+SHIFT+M
Paragraph, Remove Space After	WD 195		Line spacing button on Home tab | Remove Space After Paragraph	Paragraph | Indents and Spacing tab	
Paragraphs, Change Spacing Above and Below	WD 50		Spacing Before box arrow on Page Layout tab	Paragraph | Indents and Spacing tab	

Table 1 Microsoft Office Word 2007 Quick Reference Summary *(continued)*

Task	Page Number	Mouse	Ribbon	Shortcut Menu	Keyboard Shortcut
Password-Protect File	WD 685	Office Button | Save As | Tools button | General Options			
Paste	WD 191, WD 430, WD 436		Paste button on Home tab	Paste	CTRL+V
Picture Border, Change	WD 45		Picture Border button on Format tab		
Picture Style, Apply	WD 44		Picture Tools and Format tabs | More button in Picture Styles gallery		
Picture, Change Color	WD 662		Recolor button on Picture Tools Format tab		
Picture, Change Shape	WD 722		Picture Shape button on Format tab		
Picture, Insert	WD 41		Picture button on Insert tab		
Placeholder Text, Edit	WD 594		Design Mode button on Developer tab		
Print Document	WD 54	Office Button | Print | Print			CTRL+P
Print Document Properties	WD 130	Office Button | Print | Print | Print what box arrow			
Print Preview	WD 201	Office Button | Print | Print Preview			
Print Specific Pages	WD 253	Office Button | Print | Print			CTRL+P
Print, Draft	WD 347	Office Button | Word Options button | Advanced | Print area			
Protect Document	WD 620		Protect Document button on Developer tab		
Quick Access Toolbar, Add Macro as Button	WD 674	Customize Quick Access Toolbar button on Quick Access Toolbar			
Quick Access Toolbar, Delete Button	WD 677			Right-click button | Remove from Quick Access Toolbar	
Quick Style, Create	WD 90		More button in Styles gallery | Save Selection as a New Quick Style	Styles | Save Selection as a New Quick Style	
Quit Word	WD 55	Close button on right side of Word title bar			ALT+F4
Quote Style, Apply	WD 532		More button in Styles group on Home tab		CTRL+SHIFT+S
Rectangle, Draw	WD 613		Shapes button on Insert tab		
Remove Character Formatting (Plain Text)	WD 87		Font Dialog Box Launcher on Home tab | Font tab	Font | Font tab	CTRL+SPACEBAR

Table 1 Microsoft Office Word 2007 Quick Reference Summary *(continued)*

Task	Page Number	Mouse	Ribbon	Shortcut Menu	Keyboard Shortcut
Remove Paragraph Formatting	WD 87		Font Dialog Box Launcher on Home tab	Font | Font tab	CTRL+Q
Research Task Pane, Use	WD 128	Hold down ALT key, click word to look up			
Reveal Formatting	WD 248				SHIFT+F1
Reviewer Information, Change	WD 490	Office Button | Word Options button	Track Changes button arrow on Review tab | Change User Name on Track Changes menu		
Reviewing Pane, Display Vertically	WD 493		Reviewing Pane button arrow on Review tab | Reviewing Pane Vertical		
Right-Align Paragraph	WD 81		Align Text Right button on Home tab	Paragraph | Indents and Spacing tab	CTRL+R
Rulers, Display	WD 87	View Ruler button on vertical scroll bar	View Ruler on View tab		
Save Document as Template	WD 574	Office Button | Save As | Word Template			F12
Save Document as Web Page	WD 218	Office Button | Save As | Other Formats			F12
Save Document, Previous Word Format	WD 477	Office Button | Save As | Word 97-2003 Document			F12
Save Document, Same Name	WD 53	Save button on Quick Access Toolbar			CTRL+S
Save New Document	WD 19	Save button on Quick Access Toolbar			CTRL+S
Save, as XML File	WD 697	Office Button | Save As			
Save, as XPS File	WD 694	Office Button | Save As			
Save, Macro-Enabled Template	WD 645	Office Button | Save As			
Schema, Attach File	WD 697		Schema button on Developer tab		
Schema, Delete	WD 700		Schema button on Developer tab | Schema Library button		
Search for and Highlight Text	WD 514	Click Select Browse Object button on vertical scroll bar | Find icon	Find button on Home tab | entered desired text | Reading Highlight button | Highlight All		CTRL+F
Section Break, Continuous	WD 409		Insert Page and Section Breaks button on Page Layout tab | Continuous		
Section Break, Delete	WD 251			Cut	DELETE or BACKSPACE
Section Break, Next Page	WD 250, WD 418		Breaks button on Page Layout tab		

Table 1 Microsoft Office Word 2007 Quick Reference Summary *(continued)*

Task	Page Number	Mouse	Ribbon	Shortcut Menu	Keyboard Shortcut
Section Number, Display on Status Bar	WD 249			Section	
Section, Formatting	WD 259	Double-click section break notation			
Select Block of Text	WD 33	Click at beginning of text, hold down SHIFT key and click at end of text to select; or drag through text			CTRL+SHIFT+RIGHT ARROW and/or DOWN ARROW
Select Browse Object Menu, Use	WD 118	Select Browse Object button on vertical scroll bar			ALT+CTRL+HOME
Select Character(s)	WD 120	Drag through character(s)			CTRL+SHIFT+RIGHT ARROW
Select Entire Document	WD 120	Point to left of text and triple-click			CTRL+A
Select Graphic	WD 46	Click graphic			
Select Line	WD 27	Point to left of line and click			SHIFT+DOWN ARROW
Select Lines	WD 30	Point to left of first line and drag up or down			CTRL+SHIFT+DOWN ARROW
Select Nonadjacent Text	WD 277	Drag through text, press and hold CTRL key, drag through more text			
Select Paragraph	WD 90	Triple-click paragraph			SHIFT+DOWN ARROW
Select Paragraphs	WD 30	Point to left of first paragraph, double-click, and drag up or down			
Select Sentence	WD 120	Press and hold down CTRL key and click sentence			CTRL+SHIFT+RIGHT ARROW
Select Word	WD 59	Double-click word			CTRL+SHIFT+RIGHT ARROW
Select Words	WD 33	Drag through words			CTRL+SHIFT+RIGHT ARROW
Shade Paragraph	WD 232		Shading button arrow on Home tab		
Shape, 3-D Effect, Change Color	WD 660		3-D Effects button on Format tab | 3-D Color		
Shape, 3-D Effect, Change Direction	WD 659		3-D Effects button on Format tab | Direction		
Shape, Add Text	WD 319		Edit Text button on Drawing Tools Format tab	Add Text	
Shape, Add 3-D Effect	WD 658		3-D Effects button on Format tab		
Shape, Add Shadow	WD 617		Shadow Effects button on Format tab		
Shape, Apply Style	WD 318, WD 616		Advanced Tools Dialog Box Launcher in Shape Styles group	Format AutoShape	

Table 1 Microsoft Office Word 2007 Quick Reference Summary *(continued)*

Task	Page Number	Mouse	Ribbon	Shortcut Menu	Keyboard Shortcut
Shape, Fill with Picture	WD 660		Shape Fill button arrow on Format tab | Picture		
Shape, Insert	WD 316		Shapes button on Insert tab		
Shape, Remove 3-D Effect	WD 658		3-D Effects button on Format tab | No 3-D Effect		
Show First Line Only	WD 527		Show First Line Only check box on Outlining tab		
Signature Line, Add to a Document	WD 691		Signature Line button on Insert tab		
Single-Space Lines	WD 86		Line spacing button on the Home tab	Paragraph | Indents and Spacing tab	CTRL+1
Small Uppercase Letters	WD 86		Font Dialog Box Launcher on Home tab | Font tab	Font | Font tab	CTRL+SHIFT+K
SmartArt Graphic, Add Shape	WD 441		Add Shape button on Design tab		
SmartArt Graphic, Add Text	WD 237, WD 442	Click Text Pane control on SmartArt graphic	Text Pane button on SmartArt Tools Design tab		
SmartArt Graphic, Apply Style	WD 239		More button in SmartArt Styles gallery		
SmartArt Graphic, Change Colors	WD 238		Change Colors button on SmartArt Tools Design tab		
SmartArt Graphic, Change Layout	WD 440		Click selection in Layouts gallery on SmartArt Tools Design tab	Change Layout	
SmartArt Graphic, Insert	WD 235		Insert SmartArt Graphic button on Insert tab		
SmartArt Graphic, Outline	WD 446		Shape Outline button on Format tab		
SmartArt Graphic, Remove Formats	WD 240		Reset Graphic button on SmartArt Tools Design tab		
Sort Paragraphs	WD 200		Sort button on Home tab		
Source, Edit	WD 104	Click citation, Citation Options box arrow | Edit Source			
Spelling and Grammar	WD 125	Spelling and Grammar Check icon on status bar | Spelling	Spelling & Grammar button on Review tab	Right-click flagged text | Spelling	F7
Spelling and Grammar Check as You Type	WD 16	Spelling and Grammar Check icon on status bar		Correct word on shortcut menu	
Split Window	WD 434	Double-click split box	Split button on View tab		
Split Window, Remove	WD 437	Double-click split bar	Remove Split button on View tab		

Table 1 Microsoft Office Word 2007 Quick Reference Summary *(continued)*

Task	Page Number	Mouse	Ribbon	Shortcut Menu	Keyboard Shortcut
Status Bar, Customize	WD 249			Right-click status bar | click desired element	
Style Set, Change	WD 37		Change Styles button on Home tab | Style Set on Change Styles menu		
Styles Task Pane, Open	WD 25		Styles Dialog Box Launcher on Home tab		ALT+CTRL+SHIFT+S
Styles, Apply	WD 24		Styles gallery on Home tab		
Styles, Modify	WD 90, WD 405, WD 424, WD 656		Styles Dialog Box Launcher on Home tab	Update [*style name*] to Match Selection	
Style, Modify Using Manage Styles Button	WD 669		Styles Dialog Box Launcher on Home tab		
Subdocument, Insert	WD 528		Insert Subdocument button on Outlining tab		
Subscript	WD 86		Font Dialog Box Launcher on Home tab	Font | Font tab	CTRL+EQUAL SIGN
Superscript	WD 86		Font Dialog Box Launcher on Home tab	Font | Font tab	CTRL+SHIFT+PLUS SIGN
Symbol, Insert	WD 398		Symbol button on Insert tab		ALT | NUM LOCK key | type ANSI code
Synonym, Find	WD 124		Thesaurus on Review tab	Synonyms | desired word	SHIFT+F7
Tab Stops, Set	WD 158, WD 167	Click tab selector, click ruler on desired location	Paragraph Dialog Box Launcher | Tabs button	Paragraph | Tabs button	
Table of Authorities, Create	WD 547		Insert Table of Authorities button on References tab		
Table of Contents, Add Text to	WD 538		Add Text button on References tab		
Table of Contents, Change Format	WD 541	Select table | Table of Contents button on table	Select table | Table of Contents button on References tab		
Table of Contents, Create	WD 536		Table of Contents button on References tab		
Table of Contents, Update	WD 540	Select table | Update Table button on table	Select table | Update Table button on References tab		Select table, F9
Table of Figures	WD 542, WD 543		Insert Table of Figures button on References tab		
Table of Figures, Update	WD 543		Select table of figures | click Update Table of Figures button on References tab		Select table, F9

Table 1 Microsoft Office Word 2007 Quick Reference Summary *(continued)*

Task	Page Number	Mouse	Ribbon	Shortcut Menu	Keyboard Shortcut
Table, Add Column	WD 264		Insert Columns to the Left (or Right) button on Layout tab		
Table, Align Data in Cells	WD 268		Align [location] button on Layout tab		
Table, Apply Style	WD 176		More button in Table Styles gallery		
Table, Border	WD 267		Line Weight box arrow on Design tab | Borders button arrow		
Table, Change Row Height	WD 290	Drag border	Table Properties button on Layout tab	Table Properties	
Table, Convert Text to Table	WD 361		Table button on Insert tab | Convert Text to Table		
Table, Convert to Text	WD 653		Convert to Text button on Layout tab		
Table, Delete Column	WD 263		Delete button on Layout tab	Delete Columns	
Table, Delete Contents	WD 283				DELETE
Table, Delete Rows	WD 186, WD 264		Delete button on Layout tab | Delete Rows		
Table, Display Text Vertically in Cell	WD 284		Text Direction button on Layout tab		
Table, Distribute Rows	WD 283		Select Table button on Layout tab | Select Table		
Table, Draw	WD 280		Table button on Insert tab | Draw Table		
Table, Erase Lines	WD 282		Eraser button on Design tab		
Table, Insert	WD 173		Table button on Insert tab		
Table, Insert Borderless	WD 589		Table button on Insert tab | Borders button arrow on Design tab | No Border		
Table, Merge Cells	WD 287		Merge Cells button on Layout tab	Merge Cells	
Table, Modify Properties	WD 364		Table Properties button on Layout tab		
Table, Move	WD 267	Drag move handle			
Table, Non-Breaking Across Pages	WD 279		Table Properties button on the Table Tools Layout tab | Row tab		
Table, Resize Columns	WD 177	Double-click column boundary	AutoFit button on Layout tab	AutoFit | AutoFit to Contents	

Table 1 Microsoft Office Word 2007 Quick Reference Summary *(continued)*

Task	Page Number	Mouse	Ribbon	Shortcut Menu	Keyboard Shortcut
Table, Select	WD 179	Click table move handle	Select button on Layout tab | Select Table on Select menu		
Table, Select Cell	WD 178	Click left edge of cell			
Table, Select Column	WD 178	Click border at top of column			
Table, Select Multiple Adjacent Cells, Rows, or Columns	WD 178	Drag through cells, rows, or columns			
Table, Select Multiple Nonadjacent Cells, Rows, or Columns	WD 178	Select first cell, row, or column, hold down CTRL key while selecting next cell, row, or column			
Table, Select Next Cell	WD 178	Drag through cell			TAB
Table, Select Previous Cell	WD 178	Drag through cell			SHIFT+TAB
Table, Select Row	WD 178	Click to left of row			
Table, Shade Cells (Remove Shade)	WD 288		Shading button arrow on Design tab		
Table, Sort	WD 365		Sort button on Layout tab		
Table, Split Cells	WD 287		Split Cells button on Layout tab	Split Cells	
Table, Sum Columns	WD 265		Formula button on Layout tab		
Table, Wrapping	WD 284			Table Properties | Table tab	
Tag, Remove	WD 702			Remove tag	
Text Box, Fill	WD 523		Select text box | Shape Fill button arrow on Format tab		
Text Box, Insert	WD 427		Text Box button on Insert tab		
Text Box, Position	WD 431	Drag text box			
Text Boxes, Link	WD 521		Select first text box | Create Link button on Format tab | click the second text box		
Theme Colors, Change	WD 39		Change Styles button on Home tab | Colors on Change Styles menu		
Theme Colors, Create New	WD 618		Theme Colors button on Page Layout tab | Create New Theme Colors		
Theme Fonts, Change	WD 40		Change Styles button on Home tab | Fonts on Change Styles menu		

Table 1 Microsoft Office Word 2007 Quick Reference Summary *(continued)*

Task	Page Number	Mouse	Ribbon	Shortcut Menu	Keyboard Shortcut
Theme Fonts, Customize	WD 255		Change Styles button on Home tab | Fonts on Change Styles menu | Create new Theme Fonts		
Theme, Change	WD 467		Themes button on Page Layout tab		
Theme, Save New	WD 648		Themes button on Page Layout tab | Save Current Theme		
Theme, Set as Default	WD 650		Change Styles button on Home tab | Set as Default		
Thumbnails, Display	WD 538		Thumbnails check box on View tab		
Track Changes, Turn On/Off	WD 491, WD 492	Click Tracking Changes button on status bar	Track Changes button arrow on Review tab | Track Changes		CTRL+SHIFT+E
Tracked Change, Accept	WD 496		Accept and Move to Next button on Review tab	Right-click tracked change | Accept Change	
Tracked Change, Reject	WD 496		Reject and Move to Next button on Review tab	Right-click tracked change | Reject Change	
Tracked Changes, Accept All	WD 507		Accept and Move to Next button arrow on Review tab | Accept All Changes in Document		
Tracked Changes, Change Options	WD 499		Track Changes button arrow on Review tab | Change Tracking Options		
Tracked Changes, Display All Reviewers	WD 506		Show Markup button on Review tab | Reviewers | All Reviewers		
Tracked Changes, Display One Reviewer	WD 506		Show Markup button on Review tab | Reviewers | deselect non-target reviewers		
Tracked Changes, Reject All	WD 507		Reject and Move to Next button arrow on Review tab | Reject All Changes in Document		
Tracking Changes Button, Display on Status Bar	WD 490			Right-click status bar | Track Changes	
Underline	WD 35		Underline button on Home tab	Font | Font tab	CTRL+U
Underline Words, Not Spaces	WD 86				CTRL+SHIFT+W

Table 1 Microsoft Office Word 2007 Quick Reference Summary *(continued)*

Task	Page Number	Mouse	Ribbon	Shortcut Menu	Keyboard Shortcut
Unprotect Document	WD 646		Protect Document button on Developer tab		
User Information, Change	WD 312	Office Button | Word Options button			
Watermark, Create	WD 245		Watermark button on Page Layout tab		
White Space, Hide	WD 486	Double-click Hide White Space button			
White Space, Show	WD 487	Double-click Show White Space button			
WordArt, Fill Color	WD 393		Shape Fill button arrow on WordArt Tools Format tab	Format WordArt | Fill Effects button	
WordArt, Insert	WD 391		WordArt button on Insert tab		
WordArt, Shape	WD 395		Change WordArt Shape button on Format tab		
XML Element, Add Parent and Child	WD 700	Open XML Structure task pane | select element			

Table 2 Microsoft Office Excel 2007 Quick Reference Summary

Task	Page Number	Mouse	Ribbon	Shortcut Menu	Keyboard Shortcut
Advanced Filter	EX 386		Advanced button on Data tab		ALT+A | Q
AutoCalculate	EX 62	Select range | right-click AutoCalculate area | click calculation			
AutoFilter	EX 380		Filter button on Data tab		ALT+A | T
Bold	EX 38	Bold button on Mini toolbar	Bold button on Home tab or Font Dialog Box Launcher on Home tab | Font tab	Format Cells | Font tab | Bold in Font style list	CTRL+B
Borders	EX 111	Borders button on Mini toolbar	Borders button on Home tab or Alignment Dialog Box Launcher on Home tab | Border tab	Format Cells | Border tab	CTRL+1 | B
Cell Style, Change	EX 35		Cell Styles button on Home tab		
Cell Watch, Add	EX 641	Add Watch button on Watch Window toolbar			
Center	EX 113	Right-click cell | Center button on Mini toolbar	Center button on Home tab or Alignment Dialog Box Launcher on Home tab	Format Cells | Alignment tab	CTRL+1 | A

Task	Page Number	Mouse	Ribbon	Shortcut Menu	Keyboard Shortcut
Center Across Columns	EX 40	Right-click selection | Merge & Center button on Mini toolbar	Merge & Center button on Home tab or Alignment Dialog Box Launcher on Home tab	Format Cells | Alignment tab	CTRL+1 | A
Chart, Add	EX 50, 205		Dialog Box Launcher in Charts group on Insert tab		F11
Check Compatibility	EX 686		Prepare command on Office Button menu | Run Compatibility Checker		ALT+F | E | C
Clear Cell	EX 66	Drag fill handle back	Clear button on Home tab	Clear Contents	DELETE
Clear Worksheet	EX 66		Select All button on worksheet | Clear button on Home tab		
Close All Workbooks	EX 69	Office Button | Exit Excel			ALT+F | X
Close Workbook	EX 59		Close button on Ribbon or Office Button | Close		CTRL+W
Color Background	EX 110		Fill Color button on Home tab or Font Dialog Box Launcher on Home tab	Format Cells | Fill tab	CTRL+1 | F
Color Tab	EX 216			Tab Color	
Column Width	EX 46, 122	Drag column heading boundary	Home tab | Format button | Column Width	Column Width	ALT+O | C | W
Comma Style Format	EX 44		Comma Style button on Home tab or Number Dialog Box Launcher on Home tab | Accounting	Format Cells | Number tab | Accounting	CTRL+1 | N
Comment			New Comment button on Review tab	Insert Comment	ALT+R | C
Conditional Formatting	EX 119, 362		Conditional Formatting button on Home tab		ALT+H | L ALT+O | D
Convert Text to Columns	EX 729		Text to Columns button on Data tab		ALT+A | E
Copy and Paste	EX 175		Copy button and Paste button on Home tab	Copy to copy; Paste to paste	CTRL+C; CTRL+V
Copy and Transpose	EX 725		Paste button on Home tab | Transpose		ALT+H | V | T
Copy to adjacent cells	EX 27	Select source area | drag fill handle through destination cells	Select source area | click Copy button on Home tab | select destination area | click Paste button on Home tab	Right-click source area | click Copy | right-click destination area | click Paste	

Table 2 Microsoft Office Excel 2007 Quick Reference Summary *(continued)*

Task	Page Number	Mouse	Ribbon	Shortcut Menu	Keyboard Shortcut
Currency Style Format	EX 116		Currency Style button on Home tab or Format Cells | Number | Currency	Format Cells | Number | Currency	CTRL+1 | N
Custom Formats	EX 438		Number Dialog Box Launcher on Home tab | Custom	Format Cells | Number | Custom	ALT+H | FM
Custom View, Save	EX 767		Custom Views button on Views tab		ALT+W | C
Cut	EX 64		Cut button on Home tab	Cut	CTRL+X
Data Table	EX 288		What-If Analysis button on Data tab | Data Table		ALT+A | W | T
Data Validation, Cell	EX 348		Data Validation button on Data tab		ALT+A | V | V
Data Validation, Cell	EX 639		Data Validation button on Data tab		ALT+A | V | V
Date	EX 184	Insert Function button in formula bar | Date & Time | NOW	Date & Time button on Formulas tab | NOW		CTRL+SEMICOLON
Date, Format	EX 113		Font Dialog Box Launcher on Home tab | Number tab | Date	Format Cells | Number tab | Date	
Decimal Place, Decrease	EX 115		Decrease Decimal button on Home tab or Number Dialog Box Launcher on Home tab | Number tab | Currency	Format Cells | Number tab | Currency	CTRL+1 | N
Decimal Place, Increase	EX 118		Increase Decimal button on Home tab or Number Dialog Box Launcher on Home tab | Number tab | Currency	Format Cells | Number tab | Currency	CTRL+1 | N
Delete Rows or Columns	EX 180		Home tab | Delete button arrow | Delete Sheet Rows or Home tab | Delete button arrow | Delete Sheet Columns	Delete | Entire row or Delete | Entire column	
Digital Signature, Add	EX 602		Signature Line button on Insert tab		ALT+N | G
Digital Signature, Review	EX 603	Prepare command on Office Button menu | View Signature			ALT+F | E | R
Document Properties, Set or View	EX 55	Office Button | Prepare | Properties			ALT+F | E | P
Draft Quality	EX 309		Page Setup Dialog Box Launcher on Page Layout tab | Sheet tab		ALT+P | SP | S

Table 2 Microsoft Office Excel 2007 Quick Reference Summary (continued)

Task	Page Number	Mouse	Ribbon	Shortcut Menu	Keyboard Shortcut
E-Mail from Excel	EX 142	Office Button | Send | E-Mail			ALT+F | D | E
Embedded Chart, Delete	EX 67				Select chart, press DELETE
File Management	EX 259	Office Button | Save As | right-click file name			ALT+F | A | right-click file name
File Passwords, Saving	EX 602	Office Button | Save As | Tools | General Options			ALT+F | F then ALT+L | G
Find	EX 481		Find & Select button on Home tab | Find		CTRL+F
Fit to Print	EX 156		Page Setup Dialog Box Launcher on Page Layout tab		ALT+P | SP
Folder, New	EX 259	Office Button | Save As | Create New Folder button			ALT+F | A
Font Color	EX 39	Font Color box arrow on Mini toolbar	Font Color button arrow on Home tab or Font Dialog Box Launcher on Home tab	Format Cells | Font tab	CTRL+1 | F
Font Size, Change	EX 38	Font Size box arrow on Mini toolbar	Font Size box arrow on Home tab or Font Dialog Box Launcher on Home tab	Format Cells | Font tab	CTRL+1 | F
Font Size, Increase	EX 39	Increase Font Size button on Mini toolbar	Increase Font Size button on Home tab		
Font Type	EX 36	Font box arrow on Mini toolbar	Font box arrow on Home tab or Font Dialog Box Launcher on Home tab	Format Cells | Font tab	CTRL+1 | F
Formula Assistance	EX 101	Insert Function button in formula bar	Insert Function button on Formulas tab		CTRL+A after you type function name
Formulas Version	EX 136				CTRL+ACCENT MARK
Freeze Worksheet Titles	EX 182		Freeze Panes button on the View tab | Freeze Panes		ALT+W | F
Full Screen	EX 9		Full Screen button on View tab		ALT+V | U
Function	EX 101	Insert Function button in formula bar	Insert Function button on Formulas tab		SHIFT+F3
Go To	EX 48	Click cell	Find & Select button on Home tab		F5
Goal Seek	EX 225		What-If Analysis button on Data tab | Goal Seek		ALT+T | G
Gridlines	EX 309, 510		Gridlines check box on View tab or Page Setup Dialog Box Launcher on Layout tab | Sheet tab		ALT+W | V | G ALT+P | V | G

Table 2 Microsoft Office Excel 2007 Quick Reference Summary *(continued)*

Task	Page Number	Mouse	Ribbon	Shortcut Menu	Keyboard Shortcut
Header	EX 130, 472		Page Setup Dialog Box Launcher on Page Layout tab | Header/ Footer tab		ALT+P | SP | H
Help	EX 67 and Appendix C		Microsoft Office Excel Help button on Ribbon		F1
Hide Column	EX 122	Drag column heading boundary	Format button on Home tab | Hide & Unhide or Hide & Unhide button on View tab	Hide	CTRL+0 (zero) to hide CTRL+SHIFT+RIGHT PARENTHESIS to display
Hide Row	EX 126	Drag row heading boundary	Format button on Home tab | Hide & Unhide | Hide Rows	Hide	CTRL+9 to hide CTRL+SHIFT+LEFT PARENTHESIS to display
Hide Sheet	EX 316			Hide	
Hide Workbook	EX 317		Hide button on View tab		ALT+W | H
Import Data from Access Table	EX 718		From Access button on Data tab		ALT+A | FA
Import Data from Text File	EX 713		From Text button on Data tab		ALT+A | FT
Import Data from Web Page	EX 721		From Web button on Data tab		ALT+A | FW
In-Cell Editing	EX 63	Double-click cell			F2
Insert Rows or Columns	EX 178		Home tab | Insert button arrow | Insert Sheet Rows or Home tab | Insert button arrow | Insert Sheet Columns	Insert	ALT+I | R or C
Insert Single Cell or Range of Cells	EX 179		Home | Insert button arrow | Insert Cells		
Invalid Data, Circle	EX 647		Data Validation button on Data tab | Circle Invalid Data		ALT+A | V | I
Italicize	EX 203		Italic button on Home tab or Font Dialog Box Launcher on Home tab | Font tab	Format Cells | Font tab	CTRL+I
Link Update	EX 138		Existing Connections button on Data tab		ALT+A | X
Macro, Execute	EX 546		Macros button on Developer tab		ALT+L | PM
Macro, Record	EX 542		Record Macro button on Developer tab		ALT+L | R
Macro, View Code	EX 548		View Code button on Developer tab		ALT+L | V
Margins, Change	EX 130, 472	In Page Layout view, drag margin in ruler	Margins button on Page Layout tab or Page Setup Dialog Box Launcher | Margins tab		ALT+P | M

Table 2 Microsoft Office Excel 2007 Quick Reference Summary *(continued)*

Task	Page Number	Mouse	Ribbon	Shortcut Menu	Keyboard Shortcut
Mark as Final	EX 686	Prepare command on Office Button menu | Mark as Final			ALT+F | E | F
Merge Cells	EX 41		Merge & Center button on Home tab or Alignment Dialog Box Launcher on Home tab	Format Cells | Alignment tab	ALT+O | E | A
Move Cells	EX 177	Point to border and drag	Cut button on Home tab; Paste button on Home tab	Cut; Paste	CTRL+X; CTRL+V
Move Sheet	EX 217	Drag sheet tab to desired location		Move or Copy	
Name Cells	EX 276	Click Name box in formula bar and type name	Define Name button on Formulas tab or Create from Selection button on Formula tab or Name Manager button on Formula tab	Name a Range	ALT+M | M | D
New Workbook	EX 67	Office Button | New			CTRL+N
Open Workbook	EX 61	Office Button | Open			CTRL+O
Outline a Range	EX 273		Border button on Home tab	Format Cells | Border tab	CTRL+1 | B
Outline a Worksheet	EX 377		Group button on Data tab		ALT+A | G | G
Page Break, Insert	EX 478		Breaks button on Page Layout tab | Insert Page Break		ALT+P | B | I
Page Break, Move	EX 479	Click Page Break Preview button on status bar, drag page breaks	Page Break Preview button on View tab | drag page breaks		ALT+ W | I
Page Break, Remove	EX 478		Breaks button on Page Layout tab | Remove Page Break		ALT+P | B | R
Paste Options	EX 176		Paste button arrow on Home tab		
Percent Style Format	EX 118		Percent Style button on Home tab or Number Dialog Box Launcher on Home tab | Percentage	Format Cells | Number tab | Percentage	CTRL+1 | N Or CTRL+SHIFT+%.
Picture, Insert	EX 522		Insert Picture from File button on Insert tab		ALT+N | P
PivotChart, Add Data To	EX 756	Drag field from PivotTable Field List to PivotChart			
PivotChart, Change View	EX 759	Click field buttons in PivotTable Field List			
PivotChart, Create	EX 756		PivotChart button on Insert tab		ALT+N | V | C

Table 2 Microsoft Office Excel 2007 Quick Reference Summary *(continued)*

Task	Page Number	Mouse	Ribbon	Shortcut Menu	Keyboard Shortcut
PivotChart, Format	EX 756		Select chart | use button on Layout and Format contextual tabs		ALT+JO
PivotTable, Change View	EX 749	Drag buttons from PivotTable Field List to PivotTable			
PivotTable, Create	EX 746		PivotTable button arrow on Insert tab | PivotTable		ALT+N | V | T
PivotTable, Format	EX 753		PivotTable Styles More button on Design contextual tab	Format Cells	ALT+JY | S
Preview Worksheet	EX 132	Office Button | Print | Print Preview			ALT+F | W | V
Print Area, Clear	EX 310		Print Area button on Page Layout tab | Clear Print Area		ALT+P | R | C
Print Area, Set	EX 309		Print Area button on Page Layout tab | Set Print Area		ALT+F | T | S
Print Row and Column Headings	EX 309		Page Setup Dialog Box Launcher on Page Layout tab | Sheet tab		ALT+P | SP | S
Print Worksheet	EX 132	Office Button | Print			CTRL+P
Protect Worksheet	EX 313		Protect Sheet button on Review tab	Protect Sheet	ALT+R | PS
Quick Access Toolbar, Customize	EX 763		Customize Quick Access Toolbar button | More Commands		
Quick Style, Add	EX 440		Cell Styles button on Home tab | New Cell Style		ALT+H | J | N
Quick Style, Apply	EX 443		Cell Styles button on Home tab		ALT+H | J
Quit Excel	EX 59	Close button on title bar Office Button | Exit Excel			ALT+F4
Range Finder	EX 106	Double-click cell			
Redo	EX 65	Redo button on Quick Access Toolbar			ALT+3 or CTRL+Y
Remove All Arrows, Formula Auditing	EX 637		Remove Arrows button on Formulas tab		ALT+M | A | A
Remove Precedent Arrows	EX 635		Remove All Arrows button arrow on Formulas tab | Remove Precedent Arrows		ALT+M | A | P
Remove Splits	EX 223	Double-click split bar	Split button on View tab		ALT+W | S
Rename Sheet tab	EX 217	Double-click sheet tab | type sheet name		Rename	
Replace	EX 483		Find & Select button on Home tab | Replace		CTRL+H

Table 2 Microsoft Office Excel 2007 Quick Reference Summary *(continued)*

Task	Page Number	Mouse	Ribbon	Shortcut Menu	Keyboard Shortcut
Rotate Text	EX 169		Alignment Dialog Box Launcher on Home tab	Format Cells | Alignment tab	ALT+O | E | A
Row Height	EX 125	Drag row heading boundary	Format button on Home tab | Row Height	Row Height	ALT+O | R | E
Save Workbook, Different Format	EX 395	Office Button | Save As, choose from Save as type list			ALT+F | F | O
Save Workbook, New Name	EX 57	Office Button | Save As			ALT+F | A
Save Workbook, Same Name	EX 57	Save button on Quick Access Toolbar or Office Button | Save			CTRL+S
Scenario Manager	EX 663		What-If Analysis button on Data tab | Scenario Manager		ALT+A | W | S
Scenario PivotTable	EX 680	Summary button in Scenario Manager dialog box, choose Scenario PivotTable	What-If Analysis button on Data tab | Scenario Manager		ALT+A | W | S | ALT+U | ALT+P
Scenario Summary	EX 678	Summary button in Scenario Manager dialog box, choose Scenario Summary	What-If Analysis button on Data tab | Scenario Manager		ALT+A | W | S | ALT+U | ALT+S
Scenario, Add	EX 663	Add button in Scenario Manager dialog box	What-If Analysis button on Data tab | Scenario Manager		ALT+A | W | S | ALT+A
Scenario, Show	EX 675	Show button in Scenario Manager dialog box	What-If Analysis button on Data tab | Scenario Manager		ALT+A | W | S | ALT+S
Select All of Worksheet	EX 67	Select All button on worksheet			CTRL+A
Select Cell	EX 15	Click cell or click Name box, type cell reference, press ENTER			Use arrow keys
Select Multiple Sheets	EX 218	CTRL+click tab or SHIFT+click tab		Select All Sheets	
Series	EX 169, 286	Drag fill handle	Fill button on		
Shortcut Menu	EX 12	Right-click object			SHIFT+F10
SmartArt	EX 510		SmartArt button on Insert tab		ALT+N | M
Solver	EX 651		Solver button on Data tab		ALT+A | Y2
Solver, Solve Problem	EX 655	Solve button in Solver Parameters dialog box	Solver button on Data tab		ALT+A | Y2 | ALT+S
Spell Check	EX 127	Spelling button on Review tab			F7

Table 2 Microsoft Office Excel 2007 Quick Reference Summary *(continued)*

Task	Page Number	Mouse	Ribbon	Shortcut Menu	Keyboard Shortcut
Split Cell	EX 41		Merge & Center button on Home tab or Alignment Dialog Box Launcher on Home tab | click Merge cells to deselect	Format Cells | Alignment tab | click Merge cells to deselect	ALT+O | E | A
Split Window into Panes	EX 222	Drag vertical or horizontal split box	Split button on View tab		ALT+W | S
Stock Quotes	EX 138		Existing Connections button on Data tab		ALT+D | D | D ALT+A | X
Subtotals	EX 375		Subtotal button on Data tab		ALT+A | B
Subtotals, Remove	EX 379		Subtotal button on Data tab | Remove All button		ALT+A | B | ALT+R
Sum	EX 25	Function Wizard button in formula bar | SUM	Sum button on Home tab	Insert Function button on Formulas tab	ALT+=
Switch Summary Functions	EX 755	Drag fields to Values area of PivotTable Field List		Summarize Data by	
Table, Create	EX 346		Format as Table button on Home tab or Table button on Insert tab		ALT+H | T
Table, Sort	EX 369		Sort & Filter button on Home tab or Sort A to Z button on Data tab	Sort	ALT+A | A
Table Total Row, Add	EX 365		Total Row check box on Design tab of Table Tools contextual tab		ALT+J | T | T
Table Quick Style, Modify	EX 351		Format as Table button on Home tab | right-click style | Duplicate	Duplicate	ALT+H | T
Trace Dependents, Formula Auditing	EX 636		Trace Dependents button on Formulas tab		ALT+M | D
Trace Precedents, Formula Auditing	EX 633		Trace Precedents button on Formulas tab		ALT+M | P
Track Changes, Disable	EX 745		Track Changes button on Review tab | Highlight Changes | remove check mark		ALT+R | G | H
Track Changes, Enable	EX 740		Track Changes button on Review tab | Highlight Changes		ALT+R | G | H
Track Changes, Review	EX 742		Track Changes button on Review tab | Accept/Reject Changes		ALT+R | G | C
Trendline, Create	EX 765		Trendline button on Layout tab | select trendline type		ALT+JA | N

Table 2 Microsoft Office Excel 2007 Quick Reference Summary *(continued)*

Task	Page Number	Mouse	Ribbon	Shortcut Menu	Keyboard Shortcut
Underline	EX 203		Underline button on Home tab or Font Dialog Box Launcher on Home tab	Format Cells | Font tab	CTRL+U
Undo	EX 65	Undo button on Quick Access Toolbar			ALT+2, CTRL+Z
Unfreeze Worksheet Titles	EX 194		Freeze Panes button on View tab | Unfreeze Panes		ALT+W | F
Unhide Column	EX 122	Drag hidden column heading boundary to right	Unhide button on View tab	Unhide	ALT+O | C | U
Unhide Row	EX 127	Drag hidden row heading boundary down	Unhide button on View tab	Unhide	ALT+O | R | U
Unhide Sheet	EX 316			Unhide	
Unhide Workbook	EX 317		Unhide button on View tab		ALT+W | H
Unlock Cells	EX 313		Font Dialog Box Launcher on Home tab | Protection tab	Format Cells | Protection tab	CTRL+1 | SHIFT+P
Unprotect Worksheet	EX 315		Unprotect Sheet button on Review tab	Unprotect Sheet	ALT+R | PS
Validation Circles, Show	EX 647		Data Validation button arrow on Data tab | Circle Invalid Data		ALT+A | V | I
Validation Circles, Clear	EX 647		Data Validation button arrow on Data tab | Clear Validation Circles		ALT+A | V | R
Visual Basic Editor	EX 559		Visual Basic button on Developer tab or View Code button on Developer tab	View Code	ALT+L | V
Watch Window, Open	EX 641		Watch Window button on Formulas tab		ALT+M | W
Web Page, Save Workbook As	EX 256	Office button | Save As | Save as type: arrow | Single File Web Page or Office button | Save As | Save as type: arrow | Web Page			
WordArt	EX 466		WordArt button on Insert tab		ALT+N | W
Workbook Theme, Change	EX 109		Themes button on Page Layout tab		
Workbooks, Compare	EX 761		View Side by Side button on View tab		ALT+W | B
Worksheet Background, Format	EX 768		Background button on Page Layout tab		ALT+P | G
Worksheet Name, Change	EX 141	Double-click sheet tab, type new name		Rename	

Table 2 Microsoft Office Excel 2007 Quick Reference Summary *(continued)*

Task	Page Number	Mouse	Ribbon	Shortcut Menu	Keyboard Shortcut
Workspace, Save	EX 488		Save Workspace button on View tab		ALT+W | K
Zoom	EX 220	Zoom box on status bar or Zoom In and Zoom Out buttons on status bar	Zoom button on View tab		ALT+V | Z

Table 3 Microsoft Office Access 2007 Quick Reference Summary

Task	Page Number	Mouse	Ribbon	Shortcut Menu	Keyboard Shortcut
Add Additional Field Control	AC 316	Drag field name from field list to form			
Add Calculated field to form	AC 531		Text Box tool on Design tab		
Add Chart to Form	AC 575		Insert Chart tool on Design tab		
Add Combo Box	AC 534		Use Controls Wizard on Design tab | Combo Box (Form Control) tool		
Add Date and Time to Report	AC 490		Date & Time button on Design tab		
Add Date and Time to Form	AC 274		Date and Time button on Format tab		
Add Fields to Form	AC 279, 530		Add Existing Fields button on Format or Design tab | select field in field list | drag field to form		
Add Fields to Report	AC 265, 469		Add Existing Fields button on Format or Design tab | drag new field to report		
Add Fields to Table	AC 302			Right-click table in Navigation Pane | click Design View | click first open field	
Add Form Command Buttons	AC 541		Use Control Wizards button on Design tab | Button (Form Control) tool		
Add Form Option Group	AC 558		Use Control Wizards button on Design tab | Option group tool		
Add Form Rectangle	AC 547		Rectangle tool on Design tab		
Add Form Title	AC 323		Title button on Design tab		
Add Macro Actions	AC 368	In macro action column click box arrow | select action			

Table 3 Microsoft Office Access 2007 Quick Reference Summary *(continued)*

Task	Page Number	Mouse	Ribbon	Shortcut Menu	Keyboard Shortcut
Add New Field	AC 24	Right-click Add New Field in Datasheet	Insert Rows button on Design Tab	Design View | INSERT	
Add Page Number to Report	AC 490		Insert Page Number button on Design tab		
Add Record	AC 30, 38	New (blank) record button	New button on Home tab	Open | Click in field	CTRL+PLUS SIGN (+)
Add Smart Tag to Field	AC 636		Open table in Design view | select field | select Smart Tags text box | click Build button | select desired smart tag(s)		
Add Smart Tag to Form Control	AC 640		Open form in Design view | select control | click Property Sheet button on Design tab | click All tab | click Smart Tags property | click Build button | select desired smart tag(s)		
Add Subform	AC 324, 572		Subform/Subreport tool on Design tab | Control Wizards tool | click form		
Add Subreport	AC 482		Subform/Subreport tool on Design tab | click report		
Add Text Box to Report or Form	471		Text Box tool on Design tab | click report or form | enter text box text		
Add Title to Report	AC 490		Title button on Design tab		
Add Total and Subtotals to Report	AC 498		Group & Sort button on Design tab		
Align Controls	AC 319		Select controls | click desired alignment button on Arrange tab		
Allow Zero-Length Strings	AC 626		Open table in Design view | select field | click Allow Zero Length property | change Allow Zero Length property to Yes		

Table 3 Microsoft Office Access 2007 Quick Reference Summary *(continued)*

Task	Page Number	Mouse	Ribbon	Shortcut Menu	Keyboard Shortcut
Assign Conditional Value	AC 503		Text Box tool on the Design tab | place text box on form | delete text box label | select text box | click Property Sheet button | click Control Source property | click Build button | assign conditions using Expression Builder dialog box		
AutoFormat Report or Form	AC 284		More button in AutoFormat group on Format tab		
Calculate Statistics	AC 118		Totals button on Design tab		
Change Control's Color	AC 275		Select control | click Font Color arrow on Format tab | click desired color		
Change Back Color on Form	AC 322			Right-click form | point to Fill/Back Color arrow | click desired color	
Change Can Grow Property	AC 487		Select control | Property Sheet button on Design tab | All tab | change Can Grow property to Yes		
Change Caption	462	Select row | Caption property			
Change Chart Orientation	AC 407		Switch Row/Column button on Design tab		
Change Chart Type	AC 405		Change Chart Type button on Design tab | Type tab | select desired chart		
Change Colors and Font	AC 180		Alternate Fill/Back Color button arrow or Font Color button arrow or Font box arrow on Home tab		
Change Column Size	AC 309	Drag column boundary			
Change Database Properties	AC 60	Office button | Manage | Database Properties			
Change Field Format	AC 532		Select field | Property Sheet button on Design tab |		
Change Form Background Color	AC 537		Click form | Fill/Back Color button arrow on Design tab		

Table 3 Microsoft Office Access 2007 Quick Reference Summary *(continued)*

Task	Page Number	Mouse	Ribbon	Shortcut Menu	Keyboard Shortcut
Change Form Label Color	AC 330		View button on Design tab | select label | click Font Color arrow | select color		
Change Form Tab Order	AC 336		Tab Order button on Arrange tab | Tab Order dialog box		
Change Form Title Format	AC 333		Design View on View Button menu on Design tab | select control | Property Sheet button		
Change Gridlines	AC 179		Gridlines button on Home tab		
Change PivotTable Properties	AC 398		Property Sheet button on Design tab		
Change Primary Key	AC 28	Delete field | Primary Key button	Design View button on Design tab | select field | Primary Key button		
Change Report Margins	AC 508		Page Setup button on Design tab | Margins		
Change Row Size	AC 309	Drag record selector boundary		Right-click field or record selector | click Column Width or Row Height	
Change Size Mode	AC 330		Click control | Property Sheet button on Design tab | Size Mode		
Chart Axis Title	AC 408		Select axis title | Property Sheet button on Design tab | Format tab | Caption box | replace caption		
Chart Title	AC 409		Select chart | Property Sheet button on Design tab | General tab | Add title button | close property sheet | click title | Property Sheet button on design tab | Format tab | replace title (caption)		
Clear Form Filter	AC 282				
Clear Query	AC 98				Select all entries | DELETE
Clear Report Filter	AC 254			Right-click field | clear selected filter	
Close Object	AC 35	Close button for object		Right-click item | Close	
Close Switchboard	AC 388	Close button			
Completely Hide Navigation Pane	AC 645	Microsoft Office Button | click Access Options | click Current Database | clear Display Navigation Pane check box			

Table 3 Microsoft Office Access 2007 Quick Reference Summary *(continued)*

Task	Page Number	Mouse	Ribbon	Shortcut Menu	Keyboard Shortcut
Composite Primary Key	AC 391	Click row selector for first field | press and hold SHIFT | click row selector for second field | Primary key button			
Conditionally Format Controls	AC 250		Select field | Conditional button on Format tab		
Convert Database from an Earlier Version of Access	AC 607	Open database to convert | Microsoft Office button | Convert			
Convert Database to an Earlier Version of Access	AC 606-607	Open database to convert | Microsoft Office button | Save As			
Create Calculated Field	AC 113			Zoom	SHIFT+F2
Create Crosstab Query	AC 123		Query Wizard button on Create tab | Crosstab Query Wizard		
Create Custom Categories for Navigation Pane	AC 614	Show Navigation Pane | right-click Navigation Pane | Navigation Options | Add Item button or Add Group button | OK button			
Create Custom Input Mask	AC 625		Open table in Design view | select field for mask | click Input Mask property | enter mask		
Create Custom Properties	AC 621	Microsoft Office button | point to Manage arrow | click Database Properties | click Custom tab | revise properties as needed			
Create Database	AC 14	Blank Database button or Office Button | Save			CTRL+S or SHIFT+F12 or ALT+I
Create Form	AC 142		Form button on Create tab		
Create Form in Design View	AC 315, 529		Form Design button on Create tab		
Create Form with Datasheet	AC 343		Select "one" table in Navigation Pane | Form button on Create tab		

Table 3   Microsoft Office Access 2007 Quick Reference Summary *(continued)*

Task	Page Number	Mouse	Ribbon	Shortcut Menu	Keyboard Shortcut
Create Form with Datasheet in Layout View	AC 345		Blank Form button on Create tab | Show All Tables | plus sign for "one" table | drag fields to form | plus sign for "many" table | drag first field to form | select datasheet | drag remaining fields		
Create Form with Form Wizard	AC 269		More Forms button on Create tab | Form Wizard		
Create Initial Report in Design View	466		Report Design button on Create tab | select entire report | Property sheet button | select record source		
Create Labels	AC 509		Labels button on Create tab		
Create Macro	AC 366		Macro button arrow on Create tab | Macro		
Create Multipage Form Using Tabs	AC 571		Design tab | create new form | Tab control tool		
Create Multiple-Field Index	AC 630		Indexes button on Design tab		
Create Multi-Table Report	AC 257		Report Wizard button on Create tab | add fields for first table | click Tables/Queries arrow | select second table | add fields for second table		
Create PivotChart	AC 404	Open query | View button arrow | PivotChart View		PivotChart view on status bar	
Create PivotChart Legend	AC 404		Legend button on Design tab		
Create PivotTable	AC 396	Open query | View button arrow | PivotTable View | add fields to drop zones		PivotTable view on status bar	
Create Query	AC 78		Query Design button on Create tab		
Create Report	AC 51		Report Wizard button on Create tab		
Create Report using Report Wizard	AC 239		Report Wizard button on Create tab		

Table 3 Microsoft Office Access 2007 Quick Reference Summary *(continued)*

Task	Page Number	Mouse	Ribbon	Shortcut Menu	Keyboard Shortcut
Create Self-Signed Certificate	AC 650	Start button on Windows Vista taskbar | All Programs | Microsoft Office | Microsoft Office tools | click Digital Certificate for VBA Projects | type your name | OK button | OK button			
Create Space on Report by Moving Controls	AC 508	Select controls | drag controls to new location			
Create SQL Query	AC 430		Query Design button on Create tab | close Show Table dialog box | View button arrow | SQL View		
Create Switchboard	AC 380		Switchboard Manager button on Database Tools tab		
Create Table	AC 23	Office Button | Save button	Table button on Create tab		CTRL+S or SHIFT+F12
Create Validation Rules for Tables	AC 620		Open table in Design view | Property Sheet button on Design tab | Validation Rule property | type rule		
Customize Navigation Pane	AC 126	Navigation Pane arrow | Object Type			
Decrypt Database and Remove Password	AC 649		Close database | More button | Computer | click file name | click Open button arrow | Open Exclusive | OK button | Decrypt Database button on Database Tools tab | type password | click OK button		
Define Fields in a Table	AC 24		Right-click Add New Field on Datasheet tab | Rename Column	Right-click Add New Field | Rename Column	
Delete Record	AC 148	Click Record Selector | DELETE	DELETE button		
Enable Error Checking	AC 632	Microsoft Office Button | click Access Options | click Object Designers | check Enable error checking check box			

Table 3 Microsoft Office Access 2007 Quick Reference Summary *(continued)*

Task	Page Number	Mouse	Ribbon	Shortcut Menu	Keyboard Shortcut
Encrypt Database with Password	AC 648		Encrypt with Password button on Database Tools tab | type password | verify password | click OK button		
Enter Data in Attachment Field	AC 312			Right-click field | click Manage Attachments | click Add | navigate to file to add	
Enter Data in Date Field	AC 308	Type date in date field			Calendar button | select date
Enter Data in Hyperlink Field	AC 314			Right-click field | click Hyperlink | click Edit Hyperlink | enter desired Web address	
Enter Data in Memo Field	AC 308	Type data in memo field			
Enter Data in OLE Field	AC 310			Right-click field | click Insert Object	
Enter Data in Yes/No Field	AC 307	Click field's check box to indicate Yes			
Exclude Field from Query Results	AC 112	Show check box			
Export Query	AC 221		Select query | desired application button in Export group on External Data tab		
Field Size	AC 46		Design View button on Design tab | select field | Field Size box		
Filter by Selection	AC 149		Selection button on Home tab | select criterion		
Filter Records in Report	AC 252			Right-click field | click selected filter	
Form Filter and Sort	AC 280		Advanced button on Home tab | Advanced Filter/Sort | select fields on which to sort | enter sort criteria | Toggle Filter button		
Format Calculated Field	AC 116		Property Sheet button on Design tab		
Format Chart	AC 583	Right-click chart | point to Chart Object | click Edit			
Format Control	475, 538		Select control | Property Sheet button on Design tab | Format property box | select desired format		

Table 3 Microsoft Office Access 2007 Quick Reference Summary *(continued)*

Task	Page Number	Mouse	Ribbon	Shortcut Menu	Keyboard Shortcut
Format Field	AC 168	Select field | Format property box			
Gridlines in Form	AC 273		Gridlines button on Format tab		
Group Controls	476		Select controls | Group button on Arrange tab		
Group in Query	AC 121	Total row or include multiple fields in query			
Group in Report	AC 244		Group & Sort button on Format tab | Add a group button		
Hide Smart Tags	AC 638	Microsoft Office Button | click Access Options | click Advanced | clear Show Smart Tags on Forms and Reports or Show Smart Tags on Datasheet check box			
Import Data	AC 212		Desired application in Import group on External Data tab		
Include All Fields in Query	AC 85	Double-click asterisk in field list	Query Design button on Create tab | Add All Fields button		
Include Field in Query	AC 85		Query Design button on Create tab | select field | Add Field button		
Input Mask	AC 304	In Design View | Input Mask property box | Build button			
Join Tables	AC 105		Query Design button on Create tab | bring field lists for tables into upper pane		
Link Tables	AC 217		Access button on External Data tab | select database | OK button		
Lock Database	AC 659		Make ACCDE button on Database Tools tab | select location and name for ACCDE file | Save button		
Lookup Field	AC 172	Data Type column for field | Lookup Wizard			
Macro Group	AC 377		Macro button arrow on Design tab | Macro | Macro Names button | enter macro names		
Modify Chart Type	AC 587			Right-click chart | Chart object | Edit | right-click chart	

Table 3 Microsoft Office Access 2007 Quick Reference Summary *(continued)*

Task	Page Number	Mouse	Ribbon	Shortcut Menu	Keyboard Shortcut
Modify Controls in Subreport	AC 486	Click controls in report | resize using sizing handles or delete using DELETE key			
Modify Macro	AC 373			Right-click macro | Design view | insert new row | select new action	
Modify Section Properties	AC 489	Select section header | Property Sheet button on Design tab			
Modify Switchboard Page	AC 383, 385		Switchboard Manager button on Database Tools tab | Edit | New | select item to add to switchboard		
Move Controls in Stacked or Tabular Control Layout	AC 277	Select controls | drag to new location			
Move Field List	AC 320	Drag field list title bar			
Move Form Control	AC 276	Point to control | drag to desired location			
Move to First Record	AC 39	First Record button			
Move to Last Record	AC 39	Last Record button			
Move to Next Record	AC 39	Next Record button			
Move to Previous Record	AC 39	Previous Record button			
New Item	various	Office button | Open			
Object Dependencies	AC 339		Select object in Navigation Pane | Object Dependencies button on the Database Tools tab | Objects that depend on me button		
Omit Duplicates	AC 100	Open Property Sheet, set Unique Values to Yes	Property Sheet button on Design tab | Unique Values	Properties | Unique Values	
Open Database	AC 37	More button | Open button or Office button | double-click file name			CTRL+O
Open Database in Exclusive Mode	AC 646	Close database | More button | Computer | click file name | click Open button arrow | Open Exclusive | OK button			

Task	Page Number	Mouse	Ribbon	Shortcut Menu	Keyboard Shortcut
Open Signed Package	AC 653	Close database | More button | select package location | click Files of Type box arrow | click Microsoft Office Access Signed Packages | select package | click Open button | select location | click OK button			
Open Subreport in Design View	484	Right-click report in Navigation Pane | click Design View			
Open Switchboard	AC 387			Right-click switchboard in Navigation Pane | Open	
Open Table	AC 26	Open button		Open	
Package and Sign Database	AC 651	Microsoft Office Button | Publish arrow | click Package and Sign | select desired certificate | name package | click Create button | close database			
Preview Table	AC 41	Office button | Print | Print Preview			ALT+F, W, V
Print Form	AC 282	Office button | Print | Quick Print			
Print Labels	AC 512	Select labels report in Navigation Pane | Office Button menu | Print | Quick Print			
Print Report	AC 256	Office button | Print | Quick Print			
Print Object	AC 41, 56	Office button | Print | Quick Print or Print			CTRL+P
Quit Access	AC 36	Close button			
Referential Integrity	AC 186		Relationships button on Database Tools tab		
Remove Chart Drop Zones	AC 409		Drop Zones button on Design tab		
Remove Form Tab Stops	AC 335		Select controls | Property Sheet button on Design tab | select All tab | change Tab Stop property to No		
Resize Column	AC 175	In Datasheet view, double-click right boundary of the field selector		Right-click field name | Column Width	
Resize Column Headings	AC 263	Select column header | drag upper or lower boundary			
Resize Column in Report	AC 249	Select column | drag right column boundary			

Table 3 Microsoft Office Access 2007 Quick Reference Summary *(continued)*

Task	Page Number	Mouse	Ribbon	Shortcut Menu	Keyboard Shortcut
Resize Detail Section	AC 497	Drag section boundary			
Resize Multiple Controls	AC 540	Select controls to resize | use resizing handle to resize any control			
Resize Subform	AC 575	Drag form borders			
Resize Subreport and Report	AC 488	Open report in Design view | resize with sizing handles | drag subreport			
Run Macro	AC 372			Select macro in Navigation Pane | right-click macro | click Run	
Save Form	AC 58	Office button | Save			CTRL+S
Save Query	AC 91	Save button or Office button | Save			CTRL+S
Save Report	AC 254	Save button			
Save Table	AC 27	Save button	Office button | Save	Save	CTRL+S
Search for Access Help	AC 62	Microsoft Office Access Help button			F1
Search for Record	AC 145		Find button on Home tab		CTRL+F
Search Memo Field in Query	AC 340	In Datasheet view, include wildcards in criterion			
Select Fields for Report	AC 51		Report Wizard button on Create tab | Add Field button		
Select Startup Form	AC 644	Microsoft Office Button | click Access Options | click Current Database | click Display Form | select form to display			
Show Navigation Pane that has been Completely Hidden	AC 646	Microsoft Office Button | click Access Options | click Current Database | check Display Navigation Pane check box			
Show Smart Tags	AC 638	Microsoft Office Button | click Access Options | click Advanced | check Show Smart Tags on Forms and Reports check box Or Show Smart Tags on Datasheet check box			
Simple Query Wizard	AC 78		Query Wizard button on Create tab		
Single-Field Index	AC 629		Open table in Design view | select field for index | Indexed property box | select Yes (Duplicates OK) or Yes (No Duplicates)		

Table 3 Microsoft Office Access 2007 Quick Reference Summary *(continued)*

Task	Page Number	Mouse	Ribbon	Shortcut Menu	Keyboard Shortcut
Single-Step Macro	AC 371		Single Step button on Design tab | Run button in Design view		
Sort Data in Query	AC 98		Select field in Design grid | Ascending		
Sort in Report	AC 244		Group & Sort button on Format tab | Add a sort button		
Sort on Multiple Keys	AC 101	Assign two sort keys			
Special Effects for Form Labels	AC 330		Select label | Property Sheet button on Design tab | Special Effect property box arrow		
Split Database	AC 662		Access Database button on Database tools tab | click Split Database button | select file location | click Split button | click OK button		
Split Form	AC 57		Split Form button on Create tab		
Start Access	AC 12	Start button | All Programs | Microsoft Office | Microsoft Office Access 2007			
Subtotals in Reports	AC 268		For each subtotal, select field to sum | Totals button on Format tab | Sum		
Summary Report	AC 256		Group report on desired field | include calculations | Hide Details button on Format tab		
Switch Between Form and Datasheet Views	AC 57	Form View or Datasheet View button			
Totals in Report	AC 248		Select field | Totals button on Format tab | Sum		
Ungroup Controls	476		Select any control in group | Ungroup button on Arrange tab		
Update Grouped Controls	478		Select any control in group | Design tab | use buttons in Font group or options in property sheet		
Update Query	AC 162		Update button on Design tab | select field, Update To row, enter new value	Query Type | Update Query	
Use Advanced Filter/Sort	AC 155		Advanced button on Home tab | Advanced/Filter Sort		
Use AND Criterion	AC 95				Place criteria on same line

Table 3 Microsoft Office Access 2007 Quick Reference Summary *(continued)*

Task	Page Number	Mouse	Ribbon	Shortcut Menu	Keyboard Shortcut
Use Criterion	AC 81	Right-click query	Design View	Criteria row			
Use Date Field in Query	AC 340	In Datasheet view, type date with slashes as criterion			
Use Documenter	AC 612		Database Documenter button on Database Tools tab		
Use Form	AC 337			Right-click form in Navigation Pane	Open	click navigation buttons	
Use Format Painter	AC 539		Select control whose format to copy	double-click Format Painter on Design tab	click control to format		
Use Navigation Pane Search Bar	AC 619	Right-click Navigation Pane	click Search Bar	enter search term			
Use OR Criterion	AC 96				Place criteria on separate lines
Use Performance Analyzer	AC 611		Analyze Performance button on Database Tools tab		
Use PivotChart	AC 411		Open query in PivotChart view	Drop Zones button on Design tab	click arrows and check boxes to experiment		
Use PivotTable	AC 400	View button arrow	PivotTable View	click plus or minus signs			
Use Table Analyzer	AC 608		Analyze Table button on Database Tools tab		
Use Yes/No Field in Query	AC 340	In Datasheet view, type Yes or No as criterion			
View Report in Print Preview	475		View button on Design tab	Print Preview		

Table 4 Microsoft Office PowerPoint 2007 Quick Reference Summary

Task	Page Number	Mouse	Ribbon	Shortcut Menu	Keyboard Shortcut
Action Button, Change Fill Color	PPT 273		Shape Fill button on Format tab	Format Shape	Fill	
Action Button, Edit Hyperlink	PPT 278		Hyperlink button on Insert tab	Edit Hyperlink	
Action Button, Insert	PPT 271		Shapes button on Insert tab		
Add Shapes	PPT 119		Shapes button on Home tab	select shape		

Table 4 Microsoft Office PowerPoint 2007 Quick Reference Summary

Task	Page Number	Mouse	Ribbon	Shortcut Menu	Keyboard Shortcut
Add Transition	PPT 122		Transition effect on Animations tab or More button in Transition to This Slide group on Animations tab | select transition		ALT+A | T
Animate a Shape Using a Motion Path	PPT 420		Custom Animation on Animations tab | Add Effects button | Motion Paths | More Motion Paths		
Animate Text	PPT 114		Animations tab or Transition button on Animation tab | More button in Transition to this Slide		ALT+D | M
Assign a Macro to a Shape	PPT 487		Action button on Insert tab | Run macro on Mouse Click tab		
Background, Insert Picture	PPT 171		Background Styles button on Design tab | Format Background | Picture or texture fill | File button | select picture | Insert button	Format Background | Picture or texture fill | File button | select picture | Insert button	
Bullet Character, Animate with Entrance Effect	PPT 409		Custom Animation on Animations tab | Add Effect button | Entrance Effects | More Effects		
Bullet Character, Change to a Number	PPT 397		Numbering button arrow on Home tab	Numbering	
Bullet Character, Change to a Picture	PPT 340		Bullets arrow on Home tab | Bullets and Numbering | Picture button | Picture bullet or Import button | picture file | Add button	Bullets and Numbering | Picture button | Picture bullet or Import button | picture file | Add button	
Bullet Character, Change to a Symbol	PPT 344		Bullets arrow on Home tab | Bullets and Numbering | Customize	Bullets and Numbering | Customize	
Bullet Character, Format Color	PPT 349		Bullets arrow on Home tab | Color arrow	Bullets and Numbering | Color arrow	
Bullet Character, Format Size	PPT 346		Bullets arrow on Home tab | Bullets and Numbering | Size Up or Down arrow	Bullets and Numbering | Size up or down arrow	

Table 4 Microsoft Office PowerPoint 2007 Quick Reference Summary *(continued)*

Task	Page Number	Mouse	Ribbon	Shortcut Menu	Keyboard Shortcut
Change Animation Grouping	PPT 411		Custom Animation button on Animations tab | Start box arrow | select desired start | Animations Order list arrow | Effect Options | Text Animation tab | Group text list arrow		
Change Animation Speed	PPT 411		Custom Animation button on Animations tab | Speed box arrow		
Change Line Shape Color	PPT 467		Shape Outline button on Format tab		
Change Line Spacing	PPT 401		Line Spacing button on Home tab | *or* Paragraph Dialog Box Launcher | Indents and Spacing tab | Line Spacing box arrow	Paragraph | Indents and Spacing | Line Spacing box arrow	
Change Size, Clip Art, Photo, or Shape	PPT 101, 103, 117	Drag sizing handles	Dialog Box Launcher in Size group of Format tab | Size tab | enter height and width values or Size group of Format tab | enter height and width values		
Chart, Apply Style	PPT 260		More button in Chart Styles gallery		
Chart, Change Layout	PPT 261		More button in Chart Layouts gallery		
Chart, Insert	PPT 255	Insert Chart button in content placeholder | select chart | OK button	Chart button on Insert tab | select chart | OK button		
Chart Shape, Change Outline Color	PPT 263		Shape Outline button arrow on Format tab		
Chart Shape, Change Outline Weight	PPT 262		Shape Outline button arrow on Format tab | Weight		
Clip Art Border Color, Change	PPT 241		Picture Border button on Format tab		
Clip Art Brightness, Change	PPT 242	Drag Brightness slider or click increase or decrease Brightness arrow in Format Picture dialog box	Brightness button on Format tab		
Clip Art, Insert into Slide with Content Placeholder	PPT 96	ClipArt icon in slide	Clip Art button on Insert tab		
Clip Art, Insert into Slide without Content Placeholder	PPT 234		Clip Art button on Insert tab | type search term | Go button | click clip | Close button		

Table 4 Microsoft Office PowerPoint 2007 Quick Reference Summary (continued)

Task	Page Number	Mouse	Ribbon	Shortcut Menu	Keyboard Shortcut
Clip Art, Regroup	PPT 203		Group button on Drawing Tools Format tab | Regroup	Group | Regroup	
Clip Art, Ungroup	PPT 198		Group button on Format tab | Ungroup | Yes	Group | Ungroup	
Color, Change Object	PPT 199	Shape Fill arrow | select color		Format Shape | Color	
Comment, Delete	PPT 305		Delete Comment button on Review tab		
Comment, Insert	PPT 300		Insert Comment button on Review tab		
Comment, Modify	PPT 303		Edit Comment button on Review tab		
Compatibility Checker, Start	PPT 306	Office Button | Prepare | Run Compatibility Checker			
Compress Presentation	PPT 312		Compress Pictures button on Format tab		
Copy	PPT 276		Copy button on Home tab	Copy	CTRL+C
Create a Self-Running Presentation	PPT 429		Set Up Show button on Slide Show tab | Browsed at kiosk option		
Cut	PPT 188			Cut	CTRL+X
Date and Time, Add	PPT 173		Date & Time button on Insert tab | Date and time | Update automatically arrow | select date and time format | Apply button or Apply to All button		
Demote a Paragraph	PPT 34	Increase List Level button on Mini toolbar	Increase List Level button on Home tab		TAB or ALT+SHIFT+ RIGHT ARROW
Digital Signature, Create	PPT 313	Office Button | Prepare | Add a Digital Signature			
Dim Text after Animation	PPT 414		Animations tab | Custom Animation button | Animation Order list arrow | Effect Options | Effect tab | After animation list arrow		
Display Gridlines	PPT 479		Gridlines check box on View tab	Grid and Guides | Display grid on screen check box	SHIFT+F9
Display a Presentation in Grayscale	PPT 59		Grayscale button on View tab		ALT+V | C | U
Document Inspector, Start	PPT 307	Office Button | Prepare | Inspect Document | Inspect			

Table 4 Microsoft Office PowerPoint 2007 Quick Reference Summary *(continued)*

Task	Page Number	Mouse	Ribbon	Shortcut Menu	Keyboard Shortcut
Document Properties	PPT 44	Office Button | Prepare | Properties			
Document Theme, Choose	PPT 16		More button on Design tab | theme		
End Slide Show	PPT 54			End Show	ESC or HYPHEN
Fill, Insert Texture	PPT 168		Background Styles button on Design tab | Format Background | Picture or texture fill | Texture arrow | select background | Apply to All button	Format Background | Picture or texture fill | Texture arrow | select background | Apply to All button	
Final, Mark Presentation as	PPT 316	Office Button | Prepare | Mark as Final | Yes button			
Find and Replace Text	PPT 267		Replace button on Home tab		CTRL+H
Font, Change	PPT 109	Font button or Font box arrow on Mini toolbar	Font button on Home tab or Font arrow on Home tab | select font or Font Dialog Box Launcher on Home tab | Latin text font arrow on Font tab	Font | Latin text font arrow on Font tab	CTRL+SHIFT+F | Font tab | Latin text font arrow
Font Color	PPT 23, 110	Font Color button or Font Color arrow on Mini toolbar	Font Color button on Home tab or Font Color arrow on Home tab | select color or Font Dialog Box Launcher on Home tab | Font color button on Font tab | select color	Font | Font color button on Font tab | select color	CTRL+SHIFT+F | Font tab | Font color button | select color
Font Size, Decrease	PPT 25	Decrease Font Size button or Font Size arrow on Mini toolbar	Decrease Font Size button on Home tab or Font Size arrow on Home tab | size	Font Size arrow | Size	CTRL+SHIFT+LEFT CARET (<)
Font Size, Increase	PPT 24	Increase Font Size button or Font Size arrow on Mini toolbar	Increase Font Size button on Home tab or Font Size arrow on Home tab | size	Font size arrow | Size	CTRL+SHIFT+RIGHT CARET (>)
Guides, Display	PPT 274			Grid and Guides | Display drawing guides on screen	
Guides, Hide	PPT 279			Grid and Guides | Display drawing guides on screen	
Help	PPT 63 and Appendix A		Office PowerPoint Help button		F1
Hide Slide	PPT 266		Hide Slide button on Slide Show tab	Right-click desired slide thumbnail in Slides tab or in Slide Sorter view | Hide Slide	
Highlight Item	PPT 319	Pointer arrow on Slide Show toolbar | Highlighter		Pointer Options | Highlighter	

Table 4 Microsoft Office PowerPoint 2007 Quick Reference Summary *(continued)*

Task	Page Number	Mouse	Ribbon	Shortcut Menu	Keyboard Shortcut
Hyperlink, Add	PPT 243		Insert Hyperlink button on Insert tab | type hyperlink text | OK button	Hyperlink | type hyperlink text | OK button	CTRL+K
Ink Color, Change	PPT 320	Pointer arrow on Slide Show toolbar | Ink Color		Pointer Options | Ink Color	
Insert Movie File	PPT 353	Insert Media Clip button | select movie file | OK button | how to start movie	Movie from File button on Insert tab | select movie file | OK button | how to start movie		
Insert Picture under Slide Objects	PPT 482		Picture button on Insert tab | select picture | Open button | size picture to fill entire slide | Send to Back button	Right-click picture | Send to Back	
Insert Photograph	PPT 98, 99	Insert Picture from File icon on slide	Picture button on Insert tab		
Insert Slide	PPT 404		New Slide button arrow on Home tab | Reuse Slides | Browse button | Browse File | presentation with desired slide | Open button | Keep source formatting check box		
Insert Sound Clip	PPT 355		Sound from File button on Insert tab | sound file | OK button | how to start sound		
Markup, Show	PPT 304		Show Markup button on Review tab		
Next Slide	PPT 47	Next Slide button on vertical scroll bar			PAGE DOWN
Normal View	PPT 91	Normal View button at lower-right PowerPoint window	Normal button on View tab		ALT+V | N
Object, Delete	PPT 202				DELETE
Open Presentation	PPT 54	Office Button | Open | select file			CTRL+O
Open Word Outline as Presentation	PPT 165	Office Button | Open | All Outlines | select file | Open	New Slide button arrow on Home tab | Slides from Outline | select file | Insert		CTRL+O
Package for CD	PPT 321	Office Button | Publish | Package for CD			
Password, Set	PPT 310	Office Button | Save As | Tools | General Options			
Paste	PPT 277		Paste button on Home tab	Paste	CTRL+V
Paste Special	PPT 468		Paste button arrow on Home tab | Paste Special		

Table 4 Microsoft Office PowerPoint 2007 Quick Reference Summary *(continued)*

Task	Page Number	Mouse	Ribbon	Shortcut Menu	Keyboard Shortcut
Picture, Apply a Shape	PPT 337		Picture Shape button on Format tab		
Picture, Insert into Slide without Content Placeholder	PPT 234		Picture button on Insert tab | select file | Insert button		
Picture Border Color, Change	PPT 237		Picture Border button on Format tab		
Picture Contrast, Change	PPT 238	Drag Contrast slider or click increase or decrease Contrast arrow in Format Picture dialog box	Contrast button on Format tab		
Picture, Recolor	PPT 333		Recolor button on Format tab	Format Picture | Picture in left pane | select color | Close button	
Picture, Resize	PPT 335	Drag sizing handle in or out	Shape Height or change Shape Width up or down arrow on Format tab	Size and Position | Size tab | change Height or change Width	
Picture, Set Transparent Color	PPT 334		Recolor button on Format tab | Set Transparent Color		
Picture Style, Apply to Clip	PPT 240		More button in Picture Styles gallery on Format tab		
Picture Style, Insert in Picture	PPT 236		More button in Picture Styles gallery on Format tab		
Preview Presentation as Web Page	PPT 151	[Assumes Web Page Preview button has been added to Quick Access toolbar] Web Page Preview button			
Previous Slide	PPT 50, 51	Previous Slide button on vertical scroll bar			PAGE UP
Print a Presentation	PPT 61	Office Button | Print			CTRL+P
Print an Outline	PPT 122	Office Button | point to Print | Print Preview | Print What arrow | Outline View			
Print Speaker Notes	PPT 363	Office Button | Print arrow | Print Preview | Print What arrow | OK button | Close Print Preview button			
Promote a Paragraph	PPT 34	Decrease List Level button on Mini toolbar	Decrease List Level button on Home tab		SHIFT+TAB or ALT+SHIFT+LEFT ARROW
Quick Access Toolbar, Add Buttons	PPT 148	Customize Quick Access Toolbar button | select from command options			

Table 4 Microsoft Office PowerPoint 2007 Quick Reference Summary *(continued)*

Task	Page Number	Mouse	Ribbon	Shortcut Menu	Keyboard Shortcut
Quick Access Toolbar, Reset	PPT 154	Customize Quick Access Toolbar button | More Commands | Reset button			
Quit PowerPoint	PPT 53	Double-click Office Button or Close button on title bar or Office Button | Exit PowerPoint		Right-click Microsoft PowerPoint button on taskbar | Close	ALT+F4 or CTRL+Q
Record Narration	PPT 475		Record Narration button on Slide Show tab | microphone level | OK button | Change Quality button | Name arrow | desired recording quality | OK button | Link narrations in check box for lengthy narrations | Current Slide to match narration to particular part of the presentation | speak into microphone | Save button		
Save a Presentation	PPT 27	Save button on Quick Access toolbar or Office Button | Save			CTRL+S or SHIFT+F12
Save a Presentation with a Macro	PPT 489	Office Button | Save As | PowerPoint Macro-Enabled Presentation in Save as type list | presentation name | Save button			
Save as Web Page	PPT 152	Office Button | Save As | add File name | change Save as type to Single File Web Page | Save button			ALT+F | G or F12
Save in .PPS Format	PPT 317	Office Button | Save As | PowerPoint Presentation | type file name | Save as type arrow | PowerPoint Show | Save			
Set Margins, Text Box	PPT 457			Right-click text box | Format Shape | Text Box in left pane | set margins in Internal margins area	
Set Presentation Resolution	PPT 474		Set Up Slide Show button on Slide Show tab | Slide show resolution arrow		

Table 4 Microsoft Office PowerPoint 2007 Quick Reference Summary *(continued)*

Task	Page Number	Mouse	Ribbon	Shortcut Menu	Keyboard Shortcut
Show a Presentation with or without Narration	PPT 475		Set Up Slide Show button on Slide Show tab *or* Show without narration		
Slide, Add	PPT 29		New Slide button on Home tab or New Slide arrow on Home tab | choose slide type		CTRL+M
Slide, Arrange	PPT 41	Drag slide in Slides tab to new position or in Slide Sorter View drag slide to new position			
Slide, Background	PPT 89		Background Styles button on Design tab | select style	Format Background	
Slide, Delete	PPT 419		Delete button on Home tab	Right-click thumbnail in left pane | Delete Slide	
Slide, Duplicate	PPT 40		New Slide arrow on Home tab | Duplicate Selected Slides		
Slide, Save as Image	PPT 475	Office Button | Save As | Other Formats | type desired name | Save as type arrow | select format | Save button | Current Slide Only button			
Slide, Set Size	PPT 473		Page Setup button on Design tab | Slides sized for arrow		
Slide Layout	PPT 92, 94		Layout button on Home tab		
Slide Master, Add a Background Graphic	PPT 389		Insert Picture from File button on Insert tab | graphic file | Insert button		
Slide Master, Add Text to Placeholder	PPT 392	Select text | delete | type new text | drag sizing handles			
Slide Master, Apply a Quick Style	PPT 387		Quick Styles button on Home tab		
Slide Master, Apply Slide Theme Colors	PPT 383		Themes Color button on Slide Master tab		
Slide Master, Apply Slide Themes	PPT 383		Themes button on Slide Master tab | select theme | Theme		
Slide Master, Copy and Paste a Placeholder	PPT 394		Copy button on Home tab | different Slide Master thumbnail in left pane | Paste button		

Task	Page Number	Mouse	Ribbon	Shortcut Menu	Keyboard Shortcut
Slide Master, Close Master View	PPT 396		Close Master View button on Slide Master tab		
Slide Master, Customize Slide Theme Fonts	PPT 383		Theme Fonts button on Slide Master tab | Create New Theme Fonts | heading font | body font | default font name | Save button		
Slide Master, Display	PPT 382		Slide Master button on View tab		
Slide Master, Format Background	PPT 387		Background Styles button on Slide Master tab		
Slide Master, Format Placeholder Text	PPT 399		Text Direction button on Home tab | select direction | Align Text button		
Slide Master, Insert a Placeholder	PPT 391		Content button arrow on Slide Master tab | select placeholder | click slide		
Slide Numbers, Add	PPT 173		Slide Number button on Insert tab | Slide number | Apply button or Apply to All button		
Slide Show View	PPT 49	Slide Show button at lower-right PowerPoint window	Slide Show button on View tab or From Beginning button on Slide Show tab		F5 or ALT+V | W
Slide Sorter View	PPT 91	Slide Sorter View button at lower-right in PowerPoint window	Slide Sorter button on View tab		ALT+V | D
SmartArt Graphic, Add SmartArt Style	PPT 184		More button in SmartArt Styles group on Design tab		
SmartArt Graphic, Adjust Size	PPT 210	Drag sizing handle to desired location			
SmartArt Graphic, Animate	PPT 418		Animate button arrow on Animations tab		
SmartArt Graphic, Change Color	PPT 186		Change Colors button on Design tab		
SmartArt Graphic, Insert	PPT 205		SmartArt button on Insert tab | select category | select graphic		
SmartArt Graphic, Insert Image	PPT 183	Double-click icon in shape | select picture | Insert button			

Table 4 Microsoft Office PowerPoint 2007 Quick Reference Summary *(continued)*

Task	Page Number	Mouse	Ribbon	Shortcut Menu	Keyboard Shortcut
Spelling Check	PPT 55		Spelling button on Review tab		F7
Table, Add an Image	PPT 460			Right-click cell	Format Shape	Insert from File	desired image file	Insert button	Close button	
Table, Add Borders	PPT 251		No Border button arrow on Design tab	All Borders		
Table, Add Effect	PPT 252		Effects button on Design Tab		
Table, Apply Style,	PPT 250		More button in Table Styles gallery on Design tab		
Table, Center Text Alignment	PPT 458		Center Vertically button on Layout tab	Right-click selected cells	Format Shape	Text Box	Vertical Alignment arrow	
Table, Insert	PPT 246	Insert Table button in content placeholder	click Number of columns and Number of rows up or down arrows	OK button	Table button on Insert tab	drag to select columns and rows		
Table, Text Change Orientation	PPT 459		Text Direction button on Layout tab	Right-click desired cells	Format Shape	Text Box	Text direction arrow	
Text, Align	PPT 402		Align Text button on Home tab		
Text, Add Shadow	PPT 110		Text Shadow button on Home tab		
Text, Bold	PPT 25	Bold button on Mini toolbar	Bold button on Home tab		CTRL+B
Text, Change Color	PPT 23	Font Color button or Font Color arrow on Mini toolbar	Font color arrow on Home tab	choose color	Font	Font color button	choose color	
Text, Convert to SmartArt Graphic	PPT 181		SmartArt button on Insert tab	Convert to SmartArt	
Text, Delete	PPT 42		Cut button on Home tab	Cut	DELETE or CTRL+X or BACKSPACE
Text, Formatting with Quick Styles	PPT 119		Quick Styles button on Home tab	select style		
Text, Italicize	PPT 22	Italic button on Mini toolbar	Italic button on Home tab	Font	Font style arrow	Italics	CTRL+I
Text, Select	PPT 21	Drag to select	double-click to select word	triple-click to select paragraph			SHIFT+DOWN ARROW or SHIFT+RIGHT ARROW
Text Box, Adjust Column Spacing	PPT 351		Columns button on Home tab	More Columns		

Table 4 Microsoft Office PowerPoint 2007 Quick Reference Summary *(continued)*

Task	Page Number	Mouse	Ribbon	Shortcut Menu	Keyboard Shortcut
Text Box, Apply Quick Style	PPT 352		Quick Styles button on Home tab		
Text Box, Create Columns	PPT 350		Columns button on Home tab | number of columns | drag sizing handle up to reduce text box height		
Text Box, Format	PPT 191		Shape Fill button or Shape Outline button or Shape Effects button on Format tab		
Text Box, Insert	PPT 188		Text Box button on Insert tab | click in desired location		
Text Box, Order	PPT 457			Right-click text box | Send to Back | Send to Back	
Text Box, Remove Border	PPT 457		Shape Outline button on Home tab | No Outline		
Text Box, Rotate	PPT 189	Drag Free Rotate pointer	Rotate button on Format Tab		
Texture Fill, Insert	PPT 168		Background Styles on Design tab | Format Background		
Theme Colors, Change	PPT 233		Theme Colors button on Design tab		
Thesaurus	PPT 269		Thesaurus button on Review tab	Synonyms	SHIFT+F7
Timings, Adjust Manually	PPT 362		Automatically After up or down arrow on Animations tab		
Timings, Rehearse	PPT 360		Rehearse Timings button on Slide Show tab | Next button | repeat for all remaining slides | Yes button		
Transparency, Change	PPT 172	Drag Transparency slider in Transparency text box or click increase or decrease Transparency arrow in Format Background dialog box			
Use Format Painter	PPT 112	Format Painter button on Mini toolbar	Double-click Format Painter button on Home tab | select text with a format you want to copy | select other text to apply previously selected format | press ESC to turn off Format Painter		

Table 4 Microsoft Office PowerPoint 2007 Quick Reference Summary *(continued)*

Task	Page Number	Mouse	Ribbon	Shortcut Menu	Keyboard Shortcut
WordArt, Apply Style	PPT 175		More button on Format tab		
WordArt Outline Weight, Change	PPT 178		Text Outline arrow on Format tab | Weight		
WordArt Text Effect, Add	PPT 179		Text Effects button on Format tab		
WordArt Text Fill, Format	PPT 176		Text Fill arrow on Format tab		
Zoom for Printing	PPT 128	Drag Zoom slider on status bar or Office Button | point to Print | Print Preview |	Zoom button on View tab | select zoom		
Zoom for Viewing Slides	PPT 127, 462	Drag Zoom slider on status bar	Zoom button on View tab | select zoom		

Table 5 Microsoft Office Outlook 2007 Quick Reference Summary

Task	Page Number	Mouse	Ribbon	Shortcut Menu	Keyboard Shortcut
Accept Meeting	OUT 114		Open message | Accept button | send response | OK button		
Accept Task	OUT 108		Double-click Task Request | Accept		
Address E-Mail Message	OUT 27	Mail button in Inbox window	New Mail Message button on Message tab | To button		
Assign Task	OUT 106, 110		Assign Task button in Task window	Assign Task	
Attach File to E-Mail Message	OUT 31	Attach File button on Standard toolbar in Message window	Attach File button on Insert tab		
Categorize Calendar	OUT 124		Categorize button | All Categories *		
Change Appointment Date	OUT 92	Drag appointment to new date			
Change Appointment Month	OUT 93			Select appointment | Edit | Cut |scroll | click selected date | Paste	
Change Appointment Time	OUT 91	Drag appointment to new time or double-click appointment | edit Start time			
Change Meeting Time	OUT 117	Drag meeting to new time | Yes button | Send Update button			

Table 5 Microsoft Office Outlook 2007 Quick Reference Summary *(continued)*

Task	Page Number	Mouse	Ribbon	Shortcut Menu	Keyboard Shortcut
Change Work Week	OUT 121	Open Calendar | Tools | Options | Calendar Options button | change dates in work week area			ALT+T, O, C
Close an E-Mail Message	OUT 15	Click Close button on title bar in Message window			ALT+F, C
Compose E-Mail Message	OUT 27	New button on Standard toolbar	New | Mail Message*		CTRL+N
Create Contact List	OUT 47	New button on Standard toolbar	Actions | New Contact*	New Contact	CTRL+SHIFT+C
Create Distribution List	OUT 58	New Contact button on Standard toolbar	New Contact button | Distribution List*		CTRL+SHIFT+L
Create E-Mail Signature	OUT 24		Tools | Options | Mail Format tab | Signatures button*		ALT+T, O
Create Event	OUT 95	Double-click appointment area day heading			
Create Personal Folder	OUT 44	Contacts button in Navigation pane	File | New | Folder*	New Contacts | New Folder	CTRL+SHIFT+E
Create Note	OUT 118		New Note button*		
Create View Filter	OUT 36		View | Arrange By*	Custom	
Delete Appointment	OUT 90		Select appointment | Delete button | OK*		
Delete E-Mail Message	OUT 21	Delete button on Standard toolbar	Select message | Delete*		CTRL+D or DELETE
Delete Subfolder	OUT 103			Right-click date banner | Delete | Yes	ALT+F, F, D
Display Contacts	OUT 52	Find a Contact box on Standard toolbar	Tools | Instant Search*		CTRL+E or ALT+T, I
Enter Appointment in Appointment Area	OUT 81	Select date in Date Navigator | select time | type appointment		File | Import and Export | Export to a file	
Enter Appointment in Appointment Window	OUT 82		Select date in Date Navigator | select time | click New Appointment button*	Actions menu | New Appointment	CTRL+N
Export Subfolder	OUT 101				
Find a Contact	OUT 50	Find a Contact box on Standard toolbar	Tools | Instant Search | Advanced Find*		CTRL+SHIFT+F
Flag E-Mail Messages	OUT 34	Follow Up button on Standard toolbar	Actions | Follow Up*	Follow Up	ALT+A, U
Forward E-Mail Message	OUT 20	Forward button on Standard toolbar		Forward	CTRL+F
Import Subfolder	OUT 104			File | Import and Export | Import from another program or file	
Month View	OUT 98	Month tab			
Move to Next Day	OUT 86		Go | Go to Date*	Go to Date	CTRL+G

Table 5 Microsoft Office Outlook 2007 Quick Reference Summary (continued)

Task	Page Number	Mouse	Ribbon	Shortcut Menu	Keyboard Shortcut
Natural Language Phrasing	OUT 88			New Appointment button | enter time as natural language	
Open E-Mail Message	OUT 10	Double-click message	File | Open*	Open	CTRL+O
Print Calendar	OUT 127		Select calendar view | Print button | select style | OK*	File | Print	CTRL+P
Print Contact List	OUT 53	Print button on Standard toolbar	File | Print* or File | Print Preview | Print*		CTRL+P
Print E-Mail Message	OUT 15	Print button on Standard toolbar	File | Print | OK button*		CTRL+P, ENTER
Print Task List	OUT 127		Display task list | Print button | OK*		
Propose New Meeting Time	OUT 117		Propose New Time button in Meeting window	Propose New Time	ALT+A, S
Recurring Appointment	OUT 84		Recurrence button | Appointment Recurrence dialog box		
Reply to E-Mail Message	OUT 16	Reply button on Standard toolbar	Reply button on Message tab		CTRL+R
Save Contact List as Text File	OUT 60	Select name bar of contact | CTRL+A | File | Save As	File | Save As*		
Schedule Meeting	OUT 111		Open appointment | Scheduling button | Add Others button		
Send E-Mail Message	OUT 31	Send button in Message window	Send button on Insert tab		
Send Instant Message	OUT 139			Reply with Instant Message	
Send Meeting Update	OUT 117	Send Update button in Meeting window			
Set Message Importance, Sensitivity, and Delivery Options	OUT 38	New Mail Message button on Standard toolbar in Message window	Options dialog box launcher in the Options group on the Message tab		
Sort E-Mail Messages	OUT 35	Arrange By Command on View menu			ALT+V, A, E
Task List	OUT 99	Tasks button | New Task	New Task*	New | Task	CTRL+N
Work Week View	OUT 96	Week tab	Work Week on View menu*		ALT+V, R or CTRL+ALT+2